Les canadianismes sont clairement indiqués *Canadianisms clearly labelled*	**aubaine** *nf Can (achat ava*

auditeur, -trice *nm,f* (**a**) *(chargé de l'audit)* auditor ◻ **auditeur externe** external auditor; **auditeur interne** internal auditor; **auditeur marketing, auditeur mercatique** marketing auditor (**b**) ADMIN **auditeur à la Cour des Comptes** = junior official at the French Audit Office

Le signe = explication quand il n'y a pas de traduction possible

Explanations introduced by = when no translation possible

Chaque nouvelle catégorie sémantique est précédée d'une lettre en gras entre parenthèses *New sense category introduced by bold letter in brackets*	**avancer** *vt* (**a**) *(dans le temps)* to advance, to bring forward; **la réunion a été avancée du 14 au 7** the meeting has been brought forward from the 14th to the 7th (**b**) *(financièrement)* **avancer de l'argent à qn** to advance money to sb; *(prêter)* to lend sb money; **avancer un mois d'appointements à qn** to advance sb a month's salary, to pay sb a month's salary in advance

avilir **1** *vt (monnaie)* to depreciate, to devalue; *(prix)* to bring down **2 s'avilir** *vpr (biens)* to depreciate, to decrease in value

Les verbes pronominaux ressortent clairement

French reflexive verbs given special status

Les équivalents culturels sont précédés du signe ≃ *Cultural equivalents introduced by ≃*	**avoué** *nm* JUR *Br* ≃ solicitor, *Am* ≃ attorney

bailleur, -eresse *nm,f* (**a**) *bailleur de fonds (investisseur)* (financial) backer; *(associé passif) Br* sleeping partner, *Am* silent partner (**b**) JUR lessor

La différence entre les termes britanniques et américains donnés en traduction est clairement indiquée

Differences in British and American translations clearly labelled

Chaque nouvelle catégorie grammaticale est traitée à la ligne et précédée d'un numéro en gras *New grammatical category introduced by bold numeral, placed on a new line*	**baisser** **1** *vt (prix, loyer)* to lower, to reduce, to bring down; **faire baisser le coût de la vie** to lower *or* reduce *or* bring down the cost of living; **la concurrence fait baisser les prix** competition brings prices down **2** *vi (prix, actions)* to fall; *(stocks)* to be running low; **le dollar a baissé** the dollar has weakened

banquable = **bancable**

Les variantes orthographiques renvoient à la forme la plus courante

Alternative spellings are cross-referred to the most common form

Des informations supplémentaires apparaissent en italiques entre parenthèses *Additional information shown in italic in brackets*	**banqueroute** *nf* JUR bankruptcy; **faire banqueroute** to go bankrupt ◻ **banque-route frauduleuse** fraudulent bankruptcy; **banqueroute simple** bankruptcy *(with irregularities amounting to a breach of the law)*

bénef *nf Fam (abrév* **bénéfice***)* profit

Les indicateurs de registre renseignent sur le niveau de langue

Level of language labels mark informal usages

HARRAP

FRENCH
BUSINESS
DICTIONARY

HARRAP

FRENCH BUSINESS DICTIONARY

English-French
French-English

HARRAP

First published in Great Britain in 1999
by Chambers Harrap Publishers Ltd
7 Hopetoun Crescent
Edinburgh EH7 4AY

ISBN 0245 503757 (France)
ISBN 0245 60656 4 (UK)

Dépôt légal : mars 1999

Typeset by Chambers Harrap Publishers Ltd, Edinburgh
Printed in France by MAME

Project manager and English lexicographer/
Directrice de projet et lexicographe anglophone
Anna Stevenson

French lexicographer/Lexicographe francophone
Georges Pilard

with/avec
Gearóid Cronin
Nicolas Dupuy
José A. Gálvez

Publishing manager/Direction éditoriale
Patrick White

Specialist consultants/Consultants spécialistes
Barbara Campbell
Teacher of Business English,
Institute of Applied Linguistics, Edinburgh

Iain Davidson BA Hons, MA, TESOL
Business Communication Consultant

Marc Fermin DEA
Lecturer in Modern Languages,
Glasgow Caledonian University, University of Paisley

Maddy Glas, Docteur de la Sorbonne
Professeur de Français des Affaires, INSEAD

Bob Norton
Head of Information Services,
Institute of Management, Corby, UK

Cathy Smith
Systems Controller,
Institute of Management, Corby, UK

Trademarks

Words considered to be trademarks have been designated in this dictionary by the symbol ®. However, no judgement is implied concerning the legal status of any trademark by virtue of the presence or absence of such a symbol.

Marques déposées

Les termes considérés comme des marques déposées sont signalés dans ce dictionnaire par le symbole ®. Cependant, la présence ou l'absence de ce symbole ne constitue nullement une indication quant à la valeur juridique de ces termes.

Contents
Table des Matières

Preface

Developed from Harrap's language databases and with the assistance of experts in business French and English, this completely new edition of the **Harrap French Business Dictionary** will prove an invaluable resource for students of business French and for all businesspeople who work with companies in the French-speaking world. It brings together in one volume terms from all areas that fall under the very broad heading of business: from sales and marketing, finance, accounting and computing, to the Stock Exchange, human resources and business management. Even the language of everyday office life - paper clips and correction fluid - is covered.

The growth of the Internet as a business tool and Britain's increasingly important role within the European Union are just two examples of how the business world is constantly evolving and is therefore a very productive area for new words and expressions. **Tiger economy**, **e-commerce**, **call centre** and **externalisation**, **site Web**, **monnaie unique**, which are now commonplace terms in the business world, can all be found in this book.

Our two main aims in this dictionary are:

- to put business language in **context**
- to provide **practical help** for businesspeople and students

Context is provided by giving many translated examples within entries, and hundreds of quotations from French and English books, newspapers and magazines. These quotations are presented in boxes after the relevant entry and show the application of the word or expression in the real business world.

Practical help is provided in the form of a unique two-colour 68-page supplement comprising:

- **Doing Business on the Internet**: a 26-page article guides you through the implications for businesspeople of the growth of the Internet. Advice is given on setting up your own Web site, buying and selling on the Internet, the Internet and the law, and the use of e-mail.

- E-mail also features in our French business communication section alongside more traditional forms of communication: letters, the telephone, faxes and memos. Annotated sample letters pick out the important points so that you can draft your own business letters in French.

- A lively description of the differences between business meetings in French- and English-speaking countries, including the key phrases you will hear and want to use.

- Advice on working with an interpreter that will help make both your and the interpreter's job easier.

- Table of countries and currencies.

- Table of information on French départements.

Préface

Pour l'homme d'affaires d'aujourd'hui, la maîtrise de l'anglais n'est plus un simple atout : elle est devenue une nécessité absolue.

Cette nouvelle édition entièrement revue et corrigée du **Harrap's Business** est un outil irremplaçable pour quiconque s'intéresse à l'anglais des affaires. Cet ouvrage a été conçu à partir des bases de données de la société Harrap, avec l'aide de spécialistes du français et de l'anglais des affaires. L'ouvrage couvre des domaines aussi variés que le marketing, la vente, la finance, la comptabilité, la Bourse, l'informatique, les ressources humaines et la gestion. Y figurent également des termes non spécialisés mais néanmoins essentiels lorsque l'on travaille dans un bureau, tels que trombone et surligneur.

L'importance grandissante de l'Internet dans le monde du commerce ainsi que l'expansion de l'Union européenne contribuent considérablement à l'enrichissement du vocabulaire des affaires. Des termes tels que **tiger economy**, **e-commerce**, **call centre** et **externalisation**, **site Web**, **monnaie unique**, aujourd'hui d'un usage courant, sont tous traités dans cet ouvrage.

Lors de la rédaction de ce dictionnaire, nos deux priorités furent les suivantes :

- présenter les termes et les expressions **en contexte**
- apporter une **aide pratique** à l'utilisateur

La **mise en contexte** est assurée par de nombreux exemples qui figurent avec leur traduction dans le corps des entrées, ainsi que par la présence de centaines de citations extraites de livres, de journaux et de magazines. Ces citations sont présentées dans des encadrés à la fin des entrées correspondantes et montrent comment les termes en question sont réellement utilisés dans le monde des affaires.

L'**aide pratique** à l'utilisateur est constituée d'un supplément de 69 pages entièrement nouveau qui comprend les rubriques suivantes :

- **L'Internet et le Monde des Affaires** : **Mode d'Emploi**, un article de 27 pages qui étudie les répercussions du développement de l'Internet sur le monde des affaires. L'utilisateur y trouvera de nombreux conseils sur la façon de créer son propre site Web, sur le commerce électronique, sur le droit et l'Internet, et sur l'utilisation du courrier électronique.

- Un guide de communication commerciale en anglais qui aborde les moyens de communication traditionnels tels que le courrier, le téléphone, le fax, et les notes de service et qui fournit à l'utilisateur de plus amples informations sur le courrier électronique. Des modèles de lettres avec annotations montrent à l'utilisateur comment rédiger des lettres d'affaires en anglais.

- Un article sur les différences entre les réunions d'affaires dans les pays francophones et anglophones, dans lequel l'utilisateur trouvera également les expressions les plus utiles et les plus fréquemment utilisées.

- Un article contenant de nombreux conseils pour faciliter la tâche de l'homme d'affaires travaillant avec un interprète.

- Un tableau des états du monde et de leur monnaie.

- Une liste des cinquante états américains.

Labels

Indications d'Usage

gloss [introduces an explanation]	=	glose [introduit une explication]
cultural equivalent [introduces a translation which has a roughly equivalent status in the target language]	≃	équivalent culturel [introduit une traduction dont les connotations dans la langue cible sont comparables]
abbreviation	*abbr, abrév*	abréviation
accounting	ACCT	comptabilité
adjective	*adj*	adjectif
administration	ADMIN	administration
adverb	*adv*	adverbe
North American English	*Am*	anglais américain
no longer in existence or renamed	*Anciennement*	terme n'ayant plus cours
insurance	ASSUR	assurances
auxiliary	*aux*	auxiliaire
banking	BANKING, BANQUE	banque
Belgian French	*Belg*	belgicisme
Stock Exchange	BOURSE	Bourse
British English	*Br*	anglais britannique
Canadian French	*Can*	canadianisme
accounting	COMPTA	comptabilité
computing	COMPTR	informatique
customs	CUSTOMS	douanes
conjunction	*conj*	conjonction
customs	DOUANES	douanes
economics	ECON, ÉCON	économie
European Union	EU	Union européenne
feminine	*f*	féminin
familiar	*Fam*	familier
finance	FIN	finance
no longer in existence or renamed	*Formerly*	terme n'ayant plus cours
insurance	INS	assurances
law	JUR, LAW	droit
masculine	*m*	masculin
masculine and feminine noun [same form for both genders, eg comptable *mf*]	*mf*	nom masculin et féminin [formes identiques]
masculine and feminine noun [different form in the feminine, eg conseiller(ère) *m,f*]	*m,f*	nom masculin et féminin [formes différentes]
marketing	MKTG	marketing
noun	*n*	nom
feminine noun	*nf*	nom féminin
feminine plural noun	*nfpl*	nom féminin pluriel

masculine noun	*nm*	nom masculin
masculine and feminine noun [same form for both genders, eg **comptable** *nmf*]	*nmf*	nom masculin ou féminin [formes identiques]
masculine and feminine noun [different form in the feminine, eg **conseiller, -ère** *nm,f*]	*nm,f*	nom masculin et féminin [formes différentes au féminin]
masculine plural noun	*nmpl*	nom masculin pluriel
computing	ORDINAT	informatique
plural	*pl*	pluriel
prefix	*pref, préf*	préfixe
preposition	*prep, prép*	préposition
pronoun	*pron*	pronom
Stock Exchange	ST EXCH	Bourse
suffix	*suff*	suffixe
Swiss French	*Suisse*	helvétisme
telephone and telecommunications	TEL, TÉL	téléphone et télécommunications
European Union	UE	Union européenne
verb	*v*	verbe
intransitive verb	*vi*	verbe intransitif
impersonal verb	*v impersonnel*	verbe impersonnel
reflexive verb	*vpr*	verbe pronominal
transitive verb	*vt*	verbe transitif
transitive verb used with a preposition [eg **postuler à** (to apply for); il a **postulé à** ce poste (he has applied for this job)]	*vt ind*	verbe transitif indirect [par exemple: **postuler à**; il a **postulé à** ce poste]
inseparable phrasal verb [phrasal verb where the verb and the adverb or preposition cannot be separated, eg **sign for**; to **sign for** goods received]	*vt insep*	verbe transitif à particule inséparable [par exemple: **sign for** (signer un reçu pour); to **sign for** goods received (signer à la réception des marchandises)]
separable phrasal verb [phrasal verb where the verb and the adverb or preposition can be separated, eg **lay off**; **they laid off** the workers]	*vt sep*	verbe transitif à particule séparable [par exemple: **lay off** (licencier); they **laid off** the workers (ils ont licencié les ouvriers)]

English-French
Anglais-Français

A3 1 *n (paper format)* A3 *m*; **a sheet of A3** une feuille de format A3

2 *adj* **A3 paper** papier *m* (format) A3

A4 1 *n (paper format)* A4 *m*; **a sheet of A4** une feuille de format A4

2 *adj* **A4 paper** papier *m* (format) A4

AA *n (abbr* **Advertising Association**) = organisme britannique dont le rôle est de veiller à la qualité des publicités et de défendre les intérêts des annonceurs et des agences de publicité

abandon *vt* (**a**) *(idea, project)* abandonner; **they have had to abandon expansion plans due to a fall in profits** ils ont été contraints d'abandonner leurs projets de développement à la suite d'une baisse des bénéfices

(**b**) INS *(ship, cargo)* abandonner (**to** à); **it was decided to abandon the ship to the insurers** il a été décidé d'abandonner le navire aux assureurs

(**c**) COMPTR *(file, routine)* abandonner

abandonment *n* (**a**) *(of idea, project)* abandon *m* (**b**) INS *(of ship, cargo)* délaissement *m*; **the shipping company issued a notice of abandonment to their insurers** la compagnie maritime a donné un avis de délaissement à ses assureurs

abeyance *n (suspense)* **the matter is still in abeyance** la question est toujours pendante *ou* en suspens; **the final decision on the project is still in abeyance** la décision finale concernant le projet reste en suspens

abort COMPTR 1 *n (of program)* suspension *f* d'exécution, abandon *m*

2 *vt (program)* suspendre l'exécution de, abandonner

above *adj* ci-dessus; **please contact me at the above address** veuillez me contacter à l'adresse ci-dessus

above-mentioned *adj* susmentionné(e); **this applies to the above-mentioned employees** ceci concerne les employés susnommés

above-the-line *adj* (**a**) MKTG **above-the-line advertising** coût *m* média (**b**) ACCT *(expenses)* au-dessus de la ligne ❑ **above-the-line accounts** comptes *mpl* de résultats courants

abroad *adv* à l'étranger; **to be abroad on business** être en voyage d'affaires à l'étranger

absentee *n* absent(e) *m,f*

absenteeism *n* absentéisme *m*

absolute *adj* (**a**) MKTG **absolute frequency** fréquence *f* absolue (**b**) ECON **absolute advantage** avantage *m* absolu; **absolute efficiency** efficience *f* absolue

absorb *vt (company)* absorber; **the business has been absorbed by a competitor** l'entreprise a été absorbée par un concurrent

absorption *n* (**a**) *(of company)* rachat *m*, absorption *f* (**b**) ACCT **absorption costing** méthode *f* du coût de revient complet

abstract *n (of article)* résumé *m*, abrégé *m*

A/C, a/c *n (abbr* **account**) c.

ACAS *n (abbr* **Advisory, Conciliation and Arbitration Service**) = organisme britannique indépendant d'arbitrage des conflits du travail

accelerated depreciation *n* ACCT amortissement *m* dégressif

acceleration *n* (**a**) FIN **acceleration clause** clause *f* accélératrice (**b**) **acceleration premium** prime *f* de rendement

accelerator *n* COMPTR accélérateur *m* ❑ **accelerator card** carte *f* accélératrice

accept *vt* (**a**) *(sum, offer)* accepter; FIN **to accept a bill** accepter un effet; **do you accept credit cards?** est-ce que vous prenez les cartes de crédit? (**b**) **to accept (delivery** *or* **shipment of) goods** réceptionner des marchandises, prendre livraison de marchandises

acceptance *n* (**a**) *(agreement)* acceptation *f*; FIN *(document)* effet *m* accepté, effet à payer; **to present a bill for acceptance** présenter une traite à l'acceptation ❑ *Am* **acceptance bank** banque *f* d'acceptation, banque d'escompte d'effets étrangers; **acceptance bill** effet contre acceptation;

acceptance fee commission *f* d'acceptation; *Am* **acceptance house** banque d'acceptation, maison *f* d'acceptation
(**b**) *(of something ordered)* réception *f*
(**c**) **acceptance sampling** contrôle *m* de qualité par échantillonnage pour acceptation

accepted *adj* FIN *(written on accepted bill)* accepté, bon pour acceptation □ **accepted bill** effet *m* accepté, acceptation *f*

accepting house *n Br* FIN banque *f* d'acceptation, maison *f* d'acceptation

acceptor *n* FIN *(of bill)* accepteur *m*, tiré *m*

access 1 *n* (**a**) *(right to contact, use)* accès *m*; **to have access to sth** avoir accès à qch; **I don't have access to that information** je n'ai pas accès à ce genre d'informations
(**b**) COMPTR accès *m*; **access denied** *(DOS message)* accès refusé □ **access code** code *m* d'accès; **access level** *(in network)* niveau *m* d'accès; **access provider** fournisseur *m* d'accès; **access time** temps *m* d'accès
2 *vt* COMPTR *(data)* accéder à; **can you access last year's figures?** est-ce que tu as accès aux chiffres de l'année dernière?

accident *n* accident *m* □ **accident insurance** assurance *f* (contre les) accidents; **accident policy** police *f* d'assurance accidents

accommodation *n* (**a**) FIN *(of money)* avance *f*, prêt *m* □ **accommodation bill** traite *f* ou effet *m* de complaisance (**b**) *(lodging)* logement *m* □ **accommodation allowance** indemnité *f* de logement

accord *n Am (agreement)* convention *f*, accord *m*

accordance *n* **in accordance with** en conformité avec, conformément à; **we must work in accordance with current regulations** il nous faut agir conformément à la réglementation en vigueur

according to *prep* (**a**) *(on the evidence of)* selon, d'après; **according to the latest report, profits have risen** selon le dernier rapport, les bénéfices ont augmenté (**b**) *(in accordance with)* suivant, conformément à; **according to instructions** suivant les ordres, conformément aux ordres

account *n* (**a**) FIN *(statement)* compte *m*, note *f*; **account payable** compte créditeur, dette *f* fournisseur; **accounts payable** dettes passives *ou* fournisseurs; **account receivable** compte client *ou* débiteur; **accounts receivable** dettes actives, créances *fpl* (clients); **to pay a sum on account** payer une somme en acompte; **as per** *or* **to account rendered** *(on statement)* suivant

compte *ou* relevé remis
(**b**) *(in shop)* compte *m*; **to have an account with John Lewis** avoir un compte chez John Lewis, être en compte avec John Lewis; **to settle an account** régler un compte; **put it on** *or* **charge it to my account** inscrivez-le *ou* mettez-le à mon compte; **cash or account?** vous payez *ou* réglez comptant ou est-ce que vous avez un compte chez nous?
(**c**) ACCT **accounts** *(of company)* comptabilité *f*; **to keep the accounts** tenir les livres *ou* les écritures *ou* la comptabilité □ **account balance** *(status)* situation *f* de compte; *(after audit)* reliquat *m* de compte; **account book** livre *m* de comptes, registre *m* de comptabilité; **accounts department** (service *m* de la) comptabilité
(**d**) BANKING compte *m*; **to open an account** (se faire) ouvrir un compte; **to close an account** fermer un compte; **to pay money into one's account** verser de l'argent à son compte; **to pay sb's salary directly into his/her account** verser le salaire de qn par virement direct sur son compte; **to overdraw an account** mettre un compte à découvert □ **account charges** frais *mpl* de tenue de compte; **account fee** commission *f* de compte; **account handling fee** commission de tenue de compte; **account holder** titulaire *mf* d'un compte; **account manager** chargé *m* de compte; **account number** numéro *m* de compte; **account statement** relevé *m* ou état *m* ou bordereau *m* de compte
(**e**) *(in advertising, marketing, PR)* budget *m*, compte-client *m*, client *m*; **we lost the Guinness account** nous avons perdu la clientèle de Guinness *ou* le budget Guinness □ **account director** directeur(trice) *m,f* des comptes-clients; **account executive** *(in advertising, marketing)* responsable *mf* de budget; *(in PR)* relationniste-conseil *mf*; **account handler** responsable des comptes-clients; **account manager** responsable client *ou* des comptes-clients
(**f**) ST EXCH **the account** la liquidation (mensuelle) □ **account day** (jour *m* de) règlement *m*; *Am* **account executive** agent *m* de change
(**g**) FIN *(of expenses)* état *m*, note *f*; *(of transactions)* exposé *m*
(**h**) **to set up in business on one's own account** s'installer à son compte, se mettre à son compte

▶ **account for** *vt insep* (**a**) *(explain)* **to account for sth** comptabiliser qch, justifier qch; **the strong pound accounts for the drop in exports** la solidité de la livre explique la baisse des exportations (**b**) *(make up)* représenter; **wine accounts for 5% of all exports** le vin représente 5% des exportations totales

accountable *adj (person)* responsable (**to sb** envers qn; **for sth** de qch); *(for sum of money)* redevable (**for** de); **he's directly accountable to the managing director** il rend compte directement au président-directeur général

accountancy *n Br* comptabilité *f*, expertise *f* comptable

accountant *n* comptable *mf*, agent *m* comptable

accounting *n* comptabilité *f*, expertise *f* comptable ❑ *accounting control* contrôle *m* de la comptabilité; *accounting day* journée *f* comptable; *accounting entry* écriture *f* comptable; *accounting entry sheet or form* bordereau *m* de saisie; *accounting method* méthode *f* de comptabilité; *accounting period* exercice *m* (financier), période *f* comptable; *accounting procedure* pratique *f* comptable; *accounting system* système *m* comptable, plan *m* comptable; *accounting year* exercice (financier), période comptable

accredited *adj* accrédité(e), autorisé(e), attitré(e)

accrual *n* (**a**) FIN *(of interest, debt, cost)* accumulation *f* (**b**) ACCT *accruals (expenses)* charges *fpl* à payer; *(income)* produits *mpl* à recevoir; **accrual of dividend** échéance *f* de dividende

accrue FIN 1 *vt (interest)* produire
2 *vi (of interest)* s'accumuler, courir; **interest accrues (as) from the 5th of the month** les intérêts courent à partir du 5 du mois

accrued *adj* FIN *accrued benefits (under pension scheme)* points *mpl* de retraite; ACCT *accrued charges* effets *mpl* à payer; FIN *accrued dividends* dividendes *mpl* accrus; ACCT *accrued expenses* frais *mpl* cumulés *ou* accumulés; ACCT *accrued income* effets *ou* produit *m* à recevoir; ST EXCH *accrued interest* intérêts *mpl* courus

> Throughout this year building societies have faced strong competition from National Savings and throughout the summer months, new savings flowed away from building society accounts, although **accrued interest** of £8bn helped offset the immediate impact of this outflow.

ACH *n* BANKING *(abbr* **automated clearing house**) chambre *f* de compensation automatisée

achieve *vt (aim, goal)* atteindre, parvenir à; **the company achieved all its objectives for the year** la société a atteint tous les objectifs qu'elle s'était fixés pour l'année; **the new marketing strategy achieved very little** la nouvelle stratégie de marketing a été peu efficace

achievement *n* réussite *f*; **the company is proud of its achievements this year** la société est fière des résultats obtenus cette année

acid test ratio *n* ACCT ratio *m* de liquidité immédiate

acknowledge *vt* **to acknowledge (receipt of) a letter** accuser réception d'une lettre; **we acknowledge receipt of your letter of 19 April** nous accusons réception de votre lettre du 19 avril, nous avons bien reçu votre lettre du 19 avril

acknowledg(e)ment *n* (**a**) acknowledgement (of receipt) *(of letter, e-mail)* accusé *m* de réception; *(of payment)* reçu *m*, récépissé *m*, quittance *f* ❑ *acknowledgement slip* accusé de réception (**b**) *acknowledgement of debt* reconnaissance *f* de dette

ACORN *n* MKTG *(abbr* **A Classification of Residential Neighbourhoods**) = classement des différents types de quartiers résidentiels existant en Grande-Bretagne en 39 catégories, utilisé par les entreprises pour mieux cibler leurs clients potentiels lors de campagnes commerciales

acquire *vt (goods, right)* acquérir; *(company, property)* faire l'acquisition de

acquired *adj* acquis(e) ❑ *acquired surplus* surplus *m* acquis

acquisition *n* acquisition *f* ❑ ACCT *acquisition cost* coût *m* d'acquisition

acquisitive *adj (company)* en (phase de) croissance externe; *(society)* d'acquisition

acquit *vt* FIN *(debt)* acquitter, s'acquitter de, régler

acquittance *n* FIN *(of debt)* acquittement *m*, décharge *f*, quittance *f*

across-the-board 1 *adj* général(e); **an across-the-board increase** une augmentation générale
2 *adv* à tous les niveaux; **this applies across-the-board** ceci s'applique à tous les niveaux; **we have had to cut salaries across-the-board** il nous a fallu procéder à une réduction générale des salaires

act 1 *n* (**a**) LAW *act (of parliament)* loi *f* (**b**) INS *act of God* (cas *m* de) force *f* majeure
2 *vi* **to act as secretary/chairperson** exercer les fonctions de secrétaire/président; **to act**

on behalf of or for sb agir au nom de qn, représenter qn

▶ **act on** vt insep to act on a letter donner suite à une lettre; **to act on sb's instructions** agir selon les instructions de qn

acting adj (temporary) suppléant(e), intérimaire ❑ **acting manager** directeur(trice) m,f intérimaire

action n (a) (activity) to take action prendre des mesures (b) LAW action f, procès m; **to bring an action against sb** intenter une action en justice contre qn, poursuivre qn en justice; **action for libel** procès ou plainte f en diffamation; **action for damages** action en dommages et intérêts

active adj (a) BANKING **active money** monnaie f circulante; **active partner** (in company) associé(e) m,f gérant(e), commandité(e) m,f
(b) ST EXCH (shares) actif(ive); (market) animé(e), actif; **there is an active demand for oils** les valeurs pétrolières sont très recherchées, il y a une forte demande de valeurs pétrolières
(c) COMPTR **active file** fichier m actif; **active matrix screen** écran m à matrice active; **active program** programme m en cours d'exécution; **active window** fenêtre f active ou activée

activity n (in business, market) activité f; **this week has seen a lot of activity on the Stock Market** la Bourse a été très active cette semaine ❑ **activity chart** graphique m des activités

actual 1 npl (a) **actuals** (real figures) chiffres mpl réels (b) ST EXCH **actuals** livraisons fpl physiques, marchandises fpl livrées au comptant
2 adj réel(elle) ❑ **actual cost** prix m de revient ou d'achat; **actual employment** emploi m effectif; **actual figures** chiffres mpl réels; ST EXCH **actual quotations** cours mpl effectifs; INS **actual total loss** perte f totale effective; **actual value** valeur f réelle

> **"**
> In the event of an **actual total loss** being paid the remains or salvage will be the property of the Corporation. If the salvage is not economically worthwhile then it should be made clear to the policyholder when the **actual total loss** is paid that the remains are their property and it is up to the policyholder to dispose of them.
> **"**

actuarial adj actuariel(elle) ❑ **actuarial tables** tables fpl de mortalité

actuary n actuaire mf

ad n Fam (for product, service) pub f; (for job) annonce f; **to put an ad in the paper** mettre ou insérer une annonce dans le journal ❑ **ad agency** agence f publicitaire ou de publicité

adapter card n COMPTR carte-adaptateur f

add vt ajouter (to à); (figures) additionner, totaliser; **to add the interest to the capital** ajouter l'intérêt au capital ❑ **added value** valeur f ajoutée

▶ **add to** vt insep (increase) augmenter; **this adds to our expenses** cela augmente (le montant de) nos dépenses; **next year we hope to add to our range of products** nous espérons élargir notre gamme de produits l'année prochaine

▶ **add up** 1 vt sep (figures) additionner, totaliser
2 vi (give correct total) être juste ou exact(e); **the figures don't add up** les chiffres sont faux; **the accounts won't add up** il y a quelque chose qui ne va pas dans les comptes

▶ **add up to** vt insep (amount to) s'élever à; **the assets add up to two million** l'actif s'élève à deux millions

addition n (a) (action) addition f; (thing added) ajout m (to à); (person) nouveau venu (nouvelle venue) m,f; **additions to the staff** adjonction f de personnel; **she's the latest addition to the marketing team** c'est la dernière recrue de l'équipe du marketing
(b) **in addition (to)** en plus (de); **personnel staff in addition to the management will be attending the meeting** la direction ainsi que les employés du service du personnel assisteront à la réunion

additional adj (investment, expenses) supplémentaire; **this will require additional investment** cela nécessitera un investissement supplémentaire ❑ **additional charge** supplément m (de prix); **at no additional charge** sans supplément; **additional clause** avenant m; **additional discount** surremise f; **additional expenditure** surcroît m de dépenses; FIN **additional payment** supplément; ADMIN **additional tax** impôt m additionnel; (because of underpayment) supplément d'imposition; **additional tax assessment** redressement m fiscal; **additional voluntary contribution** supplément m de cotisation retraite (payé volontairement)

add-on *n* COMPTR produit *m* supplémentaire *ou* complémentaire, extension *f*

address 1 *n* (a) *(of person, company)* adresse *f* ❑ **address book** carnet *m* d'adresses; **address label** étiquette-adresse *f*
(b) COMPTR adresse *f* ❑ **address file** fichier *m* d'adresses
2 *vt* (a) *(write address on)* **to address an envelope** mettre *ou* écrire l'adresse sur une enveloppe; **who's the letter addressed to?** à qui la lettre est-elle adressée?; **the letter was addressed to the personnel manager** la lettre était adressée au directeur du personnel
(b) *(direct)* adresser (**to** à); **please address all enquiries to the personnel department** faire parvenir toute demande de renseignements au service du personnel
(c) *(speak to)* s'adresser à; **to address a meeting** prendre la parole lors d'une réunion
(d) COMPTR adresser, accéder à

addressable *adj* MKTG *(audience, market)* utile

addressee *n* destinataire *mf*

adjourn 1 *vt (meeting)* ajourner
2 *vi (of meeting)* être ajourné(e); **the meeting adjourned at 11 o'clock** on a levé la séance à 11 heures; **to adjourn to another room** passer dans une autre pièce

adjudicate 1 *vt* juger, arbitrer; ADMIN *(claim)* adjuger; **to adjudicate sb bankrupt** déclarer qn en faillite
2 *vi (in dispute)* arbitrer

adjudication *n* jugement *m*, décision *f*, arrêt *m*; ADMIN *(of claim)* adjudication *f* ❑ **adjudication of bankruptcy, adjudication order** jugement déclaratif de faillite

adjudicative *adj* LAW déclaratif(ive), déclaratoire

adjudicator *n* juge *m*, arbitre *m*

adjust 1 *vt* (a) *(prices)* ajuster; *(figures, salaries)* rajuster, réajuster; *(accounts)* régulariser; **the figures have been seasonally adjusted** les chiffres sont les données corrigées des variations saisonnières; **pensions have been adjusted upwards/downwards** les pensions ont été revues à la hausse/à la baisse *ou* ont été augmentées/diminuées; **income adjusted for inflation** revenu réel compte tenu de l'inflation
(b) *(modify)* modifier; **the terms of the contract have been adjusted** les termes du contrat ont été modifiés; **production has been adjusted to meet demand** on a aligné la production sur la demande
(c) INS **to adjust an average** répartir une avarie; **to adjust a claim** régler une demande d'indemnité

adjustable *adj (rate)* variable

adjuster, *Am* **adjustor** *n* INS inspecteur *m* régleur

adjusting entry *n* ACCT écriture *f* de régularisation

adjustment *n (of prices)* ajustement *m*; *(of figures, salaries)* rajustement *m*, réajustement *m*; **no adjustment was made for seasonal variation** il n'y a pas eu de corrigé des variations saisonnières ❑ ACCT **adjustment account** compte *m* collectif

adjustor *Am* = **adjuster**

adman *n Fam* publicitaire *m*

admin *n Fam* (a) *(work)* travail *m* administratif; **there's a lot of admin in this job** il y a beaucoup de paperasserie dans ce travail (b) *(department)* administration *f*; **admin will take care of it** le personnel administratif *ou* l'administration s'en occupera ❑ **admin department** service *m* administratif

administer *vt (territory, region)* administrer; *(business, property)* administrer, gérer; *(laws)* appliquer ❑ *Am* **administered price** prix *m* imposé

administration *n* (a) *(management) (of territory, region)* administration *f*; *(of business, property)* administration, gestion *f* ❑ ACCT **administration costs, administration expenses** frais *mpl* d'administration *ou* de gestion; BANKING **administration fee** frais de dossier
(b) *(work)* travail *m* administratif; *(department)* administration *f* ❑ **administration department** service *m* administratif
(c) *Am (government)* **the Administration** le gouvernement (fédéral)

administrative *adj (work, skills)* administratif(ive); *(error)* d'administration; **for administrative convenience** pour faciliter le travail administratif ❑ ACCT **administrative costs** frais *mpl* d'administration *ou* de gestion; **administrative details** détails *mpl* d'ordre administratif; **administrative expenses** frais d'administration *ou* de gestion; **administrative headquarters** siège *m* administratif; **administrative staff** personnel *m* administratif; **administrative unit** unité *f* administrative

administrator *n* (**a**) *(of company)* administrateur(trice) *m,f*, gérant(e) *m,f*, gestionnaire *mf* (**b**) *(of liquidation of a company's assets)* administrateur(trice) *m,f* judiciaire

adopt *vt (measures, approach, design)* adopter; *(minutes)* approuver; **the company must adopt new working practices for an increase in efficiency** la société doit adopter de nouvelles méthodes de travail de façon à être plus performante

ADP *n* COMPTR *(abbr* **automatic data processing**) traitement *m* automatique des données

ad valorem *adj (duty, tax)* sur la valeur, ad valorem, proportionnel(elle)

advance **1** *n* (**a**) **in advance** *(book, apply, inform)* à l'avance; *(pay)* d'avance; **payable in advance** payable d'avance; **fixed in advance** fixé à l'avance; **thanking you in advance** *(in letter)* en vous remerciant à l'avance, avec mes remerciements anticipés □ **advance booking** réservation *f* à l'avance; **advance booking charter** achat *m* de bloc-sièges; **advance notice** préavis *m*; **advance payment** *(payment in full)* paiement *m* anticipé *ou* par anticipation; *(part payment)* arrhes *fpl*; **advance warning** préavis

(**b**) FIN *(of funds)* avance *f*, acompte *m*; **he asked for an advance of £200 on his salary** il a demandé une avance de 200 livres sur son salaire; **advances on securities** *or* **against collateral** prêts *mpl* sur titres □ **advance account** compte *m* d'avances

2 *vt* (**a**) FIN *(money)* avancer (**to** à); **we will advance him £500 before completion of the contract** nous lui verserons un acompte de 500 livres avant l'achèvement des travaux □ **sum advanced** avance *f*, acompte *m*

(**b**) *(prices)* augmenter, hausser

3 *vi (of shares)* augmenter (de prix), monter; **the stocks advanced to their highest point in May** les actions ont atteint leur valeur la plus haute au mois de mai

> ❝
> You will have to pay an arrangement fee of 0.5% of the **sum advanced** on all mortgages, except where an endowment mortgage is agreed and an insurance policy is taken out to cover the entire mortgage.
> ❞

advantage *n* avantage *m*; **knowledge of French is an advantage** la connaissance du français est un avantage; **to take advantage**

of sth *(offer, situation, opportunity)* profiter de qch

adverse *adj* FIN *(balance, budget)* déficitaire; **the stock markets showed an adverse reaction to the Chancellor's budget** les différentes places financières ont mal réagi au budget annoncé par le Chancelier de l'Échiquier

advert *n Fam (for product, service)* publicité *f*, réclame *f*; *(for job)* annonce *f*

advertise **1** *vt (product, service)* faire de la publicité *ou* de la réclame pour; *(job)* mettre une annonce pour; **as advertised on TV** vu(e) à la télé

2 *vi (to sell product, service)* faire de la publicité *ou* de la réclame; *(for job)* mettre une annonce; **to advertise for sb** passer une annonce pour trouver qn

advertisement *n (for product, service)* publicité *f*, réclame *f*; *(for job)* annonce *f*

advertising *n* publicité *f* □ **advertising account** budget *m* de publicité; **advertising agency** agence *f* publicitaire *ou* de publicité; **Advertising Association** = organisme britannique dont le rôle est de veiller à la qualité des publicités et de défendre les intérêts des annonceurs et des agences de publicité; **advertising campaign** campagne *f* de publicité; **advertising director** directeur(trice) *m,f* de la publicité; **advertising expenses** dépenses *fpl* de la publicité; **advertising medium** organe *m* de publicité; **advertising schedule** programme *m* des annonces; **advertising space** espace *m* ou emplacement *m* réservé à la publicité

advice *n* (**a**) *(opinion)* conseils *mpl*; **to take legal advice** consulter un avocat (**b**) *(notice)* avis *m*; **as per advice** suivant avis; **until further advice** jusqu'à nouvel avis □ **advice note** lettre *f* ou note *f* d'avis

advise *vt* (**a**) *(give advice to)* conseiller; **to advise sb to do sth** conseiller à qn de faire qch; **the company lawyer has advised caution** l'avocat de l'entreprise a recommandé la prudence

(**b**) *(inform)* aviser, informer; **we are pleased to advise you that…** nous avons le plaisir de vous informer que…; **we should advise you that you have exceeded your credit limit** nous vous informons que vous avez dépassé votre découvert autorisé

(**c**) BANKING, FIN **to advise a draft** aviser d'une traite, donner avis d'une traite

adviser, advisor *n* conseiller(ère) *m,f*

advisory *adj* consultatif(ive) □ **advisory board** comité *m* consultatif; BANKING **ad-**

visory **committee** comité de restructuration; **advisory service** service *m* de renseignements

> ❝
> For important projects, one may also use an **advisory board** representing those who will be most influenced by the project.
> ❞

affidavit *n* LAW affidavit *m*

affiliate *n Am* société *f* affiliée, filiale *f*

affiliated *adj (member, organization)* affilié(e) ❑ **affiliated company** société *f* affiliée, filiale *f*

affiliation *n* société *f* affiliée, filiale *f*

affirmative *adj* (**a**) **to take affirmative action (to do sth)** prendre des mesures (pour faire qch); **we should take affirmative action to make our intentions clear in this marketplace** il nous faut prendre des mesures de façon à faire connaître clairement nos intentions sur ce marché (**b**) *Am* **to take affirmative action** prendre des mesures anti-discriminatoires

affluence *n* richesse *f*; **the affluence of the company's assets is well known** la société est connue pour l'importance de son actif

affluent *adj* riche ❑ **the affluent society** la société d'abondance

afford *vt* (**a**) *(have enough money for)* **to be able to afford sth** avoir les moyens d'acheter qch; **we can afford to pay all our creditors by the end of the year** nous avons les moyens de payer nos créanciers d'ici la fin de l'année; **the company cannot afford any more new software** la société n'a pas les moyens d'investir davantage dans l'achat de logiciels (**b**) *(allow oneself)* **we cannot afford to lose these members of staff** on ne peut pas se permettre de perdre ces employés; **we can afford to wait another few days** on peut se permettre d'attendre quelques jours de plus

afloat *adv* **to keep sb afloat** renflouer qn; **to keep a business/the economy afloat** maintenir une entreprise/l'économie à flot; FIN **to keep bills afloat** faire circuler des effets; **many small businesses are struggling to stay afloat** de nombreuses petites entreprises ont du mal à se maintenir à flot

> ❝
> When the company's credit is exhausted the directors may attempt to **keep** the company **afloat** by themselves by making unsecured loans to it.
> ❞

aforementioned *adj* susmentionné(e); **with reference to the aforementioned items,...** en ce qui concerne les articles susmentionnés,...

aforesaid *adj* susmentionné(e), susdit(e)

after-hours dealing *n* ST EXCH transactions *fpl* hors bourse

aftermarket *n* ST EXCH = état du marché pour une action après son entrée en Bourse

after-sales *adj* après-vente ❑ **after-sales (department)** service *m* après-vente; **after-sales marketing** mercatique *f* ou marketing *m* après-vente; **after-sales service** service après-vente

> ❝
> It is worth considering whether or not the supplier can offer the level of **after-sales service** that you require, since like any other type of equipment a photocopier requires regular servicing and maintenance in order to keep it operating at peak efficiency.
> ❞

after-tax *adj* **after-tax profit** bénéfices *mpl* après impôts; **after-tax salary** salaire *m* après impôts

against *prep* (**a**) *(in opposition to)* contre; **the workers are against the idea of striking** les travailleurs ne veulent pas se mettre en grève; **to be insured against fire/theft** être assuré(e) contre l'incendie/le vol; INS **against all risks** contre tous les risques (**b**) *(in relation to)* par rapport à; **the pound rose/fell against the dollar** la livre a augmenté/baissé par rapport au dollar; **to get an advance against one's salary** recevoir une avance sur son salaire

agency *n* agence *f* ❑ **agency account** compte *m* agence; **agency agreement** contrat *m* de mandat, accord *m* de représentation; **agency contract** contrat d'agence; **agency fee** commission *f* de gestion, frais *mpl* d'agence

agenda *n* *(of meeting)* ordre *m* du jour, programme *m*; **to draw up an agenda** dresser l'ordre du jour; **to place a question on the agenda** inscrire une question à l'ordre du jour; **the first item on the agenda** la première question à l'ordre du jour

agent *n* agent *m*, représentant(e) *m,f*; **agent for Mercury Ltd** représentant de Mercury Ltd; **he is our agent in the Far East** c'est notre agent pour l'Extrême-Orient ❑ **sole agent** agent exclusif; **to be sole agent for Rover** avoir la représentation exclusive de Rover

aggregate 1 *n* somme *f* totale, montant *m* global

2 *adj* total(e), global(e); **for an aggregate period of three years** pendant trois ans en tout □ **aggregate demand** demande *f* globale; **aggregate economic activity** ensemble *m* des activités économiques; **aggregate net increment** accroissement *m* global net; **aggregate output** production *f* globale; **aggregate supply** offre *f* globale

agio *n* FIN **(a)** *(price)* agio *m*, prix *m* du change □ **agio account** compte *m* d'agio **(b)** *(business)* commerce *m* du change

agiotage *n* agiotage *m*

AGM *n* *(abbr* **annual general meeting)** AGA *f*

agree 1 *vt* **(a)** *(reach agreement on)* *(price, conditions)* s'accorder *ou* se mettre d'accord sur; **to be agreed** *(date)* à convenir; *(price)* à débattre; **unless otherwise agreed** sauf arrangement contraire; **as agreed** comme convenu **(b)** *(approve)* **to agree the accounts** *or* **the books** faire accorder les livres; **the figures were agreed between the accountants** les chiffres ont été acceptés (d'un commun accord) par les experts-comptables

2 *vi* **(a)** *(of books, figures)* s'accorder **(b)** MKTG **to agree and counter** approuver et contre-argumenter d'un commun accord

▶ **agree on** *vt insep (price, date)* convenir de

agreed *adj (price)* convenu(e), forfaitaire

agreement *n* **(a)** *(arrangement, contract)* accord *m* **(on** *or* **about** sur); **to break an agreement** rompre un accord; **to have an agreement with sb** avoir conclu *ou* passé un accord avec qn; **to enter into** *or* **conclude an agreement with sb** passer un accord avec qn; **an agreement has been concluded between the two parties** un accord est intervenu entre les deux parties; **to come to an agreement** parvenir à un accord; **to sign an agreement** signer un accord; **to sign a legal agreement (to do sth)** s'engager (par) devant notaire (à faire qch); **to abide by the agreement** s'en tenir à ce qui a été convenu; **our agreement was that...** nous avions convenu que...

(b) *(understanding)* accord *m*, entente *f*; **as per agreement** comme (il a été) convenu; **by mutual agreement** de gré à gré, à l'amiable, d'un commun accord

agribusiness *n* agrinégoce *m*

agriculture *n* agriculture *f*

aid *n* aide *f*, assistance *f*; **in aid of** au profit de

AIDA *n* MKTG *(abbr* **attention-interest-desire-action)** AIDA *m*

AIO *n* MKTG *(abbr* **activities, interests and opinions)** AIO *mpl* □ **AIO research** étude *f* AIO

air *n* **by air** par avion □ **air cargo** fret *m* aérien; **air letter** aérogramme *m*; **air transport** transports *mpl* aériens

aircraft *n* avion *m*

airfreight 1 *n* transport *m* par avion; *(price)* fret *m*, frais *mpl* (de transport par avion); *(cargo)* fret aérien

2 *vt (goods)* transporter par avion

airline *n* compagnie *f* aérienne

airmail 1 *n (service)* poste *f* aérienne; **by airmail** par avion □ **airmail letter** aérogramme *m*

2 *adv* **to send sth airmail** envoyer qch par avion

3 *vt (letter, parcel)* envoyer par avion

airport *n* aéroport *m* □ **airport tax** taxe *f* d'aéroport

align *vt* **(a)** COMPTR *(characters, graphics)* aligner, cadrer **(b)** FIN *(currency)* aligner **(on** sur); **to align two different strategies** harmoniser deux stratégies différentes, rendre deux stratégies différentes compatibles

alignment *n* **(a)** COMPTR *(of characters, graphics)* alignement *m*, cadrage *m* **(b)** FIN *(of currencies)* alignement *m*

all-in 1 *adj (price)* tout compris, forfaitaire □ **all-in insurance** assurance *f* tous risques; INS **all-in policy** police *f* tous risques

2 *adv* tout compris; **the computing system costs £3,000 all-in** le système informatique coûte 3000 livres, tout compris

allocate *vt* **(a)** *(resources, money, capital)* affecter, attribuer **(to** à); *(duties)* assigner **(to** à); *(time)* prévoir **(to** pour) **(b)** ST EXCH *(shares)* attribuer, allouer

allocation *n* **(a)** *(of resources, money, capital)* affectation *f*, attribution *f*; *(of duties)* assignation *f*; *(of time)* prévision *f* **(b)** ST EXCH *(of shares)* attribution *f*, allocation *f*

allot *vt* **(a)** *(sum of money)* affecter **(to** à); *(job, task)* assigner **(to** à); **the funds have been allotted to the R&D department** les fonds ont été affectés au service recherche et développement **(b)** ST EXCH *(shares)* attribuer, allouer

allotment *n* **(a)** *(of sum of money)* affectation *f*; *(of job, task)* assignation *f* **(b)** ST EXCH *(of shares)* attribution *f*, allocation *f* □ **allotment letter** avis *m* d'attribution

all-out *adj (strike)* tous azimuts; *(effort)* acharné(e); **to make an all-out effort to do sth** faire tout son possible pour faire qch

allow *vt* (**a**) *(give)* **to allow sb a discount** faire un escompte *ou* une remise à qn; **the bank allows 5% interest on deposits** la banque alloue *ou* attribue 5% d'intérêt sur les dépôts (**b**) *(accept) (claim)* admettre (**c**) *(take into account)* prévoir, compter; **allow a week for delivery** il faut prévoir *ou* compter une semaine pour la livraison

▸ **allow for** *vt insep* tenir compte de; *(difficulties, delay)* prévoir; **after allowing for** *(discount, expenses)* déduction faite de; **to allow for some wastage** prévoir plus large; **we have to allow an extra 10% for carriage** il faut prévoir un supplément de 10% pour le transport; **has that been allowed for in your figures?** en avez-vous tenu compte dans vos estimations?

allowable *adj* admissible, permis(e); *(claim)* recevable; *(expense)* déductible, remboursable

allowance *n* (**a**) ADMIN *(grant)* allocation *f*; *(for housing, travel, food)* indemnité *f* (**b**) FIN *(discount)* déduction *f*, concession *f*; *(for bad quality)* réfraction *f*

all-time *adj* **unemployment is at an all-time low** le chômage n'a jamais été aussi bas; **sales have reached an all-time high** les ventes ont atteint un niveau record

alphasort COMPTR **1** *n* tri *m* alphabétique; **to do an alphasort on sth** trier qch par ordre alphabétique

   2 *vt* trier par ordre alphabétique

alpha stocks *npl* ST EXCH valeurs *fpl* de père de famille *ou* de premier ordre

alt *n* COMPTR **alt (key)** touche *f* alt

amalgamate 1 *vt (companies)* fusionner; *(industries)* unifier

   2 *vi (of companies)* fusionner

amalgamation *n (of companies)* fusion *f*

amend *vt (resolution, motion, text)* amender; **the report has been amended to include the latest sales figures** le rapport a été modifié de façon à faire figurer le dernier chiffre des ventes

amendment *n (to resolution, motion, text)* amendement *m*

American Express card *n* carte *f* American Express

American-style option *n* ST EXCH option *f* américaine

Amex *n* (**a**) *(abbr* **American Stock Exchange**) = deuxième place boursière des États-Unis (**b**) *(abbr* **American Express**) American Express

amortizable *adj* FIN *(debt)* amortissable

amortization *n* FIN *(of debt)* amortissement *m*

amortize *vt* FIN *(debt)* amortir

amount *n (sum of money)* somme *f*; *(total)* montant *m*, total *m*; **amount due** montant dû, somme due; **she billed us for the amount of £50** elle nous a présenté une facture d'un montant de 50 livres; **you're in credit to the amount of £100** vous avez un crédit de 100 livres; **please find enclosed a cheque to the amount of $100** veuillez trouver ci-joint un chèque de 100 dollars

▸ **amount to** *vi* s'élever à, se monter à; **profits last year amounted to several million dollars** les bénéfices pour l'année dernière se chiffrent à plusieurs millions de dollars; **the company has debts amounting to over £200,000** les dettes de la société se montent à plus de 200 000 livres

analog *adj* COMPTR analogique

analyse *vt* analyser; *(account)* dépouiller, décomposer

analysis *n* analyse *f*; *(of account)* dépouillement *m*, décomposition *f*

analyst *n* analyste *mf*

annual *adj (holiday, payment, report)* annuel(elle) ❑ *annual accounts* bilan *m* annuel, comptes *mpl* de clôture *ou* de fin d'exercice; *annual budget* budget *m* annuel; *annual contribution (to pension scheme)* cotisation *f* annuelle; ACCT *annual depreciation* dépréciation *f* annuelle, amortissement *m* annuel; *annual earnings (of company)* recette(s) *f(pl)* annuelle(s); *(of person)* revenu *m* annuel; *annual general meeting* assemblée *f* générale (annuelle); *annual guaranteed salary* salaire *m* annuel garanti; *annual income* revenu annuel; FIN *annual instalment* annuité *f*; *annual leave* congé *m* annuel; *annual percentage rate* taux *m* effectif global; *annual profit* profit *m* annuel; *annual report* rapport *m* annuel de gestion; *annual returns* déclarations *fpl* annuelles; *annual salary* salaire annuel; **he has an annual salary of £50,000** il gagne 50 000 livres par an; *annual sales figures* chiffre *m* d'affaires annuel; *annual turnover* chiffre d'affaires annuel

annualize *vt* annualiser; **the annualized figures** le montant total pour un an ❑ *annualized percentage rate* taux *m* effectif global

annually *adv* annuellement, tous les ans

annuity *n (regular income)* rente *f* (annuelle); *(for life)* viager *m*, rente viagère; *(investment)* viager; **to invest money in an annuity, to buy an annuity** placer son argent en viager; **to pay sb an annuity** servir *ou* faire une rente à qn

annul *vt (contract)* annuler, résilier, résoudre

annulment *n (of contract)* annulation *f*, résiliation *f*, résolution *f*

anonymous FTP *n* COMPTR protocole *m* de transfert anonyme

answer **1** *n* réponse *f*; **in answer to your letter** en réponse à votre lettre; **there's no answer** *(on telephone)* ça ne répond pas
2 *vt (letter)* répondre à; **to answer the telephone** répondre au téléphone

answering *adj* **answering machine** répondeur *m* (téléphonique); **answering service** service *m* de répondeur téléphonique

answerphone *n* répondeur *m* (téléphonique)

anticipate *vt* **(a)** *(expect)* prévoir; **we anticipate a good response to our advertisement** nous attendons de bons résultats de notre annonce publicitaire □ **anticipated sales** (taux *m* de) ventes *fpl* prévues
(b) *(be prepared for)* anticiper; **we anticipated our competitors by launching our product first** nous avons devancé la concurrence en lançant notre produit les premiers; **he anticipated the fall in price and sold early** il a anticipé la baisse des prix et a vendu avant

anticipation *n* **in anticipation of** en prévision de; **they raised their prices in anticipation of increased inflation** ils ont augmenté leurs prix en prévision d'une hausse de l'inflation

anti-dumping *adj (laws, legislation)* antidumping

anti-glare *adj* COMPTR *(filter, screen)* antireflet

anti-inflationary *adj (measures, policy)* anti-inflationniste

antitrust *adj Am* ECON anti-trust

> " ... Unlike the United States which takes a structural approach to **antitrust** policy, in which the possession of monopoly power is itself regarded as objectionable, the UK has taken a more open view of the benefits of promoting competition. "

antivirus *n* COMPTR antivirus *m* □ **antivirus program** programme *m* antivirus

AO(C)B *(abbr* **any other (competent) business)** divers

APEX *adj (abbr* **advanced purchase excursion)** *APEX fare* tarif *m* apex; *APEX ticket* billet *m* apex

apologize *vi* s'excuser; **to apologize to sb for sth** s'excuser de qch auprès de qn, présenter ses excuses à qn pour qch; **we apologize for any inconvenience** veuillez nous excuser pour les désagréments occasionnés

apology *n* excuses *fpl*; **please accept our apologies for the delay** veuillez accepter nos excuses pour ce retard; **the director sends his apologies** le directeur vous prie de l'excuser

append *vt (list, document)* joindre **(to** à); *(signature)* apposer **(to** à); *(notes, comments)* ajouter **(to** à); COMPTR *(to database)* ajouter **(to** à); **to append a document to a file** annexer *ou* joindre un document à un dossier; **please refer to the lists appended to this document** veuillez vous reporter aux listes jointes au présent document

appendix *n (to document, report, book)* appendice *m*

applicant *n (for job)* candidat(e) *m,f*, postulant(e) *m,f* **(for** a); *(for loan, funding, patent)* demandeur(euse) *m,f* **(for** de); FIN *(for shares)* souscripteur(trice) *m,f* **(for** de); *(for trademark)* déposant(e) *m,f* **(for** de)

application *n* **(a)** *(for help, loan, funding, patent)* demande *f* **(for** de); *(for job)* demande, candidature *f* **(for** de); **to submit an application** *(for help, loan, funding, patent)* faire une demande; *(for job)* présenter sa candidature; **to make an application for sth** formuler une demande pour obtenir qch; **closing date for applications** date limite de dépôt de candidatures; **full details on application** informations complètes sur demande □ **application form** *(for job)* formulaire *m* de candidature; *(for subscription)* bulletin *m* d'abonnement
(b) ST EXCH **application for shares** demande *f* de titres en souscription, souscription *f* d'actions; **to make an application for shares** souscrire (à) des actions; **payable on application** payable à la souscription □ **application form** *(for shares)* bulletin *m* de souscription
(c) COMPTR application *f*

apply *vi* **(a) to apply to sb for sth** s'adresser *ou* recourir à qn pour obtenir qch; **apply to**

the **personnel office** adressez-vous au service du personnel; **to apply for a job** faire une demande d'emploi; **she has decided to apply for the job** elle a décidé de poser sa candidature pour cet emploi; **to apply for a grant** faire une demande de bourse; **apply within** (sign) s'adresser ici; **to apply in writing** écrire; **to apply in person** se présenter

(**b**) ST EXCH **to apply for shares** souscrire (à) des actions

appoint vt (**a**) (person) nommer; (committee) constituer; **to appoint sb to a post** nommer qn à un poste; **Mr Johnston has been appointed general manager** M. Johnston a été nommé directeur général; **he's our newly appointed sales manager** c'est notre nouveau chef de vente, c'est le chef de vente que nous venons de nommer (**b**) (date, time, place) fixer; **let's appoint a time for the meeting** fixons une heure pour la réunion

appointed adj (**a**) (date, time, place) fixé(e) (**b**) *appointed agent* agent m attitré

appointee n candidat(e) retenu(e) m,f

appointment n (**a**) (meeting) rendez-vous m; **to make** or **fix an appointment with sb** prendre rendez-vous avec qn; **to break an appointment** ne pas se présenter à un rendez-vous; **to cancel an appointment** annuler un rendez-vous; **please telephone if you cannot make** or **keep your appointment** veuillez téléphoner s'il vous est impossible de venir à votre rendez-vous; **to meet** or **see sb by appointment** recevoir qn sur rendez-vous; **by appointment only** sur rendez-vous; **have you got an appointment?** avez-vous un rendez-vous? □ *appointments diary* carnet m de rendez-vous, agenda m

(**b**) (to job) nomination f, désignation f

(**c**) (job held) poste m, emploi m; **to hold an appointment** être préposé(e) à un emploi; **he's been offered an appointment on the board** on lui a proposé un poste au conseil d'administration

apportion vt (taxes, expenses) répartir

apportionment n (of taxes, expenses) répartition f

appraisal n (of standards, personnel) évaluation f; (of object for insurance purposes) estimation f, appréciation f; (before auction) prisée f; **to carry out an appraisal** conduire une expertise

appraise vt (standards, personnel) évaluer; (object for insurance purposes, before auction) estimer

appreciate vi (of goods, investment, shares) prendre de la valeur; (of value, price) augmenter; **the euro has appreciated in terms of other currencies** l'euro s'est apprécié vis-à-vis des autres monnaies

appreciation n (of goods, investment, shares) augmentation f de la valeur; (of value, price) augmentation

apprentice **1** n apprenti(e) m,f
2 vt **to apprentice sb to sb** placer qn en apprentissage chez qn

apprenticeship n apprentissage m; **to serve one's apprenticeship (with sb)** faire son apprentissage (chez qn); **she did an apprenticeship as a carpenter** elle a fait un apprentissage de charpentier

appro n Br Fam (abbr **approval**) **on appro** à l'essai; **to buy sth on appro** acheter qch à l'essai; **to send sth on appro** envoyer qch à titre d'essai

appropriate vt (funds) affecter (**to/for** à); **£4,000 has been appropriated to upgrading computers** 4000 livres ont été affectées à l'augmentation de mémoire des ordinateurs

appropriation n (of funds) affectation f; (of payment) imputation f; **appropriation to the reserve** dotation f au compte de provisions □ *appropriation account* compte m d'affectation

approval n (**a**) (sanction) approbation f; **subject to approval** soumis(e) à l'approbation; **to submit sth for approval (by sb)** soumettre qch à l'approbation (de qn); **for (your) approval** (on document) pour approbation

(**b**) (of document) ratification f, homologation f

(**c**) **on approval** à l'essai; **to buy sth on approval** acheter qch à l'essai; **to send sth on approval** envoyer qch à titre d'essai; Am **approvals** (goods) marchandises fpl envoyées à l'essai

approve vt (action, plan, proposal, accounts) approuver; (document) ratifier, homologuer; (contract) agréer; (proposal) approuver, agréer; **read and approved** (on document) lu et approuvé; **the plan must be approved by the committee** il faut que le projet reçoive l'approbation du comité

approved adj ADMIN (officially) approuvé homologué(e) □ *approved dealer* concessionnaire mf agréé(e)

approx adv (abbr **approximately**) env.

approximately adv environ

approximation *n* approximation *f*

APR *n* (*abbr* **annual** *or* **annualized percentage rate**) TEG *m*

aptitude test *n* test *m* d'aptitude

arbitrage *n* FIN, ST EXCH arbitrage *m*

> ❝
> They had been playing in a high stakes financial game known as risk **arbitrage**, hoping to get ahead of the rapid run-up in a company's share price when it became the object of a takeover (or the reversal of fortune that occurred when a takeover fell apart).
> ❞

arbitrager *n* FIN, ST EXCH arbitragiste *mf*

arbitrate 1 *vt* arbitrer, juger, trancher
2 *vi* décider en qualité d'arbitre, arbitrer

arbitration *n* arbitrage *m*; **to go to arbitration** recourir à l'arbitrage; **they referred the dispute to arbitration** ils ont soumis le conflit à l'arbitrage; **procedure by arbitration** procédure *f* arbitrale; **settlement by arbitration** règlement *m* par arbitrage ❑ **arbitration board** commission *f* paritaire d'arbitrage; **arbitration clause** clause *f* d'arbitrage; **arbitration court** tribunal *m* arbitral; **arbitration tribunal** tribunal *m* arbitral

arbitrator *n* arbitre *m*, médiateur(trice) *m,f*; **the dispute has been referred to the arbitrator** le conflit a été soumis à l'arbitrage

archive *vt* COMPTR archiver

area *n* (*region*) région *f*; **the London area** la région de Londres ❑ *Am* TEL **area code** indicatif *m*; **area manager** directeur(trice) *m,f* régionale

Ariel *n* ST EXCH= système informatique qui rend possible les operations boursières entre souscripteurs sans passer par la Bourse de Londres

arrange 1 *vt* (*meeting, trip*) arranger; (*time, date*) fixer
2 *vi* **to arrange to do sth** s'arranger pour faire qch; (*with someone else*) convenir ou prévoir de faire qch; **let's arrange a time to meet** fixons une heure pour un rendez-vous; **the meeting is arranged for noon tomorrow** la réunion est prévue pour demain midi

arrangement *n* (*understanding, agreement*) arrangement *m*; FIN (*with creditors*) accommodement *m*; **to come to an arrangement with sb** faire un arrangement avec qn; **he came to an arrangement with the bank** il est parvenu à un accord avec la banque; **price by arrangement** prix *m* à débattre; (*after bankruptcy*) concordat *m*; **special designs by arrangement** autres modèles sur demande; **by prior arrangement** sur accord préalable

arrears *npl* arriéré *m*; **we're three months in arrears on the loan payments** nous devons trois mois de traites; **to get into arrears** s'arriérer; **to be paid a month in arrears** être payé(e) en fin du mois; **interest on arrears** intérêts *mpl* moratoires; **salary with arrears effective as from 1 March** augmentation avec effect rétroactif au 1 mars; **arrears of interest** intérêts non payés; **arrears of work** travail *m* en retard

arrival *n* (*of goods*) arrivage *m*; (*of person, aeroplane*) arrivée *f*; **to await arrival** (*on letter*) prière d'attendre l'arrivée

arrive *vi* **to arrive at sth** (*solution, decision*) arriver à qch, parvenir à qch; **to arrive at a price** se mettre d'accord sur un prix

arrow key *n* COMPTR touche *f* fléchée, touche de direction

article 1 *n* (**a**) LAW (*in agreement, treaty*) article *m*, clause *f*; (*in contract*) stipulation *f* ❑ **articles of apprenticeship** contrat *m* d'apprentissage; **articles of association** statuts *mpl* (*d'une société à responsabilité limitée*); **articles and conditions** (*of sale, contract*) cahier *m* des charges
(**b**) (*item*) article *m*
2 *vt* (*to trade*) mettre en apprentissage; (*to profession*) mettre en stage; **to article sb to a tradesman** mettre qn en apprentissage chez un commerçant ❑ **articled clerk** clerc *m* d'avoué (*lié par un contrat d'apprentissage*)

> ❝
> Neither a sole trader nor a partnership is inhibited by legal formalities when commencing trading. For a company, sizeable fees may be payable because of the need for legal formalities to be followed. A solicitor may be instructed to draft the company's memorandum and **articles of association**, and a registration fee is payable.
> ❞

artificial person *n* personne *f* morale

asap *adv* (*abbr* **as soon as possible**) dès que possible; **we need to reply asap** il faut qu'on réponde dès que possible

ascending sort *n* COMPTR tri *m* en ordre croissant

ASCII *n* COMPTR (*abbr* **American Standard Code for Information**

Interchange) ASCII *m* ◻ **ASCII code** code *m* ASCII; **ASCII file** fichier *m* ASCII

ASEAN *n* (*abbr* **Association of South East Asian Nations**) ANASE *f*

> "
> If the more economically puny **ASEAN** countries (Indonesia, Malaysia, Singapore, Brunei, Thailand and the Philippines) were to bury their reservations, then the high growth from other partners, including such tigers as Thailand and South Korea alongside the more mature economies of Japan and Australia, could mean a dynamic coalition.
> "

asked price *n Am* ST EXCH cours *m* offert, cours vendeur

asking price *n* prix *m* demandé

aspirational group *n* MKTG groupe *m* de référence

assembly *n* (**a**) (*meeting*) assemblée *f*, réunion *f* (**b**) (*of machine, furniture*) assemblage *m*, montage *m* ◻ **assembly line** chaîne *f* de montage; **to work on an assembly line** travailler à la chaîne (**c**) COMPTR assemblage *m* ◻ **assembly language** langage *m* d'assemblage.

assess *vt* (**a**) (*damage*) évaluer; (*value*) estimer; **to assess a property for taxation** évaluer *ou* calculer la valeur imposable d'une propriété; **they assessed the damages at £500** ils ont fixé les dommages et intérêts à 500 livres (**b**) (*tax*) établir; **to assess sb's income** (*for tax purposes*) évaluer les revenus de qn ◻ **assessed income** revenu *m* imposable

assessable income *n* assiette *f* de l'impôt

assessment *n* (**a**) (*of damage*) évaluation *f*; (*of value*) estimation *f* (**b**) · (*of tax*) établissement; (*of income*) evaluation *f*

assessor *n* expert *m*; *Am* **assessor of taxes** inspecteur(trice) *m,f* des contributions directes

asset *n* (**a**) FIN **assets** (*of company*) actif *m*; (*personal*) patrimoine *m*; LAW (*of inheritance, company*) masse *f*; (*on liquidation after bankruptcy*) masse active; **assets and liabilities** actif et passif; **total assets** total de l'actif; **excess of assets over liabilities** excédent *m* de l'actif sur le passif ◻ **asset management** gestion *f* de capital; **asset stripper** dépeceur *m* d'entreprise; **asset stripping** démantèlement *m* d'entreprise; **asset turnover** rotation *f* des capitaux;

asset valuation réserve *f*, provision *f* pour évaluation d'actif; ACCT **asset value** valeur *f* de l'actif

(**b**) (*advantage*) atout *m*; **she's a real asset to the company** elle apporte beaucoup à l'entreprise

assign *vt* (*task*) assigner (**to** à); (*funds*) affecter (**to** à); (*goods, debts*) céder, transférer (**to** à); (*shares*) attribuer (**to** à); **to assign sb to do sth** charger qn de faire qch; **Robert has been assigned to the marketing department** Robert a été nommé au marketing

assignment *n* (*of task*) attribution *f*; (*of funds*) affectation *f*; (*of goods, debts*) cession *f*, transfert *m*; (*of shares*) attribution *f*; ACCT **assignment of accounts receivable, assignment of debts** transfert *m* de créances

assistant **1** *n* assistant(e) *m,f*
2 *adj* adjoint(e) ◻ **assistant general manager** directeur(trice) *m,f* général(e) adjoint(e); **assistant manager** sous-directeur(trice) *m,f*

associate **1** *n* (*in business*) associé(e) *m,f*, partenaire *mf*
2 *adj* associé(e) ◻ **associate company** société *f* affiliée, filiale *f*; **associate director** directeur(trice) *m,f* adjoint(e)

association *n* association *f*, société *f*; **to form an association** constituer une société

assume *vt* (*undertake*) assumer; **he will assume responsibility for the new department** il sera responsable du nouveau service; INS **to assume all risks** assumer tous les risques

assurance *n Br* assurance *f* ◻ **assurance company** compagnie *f* d'assurances; **assurance policy** police *f* d'assurance

assured *n* assuré(e) *m,f*

assurer, assuror *n* assureur *m*

ATM *n* (**a**) BANKING (*abbr* **automated teller machine**) DAB *m* (**b**) COMPTR (*abbr* **asynchronous transfer mode**) ATM *m*, commutation *f* temporelle asynchrone

at sign *n* (*in e-mail address*) arrobase *m*

attach *vt* (**a**) (*appendix, document*) joindre; **the attached letter** la lettre ci-jointe (**b**) COMPTR joindre (**to** à)

attachment *n* (**a**) (*secondment*) détachement *m*; **he's on attachment to the Manchester branch** il est en détachement à l'antenne de Manchester (**b**) LAW saisie *f*, saisie-arrêt *f*; **attachment of property** saisie immobilière (**c**) COMPTR (*of e-mail*) fichier *m* joint

attain *vt (goals, results)* réaliser; **to attain a high standard** atteindre un haut niveau

attend *vt (meeting, conference)* assister à; **the conference was well attended this year** la conférence a attiré beaucoup de monde cette année

attention *n* **for the attention of Mr Harvey** *(in letter)* à l'attention de M. Harvey; **it has been brought to our attention that you have exceeded your overdraft limit** il a été porté à notre connaissance que vous avez dépassé votre autorisation de découvert; **may I have your attention for a moment?** pourriez-vous m'accorder votre attention un instant?

attested copy *n* copie *f* certifiée conforme

attitude research *n* MKTG enquête *f*

attn *(abbr* **for the attention of***)* à l'attention de

attorney *n* **(a)** *(representative)* représentant(e) *m,f,* mandataire *mf* **(b)** *Am (lawyer)* avocat(e) *m,f*

attract *vt* attirer; **the proposal attracted a lot of attention** la proposition a attiré l'attention de beaucoup de gens; **the campaign should attract many new investors** cette campagne devrait attirer un grand nombre de nouveaux investisseurs

attractive *adj (price, offer, proposition)* intéressant(e), attractif(ive)

auction **1** *n* **(sale by) auction** (vente *f* aux) enchères *fpl*; **to sell goods** *Br* **by** *or Am* **at auction** vendre des marchandises aux enchères; **to put sth up for auction** mettre qch à l'enchère *ou* aux enchères; **the property was bought at auction** la propriété a été achetée à une vente aux enchères □ ***auction room*** salle *f* des ventes; ***auction sale*** (vente aux) enchères **2** *vt* vendre aux enchères

▸ **auction off** *vt sep* vendre aux enchères

audience *n* MKTG *(for product, advertisement)* public *m* □ ***audience exposure*** exposition *f* au public; ***audience size*** audience *f* cumulée

audio-typing *n* dactylographie *f* audio-magnéto

audio-typist *n* audiotypiste *mf*

audit **1** *n* FIN vérification *f* des comptes, audit *m* □ ***audit manager*** directeur(trice) *m,f* du service d'audit; ADMIN ***Audit office*** ≃ Cour *f* des Comptes **2** *vt* FIN *(accounts)* vérifier, apurer, examiner

auditing *n* FIN vérification *f* des comptes, audit *m*

auditor *n* *(of company)* commissaire *m* aux comptes; ADMIN *(of public body)* vérificateur(trice) *m,f* des comptes, audit *m,* auditeur(trice) *m,f*; **firm of auditors** cabinet *m* d'audit, cabinet comptable □ ***auditor's report*** rapport *m* du commissaire aux comptes

augmented product *n* MKTG produit *m* augmenté

authenticate *vt* **(a)** *(document, signature)* authentifier **(b)** COMPTR authentifier

authentication *n* **(a)** *(of document, signature)* authentification *f,* certification *f* **(b)** COMPTR authentification *f*

authority *n* **(a)** *(power)* autorité *f*; **the authorities** les autorités *fpl*; **I'd like to speak to someone in authority** je voudrais parler à un responsable; **she has authority over all the staff** elle a autorité sur tout le personnel **(b)** *(permission)* autorisation *f*; **to give sb authority to do sth** autoriser qn à faire qch

authorization *n* autorisation *f*; **you can't do anything without authorization from the management** vous ne pouvez rien faire sans l'autorisation de la direction

authorize *vt* autoriser; *(loan)* consentir; **to authorize sb to do sth** autoriser qn à faire qch

authorized *adj* autorisé(e); **authorized to sign** habile à signer □ ***authorized agent*** mandataire *mf*; ST EXCH ***authorized capital*** capital *m* autorisé *ou* social *ou* nominal; ADMIN ***authorized charges*** prix *mpl* homologués; ***authorized dealer*** distributeur *m* agréé; ***authorized distributor*** distributeur agréé; ***authorized representative*** *(of company)* agent *m* autorisé *ou* mandataire; ST EXCH ***authorized share capital*** capital *m* autorisé; ***authorized signatory*** signataire *mf* autorisé(e) *ou* accrédité(e)

automated *adj* automatisé(e) □ BANKING ***automated clearing house*** chambre *f* de compensation automatisée; ***automated reservation*** réservation *f* télématique; ***automated teller machine*** distributeur *m* automatique de billets; ***automated ticket*** billet *m* informatisé; ***automated withdrawal*** retrait *m* automatique

automatic *adj* automatique □ ***automatic accounting*** comptabilité *f* mécanographique; COMPTR ***automatic data processing*** traitement *m* automatique des données

automation *n* automatisation *f*

autonomy *n* autonomie *f* (financière); **the department has autonomy in this area** le service a toute liberté d'action dans ce domaine

autosave COMPTR **1** *n* sauvegarde *f* automatique
    2 *vt* sauvegarder automatiquement

availability *n* disponibilité *f*; **this offer is subject to availability** cette offre est valable selon disponibilité

available *adj* disponible; *(person)* libre; **available at all branches** en vente dans toutes nos succursales; **we regret that this offer is no longer available** nous avons le regret de vous annoncer que cette offre n'est plus valable; **these items are available in stock** nous avons ces articles en magasin; **sum available for dividend** affectation *f* aux actions □ **available assets** actif *m* disponible *ou* liquide; **available capital** capitaux *mpl* disponibles; **available funds** fonds *mpl* liquides *ou* disponibles, disponibilités *mpl*; MKTG **available market** marché *m* effectif

---
"

And they indicate there that there are excellent opportunities opening up in the United Kingdom bottled water market ... The total **available market** consists of thirty percent of the total population of the United Kingdom. But this market is expanding at a rate of at least five percent and predictions and calculations show that this is far in excess of this base rate.

"

AVC *n* (*abbr* **additional voluntary contribution**) supplément *m* de cotisation retraite *(payé volontairement)*

average 1 *n* **(a)** moyenne *f*; **rough average** moyenne approximative; **sales average** moyenne des ventes
    (b) INS avarie(s) *f(pl)* □ **average adjuster** répartiteur(trice) *m,f* d'avaries; **average bond** compromis *m* d'avarie
    (c) ST EXCH indice *m*
    2 *adj* moyen(enne) □ **average cost per unit** coût *m* unitaire moyen; **average due date** échéance *f* moyenne; **average price** prix *m* moyen; *Am* **average tax rate** taux *m* d'imposition effectif *ou* moyen; **average yield** rendement *m* moyen

▸ **average out at** *vi* s'élever en moyenne à; **profits average out at 10%** les bénéfices s'élèvent en moyenne à 10%; **production averages out at 120 units per day** la production est en moyenne de 120 unités par jour

await *vt* **awaiting your instructions** *(in letter, memo)* dans l'attente de vos instructions; **awaiting delivery** *(of parcel, mail)* en souffrance

award 1 *n* *(damages)* dommages-intérêts *mpl*; *(decision)* arbitrage *m*, adjudication *f*
    2 *vt* *(contract)* adjuger; *(pay rise, damages)* accorder

awareness study *n* MKTG étude *f* de notoriété

AWB *n* (*abbr* **air waybill**) LTA *f*

axe, *Am* **ax 1** *n* **to get the axe** *(of person)* être licencié(e); *(of project)* être abandonné(e); **to give sb the axe** licencier qn; **to give sth the axe** supprimer qch
    2 *vt* *(person)* licencier; *(project)* supprimer; *(job, position)* supprimer; **the service has been axed for economic reasons** le service a été supprimé pour raisons économiques

AZERTY keyboard *n* COMPTR clavier *m* AZERTY

back 1 n (of cheque) dos m, verso m

2 adj (a) (overdue) **back interest** arrérages mpl, intérêts mpl arriérés; BANKING **back office** back-office m; **back orders** commandes fpl en souffrance ou en attente; **back pay** rappel m de salaire; **back tax** arriéré m d'impôt

(b) **to put sth on the back burner** remettre qch à plus tard; **pay increases will have to be put on the back burner** les augmentations de salaire devront attendre

(c) FIN **back door** financement m déguisé

3 vt (support) soutenir, appuyer; (financially) financer; FIN (bill) avaliser, endosser, donner son aval à

▸ **back up** COMPTR 1 vt sep (data, file) sauvegarder

2 vi sauvegarder

backdate vt (cheque, document) antidater; **the pay increase is backdated to 1 May** l'augmentation de salaire a un effet rétroactif à compter du 1 mai

backer n (a) FIN (of bill) donneur m d'aval, avaliseur m (b) (financial supporter) bailleur(eresse) m,f de fonds

background n (a) (of person) (relating to qualifications, experience) expérience f; **what is the candidate's background?** quels sont les antécédents du candidat?; **we need someone with a background in computers** il nous faut quelqu'un qui s'y connaisse en informatique

(b) COMPTR arrière-plan m ▫ **background job** tâche f d'arrière-plan; **background (mode) printing** impression f en arrière-plan; **background task** tâche d'arrière-plan

backhander n Br Fam (bribe) pot-de-vin m, dessous-de-table m

backing n (a) (of currency) couverture f, garantie f (b) (support) soutien m, appui m; (financial support) financement m

backlit adj COMPTR (screen) rétro-éclairé(e)

backlog n arriéré m; **a backlog of orders** des commandes non exécutées ou en souffrance; **a backlog of work** une accumulation de travail (en retard), un arriéré de travail

backslash n COMPTR barre f oblique inversée

backspace n COMPTR retour m arrière

back-to-back adj FIN **back-to-back credit** crédit m dos-à-dos; **back-to-back operation** opération f de face à face

backup n (a) (support) soutien m, appui m ▫ **backup service** service m après-vente (b) COMPTR sauvegarde f; **to do the backup** faire la sauvegarde ▫ **backup copy** copie f de sauvegarde; **backup file** fichier m de sauvegarde; **backup system** (for doing the backup) système m de sauvegarde; (auxiliary system) système de secours

backward adj ECON **backward integration** intégration f en amont ou ascendante; **backward pricing** rajustement m des prix

BACS n (abbr **Bankers' Automated Clearing System**) = système électronique de compensation de chèques

> "
> One submission to **BACS** can initiate a number of payments to beneficiaries who then receive value two working days later, the same day that the company account is debited.
> "

bad 1 n **he is £5,000 to the bad** (overdrawn) il a un découvert de 5000 livres; (after a deal) il a perdu 5000 livres

2 adj **bad debt** créance f irrécouvrable ou douteuse; **bad management** mauvaise gestion f; **bad name** mauvaise réputation f; **that company has a bad name in the business** la société a mauvaise réputation dans le milieu

bail n LAW caution f; **to go** or **stand bail for sb** se porter garant(e) de qn

▸ **bail out** vt sep (a) (person, company) renflouer (b) LAW **to bail sb out** se porter garant(e) de qn

balance 1 n (a) FIN (of account) solde m; ACCT balance f, bilan m; **balance in hand** solde en caisse; **balance carried forward** solde à reporter; (on balance sheet) report m à nouveau; **balance brought forward** solde reporté; (on balance sheet) report; **balance due** solde débiteur; **to pay the balance** régler le solde; **off the balance sheet** hors de bilan ▫ **balance book** livre m d'inventaire; **balance sheet** bilan m; **balance sheet auditing** contrôle m du bilan; **balance sheet consolidation** consolidation f de bilan; **balance sheet**

item poste *m* de bilan; *balance sheet value* valeur *f* bilantielle

(**b**) *(remainder)* reste *m*; **the balance of your order will be supplied within ten days** le reste de votre commande vous sera livré dans les dix jours

(**c**) ECON *balance of payments* balance *f* des paiements; *balance of trade* balance commerciale

2 *vt* FIN *(account)* équilibrer, balancer; *(debt)* compenser; *(budget)* équilibrer; **to balance the books** dresser *ou* établir le bilan, arrêter les comptes; **to balance the budget** équilibrer le budget; **to balance an adverse budget** rétablir un budget déficitaire

3 *vi* FIN *(of accounts)* s'équilibrer, balancer; **I can't get the accounts to balance** je n'arrive pas à équilibrer les comptes

▶ **balance out** *vi (of figures)* correspondre; **debits and credits should balance out** les débits et les crédits devraient s'équilibrer

balancing *n* FIN *(of accounts)* solde *m*, alignement *m*, arrêté *m*

balloon *vi (increase dramatically)* monter en flèche; **exports have ballooned in the last twelve months** les exportations ont monté en flèche au cours des douze derniers mois

ballot 1 *n* (**a**) *(vote)* scrutin *m*; **to hold a ballot** organiser des élections (**b**) ST EXCH *(when shares are oversubscribed)* allocation *f* d'actions par tirage au sort

2 *vt* consulter par voie de scrutin; **union members will be ballotted on Tuesday** les membres du syndicat décideront par voie de scrutin mardi

ballpark figure *n* chiffre *m* approximatif; **a ballpark figure of £3,000** une somme qui avoisine les 3000 livres

bancassurance *n* BANKING bancassurance *f*

band *n (of ages, tax)* tranche *f*; *(of salaries)* catégorie *f*

banded pack *n* lot *m* □ *banded pack selling* vente *f* par lot

bandwidth *n* COMPTR largeur *f* de bande

bang *vt* ST EXCH **to bang the market** faire baisser les prix, écraser le marché

bank 1 *n* banque *f*; **the High Street banks** les grandes banques centrales; **the World Bank** la Banque Mondiale; **the Bank of England/France** la Banque d'Angleterre/de France □ *bank account* compte *m* en banque, compte bancaire; **to open/close a bank account** ouvrir/fermer un compte bancaire; *bank balance* solde *m*; *bank base rate* taux *m* de base bancaire; *bank bill* effet *m*

(tiré par une banque sur une autre); *bank borrowings* emprunts *mpl* bancaires, concours *m* bancaire; *bank branch code* code *m* guichet; *bank card* carte *f* d'identité bancaire; *bank charges* frais *mpl* bancaires; *bank clerk* employé(e) *m,f* de banque; *bank credit* avoir *m* en banque, crédit *m* bancaire; *bank deposit* dépôt *m* bancaire *ou* en banque; *bank details* relevé *m* d'identité bancaire, RIB *m*; *bank discount rate* escompte *m* officiel; *bank draft* traite *f* bancaire; *bank guarantee* garantie *f* bancaire, caution *f* de banque; Br *bank holiday* jour *m* férié; *bank interest* intérêt *m* bancaire; *bank lending* concours bancaire; *bank loan* prêt *m* bancaire; *bank manager* directeur(trice) *m,f* de banque; *bank overdraft* découvert *m* bancaire; ACCT *bank reconciliation* rapprochement *m* bancaire; *bank reserves* réserves *fpl* bancaires; *bank selling rate* taux de change à la vente; *bank sort code* code guichet; *bank teller* guichetier(ère) *m,f*; *bank transactions* transactions *fpl* bancaires; *bank transfer* virement *m* bancaire

2 *vt (cheque, money)* mettre *ou* déposer à la banque

3 *vi* **to bank with sb** avoir un compte (bancaire) chez qn; **where do you bank?, who do you bank with?** à quelle banque êtes-vous *ou* avez-vous votre compte?, quelle est votre banque?

bankable *adj* bancable

banker *n* banquier(ère) *m,f* □ *banker's acceptance* acceptation *f* bancaire; *Bankers' Automated Clearing System* = système électronique de compensation de chèques; *banker's card* carte *f* d'identité bancaire; *banker's draft* traite *f* bancaire; *banker's order* ordre *m* de virement bancaire

banking *n (activity)* opérations *fpl* bancaires; *(profession)* profession *f* de banquier; **she's in banking** elle travaille dans la banque □ Am *banking account* compte *m* en banque, compte bancaire; *banking business* trafic *m* bancaire; *banking hours* heures *fpl* d'ouverture de la banque; *banking house* maison *f* de banque, établissement *m* bancaire; *banking mechanism* mécanisme *m* bancaire

banknote *n* billet *m* de banque

bankroll Am **1** *n* fonds *mpl*, finances *fpl*
2 *vt (deal, project)* financer

bankrupt 1 *n* failli(e) *m,f* □ *bankrupt's certificate* concordat *m*
2 *adj* failli(e); **to go bankrupt** faire faillite; **to**

be bankrupt être en faillite; **to adjudicate** or **declare sb bankrupt** déclarer qn en faillite

3 vt (company, person) mettre en faillite; **the deal bankrupted the business** la transaction a mis l'entreprise en faillite

bankruptcy n faillite f; **to present** or **file one's petition for bankruptcy** déposer son bilan◻ Br **bankruptcy court** ≃ tribunal m de commerce; **bankruptcy proceedings** procédure f de faillite

bar n (**a**) **bar chart** graphique m à bâtons; **bar code** code-barre m (**b**) COMPTR (menu bar) barre f

bargain **1** n (**a**) (agreement) marché m, affaire f; **a bad bargain** une mauvaise affaire; **to strike** or **make a bargain with sb** conclure ou faire un marché avec qn; **to drive a hard bargain** être dur(e) en affaires
  (**b**) (good buy) affaire f, occasion f◻ **bargain counter** rayon m des soldes; **bargain offer** offre f exceptionnelle; **bargain price** prix m de solde ou exceptionnel

2 vi (**a**) (negotiate) négocier (**with** avec); **the unions are bargaining with management for an 8% pay rise** les syndicats négocient une hausse de salaire de 8% avec la direction
  (**b**) (haggle) **to bargain with sb** marchander avec qn; **to bargain over sth** marchander qch

bargaining n marchandage m ◻ **bargaining position** situation f permettant de négocier; **we are in a strong bargaining position** nous sommes en position de force pour négocier; **bargaining power** pouvoir m de négociation; **they have considerable bargaining power** ils ont beaucoup de poids dans les négociations; **bargaining table** table f des négociations

> **"**
> Ways of trying to increase your **bargaining power** include delaying negotiations or confrontation until you are in a stronger position or initiating action in another area which raises the costs to your opponent if he disagrees with your offer.
> **"**

barrier n barrière f, obstacle m; **barrier to entry** barrières fpl à l'entrée

barrister n Br LAW **barrister (at law)** ≃ avocat(e) m,f

base **1** n BANKING **base date** date f de base; **base rate** taux m de base (bancaire)

2 vt (locate) **to be based in** être basé(e) à; **where are you based?** où êtes-vous installé?; **the job is based in Tokyo** le poste est basé à Tokyo

baseline n **baseline costs** coûts mpl de base; **baseline sales** ventes fpl de base

BASIC n COMPTR (abbr **Beginners' All-Purpose Symbolic Instruction Code**) Basic m

basic adj **basic commodity** denrée f témoin, denrée de base; **basic pay** salaire m de base ou de départ; **basic statistics** statistiques fpl fondamentales

basis n (**a**) (foundation) base f; **basis of assessment** (of income tax) assiette f de l'impôt; **on the basis of these figures** sur la base de ces chiffres (**b**) (system) **employed on a part-time basis** employé(e) à mi-temps; **paid on a weekly basis** payé(e) à la semaine

batch n (of goods) lot m ◻ **batch production** production f par lots

baud n COMPTR baud m; **at 28,800 baud** à (une vitesse de) 28 800 bauds ◻ **baud rate** débit m en bauds

bay n COMPTR baie f

BBS n COMPTR (abbr **bulletin board system**) BBS m, serveur m télématique

BCE n (abbr **Board of Customs and Excise**) = douane britannique

BE n (abbr **Bank of England**) Banque f d'Angleterre

b/e n (abbr **bill of exchange**) lettre f de change

bear **1** n (**a**) ST EXCH baissier(ère) m,f, spéculateur(trice) m,f à la baisse; **to go a bear** spéculer à la baisse ◻ **bear closing** arbitrage m à la baisse; **bear market** marché m à la baisse ou baissier; **bear sale** vente f à découvert; **bear speculation** spéculation f à la baisse; **bear trading** spéculation à la baisse
  (**b**) Fam **bear hug** = communiqué d'information annonçant une OPA immédiate

2 vt (**a**) ST EXCH **to bear the market** chercher à faire baisser les cours
  (**b**) **to bear interest** porter intérêt; **to bear the costs (of sth)** prendre les frais (de qch) à sa charge

3 vi ST EXCH spéculer à la baisse

bearer n (of news, letter, cheque) porteur(euse) m,f; (of passport) titulaire mf; **cheque made payable to bearer** chèque m (payable) au porteur ◻ FIN **bearer bill** effet m au porteur; **bearer bond** titre m ou obligation f au porteur; **bearer cheque** chèque au porteur; BANKING **bearer paper** papier m au porteur; **bearer share** action f au porteur

bearish *adj* ST EXCH *(market)* à la baisse, baissier(ère); **to be bearish** spéculer à la baisse □ *bearish tendency* tendance *f* à la baisse

bed *n* (**a**) *Fam* **to get into bed with sb** *(form partnership with)* travailler en collaboration avec qn (**b**) ST EXCH *bed and breakfasting* aller et retour *m*

behalf *n* **to do sth on behalf of sb** *(write, phone)* faire qch de la part de qn; **to make a payment on behalf of sb** effectuer un versement au nom de qn

belly *n Fam* **to go belly up** *(of company)* faire faillite

below-the-line *adj* (**a**) MKTG *below-the-line advertising* publicité *f* directe; *below-the-line costs* coûts *mpl* hors-médias (**b**) ACCT *(expenses)* au-dessous de la ligne □ *below-the-line accounts* comptes *mpl* de résultats exceptionnels

benchmark *n* point *m* de repère □ *benchmark market* marché *m* de référence; *Can* ADMIN *benchmark position* poste-repère *m*

beneficiary *n* bénéficiaire *mf*

benefit 1 *n* (**a**) *Br* ADMIN *(state payment)* allocation *f*, prestation *f*; **to be on benefit** toucher l'aide sociale; **to pay out benefits** verser des prestations (**b**) **benefits (package)** *(to employee)* avantages *mpl* sociaux

2 *vt* *(person, country)* profiter à; *(trade)* favoriser; **a steady exchange rate benefits trade** un taux d'échange stable est avantageux au commerce *ou* favorise le commerce; **the change will benefit all employees** tous les employés bénéficieront de ce changement

3 *vi* **to benefit from sth** profiter de qch, tirer profit de qch; **to benefit from a rise in prices** profiter de *ou* tirer profit d'une hausse de prix

bequeath *vt* LAW léguer (**to** à)

bequest *n* LAW legs *m*

best-in-class *n* MKTG chef *m* de file

best-of-breed *n* MKTG nec plus ultra *m*

best price *n* meilleur prix *m*

best-selling *adj* à grand succès, de grosse vente

better *vt* *(improve)* améliorer; *(surpass)* faire mieux que; **we must try to better last year's figures** nous devons essayer d'obtenir de meilleurs résultats que l'an dernier; **the company has bettered the competition for the second year running** c'est la deuxième année consécutive que l'entreprise a fait mieux que la concurrence

b/f ACCT *(abbr* **brought forward***)* reporté

biannual *adj* semestriel(elle)

bid 1 *n* (**a**) *(offer)* offre *f*; *(at auction)* enchère *f*; **to make a bid of £250,000 for a property** faire une offre de 250 000 livres pour une propriété; *(at auction)* mettre une enchère de 250 000 livres sur une propriété; **to make the first** *or* **opening bid** faire la première enchère

(**b**) *(tender)* soumission *f*; **the firm made** *or* **put in a bid for the contract** l'entreprise a fait une soumission *ou* a soumissionné pour le contrat

(**c**) ST EXCH *Am* **the bid and asked** les cours *mpl* d'achat et de vente □ *bid price* cours acheteur

(**d**) *(attempt)* tentative *f*; **in a bid to reopen negotiations** dans une tentative de relancer les négociations

2 *vt* *(at auction)* faire une enchère de; **we had to bid another thousand pounds** il nous a fallu surenchérir de mille livres

3 *vi* (**a**) **to bid for sth** faire une offre pour qch; *(at auction)* mettre une enchère sur qch; **to bid a high price** offrir une grosse somme; **to bid over sb** *or* **more than sb** enchérir sur qn

(**b**) *(tender)* faire une soumission, répondre à un appel d'offres; **to bid for** *or* **on a contract** soumissionner à une adjudication; **several firms bid for** *or* **on the project** plusieurs entreprises ont soumissionné pour le projet

▸ **bid up** *vt sep* *(price, goods)* enchérir sur

bidder *n* (**a**) *(at auction)* enchérisseur(euse) *m,f*; **the lowest bidder** le moins disant; **the highest bidder** le plus offrant (**b**) *(for tender)* soumissionnaire *mf*

bidding *n* (**a**) *(at auction)* enchères *fpl*, mises *fpl*; **the bidding was very brisk** les enchères étaient vives; **to start the bidding for sth at £5,000** mettre qch à prix 5000 livres (**b**) *(tenders)* soumissions *fpl*; **the cheapest** *or* **best bidding** la soumission la plus basse *ou* la plus favorable

biennial *adj* bisannuel(elle)

big *adj* **to earn big money** gagner gros □ *Br Fam* ST EXCH *Big Bang* = déréglementation de la Bourse de Londres en octobre 1986; *Am the big board* la Bourse de New York; *big business* les grandes entreprises; *Br the Big Four* = les quatre grandes banques anglaises *(Lloyds, National Westminster, Barclays, Midland)*

> **❝**
>
> In this day governments handle astronomical sums and a multitude of people. In effect, a government today is **big business**.
>
> **❞**

bilateral *adj* bilatéral(e)

bill **1** *n* (**a**) *(notice of payment due)* facture *f*; *(for gas, electricity)* facture, note *f*; *(in hotel)* note; *Br (in restaurant)* addition *f*; **can we have the bill, please?** *(in restaurant)* l'addition, s'il vous plaît; **to make out a bill** dresser *ou* rédiger une facture; **to pay a bill** payer *ou* régler une facture; **to foot the bill** payer la note *ou* les dépenses

(**b**) *Am (banknote)* billet *m* de banque; **five-dollar bill** billet de cinq dollars

(**c**) FIN *(promissory note)* effet *m* (de commerce), traite *f*; **bills for collection** effets à l'encaissement; **bills in hand** effets en portefeuille □ **bill broker, bill discounter** courtier(ère) *m,f* de change; CUSTOMS **bill of entry** déclaration *f* d'entrée (en douane); **bill of exchange** lettre *f* de change; **bill of lading** connaissement *m*; **through bill of lading** connaissement direct *ou* à forfait; **bills payable** effets à payer; **bill payable at sight** effet payable à vue *ou* à présentation; **bills receivable** effets à recevoir; **bill of sale** acte *m ou* contrat *m* de vente; CUSTOMS **bill of sight** déclaration (en douane) provisoire

2 *vt* facturer; **they billed me twice for the spare parts** les pièces de rechange m'ont été facturées deux fois; **he bills his company for his travelling expenses** il se fait rembourser ses frais de voyage par son entreprise

billboard *n* panneau *m* d'affichage

billing *n* facturation *f*

billion *n* milliard *m*; **10 billion dollars** 10 milliards de dollars

BIM *n* *(abbr* **British Institute of Management**) = organisme britannique dont la fonction est de renseigner et de conseiller les entreprises en matière de gestion, ainsi que de promouvoir l'enseignement de cette discipline

bimonthly **1** *adj (twice a month)* bimensuel(elle); *(every two months)* bimestriel(elle)

2 *adv (twice a month)* deux fois par mois; *(every two months)* tous les deux mois

binder *n* *(for papers)* classeur *m*

binding *adj* obligatoire; *(contract, promise)* qui engage *ou* lie; **the contract is legally binding** ce contrat est juridiquement contraignant; **the agreement is binding on all parties** l'accord engage chaque partie; **it is binding on the buyer to make immediate payment** l'acheteur est tenu de payer immédiatement

bit *n* COMPTR bit *m*; **bits per second** bits par seconde

bitmap COMPTR **1** *n* bitmap *m*

2 *adj* pixélisé(e), bitmap

bit-mapped *adj* COMPTR pixélisé(e), bitmap

biweekly **1** *adj (twice a week)* bimensuel(elle); *(every two weeks)* bihebdomadaire

2 *adv (twice a week)* deux fois par semaine; *(every two weeks)* tous les quinze jours

B/L, b/l *n* *(abbr* **bill of lading**) connt.

black **1** *n* **to be in the black** *(of person)* être solvable; *(of account)* être créditeur(trice)

2 *adj* **black book** plan *m* de défense contre une OPA *ou* anti-OPA; **black economy** économie *f* souterraine *ou* parallèle; ST EXCH **black knight** chevalier *m* noir; **black market** marché *m* noir; **to buy on the black market** acheter au noir; **black marketeer** = personne qui fait du marché noir; **Black Monday** jour *m* du krach (boursier) *(le lundi 19 octobre 1987)*; **black money** *(earned on black market)* argent *m* du marché noir; *(undeclared)* argent non déclaré au fisc

blackleg *n* Fam *(strikebreaker)* jaune *m*

blacklist **1** *n* liste *f* noire

2 *vt* inscrire *ou* mettre sur la liste noire

blank **1** *n* *(in document)* blanc *m*, (espace *m*) vide *m*; **fill in the blanks** remplissez les blancs *ou* les (espaces) vides

2 *adj* (**a**) **blank cheque** chèque *m* en blanc; FIN **blank credit** crédit *m* en blanc

(**b**) COMPTR *(disk, screen)* vide; *(unformatted)* vierge □ **blank unformatted disk** disquette *f* vierge

blanket *adj* général(e), global(e); **a blanket rule for all employees** un règlement qui s'applique à tout le personnel; **our insurance policy guarantees blanket coverage** notre police d'assurance couvre tous les risques □ **blanket agreement** accord-cadre *m*; **blanket mortgage** hypothèque *f* générale; **blanket order** commande *f* globale *ou* d'une portée générale; INS **blanket policy** police *f* globale (tous risques)

blind-testing *n* MKTG tests *mpl* en aveugle

blink rate *n* COMPTR *(of cursor)* vitesse *f* de clignotement

blip *n* *(temporary problem)* contretemps *m*; **the company suffered a blip in February when it lost that contract** l'entreprise a subi un contretemps en février lorsqu'elle a perdu ce contrat

blister pack *n* blister *m*

blitz *n* MKTG campagne *f* de marketing intensive

block 1 *n* (**a**) *(of shares)* paquet *m* ❑ *block booking* location *f* en bloc; ST EXCH *block issue* émission *f* par série; *block purchase* achat *m* en bloc; *block trading* négociations *fpl* de bloc (**b**) FIN **to put a block on sth** *(cheque, account, prices, imports)* bloquer qch (**c**) COMPTR bloc *m* ❑ *block copy* copie *f* de bloc

2 *vt* (**a**) FIN *(cheque, account, prices, imports)* bloquer ❑ *blocked currency* monnaie *f* bloquée *ou* non convertible (**b**) COMPTR *(text)* bloquer

blue chip *n* ST EXCH valeur *f* de père de famille *ou* de premier ordre

blue-chip *adj* FIN *blue-chip company* affaire *f* de premier ordre; ST EXCH *blue-chip stocks* or *shares* valeurs *fpl* de père de famille *ou* de premier ordre

blue-collar *adj* ouvrier(ère) ❑ *blue-collar union* syndicat *m* ouvrier; *blue-collar worker* col *m* bleu

blue-sky security *n* titre *m* hautement speculatif *ou* à haut risque

blurb *n* baratin *m* publicitaire; *(on book jacket)* texte *m* publicitaire

board 1 *n* (**a**) *(of company)* conseil *m*, comité *m*, commission *f*; **to be on the board** faire partie *ou* être membre du conseil d'administration; **the bank is represented on the board** la banque fait partie du conseil ❑ *Board of Customs and Excise* = douane britannique; *board (of directors)* conseil d'administration; *board of enquiry* commission d'enquête; *board meeting* réunion *f* du conseil d'administration; *board member* membre *m* du conseil d'administration; *Br Formerly Board of Trade* ≃ Ministère *m* du Commerce; *board of trustees* conseil de gestion (**b**) COMPTR *(in PC)* carte *f*; *(in mainframe)* panneau *m*; **on board** installé(e)

2 *vt* ADMIN *(ship) (for inspection)* arraisonner

boardroom *n* salle *f* de réunion *(du conseil d'administration)*

bogus company *n* société *f* fantôme

boiler room *n Am* = organisation qui vend illégalement au public des produits financiers très spéculatifs ou sans valeur

► **bolster up** *vt sep* FIN *(currency, economy)* soutenir

bona fide *adj* *(genuine)* véritable, authentique; *(offer, agreement)* sérieux(euse)

bonanza *adj* prospère, favorable; **1997 was a bonanza year for us** nous avons connu une année exceptionnelle en 1997

bond 1 *n* (**a**) FIN obligation *f*; **long/medium/short bond** obligation longue/moyenne/courte ❑ *bond investment* placement *m* obligataire; *bond issue* émission *f* obligataire *ou* d'obligations; **to make a bond issue** émettre un emprunt; *bond market* marché *m* obligataire *ou* des obligations (**b**) CUSTOMS **to be in bond** être à l'entrepôt (de la douane); **to put goods in bond** entreposer des marchandises, mettre des marchandises à l'entrepôt; **to take goods out of bond** dédouaner des marchandises, faire sortir des marchandises de l'entrepôt ❑ *bond note* acquit-à-caution *m* (**c**) LAW obligation *f*, engagement *m*; **to enter into a bond (with sb)** contracter une obligation *ou* un engagement (avec qn)

2 *vt* CUSTOMS *(goods)* entreposer, mettre à l'entrepôt

bonded *adj* CUSTOMS *(goods)* entreposé(e), en entrepôt ❑ *bonded warehouse* entrepôt *m* de *ou* en douane

bondholder *n* FIN obligataire *mf*, détenteur(trice) *m,f* ou porteur(euse) *m,f* d'obligations

bonus *n* (**a**) *(on salary)* prime *f*; **to work on a bonus system** travailler à la prime; **to get a Christmas bonus** toucher une prime de fin d'année (**b**) ST EXCH *(on shares)* dividende *m* supplémentaire, bonification *f* ❑ *bonus issue* émission *f* d'actions gratuites; *bonus share* action *f* gratuite *ou* donnée en prime (**c**) INS *(to policy holder)* bénéfice *m* additionnel

book 1 *n* registre *m*; **the books** *(of company)* les comptes *mpl*; **to keep the books** tenir la comptabilité *ou* les comptes; **he's on our books** *(employee)* il est dans nos fichiers ❑ *book debts* comptes fournisseurs; *book value* valeur *f* comptable

2 *vt* (**a**) *(engage)* embaucher, engager; **we are heavily booked** nous sommes très pris (**b**) *(seat, room, table, ticket)* réserver; **to book sb into a hotel** retenir une chambre d'hôtel pour qn; **fully booked** complet(ète)

► **book up** *vt sep* **the restaurant/hotel is booked up** le restaurant/l'hôtel est complet

booking *n* location *f*, réservation *f* ❑ *booking clerk* préposé(e) *m,f* à la location; *booking office* guichet *m* ou bureau *m* de réservation

bookkeeper *n* comptable *mf*

bookkeeping *n* tenue *f* de(s) livres, comptabilité *f*

booklet *n* livret *m*, brochure *f*

bookmark COMPTR **1** n signet m
2 vt créer un signet sur

bookwork n tenue f de(s) livres ou des écritures

boom **1** n boom m, essor m économique; **boom and bust** cycle m expansion-récession ▫ **boom town** (growing) ville f champignon; (prosperous) ville prospère
2 vi prospérer, être en plein essor; (of Stock Market) être en hausse; **business is booming** les affaires marchent bien ou sont en plein essor; **car sales are booming** les ventes de voitures connaissent une forte progression

booming adj (economy, business) prospère, en plein essor

boost **1** n **to give sth a boost** (sales) augmenter qch, faire monter qch; (productivity) développer qch, accroître qch; (economy) relancer qch; (morale) remonter qch; **the announcement gave the pound a boost on the foreign exchanges** la nouvelle a fait grimper la livre sur le marché des changes
2 vt (sales) augmenter, faire monter; (productivity) développer, accroître; (economy) relancer; **we must do something to boost staff morale** il faut faire quelque chose pour remonter le moral du personnel

▸ **boot up** COMPTR **1** vt sep (computer) amorcer, faire démarrer
2 vi (of computer) s'amorcer, démarrer; (of person) démarrer

boot disk n COMPTR disquette f de démarrage

booth n stand m (d'exposition)

border n frontière f

borrow **1** vt emprunter; **to borrow money from sb** emprunter de l'argent à qn; **you can borrow up to three times your salary** vous pouvez emprunter jusqu'à trois fois le montant de votre salaire
2 vi emprunter (**from** à); **to borrow on** or **at interest** emprunter à intérêt

▸ **borrow against** vt insep FIN (salary, property) emprunter sur

> ❝ If you **borrow against** inflated values, you over-borrow in the sense that available cash-flow will ultimately not service the debt. Hence the industry's present problems. ❞

borrowed adj emprunté(e), d'emprunt ▫ **borrowed capital** capitaux mpl empruntés ou d'emprunt

borrowing n emprunts mpl; **financed by borrowing** financé(e) par des emprunts ▫ **borrowing power** capacité f de crédit; **borrowing requirements** besoins mpl de crédit

boss n Fam patron(onne) m,f; **to be one's own boss** être son propre patron

bottleneck n (in production) goulot m d'étranglement

bottom **1** n **the bottom has fallen out of the market** le marché s'est effondré
2 adj FIN **bottom line** solde m final, résultat m financier; **black bottom line** solde créditeur; **red bottom line** solde débiteur

▸ **bottom out** vi (of recession, slump) atteindre son maximum; (of price) atteindre son minimum; **the dollar has bottomed out** le dollar s'est effondré; **sales bottomed out at £40,000** à leur niveau le plus bas, les ventes sont tombées à 40 000 livres

bounce Fam **1** vt (a) (cheque) refuser d'honorer (b) **to bounce an idea off sb** soumettre une idée à qn
2 vi (of cheque) être refusé(e) pour non-provision; **I hope this cheque won't bounce** j'espère que ce n'est pas un chèque sans provision

▸ **bounce back** vi (of Stock Exchange) reprendre, remonter; **the pound has bounced back against the dollar** la livre a regagné du terrain par rapport au dollar

bound adj (obliged) obligé(e); **bound by contract** lié(e) par contrat

Bourse n Bourse f (de valeurs)

box **1** n (a) (container) boîte f; (crate) caisse f ▫ **box file** boîte de classement (b) (postal address) boîte f postale; **PO Box 301** boîte postale 301, BP 301; **Box number 301** (in advertisements) Référence 301, Ref. 301 (c) (on form) case f
2 vt (goods) mettre en boîte; (put in crate) mettre en caisse

boxed adj (goods) en boîte; (in crate) en caisse

bps n COMPTR (abbr **bits per second**) bps

bracket n ADMIN (of income, tax) tranche f; (of salaries) fourchette f; **the fifteen to twenty age bracket** le groupe ou la classe des quinze à vingt ans; **the high/low income bracket** la tranche des gros/petits revenus; **my pay rise put me in the £40,000 bracket** mon augmentation de salaire m'a placé dans la tranche (de revenus) des 40 000 livres annuelles; **what tax bracket**

are you in? dans quelle tranche d'imposition es-tu?

brain drain n fuite f des cerveaux

> **❝**
>
> It is quite clear that there is a major shortage of trained manpower in computer science in the US, which is threatening the technological progress of that country, and the **brain drain** from India is helping to mitigate this problem.
>
> **❞**

brainstorming n MKTG remue-méninges m, brainstorming m

branch n (a) (of shop) succursale f; (of company) agence f, succursale, filiale f; (of bank) agence; **this shop has branches all over the country** ce magasin a des succursales dans tout le pays ❑ **branch banking** banque f à réseau; **branch manager** directeur(trice) m,f de succursale; **branch office** agence (b) COMPTR branchement m

▸ **branch out** vi se diversifier, étendre ses activités; **they're branching out into CD-ROMs** ils se lancent dans la production de CD-ROM

brand n MKTG (of product) marque f ❑ **brand acceptance** acceptabilité f de la marque; **brand advertising** publicité f de marque ou sur la marque; **brand awareness** notoriété f de la marque; **brand competition** concurrence f entre marques; **brand concept** concept m de marque; **brand extension** extension f de la marque; **brand familiarity** connaissance f de la marque; **brand identifier** identificateur m de marque; **brand image** image f de marque; **brand imitation** imitation f de marque; **brand leader** marque de tête; **brand lifecycle** cycle m de vie de la marque; **brand loyalty** (of consumer) fidélité f à la marque; **brand management** gestion f de la marque; **brand manager** chef m de produit ou de marque; **brand mapping** carte f perceptuelle des marques, carte des positions de marques; **brand mark** emblème m de marque; **brand name** marque (de fabrique); **brand name recall** mémomarque f; **brand piracy** contrefaçon f; **brand positioning** positionnement m de la marque; **brand preference** préférence f pour une marque; **brand recognition** identification f de la marque; **brand sensitivity** sensibilité f aux marques; **brand switching** changement m de marque

branded goods npl MKTG produits mpl de marque

branding n MKTG marquage m

brand-loyal adj MKTG fidèle à la marque

breach n **breach of contract** rupture f de contrat; **to be in breach of contract** violer un contrat; **breach of trust** abus m de confiance; **breach of warranty** violation f de garantie

break 1 n (a) (in negotiations) rupture f (b) (interval, rest) pause f; **all employees are entitled to two fifteen-minute breaks** tous les employés ont droit à deux pauses de quinze minutes (c) COMPTR **break key** touche f d'interruption **2** vt (agreement, contract) rompre

▸ **break down 1** vt sep FIN (account, figures, expenses) décomposer, ventiler; (statistics) analyser; (bill, estimate) détailler; **to break down bulk** ventiler un lot **2** vi (a) (of negotiations, relations) échouer; **talks between unions and management have broken down** les négociations entre les syndicats et la direction ont échoué (b) (of machine) tomber en panne

▸ **break even** vi (of person, company) rentrer dans ses frais

▸ **break into** vt insep (market) percer sur; **many companies are trying to break into the Japanese market** de nombreuses entreprises essaient de percer sur le marché japonais

▸ **break up 1** vt sep (conglomerate, trust) scinder, diviser; (company) scinder; (coalition) rompre **2** vi (of meeting) se terminer, prendre fin; (of partnership) cesser, prendre fin; (of talks, negotiations) cesser

breakage n (damage) casse f, avarie f; **to pay for breakages** payer la casse

breakdown n (of account, figures, expenses) décomposition f, ventilation f; (of statistics) analyse f; (of bill, estimate) détail m; BANKING (of charges, interest) décompte m

break-even 1 n seuil m de rentabilité; ACCT point m mort, point m d'équilibre; **to reach break-even** atteindre le seuil de rentabilité **2** adj FIN **break-even analysis** analyse f du point mort; **break-even deal** affaire f blanche; **break-even point** seuil m de rentabilité; ACCT point m mort;

break- even price prix *m* minimum rentable

> ❝
> The **break-even point** is achieved when a sales volume of about £32,000 is reached. Sales in excess of this figure begin to produce a profit.
> ❞

break-up *n* *(of company)* scission *f* ❑ *break-up price* prix *m* de liquidation; ACCT *break-up value* valeur *f* d'inventaire, VI *f*

bribe 1 *n* pot-de-vin *m* 2 *vt* offrir un pot-de-vin à

bribery *n* corruption *f*

bridge loan *n Am* prêt-relais *m*

bridging *adj Br* **bridging loan** prêt-relais *m*; *bridging value* valeur *f* de récupération

brief 1 *n* (**a**) LAW dossier *m* (**b**) *(instructions)* mission *f*; **my brief was to develop sales** la tâche *ou* la mission qui m'a été confiée était de développer les ventes 2 *vt (inform)* mettre au courant (**on** de); *(instruct)* donner des instructions *ou* des directives à; **have you been briefed?** *(brought up to date)* est-ce que vous avez été mis au courant?; *(given instructions)* est-ce qu'on vous a donné vos instructions?

briefcase *n* serviette *f*

briefing *n* briefing *m*

▸ **bring down** *vt sep (prices, rate of inflation)* faire baisser

▸ **bring forward** *vt sep* (**a**) ACCT *(item)* reporter; **brought forward** reporté(e) (**b**) *(date, meeting)* avancer; **the conference has been brought forward to the 28th** la conférence a été avancée au 28

▸ **bring in** *vt sep (of investment, sale)* rapporter; **to bring in interest** rapporter des intérêts; **this investment has brought in 6%** ce placement a rapporté 6% d'intérêts; **tourism brings in millions of dollars each year** le tourisme rapporte des millions de dollars tous les ans

▸ **bring out** *vt sep (shares)* émettre; *(product)* lancer, sortir; *(book)* publier

brisk *adj (market, trade)* actif(ive), animé(e); *(competition)* dynamique; **business is brisk** les affaires marchent bien

British Institute of Management *n* = organisme britannique dont la fonction est de renseigner et de conseiller les entreprises en matière de gestion, ainsi que de promouvoir l'enseignement de cette discipline

brochure *n* brochure *f*, dépliant *m*

broker *n* (**a**) FIN *(for insurance, goods)* courtier(ère) *m,f* (de commerce) ❑ *broker's commission* (frais *mpl* de) courtage *m*; *broker's contract* courtage (**b**) ST EXCH agent *m* de change, courtier(ère) *m,f* (en Bourse)

brokerage *n* FIN (**a**) *(profession of broker)* courtage *m* ❑ *brokerage house* maison *f* de courtage (**b**) *(fee)* (frais *mpl* de) courtage *m*

broking *n* FIN *(profession)* courtage *m*

brown goods *npl* MKTG produits *mpl* électroménagers *(tel que télévisions, magnétoscopes)*

browse COMPTR 1 *n* **browse mode** mode *m* survol 2 *vt* **to browse the Web** naviguer sur le Web 3 *vi* se promener

▸ **browse through** *vt insep* COMPTR se promener dans, survoler

browser *n* COMPTR navigateur *m*, logiciel *m* de navigation

BS *n (abbr* **British Standard***)* = indique que le chiffre qui suit renvoie au numéro de la norme fixée par l'association britannique de normalisation

b/s *n (abbr* **bill of sale***)* acte *m* ou contrat *m* de vente

BSI *n (abbr* **British Standards Institution***)* = association britannique de normalisation

bt/fwd *adj* ACCT *(abbr* **brought forward***)* reporté(e)

bubblejet printer *n* imprimante *f* à jet d'encre

bubble pack, bubble wrap *n (for large item)* emballage-bulle *m*

buck *n Fam (dollar)* dollar *m* (américain); **to make a fast** *or* **quick buck** faire du fric; **bucks** *(money)* fric *m*

bucket shop *n Fam* (**a**) FIN bureau *m* de courtier marron (**b**) *(travel agency)* agence *f* de voyages à prix réduits

budget 1 *n* (**a**) *(financial plan)* budget *m*; *(allocated ceiling)* enveloppe *f* budgétaire; **to balance the budget** équilibrer le budget; **to be within budget** être dans les limites du budget; **the project was finished within budget** le projet a été fini sans dépasser le budget; **we are already well over budget** on a déjà largement dépassé le budget qui était alloué pour le projet ❑ *budget constraint* contrainte *f* budgétaire; *budget cuts* coupes *fpl* budgétaires; *budget deficit* déficit *m* budgétaire; *budget estimates* prévisions *fpl* budgétaires; ***budget forecast*** prévisions budgétaires; ***budget surplus*** excédent *m* budgétaire

(b) ***budget account*** *(with shop)* compte *m* (crédit); *(with bank)* compte permanent

2 *vi* **to budget for sth** budgetiser qch

budgetary *adj* budgétaire □ ***budgetary control*** contrôle *m* budgétaire; ***budgetary policy*** politique *f* budgétaire

buffer *n* **(a)** *(protection)* **a buffer against inflation** une mesure de protection contre l'inflation □ ***buffer stock*** *(of shares)* matelas *m*; *(of raw materials)* stock *m* tampon **(b)** COMPTR tampon *m*, mémoire *f* intermédiaire □ ***buffer memory*** mémoire tampon

bug *n* COMPTR bogue *f*

bug-ridden *adj* COMPTR bogué(e)

▸ **build into** *vt sep* **to build sth into a product** incorporer qch dans un produit; **the alarm will be built into the system** le système sera doté d'une alarme incorporée

▸ **build up** *vt sep* **(a)** *(develop)* *(business)* développer; *(reputation)* bâtir, établir; *(production)* accroître, augmenter **(b)** *(advertise)* faire de la publicité pour

building *n* **(a)** *(structure)* bâtiment *m*, immeuble *m* □ ***buildings insurance*** assurance *f* habitation **(b)** *(action)* construction *f* □ ***building contract*** contrat *m* d'entreprise; ***building contractor*** entrepreneur(euse) *m,f* de bâtiments; *Br* ***building plot*** lotissement *m*; *Br* FIN ***building society*** ≃ société *f* de crédit immobilier; **the building trade** l'industrie *f* du bâtiment, le bâtiment

build-up *n* **(a)** *(advertising)* publicité *f*; **to give sth a big build-up** faire beaucoup de publicité pour qch **(b)** *(of stock)* accumulation *f*

built-in obsolescence *n* obsolescence *f* programmée

bulk *n* **(a)** **in bulk** en gros; **to buy in bulk** acheter en gros; **to ship sth in bulk** transporter qch en vrac □ ***bulk buying*** achat *m* en gros; ***bulk carrier*** vraquier *m*; ***bulk discount*** remise *f* quantitative; ***bulk order*** grosse commande *f*, commande par quantité; ***bulk rate*** *(for sending letters)* affranchissement *m* à forfait **(b)** COMPTR *(of information)* volume *m*, masse *f*

bull 1 *n* ST EXCH spéculateur(trice) *m,f* à la hausse □ ***bull market*** marché *m* à la hausse *ou* haussier; ***bull trading*** spéculation *f* à la hausse; ***bull transaction*** opération *f* à la hausse

2 *vt* **to bull the market** chercher à faire hausser les cours

3 *vi* *(of person)* spéculer à la hausse; *(of stocks)* être en hausse

bulldog bond *n* FIN obligation *f* bulldog

bullet *n* COMPTR puce *f*

bulletin board *n* COMPTR serveur *m* télématique

bullion *n* or *m* en barres *ou* en lingots; FIN métal *m* □ ***bullion reserve*** réserve *f* métallique

bullish *adj* ST EXCH *(market, trend)* à la hausse, haussier(ère); **to be bullish** *(of person)* spéculer à la hausse □ ***bullish tendency*** tendance *f* à la hausse

> **"**
>
> Part of the charm of an auction is that the financial result is in itself a sort of critical judgement, reflecting even if not defining the taste and mood of the moment. But an auction is mainly a **bullish** market; vendors are trying to improve their prices, and few except dealers are selling on the market's way down, in order to rebuy.
>
> **"**

bumf *n Fam (documentation)* doc *f*; *(useless papers)* paperasse *f*

bumper *adj (profits, year)* exceptionnel(elle)

bundle *vt* MKTG **to bundle sth with sth** offrir qch en plus de qch; **to come bundled with sth** être vendu(e) avec qch

> **"**
>
> Recently, this computer has been selling **bundled** with £400–£500 worth of software for £1000. At this price it has come under increasing pressure from its main competitor, which starts at the same price and attracts similar discounts.
>
> **"**

buoyancy *n* ST EXCH *(of market)* fermeté *f*; *(of prices, currency)* stabilité *f*

buoyant *adj* ST EXCH *(market)* ferme; *(prices, currency)* stable

burden *vt* charger; **burdened with tax/ debts** accablé(e) d'impôts/de dettes

bureau *n* bureau *m*, agence *f* □ ***bureau de change*** bureau *m* de change

bureaucracy *n* bureaucratie *f*

bureaucratic *adj* bureaucratique

burn rate *n (of company)* point *m* mort

bus *n* COMPTR bus *m* □ ***bus board*** carte *f* bus; ***bus controller*** contrôleur *m* de bus

business n (a) *(trade)* affaires *fpl*; *(commerce)* commerce *m*; **to be in the antiques/restaurant business** être dans les antiquités/la restauration; **what's his line of business?, what business is he in?** qu'est-ce qu'il fait (comme métier)?; **to set up in business** ouvrir un commerce; **to be in/go into business for oneself** être/s'établir *ou* s'installer à son compte; **she's in business** elle est dans les affaires; **the company has been in business for twenty years** la société existe depuis vingt ans; **they've been in business together for twenty years** ils sont associés depuis vingt ans; **to go out of business** faire faillite; **business is slow** les affaires ne marchent pas; **I've got some business to discuss with him** il faut que je discute affaires avec lui; **to be away on business** être en déplacement (pour affaires); **to go to London on business** aller à Londres pour affaires; **to lose business** perdre de la clientèle; **to do business with sb** faire affaire *ou* des affaires avec qn; **to do good business** faire de bonnes affaires; **it's good/bad for business** c'est bon/mauvais pour les affaires; **how's business?** comment vont les affaires?; **business is business** les affaires sont les affaires □ FIN **business account** compte *m* professionnel *ou* commercial; **business acumen** sens *m* des affaires; **business address** *(of company)* (adresse *f* du) siège *m* social; *(of person)* adresse du bureau; **business administration** gestion *f* commerciale; **business agent** agent *m* d'affaires; **business associate** associé(e) *m,f*; **business bank** banque *f* d'affaires; **business banking** opérations *fpl* des banques d'affaires; **business buyer** acheteur(euse) *m,f* industriel(elle); **business call** visite *f* d'affaires; **business card** carte *f* (de visite) d'affaires; **business centre** centre *m* des affaires; **business class** *(in air travel)* classe *f* affaires; **business college** école *f* (supérieure) de commerce; **business concern** entreprise *f* commerciale; **business enterprise** entreprise commerciale; **business ethics** déontologie *f* professionnelle; **business expenses** frais *mpl* professionnels; **business failure** défaillance *f* d'entreprise; COMPTR **business graphics** graphiques *mpl* de gestion; **business hotel** hôtel *m* d'affaires; **business hours** *(of office)* heures *fpl* de bureau; *(of shop)* heures d'ouverture; **business intelligence system** réactique *f*; **business letter** lettre *f* commerciale; **business lunch** déjeuner *m* d'affaires; **business management** gestion d'entreprise; *(study)* économie *f* d'entreprise; **business manager** directeur(trice) *m,f* commercial(e); **business meeting** rendez-vous *m* d'affaires; MKTG **business mission** mission *f* d'activité *ou* de l'entreprise; **business news** chronique *f* économique; **business plan** projet *m* d'entreprise; **business premises** locaux *mpl* commerciaux; **business relations** relations *fpl* d'affaires *ou* commerciales; **business school** école (supérieure) de commerce; ECON **business sector** secteur *m* tertiaire *ou* d'affaires; **business services** services *mpl* du secteur tertiaire, services aux entreprises; **business strategy** stratégie *f* d'entreprise; **business trend** courant *m* d'affaires; **business trip** voyage *m* d'affaires; **business world** monde *m* des affaires

(b) *(company, firm)* affaire *f*, entreprise *f*; **to run a business** gérer une entreprise, diriger un commerce; **to have one's own business** travailler à son compte; **business for sale** commerce *m* à vendre; **a profitable business** une entreprise lucrative *ou* rentable; **the small business sector** la petite entreprise

businessman n homme *m* d'affaires; **to be a good businessman** s'entendre aux affaires

businesswoman n femme *f* d'affaires; **to be a good businesswoman** s'entendre aux affaires

bust adj Fam **to go bust** faire faillite; **the company went bust after a year** l'entreprise a fait faillite au bout d'un an

busy adj (a) *(person)* occupé(e); **the manager is busy with a customer** le directeur est occupé avec *ou* en rendez-vous avec un client (b) *(period)* chargé(e); **the summer is our busiest period** c'est en été que nous travaillons le plus (c) Am *(telephone line)* occupé(e); **I keep getting the busy signal** ça sonne toujours occupé

button n COMPTR *(on mouse)* bouton; *(for menu selection)* case *f*

buy 1 n (a) *(purchase)* **a good/bad buy** une bonne/mauvaise affaire; **to make a good/bad buy** faire une bonne/mauvaise affaire (b) ST EXCH **buy order** ordre *m* d'achat; **to give a buy order** donner un ordre d'achat

2 vt acheter; **to buy sth from sb** acheter qch à qn; **to buy earnings** investir en valeurs de croissance

3 vi FIN **to buy spot** acheter au comptant; **to buy wholesale** acheter en gros; **to buy in**

bulk acheter en grande quantité; **to buy on credit** acheter à crédit *ou* à terme

▸ **buy in** 1 *vt sep* (**a**) *(goods, commodities)* s'approvisionner de (**b**) ST EXCH acheter, acquérir

  2 *vi* ST EXCH **to buy in against a client** exécuter un client

▸ **buy into** *vt insep (company, sector)* acheter des actions de; **we hope to buy into telecommunications next year** nous espérons pouvoir acheter des parts dans les télécommunications l'an prochain

▸ **buy out** *vt sep (partner)* racheter la part de, désintéresser; **he was bought out for £50,000** on lui a racheté sa part dans l'affaire pour 50 000 livres; **she bought out all the other shareholders** elle a racheté les parts de tous les autres actionnaires

▸ **buy up** *vt sep* (**a**) *(goods, supplies)* acheter en masse (**b**) FIN *(company, shares, stock)* racheter; **the company bought up £50,000 worth of shares** la société a racheté des actions pour une valeur de 50 000 livres

buyer *n* (**a**) *(consumer)* acheteur(euse) *m,f*; **first time buyers** *(of property)* = personnes achetant un logement pour la première fois □ *buyer credit* crédit-acheteur *m*; FIN *buyer's market* marché *m* à la baisse, marché demandeur; *buyer's option* prime *f* acheteur (**b**) *(for company, shop)* acheteur(euse) *m,f* □ *head buyer* acheteur principal

buyer-readiness *n* MKTG prédisposition *f* à l'achat

buy-in *n* ST EXCH exécution *f*

buying *n* achat *m*; **buying and selling** l'achat et la vente; **buying back** rachat *m*; **buying in** MKTG approvisionnement *m*; ST EXCH exécution *f* □ *buying behaviour* comportement *m* d'achat; *buying department* service *m* (des) achats; MKTG *buying motive* motif *m* *ou* motivation *f* d'achat; *buying order* ordre *m* d'achat; *buying power* pouvoir *m* d'achat; ST EXCH *buying quotation, buying rate (of shares)* cours *m* d'achat

buy-out *n (of company)* rachat *m*; *(of partner)* rachat, désintéressement *m*

> **"**
>
> Many business experts hold the view that selling off a business to a management **buy-out** team is the easy way out and is not in the best interests of a company's shareholders. We had to weigh up the bid which the managers put forward against outside bids and they're never in exactly the same terms. So, in a sense, you're comparing apples with pears.
>
> **"**

bye-laws, by-laws *npl (of company)* statuts *mpl*, règlements *mpl*

by-product *n* sous-produit *m*, (produit *m*) dérivé *m*

byte *n* COMPTR (**eight-bit**) **byte** octet *m*

CA *n Br* (*abbr* **chartered accountant**) expert *m* comptable

C/A, c/a *n* BANKING (*abbr Br* **current** or **cheque** or *Am* **checking account**) C/C *m*, CCB *m*

CAC 40 index *n* ST EXCH indice *m* CAC 40

cache *n* COMPTR **cache (memory)** antémémoire *f*, mémoire-cache *f*

cachet *n* MKTG label *m*

CAD *n* (**a**) COMPTR (*abbr* **computer-assisted design**) CAO *f* (**b**) (*abbr* **cash against documents**) comptant *m* contre documents

CAD/CAM *n* COMPTR (*abbr* **computer-assisted design/computer-assisted manufacture**) CFAO *f*

CAE *n* COMPTR (*abbr* **computer-assisted engineering**) IAO *f*

CAL *n* COMPTR (*abbr* **computer-assisted learning**) EAO *m*

calculate 1 *vt* calculer
2 *vi* faire un calcul

calculated risk *n* risque *m* calculé

calculation *n* calcul *m*; **to make a calculation** faire un calcul; **to be out in one's calculations** être loin de son compte

calculator *n* calculatrice *f*

calendar *n* calendrier *m* ▫ *calendar month* mois *m* civil; *calendar year* année *f* civile

call 1 *n* (**a**) FIN (*claim*) demande *f* (d'argent); **call (up)** appel *m* de fonds *ou* de versement; **call for capital** appel de fonds; **payable at call** payable sur demande *ou* à présentation *ou* à vue ▫ *call letter* avis *m* d'appel de fonds; *call loan* prêt *m* à vue, prêt remboursable sur demande
(**b**) ST EXCH **call (option)** option *f* d'achat, call *m*; **call on a hundred shares** option de cent actions ▫ *call price* cours *m* du dont
(**c**) (**telephone**) **call** appel *m*, communication *f* (téléphonique); **to receive a call** recevoir un appel; **to make a call** passer un coup de téléphone; **to give sb a call** téléphoner à qn, appeler qn; **you have a call from Canada** on vous appelle du Canada; **there was a call for you** il y a eu un coup de téléphone *ou* un appel pour toi; **he's on a call** il est en ligne; **will you accept the call?** (*when charges are reversed*) est-ce que vous prenez *ou* acceptez l'appel?; **to put a call through** passer la communication; **to return sb's call** rappeler qn ▫ *call centre* centre *m* d'appels
(**d**) (*of representative*) visite *f*, passage *m*; **to pay** or **make a call on sb** rendre visite à qn

2 *vt* (**a**) FIN **to call a loan** demander le remboursement d'un prêt
(**b**) (*on telephone*) téléphoner à, appeler
(**c**) (*order*) **to call a strike** ordonner une grève, lancer un ordre de grève; **to call a meeting** convoquer une réunion

3 *vi* (*on telephone*) appeler; **who's calling, please?, may I ask who's calling?** c'est de la part de qui, s'il vous plaît?; **could you call again later?** est-ce que vous pouvez rappeler plus tard?

▸ **call back** 1 *vt sep* rappeler; **I'll call you back later** je vous rappellerai plus tard
2 *vi* rappeler; **could you call back later, please?** est-ce que vous pouvez rappeler plus tard?

▸ **call for** *vt insep* (*demand*) réclamer; **workers are calling for a wage increase** les travailleurs demandent une augmentation de salaire

▸ **call in** *vt sep* (**a**) (*person*) (*into building, office*) faire entrer; **call Miss Smith in, please** faites entrer Mlle Smith, s'il vous plaît; **an accountant was called in to look at the books** on a fait venir un comptable pour examiner les livres de comptes
(**b**) FIN **to call in one's money** faire rentrer ses fonds; **to call in a loan** demander le remboursement d'un prêt
(**c**) (*currency*) retirer de la circulation

▸ **call off** *vt sep* (*meeting, strike, deal*) annuler

▸ **call on** *vt insep* (**a**) (*request*) **to call on sb to do sth** demander à qn de faire qch; **they are calling on the government to take action** ils demandent au gouvernement d'agir
(**b**) (*visit*) rendre visite à; **the sales reps call on their clients monthly** les représentants de commerce rendent visite à leurs clients une fois par mois

▸ **call up** *vt sep* (**a**) (*on telephone*) téléphoner à, appeler (**b**) COMPTR (*help screen, file*) rappeler

callable *adj* FIN (*debt, loan*) remboursable avant échéance

calling in n (a) FIN (of debt, loan) demande f de remboursement immédiat (b) (of currency) retrait m

CAM n COMPTR (abbr **computer-assisted manufacture**) FAO f

campaign 1 n campagne f
2 vi faire campagne (**for/against** pour/contre); **workers are campaigning against the closure of the factory** les travailleurs font campagne contre la fermeture de l'usine

cancel 1 vt (a) (order, meeting, reservation, flight) annuler; (debt) faire remise à; (cheque) faire opposition à; (goods) décommander; LAW (agreement, contract) annuler, résilier (b) ACCT contrepasser; **to cancel each other** (of two entries) s'annuler (c) COMPTR annuler ▫ **cancel button** case f 'annuler'
2 vi COMPTR s'annuler

cancellation n (of order, meeting, reservation, flight) annulation f; (of debt) règlement m; (of cheque) opposition f; LAW (of agreement, contract) annulation, résiliation f ▫ **cancellation charge** frais mpl d'annulation; **cancellation clause** clause f d'annulation ou de résiliation; **cancellation fee** frais d'annulation

C and F (abbr **cost and freight**) coût et fret

C and I (abbr **cost and insurance**) C&A

candidate n (for job) candidat(e) m,f

cannibalization n MKTG cannibalisation f

cannibalize vt MKTG cannibaliser

canteen n cantine f

canvass 1 vt (person) démarcher, solliciter des commandes de; (area) prospecter
2 vi faire du démarchage; **to canvass for customers** prospecter la clientèle

canvasser n placier m, démarcheur(euse) m,f

canvassing n (for orders) sollicitation f; (for custom) prospection f, démarchage m

CAP n EU (abbr **Common Agricultural Policy**) PAC f

cap 1 n taux m plafond
2 vt (spending) plafonner, fixer un plafond à

capacity n (a) (output) rendement m; **to work at full capacity** travailler à plein rendement; **the factory has not yet reached capacity** l'usine n'a pas encore atteint son rendement maximum ▫ **capacity output** rendement m maximum
(b) (of container) capacité f
(c) (position) **in the capacity of** en qualité de;

to act in one's official capacity agir dans l'exercice de ses fonctions; **he's acting in an advisory capacity** il a un rôle consultatif

capital n capital m, capitaux mpl, fonds mpl; (assets) avoir m; **to live on one's capital** vivre sur son capital ▫ **capital accumulation** accumulation f de capital; **capital allowances** déductions fpl (fiscales) sur frais d'établissement; **capital assets** actif m immobilisé; **capital budget** budget m d'investissement; **capital charge** intérêt m des capitaux (investis); **capital clause** (in memorandum of association) constitution f du capital social; **capital contribution** apport m ou dotation f en capital; ACCT **capital employed** capital engagé; **capital equipment** biens mpl d'équipement, capitaux fixes; **capital expenditure** mise f de fonds, investissements mpl industriels; **capital gains** plus-value f; **capital gains tax** impôt m sur les plus-values; **capital goods** biens d'équipement; **capital growth** croissance m du capital; **capital injection** injection f de capital ou de capitaux; ACCT **capital items** biens capitaux; **capital loss** moins-value f; **capital market** marché m financier ou des capitaux; **capital movements** mouvements mpl des capitaux; **capital outlay** dépenses fpl en capital; **capital profits** plus-value; **capital share** part f sociale; Am **capital stock** capital social, capital-actions m; **capital structure** plan m financier; **capital tax** impôt sur le capital; **capital turnover** rotation f des capitaux

capital-intensive adj à forte intensité capitalistique

capitalism n capitalisme m

capitalist n & adj capitaliste mf

capitalization n FIN capitalisation f ▫ **capitalization issue** attribution f d'actions gratuites; **capitalization of reserves** incorporation f de réserves au capital

capitalize vt (a) (convert into capital) capitaliser; (raise capital from) constituer le capital social de (par émission d'actions); (provide with capital) pourvoir de capital ou de fonds ▫ **capitalized value** valeur f capitalisée
(b) (estimate value of) capitaliser; **they capitalized her investments at £50,000** ils ont capitalisé ses investissements à 50 000 livres; **the company is capitalized at £100,000** la société dispose d'un capital de 100 000 livres

caps *npl* COMPTR *(abbr* **capital letters***)* *caps lock* verrouillage *m* des majuscules; *caps lock key* touche *f* de verrouillage des majuscules

captive *adj* MKTG captif(ive) □ *captive audience* audience *f* captive; *captive market* clientèle *f* captive, marché *m* captif

captive-product pricing *n* MKTG fixation *f* du prix des produits liés

capture *vt* *(market)* accaparer; **in one year they have captured a large part of the mail-order market** en un an ils se sont emparés d'une part importante du marché de la vente par correspondance

card *n* (**a**) *(with printed information)* carte *f*; *(for card index)* fiche *f* □ *card index* fichier *m* (**b**) COMPTR carte *f* □ *card slot* emplacement *m* pour carte

card-index *vt* mettre sur fiches

cardphone *n* TEL publiphone *m* *ou* téléphone *m* à carte

career *n* carrière *f*; **a career in banking/engineering** une carrière dans la banque/l'ingénierie; **it was a good/bad career move** ça a été bon/mauvais pour ma/sa/*etc* carrière □ *career counselling* orientation *f* professionnelle; *careers service* service *m* d'orientation professionnelle

care of *prep* *(in addresses)* **care of Mr McLean** aux (bons) soins de M. McLean, chez M. McLean

cargo *n* cargaison *f*, chargement *m*; **to take on** *or* **embark cargo** charger des marchandises; **cargo outward** chargement d'aller; **cargo homeward** chargement de retour □ *cargo boat* cargo *m*; *cargo plane* avion-cargo *m*; *cargo ship* cargo

carnet *n* CUSTOMS *(pass)* carnet *m* de passage en douanes

carriage *n* *(transportation)* transport *m*; *(cost of transportation)* (frais *mpl* de) port *m*; **to pay the carriage** payer le transport; **carriage forward** (en) port dû, port avancé; **carriage free** franc de port, franco; **carriage insurance paid** port payé, assurance comprise; **carriage paid** (en) port payé □ *carriage expenses* frais de port

carrier *n* (**a**) *(company)* entrepreneur *m* de transports, transporteur *m* (**b**) COMPTR, TEL opérateur *m*

carry 1 *vt* (**a**) *(keep in stock)* vendre, avoir; **do you carry computer accessories?** est-ce que vous vendez des accessoires pour ordinateurs?
(**b**) *(interest)* rapporter; **the investment carries 10% interest over three years** l'investissement rapporte 10% d'intérêts pendant trois ans
(**c**) *(proposal, motion)* voter; **the motion was carried unanimously** la motion a été votée à l'unanimité
(**d**) *(goods)* transporter

▶ **carry forward** *vt sep* ACCT *(item)* reporter; **carried forward** report, à reporter

▶ **carry on** *vt sep* *(trade, business)* exercer

▶ **carry out** *vt sep* *(market research)* effectuer; *(instructions)* exécuter; *(order)* donner suite à

▶ **carry over** *vt sep* (**a**) ACCT *(balance)* faire un report de, reporter; **to carry over a loss to the following year** reporter une perte sur l'année suivante
(**b**) ST EXCH *(shares)* reporter, prendre en report; **carried over** *(stock)* en report
(**c**) *(defer)* reporter; **you may carry over your holiday entitlement to the following year** vous avez la possibilité de reporter vos congés sur l'année suivante; **that will have to be carried over to the next meeting** il faudra poursuivre ce point lors de la prochaine réunion

carrying *n* (**a**) *(transport)* transport *m* □ *carrying charges, carrying cost* frais *mpl* de port (**b**) *Am* ACCT *carrying cost, carrying value* valeur *f* comptable

cartage *n* *(transport)* transport *m*, camionnage *m*; *(cost)* frais *mpl* de transport □ *cartage note* bordereau *m* d'expédition

cartel *n* cartel *m*; **to form a cartel** former un cartel; **an oil/steel cartel** un cartel du pétrole/de l'acier □ *cartel laws* lois *fpl* anti-trust

cart note *n* (**a**) *(for transporting goods)* bordereau *m* d'expédition (**b**) *(for taking goods from customs)* permis *m* de sortie de marchandises

CASE *n* COMPTR *(abbr* **computer-assisted software engineering***)* ingénierie *f* des systèmes assistée par ordinateur

case *n* (**a**) *(container)* **(packing) case** caisse *f* (**b**) LAW affaire *f* (**c**) COMPTR **case sensitive** qui distingue les majuscules des minuscules; **this e-mail address is case sensitive** cette adresse électronique tient compte des majuscules

cash *n* *(coins, banknotes)* liquide *m*, espèces *fpl*; *Fam (money in general)* argent *m*; **to pay (in) cash** *(not credit)* payer comptant; *(money as opposed to cheque)* payer en liquide *ou* en espèces; **cash against documents** comptant contre documents; ACCT **cash at bank** avoir

m en banque; **cash on delivery** paiement *m* à la livraison, livraison *f* contre remboursement; ACCT **cash in till** encaisse *f*; **cash with order** paiement à la commande, envoi *m* contre paiement □ *cash account* compte *m* de caisse; *cash advance* avance *m* en numéraire; *cash balance* (status) situation *f* de caisse; (amount remaining) solde *m* actif, solde de caisse; *cash bonus* prime *f* en espèces; *cash book* livre *m* de caisse; *cash box* caisse *f*; *cash budget* budget *m* de trésorerie; *cash and carry* libre-service *m* de demi-gros; ACCT *cash contribution* apport *m* en numéraire; MKTG *cash cow* (product) vache *f* à lait; *cash deal* marché *m* au comptant; FIN *cash deposit* versement *m* ou dépôt *m* d'espèces; *cash desk* caisse; *cash discount* escompte *m* de caisse, remise *f* sur paiement (au) comptant; *cash dispenser* distributeur *m* (automatique) de billets; *cash dividend* dividende *m* en espèces; ACCT *cash expenditure* dépenses *fpl* de caisse; *cash flow* FIN cash-flow *m*, trésorerie *f*; ACCT (in cash flow statement) marge *f* brute d'autofinancement; *cash flow forecast* prévision *f* de trésorerie; *cash flow management* gestion *f* de trésorerie; *cash flow problems* problèmes *mpl* de trésorerie; ACCT *cash flow statement* état *m* des mouvements de la trésorerie; FIN *cash incentive* stimulation *f* financière; ACCT *cash item* article *m* de caisse; ACCT *cash order* ordre *m* au comptant; ACCT *cash outflow* sorties *fpl* de trésorerie; *cash payment* paiement (au) comptant *ou* en espèces; *cash point* distributeur (automatique) de billets; *cash price* prix *m* au comptant; *cash purchase* achat *m* au comptant, achat contre espèces; ACCT *cash ratio* ratio *m* de trésorerie; ACCT *cash receipt* reçu *m* pour paiement en espèces, reçu d'espèces; ACCT *cash received* (balance sheet item) entrée *f* d'argent; *cash register* caisse (enregistreuse); ACCT *cash report (form)* situation *f* de caisse; *cash reserves* réserves *fpl* en espèces; *cash sale* vente *f* au comptant; *cash settlement* liquidation *f* en espèces; *cash shortage* insuffisance *f* d'espèces; ACCT *cash statement* état *m* ou bordereau *m* ou relevé *m* de caisse; ACCT *cash surplus* restant *m* en caisse; *cash terms* payable au comptant; ACCT *cash voucher* pièce *f* de caisse, PC *f*; *cash withdrawal* retrait *m* d'espèces
2 *vt* (cheque) toucher, encaisser; (bill) encaisser, escompter

▸ **cash in** *vt sep* (bond, savings certificate) se faire rembourser, réaliser

▸ **cash up** *vi Br* faire les comptes, faire la caisse

cashier *n* caissier(ère) *m,f*, préposé(e) *m,f* à la caisse

cashless society *n* société *f* sans argent (où toutes les transactions sont effectuées en argent électronique)

cask *n* fût *m*, tonneau *m*

CASM *n* COMPTR (abbr **computer-assisted sales and marketing**) vente *f* et marketing assistés par ordinateur

cassette drive *n* COMPTR lecteur *m* de cassettes

casting vote *n* voix *f* prépondérante; **the chairman has the casting vote** la voix du président est prépondérante; **to give the casting vote** départager les voix

casual *adj* (employment, worker) occasionnel(elle), temporaire; **to employ sb on a casual basis** employer qn de façon épisodique

casualisation of labour *n* ECON précarisation *f* de l'emploi

catalogue, *Am* **catalog 1** *n* catalogue *m*; **to buy sth by catalogue** acheter qch sur catalogue
2 *vt* cataloguer

catch *vt Fam* ST EXCH **to catch a cold** perdre de l'argent lors d'une transaction

category leader *n* MKTG chef *m* de file dans sa catégorie

▸ **cater for** *vt insep* (**a**) (deal with, provide for) s'occuper de; **we cater for the needs of small companies** nous répondons aux besoins des petites entreprises; **does the building cater for disabled staff?** le bâtiment dispose-t-il de l'équipement nécessaire pour l'accueil d'employés handicapés? (**b**) (provide meals for) préparer les repas pour

caveat *n* LAW avertissement *m*; **to enter a caveat (against)** former *ou* mettre opposition (à); **caveat against unfair practices** avertissement contre la concurrence déloyale; **caveat emptor** aux risques de l'acheteur; **caveat subscriptor** aux risques du signataire

CBI *n* (abbr **Confederation of British Industry**) = patronat britannique, ≃ CNPF *m*

cc (abbr **carbon copy**) pcc

cd/fwd ACCT (abbr **carried forward**) reporté(e)

CDI *n* COMPTR (*abbr* **compact disc interactive**) CD-I *m*

CD-ROM *n* COMPTR (*abbr* **compact disc-read only memory**) CD-ROM *m*; **available on CD-ROM** existe en CD-ROM □ *CD-ROM burner* graveur *m* de CD-ROM; *CD-ROM drive* lecteur *m* de CD-ROM, lecteur de disque optique; *CD-ROM newspaper* journal *m* sur CD-ROM; *CD-ROM reader* lecteur de CD-ROM; *CD-ROM writer* graveur *m* de CD-ROM

cease *vt* **to cease trading** cesser ses activités, cesser toute activité commerciale

ceiling *n* ECON plafond *m*; **to reach a ceiling** (*of prices, interest rates*) plafonner; **to have a ceiling of** être plafonné(e) à; **to fix a ceiling to sth** fixer un plafond à qch; **the government has set a 3% ceiling on wage rises** le gouvernement a limité à 3% les augmentations de salaire □ *ceiling price* prix *m* plafond

> **"**
> "We are not against pay rises, but people have got to be sensible," he said, defending the three per cent **ceiling** on pay rises which has just come into force here.
> **"**

cell *n* COMPTR (*on spreadsheet*) cellule *f*

center *Am* = **centre**

central *adj* (**a**) FIN **central bank** banque *f* centrale (**b**) COMPTR **central processing unit** unité *f* centrale (de traitement), processeur *m* central

centralized *adj* centralisé(e) □ *centralized management* gestion *f* intégrée; *centralized purchasing* achats *mpl* centralisés

centre, *Am* **center** *n* (*place, building*) centre *m*

CEO *n Am* (*abbr* **chief executive officer**) directeur(trice) *m,f* général(e); **President and CEO** président-directeur *m* général, PDG *m*

certificate *n* certificat *m* □ BANKING *certificate of damage* certificat d'avarie; *certificate of deposit* bon *m* de caisse; *certificate of incorporation* certificat d'enregistrement de société; *certificate of insurance* attestation *f* d'assurance; *certificate of origin* certificat d'origine; *certificate of quality* certificat de qualité; *certificate of registration* (*of ship*) certificat d'inscription maritime

certified *adj* (**a**) *Am* **certified public accountant** expert *m* comptable (**b**) *certified cheque* chèque *m* certifié (**c**) LAW *certified copy* copie *f* certifiée conforme; *certified true copy* (*on document*) pour copie conforme

certify *vt* (**a**) (*confirm*) certifier (**b**) (*cheque*) certifier

CET *n* EU (*abbr* **common external tariff**) tarif *m* externe commun

> **"**
> The 13 member countries also set a new target date of October 1991 for the implementation of a common external tariff (**CET**) on imports. They insisted that there was no long-term contradiction between a common tariff structure to protect fledgling industries, and CARICOM taking advantage of such free trade areas as that proposed in the US Enterprise for the Americas Initiative.
> **"**

CF (*abbr* **carriage forward**) (en) port dû, port avancé

CFO *n Am* (*abbr* **Chief Financial Officer**) chef *m* comptable, chef de la comptabilité

CGI *n* COMPTR (**a**) (*abbr* **common gateway interface**) interface *f* commune de passerelle, CGI *f* (**b**) (*abbr* **computer-generated images**) images *fpl* créées par ordinateur

chain *n* (**a**) (*of stores, restaurants*) chaîne *f* □ *chain store* magasin *m* à succursales (multiples) (**b**) *chain of distribution* circuit *m ou* réseau *m* de distribution

chair 1 *n* (*chairperson*) président(e) *m,f*; **to be in the chair** présider; **to support the chair** se ranger à l'avis du président; **to address the chair** s'adresser au président
2 *vt* (*meeting*) présider

chairman *n* (*of meeting*) président(e) *m,f*; (*of company*) président-directeur *m* général, PDG *m*; **to act as chairman** présider (la séance); **chairman and managing director** président-directeur général, PDG; **Mr Chairman** Monsieur le Président; **Chairman of the Board** Président du Conseil d'Administration □ *chairman's report* rapport *m* (annuel) du président

chairmanship *n* présidence *f*; **under the chairmanship of Mr Greene** sous la présidence de M. Greene

chairperson *n* président(e) *m,f*

chairwoman *nf* présidente *f*; **Madam Chairwoman** Madame la Présidente

challenger n MKTG challengeur m, prétendant(e) m,f

chamber n Chamber of Commerce Chambre f de commerce; **Chamber of Trade** Chambre de métiers

Chancellor of the Exchequer n Br
Chancelier m de l'Échiquier, ≃ ministre m des finances

change 1 n **(small) change** (petite) monnaie f; **to give change for £20** donner ou rendre la monnaie de 20 livres

2 vt (money) changer; **to change dollars into francs** changer des dollars en francs

channel n (a) (means) canal m, voie f; **to go through the official channels** suivre la filière officielle; **to open up new channels for trade** créer de nouveaux débouchés pour le commerce □ **channel of distribution** circuit m ou canal de distribution; MKTG **channel management** gestion f du circuit de distribution (b) COMPTR canal m

Chaps n Br BANKING (abbr **clearing house automated payment system**) SIT m

character n COMPTR caractère m; **characters per inch** caractères par pouce; **characters per second** caractères par seconde □ **character code** code m de caractère; **character generator** générateur m de caractères; **character insert** insertion f de caractère; **character recognition** reconnaissance f de caractères; **character set** jeu m de caractères; **character smoothing** lissage m de caractères; **character space** espace m; **character spacing** espacement m des caractères

charge 1 n (cost) frais mpl, prix m; (to an account) imputation f; **to make a charge for sth** compter qch, faire payer qch; **there is no extra charge for installation** l'installation est comprise dans le prix; **what's the charge?** combien est-ce que ça coûte?; **at a small charge** moyennant une faible rétribution; Am **will that be cash or charge?** vous payez comptant ou vous le portez à votre compte? □ Am **charge account** compte m crédit d'achats; **charge card** carte f de paiement

2 vt (a) (defer payment of) **charge it** mettez-le sur mon compte; **charge it to the company's account** mettez-le sur le compte de l'entreprise; **I charged all my expenses to the company** j'ai mis tous mes frais sur le compte de la société

(b) (person) faire payer; (sum) faire payer, prendre; (commission) prélever; **they**

charged us $50 for delivery ils nous ont fait payer 50 dollars pour la livraison; **how much will you charge for the lot?** combien demandez-vous pour le tout?; **you will be charged for postage** les frais postaux seront à votre charge

3 vi (demand payment) faire payer; **they don't charge for postage and packing** ils ne font pas payer le port et l'emballage

▸ **charge off** vt Am (capital) réduire, amortir

▸ **charge up** vt sep **to charge sth up to sb's account** mettre qch sur le compte de qn; **could you charge it up?** pourriez-vous le mettre sur mon compte?

chargeable adj (a) (to an account) imputable; **to be chargeable to sb** (payable by) être à la charge de qn, être pris(e) en charge par qn; **who is it chargeable to?** c'est à la charge de qui?; **could you make that chargeable to Crown Ltd?** est-ce que vous pourriez facturer Crown Ltd? □ **chargeable expenses** frais mpl facturables (b) FIN imposable □ **chargeable asset** actif m imposable sur les plus-values; **chargeable gain** bénéfice m imposable

> **"**
> In the first three years of trading, the haulier should be careful not to make any **chargeable gains** for tax purposes. Liability to capital gains tax arises where a **chargeable gain** is made on the disposal of company assets.
> **"**

chargehand n chef m d'équipe

charitable trust n fondation f d'utilité publique

chart 1 n (diagram) graphique m □ ACCT **chart of accounts** plan m comptable général; **chart analyst** analyste mf sur graphiques

2 vt (a) (on diagram) faire le graphique de; **this graph charts sales over the last ten years** ce graphique montre l'évolution des ventes au cours des dix dernières années

(b) (follow) (progress, rise) retracer; **the director charted a way out of financial collapse** le directeur a établi ou mis au point un plan pour éviter un effondrement financier

charter 1 n (a) (of company) statuts mpl (b) (of aeroplane, boat) affrètement m □ **charter flight** vol m charter; **charter plane** (avion m) charter m

2 vt (a) (company) accorder une charte à (b) (aeroplane, boat) affréter

chartered *adj* (**a**) *Br* **chartered accountant** expert *m* comptable, *Can* comptable *mf* agréé(e); **chartered bank** banque *f* privilégiée; **chartered company** compagnie *f* privilégiée *ou* à charte (**b**) *(aeroplane, boat)* affrété(e)

▸ **chase up** *vt sep (debt)* essayer de se faire rembourser; *(person)* essayer de contacter; **can you chase up the manager for me?** pouvez-vous relancer le directeur à propos de ce que je lui ai demandé?

chat COMPTR **1** *n* bavardage *m*
2 *vi* bavarder

cheap *adj* bon marché, pas cher (chère); **to buy sth cheap** acheter qch (à) bon marché; **it works out cheaper to buy 10 kilos** cela revient moins cher d'acheter 10 kilos à la fois □ **cheap money** argent *m* à bon marché; **cheap rate** tarif *m* réduit

cheaply *adv* (à) bon marché; **they can manufacture more cheaply than we can** ils sont à même de fabriquer à meilleur marché que nous

check 1 *n* (**a**) *(restraint)* frein *m*; **to put a check on production** freiner la production (**b**) *(verification)* contrôle *m*, vérification *f* □ **check sample** échantillon *m* témoin (**c**) *Am (bill)* addition *f*, facture *f* (**d**) *Am (cheque)* chèque *m* (**e**) COMPTR **check box** case *f* de pointage *ou* d'option
2 *vt* (**a**) *(price increases, inflation)* enrayer; *(production)* freiner (**b**) *(verify, examine) (accounts, figures)* vérifier; *(document)* examiner; **to check the books** pointer les écritures; **all the sales are checked** toutes les ventes sont contrôlées (**c**) *Am (baggage)* mettre à la consigne

▸ **check in 1** *vt sep (baggage) (at airport)* (faire) enregistrer; *(at left-luggage)* mettre à la consigne
2 *vi (at hotel)* se présenter à la réception; *(at airport)* se présenter à l'enregistrement

▸ **check off** *vt sep (goods)* recenser; **to check sth off a list** cocher qch dans une liste

▸ **check out** *vi (leave hotel)* quitter l'hôtel

▸ **check over** *vt sep (goods)* examiner, vérifier

checkbook *Am* = **chequebook**

check-in *n (at airport)* **check-in time is 30 minutes prior to departure** les voyageurs sont priés de se présenter à l'enregistrement 30 minutes avant l'heure du départ □ **check-in desk** guichet *m* d'enregistrement

checking account *n Am* compte *m* courant

checkless society *Am* = **chequeless society**

check-out *n* (**a**) *(in supermarket)* caisse *f* (**b**) *(in hotel)* **check-out time is at 12 noon** les clients doivent quitter la chambre avant midi (le jour du départ)

cheque, *Am* **check** *n* chèque *m*; **a cheque for ten pounds** un chèque de dix livres; **cheque to order** chèque à ordre; **cheque to bearer** chèque au porteur; **to cash a cheque** toucher un chèque; **to endorse a cheque** endosser un chèque; **to make out a cheque (to sb)** établir *ou* faire un chèque (à l'ordre de qn); **who should I make the cheque out to?** à quel ordre dois-je faire *ou* écrire le chèque?; **will you take a cheque?** est-ce que vous acceptez les chèques?; **to pay by cheque** régler par chèque; **to pay a cheque into the bank** déposer un chèque à la banque; **to stop a cheque** faire opposition à un chèque □ **cheque account** compte *m* (de) chèques; **cheque counterfoil** talon *m* de chèque, souche *f*; *Br* **cheque (guarantee) card** carte *f* bancaire *(sans laquelle un chéquier n'est pas valable)*; **cheque number** numéro *m* de chèque; **cheque stub** talon de chèque, souche

chequebook, *Am* **checkbook** *n* carnet *m* de chèques, chéquier *m* □ **chequebook account** compte *m* (de) chèques

chequeless society, *Am* **checkless society** *n* société *f* sans chèques

chief *adj Br* **chief accountant,** *Am* **Chief Financial Officer** chef *m* comptable, chef de la comptabilité; *Br* **chief executive,** *Am* **Chief Executive Officer** directeur(trice) *m,f* général(e)

Chinese walls *npl* = murs imaginaires qui symbolisent la confidentialité indispensable dans certains milieux financiers et séparent des services qui, par ailleurs, travaillent côte à côte

chip *n* COMPTR puce *f*

CHIPS *n Am* BANKING *(abbr* **Clearing House Interbank Payment System)** SIT *m*

choice 1 *n* MKTG *(selection)* choix *m*; **the product of choice** le premier choix □ **choice**

set ensemble *m* de considérations, éventail *m* de choix

2 *adj (food, product)* de choix, de première qualité

chooser *n* COMPTR sélecteur *m*

Christmas bonus *n* prime *f* de fin d'année

chronic *adj (shortage, unemployment)* chronique

churn *vt Fam* ST EXCH *(portfolio)* faire tourner

> "
>
> In August 1990, the Securities Association, the self-regulatory body covering share dealers and advisers, acted for the first time against a broker found guilty of "**churning**" his clients' portfolios. This involves brokers generating income by constantly and needlessly buying and selling investments for their clients in order to collect the heavy commissions which accrue. It is virtually impossible to prove because guilty brokers tend to "**churn**" the portfolios of inexperienced clients.
>
> "

churning *n Fam* ST EXCH rotation *f* de portefeuille *m*

CIF, cif *n (abbr* **cost, insurance and freight**) CAF *m*

CIM waybill *n* lettre *f* de voiture CIM

circular **1** *n* **(a)** *(letter)* circulaire *f* **(b)** *(advertisement)* prospectus *m*
2 *adj* **circular letter** circulaire *f*; **circular letter of credit** lettre *f* de crédit circulaire

circulate **1** *vt* **(a)** *(banknotes)* mettre en circulation, émettre **(b)** *(document, prospectus) (from person to person)* faire circuler; *(by mass mailing)* diffuser; **please circulate the minutes of this morning's meeting** veuillez faire circuler le compte-rendu de la réunion de ce matin
2 *vi (of money)* circuler; **to circulate freely** circuler librement, rouler

circulating *adj* circulant(e) □ ACCT **circulating assets** actif *m* circulant; FIN **circulating capital** capitaux *mpl* circulants

circulation *n* **(a)** *(of capital)* roulement *m*, circulation *f* **(b)** **to be in circulation** *(of money)* circuler; **notes in circulation** billets *mpl* en circulation **(c)** *(of newspaper)* tirage *m*;

a newspaper with a large circulation un journal à grand *ou* gros tirage

City *n* **the City** la Cité *ou* City (de Londres) *(centre des affaires)*; **he's in the City** il est dans la finance *(dans la Cité de Londres)* □ **the City Companies** les corporations *fpl* de la Cité de Londres

civil *adj* **civil servant** fonctionnaire *mf*; **civil service** administration *f*

claim **1** *n* **(a)** *(demand) (for damages, compensation)* demande *f* d'indemnisation; *(as a right)* revendication *f*, réclamation *f*; **to put in a claim for sth** demander une indemnisation pour qch; **to make a legal claim for sth** revendiquer qch; **they're putting in a claim for better working conditions** ils demandent de meilleures conditions de travail
(b) INS demande *f* d'indemnité, déclaration *f* de sinistre; **to make** *or* **put in a claim (for sth)** demander une indemnité (pour qch) □ **claim form** formulaire *m* de demande d'indemnité
2 *vt (as a right)* réclamer, revendiquer; **to claim damages (from sb)** réclamer des dommages-intérêts (à qn); **workers are claiming the right to strike** les ouvriers revendiquent le droit de (faire) grève

▸ **claim back** *vt sep (VAT)* récupérer

claimant *n (for social security, insurance)* demandeur(eresse) *m,f*

clampdown *n* répression *f* (**on** de); **there has been a clampdown on credit** il y a eu un resserrement du crédit

classified *adj* **(a)** *(secret)* classé(e) secret(ète), confidentiel(elle) □ **classified information** renseignements *mpl* classés secrets **(b)** **classified advertisements** *(in newspaper)* annonces *fpl* classées, petites annonces

clause *n (of contract, law, treaty)* clause *f*; INS *(of policy)* avenant *m*

▸ **claw back** *vt sep* FIN *(expenditure)* récupérer

clawback *n* FIN récupération *f*

clean *adj (bill of lading)* sans réserves, net (nette)

clear **1** *adj* **(a)** *(net)* net (nette); **clear of taxes** net d'impôt □ **clear loss** perte *f* sèche; **clear profit** bénéfice *m* net
(b) **three clear days** trois jours francs; **ten clear days' notice** préavis *m* de dix jours francs
(c) *(accounts)* en règle
2 *vt* **(a)** *(debt)* liquider, acquitter; *(mortgage)* purger; *(account)* solder

(**b**) *(authorize)* *(ship)* expédier; *(goods through customs)* dédouaner; **to clear customs** *(of person)* passer la douane; *(of goods)* être dédouané(e)

(**c**) *(make profit of)* **she cleared 10% on the deal** l'affaire lui a rapporté 10% tous frais payés *ou* 10% net; **I clear a thousand pounds monthly** je fais un bénéfice net de mille livres par mois

(**d**) BANKING *(cheque)* compenser, virer; FIN *(bill)* régler

(**e**) COMPTR **to clear the screen** vider l'écran
3 *vi (of cheque)* être encaissé(e); **it takes three working days for cheques to clear** il y a trois jours ouvrables de délai d'encaissement

▸ **clear off** *vt sep (debt)* liquider, acquitter; *(stock)* liquider

clearance *n* (**a**) CUSTOMS *(of goods)* dédouanement *m*; **to effect customs clearance** procéder aux formalités de la douane; **clearance inward(s)** déclaration *f* d'entrée; **clearance outward(s)** déclaration de sortie □ *clearance certificate* lettre *f* de mer (**b**) *(of cheque)* compensation *f*

clearing *n (of cheque)* compensation *f*; *(of account)* liquidation *f*, solde *m*; *(of debt)* acquittement *m*; **general clearing** compensation de chèques en dehors de Londres; **under the clearing procedure** par voie de compensation □ *clearing account* compte *m* de compensation; *clearing bank* banque *f* de clearing; *clearing house* chambre *f* de compensation; **to pass a cheque through the clearing house** compenser un chèque

clerical *adj clerical error (in document)* faute *f* de copiste; *(in accounting)* erreur *f* d'écriture; *clerical job* emploi *m* de bureau; *clerical staff* personnel *m ou* employés *mpl* de bureau; *clerical work* travail *m* de bureau; *clerical worker* employé(e) *m,f* de bureau

clerk 1 *n* (**a**) *(in office)* employé(e) *m,f* de bureau, commis *m*; *(in bank)* employé de banque (**b**) *Am (in shop)* vendeur(euse) *m,f* (**c**) *Am (receptionist)* réceptionniste *mf*
2 *vi Am* travailler comme vendeur(euse)

click COMPTR **1** *n* clic
2 *vt* cliquer
3 *vi* cliquer; **to click and drag** cliquer et glisser

client *n* (**a**) *(of shop, lawyer)* client(e) *m,f* □ BANKING *client account* compte *m* client; *client confidence* confiance *f* de la clientèle *ou* du client; *client file* dossier *m ou*

fichier *m* client; *client list* liste *f* de clients
(**b**) COMPTR client(e) *m,f*

clientele *n* clientèle *f*

client-server database *n* COMPTR base *f* de données client-serveur

clinch *vt (deal)* conclure

clip art *n* COMPTR clipart *m*

clipboard *n* écritoire *m* à pince; COMPTR presse-papiers *m*, bloc-notes *m*

clock *n* COMPTR horloge *f* □ *clock speed* fréquence *f* d'horloge

▸ **clock in** *vi* pointer (à l'arrivée)

▸ **clock off** *vi* pointer (à la sortie)

▸ **clock on** *vi* = **clock in**

▸ **clock out** *vi* = **clock off**

clone *n* COMPTR clone *m*

close 1 *n* ST EXCH *(on financial futures market)* clôture *f*; *(closing price)* cours *m* de clôture; **at close of business** à la *ou* en clôture
2 *vt* (**a**) ACCT **to close the books** balancer les comptes, régler les livres; **to close the yearly accounts** arrêter les comptes de l'exercice (**b**) *(meeting)* clore; *(account)* fermer; *(deal)* conclure, clore (**c**) ST EXCH *(operation)* liquider; **to close a position** couvrir une position
3 *vi* ST EXCH clôturer; **the shares closed at 420p** les actions ont clôturé *ou* terminé à 420 pence; **the share index closed two points down** l'indice (boursier) a clôturé en baisse de deux points

▸ **close down 1** *vt sep* fermer (définitivement); **the factory was closed down after a drop in orders** l'usine a fermé ses portes à la suite d'une baisse des commandes
2 *vi (of factory, business)* fermer

▸ **close off** *vt sep (account)* arrêter

▸ **close out** *vt sep Am (goods)* solder, liquider *(avant fermeture)*

▸ **close with** *vt insep (finalize agreement with)* conclure un marché avec

closed *adj* (**a**) *(shop, factory)* fermé(e) (**b**) *closed shop* = entreprise ou usine qui n'embauche que du personnel syndiqué

closed-end *adj closed-end (investment) fund* société *f* d'investissement à capital fixe; *closed-end mortgage* prêt *m* hypothécaire à montant fixe

closing 1 *n* (**a**) *(of shop)* fermeture *f*
(**b**) *(of meeting, account)* clôture *f*; *(of deal)* clôture, conclusion *f*

(**c**) ST EXCH *(of position)* clôture *f*
2 *adj* (**a**) *(concluding)* dernier(ère), final(e) ❏ **closing speech** discours *m* de clôture
(**b**) *(final)* dernier(ère) ❏ **closing bid** dernière enchère *f*; **closing date** *(for application)* date *f* limite; **closing stock** stock *m* à l'inventaire
(**c**) ST EXCH **closing prices** cours *mpl* de clôture; **closing quotations** cotes *fpl* en clôture; **closing trade** transactions *fpl* de clôture

closing-down *n (of factory, business, shop)* fermeture *f* ❏ **closing-down sale** solde *m* de fermeture

closing-off *n* ACCT *(of accounts)* arrêt *m*

closing-out *n Am* fermeture *f*, liquidation *f* ❏ **closing-out sale** solde *m* de fermeture

closure *n (of factory, business, shop)* fermeture *f*; ST EXCH **closure by repurchase** clôture *f* par rachat

cluster *n* (**a**) COMPTR cluster *m*, bloc *m*; *(of terminals)* grappe *f* (**b**) MKTG **cluster analysis** analyse *f* par segments; **cluster sampling** sondage *m* aréolaire *ou* par grappes

> 66
>
> A further way of reducing the spread of sampling is to use what is called **cluster sampling**, a device by which sub-units are grouped together and work concentrated on them. A simple example in the case of the university student population would be to take the faculties of the university ... and take a sample of two of them. These two faculties, randomly chosen, would then be used for the sample with perhaps all the students, or a high proportion of them, being the sample.
>
> 99

CMR waybill *n* lettre *f* de voiture CMR

Co, co *n (abbr* **company**) Cie

c/o *(abbr* **care of**) chez, aux bons soins de

COBOL *n* COMPTR *(abbr* **Common Business-Oriented Language**) Cobol *m*

COD, cod *adv (abbr Br* **cash** *or Am* **collect on delivery**) contre remboursement, paiement à la livraison; **all goods are sent COD** toutes les marchandises doivent être payées à la livraison

code 1 *n* (**a**) (**dialling**) **code** indicatif *f* (**b**) *(rules)* code *m*; **code of ethics** *(in profession)* déontologie *f*
2 *vt* COMPTR coder

coded *adj* COMPTR codé(e)

coding *n* COMPTR codes *mpl*

co-director *n* codirecteur(trice) *m,f*

coinage *n* (**a**) *(monetary system)* système *m* monétaire (**b**) *(coins)* monnaie *f*

co-insurance *n* coassurance *f*

cold *adj* (**a**) MKTG **cold call** visite *f* à froid; *(on phone)* appel *m* à froid; **cold call sales** ventes *fpl* par approche directe (**b**) COMPTR **cold start** démarrage *m* à froid

collaborate *vi* collaborer; **she collaborated with us on the project** elle a collaboré avec nous au projet

collaboration *n* collaboration *f*

collapse 1 *n (of market, prices)* effondrement *m*; *(of currency)* dégringolade *f*
2 *vi (of market, prices)* s'effondrer; *(of currency)* dégringoler

collate *vt (documents, data)* rassembler

collateral FIN **1** *n* nantissement *m*; **what can you provide as collateral?** qu'est-ce que vous pouvez fournir en nantissement?; **to lodge sth as collateral** déposer qch en nantissement; **the bank prefers not to lend without collateral** de préférence, la banque ne prête pas sans nantissement
2 *adj* subsidiaire ❏ **collateral loan** prêt *m* avec garantie; **collateral security** nantissement *m*

> 66
>
> The steps that may be taken by LCH are extensive and diverse. They include the compulsory closing-out or invoicing back of the defaulting member's contracts, the liquidation of his **collateral security** and the substitution of a settlement amount ... for the member's rights and liabilities in respect of an uncompleted delivery contract.
>
> 99

collateralize *vt Am* FIN garantir

colleague *n* collègue *mf*

collect 1 *adj Am* **collect call** appel *m* en PCV; **to make a collect call** faire un appel *ou* téléphoner en PCV
2 *vt (salary)* toucher; *(debt)* recouvrer; *(taxes)* percevoir, lever; *Am* **collect on delivery** paiement *m* à la livraison, livraison *f* contre remboursement
3 *adv Am* **to call collect** faire un appel *ou* téléphoner en PCV; **to send a parcel collect** envoyer un colis en port dû *ou* payable à destination

collecting *adj* **collecting agency, collecting bank** banque *f* de recouvrement;

collecting banker banquier *m* encaisseur; *collecting department* service *m* de recouvrement

collection *n* (**a**) *(of debts)* recouvrement *m*; *(of taxes)* perception *f*, levée *f* (**b**) FIN *(of bill)* encaissement *m*; **to hand sth in for collection** donner qch à l'encaissement; **a bill for collection** un effet à l'encaissement □ *collection bank* banque *f* d'encaissement; *collection charges, collection fees* frais *mpl* d'encaissement; *collection rate* tarif *m* d'encaissement

collective *adj* collectif(ive) □ *collective bargaining* négociation *f* de convention collective; *collective bargaining agreement* convention *f* collective; *collective liability* responsabilité *f* collective; *collective ownership* propriété *f* collective

> ❝
> Both free **collective bargaining** and incomes policies were difficult to operate in a situation where there were powerful public-sector trade unions, conducting centralized wage bargaining and virtually monopolizing. key services.
> ❞

collectivism *n* ECON collectivisme *m*

collector *n* (**a**) *(of cheque)* encaisseur *m* (**b**) *(of taxes)* percepteur *m*

colour, *Am* **color** *n* COMPTR *colour graphics* graphisme *m* en couleur; *colour monitor* moniteur *m* couleur; *colour printer* imprimante *f* couleur

column *n* ACCT colonne *f*

combination *n* *(of lock)* combinaison *f* □ *combination lock* serrure *f* ou fermeture *f* à combinaison

combine *n* FIN cartel *m*, trust *m*

command *n* COMPTR commande *f*; *(from menu options)* article *m*

commerce *n* commerce *m*

commercial 1 *n* *(advertisement)* publicité *f* 2 *adj* commercial(e) □ *commercial agency* agence *f* commerciale; *commercial attaché* attaché(e) *m,f* commercial(e); *commercial bank* banque *f* commerciale; *commercial bill* titre *m* commercial; *commercial centre* centre *m* commercial; *commercial contract* contrat *m* commercial; *commercial designer* dessinateur(trice) *m,f* de publicité; *commercial directory* annuaire *m* du commerce; *commercial dispute* litige *m* commercial; *commercial district*

quartier *m* commerçant; *commercial documents* papiers *mpl* d'affaires; *commercial law* droit *m* commercial; *commercial monopoly* monopole *m* commercial; *commercial paper* effet *m* commercial; *commercial port* port *m* de commerce; *commercial value* valeur *f* marchande; *commercial vehicle* véhicule *m* utilitaire

commercialization *n* commercialisation *f*

commercialize *vt* commercialiser

commercially *adv* commercialement

commission 1 *n* (**a**) *(payment)* commission *f*; **to get 3% commission** toucher 3% de commission; **to work on a commission basis** travailler à la commission □ *commission agent* commissionnaire *mf*; ACCT *commission note* note *f* de commission; *commission sale* vente *f* à (la) commission

(**b**) *(committee)* commission *f* □ *commission of inquiry* commission d'enquête

(**c**) *(order)* commande *f*; **work done on commission** travail *m* fait sur commande; **to carry out a commission** s'acquitter d'une commande

2 *vt* *(order)* commander; **to commission sb to do sth** charger qn de faire qch

Commissioner of the Inland Revenue *n Br* ≃ Inspecteur *m* des impôts

commitment *n* FIN engagement *m* financier □ *commitment fee* commission *f* d'engagement

committee *n* comité *m*, commission *f*; **to be** *or* **sit on a committee** être membre de *ou* faire partie d'un comité

commodity *n* (**a**) ECON *(product)* marchandise *f*, produit *m*; *(foodstuff)* denrée *f*; **rice is the staple commodity of China** le riz est la ressource principale de la Chine

(**b**) ST EXCH matière *f* première; **to trade commodities** spéculer sur les marchés à terme des matières premières □ *commodity broker, commodity dealer* courtier(ère) *m,f* en matières premières; *commodity exchange* marché *m* des matières premières; *commodity futures* opérations *fpl* à terme sur matières premières; *commodity market* marché des matières premières

common *adj* (**a**) EU *Common Agricultural Policy* politique *f* agricole commune; *common budget* budget *m* de la communauté européenne; *common customs tariff* tarif *m* douanier commun; *common external tariff* tarif externe commun; ***Common Fisheries Policy*** politique commune de la pêche; ***the Common Market*** le marché commun

(**b**) *Am* ST EXCH ***common equities, common stock*** actions *fpl* ordinaires

comms *n* COMPTR ***comms package*** logiciel *m* de communication; ***comms port*** port *m* de communication

communicate *vi (be in touch)* communiquer; *(get in touch)* prendre contact, se mettre en contact

communication *n* (**a**) *(contact)* communication *f*; **to enter into communication with sb** se mettre en contact avec qn ❑ ***communication network*** réseau *m* de communication; ***communication skills*** techniques *fpl* de communication; **to have good communication skills** savoir communiquer, avoir le sens de la communication; COMPTR ***communications software*** logiciel *m* de communication; ***communication strategy*** stratégie *f* de communication

(**b**) *(message)* communication *f*, message *m*

Community *n* EU **the (European Economic) Community** la communauté (économique) européenne ❑ ***Community law*** droit *m* communautaire

commute *vi* faire la navette; **to commute to work** faire la navette pour se rendre à son travail

commuter *n* = personne qui fait la navette entre son domicile et son travail ❑ ***commuter belt*** banlieue *f*; ***commuter train*** train *m* de banlieue

Companies House, Companies Registration Office *n Br* = institut où sont enregistrées toutes les informations concernant les entreprises du pays

company *n* société *f*, entreprise *f*; **to form** *or* **incorporate a company** constituer une société; **to liquidate a company** liquider une société; **in company time** pendant les heures de travail; **Richardson and Company** Richardson et Compagnie ❑ ***Companies Act*** loi *f* sur les sociétés; ***company car*** voiture *f* de fonction; ***company credit card*** carte *f* de crédit professionnelle; ***company director*** directeur(trice) *m,f* général(e); ***company doctor*** *(doctor)* médecin *m* d'entreprise; *(businessperson)* redresseur *m* d'entreprises; ***company funds*** fonds *m* social; ***company law*** droit *m* des sociétés; ***company policy*** politique *f* de la société; ***company rules*** règlements *mpl* internes; ***company savings scheme*** plan *m*

d'épargne d'entreprise; ***company secretary*** secrétaire *mf* général(e)

comparative advantage *n* MKTG avantage *m* comparatif

compare **1** *vt* comparer (**with** *or* **to** avec *ou* à); **we must compare last year's figures with this year's** nous devons comparer les chiffres de l'année dernière avec ceux de cette année

2 *vi* être comparable (**with** à); **how does last month's output compare with this month's?** la production du mois dernier était-elle inférieure ou supérieure à celle de ce mois-ci?; **we compare well with our competitors** nous n'avons rien à envier à la concurrence

comparison advertising *n* MKTG publicité *f* comparative

compatibility *n* COMPTR compatibilité *f*

compatible *adj* COMPTR compatible (**with** avec); **IBM-compatible** compatible IBM

compensate *vt (for loss, injury)* dédommager; *(for damage)* indemniser (**for** de)

compensation *n* (**a**) *(for loss, injury)* dédommagement *m*; *(for damage)* indemnité *f* compensatrice, indemnisation *f*; LAW réparation *f* civile, composition *f* ❑ ***compensation fund*** caisse *f* de garantie

(**b**) ***compensation package*** *Br (for redundancy)* prime *f* de licenciement; *Am (when starting new job)* avantages *mpl* sociaux

compete *vi (of one company)* faire de la concurrence (**with** à); *(of two companies)* se faire concurrence; **they compete with foreign companies for contracts** ils sont en concurrence avec des entreprises étrangères pour obtenir des contrats; **we have to compete on an international level** nous devons être à la hauteur de la concurrence sur le plan international

competence, competency *n* (**a**) *(ability)* compétence *f*; **this lies within his competence** cela rentre dans ses attributions (**b**) **competencies** *(skills)* compétences *fpl*; **her competencies were re-assessed at her annual appraisal** ses compétences ont été réexaminées dans le cadre de l'évaluation annuelle du personnel

competent *adj (capable)* compétent(e) (**in** en); *(qualified)* qualifié(e); **is she competent to handle the accounts?** est-elle compétente *ou* qualifiée pour tenir la comptabilité?

competing *adj* *(companies)* concurrentiel(elle); *(products)* concurrent(e)

competition *n* *(between companies, candidates)* concurrence *f*; **the competition** *(rivals)* la concurrence

competitive *adj* ECON *(product)* concurrentiel(elle); *(company, price)* compétitif(ive); **to offer competitive terms** proposer des prix très compétitifs; **industry must become more competitive** l'industrie doit devenir plus compétitive □ **competitive advantage** avantage *m* concurrentiel; **competitive analysis** analyse *f* des concurrents; **competitive awareness** sensibilité *f* compétitive; **competitive bidding** appel *m* d'offres; **competitive edge** avance *f* sur la concurrence; **competitive marketplace** marché *m* de concurrence; **competitive position** position *f* concurrentielle

> **"**
> Some factors in the **competitive analysis** will relate to market attractiveness. If the competition offered no alternative to the proposed new product it would score highly. Since the competition is the market leader (...) it attracts a low score.
> **"**

competitively *adv* **to be competitively priced** être vendu(e) à un prix compétitif

competitiveness *n* *(of product)* concurrence *f*; *(of company, price)* competitivité *f*

competitor *n* concurrent(e) *m,f*; **we must keep up with our main competitors** nous ne devons pas nous laisser distancer par la concurrence

complain *vi* *(make formal protest)* formuler une plainte *ou* une réclamation, se plaindre; **several customers have complained about the quality of service** plusieurs clients se sont plaints du service

complaint *n* plainte *f*, réclamation *f*; **to lodge** *or* **make a complaint (against sb/about sth)** déposer une plainte (contre qn/à propos de qch) □ **complaints department, complaints office** service *m* des réclamations

complete 1 *adj* complet(ète); **the new software offers a complete service for the business user** le nouveau logiciel répond à tous les besoins de l'homme d'affaires
2 *vt* *(order, contract, work)* exécuter

completion *n* *(of work)* achèvement *m*; **the project is nearing completion** le projet s'achève *ou* est près de son terme; **payment on completion of contract** paiement à l'exécution du contrat □ **completion date** *(of work)* date *f* d'achèvement; *(of sale)* date d'exécution

complex *n* complexe *m* (industriel)

compliance test *n* test *m* de conformité

compliments slip *n* papillon *m* à en-tête *(joint aux envois et portant la mention ''avec les compliments de'')*

compound 1 *adj* FIN **compound interest** intérêts *mpl* composés; **compound (net) annual return** annuités *fpl* composées
2 *vt* *(debt)* régler à l'amiable

comprehensive *adj* *(insurance)* multirisque, tous risques

compress *vt* COMPTR *(data, file)* comprimer

comptroller *n* *Am* contrôleur(euse) *m,f*; *(of accounts)* vérificateur(trice) *m,f*

compulsory *adj* obligatoire □ **compulsory liquidation** liquidation *f* forcée; **compulsory purchase order** (ordre *m* d')expropriation *f*

computer *n* ordinateur *m*; **to be computer literate** avoir des connaissances en informatique □ **computer analyst** analyste-programmeur(euse) *mf*; **computer department** service *m* informatique; **computer engineer** ingénieur-informaticien(enne) *m,f*; **computer expert** informaticien(enne) *m,f*; **computer printout** impression *f*; **computer program** programme *m* informatique; **computer programmer** programmeur(euse) *m,f*; **computer science** informatique *f*; **computer scientist** informaticien(enne) *m,f*

computer-aided, computer-assisted *adj* assisté(e) par ordinateur □ **computer-aided audit techniques** techniques *fpl* d'audit assistées par ordinateur; **computer-aided design** conception *f* assistée par ordinateur; **computer-aided engineering** ingénierie *f* assistée par ordinateur; **computer-aided learning** enseignement *m* assisté par ordinateur; **computer-aided manufacturing** fabrication *f* assistée par ordinateur; **computer-aided trading** commerce *m* assisté par ordinateur

computer-based training *n* enseignement *m* assisté par ordinateur

computer-integrated manufac-turing *n* fabrication *f* intégrée par ordinateur

computerize *vt (company, organization)* informatiser

computerized *adj* informatisé(e)

computing *n* informatique *f*

concealment *n* LAW *(of facts)* non-divulgation *f* ❑ FIN **concealment of assets** dissimulation *f* d'actif

concept testing *n* MKTG tests *mpl* de concept

concern *n* entreprise *f*, affaire *f*; **a manufacturing concern** une entreprise industrielle; **the whole concern is for sale** toute l'entreprise est à vendre
   2 *vt* intéresser; **to whom it may concern** *(on letter)* à qui de droit; **the persons concerned** les intéressés; **the department concerned** le service compétent

concession *n* **(a)** *(right)* concession *f*; **a mining concession** une concession minière **(b)** *(discount)* réduction *f*

conciliation *n* médiation *f* ❑ **conciliation board** commission *f* d'arbitrage; **conciliation service** service *m* de médiation

conciliator *n* médiateur(trice) *m,f*

condition *n* **(a)** *(stipulation)* condition *f*; **on condition** sous réserve ❑ **conditions of contract** cahier *m* des charges; **conditions of employment** conditions d'embauche; **conditions of sale** conditions de vente **(b)** *(state)* état *m*; **in good/bad condition** *(goods, machine)* en bon/mauvais état

conditional *adj (offer)* conditionnel(elle); **the offer is conditional on your acceptance of our terms of employment** cette offre d'emploi n'est valable que dans la mesure où vous acceptez nos conditions d'embauche

confederation *n* confédération *f* ❑ **Confederation of British Industry** = patronat britannique, ≃ CNPF *m*

conference *n* **(a)** *(meeting)* conférence *f*; **to be in conference** être en conférence (**with** avec) ❑ TEL **conference call** télé-conférence *f*; **conference room** salle *f* de conférence; **conference table** table *f* de conférence; **we hope to get management to the conference table** nous espérons réunir la direction en table ronde
   (b) *(convention)* congrès *m* ❑ **conference centre** centre *m* de conférences; **conference coordinator** responsable *mf* des conférences *ou* des congrès; **conference delegate** congressiste *mf*; **conference or-**

ganizer organisateur(trice) *m,f* des conférences *ou* des congrès; **conference pack** = dossier offert aux conférenciers avec informations générales sur la conférence, petits cadeaux etc

config.sys *n* COMPTR fichier *m* config.sys

configure *vt* COMPTR configurer, paramétrer

confirm *vt* confirmer; **we confirm receipt of** *or* **that we have received your letter** nous accusons réception de votre lettre

confirmation *n* confirmation *f*; **to receive confirmation of sth** recevoir confirmation de qch ❑ **confirmation of receipt** accusé *m* de réception

confirmed letter of credit *n* lettre *f* de crédit irrévocable

confirming house *n* BANKING organisme *m* confirmateur

conflict *n* conflit *m*; **the unions are in conflict with the management** les syndicats sont en conflit avec la direction; **a conflict of interests** un conflit d'intérêts; **her presence on the boards of two competing companies led to a conflict of interests** le fait qu'elle siège au conseil d'administration de deux entreprises concurrentes a débouché sur un conflit d'intérêts

conglomerate *n* conglomérat *m*

congress *n* congrès *m*

con man *n* Fam escroc *m*

connect **1** *n* COMPTR connexion *f* ❑ **connect time** durée *f* (d'établissement) de la connexion
   2 *vt* TEL mettre en ligne *ou* en communication (**with** avec); **will you connect me with reservations, please?** est-ce que vous pouvez me passer votre service des réservations?

connection *n* **(a)** COMPTR connexion *f*, liaison *f* ❑ **connection kit** kit *m* d'accès *ou* de connexion **(b)** TEL communication *f*; **we had a very bad connection** la communication était très mauvaise

consensus *n* consensus *m*; **there was a consensus of opinion to reject the board's offer** il y avait un consensus en faveur du rejet de la proposition du conseil d'administration

consign *vt (goods)* envoyer, expédier

consignee *n* consignataire *mf*

consignment *n* **(a)** *(goods)* arrivage *m*, livraison *f*; **a consignment of machinery** un arrivage de machines **(b)** *(despatch)* envoi *m*, expédition *f*; **on consignment** en consignation, en dépôt (permanent); **goods for consignment abroad** marchandises *fpl* à destination de l'étranger ▫ *consignment note* bordereau *m* d'expédition

consignor *n* consignateur(trice) *m,f*, expéditeur(trice) *m,f*

console *n* COMPTR pupitre *m* de commande

consolidate *vt* FIN *(companies)* fusionner, réunir; *(shares)* regrouper; *(debts, funds, loans)* consolider, unifier; **the company has consolidated its position as the market leader** la société a conforté sa position de leader sur le marché

consolidated *adj* *consolidated accounts* comptes *mpl* consolidés *ou* intégrés; *consolidated annuities* fonds *mpl* consolidés; *consolidated balance sheet* bilan *m* consolidé; FIN *consolidated debt* dette *f* consolidée; *consolidated fund* fonds consolidés; *consolidated loan* emprunt *m* consolidé; *consolidated profit and loss account* bilan consolidé

consolidation *n* FIN *(of companies)* fusion *f*; *(of shares)* regroupement *m*; *(of debts, funds, loans)* consolidation *f*, unification *f*

consols *npl Br* FIN (fonds *mpl*) consolidés *mpl*

consortium *n* FIN consortium *m*

constant *adj (currency)* constant(e)

consular invoice *n* facture *f* consulaire

consult 1 *vt* consulter (**about** sur *ou* au sujet de); **I have to consult my superior before taking a decision** il faut que je consulte mon supérieur hiérarchique avant de prendre une décision
2 *vi* s'entretenir, discuter (**with** avec); **we have to consult with our supplier about this problem** il faut que l'on discute de ce problème avec notre fournisseur

consultancy *n (company)* cabinet *m* d'expert-conseil; *(advice)* assistance *f* technique ▫ *consultancy fee* frais *mpl* d'expertise; *consultancy service* service *m* d'assistance technique

consultant *n* expert-conseil *m*, consultant(e) *m,f*

consultation *n (discussion)* consultation *f*, délibération *f*; **the matter will be decided in consultation with our colleagues** la décision sera prise en consultation *ou* en concertation avec nos collègues; **he was asked to leave without prior consultation** on l'a renvoyé sans préavis

consumable 1 *n* **consumables** produits *mpl* de consommation; COMPTR consommables *mpl*
2 *adj* consommable ▫ *consumable goods* produits *mpl* de consommation

consumer *n* consommateur(trice) *m,f* ▫ MKTG *consumer acceptance* réceptivité *f* des consommateurs; *Consumers' Assocation* = association britannique de consommateurs; *consumer credit* crédit *m* à la consommation; *consumer demand* demande *f* des consommateurs; *consumer durables* biens *mpl* de consommation; *consumer goods* biens de (grande) consommation; *consumer industry* industrie *f* de consommation; *consumer market* marché *m* de la consommation; *consumer panel* groupe-témoin *m*, panel *m* de consommateurs; *consumer preference* préférence *f* du consommateur; *Am consumer price index* indice *m* des prix à la consommation; *consumer profile* profil *m* du consommateur; *consumer protection* défense *f* du consommateur; *consumer research* recherche *f* des besoins des consommateurs; *consumer society* société *f* de consommation; *consumer spending* dépenses *fpl* de consommation *ou* des ménages

> ❝
> It is important to recognise that whilst the UK business economy may soon see a recovery, the adverse effects of the current recession on the **consumer market** will continue to be felt long after the economy has begun to recover.
> ❞

consumerism *n (consumer protection)* consumérisme *m*; ECON *(consumption)* consommation *f* à outrance

consumption *n* consommation *f*

contact 1 *n* (a) *(communication)* contact *m*; **to be in contact with sb** être en contact avec qn; **to get in contact with sb** contacter qn, se mettre en contact avec qn (b) *(acquaintance)* relation *f*; **she has some useful business contacts** elle a quelques bons contacts (professionnels) ▫ *contact man* agent *m* de liaison
2 *vt* contacter, se mettre en contact avec; **we'll contact you later on this week** nous vous contacterons cette semaine

container *n* (a) *(for storage)* récipient *m*; *(for transport)* conteneur *m* ▫ *container berth* poste *m* à quai pour porte-conteneurs; *container ship* (navire *m*) porte-conteneurs *m*; *container shipping* transports *mpl* maritimes par conteneurs (**b**) MKTG *container premium* prime *f* contenant

containerization *n* conteneurisation *f*

containerize *vt* conteneuriser

contango ST EXCH **1** *n* report *m*; *(percentage)* taux *m* de report; **money on contango** capitaux *mpl* en report; **contangoes are low** les reports sont bon marché ❏ *contango day* jour *m* des reports
  2 *vt* reporter
  3 *vi* reporter une position

contents insurance *n* assurance *f* mobilier

contingency *n* éventualité *f*; **to allow for every contingency** parer à toute éventualité ❏ *contingency fund* fonds *mpl* de prévoyance; *contingency plan* plan *m* d'urgence; ACCT *contingency theory* théorie *f* de la contingence

contingent *adj* (**a**) *(possible)* éventuel(elle) ❏ *contingent liability* passif *m* éventuel *ou* exigible; *contingent profit* profit *m* aléatoire (**b**) *(dependent)* contingent(e); **to be contingent on** *or* **upon sth** dépendre de qch; **a salary increase is contingent upon group performance** l'augmentation des salaires dépend des résultats du groupe

continuous processing *n* production *f* en continu

contra ACCT **1** *n* **per contra** par contre; **as per contra** en contrepartie, porté ci-contre
  2 *adj* *contra account* compte *m* de contrepartie *ou* d'autre part; *contra entry* article *m* *ou* écriture *f* inverse, contre-passation *f*
  3 *vt* contrepasser

contraband *n* contrebande *f* ❏ *contraband goods* marchandises *fpl* de contrebande

contract *n* (**a**) *(agreement)* contrat *m*; **to draw up a contract** dresser *ou* rédiger un contrat; **to sign a contract** signer un contrat; **to cancel a contract** résilier *ou* annuler un contrat; **to be bound by contract** être lié(e) par contrat; **to break one's contract** rompre son contrat; **to be under contract** être sous contrat (**to** avec) ❏ *contract of employment* contrat de travail; *contract law* droit *m* des obligations; *contract note* note *f ou* bordereau *m* de contrat; ST EXCH avis *m* d'exécution
  (**b**) *(to supply goods, services)* soumission *f*, adjudication *f*; **to put work out to contract** sous-traiter du travail, faire effectuer un

travail en sous-traitance; **to give** *or* **award a contract to sb** accorder un contrat à qn; **to tender for a contract** soumissionner à une adjudication; **to secure a contract for sth** obtenir un contrat pour qch; **they were given a contract to build the new road** ils se sont vu attribuer le contrat pour construire la nouvelle route; **to enter into a contract** *(of person)* passer un contrat (**with** avec) ❏ *contract date* date *f* contractuelle; *contract labour* main-d'œuvre *f* contractuelle; *contract staff* personnel *m* en contrat à durée déterminée; *contract work* travail *m* en sous-traitance
  2 *vt* **to contract to do sth** s'engager (par contrat) à faire qch, entreprendre de faire qch

▸ **contract in** *vi* s'engager par contrat; *(into insurance policy, pension plan)* souscrire

▸ **contract out 1** *vt sep (work)* donner en sous-traitance (**to** à); **the work was contracted out** on a donné le travail à un sous-traitant
  2 *vi Br* se dégager d'un contrat; *(of insurance policy, pension plan)* arrêter de souscrire (**of** à)

contractor *n* entrepreneur *m*

contractual *adj* *(agreement, obligations)* contractuel(elle); **on the present contractual basis** selon les stipulations actuelles du contrat ❏ *contractual agreement* contrat *m*; *contractual claims* créances *fpl* contractuelles; *contractual liability* responsabilité *f* contractuelle

contribute *vt* donner, verser; **she contributes 10% of her salary to the pension scheme** elle verse 10% de son salaire dans son plan de retraite

contribution *n* contribution *f*, cotisation *f*; **employer's and employee's contributions** cotisations patronales et ouvrières ❏ ACCT *contribution margin* marge *f* sur les coûts variables

contributory 1 *n* ST EXCH = actionnaire responsable proportionnellement à son apport
  2 *adj* *contributory pension plan* système *m* de retraite par répartition

control *n* (**a**) *(of company, organization)* autorité *f*; **to have control of a business** être à la tête d'une entreprise, diriger une entreprise; **public spending is under the control of our department** le budget national relève de notre département; **the control process showed that objectives were being met** les contrôles effectués montraient que l'on était en train d'atteindre les objectifs fixés
  (**b**) *(of exchange rates, prices)* contrôle *m*; **to**

impose controls on sth contrôler qch; **there are to be new government controls on financial practices** il y aura de nouvelles réglementations gouvernementales sur les pratiques financières; **inflation must be kept under control** il faut maîtriser l'inflation □ **control commission** commission *f* de contrôle; MKTG **control group** groupe *m* témoin

(**c**) COMPTR **control (key)** touche *f* contrôle

2 *vt* (**a**) *(company, organization)* diriger

(**b**) *(exchange rates, prices)* contrôler; *(inflation)* contrôler, juguler; **to control the rise in the cost of living** enrayer la hausse du coût de la vie

controllable costs *npl* coûts *mpl* contrôlables

controlled economy *n* économie *f* dirigée

    ❝

The Labour government proved unwilling to pursue a more overtly socialist approach; physical controls acquired during wartime were eventually discarded and those industries that were nationalized, such as steel and the railways, were basically essential and loss-making concerns. Government was prepared to pursue a managed rather than a **controlled economy**.

    ❞

controller *n* FIN contrôleur(euse) *m,f*

controlling *adj* **controlling factor** facteur *m* déterminant; **controlling interest, controlling share** *(in company)* participation *f* majoritaire; **controlling shareholding** bloc *m* de contrôle

convene 1 *vt* *(conference, meeting)* convoquer; **to convene a meeting of shareholders** convoquer une assemblée d'actionnaires

2 *vi* *(of meeting, board, people)* se réunir

convener *n* convocateur(trice) *m,f*

convenience *n* **at your earliest convenience** *(in letter)* dans les meilleurs délais; **please reply at your earliest convenience** veuillez répondre dans les meilleurs délais

convenor = **convener**

convention *n* (**a**) *(agreement)* convention *f*; **to sign a convention (on sth)** signer une convention (sur qch) (**b**) *(conference)* convention *f*, congrès *m*

conversational *adj* COMPTR *(mode)* dialogue

conversion *n* (**a**) FIN *(of securities)* conversion *f* □ **conversion issue** émission *f* de conversion; **conversion loan** emprunt *m* de conversion; **conversion rate** taux *m* de conversion (**b**) COMPTR **conversion program** programme *m* de conversion; **conversion software** logiciel *m* de conversion

convert 1 *n Am* FIN obligation *f* convertible (en actions)

2 *vt* (**a**) convertir; **to convert pounds into francs** *(as calculation)* convertir des livres en francs; *(by exchanging them)* changer des livres en francs (**b**) COMPTR *(file)* convertir

convertibility *n* convertibilité *f*

convertible *adj* FIN *(loan, security)* convertible □ **convertible bond** obligation *f* convertible (en actions); **convertible currency** monnaie *f* convertible; **convertible loan stock** obligation convertible (en actions); **convertible money of account** monnaie de compte convertible

convey *vt* *(goods)* transporter

conveyance *n* LAW *(transfer)* cession *f*, transfert *m*; *(deed)* acte *m* de cession

conveyancing *n* LAW procédure *f* translative (de propriété)

cook *vt Fam* **to cook the books** falsifier les comptes

cookie *n* COMPTR cookie *m*, mouchard *m* électronique

cooling-off period *n* période *f* de réflexion

    ❝

Companies are not regarded as individuals under the Act and are therefore unable to break contracts once signed. Crucially, they cannot take advantage of the two week **cooling-off period** available to individuals.

    ❞

co-op *n* *(abbr* **co-operative***)* coop *f*

co-operative 1 *n* coopérative *f*

2 *adj* coopératif(ive) □ **co-operative group** coopérative *f* (de consommateurs); **co-operative society** (société *f*) coopérative

co-owner *n* copropriétaire *mf*

co-ownership *n* copropriété *f*

copartner *n* coassocié(e) *m,f*

copartnership *n* coassociation *f*

co-processor *n* COMPTR coprocesseur *m*

coproprietor *n* copropriétaire *mf*

copy 1 *n* (**a**) *(of document, letter)* copie *f*; **to make a copy of sth** faire une copie de qch ❑ *copy typist* dactylo *mf*
(**b**) *(written material)* copie *f*; *(in advertising)* texte *m*
(**c**) LAW expédition *f*
(**d**) MKTG *copy testing* pré-tests *mpl* publicitaires
(**e**) COMPTR **copy and paste** copier-coller *m* ❑ *copy block* copie *f* de bloc; *copy disk* disquette *f* de copie; *copy protection* protection *f* contre la copie
2 *vt* (**a**) *(document, letter)* copier; *(photocopy)* photocopier
(**b**) COMPTR copier; **to copy sth to disk** copier qch sur disquette; **to copy and paste sth** faire un copier-coller sur qch
3 *vi* COMPTR **to copy and paste** faire un copier-coller

copy-protected *adj* COMPTR protégé(e) contre la copie

copyright 1 *n* droit *m* de reproduction *ou* d'auteur, copyright *m*; **copyright reserved** tous droits réservés; **to be out of copyright** être (tombé(e)) dans le domaine public; **she has the sole copyright to her invention** elle est seule détentrice du copyright de son invention ❑ *copyright infringement* violation *f* du droit de reproduction
2 *adj* protégé(e) par les droits d'auteur
3 *vt* obtenir le copyright de

copywriter *n* rédacteur(trice) *m,f* publicitaire

cordless *adj* sans fil ❑ COMPTR *cordless mouse* souris *f* sans fil; *cordless telephone* téléphone *m* sans fil

core *n* *core business* activité *f* centrale; *core competence* principale compétence *f*; *core holding* investissement *m* de base *(dans le portefeuille des investisseurs institutionnels)*; *core market* marché *m* principal *ou* de référence; *core message* *(in advertising)* message *m* principal; *core skills* compétences *fpl* de base; *core time* *(in flexitime)* plage *f* fixe

corner 1 *n* monopole *m*; **to make** *or* **have a corner in sth** accaparer qch
2 *vt* *(market)* accaparer; **in two years they've cornered the market in software packages** en deux ans, ils ont accaparé le marché du progiciel

cornering *n (of market)* accaparement *m*

Corp, corp *n (abbr* **corporation**) Cie

corporate *adj* corporatif(ive), d'entreprise ❑ *corporate banking* banque *f* d'entreprise; *corporate body* personne *f* morale;

corporate bond obligation *f* de sociétés; *corporate buy-out* rachat *m* d'une entreprise par les salariés; *corporate culture* culture *f* d'entreprise; *corporate finance* finance *f* d'entreprise; *corporate hospitality* invitations *fpl* de complaisance; *corporate identity, corporate image* image *f* de marque; **the company cares about its corporate image** la société se soucie de son image; *corporate income* revenu *m* de société; *corporate income tax* impôt *m* sur les bénéfices des sociétés; *Am corporate licensing* marchandisage *m*; *corporate literature* brochures *fpl* décrivant une société; *corporate member (of association)* société-membre *f*; *corporate name* raison *f* sociale; *corporate planning* planification *f* de l'entreprise; *corporate raider* attaquant(e) *m,f*; *corporate sector* secteur *m* des grandes entreprises; *corporate strategy* stratégie *f* de l'entreprise

corporation *n* *Am* société *f*, compagnie *f* ❑ *Br corporation tax* impôt *m* sur les sociétés

correct 1 *adj (accurate)* exact(e); **these sales figures are not correct** le chiffre des ventes n'est pas exact
2 *vt (mistake, spelling)* corriger

correction *n* (**a**) *(of error, in document)* correction *f* ❑ *correction fluid* liquide *m* correcteur (**b**) ST EXCH *(adjustment)* correction *f*

correspond *vi* (**a**) *(be equivalent)* correspondre (**with** *or* **to** à); **the two sets of figures don't correspond** les deux séries de chiffres ne correspondent pas (**b**) *(write letters)* correspondre (**with** avec)

correspondence *n* (**a**) *(letterwriting)* correspondance *f*; **to be in correspondence with sb** être en correspondance avec qn (**b**) *(letters)* correspondance *f*, courrier *m*; **to read one's correspondence** lire son courrier

correspondent *n* correspondant(e) *m,f*

corrupt COMPTR **1** *adj (disk, file)* altéré(e)
2 *vt (disk, file)* altérer

co-signatory *n* LAW co-signataire *mf*

cost 1 *n* (**a**) *(price)* coût *m*, frais *mpl*; **cost, insurance and freight** coût, assurance, fret ❑ *cost accounting* comptabilité *f* analytique *ou* d'exploitation; *cost analysis* analyse *f* des coûts; ACCT *cost centre* centre *m* d'analyse; *cost factor* facteur *m* coût; *cost of living* coût de la vie; *cost management* gestion *f* des coûts; *cost price* prix *m* coûtant *ou* de revient; ACCT *cost of sales* coût de revient des produits vendus; *cost unit* unité *f* de coût

(**b**) LAW **costs** frais *mpl* d'instance, dépens *mpl*; **to pay costs** payer les frais et dépens

2 *vt* (**a**) *(be priced at)* coûter; **how much does it cost?** combien cela coûte-t-il?; **it costs $25** ça coûte 25 dollars

(**b**) *(estimate cost of)* *(article)* établir le prix de revient de; *(job)* évaluer le coût de; **how much was it costed at?** *(of job)* à combien est-ce que le coût a été évalué?

cost-benefit *adj cost-benefit analysis* analyse *f* coûts-bénéfices; *cost-benefit ratio* rapport *m* coût-profit

cost-effective *adj* rentable

cost-effectiveness *n* rentabilité *f*

costing *n (of article)* établissement *m* du prix de revient; *(of job)* évaluation *f* du coût

cost-of-living *adj cost-of-living allowance* indemnité *f* de vie chère; *cost-of-living increase (in salary)* augmentation *f* de salaire indexée sur le coût de la vie; *cost-of-living index* indice *m* du coût de la vie

cost-plus 1 *n* taux *m* de marque
2 *adj* FIN à coût majoré ❏ *cost-plus pricing* fixation *f* du prix en fonction du coût

> ❝
> The pricing method used in the above example is a very common one in practice. The addition of a profit margin to an estimate of average cost to determine price is called **cost-plus pricing**, mark-up pricing or full-cost pricing.
> ❞

co-trustee *n* LAW co-administrateur(trice) *m,f*

cottage industry *n* industrie *f* artisanale

council *n* (**a**) *(local government)* municipalité *f*; **to be on the council** être au conseil municipal (**b**) *(assembly)* conseil *m* ❏ *Council of Europe* Conseil *m* de l'Europe

counsel *n* LAW avocat-conseil *m*; **counsel for the defence** avocat *m* de la défense; **counsel for the prosecution** procureur *m*

counter *n (in shop)* comptoir *m*; *(in supermarket)* rayon *m*; *(in bank)* guichet *m*; FIN **to buy shares over the counter** acheter des actions sur le marché hors cote; **to buy/ sell sth under the counter** acheter/vendre qch sous le manteau ❏ BANKING *counter services* services *mpl* de caisse; *counter transactions* opérations *fpl* de caisse

counterbid *n* suroffre *f*, surenchère *f*

counterclaim *n* LAW demande *f* reconventionnelle; **to make a counterclaim (against sb)** opposer une demande reconventionnelle (à qn)

counterfeit 1 *n* faux *m*, contrefaçon *f*
2 *adj* faux (fausse)
3 *vt* contrefaire

counterfoil *n (of cheque)* talon *m*, souche *f* ❏ *counterfoil book* carnet *m* à souche

counter-guarantee *n* ST EXCH contre-garantie *f*

countermand *vt (order)* annuler

counterpart *n (document)* duplicata *m*, double *m*; *(person)* homologue *mf*

counterparty risk *n* BANKING risque *m* de contrepartie

counterproductive *adj* contre-productif(ive); **closing the factory will be counterproductive to the region's economy** la fermeture de l'usine aura des effets néfastes sur l'économie de la région

countersign *vt* contresigner

countertrade *vt (goods)* échanger, troquer

countertrading *n* troc *m*

countervailing *adj* FIN compensateur(trice), compensatoire

coupon *n* FIN *(on bearer bond)* coupon *m* ❏ *coupon bond* obligation *f* au porteur; *coupon yield* rendement *m* coupon

courier *n* coursier(ère) *m,f*; **to send sth/to arrive by courier** envoyer qch/arriver par coursier

course *n (of study)* stage *m*, cours *m*; **she's doing a course to improve her computer skills** elle fait un stage pour apprendre à mieux se servir d'un ordinateur

court *n* cour *f*, tribunal *m*; **to go to court** aller en justice; **to take sb to court** faire un procès à qn; **to settle out of court** parvenir à un règlement à l'amiable

covenant LAW **1** *n* convention *f*
2 *vt* s'engager (par contrat) à payer

cover 1 *n* (**a**) *(in insurance)* couverture *f*; **to have cover against sth** être couvert(e) contre qch ❏ *cover note* lettre *f* de couverture, certificat *m* provisoire d'assurance

(**b**) FIN marge *f* de sécurité; **to operate with/ without cover** opérer avec couverture/à découvert

(**c**) **to send sth under separate cover** faire parvenir qch sous pli séparé

2 *vt* (**a**) *(insure)* couvrir (**for** *or* **against**

contre); **to be fully covered** être entière-ment couvert(e); **the insurance covers serious illness** cet assurance couvre l'assuré en cas de maladie grave

(**b**) **to be covered** (of creditor) être (à) couvert; **to cover a bill** faire la provision d'une lettre de change; ST EXCH **to cover a position** couvrir une position

(**c**) (be enough for) couvrir; **to cover one's expenses** rentrer dans ses frais; **to cover a deficit** combler un déficit; ACCT **to cover a loss** couvrir un déficit

covered adj (position) couvert(e) ❑ ST EXCH *covered (short) position* position *f* (courte) couverte

covering adj (**a**) *covering letter* lettre *f* explicative (**b**) ST EXCH *covering purchases* rachats *mpl*

co-worker n Am collègue *mf*

CPA n Am (abbr **Certified Public Accountant**) expert-comptable *m*

cpa n (abbr **critical path analysis**) analyse *f* du chemin critique

cps COMPTR (abbr **characters per second**) cps

CPU n COMPTR (abbr **central processing unit**) unité *f* centrale

crack vt (market) percer sur

▶ **crack open** vt sep (market) percer sur

crash 1 n (**a**) (financial) krach *m* (**b**) (of computer) panne *f*

2 adj *crash course* cours *m* intensif; *crash programme* programme *m* choc *ou* d'urgence

3 vi (**a**) (of business) faire faillite; (of prices, shares, economy) s'effondrer (**b**) (of computer network, system) sauter; (of computer) tomber en panne

crate n (for storage, transport) caisse *f*

crawler n COMPTR araignée *f*

cream vt Am **to cream the market** écrémer le marché

▶ **cream off** vt sep (money, profits) écrémer

create vt créer; **foreign investment has created many new jobs in the area** les investissements étrangers ont permis la création de nombreux emplois dans la région; **new markets are constantly being created** de nouveaux marchés sont sans cesse en train de se créer

creation n (of jobs, new markets) création *f*

creative adj *creative accounting* manipulations *fpl* comptables; *creative marketing* créativité *f* commerciale

credit n (**a**) (for future payment) crédit *m*; **to give sb credit** faire crédit à qn; **to buy/sell sth on credit** acheter/vendre qch à crédit; ❑ *credit account* compte *m* crédit d'achats; *credit agency,* Am *credit bureau* agence *f* de notation; *credit call* appel *m* téléphonique effectué avec une carte de crédit; *credit card* carte *f* de crédit; *credit ceiling* plafond *m* de crédit; *credit control* encadrement *m* des crédits; *credit facilities* facilités *fpl* de paiement **to give sb credit facilities** accréditer qn (auprès d'une banque); *credit freeze* blocage *m* du crédit; *credit insurance* assurance *f* contre les mauvaises créances; *credit limit* limite *f* ou plafond de crédit; *credit rating* degré *m* de solvabilité; FIN notation *f*; *credit rating agency* agence de notation

(**b**) **to be in credit** (of person) avoir un compte créditeur; (of account) être créditeur(trice); ACCT **debit and credit** doit *m* et avoir *m* ❑ *credit balance* solde *m* créditeur; BANKING *credit entry* article *m* porté au crédit d'un compte; ACCT *credit item* poste *m* créditeur; *credit line* ligne *f* de crédit, autorisation *f* de crédit; *credit note* BANKING note *f* d'avoir; (in shop) avoir *m*; *credit side* (of account) avoir *m*; *credit transfer* virement *m*

2 vt (account) créditer; **to credit an account with £200, to credit £200 to an account** créditer un compte de 200 livres

creditor n créancier(ère) *m,f* ❑ *creditors' meeting* réunion *f* des créanciers; ECON *creditor nation* pays *m* créditeur

creditworthiness n solvabilité *f*

creditworthy adj solvable

creeping adj (inflation) rampant(e)

crisis n crise *f*; **to take crisis measures** prendre des mesures exceptionnelles ❑ *crisis management* gestion *f* des crises

critical adj *critical path analysis* analyse *f* du chemin critique; *critical path method* méthode *f* du chemin critique

CRN n (abbr **customs registered number**) numéro *m* d'enregistrement doua-nier

CRO n (abbr **Companies Registration Office**) = institut britannique où sont enregistrées toutes les informations con-cernant les entreprises du pays

cross vt (cheque) barrer

cross-currency adj *cross-currency interest rate* taux *m* d'intérêt croisé; ST EXCH *cross-currency swap* crédit *m* croisé

cross-holding n FIN participation f croisée

cross-impact analysis n MKTG analyse f d'interférence

crunch vt COMPTR (numbers, data) traiter à grande vitesse

cumulative adj (error) cumulé(e) ❏ **cumulative balance** solde m cumulé; FIN **cumulative interest** intérêts mpl cumulatifs; **cumulative preference share** action f privilégiée

curb vt (expenditure, inflation) contenir; (imports) freiner

currency n monnaie f; (foreign) devise f ❏ **currency conversion** conversion f de monnaies; **currency dealer** cambiste mf; **currency exposure** risque m de change; **currency fluctuation** mouvement m des devises; **currency interest-rate swap** échange m d'intérêts et de monnaies

current adj **current account** (in bank) compte m courant; ST EXCH liquidation f courante; **current assets** actif m de roulement; **current cost** prix m courant ou du marché; ST EXCH cours m instantané; **current cost accounting** comptabilité f en coûts actuels; **current earnings** bénéfices mpl de l'exercice, revenu m actuel; **current expenditure** dépenses fpl courantes; **current** Br **financial** or Am **fiscal year** exercice m en cours; **current income** (in accounts) produits mpl courants; (actual earnings) revenu actuel; **current liabilities** passif m exigible; **current rate of exchange** taux m de change en cours; ACCT **current ratio** coefficient m de liquidité; **current value** valeur f actuelle; **current year** exercice en cours

curriculum vitae n curriculum vitae m

cursor n COMPTR curseur m

curve n courbe f; **the graph shows an upward/downward curve** la courbe accuse une hausse/une baisse; Am Fam **to throw sb a curve (ball)** prendre qn à contre-pied; **he threw me a curve (ball) when he accepted their higher offer** il m'a fait un sale coup en acceptant leur surenchère

custom n (of business) clientèle f; **to lose sb's custom** perdre la clientèle de qn

customer n client(e) m,f ❏ **customer care** = qualité du service fourni à la clientèle; **customer profile** profil m de la clientèle; **customer service department** service m clientèle

customer-driven, customer-focused adj (company) tributaire du consommateur

❝
Major growth, international development, innovations in many areas, a strong **customer-driven** marketing strategy, backed by precisely targeted, high-calibre research and technical services, plus a clear vision of the future in an expanding but highly competitive sector. All of these things are already well established features of the Resins Group.
❞

customize vt faire sur mesure(s); **we provide a customized service for all our clients** nous fournissons à nos clients un service adapté à leurs besoins

customs npl douane f; **to go through customs** passer (à) la douane; **to take sth through customs** faire passer qch à la douane ❏ **customs agency** agence f en douane; **customs agent** commissionnaire m en douane; **customs allowance** tolérance f ou franchise f douanière; **customs barriers** barrières fpl douanières; **customs broker** agréé m en douane, agent m en douane; **customs charges** frais mpl de douane; **customs clearance** dédouanement m; **customs clearance area** aire f de dédouanement; **customs clearance authorization** autorisation f de dédouanement; **customs control** contrôle m douanier; **customs declaration** déclaration f de ou en douane; **customs duty** droits mpl de douane; Br **Customs and Excise** ≃ la Régie; **customs formalities** formalités fpl douanières; **customs inspector** inspecteur(trice) m,f des douanes; **customs invoice** facture f douanière; **customs note** bordereau m de douanes; **customs office** bureau m de douane; **customs officer** douanier(ère) m,f, préposé(e) m,f de la douane; **customs papers** dossier m de douane; **customs permit** permis m de douane; **customs procedure** procédure f douanière; **customs receipt** acquit m de douane; **customs regulations** réglementation f douanière; **customs tariff** tarif m douanier; **customs union** union f douanière

cut 1 n (**a**) (in wages, prices, costs, staff) réduction f; (in taxes, production) baisse f, diminution f; **he took a cut in pay** il a été obligé d'accepter une réduction de salaire
(**b**) COMPTR **cut and paste** couper-coller m
2 vt (**a**) (wages, prices, costs, staff) réduire; (taxes, production) diminuer, réduire

(**b**) COMPTR couper; **to cut and paste sth** faire un couper-coller sur qch ❑ *cut sheet feed* dispositif *m* d'alimentation feuille à feuille; *(act)* alimentation *f* feuille à feuille
  3 *vi* COMPTR **to cut and paste** faire un couper-coller

▸ **cut back 1** *vt sep (prices)* baisser; *(production)* diminuer; **arms spending has been cut right back** les dépenses d'armement ont été nettement réduites
  2 *vi (financially)* économiser, réduire les dépenses

▸ **cut back on** *vt insep* économiser sur; *(time)* réduire; *(production)* diminuer

▸ **cut down** *vt sep (spending)* couper, réduire

▸ **cut down on** *vt insep* réduire

▸ **cut in** *vt sep Fam* **to cut sb in (on a deal)** donner à qn sa part du gâteau; **we could cut him in for £5,000** nous pourrions lui filer 5 000 livres

▸ **cut off** *vt sep* (**a**) *(stop)* suspendre; **we are cutting off all overseas investment** nous suspendons tous les investissements à l'étranger (**b**) *(on telephone)* couper; **I was cut off** *(during conversation)* j'ai été coupé; *(disconnected)* on m'a coupé le téléphone

▸ **cut out** *vt sep (oust)* **to cut sb out of a deal** évincer qn dans une affaire

cutback *n (in production, budget)* réduction *f*, diminution *f*

cut-price, *Am* **cut-rate** *adj (goods)* à prix réduit; *(as special offer)* bradé(e)

cut-throat *adj (competition)* acharné(e)

cutting edge *n* **to be at the cutting edge of technology** être à la pointe du progrès

CV *n Br (abbr* **curriculum vitae***)* CV *m*

cwo *(abbr* **cash with order***)* envoi contre paiement

cyber *n* COMPTR cyber *m*

cyberspace *n* COMPTR cyberespace *m*; **in cyberspace** dans le cyberespace

cycle *n (in economy, trade)* cycle *m*

> **"**
> Whichever party succeeds in winning enough support may, once the uncertainty has passed, reap the benefit of the long-awaited upturn in the economic **cycle**.
> **"**

cyclical 1 *n* **cyclicals** valeurs *fpl* cycliques
  2 *adj* **cyclical variations** variations *fpl* cycliques

D/A *npl* (*abbr* **documents against acceptance**) documents *mpl* contre acceptation

dabble *vi* **to dabble on the Stock Exchange** boursicoter

daily *adj* quotidien(enne) □ ST EXCH *Daily Official List* cours *mpl* de clôture quotidiens; FIN *daily trading report* rapport *m* de situation journalière

daisy wheel *n* marguerite *f* □ *daisy wheel printer* imprimante *f* à marguerite

damage **1** *n* (**a**) *(to goods)* dommages *mpl*, dégâts *mpl*; *(to ship, cargo)* avaries *fpl*; **the insurance will pay for the damage** l'assurance paiera les dommages □ INS *damage certificate* attestation *f* de sinistre; *damage claim* déclaration *f* de sinistre; *damage survey* expertise *f* des dégâts

(**b**) LAW **damages** dommages-intérêts *mpl*, dommages *mpl* et intérêts *mpl*; **to award damages to sb for sth** accorder des dommages-intérêts à qn pour qch; **to sue sb for damages** poursuivre qn en dommages-intérêts; **to be liable for damages** être tenu(e) des dommages-intérêts; **to claim £1,000 damages** réclamer des dommages-intérêts de 1000 livres

(**c**) *damage limitation* limitation *f* des dégâts; **the redundancies are an exercise in damage limitation** c'est pour essayer de limiter les dégâts qu'ils ont licencié du personnel

2 *vt (goods)* avarier, endommager

damaged *adj (goods)* avarié(e), endommagé(e); **damaged in transit** endommagé en cours de route

▸ **damp down** *vt sep (market)* freiner; *(consumption)* réduire

DAT *n* COMPTR (*abbr* **digital audio tape**) DAT *f*, bande *f* audionumérique □ *DAT cartridge* cartouche *f* DAT; *DAT drive* lecteur *m* DAT, lecteur de bande audionumérique

data *n* informations *fpl*; COMPTR données *fpl*; **an item of data** une information; **to collect data on sb/sth** recueillir des informations sur qn/qch □ *data acquisition* collecte *f* *ou* saisie *f* de données; *data capture* saisie de données; *data carrier* support *m* de données; *data collection* recueil *m* *ou* collecte de données; *data entry* entrée *f* de données; *data management* gestion *f* de données; *data memory* mémoire *f*; *data path* chemin *m* d'accès aux données; *data privacy* confidentialité *f* des données *ou* de l'information; *data processing* informatique *f*, traitement *m* de l'information *ou* des données; *data processor* machine *f* de traitement de l'information, processeur *m* de données; *data protection* protection *f* de l'information; *data security* sécurité *f* des données; *data storage* stockage *m* de données; *data transfer* transfert *m* *ou* transmission *f* de données

database *n* COMPTR base *f* de données □ *database management* gestion *f* de base de données; *database management system* système *m* de gestion de base de données

datacomms *n* COMPTR communication *f* *ou* transmission *f* de données, télématique *f* □ *datacomms software* logiciel *m* de communication

date **1** *n* (**a**) date *f*; **date of delivery** date de livraison □ *date stamp (object)* (tampon *m*) dateur *m*; *(mark)* cachet *m*

(**b**) **up to date** à jour; *(well-informed)* au courant (**on** de); **I'm up to date with my work** mon travail est à jour; **to bring/keep sth up to date** mettre/tenir qch à jour

(**c**) **to date** à ce jour; **interest to date** intérêts *mpl* à ce jour

(**d**) **out of date** *(passport, cheque)* périmé(e)

(**e**) FIN *(of bill)* terme *m*, échéance *f*; **three months after date, at three months' date** à trois mois de date *ou* d'échéance; **date of maturity** (date *f* d') échéance

2 *vt (letter, cheque)* dater; **the cheque is dated 24 March** le chèque est daté du 24 mars

datebook *n* Am agenda *m*

dawn *n* ST EXCH *dawn raid* raid *m*; *dawn raider* raider *m*

> "
> During April 1988, Suchard, the Swiss-based chocolate manufacturer, launched a **dawn raid** on Rowntree, the York-based company, quickly scooping up a stake of 14.9 per cent as a 'strategic investment', but claiming that it had no intention of launching a full-scale takeover bid.
> "

day n (**a**) jour m; (working hours) journée f; **to have/take a day off** avoir/prendre un jour de congé; **to work an eight-hour day** travailler huit heures par jour; **to be paid by the day** être payé(e) à la journée □ **day shift** équipe f de jour; **to be on day shift** être de jour
(**b**) ST EXCH **day order** ordre m valable pour la journée
(**c**) **we can give you four days' grace** nous pouvons vous accorder un délai de quatre jours □ **day of grace** jour m de grâce; **days of grace** délai m de grâce

daybook n ACCT brouillard m

day-to-day adj courant(e), quotidien(enne); **he is responsible for the day-to-day running of the business** c'est lui qui est chargé d'expédier les affaires courantes; **we can barely afford the day-to-day expenses** on arrive à peine à faire face aux dépenses quotidiennes

DCF n ACCT (abbr **discounted cash flow**) valeur f actualisée nette

DD n COMPTR (abbr **double density**) double densité f

dead adj FIN **dead account** compte m inactif; **dead loss** perte f sèche; **dead market** marché m mort; **dead money** argent m mort, argent qui dort; **dead period** période f d'inactivité; **dead season** morte-saison f

deadline n (day) date f limite; (time) heure f limite; **to meet/miss a deadline** respecter/laisser passer une date/heure limite; **to work to a deadline** avoir un délai à respecter

deadlock 1 n impasse f; **to reach a deadlock** aboutir à une impasse; **talks with the union were in deadlock** les négociations avec le syndicat étaient au point mort ou étaient dans l'impasse; **they have succeeded in breaking the deadlock** ils ont réussi à sortir de l'impasse
2 vt **to be deadlocked** (of talks, negotiations) être au point mort

deadweight n chargement m en lourd, port m en lourd □ **deadweight cargo** marchandises f pl lourdes

deal 1 n affaire f, marché m; (on Stock Exchange) opération f, transaction f; **to do** or **make a deal with sb** conclure une affaire ou un marché avec qn; **to negotiate a deal** négocier une affaire ou un marché; **to call off a deal** annuler une affaire ou un marché; **it's a deal!** marché conclu!
2 vi négocier, traiter; **our firm has been dealing for over 50 years** notre société est en activité depuis plus de 50 ans; **to deal in leather** faire le commerce des cuirs; **to deal on the Stock Exchange** faire des opérations ou des transactions en Bourse; FIN, ST EXCH **to deal in options** faire le commerce des primes

▸ **deal with** vt insep (**a**) (do business with) traiter ou négocier avec (**b**) (get supplies from) se fournir chez (**c**) (handle) (problem, query, order, complaint) s'occuper de

dealer n (trader) négociant(e) m,f, marchand(e) m,f (**in** en); (in cars) concessionnaire mf; (on Stock Exchange) courtier(ère) m,f, cambiste mf

dealership n concession f

dealing n (**a**) ST EXCH opérations f pl, transactions f pl □ **dealing room** salle f des changes, salle de marchés (**b**) (commerce) commerce m; **dealings** transactions f pl; **to have dealings with sb** faire des affaires avec qn

dear adj (**a**) (expensive) cher (chère) □ **dear money** argent cher (**b**) (in letter) **Dear Sir** Monsieur; **Dear Sirs** Messieurs; **Dear Madam** Madame/Mademoiselle; **Dear Sir or Madam** Madame, Monsieur; **Dear Mr Martin** Monsieur; **Dear Ms Carrington** Madame

death n décès m, mort f; **death in service (benefit)** capital-décès m □ FIN **death benefit** capital-décès; **death duties, Am death tax** droits m pl de succession

debenture n FIN obligation f □ **debenture bond** obligation; **debenture holder** porteur(euse) m,f d'obligations, obligataire mf; **debenture issue** émission f d'obligations; **debenture loan** emprunt m obligataire; **debenture stock** obligations (sans garantie)

> "
> A **debenture** includes **debenture stock**, bonds and other securities of a company, whether amounting to a charge on the assets or not. It is a document which sets out the terms of a loan and is usually issued under authority of a company's seal, Repayment is provided for at some future date. Payment of interest is made to the **debenture holder** at a specified rate and at clearly defined intervals.
> "

debit 1 *n* débit *m*; ACCT **debit and credit** doit *m* et avoir *m* □ **debit account** compte *m* débiteur; **debit balance** solde *m* débiteur *ou* déficitaire; **debit card** carte *f* de débit; **debit column** colonne *f* débitrice *ou* des débits; **debit entry** article *m* au débit; **debit interest** intérêts *mpl* débiteurs; ACCT **debit item** poste *m* débiteur; **debit note** facture *f ou* note *f ou* bordereau *m* de débit; **debit side** *(of account)* débit

2 *vt (account)* débiter; **to debit an account with £200, to debit £200 to an account** débiter un compte de 200 livres; **has this cheque been debited to my account?** est-ce que ce chèque a été débité de mon compte?

debt *n* dette *f; (to be recovered)* créance *f*; **to be in debt** être endetté(e), avoir des dettes; **to be £12,000 in debt** avoir 12 000 livres de dettes; **to be in debt to sb** être en dette envers qn; **to pay off a debt** rembourser *ou* payer une dette; **to be out of debt** n'avoir plus de dettes; **to get** *or* **run into debt** s'endetter, faire des dettes; **to reschedule** *or* **restructure a debt** rééchelonner une dette; *Fam* **to be up to the neck** *or* **one's ears in debt** être criblé(e) de dettes; **debt owed by us** dette passive; **debt owed to us** dette active □ **debt capacity** capacité *f* d'endettement; **debt collection** recouvrement *m* de créances; **debt collection agency** agence *f* de recouvrements; **debt collector** agent *m* de recouvrements; **debt due** créance exigible; **debt financing** financement *m* par endettement; **debt instrument** titre *m* de créance; **debt limit** limite *f* d'endettement; **debt rescheduling, debt restructuring** rééchelonnement *m* des dettes; **debt servicing** service *m* de la dette; **debt swap** échange *m* de créances

debt-equity ratio *n* rapport *m* dettes-actions

debtor *n* débiteur(trice) *m,f* □ ACCT **debtor account** compte *m* débiteur; ECON **debtor nation** pays *m* débiteur; **debtor side** *(of account)* débit *m*, doit *m*

> ❝
> It was the products of American factories that kept the Allies supplied in the First World War; it was American money that financed the Allied war effort and made the USA a creditor rather than a **debtor nation** by 1918.
> ❞

debug *vt* COMPTR *(program)* déboguer

decentralization *n* décentralisation *f*

decentralized *vt* décentralisé(e)

decision *n* décision *f*; **to make a decision** prendre une décision □ **decision model** modèle *m* décisionnel; **decision tree** arbre *m* décisionnel *ou* de décision

decision-maker *n* décideur(euse) *m,f*, décisionnaire *mf*; **to be a good/bad decision-maker** savoir/ne pas savoir prendre des décisions

decision-making *n* prise *f* de décision(s); **this job calls for a lot of decision-making** ce travail demande qu'on prenne beaucoup de décisions □ **the decision-making process** le processus de prise de décision(s); **decision-making unit** unité *f* de prise de décision(s)

> ❝
> One way round this, that remains consistent with the democratic spirit of the peer group, is to have a central **decision-making unit** comprising, at any one time, only a few people, but to rotate membership of this unit, each person taking a turn.
> ❞

declaration *n* déclaration *f* □ **declaration of bankruptcy** jugement *m* déclaratif de faillite; **declaration of dividend** déclaration de dividende; **declaration of income** déclaration de revenu; **declaration of intent** déclaration *f* d'intention; ST EXCH **declaration of options** réponse *f* des primes; **declaration of solvency** déclaration de solvabilité

declare *vt* **(a)** CUSTOMS *(goods)* déclarer **(b) to declare sb bankrupt** constater *ou* prononcer l'état de faillite *ou* la faillite de qn; FIN **to declare a dividend of 10%** déclarer un dividende de 10%; ST EXCH **to declare an option** répondre à *ou* donner la réponse à une prime

decline 1 *n* déclin *m*; **to be on the decline** être en baisse; *(of industry)* être en déclin □ MKTG **decline stage** phase *f* de déclin

2 *vi* **(a)** *(decrease)* être en baisse; *(of industry)* être en déclin **(b)** *(refuse)* décliner, refuser

declining *adj* en baisse; *(industry)* déclinant

decontrol 1 *n (of prices)* libération *f*

2 *vt* libérer des contraintes du gouvernement; *(prices, wages)* débloquer

> Nobody has forgotten the rapid descent into currency chaos, rampant inflation and food riots which greeted a short-lived move to **decontrol** prices and foreign exchanges during the closing stages of the previous government last spring.

decrease 1 *n* baisse *f*; **sales are on the decrease** les ventes sont en baisse
2 *vi* diminuer, baisser

decreasing *adj* en baisse; *(number, value, strength)* décroissant(e) ❑ ACCT **decreasing rate** taux *m* dégressif

decrypt *vt* COMPTR déchiffrer

decryption *n* COMPTR déchiffrement *m*

dedicated *adj* COMPTR *(terminal)* spécialisé(e), dédié(e) ❑ **dedicated word processor** machine *f* servant uniquement au traitement de texte

deduct *vt* déduire; *(tax)* prélever; **to deduct £10 from the price** déduire 10 livres du prix; **to be deducted at source** *(of tax)* être prélevé(e) à la source; **after deducting expenses** après déduction des frais

deductible 1 *n Am* INS franchise *f*
2 *adj* déductible

deduction *n* déduction *f* (**from** sur); *(from salary)* prélèvement *m*, retenue *f*; **after deduction of taxes** après déduction des impôts; **after deductions, I'm left with a salary of £20,000** une fois les prélèvements *ou* les retenues décompté(e)s, il me reste un salaire de 20 000 livres

deed *n* LAW acte *m* notarié; **to draw up a deed** rédiger un acte ❑ **deed of arrangement, deed of assignment** acte de transfert; **deed of covenant** pacte *m*, contrat *m*; **deed of partnership** acte constitutif *ou* de société; **deed of title** titre *m* (constitutif) de propriété; **deed of transfer** feuille *f* de transfert

deep discount *n* forte remise *f*

deep-discount bond *n* obligation *f* à forte décote

> **Deep-discount bonds** are bonds which carry a low nominal rate of interest and accordingly are issued at a discount to the value at which they will be redeemed. In the extreme case where no interest at all is payable they are sometimes referred to as zero coupon bonds.

de facto *adj & adv* de facto

defalcation *n* détournement *m* de fonds

default 1 *n* (**a**) LAW *(failure to appear in court)* défaut *m*, non-comparution *f* (**b**) FIN **in default of payment** à defaut de paiement (**c**) COMPTR défaut *m* ❑ **default drive** lecteur *m* par défaut; **default font** police *f* par défaut; **default setting** configuration *f* par défaut
2 *vi* (**a**) LAW *(fail to appear in court)* ne pas comparaître (**b**) FIN manquer à ses engagements; **to default on a payment** ne pas honorer un paiement

> Because they are more likely to **default** on repayments, they would have to pay higher rates of interest than older married couples with small families.

defaulter *n* débiteur(trice) *m,f* défaillant(e)

defeasance *n* LAW abrogation *f*

defect *n* défaut *m*

defective *adj* défectueux(euse)

defend *vt* défendre; **the company must defend its share of the market** l'entreprise doit défendre sa part de marché; **they are defending themselves against the takeover bid** ils essaient de résister à l'OPA

defended takeover bid *n* OPA *f* sauvage

defer *vt* *(decision, meeting)* remettre, reporter; *(payment)* différer, retarder; *(judgement)* suspendre

deferment *n* *(of decision, meeting)* report *m*; *(of payment)* recul *m*; *(of judgement)* suspension *f*

deferred *adj* différé(e) ❑ **deferred annuity** annuité *f* différée; **deferred asset** actif *m* différé; **deferred charges** frais *mpl* différés; **deferred credit** paiement *m* différé; **deferred income** produit *m* constaté d'avance; **deferred liabilities** passif *m* reporté; **deferred ordinary share** action *f* ordinaire différée; **deferred payment** paiement différé; **deferred rebate** rabais *m* différé; **deferred results** résultats *mpl* à longue échéance; **deferred share** action différée; **deferred taxation** impôts *mpl* différés

deficit *n* FIN déficit *m*; **to be in deficit** être en déficit; **the balance of payments shows a deficit of £800 million** la balance des paiements indique un déficit de 800 millions de livres

definite *adj (order, price)* ferme

deflate FIN, ECON *vt (prices)* faire baisser; **to deflate the economy** pratiquer une politique déflationniste; **this measure is intended to deflate the economy** cette mesure est destinée à faire de la déflation

deflation *n* FIN, ECON déflation *f*

deflationary *adj* FIN, ECON *(measures)* déflationniste; *(policy)* de désinflation

defragmentation *n* COMPTR défragmentation *f*

defraud *vt (the state)* frauder; *(company, person)* escroquer; **he defrauded the government of £15,000 in unemployment benefit** il a frauduleusement perçu 15 000 livres d'allocations chômage

defray *vt* **to defray sb's expenses** défrayer qn; **to defray the cost of sth** rembourser les frais de qch; **all charges to be defrayed by the purchaser** tous les frais sont à la charge de l'acheteur

defunct *adj (company)* dissous(oute)

degearing *n* désendettement *m*

deinstall *vt* COMPTR désinstaller

deinstallation *n* COMPTR désinstallation *f*

deinstaller *n* COMPTR désinstallateur *m*

delay 1 *n* retard *m*; **we apologize for the delay in dealing with your complaint** veuillez excuser notre retard dans le traitement de votre réclamation; **there will be a 20-minute delay before the meeting** la réunion aura lieu vingt minutes plus tard que prévu; **all flights are subject to delay** tous les vols risquent d'avoir du retard

2 *vt (project, decision)* retarder; **to be delayed** *(of flight, train)* avoir du retard

delayering *n* suppression *f* d'échelons; **middle management has been cut back through delayering** la suppression d'échelons a réduit la hiérarchie intermédiaire

del credere *n* ducroire *m* □ *del credere agent* commissionnaire *m* ducroire, agent *m* ducroire; *del credere clause* clause *f* ducroire; *del credere commission* commission *f* ducroire

delegate 1 *n* délégué(e) *m,f*

2 *vt* déléguer; **to delegate sb to do sth** déléguer qn pour faire qch; **he must learn to delegate more work to his team** il faut qu'il apprenne à déléguer davantage de travail à son équipe

delegation *n (of person, powers)* délégation *f*; **to send a delegation** envoyer une délégation

delete 1 *n* COMPTR **delete (key)** touche *f* d'effacement

2 *vt* (**a**) COMPTR effacer, supprimer (**b**) **delete where applicable, delete as appropriate** *(on form)* rayer la/les mention(s) inutile(s)

3 *vi* COMPTR effacer

deliver 1 *vt* (**a**) *(letter, parcel)* remettre, distribuer (**to** à); *(goods)* livrer (**to** à); **to have sth delivered** faire livrer qch

(**b**) *(provide) (service)* assurer; FIN **to deliver a profit** rapporter *ou* faire un profit; FIN **to deliver shares** délivrer des valeurs

2 *vi (of supplier)* livrer

delivery *n (of letter, parcel)* remise *f*, distribution *f*; *(of goods)* livraison *f*; **to accept** *or* **take delivery of sth** prendre livraison de qch, réceptionner qch; **awaiting delivery** en souffrance; **for immediate delivery** à livrer de suite; **to pay on delivery** payer à *ou* sur livraison; **free delivery** *(envoi)* livraison franco; **next day delivery** livraison lendemain □ *delivery address* adresse *f* de livraison; *delivery charges* frais *mpl* d'expédition *ou* de livraison; *delivery date* date *f* de livraison; ST EXCH *delivery month* mois *m* de livraison; *delivery note* bon *m* ou bordereau *m* de livraison; *delivery order* bon de livraison; *delivery point* lieu *m* de livraison; *delivery schedule* planning *m* de livraison; *delivery time* délai *m* de livraison

demand *n* (**a**) *(request)* demande *f*, réclamation *f*; *(for taxes, rates)* avertissement *m*; **payable on demand** payable sur demande; **there have been demands for the director's resignation** certains ont réclamé la démission du directeur

(**b**) ECON demande *f*; **supply and demand** l'offre *f* et la demande; **to be in (great) demand** être (très) demandé(e) *ou* recherché(e); **there isn't much demand for this product** ce produit n'est pas très demandé □ MKTG *demand curve* courbe *f* (d'évolution) de la demande; *demand factor* facteur *m* de consommation

demand-led *adj* ECON tiré(e) par la demande

> **❝**
> This was the early eighties and Britain was clawing its way out of recession on the back of a **demand-led** boom. Legal aid is the fastest growing social service in Britain. Whilst practitioners argue that still more monies need to be spent, government concern over **demand-led** expenditure has increased.
> **❞**

demand-pull inflation *n* ECON inflation *f* par la demande

demarcation *n* démarcation *f*; **a clear demarcation of responsibilities is essential in any organization** dans toute organisation, il est essentiel de délimiter les attributions de chacun ▫ **demarcation dispute** conflit *m* d'attributions

demerger *n* scission *f*; **several new companies were formed after the demerger of the holding group** plusieurs entreprises nouvelles ont été créées à la suite de la scission du holding

demo *n* (*abbr* **demonstration**) démonstration *f*; **we received a demo of the new software system** quelqu'un est venu nous faire une démonstration du nouveau logiciel ▫ COMPTR **demo disk** disquette *f* de démonstration *ou* d'évaluation

demographic *adj* MKTG démographique ▫ **demographic analysis** analyse *f* démographique; **demographic segmentation** segmentation *f* démographique du marché

> **Demographic segmentation** involves the sub-division of markets on the basis of variables such as age, sex, occupation and class, for example. Magazines and journals are examples of products which are directed towards carefully segmented markets (readership). In addition to the basic reading material, the advertising contained in each edition reflects the segmentation.

demonetization *n* FIN (*of currency*) démonétisation *f*

demonetize *vt* FIN (*currency*) démonétiser

demonstrate *vt* (*system, equipment*) faire une démonstration de; **he demonstrated how the new system worked** il nous a montré comment le nouveau système fonctionne

demonstration *n* (*of system, equipment*) démonstration *f*; **they gave us a demonstration of the new model** il nous ont fait une démonstration du nouveau modèle ▫ **demonstration model** appareil *m* de démonstration

demote *vt* rétrograder; **he was demoted from area manager to sales representative** du poste de directeur régional, il a été rétrogradé au poste de représentant de commerce

demotion *n* rétrogradation *f*

demotivate *vt* démotiver

demotivating *adj* démotivant(e); **the spate of redundancies has been very demotivating for the workforce** la série de licenciements a eu un effet très démotivant sur le personnel

demurrage *n* surestarie(s) *f(pl)*

denationalization *n* dénationalisation *f*

denationalize *vt* dénationaliser

denomination *n* FIN valeur *f*; (*of share, banknote*) coupure *f*; **coins of all denominations** pièces *fpl* de toutes valeurs; **small/large denominations** petites/grosses coupures

department *n* (*in company*) service *m*; (*in shop*) rayon *m*; (*of government*) ministère *m*; *Br* **Department of Employment** ≃ ministère *m* du Travail; *Br* **Department of the Environment** ≃ ministère de l'Environnement; *Br* **Department of Social Security** ≃ Sécurité *f* sociale; *Br* **Department of Trade and Industry** ≃ ministère du Commerce et de l'Industrie ▫ **department manager** (*in company*) chef *m* de service; (*in shop*) chef de rayon; **department store** grand magasin *m*

departmental *adj* (*in company*) de service; (*in shop*) de rayon; (*of government*) de ministère ▫ **departmental manager** (*in company*) chef *m* de service; (*in shop*) chef de rayon

departure *n* (*from place*) départ *m*; (*from tradition*) écart *m*; (*from plan*) modification *f*; **our departure was delayed for three hours** notre départ a été retardé de trois heures; **the introduction of bonuses was a departure from standard company policy** l'introduction de primes représentait une entorse à la politique habituelle de l'entreprise ▫ **departure lounge** (*in airport*) salle *f* d'embarquement; **departure time** heure *f* de départ

deplete *vt* (*stock*) épuiser

depletion *n* (*of stock*) épuisement *m*

deposit *n* (a) BANKING dépôt *m*; **to make a deposit** déposer de l'argent; **to make a deposit of £500** déposer 500 livres en banque; **on deposit** en dépôt ▫ *Br* **deposit account** compte *m* livret, compte de dépôt; (*when notice has to be given before withdrawal*) compte à terme; **deposit slip** bordereau *m* *ou* bulletin *m* de versement (**b**) *(down payment)* acompte *m*; *(not returnable, for contract)* arrhes *fpl*; *(against damage)* caution *f*; **to pay** or **put down a deposit on sth** verser un acompte/des arrhes sur qch; **he left £10 as a deposit** il a versé un acompte de 10 livres ◻ **deposit receipt** récépissé *m* de dépôt

2 *vt (money)* déposer; *(document) (with a bank)* mettre en dépôt (**with** dans); *(with a solicitor)* confier (**with** à); FIN **to deposit sth as security** nantir qch, gager qch

depositary *n* dépositaire *mf*

deposition *vt* MKTG *(product)* dépositionner

depositor *n* BANKING déposant(e) *m,f*

depository *n* (**a**) *(warehouse)* dépôt *m*, entrepôt *m* (**b**) *(person)* dépositaire *mf*

depot *n* dépôt *m*, entrepôt *m*

depreciable base *n Am* assiette *f* de l'amortissement

depreciate **1** *vt* (**a**) *(value)* déprécier, rabaisser; *(goods)* faire perdre de la valeur à; *(property, equipment)* amortir

2 *vi (of goods, money, currency, property, equipment)* se déprécier, se dévaloriser; *(of shares)* baisser; **the pound has depreciated against the dollar** la livre a reculé par rapport au dollar

> With flexible exchange rates, any tendency towards a deficit on the UK balance of payments (which would imply an excess supply of pounds on the foreign exchange market) will cause sterling to **depreciate** in value against other currencies. This depreciation should tend to offset the effects of the domestic inflation. it makes exports cheaper to foreign buyers and imports more expensive to domestic buyers.

depreciated *adj* ACCT amorti(e); *(currency)* déprécié(e)

depreciation *n (of goods, money, currency, property, equipment)* dépréciation *f*, dévalorisation *f*; *(amount)* moins-value *f*; *(of shares)* moins-value, décote *f* ◻ ACCT **depreciation rate** taux *m* d'amortissement

depressed *adj (market, trade)* déprimé(e); *(area, industry)* touché(e) par la crise; **this is one of the most depressed sectors of the economy** c'est l'un des secteurs économiques les plus touchés par la crise; **the economy has been in a depressed state for**

nearly three years l'économie est dans un état de marasme depuis bientôt trois ans

depression *n* dépression *f*, crise *f* économique; **the country's economy is in a state of depression** l'économie du pays est en crise

dept *n* (*abbr* **department**) service *m*

depth *n* MKTG *(of product)* profondeur *f* ◻ **depth interview** entretien *m* en profondeur

> Not a great deal in the way of interpretation or conclusion should be hung on answers to a single question about "liking" a product. Only a **depth interview** of several hours can be expected to provide a complete picture of overall positive and negative feelings experienced by the consumer in relation to that product.

deputize **1** *vt* députer; **to deputize sb to do sth** députer qn pour faire qch

2 *vi* assurer l'intérim; **to deputize for sb** remplacer qn, assurer l'intérim de qn

deputy *n (assistant)* adjoint(e) *m,f*; *(temporary replacement)* remplaçant(e) *m,f*; **to act as deputy for sb** suppléer *ou* remplacer qn ◻ **deputy chairman** vice-président(e) *m,f*; **deputy director** directeur(trice) *m,f* adjoint(e); **deputy manager** sous-directeur(trice) *m,f*, directeur(trice) *m,f* adjoint(e); **deputy managing director** directeur(trice) *m,f* général(e) adjoint(e)

deregulate *vt (industry, transport)* déréglementer, déréguler; *(prices, wages)* libérer

deregulation *n (of industry, transport)* déréglementation *f*, dérégulation *f*; *(of prices, wages)* libération *f*

derivative *n* ST EXCH produit *m* dérivé ◻ **derivative market** marché *m* à terme des instruments financiers

descending sort *n* COMPTR tri *m* en ordre décroissant

description *n (of goods)* désignation *f*

design **1** *n (planning)* conception *f*; *(style)* modèle *m*; **our latest design** notre dernier modèle

2 *vt (plan)* concevoir; **they have designed a product to appeal to younger customers** ils ont conçu un produit ciblé sur le marché de la jeunesse; **this financial package is designed to meet the needs of small businesses** ces produits financiers ont été conçus pour répondre aux besoins des petites entreprises

designer n styliste mf

desk n (in office) bureau m ❑ **desk diary** agenda m de bureau; **desk job** emploi m de bureau; MKTG **desk research** recherche f documentaire

deskill vt déqualifier

deskilling n déqualification f

> **"**
>
> He claims that **deskilling** has taken place in many white-collar jobs. As the skill content of the work has been reduced, then some white-collar workers have lost the advantages they previously enjoyed over manual employees.
>
> **"**

desktop n **desktop calculator** calculatrice f; COMPTR **desktop computer** ordinateur m de bureau ou de table; **desktop publishing** publication f assistée par ordinateur, microédition f; **desktop publishing operator** opérateur(trice) m,f de publication assistée par ordinateur; **desktop publishing package** logiciel m de mise en page

despatch, despatcher etc = **dispatch, dispatcher** etc

destination n destination f ❑ COMPTR **destination disk** (hard disk) disque m de destination; (floppy disk) disquette f de destination; **destination drive** lecteur m de destination; MKTG **destination purchase** achat m prévu

destock vt & vi déstocker

detail 1 n détail m; **details** (information) renseignements mpl; (name and telephone number) coordonnées fpl; **for further details** pour tous renseignements supplémentaires, pour de plus amples renseignements; **please send me details of your range of products** veuillez me faire parvenir une documentation sur votre gamme de produits; **let me take down your details** laissez-moi vos coordonnées

2 vt (enumerate, specify) détailler

determine vt (date, price) déterminer, fixer; (conditions) fixer

Deutschmark n (deutsche) mark m

devaluation n ECON dévaluation f

devalue vt ECON dévaluer; **the franc has been devalued by 3%** le franc a été dévalué de 3%

develop 1 vt (a) (skills, idea, market) développer; (product) mettre au point
(b) ECON (country, region) mettre en valeur, développer

2 vi (a) (evolve) se développer; **we have developed into one of the leading companies in the field** nous sommes devenus l'une des entreprises les plus importantes dans ce domaine
(b) ECON (of country, region) se développer

developer n ECON promoteur(trice) m,f

developing country n pays m en voie de développement

development n (a) (of skills, idea, market) développement m; (of product) mise f au point
(b) ECON (of country, region) mise f en valeur, développement m ❑ Br **development area** = zone à fort taux de chômage où l'État incite les industries à venir s'installer; **development assistance** crédits mpl de développement; **development costs** coûts mpl de développement; **development stage** (of product) phase f de développement

device n COMPTR (peripheral) unité f périphérique, périphérique m

DG n ADMIN (abbr **Director General**) directeur(trice) m,f général(e)

DHSS n Br ADMIN Formerly (abbr **Department of Health and Social Security**) ≃ Ministère m de la Santé

diagnostic audit n audit m de diagnostic

diagram n schéma m; (graph) diagramme m, schéma

diagrammatic adj schématique

dial 1 n Am **dial tone** tonalité f
2 vt (number) composer, faire; (operator, country) appeler
3 vi composer ou faire le numéro; **to dial direct** obtenir une communication ou appeler par l'automatique

dial-up account n COMPTR compte m d'accès par ligne commutée

dialling n Br **dialling code** indicatif m; **dialling tone** tonalité f

dialogue, Am dialog n dialogue m ❑ COMPTR **dialogue box** boîte f de dialogue; **dialogue mode** mode m dialogue

diary n agenda m

Dictaphone® n Dictaphone® m, appareil m à dicter

dictate 1 vt (a) (letter) dicter; **to dictate sth to sb** dicter qch à qn
(b) (determine) imposer; **market conditions are dictated by the economic situation** la

conjoncture du marché dépend de la situation économique

2 vi **(a)** (dictate text) dicter
(b) (give orders) **to dictate to sb** donner des ordres à qn

dictating machine n appareil m à dicter

dictation n dictée f

differential 1 n écart m

2 adj différentiel(elle) ❑ **differential pricing** établissement m des prix différentiels, tarification f différentielle; **differential tariff** tarif m différentiel

differentiated marketing n MKTG marketing m de différenciation

digital adj COMPTR numérique ❑ **digital audio tape** cassette f numérique; **digital display** affichage m numérique; **digital readout** affichage numérique; **digital signal** signal m numérique; **digital signature** signature f numérique

digitize vt COMPTR (data) convertir en numérique, numériser

diluted adj FIN, ST EXCH **fully diluted earnings per share** bénéfice m net dilué par action

dilution n FIN, ST EXCH dilution f ❑ **dilution of equity** dilution du bénéfice par action; **dilution of shareholding** dilution des actions

> ❝
> Another stimulus to the market has come from issuers buying back bonds, to retire the debt entirely or swap it for new equity. Though such a swap is a better deal for a company's bondholders than for shareholders, shareholders have been prepared to accept the **dilution**, reckoning that cutting debt more than offsets it.
> ❞

diminish 1 vt (price, quality, value) diminuer, réduire
2 vi diminuer, se réduire; **their profits have diminished** leurs bénéfices ont diminué

diminishing adj décroissant(e); (price, quality, value) en baisse ❑ ACCT **diminishing balance (method)** amortissement m linéaire; **diminishing marginal product, diminishing returns** rendements mpl décroissants; **law of diminishing returns** loi f des rendements décroissants

dinosaur n MKTG poids m mort, produit m dodo

dip 1 n (in prices, value, figures) baisse f; **the winter months saw a sharp dip in profits** les bénéfices ont fortement baissé pendant l'hiver
2 vi (of prices, value, figures) baisser; **shares dipped on the London Stock Market yesterday** les actions ont baissé à la Bourse des valeurs de Londres hier

dir n **(a)** ADMIN (abbr **director**) directeur(trice) m,f **(b)** COMPTR (abbr **directory**) répertoire m

direct 1 adj **direct action** prise f de contrôle; **direct advertising** publicité f directe; **direct banking** banque f à distance; **direct competition** concurrence f directe; **direct costs** charges fpl directes; **direct cost accounting** (méthode f de) comptabilité f des coûts variables; **direct costing** méthode de coût variable ou proportionnel; Br BANKING **direct debit** prélèvement m (bancaire) automatique; **to pay by direct debit** payer par prélèvement automatique; **direct expenses** coûts mpl directs; **direct investment** investissement m direct; **direct labour** main-d'œuvre f directe; **direct labour cost** charges fpl de main-d'œuvre directes; **direct letter of credit** lettre f de crédit directe; **direct mail** publipostage m, publicité f directe; **direct mail advertising** publicité f directe ou par publipostage; **direct marketing** marketing m direct, mercatique f directe; **direct response advertising** publicité f à réponse directe; **direct sale** vente f directe; **direct selling** vente f directe; **direct tax** impôt m direct; **direct taxation** contribution f directe
2 vt (company, work) diriger; **to direct sb to do sth** ordonner à qn de faire qch

direction n (of company) direction f; **he will take over the direction of the group** il va prendre la direction du groupe

directive n directive f, instruction f

director n (of company) directeur(trice) m,f; (board member) administrateur(trice) m,f ❑ **directors' remuneration** rémunération f des administrateurs; **directors' report** rapport m annuel

directorate n (conseil m d')administration f

directorship n direction f; **during his directorship** pendant sa direction; **he has been offered a directorship** on lui a proposé un poste de directeur

directory n (of telephone numbers) annuaire m; (of addresses) répertoire m (d'adresses); COMPTR répertoire ❑ **(street) directory** guide m des rues; Br **directory enquiries** renseignements mpl

dirty adj **(a)** (bill of lading) clausé(e) **(b)** **dirty money** argent m mal acquis ou de source douteuse

disability *n* invalidité *f* ❏ INS **disability clause** = clause d'une police d'assurance-vie permettant à l'assuré de cesser tout paiement et de recevoir une pension en cas d'invalidité; **disability pension** pension d'invalidité

disburse *vt* débourser

disbursement *n* déboursement *m*

discharge 1 *n* (**a**) FIN *(of bankrupt)* réhabilitation *f* ❏ **discharge in bankruptcy** réhabilitation
(**b**) *(dismissal)* renvoi *m*
(**c**) FIN *(of debt)* liquidation *f*, acquittement *m*; *(of account, obligation)* paiement *m*, apurement *m*; **in full discharge** *(on bill)* pour acquit
(**d**) *(of ship)* déchargement *m*; *(of cargo)* déchargement, débarquement *m*
2 *vt* (**a**) FIN *(bankrupt)* réhabiliter, décharger
(**b**) *(dismiss)* congédier, renvoyer
(**c**) FIN *(debt)* liquider, acquitter; *(fine)* payer; *(account, obligation)* apurer, payer, faire l'apurement de
(**d**) *(ship)* décharger; *(cargo)* décharger, débarquer

discharged bankrupt *n* failli(e) *m,f* réhabilité(e)

disciplinary *adj* disciplinaire ❏ **disciplinary action** mesures *fpl* disciplinaires; **to take disciplinary action (against sb)** prendre des mesures disciplinaires (contre qn); **disciplinary board** conseil *m* de discipline; **disciplinary hearing** séance *f* du conseil de discipline; **disciplinary procedure** procédure *f* disciplinaire

disclaimer *n* (**a**) *(denial)* démenti *m*, désaveu *m*; **to issue a disclaimer** publier un démenti
(**b**) LAW désistement *m*, renonciation *f*

disclosure *n* ST EXCH information *f* aux actionnaires

discontinue *vt (production)* abandonner; *(product)* interrompre; **that item has been discontinued** cet article n'est plus suivi ❏ **discontinued line** fin *f* de série

discount 1 *n* (**a**) *(reduction in price)* remise *f*, rabais *m*; **to give sb a discount** faire une remise à qn; **to buy/sell sth at a discount** acheter/vendre qch au rabais; **to allow a discount of 10% (on sth)** consentir un rabais de 10% (sur qch) ❏ **discount price** prix *m* réduit *ou* faible; **discount rate** taux *m* d'escompte; **discount store** magasin *m* de discount
(**b**) FIN escompte *m*; **discounts and allowances** remise, rabais, ristourne, RRR ❏ **discount bank** banque *f* d'escompte; **discount house** comptoir *m* d'escompte; **discount market** marché *m* de l'escompte; **discount mechanism** mécanisme *m* de l'escompte; **discount rate** taux *m* d'escompte
2 *vt* (**a**) *(price)* baisser; *(goods)* solder
(**b**) FIN *(bill)* escompter

discountable *adj* FIN escomptable

discounted *adj* ACCT **discounted cash flow** valeur *f* actualisée nette; **discounted rate** taux *m* d'escompte; **discounted value** valeur actualisée

discounting *n* FIN escompte *m* ❏ **discounting bank** banque *f ou* maison *f* d'escompte

discrepancy *n* écart *m*, différence *f*; **there is a discrepancy in the accounts** les comptes ne sont pas justes

discretion *n (judgement)* jugement *m*; **at the manager's discretion** à la discrétion du directeur

discretionary *adj* BANKING **discretionary account** compte *m* avec procuration, compte sous mandat de gestion; **discretionary costs** coûts *mpl* discrétionnaires; **discretionary fund** compte sous mandat de gestion; ST EXCH **discretionary order** ordre *m* à appréciation; **discretionary powers** pouvoirs *mpl* discrétionnaires

discriminate *vi* **to discriminate in favour of sb/sth** favoriser qn/qch; **to discriminate against sb/sth** faire de la discrimination envers qn/qch; **to be discriminated against** être victime de discrimination

discriminating *adj* ADMIN *(duty, tariff)* différentiel(elle)

discrimination *n (bias)* discrimination *f*

discuss *vt* discuter de; **we can discuss the matter of pay rises at the next meeting** nous pourrons discuter des augmentations de salaires au cours de la prochaine réunion

discussion n discussion f; **to be under discussion** être en discussion; **to come up for discussion** être discuté(e)

dishonour, Am **dishonor** vt FIN (bill, cheque) ne pas accepter, ne pas honorer, refuser de payer; **dishonoured cheque** chèque impayé ou non honoré

disincentive n ECON facteur m décourageant; **heavy taxation is a disincentive to expansion** les taxes élevées découragent toute expansion; **to act as a disincentive to sth** avoir un effet dissuasif sur qch

disinflation n ECON désinflation f, déflation f

disinflationary adj ECON désinflationniste

disintermediation n désintermédiation f

disinvestment n désinvestissement m

disk n COMPTR disque m; (floppy) disquette f; **to put sth on disk** enregistrer qch sur disque/disquette □ **disk access time** temps m d'accès disque; **disk box** boîte f à disquettes; **disk capacity** capacité f de disque/disquette; **disk controller** contrôleur m de disque; **disk controller card** carte f contrôleur de disque; **disk drive** unité f ou lecteur m de disque/disquette; **disk file** fichier m disque; **disk mailer** pochette f d'expédition de disquette; **disk memory** mémoire f à disque; **disk operating system** système m d'exploitation de disques; **disk space** espace m disque

diskette n COMPTR disquette f □ **diskette box** boîte f à disquettes

dismiss vt (a) (from job) renvoyer, licencier (b) LAW (case) classer; (appeal) rejeter

dismissal n (a) (from job) renvoi m, licenciement m (b) LAW (of case) classement m; (of appeal) rejet m

dispatch 1 n (of letter, parcel, goods) expédition f, envoi m □ **dispatch department** (service m des) expéditions; **dispatch note** bulletin m ou bordereau m d'expédition; **dispatch rider** coursier(ère) m,f (à motocyclette)
2 vt (letter, parcel, goods) expédier, envoyer; (messenger) envoyer, dépêcher

dispatcher n expéditeur(trice) m,f

dispatching n (of letter, parcel, goods) expédition f, envoi m

dispenser n (for cash, drinks) distributeur m

displaced share n ST EXCH action f déclassée

displacement n ST EXCH déclassement m

display 1 n (a) (of goods) étalage m, exposition f □ **display area** espace m d'exposition; **display pack** emballage m de présentation ou présentoir m; **display space** surface f d'exposition; **display stand, display unit** présentoir m; **display window** vitrine f, étalage m
(b) COMPTR (screen) écran m; (screen, display unit) afficheur m □ **display area** surface f ou zone f d'affichage; **display unit** unité f de visualisation
2 vt (a) (goods) étaler, exposer
(b) COMPTR afficher, visualiser

disposable 1 n disposables biens mpl de consommation non durables
2 adj (a) (available) disponible □ **disposable funds** disponibilités fpl, fonds mpl disponibles; **disposable income** surplus m, revenu m disponible (b) **disposable goods** biens mpl de consommation non durables

disposal n (a) (of goods) vente f; (of property) cession f (onéreuse), vente; (of securities) cession; **for disposal** à vendre, à céder (b) (availability) **to have sth at one's disposal** disposer de qch, avoir qch à sa disposition

dispute 1 n dispute f, différend m; (between management and workers) conflit m; LAW litige m; **to be in dispute with sb over sth** être en conflit avec qn sur qch; **in dispute is the right of employees to strike** l'enjeu des discussions est le droit des employés à faire grève
2 vt (debate) discuter, débattre; (call into question) contester

dissolution n (of company, partnership) dissolution f

dissolve vt (company, partnership) dissoudre

distressed area n = région frappée par la crise économique

distributable adj (profits, reserves) distribuable

distribute vt (goods, work, profits) distribuer; **Hammond Ltd is the only company allowed to distribute our products** l'entreprise Hammond Ltd est notre distributeur exclusif

distribution n distribution f; **wholesale and retail distribution** commerce m de gros et de détail □ **distribution centre** centre m de distribution; **distribution chain** chaîne f de distribution; **distribution channel** canal *m* de distribution; **distribution costs** frais *mpl* de distribution, coût *m* de la distribution; **distribution depot** dépôt *m* de distribution; **distribution network** réseau *m* de distribution; **distribution outlet** point *m* de distribution

distributor *n* distributeur(trice) *m,f* ❑ **distributor's margin** marge *f* du distributeur

district *n* région *f* ❑ *Am* **district attorney** ≃ procureur *m* de la République; **district manager** directeur(trice) *m,f* régional(e)

disturbed *adj* ST EXCH *(market)* agité(e)

div *n (abbr* **dividend**) div.

diversification *n* diversification *f*; **the company's recent diversification into cosmetics** la diversification qu'a récemment entreprise la société en pénétrant le marché des cosmétiques

diversify **1** *vt (production)* diversifier; **we must aim to diversify our product portfolio** il nous faut essayer de diversifier notre portefeuille de produits
   2 *vi (of company)* se diversifier; **to diversify into a new market** se diversifier en pénétrant un nouveau marché; **to diversify into a new product** se diversifier en fabriquant un nouveau produit

divestment *n* FIN *(of assets)* scission *f*

dividend *n* FIN dividende *m*; *(from cooperative society)* ristourne *f*; **the company has declared a dividend of 10%** la société a déclaré un dividende de 10%; **dividend on shares** dividende d'actions; **cum dividend,** *Am* **dividend on** avec le dividende attaché; **ex dividend,** *Am* **dividend off** ex-dividende ❑ **dividend cover** taux *m* de couverture du dividende; **dividend mandate** ordonnance *f* de paiement; **dividend tax** impôt *m* sur les dividendes; **dividend warrant** chèque-dividende *m*, coupon *m* d'arrérages; **dividend yield** taux de rendement (en dividendes)

dividend-price ratio *n Am* ST EXCH ratio *m* cours-bénéfice

division *n (of company)* division *f*

DNS *n* COMPTR *(abbr* **Domain Name System**) système *m* de nom de domaine, DNS *m*

dock **1** *n* dock *m* ❑ *Br* **dock worker** docker *m*
   2 *vt* **(a)** *(ship)* mettre à quai **(b)** *(wages)* faire une retenue sur; **you'll be docked £25** on retiendra 25 livres sur votre salaire
   3 *vi (of ship)* se mettre à quai

docker *n Br* docker *m*

docket *n (on package)* fiche *f*; *(on delivery)* bordereau *m*; *(at customs)* récépissé *m*

docking station *n* COMPTR *(for notebook)* station *f* d'accueil

document *n* document *m*; **documents against acceptance** documents contre acceptation ❑ COMPTR **document file** fichier *m* document; **document handling** manipulation *f* de documents; **document reader** lecteur *m* de documents

documentation *n* documentation *f*

DoE *n Br (abbr* **Department of the Environment**) ≃ ministère *m* de l'Environnement

dog *n* MKTG *(product)* poids *m* mort, gouffre *m* financier

dollar *n* dollar *m* ❑ ECON **dollar area** zone *f* dollar; **dollar crisis** crise *f* du dollar; **dollar premium** prime *f* sur le dollar; **dollar rate** cours *m* du dollar; **dollar sign** signe *m* dollar

> **"**
>
> At one level the Ministry of Defence argument about the dollar costs of overseas expenditure was not absurd. Most of the expenditure was outside the **dollar area**, and did not give rise to immediate dollar payments. But, other things being equal, such financial transfers would ultimately lead to a real transfer of resources to the recipients of expenditure.
>
> **"**

domain *n* COMPTR domaine *m* ❑ **domain name** nom *m* de domaine

domestic *adj (affairs, trade, policy)* intérieur(e); *(currency, economy)* national(e) ❑ **domestic market** marché *m* intérieur; **domestic products** denrées *fpl* du pays

donation *n* LAW donation *f*

donor *n* LAW donateur(trice) *m,f*

door-to-door *adj* **door-to-door salesman** démarcheur *m*; **door-to-door selling** porte-à-porte *m*

dormant *adj* BANKING *(account)* sans mouvement

DOS *n* COMPTR *(abbr* **disk operating system**) DOS *m* ❑ **DOS prompt** indicatif *m* (du) DOS, invite *f* du DOS

dosh *n Br Fam (money)* fric *m*

dossier *n* dossier *m*

dot-matrix printer *n* imprimante *f* matricielle

double *adj* (**a**) COMPTR *double click* double-clic *m*; *double density disk* disquette *f* (à) double densité
  (**b**) ST EXCH *double option* stellage *m*
  (**c**) FIN *double taxation* double imposition *f*; *double taxation agreement* convention *f* de double imposition
  (**d**) *double time* *(pay)* salaire *m* double; **I get double time on Sundays** je suis payé le double le dimanche
  (**e**) **to be in double figures** avoir atteint plus de dix; **inflation is now in double figures** l'inflation a passé la barre des 10%

double-click *vi* COMPTR cliquer deux fois, faire un double-clic

double-entry bookkeeping *n* ACCT comptabilité *f* en partie double

doubtful *adj* FIN *doubtful debt* créance *f* douteuse; *doubtful loan* prêt *m* douteux

Dow-Jones *n* ST EXCH *Dow Jones (Industrial) Average* or *Index* indice *m* Dow Jones

down 1 *adv* *(reduced, lower)* **the price of gold is down** le prix de l'or a baissé; **the pound is down two cents against the dollar** la livre a baissé de deux cents par rapport au dollar; **takings are several hundred pounds down on last year** les recettes ont baissé de plusieurs centaines de livres par rapport à l'année dernière; FIN **to be down 12% as against last year** être en baisse de 12% par rapport à l'année précédente
  2 *adj* (**a**) COMPTR *down arrow* flèche *f* vers le bas (**b**) *down payment* acompte *m*; **to make a down payment on sth** verser un acompte sur qch; **he made a down payment of £500** il a versé un acompte de 500 livres

downgrade *vt* *(job)* dévaloriser, déclasser; *(person)* rétrograder

download COMPTR *vt* télécharger

downloadable *adj* COMPTR téléchargeable

downside *n* *(trend)* **prices have tended to be on the downside** la tendance des prix est plutôt à la baisse ◻ ST EXCH *downside risk* risque *m* de baisse

> " Each fund aims to provide most of the upside potential of the relevant stockmarket but to reduce the **downside risk** considerably by using futures and options. "

downsize *vt* *(company)* réduire les effectifs de

downsizing *n* réduction *f* des effectifs

downstream *adj* *(company)* en aval

downtime *n* (**a**) *(of machine, factory, worker)* période *f* de non-productivité (**b**) *(time spent on task)* temps *m*; **how much downtime have you spent on this project?** combien de temps est-ce que tu as passé sur ce projet?

downturn *n* baisse *f*; **there has been a recent downturn in profits** depuis peu les bénéfices sont en baisse

downward *adj* **the economy is on a downward path** l'économie est sur une mauvaise pente ◻ FIN *downward movement* mouvement *m* de baisse; *downward trend* tendance *f* à la baisse

downward-compatible *adj* COMPTR compatible vers le bas

DP *n* COMPTR *(abbr* **data processing***)* traitement *m* des données, informatique *f*

drachma *n* drachme *f*

draft *n* (**a**) *(of letter)* brouillon *m*; *(of law, proposal)* avant-projet *m*; *(of speech)* premier jet *m* ◻ *draft agreement* projet *m* de contrat; COMPTR *draft mode* mode *m* brouillon; COMPTR *draft printout* brouillon *m*; COMPTR *draft quality* *(of printout)* qualité *f* brouillon; COMPTR *draft quality printing* impression *f* en qualité brouillon (**b**) FIN traite *f*; **to make a draft on sb** tirer sur qn
  2 *vt* rédiger; *(letter)* faire le brouillon de; *(proposal)* rédiger; *(law, bill, contract)* préparer

drag COMPTR 1 *n* *drag and drop* glisser-lâcher *m*
  2 *vt* *(icon)* faire glisser; **to drag and drop sth** faire un glisser-lâcher sur qch
  3 *vi* **to drag and drop** faire un glisser-lâcher

drain *n* *(depletion)* perte *f*, épuisement *m*; **a drain on resources** une ponction sur les ressources

DRAM *n* COMPTR *(abbr* **dynamic random access memory***)* DRAM *f*

draw *vt* (**a**) *(salary)* toucher; **to draw money from the bank** retirer de l'argent de la banque (**b**) FIN *(cheque, bill)* tirer; **to draw a cheque on one's account** tirer un chèque sur son compte (**c**) *(interest)* produire
  2 *vi* FIN **to draw at sight** tirer à vue

▸ **draw out** *vt sep* *(money)* retirer

▸ **draw up** *vt sep* *(document, bill)* dresser,

rédiger; *(account, budget, itinerary)* établir; *(programme, procedure)* dresser, établir; *(plan)* élaborer; *(bill of exchange)* créer

drawback *n* CUSTOMS remboursm

drawdown *n* FIN tiragem

drawee *n* FIN *(of bill)* tiré m, payeurm

drawer *n* FIN tireur m; *(of bill)* souscripteur m; **to refer a cheque to drawer** refuser d'honorer un chèque

drawing *n* (**a**) *(of sum)* prélèvement m, retrait m (**b**) FIN *(of cheque, bill)* traite f ▫ *drawing account* compte m courant, compte de dépôt à vue; *drawing rights* droits mpl de tirage

drift *n (of prices, salaries)* tendance f à la hausse

drip advertising *n* MKTG publicité f continue, publicité goutte à goutte

drip-feed *vt (company)* perfuser

drive *n* (**a**) *(campaign)* campagne f; **the company is having a sales drive** la société fait une campagne de vente (**b**) COMPTR *(for disk)* lecteur m, unité f; **drive a:/b:** unité de disque a:/b:

▸**drive down** *vt sep* ECON *(prices, inflation)* faire baisser

▸**drive up** *vt sep* ECON *(prices, inflation)* faire monter

driver *n* COMPTR programme m de gestion, pilote m

drop **1** *n* (**a**) *(in prices, inflation)* chute f, baisse f (**in** de); **sales show a drop of 10%** les ventes accusent une baisse de 10% (**b**) *(delivery)* livraisonf; **I have four drops to make** j'ai quatre livraisons à faire
  2 *vt* COMPTR *(icon)* lâcher
  3 *vi (of prices, inflation)* baisser; **sales have dropped by 10%** les ventes ont baissé de 10%; ST EXCH **shares dropped a point** les actions ont reculé d'un point; **the pound dropped three points against the dollar** la livre a reculé de *ou* a perdu trois points par rapport au dollar

drop-dead fee *n* commission f de désintéressement

drop-down menu *n* COMPTR menu m déroulant

dry *adj* *dry cargo* cargaison f sèche; *dry goods* marchandises *fpl* sèches

DSS *n* *Br* ADMIN *(abbr* **Department of Social Security**) ≃ Sécurité f sociale

DTI *n* *Br* *(abbr* **Department of Trade and Industry**) ≃ ministère m du Commerce et de l'Industrie

DTP *n* COMPTR *(abbr* **desktop publishing**) PAO *f* ▫ *DTP operator* opérateur(trice) *m,f* de PAO

dual pricing *n* fixation f des prix

due **1** *n* **dues** *(membership fees)* cotisationf
  2 *adj (owed)* dû (due); *(debt)* exigible; *(bill)* payable; **I'm due three days' holiday** j'ai trois jours de congé à prendre; **I'm due a rise** j'attends une augmentation de salaire ▫ *due date* date f d'échéance, date d'exigibilité

due-date *vt* coter

dull *adj* FIN *(market)* calme, inactif(ive); **business is dull** les affaires ne marchent pas fort ▫ *dull season* morte-saisonf

duly *adv (properly)* dûment; *(as expected)* comme prévu; **a duly authorized representative** un(e) représentant(e) dûment accrédité(e); **I duly received your letter of 8 March** j'ai bien reçu votre lettre du 8 mars

dummy **1** *n (product)* objetm factice; *(book)* maquettef
  2 *adj* factice ▫ *dummy pack* emballage m factice

dump **1** *n* *dump bin* panier m de présentation en vrac, panier présentoir
  2 *vt* **to dump goods** faire du dumping
  3 *vi* faire du dumping

dumping *n (of goods)* dumpingm

duopoly *n* duopolem

duplicate **1** *n (of document, receipt)* duplicata m, double m; **in duplicate** en double, en deux exemplaires
  2 *adj* double, en double; **a duplicate receipt** un duplicata du reçu ▫ *duplicate copy* duplicatam
  3 *vt (document, receipt)* faire un duplicata *ou* un double de; *(on photocopier)* faire une photocopie de

durable **1** *n* **durables** biens *mpl* (de consommation) durables
  2 *adj* durable ▫ *durable goods* biens *mpl* (de consommation) durables

duration *n (of lease)* duréef

dutiable *adj* taxable; CUSTOMS soumis(e) aux droits de douane

duty *n* droitm; **to pay duty on sth** payer une taxe sur qch; **liable to duty** passible de droits, soumis(e) aux droits; **duty paid** franc de douane, droits acquittés

duty-free *adj (goods)* hors taxe, en franchise ❏ *duty-free allowance* = quantité de produits hors taxe autorisée; *duty-free shop* magasin *m* hors taxe

duty-paid *adj (goods)* acquitté(e), dédouané(e)

DVD *n* COMPTR (*abbr* **Digital Versatile Disk**, **Digital Video Disk**) DVD *m*, disque *m* vidéo numérique

dynamic *adj (company, economy)* dynamique ❏ COMPTR *dynamic RAM* mémoire *f* RAM dynamique

E & OE *Br* ACCT (*abbr* **errors and omissions excepted**) SE & O

early *adj* (**a**) **at your earliest convenience** (*in correspondence*) dans les meilleurs délais; **what is your earliest possible delivery date?** quelle est votre première possibilité de livraison? (**b**) MKTG *early adopter* réceptif *m* précoce; *early majority* majorité *f* innovatrice

earmark *vt* (*funds*) assigner, affecter (**for** à); **this money has been earmarked for research** cet argent a été affecté à la recherche

earn *vt* (*money*) gagner; (*interest*) rapporter; **how much do you earn?** combien gagnez-vous?; **to earn a** *or* **one's living** gagner sa vie; **their money is earning a high rate of interest** leur argent est rémunéré à un taux élevé

earned *adj* FIN *earned income* revenus *mpl* salariaux; *earned income allowance* = déduction au titre de revenus salariaux ou professionnels

> **"**
> A dependent wife's pension is included in her husband's income and is offset against the married man's tax allowance. A pension in your own right is automatically offset against the wife's **earned income allowance**.
> **"**

earner *n* (*person*) salarié(e) *m,f*; **one of the biggest earners in the company** un des plus gros salaires de l'entreprise; **this product is the biggest profit earner in our range** de toute notre gamme, ceci est le produit qui rapporte le plus

earning *adj* *earning capacity*, *earning potential* (*of person*) potentiel *m* de revenu; (*of company*) rentabilité *f*, capacité *f* bénéficiaire

earnings *npl* (*of person*) salaire *m*, revenus *mpl*; (*of company*) revenus; **earnings per share** bénéfice *m* par action ▫ *earnings forecast* résultats *mpl* prévisionnels; *earnings growth* accroissement *m* ou augmentation *f* des bénéfices; *earnings retained* bénéfices *mpl* non distribués

earnings-related *adj* proportionnel(elle) au revenu

EAS *n Br* (*abbr* **Enterprise Allowance Scheme**) fonds *m* d'aide à la création d'entreprise

easy *adj* (**a**) **by easy payments, on easy terms** avec facilités de paiement (**b**) ST EXCH (*market*) tranquille (**c**) *Fam* *easy money* argent *m* facile

EBIT *npl* (*abbr* **earnings before interest and tax**) bénéfices *mpl* avant impôts et charges

EBRD *n* (*abbr* **European Bank of Reconstruction and Development**) BERD *f*

> **"**
> Representatives of 40 countries … met at the Elysée Palace in Paris on May 29 to sign the founding charter of the European Bank for Reconstruction and Development (**EBRD** or, by its French acronym, BERD), a new international organization intended to finance industrial and economic development in the countries of Eastern Europe, using loans, guarantees, equity investment and underwriting to promote the transition to free-market economic systems in those countries.
> **"**

EC *n* (*abbr* **European Community**) CE *f*

e-cash *n* COMPTR argent *m* électronique, argent virtuel, e-cash *m*

ECB *n* (*abbr* **European Central Bank**) BCE *f*

ECGD *n Br* (*abbr* **Export Credit Guarantee Department**) ≃ COFACE *f*

echelon *n* échelon *m*; **the higher echelons of industry** les échelons supérieurs de l'industrie

e-commerce *n* COMPTR commerce *m* électronique

econometrics *n* économétrie *f*

economic *adj* (**a**) (*relating to the economy*) économique ▫ *economic adviser* conseiller(ère) *m,f* économique; *economic aid* aide *f* économique; *economic analysis* analyse *f* économique; *economic appraisal* évaluation *f* économique; *economic climate* climat *m* économique; *economic cost* coût *m* économique; *economic crisis* crise *f* économique; *economic development*

croissance *f* par habitant *ou* per capita; **economic forecast** prévisions *fpl* économiques; **economic growth** croissance *f* économique; **economic indicators** indicateurs *mpl* économiques; **economic measure** mesure *f* économique; EU **Economic and Monetary Union** union *f* économique et monétaire; **economic policy** politique *f* économique; **economic prospects** prévisions *fpl* conjoncturelles *ou* économiques; **economic recovery** reprise *f ou* redressement *m* économique; **economic sanctions** sanctions *fpl* économiques; **economic situation** conjoncture *f* économique; **economic strategy** stratégie *f* conjoncturelle; **economic trend** tendance *f ou* conjoncture *f* économique

(b) *Br (profitable)* rentable; **to make sth economic** rentabiliser qch

economical *adj (person)* économe; *(machine, method, approach)* économique

economics 1 *n (science)* économie *f*
2 *npl (profitability)* rentabilité *f; (financial aspects)* aspects *mpl* financiers; **we must consider the economics of the project before making any decisions** nous devons considérer l'aspect financier du projet avant de prendre une décision

economist *n* économiste *mf*

economize *vi* économiser, faire des économies (**on** sur); **the recession has led to a need to economize throughout the company** la récession a conduit au besoin d'économiser dans toute l'entreprise

economy *n* économie *f*; **economies of scale** économies d'échelle ❑ *economy class (in air travel)* classe *f* touriste

ECSC *n (abbr* **European Coal and Steel Community***)* CECA *f*

ECU, ecu *n* EU *(abbr* **European Currency Unit***)* ÉCU *m*, écu *m*

edit *vt* COMPTR *(text)* éditer

editing *n* COMPTR édition *f*

editor *n* COMPTR *(software)* éditeur *m*

EEA *n* EU *(abbr* **European Economic Area***)* EEE *m*

EEC *n* Formerly *(abbr* **European Economic Community***)* CEE *f*

EEOC *n* Am *(abbr* **Equal Employment Opportunity Commission***)* = commission pour l'égalité des chances d'emploi aux États-Unis

effect 1 *n* (a) **to put sth into effect** *(regulation, law)* mettre qch en pratique *ou* en application; **to come into** *or* **take effect** entrer en vigueur; **to remain in effect** demeurer en vigueur; *Br* **with effect from 1 January** applicable à compter du 1 janvier
(b) *(meaning)* sens *m*, teneur *f*; **we have made provisions to this effect** nous avons pris des dispositions dans ce sens
2 *vt (payment)* effectuer; *(sale, purchase)* réaliser, effectuer

effective *adj* (a) ECON *(yield, return, production)* effectif(ive); *(value)* réel(elle) ❑ *effective annual rate* taux *m* annuel effectif; *effective capacity* capacité *f* effective; *effective management* direction *f ou* gestion *f* efficace; *effective tax rate* taux *m* d'imposition effectif
(b) *(regulation, law)* **to become effective** entrer en vigueur; **effective as from 10 October** applicable à compter du 10 octobre ❑ *effective date* date *f* d'entrée en vigueur

efficiency *n (of person, company, method)* efficacité *f; (of machine)* rendement *m*

efficient *adj (person, company, method)* efficace; *(machine)* à haut rendement; **we must make more efficient use of the marketing team** nous devons utiliser notre équipe de marketing de manière plus efficace

EFT *n* COMPTR *(abbr* **electronic funds transfer***)* transfert *m* de fonds électronique

EFTA *n (abbr* **European Free Trade Association***)* AELE *f*

EFTPOS *n* COMPTR *(abbr* **electronic funds transfer at point of sale***)* transfert *m* de fonds électronique sur point de vente

EGM *n (abbr* **extraordinary general meeting***)* AGE *f*

elastic *adj* ECON *(market, supply, demand)* élastique

elasticity *n* ECON *(of market, supply, demand)* élasticité *f*

electronic *adj* électronique ❑ *electronic banking* bancatique *f*; COMPTR *electronic catalogue* catalogue *m* en ligne; *electronic computer* calculateur *m* électronique; *electronic data interchange* échange *m* de données informatisé; *electronic data processing* traitement *m* électronique de l'information; *electronic directory* annuaire *m* électronique; *electronic funds transfer* transfert *m* de fonds électronique;

electronic funds transfer at point of sale transfert *m* de fonds électronique au point de vente; COMPTR **electronic mail** courrier *m* électronique; COMPTR **electronic mailbox** boîte *f* à *ou* aux lettres électronique; **electronic money** argent *m* électronique, argent virtuel; COMPTR **electronic office** bureau *m* informatisé; **electronic point of sale** point *m* de vente électronique; COMPTR **electronic shopping** achats *mpl* par Internet

❝
When we speak of the **electronic office** we are now referring to an administrative system based largely on computers, word processors and associated communication devices.
❞

eligibility *n (for job)* admissibilité *f* (**for** à); *(for grant, benefit)* droit *m* (**for** à)

eligible *adj* (**a**) *(for job)* admissible (**for** à); **to be eligible for a pension/a tax rebate** avoir droit à une retraite/un dégrèvement fiscal (**b**) FIN **eligible list** effet *m* bancable; **eligible paper** effet escomptable

e-mail COMPTR **1** *n* courrier *m* électronique □ **e-mail account** compte *m* de courrier électronique
2 *vt (person)* envoyer un courrier électronique à; *(document)* envoyer par courrier électronique

embargo 1 *n* embargo *m*; **to lay** *or* **put an embargo on sth** mettre l'embargo sur qch; **to be under an embargo** *(of ship, goods)* être séquestré(e); **to lift an embargo** lever un embargo
2 *vt* mettre l'embargo sur

embark *vt* prendre à bord, embarquer

embarkation *n* embarquement *m*

embezzle 1 *vt (money, funds)* détourner
2 *vi* commettre des détournements de fonds; **to embezzle from a company** détourner les fonds d'une société

embezzlement *n* **embezzlement (of funds)** détournement *m* de fonds

embezzler *n* auteur *m* d'un détournement de fonds

emerging *adj (market)* émergent(e)

EMI *n (abbr* **European Monetary Institute)** IME *m*

e-money *n* COMPTR argent *m* électronique, argent virtuel

employ 1 *n* **to be in sb's employ** travailler pour qn, être au service de qn
2 *vt* (**a**) *(give work to)* employer; *(new staff)* embaucher; **they employ twenty staff** ils

ont vingt employés; **to employ sb as a receptionist** employer qn comme réceptionniste; **he has been employed with the firm for fifteen years** il travaille pour cette entreprise depuis quinze ans
(**b**) *(make use of)* utiliser; **we must employ all our resources to tackle this problem** nous devons utiliser toutes nos ressources pour aborder ce problème

employed 1 *npl* personnes *fpl* qui ont un emploi; **the employers and the employed** le patronat et le salariat
2 *adj* employé(e)

employee *n* employé(e) *m,f*; **management and employees** la direction et le personnel □ **employee buy-out** rachat *m* par les employés; **employee's contribution** *(to benefits)* cotisation *f* des salariés; *Br* **employee share ownership plan,** *Am* **employee stock ownership plan** plan *m* d'actionnariat des salariés

employer *n* employeur(euse) *m,f* □ **employers' association** organisation *f* patronale; **employer's contribution** cotisation *f* patronale; **employer's liability** *(for accidents at work)* responsabilité *f* patronale; **employers' liability insurance** assurance *f* des patrons contre les accidents du travail

employment *n (occupation)* emploi *m*; **to be without employment** être sans emploi; **to give sb employment** donner un emploi à qn; **to seek employment** chercher un emploi □ **employment agency, employment bureau** agence *f ou* bureau *m* de placement; **employment costs** coûts *mpl* salariaux; **employment protection** protection *f* de l'emploi

❝
A majority of overseas workers are disqualified from the **employment protection** rights laid down in UK legislation. The precise formula for working out who is eligible depends upon the legal entitlement in question. The most important is the right not to be unfairly dismissed, from which employees who ordinarily work outside Great Britain are excluded.
❞

EMS *n (abbr* **European Monetary System)** SME *m*

EMU *n (abbr* **Economic and Monetary Union)** UME *f*

emulation *n* COMPTR émulation *f*

enc (**a**) *(abbr* **enclosure)** P.J. (**b**) *(abbr* **enclosed)** ci-joint

encash *vt Br (cheque)* encaisser

encashment *n Br (of cheque)* encaissement *m*

enclose *vt (in letter)* joindre; **to enclose sth in a letter** joindre qch à une lettre; **please find enclosed my CV, enclosed please find my CV** veuillez trouver ci-joint *ou* ci-inclus mon CV; **I enclose a cheque for £20** je joins un chèque de 20 livres; **the enclosed cheque** le chèque ci-joint *ou* ci-inclus

enclosure *n (in letter)* pièce *f* jointe

encode *vt* COMPTR encoder

encoder *n* COMPTR encodeur *m*

encoding *n* COMPTR codage *m*, encodage *m*

encrypt *n* COMPTR crypter, chiffrer

encryption *n* COMPTR chiffrement *m*

end **1** *n (of month, year, meeting)* fin *f*; **to bring sth to an end** *(speech)* conclure qch; *(meeting)* clore qch; **at the end of the month/of the year** à la fin du mois/de l'année □ COMPTR **end key** touche *f* fin; *Am* **end price** prix *m* de détail; **end product** produit *m* fini
2 *vt (speech)* conclure; *(meeting)* clore
3 *vi* finir, se terminer; *(of subscription)* expirer

end-consumer *n* utilisateur(trice) *m,f* final(e)

endgame *n* MKTG objectif *m*

endnote *n* COMPTR note *f* de fin de document, NfD *f*

endorse *vt* (**a**) FIN *(document, cheque)* endosser; *(bill of exchange)* avaliser, endosser, donner son aval à (**b**) *(approve) (action)* approuver; *(candidature)* appuyer

endorsee *n* FIN endossataire *mf*

endorsement *n* (**a**) FIN *(of document, cheque)* endossement *m*, endos *m*; *(of bill of exchange)* aval *m*; *(in insurance policy)* avenant *m* □ FIN **endorsement fee** commission *f* d'endos (**b**) *(approval) (of action)* approbation *f*; *(of candidature)* appui *m*

endorser *n* FIN *(of document, cheque)* endosseur *m*, cessionnaire *mf*; *(of bill of exchange)* avaliste *mf*, avaliseur *m*

endow *vt* FIN *(person, company)* doter (**with** de)

endowment *n* FIN *(action, fund)* dotation *f* □ **endowment assurance** assurance *f* en cas de vie *ou* à dotation; **endowment mortgage** prêt-logement *m* lié à une assurance-vie

> **"**
> The **endowment mortgage** has become the most common form of loan, where life assurance protection and saving for repayment of the mortgage are conveniently combined. In making a payment of interest to the lender and a contribution to a life assurance company, the debt remains constant and the borrower is offered the prospect of a maturing policy that will not only repay the mortgage but also provide a lump sum.
> **"**

end-user *n* utilisateur(trice) *m,f* final(e)

energy énergie *f* □ **energy consumption** consommation *f* d'énergie; **energy consumption bill** facture *f* énergétique

engage *vt (staff)* engager; **to engage the services of sb** employer les services de qn

engaged *adj* (**a**) *(busy)* occupé(e); **I'm otherwise engaged** je suis déjà pris; **to be engaged in discussions** être engagé(e) dans des discussions (**b**) *Br (telephone)* occupé(e); **the line** *or* **number is engaged** la ligne est occupée; **I got the engaged tone** *or* **signal** ça sonnait occupé

engagement *n* (**a**) *(meeting, appointment)* rendez-vous *m*; **to have a previous** *or* **prior engagement** être déjà pris(e) (**b**) *(promise, obligation)* engagement *m*; **to carry out** *or* **meet one's engagements** faire face à ses engagements, remplir ses engagements

engineer *n* ingénieur *m*

engineering *n* ingénierie *f* □ **engineering company** compagnie *f* d'ingénieurs-conseils; **engineering department** service *m* technique

enhance *vt* (**a**) FIN *(pension, value)* augmenter (**b**) COMPTR améliorer

enhanced *adj* (**a**) FIN *(pension, value)* augmenté(e) (**b**) COMPTR amélioré(e) □ **enhanced keyboard** clavier *m* étendu

enhancement *n* (**a**) FIN *(of pension, value)* augmentation *f* (**b**) COMPTR amélioration *f*

enquire, enquiry = **inquire, inquiry**

enter **1** *n* COMPTR touche *f* (d')entrée □ **enter key** touche (d')entrée
2 *vt* (**a**) ACCT *(item)* comptabiliser; **to enter an item/figures in the ledger** porter un article/des chiffres sur le livre de comptes (**b**) COMPTR *(data)* entrer, introduire

► **enter into** *vt insep (business, dispute)* entrer dans; *(negotiations)* engager; *(contract)* passer; **to enter into partnership** with sb s'associer avec qn; **to enter into an agreement with sb** conclure un accord avec qn

▶ **enter up** *vt sep* ACCT **to enter up an item/ figures in the ledger** porter un article/des chiffres sur le livre des comptes

enterprise *n (business)* entreprise *f* ❑ *Br Enterprise Allowance Scheme* fonds *m* d'aide à la création d'entreprise; *enterprise culture* culture *f* d'entreprise; *Br enterprise zone* = zone d'encouragement à l'implantation d'entreprises dans les régions économiquement défavorisées

> ❝
> The "**enterprise culture**", the opening up of markets and the need to survive competition all place businesses under great pressure. The scale and pace of technological change mean that the public as well as employees are crucially at risk.
> ❞

enterprising *adj (person)* entreprenant(e); *(idea, project)* audacieux(euse)

entertainment *n entertainment allowance* indemnité *f* de fonction; *entertainment expenses* frais *mpl* de représentation

entitle *vt* **to be entitled to sth** *(allowance, benefit)* avoir droit à qch; **his disability entitles him to a pension** son infirmité lui donne droit à une pension

entitlement *n* droit *m*

entrant *n (on market)* acteur *m*; **stocks in two new entrants to the market performed well** les actions de deux sociétés nouvellement introduites en Bourse se sont bien comportées

entrepôt *n* entrepôt *m* ❑ *entrepôt port* port *m* franc

entrepreneur *n* entrepreneur(euse) *m,f*

entrepreneurial *adj (activities, decision)* d'entrepreneur; *(person, society)* qui a l'esprit d'entreprise

entrepreneurship *n* entreprenariat *m*

entry *n* **(a)** ACCT *(action)* passation *f* d'écriture, inscription *f*; *(item)* article *m*, écriture *f*; **to make an entry** passer une écriture, porter un article à compte **(b)** COMPTR *(of data)* entrée *f* **(c)** *(of company on market)* entrée *f*, pénétration *f*

envelope *n* enveloppe *f*; **in a sealed envelope** sous pli cacheté ❑ *envelope file* chemise *f* (de carton)

environment *n* COMPTR, ECON environnement *m*; **a pleasant working environment** des conditions de travail agréables

environmental *adj environmental audit* = rapport sur l'impact des activités d'une entreprise sur l'environnement; *environmental damage* dégâts *mpl* causés à l'environnement; *environmental economics* économie *f* de l'environnement; *environmental policy* politique *f* de l'environnement

environmentally-friendly *adj* qui ne nuit pas à l'environnement

EOC *n* ADMIN *(abbr* **Equal Opportunities Commission***)* = organisme britannique gouvernemental qui veille à l'égalité des chances sur le lieu de travail

EPOS *n (abbr* **electronic point of sale***)* point *m* de vente électronique

EPS *n (abbr* **earnings per share***)* BPA *m*

equal *adj* égal(e) ❑ *equal opportunities* égalité *f* des chances; ADMIN *Equal Opportunities Commission* = organisme britannique qui veille à l'égalité des chances sur le lieu de travail; *equal opportunity employer* = entreprise s'engageant à respecter la législation sur la non-discrimination dans l'emploi; *equal pay* égalité *f* des salaires; *equal rights* égalité *f* des chances

equality *n* égalité *f* ❑ *equality of opportunity* égalité des chances

equalization *n* FIN *(of dividends)* régularisation *f*

equalize *vt* FIN *(dividends)* régulariser

equip *vt (factory)* outiller, équiper **(with** de); *(person)* équiper, pourvoir **(with** de); **we must equip our staff with the tools to tackle new technology** nous devons équiper notre personnel des outils nécessaires pour aborder les nouvelles technologies

equipment *n* équipement *m*; *(in factory)* installations *fpl*, matériel *m* ❑ *equipment leasing* crédit-bail *m* mobilier

equity *n* FIN, ST EXCH *(of shareholders)* capitaux *mpl* ou fonds *mpl* propres; *(of company)* capital *m* actions; **equities** actions *fpl* ordinaires ❑ *equity capital* capital actions; *equity dilution* dilution *f* du capital; *equity investment* placement *m* en actions; *equity issue* augmentation *f* du capital par émission d'actions; *equity leader* valeur *f* vedette; *equity or equities market* marché *m* des actions (ordinaires); *equity share capital* capital *m* en actions ordinaires; *equities trader* courtier(ère) *m,f* sur actions; *equity trading* courtage *m* sur actions

equity-linked *adj* FIN, ST EXCH *(policy)* libellé(e), investi(e) en actions

equivalences of exchange *npl* FIN parités *fpl* de change

equivalent *adj* équivalent(e); **to be equivalent to sth** être équivalent à qch, équivaloir à qch

erase *vt* COMPTR, FIN effacer

ERDF *n* FIN *(abbr* **European Regional Development Fund)** FEDER *m*

"

The European Regional Development Fund (**ERDF**) was finally established in 1975, together with general agreement on the definition of a region, on the criteria for determining eligibility for assistance and upon the general characteristics that policies should possess.

"

ergonomic *adj* ergonomique

ergonomics *n* ergonomie *f*

ERM *n* FIN *(abbr* **Exchange Rate Mechanism)** mécanisme *m* de change

error *n* erreur *f*; ACCT **errors and omissions excepted** sauf erreur ou omission □ COMPTR *error message* message *m* d'erreur

escalate *vi (of prices)* monter en flèche

escalation clause, escalator clause *n (in contract)* clause *f* d'indexation

escape *n* (**a**) COMPTR échappement *m* □ *escape key* touche *f* d'échappement (**b**) *escape clause (in contract)* clause *f* échappatoire

escrow *n* LAW dépôt *m* fiduciaire *ou* conditionnel; **to be held in escrow** être placé(e) en dépôt fiduciaire *ou* en main tierce; **to put sth in escrow** placer qch en dépôt fiduciaire *ou* en main tierce □ *Am escrow account* compte *m* bloqué; *escrow agent* dépositaire *mf* légal(e)

escudo *n* escudo *m*

ESOP *n (abbr* **employee** *Br* **share** or *Am* **stock ownership plan)** plan *m* d'actionnariat des salariés

est *adj (abbr* **established)** établi(e), fondé(e); **A. Jones, est 1885** A. Jones, établi en 1885

establish *vt (system)* établir, édifier; *(business)* fonder; *(agency)* créer; **to establish oneself in business** s'établir dans les affaires

establishment *n* (**a**) *(company)* établissement *m* (**b**) *(creation) (of system)* établissement *m*; *(of business)* fondation *f*; *(of agency)* création *f* (**c**) **the Establishment** *(dominant group)* l'establishment *m*; **the**

financial establishment ceux qui comptent dans le monde financier

estate *n* (**a**) LAW *(possessions)* biens *mpl* (**b**) *(land)* terre *f*, propriété *f* □ *Br estate agency* agence *f* immobilière; *Br estate agent* agent *m* immobilier (**c**) *(inheritance)* succession *f* □ *Br estate duty, Am estate tax* droits *mpl* de succession (**d**) *(of bankrupt)* actif *m*

estimate **1** *n* (**a**) *(calculation)* évaluation *f*, calcul *m*; **these figures are only a rough estimate** ces chiffres sont très approximatifs; **give me an estimate of how much you think it will cost** donnez-moi une idée de ce que ça coûtera; **at the lowest estimate it will take three months to complete** au bas mot, cela prendra trois mois pour terminer (**b**) *(of cost)* devis *m*; **to put in an estimate (for sth/for doing sth)** établir un devis (pour qch/pour faire qch); **to ask for an estimate (for sth/doing sth)** demander un devis (pour qch/pour faire qch); **get several estimates before deciding which company to use** faites faire plusieurs devis avant de décider quelle entreprise choisir **2** *vt* estimer, évaluer; **the cost of the project was estimated at £2,000** le coût du projet était évalué à 2 000 livres

estimation *n* estimation *f*, évaluation *f*

estimator *n* expert *m*

Ethernet® *n* COMPTR Ethernet *m*

EU *n (abbr* **European Union)** UE *f*

euro *n* EU euro *m*

Eurobank *n* EU eurobanque *f*

eurobond *n* euro-obligation *f*

eurocard *n* eurocarte *f*

eurocheque *n* eurochèque *m*

euro-commercial paper *n* EU billet *m* de trésorerie *(émis sur le marché des eurodevises)*

eurocrat *n* eurocrate *mf*

eurocredit *n* eurocrédit *m*

euro-currency *n* eurodevise *f*, euromonnaie *f* □ *euro-currency market* marché *m* des eurodevises

"

The **euro-currency markets** have altered the structure and operations of most major banks by encouraging overseas representation and making them innovative and adaptable to changing economic circumstances and customer needs.

"

eurodollar n eurodollar m

euromarket n euromarché m

European adj européen(enne) ❏ *European Bank of Reconstruction and Development* Banque f européenne de reconstruction et de développement; *European Central Bank* banque f centrale européenne; ADMIN *European Coal and Steel Community* Communauté f européenne de charbon et de l'acier; *European Commission* Commission f européenne; *European Community* Communauté f européenne; *European Court of Human Rights* Cour f européenne des droits de l'homme; *European Court of Justice* Cour f européenne de justice; *European Currency Unit* unité f monétaire européenne; *European Economic Area* espace m économique européen; *Formerly European Economic Community* Communauté f économique européenne; *European Free Trade Association* Association f européenne de libre-échange; *European Investment Bank* Banque f européenne d'investissement; *European Monetary Cooperation Fund* fonds m européen de coopération monétaire; *European Monetary Institute* Institut m monétaire européen; *European Monetary System* système m monétaire européen; *European Parliament* Parlement m européen; *European Regional Development Fund* fonds m européen de développement régional; *European Union* Union f européenne

European-style option n ST EXCH option f européenne

euroyen n euroyen m

evaluate vt (damages, value, cost) évaluer

evaluation n (of damages, value, cost) évaluation f

evergreen adj FIN *evergreen facility* possibilité f de crédit permanent; *evergreen fund* fonds m de crédit permanent non confirmé

ex prep (a) (out of) **ex quay** à quai; **ex ship** à bord; **ex warehouse** à (prendre à) l'entrepôt, en entrepôt; **ex wharf** à quai; **ex works** départ usine, sortie d'usine

(b) FIN, ST EXCH (without) **ex all, ex allotment** ex-répartition f; **ex bonus** ex-capitalisation f; **ex cap, ex capitalisation** ex-capitalisation; **ex coupon** ex-coupon m, coupon m détaché; **this stock goes ex coupon on 1 August** le coupon de cette action se détache le 1 août; **ex dividend** ex-dividende m, dividende m détaché; **ex new, ex rights** ex-droit m; **ex scrip** ex-répartition f

exceed vt excéder, dépasser; **demand exceeds supply** la demande excède ou dépasse l'offre; **her salary exceeds mine by £4,000 a year** son salaire annuel dépasse le mien de 4 000 livres

exceptional item n ACCT poste m extraordinaire

excess n (in weight, expenditure) excédent m; **there has been an excess of expenditure over revenue** les dépenses ont excédé les recettes ❏ *excess capacity* surcapacité f, capacité f excédentaire; *excess charges* supplément m; Br INS *excess (clause)* franchise f; *excess demand* demande f excédentaire; Br INS *excess policy* police f complémentaire; *excess profits* surplus m des bénéfices; (unexpected) bénéfices mpl exceptionnels ou extraordinaires; BANKING *excess reserves* réserves fpl excédentaires; ST EXCH *excess shares* actions fpl détenues en surnombre; *excess supply* surproduction f; *excess weight* poids m excédentaire

exchange 1 n (a) FIN (of currency) change m; Am **exchanges** (bills) lettres fpl de change, traites fpl ❏ *exchange broker* agent m de change, cambiste mf; *exchange control* contrôle m des changes; *exchange cross rate* taux m de change entre devises tierces; *exchange dealer* agent m de change, cambiste mf; *exchange equalization account* fonds m de stabilisation des changes; *exchange index* indice m boursier; *exchange market* marché m des changes; *exchange premium* prime f de change; *exchange rate* cours m ou taux m de change; **at the current exchange rate** au cours du jour; EU *Exchange Rate Mechanism* mécanisme m de change; *exchange reserves* réserves fpl en devises (étrangères); *exchange restrictions* contrôle m des changes

(b) (of goods, shares, commodities) échange m

2 vt (a) (goods, shares, commodities) échanger

(b) **to exchange contracts** (when buying property) signer les contrats de vente et d'achat d'une propriété

exchequer n Br ADMIN **the Exchequer** (money) le Trésor public; (government department) ≃ le Ministère des Finances ❏ *exchequer bill* bon m du Trésor

excise n ADMIN (tax) contribution f indirecte, taxe f, Belg accise f; Br (department) service m des contributions indirectes, régie f ❏ *excise bond* acquit-à-caution m; *excise documents* documents mpl administratifs de régie; **excise duty** contribution *f* indirecte

exclusive 1 *adj* exclusif(ive) ❑ **exclusive distribution** distribution *f* exclusive; **exclusive rights** droits *mpl* exclusifs (de vendre), exclusivité *f*; **exclusive territory** territoire *m* exclusif

2 *adv* **exclusive of tax** hors taxe; **exclusive of delivery** frais de livraison non compris

exclusivity *n* exclusivité *f* ❑ **exclusivity clause** clause *f* d'exclusivité

> ❝
>
> An example of an **exclusivity clause** is given below: For the period of [3] months from the date hereof neither you [the vendor] nor the subsidiaries (and their management) will approach or enter into discussions with any other prospective purchasers for the sale of your shareholding in the [Company] or a disposal of any of the business and/or assets of any part of the [Group].
>
> ❞

ex-directory *adj* Br *(telephone number)* sur la liste rouge

executable file *n* COMPTR fichier *m* exécutable

execute *vt* (**a**) FIN *(transfer)* effectuer (**b**) COMPTR exécuter

executive 1 *n (person)* directeur(trice) *m,f*, cadre *m*; *(board, committee)* bureau *m*, comité *m* central

2 *adj (power)* exécutif(ive); *(ability)* d'exécution; *(job)* de cadre; *(car, plane)* de direction ❑ **executive board** conseil *m* d'administration; **executive director** cadre *m* supérieur *ou* dirigeant; **executive member** membre *m* du comité de direction; **executive officer** cadre *m* supérieur; **executive pension plan** caisse *f* de retraite des cadres; **executive share option scheme** plan *m* d'investissement en actions pour cadres

executor *n* LAW *(of will)* exécuteur(trice) *m,f* testamentaire

exempt 1 *adj* exempté(e), dispensé(e) (**from** de); **exempt from taxes** exonéré(e) *ou* exempt(e) d'impôt

2 *vt* exempter, dispenser (**from** de); *(from taxes)* exonérer, exempter (**from** de)

exemption *n* exemption *f*, dispense *f*; *(from tax)* exonération *f*, exemption

exercise 1 *n* (**a**) *(of one's duties)* exercice *m* (**b**) ST EXCH *(of option)* levée *f* ❑ **exercise date** date *f* d'échéance; **exercise notion** assignation *f*; **exercise price** cours *m* de

base, prix *m* d'exercice

2 *vt* (**a**) *(duties)* exercer (**b**) ST EXCH **to exercise an option** lever une prime

ex gratia *adj (payment)* à titre de faveur

ex-growth *n (decline)* baisse *f*; **to go ex-growth** être en déclin

> ❝
>
> Siemens Nixdorf's biggest problem is that it is a combination of a company that was just about to go **ex-growth** with one that was already failing, so it very much needs any partner to be a firm seen to be strong and a winner: Hewlett-Packard and ICL presently best fit that profile.
>
> ❞

exhibit 1 *n* objet *m* exposé

2 *vt (object, goods)* exhiber, montrer

exhibition *n* (**a**) *(of goods)* étalage *m* (**b**) *(show)* exposition *f* ❑ **exhibition hall** salon *m* d'exposition; **exhibition stand** stand *m* (d'exposition)

exhibitor *n (at exhibition)* exposant(e) *m,f*

existing *adj* MKTG **existing customer** client(e) *m,f* actuel(elle); **existing market** marché *m* existant *ou* actuel

exit 1 *n* (**a**) **exit interview** entrevue *f* de départ (**b**) COMPTR sortie *f*

2 *vt* COMPTR *(program, session)* sortir de

3 *vi* COMPTR sortir

ex officio ADMIN 1 *adj (member)* de droit

2 *adv (act)* d'office

expand 1 *vt (company, business, staff)* agrandir, développer; COMPTR *(memory)* étendre; **to expand a company into a multinational** agrandir une société pour en faire une multinationale

2 *vi (of company, business, staff)* s'agrandir, se développer; **we are looking to expand into the cosmetics industry** nous envisageons de nous diversifier en nous lançant dans l'industrie des cosmétiques

expandable *adj* COMPTR *(memory)* extensible; **4MB expandable to 64MB** 4 Mo extensible à 64 Mo

expanding *adj (company, market)* en expansion

> ❝
>
> Given this favourable outlook and the marketing efforts of the British Gas Corporation, an **expanding** market must be supplied. How it is to be supplied is however a matter of controversy.
>
> ❞

expansion n (**a**) *(of company, business, market)* expansion f; *(of economy)* relance f (**b**) COMPTR *(of memory)* extension f □ *expansion card* carte f d'extension; *expansion slot* emplacement m pour carte d'extension

expansionist adj expansionniste

expectation n prévision f; **performance did not confirm City expectations** les résultats n'ont pas répondu à l'attente de la City; **we have certain expectations of our employees** nous avons certaines exigences envers nos employés

expected adj attendu(e) □ *expected monetary value* valeur f monétaire escomptée; *expected value* valeur attendue

expenditure n (**a**) *(spending)* dépense f (**b**) *(amount spent)* dépenses fpl; **it entails heavy expenditure** cela entraîne de fortes dépenses

expense n (**a**) *(cost)* dépense f, frais mpl; **at great expense** à grands frais; **it's not worth the expense** c'est trop cher pour ce que c'est □ *expense account* note f de frais; **to put sth on the expense account** mettre qch sur la note de frais (**b**) **expenses** frais mpl; **to meet/cover sb's expenses** rembourser/couvrir les frais de qn; **to put sth on expenses** mettre qch sur la note de frais; **it's on expenses** c'est la société qui paie, ça va sur la note de frais; **to cut down on expenses** réduire les frais; **to incur expenses** faire des dépenses; **to have all expenses paid** être défrayé de tout □ *expenses claim form* note f de frais

expensive adj coûteux(euse), cher (chère); **to be expensive** coûter cher

experience n expérience f; **do you have any experience of dealing with the public?** avez-vous déjà travaillé près du public?; **she has considerable management experience** elle a une expérience considérable dans la gestion □ MKTG *experience curve* courbe f d'expérience

expert n expert m; **he is an expert in this field** il est expert en la matière □ COMPTR *expert system* système m expert

expertise n expertise f

expiration n *(of options market)* échéance f; *(of term)* fin f; *(of lease)* expiration f; *(of insurance policy)* expiration, échéance f

expire vi *(of deadline, lease, insurance policy)* expirer

expiry n expiration f, fin f, échéance f □ *expiry date* date f d'échéance

explore vt *(market)* prospecter

export 1 n (**a**) *(product)* article m d'exportation; **exports** *(of country)* exportations fpl (**b**) *(activity)* exportation f; **for export only** réservé à l'exportation □ *export agent* commissionnaire mf exportateur(trice); *export ban* interdiction f d'exporter; **to impose an export ban on sth** interdire qch d'exportation; *export credit* crédit m à l'exportation; Br *Export Credit Guarantee Department* ≃ Compagnie f française d'assurances pour le commerce extérieur; *export department* service m des exportations; *export duty* droit(s) m(pl) de sortie; *export incentive* prime f à l'exportation; *export licence* licence f d'exportation; *export price* prix m à l'export; *export quotas* contingents mpl d'exportation; *export trade* commerce m d'exportation
2 vt (**a**) *(goods)* exporter (**b**) COMPTR exporter (**to** vers)
3 vi exporter; **the firm exports all over the world** l'entreprise exporte dans le monde entier

exportation n *(of goods)* exportation f

exporter n exportateur(trice) m,f; **Britain is now one of the world's biggest exporters of aircraft** la Grande-Bretagne est maintenant l'un des plus grands exportateurs d'avions du monde

exporting adj exportateur(trice) □ *exporting country* pays m exportateur

> **❝**
> An agreement was reached in July 1991 to collect VAT at the country of origin rather than in the country of destination. This will mean that goods will cross borders at the rate of VAT levied by the **exporting country**, and then become subject to the VAT rate of the importing country.
> **❞**

exposure n *(publicity)* couverture f; **to get a lot of exposure** *(of company, product)* faire l'objet d'une couverture médiatique importante; **exposure to the media is important for a new product** il est important de bénéficier d'une couverture médiatique pour un nouveau produit

express adj *(letter, delivery)* exprès

ext n *(abbr* **extension***)* poste m

extend vt (**a**) **to extend credit to sb** accorder un crédit ou des facilités de crédit à qn (**b**) *(deadline, contract)* prolonger; *(expiry of bill)* proroger

extended *adj* (**a**) *extended credit* accréditif *m* prolongé; *extended guarantee* prolongation *f* de garantie (**b**) COMPTR *extended keyboard* clavier *m* élargi

extension *n* (**a**) ACCT *(of balance)* transport *m*, report *m*

(**b**) *(of credit, deadline, contract)* prolongation *f*; **we need an extension to complete the project** nous avons besoin d'un délai pour terminer le projet

(**c**) *(for telephone)* poste *m*; **extension 35** poste 35 ❑ *extension number* numéro *m* de poste

(**d**) COMPTR *(of file)* extension *f*

external *adj* (**a**) *(trade, debt)* extérieur(e) ❑ *external account* compte *m* d'étranger, *Can* compte de non-résident; *external audit* audit *m* externe; *external auditor* audit *ou* auditeur(trice) *m,f* externe; FIN *external financing* fonds *mpl* extérieurs; *external*

growth croissance *f* externe

(**b**) COMPTR *external device* dispositif *m* externe, périphérique *m*; *(printer)* imprimante *f*; *external drive* unité *f* (de disque) externe; *external modem* modem *m* externe

extn *n* *(abbr* **extension**) poste *m*

extra **1** *n* *(additional charge)* supplément *m*
2 *adj* supplémentaire, de plus; **to charge extra** percevoir un supplément ❑ *extra charge* supplément *m*; *extra cost* surcoût *m*

extraordinary *adj* (**a**) FIN *extraordinary general meeting* assemblée *f* générale extraordinaire; **to call an extraordinary general meeting of the shareholders** convoquer d'urgence les actionnaires

(**b**) ACCT *extraordinary income* produits *mpl* exceptionnels; *extraordinary item* poste *m* extraordinaire

faa adj (abbr **free of all average**) franc de toute avarie

face n (a) *face value, Am face amount* (of banknote, traveller's cheque) valeur f nominale; (of stamp) valeur faciale (**b**) (of document) recto m

facilitate vt faciliter; **to facilitate a meeting** faciliter une réunion

facilitator n MKTG auxiliaire mf

facility n (**a**) (service) service m; **facilities for payment** facilités fpl de paiement; **we offer easy credit facilities** nous offrons des facilités de paiement ou de crédit (**b**) **facilities** (equipment) installations fpl; **we don't have the facilities to hold a conference here** nous ne sommes pas équipés pour organiser une conférence ici

facsimile n fac-similé m

factor n (**a**) (in multiplication) indice m, coefficient m; **the sales increased by a factor of ten** les ventes sont dix fois plus élevées, l'indice des ventes est dix fois plus haut (**b**) ECON **factor of production** facteur m de production (**c**) (factoring company) société f d'affacturage

factorage n (charge) commission f d'affacturage

factoring n affacturage m, factoring m ❑ *factoring company* société f d'affacturage; *factoring charges* commission f d'affacturage

> **❝**
> The more we expanded, the worse our cashflow got till, in the end, our very success threatened us with bankruptcy. The simple answer is **factoring**. We get paid up front, we've got credit protection, and we save a huge amount of work chasing payments.
> **❞**

factory n usine f ❑ *factory inspection* inspection f du travail; *factory inspector* inspecteur(trice) m,f du travail; *factory overheads* frais mpl généraux de fabrication; *factory price* prix m (sortie) usine; *factory shop* magasin m d'usine; *factory unit* unité f de fabrication; *factory worker* ouvrier(ère) m,f d'usine

fail vi (of project, scheme, negotiations) échouer; (of company) faire faillite

failure n (of project, scheme, negotiations) échec m; (of company) faillite f ❑ Am *failure investment* investissement m en valeurs de redressement; *failure rate* taux m de panne

fair 1 n (exhibition) foire f
2 adj *fair average quality* qualité f loyale et marchande; *fair copy* (of document) copie f au net ou au propre; *fair deal* arrangement m équitable; *fair trading* pratique f commerciale loyale; *fair wage* salaire m équitable; *fair wear and tear* usure f normale

faith n **in good faith** de bonne foi; **to buy sth in good faith** acheter qch de bonne foi

faithfully adv **yours faithfully** (in letter) veuillez agréer nos meilleures salutations ou nos salutations distinguées

fake 1 n (product, document) faux m
2 adj faux (fausse)
3 vt (document) falsifier; (signature) contrefaire

fall 1 n (of prices, shares, interest rate, value) baisse (**in** de); (of currency) dépréciation f (**in** de)
2 vi (of prices, shares, interest rate, value) baisser; (of currency) se déprécier

▸ **fall back** vi (of shares) se replier; **shares fell back one point** les actions se sont repliées d'un point

▸ **fall off** vi (of profits, takings, sales) diminuer

fallen angel n ST EXCH ange m déchu

falling adj (prices, shares, interest rate, value) qui baisse; (currency) en baisse; (market) baissier(ère), en baisse

falling-off n baisse f, réduction f (**in** de); **there has been a recent falling-off in production** il y a eu récemment une baisse de la production

falsification n falsification f

falsify vt (document) falsifier; (balance sheet) fausser

family n MKTG *family brand* marque f générale; *family lifecycle* cycle m de vie familiale

FAO 1 n (abbr **Food and Agriculture Organization**) FAO f

2 *prep* (*abbr* **for the attention of**) à l'attention de

FAQ *n* COMPTR (*abbr* **frequently asked questions**) FAQ ❑ *FAQ file* fichier *m* FAQ

faq *n* (*abbr* **fair average quality**) qualité *f* loyale et marchande

FAS *adj* (*abbr* **free alongside ship**) FLQ, FAS, franco quai

fast mover *n* MKTG article *m* à forte rotation

fast-moving *adj* MKTG à forte rotation ❑ *fast-moving consumer goods* biens *mpl* de (grande) consommation à forte rotation

fat cat *n* (*in industry*) = personne touchant un salaire extrêmement élevé de façon injustifiée

❝ What environmentalists are saying is that change should not be made for the benefit of a few and to the detriment of many. Rather than **fat cat** developers benefiting from the countryside, small businesses and local people should have the main part to play in sensitive development. ❞

fault tree *n* arbre *m* de défaillances

faulty *adj* défectueux(euse)

favourable, *Am* **favorable** *adj* (*terms*) bon (bonne), avantageux(euse); **on favourable terms** à des conditions avantageuses, à bon compte

fax **1** *n* (*machine*) fax *m*, télécopieur *m*; (*message*) fax, télécopie *f*; **to send sb a fax** envoyer un fax à qn ❑ COMPTR *fax modem* modem-fax *m*; *fax number* numéro *m* de fax
2 *vt* (*message, document*) faxer, envoyer par fax; (*person*) envoyer un fax à

FCFS (*abbr* **first come, first served**) premier arrivé, premier servi

FCL-FCL (*abbr* **full container load-full container load**) FCL-FCL

FCL-LCL (*abbr* **full container load-less than container load**) FCL-LCL

feasibility *n* (*of plan*) faisabilité *f* ❑ *feasibility report* rapport *m* de faisabilité; MKTG *feasibility stage* phase *f* de faisabilité; *feasibility study* étude *f* de faisabilité; *feasibility test* essai *m* probatoire

featherbed *vt* ECON (*industry, business*) subventionner excessivement

❝ The more resources that Japan devoted to its basic comforts, reasoned the Americans, the less it would have for **featherbedding** its export industries — and thus, just possibly, Japan's trade surplus with America might fall. ❞

featherbedding *n* ECON subventionnement *m* excessif

Fed *n Am* (**a**) (*abbr* **Federal Reserve Board**) banque *f* centrale (des États-Unis) (**b**) (*abbr* **Federal Reserve (System)**) (système *m* de) Réserve *f* fédérale (**c**) (*abbr* **Federal**) *Fed funds* fonds *mpl* fédéraux

❝ City economists said yesterday that the American decision to cut the **Fed funds** rate by point to 33/4 p.c. may have been taken with the international as well as the domestic situation in mind. ❞

federal *adj Am Federal Debt* dette *f* publique *ou* de l'État; *Federal funds* fonds *mpl* fédéraux; *Federal Reserve Bank* banque *f* membre de la Réserve fédérale; *Federal Reserve Board* conseil *m* d'administration des banques centrales américaines; *Federal Reserve (System)* (système *m* de) Réserve *f* fédérale; *Federal Trade Commission* = commission fédérale chargée de veiller au respect de la concurrence sur le marché

❝ Wall Street soared yesterday after the **Federal Reserve Board**, the nation's central bank, lowered short-term interest rates to prevent the economic recovery from stalling. ❞

federation *n* fédération *f*

fee *n* droits *mpl*; (*of lawyer, doctor*) honoraires *mpl*; (*for services*) prestation *f*, redevance *f*; **to draw one's fees** toucher ses honoraires; **to do sth for a small fee** faire qch contre une somme modique; **to charge a fee** demander une prestation de service

feed *vt* COMPTR (*paper*) faire avancer, alimenter; **to feed data into a computer** entrer des données dans un ordinateur

feedback *n* réaction *f*, écho *m*; **we welcome feedback from our customers** nous sommes toujours heureux d'avoir les impressions *ou* les réactions de nos clients; **we need more feedback** nous avons besoin de plus d'informations *ou* d'informations en retour; **this will provide us with much-needed feedback on public opinion** ceci nous fournira des informations dont nous avons grand besoin sur l'opinion publique

fetch vt (be sold for) rapporter; (specific price) atteindre; **it fetched a high price** cela s'est vendu cher; **it fetched £100,000** cela a atteint les 100 000 livres

fiat money n Am monnaie f fiduciaire

> **"**
>
> In most of the models of temporary equilibrium the only financial asset which is explicitly modelled is the stock of **fiat money** – effectively notes and coins in circulation. Other financial assets – bonds, equities, inside money – scarcely feature at all.
>
> **"**

fictitious adj **fictitious assets** actif m fictif; **fictitious person** personne f fictive

fidelity guarantee n INS assurance f contre les détournements

fiduciary FIN **1** n (trustee) dépositaire mf **2** adj fiduciaire □ **fiduciary issue** émission f fiduciaire

field n (**a**) MKTG (for product) marché m □ **field experiment** expérience f sur le terrain; **field research** études fpl sur le terrain; **field work** démarchage m auprès de la clientèle
(**b**) (sphere of activity, knowledge) domaine m; **what field are you in?, what's your field?** quel est votre domaine?; **to be an expert in one's field** être expert dans son domaine □ **field of activity** sphère f ou secteur m d'activité
(**c**) COMPTR (in database) champ m

FIFO (abbr **first in, first out**) PEPS

fifty-fifty 1 adj **a fifty-fifty venture** un accord d'entreprise en coparticipation à 50% **2** adv **to share the costs fifty-fifty** partager les frais moitié-moitié

figure n chiffre m; **figures** (statistics) statistiques fpl; **the figures for next year look good** les statistiques pour l'année prochaine semblent favorables; **to work out the figures** faire les calculs; **to find a mistake in the figures** trouver une erreur de calcul; **his income runs into six figures** ≃ il a un revenu de plus d'un million de francs

file 1 n (**a**) (folder) chemise f; (ring binder) classeur m
(**b**) (documents) dossier m; **to have/keep sth on file** avoir/garder qch dans ses dossiers; **it's on file** c'est dans les dossiers, c'est classé; **we will keep your name on file** nous

garderons votre dossier (de candidature) □ Am **file clerk** documentaliste mf; **file copy** exemplaire m ou pièce f d'archives
(**c**) COMPTR fichier m □ **file compression** compression f de fichiers; **file (name) extension** extension f du nom de fichier; **file conversion** conversion f de fichiers; **file format** format m de fichier; **file management** gestion f ou tenue f des fichiers; **file manager** gestionnaire m des fichiers; **file name** nom m de fichier; **file server** serveur m de fichiers; **file sharing** partage m de fichiers; **file transfer** transfert m de fichier; **file transfer protocol** protocole m de transfert de fichier
2 vt (**a**) (documents) classer; **file these documents under 'sales'** classez ces documents sous la rubrique 'ventes'; **what name is it filed under?** sous quel nom est-il classé?
(**b**) (complaint, claim, request) déposer; FIN **to file one's petition in bankruptcy** déposer son bilan; **to file an application for a patent** déposer une demande de brevet; Am **to file one's tax return** remplir sa déclaration d'impôts
3 vi (classify documents) faire du classement

filing n (**a**) (of documents) classement m; **there is a lot of filing to be done** il y a beaucoup de classement à faire □ **filing cabinet** classeur m; **filing system** (méthode f de) classement; **filing tray** corbeille f pour documents à classer (**b**) (of complaint, claim, request) dépôt m

fill vt (post, vacancy) pourvoir à; **the post has already been filled** le poste est déjà pourvu

▸ **fill in** vt sep (form, cheque stub, application) remplir; (date) insérer

▸ **fill out** vt sep (form, cheque stub, application) remplir

filter n COMPTR filtre m

final adj dernier(ère) □ **final acceptance** réception f définitive; **final accounts** compte m définitif; **final copy** copie f au net ou au propre; FIN **final date** (for payment) date f limite; **final demand** (for payment) dernier avis m, dernier rappel m; ST EXCH **final dividend** dividende m définitif; **final instalment** dernier versement m, versement libératoire; **final offer** dernière proposition f; **final product** produit m fini; FIN **final settlement** solde m de tout compte

finance 1 n (**a**) (money, field) finance f; **we don't have the necessary finance** nous n'avons pas les fonds nécessaires □ **finance company, finance house** société f financière

(b) finances *(funds)* finances *fpl*; **the company's finances are a bit low just now** les finances de l'entreprise sont un peu basses en ce moment

2 *vt (project)* financer; *(person, company)* financer, commanditer; **the company has agreed to finance staff training** l'entreprise a donné son accord pour financer la formation du personnel

financial *adj* financier(ère) ❑ *financial accountant* compatable *mf* financier(ère); *financial accounting* comptabilité *f* générale; *financial adviser* conseiller(ère) *m,f* financier(ère); *financial analyst* analyste *mf* financier(ère); *financial appraisal* évaluation *f* financière; *financial assistance* appui *m* financier; *financial backer* bailleur(eresse) *m,f* de fonds; *financial backing* financement *m*, aide *f* financière; *financial centre* place *f* financière; *financial consultant* conseiller(ère) financier(ère); *financial controller* contrôleur *m* financier, ACCT *financial deal* opération *f* financière; *financial director* directeur(trice) *m,f* financier(ère); ST EXCH *financial future* instrument *m* financier à terme; *financial gearing* effet *m* de levier financier; *financial healthcheck* diagnostic *m* financier; *financial institution* établissement *m* financier; *financial instrument* instrument *m* financier; *financial intermediary* intermédiaire *mf* financier(ère); *financial management* direction *f ou* gestion *f* financière; *financial manager* directeur(trice) *m,f* financier(ère); *financial market* marché *m* financier; *financial ombudsman* arbitre *m* financier; *financial planning* planification *f* financière; *financial position* position *f ou* situation *f* financière; *financial pressure* problèmes *mpl* financiers; *Br* **Financial Reporting Council** = commission de contrôle de la qualité de l'information financière publiée par les entreprises; *financial resources* ressources *fpl*; *financial services* services *mpl* financiers; *financial statement* bilan *m* financier; *Financial Times All-Share Index* = indice boursier du *Financial Times* basé sur la valeur de 700 actions cotées à la Bourse de Londres; *Financial Times-(Industrial) Ordinary Share Index* = indice boursier du *Financial Times* basé sur la valeur de 30 actions cotées à la Bourse de Londres; *Financial Times-Stock Exchange 100 Share Index* = principal indice boursier du *Financial Times* basé sur la valeur de 100 actions cotées à la Bourse de Londres; *financial transaction* opération *f* financière; *Br* **financial year** exercice *m* (comptable)

financially *adv* financièrement; **financially sound** solvable

financier *n* financier *m*

financing *n* financement *m*

find COMPTR **1** *n* **find command** commande *f* de recherche

2 *vt* **to find and replace** trouver et remplacer

fine *adj* **fine bill** beau papier *m*; **fine trade bill** papier de haut commerce *ou* de première catégorie

finish *n* ST EXCH **price at the finish** prix *m* de clôture; **trading at the finish** opérations *fpl* de clôture; **shares were up at the finish** les actions étaient en hausse à la clôture

fire *vt (dismiss)* virer; **to get fired** se faire virer

firewall *n* COMPTR mur *m* coupe-feu, garde-barrière *f*

> **“**
>
> The domain is an important part of one's Internet mailing address. Access to participants is not completely open. Companies tend to use a "**firewall**" along their route into Internet so that individuals cannot be looked up in the directory of users — a sort of ex directory. This would parallel any company policy on not giving out personal telephone numbers but instead routing calls through the switchboard.
>
> **”**

firm **1** *n* entreprise *f*, firme *f*; *(of lawyers, consultants)* cabinet *m*

2 *adj (market, offer, sale, deal)* ferme; *(contango rates)* tendu(e); **oil shares remain firm at $20** les valeurs pétrolières se maintiennent à 20 dollars; **to place a firm order for sth** passer une commande ferme de qch

first **1** *n* **(a)** BANKING, FIN **first of exchange** première *f* de change **(b)** **first in, first out** premier entré, premier sorti; **first come, first served** premier arrivé, premier servi

2 *adj* premier(ère) ❑ *first quarter* *(of year)* premier trimestre *m*

first-class paper *n* effet *m* de première catégorie

first-loss *n* INS premier risque *m* ❑ *first-loss insurance* assurance *f* au premier risque

first-notice day *n* ST EXCH premier jour *m* de notification

first-time *adj* **first-time buyer** *(of property)* = personne achetant une propriété pour la première fois; **first-time user** nouvel(elle) utilisateur(trice) *m,f*

fiscal *adj* fiscal(e) □ *fiscal agent* représentant(e) *m,f* fiscal(e); *fiscal policy* politique *f* budgétaire; *fiscal year* exercice *m* (financier)

Five-Year Plan *n* ECON Plan *m* quinquennal

fix *vt (price, interest rate)* fixer; **to fix the budget** déterminer le budget

▸ **fix up** *vt sep* organiser

fixed *adj (price, rate)* fixe □ ACCT *fixed asset* actif *m* immobilisé; ACCT *fixed assets* immobilisations *fpl*; *fixed capital* capital *m* fixe; *fixed charge* frais *mpl* fixes; *fixed cost* coût *m* fixe *ou* constant; *fixed deposit* dépôt *m* à terme (fixe) *ou* à échéance fixe; COMPTR *fixed disk* disque *m* fixe; *fixed interest* intérêt *m* fixe; *fixed investment* immobilisations *fpl*; *fixed wage* salaire *m* fixe

fixed-interest *adj (investments, securities)* à intérêt fixe □ *fixed-interest market* marché *m* des obligations

fixed-rate *adj (loan, mortgage)* à taux fixe

fixed-term *adj* à terme fixe □ *fixed-term contract* contrat *m* à durée déterminée

fixture *n* installation *f* fixe □ *fixtures and fittings* reprise *f*; **"fixtures and fittings £2,000"** "reprise 2 000 livres"

flag *n* **flag airline** compagnie *f* aérienne nationale; *flag of convenience* pavillon *m* de complaisance

flagging *adj (economy)* languissant(e)

flame COMPTR **1** *n* **flame war** guerre *f* d'insultes
2 *vt* descendre en flammes

flat *adj (market)* calme, languissant(e) □ *flat fee* commission *f* immédiate; *flat rate* tarif *m* fixe

flatbed scanner *n* COMPTR scanner *m ou* scanneur *m* à plat

flat-rate *adj* à taux fixe □ *flat-rate subscription* (to Internet) abonnement *m* à forfait

fledgling *adj (company, industry)* naissant(e)

fleet rating *n* INS barème *m* des flottes

flexibility *n (of budget, prices, approach)* flexibilité *f*

flexible *adj (budget, prices, approach)* flexible □ *flexible manufacturing system* système *m* de fabrication flexible; *flexible working hours* horaires *mpl* flexibles *ou* à la carte

flexitime, flextime *n* horaires *mpl* flexibles *ou* à la carte

flip chart *n* tableau *m* à feuilles

float 1 *n* (a) *Am (petty cash)* petite caisse *f*; *Br (in cash register)* fonds *m* de caisse; *(cash advance)* avance *f*
(b) ST EXCH flottant *m* □ *clean float* taux *mpl* de change libres *ou* flottants; *dirty float* taux de change concertés
2 *vt* (a) FIN, ST EXCH *(company)* introduire en Bourse; *(loan, bonds, share issue)* émettre, lancer
(b) *(currency)* laisser flotter
(c) *(idea, proposal)* émettre

floatation = flotation

floater *n* effet *m* à taux flottant

floating 1 *n* (a) FIN, ST EXCH *(of company)* introduction *f* en Bourse; *(of loan, bonds, share issue)* émission *f*, lancement *m*
(b) *(of currency)* flottement *m*
(c) *(of idea, proposal)* lancement *m*
2 *adj* FIN *(currency, exchange rate)* flottant(e); *(capital)* circulant(e), mobile □ ACCT *floating assets* actif *m* circulant, capital *m* disponible; BANKING *floating charge* nantissement *m* général; *floating debt* dette *f* flottante *ou* non consolidée; COMPTR *floating point* virgule *f* flottante; INS *floating policy* police *f* d'abonnement *ou* flottante; *floating rate* taux *m* flottant

floating-rate *adj* à taux flottant □ BANKING *floating-rate certificate of deposit* certificat *m* de dépôt à taux flottant; *floating-rate interest* intérêt *m* à taux flottant; *floating-rate note* effet *m* à taux flottant

floor *n* (a) *(in department store)* *floor manager* chef *m* de rayon (b) *(of Stock Exchange)* parquet *m* □ *floor trader* commis *m*; *floor trading* cotation *f* à la corbeille

floorwalker *n (in department store)* chef *m* de rayon

floppy COMPTR **1** n disquette f
  2 adj **floppy disk** disquette f; **floppy (disk) drive** unité f de disquettes

florin n florin m

flotation n (**a**) FIN, ST EXCH (of company) lancement m; (of loan, bonds, share issue) émission f, lancement m (**b**) (of currency) flottement m

flourish vi (of business, economy, trade) prospérer

flourishing adj (business, economy, trade) prospère

flow 1 n FIN (of capital) mouvement m; (of information) circulation f; **flow of money** flux m monétaire ou financier ❑ **flow chart** graphique m d'évolution, organigramme m
  2 vi (of capital, money) circuler

flow-through method n Am (of accounting) méthode f de l'impôt exigible

fluctuate vi (of market, currency, value) fluctuer; (of price) flotter, varier

fluctuating adj (market, currency, value) fluctuant(e); (price) flottant(e), variable

fluctuation n (of market, currency, value) fluctuation f; (of price) variation f

flurry n agitation f; **there has been a late flurry of activity on the Stock Market** à la Bourse on a assisté à une reprise soudaine de l'activité en fin de journée

fly-by-night adj (company) véreux(euse)

FMCG npl MKTG (abbr **fast-moving consumer goods**) biens mpl de (grande) consommation à forte rotation

FO n Br ADMIN (abbr **Foreign Office**) Ministère m des affaires étrangères

FOB, fob adj (abbr **free on board**) FOB, FAB ❑ **FOB port of embarkation** FAB port m d'embarquement

focus group n MKTG groupe-témoin m ❑ **focus group interviewing** entretien m avec les membres du groupe-témoin

> **❝**
> ... that these groups work best at the initial stages of research when concepts still have to be clarified; they can never replace a properly constituted sample. The danger is that sometimes people who observe **focus groups** or read the reports on their discussions fall into the trap of saying that "the majority" of members favoured a certain viewpoint, when this simply means five out of eight selected individuals.
> **❞**

fold vi Fam (of business) fermer ses portes, faire faillite

folder n (**a**) (file, document wallet) chemise f; (ring binder) classeur m (**b**) COMPTR (directory) répertoire m

folio ACCT **1** n (sheet) folio m, feuillet m; (book) (livre m) in-folio m
  2 vt paginer à livre ouvert

▸ **follow up 1** vt sep (letter) faire suivre d'une seconde lettre; (person) relancer; (advantage) poursuivre; (enquiry, order) donner suite à; (opportunity) saisir; (success) exploiter; **follow up your initial phone call with a letter** confirmez votre coup de téléphone par écrit
  2 vi (in selling) faire de la relance

follower n MKTG suiveur m

follow-me product n MKTG produit m tactique

follow-up n suite f; (of advertising, client) relance f; (of orders) suivi m ❑ **follow-up letter** lettre f de relance; **follow-up visit** visite f de relance; **follow-up work** travail m complémentaire

font n COMPTR police f, fonte f

food n aliments mpl ❑ **the food industry** l'industrie f alimentaire; **food manufacturer** fabricant m de produits comestibles; **food packaging** emballage m des produits alimentaires; **food products** produits mpl alimentaires, comestibles mpl, denrées fpl

foodstuffs npl produits mpl alimentaires, comestibles mpl, denrées fpl

footer n COMPTR bas m de page

footfall n MKTG (people entering shop) = nombre de personnes qui entrent dans un magasin

footprint n (of building) surface f au sol

FOOTSIE, Footsie n (abbr **Financial Times-Stock Exchange 100 Index**) = principal indice boursier du *Financial Times* basé sur la valeur de 100 actions cotées à la Bourse de Londres

> **❝**
> An eventual 9.5 point gain on the **Footsie** to 2600.5 was mainly due to a strong early-session bounce on Wall Street.
> **❞**

FOR adj (abbr **free on rail**) franco wagon

force n (**a**) **to be in force** (of law, regulation) être en vigueur; **to come into force** entrer en vigueur (**b**) INS **force majeure** (cas m de) force *f* majeure; **force majeure clause** clause *f* de force majeure

▶ **force down** *vt sep (prices, inflation)* faire baisser

▶ **force up** *vt sep (prices, inflation)* faire monter

forced *adj* **forced sale** vente *f* forcée; **forced saving** épargne *f* forcée

forecast 1 *n* prévisions *fpl* ❏ **forecast operating budget** budget *m* d'exploitation prévisionnel; **forecast plan** plan *m* prévisionnel

2 *vt* prévoir; **he forecasts sales of £2m** il prévoit un chiffre de vente de 2 millions de livres

forecaster *n* ECON expert *m*

foreclose LAW **1** *vt* saisir; **to foreclose a mortgage** saisir un bien hypothéqué

2 *vi* saisir le bien hypothéqué; **to foreclose on sb** saisir les biens de qn; **to foreclose on a mortgage** saisir un bien hypothéqué

foreclosure *n* LAW forclusion *f*, saisie *f*

foreign *adj* étranger(ère) ❏ **foreign bill** effet *m* sur l'extérieur; **foreign currency** devises *fpl* étrangères; **foreign currency assets** avoirs *mpl* en devises étrangères; **foreign debt** dette *f* extérieure; **foreign exchange** devises *fpl* étrangères; **foreign exchange broker, foreign exchange dealer** cambiste *mf*, courtier(ère) *m,f* en devises; **foreign exchange market** marché *m* des changes; **foreign exchange option** option *f* sur devises; **foreign exchange transfer** transfert *m* de devises; **foreign goods** marchandises *fpl* qui viennent de l'étranger; **foreign investments** investissements *mpl* à l'étranger; **foreign market** marché *m* extérieur; *Br* **Foreign Office** Ministère *m* des affaires étrangères; **foreign trade** commerce *m* extérieur

> **"**
> It is important for the reader to realise that no physical **foreign exchange market** exists. Instead it consists of telephones, telexes, visual display units and other electronic gadgetry which link together the foreign exchange departments of banks in London and overseas. Modern communications have created a truly worldwide market for major currencies.
> **"**

foreman *n* contremaître *m*, chef *m* d'équipe

forementioned *adj* LAW, ADMIN précité(e)

forfaiting *n* BANKING forfaitage *m*, forfaitisation *f*

forfeit 1 *n* **(a)** LAW *(for non-performance of contract)* dédit *m* ❏ **forfeit clause** clause *f* de dédit

(b) ST EXCH **to relinquish the forfeit** abandonner la prime

(c) LAW **to declare goods forfeit** confisquer des marchandises

2 *vt* LAW *(lose)* perdre par confiscation; *(confiscate)* confisquer; **to forfeit a deposit** perdre les arrhes; **to forfeit a patent** déchoir d'un brevet

forfeiture *n* ST EXCH *(of shares)* déchéance *f*, forfaiture *f*

forge *vt* contrefaire

forged *adj* faux (fausse)

forgery *n* **(a)** *(activity)* contrefaçon *f*; *(of document, banknote)* falsification *f* **(b)** *(thing forged)* faux *m*; **the signature was a forgery** la signature était contrefaite

form 1 *n* **(a)** *(for applications, orders)* formulaire *m* **(b)** COMPTR **form feed** avancement *m* du papier

2 *vt (company)* fonder, créer; *(committee)* former

formal *adj (official)* officiel(elle) ❏ **formal agreement** accord *m* en bonne et due forme; **formal demand** demande *f* officielle; **formal notice** mise *f* en demeure

format COMPTR **1** *n* format *m*

2 *vt (disk)* formater; *(page, text)* mettre en forme, formater

formation *n (of company)* constitution *f*

formatting *n* COMPTR *(of disk)* formatage *m*; *(of page, text)* mise *f* en forme, formatage

Fortune 500 *npl* = les cinq cents plus grosses entreprises américaines (dont la liste est établie, chaque année, par le magazine Fortune)

> **"**
> California's Amgen, the jewel in the crown of American biotechnology, is set to become the industry's first to enter the **Fortune 500** list of America's top companies, with revenue of $1 billion expected this year.
> **"**

forum *n* COMPTR forum *m* de discussion

forward 1 *adj* FIN à terme ❏ **forward account** compte *m* à terme; **forward buying** achat *m* à terme; **forward contract** contrat *m* à terme; **forward dealing** opérations *fpl* à terme; **forward delivery** livraison *f* à terme; **forward exchange**

market marché *m* des changes à terme; MKTG *forward integration* intégration *f* en aval *ou* descendante; *forward market* marché *m* à terme; *forward price* prix *m* à terme; *forward rate* cours *m* à terme, taux *m* pour les opérations à terme; *forward rate agreement* accord *m* de taux à terme; *forward trading* opérations à terme

2 *adv* ACCT **to carry the balance forward** reporter le solde à nouveau; **(carried) forward** report *m*

3 *vt* (**a**) *(goods)* expédier, envoyer; **to forward sth to sb** faire parvenir qch à qn; **to forward goods to Paris** acheminer des marchandises sur *ou* vers Paris

(**b**) *(letter)* faire suivre; **please forward** *(on letter)* (prière de) faire suivre, faire suivre s.v.p.

forwardation *n* report *m*

forwarding *n* expédition *f*, envoi *m* ❏ *forwarding address* *(for goods)* adresse *f* pour l'expédition; *(for letter)* adresse pour faire suivre le courrier; *forwarding agent* (agent *m*) transitaire *m*; *forwarding charges* frais *mpl* d'expédition; *forwarding instructions* indications *fpl* concernant l'expédition

FOT *adj* *(abbr* **free on truck**) franco camion

foul *adj* *(bill of lading)* avec réserves

founder *n* *(of company)* fondateur(trice) *m,f* ❏ *founder member* membre *m* fondateur; *founder's share* part *f* bénéficiaire *ou* de fondateur

fourth *adj* quatrième ❏ *fourth quarter* *(of year)* quatrième trimestre *m*

Fr *(abbr* **franc**) F

fraction *n* FIN *(of share)* fraction *f*

fractional money *n* monnaie *f* divisionnaire

fragile *adj* *(goods)* fragile

fragmentation *n* COMPTR *(of hard disk)* fragmentation *f*

franc *n* franc *m*

franchise **1** *n* franchise *f* ❏ *franchise outlet* boutique *f* franchisée

2 *vt* franchiser, accorder une franchise à

franchisee *n* franchisé(e) *m,f*

franchiser *n* franchiseur *m*

franchising *n* franchisage *m* ❏ *franchising operation* franchisage

franchisor = **franchiser**

franco **1** *adj* franco ❏ *franco price* prix *m* franco

2 *adv* franco

frank *vt* *(letter)* affranchir

franking machine *n* Br machine *f* à affranchir

fraud *n* fraude *f*; **to obtain sth by fraud** obtenir qch par fraude *ou* frauduleusement

fraudulent *adj* frauduleux(euse) ❏ *fraudulent balance sheet* faux bilan *m*; *fraudulent trading* commerce *m* frauduleux; *fraudulent transaction* transaction *f* frauduleuse

fraudulently *adv* frauduleusement

FRB *n* *(abbr* **Federal Reserve Board**) conseil *m* d'administration des banques centrales américaines

FRCD *n* BANKING *(abbr* **floating-rate certificate of deposit**) certificat *m* de dépôt à taux flottant

free **1** *adj* (**a**) *(without charge)* gratuit(e); *free overside* franco allège; *free in and out* bord à bord; *free alongside ship, free at quay, free on wharf* franco long du quai, franco long du bord; *free at frontier* franco frontière; *free of all average* franc de toute avarie; CUSTOMS *free of duty* exempt(e) de droits d'entrée; *free of tax* franc d'impôts; *free on board* franco à bord; *free carrier* franco transporteur; *free on rail* franco wagon, franco de rail; *free on truck* franco camion ❏ *free credit* crédit *m* gratuit; *free delivery* livraison *f* gratuite; *free gift* prime *f*, cadeau *m*; ST EXCH *free issue* attribution *f* d'actions gratuites; *free list* liste *f* d'exemptions, liste des marchandises importées en franchise; *free sample* échantillon *m* gratuit; *free trial* essai *m* gratuit; *free trial period* période *f* d'essai gratuit

(**b**) *(unrestricted)* libre ❏ *free agent* agent *m* indépendant; *free competition* libre concurrence *f*; *free enterprise* libre entreprise *f*; *free market* marché *m* libre; *free market economy* économie *f* de marché; *free port* port *m* franc; *free trade* libre-échange *m*; *free trade area* zone *f* de libre-échange; *free trade policy* politique *f* antiprotectionniste, politique de libre-échange; *free trader* libre-échangiste *mf*, antiprotectionniste *mf*; *free trade zone* zone *f* de libre-échange; *free zone* zone *f* franche

2 *adv* gratuitement; **they will deliver free of charge** ils livreront gratuitement

3 *vt* *(prices, trade)* libérer

> **"**
> Europe does not have a **free market economy** in agricultural and other primary products. The essence of government intervention has been to limit and distort competition rather than to encourage it, to the detriment of the poorer areas.
> **"**

free-flowing *adj (capital)* flottant(e)

Freefone® *n Br* TEL appel *m* gratuit, ≃ numéro *m* vert; **call Freefone 400** ≃ appelez le numéro vert 400

freehold *n* propriéte *f* foncière perpétuelle et libre

freeholder *n* propriétaire *mf* foncier(ère)

freelance 1 *n* travailleur(euse) *m,f* indépendant(e)
2 *adj* indépendant(e), free-lance
3 *adv* **to work freelance** travailler en indépendant(e) *ou* en free-lance
4 *vi* travailler en indépendant(e) *ou* en free-lance

freenet *n* COMPTR libertel *m*

Freepost® *n Br* franchise *f* postale

freeze 1 *n (of credit, wages)* blocage *m*, gel *m*; *(of currency, prices, assets)* gel
2 *vt (credit, wages)* geler, bloquer; *(currency, prices, assets)* geler

freezing *n (of credit, wages)* blocage *m*, gel *m*; *(of currency, prices, assets)* gel

freight 1 *n* (**a**) *(transport)* fret *m*, transport *m* de marchandises; **to send goods by freight** envoyer des marchandises par régime ordinaire
(**b**) *(cargo, load)* fret *m*, cargaison *f*; **to take in freight** prendre du fret
(**c**) *(goods)* marchandises *fpl* (transportées) ❑ *Am* **freight car** wagon *m* de marchandises; **freight depot** gare *f* de marchandises; **freight insurance** assurance *f* sur fret; **freight note** note *f* de fret; **freight plane** avion *m* de fret; **freight release** bon *m* à délivrer; **freight shipping** messageries *fpl* maritimes; **freight ton** tonne *f* d'affrètement; *Am* **freight train** train *m* de marchandises; **freight vehicle** véhicule *m* de transport de marchandises
(**d**) *(cost)* (frais *mpl* de) port *m*; **freight by weight** fret *m* au poids; **freight charges paid** port payé; **freight forward** port avancé
2 *vt (goods)* transporter

freightage *n* (frais *mpl* de) port *m*

freighter *n* (**a**) *(of ship)* affréteur *m* (**b**) *(ship)* cargo *m*; *(aeroplane)* avion *m* de fret

freightliner *n* train *m* de marchandises en conteneurs

frequent *adj* MKTG **frequent flyer club** club *m* de fidélité de compagnie aérienne; **frequent flyer programme** programme *m* de fidélisation des passagers de compagnies aériennes; **frequent user card** carte *f* de fidélité

friction feed *n* COMPTR avancement *m* par friction

friendly society *n Br* FIN société *f* de mutualité

fringe *n Am* **fringes** avantages *mpl* accessoires ❑ *Br* **fringe benefits** avantages accessoires; **fringe market** marché *m* marginal

FRN *n* BANKING *(abbr* **floating-rate note***)* effet *m* à taux flottant

front *n* (**a**) **front man** *(figurehead)* prête-nom *m*; BANKING **front office** front-office *m* (**b**) *Fam* **to pay up front** payer d'avance; **they want £5,000 up front** ils veulent 5 000 livres d'avance

front-end *adj* **front-end fee** frais *mpl* d'entrée; **front-end loading** = système de prélèvement des frais sur les premiers versements

> **"**
> The charges for buying into a trust are usually at the standard rate. Dunedin, however, has no **front-end fee** for its share plan other than stamp duty.
> **"**

front-runner *n* candidat(e) *m,f* favori(ite)

frozen *adj* (**a**) FIN *(credit, wages)* gelé(e), bloqué(e); *(currency, prices, assets)* gelé (**b**) COMPTR bloqué(e)

frustration of contract *n* LAW résolution *f* de contrat

FT index *n* (**a**) *(abbr* **Financial Times-(Industrial) Ordinary Share Index***)* = indice boursier du *Financial Times* basé sur la valeur de 30 actions cotées à la Bourse de Londres (**b**) *(abbr* **Financial Times-Stock Exchange 100 Index***)* = principal indice boursier du *Financial Times* basé sur la valeur de 100 actions cotées à la Bourse de Londres

FTC *n Am (abbr* **Federal Trade Commission***)* = commission fédérale chargée de veiller au respect de la concurrence sur le marché

FTP *n* COMPTR *(abbr* **File Transfer Protocol***)* protocole *m* de transfert de fichier

FT-SE index *n (abbr* **Financial Times-Stock Exchange 100 Index***)* = principal indice boursier du *Financial Times* basé sur la valeur de 100 actions cotées à la Bourse de Londres

fulfil, *Am* **fulfill** *vt (contract, order)* exécuter; *(obligation)* remplir

fulfilment, *Am* **fulfillment** *n (of contract, order)* exécution *f*; *(of obligation)* remplissement *m*

full 1 *n* **to pay in full** payer intégralement; **we paid the bill in full** nous avons payé la facture dans son intégralité; **they refunded my money in full** ils m'ont entièrement remboursé

2 *adj* ACCT *full consolidation* intégration *f* globale; *full container load* conteneur *m* chargé complètement; *full costing* méthode *f* du coût de revient complet; INS *full cover* garantie *f* totale; FIN *full discharge* quitus *m*; *full employment* plein emploi *m*; *full fare (in air travel)* plein tarif *m*; *full pay* paie *f* entière; *full payment* paiement *m* intégral; *full price* prix *m* fort; *full rate* plein tarif *m*; *full weight* poids *m* juste

full-cost pricing *n* MKTG fixation *f* du prix en fonction du coût

full-line strategy *n* MKTG stratégie *f* de gamme complète

full-time 1 *adj (job, employee)* à plein temps, à temps complet; **to be in full-time employment** travailler à plein temps *ou* à temps complet

2 *adv* à plein temps, à temps complet

fully *adv* *fully diluted earnings per share* bénéfice *m* par action entièrement dilué; *fully paid capital* capital *m* entièrement versé; *fully paid-up share* action *f* entièrement libérée

function *n* (a) *(role) (of machine)* fonction *f*; *(of person)* fonction, charge *f*; **in his function as a magistrate** en sa qualité de magistrat; **to resign one's functions** se démettre de ses fonctions □ COMPTR *function key* touche *f* de fonction (b) *(ceremony)* cérémonie *f*; *(reception)* réception *f*

functional *adj* fonctionnel(elle); *(approach)* pragmatique □ *functional budget* budget *m* fonctionnel; *functional organization* organisation *f* fonctionnelle *ou* horizontale; *functional strategy* stratégie *f* fonctionnelle

fund FIN 1 *n* (a) *(reserve of money)* fonds *m*, caisse *f*; **fund of funds** fonds de fonds □ *fund management* gestion *f* de fonds; *fund manager* gestionnaire *mf* de fonds

(b) **funds** *(cash resources)* fonds *mpl*; *(of government)* fonds publics; **to be short of** *or* **low on funds** être à court d'argent; *Br* **the Funds** les bons *mpl* du Trésor; **to make a call for funds** faire un appel de capital

2 *vt (project)* financer; *(company)* pourvoir de fonds; *(public debt)* consolider; **to fund money** placer de l'argent dans les fonds publics

fundamental market analyst *n* analyste *mf* fondamental(e)

funded *adj* FIN *(assets)* en rentes □ *funded capital* capitaux *mpl* investis; *funded debt* dette *f* consolidée; *funded pension scheme* régime *m* de retraite par capitalisation

fundholder *n* rentier(ère) *m,f*

funding *n* *(of project)* financement *m*; *(of debt)* consolidation *f*; *(of income)* assiette *f*; **BP will put up half of the funding** BP financera le projet à 50% □ *funding loan* emprunt *m* de consolidation; *funding operation* opération *f* de financement

fungible ST EXCH 1 *n* **fungibles** fongibles *mpl*

2 *adj* fongible □ *fungible securities* titres *mpl* en suspens

funnelling *n* MKTG *(in questionnaire construction)* entonnoir *m*

> **"**
>
> A technique known as "**funnelling**" in which more general questions are followed by more specific ones amplifying the general ones can be useful in guiding the interviewer through the schedule and encouraging the respondent to give fuller answers. ... For example, questions of relevance only to married women can be prefaced by a general question about marital status followed by an instruction for those who have answered in a particular way to move to the relevant subset.
>
> **"**

furnish *vt (supply) (provisions)* fournir; *(information, reason)* fournir, donner; **to furnish sb with sth** fournir qch à qn

further 1 *adj* **for further information, phone this number** pour tout renseignement complémentaire, appelez ce numéro; **please send me further information concerning the project** veuillez m'envoyer de plus amples renseignements concernant le projet; **I would like further details of the programme** j'aimerais avoir quelques précisions supplémentaires sur le programme; **until further notice** jusqu'à nouvel ordre

2 *adv* **further to** *(in letter)* suite à; **further to your letter of 15 June** suite à votre lettre du 15 juin; **further to our telephone call** suite à notre conversation téléphonique

future 1 *n* (a) *(of person)* avenir *m*; **a job with a (good) future** une situation pleine d'avenir; **there is a future ahead for bilingual people in publishing** le monde de l'édition offre des possibilités d'avenir pour les personnes bilingues

(b) ST EXCH **futures** opérations *fpl* à terme ❏ *futures contract* contrat *m* à terme; *futures exchange* marché *m* à terme; *futures market* marché *m* à terme; *futures option* option *f* sur contrats à terme; *futures trading* négociations *fpl* à terme

2 *adj* FIN *future delivery* livraison *f* à terme; **goods for future delivery** marchandises *fpl* livrables à terme; *future value* valeur *f* capitalisée

> **"**
>
> The London **futures market** had its bus-iest day with 650,000 contracts changing hands — 60 per cent more than on the previous record day. Most of the business was in shorter-term sterling **futures** as the pound gained against other currencies.
>
> **"**

FX *n* (*abbr* **foreign exchange**) devises *fpl* étrangères ❏ *FX broker, FX dealer* cambiste *mf*, courtier(ère) *m,f* en devises; *FX market* marché *m* des changes; *FX option* option *f* sur devises; *FX transfer* transfert *m* de devises

G7 *n* G7 *m*, groupe *m* des 7 ❑ ***G7 meeting*** réunion *f* du G7; ***G7 summit*** sommet *m* du G7

G8 *n* G8 *m*, groupe *m* des 8 ❑ ***G8 meeting*** réunion *f* du G8; ***G8 summit*** sommet *m* du G8

GA *n* INS (*abbr* **general average**) avarie *f* commune

GAAP *npl* ACCT (*abbr* **generally-accepted accounting principles**) PCGR *mpl*

gain 1 *n* (**a**) *(profit)* gain *m*, profit *m*, avantage *m* (**b**) *(increase)* accroissement *m*, augmentation *f*; FIN **gain in value** plus-value *f*; **there has been a net gain in profits this year** il y a eu une augmentation nette des bénéfices cette année; **there has been a gain of 100 points on the Dow Jones** l'indice Dow Jones a gagné 100 points
2 *vt* gagner, bénéficier de; **the share index has gained two points** l'indice des actions a gagné deux points

galloping inflation *n* ECON inflation *f* galopante

gamble *vi* **to gamble on the Stock Exchange** boursicoter, jouer à la Bourse

gameplan *n* MKTG stratégie *f* (de marketing)

game theory *n* MKTG théorie *f* des jeux

gap *n* écart *m*; **a gap in the market** un créneau ❑ MKTG ***gap analysis*** étude *f* des créneaux; MKTG ***gap level*** écart de performance; ***gap study*** étude *f* des écarts

> " ————
> The mother and baby specialist retail chain had been very successful in identifying **a gap in the market** and had filled it very efficiently, but it lacked the flair and creative genius that Conran had brought to Habitat and was losing business as a consequence.
> ———— "

garnishee *n* LAW tiers *m* saisi ❑ ***garnishee order*** ordonnance *f* de saisie-arrêt

gatekeeper *n* MKTG contrôleur *m*, relais *m*, filtre *m*

gateway *n* COMPTR passerelle *f* de connexion

GATT *n* (*abbr* **General Agreement on Tariffs and Trade**) agétac *m*

gazump *vt* = revenir sur une promesse de vente de maison pour accepter l'offre plus élevée d'une tierce personne

GB *n* COMPTR (*abbr* **gigabyte**) GO *m*

GDP *n* ECON (*abbr* **gross domestic product**) PIB *m*

gear *vt* *(link)* indexer; **salaries are geared to the cost of living** les salaires sont indexés au coût de la vie

▸ **gear up** *vt sep* (**a**) *(prepare)* préparer; **the company is geared up for expansion** la société est orientée vers l'expansion (**b**) *(increase)* augmenter; **we must gear up production to meet the demand** il nous faut augmenter la production pour faire face à la demande

> " ————
> … if there is going to be a high level of unemployment because productivity is rising faster than output, this means that the cost of goods and services is falling fast and either consumer demand is not increasing fast enough or industry cannot **gear up** production fast enough to create the demanded extra output.
> ———— "

gearing *n* FIN *(leverage)* effet *m* de levier; *(as percentage)* ratio *m* d'endettement ❑ ***gearing adjustment*** redressement *m* financier

> " ————
> Strong cashflow allowed borrowings to fall. Interest paid was down from £3.1m to £1.2m and **gearing** at the year-end was 9 per cent.
> ———— "

general *adj* BANKING ***general account manager*** chargé(e) *m,f* de clientèle grand public; ***general and administrative expenses*** frais *mpl* généraux et frais de gestion; ***general agent*** agent *m* d'affaires; ***General Agreement on Tariffs and Trade*** Accord *m* général sur les tarifs douaniers et le commerce; INS ***general average*** avarie *f* commune; ***general business*** *(on agenda)* questions *fpl* diverses; ***general expenses*** frais *mpl* généraux; LAW ***general lien*** privilège *m* général; ***general manager*** directeur(trice) *m,f* général(e); ***general meeting*** assemblée *f* générale; ***general***

overheads frais *mpl* d'administration générale; **general price level** niveau *m* général des prix; **general trend** tendance *f* générale; **general wage level** niveau *m* général des salaires

generate *vt* (**a**) COMPTR créer, générer (**b**) *(income)* créer, produire; **we must try to generate new sources of income** nous devons essayer de créer de nouvelles sources de revenus

generic MKTG **1** *n* produit *m* générique **2** *adj* générique □ **generic advertising** publicité *f* générique; **generic market** marché *m* générique; **generic product** produit *m* générique

gentleman's agreement *n* gentleman's agreement *m*

genuine *adj* *(article)* garanti(e) d'origine; *(diamond, gold, leather)* véritable

geodemographic *adj* MKTG géodémographique □ **geodemographic segmentation** segmentation *f* géodémographique

geographic pricing *n* MKTG tarification *f* géographique

get *vt* (**a**) *(obtain)* se procurer, obtenir; *(buy)* acheter; **I got this computer cheap** j'ai eu *ou* acheté cet ordinateur bon marché (**b**) *(earn)* gagner; **to get £35,000 a year** gagner 35 000 livres par an (**c**) *(letter, phone call, reply)* recevoir; **I got his answer this morning** j'ai eu *ou* reçu sa réponse ce matin (**d**) *(contact by telephone)* joindre; **I couldn't get her at the office** je n'ai pas pu l'avoir au bureau; **get me Washington 330 330** *(to operator)* appelez-moi Washington 330 330

▸ **get through** *vi* **to get through to sb** *(on telephone)* obtenir la communication avec qn

GIF *n* COMPTR *(abbr* **Graphics Interchange Format**) GIF *m*

gift *n* (**a**) LAW *(donation)* don *m*, donation *f*; **as a gift** à titre d'avantage □ **gift inter vivos** donation *f* entre vifs (**b**) *(present)* cadeau *m*

gigabyte *n* COMPTR gigaoctet *m*

gilt *n* ST EXCH fonds *m* d'État, valeur *f* de tout repos *ou* de père de famille

gilt-edged *adj* ST EXCH (**a**) **gilt-edged stock, gilt-edged securities** fonds *mpl* d'État, valeurs *fpl* de tout repos *ou* de père de famille (**b**) *Am* **gilt-edged bond** valeur *f* du Trésor américain

> " The Chancellor is expected to modify the Government's policy of buying in enough long-dated **gilt-edged stock** in a single fiscal year to offset the financial drain on the economy created by the budget surplus and foreign exchange intervention to support the pound — the so-called full funding rule. "

giro *n Br* (**a**) *(system)* = système de virement interbancaire introduit par la Poste britannique □ **giro account** compte *m* chèque postal, CCP *m*; **giro cheque** chèque *m* de virement; **giro transfer** transfert *m* par CCP (**b**) *Fam (unemployment benefit)* allocation *f* (de) chômage

Girobank *n Br* service *m* de chèques postaux

give *vt (pay)* donner; **to give a good price for sth** donner *ou* payer un bon prix pour qch; **I'll give you £500 for it** je vous en donnerai 500 livres; **what will you give me for it?** combien m'en offrez-vous?

giveaway *n Fam (free gift)* prime *f*, cadeau *m* □ **giveaway paper** journal *m* gratuit

given *adj* donné(e); **at a given price** à un cours donné *ou* déterminé

glare *n* COMPTR **glare filter** filtre *m* anti-reflet; **glare screen** écran *m* anti-reflet

glass ceiling *n* = plafond de verre qui désigne métaphoriquement l'ensemble des facteurs qui empêchent les femmes de parvenir aux postes les plus élevés dans le monde professionnel

> " The fact that a woman, Margaret Thatcher, smashed the biggest **glass ceiling** of all in 1979 and that women have been storming into business and Government with ever more determination and success than before, should point the way for the hospitality industry. "

global *adj* (**a**) *(worldwide)* mondial(e) □ FIN **global bond** obligation *f* multimarchés; **global custody** conservation *f* globale; FIN **global equities market** marché *m* mondial des actions; MKTG **global market** marché *m* global; MKTG **global marketing** marketing *m* global *ou* international; MKTG **global player**

acteur *m* international; *global village* village *m* planétaire

　(**b**) *(comprehensive)* global(e) ▫ *global finance* financement *m* aux entreprises

globalize *vt (production, strategy)* globaliser

> Production has been increasingly **globalized**, with processes located where it is most advantageous in terms of profit maximization. This has resulted in regional specialization and, effectively, the creation of a global division of labour.

glut **1** *n (on market)* encombrement *m*; *(of commodity)* surabondance *f*; **there is a glut of oil on the market** il y a une surabondance de pétrole sur le marché; FIN **glut of money** pléthore *f* de capitaux

　2 *vt (market, economy)* encombrer, inonder; **the market is glutted with luxury goods** il y a une surabondance d'objets de luxe sur le marché

gnome *n Fam* **the gnomes of Zurich** les grands banquiers *mpl* suisses

GNP *n* ECON *(abbr* **gross national product***)* PNB *m*

▸ **go down** *vi (of prices, value)* baisser

▸ **go up** *vi (of prices, value)* monter, augmenter; **the cost of living is going up** le coût de la vie augmente

go-between *n* intermédiaire *mf*

gofer *n Fam* factotum *m*

going *adj* (**a**) *(profitable)* **going concern** affaire *f* qui marche; **for sale as a going concern** à vendre avec fonds (**b**) *(current) (price)* courant(e), actuel(elle); **she's getting the going rate for the job** elle touche le tarif normal pour ce genre de travail

going-concern *adj* ACCT **going-concern concept** principe *m* de la continuité de l'exploitation; **going-concern status** continuité *f* d'exploitation

going-rate pricing *n* MKTG alignement *m* sur les prix du marché

gold *n or m* ▫ FIN **gold bond** obligation *f* or; **gold bullion** encaisse *f* or; **gold bullion standard** étalon *m* or-lingot; **gold card** carte *f* de crédit illimitée; **gold currency** monnaie *f* d'or; **gold ingot** lingot *m* d'or; **gold market** marché *m* de l'or; **gold reserves** réserve *f* d'or; **gold share** valeur *f* aurifère; **gold standard** étalon-or *m*

gold-collar worker *n* col *m* doré

golden *adj* **golden handcuffs** contrat *m* alléchant *(qui encourage les employés à rester avec le même employeur)*; **golden handshake** indemnité *f* de départ; **golden hello** pont *m* d'or; **golden parachute** indemnité *f* contractuelle de départ; **golden share** participation *f* majoritaire *(souvent détenue par le gouvernement britannique dans les entreprises privatisées)*

good *adj (cheque, debt)* bon (bonne); *(investment, securities)* sûr(e); **their credit is good for £5,000** on peut leur faire crédit jusqu'à 5 000 livres

goods *npl* (**a**) LAW *(possessions)* biens *mpl*; **goods and chattels** biens et effets (**b**) *(articles)* marchandises *fpl*, articles *mpl*; **send us the goods by rail** envoyez-nous la marchandise par chemin de fer ▫ *goods train* train *m* de marchandises; *goods vehicle* véhicule *f* de transport de marchandises

goodwill *n* fonds *m* de commerce, biens *mpl* incorporels

> Much of the concern is levelled at agency balance sheets which have been weakened by the sector's lust for acquisitions. Quoted advertising agencies wrote off **goodwill** totalling £1.7bn in the year to November 1988, leaving aggregate shareholders' funds in the sector below £39m.

gopher *n* (**a**) COMPTR (serveur *m*) gopher *m* (**b**) *Fam (person)* factotum *m*

go-slow **1** *n* grève *f* perlée

　2 *adj* **go-slow strike** grève *f* perlée

government *n* gouvernement *m* ▫ *government bonds* obligations *fpl* d'État; *government borrowings* emprunts *mpl* de l'État; *Br government broker* agent *m* du trésor; *government grant* subvention *f* de l'État; *government loan* emprunt *m* public *ou* d'État; *government securities, government stock* effets *mpl* publics

grade **1** *n* (**a**) *(in profession)* échelon *m*; **the top grades of the civil service** les échelons supérieurs *ou* les plus élevés de la fonction publique (**b**) *(of product)* qualité *f* ▫ *grade label* étiquette *f* de calibrage

　2 *vt (products)* classer, calibrer

graded *adj (advertising rates)* dégressif(ive); *(tax)* progressif(ive)

graduate *Br* **1** *n* diplômé(e) *m,f*, licencié(e) *m,f* ▫ *graduate entry* échelon *m* d'entrée pour les diplômés; *graduate training scheme* programme *m* de formation professionnelle pour les diplômés

2 *vi* obtenir sa licence; **she has recently graduated in economics** elle a récemment obtenu sa licence en économie

graduated *adj (tax)* progressif(ive)

grain *n* céréales *fpl* ❑ **grain market** marché *m* des céréales

grammar checker *n* COMPTR correcteur *m* grammatical

granny bond *n Br Fam* FIN = type d'obligation visant le marché des retraités

grant 1 *n* (**a**) *(financial aid)* subvention *f*, allocation *f* (**b**) *(transfer) (of property)* cession *f*; *(of land)* concession *f*
2 *vt (subsidy, loan, overdraft)* accorder

grant-aided *adj* subventionné(e) par l'État

graph *n* graphique *m*, diagramme *m*; **to plot a graph** tracer un graphique ❑ **graph paper** papier *m* quadrillé

graphical user interface *n* COMPTR interface *f* utilisateur graphique

graphic interface *n* COMPTR interface *f* graphique

graphics *npl* COMPTR graphismes *mpl*, graphiques *mpl* ❑ **graphics accelerator** accélérateur *m* graphique; **graphics accelerator card** carte *f* accélérateur graphique; **graphics card** carte *f* graphique; **graphics mode** mode *m* graphique; **graphics software** logiciel *m* graphique; **graphics tablet** tablette *f* graphique

grass-roots *adj* de base, qui émane de la base; **there is no grass-roots support for their policy** il n'y a pas de soutien de la base pour leur politique; **the grass-roots feeling is that...** le sentiment à la base est que...; **at grass-roots level** à la base ❑ MKTG **grass-roots forecasting** prévision *f* de la base

gratis 1 *adj* gratuit(e)
2 *adv* gratis, gratuitement

gratuity *n* (**a**) *(tip)* pourboire *m*, gratification *f* (**b**) *Br (payment to employee)* prime *f*

gray *Am* = **grey**

green *adj* **green audit** = rapport sur l'impact des activités d'une entreprise sur l'environnement; ADMIN **green card** ≃ permis *m* de travail; *(in insurance)* carte *f* verte, attestation *f* d'assurance; EU **green currency** monnaie *f* verte; EU **green pound** livre *f* verte; MKTG **green product** produit *m* vert *ou* écologique; **green rate** taux *m* vert; **green tourism** tourisme *m* vert

greenback *n Am Fam* billet *m* vert

greenfield site *n* terrain *m* à bâtir *(sur lequel rien n'a jamais été construit)*

> **"**
> There is great public concern about design and quality, especially when development takes place on a **greenfield site**. Although screening and landscaping can help reduce visual impact, it is not on its own an adequate response to design issues.
> **"**

greenmail *n* FIN greenmail *m*

grey, *Am* **gray 1** *n* COMPTR **shades of grey** niveaux *mpl* de gris
2 *adj* **grey import** importation *f* grise; ST EXCH **grey knight** chevalier *m* gris; ST EXCH **grey market** marché *m* gris; **grey zone** zone *f* grise

greyscale *n* COMPTR niveau *m* de gris

grievance *n (complaint)* réclamation *f*; **the workers put forward a list of grievances** les travailleurs ont présenté un cahier de revendications ❑ **grievance procedure** = procédure permettant aux salariés de faire part de leurs revendications

gross 1 *n* douze douzaines *fpl*, grosse *f*
2 *adj (weight, price, profit, interest)* brut(e) ❑ **gross amount** montant *m* brut; INS **gross average** grosse(s) avarie(s) *f(pl)* commune(s); **gross domestic product** produit *m* intérieur brut; **gross income** *(in accounts)* produit *m* brut; *(of individual)* revenu *m* brut; **gross margin** marge *f* brute; **gross national income** revenu *m* national brut; **gross national product** produit *m* national brut; **gross profit** bénéfice *m* brut; **gross profit margin** marge *f* commerciale brute; **gross receipts** recettes *fpl* brutes; **gross redemption yield** rendement *m* actuarial brut; **gross return** rendement *m* brut
3 *vt (of person, company)* gagner brut; *(of sale)* produire brut; **they grossed £10 million** cela leur a rapporté brut 10 millions de livres

ground *n* terrain *m* ❑ **ground rent** rente *f* foncière

group *n (of people, companies)* groupe *m*; **the Shell Group** le Groupe Shell; **Group of Seven** groupe des sept; **Group of Eight** groupe des huit ❑ **group insurance** assurance *f* collective; **group leader** responsable *mf* de groupe; **group manager** chef *m* de groupe; **group meeting** *(for marketing survey)* réunion *f* de groupe; FIN **group turnover** chiffre *m* d'affaires du groupe

grouped consignment *n* envoi *m* groupé

growth n *(of business, market, industry)* croissance f, expansion f; **the experts predict a 2% growth in imports** les experts prédisent une croissance des importations de 2%; **to go for growth** favoriser la croissance; **the recent growth in the number of small businesses** l'augmentation récente du nombre de petites entreprises ❑ *growth area* secteur m en expansion; *growth curve* courbe f de croissance; *growth index* indice m de croissance; *growth industry* industrie f en plein essor; *growth market* marché m porteur; *growth rate* taux m de croissance *ou* d'expansion; *growth sector* secteur m de croissance; ST EXCH *growth shares, growth stock* actions fpl d'avenir *ou* de croissance; *growth strategy* stratégie f de croissance

growth-share matrix n MKTG matrice f croissance-part de marché

guarantee 1 n (a) *(document, promise)* garantie f; **this computer has a five-year guarantee** cet ordinateur est garanti cinq ans; **under guarantee** sous garantie ❑ *guarantee certificate* certificat m de garantie
(b) *(security)* garantie f, caution f, cautionnement m; **to secure all guarantees** s'assurer toutes les garanties nécessaires; **to leave sth as a guarantee** laisser qch en garantie ❑ *guarantee company* société f de sécurité; *guarantee fund* fonds m de garantie
(c) *(person)* garant(e) m,f, caution f; **to act as guarantee (for sb)** se porter garant (de qn)
2 vt (a) *(product, appliance)* garantir; **this computer is guaranteed for five years** cet ordinateur est garanti cinq ans
(b) *(loan, cheque, debt)* garantir, cautionner

guaranteed adj *(bond, stocks)* garanti(e) ❑ *guaranteed minimum wage* salaire m minimum interprofessionnel garanti

guarantor n garant(e) m,f; **to stand as guarantor for sb** se porter garant de qn

guerilla attack n MKTG guérilla f

GUI n COMPTR *(abbr* **graphical user interface***)* interface f utilisateur graphique

guilder n florin m

guillotine n *(for cutting paper)* massicot m

gyrations npl *(in market)* fluctuations fpl

habitual buying behaviour *n* MKTG comportement *m* d'achat habituel

hack *vi* COMPTR **to hack into sth** s'introduire en fraude dans qch

hacker *n* COMPTR pirate *m* informatique

haggle *vi* marchander; **to haggle over sth** marchander qch; **to haggle over the price of sth** marchander qch

half-commission man *n* remisier *m*

half-day *n* demi-journée *f*; **tomorrow is my half-day** demain c'est ma demi-journée de congé; **to work half-days** faire des demi-journées

half-yearly **1** *adj* semestriel(elle)
2 *adv* tous les six mois

halo effect *n* MKTG effet *m* de halo

▸ **hammer out** *vt sep* (agreement, contract) élaborer

hammered *adj* ST EXCH (stockbroker) déclaré(e) insolvable

hammering *n* ST EXCH (of stockbroker) déclaration *f* d'insolvabilité

hand *n* **to change hands** (of business) changer de propriétaire

▸ **hand in** *vt sep* remettre, déposer; **to hand in one's resignation** démissionner, donner sa démission

handbook *n* manuel *m*

hand-held scanner *n* COMPTR scanner *m ou* scanneur *m* à main

handle *vt* (**a**) (deal with) s'occuper de; **we can handle orders for overseas** nous prenons des commandes pour l'étranger; **we're too small to handle an order of that size** notre entreprise est trop petite pour traiter une commande de cette importance; **she's good at handling difficult customers** elle sait bien s'occuper des clients difficiles
(**b**) (trade in) faire, vendre; **we don't handle chemical products** nous ne faisons pas de produits chimiques
(**c**) **handle with care** (on parcel) ≃ fragile

handler *n* manutentionnaire *mf*

handling *n* (**a**) (of goods) manutention *f*, distribution *f* □ **handling capacity** capacité *f* de traitement; **handling charges** frais *mpl* de manutention (**b**) (of order, contract) traitement *m*, exécution *f*

hand-made *adj* fait(e) à la main

handout *n* (brochure) prospectus *m*; (sample) cadeau *m* publicitaire

handshake *n* COMPTR dialogue *m* d'établissement de liaison

hands-off *adj* (approach, manager) non-interventionniste

hands-on *adj* pratique; **the director has a hands-on style of management** le directeur n'a pas peur de mettre la main à la pâte □ **hands-on training** formation *f* pratique

> All six departments obtain specific company annual accounts which they analyse themselves for their own particular uses. It is felt that this "**hands-on**" approach is the only way of getting sufficiently reliable information. But, for less detailed examinations or as back-up information, the analyses presented in stockbroker reports are considered extremely useful.

handwork *n* travail *m* manuel

Hang Seng index *n* ST EXCH indice *m* Hang Seng, indice Hong Kong

harbour, *Am* **harbor** *n* port *m* □ **harbour dues** droits *mpl* de port

hard *adj* (**a**) **hard sell** vente *f* agressive; **to give sb the hard sell** imposer une vente à qn; **to give sth the hard sell** promouvoir qch de façon agressive; **hard sell techniques** méthode *f* de vente agressive
(**b**) FIN (stock, rates) soutenu(e), ferme □ **hard loan** prêt *m* aux conditions du marché
(**c**) **hard commodities** minerais *mpl*; **hard currency** devise *f* ou monnaie *f* forte
(**d**) COMPTR **hard copy** copie *f* sur papier; **hard disk** disque *m* dur; **hard drive** unité *f* de disque dur

hard-core loyal *n* MKTG fidèle *mf* absolu(e)

hardware *n* COMPTR matériel *m*, hardware *m*

haul **1** *n* (transport) transport *m*
2 *vt* (transport) transporter par camion

haulage *n* (**a**) (transportation) transport *m* (routier) □ **haulage contractor** entrepreneur *m* de transports, transporteur *m* (**b**) *(costs)* frais *mpl* de transport

haulier, *Am* **hauler** *n* entrepreneur *m* de transports, transporteur *m* ; *(driver)* routier *m*

hazard forecasting *n* MKTG prévision *f* événementielle

HD COMPTR (**a**) *(abbr* **hard disk**) DD (**b**) *(abbr* **high density**) HD

head *n* (**a**) *(person)* chef *m* ; **head of department** chef de service ; *(in shop)* chef de rayon ❑ *head foreman* chef d'atelier ; *head office* siège *m* social (**b**) *heads of agreement* *(draft)* protocole *m* d'accord

headed (note)paper *n* papier *m* à en-tête

header *n* COMPTR en-tête *m*

headhunt *vt* recruter ; **to be headhunted** être recruté(e) par un chasseur de têtes

> 〝
> More recently 3i has become involved in the fashionable technique of "buy-ins", where teams of successful managers are **headhunted** from larger companies to run smaller struggling firms and turn them around.
> 〞

headhunter *n* chasseur *m* de têtes

heading *n* (**a**) *(of letter, bill)* en-tête *m* (**b**) *(subject)* rubrique *f* ; **see under the heading 'sales'** voir sous la rubrique 'vente'

head-on attack *n* MKTG attaque *f* frontale

headquarters *npl* siège *m* social ; **the company has its headquarters in Zurich** l'entreprise a son siège social à Zurich

health *n* *health cover* couverture *f* santé ; *health insurance* assurance *f* maladie ; *Health and Safety Executive* ≃ inspection *f* du travail ; *health and safety regulations* réglementation *f* sur l'hygiène et la sécurité ; *Br* *Health and Safety at Work Act* loi *f* sur les accidents du travail

heart share *n* MKTG préférence *f*

heavy *adj* *(loss, tax)* lourd(e) ; *(expenditure, payments)* gros (grosse), considérable ; **they expect heavy trading on the Stock Exchange** ils s'attendent à ce que le marché soit très actif ; **closures have resulted in heavy job losses** les fermetures ont conduit à des pertes d'emplois élevées ❑ *heavy equipment* matériel *m* lourd ; *Br* *heavy goods vehicle* poids *m* lourd ; *heavy industry* industrie *f* lourde ; ST EXCH *heavy market* marché *m* lourd

hedge ST EXCH **1** *n* **hedge fund** société *f* d'investissement

2 *vt* *(shares)* arbitrer ; *(transactions)* couvrir

3 *vi* se couvrir ; **to hedge against currency fluctuations** se couvrir contre les fluctuations monétaires

> 〝
> There are ways of **hedging** against the exchange rate risk. One method is to switch the foreign currency loan back into sterling if you think that sterling will weaken significantly — more than a possibility. This again is a strategy to be pursued only by those with considerable financial sophistication.
> 〞

hedger *n* ST EXCH opérateur(trice) *m,f* en couverture

hedging *n* ST EXCH opérations *fpl* de couverture

help *n* COMPTR *help menu* menu *m* d'aide ; *help screen* écran *m* d'aide

hereafter *adv* *(in legal document)* ci-après

hereby *adv* *(in legal document)* par la présente ; **we hereby declare that...** nous déclarons par la présente que...

HGV *n* *Br* *(abbr* **heavy goods vehicle**) poids *m* lourd ❑ *HGV licence* permis *m* poids lourd

hidden *adj* FIN *hidden cost* coût *m* caché ; *hidden defects* défauts *mpl* ou vices *mpl* cachés ; *hidden extras* dépenses *fpl* supplémentaires inattendues ; *hidden reserves* réserves *fpl* occultes ; *hidden tax* impôt *m* déguisé

high **1** *n* *(peak)* haut *m*, sommet *m* ; **the Stock Market reached a new high** la Bourse a atteint un nouveau record *ou* maximum ; **prices are at an all-time high** les prix ont atteint un record *ou* leur maximum ; ST EXCH **the highs and lows** les hauts et les bas

2 *adj* (**a**) *(cost, price, interest rate)* élevé(e) ; *(salary)* élevé, gros (grosse) ; **to fetch a high price** se vendre cher ; **areas of high unemployment** des régions à fort taux de chômage

(**b**) *(important)* haut(e) ; **to hold a high position** être haut placé(e)

(**c**) *Br* **the high street** la grand-rue, la rue principale ; **the high street has been badly hit by the recession** les petits commerçants ont été durement touchés par la récession

3 *adv* **to run high** *(of prices)* être élevé(e)

high-density *adj* COMPTR *(disk, graphics, printing)* haute densité

high-end *adj* *(goods)* haut de gamme

higher-income group *n* groupe *m* de contribuables à revenus élevés

high-grade *adj (goods)* de première qualité, de (premier) choix

high-involvement *adj* MKTG à forte participation des consommateurs

high-level *adj (talks, meeting)* à haut niveau □ *high-level decision* décision *f* prise à un niveau supérieur; *high-level staff* cadres *mpl* supérieurs

highlight *vt (with highlighter pen)* surligner; COMPTR *(text)* sélectionner

highlighter *n (pen)* surligneur *m*

highly *adv* (a) *(at an important level)* haut; **a highly placed official** un officiel de haut rang; ADMIN un haut fonctionnaire (b) *(very well)* très bien; **his employees are highly paid** ses employés sont très bien payés *ou* touchent de gros salaires

highly-geared *adj* à ratio d'endettement élevé

> The attractions of ordinary shares can often depend upon the economic environment and the company's potential for growth. In periods of rising profits a company which is geared at a low level may not have the growth potential to give ordinary shareholders the returns expected from a more **highly-geared** company.

high-powered *adj (person)* qui occupe un poste à hautes responsabilités; *(job)* à hautes responsabilités

high-quality *adj (product)* de première qualité, de (premier) choix

high-resolution *adj* COMPTR de haute résolution

high-speed *adj* COMPTR de haute vitesse

high-street *adj Br* **the high-street banks** les grandes banques; *high-street shops* le petit commerce

high-tech *adj (product)* perfectionné(e); *(industry)* de pointe; *(approach, solution)* qui a recours à une technologie de pointe

hire 1 *n* (a) *Br (of car, equipment)* location *f* □ *hire car* voiture *f* de location
(b) *hire purchase* achat *m* à crédit *ou* à tempérament; **to buy sth on hire purchase** acheter qch à crédit *ou* à tempérament; *hire purchase agreement* contrat *m* de location-vente
2 *vt* (a) *(worker)* engager
(b) *Br (car, equipment)* louer, prendre en location; **to hire sb's services** employer les services de qn

3 *vi (engage workers)* engager du personnel; **the personnel manager has the power to hire and fire** le chef du personnel a tous droits d'embauche et de renvoi

▸ **hire out** *vt sep Br (car, equipment)* donner en location; **to hire out one's services** offrir ses services

hired *adj Br (car, equipment)* de location

historical cost *n* ACCT coût *m* historique *ou* à l'origine

hit COMPTR 1 *n* hit *m*, contact *m* (de page); **this Web site counted 20,000 hits last week** ce site Web a été consulté 20 000 fois la semaine dernière
2 *vt (key)* appuyer sur

hi-tech = **high-tech**

▸ **hive off** *vt sep (money, profits)* séparer; **part of the industry was hived off to private ownership** une partie de cette industrie a été privatisée; **the subsidiary companies will be hived off** les filiales deviendront indépendantes

HNC *n Br (abbr Higher National Certificate)* = diplôme technique préparé en un an

HND *n Br (abbr Higher National Diploma)* = diplôme technique préparé en deux ans

hoarding *n Br (billboard)* panneau *m* d'affichage

hold 1 *n* **to put sb on hold** *(on telephone)* mettre qn en attente; **to be on hold** être en attente
2 *vt* (a) *(possess)* **to hold shares** détenir *ou* avoir des actions; **to hold 5% of the shares in a company** détenir 5% du capital d'une société; **to hold office** *(of chairperson, deputy)* être en fonction, remplir sa fonction; **to hold a seat on the board** avoir un siège au conseil d'administration; **she holds the post of treasurer** elle occupe le poste de trésorière
(b) *(conversation)* avoir; *(negotiations)* mener; **the meeting will be held at 2 o'clock** la réunion aura lieu à 14 heures; **interviews will be held in early May** les entretiens auront lieu début mai
(c) COMPTR *(store)* stocker; **how much data will this disk hold?** quelle quantité de données cette disquette peut-elle stocker?; **the commands are held in the memory** les instructions sont gardées en mémoire
(d) *(on telephone)* **hold the line please** ne quittez pas, s'il vous plaît; **hold all my calls** ne me passez aucun appel
3 *vi* (a) *(on telephone)* attendre; **the line's** *Br* **engaged** *or Am* **busy, will you hold?** la ligne est occupée, voulez-vous patienter?

(b) *(remain)* se maintenir; **prices held at the same level as last year** les prix se sont maintenues au même niveau que l'année dernière; **the pound held firm against the dollar** la livre s'est maintenue par rapport au dollar

▶ **hold over** *vt sep (payment)* arriérer, différer; *(meeting)* remettre, reporter; **payment was held over for six months** le paiement a été différé pendant six mois; **we'll hold these items over until the next meeting** on va remettre ces questions à la prochaine réunion

▶ **hold up** 1 *vt sep (delay)* retarder; **the goods were held up at customs** les marchandises ont été immobilisées à la douane
2 *vi* se maintenir; **the shares held up well** les actions se sont bien défendues; **the market is holding up well** le marché tient toujours

holder *n (of passport, permit, post, account, degree)* titulaire *mf*; *(of shares)* détenteur(trice) *m,f*; FIN *(of bonds, bill)* porteur (euse) *m,f*; *(of patent)* concessionnaire *mf*; *(of land)* propriétaire *mf*; *(of insurance policy)* assuré(e) *m,f*

holding *n* FIN *(shares in company)* participation *f*; **he has holdings in several companies** il est actionnaire de plusieurs sociétés ❏ *holding company* (société *f* en) holding *m*

> "
> A preferable alternative for both sides would be a merger. One way would be to form a **holding company** to which both banks would issue shares in proportion to their shareholders' funds. This would enable Hongkong Bank to avoid paying a packet for goodwill and for it to remain a Hongkong bank while Midland remained British.
> "

hole-in-the-wall machine *n Fam* BANKING distributeur *m* (de billets)

holiday *n* **(a)** *Br (vacation)* vacances *fpl*; **a month's holiday** un mois de vacances; **to be on/go on holiday** être/aller en vacances; **to get paid holidays** avoir les congés payés ❏ *holiday entitlement* congés *mpl* annuels
(b) *(day off)* (jour *m* de) congé *m*
(c) *(public)* jour *m* férié

home *n* **(a)** *(house)* **to work at** *or* **from home** travailler à domicile ❏ *home address* adresse *f* personnelle, domicile *m*; *home banking* banque *f* à domicile; *home loan* prêt *m* immobilier; *home ownership* accession *f* à la propriété; MKTG *home party*

selling vente *f* domiciliaire; *home shopping* téléachat *m*
(b) *(country)* ECON *home consumption* consommation *f* intérieure; *home market* marché *m* intérieur; *Br Home Office* ≃ Ministère *m* de l'Intérieur; *home products* produits *mpl* nationaux *ou* domestiques; *home sales* ventes *fpl* sur le marché intérieur; *home trade* commerce *m* intérieur
(c) COMPTR début *m* ❏ *home key* touche *f* début; *home page* page *f* d'accueil
(d) *Am home office (of company)* siège *m* social

homeowner *n* propriétaire *mf*

homeward *adj* de retour ❏ *homeward freight* fret *m* de retour; *homeward journey* voyage *m* de retour

homeworker *n* travailleur(euse) *m,f* à domicile

homeworking *n* travail *m* à domicile

homogeneous *adj* homogène ❏ MKTG *homogeneous shopping goods* produits *mpl* d'achat réfléchi homogènes

honour, *Am* **honor** *vt (cheque, bill of exchange)* honorer, payer; *(agreement, contract)* honorer

horizontal *adj horizontal communication* communication *f* horizontale; *horizontal integration* intégration *f* horizontale

horse-trading *n* négociations *fpl* acharnées; **a lot of horse-trading was required to clinch the deal** l'accord a été conclu à l'issu de négociations acharnées

host COMPTR 1 *n host computer* ordinateur-serveur *m*
2 *vt (Web site)* héberger

hostile takeover bid *n* OPA *f* hostile

> "
> The board of directors of the target company have to give their opinion on the offer and make it clear whether or not they recommend it. However, restrictions are placed on the power of management to combat a **hostile takeover bid**, for fear that they might act only in their own interests rather than for those of the company or its shareholders.
> "

hosting *n* COMPTR *(of Web site)* hébergement *m*

hot *adj* **(a)** TEL *hot line* numéro *m* d'urgence
(b) FIN *hot money* capitaux *mpl* fébriles *ou* flottants **(c)** COMPTR *hot key* touche *f* personnalisée

hotel *n* hôtel *m* ❑ *hotel accommodation* chambre *f* d'hôtel; *hotel bill* frais *mpl* de séjour à l'hôtel; *hotel manager* directeur(trice) *m,f* d'hôtel; *the hotel trade* l'industrie *f* hôtelière

hour *n* heure *f*; **to pay sb by the hour** payer qn à l'heure; **to be paid £5 an hour** être payé(e) 5 livres (de) l'heure; **an eight-hour day** une journée *f* (de travail) de huit heures

hourly *adj (rate, pay)* à l'heure, horaire

house *n* (a) *(company)* maison *f* ❑ FIN *house bill* double *m* de connaissement, lettre *f* de change creuse; *house magazine* journal *m* (interne) d'entreprise (b) ST EXCH **the House** la Bourse (de Londres)

household *n* ECON ménage *m* ❑ *household expenses* budget *m* du ménage; *household goods* biens *mpl* d'équipement ménagers; *household name* nom *m* de marque connu

householder *n (owner)* propriétaire *mf*; *(tenant)* locataire *mf*

house-to-house *adj (selling)* à domicile ❑ *house-to-house canvassing* porte-à-porte *m*, démarchage *m*

housing *n Br* ADMIN *housing association* = organisme d'aide au logement; *Br* ADMIN *housing benefit* ≃ allocation *f* logement; *housing market* marché *m* de l'immobilier

HP *n (abbr* **hire purchase**) achat *m* à crédit *ou* à tempérament

HQ *n (abbr* **headquarters**) QG *m*

HR *npl (abbr* **human resources**) RH *fpl*

HRM *n (abbr* **human resource management**) GRH *f*

HTML *n* COMPTR *(abbr* **Hyper Text Markup Language**) HTML

HTTP *n* COMPTR *(abbr* **Hyper Text Transfer Protocol**) protocole *m* HTTP

huckster *n Am Fam* agent *m* de publicité agressif

human *adj human resources* ressources *fpl* humaines; *human resource management* gestion *f* de ressources humaines

hype *Fam* **1** *n (publicity)* battage *m* publicitaire
2 *vt (publicize)* faire du battage publicitaire pour

▸ **hype up** *vt sep Fam (publicize)* faire du battage publicitaire pour

hyperinflation *n* hyperinflation *f*

hyperlink *n* COMPTR hyperlien *m*

hypermarket *n* hypermarché *m*

hypermedia *n* COMPTR hypermédia *m*

hypertext *n* COMPTR hypertexte *m*

hyphenation *n* COMPTR césure *m*

IAP n COMPTR (abbr **Internet Access Provider**) fournisseur m d'accès Internet

IBOR n (abbr **interbank offered rate**) taux m interbancaire offert

IBRD n (abbr **International Bank for Reconstruction and Development**) BIRD f

ICC n (abbr **International Chamber of Commerce**) CCI f

icon n COMPTR icône f

IDE n COMPTR (abbr **intelligent disk enhancement**) IDE

identifier n COMPTR identificateur m

idle adj (**a**) (employee) désœuvré(e); (factory, machine) arrêté(e); ST EXCH (markets) improductif(ive), dormant(e) (**b**) **to lie idle** (of money) dormir; **to let one's money lie idle** laisser dormir son argent (**c**) *idle time* temps m mort

IFA n (abbr **independent financial adviser**) conseiller(ère) m,f financier(ère) indépendant(e)

“

If you're considering making an investment, it's nearly always better to talk to an independent financial adviser (**IFA**). A company representative or agent will only tell you about his own firm's plans and so his advice will be limited. But an **IFA** can shop around for the best deals.

”

---

illegal adj illégal(e); COMPTR (character, file name, instruction) non autorisé(e)

illegally adv illégalement

illicit adj (trading, profits) illicite

illiquid adj non liquide □ *illiquid assets* actif m non-disponible ou immobilisé

illiquidity n non-liquidité f

ILO n (abbr **International Labour Organization**) OIT f

image n image f □ MKTG *image pricing* fixation f de prix en fonction de l'image; *image refresh rate* taux m de rafraîchissement d'images

IMF n ECON (abbr **International Monetary Fund**) FMI m

“

The European Investment Bank will make available up to Ecu 1bn (£685m) for loans to Poland and Hungary — another first. The traditional multilateral institutions, **IMF** and World Bank, are gearing up for a major contribution.

”

---

imitative product n MKTG produit m d'imitation

immobilization n FIN (of capital) immobilisation f

immobilize vt FIN (capital) immobiliser

immovable LAW **1** n **immovables** biens mpl immobiliers ou immeubles
2 adj *immovable property* biens mpl immobiliers ou immeubles

immunity n exemption f, exonération f (**from** de); **immunity from taxation** exemption ou exonération d'impôts

impact n impact m; **high wages have had a considerable impact on production costs** les salaires élevés ont eu un impact considérable sur les coûts de production □ ST EXCH *impact day* = jour où l'on annonce une nouvelle émission d'actions

imperfect adj imparfait(e) □ *imperfect competition* concurrence f imparfaite

impersonal accounts npl ACCT comptes mpl impersonnels

implement vt (plan, strategy, policy) exécuter, mettre en application; (law) appliquer

implementation n (of plan, strategy, policy) exécution f, application f; (of law) application; MKTG (of product) mise f en œuvre

implicit adj (cost, interest) implicite

import 1 n (**a**) (product) article m d'importation; **imports** (of country) importations fpl (**b**) (activity) importation f; **import and export** l'importation et l'exportation f □ *import agent* commissionnaire mf importateur(trice); *import ban* interdiction f d'importation; **to impose an import ban on sth** interdire qch d'importation; *import controls* contrôles mpl à l'importation; *import duty* droit m de douane à l'importation; *import firm* maison f

d'importation; **import licence** licence *f* d'importation; **import list** liste *f* des importations; *(of prices)* tarif *m* d'entrée; **import permit** permis *m* d'importer *ou* d'importation; **import quotas** contingents *mpl* d'importation; **import restrictions** restrictions *fpl* à l'importation; **import trade** commerce *m* d'importation; **import wholesaler** grossiste *m* importateur
2 *vt* **(a)** *(goods)* importer (**from** de)
(b) COMPTR importer (**from** depuis)

importation *n* **(a)** *(of goods)* importation *f*; **for temporary importation** en franchise temporaire **(b)** *Am (imported article)* article *m* d'importation, importation *f*

importer *n* *(person)* importateur(trice) *m,f*; *(country)* pays *m* importateur; **an oil importer** un pays importateur de pétrole

import-export *n* import-export *m* ❑ **import-export company** société *f* d'import-export

importing *adj* importateur(trice) ❑ **importing country** pays *m* importateur; **importing house** maison *f* d'importation

impose *vt* **to impose a tax on sth** taxer qch; **to impose a ban on sth** interdire qch; **the EU is in favour of imposing a ban on tobacco advertising** l'UE est en faveur d'interdire la publicité pour le tabac

imposition *n* *(of tax, ban)* imposition *f*

impound *vt* LAW *(goods)* confisquer, saisir; *(documents)* faire déposer au greffe

imprest *n* avance *f* ❑ **imprest account** compte *m* d'avances (à montant fixe); **imprest system** comptabilité *f* de prévision

“
In most businesses it is usual to keep a petty cash book for the payment of small expenses. This petty cash is kept on the **imprest system**, whereby the petty cashier is entrusted with a fixed sum of money. This is called the **imprest**, and out of this he or she makes all small payments.
„

improve *vi* s'améliorer; *(of prices, markets)* monter, être en hausse; **business is improving** les affaires reprennent; **the pound improved against the dollar** la valeur de la livre a augmenté par rapport à celle du dollar

▸ **improve on, improve upon** *vt insep* **to improve on sb's offer** offrir plus que qn

impulse buying *n* MKTG achats *mpl* spontanés *ou* d'impulsion

inactive *adj (money, bank account, Stock Market)* inactif(ive)

Inc *adj Am (abbr* **Incorporated**) ≃ SARL

incentive *n* *(payment)* prime *f*; MKTG stimulation *f*; *(reduction, free gift)* stimulant *m*, stimulateur *m* ❑ **incentive bonus** prime *f* d'encouragement *ou* de rendement; **incentive marketing** marketing *m* *ou* mercatique *f* de stimulation; **incentive pay** primes *fpl* de rendement; **incentive scheme** *(for buyers)* programme *m* de stimulation; *(for workers)* système *m* de primes

incidental 1 *n* **incidentals** faux frais *mpl*
2 *adj* **incidental costs, incidental expenses** faux frais *mpl*

in-clearing book *n* BANKING livre *m* du dedans, registre *m* des chèques à rembourser

include *vt* comprendre, inclure; *(in letter)* joindre; **up to and including 31 December** jusqu'au 31 décembre inclusivement; **the price includes VAT** la TVA est comprise (dans le prix)

inclusive *adj (price, sum)* net (nette); **from 4 to 12 February inclusive** du 4 au 12 février inclusivement; **inclusive of all taxes** toutes taxes comprises; **inclusive of VAT** TVA comprise

income *n* **(a)** *(of person)* revenu *m*; **to be on a low/high income** avoir un faible revenu/un revenu élevé; **their combined income totals $200,000** leurs revenus additionnés s'élèvent à 200 000 dollars; **the income from her investments** les revenus provenant de ses placements ❑ **income bracket, income group** tranche *f* de salaire *ou* de revenu; *Br* ADMIN **income support** ≃ RMI *m*; **income tax** impôt *m* sur le revenu; **income tax allowance** déduction *f* avant impôt, déduction fiscale; **income tax return** déclaration *f* de revenu; *(form)* feuille *f* d'impôt
(b) *(of company)* recettes *fpl*, revenus *mpl*; ACCT **income from operations** produits *mpl* de gestion courante *ou* d'exploitation ❑ ACCT **income account** compte *m* de produits; **income bond** valeur *f* de rendement; **income and expenditure account** compte *m* de dépenses et recettes; **incomes policy** politique *f* des revenus; **income smoothing** manipulations *fpl* comptables; *Am* ACCT **income statement** compte *m* de résultat; **income stock** valeurs *fpl* de placement

incoming 1 *n* FIN **incomings** recettes *fpl*, revenus *mpl*; **incomings and outgoings** dépenses *fpl* et recettes
2 *adj (telephone call)* de l'extérieur; *(fax)* en entrée; *(mail)* à l'arrivée

inconvenience *n* désagrément *m*; **we apologize for any inconvenience** veuillez nous excuser pour les désagréments occasionnés

inconvertible *adj* FIN inconvertible

incorporate 1 *vt (company)* constituer en société commerciale; *(banks)* réunir en société

2 *vi (form a corporation)* se constituer en société commerciale; *(merge)* fusionner

incorporated *adj Am* **Ross and Greene Incorporated** ≃ Ross and Greene SARL ❑ *incorporated company* ≃ société *f* à responsabilité limitée

incorporation *n (of company)* constitution *f* en société commerciale

incoterm *n (abbr* **international commercial term***)* incoterm *m*, terme *m* de commerce international

increase 1 *n (in price, rate, sales)* augmentation *f*, hausse *f* (**in** de); *(in salary)* augmentation (de salaire); **the increase in productivity/in the cost of living** l'augmentation de la productivité/du coût de la vie; **to be on the increase** être en hausse

2 *vt* augmenter; **we must increase output to 500 units a week** il faut augmenter la production à 500 unités par semaine

3 *vi* augmenter; **to increase by 10%** augmenter de 10%; **to increase in value** augmenter de valeur; **to increase in price** devenir plus cher (chère), augmenter de prix; **the growth rate is likely to increase** le taux de croissance va probablement augmenter

increased *adj* accru(e); **increased demand will lead to increased productivity** un accroissement de la demande entraînera une augmentation de la productivité

increment *n* augmentation *f*; **a salary of £36,000 plus annual increments of £4,000** un salaire de 36 000 livres avec augmentation annuelle de 4 000 livres

incremental *adj* croissant(e) ❑ *incremental cost* coût *m* marginal; *incremental increase* augmentation *f* régulière

incur *vt (risk)* courir; *(loss)* subir; *(debts)* contracter; *(expenses)* engager; **the expenses incurred amount to several thousand pounds** les dépenses engagées s'élèvent à plusieurs milliers de livres

indebted *adj* endetté(e); **to be heavily indebted to sb** devoir une forte somme à qn

indemnification *n* (**a**) *(act of compensation)* indemnisation *f*, dédom-

magement *m* (**b**) *(sum reimbursed)* indemnité *f*, dédommagement *m*

indemnify *vt* (**a**) *(compensate)* indemniser, dédommager (**for** de); **you will be indemnified for any losses incurred** vous serez indemnisé *ou* dédommagé de toutes les pertes subies (**b**) *(insure)* assurer, garantir (**against** contre); **to be indemnified against sth** être assuré(e) contre qch

> ❝
> A typical formula provides that the parent company will **indemnify** an expatriate against any loss or expense he may suffer as a result of a breach of contract by the subsidiary, for instance if the employment is terminated before the expiry of a specified fixed term.
> ❞

indemnity *n* (**a**) *(compensation)* indemnité *f*, dédommagement *m* (**b**) *(insurance)* assurance *f*, garantie *f*

indent 1 *n* (**a**) *Br (order)* commande *f* de marchandises ❑ *closed indent* commande spécifiant le fournisseur; *open indent* commande ne spécifiant pas le fournisseur (**b**) *(in text)* alinéa *m*

2 *vt (line of text)* mettre en retrait; **indent the first line** commencez la première ligne en retrait

3 *vi (at start of paragraph)* faire un alinéa

independent *adj* indépendant(e) ❑ *independent financial adviser* conseiller(ère) *m,f* financier(ère) indépendant(e); *independent income* revenus *mpl* indépendants; *independent retailer* détaillant(e) *m,f* indépendant(e)

index 1 *n* (**a**) *(in book, database)* index *m* (**b**) *(on index cards)* fichier *m* (**c**) *Am* FIN, ST EXCH *index arbitrage* arbitrage *m* sur indice; *index option* option *f* sur indice

2 *vt* (**a**) COMPTR *(database)* indexer (**b**) FIN *(wages, pension, payment)* indexer (**to** sur)

indexation *n* FIN indexation *f*

index-linked *adj* FIN indexé(e)

index-linking *n* FIN indexation *f*

indicator *n (sign)* indice *m*

> ❝
> The market often anticipates interest changes likely to come as a result of changes in economic **indicators** such as the inflation rate or the exchange rate. Thus, often gilt prices start to change direction before interest rate movements take place, as investors successfully anticipate the government's intentions.
> ❞

indirect *adj* indirect(e) ❏ *indirect costs* coûts *mpl* indirects; MKTG *indirect promotional expenditure* coûts de promotion indirects; *indirect selling* vente *f* indirecte; *indirect tax* impôt *m* indirect

indorse = **endorse**

induction course *n* stage *m* préparatoire *ou* de formation

industrial 1 *adj* (**a**) industriel(elle) ❏ *industrial accident* accident *m* du travail; *industrial action* grève *f*; **to take industrial action** se mettre en grève, faire grève; *industrial centre* centre *m* industriel; *industrial design* dessin *m* industriel; *industrial dispute* conflit *m* entre la direction et les travailleurs; *industrial espionage* espionnage *m* industriel; *industrial estate* zone *f* industrielle; *industrial injury* accident *m* du travail; *industrial injuries benefit* indemnité *f* pour accidents du travail; *industrial insurance* assurance *f* contre les accidents du travail; *the industrial machine* la machine industrielle; *industrial relations* relations *fpl* entre le patronat et les employés; *industrial training* formation *f* en entreprise; *industrial tribunal* ≃ conseil *m* de prud'hommes

(**b**) ECON *industrial unit* atelier *m*
(**c**) FIN *industrial bank* banque *f* industrielle; ST EXCH *industrial shares* valeurs *fpl* industrielles

2 *n* ST EXCH **industrials** valeurs *fpl* industrielles

industrialist *n* industriel *m*

industrialization *n* industrialisation *f*

industrialize 1 *vt* industrialiser
2 *vi* s'industrialiser

industrialized *adj* industrialisé(e) ❏ *industrialized countries* pays *mpl* industrialisés

> **44**
> National income, or its rate of growth, has most often been used in the West to indicate success. To many poorer countries, however, the idea of turning into a replica of one of the **industrialized countries**, pursuing high money incomes and high growth rates as goals in their own right, appears neither feasible nor desirable.
> **77**

industry *n* industrie *f*; **the building industry** l'industrie du bâtiment

inefficiency *n* inefficacité *f*

inefficient *adj* inefficace

inelastic *adj* (*demand*) fixe

inertia selling *n* MKTG vente *f* forcée

inexpensive *adj* bon marché, pas cher(chère)

infect *vt* COMPTR infecter

inferior *adj* (*goods, quality*) inférieur(e)

inflate *vt* (**a**) (*account*) grossir, charger; (*expense account, figures*) gonfler (**b**) ECON (*prices*) faire monter; **to inflate the currency** provoquer l'inflation monétaire

inflated *adj* ECON (*price*) exagéré(e); (*salaries*) gonflé(e) ❏ *inflated currency* inflation *f* monétaire

inflation *n* ECON inflation *f*; **inflation is down/up on last year** l'inflation est en baisse/en hausse par rapport à l'année dernière; **inflation now stands at 5%** l'inflation est maintenant à 5% ❏ *inflation tax* impôt *m* à la production

inflationary *adj* ECON inflationniste ❏ *inflationary spiral* spirale *f* inflationniste

> **44**
> ... the Finance Minister ... had said that it was not possible suddenly to remove controls on prices without creating an **inflationary spiral** in the ensuing price-wage explosion, although he agreed that the current pricing mechanism distorted prices and adversely affected supply and demand.
> **77**

inflation-proof *adj* protégé(e) contre les effets de l'inflation

inflow *n* afflux *m*; **the inflow of capital/of cheap imports** l'afflux de capitaux/de produits importés de mauvaise qualité

influencer *n* MKTG préconisateur *m*

influx *n* afflux *m*

info *n* Fam informations *fpl*, renseignements *mpl*; **a piece of info** une information, un renseignement

infoaddict *n* Fam COMPTR accro *mf* de l'Internet

infomercial *n* = publicité télévisée sous forme de débat sur l'annonceur et son produit

inform *vt* (*in letter*) **I am pleased to inform you that...** j'ai le plaisir *ou* l'honneur de vous informer que...; **I regret to inform you that...** j'ai le regret de vous faire savoir que...; **we are informed that...** on nous informe que...

information *n* (**a**) (*news, facts*) informations *fpl*, renseignements *mpl*; **a piece of information** une information, un renseignement; **I am sending you for your**

information... je vous envoie à titre d'information *ou* de renseignement... ❑ ADMIN *information copy* copie *f* pour information; *information services* marché *m* de l'information

(**b**) COMPTR information *f* ❑ *information retrieval* recherche *f* documentaire; *information society* société *f* de l'information; *information storage* mémorisation *f* des informations; *information superhighway* autoroute *f* de l'information; *information technology* informatique *f*

(**c**) *Am* TEL renseignements *mpl*

❝ ────────────
In addition the **information society** substitutes brain for brawn: 70 per cent of its jobs require intellectual skills and at least half of them require a professional qualification or education to degree standard.
──────────── ❞

informative advertising *n* MKTG publicité *f* informative

infrastructure *n* ADMIN infrastructure *f*

infringe *vt (agreement, rights)* violer, enfreindre; **to infringe a copyright** violer les droits d'auteur; **to infringe a patent** contrefaire un objet breveté

infringement *n (of agreement, rights)* violation *f*; **infringement of copyright** violation des droits d'auteur; **infringement of a patent** contrefaçon *f* d'un objet breveté

ingot *n* lingot *m*

inherent vice *n* INS vice *m* inhérent

inheritance *n* héritage *m* ❑ *inheritance tax* droits *mpl* de succession

inhibitor *n* MKTG inhibiteur *m*

in-home placement testing *n* MKTG test *m* à domicile par des consommateurs-témoins

in-house **1** *adj* interne; *(staff)* qui travaille sur place ❑ *in-house magazine* magazine *m* d'entreprise; *in-house training* formation *f* interne

2 *adv* sur place; **we prefer to train our staff in-house** nous préférons former notre personnel au sein de l'entreprise

initial **1** *adj* initial(e) ❑ *initial capital* capital *m* initial *ou* d'apport; *initial cost* coût *m* initial; *(of manufactured product)* prix *m* de revient; *initial expenditure* frais *mpl* de premier établissement; ST EXCH *initial margin* marge *f* initiale; *Am* ST EXCH *initial public offering* introduction *f* en Bourse; *initial stock* stock *m* de départ; *initial*

value valeur *f* de départ

2 *vt (letter, document, changes)* parapher

❝ ────────────
Software Etc Stores Inc, Edina, Minnesota filed with the Securities & Exchange Commission for an **initial public offering** of up to 800,000 common shares, all new at a target price of $15.50 a share and says it wants the $12m or so net proceeds to finance expansion.
──────────── ❞

initialization *n* COMPTR initialisation *f*

initialize *vt* COMPTR initialiser

initiator *n* MKTG initiateur *m*

inject *vt (money)* injecter (**into** dans); **they've injected billions of dollars into the economy** ils ont injecté des milliards de dollars dans l'économie

injection *n (of money)* injection *f* (**into** dans); **an injection of capital** une injection de capitaux

injunction *n* LAW injonction *f*; **to take out an injunction against sb** faire une demande d'injonction contre qn

injured party *n* LAW partie *f* lésée

ink *n* encre *f*

inkjet printer *n* COMPTR imprimante *f* à jet d'encre

Inland Revenue *n* *Br* **the Inland Revenue** ≃ le fisc

innovating company *n* MKTG entreprise *f* innovatrice

innovation *n* innovation *f*; **innovations in management techniques** des innovations en matière de gestion

innovative *adj* novateur(trice), innovateur(trice) ❑ MKTG *innovative product* produit *m* novateur

input **1** *n* (**a**) *(of production)* input *m*, entrée *f* ❑ ACCT *input tax* TVA *f* récupérée

(**b**) COMPTR *(action)* entrée *f*, introduction *f*; *(data)* données *fpl* (en entrée) ❑ *input device* périphérique *m* d'entrée

(**c**) *(during meeting, discussion)* contribution *f*; **we'd like some input from marketing before committing ourselves** nous aimerions consulter le service marketing avant de nous engager

2 *vt* COMPTR *(data)* entrer

input/output *n* COMPTR entrée/sortie *f* ❑ *input/output device* périphérique *m* d'entrée/sortie

inquire 1 *vt* demander
2 *vi* se renseigner (**about** sur)

inquiry *n* demande *f* de renseignements; **to make inquiries (about sth)** se renseigner (sur qch); **with reference to your inquiry of 5 May,...** *(in letter)* en réponse à votre demande du 5 mai,... ◻ *inquiry office* bureau *m* de renseignements

insert COMPTR 1 *n* insertion *f* ◻ *insert key* touche *f* d'insertion; *insert mode* mode *m* (d')insertion
2 *vt* insérer

insider *n* FIN, ST EXCH **the insiders** les initiés *mpl* ◻ *insider dealing, insider trading* délit *m* ou opération *f* d'initié

"

Leaving aside for one moment the arguments advanced earlier about the morality of **insider dealing**, the use of inside information to compensate managers and entrepreneurs is not without its practical difficulties. First, **insider dealing** is an unpredictable form of reward; in fact the opportunity to exploit inside information may come only "once every ten years for each listed company".

"
---

insolvency *n (of person)* insolvabilité *f*; *(of company)* faillite *f*

insolvent *adj (person)* insolvable; *(company)* en faillite; **to declare oneself insolvent** *(of person)* se déclarer insolvable; *(of company)* déposer son bilan

inspect *vt (documents, goods)* examiner; *(premises, factory, staff)* inspecter; *(equipment)* vérifier, inspecter; *(books)* contrôler

inspection *n (of documents, goods)* examen *m*; *(of premises, factory, staff)* inspection *f*; *(of equipment)* vérification *f*, inspection; *(of books)* contrôle *m*; **to buy goods on inspection** acheter des marchandises sur examen ◻ CUSTOMS *inspection order* bon *m* de visite

inspector *n* inspecteur(trice) *m,f* ◻ *Am inspector general* inspecteur général; *Br Inspector of Taxes* inspecteur des impôts

instability *n* instabilité *f* (financière)

install, *Am* **instal** *vt* (**a**) *(machinery, equipment)* installer; **to install sb in a post** mettre qn à un poste (**b**) COMPTR *(software)* installer

instalment, *Am* **installment** *n (part payment)* acompte *m*, versement *m*; **to pay in** or **by instalments** payer par versements échelonnés ◻ *Am installment plan* vente *f* à tempérament; **to buy sth on the installment plan** acheter qch à tempérament *ou* à crédit

installer *n* COMPTR programme *m* d'installation

installment *Am* = **instalment**

instant *adj (access to savings)* immédiat(e)

instant-access *adj (bank account)* à accès immédiat

"

The distinction between sight and time deposits has become increasingly blurred in recent years, with interest being paid on current accounts and with **instant-access**, no-penalty, high-interest accounts.

"
---

institute *vt* **to institute proceedings against sb** intenter un procès contre qn

institution *n (organization)* institution *f*; *(public, financial)* établissement *m*

institutional *adj* **institutional advertising** publicité *f* institutionnelle; FIN **institutional buying** achats *mpl* institutionnels; *institutional investors* investisseurs *mpl* institutionnels

in-store *adj* MKTG **in-store advertising** PLV *f*, publicité *f* sur le lieu de vente; *in-store advertising space* espace *m* de PLV, espace de publicité sur le lieu de vente; *in-store demonstration* démonstration *f* sur le lieu de vente

instruction *n* COMPTR **instructions** *(in program)* instructions *fpl* ◻ *instruction manual* guide *m* de l'utilisateur

instrument *n* FIN effet *m*, titre *m*; LAW instrument *m*, acte *m* juridique ◻ *instrument of incorporation* statut *m*, acte *m* de constitution; *instrument to order* papier *m* à ordre

insufficient *adj* insuffisant(e) ◻ BANKING *insufficient funds* provision *f* insuffisante, insuffisance *f* de provision

insurable *adj* assurable ◻ *insurable interest* intérêt *m* pécuniaire

insurance *n* assurance *f*; *(cover)* garantie *f* (d'assurance), couverture *f*; *(premium)* prime *f* (d'assurance); **to take out insurance (against sth)** prendre une assurance (contre qch); **how much do you pay in insurance?** combien payez-vous (de prime) d'assurance? ◻ *insurance adviser* assureur-conseil *m*; *insurance agent* agent *m* d'assurance(s); *insurance broker* courtier(ère) *m,f* d'assurance(s); *insurance charges* frais *mpl* d'assurance; *insurance claim* demande *f* d'indemnité; *(for more serious damage)* déclaration *f* de sinistre; **to make an**

insurance claim faire une demande d'indemnité; *(for more serious damage)* faire une déclaration de sinistre; *insurance company* société *f* d'assurances; *insurance cover* couverture *f*; *insurance group* groupe *m* d'assurance; *insurance money* indemnité *f* d'assurance; *insurance policy* police *f* d'assurance; **to take out an insurance policy** contracter une assurance; *insurance portfolio* portefeuille *m* d'assurances; *insurance premium* prime *f* d'assurance; *insurance value* valeur *f* d'assurance

insure 1 *vt* assurer (**against** contre); **to insure one's life** s'assurer sur la vie; **we're insured against flooding** nous sommes assurés contre les inondations
2 *vi* **to insure against sth** s'assurer *ou* se faire assurer contre qch

insured 1 *n* assuré(e) *m,f*
2 *adj* assuré(e) (**against** contre) ❑ *insured value* valeur *f* assurée

insurer *n* assureur *m*

intangible 1 *n* **intangibles** valeurs *fpl* immatérielles, actif *m* incorporel
2 *adj* ACCT *intangible asset* valeur *f* immatérielle, actif *m* incorporel; *intangible fixed assets* immobilisations *fpl* incorporelles

integrated *adj* COMPTR *integrated package* logiciel *m ou* progiciel *m* intégré; *integrated software* logiciel *m* intégré

integration *n* intégration *f*, concentration *f*

> **"**
> Formerly, East German companies had strong vertical and horizontal **integration** with activities separate from the core business, and large numbers of employees. There were no separately managed service industries other than those dictated by the core business such as agriculture and manufacturing.
> **"**

integrative growth *n* croissance *f* par intégration

intellectual property *n* propriété *f* intellectuelle

intelligent terminal *n* COMPTR terminal *m* intelligent

intensive distribution strategy *n* MKTG stratégie *f* de distribution intensive

intention-to-buy-scale *n* MKTG échelle *f* des intentions d'achat

interactive *adj* COMPTR interactif(ive)

interbank *adj* interbancaire ❑ *interbank loan* prêt *m* de banque à banque *ou* entre banques; *interbank market* marché *m* interbancaire; *interbank offered rate* taux *m* interbancaire offert

interbranch *adj* entre succursales *(d'une même entreprise)*

intercept interview *n* MKTG entretien *m* spontané

intercompany *adj* intersociété ❑ *intercompany transactions* transactions *fpl* inter-sociétés

interdepartmental *adj* interdéparte-mental(e)

interest *n* (**a**) FIN *(on loan, investment)* intérêt(s) *m(pl)* (**on** sur); **interest paid** intérêts versés; **interest payable** intérêt exigible; **to bear** *or* **yield interest** porter intérêt, rapporter; **to bear** *or* **yield 5% interest** rapporter du 5% *ou* un intérêt de 5%; **to pay interest** payer des intérêts ❑ *interest charges* intérêts (à payer); *(on overdraft)* agios *mpl*; *interest and dividend income* produits *mpl* financiers; *interest rate* taux *m* d'intérêt; **the interest rate is 4%** le taux d'intérêt est de 4%; ST EXCH *interest rate swap* échange *m* de taux d'intérêt
(**b**) *(stake)* intérêts *mpl*; **our firm's interests in Europe** les intérêts de notre société en Europe; **to have a financial interest in sth** avoir investi financièrement dans qch; **to have an interest in the profits** participer aux bénéfices; **his interest in the company is £10,000** il a une commandite de 10 000 livres

interest-bearing *adj* productif(ive) d'intérêts ❑ *interest-bearing capital* capital *m* productif d'intérêts; *interest-bearing loan* prêt *m* à intérêt; *interest-bearing securities* titres *mpl* qui produisent des intérêts

interested party *n* LAW partie *f* intéressée

interest-free *adj* sans intérêt ❑ *interest-free credit* crédit *m* gratuit; *interest-free loan* prêt *m* sans intérêt

interface *n* COMPTR interface *f*

interim *adj* intérimaire ❑ *interim accounts* comptes *mpl* semestriels; FIN *interim dividend* dividende *m* intérimaire; ACCT *interim profit and loss statement* compte *m* de résultat prévisionnel; *interim report* rapport *m* intérimaire; ACCT *interim statement* bilan *m* intérimaire

intermediary *n* intermédiaire *mf*

intermediate *adj* FIN *intermediate broker* intermédiaire *mf*, remisier *m* (en

Bourse); *intermediate credit* crédit *m* à moyen terme; *intermediate goods* biens *mpl* intermédiaires

internal *adj* (a) *(trade, flight)* intérieur(e) ❏ *internal audit* audit *m* interne; *internal auditor* audit *ou* auditeur(trice) *m,f* interne; *internal check* contrôle *m* interne; *internal company document* document *m* interne à l'entreprise; *internal mail* courrier *m* interne; *Am internal rate of return* taux *m* de rentabilité interne; *internal revenue* recettes *fpl* fiscales; *Am the Internal Revenue Service* ≃ le fisc

(b) COMPTR *internal drive* unité *f* (de disque) interne; *internal modem* modem *m* interne

international *adj* international(e) ❏ *International Bank for Reconstruction and Development* Banque *f* internationale pour la reconstruction et le développement; *International Chamber of Commerce* Chambre *f* de commerce internationale; *International Labour Organization* Bureau *m* international du travail; *international law* droit *m* international; *International Monetary Fund* Fonds *m* monétaire international; *international money market* marché *m* monétaire international; *international reply coupon* coupon-réponse *m* international; *International Standards Organization* Organisation *f* internationale de normalisation; *international trading corporation* société *f* de commerce international

> **"**
> At international level, the **International Labour Organization** (ILO) and the World Health Organization (WHO) collaborate to produce various recommendations which seek to establish worldwide standards of safety with the purpose of preventing avoidable accidents at work.
> **"**

Internet *n* COMPTR Internet *m*; to surf the Internet naviguer sur l'Internet ❏ *Internet access provider* fournisseur *m* d'accès Internet; *Internet account* compte *m* Internet; *Internet address* adresse *f* Internet; *Internet banking* opérations *fpl* bancaires par l'Internet; *Internet connection* connexion *f* à l'Internet; *Internet number* numéro *m* Internet; *Internet phone* téléphone *m* Internet; *Internet protocol* protocole *m* Internet; *Internet Relay Chat* service *m* de bavardage Internet, canal *m* de dialogue en direct; *Internet service provider* fournisseur *m* de services Internet; *Internet surfer* internaute *mf*; *Internet surfing*

navigation *f* sur l'Internet, surf *m* sur l'Internet; *Internet telephone* téléphone *m* Internet

interpret 1 *vt* interpréter
2 *vi* faire l'interprète

interpreter *n* interprète *mf*

intervention price *n* EU prix *m* d'intervention

interview 1 *n* *(for job)* entretien *m*; to give sb an interview faire passer un entretien à qn; to call sb for interview convoquer qn pour un entretien; interviews will be held at our London offices les entretiens se dérouleront dans nos bureaux de Londres
2 *vt* *(for job)* faire passer un entretien à; shortlisted candidates will be interviewed in March les candidats sélectionnés seront convoqués pour un entretien en mars

interviewee *n* *(for job)* candidat(e) *m,f* (à qui l'on fait passer un entretien)

interviewer *n* *(for job)* = personne qui fait passer un entretien

intestate *adj* to die intestate mourir intestat

Intranet *n* COMPTR Intranet *m*

intrapreneur *n* = personne chargée de lancer de nouveaux projets au sein d'une entreprise

in-tray *n* corbeille *f* du courrier à traiter

intrinsic value *n* ST EXCH valeur *f* intrinsèque

introduce *vt* *(product)* lancer; ST EXCH *(shares)* introduire

introduce-a-friend scheme *n* MKTG offre-ami *f*

introduction *n* (a) ST EXCH introduction *f* au marché hors cote (b) MKTG *introduction stage* *(of product)* phase *f* d'introduction

introductory *adj* MKTG *introductory offer* offre *f* de lancement; *introductory price* prix *m* de lancement

intruder *n* COMPTR intrus(e) *m,f*

invalid *adj* *(argument, objection, document)* non valable; COMPTR *(file name)* invalide

invalidate *vt* *(contract, document)* invalider

invalidity *n* (a) *Br* ADMIN *invalidity benefit* prestation *f* d'invalidité; *invalidity pension* pension *f* d'invalidité (b) *(of contract, document)* invalidité *f*

inventory *n* (a) *(list)* inventaire *m*; to draw up *or* take an inventory dresser *ou* faire un inventaire ❏ *inventory book* livre *m* d'inventaires; *inventory of fixtures* état *m* des lieux; *inventory management* gestion *f* de l'inventaire

(b) *(stock)* stock(s) *m(pl)* ❏ *inventory account* compte *m* de stock; *inventory control* contrôle *m* des stocks; *inventory level* niveau *m* des stocks; *inventory management* gestion *f* des stocks; *inventory turnover* rotation *f* des stocks; *inventory valuation* valorisation *f* des stocks

invest FIN **1** *vt (money)* placer, investir; *(capital)* investir; **to invest money in a business** mettre de l'argent *ou* placer des fonds dans un commerce; **they invested five million dollars in new machinery** ils ont investi cinq millions de dollars dans de nouveaux équipements

2 *vi* investir, faire des placements; **to invest in shares/in the oil industry** investir en actions/dans l'industrie pétrolière; **to invest in property** faire des placements dans l'immobilier; **we're going to invest in three new machines** nous allons investir dans trois nouvelles machines; **she's been investing on the Stock Market** elle a investi en Bourse

investment *n* FIN placement *m*, investissement *m*; *(money invested)* investissement, mise *f* de fonds; **are these shares a good investment?** ces actions sont-elles un bon placement?; **property is no longer such a safe investment** l'immobilier n'est plus un placement aussi sûr; **I'd prefer a better return on investment** je préférerais un investissement plus rentable; **the company has investments all over the world** la société a des capitaux investis dans le monde entier ❏ *investment account* compte *m* d'investissement; *investment adviser* conseiller(ère) *m,f* en placements; *investment analyst* analyste *mf* en placements; *investment appraisal* appréciation *f* des investissements; *Am investment bank* banque *f* d'affaires; *Am investment banking* banque *f* d'affaires; *investment company* société *f* d'investissements; *investment fund* fonds *m* commun de placement; *investment grant* subvention *f* d'investissement; *investment income* revenu *m* provenant d'investissements; *investment institution* société *f* d'investissements; *investment instrument* instrument *m* de placement; *investment market* marché *m* des capitaux; *investment portfolio* portefeuille *m* d'investissements; *investment securities, investment stock* valeurs *fpl* en portefeuille *ou* de placement; *investment trust* société *f* de placement

investor *n* FIN investisseur *m*; *(shareholder)* actionnaire *mf*

invisible ECON **1** *n* invisibles invisibles *mpl* **2** *adj invisible asset* actif *m* incorporel,

immobilisation *f* (incorporelle); *invisible earnings* gains *mpl* invisibles; *invisible exports* exportations *fpl* invisibles; *invisible imports* importations *fpl* invisibles; *invisible trade* commerce *m* de services

> **❝**
>
> Payments for actual physical goods are not the only items involved in international trade. Debts also arise between countries because of services performed by one country for another. Because one cannot actually see such services they are referred to as "**invisible**" exports or imports. ... Payment for shipping services, income from tourism, banking services and interest payments from international loans are other examples of **invisibles**.
>
> **❞**

invite *vt* **(a)** *(ask)* **to invite sb for interview** convoquer qn pour un entretien; **we invite applications from all qualified candidates** nous invitons tous les candidats ayant le profil requis à postuler **(b)** FIN **to invite bids** *or* **tenders** faire un appel d'offres

invoice 1 *n* facture *f*; **to make out an invoice** établir *ou* faire une facture; **to settle an invoice** régler une facture; **as per invoice** conformément à la facture; **payment should be made within 30 days of invoice** les factures doivent être réglées sous 30 jours; **payable against invoice** à payer à réception de la facture ❏ *invoice date* date *f* de facturation; *invoice of origin* facture originale; *invoice price* prix *m* facturé *ou* de facture

2 *vt (goods)* facturer, porter sur une facture; *(person, company)* envoyer la facture à; **to invoice sb for sth** facturer qch à qn

invoicing *n (of goods)* facturation *f* ❏ *invoicing machine* machine *f* à facturer

inward *adj inward bill of lading* connaissement *m* d'entrée; *inward charges (of ship)* frais *mpl* à l'entrée; *inward customs clearance* entrée *f* en douane; *inward investment* investissements *mpl* étrangers; ACCT *inward payment* paiement *m* reçu

I/O *n* COMPTR *(abbr* **input/output***)* E/S *f*

IOU *n (abbr* **I owe you***)* reconnaissance *f* de dette

IP *n* COMPTR *(abbr* **Internet Protocol***)* IP *address* adresse *f* IP; *IP number* numéro *m* IP

IPO *n Am* ST EXCH *(abbr* **initial public offering***)* introduction *f* en Bourse

IRC *n* COMPTR *(abbr* **Internet Relay Chat***)* IRC, service *m* de bavardage Internet, canal *m* de dialogue en direct

irrecoverable *adj (debt)* irrécouvrable

irredeemable FIN **1** *n* **irredeemables** obligations *fpl* non amortissables
2 *adj (funds, share)* non remboursable; *(bill)* non convertible ❑ ***irredeemable bond*** obligation *f* non amortissable

irregularity *n (in accounts)* irrégularité *f*; **there were some irregularities in the paperwork** il y avait quelques irrégularités dans les écritures

irregulars *npl Am* articles *mpl* de deuxième qualité *ou* de qualité moyenne

irrevocable *adj* BANKING *(letter of credit)* irrévocable

IRS *n Am (abbr* **Internal Revenue Service)** **the IRS** ≃ le fisc

ISDN 1 *n* COMPTR *(abbr* **integrated services digital network)** RNIS *m* ❑ ***ISDN line*** ligne *f* RNIS
2 *vt Fam* **to ISDN sth** envoyer qch par RNIS

> **"**
> Digital networks, in the form of **ISDN** (integrated services digital network) have been talked about for many years, and in mainly technical terms. But most major countries have now digitised at least parts of their telephone networks, and international services are increasingly compatible. So it is getting cheaper for carriers to connect their large customers via **ISDN** rather than leased lines or conventional analogue links.
> **"**

ISO *n (abbr* **International Standards Organization)** ISO *f*

ISP *n* COMPTR *(abbr* **Internet Service Provider)** fournisseur *m* de services Internet

issue 1 *n* **(a)** FIN, ST EXCH *(of banknotes, money orders, shares)* émission *f* ❑ ***issue premium*** prime *f* d'émission; ***issue price*** prix *m* d'émission **(b)** ADMIN ***issue card*** carte *f* (de) sortie de stock
2 *vt* FIN, ST EXCH *(banknotes, money orders, shares)* émettre; *(bill)* créer; *(new edition, prospectus)* publier; *(letter of credit)* fournir; **to issue a draft on sb** fournir une traite sur qn

issued *adj* FIN, ST EXCH ***issued capital*** capital *m* émis; ***issued securities*** titres *mpl* émis

issuing *adj* FIN, ST EXCH émetteur(trice) ❑ ***issuing bank*** banque *f* émettrice; ***issuing company*** société *f* émettrice; ***issuing house*** banque *f* émettrice

IT *n* COMPTR *(abbr* **information technology)** l'informatique *f*

item *n* **(a)** *(article)* article *m*; **please send us the following items** prière de nous envoyer les articles suivants **(b)** ACCT article *m*, écriture *f*; ***item of expenditure*** article *m* de dépense **(c)** *(in list, contract)* article *m*; *(on agenda)* question *f*

itemize *vt (bill, account)* détailler ❑ ***itemized bill*** facture *f* détaillée

J/A, j/a *n* BANKING (*abbr* **joint account**) compte *m* joint

Java *n* COMPTR Java *m* □ *Java script* langage *m* Java

jet lag *n* fatigue *f* due au décalage horaire

jet-lagged *adj* fatigué(e) par le décalage horaire

jingle *n* MKTG jingle *m*, sonal *m*

JIT *adj* (*abbr* **just in time**) juste à temps, JAT □ *JIT production* production *f* juste à temps ou JAT

job *n* (**a**) (*employment, post*) travail *m*, emploi *m*; **to look for a job** chercher du travail ou un emploi; **to lose one's job** perdre son emploi; **to be out of a job** être sans travail ou emploi □ ADMIN *job analysis* analyse *f* de la tâche; *job assignment* assignation *f* des tâches; *job classification* classification *f* des emplois; *job creation* création *f* d'emplois; *job description* description *f* de poste; *job enrichment* enrichissement *m* des tâches; *job evaluation* évaluation *f* des tâches; *job offer* offre *f* d'emploi; *job opportunities* débouchés *mpl*; *job rotation* rotation *f* des postes; *job satisfaction* satisfaction *f* dans le travail; *job security* sécurité *f* d'emploi; *job sharing* partage *m* d'emploi; *job specification* spécification *f* de la fonction; *job title* fonction *f*

(**b**) (*piece of work, task*) tâche *f*, travail *m*; **to do a job** faire un travail

(**c**) *job lot* lot *m*; **to buy sth as a job lot** acheter qch en lot; **they sold off the surplus as a job lot** ils ont vendu tout l'excédent en un seul lot

> These costs were attributed to job dissatisfaction caused by boring, repetitive work. A senior manager at AT&T, one American organization which experimented extensively with **job enrichment**, was quoted as saying, "This company has lost too many people who are still with us" (Ford, 1969).

▸ **job out** *vt sep* sous-traiter; **they jobbed out the work to three different firms** ils ont confié le travail à trois sous-traitants

jobber *n* (*piece worker*) ouvrier(ère) *m,f* à la tâche

jobbing *n* ouvrage *m* à la tâche

Jobcentre *n Br* ≃ agence *f* nationale pour l'emploi, ANPE *f*

jobless **1** *npl* **the jobless** les sans-emploi *mpl*
2 *adj* sans emploi

Jobseekers allowance *n Br* allocation *f* (de) chômage

job-share **1** *n* emploi *m* partagé
2 *vi* partager un emploi

join *vt* (*company*) entrer dans; (*union*) devenir membre de

joining fee *n* COMPTR frais *mpl* d'accès au service

joint *adj* (*statement, decision, agreement, responsibility*) commun(e); (*contract*) (*between two parties*) bilatéral(e); (*between more than two parties*) collectif(ive) □ BANKING *joint account* compte *m* joint; *joint beneficiary* bénéficiaire *mf* conjoint(e); *joint commission* commission *f* mixte; *joint creditor* cocréancier(ère) *m,f*; *joint debtor* codébiteur(trice) *m,f*; *joint enterprise* entreprise *f* en participation; LAW *joint liability* responsabilité *f* conjointe; *joint obligation* coobligation *f*; *joint ordering* groupage *m* de commandes; *joint owner* copropriétaire *mf*; **to be joint owners of sth** posséder ou détenir qch en commun; *joint ownership* copropriété *f*; *joint partnership* coassociation *f*; INS *joint policy* police *f* conjointe; *joint production* coproduction *f*; *joint purchase* coacquisition *f*; *joint report* rapport *m* collectif; LAW *joint and several liability* responsabilité *f* solidaire et indivise; *joint shares* actions *fpl* indivises; *joint stock* capital *m* social; *joint surety* cautionnement *m* solidaire; *joint tenant* colocataire *mf*; *joint venture* entreprise *f* commune; *joint venture agreement* accord *m* de partenariat; *joint venture company* société *f* d'exploitation en commun

jointly *adv* conjointement; **we manage the firm jointly** nous sommes cogérants de la maison; LAW **jointly liable** conjointement responsable; **jointly and severally liable** responsables conjointement et solidairement

joint-stock *adj Br* FIN *joint-stock bank* banque *f* de dépôt; *joint-stock company* société *f* (anonyme) par actions

journal *n* (**a**) ACCT *(for transactions)* livre *m* de comptes, (livre) journal *m* □ *journal entry* écriture *f* comptable (**b**) *(magazine)* revue *f*

judg(e)ment *n* (**a**) LAW jugement *m*; **to pass judgement on sb/sth** porter un jugement sur qn/qch (**b**) MKTG *judgement sample* échantillon *m* discrétionnaire

judg(e)mental *adj* MKTG *judgemental forecasting* prévision *f* par estimation; *judgemental method* méthode *f* estimative

judicial *adj* judiciaire □ *judicial enquiry* enquête *f* judiciaire; *Am judicial review* examen *m* d'une décision de justice

jumbo trade *n* ST EXCH opération *f* jumbo

jump **1** *n (rise)* hausse *f* (**in** de); **there has been a sudden jump in house prices** il y a eu une flambée des prix de l'immobilier
2 *vi (rise)* faire un bond, monter en flèche

junior **1** *n (in rank)* subalterne *mf*
2 *adj (in rank)* subalterne; **to be junior to sb** être au-dessous de qn □ *junior executive* jeune cadre *m*; *Br junior partner* jeune associé(e) *m,f*

junk *n* FIN, ST EXCH *junk bond* obligation *f* à haut rendement mais à haut risque; *junk mail* courrier *m* publicitaire

> Corporate restructuring on a large scale began with the development of the **junk bond** market in the USA in the 1980s. **Junk bonds** were used to finance leveraged buyouts and takeovers, with the aim of extracting value from existing bondholders and shareholders.

jurisdiction *n* juridiction *f*; **this matter does not come within our jurisdiction** cette matière n'est pas de notre compétence

justification *n* COMPTR justification *f* □ *left justification* justification *f* à gauche; *right justification* justification *f* à droite

justified *adj* COMPTR justifié(e); **left/right justified** justifié à gauche/droite

justify *vt* COMPTR justifier

just-in-time *adj* juste à temps □ *just-in-time production* production *f* juste à temps; *just-in-time purchasing* achat *m* juste à temps

> Production cannot be "**just-in-time**" when parts are imported from thousands of miles away in Japan. At Georgetown, Toyota keeps three days' worth of stocks of imported parts, compared with 1.5 days' worth of American parts — or four hours' worth at its Japanese plants.

K *n* (**a**) (*abbr* **thousand, thousand pounds**) **he earns 30K** il gagne 30 000 livres (**b**) COMPTR (*abbr* **kilobyte**) KO *m*; **how many K are left?** combien de KO reste-t-il?; **720K diskette** disquette *f* de 720 KO

kaffir *n Fam* ST EXCH valeur *f* or sudafricaine

kangaroo *n Fam* ST EXCH valeur *f* australienne

KB *n* COMPTR (*abbr* **kilobyte**) KO *m*

kbps COMPTR (*abbr* **kilobytes per second**) ko/s

keen *adj* (*competition*) acharné(e); (*prices*) compétitif(ive)

keep *vt* (**a**) **to keep the books** tenir la comptabilité *ou* les comptes; **to keep a note of sth** noter qch (**b**) (*have in stock*) vendre; **we don't keep computer accessories** nous ne vendons pas d'accessoires informatiques

▸ **keep down** *vt sep* (*prevent from increasing*) empêcher d'augmenter; **we must keep our expenses down** il faut que nous limitions nos dépenses; **our aim is to keep prices down** notre but est d'empêcher les prix d'augmenter

▸ **keep up** *vt sep* (*prices*) maintenir ferme

kerb *n Fam* ST EXCH **to buy/sell on the kerb** acheter/vendre après la clôture officielle de la Bourse; **business done on the kerb** opérations *fpl* effectuées en coulisse *ou* après clôture de Bourse ▫ **kerb broker** coulissier *m*, courtier(ère) *m,f* en valeurs mobilières; **kerb market** marché *m* hors cote, coulisse *f*

> But the occasional $500m-worth of speculative trading on the Korean Stock Exchange on a single day — as happened on January 17th — and a booming **kerb market** make it clear that a great deal of loose cash is still swirling around.

kerbstone market *n Fam* ST EXCH marché *m* hors cote, coulisse *f*

key **1** *n* COMPTR (*of sort, identification*) indicatif *m*, critère *m*; (*button*) touche *f* ▫ **key combination** combinaison *f* de touches
2 *adj* clé ▫ MKTG **key account** compte-clé *m*; **key factor** facteur *m* clé; **key industry** industrie *f* clé; **key person** pivot *m*; **key post** poste *m* clé; **key staff** personnel *m* de base
3 *vt* COMPTR (*data, text*) taper, saisir

▸ **key in, key up** *vt sep* COMPTR (*data, text*) taper, saisir

key-account *adj* MKTG **key-account management** gestion *f* de comptes-clés; **key-account sales** ventes *fpl* aux comptes-clés

keyboard **1** *n* (*of typewriter, computer*) clavier *m* ▫ **keyboard layout** disposition *f* de clavier; **keyboard skills** compétences *fpl* de claviste
2 *vt* (*data, text*) taper, saisir
3 *vi* introduire des données par clavier

keyboarder *n* COMPTR claviste *mf*, opérateur(trice) *m,f* de saisie

keypad *n* COMPTR pavé *m*

keystroke *n* COMPTR frappe *f* (de touche); **keystrokes per minute/hour** vitesse *f* de frappe à la minute/à l'heure

keyword *n* COMPTR mot *m* clé

kick *vt Fam* **to kick sb upstairs** = donner une promotion à qn dont on veut se débarrasser

kickback *n Fam* dessous-de-table *m*, pot-de-vin *m*

killing *n Fam* **to make a killing** s'en mettre plein les poches

kilobyte *n* COMPTR kilo-octet *m*

kindly *adv* (*in letter*) **kindly remit by cheque** prière de nous couvrir par chèque; **kindly reply by return of post** prière de répondre par retour de courrier

kite *n Fam* FIN traite *f* en l'air, billet *m* de complaisance; **to fly** *or* **to send up a kite** tirer en l'air *ou* à découvert ▫ **kite flyer** tireur *m* en l'air *ou* à découvert

kiting *n Fam* FIN tirage *m* en l'air *ou* à découvert

▸ **knock down** *vt sep* (*price*) baisser; (*salesman*) faire baisser; **I managed to knock him down to $500** j'ai réussi à le faire baisser à 500 dollars

knockdown price *n Br Fam* **for sale at knockdown prices** en vente à des prix imbattables; **I got it for a knockdown price** je l'ai eu pour trois fois rien

knocking copy *n* MKTG publicité *f* comparative dénigrante

knock-on effect *n* répercussions *fpl*, contrecoup *m*; **businesses are feeling the knock-on effect of a strong pound** les entreprises subissent le contrecoup d'une livre forte

know-how *n* savoir-faire *m*; *(technical)* know-how *m*

krona *n* couronne *f* (suédoise)

krone *n* *(in Norway)* couronne *f* (norvégienne); *(in Denmark)* couronne (danoise)

label 1 *n* étiquette *f*
  2 *vt* étiqueter

labelling, *Am* **labeling** *n* étiquetage *m*

labor, laborer *etc Am* = **labour, labourer** *etc*

labour, *Am* **labor** *n* (**a**) *(work)* travail *m* (**b**) *(workers)* main-d'œuvre *f* □ *Am* **labor contract** contrat *m* de travail; **labour costs** (coût *m* de la) main-d'œuvre; **labour dispute** conflit *m* du travail; **labour force** effectifs *mpl*; ECON *(of country)* population *f* active; **labour market** marché *m* du travail; **labour relations** relations *fpl* sociales

labourer, *Am* **laborer** *n* ouvrier(ère) *m,f*

labour-intensive, *Am* **labor-intensive** *adj* qui dépend d'une main-d'œuvre considérable

labour-saving, *Am* **labor-saving** *adj* qui facilite le travail □ **labour-saving device** appareil *m* facilitant le travail

lack 1 *n* *(of capital, workers)* manque *m* (**of** de)
  2 *vt* manquer de; **we lack the necessary resources** nous n'avons pas les ressources nécessaires

lading *n* (**a**) *(of ship)* chargement *m* (**b**) *(of goods)* embarquement *m*, mise *f* à bord

lag *n* retard *m*, décalage *m*; **there was a lag between completion and publication** il y a eu un décalage entre l'achèvement de l'œuvre et sa publication

laggard *n* MKTG traînard(e) *m,f*

laisser-faire, laissez-faire *n* ECON laisser-faire *m* □ **laisser-faire policy** politique *f* de laisser-faire

lame duck *n* *(company)* canard *m* boîteux

> **❝**
> Anglo-Welsh claim that their offer is "extremely generous". However, they know that your Company is not a **lame duck**, but widely described as one of the best managed in the industry.
> **❞**

LAN *n* COMPTR *(abbr* **local area network***)* réseau *m* local

land 1 *n* LAW terre(s) *f(pl)* □ **land register** cadastre *m*; **land registry (office)** bureau *m* du cadastre; **land tax** impôt *m* foncier
  2 *vt (goods)* décharger, débarquer

landed *adj* (**a**) ACCT **landed costs** coûts *mpl* fonciers; **landed property** propriété *f* foncière *ou* territoriale; **landed proprietor** propriétaire *mf* terrien(enne) (**b**) **landed cost** *(of goods)* prix *m* à quai

landing *n* *(of goods)* déchargement *m* □ **landing certificate** certificat *m* de déchargement; **landing charges** frais *mpl* de déchargement; **landing order** permis *m* de débarquement

landscape *n* COMPTR paysage *m*; **to print sth in landscape** imprimer qch en paysage □ **landscape mode** mode *m* paysage

lapse 1 *n* LAW (**a**) *(of right, patent)* déchéance *f* (**b**) **lapse of time** laps *m* de temps; **after a lapse of three months** après un délai de trois mois
  2 *vi* (**a**) LAW *(of right, patent)* se périmer, tomber en désuétude (**b**) *(of subscription, insurance policy)* expirer

laptop *n* COMPTR portable *m*

laser *n* COMPTR laser *m* □ **laser disk** disque *m* laser; **laser printer** imprimante *f* laser

last *adj* (**a**) ST EXCH **last trading day** dernier jour *m* de cotation (**b**) **last in, first out** dernier entré premier sorti

late *adj* (**a**) *(behind schedule)* en retard □ **late delivery** livraison *f* retardée; **late payment** retard *m* de paiement
  (**b**) MKTG **late adopter** utilisateur(trice) *m,f* tardif(ive); **late entrant** concurrent(e) *m,f* tardif(ive); **late entry** lancement *m* tardif
  (**c**) ST EXCH **late trading** opérations *fpl* de clôture

latent defect *n* vice *m* caché

launch 1 *n* *(of product, project)* lancement *m*; **the launch of a new job creation scheme** le lancement d'un nouveau programme de création d'emplois
  2 *vt* (**a**) *(product, project)* lancer; **to launch a £3m cash bid** lancer une offre au comptant de 3 millions de livres (**b**) ST EXCH *(company)* introduire en Bourse; *(shares)* émettre

launching *n* *(of product, project)* lancement *m*

launder *vt (money)* blanchir

> **"**
>
> Unlike the rest of Europe, including even Switzerland, it is not a criminal offence to **launder** money in Germany, although a bill proposed last week would force credit institutes to identify customers who make transactions worth more than £10,500, or place deposits above £17,500.
>
> **"**

LAUTRO n INS (abbr **Life Assurance and Unit Trust Regulatory Organization**) = organisme britannique chargé d'établir des codes de conduite à l'usage des compagnies d'assurance-vie et des sociétés d'investissement, et de veiller à leur respect

law n (**a**) (rule) loi f; ECON **the law of supply and demand** la loi de l'offre et de la demande (**b**) (system of justice) droit m; Br **to go to law** aller en justice □ **law court** cour f de justice; **law department** service m du contentieux

lawful adj (legal) légal(e); (rightful) légitime □ **lawful currency** cours m légal; **lawful owner** possesseur m légitime; **lawful trade** commerce m licite

lawsuit n action f en justice; **to bring a lawsuit against sb** intenter une action (en justice) contre qn

lawyer n avocat(e) m,f; (for wills, conveyancing) notaire m; (in company) conseiller(ère) m,f juridique

▸ **lay in** vt sep (goods, stock) faire provision de

▸ **lay off** vt sep (**a**) (make redundant) licencier; (temporarily) mettre en chômage technique (**b**) INS **to lay off a risk** effectuer une réassurance

lay-away plan n Am vente f réservée ou à terme

lay-off n licenciement m; (temporary) chômage m technique □ Am **lay-off pay** indemnité f de licenciement

layout n (**a**) (of building) agencement m (**b**) (of plan) étude f, tracé m

LBO n FIN (abbr **leveraged buy-out**) OPA f à crédit

L/C n (abbr **letter of credit**) l/c f

LCD n COMPTR (abbr **liquid crystal display**) affichage m à cristaux liquides, LCD m □ **LCD screen** écran m LCD

LCL n (abbr **less-than-container load**) conteneur m chargé en partie

lead n (**a**) **lead time** (for production) délai m de production; (for delivery) délai m de livraison (**b**) MKTG **lead user** utilisateur(trice) m,f pilote

leader n (**a**) MKTG (product) numéro m un (sur le marché); (company) chef m de file, leader m; Am (loss leader) produit m d'appel (**b**) ST EXCH valeur f vedette

leading adj principal(e); **a leading shareholder** un des principaux actionnaires; **one of the leading firms in the country** une des plus importantes entreprises du pays □ **leading indicators** principaux indicateurs mpl économiques; Am **leading price indicator** indice m composite des principaux indicateurs; **leading share** valeur f dirigeante ou vedette

leaflet n prospectus m □ **leaflet drop** distribution f de prospectus

learning curve n courbe f d'assimilation

> **"**
>
> The process of making anything from a switch to a civil airliner is subject to improvements in speed, quality and cost reduction which follow the characteristic **learning curve**. It is obviously important to the managers of such organisations to be able to predict by how much the process will improve after particular lengths of time and numbers of products made.
>
> **"**

lease **1** n (of property) bail m; (of equipment) location f; (of land) affermage m; (document) (contrat m de) bail; **the lease runs out in May** le bail expire en mai; **to sign a lease** signer un bail □ ACCT **lease charges** charges fpl locatives; **lease contract** (for property) contrat de bail; (for equipment) contrat en location; **lease financing** leasing m, location f avec option d'achat; ACCT **lease revenue** loyers mpl

2 vt (**a**) (of owner) (property) louer ou céder à bail; (equipment) louer; (land) affermer (**b**) (of leaseholder) (property) prendre à bail, louer; (equipment) louer; (land) prendre en fermage

▸ **lease back** vt sep = prendre en location quelque chose que l'on a vendu

▸ **lease out** vt sep (property) louer ou céder à bail; (equipment) louer; (land) affermer

lease-back n cession-bail f

leased line n COMPTR ligne f louée

leasehold **1** n (contract) bail m; (property) location f à bail **2** adj loué(e) à bail

leaseholder n locataire mf

leasing n (of property) location f à bail; (of equipment) location; (of land) affermage m; (system) crédit-bail m, leasing m □ **leasing company** société f de leasing

leave n (holiday) congé m; **to be on leave** être en congé; **to take two weeks' leave** prendre deux semaines de congé ❑ **leave of absence** congé m exceptionnel; **leave pay** salaire m de congé

LED n COMPTR (abbr **light-emitting diode**) DEL f

ledger n ACCT grand-livre m

left arrow n COMPTR flèche f vers la gauche ❑ **left arrow key** touche f de déplacement à gauche

leftover stock n restes mpl

legacy n LAW legs m; **to leave sb a legacy** faire un legs ou laisser un héritage à qn; **to come into a legacy** faire un héritage

legal 1 adj (lawful) légal(e); (judicial) juridique ❑ **legal action** action f en justice; **to take legal action against sb** intenter une action (en justice) contre qn; **to take legal advice** consulter un avocat; **legal adviser** conseiller(ère) m,f juridique; **to have a legal claim to sth** avoir légalement droit à qch; **legal department** (in company) service m du contentieux; **legal dispute** litige m; **legal document** acte m authentique, document m juridique; **legal entity** personne f morale; **legal expenses** frais mpl de justice; **legal owner** propriétaire mf légitime; **legal proceedings** poursuites fpl judiciaires; **to take legal proceedings against sb** engager des poursuites judiciaires contre qn; **legal status** statut m légal, statut juridique; **to be legal tender** avoir cours (légal)

2 n Am (paper size) légal m (216mm × 356mm)

legality n légalité f

legalization n légalisation f

legalize vt légaliser

legally adv légalement; **to act legally** agir légalement ou dans la légalité; **to be legally binding** avoir force de loi; **legally responsible** responsable en droit

leisure industry n industrie f du temps libre ou des loisirs

lend vt prêter; **to lend sth to sb, to lend sb sth** prêter qch à qn; **to lend money at interest** prêter de l'argent à l'intérêt

lender n (person) prêteur(euse) m,f; (institution) organisme m de crédit; **lender of last resort** prêteur m en dernier ressort

lending n prêt m ❑ **lending bank** banque f de crédit; **lending limit** plafond m de crédit

less prep **the purchase price less 10%** le prix d'achat moins 10%; **interest less tax amounts to £50** les intérêts nets s'élèvent à 50 livres

lessee n locataire mf (à bail)

lessor n bailleur(eresse) m,f

let 1 n location f; **a short/long let** une location de courte/longue durée
2 vt louer; **to let** (sign) à louer

let-out clause n clause f échappatoire

letter n (a) (communication) lettre f; **to notify sb by letter** informer qn par lettre; **your letter of 4 October** votre lettre (en date) du 4 octobre ❑ **letter of acknowledgement** accusé m de réception; ST EXCH **letter of allotment** avis m d'attribution ou de répartition; **letter of apology** lettre d'excuse; **letter of application** (for job) lettre de demande d'emploi; ST EXCH (for shares) lettre de souscription; **letter of appointment** lettre de nomination ou d'affectation; **letter of complaint** lettre de réclamation; **letter of confirmation** lettre de confirmation; **letter of dismissal** lettre de licenciement; **letter of indemnity** cautionnement m, lettre de garantie; **letter of reference** lettre de recommandation
(b) **letters patent** brevet m d'invention, lettres fpl patentes
(c) BANKING **letter of advice** lettre f d'avis; **letter of credit** lettre de crédit; **letter of exchange** lettre de change; **letter of guaranty** lettre d'aval; **letter of intent** lettre d'intention
(d) Am (paper size) lettre f (216mm × 279mm)

letterhead n en-tête m; (paper) papier m à en-tête

letting adj location f ❑ **letting agency** agence f de location

level 1 n (of salaries, prices) niveau m; **to maintain prices at a high level** maintenir les prix à un niveau élevé
2 vt niveler

▶ **level off, level out** vi (of prices, demand, sales) se stabiliser, s'équilibrer

leverage n FIN (gearing) effet m de levier; (as percentage) ratio m d'endettement

leveraged adj **the company is highly leveraged** la société est fortement endettée ❑ **leveraged buy-out** rachat m d'entreprise financé par l'endettement; **leveraged management buy-out** rachat d'entreprise par les salariés

> ❝
> AMI is 65 per cent owned by American Healthcare International, the US group. The parent company is subject of a £1.3bn **leveraged buy-out** from IMA, an investor group.
> ❞

levy 1 n (**a**) *(activity)* prélèvement m; **a capital levy of 10%** un prélèvement de 10% sur le capital (**b**) *(tax)* impôt m, droit m; **to impose a levy on imports** taxer les importations

2 vt *(tax)* prélever; **to levy a duty on goods** imposer des marchandises, prélever une taxe sur les marchandises

liability n (**a**) LAW *(responsibility)* responsabilité f (**for** de); **to admit liability for sth** reconnaître être responsable de qch (**b**) ACCT, FIN **liabilities** *(debts)* passif m

liable adj (**a**) LAW *(responsible)* responsable (**for** de); **to be held liable for sth** être tenu(e) (pour) responsable de qch; **to be liable for sb's debts** répondre des dettes de qn; **employers are liable for their staff's mistakes** les employeurs sont responsables des erreurs de leur personnel (**b**) *(to tax)* assujetti(e) (**to** à)

liaise vi **to liaise with sb** *(be in contact with)* assurer la liaison avec qn; *(work together with)* collaborer avec qn

liaison n *(contact)* liaison f; *(co-operation)* collaboration f

libel n LAW diffamation f; **to sue for libel** intenter un procès en diffamation □ *libel laws* lois fpl contre la diffamation

LIBOR n Br FIN *(abbr* **London Inter-Bank Offer Rate**) ≃ TIOP m

licence, Am **license**[1] n *(to manufacture, sell)* licence f; **to manufacture/sell sth under licence** fabriquer/vendre qch sous licence □ *licence agreement* contrat m de concession; *licence holder* titulaire mf d'une licence

license[2] vt accorder une licence à; **to be licensed to manufacture/sell sth** avoir l'autorisation de fabriquer/vendre qch

licensed adj sous licence □ *licensed brand name* nom m de marque sous licence; *licensed product* produit m sous licence

licensee n titulaire mf d'une licence

licensing n autorisation f □ *licensing requirements* conditions fpl d'autorisation

lien n LAW privilège m, droit m de rétention; **vendor's lien** privilège du vendeur; **lien on shares** nantissement m d'actions

lieu n **in lieu** à la place; **in lieu of** au lieu de; **take Thursday off in lieu** prenez jeudi à la place; **we get days off in lieu of overtime** on nous accorde des jours de congé en plus pour compenser les heures supplémentaires

life n (**a**) *life annuity* rente f viagère; *life pension* pension f à vie; *life tenant* usufruitier(ère) m,f

(**b**) INS *life assurance, life insurance* assurance f sur la vie, assurance-vie f (**c**) FIN *(of loan)* durée f □ *life expectancy (of product)* durée f (utile)

lifecycle n MKTG *(of product)* cycle m de vie □ *lifecycle chart* courbe f du cycle de vie

lifestyle n MKTG *lifestyle analysis* analyse f du style de vie; *lifestyle segmentation* segmentation f par styles de vie

LIFFE n *(abbr* **London International Financial Futures Exchange**) = marché à terme d'instruments financiers

> 〈〈
>
> In the UK, all financial futures contracts are traded on the London International Financial Futures Exchange (**LIFFE**) which opened in 1982. Members of **LIFFE** include banks, member firms of the ISE, money and commodity brokers, discount houses and individual traders (known as locals) who trade on their own account.
>
> 〉〉

LIFO *(abbr* **last in, first out**) DEPS

light 1 n COMPTR *light pen* stylo m optique **2** adj (**a**) *(market, trading)* faible □ *light industry* industrie f légère (**b**) MKTG *light user* faible utilisateur(trice) m,f

limit 1 n (**a**) *(restriction)* limitation f; **to put** or **set a limit on sth** limiter qch; **the limit on Japanese imports** la limitation des importations japonaises (**b**) ST EXCH *limit order* ordre m limite

2 vt limiter; **we're trying to limit costs** nous essayons de limiter les coûts

limitation n *(restriction)* limitation f

limited adj (**a**) *(market)* étroit(e), restreint(e); *(expenditure)* réduit(e) □ *limited edition* (édition f à) tirage m limité; LAW *limited liability* responsabilité f limitée (**b**) *limited company* ≃ société f à responsabilité limitée; *limited partner* commanditaire m; *limited partnership* société f en commandite

line n (**a**) *(telephone connection)* ligne f; **hold the line please** ne quittez pas; **the line's very bad** la communication est mauvaise; **she's on the other line** elle est sur l'autre ligne (**b**) *(of goods)* ligne f, série f; **a new line of office furniture** une nouvelle ligne de meubles de bureau; **line of credit** ligne f de crédit □ MKTG *line addition* ajout m à la ligne; *line extension* extension f de ligne; *line filling* consolidation f de ligne; *line stretching* extension de ligne (**c**) *(in hierarchy)* *line management* organisation *f* hiérarchique; *line manager* chef *m* hiérarchique; *line organization* organisation *f* hiérarchique; *line and staff management* structure *f* mixte

(d) COMPTR *line feed* changement *m* de ligne; *line spacing* interlignage *m*, espacement *m* de lignes

link *n* COMPTR lien *m*

liquid *adj* (a) FIN liquide □ *liquid assets, liquid capital* actif *m* liquide, liquidités *fpl*; *liquid debt* dette *f* liquide (b) *liquid paper (correction fluid)* liquide *m* correcteur

liquidate *vt* FIN *(company, debt)* liquider; *(capital)* mobiliser; ST EXCH *to liquidate a position* liquider une position

liquidation *n* FIN *(of company, debt)* liquidation *f*; *(of capital)* mobilisation *f*; *to go into liquidation (of company)* entrer en liquidation, déposer son bilan

liquidator *n (of company)* liquidateur(trice) *m,f*

liquidity *n* FIN *(of company, debt)* liquidité *f* □ BANKING *liquidity ratio* ratio *m* de liquidité

> **"**
>
> The ratio of an institution's liquid assets to illiquid assets is known as its **liquidity ratio**. For example, if a bank had £100 million of assets, of which £10 million were liquid and £90 million were illiquid, the bank would have a 10 per cent **liquidity ratio**. If a financial institution's **liquidity ratio** is too high, it will make too little profit. If the ratio is too low, there will be the risk that customers' demands may not be able to be met.
>
> **"**

lira *n* lire *f*

list 1 *n* (a) *(of bills, assets, liabilities)* liste *f*; FIN, ST EXCH **list of applicants** *(for loan, shares)* liste des souscripteurs

(b) ST EXCH **list of quotations** bulletin *m* des cours

(c) BANKING **list of investments** (bordereau *m* de) portefeuille *m*; **list of bills for collection/for discount** bordereau d'effets à l'encaissement/à l'escompte

(d) *list price (of product)* prix *m* (de) catalogue

2 *vt* (a) *(enter in list)* faire une liste de; *(goods)* inventorier; ST EXCH **to be listed on the Stock Exchange** être coté(e) en Bourse

(b) COMPTR lister

listed *adj* ST EXCH *listed company* société *f* cotée en Bourse; *listed securities, listed stock* valeurs *fpl* admises *ou* inscrites à la cote officielle

listing *n* (a) ST EXCH admission *f* à la cote officielle; **to have a listing** être coté(e) en Bourse □ *listing agreement* dossier *m* de demande d'introduction en Bourse (b) COMPTR listing *m* □ *listing paper* papier *m* continu, papier listing

literature *n (information)* documentation *f*

litigant *n* LAW partie *f*

litigate LAW 1 *vt* contester (en justice)
2 *vi* intenter une action en justice

litigation *n* LAW action *f* en justice

livelihood *n* moyens *mpl* de subsistance, gagne-pain *m*; **to lose one's livelihood** perdre son gagne-pain

lively *adj* FIN *(market)* animé(e)

living *n (livelihood)* vie *f*; **what do you do for a living?** qu'est-ce que vous faites dans la vie? □ *living allowance* indemnité *f* de séjour; *living expenses* frais *mpl* de séjour; *living wage* minimum *m* vital

Lloyd's name *n* Br INS membre *m* du syndicat d'assurances Lloyds

LMBO *n (abbr* **leveraged management buy-out***)* rachat *m* d'entreprise par les salariés

load 1 *n (of ship, lorry)* charge *f*, chargement *m* □ *load carrying capacity* charge utile; *load limit* charge limite

2 *vt* (a) *(ship, lorry)* charger; *(goods)* embarquer; **the ship is loading grain** on est en train de charger le navire de céréales

(b) INS *(premium)* majorer

(c) COMPTR charger

3 *vi* (a) *(of ship, lorry)* charger; **the ship is loading** le navire est en cours de chargement

(b) COMPTR *(of software, program)* se charger

▸**load up** *vt sep* (a) *(ship, lorry)* charger
(b) COMPTR charger

loaded *adj* (a) *(ship, lorry)* chargé(e) (b) INS *loaded premium* prime *f* majorée, surprime *f*

loading *n (of ship, lorry)* chargement *m*; *(of goods)* embarquement *m* □ *loading bay* aire *f* de chargement; *loading dock* embarcadère *m*; *loading point* point *m* de chargement

loan 1 *n (money lent)* prêt *m*; *(money borrowed)* emprunt *m*; **to take out a loan** faire un emprunt; **to apply for a loan** demander un prêt; **to repay a loan** rembourser un emprunt; ACCT **loans and advances to customers** créances *fpl* clients; ACCT **loans outstanding** encours *m*; **loan at interest** prêt à intérêt; **loan at call, loan repayable on demand** prêt remboursable sur demande; **loan at notice** prêt à terme;

loan on collateral prêt sur gage *ou* sur nantissement; **loan on mortgage** prêt hypothécaire *ou* sur hypothèque; **loan on overdraft** prêt à découvert; **loan on securities** emprunt sur titres ❑ BANKING *loan account* compte *m* de prêt; *loan agreement* contrat *m* de prêt; *loan back* cession-bail *f*; ACCT *loan capital* capital *m* sur prêt; *loan certificate* titre *m* de prêt; *loan charges* frais *mpl* financiers; *loan company* société *f* de crédit; *loan department* service *m* des crédits; *loan guarantee scheme* prêts bonifiés d'aide au développement des entreprises; *loan market* marché *m* des prêts; *loan maturity* échéance *f* emprunt; FIN *loan note* titre *m* d'obligation, titre de créance; *loan office* organisme *m* de crédit; *loan repayment insurance* assurance *f* crédit; *loan risk cover* couverture *f* du risque de crédit; *loan stock* emprunt *m* obligataire
2 *vt* prêter

local *adj* local(e) ❑ *local agent* agent *m* sur le terrain; COMPTR *local area network* réseau *m* local; *local authority* administration *f* locale; *(in town)* municipalité *f*; TEL *local call* communication *f* locale; *local currency* monnaie *f* locale

> ❝
> The **local area network** (LAN) arrived in the early 80s as a means of sharing expensive equipment. But over the last decade the cost of hardware has dropped, the perceived value of information has risen, and the LAN has become most significant for its information-sharing capabilities.
> ❞

localization *n* COMPTR localisation *f*

localize *vt* COMPTR localiser

locate *vi (of company, factory)* s'installer, s'établir

location *n (of company, factory)* emplacement *m*; **the company has moved to a new location** la société a déménagé ❑ MKTG *location pricing* fixation *f* des prix selon l'endroit

lock *vt* COMPTR verrouiller

▸ **lock into** *vt sep* **to be locked into sth** *(pension scheme)* ne pas pouvoir changer de qch; *(contract)* être lié(e) par qch; *(company)* être totalement dépendant(e) de qch

▸ **lock out** *vt sep (workers)* lock-outer

▸ **lock up** *vt sep (capital)* immobiliser, bloquer

lockout *n (of workers)* lock-out *m*

loco 1 *adj* loco ❑ *loco price* prix *m* loco
2 *adv* loco; **the prices are loco Hull** les prix incluent le transport jusqu'à Hull

lodge *vt* (**a**) *(claim)* déposer; **to lodge a complaint** porter plainte; **she lodged a formal complaint with the authorities** elle a déposé une plainte officielle auprès de l'administration (**b**) *(money)* consigner, déposer; **to lodge securities with a bank** déposer des titres dans une banque

log file *n* COMPTR fichier *m* compte-rendu

▸ **log in** = **log on**

▸ **log off** COMPTR 1 *vt sep* faire sortir
2 *vi* sortir

▸ **log on** COMPTR 1 *vt sep* faire entrer
2 *vi (of user)* entrer, ouvrir une session; *(to remote system)* entrer en communication; **to log onto a system** se connecter à un système

▸ **log out** = **log off**

logical *adj* COMPTR logique

logic circuit *n* COMPTR circuit *m* logique

logo *n* logo *m*

Lombard rate *n* BANKING taux *m* Lombard

long 1 *n* ST EXCH **longs** titres *mpl* longs, obligations *fpl* longues
2 *adj* *long credit* crédit *m* à long terme; ST EXCH *long position* position *f* acheteur *ou* longue; **to take a long position** acheter à la hausse, prendre une position longue
3 *adv* ST EXCH **to go long** acheter à la hausse, prendre une position longue

long-dated *adj* FIN à longue échéance ❑ *long-dated bill* billet *m* à longue échéance; *long-dated securities* titres *mpl* longs, obligations *fpl* longues

long-distance 1 *adj (telephone call)* longue distance
2 *adv* **to telephone long-distance** faire un appel longue distance

long-range *adj (forecast)* à long terme

longshoreman *n Am* docker *m*

longstanding *adj* de longue date ❑ *longstanding accounts* vieux comptes *mpl*

long-term *adj (loan, policy)* à long terme ❑ FIN *long-term bond* obligation *f* à long terme; ACCT *long-term borrowings* emprunts *mpl* à long terme; ACCT *long-term capital* capitaux *mpl* permanents; *long-term credit* crédit *m* à long terme; *long-term financing* financement *m* à long terme; *long-term interest rate* taux *m* d'intérêt à long terme; ACCT *long-term investments* immobilisations *fpl* financières; ***long-term planning*** planification *f* à long terme

look-up table *n* COMPTR table *f* de recherche *ou* de référence

loophole *n* *(in law, contract)* vide *m* juridique

loose *adj* (**a**) *(goods)* en vrac (**b**) ***loose insert*** encart *m* libre

lorry *n* Br camion *m* ❑ ***lorry driver*** chauffeur *m* de poids lourd

lose **1** *vt* *(custom, market share, job, money)* perdre; **his shop is losing money** son magasin perd de l'argent; **they are losing their markets to the Koreans** ils perdent leurs marchés au profit des Coréens
2 *vi* perdre; **the dollar is losing in value** le dollar baisse

▸ **lose out** *vi* perdre; **to lose out on a deal** être perdant(e) dans une affaire; **will the Americans lose out to the Japanese in computers?** les Américains vont-ils perdre le marché de l'informatique au profit des Japonais?

loser *n* FIN valeur *f* en baisse

loss *n* (**a**) *(of custom, market share, job)* perte *f*; **she's seeking compensation for loss of earnings** elle cherche à se faire rembourser le manque à gagner; **the closure will cause the loss of hundreds of jobs** la fermeture provoquera la disparition de centaines d'emplois
(**b**) *(financial)* déficit *m*; **to make a loss** perdre de l'argent, être déficitaire; **to run at a loss** *(of business)* tourner à perte; **to sell sth at a loss** vendre qch à perte; **the company announced losses** *or* **a loss of £4m** la société a annoncé un déficit de 4 millions de livres; **we made a loss of 10% on the deal** nous avons perdu 10% dans l'affaire ❑ MKTG ***loss leader*** produit *m* d'appel; ***loss leader price*** prix *m* d'appel; ***loss leader pricing*** fixation *f* d'un prix d'appel
(**c**) INS sinistre *m*; **to estimate the loss** évaluer le sinistre ❑ ***loss adjuster*** expert *m* en assurances; ***loss assessment*** fixation *f* des dommages;
(**d**) *(of product being manufactured or transported)* freinte *f* ❑ ***loss in transit*** freinte de route

loss-making *adj* déficitaire

lot *n* (**a**) FIN, ST EXCH *(of bonds, shares)* paquet *m*; **in lots** par lots; **to buy/sell in one lot** acheter/vendre en bloc ❑ ***lot number*** numéro *m* de lot; ***lot size*** unité *f* de transaction
(**b**) *(at auction)* lot *m*; **lot 49 is a set of five paintings** le lot 49 est un ensemble de cinq tableaux
(**c**) *(piece of land)* terrain *m*

lottery *n* (**a**) FIN ***lottery loan*** emprunt *m* à lots (**b**) Br ***lottery funding*** *(from National Lottery)* = fonds provenant de la loterie nationale

low **1** *n* niveau *m* bas; **the share index has reached a new low** l'indice des actions est descendu à son plus bas niveau; **inflation is at an all-time low** l'inflation est à son niveau le plus bas; ST EXCH **the highs and lows** les hauts et les bas
2 *adj* *(cost, price, interest rate)* bas (basse), faible; *(salary)* peu élevé(e); **prices are at their lowest** les prix sont au plus bas

low-end *adj* MKTG bas de gamme

lower¹ *vt* *(prices, interest rate)* baisser

lower² *adj* ***lower case*** bas *m* de casse, (lettres *fpl*) minuscules *fpl*; ***lower limit*** plancher *m*

lower-case *adj* en bas de casse, en (lettres) minuscules

lower-income group *n* groupe *m* de contribuables à revenus moyens

low-grade *adj* de qualité inférieure

low-involvement *adj* MKTG *(purchasing)* à faible participation des consommateurs

loyal-customer discount *n* MKTG remise *f* de fidélité au client

loyalty *n* MKTG ***loyalty card*** carte *f* de fidélité; ***loyalty discount*** remise *f* de fidélité

Ltd Br *(abbr* **limited***)* ≃ SARL; **Dragon Software Ltd** ≃ Dragon Software SARL

lucrative *adj* lucratif(ive)

lump sum *n* somme *f* forfaitaire; **to be paid in a lump sum** être payé(e) en une seule fois

luncheon voucher *n* Br ticket restaurant *m*, ticket-repas *m*

luxury *adj* de luxe ❑ ***luxury goods*** articles *mpl* de luxe; ***luxury tax*** taxe *f* de luxe

machine *n (device, computer)* machine *f* □ COMPTR **machine code** code *m* machine; **machine hour** heure *f* machine; COMPTR **machine language** langage *m* machine; **machine production** production *f* en série; **machine shop** atelier *m* d'usinage; **machine tool** machine-outil *f*; **machine work** travail *m* à la machine

machine-down time *n* = durée d'immobilisation d'une machine

machine-produced *adj* fait(e) à la machine *ou* en série

machine-readable *adj* COMPTR lisible par ordinateur

machinery *n* **(a)** *(machines)* machines *fpl*, machinerie *f* **(b)** *(of organization, government)* rouages *mpl*

machining *n* usinage *m*

macro *n* COMPTR macro *f* □ **macro language** macrolangage *m*

macroeconomics *n* macroéconomie *f*

macroenvironment *n* macroenvironnement *m*

MAD *n* ACCT *(abbr* **mean absolute deviation**) écart *m* moyen absolu

mad dog *n Fam (company)* société *f* en pleine expansion; **there are several rising mad dogs in the IT sector** il existe plusieurs sociétés en pleine expansion dans le secteur de l'informatique

made *adj* fait(e), fabriqué(e); **made in France** *(on product)* fabriqué en France

magnate *n* magnat *m*; **he's one of the biggest computer magnates** c'est un des plus grands magnats de l'informatique

magnetic *adj* COMPTR **magnetic card** carte *f* magnétique; **magnetic card reader** lecteur *m* de cartes magnétiques; **magnetic disk** disque *m* magnétique; *(floppy)* disquette *f* magnétique; **magnetic strip** *(on card)* piste *f* magnétique; **magnetic tape** bande *f* magnétique

mail 1 *n* **(a)** *(letters, parcels)* courrier *m*; **has the mail arrived?** est-ce que le courrier est arrivé?

(b) *(postal service)* poste *f*; **to put sth in the mail** mettre qch à la poste; **by mail** par la poste □ **mail order** vente *f* par correspondance; **to buy sth by mail order** acheter qch par correspondance; **mail order**

catalogue catalogue *m* de vente par correspondance; **mail order company** maison *f* de vente par correspondance; **mail specialist** vépéciste *m*; MKTG **mail survey** enquête *f* postale

(c) COMPTR courrier *m* électronique □ **mail forwarding** réexpédition *f* du courrier électronique; **mail gateway** passerelle *f* (de courrier électronique); **mail path** chemin *m* du courrier électronique

2 *vt (letter, parcel)* poster

mailbox *n* COMPTR boîte *f* à *ou* aux lettres

mailing *n* MKTG, COMPTR *(mailshot)* publipostage *m*, mailing *m* □ **mailing list** fichier *m* d'adresses; **mailing shot** publipostage, mailing

mailmerge *n* COMPTR publipostage *m*

mailshot *n* MKTG publipostage *m*, mailing *m*

main *adj* principal(e) □ **main branch** *(of shop, bank)* établissement *m* principal; ST EXCH **main market** = marché principal de la Bourse de Londres; **main office** bureau *m* principal; *(headquarters)* siège *m* (social); ECON **main product** produit *m* principal

mainframe *n* COMPTR mainframe **(computer)** ordinateur *m* central

maintain *vt (relations, contact)* entretenir; *(exchange rate, output)* maintenir; **we must maintain our position as market leader** nous devons maintenir notre position de leader sur le marché

maintenance *n (of building, equipment)* entretien *m* □ **maintenance costs** frais *mpl* d'entretien; **maintenance equipment** matériel *m* d'entretien; **maintenance staff** personnel *m* d'entretien

major 1 *n Am (big company)* société *f* de premier ordre; **the oil majors** les grandes

compagnies pétrolières
2 *adj* majeur(e) ❑ ***major shareholder***
actionnaire *mf* majoritaire

majority *n* majorité *f* ❑ ***majority decision***
décision *f* prise à la majorité; ***majority***
interest participation *f* majoritaire;
majority shareholder actionnaire *mf*
majoritaire

majority-owned subsidiaries *npl*
= filiales dans lesquelles une personne ou
une compagnie détient une participation
majoritaire

make 1 *n* *(of product)* marque *f*; **what make**
of computer is it? c'est quelle marque
d'ordinateur?
2 *vt* **(a)** *(construct)* fabriquer, faire **(b)** *(earn)*
gagner; *(profit)* gagner, réaliser; **to make**
£50,000 a year gagner 50 000 livres par an

▸ **make out** *vt sep* *(list)* faire, dresser; *(bill)*
établir, dresser; **to make out a cheque (to sb)**
faire un chèque (à l'ordre de qn)

▸ **make over** *vt sep* céder (**to** à)

▸ **make up** *vt sep* **(a)** *(deficit, loss)* combler
(b) *(parcel)* faire; *(order)* exécuter, préparer;
(list) faire, dresser; *(bill)* établir, dresser

▸ **make up for** *vt insep* compenser;
European sales made up for our losses in
the UK les ventes en Europe ont compensé
nos pertes au Royaume-Uni

maker *n* *(manufacturer)* fabricant *m*; *(of*
machinery, cars) constructeur *m* ❑ ***maker's***
price prix *m* de fabrique

making-up *n* ST EXCH ***making-up day***
jour *m* de liquidation; ***making-up price***
cours *m* de compensation

maladjustment *n* ECON déséquilibre *m*

maladministration *n* mauvaise administration *f*

malpractice *n* faute *f* professionnelle

man *vt* *(organization)* fournir du personnel à;
(switchboard) assurer le service de; *(machine)*
assurer le fonctionnement de; **to man a**
nightshift composer une équipe de nuit; **to**
man the phone répondre au téléphone; **the**
office is manned by a skeleton staff le
bureau tourne à effectif réduit

manage *vt* **(a)** *(company, factory, project,*
bank) diriger; *(shop, hotel)* être le gérant de;
(property, estate) gérer **(b)** *(economy, money,*
resources) gérer; **to manage sb's affairs**
gérer les affaires de qn

managed *adj* FIN ***managed currency***
devise *f* contrôlée; ***managed fund*** fonds *m*
géré; ***managed unit trust*** fonds *m* commun
de placement géré

management *n* **(a)** *(action)* *(of company,*
factory, project) gestion *f*, direction *f*; *(of*
economy, money, resources, shop, hotel)
gestion; **all their problems are due to bad**
management tous leurs problèmes sont dus
à une mauvaise gestion ❑ ***management***
accountant contrôleur *m* de gestion;
management accounting comptabilité *f*
de gestion; ***management audit*** contrôle *m*
de gestion; ***management committee***
comité *m* de direction; ***management***
company société *f* de gestion; ***man-***
agement consultancy *(activity)* conseils
mpl en gestion; *(firm)* cabinet *m* (de) conseils;
management consultant conseiller(ère)
m,f en gestion; *Am* ***management***
expenses frais *mpl* de gestion;
management fee frais *mpl* de gestion;
management function fonction *f*
d'encadrement; COMPTR ***management***
information system système *m* intégré de
gestion; ***management by objectives***
gestion *f* par objectifs; ***management***
operating system système *m* intégré de
gestion; ***management science*** science *f*
de la gestion; ***management theory*** théorie
f de la gestion de l'entreprise; ***management***
skills qualités *fpl* de gestionnaire;
management style mode *m* de gestion;
management technique technique *f* de
gestion; ***management theory*** théorie *f* de
la gestion de l'entreprise; ***management***
tool outil *m* de gestion; ***management***
training formation *f* des cadres
(b) *(managers, employers)* administration *f*,
direction *f*; **negotiations between**
management and unions have broken
down les négociations entre le patronat et
les syndicats ont échoué ❑ ***management***
buy-in apport *m* de gestion; ***management***
buy-out rachat *m* d'une société par la
direction; ***management team*** équipe *f*
dirigeante *ou* de direction

> **❝**
> … in 1973 the US government adopted
> a system of **management by**
> **objectives** (MBO). This was another
> system adopted from the private sector
> and was essentially one in which
> objectives were specified and
> quantified, potential conflicts iden-
> tified, and opportunities provided to
> management to monitor progress and
> to evaluate results.
> **❞**

manager *n* **(a)** *(of company, factory, project,*
bank) directeur(trice) *m,f*; *(of shop, hotel)*
gérant(e) *m,f*; *(of funds, money)* gestionnaire

mf; *(of assets)* administrateur(trice) *m,f*
(**b**) COMPTR *(of disk)* gestionnaire *m*

manageress *n* *(of company, bank)*
directrice *f*; *(of shop, hotel)* gérante *f*

managerial *adj* directorial(e) ❑ *managerial skills* qualités *fpl* de gestionnaire; *managerial staff* cadres *mpl*; *managerial structure* hiérarchie *f*

managing director *n* directeur(trice) *m,f* général(e)

mandate *n* mandat *m* ❑ BANKING *mandate form* lettre *f* de signatures autorisées

mandatory *adj* obligatoire ❑ BANKING *mandatory liquid assets* liquidités *fpl* obligatoires

man-hour *n* heure *f* de travail *(d'un employé)*

manifest *n* *(of ship, aeroplane)* manifeste *m*

manipulate *vt* **to manipulate the accounts** trafiquer les comptes; ST EXCH **to manipulate the market** agir sur le marché

manpower *n* main-d'œuvre *f*; **we don't have the necessary manpower** nous n'avons pas la main-d'œuvre nécessaire ❑ *manpower forecasting* prévision *f* de l'emploi; *manpower management* gestion *f* de l'emploi; *manpower planning* planification *f* de l'emploi

manual 1 *n* *(handbook)* manuel *m* (d'utilisation)
2 *adj* manuel(elle) ❑ *manual labour* travail *m* manuel; *manual operation* fonctionnement *m* manuel; *manual work* travail *m* manuel; *manual worker* travailleur(euse) *m,f* manuel(elle)

manually *adv* manuellement, à la main

manufacture 1 *n* fabrication *f*; *(of machinery, cars)* construction *f*
2 *vt* fabriquer; *(machinery, cars)* construire ❑ *manufactured goods* produits *mpl* manufacturés

manufacturer *n* fabricant(e) *m,f*; *(of machinery, cars)* constructeur *m* ❑ *manufacturer's agent* agent *m* exclusif; *manufacturer's brand* marque *f* de fabricant; *manufacturer's liability* responsabilité *f* du fabricant; MKTG *manufacturer's recommended price* prix *m* conseillé par le fabricant

manufacturing *n* fabrication *f* ❑ ACCT *manufacturing account* compte *m* de production; *manufacturing capacity* capacité *f* de production; *manufacturing costs* frais *mpl* de fabrication; *manufacturing industry* industrie *f* de

fabrication; *manufacturing licence* brevet *m* ou licence *f* de fabrication; *manufacturing overheads* frais *mpl* de fabrication; *manufacturing process* procédé *m* de fabrication; *manufacturing rights* droits *mpl* de fabrication; *manufacturing town* ville *f* industrielle

margin *n* (**a**) FIN marge *f*; **the margins are very tight** les marges sont très réduites ❑ *margin of error* marge d'erreur (**b**) ST EXCH marge *f* de garantie ❑ *margin call* appel *m* de couverture *ou* de marge *ou* de garantie; *margin dealing* *(method of dealing commodities or financial futures)* cotation *f* par appel de marge; *(high-gear dealing)* arbitrage *m* à la marge *ou* marginal; *(transactions on margin of loan)* arbitrage *m* sur dépôt de titres de garantie

marginal *adj* *(business, profit)* marginal(e) ❑ *marginal cost* coût *m* marginal; *marginal costing* méthode *f* des coûts marginaux; *marginal profit* bénéfice *m* marginal; *marginal productivity* productivité *f* marginale; *marginal relief* dégrèvement *m* marginal; *marginal return on capital* rendement *m* marginal du capital; *marginal revenue* revenu *m* marginal; *marginal utility* utilité *f* marginale

> **❝**
>
> Another duty of the accounts department is that of recording the costs incurred in company activities such as manufacturing. One method of doing this is the system of **marginal costing**. Marginal cost is defined as "prime cost plus variable overheads".
>
> **❞**

marine *adj* maritime ❑ *marine bill of lading* connaissement *m* maritime; *marine insurance* assurance *f* maritime

maritime *adj* maritime ❑ *maritime law* droit *m* maritime

mark¹ *n* *(currency)* mark *m*, Deutschmark *m*

mark² 1 *n* *(level)* niveau *m*; **sales topped the 5 million mark** les ventes ont dépassé la barre des 5 millions
2 *vt* *(goods)* marquer

▸ **mark down** *vt sep* *(price)* baisser; *(goods)* baisser le prix de, démarquer; **everything has been marked down to half price** tout a été réduit à moitié prix; ST EXCH **prices have been marked down** les cours sont en baisse

▸ **mark up** *vt sep* *(price)* augmenter; *(goods)* augmenter le prix de, majorer; ST EXCH **prices have been marked up** les cours sont en hausse

markdown n réduction f

marker barrel n prix m du baril de pétrole

market 1 n **(a)** ECON, MKTG marché m; **to be on the market** être en vente; **to come onto the market** arriver sur le marché; **to put sth on the market** mettre qch sur le marché; **to take sth off the market** retirer qch du marché; **to be in the market for sth** être acheteur de qch, chercher à acheter qch; **to find a market for sth** trouver un débouché ou des acheteurs pour qch; **to corner a market** accaparer un marché; **to find a ready market** trouver à vendre facilement; **to price oneself out of the market** perdre sa clientèle en demandant trop cher; **the bottom has fallen out of the market** le marché s'est effondré ▫ **market analysis** analyse f du marché; **market analyst** analyste mf du marché; **market appraisal** évaluation f du marché; **market challenger** challengeur m; **market choice** choix m sur le marché; (product) choix du marché; **market conditions** conditions fpl du marché; **market correction** correction f du marché; **market development** développement m du marché; **market entry** lancement m sur le marché; **market exposure** exposition f sur le marché; **market follower** suiveur m (sur le marché); **market forces** tendances fpl du marché; **market forecast** prévisions fpl du marché; **market growth** croissance f du marché; **market intelligence** information f commerciale; **market leader** leader m sur le marché; **market maker** teneur m de marché; **market mechanism** mécanisme m du marché; **market penetration** pénétration f du marché; **market penetration pricing** tarification f de pénétration du marché; **market positioning** positionnement m sur le marché; **market potential** (of product) potentiel m sur le marché; (of market) potentiel m du marché; **market price** prix m du marché; **market profile** profil m du marché; **market prospects** perspectives fpl commerciales; **market rate** taux m du marché; **market rate of discount** taux m d'escompte hors banque; **market report** étude f de marché, rapport m ou bilan m commercial; **market research** étude f de marché; **market researcher** = personne qui fait une étude de marché; Br **Market Research Society** = société d'étude de marché britannique; **market segment** segment m de marché; **market segmentation** segmentation f du marché; **market share** part f de marché; **market size** (of product) part f de marché;

(of market) taille f du marché; **market survey** étude f de marché; **market trends** tendances fpl du marché; **market value** valeur f marchande

(b) ST EXCH marché m; **to play the market** spéculer ▫ **market capitalization** capitalisation f boursière; **market commentator** chroniqueur m boursier; **market crisis** choc m boursier; **market indicator** indicateur m de marché; **market maker** intermédiaire mf; **market order** ordre m au mieux; **market price** cours m (de la Bourse); **market price list** mercuriale f; **market quotation** cotation f au cours du marché; **market rating** cours m en Bourse; **market risk** risque m du marché; **market trend** conjoncture f boursière

2 vt commercialiser; (launch) lancer

> **❝**
>
> A **market maker** does not have complete control over his portfolio because he is always required to make a market. We are therefore left with the unsatisfactory position that the **market maker** may well be harmed but be the very person who is unable to prove that this was caused by the inside trade.
>
> **❞**

marketability n MKTG possibilité f de commercialisation

marketable adj **(a)** MKTG (goods) commercialisable **(b)** ST EXCH (shares, securities) négociable

marketer n MKTG mercaticien(enne) m,f, spécialiste mf en marketing

marketing n (study, theory) marketing m, mercatique f; (of product) commercialisation f ▫ **marketing agreement** accord m de commercialisation; **marketing consultant** conseil m en marketing; **marketing costs** frais mpl de commercialisation; **marketing department** service m du marketing; **marketing environment** environnement m commercial ou mercatique; **marketing implementation** mise f en place mercatique; COMPTR **marketing information system** système m d'information marketing; **marketing intelligence system** système m d'intelligence marketing; **marketing manager** directeur(trice) m,f du marketing; **marketing mix** marchéage m; **marketing myopia** myopie f mercatique; **marketing policy** politique f de commercialisation; **marketing research** recherche f commerciale; **marketing strategy** stratégie f marketing

marketplace *n* ECON marché *m*; **the products in the marketplace** les produits sur le marché

marking *n* ST EXCH *(of shares)* cotation *f*

markka *n* mark *m* finlandais

mark-up *n* majoration *f*; **we operate a 2.5 times mark-up** nous appliquons une marge de 2,5 □ *mark-up pricing* fixation *f* du prix au coût moyen majoré; *mark-up ratio* taux *m* de marge

mart *n* (**a**) *(market)* marché *m* (**b**) *(auction room)* salle *f* des ventes

marzipan layer *n* Fam cadres *mpl* moyens

mass *n* *mass dismissal* licenciement *m* collectif; *mass media* mass médias *mpl*; *mass production* fabrication *f* en série; *mass unemployment* chômage *m* sur une grande échelle

mass-produce *vt* fabriquer en série

master *n* (**a**) *(expert)* maître *m*, expert *m* □ *master builder* maître *m* bâtisseur (**b**) COMPTR *master file* fichier *m* maître; *master production schedule* plan *m* de production principal

matched *adj* ST EXCH *matched bargain* mariage *m*; Am *matched orders* ordres *mpl* couplés d'achat et de vente *(pour stimuler le marché)*

matching *n* Am ST EXCH application *f*

material *n* materials *(equipment)* matériel *m* □ *materials cost* coût *m* du matériel; *materials management* gestion *f* du matériel; *material requirements planning* prévision *f* des besoins matériels

maternity *n* *maternity benefit* allocation *f* de maternité; *maternity leave* congé *m* de maternité

maths co-processor *n* COMPTR coprocesseur *m* mathématique

matrix organization *n* organisation *f* matricielle

mature 1 *adj* (**a**) *mature economy* économie *f* en pleine maturité (**b**) FIN *(bill, investment, insurance policy)* échu(e)
2 *vi* FIN *(of bill, investment, insurance policy)* échoir, arriver à échéance

maturity *n* FIN *(of bill, investment, insurance policy)* échéance *f* □ *maturity date* date *f* d'échéance; *maturity value* valeur *f* à l'échéance

maximization *n* maximisation *f*; **our aim for this year is the maximization of profits** notre but pour cette année est la maximisation des bénéfices

maximize *vt* maximaliser

maximum 1 *n* maximum *m*; **to raise production to a maximum** porter la production au maximum; **the space has been used to the maximum** l'espace a été utilisé au maximum
2 *adj* maximum, maximal(e) □ *maximum efficiency* rendement *m* maximum; *maximum load* charge *f* maximale; *maximum output* rendement *m* maximum; *maximum price* prix *m* maximum

MB *n* COMPTR *(abbr* **megabyte***)* Mo

Mb *n* COMPTR *(abbr* **megabit***)* Mb

MBA *n* *(abbr* **Master of Business Administration***)* MBA *m*

MBI *n* *(abbr* **management buy-in***)* apport *m* de gestion

> " —————
>
> In the last few months, we have seen more managers taking advantage of the bottom of the economic cycle to buy into businesses. As companies continue to dispose of non-core subsidiaries, this next generation of **MBI** managers will have golden opportunities to acquire companies at realistic prices.
>
> ————— "

MBO *n* (**a**) *(abbr* **management buy-out***)* rachat *m* d'une société par la direction (**b**) *(abbr* **management by objectives***)* gestion *f* selon objectifs

MBps COMPTR *(abbr* **megabytes per second***)* mops

Mbps COMPTR *(abbr* **megabits per second***)* mbps

MD *n* *(abbr* **managing director***)* directeur(trice) *m,f* général(e)

meal ticket *n* Am ticket-restaurant *m*

mean 1 *n* *(average)* moyenne *f*
2 *adj* *(average)* moyen(enne) □ *mean absolute deviation* écart *m* moyen absolu; *mean price* prix *m* moyen

means 1 *n* *(method)* moyen *m*; **means of payment** moyen de paiement; ECON **means of production** moyen de production
2 *npl* *(income, wealth)* moyens *mpl*, ressources *fpl* □ ADMIN *means test (for state benefit)* enquête *f* sur les revenus; **the grant is subject to a means test** l'allocation est assujettie à des conditions de ressources

means-test *vt* ADMIN to means-test sb = faire une enquête sur les revenus de quelqu'un avant de lui accorder une aide sociale; **all applicants are means-tested** tous les candidats font l'objet d'une enquête sur leurs revenus

measure *n* *(action, step)* mesure *f*, démarche *f*; **to take measures to do sth** prendre des mesures pour faire qch

measurement *n* **(a)** *(of performance, productivity)* mesure *f* **(b)** *(of freight)* cubage *m*, encombrement *m* ❑ *measurement tonnage* jaugeage *m*

mechanical *adj* mécanique ❑ *mechanical fault* défaut *m* mécanique

mechanism *n* mécanisme *m*

mechanization *n* mécanisation *f*

mechanize *vt* mécaniser

media *n* médias *mpl* ❑ *media analysis* analyse *f* des médias; *media coverage* couverture *f* médiatique; *media mix* mixte média; *media planner* médiaplaneur *m*, médialiste *mf*; *media planning* médialisation *f*, plan *m* média; *media research* médialogie *f*; *media schedule* calendrier *m* de campagne; *media vehicle* véhicule *m* médiatique

> 66 ───────────────
> Carlton will use a wide-ranging **media mix** of radio, posters, press and television … to inform the public, advertising and business communities of its programme and corporate format prior to launch.
> ─────────────── 99

mediate *vi* servir de médiateur (**for/between** pour/entre)

mediation *n* médiation *f*; **to go to mediation** recourir à une médiation

mediator *n* médiateur(trice) *m,f*

medical *adj* *medical certificate* certificat *m* médical; *medical officer* médecin *m* du travail

medium-dated *adj* *(gilts, securities)* à échéance moyenne

medium of exchange *n* ECON moyen *m* d'échange

medium-sized *adj* de taille moyenne

medium-term *adj* *(forecast, loan)* à moyen terme ❑ EU *medium-term financial assistance* aide *f* financière à moyen terme; *medium-term liabilities* dettes *fpl* à moyen terme; FIN *medium-term note* billet *m* à moyen terme

meet **1** *vt* **(a)** *(by arrangement)* rejoindre, retrouver; **to arrange to meet sb** donner rendez-vous à qn, prendre rendez-vous avec qn; **I arranged to meet him at 3 o'clock** j'ai pris rendez-vous avec lui pour 15 heures **(b)** *(become acquainted with)* faire la connaissance de; **it was a pleasure to meet you** je suis enchanté d'avoir fait votre connaissance; **I hope to meet you soon** j'espère avoir bientôt le plaisir de faire votre connaissance **(c)** *(satisfy)* *(need)* satisfaire à; *(order)* satisfaire, assurer; **to meet sb's requirements** satisfaire aux besoins de qn; **to meet demand** répondre à la demande; **to meet sb's expenses** subvenir aux frais de qn; **the cost will be met by the company** les frais seront pris en charge par la société **2** *vi* *(assemble)* se réunir; **the delegates will meet in the conference room** les délégués se réuniront dans la salle de conférence; **the committee meets once a month** le comité se réunit une fois par mois

meeting *n* réunion *f*; *(of shareholders)* assemblée *f*; **to hold a meeting** tenir une réunion; **the meeting will be held tomorrow at 3 o'clock** la réunion aura lieu demain à 15 heures; **to call a meeting of shareholders/the workforce** convoquer les actionnaires/le personnel; **to open the meeting** déclarer la séance ouverte; **to close the meeting** lever la séance; **to address the meeting** prendre la parole; **to put a resolution to the meeting** mettre une résolution aux voix ❑ *meeting place* lieu *m* de réunion

meg *n* *Fam* COMPTR méga *m*

megabit *n* COMPTR mégabit *m*

megabyte *n* COMPTR méga-octet *m*; **20 megabyte memory** mémoire *f* de 20 méga-octets

megamerger *n* méga-fusion *f*

member *n* membre *m* ❑ *Am member bank* banque *f* membre de la Réserve fédérale; EU *member country* pays *m* membre; ST EXCH *member firm* société *f* membre; EU *member state* État *m* membre

membership *n* **(a)** *(state)* adhésion *f*; **to apply for membership** faire une demande d'adhésion; **they have applied for membership to the EU** ils ont demandé à entrer dans l'UE; **membership of the union will entitle you to vote in meetings** l'adhésion au syndicat vous donne le droit de voter lors des réunions; **his country's membership of UNESCO is in question** l'adhésion de son pays à l'UNESCO est remise en question ❑ *membership card* carte *f* de membre; *membership fee* cotisation *f*

(b) *(members)* membres *mpl*, adhérents *mpl*; **the opinion of the majority of our membership** l'avis de la majorité de nos membres

memo *n* note *f* de service ❑ *memo pad* bloc-notes *m*

memorandum *n* **(a)** *(in office)* note *f* de service **(b)** *(of contract, sale)* mémoire *m* **(c)** LAW *memorandum and articles of association* statuts *mpl*; *memorandum of association* acte *m* de constitution; *memorandum of satisfaction* = document certifiant le paiement d'une hypothèque

memory *n* COMPTR mémoire *f* ❑ *memory card* carte *f* mémoire

menu *n* COMPTR menu *m* ❑ *menu bar* barre *f* de menu; *menu item* élément *m* de menu

MEP *n* *(abbr* **Member of the European Parliament)** député *m* au Parlement européen

mercantile *adj* commercial(e) ❑ *mercantile agency* agence *f* commerciale; *mercantile agent* agent *m* commercial; *mercantile broker* agent *m* de change; *mercantile law* droit *m* commercial; *mercantile nation* nation *f* commerçante; *mercantile operations* opérations *fpl* mercantiles; *mercantile paper* papier *m* commercial *ou* de commerce

> 〝
> The seller must be a **mercantile agent**, i.e. a factor. Broadly, a **mercantile agent** is an independent agent acting in a way of business to whom someone else entrusts his goods and upon whom is conferred authority …
> 〞

mercantilism *n* mercantilisme *m*

merchandise **1** *n* marchandises *fpl* **2** *vt* marchandiser, commercialiser

merchandiser *n* *(object)* présentoir *m*; *(person)* marchandiseur *m*

merchandising *n* marchandisage *m*, commercialisation *f*

merchant *n* *(trader)* négociant(e) *m,f*; *(shopkeeper)* marchand(e) *m,f* ❑ Br *merchant bank* banque *f* d'affaires; *merchant banker* banquier(ère) *m,f* d'affaires; *merchant wholesaler* grossiste *mf*

merchantable quality *n* qualité *f* marchande; **all goods must be of**

merchantable quality tous les articles doivent être vendables

merge **1** *vt* *(banks, companies)* amalgamer, fusionner; COMPTR *(files)* fusionner **2** *vi* *(of banks, companies)* s'amalgamer, fusionner; **they have merged with their former competitor** ils ont fusionné avec leur ancien concurrent

merger *n* *(of banks, companies)* fusion *f*; *(takeover)* absorption *f* ❑ *merger accounting* = type de comptabilité qui fait figurer les comptes d'une filiale récemment acquise avec ceux de la société mère; *merger talks* discussions *fpl* en vue d'une fusion

merit *n* mérite *m*; **promotion is on merit alone** l'avancement se fait uniquement au mérite ❑ *merit bonus* prime *f* de rendement; *merit increase* augmentation *f* au mérite; *merit rating* notation *f* du personnel; *merit system* système *m* d'avancement fondé sur le mérite

message *n* message *m*; **to leave a message (for sb)** laisser un message (pour qn); **would you like to leave a message for him?** voulez-vous (lui) laisser un message?; **can you give her a message?** pouvez-vous lui transmettre un message? ❑ COMPTR *message handling* messagerie *f* (électronique)

messenger *n* messager(ère) *m,f*; **by special messenger** par porteur spécial ❑ *messenger boy* garçon *m* de courses

Messrs *nmpl* *(abbr* **Messieurs)** MM

method *n* méthode *f*; **method of payment** modalité *f* de paiement; **method of operation** méthode d'exploitation ❑ *method study* étude *f* des méthodes

methodical *adj* méthodique

me-too product *n* MKTG produit *m* tactique

mezzanine *n* *mezzanine debt* dette *f* subordonnée *ou* mezzanine; *mezzanine finance* = méthode de financement d'une partie du capital nécessaire pour acheter une entreprise *(utilisée principalement par ses employés)*

> 〝
> The money will be raised in a mixture of straightforward borrowing and long-term, high-interest bearing **mezzanine finance** — often referred to as junk bonds. The existing equity holders may also be asked to participate in a further round of equity raising, for around 10 per cent of the total.
> 〞

mfd (*abbr* **manufactured**) fabriqué(e)

MHz COMPTR (*abbr* **megahertz**) MHz

micro *n* COMPTR micro *m*

microchip *n* COMPTR microprocesseur *m*

microcomputer *n* micro-ordinateur *m*

micro-computing *n* micro-informatique *f*

microeconomics *n* microéconomie *f*

microfiche *n* microfiche *f*

microfilm *n* microfilm *m*

micromarketing *n* micromarketing *m*

microprocessing *n* micro-informatique *f*

microprocessor *n* microprocesseur *m*

mid *adj* **mid June** mi-juin ❑ ST EXCH **mid month account** liquidation *f* de quinzaine

middle *adj* **middle management** cadres *mpl* moyens; ST EXCH **middle.price** cours *m* moyen

middle-income group *n* groupe *m* de contribuables à revenus moyens

middleman *n* intermédiaire *mf* ❑ **middleman's market** marché *m* des intermédiaires

mileage allowance *n* ≃ indemnité *f* kilométrique

millennium bug *n* COMPTR bogue *m* de l'an 2000

minicomputer *n* mini-ordinateur *m*

MiniDisc® *n* COMPTR MiniDisc® *m*

minimal *adj* minimum, minimal(e) ❑ **minimal value** valeur *f* minimale; **minimal weight** poids *m* minimum

minimize *vt* réduire au minimum; **we must try to minimize overheads** nous devons essayer de réduire au minimum les frais généraux

minimum 1 *n* minimum *m*; **to reduce sth to a minimum** réduire qch au minimum; **keep expenses to a minimum** limitez au minimum les dépenses

2 *adj* minimum, minimal(e); **the minimum number of shares** le nombre minimum d'actions ❑ **minimum charge** tarif *m* minimum; **minimum deposit** acompte *m* minimum; *Br* FIN **minimum lending rate** taux *m* de base; **minimum rate** taux *m* minimum; **minimum stock level** stock *m* d'alerte; **minimum wage** salaire *m* minimum

mini tower *n* COMPTR mini-tour *f*

minor *adj* mineur(e) ❑ **minor shareholder** actionnaire *mf* minoritaire

minority *n* minorité *f* ❑ **minority interest** participation *f* minoritaire; **minority investor** investisseur *m* minoritaire; **minority shareholder** actionnaire *mf* minoritaire

mint 1 *n Br* FIN **the (Royal) Mint** ≃ (l'hôtel *m* de) la Monnaie ❑ **mint par** pair *m* intrinsèque

2 *vt* (*coins*) frapper, battre

minute *n* **minutes** (*of meeting*) procès-verbal *m*, compte-rendu *m*; **to confirm the minutes of the last meeting** approuver le procès-verbal de la dernière réunion; **to take the minutes of a meeting** rédiger le procès-verbal d'une réunion ❑ **minute book** registre *m* des procès-verbaux

mips *n* COMPTR (*abbr* **million instructions per second**) MIPS *m*

MIRAS *n* (*abbr* **Mortgage Interest Relief at Source**) = système par lequel les intérêts dus à une société de crédit immobilier sont déductibles des impôts

> ❝
>
> The appropriate tax rates are then applied to calculate the total income tax due and it is only at this stage that the **MIRAS** system is introduced into the assessment. The income tax relief already given under **MIRAS** should be offset against PAYE deductions, income tax deducted from dividends etc in order to arrive at the net income tax already suffered.
>
> ❞

mirror site *n* COMPTR site *m* miroir

MIS *n* (**a**) COMPTR (*abbr* **management information system**) système *m* intégré de gestion (**b**) MKTG (*abbr* **marketing information system**) système *m* d'information marketing

misapplication *n* (*of money*) détournement *m*

misapply *vt* (*money*) détourner

misappropriate *vt* (*money*) détourner

misappropriation *n* (*of money*) détournement *m*

miscalculate *vt* mal calculer

miscalculation *n* erreur *f* de calcul

miscarriage *n Br* (*of mail, goods*) perte *f*

miscellaneous *adj* divers(es) ❑ **miscellaneous expenses** frais *mpl* divers; **miscellaneous shares** valeurs *fpl* diverses

misdate *vt* mal dater

misdirect *vt* (*letter*) mal adresser

misentry *n* ACCT contre-position *f*

misleading advertising *n* publicité *f* mensongère

mismanage *vt* mal gérer

mismanagement *n* mauvaise gestion *f*

misroute *vt (parcel)* mal acheminer

mission *n* (a) *(delegation)* mission *f*; **a Chinese trade mission** une mission commerciale chinoise (b) *(of company)* mission *f* ▫ **mission statement** définition *f* de mission

> The members of any organisation should have a clear idea of its general purpose which is expressed in the form of a "**mission statement**" or "corporate objective", defining the business in which the organisation is involved.

missionary selling *n* MKTG ventes *fpl* de prospection

mistake *n* erreur *f*; **to make a mistake** faire une erreur

misuse **1** *n (of equipment, resources)* mauvais emploi *m*; *(of authority)* abus *m*; *(of funds)* détournement *m*
2 *vt (equipment, resources)* mal employer; *(authority)* abuser de; *(funds)* détourner

mixed *adj* mixte ▫ **mixed cargo** cargaison *f* mixte; **mixed costs** frais *mpl* semi-variables; **mixed economy** économie *f* mixte; INS **mixed policy** police *f* d'assurance mixte

MLR *n Br* FIN *(abbr* **minimum lending rate)** taux *m* de base

MMC *n (abbr* **Monopolies and Mergers Commission)** = commission britannique veillant au respect de la législation antitrust

MMF *n* ST EXCH *(abbr* **money market fund)** ≃ sicav *f* monétaire

mobile **1** *n (mobile phone)* portable *m*
2 *adj* **mobile phone** téléphone *m* portable

mobility *n* (a) *(of capital, workforce)* mobilité *f* (b) *Br* ADMIN **mobility allowance** allocation *f* de déplacement *(versée aux personnes handicapées)*

mobilization *n (of capital)* mobilisation *f*

mobilize *vt (capital)* mobiliser

mock-up *n* maquette *f*

mode *n* COMPTR mode *m*

model *n* (a) *(small version)* maquette *f* (b) *(example)* modèle *m*; **this is our latest**

model c'est notre dernier modèle (**c**) ECON modèle *m*

modem *n* COMPTR modem *m* ▫ **modem card** carte *f* modem

moderate *adj (price, income, rise)* modéré(e)

modernization *n* modernisation *f*

modernize *vt* moderniser

modified rebuy *n* rachat *m* modifié

monadic testing *n* MKTG test *m* monade *(portant sur un seul élément)*

monetarism *n* ECON monétarisme *m*

monetarist *n & adj* ECON monétariste *mf*

monetary *adj* monétaire ▫ ACCT **monetary area** zone *f* monétaire; **monetary assets** liquidités *fpl*; **monetary control** contrôle *m* monétaire; **monetary convention** convention *f* monétaire; **monetary policy** politique *f* monétaire; **monetary reform** réforme *f* monétaire; **monetary standard** étalon *m* monétaire; **monetary system** système *m* monétaire; **monetary unit** unité *f* monétaire

> And membership could be offered to the reforming economies of Eastern Europe. They would benefit from real exchange-rate stability within the European **monetary area** without having to surrender all discretion over **monetary policy** — which, even if desirable, would not be feasible.

money *n* argent *m*; *(currency)* monnaie *f*; **to make money** *(of person)* gagner de l'argent; *(of business)* rapporter de l'argent; **to be worth a lot of money** *(of thing)* valoir cher; *(of person)* être riche; **to get one's money back** *(get reimbursed)* se faire rembourser; *(recover one's expenses)* rentrer dans ses fonds ▫ **money broker** prêteur(euse) *m,f* sur titre; BANKING **money at call** argent au jour le jour, argent à vue; **money laundering** blanchiment *m* d'argent; **money market** marché *m* monétaire; **money market fund** ≃ sicav *f* monétaire; **money order** mandat *m* (postal); **money rate** taux *m* de l'argent; BANKING **money at short notice** argent *m* à court terme; **money supply** masse *f* monétaire; **money trader** cambiste *mf*

money-back *adj* **money-back guarantee** garantie *f* de remboursement intégral; **money-back offer** offre *f* de remboursement

moneychanger *n* (**a**) *(person)* courtier(ère) *m,f* de change (**b**) *Am (machine)* distributeur *m* de monnaie

moneylender *n* prêteur(euse) *m,f*

moneymaker *n* **to be a moneymaker** *(of shop, business, product)* rapporter

monitor **1** *n* COMPTR moniteur *m*
  2 *vt* MKTG surveiller

monitoring *n* MKTG surveillance *f*

Monopolies and Mergers Commission *n* = commission britannique veillant au respect de la législation antitrust

monopolize *vt* monopoliser

monopoly *n* monopole *m*; **to have a monopoly of** *or* **on sth** avoir le monopole de qch; **to form a monopoly** constituer un monopole ◻ *monopoly control* contrôle *m* monopolistique; *monopoly market* marché *m* monopolistique

monopsony *n* monopsone *m*

month *n* mois *m*

monthly **1** *adj* mensuel(elle) ◻ *monthly instalment, monthly payment* mensualité *f*; *monthly statement* relevé *m* de fin de mois
  2 *adv* tous les mois; *(pay)* mensuellement

moonlight *vi Fam (work illegally)* travailler au noir; *(have second job)* avoir un deuxième emploi

moratorium *n* FIN moratoire *m*; **to declare a moratorium** décréter un moratoire

mortality tables *npl* INS tables *fpl* de mortalité

mortgage **1** *n* FIN *(for house purchase)* crédit *m ou* prêt *m* immobilier; *(raised on property)* hypothèque *f*; **to take out a mortgage** prendre un crédit *ou* un prêt immobilier; **to secure a debt by mortgage** hypothéquer une créance; **to pay off a mortgage** purger une hypothèque ◻ *mortgage bond, mortgage debenture* obligation *f* hypothécaire; *mortgage rate* taux *m* de crédit immobilier; *mortgage registrar* conservateur(trice) *m,f* des hypothèques; *mortgage repayment* remboursement *m* d'emprunt
  2 *vt (land, building, title deeds)* hypothéquer

❝
Roughly half the leading building societies' borrowers repay on budget schemes. They will pay nothing more now, but will have the delayed interest on at least two **mortgage rate** rises to account for when the new yearly rates are fixed early in 1990.
❞

mortgageable *adj* hypothécable

mortgagee *n* créancier(ère) *m,f* hypothécaire

mortgagor *n* débiteur(trice) *m,f* hypothécaire

most-favoured nation, *Am* **most-favored nation** *n* nation *f* la plus favorisée; **this country has most-favoured nation status** ce pays bénéficie de la clause de la nation la plus favorisée

❝
A trade agreement provided for a reduction of customs duties on goods traded by the two countries (thus extending **most-favoured nation** status to the Soviet Union and improving the competitiveness of each country's goods in the other's markets).
❞

motherboard *n* COMPTR carte *f* mère

motion *n* (**a**) *(in meeting, debate)* motion *f*; **to propose a motion** proposer une motion; **to carry a motion** faire adopter une motion; **to second a motion** appuyer une motion (**b**) *(movement)* mouvement *m* ◻ *motion analysis* analyse *f* des mouvements (**c**) LAW *(request)* demande *f*, requête *f*

motivate *vt* motiver

motivation *n* motivation *f* ◻ MKTG *motivation research* recherche *f* de motivation

motivational research *n* MKTG recherche *f* de motivation

mouse *n* COMPTR souris *f* ◻ *mouse button* bouton *m* de souris; *mouse driver* programme *m* de commande de la souris; *mouse mat, mouse pad* tapis *m* de souris

movable LAW **1** *n* **movables** biens *mpl* mobiliers
  2 *adj* mobilier(ère) ◻ *movable assets* valeurs *fpl* mobilières; *movable effects* effets *mpl* mobiliers; *movable property* biens *mpl* mobiliers

move **1** *vt (sell)* vendre; **we must move these goods quickly** nous devons vendre ces marchandises rapidement
  2 *vi (sell)* se vendre; **the new model isn't moving as quickly as planned** le nouveau modèle ne se vend pas aussi vite que prévu

▶ **move up** *vi* ST EXCH *(of shares)* se relever, reprendre; **shares moved up three points today** les actions ont gagné trois points aujourd'hui

moveable = **movable**

movement n *(of capital)* circulation *f*; *(of share prices)* mouvement *m*; *(of market)* activité *f*

moving averages npl moyennes *fpl* mobiles

mps n *(abbr* **master production schedule***)* plan *m* de production principal

mrp n *(a)* *(abbr* **manufacturer's recommended price***)* prix *m* conseillé par le fabricant
(**b**) *(abbr* **material requirements planning***)* prévision *f* des besoins matériels

MRS n *(abbr* **Market Research Society***)* = société d'étude de marché britannique

MTFA n EU *(abbr* **medium-term financial assistance***)* aide *f* financière à moyen terme

multi-access adj COMPTR à accès multiple

multibrand n MKTG marque *f* multiple, multimarque *f*

multifunctional card n BANKING carte *f* multifonctions

multilateral adj multilatéral(e) ❑ *multilateral trade agreement* accord *m* commercial multilatéral

multimedia COMPTR **1** n multimédia *m*
2 adj multimédia

❝
Nowadays, **multimedia** means a computer using different media, such as a laser disc, a CD-ROM, cable TV and who knows what else. The most-talked-about end use is as a grandiose teaching machine.
❞

multinational 1 n multinationale *f*
2 adj multinational(e) ❑ *multinational company* société *f* multinationale; *multinational enterprise* entreprise *f* multinationale; *multinational marketing* marketing *m* multinational, mercatique *f* multinationale

multiple 1 n *(chain store)* chaîne *f* de magasins
2 adj multiple ❑ ST EXCH *multiple application* application *f* multiple; *multiple exchange rate* taux *m* de change multiple; ST EXCH *multiple options facility* ligne *f* de crédit à options multiples; *multiple ownership* multipropriété *f*; *multiple pricing* = fait d'adapter le prix de vente d'un produit au marché où on le commercialise

multiple-choice adj MKTG *(question, survey)* à choix multiples

multiple-use principle n principe *m* de polyvalence

multi-station adj COMPTR multipostes

multitasking 1 n *(a)* *(of employee)* = capacité à mener plusieurs tâches de front
(**b**) COMPTR multitâche *m*
2 adj COMPTR multitâche

multi-user adj COMPTR pour utilisateurs multiples ❑ *multi-user software* logiciel *m* multi-utilisateur; *multi-user system* système *m* multi-utilisateur

mutual adj mutuel(elle), réciproque ❑ *mutual benefit society* société *f* de secours mutuel; *Am mutual fund* fonds *m* commun de placement; *mutual insurance* assurance *f* mutuelle; *mutual insurance company* mutuelle *f*

N/A, n/a ADMIN (*abbr* **not applicable**) *(on form)* s.o.

NAFTA *n* (*abbr* **North American Free Trade Agreement**) ALENA *m*

naked *adj* sans garantie □ **naked debenture** obligation *f* chirographaire *ou* sans garantie; ST EXCH **naked option** option *f* d'achat vendue à découvert; **naked sale** vente *f* nue

name *n* (**a**) *(of person)* nom *m*; *(of company)* raison *f* sociale; *(of account)* intitulé *m*; **the shares are in my name** les actions sont à mon nom; **the company trades under the name of Scandia** la société a pour dénomination Scandia □ **name brand** marque *f*; ST EXCH **name day** deuxième jour *m* de liquidation; MKTG **name licensing** cession *f* de licence de nom; **name product** marque *f*
(**b**) *(reputation)* réputation *f*; **to have a good/bad name** avoir (une) bonne/mauvaise réputation; **they have a name for efficiency** ils ont la réputation d'être efficaces

narration, narrative *n* ACCT = note explicative dans un livre de commerce justifiant une écriture

narrow *adj (market)* étroit(e) □ **narrow money** = ensemble des billets et pièces de monnaie en circulation

nation *n* nation *f*

national *adj* national(e) □ **national debt** dette *f* publique; BANKING **National Giro** = service britannique de chèques postaux; *Br* **National Health Service** service *m* de santé publique; **national income** revenu *m* national; **National Insurance** = système britannique de sécurité sociale; *Br* **National Insurance contributions** cotisations *fpl* à la Sécurité sociale; **national product** produit *m* national; *Br* **National Savings Bank** ≃ Caisse *f* nationale d'épargne

nationalization *n* nationalisation *f*

nationalize *vt* nationaliser

natural *adj* naturel(elle) □ **natural economy** économie *f* non monétaire; **natural resources** ressources *fpl* naturelles; **natural wastage** = réduction des effectifs due aux départs d'employés non remplacés

NAV *n* (*abbr* **net asset value**) valeur *f* d'actif net

navigate COMPTR **1** *vt* naviguer sur; **to navigate the Net** naviguer sur l'Internet
2 *vi* naviguer

navigation *n* navigation *f* □ **navigation company** compagnie *f* de navigation *ou* de transports maritimes; **navigation dues** droits *mpl* de navigation

NBA *n* (*abbr* **net book agreement**) = accord entre maisons d'édition et libraires stipulant que ces derniers n'ont le droit de vendre aucun ouvrage à un prix inférieur à celui fixé par l'éditeur

NBV *n* ACCT (*abbr* **net book value**) valeur *f* comptable nette

NDP *n* ACCT (*abbr* **net domestic product**) produit *m* intérieur net

near month *n* ST EXCH échéance *f* proche

need *n* MKTG besoin *m* □ **needs analysis** analyse *f* des besoins; **needs assessment** estimation *f* des besoins; **need identification** identification *f* des besoins; **need level** niveau *m* des besoins; **need market** marché *m* des besoins; **need recognition** reconnaissance *f* des besoins; **needs study** étude *f* des besoins

needs-and-wants exploration *n* MKTG exploration *f* des besoins et des désirs

needs-based *adj* MKTG fondé(e) sur les besoins □ **needs-based market** marché *m* fondé sur les besoins; **needs-based segmentation** segmentation *f* fondée sur les besoins

negative *adj* négatif(ive) □ **negative equity** plus-value *f* immobilière négative; **negative income tax** impôt *m* négatif sur le revenu; **negative interest** intérêt *m* négatif; FIN **negative pledge** clause *f* de nantissement négative

> For homeowners who have **negative equity** — where the value of their house is less than the mortgage — the Chancellor ratified earlier proposals to make it easier for them to trade down.

neglected *adj* ST EXCH *(shares)* négligé(e)

negligence *n* négligence *f*; **through negligence** par négligence ◻ INS **negligence clause** clause *f* de négligence

negotiability *n* négociabilité *f*

negotiable *adj (salary, fee)* négociable, à débattre; FIN *(bill, document)* négociable; **not negotiable** *(on cheque)* non à ordre ◻ **negotiable instrument** instrument *m* négociable; **negotiable paper** papier *m* négociable

negotiate 1 *vt* (a) *(business deal)* négocier, traiter; *(loan, treaty, fee)* négocier; FIN *(bill, document)* négocier, trafiquer

2 *vi* négocier; **the unions will have to negotiate with the management for higher pay** il faudra que les syndicats négocient une augmentation de salaire auprès de la direction

negotiation *n* négociation *f*; **under negotiation** en négociation; **to be in negotiation with sb** être en pourparlers avec qn; **to enter into negotiations with sb** entamer des négociations avec qn; **to break off/resume negotiations** rompre/reprendre les négociations; **the pay deal is subject to negotiation** l'accord salarial est sujet à négociation

negotiator *n* négociateur(trice) *m,f*

nervous *adj (market)* agité(e), instable

Net *n* Fam COMPTR **the Net** le Net

net 1 *adj (weight, price, profit, interest)* net (nette) ◻ **net amount** montant *m* net; **net assets** actif *m* net; **net asset value** valeur *f* d'actif net; **net book agreement** = accord entre maisons d'édition et libraires stipulant que ces derniers n'ont le droit de vendre aucun ouvrage à un prix inférieur à celui fixé par l'éditeur; ACCT **net book value** valeur *f* comptable nette; **net cost** prix *m* de revient; ACCT **net current assets** actif *m* circulant net; **net dividend** dividende *m* net; ECON **net domestic product** produit *m* intérieur net; **net earnings** *(of company)* bénéfices *mpl* nets; *(of worker)* salaire *m* net; **net income** *(in accounts)* produit *m* net; *(of individual)* revenu *m* net; **net loss** perte *f* nette; **net margin** marge *f* nette; **net national product** produit *m* national net;

net operating profit rentabilité *f* nette d'exploitation; **net present value** valeur *f* actuelle nette; ACCT **net present value rate** taux *m* d'actualisation; **net profit ratio** ratio *m* de rentabilité nette; ACCT **net realizable value** valeur *f* réalisable nette; **net receipts** recettes *fpl* nettes; **net residual value** valeur *f* résiduelle nette; **net result** résultat *m* final; **net return** rendement *m* net; **net tangible assets** actif *m* corporel net; **net tonnage** jauge *f* nette; **net total** montant *m* net; ACCT **net variance** écart *m* net; **net worth** situation *f* nette

2 *n* net *m*; **net payable** net à payer

3 *vt (of person, company)* gagner net; *(of sale)* produire net; **he nets £20,000 a year** il gagne 20 000 livres net par an

4 *adv* **net of tax** net d'impôt; **net of VAT** hors TVA

nethead *n* Fam COMPTR accro *mf* de l'Internet

netiquette *n* COMPTR netiquette *f*

netizen *n* COMPTR internaute *mf*

network 1 *n* COMPTR réseau *m* ◻ **network administrator** administrateur *m* de réseau; **network card** carte *f* réseau; **network computer** ordinateur *m* en réseau; **network driver** gestionnaire *m* de réseau; **network manager** gestionnaire *m* de réseau; **network server** serveur *m* de réseau; **network software** logiciel *m* de réseau; **network traffic** trafic *m* de réseau

2 *vt* COMPTR mettre en réseau ◻ **networked systems** systèmes *mpl* en réseau

3 *vi (make contacts)* établir un réseau de contacts

networking *n* (a) COMPTR travail *m* en réseau; *(connecting as network)* mise *f* en réseau; **to have networking capabilities** *(of terminal)* offrir la possibilité d'intégration à un réseau (b) *(making contacts)* établissement *m* d'un réseau de contacts

neural network *n* COMPTR réseau *m* neuronal

new *adj* nouveau(elle); *(not used)* neuf (neuve) ◻ MKTG **new buy situation** situation *f* de nouvel achat; **new capital** capitaux *mpl* frais; **new departure** nouvelle orientation *f*; ST EXCH **new issue** nouvelle émission *f*; ST EXCH **new issue market** marché *m* des nouvelles émissions, marché *m* primaire; **new money** crédit *m* de restructuration; MKTG **new product** nouveau produit *m*; **new product development** développement *m* de nouveaux produits; **new product marketing**

marketing *m* de nouveaux produit(s); *new shares* actions *fpl* nouvelles

newbie *n Fam* COMPTR internaute *mf* novice

newly-industrialized country *n* nouveau pays *m* industrialisé

news *n* (a) *(information)* nouvelles *fpl*; *(on TV, radio)* informations *fpl* □ *news agency* agence *f* de presse (b) COMPTR nouvelles *fpl* □ *news reader* logiciel *m* de lecture de nouvelles

newsgroup *n* COMPTR forum *m* de discussion, newsgroup *m*

newsletter *n* bulletin *m* (d'informations)

new-to-the-company product *n* MKTG produit *m* nouveau dans la compagnie

new-to-the-world product *n* MKTG produit *m* nouveau dans le monde

NGO *n* (abbr **non-governmental org-anization**) ONG *f*

NHS *n Br* (abbr **National Health Service**) service *m* de santé publique

NI *n* (abbr **National Insurance**) = système britannique de sécurité sociale

NIC *n* (a) *Br* (abbr **National Insurance contributions**) cotisations *fpl* à la Sécurité sociale (b) (abbr **newly-industrialized country**) NPI *m*

niche *n* MKTG *(in market)* créneau *m* □ *niche player* acteur *m* sur un segment de marché; *niche product* produit *m* ciblé

> **"**
> Centre Re, one of Zurich's American subsidiaries, is a **niche player** par excellence. The firm ... started with capital of just $150m in 1988. ... It now commands a market niche known as "finite-risk insurance", sold mostly to multinational companies.
> **"**

night *n* nuit *f* □ *night rate* tarif *m* de nuit; BANKING *night safe* coffre(-fort) *m* de nuit; *night shift* équipe *f* de nuit; **to be on night shift** être de nuit

Nikkei Index *n* ST EXCH indice *m* Nikkei

nil 1 *n* néant *m*, zéro *m*; **the balance is nil** le solde est nul

2 *adj* nul (nulle), zéro □ *nil growth* croissance *f* zéro; *nil profit* bénéfice *m* nul

NNP *n* (abbr **net national product**) produit *m* national net

no-claims bonus *n* INS bonus *m*

node *n* COMPTR noyau *m*

no-fault insurance *n Am* assurance *f* non-responsabilité

noise *n* COMPTR bruit *m*

nominal *adj* (a) *(neglible)* nominal(e); *(rent)* insignifiant(e); *(damages)* symbolique (b) ACCT *nominal account* compte *m* d'exploitation générale; FIN *nominal capital* capital *m* nominal; FIN *nominal interest rate* taux *m* d'intérêt nominal; *nominal ledger* grand-livre *m* général; *nominal partner* associé(e) *m,f* fictif(ive); *nominal price* prix *m* nominal; *nominal value* valeur *f* nominale; *nominal wages* salaire *m* nominal; *nominal yield* taux *m* nominal

nominate *vt* (a) *(appoint)* nommer, désigner; **to nominate sb to a post** désigner qn à un poste; **he was nominated chairman** il a été nommé président (b) *(propose)* proposer; **to nominate sb for a post** proposer la candidature de qn à un poste

nomination *n* nomination *f*

nominee *n* (a) *(appointed)* personne *f* nommée (b) *(proposed)* candidat(e) *m,f* □ ST EXCH *nominee shareholding* actionnariat *m* intermédiaire

non-acceptance *n* BANKING *(of bill of exchange)* non-acceptation *f*

non-adopter *n* MKTG = consommateur qui n'essaie jamais de nouveaux produits

non-contributory pension *n* caisse *f* de retraite sans versements de la part des bénéficiaires

> **"**
> Although 70% of the 135 individuals questioned said they would prefer an equivalent salary increase to most benefits, given a choice of perks, the **non-contributory pension** narrowly defeated a company car as favourite.
> **"**

non-cumulative *adj* FIN *(shares)* non cumulatif(ive) □ *non-cumulative quantity discount* remise *f* sur quantité non cumulable

non-current liabilities *npl* ACCT passif *m* non exigible

non-delivery *n (of goods)* non-livraison *f*; **in the event of non-delivery** dans l'éventualité où les marchandises ne seraient pas livrées

non-dutiable *adj* CUSTOMS exempt(e) de droits de douane

non-equity share *n* ST EXCH action *f* sans privilège de participation

non-execution *n (of contract)* non-exécution *f*

non-executive director *n* administrateur(trice) *m,f*

non-forfeiture *n* LAW non-déchéance *f* ❏ INS ***non-forfeiture clause*** clause *f* de reconduction automatique

non-fulfilment *n (of contract)* non-exécution *f*

non-liability *n* LAW non-responsabilité *f* ❏ ***non-liability clause*** clause *f* de non-responsabilité

non-negotiable *adj* non-négociable

non-participating *adj* INS *(policy)* sans participation aux bénéfices; ST EXCH *(share)* sans droit de participation

non-payment *n* non-paiement *m*; **in case of non-payment** en cas de non-paiement, à défaut de paiement

non-performing loan *n* BANKING prêt *m* en souffrance

non-probability *adj* MKTG ***non-probability method*** *(of sampling)* méthode *f* non probabiliste; ***non-probability sampling*** échantillonnage *m* non probabiliste

non-profit-making organization *n Br* société *f* à but non lucratif

non-qualifying policy *n* régime *m* de retraite non défiscalisé

non-recourse finance *n* FIN financement *m* sans recours *ou* à forfait

non-recurring expenditure *n* frais *mpl ou* dépenses *fpl* extraordinaires

non-refundable packaging *n* emballage *m* perdu

non-returnable *adj* sans réserve de retour; *(container, packaging)* non consigné(e)

non-tariff barrier *n* barrière *f* non tarifaire

non-taxable *adj* ADMIN *(revenue)* non imposable

non-union, non-unionized *adj (worker)* non syndiqué(e)

nonvoting *adj* FIN, ST EXCH *(share)* sans droit de vote

non-warranty *n* non-garantie *f* ❏ ***non-warranty clause*** clause *f* de non-garantie

normal *adj* MKTG ***normal distribution curve*** courbe *f* de distribution normale; ST EXCH ***normal market size*** taille *f* normale du marché; ***normal retirement age*** âge *m* normal de départ à la retraite

North American Free Trade Agreement *n* accord *m* de libre-échange nord-américain

> **"**
>
> A significant delay in the signing of the **North American Free Trade Agreement** (Nafta), to create a free trade area stretching from Canada to Mexico … was expected following talks at the US presidential retreat at Camp David on Dec. 14 between President Carlos Salinas de Gortari and United States President Bush.
>
> **"**

notarial *adj* LAW *(functions, procedure)* notarial(e); *(deed)* notarié(e)

notary *n* LAW **notary (public)** notaire *m*

note **1** *n* **(a)** *(information, reminder)* note *f* **(b)** *(banknote)* billet *m*; **a ten-pound note** un billet de dix livres ❏ FIN ***note issue facility*** autorisation *f* d'émettre les billets de banque **2** *vt* noter, remarquer; *(error)* relever; *(fact)* constater; **you will note that there is an error in the account** nous vous faisons remarquer qu'il s'est glissé une erreur dans le compte

notebook *n* COMPTR agenda *m*

not-for-profit organization *n Am* société *f* à but non lucratif

notice *n* **(a)** *(notification)* avis *m*, notification *f*; **until further notice** jusqu'à nouvel ordre ❏ ***notice of receipt*** accusé *m* de réception; ***notice of withdrawal*** avis *m* de retrait de fonds

(b) *(warning)* avertissement *m*; *(of resignation, redundancy)* préavis *m*; **to give in** *or* **hand in one's notice** donner sa démission, démissionner; **to give six months' notice** donner un préavis de six mois; **to give sb notice (of sth)** prévenir *ou* avertir qn (de qch); *(of resignation, redundancy)* donner un préavis à qn (de qch); **can be delivered at three days' notice** livrable dans un délai de trois jours; BANKING **deposit at seven days' notice** dépôt *m* à sept jours de préavis

(c) *(intent to vacate premises)* **notice (to quit)** (avis *m* de) congé *m*; **to be under notice to quit** avoir reçu son congé; **to give sb notice** *(of landlord)* donner son congé à qn

notification *n* avis *m*, notification *f*; **to give sb notification (of sth)** avertir qn (de qch); **you will receive notification by mail** vous serez averti par courrier

notify *vt* annoncer, notifier; **to notify sb of sth** avertir qn de qch

notional *adj* fictif(ive) ❑ *notional income* revenu *m* fictif; *notional rent* loyer *m* insignifiant

novation *n* LAW novation *f*

NPV *n* ACCT (*abbr* **net present value**) VAN *f* ❑ *NPV rate* taux *m* d'actualisation

null *adj* LAW (*invalid*) nul (nulle); **null and void** nul et non avenu; **to declare a contract null and void** déclarer un contrat nul et non avenu

nullification *n* annulation *f*

nullify *vt* annuler

number 1 *n* (*numeral*) nombre *m* ❑ COMPTR *number crunching* calculs *mpl* (rapides); *number key* touche *f* numérique; *numbers*
lock verrouillage *m* du clavier numérique; *numbers lock key* touche *f* de verrouillage du clavier numérique
2 *vt* (*consecutively*) numéroter ❑ *numbered account* compte *m* numéroté

numeric COMPTR 1 *n* **numerics** chiffres *mpl* ou caractères *mpl* numériques
2 *adj* numérique ❑ *numeric pad* pavé *m* numérique

numerical *adj* numérique ❑ COMPTR *numerical analysis* analyse *f* numérique; *numerical data* données *fpl* numériques; *numerical keypad* pavé *m* numérique

num lock *n* COMPTR (*abbr* **numbers lock**) verr num

objective n but m, objectif m; **to achieve** or **attain one's objectives** atteindre ses objectifs

objectivity n ACCT objectivité f

object-orientated adj COMPTR orienté(e) objet

obligate vt Am FIN (funds, credits) affecter

obsolescence n obsolescence f ❑ INS **obsolescence clause** clause f de vétusté

obsolescent adj obsolescent(e)

occupancy n (**a**) (of building) occupation f (**b**) LAW possession f à titre de premier occupant

occupant n (**a**) (of building) occupant(e) m,f; (tenant) locataire mf (**b**) LAW premier(ère) occupant(e) m,f

occupation n (**a**) (profession) métier m, emploi m; **what is his occupation?** quel est son metier?; **please state your name and occupation** veuillez indiquer votre nom et votre profession (**b**) (of building) occupation f; **the offices are ready for occupation** les bureaux sont prêts à être occupés

occupational adj professionnel(elle) ❑ **occupational accident** accident m du travail; **occupational disease** maladie f professionnelle; **occupational hazard** risque m du métier; **occupational pension scheme** caisse f de retraite maison

> 〞
> Generally, an individual cannot be a member of an **occupational pension scheme** and make contributions to a personal pension scheme or retirement annuity policy in respect of the same source of income.
> 〞

occupier n occupant(e) m,f

occupy vt occuper

OCR n COMPTR (**a**) (abbr **optical character reader**) lecteur m (à reconnaissance) optique de caractères (**b**) (abbr **optical character recognition**) OCR f ❑ **OCR software** logiciel m d'OCR

OD n (abbr **overdraft**) découvert m

ODA n Br (abbr **Overseas Development Administration**) = organisme d'aide aux pays en voie de développement

odd lot n (**a**) (of goods) lot m dépareillé (**b**) ST EXCH (of shares) lot m de moins de cent actions

odd-lot adj ST EXCH **odd-lot order** ordre m de moins de cent actions; **odd-lot trading** achats mpl et ventes fpl de lots de moins de cent actions

OECD n (abbr **Organization for Economic Cooperation and Development**) OCDE f

offer **1** n offre f; **to make sb an offer (for sth)** faire une offre à qn (pour qch); **under offer** (building) en vente; **what is on offer in the negotiations?** qu'est-ce qui est proposé dans les négociations?; **£500 or nearest offer** 500 livres, à débattre ❑ **offer price** cours m ou prix m vendeur; **offer by prospectus** offre f publique de vente; **offer to purchase** offre f publique d'achat; **offer for sale** mise f sur le marché

2 vt offrir; **he was offered the post** on lui a offert le poste; **to offer goods for sale** mettre des marchandises en vente; **to offer one's services** proposer ses services

offering n (of new shares) mise f sur le marché ❑ Am **offering circular** note f d'information

office n (**a**) (place) bureau m; **for office use only** (on form) (cadre) réservé à l'administration ❑ **office automation** bureautique f; **office account** compte m professionnel ou commercial; **office block** immeuble m de bureaux; **office equipment** matériel m de bureau; **office expenses** frais mpl de bureau; **office hours** heures fpl de bureau; **office management** organisation f des bureaux; **office space** locaux mpl pour bureaux; **office supplies** articles mpl de bureau; **office staff** personnel m de bureau; **office worker** employé(e) m,f de bureau

(**b**) (position) fonctions fpl; **to be in office, to hold office** être au pouvoir; **to be out of office** ne plus être au pouvoir

(**c**) (government department) bureau m, département m; **I have to send this to the tax office** je dois envoyer ça au centre des impôts ❑ **Office of Fair Trading** = service britannique de la concurrence et des prix

officer n (in local government) fonctionnaire mf; (of trade union) représentant(e) m,f permanent(e); *(of office)* membre *m* de la direction

official 1 *n* fonctionnaire *mf*
2 *adj (statement, visit, strike)* officiel(elle); *(language) (of country)* officiel; *(bureaucratic)* administratif(ive); **his appointment will be made official tomorrow** sa nomination sera rendue officielle demain; **to go through the official channels** suivre la filière officielle; **to act in one's official capacity** agir dans l'exercice de ses fonctions ▫ **official document** document *m* officiel; **official letter** pli *m* officiel *ou* de service; FIN **Official List** cote *f* officielle; **official market** marché *m* officiel; **official quotation** cours *m* officiel; BANKING **official rate** taux *m* officiel d'escompte; **official receiver** administrateur(trice) *m,f* judiciaire; **official receivership** liquidation *f* judiciaire; *Br* **Official Secrets Act** = document relatif au secret-défense, signé par tous les fonctionnaires

officialese *n Fam* jargon *m* administratif

officially *adv* officiellement

off-line *adj* COMPTR non connecté(e); *(processing)* en différé; *(printer)* déconnecté(e); **to be off-line** ne pas être connecté; **to go off-line** se déconnecter ▫ **off-line mode** mode *m* autonome; **off-line reader** lecteur *m* non connecté

offload *vt (goods)* débarquer

off-peak 1 *adj (consumption, rate)* aux heures creuses
2 *adv* pendant les heures creuses

off-season 1 *n* morte-saison *f*
2 *adj* hors saison ▫ **off-season tariff** tarif *m* hors saison
3 *adv* pendant la morte-saison

offset 1 *n* ACCT compensation *f*, dédommagement *m* ▫ **offset agreement** accord *m* de compensation
2 *vt (compensate for)* compenser; **to offset sth against tax** déduire le montant de qch de ses impôts; **any wage increase will be offset by inflation** avec l'inflation, les augmentations de salaire n'en seront plus vraiment

offsetting entry *n* ACCT écriture *f* de compensation

offshore 1 *adj* **offshore banking** opérations *fpl* bancaires off-shore; **offshore company** société *f* off-shore; **offshore fund** fonds *m* off-shore; **offshore investment** placement *m* off-shore
2 *adv* **to keep sth offshore** garder qch offshore

> **"**
> For UK residents, the reason for considering **offshore funds**, other than if they have some special appeal … will be possible tax advantages. If an **offshore fund** does not acquire distributor status from the Inland Revenue then any gain will be taxed as income when realised.
> **"**

off-the-peg research *n* MKTG = étude de marché utilisant des données déjà rassemblées

off-the-shelf *adj (goods)* prêt(e) à l'usage ▫ **off-the-shelf company** société *f* tiroir

OFT *n (abbr* **Office of Fair Trading)** = service britannique de la concurrence et des prix

OHP *n (abbr* **overhead projector)** rétroprojecteur *m*

oil *n (petroleum)* pétrole *m* ▫ **oil company** société *f* pétrolière; **oil field** gisement *m* pétrolifère; **oil market** marché *m* pétrolier; **oil prices** prix *mpl* pétroliers; **oil products** produits *mpl* pétroliers; **oil revenu** revenu *m* pétrolier; **oil shares** valeurs *fpl* pétrolières

oil-producing countries *npl* pays *mpl* producteurs de pétrole

old-age pension *n* pension *f* de retraite

oligopoly *n* ECON oligopole *m*

ombudsman *n* ≃ médiateur *m* de la République

omnibus survey *adj* MKTG = enquête fondée sur un questionnaire envoyé régulièrement à un panel, à laquelle peuvent participer plusieurs sociétés ayant chacune quelques questions à poser

omnium *n* ST EXCH omnium *m*

on-board surcharge *n* surcharge *f* 'on-board'

oncosts *npl* frais *mpl* généraux

one *n* ST EXCH unité *f*; **to issue shares in ones** émettre des actions en unités

one-man business *n* entreprise *f* individuelle

one-off *Br* **1** *n (article)* objet *m* unique
2 *adj (article)* spécial(e), hors série; *(order, job)* unique

one-sided *adj (contract)* unilatéral(e), inégal(e)

one-stop *adj* **one-stop buying** achats *mpl* regroupés; **one-stop shop** magasin *m* où l'on trouve de tout

one-way *adj (packaging)* perdu(e)

on-line *adj* COMPTR en ligne; **to go on-line** se connecter; **to put the printer on-line** connecter l'imprimante □ *on-line cash desk terminal* terminal *m* de paiement connecté; *on-line help* aide *f* en ligne; *on-line mode* mode *m* connecté; *on-line time* durée *f* de connexion

ono *adv (abbr* **or nearest offer**) à débattre

on-screen *adj* COMPTR à l'écran

on-target earnings *npl* salaire *m* de base plus commissions

on-the-job *adj (training, experience)* sur le tas

OPEC *n (abbr* **Organization of Petroleum-Exporting Countries**) OPEP *f*

open 1 *adj* ouvert(e) □ FIN *open account* compte *m* ouvert; *open cheque* chèque *m* ouvert *ou* non barré; ST EXCH *open contract* position *f* ouverte; *open credit* crédit *m* à découvert; *open economy* économie *f* ouverte; ECON *open market* marché *m* libre; ST EXCH **to buy shares on the open market** acheter des actions en Bourse; ST EXCH *open outcry* criée *f*; INS *open policy* police *f* flottante; ST EXCH *open position* position *f* ouverte
2 *vt* ouvrir; *(negotiations, conversation, debate)* entamer; **to open a line of credit** ouvrir un crédit; **to open a loan** ouvrir un emprunt
3 *vi* (**a**) *(of shop, business)* ouvrir (**b**) ST EXCH coter à l'ouverture; **the FTSE opened at 1083** l'indice FT a ouvert à 1083

> **❝**
> The bulk of LIFFE's trade is conducted by "**open outcry**" in pits, each of which is specific to a particular type of instrument which is traded in it only during the recognised hours laid down by the Exchange. A large electronic price board displays current in-house information in the Exchange, which is relayed to outside agencies.
> **❞**

▸ **open up 1** *vt sep (office, shop)* ouvrir; **to open up a country to trade** ouvrir un pays au commerce
2 *vi (of office, shop)* ouvrir

open-door policy *n (for importing goods)* politique *f* de la porte ouverte

open-ended *adj (agreement, mortgage)* sans date limite □ *open-ended contract* contrat *m* à durée indéterminée; *open-*

ended trust société *f* d'investissement à capital variable, sicav *f*

opening *n* (**a**) *(of shop, office, account, credit, negotiations)* ouverture *f* □ ACCT *opening entry* écriture *f* d'ouverture; *opening hours* heures *fpl* d'ouverture; ACCT *opening stock* stock *m* initial *ou* d'ouverture
(**b**) *(opportunity)* occasion *f* favorable; *(job)* débouché *m*; **there are lots of good openings in industry** l'industrie offre de nombreux débouchés intéressants
(**c**) ST EXCH *opening day* jour *m* d'ouverture; *opening price (at start of trading)* cours *m* d'ouverture, premier cours *m*; *(of new shares)* cours *m* d'introduction

operate 1 *vt* (**a**) *(machine)* faire fonctionner (**b**) *(business)* gérer, diriger; **she operates her business from home** elle fait marcher son affaire depuis son domicile
2 *vi* (**a**) *(of machine)* fonctionner; **the factory is operating at full capacity** l'usine tourne à plein rendement (**b**) *(take effect)* être en vigueur; **the pay rise will operate from 1 January** l'augmentation des salaires entrera en vigueur le 1 janvier

operating *adj* (**a**) *Am operating account* compte *m* d'exploitation; *operating budget* budget *m* d'exploitation; *operating cost* charge *f* opérationnelle; *operating costs* frais *mpl ou* coûts *mpl* d'exploitation; *operating costs analysis* comptabilité *f* analytique d'exploitation; *operating expenses* frais *mpl* d'exploitation; *operating income* produits *mpl* d'exploitation; *operating loss* perte *f* d'exploitation; *operating margin* marge *f* (nette) d'exploitation; *operating profit* bénéfice *m* d'exploitation; *operating ratio* coefficient *m* d'exploitation; *operating rules* règles *fpl* d'exploitation; FIN *operating statement* compte *m* d'exploitation
(**b**) COMPTR *operating system* système *m* d'exploitation

operation *n (of company)* activité *f*; **the company is moving its soft drinks operation** la société déménage sa branche de boissons non alcoolisées □ *operations breakdown* décomposition *f* des tâches; *operations management* gestion *f* des opérations; *operations manager* directeur(trice) *m,f* des exploitations; *operations strategy* stratégie *f* opérationnelle

operational *adj* opérationnel(elle); **the design team was operational within six months** en l'espace de six mois, l'équipe de dessinateurs était opérationnelle □ *operational audit* audit *m* opérationnel;

operational costs coûts *mpl* opérationnels; ACCT **operational cost accounting** comptabilité *f* analytique d'exploitation; ACCT **operational cost centre** centre *m* d'analyse opérationnel; **operational efficiency** efficacité *f* opérationnelle; **operational marketing** marketing *m* opérationnel; **operational planning** planification *f* des opérations; **operational research** recherche *f* opérationnelle

operative 1 *n (manual worker)* ouvrier(ère) *m,f*
2 *adj* (**a**) *(law, rule, regulation)* en vigueur; **to become operative** entrer en vigueur, prendre effet (**b**) *(system, scheme)* opérationnel(elle); **the system will soon be operative** le système sera bientôt opérationnel

operator *n* (**a**) TEL opérateur(trice) *m,f* ▫ **(switchboard) operator** standardiste *mf* (**b**) *(of machine)* opérateur(trice) *m,f*

opinion *n* MKTG **opinion former, opinion leader** leader *m* d'opinion; **opinion measurement technique** technique *f* de sondage d'opinion; **opinion poll, opinion survey** sondage *m* (d'opinion)

opportunity *n* MKTG **opportunity to hear** occasion *f* d'entendre; **opportunity to see** occasion *f* de voir; **opportunity and threat analysis** analyse *f* des opportunités et des menaces

opposition *n (competitors)* concurrence *f*

optical *adj* COMPTR **optical character reader** lecteur *m* optique de caractères; **optical character recognition** reconnaissance *f* optique des caractères; **optical disk** disque *m* optique; **optical drive** lecteur *m* optique

optimal *adj* optimal(e) ▫ **optimal resource allocation** répartition *f* optimale des ressources; MKTG **optimal psychological price** prix *m* psychologique optimum

optimizer *n* COMPTR optimiseur *m*

optimum 1 *n* optimum *m*
2 *adj* optimum, optimal(e) ▫ **optimum conditions** conditions *fpl* optimales; **optimum employment of resources** emploi *m* optimum des ressources

option *n* (**a**) ST EXCH option *f*, (marché *m* à) prime *f*; **to take an option (on sth)** prendre une option (sur qch); **to declare an option** répondre à une option; **option on shares** option sur actions; **option to double** option du double ▫ **option day** (jour *m* de la) réponse *f* des primes; **option deal** opération *f* à prime; **options desk** desk *m* d'options; **options market** marché *m* à options *ou* à primes; **option money** (montant *m* de la) prime *f*; **option price** prix *m* de l'option; **options trading** négociations *fpl* à prime
(**b**) COMPTR **option box** case *f* d'option; **option button** case *f* d'option

optional *adj* facultatif(ive) ▫ **optional extra** (accessoire *m* en) option *f*

optional-feature pricing *n* MKTG fixation *f* du prix en fonction des options

optionee *n* ST EXCH bénéficiaire *mf* d'options

order 1 *n* (**a**) *(request for goods)* commande *f*; **to place an order (with sb/for sth)** passer une commande (à qn/de qch); **to make sth to order** faire qch sur commande; **to deliver an order** livrer une commande; **to fill an order** exécuter une commande; **as per order** conformément à votre commande ▫ **order book** carnet *m* de commandes; **order cycle time** durée *f* du cycle de commande; **order form** bon *m* de commande; **order number** numéro *m* de commande; **order to remittance cycle** cycle *m* commande-livraison-facturation
(**b**) FIN *(document)* mandat *m*; **pay to the order of J. Martin** payez à l'ordre de J. Martin; **pay J. Martin or order** payez à J. Martin ou à son ordre; **by order and for account of J. Martin** d'ordre et pour compte de J. Martin
(**c**) *(condition)* **in (good) working order** en (bon) état de fonctionnement *ou* de marche; **out of order** *(telephone)* en dérangement; *(lift, machine)* hors service
2 *vt (goods)* commander

ordinary *adj* ACCT **ordinary activities** *(balance sheet item)* opérations *fpl* courantes; FIN **ordinary creditor** créancier(ère) *m,f* ordinaire; *Br* FIN, ST EXCH **ordinary share** action *f* ordinaire; **ordinary share capital** capital *m* en actions ordinaires

organigram *n* organigramme *m*

organization *n* organisation *f*; **we are unhappy with the organization of the company** l'organisation de la société ne nous satisfait pas ▫ **organization chart** organigramme *m*; **Organization for Economic Cooperation and Development** Organisation de Coopération et de développement économiques; **organization and methods** organisation scientifique du travail

organizational *adj (skills, methods)* organisationnel(elle), d'organisation; *(expenses)* d'organisation ❏ ᴇᴄᴏɴ ***organizational behaviour*** comportement *m* de l'individu au sein d'une organisation

organize 1 *vt* (**a**) *(put into order)* organiser (**b**) *(workers)* syndiquer ❏ ***organized labour*** main-d'œuvre *f* syndiquée
 2 *vi (of workers)* se syndiquer

organizer *n* organisateur(trice) *m,f*

organizing *n* organisation *f* ❏ ***organizing committee*** comité *m* d'organisation

origin *n* origine *f*; **country of origin** pays *m* d'origine ❏ ***origin of goods label*** marque *f* d'origine

original 1 *n (of document)* original *m*; ꜰɪɴ *(of bill of exchange)* primata *m*
 2 *adj* original(e) ❏ ꜰɪɴ ***original capital*** capital *m* d'origine; ***original cost*** coût *m* initial; ᴀᴄᴄᴛ ***original document*** pièce *f* comptable; ***original packing*** emballage *m* d'origine; ***original value*** valeur *f* initiale

OS *n* ᴄᴏᴍᴘᴛʀ *(abbr* **operating system***)* système *m* d'exploitation

OTC *adj* ꜱᴛ ᴇxᴄʜ *(abbr* **over-the-counter***)* hors cote

OTE *npl (abbr* **on-target earnings***)* salaire *m* de base plus commissions

OTH *n* ᴍᴋᴛɢ *(abbr* **opportunity to hear***)* ODE *f*

OTS *n* ᴍᴋᴛɢ *(abbr* **opportunity to see***)* ODV *f*

out 1 *adj* ᴀᴄᴄᴛ ***out book*** livre *m* du dehors
 2 *adv* **to be out (on strike)** faire grève

outage *n (goods lost)* pertes *fpl*

outbid *vt (at auction)* enchérir sur

outbound freight *n* fret *m* de sortie

outflow *n* ꜰɪɴ *(of gold, currency)* sortie *f*; **outflow per hour** débit *m* par heure

outgoing *adj (telephone call)* sortant(e); *(mail)* à expédier, au départ

outgoings *npl* dépenses *fpl*; **the outgoings exceed the incomings** les dépenses excèdent les recettes

outlay *n* frais *mpl*, dépenses *fpl*

outlet *n (market)* débouché *m*; *(point of sale)* point *m* de vente; **there are not many sales outlets in Japan** le Japon offre peu de débouchés commerciaux

out-of-court settlement *n* ʟᴀᴡ règlement *m* à l'amiable

out-of-pocket expenses *npl* menues dépenses *fpl*

out-of-town *adj (supermarket, development)* situé(e) à la périphérie d'une ville

outplacement *n* = aide à la recherche d'un nouvel emploi, fournie par l'employeur lors d'un licenciement

output 1 *n* (**a**) *(of factory, worker)* production *f*, rendement *m*; *(of machine)* débit *m*, rendement; **this represents 25% of the total output** cela représente 25% de la production totale ❏ ***output bonus*** prime *f* de rendement; ***output ceiling*** plafond *m* de la production; ᴀᴄᴄᴛ ***output tax*** TVA *f* encaissée
 (**b**) ᴄᴏᴍᴘᴛʀ *(of data, information)* sortie *f* ❏ ***output device*** dispositif *m* ou périphérique *m* de sortie
 2 *vt* (**a**) *(of factory, worker, machine)* produire
 (**b**) ᴄᴏᴍᴘᴛʀ *(data, information)* sortir (**to** sur)

outreach *n* ᴀᴅᴍɪɴ = recherche des personnes qui ne demandent pas l'aide sociale dont elles pourraient bénéficier

outright *adv* **to buy sth outright** acheter qch au comptant

outsell *vt (of goods)* se vendre mieux que; *(of retailer)* vendre plus que

outside *adj* (**a**) ***outside worker*** travailleur(euse) *m,f* à domicile
 (**b**) ꜱᴛ ᴇxᴄʜ ***outside broker*** courtier(ère) *m,f* marron; ***outside brokerage*** affaires *fpl* de banque; ***outside market*** marché *m* hors cote; ***outside price*** prix *m* maximum
 (**c**) ᴛᴇʟ ***outside line*** ligne *f* extérieure

outsider *n* ꜱᴛ ᴇxᴄʜ courtier(ère) *m,f* marron

outsource *vt* externaliser; **computer maintenance has been outsourced to another company** l'entretien du matériel informatique a été externalisé

> Design consultancy was one of the fastest growing sectors in the UK during the 1980s. ... Consolidation and survival characterise this sector in the 1990s. But as more companies **outsource** design skills and expertise the sector is likely to continue to expand.

outsourcing *n* externalisation *f*

outstanding *adj (business)* en suspens; *(amount, account)* impayé(e), dû (due); *(payment)* en retard; *(invoice)* en souffrance; *(interest)* échu(e) □ **outstanding balance** solde *m* à découvert; BANKING **outstanding cheque** chèque *m* en circulation; **outstanding debts** créances *fpl* (à recouvrer); **outstanding shares** actions *fpl* en cours *ou* en circulation

out-supplier *n* fournisseur *m* potentiel

out-tray *n* corbeille *f* du courrier à expédier

outward *adj* **outward bill of lading** connaissement *m* de sortie; **outward cargo** cargaison *f* d'aller; **outward freight** fret *m* de sortie; ECON **outward investment** investissement *m* à l'étranger; **outward mail** courrier *m* (en partance) pour l'étranger; **outward mission** mission *f* à l'étranger; **outward voyage** voyage *m* d'aller

outwork *n* travail *m* fait à domicile

outworker *n* employé(e) *m,f* qui travaille à domicile

overage *n Am* excédent *m*, surplus *m*

overall *adj* global(e); *(size, area)* total(e); **she has overall responsibility for sales** elle est responsable de l'ensemble du service des ventes □ **overall consumption** consommation *f* totale; **overall demand** demande *f* globale; **overall plan** plan *m* d'ensemble

overassessment *n* surimposition *f*

overbook 1 *vt (flight, hotel)* surréserver **2** *vi (of airline, hotel)* surréserver

overbooking *n* surréservation *f*

overbought *adj* ST EXCH *(market)* surévalué(e), surachété(e)

overcapacity *n* ECON surcapacité *f*

overcapitalization *n* FIN surcapitalisation *f*

overcapitalize *vt* FIN surcapitaliser

overcharge 1 *vt (person)* faire payer trop cher à; **they overcharged me for the repair** ils m'ont pris trop cher pour la réparation **2** *vi* faire payer trop cher

overconsumption *n* ECON surconsommation *f*

overdevelop *vt* ECON surdévelopper

overdevelopment *n* ECON surdéveloppement *m*

overdraft *n* BANKING découvert *m*; **to have an overdraft** avoir un découvert; **to allow sb an overdraft** accorder à qn un découvert; **to pay off one's overdraft** rembourser son découvert □ **overdraft facility** autorisation *f* de découvert, facilités *fpl* de caisse; **overdraft limit** plafond *m* de découvert

> A company can borrow from its clearing bank via an **overdraft facility** attached to its current account. Large corporate customers pay interest on overdrafts at the bank's base rate plus 1%. Smaller companies will pay a higher margin.

overdraw BANKING **1** *vt (account)* mettre à découvert; **to be overdrawn** avoir un découvert, être à découvert; **your account is overdrawn** votre compte est débiteur *ou* à découvert; **I'm £100 overdrawn** j'ai un découvert de 100 livres **2** *vi* tirer à découvert

overdue *adj (account, payment)* en retard, impayé(e); **our repayments are two months overdue** nous avons un retard de deux mois dans nos remboursements

overemployment *n* ECON suremploi *m*

overestimate *vt (assets)* majorer; *(item)* surévaluer, surestimer la valeur de

overexposure *n* risque *m* accru

overflow *n* COMPTR dépassement *m* de capacité

overfreight *n* poids *m* en excès

overfunding *n* déflation *f* budgétaire

overgearing *n* FIN surendettement *m*

overhead 1 *n* charge *f* opérationnelle; *Br* **overheads,** *Am* **overhead** frais *mpl* généraux □ **overhead budget** budget *m* des charges; **overhead costs, overhead expenses** frais *mpl* généraux; FIN **overhead variance** variance *f* des frais généraux **2** *adj* **overhead projector** rétroprojecteur *m*

overindustrialization *n* surindustrialisation *f*

overinsurance *n* surassurance *f*

overinsure *vt* surassurer

overinvestment *n* FIN surinvestissement *m*

overissue **1** *n* (of paper money) surémission *f*
2 *vt* (paper money) faire une surémission de

overlap *n* MKTG débordement *m*

overload *vt* (market) surcharger

overmanned *adj* en sureffectif

overmanning *n* sureffectifs *mpl*

overnight *adj* FIN **overnight loan** prêt *m* du jour au lendemain; **overnight rate** taux *m* de l'argent au jour le jour

> This forced the Central Bank, in a 10-day period up to Sept. 13, to buy $800,000,000 in US dollars, to prevent Brazilian exports being priced out of the market. The freeze caused interest rates to rise steeply, the **overnight rate** reaching 38 per cent on Sept. 17 before settling back to 30 per cent.

over-packaging *n* MKTG suremballage *m*

overpay *vt* surpayer, trop payer

overpayment *n* (of taxes) trop-perçu *m*; (of employee) rémunération *f* excessive

over-position *vt* MKTG surpositionner

over-positioning *n* MKTG surpositionnement *m*

overprice *vt* vendre trop cher

overproduce *vt & vi* surproduire

overproduction *n* surproduction *f*

overrate *vt* ADMIN surtaxer

overriding *adj* (importance) primordial(e), capital(e); (factor) prépondérant(e) ❑ LAW **overriding clause** clause *f* dérogatoire; **overriding commission** (paid to broker) commission *f* spéciale

overrun *n* (**a**) (in cost) dépassement *m* du budget (**b**) (in production) excédent *m*, surplus *m*

overseas **1** *adj* d'outremer ❑ **overseas debt** dette *f* extérieure; *Br* **Overseas Development Administration** = organisme d'aide au pays en voie de développement; **overseas investment** investissement *m* étranger; **overseas market** marché *m* étranger
2 *adv* à l'étranger

oversold *adj* ST EXCH (market) sous-évalué(e)

overspend **1** *n* découvert *m*
2 *vt* dépenser au-delà de, dépasser
3 *vi* trop dépenser

overstaffed *adj* en sureffectif

overstaffing *n* sureffectifs *mpl*

overstock **1** *npl Am* **overstocks** surplus *m*, excédent *m*
2 *vt* (market) encombrer; (warehouse) trop approvisionner (**with** de)

overstocked *adj* (market) encombré(e); (warehouse) trop approvisionné(e); **the market is overstocked with foreign goods** le marché regorge de marchandises étrangères

oversubscribe *vt* FIN, ST EXCH (loan, share issue) sursouscrire; **the share issue was oversubscribed** la demande d'achats a dépassé le nombre de titres émis

oversubscription *n* FIN, ST EXCH (of loan, share issue) sursouscription *f*

overtax *vt* FIN (goods) surtaxer; (person) surtaxer, surimposer

over-the-counter *adj* ST EXCH hors cote

> Some companies will transfer from the Third market to the USM, some will go to the **over-the-counter** market (OTC), which is an informal market that consists of trading in small business shares by a group of brokers and licensed dealers to the public.

overtime **1** *n* heures *fpl* supplémentaires; **an hour's overtime** une heure supplémentaire; **the salary does not include overtime** les heures supplémentaires ne sont pas comprises *ou* comptées dans le salaire ❑ **overtime ban** grève *f* des heures supplémentaires
2 *adv* **to work** *or* **do overtime** faire des heures supplémentaires

overtrading *n* = emballement de l'activité d'une entreprise (au-delà des limites de son capital)

overvaluation *n* surévaluation *f*

overvalue **1** *n* (of currency) survaleur *f*
2 *vt* (assets) surestimer, majorer; (object, currency) surévaluer

overweight **1** *n* surpoids *m*, poids *m* en excès
2 *adj* (luggage, parcel) au-dessus du poids réglementaire

overwrite COMPTR **1** *n overwrite mode* mode *m* de superposition
  2 *vt (file)* écraser

owe *vt* devoir; **to owe sb sth, to owe sth to sb** devoir qch à qn; **the sum owed to her** le montant qui lui est dû

owing *adj* dû (due); **all the money owing to me** tout l'argent qui m'est dû

own *vt* posséder; **50% owned company** société détenue à 50%

own-brand MKTG **1** *n* marque *f* de distributeur
  2 *adj* **own-brand label** marque *f* de distributeur; **own-brand product** produit *m* à marque de distributeur

own-branding *n* MKTG apposition *f* de sa propre marque

owner *n* propriétaire *mf* ❑ ACCT **owner's capital account** compte *m* de l'exploitant

owner-occupied *adj* occupé(e) par le propriétaire

owner-occupier *n* propriétaire *mf* occupant(e)

ownership *n* propriété *f*; **under new ownership** *(sign)* changement de propriétaire; **to be in private/public ownership** appartenir au secteur privé/public

own-label *adj* à marque de distributeur

PA n (abbr **personal assistant**) secrétaire mf de direction

p.a. adv (abbr **per annum**) par an

pack 1 n paquet m
2 vt (**a**) (goods) emballer, empaqueter (**b**) COMPTR (database) condenser, compacter

package 1 n (**a**) (set of proposals) ensemble m; (contract) contrat m global; **the package includes a company car** l'offre comprend une voiture de société; **the offer is part of a larger package** l'offre fait partie d'un ensemble plus important; **a new package of measures to halt inflation** un nouvel ensemble visant à stopper l'inflation; **we offered them a generous package worth over £100,000** nous leur avons proposé un contrat global très avantageux de plus de 100 000 livres ▫ **package deal** contrat m global
(**b**) COMPTR (software) logiciel m
(**c**) (parcel) paquet m, colis m
2 vt emballer, conditionner

packaging n emballage m

packet n COMPTR (of data) paquet m

packing n emballage m; **postage and packing** frais mpl d'emballage et d'envoi ▫ **packing case** caisse f ou boîte f d'emballage; **packing charges, packing costs** frais mpl d'emballage; **packing list** liste f de colisage; **packing materials** matériaux mpl d'emballage; **packing slip** bon m de livraison

pad n (writing) pad bloc m

page[1] n (of book, document, computer file) page f ▫ **page design** mise f en page; COMPTR **page down** page suivante; COMPTR **page down key** touche f page suivante; **page format** format m de page; COMPTR **page layout** mise f en page; COMPTR **page preview** aperçu m avant l'impression; COMPTR **page scanner** lecteur m de pages; COMPTR **page up** page précédente; COMPTR **page up key** touche f page précédente

▸ **page down** vi COMPTR feuilleter en avant

▸ **page up** vi COMPTR feuilleter en arrière

page[2] vt (by loudspeaker) appeler par haut-parleur; (by electronic device) biper

pager n récepteur m d'appels

paid adj (**a**) (person, work) payé(e), rémunéré(e) ▫ **paid holidays** congés mpl payés (**b**) (goods, bill) payé(e); **paid** (on bill) pour acquit

paid-up adj (member) qui a payé sa cotisation ▫ FIN **paid-up capital** capital m versé; **paid-up shares** actions fpl libérées

❝
A member's liability is limited to the amount, if any, which remains unpaid upon the member's shares. Since normal practice is for a member to be issued with **paid-up shares**, the member's liability is limited to the extent that the shares which he or she has in the company are rendered valueless.
❞

paired comparison n MKTG comparaison f par paire

palette n COMPTR palette f

pallet n palette f ▫ **pallet truck** transpalette f

palmtop n COMPTR ordinateur m de poche

P & L n FIN (abbr **profit and loss**) pertes fpl et profits mpl

p & p n Br (abbr **postage and packing**) port m et emballage m

panel n MKTG (for market research) panel m ▫ **panel discussion** table f ronde, débat m; **panel member** panéliste mf; **panel research** recherches fpl par panel

panic n **panic buying** achats mpl de précaution; **panic selling** ventes fpl de précaution

paper n (**a**) (material) papier m; (document) document m
(**b**) ↘FIN **paper company** société f d'investissement; **paper loss** moins-value f; **paper profit** profit m fictif; **paper securities** titres mpl fiduciaires
(**c**) (banknotes) billets mpl (de banque) ▫ **paper money** papier-monnaie m
(**d**) COMPTR **paper advance** (on printer) entraînement m du papier; **paper feed** alimentation f en papier; **paper format** format m de papier; **paper jam** bourrage m de papier; **paper tray** bac m à feuilles

paperless adj électronique ▫ **paperless office** bureau m informatisé; ST EXCH

paperless trading marché *m ou* cotation *f* électronique

paperwork *n* travail *m* administratif

par *n* FIN *(of bills, shares)* pair *m*; **at par** au pair; **to issue shares at par** émettre des actions au pair; **above par** au-dessus du pair; **below par** au-dessous du pair □ *par of exchange* pair du change; ST EXCH *par value* valeur *f* au pair *ou* nominale

parallel *adj parallel imports* importations *fpl* parallèles; COMPTR *parallel interface* interface *f* parallèle; *parallel market* marché *m* parallèle; COMPTR *parallel port* port *m* parallèle; *parallel rate of exchange* cours *m* parallèle; MKTG *parallel selling* vente *f* parallèle

parameter *n* COMPTR paramètre *m*

parcel *n* (**a**) *(package)* paquet *m*, colis *m*; **to make up a parcel** faire un paquet □ *parcel post* service *m* des colis postaux; **to send sth by parcel post** envoyer qch par colis postal; *parcel rates* tarif *m* colis postal (**b**) ST EXCH *(of shares)* paquet *m*

▶ **parcel up** *vt sep* empaqueter, emballer

parent company *n* société *f ou* maison *f* mère

pari passu *adj* FIN, ST EXCH pari passu (**with** avec)

> “
>
> Shares allotted following the exercise of an option will rank **pari passu** with the then issued shares of the same class of the Company (except that they will not rank for any dividend or other right having a record date prior to the allottee's entry on the Company's register of members).
>
> ”

parity *n* FIN parité *f*; **the two currencies were at parity** les deux monnaies étaient à parité; **franc-dollar parity** parité franc-dollar □ *parity of exchange* parité de change; *parity table* table *f* des parités; *parity value* valeur *f* au pair

parking *n* ST EXCH mise *f* en attente

part *n* (**a**) *(portion)* *part exchange* reprise *f*; *part load* charge *f* incomplète; *part owner* copropriétaire *mf*; *part ownership* copropriété *f*; *part payment* acompte *m*; *part shipment* expédition *f* partielle (**b**) *(for machine)* pièce *f*

partial *adj* partiel(elle) □ BANKING *partial acceptance* *(of bill)* acceptation *f* partielle; INS *partial loss* perte *f* partielle, sinistre *m* partiel

participating interest *n* intérêt *m* de participation; **to hold a participating interest in a company** avoir un intérêt de participation dans une société

partly *adv* partiellement, en partie □ FIN *partly paid-up capital* capital *m* non entièrement versé; *partly paid-up shares* actions *fpl* non entièrement libérées; *partly secured creditor* créancier(ère) *m,f* partiellement nanti(e)

partner *n* associé(e) *m,f*; **our European partners** nos partenaires européens

partnership *n* (**a**) *(association)* association *f*; **to enter into** *or* **go into partnership (with sb)** s'associer (avec qn); **to dissolve a partnership** dissoudre une association; **they've offered him a partnership** ils lui ont proposé de devenir leur associé □ *partnership agreement* accord *m* de partenariat (**b**) *(company)* ≃ société *f* en nom collectif

part-time 1 *adj (job, employee)* à temps partiel; **to be in part-time employment** travailler à temps partiel
2 *adv* à temps partiel

party *n* LAW *(participant)* partie *f*; **the contracting parties** les parties contractantes

PASCAL *n* COMPTR PASCAL *m*

pass 1 *n (permit)* laissez-passer *m* □ *pass book* livret *m* de banque
2 *vt (bill, resolution)* voter; *(invoice)* approuver; **to pass a dividend** conclure un exercice sans payer de dividende

passing trade *n* clients *mpl ou* clientèle *f* de passage

passport *n* passeport *m*

password *n* COMPTR mot *m* de passe □ *password protection* protection *f* par mot de passe

password-protected *adj* COMPTR protégé(e) par mot de passe

paste *vt* COMPTR coller

patch *n* COMPTR *(correction)* correction *f*

patent 1 *n* brevet *m* (d'invention); **to take out a patent (for sth)** prendre un brevet (pour qch); **patent applied for, patent pending** *(on product)* demande de brevet déposée □ *patent office* bureau *m* des brevets; *patent rights* propriété *f* industrielle
2 *adj (patented)* breveté(e) □ *patent goods* articles *mpl* brevetés; *patent medicine* spécialité *f* pharmaceutique
3 *vt (of authorities)* breveter; *(of inventor)* faire breveter

patented *adj* breveté(e)

patentee n titulaire mf d'un brevet

paternity leave n congé m de paternité

> **❝**
>
> We aim to guarantee every woman in employment the right to 14 weeks' maternity leave on full pay, and to give fathers **paternity leave**, bringing Britain into line with the better provision in the European Community.
>
> **❞**

path n COMPTR chemin m (d'accès)

patron n (of shop) client(e) m,f

patronage n clientèle f

patronize vt (shop) accorder sa clientèle à

pattern n (sample) échantillon m ❑ **pattern book** livre m d'échantillons

pawn 1 n to put sth in pawn mettre qch en gage; to take sth out of pawn dégager qch
  2 vt mettre en gage

pawnbroker n prêteur(euse) m,f sur gage

pawnshop n bureau m de prêt sur gage, mont-de-piété m

pay 1 n (wages) salaire m, paie f; the pay's good/bad ça paie bien/mal ❑ **pay cheque** chèque m de paie; **pay day** jour m de paie; ACCT **pay ledger** livre m de paie; **pay packet** (envelope) enveloppe f de paie; (money) paie; **pay policy** politique f salariale; **pay slip** bulletin m de paie; **pay talks** négociations fpl salariales
  2 vt (a) (person) payer; to pay sb £100 payer 100 livres à qn; to be paid by the hour/the week être payé à l'heure/la semaine; she's paid $5,000 a month elle est payée ou elle touche 5000 dollars par mois
  (b) (sum of money) payer; you pay £100 now, the rest later vous payez cent livres maintenant, le solde plus tard; to pay money into sb's account verser de l'argent au compte de qn
  (c) (bill, debt) payer, régler; (dividend) distribuer; (fine, taxes) payer; to pay cash payer (argent) comptant, payer en espèces; to pay a cheque into the bank déposer un chèque à la banque
  3 vi payer, régler; how would you like to pay? comment souhaitez-vous régler?; to pay by cheque payer ou régler par chèque; to pay in cash payer en espèces; to pay in advance payer d'avance; to pay in full payer intégralement ou en totalité; FIN to pay on demand or on presentation payer à vue ou à présentation; FIN pay to bearer payez au porteur

▸ **pay back** vt sep (loan, lender) rembourser

▸ **pay in** vt sep (money, cheque) verser sur un compte

▸ **pay off 1** vt sep (a) (workers) licencier

(b) (debt, loan, mortgage) rembourser
  2 vi (of work, efforts) porter ses fruits; moving the company out of London really paid off la transfert de la société hors de Londres a été une affaire rentable

▸ **pay out 1** vt sep débourser, dépenser
  2 vi payer

▸ **pay up** vi payer

payable 1 adj payable; **payable in 24 monthly instalments/in advance** payable en 24 mensualités/d'avance; **to make a cheque payable to sb** faire ou libeller un chèque à l'ordre de qn; **please make your cheque payable to Miss Johnston** veuillez libeller votre chèque à l'ordre de Miss Johnston; **payable at sight** payable à vue; **payable to order** payable à ordre; **payable to bearer** payable au porteur
  2 n Am **payables** factures fpl à payer

pay-as-you-earn, Am **pay-as-you-go** n prélèvement m de l'impôt à la source

payback n FIN récupération f (du capital investi) ❑ **payback period** délai m de récupération

PAYE n Br (abbr **pay-as-you-earn**) prélèvement m de l'impôt à la source

> **❝**
>
> There may be an obligation for the band members to deduct income tax (Pay As You Earn) from the salaries of any employees. In this case, it is necessary to set up a **PAYE** scheme with the Inland Revenue, to deduct tax and National Insurance, and to pay these over on a regular monthly basis.
>
> **❞**

payee n (of postal order, cheque) bénéficiaire mf; (of bill) porteur m, preneur m

paying bank n domiciliataire m, établissement m payeur, domiciliation f bancaire

paying-in n **paying-in book** carnet m de versements; **paying-in slip** bordereau m de versement

payload n (of vehicle) charge f utile

payment n paiement m, versement m; **to make a payment** effectuer un versement; **to stop payment on a cheque** faire opposition à un chèque; **on payment of £100** contre paiement de 100 livres; **payment by instalments** paiement échelonné ou par versements; **in easy payments** avec facilités de paiement; **payment on account** paiement partiel; **payment in cash** paiement en espèces; **payment by cheque** paiement par chèque; **payment on delivery** livraison *f* contre remboursement; **payment in full** paiement intégral; **payment in kind** paiement en nature

payoff *n* (**a**) *(final payment)* paiement *m*, règlement *m* (**b**) *(reward)* indemnité *f*; **executive payoffs are expected to reach £500,000** les indemnités de départ des cadres devraient atteindre 500 000 livres (**c**) *(profit)* rendement *m*

payout *n* (**a**) INS remboursement *m* (**b**) *Am (of investment)* récupération *f*

payroll *n* (**a**) *(list of employees)* liste *f* du personnel; **to be on the payroll** faire partie du personnel; **how many do you have on the payroll?** combien d'employés avez-vous?; **she's been on our payroll for over twenty years** elle fait partie de notre personnel depuis plus de vingt ans □ ACCT *payroll ledger* journal *m ou* livre *m* de paie (**b**) *(money paid)* masse *f* salariale □ *payroll tax* impôt *m* sur la masse salariale

PC *n* (*abbr* **personal computer**) PC *m*

PCMCIA *n* COMPTR (*abbr* **PC memory card international association**) PCMCIA

peak **1** *n (of price, inflation, demand)* maximum *m*; **production was at its peak** la production était à son maximum □ *peak hours* heures *fpl* de pointe; *peak output* niveau *m* record de production; *peak year* année *f* record
2 *vi (of price, inflation, demand)* atteindre un *ou* son maximum; **profits peaked in July** les bénéfices ont atteint un maximum en juillet

peg *vt* FIN, ST EXCH *(prices) (fix)* fixer; *(stabilize)* stabiliser; **to peg sth to the rate of inflation** indexer qch sur le taux de l'inflation; **oil was pegged at $20 a barrel** le prix du pétrole était fixé à 20 dollars le baril; **export earnings are pegged to the exchange rate** le revenu des exportations varie en fonction du taux de change

penalty *n (for late delivery, payment)* amende *f* □ *penalty clause (in contract)* clause *f* pénale; *penalty interest* pénalité *f* de retard, intérêts *mpl* moratoires

pending **1** *adj (negotiations)* en cours; *(documents)* en souffrance, en attente; LAW *(case)* en instance □ *pending tray* corbeille *f* pour les documents en attente
2 *prep* en attendant; **pending your decision** en attendant votre décision

penetrate *vt (market)* pénétrer

penetration *n (of market)* pénétration *f* □ *penetration strategy* stratégie *f* de pénétration

penny *n Br (coin, unit of currency)* penny *m*; *Am (coin)* cent *m* □ *Br penny shares* actions *fpl* d'une valeur de moins d'une livre sterling; *Am penny stock* actions *fpl* d'une valeur de moins d'un dollar

pen-pusher *n Fam* gratte-papier *m*

pen-pushing *n Fam* travail *m* de bureau

pension *n* pension *f*; *(after retirement)* (pension de) retraite *f*; **to be on a pension** toucher une pension; *(after retirement)* toucher une retraite □ *pension fund* caisse *f* de retraite; *pension plan* plan *m* de retraite

> ❝
> These interlocking shareholders have an interest in each other's prosperity, partly because they do business with one another, partly because they have invested in each other. Unlike a **pension fund** in either Britain, America or even Japan, these interlocking shareholders have strong economic reasons to care about the performance of the firms in which they own shares.
> ❞

▸ **pension off** *vt sep* **to pension sb off** mettre qn à la retraite

pensionable *adj (person)* qui a droit à une pension; *(after retirement)* qui a droit à sa retraite □ *pensionable age* âge *m* de la mise à la retraite

pensioner *n* **(old-age) pensioner** retraité(e) *m,f*

PEP *n* FIN (*abbr* **personal equity plan**) ≃ PEA *m*

peppercorn rent *n Br* loyer *m* nominal

per *prep* par; **per annum** par an; **per capita** par personne; **the highest per capita income in Europe** le revenu par habitant le plus élevé d'Europe; LAW **per pro** par procuration; **per pro signature** signature *f* par procuration; **per week** par semaine; **as per invoice** suivant facture; **as per your instructions** conformément à vos instructions; **as per sample** conformément à l'échantillon

p/e ratio *n* ACCT (*abbr* **price/earnings ratio**) taux *m* de capitalisation

perceived *adj* MKTG *perceived performance* résultats *mpl* perçus; *perceived quality* qualité *f* perçue; *perceived risk* risque *m* perçu; *perceived service* service *m* perçu; *perceived value* valeur *f* perçue;

perceived value pricing tarification *f* en fonction de la valeur perçue

percent 1 *n* pourcentage *m*
  2 *adv* pour cent; **a seven percent interest rate** un taux d'intérêt de sept pour cent; **prices went up ten percent** les prix ont augmenté de dix pour cent

percentage *n* pourcentage *m*; **a high percentage of the staff** une grande partie du personnel; **to get a percentage on sth** *(share of profit, commission)* toucher un pourcentage sur qch

percentile *n* centile *m*

perform *vi* (**a**) *(of company)* fonctionner; *(of shares, investment, currency)* se comporter; **the Edinburgh branch is performing very well** les résultats de la succursale d'Édimbourg sont très satisfaisants; **how did the company perform in the first quarter?** comment la société a-t-elle fonctionné au premier trimestre?; **shares performed well yesterday** les actions se sont bien comportées hier
  (**b**) *(of person) (in job, situation)* se débrouiller; **she performs well under pressure** elle se débrouille bien lorsqu'elle est sous pression

performance *n* (**a**) *(of contract, task)* exécution *f* ◻ **performance bond** garantie *f* de bonne fin (**b**) *(of company)* résultats *mpl*, performance *f*; *(of shares, investment, currency)* performance *f*; **the country's poor economic performance** les mauvais résultats économiques du pays; **sterling's performance on the Stock Exchange** le comportement en Bourse de la livre sterling ◻ **performance appraisal** *(of staff)* évaluation *f*, appréciation *f*

performance-related *adj* **performance-related bonus** prime *f* au rendement; **performance-related pay** salaire *m* au rendement

period *n* période *f*; **for a period of three months** pendant une période de trois mois; **within the agreed period** dans les délais convenus ◻ FIN **period bill** effet *m* à terme; **period of grace** délai *m* de grâce

peripheral COMPTR 1 *n* périphérique *m*
  2 *adj* périphérique ◻ **peripheral device, peripheral unit** unité *f* périphérique

perishable 1 *n* **perishables** denrées *fpl* périssables
  2 *adj* périssable ◻ **perishable cargo** chargement *m* périssable; **perishable goods** denrées *fpl* périssables

perk *n* *(of job)* avantage *m* en nature; **cheap air travel is one of the perks of his job** l'un des avantages de son travail est qu'il bénéficie de billets d'avion à prix réduit

permanent *adj* permanent(e); *(residence, address)* fixe ◻ FIN **permanent assets** actif *m* immobilisé; INS **permanent health insurance** assurance *f* longue maladie; **permanent job** emploi *m* permanent; *(in public service)* poste *m* de titulaire; **permanent staff** personnel *m* permanent; *(in public service)* personnel titulaire

permission *n* permission *f*, autorisation *f*; **to ask for permission to do sth** demander la permission de faire qch; **to give sb permission to do sth** donner à qn la permission de faire qch, autoriser qn à faire qch ◻ ST EXCH **permission to deal** visa *m* *(de la COB)*

permit 1 *n* permis *m*; CUSTOMS acquit-à-caution *m*
  2 *vt* permettre; **to permit sb to do sth** permettre à qn de faire qch, autoriser qn à faire qch; **smoking is not permitted** il est interdit de fumer

perpetual *adj* perpétuel(elle) ◻ **perpetual inventory** inventaire *m* permanent

personal *adj* personnel(elle); **personal** *(on letter)* personnel ◻ INS **personal accident insurance** assurance *f* contre les accidents corporels; **personal account** ST EXCH compte *m* de tiers; ACCT compte *m* propre; **personal assets** patrimoine *m*; BANKING **personal assets profile** profil *m* patrimonial; **personal assistant** secrétaire *mf* de direction; COMPTR **personal computer** ordinateur *m* individuel; CUSTOMS **personal effects** effets *mpl* personnels; FIN **personal equity plan** ≃ plan *m* d'épargne en actions; BANKING **personal identification number** code *m* confidentiel *(d'une carte bancaire)*; BANKING **personal loan** prêt *m* personnel; MKTG **personal observation** observation *f* en situation; **personal organizer** *(book)* agenda *m*; *(electronic)* agenda *m* électronique; MKTG **personal selling** ventes *fpl* personnelles

❝

The income is tax-free because your units are held in a **personal equity plan**. The government made PEPs tax-free to encourage people to invest in shares. A PEP should be regarded as a long-term investment though, so do not tie your money up if you think you may need it quickly.

❞

personality promotion *n* MKTG promotion *f* par une personnalité

personalty *n* LAW biens *mpl* mobiliers; **to convert realty into personalty** ameublir un bien

personnel *n* personnel *m* □ *personnel department* service *m* du personnel; *personnel manager* directeur(trice) *m,f* du personnel; *personnel management* direction *f* du personnel

peseta *n* peseta *f*

PEST *n* MKTG (*abbr* **political economic sociological technological**) = facteurs politiques, économiques, sociaux et technologiques (considérés comme les aspects les plus importants lors de l'analyse de l'environnement d'une entreprise)

petition in bankruptcy *n* demande *f* de mise en liquidation judiciaire; **to file a petition in bankruptcy** déposer son bilan

petrocurrency *n* pétromonnaies *fpl*

petrodollar *n* pétrodollar *m*

petroleum *n* pétrole *m* □ *petroleum industry* industrie *f* pétrolière; *petroleum products* produits *mpl* pétroliers

petty cash *n* petite caisse *f*; **they'll pay you back out of petty cash** ils vous rembourseront avec la petite caisse □ *petty cash book* livre *m* de petite caisse; *petty cash box* petite caisse; *petty cash voucher* bon *m* de petite caisse

phase *n* phase *f*; **the project is going through a critical phase** le projet traverse une phase critique

▶ **phase in** *vt sep* (*new methods*) adopter *ou* introduire progressivement; (*new installations, equipment*) mettre en place progressivement; **the increases will be phased in over five years** les augmentations seront échelonnées sur cinq ans; **the reforms will have to be phased in** les réformes devront être introduites progressivement

▶ **phase out** *vt sep* éliminer progressivement; **these jobs will be phased out over the next five years** ces postes seront éliminés progressivement au cours des cinq prochaines années

phone 1 *n* téléphone *m*; **to be on the phone** (*speaking*) être au téléphone; (*have a phone*) être abonné(e) au téléphone; **to answer the phone** répondre au téléphone; **you're wanted on the phone** on vous demande au téléphone □ *phone book* annuaire *m* (téléphonique); *phone call* appel *m* (téléphonique); *phone number* numéro *m* de téléphone

2 *vt* **to phone sb** téléphoner à qn; **I'll phone you** je vous téléphonerai

3 *vi* téléphoner; **to phone for sth** demander qch par téléphone

phonecard *n Br* télécarte *f*

photocopier *n* photocopieur *m*, photocopieuse *f*

photocopy 1 *n* photocopie *f*; **to make a photocopy of sth** faire une photocopie de qch

2 *vt* photocopier

physical *adj* FIN *physical capital* capital *m* existant; MKTG *physical distribution* distribution *f* physique; MKTG *physical distribution management* gestion *f* de la distribution physique; *physical inventory* inventaire *m* effectif

PIBOR *n* (*abbr* **Paris Interbank Offer Rate**) TIOP *m*

> "
> The MATIF's other French products, namely the Paris Interbank Offer Rate (**PIBOR**) contracts and the CAC 40 index future, trade at adequate volumes, though by no means as vigorously as the Government Bond derivatives.
> "

▶ **pick up** *vi* (*of business, prices*) reprendre; **the market is picking up after a slow start** le marché commence à prendre après avoir démarré doucement

picket 1 *n* (*group, individual*) piquet *m* de grève □ *picket line* piquets de grève

2 *vt* **to picket a factory** faire le piquet de grève devant une usine

piece *n* pièce *f*; **to sell sth by the piece** vendre qch à la pièce □ *piece rate* salaire *m* à la pièce; **to be paid piece rates** être payé(e) à la pièce

piecework *n* travail *m* à la pièce *ou* à la tâche

pieceworker *n* travailleur(euse) *m,f* à la pièce *ou* à la tâche

pie-chart *n* graphique *m* rond à secteurs, camembert *m*

pigeonhole *n* casier *m* (à courrier)

piggybacking *n* (a) (*in export*) exportation *f* kangourou (b) BANKING portage *m*

pilot 1 *n* *pilot factory* usine-pilote *f*; *pilot project* projet-pilote *m*; *pilot questionnaire* questionnaire-pilote *m*; *pilot scheme* projet-pilote *m*; *pilot series* présérie *f*; MKTG *pilot study* étude-pilote *f*; *pilot survey* enquête-pilote *f*

2 *vt* (*study, scheme*) piloter

PIMS n MKTG (abbr **profit impact of marketing strategy**) IRSM m

PIN n (abbr **personal identification number**) PIN (number) code m personnel

pin n COMPTR broche f

pipe vt COMPTR (commands) chaîner

pipeline n (a) (for oil) pipeline f, oléoduc m; (for gas) gazoduc m
(b) **to be in the pipeline** être en préparation; **they have a new model in the pipeline** ils sont en train de mettre un nouveau modèle au point; **important changes are in the pipeline for next year** d'importants changements sont prévus pour l'année prochaine

piracy n (of book, software) piratage m

pirate 1 n (book, software) pirate m ▫ **pirate edition** édition f pirate
2 vt (book, software) pirater

pit n ST EXCH corbeille f

pixel n COMPTR pixel m

place 1 n lieu m ▫ **place of business** lieu de travail; FIN **place of issue** lieu d'émission; **place of residence** domicile m
2 vt (a) (order) passer (**with** à); (contract) passer (**with** à) (b) ST EXCH (shares) placer, disposer

placement n (a) (work experience) stage m (en entreprise) (b) ST EXCH (of shares) placement m

plaintiff n LAW plaignant(e) m,f

plan 1 n (a) (strategy) plan m, projet m; **to draw up** or **to make a plan** dresser ou établir un plan (b) (of building, town) plan m
2 vt (a) (arrange) projeter; **to plan to do sth** projeter de faire qch; **an industrial estate is planned for this site** il est prévu d'aménager un parc industriel sur ce site; **they're planning a new venture** ils ont en projet une nouvelle entreprise (b) (building, town) faire le plan de; ECON (economy) planifier

planned adj ECON planifié(e) ▫ **planned economy** économie f planifiée; **planned obsolescence** obsolescence f planifiée

> This enables us to say therefore that competition creates a system of prices which embodies relevant information so that the wealth created within the market order is produced at least cost. In other words, a market economy is an efficient way of producing wealth; the reason it is more efficient than a **planned economy** in which prices are not competitive is that prices do not convey this information.

planner n ECON planificateur(trice) m,f

planning n (a) **planning permission** permis m de construire (b) ECON (of economy) planification f (c) **planning and allocation of resources** estimation f des besoins et répartition des moyens; **planning, programming and budgeting system** rationalisation f des choix budgétaires

plant n (equipment) matériel m; (factory) usine f ▫ **plant capacity** capacité f de l'usine; **plant hire** location f d'équipement; **plant layout** schéma m d'installation; **plant manager** directeur(trice) m,f d'usine

plastic Fam 1 n (credit cards) cartes fpl de crédit; **to put sth on the plastic** payer qch avec une carte de crédit; **do they take plastic?** est-ce qu'ils acceptent les cartes de crédit?
2 adj **plastic money** cartes fpl de crédit

platform n COMPTR plateforme f

player n MKTG acteur m; **who are the key players in this market?** qui sont les acteurs principaux sur ce marché?

PLC, plc n Br (abbr **public limited company**) ≃ SA f; **Scotia Hotels plc** ≃ Scotia Hotels SA

pledge FIN 1 n gage m, garantie f ▫ **pledge holder** détenteur(trice) m,f de gage(s)
2 vt donner en gage ou en garantie; **to pledge one's property** engager son bien; **to pledge securities** déposer des titres en garantie

plotter n COMPTR (device) traceur m

▸ **plough back,** Am **plow back** vt sep FIN réinvestir (**into** dans); **to plough the profits back into the company** réinvestir les bénéfices dans la société

▸ **plough in,** Am **plow in** vt sep (money) investir

ploughback, Am **plowback** n bénéfices mpl réinvestis

▸ **plow back, plow in** Am = **plough back, plow in**

▸ **plowback** Am = **ploughback**

plug Fam 1 n (publicity) pub f; **their products got another plug on TV** on a encore fait de la pub pour leurs produits à la télé
2 vt (product) faire du battage ou de la pub pour

plug-in n COMPTR module m d'extension

plummet vi (of price, rate, currency) dégringoler, s'effondrer; **the value of the pound has plummeted** la livre a chuté

plunge vi (a) ST EXCH risquer de grosses sommes (b) (of price, rate, currency) chuter;

sales have plunged by 30% les ventes ont chuté de 30%

PO n (a) (abbr **Post Office**) poste f ▫ **PO Box** BP f (b) (abbr **postal order**) mandat m postal

poach vt (employee) débaucher; **several of our staff have been poached by a rival company** plusieurs de nos employés ont été débauchés par un de nos concurrents

point n (a) MKTG **point of sale** point m de vente; **point of sale advertising** publicité f sur le lieu de vente, PLV f; **point of sale material** matériel m de publicité sur le lieu de vente ou de PLV; **point of sale terminal** terminal m point de vente
(b) ST EXCH point m; **the Dow Jones index is up/down two points** l'indice Dow Jones a augmenté/baissé de deux points

pointer n COMPTR pointeur m

poison pill n Fam (strategy) pilule f empoisonnée

> ❝
> The 13th Company Law Directive will put an end to the more blatant "**poison pill**" tactics that enable companies under threat of takeover to make themselves unappetising.
> ❞

policy n (a) (of company, organization) politique f; **to adopt a policy** adopter une ligne de conduite; **this is in line with company policy** ça va dans le sens de la politique de l'entreprise; **our policy is to hire professionals only** nous avons pour politique de n'engager que des professionnels ▫ **policy statement** rapport m annuel
(b) INS police f; **to take out a policy** souscrire une police (d'assurance) ▫ **policy holder** assuré(e) m,f

poll 1 n (survey) sondage m (d'opinion); **to carry out a poll (on sth)** faire un sondage (sur qch)
2 vt (person) sonder; **most of those polled were in favour of the plan** la plupart des personnes sondées étaient favorables au projet

pool 1 n (of companies) groupement m, pool m; (of company cars, computers) parc m
2 vt (capital, profits, ideas, resources) mettre en commun; (orders) grouper

POP n COMPTR (abbr **post office protocol**) protocole m POP

pop-up menu n COMPTR menu m local

port n (a) (harbour) port m ▫ **port authority** autorité f portuaire; **port**

charges, port dues droits mpl de port
(b) COMPTR port m

portable 1 n (computer) (ordinateur m) portable m
2 adj (a) (computer) portable (b) FIN (pension, mortgage) transférable

porterage n (of goods, parcels) transport m (par porteurs); (cost) prix m de transport ▫ **porterage facilities** service m de porteurs

portfolio n (a) (for holding documents) porte-documents m (b) FIN (of shares) portefeuille m ▫ **portfolio analysis** analyse f de portefeuille; **portfolio insurance** assurance f de portefeuille; **portfolio management** gestion f de portefeuille (c) MKTG **portfolio mix** portefeuille m d'activités

portrait n COMPTR portrait m; **to print sth in portrait** imprimer qch en portrait ▫ **portrait mode** mode m portrait

POS n (abbr **point of sale**) PDV m

position 1 n (a) (circumstances) état m, situation f; **the cash position is not good** la situation de la caisse laisse à désirer; **our financial position is improving** notre situation financière s'améliore
(b) (job) poste m; **it's a position of great responsibility** c'est un poste à haute responsabilité; **there were four candidates for the position of manager** il y avait quatre candidats au poste de directeur
(c) ST EXCH position f; **to take a long/short position** prendre une position longue/courte ▫ **position trader** spéculateur(trice) m,f sur plusieurs positions
2 vt MKTG (product) positionner

positioning n MKTG positionnement m ▫ **positioning study** étude f de positionnement

possession n LAW (of property) possession f, jouissance f; **to take possession (of sth)** prendre possession (de qch)

post¹ 1 n Br (mail) courrier m; **by return of post** par retour du courrier; **to send sth by post** envoyer qch par la poste; **it's in the post** c'est parti au courrier; **can you put the cheque in the post?** pouvez-vous poster le chèque? ▫ **post office** (bureau m de) poste f; **the Post Office** (organization) ≃ la Poste; **post office box** boîte f postale
2 vt (a) (letter, parcel) mettre à la poste, poster; **I'll post it to you** je vous l'enverrai par la poste
(b) ACCT (entry) passer; **to post an amount** passer un montant; **to post the books** passer les écritures

(c) ST EXCH **to post security** déposer des garanties

post² **1** n (job) poste m; **the post is still vacant** nous n'avons pas encore pourvu à ce poste; **he got a post as an economist** il a obtenu un poste d'économiste

2 vt (assign) affecter; **to be posted to a different branch** être affecté(e) à une autre succursale

postage n affranchissement m; **postage and packing** frais mpl de port et d'emballage; **postage included** port compris; **postage paid** port payé □ **postage stamp** timbre-poste m

postal adj postal(e) □ **postal charges** frais mpl d'envoi ou de port; Am **postal meter** machine f à affranchir; **postal order** mandat m postal; **postal rates** tarifs mpl postaux; **postal services** services mpl postaux

postcode n Br code m postal

postdate vt postdater

poster n MKTG affiche □ **poster advertising** publicité f par affichage; **poster campaign** campagne f d'affichage

> They point to the **poster campaign** it launched last September, through Ogilvy & Mather, which effectively relaunched Wisk as a mainstream colour care detergent, and the new label design as evidence of Lever's determination to boost its sales.

poste restante n poste f restante

post-free **1** adj (prepaid) port payé; (free of postal charges) dispensé(e) d'affranchissement

2 adv (prepaid) en port payé; (free of postal charges) en franchise postale

Post-it® n note f autocollante

postmaster n COMPTR maître m de poste

post-paid **1** adj port payé

2 adv en port payé

postpone vt remettre à plus tard, reporter; (payment) différer; **the meeting was postponed until a later date** la réunion a été remise à une date ultérieure

postponement n report m

post-purchase adj MKTG post-achat □ **post-purchase behaviour** comportement m post-achat; **post-purchase evaluation** évaluation f post-achat

post-test n MKTG post-test m

potential **1** n potentiel m; **the idea has potential** l'idée a de l'avenir; **there is little potential for development in the firm** l'entreprise offre peu de possibilités de développement

2 adj potentiel(elle) □ **potential buyer** acheteur(euse) m,f éventuel(elle)

pound n (British currency) livre f □ **pound sign** symbole m de la livre; **pound sterling** livre f sterling

poverty line n seuil m de pauvreté; **to live above/on/below the poverty line** vivre en dessus/à la limite/en dessous du seuil de pauvreté

> The government gets its data from a national survey conducted every five years. The **poverty line** is put at consumption per person of about $11 a month, just about conceivable in India though it may sound impossibly low to a westerner.

power n (a) pouvoir m; **to act with full powers** agir de pleine autorité □ **power breakfast** petit déjeuner m d'affaires; **power dressing** = façon de s'habiller qu'adoptent certaines femmes cadres dans le but de projeter une image d'autorité; **power lunch** déjeuner m d'affaires important

(b) LAW pouvoir m □ **power of attorney** procuration f

(c) COMPTR **power supply** transformateur m; **power user** = personne qui sait utiliser au mieux les ressources de son ordinateur

▸ **power down** COMPTR **1** vt sep éteindre

2 vi éteindre

▸ **power up** COMPTR **1** vt sep allumer

2 vi allumer

power-down n COMPTR mise f hors tension

pp (abbr **per procurationem**) pp

PPD adj (abbr **prepaid**) port payé par le destinataire

PPP n COMPTR (abbr **point-to-point protocol**) protocole m PPP, protocole m point à point

PR n (abbr **public relations**) RP f

pre-acquisition n acquisition f faite au préalable

prebilling n ACCT préfacturation f

predate vt (cheque) antidater

predator n (company) prédateur m

predatory pricing n MKTG fixation f de prix prédateurs

predecessor n prédécesseur m

preference n (a) ECON tarif m ou régime m de faveur; (preferential treatment) traitement m préférentiel ou de faveur
(b) ST EXCH droit m de priorité □ Br **preference share** action f privilégiée ou de priorité
(c) MKTG **preference test** test m de préférence

preferential adj (a) (treatment) préférentiel(elle) □ **preferential price** prix m de faveur; FIN **preferential rate** tarif m préférentiel; **preferential voting** vote m préférentiel
(b) CUSTOMS **preferential duty** préférences fpl douanières; **preferential tariff** tarif m préférentiel
(c) LAW **preferential claim** droit m préférentiel ou de préférence; **preferential creditor** créancier(ère) m,f privilégié(e)

❝
The agreement maintained a **preferential price** for Cuban sugar, lower than that of the previous five-year period, but higher than world prices.
❞

preferred adj (a) **preferred creditor** créancier(ère) m,f privilégié(e); FIN **preferred debt** dette f ou créance f privilégiée
(b) Am ST EXCH **preferred stock** actions fpl privilégiées ou de priorité

preformatted adj COMPTR préformaté(e)

pre-inventory balance n ACCT balance f avant inventaire

prejudice 1 n LAW (detriment) préjudice m, tort m; **without prejudice to your guarantee** sans préjudice de votre garantie; **to the prejudice of sb's rights** au préjudice des droits de qn
2 vt porter préjudice à, compromettre

preliminary adj préliminaire □ **preliminary expenses** frais mpl d'établissement; LAW **preliminary investigation** instruction f

premises npl locaux mpl, lieux mpl

premium n (a) INS (payment) prime f; **to pay an additional premium** payer une surprime
(b) (additional sum) (on price) supplément m; (on salary) prime f; ST EXCH **to pay a premium** verser ou acquitter un premium; **to sell sth at a premium** vendre qch à prime ou à bénéfice; **to issue shares at a premium** émettre des actions au-dessus du pair ou de leur valeur nominale □ **premium bonds** ≃ obligations fpl à lots

(c) **premium price** prix m de prestige; **premium rebate** ristourne f de prime; **premium selling** vente f à prime; **premium service** service m premier

prepack, prepackage vt conditionner, préemballer

prepaid adj prépayé(e); ACCT payé(e) ou constaté(e) d'avance □ **prepaid envelope** enveloppe f affranchie; **prepaid income** produit m constaté d'avance

prepayment n paiement m à l'avance; ACCT charge f constatée d'avance

preprogram vt COMPTR préprogrammer

preprogrammed adj COMPTR préprogrammé(e)

prerequisite n condition f préalable

present 1 adj actuel(elle); **the present year** l'année courante □ **present capital** capital m appelé; ACCT **present value** valeur f actuelle
2 vt (a) (report, information, proposal) présenter (b) FIN (invoice) présenter; **to present a cheque for payment** présenter un chèque à l'encaissement; **to present a bill for acceptance** présenter une traite à l'acceptation

presentation n (a) (showing) présentation f; **presentation for acceptance** présentation à l'acceptation; **presentation for payment** présentation au paiement; **payable on presentation of the coupon** payable contre remise du coupon; **on presentation of the invoice** au vu de ou sur présentation de la facture; **cheque payable on presentation** chèque m payable à vue
(b) (formal talk) présentation f; **to give a presentation (on sth)** faire une présentation (de qch) □ COMPTR **presentation graphics** graphiques mpl de présentation
(c) BANKING **presentation date** date f de présentation
(d) MKTG **presentation pack** paquet m de présentation

presentment n (of bill of exchange) présentation f

preside vi présider; **to preside over a meeting** présider une réunion

presidency n présidence f

president n (of country, organization) président(e) m,f; Am (of company) président-directeur général m, P-DG m

press n (newspapers) **the press** la presse; **to get (a) good/bad press** avoir bonne/mauvaise presse □ **press conference** conférence f de presse; MKTG **press kit**

dossier *m* de presse; ***press office*** service *m* de presse; ***press officer*** responsable *mf* des relations avec la presse; MKTG ***press pack*** dossier *m* de presse; ***press release*** communiqué *m* de presse

pressure *n* pression *f*; **copper prices came under renewed pressure** les cours du cuivre ont subi une nouvelle pression ◻ ***pressure group*** groupe *m* de pression

prestige *n* MKTG ***prestige advertising*** publicité *f* de prestige; ***prestige price*** prix *m* de prestige; ***prestige promotion*** promotion *f* de prestige

pre-tax *adj* brut(e), avant impôts ◻ ***pre-tax profit*** bénéfice *m* brut *ou* avant impôts

pre-test *n* MKTG pré-test *m*

prevailing *adj* actuel(elle); **the prevailing economic climate** le climat économique actuel

price 1 *n* prix *m*; *(of shares)* cours *m*, cote *f*; **to rise** *or* **increase** *or* **go up in price** augmenter ◻ ***price agreement*** entente *f* sur les prix; ***price ceiling*** prix plafond; ***price control*** contrôle *m* des prix; ***price cut*** réduction *f* (des prix), baisse *f* des prix; ***price cutting*** baisse *f* de prix; ***price differential*** écart *m* de prix; ***price fixing*** *(control)* contrôle *m* des prix; *(rigging)* entente *f* sur les prix; ***price freeze*** gel *m* des prix; ***prices and incomes policy*** politique *f* des prix et des salaires; ***price increase*** hausse *f* des prix; ***price index*** indice *m* des prix; ***price inflation*** inflation *f* des prix; ***price label*** étiquette *f* de prix; ***price leadership*** = position dominante en matière de fixation des prix; ***price level*** niveau *m* de prix; ***price list*** tarif *m*, liste *f* des prix; ***price markup*** majoration *f* de prix; BANKING, FIN ***price of money*** prix de l'argent; MKTG ***price plan*** plan *m* prix; MKTG ***price point*** point *m* prix; ***price policy*** politique *f* des prix; MKTG ***price positioning*** positionnement *m* des prix; ***price promotion*** promotion *f*; ***price range*** gamme *f* des prix; ***price reduction*** réduction *f* (des prix); ***price regulation*** réglementation *f* des prix; ***price ring*** monopole *m* des prix; ***price scale*** barème *m* des prix; ***price setting*** détermination *f* *ou* fixation *f* des prix; ST EXCH ***price spreads*** écarts *mpl* de cours; ***price stability*** stabilité *f* des prix; MKTG ***price step*** écart *m* de prix; ***price structure*** structure *f* des prix; ***price tag*** étiquette *f* de prix; ***price undercutting*** gâchage *m* des prix; ***price war*** guerre *f* des prix

2 *vt* (**a**) *(decide cost of)* déterminer *ou* fixer le prix de; **the book is priced at £17** le livre coûte 17 livres

(**b**) *(indicate cost of)* mettre le prix sur; **these goods haven't been priced** ces articles n'ont pas reçu de prix *ou* n'ont pas été étiquetés

(**c**) *(ascertain cost of)* s'informer du prix de; *(estimate value of)* évaluer qch, estimer la valeur de qch; **she priced it in several shops before buying it** elle a vérifié le prix dans plusieurs magasins avant de l'acheter

(**d**) **to price competitors out of the market** éliminer la concurrence en pratiquant des prix déloyaux; **to price oneself out of the market** perdre sa clientèle en pratiquant des prix trop élevés; **we've been priced out of the Japanese market** nous avons perdu le marché japonais à cause de nos prix

(**e**) ECON *(quantity)* valoriser

▶ **price down** *vt sep* baisser le prix de; **all items have been priced down by 10%** tous les articles ont été démarqués de 10%

▶ **price up** *vt sep* augmenter le prix de

price-earnings ratio *n* ST EXCH ratio *m* cours-bénéfices

price-elastic *adj* MKTG au prix élastique

> Later on, products mature and become more **price-elastic**, allowing production advantage to shift to lower-income countries that may later begin exporting on their own account.

price-inelastic *adj* MKTG au prix stable

pricing *n* détermination *f* *ou* fixation *f* du prix ◻ ***pricing policy*** politique *f* des prix

primary *adj* ECON primaire ◻ MKTG ***primary demand*** demande *f* primaire; *Am* ***primary earnings per share*** bénéfices *mpl* premiers par action; ***primary industry*** secteur *m* primaire; ST EXCH ***primary market*** marché *m* primaire; ***primary product*** matière *f* première, produit *m* brut; ***primary production*** production *f* de matières premières

prime *adj* FIN ***prime bill*** papier *m* commercial de premier ordre; ***prime bond*** obligation *f* de premier ordre; ***prime cost*** prix *m* de revient; FIN ***prime rate*** taux *m* d'escompte bancaire préférentiel

principal *n* (**a**) LAW *(employer of agent)* mandant *m*, commettant *m* (**b**) FIN *(capital)* capital *m*; *(of debt)* principal *m*; **principal and interest** capital et intérêts

print *n* COMPTR ***print format*** format *m* d'impression; ***print head*** tête *f* d'impression; ***print job*** fichier *m* à imprimer; ***print**

menu menu *m* d'impression; **print preview** aperçu *m* avant impression; **print quality** qualité *f* d'impression; **print queue** liste *f* de fichiers à imprimer; **print speed** vitesse *f* d'impression

▶ **print out** *vt sep* COMPTR imprimer

printed *adj* imprimé(e) ❏ **printed form** imprimé *m*; **printed matter** imprimés

printer *n* COMPTR imprimante *f* ❏ **printer cable** câble *m* d'imprimante; **printer driver** programme *f* de commande d'impression; **printer font** fonte *f* imprimante; **printer paper** papier *m* d'impression; **printer speed** vitesse *f* d'impression

printout *n* COMPTR sortie *f* sur papier; *(list, results of calculation)* listing *m*

prior *adj* précédent(e), antérieur(e) **(to** à); **to have a prior engagement** être déjà pris(e); **without prior notice** sans préavis

priority *n* priorité *f*; **to have** *or* **take priority (over)** avoir la priorité (sur); **the matter has top priority** l'affaire est prioritaire ❏ ST EXCH **priority share** action *f* privilégiée *ou* de priorité

private *adj* **(a)** *(not state-run)* privé(e) ❏ **private bank** banque *f* privée; **private enterprise** entreprise *f* privée; **private health insurance** assurance *f* maladie privée; **private limited company** société *f* à responsabilité limitée; **private ownership** propriété *f* privée; **private pension** retraite *f* complémentaire; **private sector** secteur *m* privé

(b) *(personal)* personnel(elle) ❏ LAW **private agreement** acte *m* sous seing privé; **private income** rentes *fpl*; **private investor** investisseur *m* privé

(c) *(confidential)* privé(e), confidentiel(elle); **private (and confidential)** *(on letter)* confidentiel

private-label brand *n* MKTG marque *f* de distributeur

privately *adv* **to sell sth privately** vendre qch de gré à gré; **privately owned** *(company)* privé(e)

privatization *n* privatisation *f*

privatize *vt* privatiser

proactive *adj* qui fait preuve d'initiative ❏ ADMIN **proactive staffing** dotation *f* par anticipation

probability method *n* MKTG *(of sampling)* méthode *f* probabiliste

probate LAW **1** *n (of document, will)* validation *f*, homologation *f*; **to value sth for probate** évaluer *ou* expertiser qch pour

l'homologation d'un testament ❏ **probate price** prix *m* moyen

2 *vt (document, will)* valider, homologuer

probation *n (trial employment)* période *f* d'essai; **to take sb on probation** prendre qn à l'essai; **to be on probation** être en période d'essai

probationary *adj (period)* d'essai

probationer *n (employee)* employé(e) *m,f* à l'essai *ou* en période d'essai

problem *n* problème *m* ❏ **problem analysis** analyse *f* de problème(s); MKTG **problem child** dilemme *m*; **problem solving** résolution *f* de problèmes

> ❝ ───
>
> Long a **problem child**, Granada Computer Services is now thriving and as of April 15, it restructured its customer support functions into two separate divisions with the aim of providing a more focussed and efficient service.
>
> ─── ❞

procedure *n* procédure *f*; **what's the correct procedure?** comment doit-on procéder?, quelle est la marche à suivre?; **you must follow the normal procedure** vous devez suivre la procédure normale

proceed *vi* **(a)** *(continue)* continuer, poursuivre; **we are now unable to proceed with our plans for expansion** nous sommes maintenant dans l'impossibilité de poursuivre nos projets d'expansion

(b) *(happen)* se passer, se dérouler; **is the meeting proceeding according to plan?** est-ce que la réunion se déroule comme prévu?

(c) *(act)* procéder, agir; **how should we proceed?** comment doit-on procéder?, quelle est la marche à suivre?

proceedings *npl* **(a)** *(meeting)* réunion *f*, séance *f*; *(record of meeting)* compte-rendu *m*, procès-verbal *m* **(b)** LAW poursuites *fpl* judiciaires *ou* en justice; **to take** *or* **institute proceedings (against sb)** engager des poursuites (contre qn)

proceeds *npl (from sale)* recette *f*

process **1** *n* **(a)** *(method)* procédé *m*, méthode *f*; **to develop a process for doing sth** mettre au point un procédé pour faire qch; **a new manufacturing process** un nouveau procédé de fabrication

(b) COMPTR procédé *m*, traitement *m*

2 *vt* **(a)** *(information, application, order)* traiter; **my insurance claim is still being processed** ma déclaration de sinistre est

toujours en cours de règlement; **we process thousands of applications every week** nous traitons des milliers de demandes chaque semaine
(**b**) COMPTR *(data)* traiter
(**c**) *(raw materials)* traiter, transformer

processing *n* (**a**) *(of information, application, order)* traitement *m* (**b**) COMPTR *(of data)* traitement *m* (**c**) *(of raw materials)* traitement *m*, transformation *f*

processor *n* COMPTR processeur *m*

procuration *n* LAW procuration *f*

procurator *n* LAW fondé *m* de pouvoir

produce 1 *n* produits *mpl*
2 *vt* (**a**) *(manufacture, make)* produire, fabriquer; **we aren't producing enough spare parts** nous ne produisons pas assez de pièces détachées; **we have produced three new models this year** nous avons sorti trois nouveaux modèles cette année
(**b**) *(interest, profit)* rapporter; **my investments produce a fairly good return** mes investissements sont d'un assez bon rapport; **this account produces a high rate of interest** ce compte rapporte des intérêts élevés
(**c**) *(raw materials)* produire

producer *n* *(of raw materials, goods)* producteur(trice) *m,f*; **this region is Europe's biggest wine producer** cette région est la plus grande productrice de vin d'Europe □ **producer goods** biens *mpl* de production

product *n* produit *m* □ **product advertising** publicité *f* de produit; **product analysis** analyse *f* de produit; MKTG **product awareness** notoriété *f* ou mémorisation *f* du produit; MKTG **product bundling pricing** fixation *f* des prix par lot; **product category** catégorie *f* de produit; **product champion** champion *m* de produit; **product design** conception *f* du produit; **product development** mise *f* au point de produit; **product features** caractéristiques *fpl* du produit; **product image** image *f* de produit; **product information sheet** fiche *f* technique; **product innovation** innovation *f* de produit; EU **product liability** responsabilité *f* du produit; **product liability insurance** assurance *f* de responsabilité du produit; **product lifecycle** cycle *m* de vie du produit; **product lifecycle curve** courbe *f* du cycle de vie du produit; **product line** ligne *f* de produits; **product management** gestion *f* de produits; **product mix** assortiment *m* ou mix *m* de produits; MKTG **product placement** placement *m* d'un produit; **product**

planning plan *m* de développement des produits; **product policy** politique *f* de lancement d'un produit; **product portfolio** portefeuille *m* de produits; **product positioning** positionnement *m* du produit; **product range** gamme *f* de produits

production *n* production *f*, fabrication *f*; **to go into/out of production** être/ne plus être fabriqué(e); **to cease production** arrêter la production □ **production capacity** capacité *f* de production; **production cost** coût *m* de production; **production department** service *m* de la production; **production engineering** productique *f*; **production incentive** prime *f* de rendement; **production line** chaîne *f* de montage; **to work on a production line** travailler à la chaîne; **this model has just come off the production line** ce modèle vient juste de sortir de la chaîne de production; **production management** gestion *f* de la production; **production manager** directeur(trice) *m,f* de la production; **production plant** usine *f*; **production schedule** programme *m* de fabrication

productive *adj* ECON *(work, capital)* productif(ive) □ **productive forces** forces *fpl* productives; **productive life** *(of machine)* vie *f* physique

productivity *n* productivité *f*, rendement *m* □ **productivity agreement** accord *m* de productivité; **productivity bargaining** négociation *f* syndicale d'un contrat de productivité; **productivity bonus** prime *f* de rendement; **productivity deal** contrat *m* de productivité; **productivity drive** campagne *f* de productivité

product/market pair *n* MKTG couple *m* produit/marché

product/price policy *n* MKTG politique *f* de produit/prix

profession *n* profession *f*; **by profession** de profession

professional 1 *n* professionnel(elle) *m,f*; *(executive, lawyer)* membre *m* des professions libérales
2 *adj* (**a**) *(relating to a profession)* professionnel(elle) □ **professional association** association *f* professionnelle; **professional body** organisation *f* professionnelle; **professional fees** frais *mpl* professionnels; **professional indemnity policy** politique *f* de responsabilité professionnelle; **professional misconduct** faute *f* professionnelle; **professional training** formation *f* professionnelle
(**b**) *(in quality, attitude)* professionnel(elle); **he**

works in a very professional manner il travaille en professionnel; **she is very professional in her approach to the problem** elle aborde le problème de façon très professionnelle

proficiency n compétence f (**in** en); **proficiency in a foreign language is essential** la compétence dans une langue étrangère est essentielle

proficient adj compétent(e) (**in** en)

profile n (of candidate, employee) profil m; **to have the right profile for the job** avoir le bon profil pour le poste

profit n bénéfice m, profit m; **profits were down/up this year** les bénéfices ont diminué/augmenté cette année; **to make a profit** faire un bénéfice ou des bénéfices; **to show a profit** rapporter un bénéfice ou des bénéfices; **to move into profit** (of business) devenir rentable; **to sell sth at a profit** faire un bénéfice sur une vente; **profit and loss** pertes fpl et profits; **profit and loss account** compte m de pertes et profits, compte de résultat □ **profit balance** solde m bénéficiaire; **profit centre** centre m de profit; **profit margin** marge f bénéficiaire; **profit motive** motivation f par le profit; **profit warning** = annonce d'une baisse prochaine des bénéfices d'une entreprise

> ❝
> It is hoped that the managers, spurred on by the **profit motive**, will have an incentive to improve efficiency, as will the workforce, aware that the state will not be there to bail out loss-making enterprises.
> ❞

profitability n rentabilité f

profitable adj (business, deal, investment) rentable; **this factory is no longer profitable** cette usine n'est plus rentable; **it wouldn't be profitable for me to sell** cela ne me rapporterait pas grand-chose de vendre

profiteer 1 n profiteur(euse) m,f
2 vi profiter d'une situation pour faire des bénéfices excessifs

profit-making adj (**a**) (aiming to make profit) à but lucratif □ **profit-making organization** association f à but lucratif
(**b**) (profitable) rentable

profit-sharing n participation f ou intéressement m aux bénéfices; **we have a profit-sharing scheme** nous avons un système de participation (aux bénéfices)

proforma 1 n (invoice) facture f pro forma
2 adj **proforma invoice** facture f pro forma

program COMPTR 1 n programme m □ **program disk** disquette f programme; **program language** langage m de programmation
2 vt programmer; **to program a computer to do sth** programmer un ordinateur pour qu'il fasse qch
3 vi programmer

programmer n COMPTR programmeur(euse) m,f

programming n COMPTR programmation f □ **programming language** langage m de programmation

progress 1 n progrès m; **to make progress** faire des progrès; **to be in progress** être en cours; **the negotiations in progress** les négociations en cours □ **progress payment** paiement m proportionnel (à l'avancement des travaux); **progress report** compte-rendu m; (on work) rapport m sur l'avancement des travaux
2 vi progresser; **the talks are progressing well** les pourparlers sont en bonne voie

prohibitive adj (price) prohibitif(ive)

project 1 n projet m; **they're working on a new building project** ils travaillent sur un nouveau projet de construction □ **project analysis** étude f de projet; **project management** gestion f de projets; **project manager** directeur(trice) m,f de projet; **project milestones** étapes fpl principales du projet
2 vt (forecast) prévoir; **he's projecting a 40% slide in May** il prévoit une baisse de 40% au mois de mai; **we have attempted to project next year's figures/output** nous avons tenté de prévoir les chiffres/la production pour l'année prochaine

projected adj (forecast) prévu(e); **the projected growth of the economy** la croissance économique prévue

projection n (forecast) projection f, prévision f; **here are my projections for the next ten years** voici mes prévisions pour les dix années à venir

promissory note n FIN billet m à ordre

promo n Fam (promotion) promo f

promote vt (**a**) (person) promouvoir, donner de l'avancement à; **to be promoted** être promu(e), recevoir de l'avancement; **she's been promoted to regional manager** elle a été promue au poste de directrice régionale
(**b**) (foster) promouvoir, favoriser; **to promote economic growth** promouvoir ou favoriser la croissance économique

(**c**) *(product)* promouvoir, faire la promotion de; **to promote a new product** faire la promotion d'un nouveau produit

promoter *n* promoteur(trice) *m,f*

promotion *n* (**a**) *(of person)* promotion *f*, avancement *m*; **to get promotion** être promu(e), recevoir de l'avancement; **there are good prospects of promotion in this company** il y a des réelles possibilités de promotion *ou* d'avancement dans cette société

(**b**) *(of product)* promotion *f*; **this week's promotion** la promotion de la semaine ❑ *promotion budget* budget *m* promotionnel; *promotion team* équipe *f* promotionnelle

promotional *adj* promotionnel(elle) ❑ *promotional campaign* campagne *f* de promotion; *promotional literature* prospectus *mpl* promotionnels; *promotional material* matériel *m* de promotion; *promotional offer* offre *f* promotionnelle; *promotional video* (cassette *f*) vidéo *f* promotionnelle

prompt 1 *n* (**a**) *(for payment)* délai *m* (de paiement) ❑ *prompt day* jour *m* de paiement; *prompt note* rappel *m* (**b**) COMPTR invite *f*; *(with wording)* message *m* d'invite

2 *adj (quick)* prompt(e), rapide ❑ *prompt payment* paiement *m* dans les délais; *prompt service* service *m* rapide

property *n* (**a**) *(land, house)* propriété *f*; *(real estate)* biens *mpl* immobilers; **he's investing his money in property** il investit son argent dans l'immobilier ❑ *property developer* promoteur(trice) *m,f* immobilier(ère); *property market* marché *m* immobilier; *property owner* propriétaire *mf*; *property tax* impôt *m* foncier (**b**) *(possessions)* biens *mpl*

proposal *n* proposition *f*; **to make a proposal** faire *ou* formuler une proposition

propose *vt* proposer; **to propose a motion** présenter *ou* soumettre une motion

proprietary *adj proprietary article* article *m* de marque (déposée); *proprietary brand* marque *f* déposée; *proprietary name* nom *m* déposé

proprietor *n* propriétaire *mf*

pro rata 1 *adj* prorata; **the salary is £21,000 pro rata** le salaire est calculé sur la base de 21 000 livres par an

2 *adv* au prorata

prosecute *vt* LAW poursuivre (en justice)

prosecution *n* LAW poursuites *fpl* (judiciaires); **to be liable to prosecution** s'exposer à des poursuites judiciaires; **to bring a prosecution against sb** poursuivre qn (en justice)

prospect *n* (**a**) *(chance, likelihood)* perspective *f*; **the prospects for the automobile industry** les perspectives d'avenir de l'industrie automobile; **it's a job without any prospects of promotion** c'est un poste qui n'offre aucune perspective d'avenir

(**b**) *(prospective customer)* client(e) *m,f* éventuel(elle); **he's a good prospect for the manager's job** c'est un candidat potentiel au poste de directeur

2 *vi* MKTG prospecter; **to prospect for new customers** rechercher *ou* démarcher de nouveaux clients

prospective *adj (buyer, client)* éventuel(elle), potentiel(elle)

prospectus *n* (**a**) *(about company, product)* prospectus *m* (**b**) ST EXCH *(about share issue)* appel *m* à la souscription publique

protectionism *n* ECON protectionnisme *m*

protectionist *n & adj* ECON protectionniste *mf*

protective *adj* ECON *(duty, measure)* protecteur(trice)

protocol *n* COMPTR protocole *m*

prototype *n* prototype *m*

provide *vt* (**a**) *(stipulate)* stipuler; **the contract provides that...** dans le contrat il est stipulé que... (**b**) *(supply)* fournir; **to provide sb with sth** fournir qch à qn; **the new plant will provide 2,000 jobs** la nouvelle usine créera 2000 emplois

▸ **provide for** *vt insep* (**a**) *(allow for)* stipuler; **the bill provides for subsidies to be reduced** le projet de loi prévoit une baisse des subventions; INS **this risk is not provided for in the policy** ce risque n'est pas prévu dans la police

(**b**) *(support)* pourvoir aux besoins de; **an insurance policy that will provide for your children's future** une assurance qui subviendra aux besoins de vos enfants

(**c**) *(prepare)* **to provide for sth** se préparer à qch

provision *n* (**a**) *(act of supplying)* approvisionnement *m*; **the provision of new jobs** la création d'emplois

(**b**) *(allowance)* provision *f*; **to make provision for sth** prévoir qch; ACCT **provision for depreciation** provision pour dépréciation; ACCT **provision for liabilities** provision pour sommes exigibles

(**c**) **provisions** *(supplies)* provisions *fpl*

(**d**) *(in treaty)* disposition *f*; *(in contract)* clause *f*; **under the provisions of the UN charter** selon les dispositions de la charte de l'ONU; **a 4% increase is included in the budget's provisions** une augmentation de 4% est prévue dans le budget

proviso *n* condition *f*, stipulation *f*; **with the proviso that the goods be delivered within one month** à condition que les marchandises soient livrées dans un délai d'un mois; **they accept, with one proviso** ils acceptent, à une condition

proxy *n* (**a**) LAW *(power)* procuration *f*; *(person)* mandataire *mf*; **by proxy** par procuration; **to vote by proxy** voter par procuration (**b**) COMPTR mandataire *m*

prudence concept *n* ACCT principe *m* de prudence

> 66 ———
> The 1987 SORP stated that the **prudence concept** has to be modified because "proper accounting practice within the legal framework" includes accounting that "best commercial practice" would find imprudent. The instance cited was where debt charges continue to be included in revenue accounts for financing assets whose useful life is over.
> ——— 99

PSBR *n Br* ECON *(abbr* **public sector borrowing requirement***)* = besoins d'emprunt du secteur public non couverts par les rentrées fiscales

psychographic segmentation *n* MKTG segmentation *f* psychographique

psychological *adj* **psychological contract** contrat *m* psychologique; MKTG **psychological price** prix *m* psychologique

public 1 *n* **the (general) public** le (grand) public; **to issue shares to the public** placer des actions dans le public

2 *adj* public(ique); ST EXCH **to go public** être coté(e) en Bourse □ **public authorities** pouvoirs *mpl* publics; *Br* **public corporation** entreprise *f* publique; **public debt** dette *f* publique *ou* de l'État; BANKING **public deposits** = avoirs des différents services du gouvernement britannique à la Banque d'Angleterre; **public enterprise** entreprise *f* publique; **public expenditure** dépenses *fpl* publiques; **public finance** finances *fpl* publiques; **public funds** fonds

mpl publics; **public holiday** fête *f* légale; **public liability** responsabilité *f* civile; **public liability insurance** assurance *f* responsabilité civile; **public limited company** ≃ société *f* anonyme; ST EXCH **public offering** offre *f* publique; **public ownership** propriété *f* publique; **public relations** relations *fpl* publiques; **public sector** secteur *m* publique; **public sector borrowing requirement** = besoins d'emprunt du secteur public non couverts par les rentrées fiscales; **public sector deficit** déficit *m* du secteur public; **public sector earnings** revenus *mpl* du secteur public; **public servant** fonctionnaire *mf*; ST EXCH **public share offer** offre *f* publique de vente; **public spending** dépenses *fpl* publiques; **public utility** service *m* public

publication *n (activity, published work)* publication *f*

publicity *n* publicité *f*; **it'll give us free publicity for the product** ça fera de la publicité gratuite pour notre produit □ **publicity campaign** campagne *f* publicitaire *ou* de publicité; **publicity department** service *m* de la publicité; **publicity manager** chef *m* de (la) publicité

publicize *vt (product)* faire de la publicité pour

publicly *adv* publiquement; ECON **publicly owned** à capitaux publics; **the company is 51% publicly controlled** la société est contrôlée à 51% par des capitaux publics

publish *vt* publier

publisher *n (person)* éditeur(trice) *m,f*; *(company)* maison *f* d'édition

publishing *n* édition *f* □ **publishing company, publishing house** maison *f* d'édition

▸ **pull down** *vt sep* COMPTR *(menu)* dérouler

pull-down menu *n* COMPTR menu *m* déroulant

pull strategy *n* MKTG stratégie *f* 'tirer'

punter *n Fam* (**a**) *(customer)* client(e) *m,f* (**b**) ST EXCH *(speculator)* boursicoteur(euse) *m,f*, boursicotier(ère) *m,f*

purchase 1 *n (act of buying, thing bought)* achat *m*; *(of company)* rachat *m*; **to make a purchase** faire un achat □ MKTG **purchase behaviour** comportement *m* d'achat; **purchase cost** coût *m* d'achat; ACCT **purchase of debts** rachat des créances; MKTG **purchase decision** décision *f* d'achat; ACCT **purchase entry** écriture *f* d'achats; MKTG *purchase frequency* fréquence *f* d'achat; ACCT *purchase invoice* facture *f* d'achat; ACCT *purchase ledger* (grand-) livre *m* d'achats; *purchase method* méthode *f* d'achat; *purchase order* *(for goods, service)* bon *m* de commande; ST EXCH *(for shares)* ordre *m* d'achat; *purchase price* prix *m* d'achat; *purchase tax* taxe *f* à l'achat

2 *vt* acheter, acquérir; **to purchase sth from sb** acheter qch à qn; **to purchase sth on credit** acheter qch à crédit; ACCT **to purchase a debt** racheter une créance

3 *vi* acheter; **now is the time to purchase** c'est maintenant qu'il faut acheter

purchaser *n* acheteur(euse) *m,f* ▫ MKTG *purchaser behaviour* comportement *m* de l'acheteur

purchasing *n* achat *m*; *(of company)* rachat *m* ▫ Am *purchasing agent* acheteur(euse) *m,f*; MKTG *purchasing behaviour* comportement *m* d'achat; *purchasing costs* frais *mpl* de passation de commande; *purchasing department* service *m* des achats; *purchasing manager* chef *m* des achats; ECON *purchasing power* pouvoir *m* d'achat

> **"**
>
> Estimating comparative levels of per capita GNP between various nations is probably best done by assessing relative levels of **purchasing power** — what a currency will buy in the country in which it is issued, using comparisons between particular products.
>
> **"**

push **1** *n* *push money* prime *f* au vendeur; MKTG *push strategy* stratégie *f* 'pousser'

2 *vt* ST EXCH **to push shares** placer des valeurs douteuses

put **1** *n* ST EXCH *put band* période *f* de validité d'une option de vente; *put and call* double option *f*, stellage *m*; *put option* option *f* de vente

2 *vt* **(a)** *(invest)* placer, investir; **she had put all her savings into property** elle avait placé ou investi toutes ses économies dans l'immobilier

(b) *(present)* *(suggestion, question)* soumettre; *(motion)* proposer, présenter; **to put a proposal to the board** présenter une proposition au conseil d'administration

▸ **put back** *vt sep* **(a)** *(postpone)* reporter, remettre; **the meeting has been put back to Thursday** la réunion a été reportée ou remise à jeudi **(b)** *(delay)* retarder; **the strike has put our schedule back at least a month** la grève nous a fait perdre au moins un mois sur notre planning

▸ **put down** *vt sep* **(a)** *(write)* écrire; **to put sth down in writing** remettre qch par écrit **(b)** *(pay as deposit)* verser; **we've already put £500 down on the computer** nous avons déjà versé un acompte de 500 livres pour l'ordinateur

▸ **put forward** *vt sep* **(a)** *(bring forward)* avancer; **the meeting has been put forward to early next week** la réunion a été avancée au début de la semaine prochaine **(b)** *(suggest)* *(proposal, idea)* avancer; *(candidate)* proposer; **she put her name forward for the post of treasurer** elle a posé sa candidature au poste de trésorière

▸ **put out** *vt sep* *(sub-contract)* donner en sous-traitance; **we put most of our work out** nous confions la plus grande partie de notre travail à des sous-traitants

▸ **put through** *vt sep* *(on phone)* **to put sb through to sb** mettre qn en ligne avec qn, passer qn à qn; **put him through, please** mettez-le en ligne ou passez-le moi, s'il vous plaît; **I'll put you through to him** je vous le passe

▸ **put up** *vt sep* **(a)** *(money)* fournir; **who's putting the money up for the new business** qui finance la nouvelle entreprise? **(b)** *(increase)* faire monter, augmenter; **this will put up the price of oil** ça va faire augmenter le prix du pétrole

pyramid selling *n* vente *f* pyramidale

QC *n* (*abbr* **quality control**) contrôle *m* de la qualité

qty *n* (*abbr* **quantity**) qté

qualification *n* (**a**) (*diploma*) diplôme *m*; **list your academic qualifications** indiquez vos diplômes scolaires et universitaires (**b**) (*skill, competence*) compétence *f*, aptitude *f*; **the main qualification we are looking for is a creative mind** ce que nous attendons avant tout du candidat, c'est qu'il fasse preuve d'un esprit créatif

qualified *adj* (**a**) (*having diploma*) diplômé(e); **our staff are highly qualified** notre personnel est hautement qualifié; **to be qualified to do sth** avoir les diplômes requis pour faire qch □ *qualified accountant* comptable *mf* diplômé(e) (**b**) (*skilled, competent*) compétent(e); **to be qualified to do sth** avoir les compétences requises pour faire qch (**c**) (*modified*) mitigé(e) □ BANKING *qualified acceptance* acceptation *f* conditionnelle *ou* sous condition; *qualified approval* approbation *f* avec réserve; ACCT *qualified report* rapport *m* réservé

qualify **1** *vt* (**a**) (*make competent*) **to qualify sb to do sth** donner les compétences nécessaires à qn pour faire qch; **her experience qualifies her for the post** son expérience lui permet de prétendre à ce poste (**b**) (*modify*) mitiger; **they qualified their acceptance of the plan** ils ont accepté le projet sous conditions

qualitative *adj* MKTG *qualitative forecasting* prévisions *fpl* qualitatives; *qualitative research* études *fpl* qualitatives

quality *n* (**a**) (*standard*) qualité *f*; **of good/poor quality** de bonne/mauvaise qualité; **we have a reputation for quality** nous sommes réputés pour la qualité de nos produits □ *quality control* contrôle *m* de la qualité; *quality goods* marchandises *fpl* de qualité; MKTG *quality positioning* positionnement *m* par la qualité (**b**) (*attribute*) qualité *f*; **these are the qualities we are looking for in our candidates** voici les qualités que nous recherchons chez nos candidats

quality-price ratio *n* rapport *m* qualité-prix

quango *n* *Br* (*abbr* **quasi-autonomous non-governmental organization**) = orga-

nisme créé par le gouvernement et doté de pouvoirs quasi autonomes

> " Exactly how many **quangos** exist is not known. … Certainly the total runs to hundreds. They have been a very popular means of dealing with a wide variety of functions which ministers want to encourage, to finance and to guide, but which would not fit easily into the structure of a government department. "

quantify *vt* quantifier, évaluer

quantitative *adj* MKTG *quantitative forecasting* prévisions *fpl* quantitatives; *quantitative research* études *fpl* quantitatives

quantity *n* quantité *f*; **to buy sth in large quantities** acheter qch en grande quantité □ *quantity rebate* remise *f* sur la quantité; *quantity surveying* métrage *m*; *quantity surveyor* métreur *m* vérificateur; ECON *quantity theory* théorie *f* quantitative

quarter *n* (*three-month period*) trimestre *m*; **profits were up during the last quarter** les bénéfices ont augmenté au cours du dernier trimestre

quarterly **1** *n* (*publication*) publication *f* trimestrielle
2 *adj* trimestriel(elle)
3 *adv* tous les trimestres

quasi-contract *n* LAW quasi-contrat *m*

quasi-money *n* FIN quasi-monnaie *f*

quay *n* quai *m*

quayage *n* droits *mpl* de quai

query *n* COMPTR interrogation *f*

question mark *n* MKTG (*product*) point *m* d'interrogation, dilemme *m*

questionnaire *n* MKTG questionnaire *m*

queue COMPTR **1** *n* file *f* d'attente
2 *vt* (*print jobs*) mettre en file d'attente

quick *adj* rapide □ ACCT *quick assets* actif *m* liquide; *quick ratio* ratio *m* de liquidité immédiate; *quick returns* profits *mpl* rapides

> " … individual businesses have to show **quick returns** on minimal outlays or be deliberately run down and liquidated as "cash cows." "

quid *n Br Fam (pound sterling)* livre *f*

quiet *adj (market, business, trading)* calme; **business is very quiet** les affaires sont très calmes

quit COMPTR **1** *vt (database, program)* sortir de, quitter
  2 *vi* sortir

quittance *n* FIN quittance *f*

quorum *n* quorum *m*; **to have a quorum** atteindre le quorum; **we don't have a quorum** le quorum n'est pas atteint

quota *n* (**a**) *(limited quantity)* quota *m*; **fishing quotas have been disputed** les quotas pour la pêche ont été contestés
  (**b**) *(share)* part *f*, quota *m* ❑ **quota sampling** échantillonnage *m* par quota

quotable *adj* ST EXCH cotable

quotation *n* (**a**) ST EXCH cotation *f*, cours *m*; **the latest quotations** les derniers cours; **to seek a share quotation** faire une demande d'admission à la cote
  (**b**) *(for work)* devis *m*; **to get a quotation** faire faire un devis; **they gave me a**

quotation of £500 ils m'ont fait un devis de 500 livres

quote 1 *n (for work)* devis *m*; **to get a quote** faire faire un devis; **they gave me a quote of £500** ils m'ont fait un devis de 500 livres
  2 *vt* (**a**) ST EXCH *(shares)* coter; **gold prices were quoted at £500** l'or a été coté à 500 livres ❑ **quoted company** société *f* cotée en Bourse; **quoted investment** valeurs *fpl* mobilières de placement; **quoted price** cours *m* inscrit à la cote officielle; **quoted share** action *f* inscrite à la cote officielle
  (**b**) *(price)* indiquer; **to quote sb a price for sth** fixer à qn un prix pour qch; **they quoted me £500 for the work** ils m'ont fait un devis de 500 livres pour le travail
  (**c**) ADMIN **please quote this number** *(in reply)* prière de rappeler ce numéro
  3 *vi* **to quote for a job** faire un devis pour un travail

quote-driven *adj* ST EXCH *(Stock Market)* gouverné(e) par les prix

QWERTY keyboard *n* COMPTR clavier *m* qwerty

radiopager n récepteur m de poche ou d'appel

raid ST EXCH **1** n raid m

2 vt **to raid the bears** chasser le découvert

raider n ST EXCH raider m

rail n (train system) chemin m de fer; **to send goods by rail** envoyer des marchandises par chemin de fer

railroad n Am (train system) chemin m de fer

railway n Br (train system) chemin m de fer

raise 1 n Am (pay increase) augmentation f (de salaire)

2 vt (**a**) (price, rate, salary) augmenter (**b**) (cheque) faire (**c**) (capital) mobiliser, procurer; (funds) collecter (**d**) (taxes) lever; (loan) lancer, émettre

▸ **rake in** vt sep Fam (money) amasser; **they must be raking it in** ils s'en mettent plein les poches

rake-off n Fam pourcentage m, commission f; **to get a rake-off on each sale** toucher un pourcentage ou une commission sur chaque vente

rally 1 n (of prices, shares, business) reprise f

2 vi (of prices, shares, business) se redresser, reprendre; **the pound rallied in the afternoon** la livre est remontée dans l'après-midi

RAM n COMPTR (abbr **random access memory**) mémoire f vive

R&D, R and D n (abbr **research and development**) R-D f

random adj (fait(e)) au hasard ▫ COMPTR **random access memory** mémoire f vive; **random check** contrôle m par sondage(s); **random error** erreur f aléatoire; **random sampling** échantillonnage m aléatoire; MKTG **random selection** sélection f au hasard

range 1 n (**a**) (of prices, colours, products) gamme f; **we stock a wide range of office materials** nous avons en stock une large gamme de matériels de bureau; **this product is the top/bottom of the range** ce produit est le modèle haut/bas de gamme

(**b**) ST EXCH fourchette f, écart m; **opening/ closing range** fourchette de cours d'ouverture/de clôture

2 vi **to range from… to…** aller de… à…; **prices range from £15 to £150** les prix vont de 15 livres à 150 livres

rank 1 n (**a**) (grade) rang m, grade m; **to pull rank** abuser de son rang

(**b**) FIN (of debt, mortgage) rang m

2 vi (**a**) (of creditor, claimant) **to rank after sb** prendre rang ou passer après qn; **to rank before sb** prendre rang ou passer avant qn; **to rank equally (with sb)** prendre ou avoir le même rang (que qn)

(**b**) LAW (of share) **to rank after sth** être primé(e) par qch; **to rank before sth** avoir la priorité sur qch; **to rank equally (with sth)** prendre le même rang (que qch)

ratable adj = **rateable**

rate n (**a**) (of inflation, tax, interest) taux m; **the rate is 20p in the pound** le taux est de 20 pence par livre ▫ MKTG **rate of adoption** (of product) taux d'adoption; MKTG **rate of churn** taux de clients passés à la concurrence; **rate of depreciation** taux d'amortissement; **rate of exchange** cours m du change; **rate of growth** taux d'accroissement ou de croissance; MKTG **rate of penetration** taux de pénétration; MKTG **rate of renewal** taux de renouvellement; **rate of return** (on investment) taux de rendement; **rate of taxation** taux d'imposition; **rate of uptake** taux de succès (**b**) (price, charge) tarif m; **the going rate** le tarif courant

▸ **rate up** vt sep INS **to rate sb up** faire payer à qn une prime plus élevée

ratification n LAW ratification f

ratify vt LAW ratifier

ratio n rapport m; **in the ratio of one to three** dans le rapport ou la proportion de un à trois

rationalization n (of industry) rationalisation f

rationalize vt (industry) rationaliser

rationing *n* *(of funds)* rationnement *m*; **banks are warning of mortgage rationing** les banques annoncent qu'elles vont limiter le nombre de prêts immobiliers

rat race *n* foire *f* d'empoigne

raw *adj* *(data, statistics)* brut(e) □ **raw materials** matières *fpl* premières

RDBMS *n* COMPTR *(abbr* **relational database management system***)* SGBDR *m*

re *prep* *(abbr* **regarding***)* concernant; **re your letter of 8 March** suite à votre lettre du 8 mars; **re: 1998 sales figures** *(in letter heading)* Réf: les ventes de 1998

reach *vt* **(a)** *(extend as far as)* arriver à, atteindre; **inflation has reached record levels** l'inflation a atteint un niveau record **(b)** *(agreement, decision)* arriver à, parvenir à **(c)** *(contact)* joindre; **you can always reach me at this number** vous pouvez toujours me joindre à ce numéro

react *vi* *(of prices)* réagir

reaction *n* *(of prices)* réaction *f*

read *vt* lire; ADMIN **read and approved** *(on document)* lu et approuvé; **to take the minutes as read** passer sur la lecture du procès-verbal

▸ **read out** *vt sep* COMPTR *(data)* sortir, extraire de la mémoire

read-me document *n* COMPTR ouvrez-moi *m*

read-only memory *n* COMPTR mémoire *f* morte

readvertise *vt* *(job, position)* repasser une annonce pour

read-write head *n* COMPTR tête *f* de lecture-écriture

ready *adj* **ready cash, ready money** argent comptant *ou* liquide; **to pay in ready cash** *or* **money** payer (au) comptant; **ready reckoner** barème *m*

real *adj* **(a)** *(actual)* réel(elle) □ **real accounts** comptes *mpl* de valeur; **real assets** biens *mpl* immobiliers; **real cost** coût *m* réel; **real income** revenu *m* réel; MKTG **real repositioning** repositionnement *m* réel; **real salary** salaire *m* réel; **real terms** termes *mpl* réels; **salaries have fallen in real terms** les salaires ont baissé en termes réels; COMPTR **real time** temps *m* réel; FIN **real value** valeur *f* effective

(b) *Am* **real estate** biens *mpl* immobiliers; **real estate agency** agence *f* immobilière; **real estate agent** agent *m* immobilier; **real estate leasing** crédit-bail *m* immobilier

> The proposal also included an offer to reduce the price of supplies in **real terms** over the first five years and a pledge that during the contract period prices would remain "within the general movement of prices in the economy".

realign *vt* FIN réaligner

realignment *n* FIN réalignement *m*; **realignment of currencies** réalignement monétaire

realizable *adj* FIN réalisable □ **realizable assets** actif *m* réalisable; **realizable securities** valeurs *fpl* réalisables

realization *n* FIN réalisation *f*

realize *vt* FIN *(convert into cash)* réaliser; *(yield financially)* rapporter; **to realize a high price** *(of goods)* atteindre un prix élevé; *(of seller)* obtenir un prix élevé; **how much did they realize on the sale?** combien est-ce qu'ils ont gagné sur la vente?; **these shares cannot be realized** il n'y a pas de marché pour ces titres

real-time *adj* COMPTR en temps réel

realtor *n Am* agent *m* immobilier

realty *n Am* biens *mpl* immobiliers

reapply *vi* *(for job)* poser à nouveau sa candidature (**for** pour); **previous candidates need not reapply** les personnes ayant déjà posé leur candidature n'ont pas besoin de le faire à nouveau

reappoint *vt* **to reappoint sb** réintégrer qn dans ses fonctions

reappraisal *n* **(a)** FIN *(of property)* réévaluation *f* **(b)** *(of policy)* réexamen *m*

reappraise *vt* **(a)** FIN *(property)* réévaluer **(b)** *(policy)* réexaminer

reasonable *adj* *(offer, price)* raisonnable

reassess *vt* **(a)** *(policy, situation)* reconsidérer, réexaminer **(b)** FIN *(damages)* réévaluer; *(taxation)* réviser; **you have been reassessed** votre situation fiscale a été réexaminée

reassessment *n* **(a)** *(of policy, situation)* réexamen *m* **(b)** FIN *(of damages)* réévaluation *f*; *(of taxation)* révision *f*

reassign *vt* *(funds)* réaffecter

reassignment *n* *(of funds)* réaffectation *f*

rebate *n* **(a)** *(refund)* remboursement *m*; *(of tax)* dégrèvement *m* **(b)** *(discount on purchase)* rabais *m*, ristourne *f*

reboot COMPTR **1** *vt* réamorcer
2 *vi* se réamorcer

rebuy *n* MKTG réachat *m* ❑ *rebuy rate* taux *m* de réachat

recall 1 *n* MKTG *recall test* test *m* de rappel *ou* de mémoire
2 *vt (faulty goods)* rappeler

> " ————————————
> … there is liable to be a very different result according to whether a **recall test** is carried out within 24 hours, or a week, or three months, of an ad appearing.
> ———————————— "

recapitalization *n* FIN *(of company)* changement *m* de la structure financière

recapitalize *vt* FIN *(company)* changer la structure financière de

receipt 1 *n* **(a)** *(act of receiving)* réception *f*; **to be in receipt of sth** avoir reçu qch; **we are in receipt of your letter of 9 June** nous avons bien reçu votre lettre du 9 juin; **to pay on receipt** payer à la réception; **to acknowledge receipt** accuser réception (**of** de); **on receipt of this letter** dès réception de cette lettre
(b) *(proof of payment)* reçu *m* (**for** de); *(in supermarket, bar)* ticket *m* de caisse; *(for letter, parcel)* récépissé *m*, accusé *m* de réception; *(for rent, insurance)* quittance *f* ❑ *receipt book* carnet *m* de quittances
(c) **receipts** *(takings)* recettes *fpl*, rentrées *fpl*; **receipts and expenditure** recettes et dépenses *fpl*
2 *vt* acquitter, quittancer; **to receipt a bill** acquitter une facture

receivable 1 *n* **receivables** *(debts)* comptes *mpl* clients, créances *fpl*; *(bills)* effets *mpl* à recevoir
2 *adj (account, bill)* à recevoir

receive *vt* recevoir; *(money, salary)* toucher; ST EXCH **to receive a premium** encaisser un premium; **received with thanks** *(on bill)* acquitté, pour acquit

receiver *n* **(a)** *(of goods, consignment)* destinataire *mf*, consignataire *mf* **(b)** FIN *(in bankruptcy)* administrateur(trice) *m,f* judiciaire; **to be in the hands of the receiver(s)** être en règlement judiciaire **(c)** *Am* **receiver general** receveur *m* des impôts

receivership *n* **to go into receivership** être placé(e) en règlement judiciaire

receiving *n* **(a)** *(of goods)* réception *f* ❑ *receiving depot* dépôt *m* de réception; *receiving office* bureau *m* de réception

(b) LAW *receiving order* ordonnance *f* de mise sous séquestre

reception *n* **(a)** *reception (desk)* *(at hotel)* réception *f*; *(in office)* accueil *m*; *Am* *reception clerk* réceptionniste *mf* **(b)** *(formal party)* réception *f*

receptionist *n* réceptionniste *mf*

recession *n* ECON récession *f*; **the economy is in (a) recession** l'économie est en récession

recessionary *adj* ECON *(conditions, policy)* de récession; **to have a recessionary effect** entraîner une récession

> " ————————————
> The most important part of his empire in the **recessionary** Nineties is the lower-priced Emporio Armani line, sold both in London and Glasgow, which takes all its inspiration from the street.
> ———————————— "

recipient *n* *(of letter)* destinataire *mf*; *(of cheque, bill)* bénéficiaire *mf*

reciprocal *adj* réciproque, mutuel(elle) ❑ *reciprocal agreement* accord *m* réciproque; MKTG *reciprocal relationships model* modèle *m* de relations réciproques; *reciprocal trading* commerce *m* réciproque

reckon 1 *vt (calculate)* calculer; **to reckon the cost of sth** calculer les frais de qch
2 *vi (calculate)* calculer

recognition test *n* MKTG test *m* de reconnaissance

recognized *adj (agent)* accrédité(e)

recommended retail price *n* prix *m* recommandé *ou* conseillé

reconcile *vt (figures, bank statements)* rapprocher; ACCT *(accounts, entries)* faire cadrer *ou* accorder

reconciliation *n* *(of figures, bank statements)* rapprochement *m*; ACCT *(of accounts, entries)* ajustement *m* ❑ *reconciliation account* compte *m* collectif; ACCT *reconciliation statement* état *m* de rapprochement

reconstruction *n* *(of company)* reconstitution *f*; *(of economy)* restauration *f*

record 1 *n* **(a)** *(account)* rapport *m*; *(file)* dossier *m*; **to make a record of sth** noter qch; **to keep a record of sth** garder une trace écrite de qch; **they keep a record of all deposits** ils enregistrent tous les versements; **do you have any record of the transaction?** avez-vous gardé une trace de la transaction?; **our records show that**

payment is overdue nos dossiers font état d'un arriéré de paiement
  (**b**) *(past history)* passé *m*; **his past record with the firm** son passé dans l'entreprise; **the makers have an excellent record for high quality** les fabricants sont très réputés pour l'excellente qualité de leurs produits
  (**c**) COMPTR *(in database)* article *m*, enregistrement *m*
  2 *adj* record; **unemployment is at a record high/low** le chômage a atteint son taux le plus haut/bas
  3 *vt (take note of)* enregistrer; **to record the minutes of a meeting** faire le procès-verbal *ou* le compte-rendu d'une réunion

recorded delivery *n Br* recommandé *m*; **to send sth recorded delivery** envoyer qch en recommandé

recoup *vt* (**a**) *(get back) (losses)* récupérer; **to recoup one's investments** rentrer dans ses fonds; **to recoup one's costs** rentrer dans *ou* couvrir ses frais (**b**) *(pay back) (person)* rembourser, dédommager

recourse *n* FIN, LAW recours *m*; **to have recourse to sb** avoir recours contre qn; **endorsement without recourse** endossement *m* à forfait

recover **1** *vt* (**a**) *(debt)* recouvrer; *(money, deposit)* récupérer; **to recover one's expenses** rentrer dans ses fonds (**b**) LAW *(damages)* obtenir (**c**) COMPTR *(file, data)* récupérer
  2 *vi (of economy, currency)* se redresser; *(of prices, shares)* se redresser, remonter; *(of market, business)* reprendre

recoverable *adj (debt)* recouvrable; *(packaging)* récupérable

recovery *n* (**a**) *(of debt)* recouvrement *m*; *(of money, deposit)* récupération *f*
  (**b**) LAW *(of damages)* obtention *f*
  (**c**) *(of economy)* relance *f*, redressement *m*; *(of prices, shares)* redressement, remontée *f*; *(of currency)* redressement; *(of market, business)* reprise *f*
  (**d**) COMPTR *(of file, data)* récupération *f*

recruit *vt* recruter

recruitment *n* recrutement *m* ❑ ***recruitment agency*** agence *f* de recrutement; ***recruitment consultant*** conseil *m* en recrutement; ***recruitment drive*** campagne *f* de recrutement

rectification *n (of mistake)* rectification *f*, correction *f*; ACCT *(of entry)* modification *f*, rectification

rectify *vt (mistake)* rectifier, corriger; ACCT *(entry)* modifier, rectifier

recurrent expenses *npl* dépenses *fpl* courantes

recycle *vt (materials)* recycler; FIN *(funds)* remettre en circulation

red **1** *n* **to be in the red** *(of person)* avoir un découvert, être dans le rouge; *(of company)* être en déficit; *(of account)* avoir un solde déficitaire; **to be £5,000 in the red** *(of person)* avoir un découvert de 5 000 livres; *(of company)* avoir un déficit de 5 000 livres; *(of account)* avoir un solde déficitaire de 5 000 livres
  2 *adj Am* FIN **to go into red ink** *(of person)* être à découvert; *(of company)* être en déficit; *(of account)* avoir un solde déficitaire ❑ ***red tape*** *(bureaucracy)* paperasserie *f*

> ❝
> He argues that the small firms sector is particularly well situated to benefit from the wider enterprise opportunities offered by the single market and should not be tied down by EC **red tape**.
> ❞

redeem *vt* FIN (**a**) *(bond, share)* réaliser; *(coupon)* échanger (**b**) *(annuity, loan, mortgage)* rembourser; *(bill)* honorer; *(debt)* amortir, se libérer de

redemption *n* FIN (**a**) *(of bond, share)* remboursement *m* ❑ ***redemption date*** date *f* d'échéance; ***redemption fee, redemption premium*** prime *f* de remboursement; ***redemption yield*** rendement *m* à l'échéance (**b**) *(of annuity, loan, mortgage)* remboursement *m*

redeploy *vt (resources)* redéployer; *(workforce)* réaffecter

redeployment *n (of resources)* redéploiement *m*; *(of workforce)* réaffectation *f*

redial TEL **1** *n* **redial (feature)** rappel *m* du dernier numéro; **the latest model has automatic redial** le dernier modèle est muni du système de rappel du dernier numéro
  2 *vt (number)* refaire
  3 *vi* refaire le numéro

redirect *vt (mail)* faire suivre

redraft *vt (document, letter, report)* rédiger de nouveau

reduce *vt* réduire; *(price)* baisser; *(output)* ralentir

reduced *adj* réduit(e); *(goods)* soldé(e), en solde; **to buy sth at a reduced price** acheter qch à prix réduit ❑ ***reduced rate*** tarif *m* réduit

reduction n (**a**) réduction f; (of prices) baisse f; (of taxes) allègement m (**b**) (discount) rabais m, remise f; **to make a reduction (on sth)** faire un rabais ou une remise (sur qch)

redundancy n Br (dismissal) licenciement m; **the strike caused over three hundred redundancies** la grève a causé le licenciement de plus de trois cents personnes □ **redundancy notice** avis m de licenciement; **redundancy pay** indemnité f de licenciement

redundant adj Br (worker) licencié(e); **to make sb redundant** (of employer) licencier qn; **to be made redundant** être licencié(e), être mis(e) au chômage

re-employ vt reprendre, réembaucher

re-employment n réembauche m

re-export 1 n (activity) réexportation f; (product) article m de réexportation; **re-exports** réexportations □ **re-export trade** commerce m de réexportation
2 vt réexporter

re-exportation n réexportation f

ref n (abbr **reference**) (at head of letter) réf; **your ref** v/réf; **our ref** n/réf

refer 1 vt (**a**) BANKING **to refer a cheque to drawer** refuser d'honorer un chèque; **refer to drawer** (on cheque) voir le tireur (**b**) (send, direct) renvoyer; **to refer a customer to another department** renvoyer un client à un autre service

▸ **refer to** vt insep (consult) (person, notes) consulter; (document) se reporter à; **I shall have to refer to the board** il faudra que je consulte le conseil de direction

referee n (**a**) (for job) répondant(e) m,f; **please give the names of two referees** veuillez fournir deux références; **you can give my name as a referee** vous pouvez me citer comme référence (**b**) LAW arbitre m (**c**) **referee in case of need** (on bill of exchange) adresse f au besoin

reference n (**a**) (consultation) référence f; **with reference to your letter of 20 March** (in letter) suite à votre lettre du 20 mars; **with reference to what was said at the meeting** à propos de ou en ce qui concerne ce qui a été dit au cours de la réunion; **reference AB** (at head of letter) référence AB □ **reference number** numéro m de commande; **please quote this reference number** (in reply) prière de rappeler cette référence
(**b**) (testimonial) (from bank) référence f; (from employer) référence, recommandation f; **to give sb a reference** fournir une référence à qn; **to have good references**

avoir de bonnes références; **to take up references** prendre contact avec les personnes dont un candidat se recommande; **you can use my name as a reference** vous pouvez me citer comme référence
(**c**) MKTG **reference customer** client(e) m,f de référence; **reference group** groupe m de référence; **reference price** prix m de référence; **reference sale** vente f de référence
(**d**) (of commission, tribunal) compétence f, pouvoirs mpl; **under these terms of reference** aux termes des instructions données; **the question is outside the tribunal's reference** la question n'est pas de la compétence du tribunal

refinance FIN **1** vt (loan) refinancer
2 vi (of company) se refinancer

refinancing n FIN refinancement m

reflate vt (economy) relancer

reflation n relance f (économique)

> 66 ———
> So when unemployment approached one million in early '72, following fiscal deflation in earlier budgets, the government went for **reflation** by means of substantial tax cuts — a course of action which had the full support of most economic commentators including the "Times".
> ——— 99

refloat vt FIN (loan) émettre de nouveau; (company) renflouer, remettre à flot

refresh COMPTR **1** n actualisation f □ **refresh rate** taux m d'actualisation
2 vt actualiser

refresher course n cours m de recyclage

refrigerate vt réfrigérer □ **refrigerated lorry** camion m frigorifique; **refrigerated ship** navire m frigorifique

refrigeration n réfrigération f; **to keep sth under refrigeration** garder qch au réfrigérateur □ **refrigeration plant** installation f frigorifique

refrigerator n (storeroom) chambre f frigorifique

refund 1 n (**a**) remboursement m; **to get a refund** se faire rembourser (**b**) LAW (of monies) restitution f
2 vt (**a**) (person, money) rembourser; **to refund sb sth, to refund sth to sb** rembourser qch à qn; **they refunded me the postage** ils m'ont remboursé les frais de port (**b**) LAW (monies) restituer
3 vi LAW faire restitution d'indu

refundable *adj* remboursable

refunding *n* remboursement *m* ❑ ***refunding clause*** clause *f* de remboursement; ***refunding loan*** prêt *m* de remboursement

refusal *n* (**a**) *(of request, proposal, offer)* refus *m*; **to meet with a refusal** essuyer un refus ❑ MKTG ***refusal rate*** taux *m* de refus (**b**) *(option to buy)* **to have first refusal (on sth)** avoir la première offre (de qch); **to give sb first refusal (on sth)** donner la priorité à qn (pour qch)

refuse *vt* (**a**) *(request, proposal, offer)* refuser; **I refused to take delivery of the parcel** j'ai refusé d'accepter le paquet (**b**) *(permission)* refuser (d'accorder); *(help, visa)* refuser; **he was refused entry** on lui a refusé l'entrée; **they were refused a loan** on leur a refusé un prêt

regard *n* **with regard to** en ce qui concerne; **with regard to your enquiry, I am happy to inform you that...** en ce qui concerne *ou* suite à votre demande, j'ai le plaisir de vous informer que...

register **1** *n* (**a**) *(book)* registre *m*; *(list)* liste *f*; **to enter sth in a register** inscrire qch dans un registre ❑ *Br* LAW ***register of companies*** registre du commerce et des sociétés; ST EXCH ***register of shareholders*** registre des actionnaires (**b**) COMPTR registre *m*
2 *vt (name, luggage)* enregistrer; *(company)* immatriculer au registre du commerce; *(shares)* immatriculer; *(trademark)* déposer; *(mortgage)* inscrire; **to register a complaint** déposer une plainte

registered *adj* (**a**) FIN ***registered bond*** obligation *f* nominative; ***registered capital*** capital *m* déclaré; ***registered charity*** organisme *m* de bienfaisance reconnu par l'État; FIN ***registered debenture*** obligation *f* nominative; ***registered design*** modèle *m* déposé; ***registered name*** nom *m* déposé; *Can* FIN ***registered retirement savings plan*** régime *m* enregistré d'épargne-retraite; ***registered share certificate*** certificat *m* nominatif d'action(s); ***registered securities, registered stock*** titres *mpl* nominatifs; ***registered tonnage*** tonnage *m* net *ou* de jauge; ***registered trademark*** marque *f* déposée; COMPTR ***registered user*** utilisateur(trice) *m,f* disposant d'une licence; ***registered value*** valeur *f* enregistrée (**b**) *(letter, parcel)* recommandé(e); **to send sth by registered post** envoyer qch en recommandé

registrar *n* (**a**) *Br* ADMIN officier *m* de l'état civil (**b**) *Br* LAW ***registrar of companies***

directeur(trice) *m,f* du registre du commerce et des sociétés

registration *n* *(of name, luggage)* enregistrement *m*; *(of shares, company)* immatriculation *f*; *(of trademark)* dépôt *m*; *(of mortgage)* inscription *f* ❑ ST EXCH ***registration body*** chambre *f* d'enregistrement; COMPTR ***registration card*** licence *f*; ***registration certificate*** matricule *f*; ***registration fees*** droits *mpl* d'inscription; COMPTR ***registration number*** numéro *m* de licence; FIN ***registration and transfer fees*** droits *mpl* d'inscription et de transfert

registry *n* bureau *m* d'enregistrement ❑ *Br* ADMIN ***registry office*** bureau *m* d'état civil

regular *adj* *(habitual, normal)* régulier(ère); **to be in regular employment** avoir un emploi régulier; **to go through the regular channels** suivre la filière normale *ou* habituelle ❑ ***regular customer*** client(e) *m,f* habitué(e); ***regular income*** revenu *m* régulier; ***regular price*** prix *m* de règle

regulate *vt* *(control)* régler; *(with rules)* réglementer; **the price is regulated by supply and demand** le prix est déterminé par l'offre et la demande

regulation *n* règlement *m*; **it's contrary to regulations** c'est contraire au règlement; **it complies with EC regulations** c'est conforme aux dispositions communautaires

regulator *n* régulateur(trice) *m,f*

regulatory *adj* régulateur(trice) ❑ ***regulatory body*** organisme *m* de réglementation

> **"**
>
> The Office of Telecommunications (OFTEL) was created to act as the **regulatory body** for the telecommunications industry in order to ensure that BT did not abuse its dominant position.
>
> **"**

reimburse *vt* rembourser; **to reimburse sb for sth** rembourser qn de qch

reimport **1** *n* réimportation *f*
2 *vt* réimporter

reimportation *n* réimportation *f*

reinitialize *vt* COMPTR réinitialiser

reinstate *vt* (**a**) *(person)* réintégrer (**b**) *(law, idea, system)* rétablir

reinstatement *n* (**a**) *(of person)* réintégration *f* (**b**) *(of law, idea, system)* rétablissement *m*

reinsurance *n* INS réassurance *f*

reinsure *vt* INS réassurer

reinvest *vt* FIN réinvestir

reinvestment *n* FIN réinvestissement *m*

reissue FIN **1** *n* *(of banknotes, shares)* nouvelle émission *f*
2 *vt* *(banknotes, shares)* émettre de nouveau

reject 1 *n* *(object)* article *m* de rebut
2 *vt* *(offer, proposal)* rejeter, repousser; *(goods, candidate, application)* refuser

related to, relating to *prep* ADMIN, LAW afférent(e) à; **questions related to official procedure** des questions afférentes à la procédure officielle

relational database *n* COMPTR base *f* de données relationnelle

relationship marketing *n* MKTG marketing *m* relationnel

relaunch 1 *n* *(of product)* relancement *m*
2 *vt* *(product)* relancer

release 1 *n* **(a)** *(of debtor)* libération *f* **(b)** CUSTOMS *(of goods from bond)* dédouanement *m* **(c)** FIN *(of credits, funds)* déblocage *m*, dégagement *m*
2 *vt* **(a)** *(debtor)* libérer **(b)** CUSTOMS *(goods from bond)* dédouaner **(c)** FIN *(credits, funds)* débloquer, dégager

reliability *n* *(of person, company)* sérieux *m*; *(of information, account, machine)* fiabilité *f*; *(of guarantee)* solidité *f*

reliable *adj* *(person, company)* sérieux(euse), à qui on peut faire confiance; *(information, account)* sûr(e); *(machine)* fiable; *(guarantee)* solide

relief *n* **(a)** *(replacement)* remplaçant(e) *m,f* **(b)** *Am* ADMIN *(state benefit)* aide *f* sociale; **to be on relief** recevoir des aides sociales

relocate 1 *vt* *(company)* transférer; *(person)* muter
2 *vi* *(of company)* être transféré(e); *(of person)* se déplacer

relocation *n* déménagement *m* ❑ *reloc-ation allowance* indemnité *f* de déménagement; *relocation expenses* frais *mpl* de déménagement

> **"**
> Whatever the source of recruitment, it is going to be expensive. The main costs are likely to be advertising space; agency fees (if an outside bureau is used); candidates' travelling and subsistence expenses; and perhaps **relocation expenses** for the successful candidate.
> **"**

reminder *n* (lettre *f* de) rappel *m*

remit 1 *n* *(area of authority)* attributions *fpl*; **that's outside their remit** cela n'entre pas dans leurs attributions
2 *vt* **(a)** *(payment)* remettre **(b)** *(cancel)* *(debt)* remettre, faire remise de; **to remit sb's fees** dispenser qn de ses frais; **to remit sb's income tax** dispenser *ou* exempter qn d'impôt
3 *vi* *(pay)* régler, payer; **please remit by cheque** veuillez régler *ou* payer par chèque

remittance *n* *(money)* paiement *m*, règlement *m*; **return the form with your remittance** renvoyez le formulaire avec votre paiement *ou* règlement ❑ *remittance advice* avis *m* de remise; *remittance date* date *f* de remise

remortgage *vt* *(house, property)* hypothéquer de nouveau, prendre une nouvelle hypothèque sur

remote *adj* COMPTR *(user)* à distance ❑ *remote access* accès *m* à distance; *remote server* serveur *m* distant; *remote terminal* terminal *m* distant

removable *adj* COMPTR *(disk)* amovible, extractible

remunerate *vt* rémunérer

remuneration *n* rémunération *f* (**for** de); **to receive remuneration for sth** être rémunéré(e) pour qch ❑ *remuneration package* = salaire et avantages complémentaires

> **"**
> This had led to the development of top executives receiving not a salary but a "total **remuneration package**" which includes a whole range of fringe benefits. For example, cheap mortgages supplied by employers are one important way in which higher income earners maintain real higher standards of living.
> **"**

remunerative *adj* rémunérateur(trice)

rename *vt* COMPTR *(file)* changer le nom de, renommer

render *vt* *(bill, account)* remettre; **as per account rendered** suivant compte remis; **for services rendered** pour services rendus

renew *vt* *(lease, passport, membership, contract)* renouveler; *(bill)* prolonger; **to renew one's subscription (to sth)** se réabonner (à qch)

renewal *n* *(of lease, passport, membership, contract)* renouvellement *m*; *(of bill)* prolongation *f*; *(of subscription)* réabonnement *m* (**to** à) ◻ INS ***renewal notice*** avis *m* de renouvellement; ***renewal premium*** prime *f* de renouvellement

rent **1** *n* loyer *m*; **for rent** *(sign)* à louer
　　2 *vt* louer; **to rent sth from sb** louer qch à qn

▸ **rent out** *vt sep* louer; **to rent sth out to sb** louer qch à qn

rental *n* (**a**) *(hire)* location *f* ◻ ***rental agreement*** contrat *m* de location (**b**) *(money)* *(for house, office)* loyer *m*; *(for equipment)* location *f*; *(for telephone)* abonnement *m* ◻ ACCT ***rental charges*** charges *fpl* locatives; ***rental income*** revenus *mpl* locatifs

rent-free **1** *adj* exempt(e) de loyer
　　2 *adv* sans payer de loyer

reopen **1** *vt* rouvrir; *(debate, negotiations)* reprendre
　　2 *vi* rouvrir; *(of debate, negotiations)* reprendre

reorder **1** *n* nouvelle commande *f* ◻ ***reorder level*** seuil *m* de réapprovisionnement
　　2 *vt* faire une nouvelle commande de

reorganization *n* réorganisation *f*

reorganize **1** *vt* réorganiser
　　2 *vi* se réorganiser

rep *n Fam* *(abbr* **representative**) VRP *m*

repackage *vt* MKTG *(goods)* reconditionner, repenser l'emballage de; *(company, image)* redorer

repair **1** *n* (**a**) *(mending)* réparation *f*; **to be under repair** être en réparation; **to carry out repairs on sth** effectuer des réparations sur qch; **closed for repairs** *(sign)* fermé pour (cause de) travaux (**b**) *(condition)* état *m*; **to be in good/bad repair** être en bon/mauvais état
　　2 *vt* réparer

repatriate *vt (funds)* rapatrier

repatriation *n (of funds)* rapatriement *m*

repay *vt (person, money, debt)* rembourser

repayable *adj* remboursable; **the amount is repayable in five years** la somme est remboursable en cinq ans

repayment *n* remboursement *m*; **repayments can be spread over 12 months** les remboursements peuvent être échelonnés sur 12 mois ◻ ***repayment mortgage*** prêt-logement *m (qui n'est pas lié à une assurance-vie)*

repeal **1** *n (of law)* abrogation *f*
　　2 *vt (law)* abroger

repeat **1** *n* COMPTR ***repeat function*** fonction *f* de répétition; ***repeat order*** commande *f* renouvelée; MKTG ***repeat purchase*** achat *m* renouvelé; MKTG ***repeat sale*** vente *f* répétée
　　2 *vt (order, offer)* renouveler

repetitive strain injury *n* = douleurs dans les bras et les mains dues à la répétition de certains mouvements, qui affectent notamment les gens qui travaillent sur ordinateur

replace *vt* remplacer; COMPTR **replace all** *(command)* tout remplacer

replacement *n* (**a**) *(person)* remplaçant(e) *m,f*; *(engine or machine part)* pièce *f* de rechange; *(product)* produit *m* de remplacement; **we are looking for a replacement for our secretary** nous cherchons quelqu'un pour remplacer notre secrétaire (**b**) *(substituting)* remplacement *m* ◻ ***replacement cost*** coût *m* de remplacement; ***replacement sale*** vente *f* de remplacement; ***replacement staff*** personnel *m* de remplacement; INS ***replacement value*** *(of item)* valeur *f* de remplacement

reply **1** *n* réponse *f*; **in reply to your letter** en réponse à votre lettre; **reply paid** réponse payée ◻ ***reply card*** carte-réponse *f*; ***reply coupon*** coupon-réponse *m*; ***reply slip*** talon *m* à retourner
　　2 *vi* répondre (**to** à)

repo *n (abbr* **repurchase**) rachat *m* ◻ ***repo agreement*** faculté *f* de rachat; ***repo rate*** taux *m* de rachat

report **1** *n* (**a**) *(account, review)* rapport *m* (**on** sur); *(of meeting, speech)* compte-rendu *m*; *(official record)* procès-verbal *m*; **to draw up** *or* **make a report on sth** faire *ou* rédiger un rapport sur qch; **to present a report to sb on sth** présenter un rapport à qn sur qch ◻ ***report of the board of directors*** *(in annual accounts)* rapport de gestion (**b**) ACCT *(balance sheet)* bilan *m* (**c**) COMPTR état *m*
　　2 *vt* (**a**) *(give account of)* rendre compte de; **to report one's findings (to sb)** faire un rapport (à qn)
　　(**b**) CUSTOMS **to report a vessel** déclarer un navire
　　3 *vi* (**a**) *(present oneself)* se présenter (**to** à); **please report to our branch in Paris** veuillez vous présenter à notre succursale de Paris; **report to my office** présentez-vous à mon bureau
　　(**b**) *(give account)* faire un rapport (**to sb** à qn; **on sth** sur qch)

(**c**) *(be accountable)* **to report to sb** rendre compte à qn; **I report directly to the sales manager** je dépends directement du chef des ventes

reporting limit *n* ST EXCH seuil *m* d'annonce obligatoire

reposition *vt* MKTG *(product)* repositionner

> 66
>
> Sales, independent for each of the four brands, operate out of new design studios, showrooms and offices. The brands have been **repositioned** with relevant distribution and marketing changes. The team is now in place but the total reorganisation task has been expensive and operational efficiency has suffered during the process of change.
>
> 99

repositioning *n* MKTG *(of product)* repositionnement *m*

repossess *vt* LAW saisir

represent *vt* représenter; **I represent the agency** je viens de la part de l'agence; **he represented the union at the meeting** il a représenté le syndicat à la réunion

representation *n* représentation *f*

representative **1** *n* *(of group, company, organization)* représentant(e) *m,f*
2 *adj* représentatif(ive) ◻ MKTG ***representative sample*** échantillon *m* type

reprocess *vt* retraiter

reprocessing *n* retraitement *m*

reprogram *vt* COMPTR reprogrammer

repurchase **1** *n* rachat *m*; **sale with option of repurchase** vente *f* avec faculté de rachat ◻ ***repurchase agreement*** faculté *f* de rachat; MKTG ***repurchase market*** marché *m* de renouvellement; ***repurchase period*** délai *m* de rachat; ***repurchase rate*** taux *m* de rachat; ***repurchase right*** droit *m* de rachat
2 *vt* racheter

request **1** *n* demande *f* (**for** de); **to make a request (for)** faire une demande (de); **samples sent on request** échantillons sur demande
2 *vt* demander; **to request sb to do sth** demander à qn de faire qch; **as requested** (comme) suite à votre demande

require *vt* (**a**) *(qualifications, standard, commitment)* exiger, réclamer; **this job requires skills and experience** ce travail demande *ou* réclame compétence et

expérience; **it is required that you begin work at 8 o'clock every morning** on exige de vous que vous commenciez votre travail à 8 heures tous les matins
(**b**) *(need)* avoir besoin de; **your presence is urgently required** on vous réclame d'urgence

requirement *n* (**a**) *(need, demand)* exigence *f*; **to meet sb's requirements** satisfaire aux exigences de qn; **this doesn't meet our requirements** ceci ne répond pas à nos exigences (**b**) *(condition, prerequisite)* condition *f* (requise); **she doesn't fulfil the requirements for the job** elle ne remplit pas les conditions requises pour le poste

requisition *n* demande *f*; **to put in a requisition for sth** passer une demande de qch ◻ ***requisition number*** numéro *m* de référence

resale *n* revente *f* ◻ ***resale price maintenance*** vente *f* au détail à prix imposé; ***resale value*** valeur *f* à la revente

reschedule *vt* (**a**) *(appointment, flight, departure)* *(change time of)* modifier l'heure de; *(change date of)* modifier la date de; **the meeting has been rescheduled for next week** la réunion a été reportée à la semaine prochaine (**b**) FIN *(debt)* rééchelonner

rescind *vt* *(agreement)* annuler; *(contract)* résilier; *(law)* abroger

rescission *n* *(of agreement)* annulation *f*; *(of contract)* résiliation *f*; *(of law)* abrogation *f*

research **1** *n* recherche *f*; **to do research (into sth)** faire des recherches (sur qch); **research and development** recherche et développement *m* ◻ ***research department*** service *m* de recherche; ***research programme*** programme *m* de recherches; ***research work*** travaux *mpl* de recherche
2 *vt* faire des recherches sur
3 *vi* faire des recherches (**into** sur)

researcher *n* chercheur(euse) *m,f*

resell *vt* revendre

reservation *n* *(booking)* réservation *f*; **to make a reservation** faire une réservation ◻ ***reservation desk*** bureau *m* des réservations

reserve **1** *n* (**a**) FIN *(of money)* réserve *f*; **to draw on the reserves** puiser dans les réserves ◻ ***reserve account*** compte *m* de réserve; ***reserve capital*** capital *m* de réserve; ***reserve currency*** monnaie *f* de réserve; ACCT ***reserve fund*** fonds *m* de réserve (**b**) ***reserve price*** *(at auction)* prix *m* minimum
2 *vt* *(room, table, seat)* réserver

> But an increase in the supply of dollars implied a persistent US balance of payments deficit (e.g. exporters to the USA accept payments in dollars, or payments overseas by US residents are made in dollars), and this would undermine confidence in the dollar as a **reserve currency** because dollar claims were growing in relation to US gold reserves.

reset *n* COMPTR réinitialisation *f* ❏ *reset button, reset switch* bouton *m* de réinitialisation

residence *n* (stay) séjour *m*; (home) demeure *f* ❏ *residence permit* permis *m* de séjour

resign 1 *vt* (job, position) démissionner de 2 *vi* démissionner; **she resigned from her job/from the committee** elle a démissionné de son emploi/du comité

resignation *n* démission *f*; **to hand in one's resignation** donner sa démission

resolution *n* (a) (formal motion) résolution *f*; **to put a resolution to the meeting** soumettre *ou* proposer une résolution; **to pass/adopt/reject a resolution (to do sth)** voter/adopter/rejeter une résolution (pour faire qch); **the statutes can only be changed by resolution** les statuts ne peuvent être modifiés que par l'adoption d'une résolution (b) COMPTR résolution *f*; **high resolution screen** écran *m* à haute résolution *ou* définition

resource *n* ressource *f*; **there's a limit to the resources we can invest** il y a une limite à la somme que nous pouvons investir ❏ *resource allocation* allocation *f* des ressources; *resource management* gestion *f* des ressources

respect *n* **with respect to, in respect of** (in letter) en ce qui concerne, concernant

respite *n* (delay) délai *m*; **we've been given a week's respite before we need to pay** on nous a accordé un délai d'une semaine pour payer

responsibility *n* (a) (control, authority) responsabilité *f*; **to have responsibility for sth** avoir la charge *ou* la responsabilité de qch; **the project is their joint responsibility** le projet relève de leur responsabilité à tous les deux; **a position of great responsibility** un poste à haute responsabilité (b) (task, duty) responsabilité *f*; **your responsibilities will include product**

development vous assurerez entre autres le développement de nouveaux produits; **they have a responsibility to the shareholders** ils ont une responsabilité envers les actionnaires

responsible *adj* (a) (in control, in authority) responsable; **who's responsible for research?** qui est chargé de la recherche?; **a responsible position** un poste à responsabilité (b) (accountable) responsable; **he is responsible only to the managing director** il n'est responsable que devant le directeur général (c) (serious, trustworthy) responsable; **the chemical industry has become more environmentally responsible** l'industrie chimique se préoccupe davantage de l'environnement; **our bank makes responsible investments** notre banque a une politique d'investissement responsable

restart COMPTR 1 *n* (of system) redémarrage *m*; (of program) reprise *f* 2 *vt* (system) redémarrer; (program) reprendre 3 *vi* (of system) redémarrer; (of program) reprendre

restore COMPTR 1 *n* restauration *f* 2 *vt* restaurer

restrict *vt* (expenses, production) restreindre; **to restrict credits** encadrer le crédit

restricted *adj* (document, information) secret(ète), confidentiel(elle)

restriction *n* (of expenses, production) restriction *f*, limitation *f*; **to place restrictions on sth** imposer des restrictions sur qch

restrictive *adj* restrictif(ive) ❏ *restrictive clause* clause *f* restrictive; *restrictive practices* pratiques *fpl* restrictives

restructure *vt* restructurer

restructuring *n* restructuration *f*

result 1 *n* résultat *m*; **the company's results are down on last year's** les résultats financiers de l'entreprise sont moins bons que l'année dernière; **to yield** *or* **show results** donner des résultats; **our policy is beginning to show results** notre politique commence à porter ses fruits 2 *vi* résulter; **to result in sth** avoir qch pour résultat, entraîner qch; **a price rise would inevitably result** il en résulterait inévitablement une augmentation des prix

résumé *n* (a) (summary) résumé *m* (b) Am (curriculum vitae) curriculum vitae *m*

retail 1 *n* (vente *f* au) détail *m*; **a wholesale and retail business** un commerce de gros et de détail ◻ ***retail bank*** banque *f* de détail; ***retail customer*** client(e) *m,f* qui achète au détail; ***retail dealer*** détaillant(e) *m,f*; ***retail outlet*** magasin *m* de détail; ***retail panel*** panel *m* de détaillants; ***retail price*** prix *m* de détail; *Br* ECON, FIN **Retail Price Index** indice *m* des prix de détail; ***retail price maintenance*** prix *m* imposé; ***retail sales*** vente *f* au détail; ***retail shipment*** expédition *f* de détail; ***retail trade*** (commerce *m* de) détail

2 *vt* vendre au détail

3 *vi* se vendre (au détail); **they retail at £50 each** ils se vendent à 50 livres la pièce

> **❝**
> Since 1966 it has operated a set of rules known as the "stabilizer" which has regulated the behaviour of tour operators and travel agents in the inclusive tour industry. This involves exclusive dealing and **retail price maintenance** in return for which consumers are guaranteed a degree of protection and recompense in the case of financial failure of a tour operator.
> **❞**

retailer *n* détaillant(e) *m,f*

retained *adj* ACCT **retained earnings** revenu *m* non distribué; ***retained profit*** bénéfices *mpl* non distribués

retainer *n* provision *f*; **to pay sb a retainer** verser une provision à qn

retaining fee *n* provision *f*

retire 1 *vt* (**a**) *(person)* mettre à la retraite (**b**) FIN *(bill, bonds, shares)* retirer

2 *vi* prendre sa retraite; **he retired at 65** il a pris sa retraite à 65 ans

retired *adj* (**a**) *(person)* retraité(e), à la retraite (**b**) FIN *(bill, bonds, shares)* retiré(e)

retiree *n Am* retraité(e) *m,f*

retirement *n* (**a**) *(of person)* retraite *f*; **to take early retirement** partir en retraite anticipée ◻ ***retirement age*** l'âge *m* de la retraite; ***retirement pension*** (pension *f* de) retraite (**b**) FIN *(of bill, bonds, shares)* retrait *m*

retiring *adj (employee)* qui prend sa retraite ◻ ***retiring age*** l'âge *m* de la retraite

retrain 1 *vt* recycler

2 *vi* se recycler

> **❝**
> It is unlikely that people training for work today will be prepared for a job for life. Instead they will have to **retrain** in future, perhaps to do jobs they cannot even imagine today.
> **❞**

retraining *n* recyclage *m*

retrench FIN **1** *vt (expenditure, costs)* restreindre

2 *vi* restreindre ses dépenses, faire des économies

retrenchment *n* FIN *(of expenditure, costs)* réduction *f*

retrieval *n* COMPTR *(of data, file)* recherche *f*; *(of lost data)* récupération *f*

retrieve *vt* COMPTR *(data, file)* rechercher; *(lost data)* récupérer

retroactive *adj* rétroactif(ive)

> **❝**
> The earliest the matter can be raised again is in January when the new Congress returns, and although if the benefit is reintroduced it may well be **retroactive** to 1 January, potential donors are biding their time for the moment.
> **❞**

retroactively *adv* rétroactivement

retry *vi* COMPTR réessayer

return 1 *n* (**a**) *(of goods)* renvoi *m*; **by return of post** par retour du courrier; **on sale or return** *(goods)* vendu(e) avec possibilité de retour ◻ ***return address*** adresse *f* de l'expéditeur; ***return cargo*** cargaison *f* de retour; ***return freight*** fret *m* de retour

(**b**) FIN *(yield)* rapport *m* (**on** de); **how much return do you get on your investment?** combien est-ce que ton investissement te rapporte?; **to bring a good return** rapporter un bon bénéfice; ACCT **return on capital** retour *m* sur capital; ACCT **return on capital employed** retour sur capital immobilisé; **return on capital invested** retour sur capitaux investis; **return on investment** retour sur investissements

(**c**) **returns** *(profit)* bénéfices *mpl* ◻ ACCT ***returns ledger*** journal *m* des rendus

(**d**) *(for declaring tax)* (formulaire *m* de) déclaration *f* d'impôts

(**e**) *Br (round trip)* aller et retour *m* ◻ ***return ticket*** (billet *m*) aller et retour

(**f**) COMPTR retour *m* ◻ ***return key*** touche *f* retour

2 *vt* (**a**) *(goods)* renvoyer; **to return sb's call** rappeler qn; **return to sender** *(on letter)* retour à l'expéditeur

(**b**) *(deposit)* rendre; *(sum paid in excess)* ristourner, rembourser

(**c**) FIN *(profit, interest)* rapporter

returnable *adj (container)* consigné(e)

revaluation *n* ECON, FIN *(of currency, property)* réévaluation *f*

revalue *vt* ECON, FIN *(currency, property)* réévaluer

revenue *n* FIN revenu *m*; *(from land, property)* revenu, rentes *fpl*; *(from sales)* recettes *fpl* □ **revenue account** compte *m* des recettes et des dépenses

reverse 1 *adj* **(a)** ACCT **reverse entry** écriture *f* inverse; FIN, ST EXCH **reverse takeover** centre-OPA *f*

(b) COMPTR **reverse sort** tri *m* en ordre décroissant

2 *vt* **(a)** *(policy)* inverser; *(decision)* revenir sur

(b) *Br* TEL **to reverse the charges** appeler en PCV

(c) ACCT *(entry)* contre-passer

reverse-charge call *n Br* TEL communication *f* en PCV

reversionary annuity *n* INS rente *f* réversible

review 1 *n (of policy, salary)* révision *f*; *(of finances, situation)* examen *m*, bilan *m*; **the annual review of expenditure** le bilan annuel des dépenses; **all our prices are subject to review** tous nos prix sont susceptibles d'être révisés; **my salary comes up for review next month** mon salaire doit être révisé le mois prochain

2 *vt (policy, salary)* réviser; *(finances, situation)* examiner; **they should review their security arrangements** ils devraient revoir leurs dispositifs de sécurité

revival *n (in economy)* relance *f*; *(in business, industry)* reprise *f*

revive 1 *vt (economy)* relancer; *(business, industry)* ranimer

2 *vi (of economy, business, industry)* reprendre

revoke *vt (law)* abroger; *(decision)* revenir sur

revolving *adj* FIN **revolving credit** crédit *m* renouvelable *ou* revolving; **revolving fund** fonds *m* de roulement

> "
> And the whole point of credit cards and other forms of **revolving credit** is that they don't come to an end. This puts a new burden on the credit user: the need to decide not to use a form of credit, or stop using it, instead of the need to decide to use it.
> "

rider *n (to document)* annexe *f*

rig ST EXCH **1** *n (rise)* hausse *f* factice; *(fall)* baisse *f* factice

2 *vt* **to rig the market** manipuler la Bourse

rigging *n* ST EXCH spéculation *f*, agiotage *m*

right 1 *n* **(a)** *(entitlement)* droit *m*; **to have the right to sth** avoir droit à qch; **she has a right to half the profits** elle a droit à la moitié des bénéfices

(b) ST EXCH droit *m* préférentiel de souscription □ **rights issue** émission *f* de nouvelles actions à taux préférentiel

2 *adj* COMPTR **right arrow** flèche *f* vers la droite; **right arrow key** touche *f* flèche vers la droite

rightful *adj* légitime □ **rightful owner** propriétaire *mf* légitime

rightsize *vt* dégraisser

rightsizing *n* dégraissage *m*

rim country *n Am* nouveau pays *m* industrialisé

ring¹ *n* **(a)** *(group)* syndicat *m*, cartel *m*
(b) ST EXCH **the Ring** le Parquet

ring² 1 *vt (on telephone)* appeler
2 *vi (on telephone)* appeler

▸ **ring back 1** *vt sep* rappeler
2 *vi* rappeler

▸ **ring off** *vi (on telephone)* raccrocher

▸ **ring up 1** *vt sep* **(a)** *(on telephone)* appeler
(b) *(on cash register)* enregistrer
2 *vi* appeler

▸ **rip off** *vt sep Fam* arnaquer

rip-off *n Fam* arnaque *f*

RISC *n* COMPTR *(abbr* **reduced instruction set chip** *or* **computer***)* RISC

rise 1 *n* **(a)** *(in price, cost of living)* hausse *f*; *(in salary, value)* augmentation *f*; *(in bank rates, interest)* relèvement *m*, hausse; **the rise in the price of petrol** la hausse du prix de l'essence; ST EXCH **to speculate on a rise** jouer à la hausse **(b)** *Br (salary increase)* augmentation *f* (de salaire)

2 *vi* monter, augmenter; **the pound has risen against the dollar** la livre s'est appréciée vis-à-vis du dollar; **gold has risen in value by 10%** la valeur de l'or a augmenté de 10%

rising star *n* MKTG produit *m* d'avenir

risk *n* **(a)** *(possibility)* risque *m*; **to run a risk** courir un risque; **it was a calculated risk** c'était un risque calculé □ **risk analysis** analyse *f* des risques; *Am* ST EXCH **risk arbitrage** arbitrage *m* risque; **risk assessment** évaluation *f* des risques; FIN **risk capital** capital *m* à risque; **risk factor**

facteur *m* de risque; ***risk management*** gestion *f* des risques; ***risk spreading*** répartition *f* des risques

(**b**) INS risque *m*; **to underwrite a risk** souscrire un risque

risk-reward ratio *n* ST EXCH ratio *m* risque-rentabilité

rival *adj & n* rival(e) *m,f*

road *n* route *f*; **to be on the road** *(of salesman)* être sur la route ◻ ***road haulage*** transports *mpl* routiers; MKTG ***road show*** tournée *f* de présentation; ***road transport*** transports *mpl* routiers

robotics *n* robotique *f*

rock bottom *n* **to reach rock bottom** *(of company, finances)* toucher le fond; **prices have reached rock bottom** les prix sont au plus bas

> ❝
>
> "Interest rates are not going to fall much more, and prices for properties under £100,000 have **reached rock bottom**."
>
> ❞

rock-bottom *adj (price)* le plus bas

rocket *vi (of prices, inflation, unemployment)* monter en flèche

ROI *n (abbr* **return on investment***)* retour *m* sur investissements

▸ **roll back** *vt sep Am (prices, inflation, unemployment)* baisser

▸ **roll over** *vi* FIN renouveler

rollback *n Am (in prices, inflation, unemployment)* réduction *f*, baisse *f* (**in** de)

rollercoaster market *n* marché *m* volatile

roll-on-roll-off *n (system)* roulage *m*; *(ship)* navire *m* roulier

rollover *adj (credit, loan)* à taux révisable

ROM *n* COMPTR *(abbr* **read only memory***)* mémoire *f* morte, (mémoire) ROM *f*

root directory *n* COMPTR racine *f*, répertoire *m* principal

RORO *n (abbr* **roll-on-roll-off***) (system)* roulage *m*; *(ship)* navire *m* roulier

rotation *n (of staff, jobs)* roulement *m*

rough **1** *n* MKTG *(of design)* crayonné *m*, esquisse *f*

2 *adj (approximate, not finalized)* approximatif(ive) ◻ ***rough calculation*** calcul *m* approximatif; ***rough copy*** brouillon *m*; ***rough estimate*** évaluation *f* en gros;

rough layout crayonné *m*, esquisse *f*; ***rough sketch*** ébauche *f* (de projet)

round **1** *n (of talks, visits)* série *f*

2 *adj (***a***) round figure* chiffre *m* rond; **in round figures** en chiffres ronds; ***round sum*** compte *m* rond (**b**) *Am* ***round trip*** aller et retour *m*; ***round trip ticket*** (billet *m*) aller et retour

▸ **round down** *vt sep* arrondir au chiffre inférieur

▸ **round up** *vt sep* arrondir au chiffre supérieur

route **1** *n (of traveller)* itinéraire *m*; *(of plane, ship)* route *f*

2 *vt (parcel, goods)* acheminer

router *n* COMPTR routeur *m*

routine *n* COMPTR sous-programme *m*

routing *n (of parcel, goods)* acheminement *m*

row *n* COMPTR *(in spreadsheet)* ligne *f*

Royal Mint *n Br* FIN ≃ (l'hôtel *m* de) la Monnaie

royalty *n (for invention)* redevance *f*; **royalties** *(for author, musician)* droits *mpl* d'auteur

RPM *n (abbr* **retail price maintenance***)* prix *m* imposé

RRP *n (abbr* **recommended retail price***)* prix *m* recommandé *ou* conseillé

RSI *n (abbr* **repetitive strain injury***)* = douleurs dans les bras et les mains dues à la répétition de certains mouvements, qui affectent notamment les gens qui travaillent sur ordinateur

> ❝
>
> For a "disease caused by typing" £45,000 may seem an awful lot of compensation, but this is the figure awarded last year to a typist suffering from **RSI** (repetitive strain injury).
>
> ❞

RTM *n (abbr* **registered trade mark***)* marque *f* déposée

rule **1** *n (law, principle)* règle *f*; *(regulation)* règlement *m*; **rules and regulations** règles

2 *vi (make decision)* statuer (**on** sur); **to rule on a dispute** statuer sur un litige

▸ **rule off** *vt sep (account)* clore, arrêter

ruler *n* règle *f* ◻ COMPTR ***ruler line*** règle

ruling **1** *n (judgement)* décision *f*, jugement *m*

2 *adj (class)* dirigeant(e)

run **1** *n* FIN *(on currency, Stock Exchange)* ruée *f* (**on** sur); *(on bank)* retrait *m* massif; **there was a run on the dollar** il y a eu une ruée sur le dollar

2 *vt* (**a**) *(business, office)* diriger; *(shop)* tenir (**b**) *(machinery)* faire marcher, faire fonctionner (**c**) COMPTR *(program)* exécuter, faire tourner; **this computer runs most software** on peut utiliser la plupart des logiciels sur cet ordinateur

3 *vi* (**a**) *(of contract, lease, bill of exchange)* courir; **the lease has another year to run** le bail n'expire pas avant un an; **your subscription will run for two years** votre abonnement sera valable deux ans

(**b**) *(of machine)* marcher, fonctionner; **the new assembly line is up and running** la nouvelle chaîne de montage est en service

(**c**) COMPTR **this software runs on DOS** ce logiciel tourne sous DOS; **do not interrupt the program while it is running** ne pas interrompre le programme en cours d'exécution

▸ **run down** *vt* *(production, stocks)* réduire, diminuer

▸ **run into** *vt insep (amount to)* s'élever à; **the debts run into millions of dollars** la dette s'élève à des millions de dollars

▸ **run out** *vi (of lease, contract)* expirer; *(of money, supplies, resources)* s'épuiser; **to run out of sth** manquer de qch; **to have run out of sth** ne plus avoir de qch

▸ **run up** *vt sep (bill, debt)* laisser accumuler; **I've run up a huge overdraft** j'ai un découvert énorme

runner *n (messenger)* coursier(ère) *m,f*

running 1 *n* (**a**) *(of machine)* marche *f*, fonctionnement *m* ❑ **running costs** frais *mpl* d'entretien (**b**) *(mangement)* direction *f*; **she leaves the day-to-day running of the department to her assistant** elle laisse son assistant s'occuper de la gestion quotidienne du service ❑ **running costs** frais *mpl* d'exploitation

2 *adj* BANKING **running account** compte *m* courant

runtime system *n* COMPTR système *m* en phase d'exécution

rush *n* (**a**) **rush hour** *(busy period)* heures *fpl* d'affluence *ou* de pointe (**b**) *(hurry)* hâte *f* ❑ **rush job** travail *m* de première urgence; **rush order** commande *f* urgente

▸ **rush out** *vt sep (new product)* sortir rapidement

▸ **rush through** *vt sep (job)* expédier; *(goods ordered)* envoyer d'urgence; *(order, application)* traiter d'urgence

sabbatical 1 *n* congé *m* sabbatique
2 *adj* sabbatique

sack *Fam* **1** *n* *(dismissal)* renvoi *m*; **to get the sack** se faire virer; **to give sb the sack** virer qn
2 *vt* *(dismiss)* virer

SAE *n* *Br* (*abbr* **stamped addressed envelope**) enveloppe *f* timbrée libellée à ses noms et adresse

safe 1 *n* coffre-fort *m*
2 *adj* (**a**) **to place sth in safe custody** *(securities, assets)* mettre qch en dépôt (**b**) *(investment)* sûr(e)

safe-deposit box *n* coffre *m* *(dans une banque)*

safe-keeping *n* garde *f*; **to place securities in the bank for safe-keeping** mettre des valeurs en dépôt à la banque

safety *n* sécurité *f* □ **safety factor** facteur *m* de sécurité; **safety margin** marge *f* de sécurité; **safety regulations** règles *fpl* de sécurité; **safety standards** normes *fpl* de sécurité; **safety stock** stock *m* tampon *ou* de sécurité; **safety vault** chambre *f* forte

sag 1 *n* *(of shares, prices, demand)* baisse *f*
2 *vi* *(of shares, prices, demand)* baisser

sagging *adj* *(shares, prices, demand)* en baisse

salaried *adj* *(personnel, job)* salarié(e) □ **salaried employee** salarié(e) *m,f*; **salaried staff** salarié(e)s

salary *n* salaire *m*; **to draw one's salary** toucher son salaire □ **salary earner** salarié(e) *m,f*; **salary grade** échelon *m* des salaires; **salary increase** augmentation *f* de salaire; **salary progression curve** courbe *f* d'augmentation de salaire; **salary scale** échelle *f* de salaires; **salary structure** structure *f* des salaires

sale *n* (**a**) *(act, event)* vente *f*; **sales** *(turnover)* chiffre *m* d'affaires; **for sale** à vendre; **to put sth up for sale** mettre qch en vente; **on sale** en vente; **sales and marketing** vente-marketing *f*; **sales and marketing department** service *m* vente-marketing; **sale at arrival** vente à l'arrivée; **sale at departure** vente au départ; **sale by private agreement** vente à l'amiable; **sale or return** vente avec faculté de retour; **sale by sealed tender** vente par soumission cachetée; **sale**

as seen vente en l'état; **sale by description** vente sur description; **sale by sample** vente sur échantillon; **sale with option of repurchase** vente avec faculté de rachat; **sale and lease-back** cession-bail *f*; **sale by auction** vente aux enchères; ST EXCH **sale for the account** vente à terme □ **sales account** compte *m* des ventes; **sales acumen** sens *m* du commerce; **sale agreement** compromis *m* de vente; **sales analysis** analyse *f* des ventes; **sales area** *(in store)* surface *f* de vente; *(district)* région *f* desservie; *Br* **sales assistant** vendeur(euse) *m,f*; **sales audit** audit *m* de vente; **sales campaign** campagne *f* de vente; *Am* **sales clerk** vendeur(euse) *m,f*; **sales commission** commission *f* de vente; **sales contract** contrat *m* de vente; **sales department** service *m* commercial; **sales drive** campagne *f* de vente; **sales figures** chiffre *m* de vente; **sales floor** surface *f* de vente; **sales force** force *f* de vente; **sales forecast** prévision *f* des ventes; **sales invoice** facture *f* de vente; ACCT **sales ledger** grand-livre *m* des ventes, journal *m* des ventes; **sales literature** brochures *fpl* publicitaires; **sales manager** directeur(trice) *m,f* commercial(e); **sales meeting** réunion *f* de représentants; **sales network** réseau *m* de vente; **sales objective** objectif *m* de vente; **sales outlet** point *m* de vente; **sales pitch** arguments *mpl* de vente; **sales policy** politique *f* de vente; **sales potential** potentiel *m* de vente; **sale price** prix *m* de vente; **sales projection** prévision *f* des ventes; **sales promotion** promotion *f* des ventes; **sales quota** quota *m* de ventes; **sales representative** représentant(e) *m,f*; **sales room** *(for auction)* salle *f* des ventes; *Am* **sales slip** ticket *m* de caisse; **sales target** objectif *m* de vente; **sales tax** taxe *f* sur le chiffre d'affaires; **sales team** équipe *f* de vente; **sales technique** technique *f* de vente; **sales territory** territoire *m* de vente; **sales tool** instrument *m* de vente; **sales volume** volume *m* des ventes; MKTG **sales wave** vague *f* de vente

(**b**) *(at reduced prices)* soldes *mpl*; *Br* **in the sale,** *Am* **on sale** *(article)* en solde; **the sales** les soldes; **I got it in a sale** je l'ai acheté en solde □ **sale price** prix *m* soldé

"

Thus it has been shown that with professional pre-planning and management, exhibitions can be a powerful **sales tool** and not the expensive luxury that many companies regard them to be.

"

saleable *adj* vendable

saleroom *n (for auction)* salle *f* des ventes

salesman *n (for company)* représentant *m*; *(in shop)* vendeur *m*

salesmanship *n* technique *f* de vente

salesperson *n (for company)* représentant(e) *m,f*; *(in shop)* vendeur(euse) *m,f*

saleswoman *n (for company)* représentante *f*; *(in shop)* vendeuse *f*

salvage 1 *n (recovery) (of cargo, waste material)* récupération *f*; *(things recovered)* objets *mpl* récupérés □ *salvage company* entreprise *f* de récupération; *salvage money* prime *f* de sauvetage; *salvage value* récupérabilité *f*
2 *vt (cargo, waste material)* récupérer

same-day delivery *n* livraison *f* le jour même

sample 1 *n* échantillon *m*; **up to sample** pareil *ou* conforme à l'échantillon; **to send sth as a sample** envoyer qch à titre d'échantillon; **to buy sth from sample** acheter qch d'après échantillon □ *sample book* catalogue *m* d'échantillons; *sample card* carte *f* d'échantillons; MKTG *sample survey* enquête *f* par sondage
2 *vt* (**a**) *(food)* goûter (**b**) MKTG *(public opinion)* sonder

sampling *n* MKTG échantillonnage *m* □ *sampling error* erreur *f* d'échantillonnage; *sampling method* méthode *f* de sondage

Samurai bond *n* ST EXCH obligation *f* Samouraï

sanction *n* (**a**) *(penalty)* sanction *f*; **to impose (economic) sanctions on a country** prendre des sanctions (économiques) à l'encontre d'un pays (**b**) *(approval)* sanction *f*; **it hasn't yet been given official sanction** ceci n'a pas encore été officiellement approuvé

sandbag *n (in takeover bid)* = tactique de temporisation utilisée par une entreprise faisant l'objet d'une OPA

sandwich course *n Br* = stage de formation professionnelle en alternance

SASE *n Am (abbr* **self-addressed stamped envelope**) enveloppe *f* timbrée libellée à ses noms et adresse

satisfaction *n* (**a**) *(of demand, conditions)* satisfaction *f*;. *(of contract)* exécution *f*, réalisation *f*; **the satisfaction of the union's demands** la satisfaction des revendications syndicales (**b**) *(of debt)* paiement *m*, liquidation *f*

satisfy *vt* (**a**) *(demand, conditions)* satisfaire à; *(contract)* remplir (**b**) *(debt)* payer, liquider

saturate *vt (market)* saturer

saturated *adj (market)* saturé(e)

saturation *n (of market)* saturation *f* □ *saturation advertising* publicité *f* intensive; *saturation campaign* campagne *f* intensive *ou* de saturation; *saturation point* point *m* de saturation; **the market has reached saturation point** le marché est saturé

"

With the main market for computer games (pre-adolescent boys) reaching **saturation point**, the big companies are casting around for ways to keep those sales figures healthy. The latest big idea is to turn girls into committed gameheads.

"

save 1 *vt* (**a**) *(money) (keep for future)* mettre de côté; *(not waste)* économiser; **I save £100 a month in a special account** j'économise 100 livres par mois sur un compte spécial; **how much money have you got saved?** combien d'argent avez-vous mis de côté?; **buying in bulk saves 10%** l'achat en gros fait économiser 10%
(**b**) COMPTR sauvegarder; **to save sth to disk** sauvegarder qch sur disquette
2 *vi* économiser, faire des économies; **to save on sth** économiser sur qch; **you save if you buy in bulk** on fait des économies en achetant en gros

save-as-you-earn *adj Br* FIN = plan d'épargne à contributions mensuelles produisant des intérêts exonérés d'impôts

saver *n* épargnant(e) *m,f*

saving *n* (**a**) *(thrift, economy)* économie *f*, épargne *f*; **measures to encourage saving** des mesures pour encourager l'épargne
(**b**) *(money saved)* économie *f*; **we made a saving of £500 on the usual price** nous avons fait une économie de 500 livres sur le prix habituel; **savings** économies *fpl*; ECON dépôts *mpl* d'épargne □ *savings account* compte *m* d'épargne; *savings bank* caisse *f*

d'épargne; *savings certificate* ≃ bon *m* d'épargne; *Am savings and loan association* ≃ caisse *f* d'épargne-logement; FIN *savings scheme* plan *m* d'épargne

SAYE *n Br* FIN (*abbr* **save-as-you-earn**) = plan d'épargne à contributions mensuelles produisant des intérêts exonérés d'impôts

SBU *n* (*abbr* **strategic business unit**) DAS *m*

scale *n* (*of salaries, taxes, prices*) échelle *f*

▶ **scale down** *vt sep* (*reduce*) réduire, baisser; **production is being scaled down** on a entrepris de réduire la production

▶ **scale up** *vt sep* (*increase*) augmenter; **allowances were scaled up by 10%** les allocations ont été augmentées de 10%

scalper *n* ST EXCH spéculateur(trice) *m,f* à la journée

scan COMPTR **1** *n* lecture *f* au scanne(u)r
2 *vt* passer au scanne(u)r, scanner

▶ **scan in** *vt sep* COMPTR (*graphics*) insérer par scanne(u)r, capturer au scanne(u)r

scanner *n* COMPTR scanner *m*, scanneur *m*

scanning *n* MKTG veille *f* technologique

scarce *adj* (*commodities*) rare, peu abondant(e); **sugar is scarce at the moment** il y a une pénurie de sucre en ce moment □ *scarce currency* devise *f* forte

scarceness, scarcity *n* manque *m*, pénurie *f*; **there is a scarcity of labour** il y a une pénurie de main-d'œuvre □ *scarcity value* valeur *f* de rareté

schedule **1** *n* (**a**) (*plan*) programme *m*, planning *m*; **a schedule was agreed for the work** on a convenu d'un planning pour le travail; **the work was carried out according to schedule** le travail a été effectué selon les prévisions; **to be on schedule** être dans les temps; **to be behind schedule** être en retard sur le programme; **to be ahead of schedule** être en avance sur le programme; **to go according to schedule** se dérouler comme prévu; **to work to a tight schedule** avoir un emploi du temps chargé
(**b**) (*list*) (*of items*) nomenclature *f*; (*of machines*) inventaire *m*; (*of prices*) barème *m*; ADMIN (*of taxes*) cédule *f*; **schedule of charges** tarif *m*
(**c**) LAW (*clause*) annexe *f*
2 *vt* (**a**) (*plan*) prévoir; **the meeting was scheduled for 3 o'clock/Wednesday** la réunion était prévue pour 15 heures/mercredi; **we're scheduled to arrive at 9pm** notre arrivée est prévue à 21 heures
(**b**) LAW (*clause*) ajouter comme annexe

scheduler *n* COMPTR (*package*) logiciel *m* de planification (de projets)

scheme *n* (**a**) (*system*) système *m*; **the company has a profit-sharing/a pension scheme** l'entreprise a un système de participation aux bénéfices/un régime de retraites complémentaires (**b**) (*plan*) plan *m*, projet *m*; **a scheme for new investment** un plan *ou* projet pour de nouveaux investissements □ LAW *scheme of arrangement* concordat *m* préventif (à la faillite)

> **"**
> … the court makes a preliminary order, called a "receiving order", which protects the debtor's property and prevents creditors from suing him without the leave of the court. The debtor may then (with the court's approval) make a composition or **scheme of arrangement** with his creditors …
> **"**

schilling *n* schilling *m*

scorched earth policy *n* (*against hostile takeover situation*) politique *f* de la terre brûlée

scrambled merchandising *n* MKTG = diversification des services proposés

scrap **1** *n* déchets *mpl*; **to sell sth for scrap** vendre qch à la casse □ *scrap dealer, scrap merchant* ferrailleur *m*; *scrap metal* ferraille *f*; *scrap value* valeur *f* à la casse
2 *vt* (**a**) (*send to scrap*) mettre à la ferraille *ou* à la casse (**b**) (*abandon*) (*idea, plans*) renoncer à, abandonner; (*system*) abandonner, mettre au rencart; (*machinery*) mettre au rebut *ou* au rencart

scratchpad *n Am* COMPTR bloc-notes *m* □ *scratchpad memory* mémoire *f* bloc-notes

screen **1** *n* COMPTR écran *m*; **on screen** sur (l')écran; **to bring up the next screen** amener l'écran suivant □ *screen display* affichage *m*; *screen dump* impression *f* écran; *screen refresh* actualisation *f* *ou* régénération *f* de l'écran; *screen saver* économiseur *m* d'écran; ST EXCH *screen trader* opérateur(trice) *m,f* sur écran; ST EXCH *screen trading* opérations *fpl* sur écran
2 *vt* (*candidates, applications*) passer au crible; **we screen all our security staff** nous faisons une enquête préalable sur tous les candidats aux postes d'agent de sécurité

screening *n* (*of candidates, applications*) sélection *f*

scrip n FIN, ST EXCH titre m ❑ **scrip certificate** certificat m d'actions provisoire; *Am* **scrip dividend** certificat de dividende provisoire; **scrip issue** attribution f d'actions gratuites

scripholder n FIN, ST EXCH détenteur(trice) m,f de titres

scroll COMPTR 1 n défilement m ❑ **scroll bar** barre f de défilement
  2 vt faire défiler
  3 vi défiler

▸ **scroll down** COMPTR 1 vt insep **to scroll down a page** passer à la page suivante
  2 vi *(of person)* faire défiler de haut en bas; *(of text)* défiler de haut en bas

▸ **scroll through** vt insep COMPTR *(text)* parcourir

▸ **scroll up** COMPTR 1 vt insep **to scroll up a page** passer à la page précédente
  2 vi *(of person)* faire défiler de bas en haut; *(of text)* défiler de bas en haut

SCSI n COMPTR *(abbr* **small computer systems interface**) SCSI f ❑ **SCSI card** carte f SCSI

SDR n *(abbr* **special drawing right**) DTS m

seal 1 n *(on deed)* sceau m; *(on letter)* cachet m; *(on goods for export)* plomb m
  2 vt *(deed)* sceller; *(envelope)* cacheter; *(goods for export)* (faire) plomber ❑ **sealed bid, sealed tender** soumission f cachetée

sealed-bid pricing n fixation f d'un prix de soumission

seaport n port m maritime

SEAQ n *(abbr* **Stock Exchange Automated Quotations System**) système m de cotation automatisé

> 66 ———
> Take the London Stock Exchange. It was dragged kicking and screaming into Big Bang in 1986, but since then it has seemed pretty effective, in the main. … It gave up its trading floor before most other exchanges; its computerised **SEAQ** trading system has been highly successful at pulling business in European blue-chip shares from continental bourses.
> ——— 99

search COMPTR 1 n recherche f; **to do a search** faire une recherche; **to do a search for sth** rechercher qch; **search and replace** recherche et remplacement m ❑ **search engine** moteur m de recherche
  2 vt *(file, directory)* rechercher dans; **to**

search and replace sth rechercher et remplacer qch
  3 vi faire une recherche

season n **(a)** *(for trade)* saison f; **it's a busy season for tour operators** c'est une époque très chargée pour les voyagistes; **in season** en saison; **out of season** hors saison; **the low/high season** la basse/haute saison **(b)** **season ticket** *(for public transport)* carte f d'abonnement

seasonal adj *(demand, fluctuations)* saisonnier(ère) ❑ **seasonal adjustment** rectification f saisonnière

seasonally adv **seasonally adjusted** *(figures)* rectifié(e) ou corrigé(e) des variations saisonnières

SEC n *(abbr* **Securities and Exchange Commission**) = commission américaine des opérations de Bourse, ≃ COB f

second¹ 1 n **seconds** articles mpl défectueux
  2 adj second(e), deuxième ❑ **second debenture** obligation f de deuxième rang; **second mortgage** deuxième hypothèque f; **second quarter** *(of year)* deuxième trimestre m

second² vt *(motion)* appuyer; *(speaker)* appuyer la motion de

second³ vt *(employee)* détacher, envoyer en détachement; **she's been seconded to head office** elle a été détachée au siège social

secondary adj secondaire ❑ **secondary industry** industrie f secondaire; ST EXCH **secondary market** marché m secondaire; *Br* **secondary picketing** piquets mpl de grève de solidarité; **secondary product** sous-produit m; **secondary production** production f manufacturée

second-hand 1 adj *(goods)* d'occasion ❑ **second-hand dealer** brocanteur(euse) m,f; **second-hand market** marché m de revente; **second-hand shop** magasin m d'occasions
  2 adv *(buy)* d'occasion

secondment n détachement m; **to be on secondment** être en détachement

second-rate adj *(goods)* de qualité inférieure

secretarial adj *(tasks)* de secrétaire, de secrétariat; **to have a secretarial job** avoir un travail de secrétaire ❑ **secretarial course** cours m de secrétariat; **secretarial school** école f de secrétariat; **secretarial skills** notions fpl de secrétariat; **secretarial work** travail m de secrétaire

secretary n secrétaire mf

section n (**a**) *(sector)* section f; **the business section of the community** les commerçants et les hommes d'affaires de notre communauté (**b**) *(of document)* section f; *(of law)* article m

sector n (**a**) ECON secteur m; **the banking sector** le secteur bancaire; **whole sectors of society live below the poverty line** des catégories sociales entières vivent en dessous du seuil de pauvreté (**b**) COMPTR *(of screen)* secteur m

secure **1** adj *(investment, job)* sûr(e)
2 vt (**a**) *(obtain)* *(agreement, loan)* obtenir (**b**) *(guarantee)* *(debt, loan)* garantir

secured adj FIN **secured bond** obligation f cautionnée; **secured creditor** créancier(ère) m,f privilégié(e); **secured debenture** obligation f cautionnée; **secured debt** créance f garantie; **secured loan** prêt m garanti

securitization n ST EXCH titrisation f

securitize vt ST EXCH titriser

security n (**a**) *(financial guarantee)* garantie f; *(for payment of debt)* caution f, cautionnement m; *(collateral)* nantissement m; *(person)* garant(e) m,f; **to give sth as security** donner qch en cautionnement; **to stand security for sb** se porter garant ou caution pour qn; **to lend money on security** prêter de l'argent sur nantissement ou sur garantie; **to lend money without security** prêter de l'argent à découvert; **what security do you have for the loan?** quelle garantie avez-vous pour couvrir ce prêt? ❑ **security of tenure** *(of property)* bail m assuré; *(of job)* sécurité f de l'emploi
(**b**) ST EXCH **securities** titres mpl, valeurs fpl ❑ **securities department** service m des titres; **Securities and Exchange Commission** = commission américaine des opérations de Bourse, ≃ COB f; **securities house** société f de Bourse; **Securities and Investment Board** = commission britannique des opérations de Bourse, ≃ COB f; **securities market** marché m des titres ou des valeurs
(**c**) COMPTR sécurité f ❑ **security level** niveau m de sécurité

> **"**
> To help the New York Stock Exchange's slipping share of global trading in equities, the **Securities and Exchange Commission** is to allow after-hours trading for a two-year trial period from June 13th.
> **"**

seed capital n FIN capital m initial

seek time n COMPTR temps m d'accès

seesaw effect n FIN effet m balançoire

segment vt MKTG *(market)* segmenter

segmentation n MKTG segmentation f

seize vt LAW *(goods)* saisir, opérer la saisie de

select vt (**a**) *(candidate)* sélectionner, choisir (**b**) COMPTR sélectionner; **select 'enter'** tapez 'entrée'; **to select an option** activer une option (**c**) MKTG sélectionner

selection n (**a**) *(of candidate)* sélection f ❑ **selection committee** comité m de sélection (**b**) COMPTR sélection f ❑ **selection box** rectangle m de sélection (**c**) MKTG sélection f ❑ **selection error** erreur f d'echantillonnage *(dans le cadre d'une étude de marché)*; **selection method** méthode f de sélection

selective adj sélectif(ive) ❑ **selective marketing** marketing m sélectif, mercatique f sélective; **selective selling** distribution f sélective

self-assessment n Br *(for tax purposes)* auto-évaluation f

self-employed **1** npl **the self-employed** les travailleurs mpl indépendants
2 adj indépendant(e), qui travaille à son (propre) compte

self-financing **1** n autofinancement m
2 adj autofinancé(e)

self-liquidating adj auto-amortissable

> **"**
> However, for a banker such loans are not directly **self-liquidating**, as little or no foreign exchange is directly generated from such projects to service external debt. Instead, the bank assumes that such schemes will boost overall economic growth and exports, thereby providing the necessary foreign currency receipts.
> **"**

self-mailer n MKTG carte f de publicité directe *(qui est mise à la poste sans enveloppe)*

self-management n autogestion f

self-regulatory organization n Br ST EXCH organisme m auto-réglementé ou autonome

self-sufficiency n *(of nation, resources)* autosuffisance f; ECON autarcie f

self-sufficient adj autosuffisant(e); ECON autarcique; **self-sufficient in oil** autosuffisant en pétrole

self-tender n FIN = proposition de rachat présentée par une entreprise à ses actionnaires

self-test n COMPTR autotest m

sell 1 n ST EXCH **sell order** injonction f à la vente; **sell price** prix m (du) comptant

2 vt vendre; ST EXCH (shares) vendre, réaliser; **to sell sth to sb, to sell sb sth** vendre qch à qn; **to sell sth for cash** vendre qch (au) comptant; **to sell sth at a loss** vendre qch à perte; **he sells computers for a living** il gagne sa vie en vendant des ordinateurs

3 vi (of product) se vendre; (of person) vendre; ST EXCH **to sell short** vendre à découvert; **to sell at best** vendre au mieux

▸ **sell forward** vt sep ST EXCH vendre à terme

▸ **sell off** vt sep (**a**) (goods) (at reduced price) solder; (to clear) liquider; **the house was sold off to pay debts** la maison a été vendue pour régler des créances (**b**) (shares) vendre

▸ **sell out 1** vt sep (**a**) ST EXCH vendre, réaliser (**b**) **to be sold out** (of book, item) être épuisé(e)

2 vi (**a**) (sell business) vendre son commerce; (sell stock) liquider (son stock); **he sold out to some Japanese investors** il a vendu à des investisseurs japonais (**b**) (run out) vendre tout le stock; **to sell out of sth** ne plus avoir de qch

▸ **sell up 1** vt sep (business) vendre, liquider; (goods) procéder à la liquidation de

2 vi (sell business) vendre son commerce

sell-by date n date f limite de vente

seller n (**a**) (person) vendeur(euse) m,f □ **seller's market** marché m à la hausse; ST EXCH **seller's option** prime f vendeur (**b**) (article) **to be a good/bad seller** se vendre bien/mal; **it's one of our biggest sellers** c'est un de nos articles qui se vend le mieux

selling n (of goods) vente f; ST EXCH (of shares) vente, réalisation f □ **selling cost** frais mpl commerciaux; **selling point** avantage m, atout m; **selling power** puissance f de vente; **selling price** prix m de vente

> Certain industries will demand regulation if it helps to improve the position of the firms within them. Thus farmers may perceive benefits in bodies such as the Milk Marketing Board through gains in **selling power**, although other aspects of the Board's operations may be undesirable to them.

sell-off n (**a**) (of goods) (at reduced price) solde m; (to clear) liquidation f (**b**) (of shares) vente f

semi-automated adj semi-automatisé(e)

semi-finished adj (goods) semi-fini(e)

semi-skilled adj spécialisé(e)

semi-variable adj (costs) semi-variable

send vt (person) envoyer; (letter, parcel, money) envoyer, expédier; **to send sb sth, to send sth to sb** envoyer qch à qn

▸ **send away** vi **to send away for sth** se faire envoyer qch; (by mail order) commander qch par correspondance

▸ **send back** vt sep (goods) renvoyer

▸ **send for** vt insep **to send for sth** se faire envoyer qch; (by mail order) commander qch par correspondance

▸ **send in** vt sep envoyer; **please send in a written application** veuillez envoyer une demande écrite; (for job) veuillez poser votre candidature par écrit

▸ **send off 1** vt sep (letter, parcel, money) envoyer, expédier

2 vi **to send off for sth** se faire envoyer qch; (by mail order) commander qch par correspondance

▸ **send on** vt sep (mail) faire suivre

▸ **send out** vt sep envoyer, expédier

sender n expéditeur(trice) m,f

senior 1 n (in rank) supérieur(e) m,f

2 adj (in rank) supérieur(e); **to be senior to sb** être le supérieur de qn □ **senior executive** cadre m supérieur; **senior partner** associé(e) m,f principal(e)

seniority n (in age) priorité f d'âge; (in length of service) ancienneté f; (in rank) supériorité f

sensitive adj FIN (market) sensible

separator n COMPTR séparateur m

sequential adj COMPTR séquentiel(elle) □ **sequential access** accès m séquentiel; **sequential processing** traitement m séquentiel

sequester, sequestrate vt LAW (goods) séquestrer, mettre sous séquestre

sequestration n LAW mise f sous séquestre □ **sequestration order** ordonnance f de mise sous séquestre

serial adj (**a**) COMPTR série □ **serial cable** câble m série; **serial interface** interface f série; **serial port** port m série; **serial printer** imprimante f série (**b**) **serial number** (of product) numéro m de série

Serious Fraud Office n Br ≃ Service m de la répression des fraudes

SERPS *n Br* FIN *(abbr* **State Earnings-Related Pension Scheme**) = retraite versée par l'État, calculée sur le salaire

> ❝
>
> At the other end of the age range employees who have not taken advantage of the incentives to contract out of the State Earnings-Related Pension Scheme (**SERPS**) should do so before they dwindle away altogether.
>
> ❞

serve *vt (customer)* servir

server *n* COMPTR serveur *m* ❑ ***server administrator*** administrateur *m* de serveur

service *n* (**a**) *(employment)* service *m*; **ten years' service** dix années de service; **promotion according to length of service** avancement *m* à l'ancienneté; **bonuses depend on length of service** les primes sont versées en fonction de l'ancienneté ❑ ***service agreement, service contract*** contrat *m* de service
(**b**) *(in shop, restaurant)* service *m*; **service included** service compris ❑ ***service charge*** service
(**c**) *(facility provided)* ***service charge*** frais *mpl* administratifs; *(paid by tenants)* prestations *fpl* locatives; ***service provider*** *(for Internet)* fournisseur *m* d'accès
(**d**) *(working order)* service *m*; **to bring sth into service** *(machine, vehicle)* mettre qch en service; **the cash dispenser isn't in service at the moment** le distributeur est hors service *ou* n'est pas en service en ce moment ❑ ***service life*** durée *f* de vie
(**e**) ECON **services** services *mpl*; **goods and services** biens *mpl* et services ❑ ***service bureau*** société *f* de services; COMPTR société *f* de traitement à façon; ***service fee*** prestation *f* de service; ***service industry*** secteur *m* tertiaire
(**f**) *Am* ***service center*** ville *f* commerciale *(qui dessert toute une région)*
2 *vt* (**a**) *(machine)* entretenir
(**b**) FIN *(loan, debt)* assurer le service de

session *n (period of activity, meeting)* séance *f*; **to hold a session** se réunir

SET® *n* COMPTR *(abbr* **secure electronic transaction**) SET *f*

> ❝
>
> Each bank or financial institution has a unique key; a trusted third party holds and issues keys that merchants and acquirers need to decrypt each other's **SET**® messages.
>
> ❞

set 1 *n* (**a**) COMPTR *(of characters, instructions)* jeu *m*, ensemble *m* (**b**) FIN *(of bills of exchange)* jeu *m*
2 *adj (price)* fixe
3 *vt (fix) (date, limit, price, schedule)* fixer, déterminer; *(rule, guideline, objective)* établir; COMPTR *(tabs, format)* poser; **to set a value on sth** évaluer qch, estimer la valeur de qch; **it's up to them to set their own production targets** c'est à eux d'établir leurs propres objectifs de production; **a deficit ceiling has been set** un plafonnement du déficit a été imposé *ou* fixé; **the price was set at $500** le prix a été fixé à 500 dollars; **how are exchange rates fixed?** comment les taux de change sont-ils déterminés?

▸ **set against** *vt sep (deduct, offset)* déduire; **to set losses against tax** déduire les pertes des impôts

▸ **set aside** *vt sep (money)* mettre de côté; *(time, place)* réserver; **this room is set aside for meetings** cette pièce est réservée aux réunions

▸ **set off** *vt sep (deduct, offset)* déduire; **some of these expenses can be set off against tax** certaines de ces dépenses peuvent être déduites des impôts

▸ **set up 1** *vt sep* (**a**) *(company)* créer, fonder; *(system, programme)* mettre en place; *(committee)* constituer; **you'll be in charge of setting up training programmes** vous serez responsable de la mise en place des programmes de formation
(**b**) *(financially, in business)* installer, établir; **he set his son up in a dry-cleaning business** il a acheté à son fils une entreprise de nettoyage à sec; **she can finally set herself up as an accountant** elle peut enfin s'installer comme comptable
2 *vi (in business)* s'installer, s'établir; **he's setting up in the fast-food business** il se lance dans la restauration rapide; **to set up on one's own** s'installer à son compte

set-aside *n* EU gel *m* des terres

setback *n* FIN, ST EXCH tassement *m*, repli *m*

settle 1 *vt* (**a**) *(day, date, place)* fixer, déterminer; *(terms)* convenir
(**b**) *(question, problem, dispute)* régler; LAW **to settle a matter out of court** régler une affaire à l'amiable
(**c**) *(account)* régler; *(bill)* acquitter, régler; *(debt, fine)* payer
(**d**) *(money, allowance, estate)* constituer; **to settle an annuity on sb** constituer une rente à qn
2 *vi* LAW **to settle out of court** régler l'affaire à l'amiable

▶ **settle up** *vi (pay bill)* régler; **I must settle up with the plumber** il faut que je règle le plombier

settlement *n* (**a**) *(of question, problem, dispute)* règlement *m*

(**b**) *(of account)* règlement *m*; *(of bill)* acquittement *m*, règlement; *(of debt, fine)* paiement *m*; **I enclose a cheque in settlement of your account** veuillez trouver ci-joint un chèque en règlement de votre compte ❑ FIN *settlement discount* remise *f* pour règlement rapide; *settlement period* délai *m* de règlement, terme *m* de liquidation; *settlement value* valeur *f* transactionnelle

(**c**) ST EXCH liquidation *f* ❑ *settlement day* jour *m* de (la) liquidation; *settlement price* cours *m* de liquidation

(**d**) *(agreement)* accord *m*; **to reach a settlement** parvenir à un accord

setup charge *n* COMPTR frais *mpl* d'inscription

sever *vt (contract)* résilier

several liability *n* LAW responsabilité *f* individuelle

severally *adv* LAW **severally liable** responsable individuellement

severance pay *n* indemnité *f* de licenciement

sexual *adj* *sexual discrimination* discrimination *f* sexuelle; *sexual harrassment* harcèlement *m* sexuel

SFO *n Br (abbr* **Serious Fraud Office**) ≃ Service *m* de la répression des fraudes

shade **1** *n* COMPTR **shades of grey** niveaux *mpl* ou tons *mpl* de gris

2 *vt Am* **to shade prices** établir des prix dégressifs; **prices shaded for quantities** tarif dégressif pour le gros

shadow printing *n* COMPTR impression *f* ombrée

shake-up *n Fam (of company, organization)* remaniement *m*, restructuration *f*

sham *adj (dividend)* fictif(ive)

share **1** *n* (**a**) FIN, ST EXCH action *f*, titre *m*; **to allot shares** attribuer des actions; **to issue shares** émettre des actions; **to transfer shares** transférer des actions; **to hold** *or* **have shares (in)** détenir des actions (dans); **to own 51% of the shares** détenir 51% du capital ❑ *share account* compte-titres *m*; *share capital* capital *m* social; *share certificate* titre *m* d'action(s), certificat *m* d'actions; *share dealing* opérations *fpl* de Bourse; *share index* indice *m* boursier; *share issue* émission *f* d'actions; *share*

ledger registre *m* des actionnaires; *share market* marché *m* des valeurs mobilières; *share option* option *f* d'achat des actions; *share premium* prime *f* d'émission; *share prices* cours *m* des actions; *share price index* indice *m* des cours d'actions; *share register* registre *m* des actions; *share splitting* division *f ou* fractionnement *m* des actions

(**b**) *(portion)* **to give sb a share of the profits** donner à qn une part des bénéfices; **to have a share in a business** avoir des intérêts dans une affaire ❑ MKTG *share point* point *m* de part de marché

2 *vt* partager; **to share an office with sb** partager un bureau avec qn; **responsibility is shared between the manager and his assistant** la responsabilité est partagée entre le directeur et son assistant

3 *vi* **to share in the profits** avoir part aux bénéfices

shareholder *n* FIN, ST EXCH actionnaire *mf* ❑ *shareholders' equity* fonds *mpl* propres, avoir *m* des actionnaires; *shareholders' meeting* réunion *f* d'actionnaires; *shareholders' register* registre *m* des actionnaires

> **ʼʼ**
>
> For small firms the cost of raising capital through public stock issues is prohibitively expensive, but in Japan this is not the main problem as firms are significantly less reliant on equity finance. Although firms are more dependent on external fundraising, the proportion of **shareholders' equity** in total assets is lower than in other advanced capitalist economies.
>
> **ʼʼ**

shareholding *n* FIN, ST EXCH actionnariat *m*; **he has a major shareholding in the company** il est un des principaux actionnaires de la société

share-out *n* partage *m*, répartition *f*

shareware *n* COMPTR shareware *m*, partagiciel *m*

shark *n Fam (in business)* raider *m*, requin *m* ❑ *shark watcher* détecteur *m* de requin

sharp *adj (rise, fall, change)* brusque, soudain(e)

sheet *n (of paper)* feuille *f*

sheetfeed *n* COMPTR avancement *m* du papier

shelf *n (in shop)* rayon *m*, étagère *f* ❑ *shelf life (of product)* durée *f* de vie; *shelf space* linéaire *m*

shift 1 n (a) *(period worked)* poste m, équipe f; *(workers)* équipe f; **to work shifts, to be on shifts** avoir un travail posté; **what shift are you on this week?** à quel poste avez-vous été affecté cette semaine?; **to be on eight-hour shifts** faire les trois-huit; **I'm on the night/morning shift** je suis dans l'équipe de nuit/du matin; **she works long shifts** elle fait de longues journées ❑ **shift work** travail m posté *ou* en équipe

(b) *(change)* changement m ❑ COMPTR **shift key** touche f des majuscules

2 vt Fam *(sell)* écouler; **how can we shift this old stock?** comment écouler ces vieilles marchandises?

3 vi Fam *(sell)* se vendre; **those TVs just aren't shifting at all** ces télés ne se vendent pas du tout

ship 1 n navire m ❑ **ship's certificate of registry** certificat m d'immatriculation d'un navire; **ship's papers** papiers mpl de bord

2 vt (a) *(send by ship)* expédier (par mer); *(carry by ship)* transporter (par mer); **we're having our luggage shipped** nous expédions nos bagages par mer

(b) *(send by any means)* expédier; *(carry by any means)* transporter; **the goods will be shipped by train** *(sent)* les marchandises seront expédiées par le train; *(transported)* les marchandises seront transportées par chemin de fer

(c) *(embark)* *(passengers, cargo)* embarquer

shipbroker n courtier m maritime

shipbrokerage n courtage m maritime

shipment n (a) *(sending of goods)* expédition f (b) *(cargo, goods shipped)* chargement m, cargaison f

shipped adj embarqué(e) ❑ **shipped bill** connaissement m embarqué; **shipped weight** poids m embarqué

shipping n *(by sea)* transport m maritime; *(by any means)* transport ❑ **shipping agency** agence f maritime; **shipping agent** agent m maritime; **shipping bill** connaissement m embarqué; **shipping charges** frais mpl de transport; **shipping company** entreprise f de transport routier; **shipping office** agence f maritime

▶ **shoot up** vi *(of prices, inflation, demand)* monter en flèche

shop 1 n (a) *(for goods)* magasin m; **to keep a shop** tenir un magasin; **to talk shop** parler boutique; **to set up shop** *(open a shop)* ouvrir un magasin; *(start a business)* s'établir, s'installer ❑ **shop assistant** vendeur(euse) m,f; **shop front** devanture f *(de magasin)*; **shop window** vitrine f

(b) *(workshop)* atelier m ❑ **the shop floor** *(place)* l'atelier; *(workers)* les ouvriers mpl; **shop foreman** chef m d'atelier; **shop steward** délégué(e) m,f syndical(e)

2 vi faire ses courses; **to shop around** comparer les prix; **I shopped around before opening a bank account** j'ai comparé plusieurs banques avant d'ouvrir un compte; **our company is shopping around for new premises** notre société est à la recherche de nouveaux locaux

shopping n courses fpl; **to do one's/the shopping** faire ses/les courses ❑ ECON **shopping basket** panier m de la ménagère; **shopping centre** centre m commercial, **shopping mall** galerie f marchande

> ❝ ──────────────
> The effects of inflation are not limited to the **shopping basket**, says Raoul Pinnell, Prudential's marketing director. Those special events are treats that we save up for, look forward to and are also subject to the ravages of inflation.
> ────────────── ❞

short 1 n ST EXCH **shorts** titres mpl courts

2 adj (a) *(lacking, insufficient)* insuffisant(e); **to be short of staff/money** manquer de personnel/d'argent; **to give short weight** ne pas donner le poids; **the weight is 50 grams short** il manque 50 grammes au poids ❑ **short delivery** livraison f partielle

(b) FIN **short bill** traite f à courte échéance; **short payment** moins-perçu m; **short rate** taux m à court terme

(c) ST EXCH **short covering** couverture f de position; **short position** position f vendeur; **short selling** vente f à découvert

3 adv ST EXCH **to sell short** vendre à découvert; **to buy short** acheter à court terme

shortage n *(of labour, resources, materials, staff)* manque m, pénurie f; *(of money)* manque

shortcut key n COMPTR touche f de raccourci

short-dated adj FIN *(bill)* à courte échéance; *(paper)* court(e)

shortfall n insuffisance f, manque m; **there's a shortfall of $100** il manque 100 dollars

shorthand n sténographie f, sténo f; **to take notes in shorthand** prendre des notes en sténo ❑ **shorthand typist** sténodactylo mf

shorthanded *adj* à court de personnel; **we're very shorthanded at the moment** nous sommes vraiment à court de personnel en ce moment

shortlist *Br* **1** *n* liste *f* des candidats présélectionnés *ou* retenus

2 *vt (candidate)* présélectionner, retenir; **to be shortlisted for sth** être parmi les candidats retenus à qch

short-staffed *adj* à court de personnel; **we're very short-staffed at the moment** nous sommes vraiment à court de personnel en ce moment

short-term *adj* à court terme ❑ *short-term borrowings* emprunts *mpl* à court terme; *short-term contract* contrat *m* à courte durée; *short-term loan* emprunt *m* à court terme

> ❝ ─────────────
>
> The move came after the company had failed to find major investors to provide an emergency loan to repay more than $100,000,000 due on **short-term borrowings**. Neither the Securities and Exchange Commission nor the Federal Reserve Bank of New York were prepared to assist, and on Feb. 17 the company ... made 5,000 employees redundant.
>
> ───────────── ❞

short-time working *n* chômage *m* partiel

show **1** *n (exhibition)* exposition *f* ❑ *show house* maison *f* témoin

2 *vt (profit, loss)* afficher; **prices show a 10% increase on last year** les prix ont augmenté de 10% par rapport à l'an dernier

showcard *n (in shop)* pancarte *f*; *(of samples)* carte *f* d'échantillons

showcase *n* vitrine *f*; **a showcase for British exports** une vitrine pour les exportations britanniques

showroom *n* salle *f* *ou* salon *m* d'exposition

shred *vt (documents)* détruire

shredder *n* destructeur *m* de documents

shrink *vi (of profits, savings, income, budget)* diminuer, se réduire; *(of economy)* se contracter

shrinkage *n (through theft)* coulage *m*; *(through damage)* casse *f*

shrink-wrap *vt* emballer sous film plastique

shrink-wrapped *adj* emballé(e) sous film plastique

shut *vi (of shop, business)* fermer

▸ **shut down** **1** *vt sep* **(a)** *(shop, business)* fermer; *(production)* arrêter **(b)** COMPTR *(system)* arrêter

2 *vi* **(a)** *(of shop, business)* fermer **(b)** COMPTR *(of system)* s'arrêter

shutdown *n* **(a)** *(of shop, business)* fermeture *f* **(b)** COMPTR fermeture *f*, arrêt *m* de fin de session

shut-out *n* lock-out *m*

SIB *n (abbr* **Securities and Investment Board)** = commission britannique des opérations de Bourse, ≃ COB *f*

sick *adj* *sick building syndrome* = maladie qu'on retrouve chez des personnes travaillant dans des bâtiments équipés de la climatisation; *sick leave* congé *m* de maladie; **to be on sick leave** être en congé de maladie; *sick pay* indemnité *f* de maladie

sickness benefit *n Br* ADMIN prestations *fpl* de l'assurance maladie, indemnités *fpl* journalières

sideline *n* **(a)** *(product)* ligne *f* de produits secondaires; **they've made recycling a profitable sideline** ils ont fait du recyclage une activité secondaire rentable; **it's only a sideline for us** ce n'est pas notre spécialité **(b)** *(job)* occupation *f* *ou* travail *m* secondaire

sight *n* **(a)** FIN *sight bill* effet *m* payable à vue; *sight deposit* dépôt *m* à vue; *sight letter of credit* crédit *m* utilisable à vue; ST EXCH *sight quotation* cotation *f* à vue **(b)** **to sell sth sight unseen** vendre qch sans inspection; **to buy sth sight unseen** acheter qch sans l'avoir vu

> ❝ ─────────────
>
> Five years ago companies that bought their personal computers **sight unseen** through the mail were few and far between. During the 1980s the business PC, like many other IT products, was best bought from a reputable dealer. But PCs are increasingly sold through "direct" channels rather than distributors, with reliable suppliers offering rapid delivery at rock bottom prices.
>
> ───────────── ❞

sighting *n* FIN *(of bill)* présentation *f*

sign **1** *vt (one's name, document, cheque)* signer; *(bill of exchange)* accepter; **to sign a deal** passer un marché; **the deal will be signed and sealed tomorrow** l'affaire sera définitivement conclue demain

2 *vi (write one's name)* signer

▸ **sign for** *vt insep (delivery, parcel)* signer un reçu pour; **to sign for goods received** signer à la réception de marchandises; **the files have to be signed for** il faut signer pour retirer les dossiers

▸ **sign on** *vi Br Fam (register as unemployed)* s'inscrire au chômage; **you have to sign on every two weeks** il faut pointer (au chômage) toutes les deux semaines

▸ **sign out** *vt sep* **to sign sth out** *(file, equipment)* signer un registre pour emprunter qch

signatory *n & adj* signataire *mf*

signature *n* signature *f*; **to put one's signature to sth** apposer sa signature sur qch; **his signature was on the letter** la lettre portait sa signature; **for signature** pour signature

silent partner *n Am* commanditaire *m*; *(who supplies capital)* bailleur(eresse) *m,f* de fonds

silver *n* argent *m* ❑ *silver export point* silver-point *m* de sortie; *silver import point* silver-point d'entrée

SIMM *n* COMPTR *(abbr* **single in-line memory module***)* SIMM *m*

simple *adj* LAW *simple contract* convention *f* verbale, acte *m* sous seing privé; FIN *simple interest* intérêts *mpl* simples; ST EXCH *simple position* position *f* élémentaire

simulation *n* simulation *f*

simultaneous product development *n* MKTG développement *m* simultané de produits

sincerely *adv* **yours sincerely** *(in letter)* veuillez agréer, Monsieur/Madame, l'expression de mes sentiments distingués

single 1 *n Br (ticket)* aller *m* simple
2 *adj* (**a**) *(one only)* EU *single currency* monnaie *f* unique; *Single (European) Market* marché *m* unique (européen); INS *single premium* prime *f* unique; COMPTR *single user licence* licence *f* individuelle d'utilisation
(**b**) *(not double)* **to be in single figures** être inférieur(e) à dix; **inflation is now in single figures** l'inflation est descendue à moins de dix pour cent

> " ────────────
> For a start, long-term interest rates are still falling … Falling oil and commodity prices have helped. So has the squeeze on government borrowing in the run-up to the launch of Europe's **single currency** next year.
> "

single-entry bookkeeping *n* ACCT comptabilité *f* en partie simple

singletasking COMPTR 1 *n* monotâche *m*
2 *adj* monotâche

singly *adv (packaged)* individuellement; **to be sold singly** se vendre à la pièce

sink 1 *vt* (**a**) *(debt, loan)* amortir (**b**) *(invest)* investir; **we sank a fortune into this company** nous avons englouti une fortune dans cette société
2 *vi (of prices, currency, rate, profits)* baisser, diminuer; **the dollar has sunk to half its normal value** le dollar a perdu la moitié de sa valeur; **profits have sunk to an all-time low** les bénéfices sont au plus bas

sinking fund *n* fonds *mpl ou* caisse *f* d'amortissement

sister company *n* société *f* sœur

sit-down strike *n* grève *f* sur le tas

site 1 *n* (**a**) *(piece of land)* terrain *m*; **the development project includes sites for small businesses** le projet immobilier prévoit des terrains pour de petites entreprises (**b**) **(building) site** chantier *m* (de construction) (**c**) COMPTR site *m*
2 *vt* situer

sit-in *n* (grève *f* avec) occupation *f* des lieux

sitting tenant *n* locataire *mf* dans les lieux *ou* en place

situation *n* (**a**) *(state of affairs)* situation *f*; **the firm's financial situation isn't good** la situation financière de la société n'est pas bonne; **the skills needed in an interview situation** les compétences dont on a besoin pour faire face à un entretien (**b**) *(job)* emploi *m*, situation *f*; **situations vacant/wanted** *(in advertisements)* offres *fpl*/demandes *fpl* d'emplois

size *n* COMPTR *(of file)* taille *f* ❑ *size box* case *f* de dimensionnement

skeleton *n* *skeleton organization* organisation *f* squelettique; *skeleton staff* personnel *m* réduit

skill *n* aptitude *f*, compétence *f*; **computer technology requires us to learn new skills** l'informatique nous oblige à acquérir de nouvelles compétences

skilled *adj (worker)* qualifié(e); *(task)* de spécialiste ❑ *skilled labour* main-d'œuvre *f* qualifiée

skim *vt* MKTG *(market)* écrémer

skip *vt* COMPTR *(command)* sauter

slack *adj (business)* calme; **the slack season for tourists** la période creuse pour le tourisme; **business is slack at the moment** les affaires marchent au ralenti en ce moment

slacken vi *(of business)* ralentir

slash vt *(prices)* casser; *(cost, taxes)* réduire considérablement; **prices have been slashed by 40%** les prix ont été réduits de 40%

sleeping partner n Br commanditaire m; *(who supplies capital)* bailleur(eresse) m,f de fonds

sliding scale n *(for prices, tax)* barème m; *(for salaries)* échelle f mobile

sliding-scale tariff n tarif m dégressif

slip 1 n *(printed paper)* bordereau m
  2 vi *(of prices)* glisser; **shares slipped to 125p** le prix des actions a baissé jusqu'à 125 pence

slogan n slogan m (publicitaire)

slot n (a) COMPTR emplacement m (b) *(opening)* créneau m

slow 1 adj *(business, market)* calme; **business is slow** les affaires ne marchent pas fort
  2 adv **to go slow** faire une grève perlée

▸ **slow down** 1 vt sep ralentir; **production is slowed down during the winter** pendant l'hiver, la production tourne au ralenti
  2 vi ralentir; **growth slowed down in the second quarter** il y a eu un ralentissement de la croissance au cours du deuxième trimestre

slowdown n Am grève f perlée

sluggish adj *(market, business, economy)* calme, stagnant(e); **trading is always rather sluggish on Mondays** les affaires ne marchent jamais très fort le lundi

slump 1 n *(in prices, sales, market)* effondrement m; *(economic depression)* crise f (économique); **there has been a slump in investment** les investissements sont en forte baisse; **a slump in prices/demand** une forte baisse des prix/de la demande
  2 vi *(of prices, currency, economy)* s'effondrer

slush fund n caisse f noire

> One of the more controversial aspects of the budget ... was an increase in the so-called "MPs' **slush fund**" (more correctly the National Development Fund) to K100,000 annually for each member. The fund was originally intended to fund small-scale enterprises and services in each constituency but MPs were virtually unaccountable for its distribution and use.

small adj (a) **small ad** petite annonce f; **the small print** *(in contract)* ce qui est écrit en petits caractères; **make sure you read the small print before you sign** lisez bien ce qui est écrit en petits caractères avant de signer (b) **small business** petite entreprise f; **small businessman** petit entrepreneur m

small-claims court n Br LAW tribunal m d'instance

smart adj **smart card** carte f à puce; **smart money** placement m astucieux

SME n *(abbr* **small and medium-sized enterprise**) PME f

SMI n *(abbr* **small and medium-sized industry**) PMI f

smuggle 1 vt passer en contrebande; **to smuggle sth through customs** passer qch en fraude à la douane
  2 vi faire de la contrebande

▸ **smuggle in** vt sep *(goods)* faire entrer en contrebande

▸ **smuggle out** vt sep *(goods)* faire sortir en contrebande

smuggler n contrebandier(ère) m,f

smuggling n contrebande f

snake n ECON serpent m (monétaire)

soar vi *(of prices, profits, inflation)* monter en flèche; **sales have soared since the advertising campaign** les ventes ont monté en flèche depuis la campagne publicitaire

soaring adj *(of prices, profits, inflation)* qui monte en flèche

social adj **social contract** convention f sociale; **social cost** coût m social; **social charges** *(levied on employers)* charges fpl sociales; Br ADMIN **social fund** caisse f d'aide sociale; **social ownership** propriété f collective; **social security** prestations fpl sociales; **to be on social security** toucher une aide sociale

soft 1 n **softs** biens mpl non durables
  2 adj **soft commodities** biens mpl non durables; COMPTR **soft copy** visualisation f sur écran; **soft currency** devise f faible; **soft loan** prêt m bonifié; **soft sell** méthode f de vente non agressive

> For that is the purpose of the muzak, is it not? It is a variant on the **soft sell** device of the supermarkets who have apparently demonstrated that people buy more when they are subjected to muzak. What is new is perhaps the idea that people have to be encouraged or influenced to spend.

software n COMPTR logiciel m, software m □ *software company* éditeur m de logiciels; *software error* erreur f de logiciel; *software house* éditeur m de logiciel; *software package* logiciel; *software problem* problème m de logiciel

sola of exchange n FIN seule f de change

sole adj unique □ *sole agency* représentation f exclusive; *sole agent* agent m exclusif; *sole contract* contrat m exclusif; *sole owner* propriétaire mf unique; *sole right* droit m exclusif; *sole trader* entreprise f unipersonnelle

solicitor n Br (in court cases) avocat(e) m,f; (for wills, property) notaire m

solus adj MKTG (position, site) isolé(e)

solvency n solvabilité f □ *solvency ratio* ratio m ou taux m de solvabilité

solvent adj solvable

sort 1 n (a) COMPTR tri m; **the program will do an alphabetical sort** le programme exécutera un tri alphabétique (b) BANKING *sort code* code m guichet
2 vt COMPTR trier
3 vi COMPTR trier; (of file, data) se trier

sorting code n BANKING code m guichet

sound[1] n COMPTR *sound card* carte f son

sound[2] adj (investment) sûr(e); (business, financial position) solide

source n (a) (of revenue) source f; (of goods) provenance f; **income is taxed at source** les impôts sont prélevés à la source □ ACCT *source and application of funds* état m de flux de trésorerie (b) COMPTR *source disk* disque m source; (floppy) disquette f source; *source document* document m de base, document source; *source file* fichier m source; *source language* langage m source; *source text* texte m de départ

spam vi COMPTR spammer

spamming n COMPTR spamming m

spare 1 n (spare part) pièce f de rechange, pièce détachée
2 adj (funds, capital) disponible □ *spare part* pièce f de rechange, pièce détachée

speak vi (on telephone) **who's speaking?** qui est à l'appareil?; (before transferring call) c'est de la part de qui?; **Mr Thomas? – yes, speaking** Mr Thomas? – lui-même

spec n (abbr **specification**) spécifications fpl

special adj Br *special delivery* (of mail) envoi m en exprès; FIN *special drawing rights* droits mpl de tirage spéciaux; *special*

offer offre f spéciale; **on special offer** en promotion; *special price* prix m spécial

specialist 1 n spécialiste mf
2 adj (skills, equipment) de spécialiste

speciality, Am **specialty** n spécialité f; **our speciality is electronic components** nous nous spécialisons dans les composants électroniques

specialization n spécialisation f; **his specialization is computers** il est spécialisé en informatique

specialize vi se spécialiser (**in** dans); **we specialize in electronics** nous nous spécialisons dans l'électronique

specialty Am = **speciality**

specie n FIN (coins) espèces fpl; **to pay in specie** payer en espèces

specification n (a) (of contract) stipulation f (b) (in construction, industry) spécifications fpl; **specifications** cahier m des charges (c) MKTG *specification buying* achats mpl spécifiés

specify vt spécifier, préciser; **unless otherwise specified** sauf indication contraire; **the rules specify a 5-minute break** le règlement spécifie une pause de 5 minutes □ *specified load* charge f prescrite

specimen n spécimen m □ *specimen invoice* modèle m de facture; *specimen signature* spécimen de signature

speculate vi FIN, ST EXCH spéculer; **to speculate on the Stock Market** spéculer ou jouer en Bourse; **to speculate in oils** spéculer sur les valeurs pétrolières; **to speculate for a fall** spéculer à la baisse; **to speculate for a rise** spéculer à la hausse

speculation n FIN, ST EXCH spéculation f; **speculation in oil** spéculation sur le pétrole

speculative adj FIN, ST EXCH spéculatif(ive) □ *speculative buying* achats mpl spéculatifs; *speculative selling* vente f spéculative; *speculative shares* valeurs *fpl* spéculatives

speculator *n* FIN, ST EXCH spécula-teur(trice) *m,f*

speech recognition *n* COMPTR recon-naissance *f* de la parole

spellcheck *n* COMPTR correction *f* orthographique; **to do** *or* **run a spellcheck on a document** effectuer une correction orthographique sur un document

spellchecker *n* COMPTR correcteur *m* orthographique *ou* d'orthographe

spend 1 *n* dépenses *fpl*; **we must increase our marketing spend** nous devons aug-menter le budget marketing
2 *vt* (**a**) *(money)* dépenser; **to spend money on sth** dépenser de l'argent en qch (**b**) *(time)* passer; **to spend time on sth/doing sth** passer du temps sur qch/à faire qch

spending *n* dépenses *fpl* ❑ *spending cuts* réductions *fpl* des dépenses; *spending money* argent *m* de poche; ECON *spending power* pouvoir *m* d'achat

sphere *n* *(of interest, activity)* sphère *f*, domaine *m*; **sphere of activity** domaine *m* d'activité; **it's not my sphere** ce n'est pas de mon domaine, ce n'est pas dans mes com-pétences; **the question is outside the committee's sphere** la question ne relève pas des compétences du comité

spin-off *n* *(by-product)* produit *m* dérivé, retombée *f*

> ❝
> Agents, meanwhile, demand ever-larger advances, which publishers have to pay years before they see a book; and unlike, say, the movie business, the publisher does not keep the rights to **spin-offs** such as television or merchandising.
> ❞

spiral *vi* *(of prices)* monter en flèche, s'envoler

split 1 *n* FIN, ST EXCH *(of shares)* division *f*, fractionnement *m*
2 *adj* COMPTR *split screen* écran *m* divisé, multi-écran *m*
3 *vt* FIN, ST EXCH **to split shares** diviser *ou* fractionner des actions; **the shares were split 50%, one new share for each two shares held** les actions ont été fractionnées à raison d'une action nouvelle pour deux anciennes

spoil 1 *vt* *(goods)* avarier
2 *vi* *(of goods)* s'avarier

spoilage *n* déchets *mpl*

sponsor 1 *n* *(of sportsman, team, tournament)* sponsor *m*; *(of film, TV pro-gramme)* sponsor, commanditaire *m*
2 *vt* sponsoriser

sponsorship *n* sponsoring *m* ❑ *spon-sorship deal* contrat *m* de sponsoring

spooler *n* COMPTR *(for printing)* spouleur *m*, pilote *m* de mise en file d'attente

spot *n* (**a**) FIN *spot buying* achats *mpl* au comptant; *spot cash* argent *m* comptant; **to pay spot cash** payer comptant; *spot credit* crédit *m* ponctuel *ou* à court terme; *spot deal* opération *f* au comptant; *spot delivery* livraison *f* au comptant *ou* immédiate; *spot goods* marchandises *fpl* livrables au comptant; *spot market* marché *m* au comtpant; *spot price* prix *m* du disponible; *spot rate* cours *m* du disponible; *spot trading* négociations *fpl* au comptant; *spot transaction* opération *f* *ou* transaction *f* au comptant
(**b**) *(in advertising)* message *m* publicitaire, spot *m*

spread 1 *n* (**a**) *(between two rates)* différence *f*; ST EXCH *(between buying and selling prices)* différence, écart *m* (**b**) ST EXCH *(range of investments)* diversification *f*
2 *vt* *(payments)* échelonner, étaler
3 *vi* ST EXCH spéculer sur les différentiels de cours

spreadsheet *n* COMPTR feuille *f* de calcul; *(software)* tableur *m*

square 1 *n* Fam **the Square Mile** = la City de Londres, dont la superficie fait environ un mile carré
2 *vt* *(account, bill)* régler; *(debt)* acquitter; *(books)* balancer

squeeze 1 *n* *(on credit)* reserrement *m*
2 *vt* *(profits, budget)* réduire

SRO *n* Br ST EXCH *(abbr* **self-regulatory organization***)* organisme *m* auto-régle-menté *ou* autonome

> ❝
> Indeed, it is something of an anomaly that there is no self-regulatory organisation for the pension fund industry. Specific areas of controversy where an **SRO** for pension funds would be useful are in disputes over investment strategies of funds, in fund surpluses, and in pension fund "holidays".
> ❞

SSP *n* Br ADMIN *(abbr* **statutory sick pay***)* = indemnité de maladie versée par l'em-ployeur

stability n (of prices, market, economy) stabilité f

stabilization n (of prices, market, economy) stabilisation f

stabilize 1 vt (prices, market, economy) stabiliser

2 vi (of prices, market, economy) se stabiliser

stabilizing adj stabilisateur(trice); **to have a stabilizing influence on prices** exercer une influence stabilisatrice sur les prix □ **stabilizing policy** politique f de stabilité

stable adj (prices, market, economy) stable

staff 1 n personnel m, employés mpl; **to be on the staff** faire partie du personnel; **staff only** (sign) réservé au personnel □ **staff management** direction f du personnel; **staff manager** chef m du personnel; **staff organization** organisation f fonctionnelle ou horizontale

2 vt **the office is staffed by volunteers** le personnel du bureau est composé de volontaires; **the desk is staffed at all times** il y a toujours quelqu'un au bureau

staffing n recrutement m; **the delay is due to staffing difficulties** le retard est dû à des problèmes de recrutement □ **staffing policy** politique f de recrutement du personnel

stag n ST EXCH loup m

stage n (phase) stade m; **the next stage in computer technology** le stade suivant du développement de l'informatique; **the changes were instituted in stages** les changements ont été introduits progressivement

stagflation n ECON stagflation f

The Government's main fear for the coming year is that the economy will enter a period of **stagflation**, with minimal growth combined with stubborn inflationary pressures.

stagger vt (payments) échelonner, répartir; (holidays) étaler; **they plan to bring in staggered working hours** ils ont l'intention de mettre en place un système d'échelonnement des heures de travail; **employees' vacation times are staggered over the summer months** les vacances du personnel sont étalées sur tout l'été

stagnant adj (economy, prices, trade) stagnant(e)

stagnate vi (of economy, prices, trade) stagner

stagnation n (of economy, prices, trade) stagnation f

stake n (interest, share) intérêt m, part f; (investment) investissement m; (shareholding) participation f; **she has a 10% stake in the company** elle a une participation de 10% dans la société; **the company has a big stake in nuclear energy** la société a fait de gros investissements dans le nucléaire

stakeholder n partie f prenante

stale adj (cheque) périmé(e), prescrit(e)

stall vi to stall (for time) essayer de gagner du temps; **I think they're stalling on the loan until we make more concessions** je crois qu'ils vont retarder le prêt jusqu'à ce que nous leur fassions davantage de concessions

stamp 1 n (a) (for letter, parcel) timbre m (b) (device) tampon m; (mark) cachet m (c) **stamp duty** droit m de timbre

2 vt (a) (document) tamponner; **he stamped the firm's name on each document** il a tamponné le nom de la société sur chaque document; **incoming mail is stamped with the date received** le courrier qui arrive est tamponné à la date de réception (b) (letter, parcel) timbrer, affranchir □ Br **stamped addressed envelope** enveloppe f timbrée libellée à ses noms et adresse

stand 1 n (at exhibition) stand m (d'exposition)

2 vi (a) (be valid) tenir; **the agreement stands** le contrat tient toujours; **even with this new plan, our objection still stands** ce nouveau plan ne remet pas en cause notre objection première (b) (of statistics) **inflation/unemployment stands at 5%** le taux d'inflation/de chômage est à 5%; **their turnover now stands at three million pounds** leur chiffre d'affaires atteint désormais les trois millions de livres

▶ **stand down** vi (resign) démissionner

▶ **stand off** vt sep Br (workers) faire chômer

stand-alone n COMPTR poste m autonome □ **stand-alone computer** ordinateur m autonome

standard 1 n (a) (level) niveau m; **to be up to/below standard** être du/en dessous du niveau requis; **most of the goods are up to standard** la plupart de marchandises sont de qualité satisfaisante □ **standard of living** niveau de vie

(b) (set requirements) norme f; (for weights, measures, currency) étalon m; **to make a product comply with standards** adapter un produit aux normes; **to set standards for a**

product fixer des normes pour un produit

2 adj (design, size) standard ❏ **standard cost accounting, standard costing** méthode f des coûts standards; INS **standard policy** police f (d'assurance) type; **standard practice** pratique f courante; **standard price** prix m standard; **standard rate** (of tax) taux m standard

standardization n standardisation f; (of methods, products, production) normalisation f

standardize vt standardiser; (methods, products, production) normaliser

standby n (**a**) FIN ligne f de crédit ❏ **standby credit** crédit m de réserve ou de soutien; **standby letter of credit** caution f bancaire (**b**) (for flight) **to be on standby** être en stand-by ❏ **standby passenger** passager(ère) m,f (en) stand-by; **standby ticket** billet m en stand-by (**c**) COMPTR **standby mode** (of printer) veille f

standing **1** n (status) réputation f; **enquiries were made into his financial standing** on a enquêté sur sa situation financière; **the scandal has damaged the company's standing** le scandale a nui à la réputation de la société

2 adj **standing charges** (on bill) frais mpl d'abonnement; Br FIN **standing order** virement m automatique; **I get paid by standing order** je reçois mon salaire par virement bancaire

standstill n **to be at a standstill** (of economy, production) être paralysé(e) ❏ **standstill agreement** moratoire m

> Hongkong Bank bought a 14.9% stake in Midland, paying £4.75 a share (Midland's shares price is now £3.43). It signed a **standstill agreement** under which it promised not to increase its holding for three years.

staple¹ **1** n (for paper) agrafe f ❏ **staple gun** agrafeuse f

2 vt agrafer (**to** à)

staple² **1** n (basic foodstuff) aliment m de base; (basic product) principale production f

2 adj (foodstuffs, products) de base; (export, crop) principal(e); **their staple commodity is cotton** le coton est leur produit de base

stapler n agrafeuse f

star n MKTG vedette f

start **1** n début m

2 vt (**a**) (machine, device) mettre en marche;

to start the printer again, press this key pour remettre en marche l'imprimante, appuyez sur cette touche (**b**) (business) fonder, créer; (project, campaign) lancer

3 vi commencer; **she started on $500 a week** elle a débuté à 500 dollars par semaine

▸ **start up** vt sep (business) fonder, créer; (project, campaign) lancer

starting n **starting date** date f d'entrée en vigueur; **starting price** prix m initial; (at auction) prix d'appel; **starting salary** salaire m de départ

start-up n (of new business) lancement m; **there have been 500 start-ups this year** il y a eu 500 créations d'entreprises cette année ❏ **start-up capital** capital m initial; **start-up costs** frais mpl de lancement; **start-up loan** prêt m initial

state¹ n (country, administrative region) État m ❏ Am **state bank** banque f de dépôts (agréée par un État); **state control** contrôle m étatique; **to be placed under state control** être nationalisé(e); **state pension** pension f de l'État

state² vt (conditions, demands, reasons) déclarer; **please state salary expectations** veuillez indiquer le salaire souhaité

state-aided adj subventionné(e) par l'État

state-controlled adj (industry) nationalisé(e); (economy) étatisé(e); **the oil company is 51% state-controlled** l'État détient 51% des actions de la compagnie pétrolière

stated adj (amount, date, price) fixé(e); (limit) prescrit(e); **it will be finished within the stated time** cela va être terminé dans les délais prescrits

statement n (**a**) (of facts, situation) exposé m, compte-rendu m (**b**) (from bank) relevé m de compte (bancaire) ❏ ACCT **statement of account** état m ou relevé de compte; **statement of affairs** bilan m de liquidation; **statement of expenses** état m ou relevé des dépenses; INS **statement of loss** certificat m d'avarie

state-of-the-art adj avancé(e); **the method incorporates state-of-the-art technology** la méthode utilise des technologies de pointe

state-owned adj nationalisé(e)

stationery n papeterie f; (writing paper) papier m à lettres ❏ ADMIN **the Stationery Office** = maison d'édition britannique publiant les documents approuvés par le

Parlement, les ministères et autres organismes officiels, ≃ l'Imprimerie f nationale

statistic n chiffre m, statistique f; **statistics** statistiques

statistical adj statistique ▫ **statistical analysis** analyse f statistique

statistician n statisticien(enne) m,f

statistics npl statistique f

status n (position) position f, statut m; **what's your status in the company?** quelle est votre position dans l'entreprise? ▫ **status inquiry** enquête f de solvabilité; COMPTR **status line** ligne f d'état; **status report** état m du projet

statute n LAW loi f, ordonnance f; **statutes** (of company) statuts mpl, règlements mpl ▫ **statute book** recueil m des lois

statutory adj (price controls, income policy) obligatoire; (rights, duties, regulations) statutaire; (holiday) légal(e) ▫ **statutory company** entreprise f de service public; **statutory report** = rapport annuel sur l'état de l'entreprise (obligatoire dans le cadre de la loi sur les sociétés); **statutory reserve** réserve f statutaire; **statutory rights** droits mpl statutaires; **statutory sick pay** = indemnité de maladie versée par l'employeur

steady 1 adj (growth, increase, decline) régulier(ère), progressif(ive); (price, rate, Stock Market) stable; **inflation remains at a steady 5%** l'inflation s'est stabilisée à 5%
2 vi (of growth, increase, decline) devenir régulier(ère); (of price, rate, Stock Market) se stabiliser

steep adj (price) élevé(e); (rise, fall) considérable; **a steep drop in share prices** une forte chute des prix des actions

steering committee n comité m de restructuration

> ❝
> A meeting of the **steering committee** of the multilateral talks was held in Lisbon, Portugal on May 27. An agreement was reached on the venues of future meetings: water in Washington; economic co-operation in Paris; arms control in Moscow; environment in The Hague; and refugees in Ottawa.
> ❞

sterling n sterling m; **in sterling** en livres sterling; **five thousand pounds sterling** cinq mille livres sterling ▫ **sterling area** zone f sterling

stevedore n docker m, débardeur m

stimulate vt (production) encourager, activer; (growth, trade) stimuler

stimulus n stimulant m ▫ MKTG **stimulus response** réponse f stimulée

stipulate vt stipuler; **it is stipulated that construction shall start next month** il est stipulé que la construction doit commencer le mois prochain; **please stipulate the quantity on your order form** veuillez stipuler la quantité sur votre commande

stipulation n stipulation f; **they accepted, but with the stipulation that the time limit be extended** ils ont accepté sous réserve que les délais soient prolongés

stock n 1 (a) (of goods) stock m; **stocks are low** il y a peu de marchandises en stock; **while stocks last** jusqu'à épuisement des stocks; **to be in stock** être en stock; **to be out of stock** être épuisé(e); **we're out of stock** nous sommes en rupture de stock ▫ **stock clearance** liquidation f de stock; **stock control** gestion f ou contrôle m des stocks; **stock in hand** marchandises fpl en stock ou en magasin; **stock valuation** évaluation f des stocks

(b) ST EXCH (en Grande-Bretagne) valeurs fpl, actions fpl, titres mpl; (aux États-Unis) actions ordinaires; **stocks and shares** valeurs boursières ou mobilières, titres ▫ Am **stock average** indice m des titres; **stock dividend** dividende m (en) action; **stock exchange** bourse f des valeurs; **the Stock Exchange** la Bourse; **Stock Exchange Daily Official List** cours mpl de clôture quotidiens; **stock index** indice m de la Bourse; **stock list** cours mpl de la Bourse; **stock market** marché m des valeurs; **the Stock Market** la Bourse; **stock market price** cours m de la Bourse; **stock market report** bulletin m des cours de la Bourse; **stock market value** valeur f en Bourse; **stock option** option f de titres; **stock option plan, stock purchase plan** plan m d'option sur titres

2 vt (a) (supply) approvisionner (**with** de); **this shop is well stocked** ce magasin est bien approvisionné

(b) (have in stock) avoir en stock; **we don't stock that item any more** nous ne vendons ou faisons plus cet article

> ❝
> ... the maximum price which may be paid for a Share shall be not more than 5% above the average of the middle market quotations derived from the London **Stock Exchange Daily Official List** for the ten business days immediately preceding the date of purchase of the Share ...
> ❞

stockbroker *n* ST EXCH agent *m* de change
❑ *stockbroker belt* = partie de la banlieue sud de Londres où habitent les agents de change et autres personnes du même milieu socio-professionnel

stockbroking *n* ST EXCH commerce *m* des valeurs en Bourse

stockholder *n* ST EXCH actionnaire *mf*

stock-in-trade *n* marchandises *fpl* en stock *ou* en magasin

stockist *n* stockiste *mf*

stockjobber *n Br* ST EXCH *Formerly* = avant 1986, intermédiaire en Bourse qui traitait directement avec les agents de change et non avec le public

stockpile **1** *n* stocks *mpl* de réserve
2 *vt* stocker

stockroom *n* magasin *m*, réserve *f*

stocktaking *n* inventaire *m* (des stocks); **to do the stocktaking** faire l'inventaire; **stocktaking is in February** on fait l'inventaire en février

stop **1** *n* ST EXCH *stop loss* ordre *m* stop
2 *vt Br* (*withhold*) **to stop payment** suspendre des paiements; **to stop a cheque** faire opposition à un chèque; **to stop sb's wages** retenir le salaire de qn; **the money will be stopped out of your wages** la somme sera retenue sur votre salaire

stop-go policy *n Br* ECON politique *f* économique en dents de scie, politique du stop-and-go

stoppage *n* (**a**) (*strike*) grève *f*, arrêt *m* de travail (**b**) *Br* (*sum deducted*) retenue *f*; **my wages are a lot less after stoppages** après les retenues, il ne reste plus grand-chose de mon salaire

storage *n* (**a**) (*action*) entreposage *m*, emmagasinage *m*; (*space available*) (espace *m* de) rangement *m*; (*state*) stockage *m*; **to put sth into storage** entreposer qch ❑ *storage capacity* capacité *f* d'emmagasinage; *storage charges* frais *mpl* de magasinage; *storage facilities* entrepôt *m* (**b**) COMPTR mémoire *f* ❑ *storage capacity* capacité *f* de stockage; *storage device* dispositif *m* de stockage

store **1** *n* (**a**) (*supply*) provision *f*, stock *m*, réserve *f* (**b**) (*warehouse*) entrepôt *m* (**c**) (*large shop*) grand magasin *m*; *Am* (*shop*) magasin *m* ❑ MKTG *store audit* contrôle *m* des points de vente; MKTG *store brand* marque *f* de magasin; *store card* carte *f* de crédit (*d'un magasin*) (**d**) COMPTR mémoire *f*

2 *vt* (**a**) (*goods*) mettre en magasin, entreposer (**b**) COMPTR stocker

storehouse *n* entrepôt *m*

storekeeper *n* (**a**) (*in warehouse*) magasinier(ère) *m,f* (**b**) *Am* (*shopkeeper*) commerçant(e) *m,f*

storeroom *n* réserve *f*

straddle *n* ST EXCH ordre *m* lié, opération *f* à cheval; **to take a straddle position** = jumeler simultanément un achat sur une époque avec une vente sur une autre

> **❝**
> There is a lower level of initial margin on straddle positions. A **straddle position** is a simultaneous long and short position in different months of the same futures contract, e.g. long one June ST3 contract and short one September ST3 contract. Because the daily price movements in a **straddle** are likely to be lower than in the individual contracts, the initial margin is lower.
> **❞**

straight-line depreciation *n* ACCT amortissement *m* linéaire

strategic *adj* stratégique ❑ *strategic business plan* plan *m* stratégique d'entreprise; *strategic business unit* domaine *m* d'activité stratégique; *strategic management* gestion *f* stratégique; *strategic marketing* marketing *m ou* mercatique *f* stratégique; *strategic planning* planification *f* stratégique

strategically *adv* stratégiquement

strategy *n* stratégie *f*

streamline *vt* (*production, methods*) rationaliser; (*company, department, industry*) dégraisser

streamlined *adj* (*production, methods*) rationalisé(e); (*company, department, industry*) dégraissé(e)

streamlining *n* (*of production, methods*) rationalisation *f*; (*of company, department*) dégraissement *m*

street *n* ST EXCH *street dealing* transactions *fpl* hors Bourse; *street market* marché *m* hors Bourse; *street price* cours *m* hors Bourse

strengthen **1** *vt* (*financial position, currency, economy*) consolider
2 *vi* (*of financial position, currency, economy*) se consolider

stress-related illness *n* maladie *f* due au stress

strike 1 *n* *(of workers)* grève *f*; **to be on strike** faire (la) grève, être en grève; **to come out** *or* **go on strike** se mettre en grève ❑ INS **strike clause** clause *f* pour cas de grève; **strike fund** = caisse de prévoyance permettant d'aider les grévistes; **strike pay** allocation *f* de grève

2 *vt* *(bargain, deal, agreement)* conclure

3 *vi* *(of workers)* faire grève; **they're striking for more pay** ils font grève pour obtenir une augmentation de salaire

strikebreaker *n* briseur(euse) *m,f* de grève

striker *n* gréviste *mf*

string *n* **(a)** COMPTR *(of characters)* chaîne *f* **(b) to pull strings** faire jouer ses relations; **somebody pulled strings to get him the job** il a eu le poste par piston; **with no strings attached** sans conditions

strong *adj* *(market)* ferme; *(currency, price)* solide; **the pound is getting stronger** la livre se raffermit

structural unemployment *n* ECON chômage *m* structurel

structure 1 *n* structure *f*
2 *vt* structurer

stub *n* *(of cheque)* souche *f*, talon *m*

study *n* *(of market, feasibility)* étude *f*

▸ **stump up** *Br Fam* 1 *vt sep* casquer
2 *vi* casquer (**for** pour)

style *n* COMPTR **style bar** barre *f* de style; **style sheet** feuille *f* de style

sub-agency *n* sous-agence *f*

sub-agent *n* sous-agent *m*

> ❝
> From the start, Copyrights placed the emphasis on the international market and, instead of using **sub-agents**, opened its own offices.
> ❞

subcommittee *n* sous-comité *m*

subcontract 1 *n* contrat *m* de sous-traitance

2 *vt* *(work, order)* sous-traiter; **they subcontract some of the work out to local firms** ils sous-traitent une partie du travail à des entreprises locales

3 *vi* travailler en sous-traitance; **they have a lot of small companies who subcontract for them** beaucoup de petites sociétés travaillent pour eux en sous-traitance

subcontracting *n* sous-traitance *f*

subcontractor *n* sous-traitant *m*

subdirectory *n* COMPTR sous-répertoire *m*

subject *adj* *(liable)* **to be subject to sth** *(fine, taxation, commission)* être passible de qch; **the terms are subject to alteration without notice** les termes peuvent être modifiés sans préavis; **the price is subject to a handling charge** les frais de manutention sont en sus

sub-lease 1 *n* sous-location *f*
2 *vt* sous-louer

sub-let 1 *n* sous-location *f*
2 *vt* sous-louer

submenu *n* COMPTR sous-menu *m*

subordinate 1 *n* subordonné(e) *mf*
2 *adj* *(job, position)* subalterne; **to be subordinate to sb** être subordonné(e) à qn

subrogation *n* LAW subrogation *f*

subroutine *n* COMPTR sous-programme *m*

subscribe 1 *vt* FIN *(shares)* souscrire ❑ **subscribed capital** capital *m* souscrit
2 *vi* **(a)** *(to newspaper, magazine, Internet)* s'abonner (**to** à); **to subscribe to the Internet** s'abonner à l'Internet **(b)** FIN *(to loan, share issue)* souscrire (**to** à)

subscriber *n* **(a)** *(to newspaper, magazine, Internet)* abonné(e) *m,f* **(b)** FIN *(to loan, share issue)* souscripteur(trice) *m,f* **(c)** *(of new company)* signataire *mf* des statuts

subscription *n* **(a)** *(to newspaper, magazine, Internet)* abonnement *m*; **to take out a subscription to sth** s'abonner à qch ❑ **subscription form** bulletin *m* d'abonnement; **subscription rate** prix *m* de l'abonnement

(b) FIN *(to loan, share issue)* souscription *f* ❑ **subscription list** liste *f* de souscriptions; **subscription right** droit *m* de souscription (d'actions)

subsidiarity *n* subsidiarité *f*

subsidiary 1 *n* *(company)* filiale *f*
2 *adj* subsidiaire, auxiliaire ❑ **subsidiary account** sous-compte *m*; **subsidiary company** filiale *f*

subsidize *vt* subventionner; **the company was subsidized to the tune of £3 million** l'entreprise a reçu trois millions de livres de subventions ❑ **subsidized industry** industrie *f* subventionnée

subsidy *n* subvention *f*

> ❝
> Particular concern surrounded US complaints over the EC **subsidies** being paid to the European Airbus project — a joint development by France, Germany, Spain and the UK.
> ❞

sub-standard *adj* *(goods)* de qualité inférieure

subtenancy *n* sous-location *f*

subtenant *n* sous-locataire *mf*

subvention *n Am* subvention *f*

sue LAW **1** *vt* poursuivre (en justice), intenter un procès à; **to sue sb for sth** poursuivre qn en justice pour qch; **he sued the factory for damages** il a poursuivi l'usine pour obtenir des dommages-intérêts
2 *vi* intenter un procès, engager des poursuites

suicide pill *n (defensive tactics in takeover)* clause *f* de suicide

suit *n* LAW action *m*, procès *m*; **to bring** *or* **file a suit against sb** poursuivre qn en justice, intenter un procès à qn

sum *n (amount of money)* somme *f*; *(total)* total *m*

summit *n (meeting)* sommet *m*; **to hold a summit** tenir un sommet

summon *vt (person, meeting)* convoquer; LAW *(witness)* assigner *ou* citer à comparaître

summons LAW **1** *n* assignation *f ou* citation *f* à comparaître
2 *vt* assigner *ou* citer à comparaître

sundry **1** *n* **sundries** *(items)* articles *mpl* divers; *(costs)* frais *mpl* divers
2 *adj* divers(e) ❑ **sundry expenses** frais *mpl* divers

sunrise industry *n* industrie *f* naissante

sunset industry *n* industrie *f* déclinante

superannuation *n (act of retiring)* mise *f* à la retraite; *(pension)* pension *f* de retraite; *(contribution)* cotisation *f* pour la retraite ❑ **superannuation fund** caisse *f* de retraite

supercomputer *n* COMPTR super-ordinateur *m*

superhighway *n* COMPTR autoroute *f*

supermarket *n* supermarché *m*

superstock *n Am* ST EXCH actions *fpl* à droit de vote double

superstore *n* hypermarché *m*

supertax *n* impôt *m* sur les grandes fortunes

supervise *vt* superviser, surveiller

supervision *n* supervision *f*, surveillance *f*

supervisor *n (in office)* chef *m* de service; *(in factory)* chef d'équipe

supplement **1** *n (additional amount)* supplément *m*; **a supplement is charged for occupying a single room** il y a un supplément à payer pour les chambres à un lit
2 *vt* compléter

supplier *n* fournisseur(euse) *m,f* ❑ **supplier code** code *m* fournisseur; ACCT **supplier credit** crédit-fournisseur *m*, avoir-fournisseur *m*

supply **1** *n* **(a)** ECON offre *f*; **supply and demand** l'offre et la demande ❑ **supply curve** courbe *f* de l'offre; **supply price** prix *m* de l'offre
(b) *(stock)* provision *f*, réserve *f*; *(act of supplying)* approvisionnement *m*; **supplies** provisions *fpl*; **we are expecting a new supply of microchips** nous espérons recevoir bientôt un nouveau stock de microprocesseurs; **this paper is in short supply** nous ne sommes à court de ce papier
2 *vt (goods, services)* fournir; **to supply sb with sth, to supply sth to sb** fournir qn de qch, fournir qch à qn; **they supply all the local retailers** ils fournissent tous les détaillants du coin

support **1** *n* **(a)** *(funding)* soutien *m*; **they depend on the government for financial support** ils sont subventionnés par le gouvernement; **what are your means of support?** quelles sont vos sources de revenus? ❑ EU **support price** prix *m* de soutien
(b) *(backing)* soutien *m*, appui *m*; **to give** *or* **lend one's support to sth** accorder son appui à qch
2 *vt* **(a)** *(financially)* subvenir aux besoins de
(b) *(back)* soutenir, appuyer
(c) COMPTR permettre l'utilisation de, supporter; **this package is supported by all workstations** ce progiciel peut être utilisé sur tous les postes de travail
(d) FIN *(price, currency)* maintenir

> **"**
>
> To be successful, farmers need to be sure of being able to sell their outputs at reasonable prices. To help them the government of the EEC, in Brussels, fixes the lowest, or minimum, price for each product each year. This is called the **support price**, or intervention price.
>
> **"**

surcharge **1** *n* supplément *m*
2 *vt* faire payer un supplément à

surety *n (person)* caution *f*, garant(e) *m,f*; *(collateral)* caution, sûreté *f*; **to stand surety (for sb)** se porter caution (pour qn)

surf *vt* COMPTR **to surf the Net** naviguer sur l'Internet

surface mail *n* courrier *m* par voie de terre; **by surface mail** par voie de terre

surfeit *n* surabondance *f*; **there is a surfeit of imported goods** il y a trop d'importations

surplus *n* surplus *m*, excédent *m*; **EU grain surpluses** excédents de céréales de l'UE; **Japan's trade surplus** l'excédent commercial du Japon ◦ *surplus stock* surplus *mpl*

surrender **1** *n* INS *(of policy)* rachat *m* ◦ *surrender value* valeur *f* de rachat
2 *vt (right)* céder; INS *(policy)* racheter

surtax **1** *n* surtaxe *f*
2 *vt* surtaxer

survey **1** *n* (**a**) *Br (of building)* expertise *f*
(**b**) *(study, investigation)* étude *f*, enquête *f*; **they carried out a survey of retail prices** ils ont fait une enquête sur les prix au détail
(**c**) *(opinion poll)* sondage *m*
2 *vt* (**a**) *Br (building)* expertiser, faire une expertise de
(**b**) *(study, investigate)* faire une étude de, étudier; **the report surveys the current state of the manufacturing industry** le rapport étudie l'état actuel de l'industrie manufacturière
(**c**) *(poll)* sonder; **65% of women surveyed were opposed to the measure** 65% des femmes interrogées étaient contre cette mesure

surveyor *n Br (of building)* expert *m*

suspect *n* MKTG client(e) *m,f* potentiel(elle) ◦ *suspect pool* clients potentiels

suspend *vt* (**a**) *(payment)* suspendre; **the government has suspended the repayment of foreign debts** le gouvernement a suspendu le remboursement de sa dette extérieure (**b**) *(employee)* suspendre

suspense account *n* compte *m* d'ordre

suspension *n* (**a**) *(of payment)* suspension *f*
(**b**) *(of employee)* suspension *f*

swap **1** *n* BANKING, ST EXCH échange *m* financier, swap *m* ◦ *swap agreements* accords *mpl* d'échanges; *swap facilities* facilités *fpl* de crédits réciproques
2 *vt* ST EXCH swaper

swingline *adj (loan, credit)* immédiatement disponible

swipe **1** *n swipe card* badge *m*
2 *vt (card)* passer dans un lecteur de cartes

switch **1** *n* (**a**) *Br* **Switch** = société de cartes de paiement britannique ◦ *Switch card* = carte de paiement utilisée en Grande-Bretagne (**b**) COMPTR *(in DOS)* clé *f* (**c**) ST EXCH *switch trading* arbitrage *m*
2 *vt* ST EXCH **to switch a position** = reporter

une position d'une échéance à une autre plus éloignée

switchboard *n* standard *m* ◦ *switchboard operator* standardiste *mf*

switching *n* ST EXCH arbitrage *m* de portefeuille

SWOT *n* MKTG *(abbr* **strengths, weaknesses, opportunities, threats)** forces, faiblesses, opportunités et menaces *fpl* ◦ *SWOT analysis* analyse *f* des forces, faiblesses, opportunités et menaces

> **"**
> Strategic planners use techniques such as **SWOT analysis**. … The idea is to improve the overall organisational performance by eliminating weaknesses and developing strengths. Opportunities are to be maximised and threats either avoided or turned into opportunities.
> **"**

sympathy *n* **to come out in sympathy** se mettre en grève par solidarité ◦ *sympathy strike* grève *f* de solidarité

syndicate **1** *n* syndicat *m*, groupement *m*; **to form a syndicate** se syndiquer; **the loan was underwritten by a syndicate of banks** le prêt était garanti par un consortium bancaire; **a syndicate of British and French companies** un groupement de sociétés françaises et britanniques
2 *vt* (**a**) *(industry)* syndiquer (**b**) FIN *syndicated credit* crédit *m* consortial; *syndicated loan* prêt *m* en participation; *syndicated shares* actions *fpl* syndiquées

syntax *n* COMPTR syntaxe *f*

SYSOP *n* COMPTR *(abbr* **Systems Operator)** sysop *m*, opérateur *m* système

system *n* (**a**) *(structure, method)* système *m*; **a new system of sorting mail** un nouveau système pour trier le courrier
(**b**) COMPTR système *m* ◦ *systems analysis* analyse *f* des systèmes; *systems analyst* analyste-programmeur(euse) *m,f*; *system crash* panne *f* du système; *system disk* disque *f* système; *systems engineering* planification *f* des systèmes; *system error* erreur *f* système; *system failure* panne *f* du système; *systems management* direction *f* systématisée; *system software* logiciel *m* d'exploitation, logiciel système

systematic *adj* systématique

tab n (on typewriter, word processor) tabulation f; **to set tabs (at)** régler ou positionner les tabulateurs (à) □ **tab key** tabulateur m, touche f de tabulation; **tab points** points mpl de tabulation; **tab setting** tabulation; **tab stop** taquet m de tabulation

table 1 n (a) (chart) table f, tableau m; (of prices) barème m; **the results are set out in the following table** les résultats sont donnés dans le tableau suivant □ **table of contents** table des matières

(b) (furniture) table f; **to get round the negotiating table** s'asseoir à la table des négociations

2 vt **to table a motion/proposal** Br (present) présenter une motion/une proposition; Am (postpone) ajourner une motion/une proposition

tabloid n Am (paper size) tabloïd m (279mm × 432mm)

tabular adj (statistics, figures) tabulaire; **in tabular form** sous forme de tableau

tabulate vt (a) (present in table form) mettre sous forme de tableau (b) (classify) classifier

tabulator n tabulateur m

tag 1 n (a) (showing price) étiquette f (de prix) (b) COMPTR (code) balise f
2 vt COMPTR baliser

take 1 n Fam (takings) recette f; (share) part f
2 vt (a) (remove) **to take an amount out of one's income** prélever une somme sur son revenu; **to take sth off the market** retirer qch du marché

(b) (receive) (money) **she takes home £3,000 a month** son salaire net est de 3000 livres par mois

(c) (accept) (cheque, credit card) accepter; **he won't take less** il refuse d'accepter un prix moins élevé; **does the machine take pound coins?** est-ce que la machine accepte les pièces d'une livre?

(d) (write down) (letter, name and address, notes) prendre; **to take the minutes** rédiger le procès-verbal

▸ **take back** vt sep (a) (employee) reprendre; **the factory took back the workers** l'usine a repris les ouvriers (b) (goods) rapporter; **take it back to the shop** rapporte-le au magasin

▸ **take off** vt sep (a) (deduct) déduire, rabattre; **he took 10% off the price** il a réduit le prix de 10%, il a déduit 10% du prix (b) (time) **to take a day off** prendre un jour

de congé; **she takes Thursdays off** elle ne travaille pas le jeudi

▸ **take on** vt sep (a) (worker) engager, embaucher (b) (responsibility, task) se charger de; (new contract, customer) accepter

▸ **take out** vt sep (permit, licence, patent) prendre, obtenir; (insurance policy) souscrire à; (subscription) prendre; **to take out a mortgage** prendre un emprunt-logement

▸ **take over** 1 vt sep (company) (become responsible for) prendre la direction de; (buy out) racheter; **they were taken over by a Japanese firm** ils ont été rachetés par une entreprise japonaise; ST EXCH **to take over an issue** absorber une émission

2 vi (of new manager) prendre la direction; **to take over from sb** (replace) relever qn dans ses fonctions

▸ **take up** vt sep (a) (offer) accepter; **to take sb up on an offer** accepter l'offre de qn

(b) FIN (bill) honorer, retirer; ST EXCH (option) lever, consolider; (shares) souscrire à

(c) (position, post) prendre; **to take up one's duties** entrer en fonctions

take-home pay n salaire m net

takeover n (of company) rachat m □ **takeover bid** offre f publique d'achat, OPA f; **to be the subject of a takeover bid** être l'objet d'une OPA

❝

At the same time as building up the 15 per cent stake, GM would make a big cash injection into Jaguar — perhaps as much as £200m — to help the Coventry-based firm to fend off Ford, which has already announced it plans to take a 15 per cent holding as a prelude to a full **takeover bid**.

❞

---

taker n (buyer) preneur(euse) m,f, acheteur(euse) m,f; **there were no takers** personne n'en voulait

takings npl recette f

talks npl (negotiations) négociations fpl, pourparlers mpl

tally 1 n (record) pointage m; **to keep a tally of goods** pointer des marchandises
2 vt (goods) pointer
3 vi (of figures, accounts) correspondre (**with** à), s'accorder, concorder (**with** avec); **these**

accounts do not tally ces comptes ne s'accordent pas

tangible ACCT **1** *n* **tangibles** actif *m* corporel

2 *adj* **tangible assets** actif *m* corporel; **tangible fixed assets** immobilisations *fpl* corporelles

tap *n* FIN valeur *f* du Trésor mise aux enchères; **long/medium/short tap** valeurs *fpl* émises à un prix déterminé par l'État à long/moyen/court terme □ **tap issue** émission *f* des valeurs du Trésor; **tap stock** valeur du Trésor mise aux enchères

tape *n* COMPTR bande *f* □ **tape backup** sauvegarde *f* sur bande; **tape backup system** système *m* de sauvegarde sur bande; **tape backup unit** unité *f* de sauvegarde sur bande; **tape unit** unité *f* de bande

tapering *adj* FIN (rate) dégressif(ive)

tare *n* tare *f*; (of lorry) poids *m* net; **to allow for the tare** faire la tare

target 1 *n* (objective) but *m*, objectif *m*; **to meet production targets** atteindre les objectifs de production; **to be on target** (of plans) se dérouler comme prévu; (of productivity) atteindre les objectifs prévus

2 *adj* MKTG **target buyer** acheteur(euse) *m,f* cible; MKTG **target company** société *f* cible; MKTG **target consumer** consommateur(trice) *m,f* cible; **target cost** coût *m* ciblé; **target date** date *f* ciblée *ou* visée; COMPTR **target disk** (hard) disque *m* cible; (floppy) disquette *f* cible; MKTG **target group** groupe *m* cible; MKTG **Target Group Index** indice *m* des groupes cibles; MKTG **target market** marché *m* cible; **target population** population *f* cible; **target price** prix *m* d'équilibre; **target pricing** fixation *f* du prix en fonction de l'objectif

3 *vt* (market) cibler; (advertising campaign) diriger; **the benefits are targeted at one-parent families** les allocations visent les familles monoparentales

targetting *n* MKTG ciblage *m*

tariff *n* (a) (list of prices) tableau *m* des prix, tarif *m* (b) (tax) tarif *m*, droit *m* de douane □ **tariff agreement** accord *m* tarifaire; **tariff barrier** barrière *f* tarifaire; **tariff laws** lois *fpl* tarifaires; **tariff level indices** taux *mpl* indices des tarifs

task *n* tâche *f* □ **task force** groupe *m* d'intervention

tax 1 *n* (on income) impôt *m*, contributions *fpl*; (on goods, services, imports) taxe *f*; **most of my income goes on tax** la plus grande partie de mes revenus va aux impôts; **I paid over $5,000 in tax** j'ai payé plus de 5000 dollars d'impôts; **there is a high tax on whisky** le whisky est fortement taxé; **to levy a tax on sth** frapper qch d'une taxe; **to be liable to tax** être assujetti(e) à l'impôt; **before tax** hors taxe; (income) avant impôt; **after tax** après impôt; **exclusive of tax** hors taxe □ **tax adjustment** redressement *m* d'impôt; **tax allowance** abattement *m* fiscal; **tax assessment** avis *m* d'imposition, fixation *f* de l'impôt; **tax avoidance** = moyen légal pour payer moins d'impôts; **tax band** tranche *f* d'imposition; **tax base** assiette *f* fiscale; **tax bite** proportion *f* du revenu pris par l'impôt; **tax bracket** tranche *f* d'imposition; **tax break** allègement *m* fiscal; **tax burden** pression *f* fiscale, poids *m* de la fiscalité; **tax code** barème *m* fiscal; **tax collector** percepteur *m* d'impôt; **tax consultant** conseiller(ère) *m,f* fiscal(e); **tax cut** baisse *f* *ou* réduction *f* des impôts; **tax deduction** déduction *f* fiscale; *Am* **tax dollars** impôts *mpl* (payés par la population); **tax evasion** évasion *f* fiscale; **tax exemption** exemption *f* d'impôt; **tax exile** = personne qui réside à l'étranger pour minimiser la responsabilité fiscale; **tax form** déclaration *f* d'impôt; **tax fraud** fraude *f* fiscale; **tax haven** paradis *m* fiscal; **tax holiday** = période de grâce accordée pour le paiement des impôts; **tax incentive** incitation *f* fiscale; **tax loophole** échappatoire *f* fiscale; **tax loss** déficit *m* fiscal reportable; **tax office** (bureau *m* de) perception *f*; **tax rate** taux *m* d'imposition; **tax reduction** abattement *m* fiscal; **tax refund** (on goods) détaxe *f*; **tax relief** dégrèvement *m* (fiscal); **tax return** déclaration *f* de revenu, feuille *f* d'impôt; **tax shelter** avantage *m* fiscal; **tax year** année *f* fiscale

2 *vt* (person, company) imposer, frapper d'un impôt; (goods, services, imports) taxer, frapper d'un taxe; **the rich will be more heavily taxed** les riches seront plus lourdement imposés; **luxury goods are taxed at 28%** les articles de luxe sont taxés à 28%; **small businesses are being taxed out of existence** accablées d'impôts, les petites entreprises disparaissent

44

What equity investment there is will be best placed in the regular savings schemes offered by unit trust and investment trust schemes with higher rate tax payers using the **tax shelter** of PEPs.

77

taxable *adj* imposable □ **taxable income** revenu *m* imposable

taxation n (**a**) *(of person, company)* imposition f; *(of goods)* taxation f (**b**) *(taxes)* impôts mpl, contributions fpl

tax-deductible adj déductible des impôts

tax-exempt, tax-free adj *(income)* exonéré(e) d'impôts; *(goods)* exonéré(e) de taxes

taxman n Br Fam **the taxman** le fisc

taxpayer n contribuable mf

TCP/IP n COMPTR *(abbr* **transmission control protocol/Internet protocol)** TCP-IP

team n équipe f; **she's a team player** elle a l'esprit d'équipe □ **team building** création f d'un esprit d'équipe; **team leader** chef m d'équipe; **team spirit** esprit m d'équipe

teamster n Am camionneur m, routier(ère) m,f; **the Teamsters** *(union)* = syndicat américain des camionneurs

teamwork n travail m d'équipe

teaser n MKTG **teaser ad** aguiche f; **teaser campaign** campagne f teasing

technical adj technique □ **technical analysis** analyse f sur graphiques; ST EXCH **technical correction** correction f d'un cours en Bourse; COMPTR **technical support** support m technique

technician n technicien(enne) m,f

technique n technique f

technology n technologie f

teething troubles npl difficultés fpl initiales ou de départ; **we're having teething troubles with the new computer** nous avons des problèmes de mise en route avec le nouvel ordinateur

telebanking n banque f à domicile

telecomms npl *(abbr* **telecommunications)** télécommunications fpl

telecommunications npl télécommunications fpl

telecommuting n télétravail m

> We may observe in the future a continued trend in the use of sub-contractors, consultants, and other external agencies, thus reducing the core size of currently large firms. This trend may be accelerated by an increase in **telecommuting** (working from home via a telecommunications link).

teleconference n téléconférence f

telegram n télégramme m; **to send sb a telegram** envoyer un télégramme à qn

telegraph **1** n télégraphe m □ **telegraph service** service m télégraphique
2 vt *(news)* télégraphier; *(person)* envoyer un télégramme à
3 vi télégraphier

telegraphic adj télégraphique □ **telegraphic address** adresse f télégraphique; FIN **telegraphic transfer** transfert m télégraphique

telemarketing n télémarketing m

telematics n télématique f

teleorder **1** n commande f par ordinateur
2 vt commander par ordinateur

telephone **1** n téléphone m; **to be on the telephone** *(have a telephone)* être abonné(e) au téléphone; *(talking)* être au téléphone; **to have a good telephone manner** savoir bien parler au téléphone; **to order sth by telephone** commander qch par téléphone; **the boss is on the telephone for you** le patron te demande au téléphone; **you're wanted on the telephone** on vous demande au téléphone □ **telephone banking** opérations fpl bancaires par téléphone; **telephone bill** facture f de téléphone; **telephone book** annuaire m (téléphonique); **telephone call** appel m téléphonique, coup m de téléphone; **telephone directory** annuaire m (téléphonique); **telephone exchange** central m téléphonique; **telephone message** message m téléphonique; **telephone number** numéro m de téléphone; **telephone order** commande f téléphonique ou par téléphone; **telephone subscriber** abonné(e) m,f du téléphone
2 vt téléphoner à; **to telephone New York** appeler New York
3 vi téléphoner

telephonist n Br téléphoniste mf

teleprinter n Br téléscripteur m, téléimprimeur m

teleprocessing n télétraitement m

telesales n téléventes fpl

teleshopping n téléachat m

teletex n COMPTR télétex m

teletypewriter n Am téléscripteur m, téléimprimeur m

teleworker n télétravailleur(euse) m,f

teleworking n télétravail m

telex **1** n télex m; **to send sth by telex** envoyer qch par télex
2 vt envoyer par télex, télexer

teller *n* caissier(ère) *m,f*, guichetier(ère) *m,f*

temp 1 *n* intérimaire *mf*
2 *vi* faire de l'intérim

temping *n* intérim *m* ❏ **temping agency** agence *f* d'intérim

template *n* COMPTR *(for keyboard)* réglette *f*; *(for program)* modèle *m*

temporary *adj (work, employee)* intérimaire, temporaire; *(measures)* temporaire, provisoire ❏ **temporary contract** *(for employment)* contrat *m* temporaire; CUSTOMS **temporary importation** importation *f* temporaire

> ❝
> There are a substantial number of boats berthed in EC waters, often under **temporary importation** arrangements and on which VAT has not been paid anywhere in the EC. In many cases, these boats have remained in EC waters for many years and have changed ownership several times. The view is almost certain to be that these tax-free boats should not remain in EC waters unless VAT is paid.
> ❞

tenable *adj* MKTG *(company)* défendable

tenancy *n* location *f*; *(period)* occupation *f*; **to take up the tenancy on a house** prendre une maison en location; **during my tenancy of the house** pendant que j'étais locataire de la maison ❏ **tenancy agreement** bail *m* (de location)

tenant *n* locataire *mf*

tendency *n* tendance *f* (**to** à); **an upward/downward tendency** *(in prices)* une tendance à la hausse/à la baisse

tender 1 *n (bid)* offre *f*, soumission *f*; **to make** *or* **put in a tender for sth** soumissionner *ou* faire une soumission pour qch; **to invite tenders for a job, to put a job out to tender** mettre un travail en adjudication; **by tender** par voie d'adjudication
2 *vt* (a) *(services)* offrir; *(bid, offer)* faire; *(resignation)* donner (b) *(money)* tendre
3 *vi* faire une soumission; **to tender for a contract** soumissionner à un appel d'offres

tenor *n* FIN *(of bill)* (terme *m* d')échéance *f*

tentative *adj (provisional)* provisoire

tenure *n (of post)* occupation *f*; *(of property)* bail *m*; *(of land)* fermage *m*; **during his tenure as chairman** pendant qu'il occupait le poste de président

term *n* (a) **terms** *(conditions)* conditions *fpl*; *(of agreement, contract)* termes *mpl*; *(rates,*

tariffs) conditions, tarifs *mpl*; **under the terms of the agreement** selon les termes de l'accord; **on easy terms** avec facilités de paiement ❏ **terms of credit** conditions de crédit; **terms of payment** conditions *ou* termes *mpl* de paiement; **terms of reference** *(of commission)* attributions *fpl*, mandat *m*; ECON **terms of trade** termes de l'échange
(b) FIN *(of bill of exchange)* (terme *m* d')échéance *f*; **to set** *or* **put a term to sth** mettre fin *ou* un terme à qch ❏ **term bill** effet *m* à terme; **term day** (jour *m* du) terme *m*; **term deposit** dépôt *m* à terme; **term draft** traite *f* à terme; **term loan** crédit *m* à terme
(c) *(duration)* terme *m*, période *f*; **the loan shall be for a term of ten years** l'emprunt sera conclu pour dix ans ❏ **term of notice** délai *m* de congé; **term of office** mandat *m*

terminal 1 *n* (a) *(at airport)* terminal *m*; *(for goods)* terminus *m* (b) COMPTR (poste *m*) terminal *m*
2 *adj* INS **terminal bonus** = bonus versé au titulaire d'une assurance-vie, au terme de celle-ci; FIN **terminal charges** charges *fpl* terminales; ACCT **terminal loss** perte *f* finale; ST EXCH **terminal market** marché *m* à terme; **terminal price** cours *m* du livrable

terminate *vt (employment, project)* mettre fin à; *(contract)* résilier

termination *n (of employment, project)* fin *f*; *(of contract)* résiliation *f*

terminator *n* COMPTR terminateur *m*

territorial waters *npl* eaux *fpl* territoriales

territory *n (of salesperson)* territoire *m*, région *f*

tertiary *adj (industry, market)* tertiaire

TESSA *n* Br *(abbr* **tax-exempt special savings account)** = plan d'épargne exonéré d'impôts

> ❝
> TESSAs are similar to personal-equity plans (PEPs), which also shelter savings from tax, but they should appeal to less sophisticated savers. That should help **TESSAs** to increase, rather than merely divert, saving. Mr King reckons that the net increase could be big: if 4m take out a **TESSA**, private saving could rise by about 30%.
> ❞

test 1 *n* (a) *(of machine, product, equipment)* essai *m*, épreuve *f*, test *m*; *(of quality)* contrôle *m*; **to carry out tests on sth** effectuer des tests sur qch ❏ **test certificate** certificat *m* d'essai

(b) *(of reaction, popularity)* évaluation *f* ❏ MKTG **test city** ville-test *f*; MKTG **test site** site-témoin *m*

2 *vt* **(a)** *(machine, product, equipment)* essayer; *(quality)* contrôler

(b) *(reaction, popularity)* mesurer, évaluer

testimonial *n (certificate)* attestation *f*; *(reference)* recommandation *f* ❏ MKTG **testimonial advertising** = publicité dans laquelle une célébrité recommande un produit

testing *n (of machine, product)* essai *m*, épreuve *f*; *(of quality)* contrôle *m*

text *n* COMPTR texte *m* ❏ **text block** bloc *m* de texte; **text buffer** mémoire *f* tampon de texte; **text editor** éditeur *m* de texte; **text file** fichier *m* texte; **text layout** disposition *f* de texte; **text mode** mode *m* texte; **text processing** traitement *m* de texte; **text processor** (unité *f* de) traitement de texte

thermal *adj* COMPTR **thermal paper** papier *m* thermique *ou* thermosensible; **thermal printer** imprimante *f* thermique *ou* thermoélectrique

think tank *n* groupe *m* d'experts

third *adj* troisième ❏ **third party** tierce personne *f*, tiers *m*; **third quarter** *(of year)* troisième trimestre *m*; **the Third World** le tiers-monde

third-party *adj* INS **third-party insurance** assurance *f* au tiers; **third-party liability** responsabilité *f* au tiers; **third-party risk** risque *m* de recours de tiers

threshold *n* seuil *m*; **the government has raised tax thresholds in line with inflation** le gouvernement a relevé les tranches de l'impôt pour tenir compte de l'inflation ❏ **threshold agreement** accord *m* d'indexation des salaires sur les prix; EU **threshold price** prix *m* du seuil

thrift *n Am* **thrift (institution)** *(savings bank)* caisse *f* d'épargne

thrive *vi (company, industry)* prospérer

thriving *adj (company, industry)* prospère, florissant(e)

through **1** *prep Am* **Monday through Friday** de lundi à vendredi

2 *adj* FIN **through bill** connaissement *m* direct; **through freight** marchandises *fpl* en transit

3 *adv (on telephone)* **to get through to sb** joindre qn; **to put sb through to sb** mettre qn en ligne avec qn, passer qn à qn

throughput *n* débit *m*, rendement *m*; COMPTR capacité *f* de traitement

thumbtack *n Am* punaise *f*

tick *Br* **1** *n* **(a)** *Fam (credit)* crédit *m*; **to buy sth on tick** acheter qch à crédit **(b)** *(mark)* coche *f*; **to put a tick against sth** cocher qch

2 *vt (on form)* cocher; **tick the appropriate box** cocher la case correspondante

ticket *n* **(a)** *(for plane, train)* billet *m*; *(for underground, bus)* ticket *m* **(b)** *(label)* étiquette *f* (de prix)

▸ **tie up** *vt sep (money)* immobiliser; **their money is all tied up in shares** leur argent est entièrement investi dans des actions

tied outlet *n* = magasin astreint par bail à vendre la marchandise d'un certain fabricant

tie-in *n* = livre, cassette etc lié à un film ou une émission ❏ MKTG **tie-in promotion** promotion *f* collective; *Am* **tie-in (sale)** vente *f* par lots

tiger economy *n* = pays à l'économie très performante; **the (Asian) tiger economies** les dragons *ou* les tigres asiatiques

> **"**
>
> Before the crisis broke, almost everybody was far too starry-eyed about East Asia's economic prospects. Now the mood has swung to the other extreme and many people are being too gloomy. Some myths about the **tiger economies'** success needed to be debunked …
>
> **"**

tight *adj* **(a)** *(schedule, deadline)* serré(e) **(b)** *(budget, credit, discount)* serré(e), resserré(e); **to work on a tight budget** travailler avec un budget serré

tighten *vt (budget, credit)* resserrer

till *n* caisse *f*; **to do the till** faire la caisse

time *n* **(a)** *(in general)* temps *m* ❏ **time frame** délai *m*; **time limit** délai; **the work must be completed within the time limit** le travail doit être terminé avant la date limite; **time management** gestion *f* du temps de travail; **time and motion consultant** organisateur-conseil *m*; **time and motion study** étude *f* de productivité *(qui se concentre sur l'efficacité des employés)*; MKTG **time pricing** fixation *f* des prix en fonction du moment; COMPTR **time sharing** partage *m* de temps; ST EXCH **time value** valeur *f* temporelle

(b) *(by clock)* heure *f*; **time of arrival/departure** heure d'arrivée/de départ ❏ **time card** feuille *f* de présence; **time difference** décalage *m* horaire; **time sheet** fiche *f* horaire; **time work** travail *m* à l'heure

(c) *(credit)* terme *m*; *Am* **to buy sth on time** acheter qch à tempérament *ou* à terme ❏ ST EXCH **time bargain** marché *m* à terme; FIN

time bill traite f à terme; *Am* **time deposit** dépôt m à terme; **time draft** traite f à terme; **time loan** emprunt m à terme; INS **time policy** police f à terme

(d) *(hourly wages)* **we pay time and a half on weekends** nous payons les heures du week-end une fois et demie le tarif normal; **overtime is paid at double time** les heures supplémentaires sont payées *ou* comptées double

timetable 1 n (a) *(for transport)* horaire m (b) *(schedule)* emploi m du temps

2 vt *(talks, meeting)* *(fix time of)* fixer une heure pour; *(fix date of)* fixer une date pour

tip 1 n *(cash)* pourboire m
2 vt donner un pourboire à

Tipp-Ex® **1** n correcteur m liquide, Tipp-Ex® m
2 vt **to Tipp-Ex sth out** effacer qch (avec du Tipp-Ex®)

TIR n *(abbr* **Transport International Routier***)* TIR m

title n (a) LAW droit m, titre m □ **title deed** titre (constitutif) de propriété (b) COMPTR **title bar** barre f de titre

toggle COMPTR **1** n **toggle key** touche f à bascule; **toggle switch** commande f à bascule
2 vi basculer; **to toggle between two applications** alterner entre deux applications

token adj *(payment, rent)* symbolique

tolerance n CUSTOMS tolérance f (permise)

toll n (a) *(on bridge, road)* péage m □ **toll bridge** pont m à péage; **toll road** route f à péage (b) *Am* TEL frais mpl d'interurbain □ **toll call** communication f interurbaine

toll-free *Am* **1** adj **toll-free number** ≃ numéro m vert
2 adv *(call)* gratuitement

tone n **leave a message after the tone** *(on answering machine)* laissez votre message après le bip sonore

toner n *(for printer, fax)* encre f □ **toner cartridge** cartouche f d'encre

tonnage n tonnage m, jauge f

tool n *(implement)* outil m; **(set of) tools** outillage m; **the computer has become an essential tool for most businesses** l'ordinateur est devenu un outil essentiel pour la plupart des entreprises; **to down tools** *(stop working)* cesser de travailler; *(go on strike)* se mettre en grève □ COMPTR **tool bar** barre f d'outils

toolbox n COMPTR boîte f à outils

top 1 n ST EXCH **to buy at the top and sell at the bottom** acheter au plus haut et vendre au plus bas; **the top of the range** le haut de gamme
2 adj **this job should be given top priority** ce travail doit être fait en priorité □ **top copy** *(of document)* original m; **top management** cadres mpl supérieurs; **top price** prix m fort; **top quality** qualité f supérieure
3 vt *(exceed)* dépasser; **production topped five tons last month** la production a dépassé les cinq tonnes le mois dernier; **to top sb's offer** renchérir sur l'offre de qn

top-down adj *(management)* contrôlé(e) par le haut □ MKTG **top-down forecasting** prévisions fpl hiérarchisées

top-heavy adj (a) *(company, structure)* trop lourd(e) du haut (b) FIN surcapitalisé(e)

> **“**
> Many corporations have **top-heavy**, vertical organization structures and new ideas just take too long to move through the business process.
> **”**

top-of-the-range adj haut de gamme

▶ **tot up** vt sep Br additionner

total 1 n total m; **the total comes to $389** cela fait au total 389 dollars
2 adj *(amount, cost, output, profit, loss)* total(e) □ **total annual expenses** consommations fpl de l'exercice; **total assets** total m de l'actif; **total asset value** valeur f de bilan; **total constructive loss** perte f totale; **total contract value** valeur f totale du contrat; **total fixed cost** coût m fixe total; **total insured value** valeur f totale assurée; **total liabilities** total m du passif; **total loss settlement** règlement m en perte totale; **total quality control** contrôle m de la qualité globale; **total quality management** gestion f de la qualité globale
3 vt (a) *(add up)* additionner (b) *(amount to)* s'élever à

totalize vt totaliser, additionner

touch n (a) *(communication)* **to be in touch with sb** être en contact avec qn; **to get in touch with sb** se mettre en contact avec qn (b) COMPTR **touch screen** écran m tactile

touch-sensitive adj COMPTR *(screen)* tactile; *(key, switch)* à effleurement

touch-tone telephone n téléphone m à touches

touch-type vi taper au toucher

tour n *(by tourist)* voyage m □ **tour operator** voyagiste m, tour-opérateur m

tourism *n* tourisme *m*

tourist *n* touriste *mf* ❏ *tourist class* (in air travel) classe *f* touriste; *tourist (information) office* bureau *m* de tourisme, syndicat *m* d'initiative; *the tourist trade* le tourisme

tower *n* COMPTR boîtier *m* vertical, tour *f* ❏ *tower system* système *m* à boîtier vertical *ou* à tour

town *n* *town planner* urbaniste *mf*; *town planning* urbanisme *m*

TQC *n* (abbr **total quality control**) QG *f*

TQM *n* (abbr **total quality management**) gestion *f* de la QG

> ❝
> The essence of **TQM** is the process of reducing costs by improving quality, so enhancing customer satisfaction. … Although, traditionally, customers are perceived as external to the organisation, **TQM** defines all working relationships in terms of customer satisfaction and quality is defined in terms of conformity to customer requirements.
> ❞

trackball *n* COMPTR boule *f* de commande, trackball *m ou f*

trade 1 *n* (**a**) (commerce) commerce *m*, affaires *fpl*; *it's good for trade* cela fait marcher le commerce; *to do a roaring trade* faire des affaires en or ❏ *trade agreement* accord *m* commercial; *trade association* association *f* professionnelle; *trade balance* balance *f* commerciale; *trade ban* interdiction *f* de commerce; *trade bills* effets *mpl* de commerce; *trade bloc* union *f* douanière; ACCT *trade credit* crédit *m* fournisseur; ACCT *trade creditor* créancier(ère) *m,f* d'exploitation; ACCT *trade debt* dettes *fpl* d'exploitation; ACCT *trade debtor* compte *m ou* créance *f* client; *trade deficit* déficit *m* commercial; *trade delegation* délégation *f* commerciale; Br *Trade Descriptions Act* = loi qui empêche la publicité mensongère; *trade exhibition* foire-exposition *f*, exposition *f* commerciale; *trade fair* foire *f* commerciale; *trade figures* chiffre *m* d'affaires; *trade gap* déficit *m* commercial; *trade practices* usages *mpl* commerciaux; ST EXCH *trade price* prix *m* de négociation

(**b**) (profession) métier *m*; *to be in the trade* être du métier; *he's a plumber by trade* il est plombier de son état *ou* métier ❏ *trade body* syndicat *m* professionnel; *trade discount*

remise *f* professionnelle; *trade name* (of product) nom *m* de marque; (of company) raison *f* commerciale; Br *trade press* presse *f* spécialisée *ou* professionnelle; *trade register* registre *m* du commerce; *trade representative* délégué(e) *m,f* commercial(e); *trade secret* secret *m* professionnel; Br *trade union* syndicat *m*; *Trades Union Congress* = confédération des syndicats britanniques; *trade unionism* syndicalisme *m*; *trade unionist* syndicaliste *mf*; *trade union tariff* tarif *m* syndical

(**c**) Am (transaction) marché *m*, affaire *f*

2 *vt* ST EXCH négocier ❏ *traded option* option *f* négociable

3 *vi* (**a**) (do business) faire du commerce, commercer; *he trades in clothing* il est négociant en confection; *the company trades under the name of Prism Ltd* l'entreprise opère sous le nom de Prism Ltd; *to trade at a loss* vendre à perte; *to trade with sb* avoir des relations commerciales avec qn

(**b**) ST EXCH (of shares, commodity, currency) s'échanger (**at** à); *corn is trading at $2.20* le maïs se négocie à 2,20 dollars

▸ **trade down** *vi* ST EXCH acheter des valeurs basses

▸ **trade in** *vt sep* faire reprendre

▸ **trade up** *vi* ST EXCH acheter des valeurs hautes

trade-in *n* reprise *f* ❏ *trade-in price* prix *m* à la reprise; *trade-in value* valeur *f* de reprise

trademark *n* marque *f* (de fabrique)

trader *n* commerçant(e) *m,f*, marchand(e) *m,f*; (on large scale) négociant(e) *m,f*; ST EXCH opérateur(trice) *m,f*

tradesman *n* (**a**) (tradesman) commerçant *m*, marchand *m* (**b**) (skilled workman) ouvrier *m* qualifié

trading *n* commerce *m*, négoce *m*; *trading on the Stock Exchange was heavy* le volume de transactions à la Bourse était important ❏ ACCT *trading account* compte *m* d'exploitation; *trading bank* banque *f* commerciale; *trading capital* capital *m* engagé *ou* de roulement; *trading company* entreprise *f* commerciale; ST EXCH *trading day* jour *m* de Bourse; Br *trading estate* zone *f* industrielle; ST EXCH *trading floor* parquet *m*, corbeille *f*; *trading hours* FIN heures *fpl* d'ouverture; ST EXCH horaires *fpl* des criées; *trading licence* carte *f* de commerce; *trading loss* perte *f*; ST EXCH *trading member* intermédiaire *m* négociateur; ST EXCH *trading order* ordre *m* de négociation; *trading partner* partenaire *m* commercial;

Am ST EXCH **trading post** parquet *m*, corbeille *f*; **trading profit** bénéfice *m* d'exploitation; ACCT **trading and profit and loss account** compte *m* de résultat; ST EXCH **trading range** écart *m* de prix; **prices are stuck in a trading range** les prix ne varient pas beaucoup; **trading results** résultats *mpl* de l'exercice; **trading standards** normes *fpl* de conformité; Br **Trading Standards Office** ≃ Direction *f* de la consommation et de la représentation des fraudes; **trading year** exercice *m* comptable

traffic 1 *n* (trade) commerce *m*; (illegal) trafic *m* ❑ MKTG **traffic builder** article *m* d'appel

2 *vi* **to traffic in sth** faire le commerce de qch; (illegally) faire le trafic de qch

train 1 *vt* (employee) former; **he's training somebody to take over from him** il forme son successeur; **she was trained in economics** elle a reçu une formation d'économiste

2 *vi* recevoir une formation; **to train as an accountant** recevoir une formation de comptable; **where did you train?** où avez-vous reçu votre formation?

trained *adj* qualifié(e); (engineer, translator) diplômé(e)

trainee *n* stagiaire *mf*; **trainee computer programmer** élève *mf* programmeur

traineeship *n* stage *f*

training *n* formation *f*; **I have had business training** j'ai suivi une formation commerciale ❑ **training centre** centre *m* de formation; **training course** stage *m* (de formation); **training officer** directeur(trice) *m,f* de formation; **training programme** programme *m* de formation; **training scheme** plan *m* de formation; **training time** temps *m* de formation

tranche *n* (of loan, payment, shares) tranche *f*

> ❝ It is noticeable that the French **tranche**, covering 50 per cent of the issue, is being sold by a general offer for sale while the British **tranche**, half as large, is split between an offer and a placing with institutions. ❞

transact *vt* (deal, purchase, sale) traiter, négocier; **to transact business (with sb)** faire des affaires (avec qn)

transaction *n* (a) (deal) opération *f* (commerciale), affaire *f*; ST EXCH, FIN transaction *f*; **cash transactions have increased** les mouvements d'espèces ont

augmenté (b) (act of transacting) conduite *f*, gestion *f*; **transaction of business will continue as normal** la conduite des affaires se poursuivra comme à l'accoutumé

transfer 1 *n* (a) (of employee) mutation *f*; (of goods) transfert *m*, transport *m*; (of air passenger) transfert; FIN, ST EXCH (of shares, funds, capital) transfert; BANKING (of money from one account to another) virement *m* ❑ **transfer cheque** chèque *m* de virement; ST EXCH **transfer duty** droits *mpl* de transfert; ST EXCH **transfer fee** frais *mpl* de transfert; ST EXCH **transfer form** formule *f* de transfert; FIN **transfer order** ordre *m* de virement; **transfer passenger** (between flights) voyageur(euse) *m,f* en transit; ST EXCH **transfer register** registre *m* des transferts

(b) ACCT (of debt) transport *m*; (of entry) contre-passation *f* ❑ **transfer entry** article *m* de contre-passation

(c) LAW (of property, ownership, rights) cession *f* ❑ **transfer deed** acte *m* de cession; acte translatif (de propriété); Br **transfer tax** droits *mpl* de succession; (between living persons) droit de mutation

(d) COMPTR (of data) transfert *m* ❑ **transfer speed** vitesse *f* de transfert

2 *vt* (a) (employee) muter; (goods) transférer, transporter; FIN (shares, funds, capital) transférer; BANKING (money) virer

(b) ACCT (debt) transporter; (entry) contre-passer

(c) LAW (property, ownership, rights) céder, faire cession de; **she will transfer the rights over to him** elle va lui céder les droits

(d) TEL (call) transférer; **I'm transferring you now** je vous mets en communication ❑ Br **transfer charge call** communication *f* en PCV

(e) COMPTR (data) transférer

3 *vi* (a) (of employee) être muté(e); **to transfer to a different department** être transféré(e) dans un autre service

(b) (of air passenger) changer

transferable *adj* (document) transmissible; LAW (property, ownership, rights) cessible ❑ **transferable bond** obligation *f* transmissible *ou* transférable; **transferable credit** crédit *m* transférable; **transferable securities** valeurs *fpl* négociables; **transferable share** action *f* au porteur

transferee *n* FIN, ST EXCH (of shares, funds, capital) bénéficiaire *mf*; LAW (of property, ownership, rights) cessionnaire *mf*

transferor *n* FIN, ST EXCH (of shares, funds, capital) vendeur(euse) *m,f*; LAW (of property, ownership, rights) cédant(e) *m,f*

tranship, transhipment = **transship, transshipment**

transit n transit m; **in transit** en transit; **goods lost in transit** marchandises perdues en cours de route □ CUSTOMS *transit visa* visa m de transit

transparency n *(for overhead projector)* transparent m

transport 1 n transport m; **means of transport** moyen m de transport □ *transport company* société f de transport; *transport costs* frais mpl de transport; *transport facilities* moyens mpl de transport
　2 vt transporter

transportation n transport m

transship vt transborder

transshipment n transbordement m □ *transshipment bill of lading* connaissement m de transbordement

trash n Am COMPTR poubelle f

travel 1 n voyages mpl □ *travel agency* agence f de voyages; *travel agent* agent m de voyages; *travel allowance* indemnité f de déplacement; *travel documents* titre m de transport; *travel expenses* frais mpl de déplacement
　2 vi voyager; **to travel on business** voyager pour affaires

traveling Am = **travelling**

traveller, Am **traveler** n voyageur(euse) m,f □ *traveller's cheque* chèque m de voyage

travelling, Am **traveling** 1 n voyages mpl □ *travelling allowance* indemnité f de déplacement; *travelling expenses* frais mpl de déplacement
　2 adj *travelling salesman* voyageur m de commerce

treasurer n trésorier(ère) m,f □ *treasurer's report* rapport m financier

treasury n *(funds)* trésor m (public); *(place)* trésorerie f; **the Treasury** *(government department)* ≃ le ministère des finances □ FIN *Treasury bill, Treasury bond* ≃ bon m du Trésor; Am *Treasury Secretary* ≃ ministre m des finances

"
Long-term **Treasury-bond** yields were as low as 7.75% towards the end of 1989. Bond prices have since fallen and yields risen, partly because of inflation worries, but more because of a worldwide liquidity squeeze which has caused bond yields to rise virtually everywhere. The 30-year **Treasury bond** yielded 8.45% on March 20th.
"

treaty n *(international)* traité m; *(between individuals)* contrat m, accord m; **they sold the property by private treaty** ils ont vendu la propriété par accord privé

trend n tendance f; **the general trend of the market** les tendances du marché; **house prices are on an upward/downward trend** les prix des maisons est à la hausse/baisse □ MKTG *trend analysis* analyse f des tendances; *trend reversal* renversement m de tendance

triad market n MKTG marché m de la triade

trial 1 n (a) *(test)* essai m; **to give sth a trial** faire l'essai de qch; **on trial** à l'essai; **give her a month's trial before you take her on** prenez-la un mois à l'essai avant de l'embaucher □ *trial lot* envoi m à titre d'essai; *trial order* commande f à l'essai; *trial period* période f d'essai
　(b) ACCT *trial balance* balance f d'inventaire
　(c) LAW procès m; **to stand trial (for sth)** passer en justice (pour qch); **to bring sb to trial (for sth)** faire passer qn en justice (pour qch)
　2 vt tester

tribunal n tribunal m

trickle-down theory n ECON = théorie selon laquelle les richesses accumulées par un petit nombre bénéficieront à tous les membres de la société

"
And on Sunday, the Archbishop of Canterbury, George Carey (at a service of dedication to mark — of all things — the advent of the single European market), inveighed against the **"trickle-down" theory** of wealth distribution, whereby ever-higher incomes for the wealthy are somehow supposed "naturally" to find their way through to the poor.
"

trigger 1 n *(of change, decision)* déclenchement m; **the strike was the trigger for nationwide protests** la grève a donné le signal d'un mouvement de contestation dans tous le pays
　2 vt déclencher; **the crisis has triggered huge numbers of closures** la crise a déclenché un grand nombre de fermetures

▸ **trigger off** vt sep déclencher

triple-A rating n ST EXCH notation f AAA

triplicate 1 *n* triplicata *m*; **in triplicate** en trois exemplaires
2 *vt (document)* rédiger en trois exemplaires

troubleshoot *vi* régler un problème

troubleshooter *n (in conflict)* média-teur(trice) *m,f*; *(in crisis)* expert *m (appelé en cas de crise)*

troubleshooting *n (in conflict)* média-tion *f*; COMPTR dépannage *m*

trough *n* ECON *(of wave, graph, cycle)* creux *m*

truck 1 *n* camion *m* ❑ **truck driver** camion-neur *m*
2 *vt* camionner, transporter par camion

trucker *n Am* camionneur *m*

true *adj* **true copy** *(of document)* copie *f* conforme; ACCT **true and fair view** *(of accounts)* image *f* fidèle

trust *n* **(a)** LAW *(investment)* fidéicommis *m*; **to set up a trust for sb** instituer un fidéicommis pour qn ❑ **trust account** compte *m* en fidéicommis; **trust deed** acte *m* de fidéicommis; **trust fund** fonds *m* en fidéicommis **(b)** FIN *(cartel)* trust *m*, cartel *m* ❑ **trust bank** banque *f* de gestion de patrimoine; **trust company** société *f* fiduciaire

trusted third party *n* COMPTR *(for Internet transactions)* tierce partie *f* de confiance

❝
At the moment a mere $200m worth of goods are sold across the Internet each year. All the estimates of this figure reaching $30 billion by the end of the decade will count for little unless somebody comes up with some kind of 'digital signature' that gives users the same assurance that face-to-face contact, a physical address or even a driving licence does in the real world. Ideally, a digital signature should be guaranteed by some **trusted third party** — eg, a credit-card firm or a government body.
❞

trustee *n* LAW *(of fund, property)* fidéicommissaire *m*; *(of charity)* adminis-trateur(trice) *mf*

TTP *n* COMPTR *(abbr* **trusted third party***)* *(for Internet transactions)* TPC *f*

TUC *n Br (abbr* **Trades Union Congress***)* = confédération des syndicats britanniques

turbomarketing *n* MKTG turbo-marketing *m*

▸ **turn down** *vt sep (applicant, job)* refuser; *(offer)* rejeter

▸ **turn out** *vt sep (goods)* produire, fabriquer

▸ **turn over** *vt sep (capital)* faire rouler; **he turns over £1,000 a week** son chiffre d'affaires est de 1000 livres par semaine

▸ **turn round** *vt sep (process, deal with)* traiter, s'occuper de; **the stocks are turned round every four months** le délai de rotation (des stocks) est de quatre mois

turnaround *n (of order)* traitement *m*; **they offer a faster turnaround** leurs délais sont plus courts ❑ **turnaround time** délai *m* d'exécution

turnkey *adj (project, operation, system)* clés en main

turnover *n* **(a)** FIN *(of company)* chiffre *m* d'affaires; **his turnover is £100,000 per annum** il fait 100 000 livres d'affaires par an ❑ **turnover tax** impôt *m* ou taxe *f* sur le chiffre d'affaires
(b) *(of stock)* écoulement *m*, rotation *f*; *(of capital)* roulement *m*; **the staff turnover there is very high** le taux de renouvellement du personnel y est très élevé ❑ **turnover rate** vitesse *f* de rotation des stocks

tutorial *n* COMPTR didacticiel *m* ❑ **tutorial program** didacticiel

tycoon *n* magnat *m*; **an oil tycoon** un magnat du pétrole

type 1 *vt* taper (à la machine); **to type sth into a computer** saisir qch à l'ordinateur
2 *vi* taper (à la machine)

▸ **type out** *vt sep* taper (à la machine)

▸ **type up** *vt sep* taper (à la machine)

typewriter *n* machine *f* à écrire

typing *n* dactylographie *f* ❑ **typing error** faute *f* de frappe; **typing paper** papier *m* machine; **typing pool** équipe *f* de dactylos; **typing speed** vitesse *f* de frappe

typist *n* dactylographe *mf*

ullage *n* = quantité de liquide perdue par l'évaporation ou par des fuites au cours du transport

ultimate *adj* **ultimate consumer** utilisateur(trice) *m,f* final(e); **ultimate holding company** holding *m* tête de groupe *(dont certaines filiales sont également des holdings)*

umbrella *n* **umbrella committee** comité *m* de coordination; **umbrella fund** fonds *m* de consolidation; **umbrella organization** organisme *m* de tutelle

> ❝
> To try to make money by switching currencies according to exchange rates is considered risky and not in general the purpose of these accounts. In such instances a managed currency fund or an **umbrella fund** offering a choice of separate currencies would be more appropriate. However, most banks will exchange currency at short notice.
> ❞

UN *n* *(abbr* **United Nations***)* ONU*f*

unabsorbed cost *n* coût *m* non-absorbé

unaccounted for *adj (money)* qui manque; **these sixty pounds are unaccounted for in the balance sheet** ces soixante livres ne figurent pas au bilan; **there is still a lot of money unaccounted for** il manque toujours beaucoup d'argent

unallotted *adj* FIN, ST EXCH *(shares)* non réparti(e)

unanimous *adj (consent, decision)* unanime ▫ **unanimous vote** vote *m* à l'unanimité

unappropriated *adj (money)* inutilisé(e), disponible ▫ **unappropriated profits** bénéfices *mpl* non distribués

unaudited *adj (figures)* non certifié(e)

unauthorized *adj* non autorisé(e) ▫ COMPTR **unauthorized access** accès *m* non autorisé

unavailable *adj (person)* indisponible, non disponible; *(goods, resources)* qu'on ne peut se procurer; **the manager is unavailable** le directeur n'est pas disponible

unbalanced *adj* **(a)** ACCT *(account)* non soldé(e) **(b)** FIN *(economy)* déséquilibré(e)

unbankable *adj* FIN *(bill)* non bancable

unbranded *adj* MKTG sans marque

unbundle *vt (company)* dégrouper

unbundling *n (of company)* dégroupage *m*

uncallable *adj (bond)* non remboursable

uncalled *adj* FIN *(capital)* non appelé(e)

unclaimed *adj (dividend)* non réclamé(e)

unconditional *adj (acceptance, offer)* sans condition ▫ FIN **unconditional order** ordre *m* (de payer) pur et simple

unconfirmed letter of credit *n* lettre *f* de crédit révocable

unconscionable bargain *n* LAW contrat *m* léonin

unconsolidated *adj* FIN *(debt)* non consolidé(e)

uncovered *adj* FIN *(purchase, sale)* à découvert; *(cheque)* sans provision ▫ **uncovered advance** avance *f* à découvert; **uncovered balance** découvert *m*; ST EXCH **uncovered position** position *f* non couverte

uncrossed *adj (cheque)* non barré(e)

UNCTAD *n* *(abbr* **United Nations Conference on Trade and Development***)* CNUCED*f*

> ❝
> Superficially, the rich countries appeared to make two concessions to the **UNCTAD** complaint of inequality in international trade. One was to acknowledge that GATT's rules should take account of levels of economic development, and that developing countries henceforward would not invariably be expected to make reciprocal concessions to the rich, developed countries.
> ❞

undated *adj* non daté(e), sans date

underbid *vt (for tender)* faire des soumissions plus avantageuses que

undercapitalization *n* sous-capitalisation*f*

undercapitalized *adj* sous-capitalisé(e)

undercut *vt (competitor)* vendre moins cher que; *(prices)* casser

underdeveloped *adj* ECON *(country)* sous-développé(e)

underemployed *adj* ECON sous-employé(e)

underemployment *n* ECON sous-emploi *m*

underequipped *adj* sous-équipé(e)

underfunded *adj* sous-capitalisé(e)

underground economy *n* économie *f* souterraine

> ""
> But the domestic parts of some countries … are riddled with regulations or government-protected monopolies that stifle competition, stunt growth and drive businesses into the **underground economy**.
> ""

underinsure *vt* sous-assurer

undermanned *adj* à court de personnel

underpaid *adj* sous-payé(e)

underpin *vt* (market) soutenir

underpriced *adj* au-dessous de la valeur

undersell *vt* (person, company) vendre moins cher que; (goods) vendre au-dessous de la valeur de

undersigned **1** *n* the undersigned le (la) soussigné(e); **I, the undersigned declare that…** je soussigné déclare que…
   2 *adj* soussigné(e)

understaffed *adj* qui manque de personnel; **to be understaffed** manquer de personnel

understanding *n* (agreement) accord *m*, entente *f*; **to come to an understanding with sb (about sth)** s'entendre avec qn (sur qch)

undertake *vt* (job, project) se charger de, entreprendre; (responsibility) assumer; **to undertake to do sth** entreprendre de faire qch

undertaking *n* (**a**) (enterprise) entreprise *f* (**b**) (promise) engagement *m*; **to give an undertaking to do sth** s'engager à faire qch

undervaluation *n* (of goods) sous-évaluation *f*

undervalue *vt* (goods) sous-évaluer

underwater *adj* Am (share prices) décoté(e) □ **underwater option** option *f* à prix glissant à la baisse

underwrite *vt* (**a**) INS (policy, risk) garantir (**b**) ST EXCH (new issue) garantir, souscrire

underwriter *n* (**a**) INS (of policy, risk) assureur *m* (**b**) ST EXCH (of new issue) syndicataire *mf* □ **underwriter agent** agent *m* souscripteur

underwriting *n* (**a**) INS (of policy, risk) garantie *f* (**b**) ST EXCH (of new issue) garantie *f*, souscription *f* □ **underwriting agent** agent *m* souscripteur; **underwriting commission** commission *f* de garantie; **underwriting contract** contrat *m* de garantie; **underwriting fee** commission *f* de placement; **underwriting share** part *f* syndicataire; **underwriting syndicate** syndicat *m* de prise ferme

undischarged *adj* (**a**) LAW (bankrupt) non réhabilité(e) (**b**) FIN (debt) non liquidé(e)

undisclosed *adj* (sum) non révélé(e) □ **undisclosed principal** acheteur(euse) *m,f* non identifié(e) *ou* anonyme

undiscountable *adj* FIN inescomptable

undistributed *adj* (money, earnings) non distribué(e) □ **undistributed profit** bénéfice *m* non distribué

undo *vt* COMPTR (command) annuler, défaire

unearned income *n* revenus *mpl* non professionels, rentes *fpl*

> ""
> Private productive property provides massive **unearned income**, and also frequently forms the basis of economic power. **Unearned income** derives from: (i) rent on buildings or land; (ii) dividends paid from profit of firms to shareholders; and (iii) interest on monetary investments such as deposit accounts or government securities.
> ""

uneconomic *adj* Br (unprofitable) peu rentable

uneconomical *adj* (person) peu économe; (machine, method, approach) peu économique

unedited *adj* COMPTR (text) non édité(e)

unemployed **1** *npl* the unemployed les chômeurs *mpl*, les sans-emploi *mpl*
   2 *adj* (**a**) (person) en chômage, sans emploi (**b**) (capital, funds) inemployé(e)

unemployment *n* chômage *m* □ Br **unemployment benefit**, Am **unemployment compensation** allocation *f* chômage, indemnité *f* de chômage; **unemployment fund** caisse *f* de chômage; **unemployment insurance** assurance *f* chômage; **unemployment level, unemployment rate** taux *m* de chômage

unendorsed *adj* (cheque) non endossé(e)

unenforceable *adj (contract)* non exécutoire

unexchangeable *adj* FIN *(securities)* impermutable, inéchangeable

unfair *adj* **unfair competition** concurrence *f* déloyale; **unfair dismissal** licenciement *m* abusif

unfavourable, *Am* **unfavorable** *adj (balance of trade, exchange rate)* défavorable

unformatted *adj* COMPTR *(disk)* non formaté(e)

unfunded *adj* sans capitaux suffisants □ FIN **unfunded debt** dette *f* flottante

ungeared *adj* sans endettement

UNIDO *n (abbr* **United Nations Industrial Development Organization)** UNIDO *f*

uniform business rate *n* Br taxe *f* professionnelle

unilateral *adj (action, decision, contract)* unilatéral(e)

uninitialized *adj* COMPTR non initialisé(e)

uninsured *adj* non assuré(e)

union *n (trade union)* syndicat *m* □ **union agreement** convention *f* collective; **union card** carte *f* syndicale; **union meeting** réunion *f* syndicale; **union member** syndiqué(e) *m,f*; **union representative** délégué(e) *m,f* syndical(e)

unionism *n* syndicalisme *m*

unionist *n* syndicaliste *mf*

unionize *vt* syndiquer

unique *adj* MKTG **unique proposition** proposition *f* unique; **unique selling point** *or* **proposition** proposition unique de vente

unissued *adj (shares, share capital)* non encore émis(e)

unit *n* unité *f*; **each lot contains a hundred units** chaque lot contient cent unités □ EU **unit of account** unité de compte; **unit of consumption** unité de consommation; **unit cost** prix *m* de revient unitaire; **unit of currency** unité monétaire; **unit of labour** unité de travail; **unit price** prix unitaire *ou* à l'unité; **unit of production** unité de production; Br **unit trust** sicav *f*, fonds *m* commun de placement

unitary *adj* unitaire

United Nations *npl* **the United Nations** les Nations *fpl* Unies

unlawful *adj* illégal(e)

unlimited *adj (funds)* inépuisable; INS *(cover)* sans limitation de somme □ **unlimited**

company société *f* à responsabilité illimitée; **unlimited liability** responsabilité *f* illimitée

unlisted *adj* **(a)** ST EXCH *(share, company)* non coté(e), non inscrit(e) à la cote □ **unlisted market** Bourse *f* coulisse; **unlisted securities market** second marché *m* **(b)** Am *(telephone number)* sur la liste rouge

> ❝ ──────────────
> … Sherwood Group (steady at 760p and now capitalised at £140m) is looking too big for the **unlisted securities market** and a move up to the main market may well accompany Tuesday's year-end profits.
> ────────────── ❞

unload 1 *vt (ship, truck, goods)* décharger **2** *vi* **(a)** *(of ship, truck)* décharger **(b)** Am *(flood market)* inonder le marché

unlock *vt (assets)* débloquer

unmarketable *adj (goods)* invendable; *(assets)* non réalisable

unmortgaged *adj* libre d'hypothèques

unnegotiable *adj (cheque, bill)* non négociable

UNO *n (abbr* **United Nations Organization)** ONU *f*

unofficial *adj (appointment, meeting)* non officiel(elle) □ **unofficial strike** grève *f* sauvage

unpaid *adj* **(a)** *(person)* non salarié(e); *(post)* non rétribué(e) □ **unpaid leave** congé *m* sans solde **(b)** *(account, bill, debt, salary)* impayé(e)

unproductive *adj (capital, work)* improductif(ive)

unproductiveness *n* improductivité *f*

unprofessional *adj* peu professionnel(elle)

unprofitable *adj (business)* peu rentable; *(discussions)* peu profitable

unquoted *adj* ST EXCH *(share)* non coté(e) □ **unquoted company** société *f* non cotée; **unquoted securities** valeurs *fpl* non cotées

unreadable *adj* COMPTR illisible

unrealizable *adj* FIN *(capital, assets)* non réalisable

unrealized *adj* FIN *(capital, assets)* non réalisé(e); *(gain, loss)* latent(e)

unredeemed *adj* FIN *(loan)* non amorti(e), non remboursé(e); *(draft)* non honoré(e); *(mortgage)* non purgé(e)

unrest *n* agitation *f*

unsaleable *adj (goods)* invendable

unsecured *adj* *(loan, overdraft)* non garanti(e), à découvert; *(debt)* sans garantie ❑ *unsecured advance* avance *f* à découvert; *unsecured creditor* créancier(ère) *m,f* ordinaire; *unsecured debenture* obligation *f* non garantie

> The position of a secured creditor is to be contrasted with that of an **unsecured creditor** who merely has a personal claim to sue for the payment of his debt and to invoke the available legal processes for the enforcement of any judgment that he may obtain.

unsettled *adj* (a) *(market)* instable (b) *(account, bill, debt)* impayé(e)

unskilled *adj* *(worker)* non qualifié(e), non spécialisé(e); *(job, work)* qui ne nécessite pas de connaissances professionnelles ❑ *unskilled labour* main-d'œuvre *f* non spécialisée; *unskilled labourer* ouvrier(ère) *m,f* non spécialisé(e)

unsocial *adj* **to work unsocial hours** travailler en dehors des heures normales

unsold *adj* invendu(e)

unsound *adj* *(enterprise, investment)* peu sûr(e), risqué(e); *(business)* peu sûr, précaire; **the project is economically unsound** le projet n'est pas sain *ou* viable sur le plan économique

unspent *adj* *(sum, balance)* non dépensé(e)

unstable *adj* *(market, prices)* instable

unstamped *adj* *(letter)* sans timbre, non affranchi(e); *(document)* non estampillé(e)

unsteady *adj* *(prices)* variable; *(market)* agité(e)

unsubscribed *adj* *(capital)* non souscrit(e)

untaxed *adj* *(income)* exempt(e) *ou* exonéré(e) d'impôt; *(goods)* non imposé(e), non taxé(e)

untradable *adj* ST EXCH incotable

unweighted *adj* ECON *(index)* non pondéré(e) ❑ *unweighted figures* chiffres *mpl* bruts

unzip *vt* COMPTR dézipper

UP *n* *(abbr* **unit price***)* PU *m*

up 1 *adj* COMPTR *up arrow* flèche *f* vers le haut
   2 *adv* (a) *(higher)* **the price of gold is up** le prix de l'or a augmenté; **the pound is up ten cents against the dollar** la livre a gagné dix cents par rapport au dollar; **profits are up**

25% on last year les profits ont augmenté de 25% par rapport à l'année dernière
   (b) **up front** *(pay)* d'avance

update COMPTR **1** *n* *(of software package)* mise *f* à jour, actualisation *f*
   2 *vt* mettre à jour, actualiser

upgradable *adj* COMPTR *(hardware, system)* évolutif(ive); *(memory)* extensible

upgrade COMPTR **1** *n* *(of hardware, system)* augmentation *f* de puissance; *(of software)* mise *f* à jour, actualisation *f* ❑ *upgrade kit* kit *m* d'évolution *ou* d'extension
   2 *vt* *(hardware, system)* optimiser; *(software)* améliorer, perfectionner

upkeep *n* *(maintenance)* entretien *m*; *(cost)* frais *mpl* d'entretien

upload *vt* COMPTR télécharger *(vers un gros ordinateur)*

upper *adj* *upper case* haut *m* de casse, (lettres *fpl*) majuscules *fpl*; *upper limit* plafond *m*

upper-case *adj* en haut de casse, en (lettres) majuscules

UPS *n* COMPTR *(abbr* **uninterruptible power supply***)* onduleur *m*

upset price *n* *(at auction)* mise *f* à prix

upside *n* *(trend)* **prices have been on the upside** les prix ont été à la hausse ❑ ST EXCH *upside risk* risque *m* de hausse

upstream *adj* *(company)* en amont

upswing *n* mouvement *m* vers la hausse; **the Stock Market is on the upswing** la Bourse est en haussse; **there has been an upswing in sales** il y a eu une progression des ventes

> We now have an outline of the reasons for an **upswing** in economic activity and for an increase in the rate of surplus-value. But the faster the **upswing**, the more bunched replacements will be and the sooner a new crisis will loom on the horizon.

up-to-date *adj* (a) *(most recent)* à jour; **to bring sb up-to-date on sth** mettre qn au courant de qch (b) *(modern)* *(machinery, methods)* moderne

uptrend *n* tendance *f* à la hausse

upturn *n* *(in economy)* redressement *m*; *(in production, sales)* reprise *f*, progression *f*; **there has been an upturn in the market** il y a eu une progression du marché

upward *adj* FIN *upward movement* mouvement *m* de hausse; *upward trend* tendance *f* à la hausse

upward-compatible *adj* COMPTR compatible vers le haut

urgent *adj* urgent(e); **it's not urgent** ce n'est pas urgent

URL *n* COMPTR (*abbr* **uniform resource locator**) (adresse *f*) URL *m*

usance *n* BANKING, FIN *(time limit)* usance *f*; **at thirty days' usance** à usance de trente jours □ *usance bill* effet *m* à usance

user *n* *(of machine, computer)* utilisateur(trice) *m,f*; *(of telephone)* abonné(e) *m,f* □ COMPTR *user ID, user identification* identification *f* de l'utilisateur; *user interface* interface *f* utilisateur; *user language* langage *m* utilisateur; *user manual* manuel *m* d'utilisation; *user name* nom *m* de l'utilisateur; *user software* logiciel *m* utilisateur; *user support* assistance *f* à l'utilisateur

user-definable *adj* COMPTR *(characters, keys)* définissable par l'utilisateur

user-friendly *adj* convivial(e)

USM *n* ST EXCH (*abbr* **unlisted securities market**) second marché *m*

USP *n* MKTG (*abbr* **unique selling point** *or* **proposition**) proposition *f* unique de vente

> **"**
>
> In other words, it should be offering the potential buyer at least one, possibly only one, clear reason for purchase. In its extreme form, this is an expression of the Unique Selling Proposition, or **USP** … Very simply, the theory behind this is that any product has some characteristic which can be developed so as to make it unique in its class.
>
> **"**

usufruct *n* LAW usufruit *m*

usury *n* usure *f*

utility *n* (**a**) *(service)* **(public) utility** service *m* public □ *Am* **utility stocks** valeurs *fpl* de services publics (**b**) COMPTR programme *m* utilitaire, utilitaire *m* □ *utility program* (logiciel *m*) utilitaire

utilization *n* utilisation *f*

utilize *vt* *(use)* utiliser, se servir de; *(make best use of)* exploiter

vacancy *n* poste *m* vacant; **to fill a vacancy** pourvoir à un emploi; **the vacancy has been filled** le poste a été pourvu; **we have a vacancy for a sales assistant** nous avons un poste de vendeur à pourvoir, nous cherchons un vendeur; **do you have any vacancies?** avez-vous des postes à pourvoir?

vacant *adj* (**a**) *(job, position)* à pourvoir, vacant(e); **there are several vacant places to be filled** il y a plusieurs postes à pourvoir; **a secretarial job has become vacant** un poste de secrétaire est devenu disponible *ou* vacant (**b**) *(room, apartment)* libre ❑ *vacant possession* libre possession *f*; **apartments sold with vacant possession** appartements libres à la vente

vacate *vt (hotel room)* quitter, libérer; *(house, property)* quitter; *(job)* démissionner de; LAW **to vacate the premises** vider les lieux

vacation *n* (**a**) *Am (holiday)* vacances *fpl*; **a month's vacation** un mois de vacances; **to be on/go on vacation** être/aller en vacances; **to get vacation with pay** avoir les congés payés ❑ *vacation leave* congés *mpl* annuels (**b**) *Br* LAW *(of courts)* vacations *fpl*, vacances *fpl* judiciaires

vacuum-packed *adj* emballé(e) sous vide

valid *adj (contract, passport)* valide, valable; **valid for six months** valable six mois

validate *vt* valider

validation *n* validation *f*

validity *n* validité *f*

valium picnic *n Am Fam (quiet day on New York Stock Exchange)* séance *f* morne

valorization *n* FIN valorisation *f*

valorize *vt* FIN valoriser

valuable **1** *n* **valuables** objets *mpl* de valeur **2** *adj* de valeur

valuation *n* FIN (**a**) *(act)* évaluation *f*, estimation *f*, expertise *f*; **to get a valuation of sth** faire évaluer *ou* estimer *ou* expertiser qch; **to make a valuation of sth** évaluer *ou* estimer *ou* expertiser qch ❑ *valuation charge* taxation *f* à la valeur (**b**) *(price)* évaluation *f*; **the valuation put on the business is £100,000** l'affaire a été

évaluée *ou* estimée *ou* expertisée à 100 000 livres

valuator *n* expert *m (en expertise de biens)*

value **1** *n* valeur *f*; **to be of value** avoir de la valeur; **to be of no value** être sans valeur; **to be good/poor value (for money)** être d'un bon/mauvais rapport qualité-prix; **to go up/down in value** prendre/perdre de la valeur; **to set** *or* **put a value on sth** estimer la valeur de qch; **they put a value of £150,000 on the property** ils ont estimé *ou* expertisé la propriété à 150 000 livres; **of no commercial value** sans valeur commerciale; **to the value of** pour une valeur de; **what will this do to the value of property?** quel effet est-ce que ça va avoir sur le prix de l'immobilier? ❑ BANKING *value in account* valeur en compte; *value added* valeur ajoutée; *value analysis* analyse *f* de valeur; MKTG *value brand* marque *f* de valeur; MKTG *value chain* chaîne *f* de valeur; FIN *value for collection* valeur à l'encaissement; FIN *value date* date *f* de valeur, jour *m* de valeur; *value engineering* analyse *f* de valeur; *value in exchange* valeur d'échange, contre-valeur *f*; BANKING *value in gold currency* valeur-or *f*; *value at maturity* valeur à l'échéance; *value for money audit* = estimation des performances d'une société à but non lucratif *ou* d'un service gouvernemental; FIN *value below rate* décote *f*; *value in use* valeur d'usage

2 *vt (goods, damage)* évaluer, estimer, expertiser; **to have sth valued** faire évaluer *ou* estimer *ou* expertiser qch; **they valued the company at $10 billion** ils ont estimé la valeur de la société à 10 milliards de dollars ❑ INS *valued policy* assurance *f* forfaitaire

> **"**
>
> **Value engineering** (VE) consists of considering the costs of producing a product together with the functions it provides. The objective is to engineer an all-round improvement in value with benefits to both user and supplier. The cost of a product is not, therefore, its value. This can only be arrived at by considering the functions it performs.
>
> **"**

value-add *n* MKTG valeur *f* ajoutée

value-added *adj* (*product, service*) à valeur ajoutée ❑ *Br* **value-added tax** taxe *f* sur la valeur ajoutée

valueless *adj* sans valeur

valuer *n* expert *m* (*en expertise de biens*)

variability *n* variabilité *f*

variable 1 *n* variable *f*
2 *adj* variable ❑ **variable cost** coût *m* variable; **variable expenses** frais *mpl* variables; EU **variable import levy** prélèvement *m* à l'importation; BANKING **variable rate** taux *m* variable; **variable yield securities** valeurs *fpl* à revenu variable

variance *n* ACCT variance *f*, écart *m* ❑ **variance analysis** analyse *f* des écarts

variation *n* variation *f*; **the level of demand is subject to considerable variation** le niveau de la demande peut varier considérablement ❑ INS **variation of risk** modification *f* de risque

VAT *n Br* (*abbr* **value-added tax**) TVA *f*; **exclusive of** *or* **excluding VAT** hors TVA; **subject to VAT** soumis(e) à la TVA; **to be VAT registered** être assujetti(e) à la TVA ❑ *Fam* **VAT man** service *m* de la TVA; **VAT return** déclaration *f* de TVA

VDU *n* COMPTR (*abbr* **visual display unit**) moniteur *m* ❑ **VDU operator** personne *f* travaillant sur écran

veep *n Am Fam* vice-président(e) *m,f*

vend *vt* LAW vendre

vending machine *n* distributeur *m* automatique

vendor *n* LAW vendeur(euse) *m,f*; COMPTR fournisseur *m* ❑ **vendor placing** = opération par laquelle une société s'engage à vendre de nouvelles actions à un investisseur en échange d'un apport en espèces; FIN **vendor's shares** actions *fpl* d'apport *ou* de fondation

venture *n* entreprise *f* ❑ **venture capital** capital-risque *m*; **venture capitalist** spécialiste *m* de la prise de risques (*dans la finance*); **venture team** équipe *f* commando

verbal *adj* (*agreement, offer, promise*) verbal(e)

verdict *n* verdict *m*

verification *n* vérification *f*

verify *vt* vérifier

vertical *adj* vertical(e) ❑ **vertical concentration** concentration *f* verticale; **vertical integration** intégration *f* verticale; **vertical merger** concentration *f* verticale; ST EXCH **vertical spread** écart *m* vertical; **vertical trust** trust *m* vertical

> **“**
> By a horizontal merger we mean the union of two firms at the same production stage in the same industry, for example the merger of two steel producers or two motor car manufacturers. By a **vertical merger** we mean the union of two firms at different production stages in the same industry, as when a car manufacturer merges with a steel producer.
> **”**

vessel *n* (*ship*) vaisseau *m*

vested interest *n* **to have a vested interest in a business** avoir des capitaux investis dans une entreprise, être intéressé(e) dans une entreprise; **vested interests** (*rights*) droits *mpl* acquis; (*investments*) capitaux *mpl* investis; (*advantages*) intérêts *mpl*; **there are vested interests in industry opposed to trade union reform** ceux qui ont des intérêts dans l'industrie s'opposent à la réforme des syndicats

vet *vt* (*person*) enquêter sur; (*application*) examiner minutieusement; (*facts, figures*) vérifier soigneusement; **she was thoroughly vetted for the job** ils ont soigneusement examiné sa candidature avant de l'embaucher; **the committee has to vet any expenditure exceeding £100** le comité doit approuver toute dépense au-delà de 100 livres

veto 1 *n* veto *m*; **right of veto** droit *m* de veto; **to use one's veto** exercer son droit de veto; **to impose** *or* **put a veto on sth** mettre *ou* opposer son véto à qch
2 *vt* mettre *ou* opposer son veto à

viability *n* viabilité *f*

viable *adj* viable; **it's not a viable proposition** cette proposition n'est pas viable

vice-chairman *n* vice-président(e) *m,f*

vice-chairmanship *n* vice-présidence *f*

vice-presidency *n* vice-présidence *f*

vice-president *n* vice-président(e) *m,f*

video *n* vidéo *f* ❑ COMPTR **video accelerator card** carte *f* vidéo accélératrice; **video clip** clip *m* (vidéo)

videoconference *n* vidéoconférence *f*

videoconferencing *n* vidéoconférence *f*

videophone *n* visiophone *m* ❑ **videophone conference** visioconférence *f*

videotex *n* COMPTR vidéotex *m*

view *vt* COMPTR (*codes, document*) visualiser

Viewdata® *n* vidéotex *m*

violate *vt (law)* violer, enfreindre; *(agreement)* violer

VIP *n (abbr* **very important person**) VIP *mf*, personnage *m* de marque ◻ *VIP lounge* = salon d'accueil dans un aéroport réservé aux personnages de marque

virtual *adj* COMPTR virtuel(elle) ◻ *virtual reality* réalité *f* virtuelle

virus *n* COMPTR virus *m*; **to disable a virus** désactiver un virus ◻ *virus check* détection *f* de virus; **to run a virus check on a disk** faire tourner le programme détecteur de virus sur une disquette; *virus detection* détection *f* de virus; *virus program* programme *m* virus

virus-free *adj* COMPTR dépourvu(e) de virus

visa 1 *n* visa *m*
   2 *vt* viser, apposer un visa à

visible ECON 1 *n* **visibles** biens *mpl* visibles
   2 *adj* **visible balance** balance *f* visible; *visible defects* défauts *mpl* apparents; *visible exports* exportations *fpl* visibles; *visible imports* importations *fpl* visibles; *visible trade* commerce *m* de biens

> **"**
> The Treasury has stuck to its earlier forecast of a £15 billion current-account deficit this year. It expects a smaller invisibles surplus than before, but the forecasters are a lot more optimistic about **visible trade**: exports are booming.
> **"**

visit 1 *vt (person)* rendre visite à; *(place)* visiter
   2 *vi* **to be visiting** être de passage; *Am* **to visit with sb** rendre visite à qn

visitor *n* visiteur(euse) *m,f*; **all visitors must report to reception** tous les visiteurs doivent se présenter à l'accueil

visual display unit *n* COMPTR écran *m ou* console *f* de visualisation

vocational *adj* professionnel(elle) ◻ *vocational guidance* orientation *f* professionnelle; *vocational training* formation *f* professionnelle

voice *n* COMPTR *voice mail* messagerie *f* vocale; *voice recognition software* logiciel *m* de reconnaissance vocale; *voice synthesizer* synthétiseur *m* de paroles

voice-activated *adj* COMPTR à commande vocale

void 1 *adj (deed, contract)* nul(nulle); **null and void** nul et non avenu; **to make sth void** annuler qch, rendre qch nul
   2 *vt (deed, contract)* annuler, rendre nul (nulle)

voidable *adj* annulable

voidance *n* annulation *f*

volatile *adj (market)* instable

volume *n* volume *m* ◻ *volume of business* volume des affaires; *volume of output* volume de la production; *volume of sales* volume de ventes, chiffre *m* d'affaires

voluntary *adj* (a) *(unpaid)* *(work, worker)* bénévole; **the shop is run on a voluntary basis** le magasin est tenu par des bénévoles
   (b) *(optional)* facultatif(ive) ◻ *voluntary arrangement* = arrangement entre une entreprise et ses créanciers de façon à éviter la mise en liquidation; *voluntary export restraint* restriction *f* volontaire des exportations; *voluntary insurance* assurance *f* facultative; *voluntary liquidation* liquidation *f* volontaire; *voluntary redundancy* départ *m* volontaire

vote 1 *n* (a) *(ballot)* vote *m*, scrutin *m*; **to put sth to the vote** soumettre qch au vote; **to take a vote on sth** voter sur qch; **to take the vote** procéder au scrutin ◻ *vote of confidence* vote de confiance; *vote of no confidence* motion *f* de censure; *vote of thanks* discours *m* de remerciement; **to propose a vote of thanks to sb** voter des remerciements à qn
   (b) *(individual vote)* voix *f*, vote *m*; **to give one's vote to sb** voter pour qn; **to cast one's vote** voter
   2 *vt* voter; **to vote to do sth** voter pour faire qch; **to vote sb in** élire qn; **to vote sb out** ne pas réélire qn
   3 *vi* voter (**for/against** pour/contre); **most of the delegates voted against the chairman** la plupart des délégués ont voté contre le président; **to vote by a show of hands** voter à main levée; **to vote by proxy** voter par procuration

voter *n* électeur(trice) *m,f*

voting 1 *n* vote *m*, scrutin *m* ◻ *voting paper* bulletin *m* de vote; ST EXCH *voting rights (of shareholders)* droit *m* de vote; *voting shares* actions *fpl* donnant droit au vote
   2 *adj (assembly, member)* votant(e)

voucher *n* (a) *(for purchase)* bon *m* (b) *(receipt)* reçu *m*, récépissé *m* (c) ACCT pièce *f* comptable

VP *n* *(abbr* **vice-president**) vice-président(e) *m,f*

VRAM *n* COMPTR *(abbr* **video random access memory**) VRAM *f*

wage n **wage(s)** salaire m, paie f ❑ **wage(s) agreement** accord m salarial; **wage(s) bill** masse f salariale, charges fpl salariales; **wage claim** revendication f salariale; **wage cut** réduction f de salaire; **wage differential** écart m salarial; **wage earner** salarié(e) m,f; **wage freeze** gel m ou blocage m des salaires; **wage increase** augmentation f de salaire; **wage packet** (envelope) enveloppe f de paie; (money) paie; **wage policy** politique f salariale ou des salaires; **wage rate** taux m des salaires; **wage restraint** restriction f salariale; **wage scale** échelle f des salaires; **wage structure** structure f des salaires; **wage zone** zone f de salaires

wage-price spiral n spirale f inflationniste prix-salaires

> « ———
>
> With its inflation still rising, the country on the verge of a perilous **wage-price spiral** and public finances deeply in the red, the Bundesbank has made it clear that it will keep the German economy locked in a vice of high interest rates for as long as it takes to squeeze out inflation.
>
> ———— "

waiter n ST EXCH coursier m

waiting time n temps m mort

waive vt (condition, requirement) abandonner; (law, rule) déroger à; (claim, right) renoncer à

waiver n (of condition, requirement) abandon m; (of law, rule) dérogation f; (of claim, right) renonciation f

▸ **walk out** vi (a) (strike) se mettre en grève (b) (leave) partir

walkout n grève f (surprise); **to stage a walkout** se mettre en grève

wallpaper n COMPTR papier m peint

Wall Street n Wall Street (quartier de la Bourse de New York) ❑ **the Wall Street Crash** le krach de Wall Street

WAN n COMPTR (abbr **wide area network**) réseau m longue distance

warehouse 1 n entrepôt m, magasin m ❑ **warehouse charges** frais mpl d'entreposage ou de magasinage; **warehouse keeper** magasinier m; **warehouse manager** responsable mf d'entrepôt; **warehouse receipt** récépissé m d'entreposage; **warehouse warrant** certificat m d'entreposage

2 vt entreposer, mettre en entrepôt

warehousing n (a) (of goods) entreposage m, magasinage m ❑ **warehousing charges** frais mpl d'entreposage ou de magasinage; **warehousing system** système m d'entrepôt (b) ST EXCH (of shares) parcage m d'actions

warrant 1 n (a) LAW (written order) mandat m (b) (for goods) certificat m d'entrepôt (c) ST EXCH bon m de souscription d'actions (d) (for payment) bon m; (guarantee) garantie f
2 vt (a) (justify) justifier; **costs are too high to warrant further investment** les frais sont trop élevés pour justifier d'autres investissements (b) (guarantee) garantir

warranted adj garanti(e)

warrantee n LAW porteur(euse) m,f d'une garantie

warrantor n LAW répondant(e) m,f, garant(e) m,f

warranty n garantie f; LAW (in contract) clause f pénale; **under warranty** sous garantie ❑ **warranty certificate** certificat m de garantie

wastage n (a) (of materials, money) gaspillage m; (wasted material) déchets mpl; **to allow for wastage** tenir compte du gaspillage (b) (reduction of workforce) départ m d'employés

waste 1 n (a) (of materials, money, resources) gaspillage m; (of time) perte f (b) (refuse) déchets mpl ❑ **waste disposal** élimination f des déchets; **waste material** déchets mpl; **waste products** produits mpl de rejet
2 vt (materials, money, resources) gaspiller; (of time) perdre

wastebasket n COMPTR corbeille f

wasting asset n ACCT actif m qui se déprécie

> « ———
>
> There is a series of complex rules for determining the true length of a lease ... A lease will usually be a **wasting asset** for the purposes of capital gains tax when its duration does not exceed fifty years.
>
> ———— "

watchdog n (organization) organisme m de contrôle ❑ COMPTR **watchdog program** programme m sentinelle

waybill n feuille f de route, connaissement m

weaken 1 vt (currency) affaiblir, faire baisser; (market, prices) faire fléchir
2 vi (of currency) s'affaiblir, baisser; (of market, prices) fléchir

wealth n richesse(s) f(pl) ❑ **wealth tax** impôt m de solidarité sur la fortune

wealthy 1 npl **the wealthy** les riches mpl
2 adj riche

wear n usure f ❑ **wear and tear** usure; **fair wear and tear** usure normale

Web n COMPTR **the Web** le Web, la Toile ❑ **Web master** Webmaster m, Webmaître m, Webmestre m; **Web page** page f Web; **Web server** serveur m Web; **Web site** site m Web; **Web space** espace m Web

week n semaine f

weekday n jour m de semaine; ADMIN jour ouvrable

weekly 1 adj hebdomadaire
2 adv chaque semaine

weight 1 n poids m; **weight when empty** poids à vide; **to sell sth by weight** vendre qch au poids ❑ **weights and measures** poids et mesures
2 vt ECON (index, average) pondérer

weighted adj ECON (index, average) pondéré(e)

weighting n ECON (of index, average) pondération f, coefficient m; ADMIN **London weighting** (in salary) indemnité f de résidence à Londres

wharf quai m ❑ **wharf dues** droits mpl de quai

wharfage n droits mpl de quai

wharfinger n gardien(enne) m,f de quai

wheeler-dealer n Fam brasseur m d'affaires (plus ou moins en marge de la loi)

wheeling and dealing n Fam magouilles fpl

> ❝
> Worsening expectations had not yet led to a collapse in investment, however. ... Their most obvious effect had been a massive increase in speculation as more capitalists tried to make money by **wheeling and dealing** rather than by productive investment: hence the huge foreign exchange dealings and the booms in share prices, gold, land, real estate and commodities.
> ❞

white adj **white goods** appareils mpl ménagers; ST EXCH **white knight** chevalier m blanc

white-collar adj d'employé de bureau ❑ **white-collar union** syndicat m d'employés; **white-collar worker** col m blanc

whizz kid n Fam jeune prodige m; **she's a computer whizz kid** c'est un vrai génie de l'informatique

whole-life policy, whole-of-life policy n INS assurance-décès f

wholesale 1 n (vente f en) gros m; **wholesale and retail** le gros et le détail
2 adj de gros ❑ **wholesale bank** banque f de gros; **wholesale co-operative** coopérative f d'achats; **wholesale dealer** grossiste mf; **wholesale goods** marchandises fpl de gros; **wholesale manufacture** fabrication f en série; BANKING **wholesale market** marché m de gré à gré entre banques; **wholesale price** prix m de gros; **wholesale price index** indice m des prix de gros; **wholesale trade** commerce m de gros
3 adv (buy, sell) en gros; **I can get it for you wholesale** je peux vous le procurer au prix de gros

wholesaler n grossiste mf

wholly-owned subsidiary n filiale f à cent pour cent

> ❝
> Multinationals face increasing scrutiny of workplace standards in their foreign suppliers. ... While it may be straightforward to impose a policy in a **wholly-owned subsidiary**, how can contractors be brought into line?
> ❞

wide area network n COMPTR réseau m longue distance

widow's pension n allocation f veuvage

wildcard n COMPTR joker m ❑ **wildcard character** caractère m joker

wildcat n (a) **wildcat strike** grève f sauvage (b) MKTG **wildcats** dilemmes mpl

will n testament m; **to make a will** faire un testament

▶ **wind up** (company) liquider, dissoudre; (account) régler, clôturer; (speech, meeting) terminer; **the business will be wound up by the end of the year** l'entreprise sera liquidée avant la fin de l'année

windbill n FIN billet m ou effet m de complaisance

windfall *n (unexpected gain)* aubaine *f*
❑ *windfall profits* profits *mpl* inattendus;
windfall tax impôt *m* sur les gains exceptionnels

winding-up *n (of company)* liquidation *f*;
(of account) clôture *f* ❑ *winding-up order*
ordre *m* de mise en règlement judiciaire

window *n* (**a**) *(of shop)* vitrine *f* ❑ *window
display* étalage *m*; *window dressing (in
shop)* présentation *f* de l'étalage; ACCT
habillage *m* de bilan
  (**b**) COMPTR fenêtre *f*
  (**c**) *Fam (in schedule)* créneau *m*, moment *m*
libre; **I've got a window at 10.30** j'ai un trou
à 10h30; **a window of opportunity** de
nouvelles possibilités

> **❝**
>
> He … began buying businesses on the
> cheap, some from distressed sellers,
> others from receivers. … He even
> bought one business from Hanson —
> shower maker Croydex for £7.7m —
> and another from his old employers,
> Williams. "The recession gave us a
> **window of opportunity**," he said at
> the time.
>
> **❞**

WIP *n (abbr* **work in progress***)* travail *m* en
cours

▶ **wipe off** *vt sep (debt)* annuler; **several
millions of pounds were wiped off the
value of shares** la valeur des actions a baissé
de plusieurs millions de livres

withdraw *vt* (**a**) *(money)* retirer; **I need to
withdraw £500 from my account** il faut que
je retire 500 livres de mon compte (**b**) *(order)*
annuler

withdrawal *n (of money)* retrait *m*; **to
make a withdrawal** faire un retrait ❑ *withdrawal limit* plafond *m* de retrait; *withdrawal notice* avis *m* de retrait; *withdrawal
slip* bordereau *m* de retrait

withholding tax *n Am* impôt *m* retenu à
la source, retenue *f* fiscale

without *prep* LAW **without prejudice** *(on
document)* sous toutes réserves; **without
recourse** *(on bill of exchange)* sans recours

with-pack premium *n* MKTG prime *f*
directe

word *n* COMPTR *word count* nombre *m* de
mots; **to do a word count** compter les mots;
word count facility fonction *f* de comptage
de mots; *word processor* machine *f* de
traitement de texte

word-of-mouth   advertising   *n*
publicité *f* de bouche à oreille

word-processing *n* COMPTR traitement
m de texte

wordwrap *n* COMPTR passage *m* automatique à la ligne suivante

work 1 *n* (**a**) *(labour)* travail *m*; **this report
needs more work** il y a encore du travail à
faire sur ce rapport; **to start work, to set to
work** se mettre au travail; **she set to work on
the contract** elle a commencé à travailler sur
le contrat ❑ COMPTR *work area* zone *f* de
travail; *work flow* déroulement *m* des
opérations; *work in progress* travail en
cours; *(sign)* travaux; *work progress*
avancement *m* des travaux
  (**b**) *(employment)* travail *m*, emploi *m*; **to look
for work** chercher du travail; **to be out of
work** être sans travail *ou* sans emploi; **to take
time off work** prendre des congés; **she's off
work today** elle ne travaille pas aujourd'hui
❑ *work experience* expérience *f* professionnelle; *work permit* permis *m* de
travail
  (**c**) *(task)* travail *m*; **to take work home**
ramener du travail à la maison; **he's trying
to get some work done** il essaie de travailler
un peu
  (**d**) **works** *(construction)* travaux *mpl*;
(factory) usine *f* ❑ *works council* comité *m*
d'entreprise
2 *vt (employee)* faire travailler; **the boss
works his staff hard** le patron exige beaucoup de travail de ses employés
3 *vi* (**a**) *(of person)* travailler; **he works in
advertising** il travaille dans la publicité; **we
have to work to a budget** nous devons
travailler avec un certain budget; **to work to
rule** faire la grève du zèle
  (**b**) *(of machine)* fonctionner
  (**c**) *(of plan, idea, method)* marcher

▶ **work out 1** *vt sep* (**a**) *(plan)* élaborer
(**b**) *(account)* examiner; *(price)* établir,
calculer
2 *vi (total)* **to work out at** s'élever à; **the
total works out at £9,000** le montant
s'élève à 9000 livres

▶ **work up** *vt sep* **to work one's way up**
faire son chemin; **she worked her way up
from secretary to managing director** elle a
commencé comme secrétaire et a fait son
chemin jusqu'au poste de P-DG

workable *adj (project, plan)* réalisable

workaholic *n Fam* bourreau *m* de travail

worker *n* travailleur(euse) *m,f*; *(in industry)*
ouvrier(ère) *m,f* ❑ *worker director* = ouvrier
qui fait partie du conseil d'administration;

worker participation participation *f* ouvrière; **worker representation** représentation *f* du personnel

> Giving employees a greater say in how their companies operate could be an important step towards such a goal, but Laing is opposed to the appointment of **worker directors**, as is the practice in Scandinavia. 'I think everybody who joins a company in any capacity should, if he's got the capability, be able to reach board level. But I don't think you should just appoint somebody and say he's a **worker director**. I just don't believe in that.''

workforce *n* main-d'œuvre *f*, personnel *m*

working *adj* (*person*) qui travaille; (*population*) actif(ive) ❏ **working account** compte *m* d'exploitation; **working agreement** accord *m*, entente *f*; **working assets** actif *m* circulant; **working capital** fonds *mpl* de roulement; **working capital fund** compte *m* d'avances; **working capital requirements** besoins *mpl* en fonds de roulement; **working class** classe *f* ouvrière; **working conditions** conditions *fpl* de travail; **working day** journée *f* (de travail); **working document** document *m* de travail; **working expenses** frais *mpl* généraux, frais d'exploitation; **working hours** heures *fpl* de travail; **working interest** participation *f* d'exploitation; **working lunch** déjeuner *m* d'affaires *ou* de travail; **working party** groupe *m* de travail; **working week** semaine *f* de travail

workload *n* travail *m* à effectuer, charge *f* de travail; **to have a heavy workload** être surchargé(e) de travail; **my workload has eased off a bit** j'ai un peu moins de travail en ce moment

workman *n* (*manual worker*) ouvrier *m*; (*craftsman*) artisan *m*

workmanlike *adj* (*efficient*) professionnel(elle); (*well made*) bien fait(e)

workmanship *n* exécution *f*; **a good/shoddy piece of workmanship** du travail bien/mal fait

workplace *n* lieu *m* de travail; **in the workplace** sur le lieu de travail

workshop *n* atelier *m*

workstation *n* COMPTR station *f* *ou* poste *m* de travail

work-to-rule *n* grève *f* du zèle

world *n* (a) (*earth*) monde *m* ❏ **World Bank** Banque *f* mondiale; **world economy** conjoncture *f* économique mondiale; **world markets** marchés *mpl* mondiaux *ou* internationaux; **world trade** commerce *m* international; **World Trade Organization** Organisation *f* mondiale du commerce; COMPTR **the World Wide Web** le World Wide Web

(b) (*domain*) monde *m*, milieu *m*; **the business world** le monde des affaires; **the financial world** le monde de la finance

> When the **World Trade Organization** was set up in 1995 to take over the policing of the world's trading system, it was given significant powers and responsibilities. Unfortunately it may be unable to afford the expense that comes with them. Since it replaced the General Agreement of Tariffs and Trade ... its annual allowance has been frozen at SFr118m ($75.5m).

worldwide **1** *adj* mondial(e)
2 *adv* partout dans le monde

WORM COMPTR (*abbr* **write once read many times**) WORM

worth **1** *n* valeur *f*; **£500 worth of damage** pour 500 livres de dégâts, des dégâts qui se montent à 500 livres; **a week's worth of supplies** suffisament de provisions pour une semaine
2 *prep* **to be worth sth** valoir qch; **how much is it worth?** combien est-ce que cela vaut?; **what is the franc worth?** combient vaut le franc?

worthless *adj* (*object, advice, suggestion*) sans valeur

WP *n* COMPTR (a) (*abbr* **word processing**) traitement *m* de texte (b) (*abbr* **word processor**) machine *f* à traitement de texte

wrap *vi* COMPTR (*of lines*) se boucler

wrist rest *n* COMPTR repose-poignets *m*

writ *n* LAW ordonnance *f*; **to serve a writ on sb** assigner qn en justice

write **1** *vt* (*letter, name, address*) écrire; (*cheque*) faire; *Am* **to write sb** écrire à qn; COMPTR **to write sth to disk** écrire qch sur disque
2 *vi* écrire; **to write to sb** écrire à qn

▸ **write away for** *vt insep* (*order by post*) commander par lettre, écrire pour commander; **I wrote away for a catalogue** j'ai écrit pour commander un catalogue; **I had to write away for spare parts** j'ai dû écrire pour commander des pièces

▶ **write down** *vt sep* (**a**) *(note)* noter; *(put in writing)* mettre par écrit (**b**) FIN *(capital, stock)* réduire; ACCT *(asset)* déprécier

▶ **write off** *vt sep* (**a**) FIN *(capital, stock)* amortir (**b**) ACCT *(bad debt, asset)* passer par profits et pertes

▶ **write up** *vt sep* FIN *(capital, stock)* augmenter; ACCT *(asset)* revaloriser

write-down *n* ACCT dépréciation *f*

write-off *n* ACCT annulation *f* par écrit

write-protected *adj* COMPTR protégé(e) en écriture

write-up *n* ACCT augmentation *f*

wrongful *adj* ***wrongful dismissal*** licenciement *m* abusif; ***wrongful trading*** = situation dans laquelle une société poursuit ses opérations en dépit du fait que la mise en liquidation est inévitable

„

The court may impose personal liability for a company's debts on … directors who ought to have realized that insolvent liquidation was inevitable, but who failed to take the necessary step to minimize the potential loss to creditors. This is known as **wrongful trading**.

„

WTO *n* (*abbr* **World Trade Organization**) OMC *f*

WWW *n* COMPTR (*abbr* **World Wide Web**) WWW, W3

WYSIWYG *n* COMPTR (*abbr* **what you see is what you get**) tel écran-tel écrit *m*, tel-tel *m*, Wysiwyg *m* ❏ ***WYSIWYG display*** affichage *m* tel écran-tel écrit *ou* tel-tel *ou* Wysiwyg

xerography n xérographie f

Xerox® **1** n (machine) photocopieur m, photocopieuse f; (copy) photocopie f □ **Xe-** rox copy photocopie; **Xerox machine** photocopieur, photocopieuse
2 vt photocopier

Yankee bond n Am FIN obligation f Yankee

year n (twelve-month period) an m; (referring to duration) année f; **to earn £40,000 a year** gagner 40 000 livres par an; **the year under review** l'exercice écoulé; ACCT **year ended 31 December 1999** exercice clos le 31 décembre 1999; COMPTR **year 2000 compliant** protégé(e) contre le bogue de l'an 2000 □ **year of assessment** année f d'imposition; **year's purchase** taux m de capitalisation des bénéfices

yearbook n annuaire m

year-end n ACCT fin f d'exercice □ **year-end accounts** compte m de résultats; **year-end audit** vérification f comptable de fin d'exercice; **year-end closing of accounts** clôture f annuelle des livres; **year-end profits** bénéfices mpl de fin d'exercice; **year-end loss** perte f de fin d'exercice

yearly 1 adj annuel(elle) □ **yearly accounts** comptes mpl annuels; **yearly payment** annuité f; **yearly premium** prime f annuelle
2 adv annuellement

yellow adj **the Yellow Pages**® les Pages fpl Jaunes; **yellow sticker** (Post-it®) note f autocollante

yen n yen m

yield 1 n (from investments) rapport m, rendement m; (from tax) recette f, rapport □ **yield capacity** productivité f; **yield curve** courbe f des taux; **yield gap** prime f de risque
2 vt (dividend, interest) rapporter; (income) créer; **the investment bond will yield 5%** le bon d'épargne rapportera 5%

yuppie n yuppie mf

Z chart *n* diagramme *m* en Z

zero *n* zéro *m* ❑ *zero base budgeting* système *m* du budget à base zéro; *zero coupon bond* obligation *f* émise à coupon zéro; MKTG *zero defects purchasing* achats *mpl* de qualité à 100%, achats zéro défaut; ECON *zero growth* croissance *f* zéro, croissance économique nulle

> 66
>
> The right wing coalition parties, RPR and UDF, are expected to triumph at the French legislative elections due to take place at the end of this month but, regardless of who wins, the French economy is set to go into recession in the first half of this year with even the most optimistic forecasters predicting **zero growth**.
>
> 99

zero-rated *adj (for VAT)* exempt(e) *ou* exonéré(e) de TVA; **in Britain, books are zero-rated** en Grande-Bretagne, les livres sont exempts *ou* exonérés de TVA

zero-rating *n* franchise *f* de TVA, taux *m* zero

zip 1 *n Am zip code* code *m* postal
2 *vt* COMPTR zipper

zone 1 *n (area)* zone *f*
2 *vt (classify)* désigner; **to zone an area as industrial/residential** classer un secteur zone industrielle/résidentielle

zoning *n* zonage *m*

zoom box *n* COMPTR case *f* zoom

SUPPLEMENT

Table des Matières

business@harrap.fr

L'INTERNET ET LE MONDE DES AFFAIRES: MODE D'EMPLOI

Petit guide de l'Internet à l'usage de l'homme d'affaires utilisant l'anglais comme langue de travail

par Bob Norton et Cathy Smith

traduit de l'anglais par Rose Rociola

Bob Norton dirige le service de documentation de l'Institut de Management de Corby, en Angleterre. Cathy Smith est chef du service informatique du centre de documentation sur le management du même institut. Bob et Cathy sont responsables de l'élaboration et de la gestion du site Internet de l'Institut. Chacun est l'auteur de nombreux articles sur la gestion de l'information et ils ont signé ensemble l'ouvrage *Understanding Business on the Internet*.

Table des Matières

business@harrap.fr

Qu'est-ce que l'Internet?

L'Internet, réseau mondial ouvert, est constitué d'une multitude de réseaux informatiques reliés entre eux par l'intermédiaire de lignes téléphoniques publiques et privées. Ces réseaux sont la propriété d'organismes divers, agences gouvernementales, universités, sociétés privées et organisations bénévoles, qui autorisent ainsi l'accès à leurs ordinateurs – appelés dans ce cas serveurs – et aux informations qu'ils contiennent.

Le courrier électronique, qui peut se substituer au courrier postal, au téléphone ou à la télécopie, est le service le plus utilisé de l'Internet. D'autres services, tels que les groupes de nouvelles ou forums et les groupes de discussion, donnent à des utilisateurs ayant un intérêt commun la possibilité de dialoguer dans le monde entier. Quant au World Wide Web, service le plus célèbre, il permet de consulter des pages d'informations pouvant contenir du texte, des graphiques, des images et du son. Ces pages, bien que situées sur différents serveurs, sont reliées entre elles.

L'Internet n'appartient à personne et n'est régi par aucun organisme. Cependant, un certain nombre d'organisations bénévoles, telles que l'ISOC (Internet Society) ou l'IETF (Internet Engineering Taskforce), veillent à son évolution.

Les origines du réseau des réseaux

Au début des années soixante, en pleine guerre froide, le gouvernement américain veut mettre au point un système de communication efficace dans l'éventualité d'une attaque nucléaire. En effet, pour l'armée du Pentagone, il est bien trop risqué de garder des informations stratégiques dans un seul site, en cas de destruction de ce site. C'est ainsi que la société Rand Corporation eut l'idée d'un réseau décentralisé qui continuerait de fonctionner même en cas de destruction partielle. Pour plus de sécurité, les informations ne circuleraient pas sur le réseau dans leur intégralité, mais seraient décomposées en paquets et reconstituées une fois arrivées à destination.

En 1969, le réseau ARPANET voit le jour. Quatre universités sont reliées au moyen de lignes et de modems à grande vitesse, permettant ainsi aux chercheurs du gouvernement et des universités de communiquer par courrier électronique. Suite au succès de ce moyen de communication rapide, d'autres centres de recherches ainsi que des sociétés, d'abord aux États-Unis puis dans le monde entier, se connectent. C'est la naissance de l'Internet.

Dans les années quatre-vingt, les grandes entreprises commencent à utiliser l'Internet pour communiquer. À partir de 1990, dans le monde entier, un grand nombre d'entreprises de toutes sortes ainsi que de plus en plus de particuliers viennent se connecter.

business@harrap.fr

Selon des estimations récentes, il y aurait plus de 50 millions d'utilisateurs aux États-Unis et ce chiffre ne cesse de croître. En Europe, on estime que de 2 à 3 % des ménages ont accès à l'Internet. Avec un million d'utilisateurs, la France vient en troisième position, après l'Allemagne et le Royaume-Uni, qui compte à ce jour trois millions d'utilisateurs en constante augmentation. La France est suivie de près par les Pays-Bas, la Suède, l'Italie et l'Espagne. À la fin des années 90, on estime que les communications sur l'Internet, et notamment la quantité de courriers électroniques échangés, doublent tous les cent jours; quant au World Wide Web, il double de volume tous les six mois. Certains estiment qu'il y aura 250 millions d'utilisateurs d'ici à l'an 2000. Pour d'autres, à ce rythme là, tous les habitants de la planète seront connectés d'ici à 2003!

Quatre facteurs expliquent ce taux de croissance exceptionnel:

- le rapprochement des technologies de l'informatique et des télécommunications;
- la baisse des prix des micro-ordinateurs et l'augmentation des ventes qui s'en est suivie;
- la médiatisation importante de l'Internet;
- l'amélioration de la convivialité de l'Internet, en particulier depuis l'apparition du World Wide Web en 1993-94.

Au départ, l'internaute type était un homme instruit de 35 ans, partisan de la liberté individuelle et de la liberté d'expression. À partir de 1995, parmi les utilisateurs types on trouve également le cadre d'entreprise, homme ou femme pouvant avoir la quarantaine et utilisant l'Internet pour communiquer à distance avec des clients et des fournisseurs ainsi que pour rechercher et envoyer des informations relatives à son travail.

Les enjeux de l'Internet

L'utilisation de l'Internet présente de nombreux avantages pour les entreprises: la possibilité de communiquer mieux et moins cher, de travailler efficacement à distance et, quelle que soit la taille de l'entreprise, de se faire connaître sur le marché international à moindre frais.

Cependant, au début des années quatre-vingt-dix, de nombreuses entreprises se sont laissé prendre par l'illusion d'un marché électronique facile où de nombreux clients les attendaient. Certains articles parus dans la presse ont contribué à répandre la peur que ceux qui ne se reliaient pas à l'Internet seraient vite dépassés et évincés de ce marché prometteur.

De nombreuses entreprises ont suivi le mouvement sans toutefois réaliser que cette nouvelle opportunité devait être planifiée, organisée et gérée, au même titre que tout projet professionnel. De nombreuses sociétés qui n'ont pas su adapter l'utilisation de l'Internet à leurs besoins réels se demandent maintenant comment y parvenir et combien de ressources y consacrer.

L'Internet peut-il vraiment être utile au monde des affaires et changer notre façon de travailler ou ne correspond-il qu'à une simple lubie? Force est de constater qu'il s'agit d'un phénomène durable. L'Internet est en pleine expansion et le grand public sait de mieux en mieux s'en servir.

- L'Internet n'est plus uniquement l'apanage de jeunes gens boutonneux toujours rivés à leur écran. La standardisation de l'équipement nécessaire, micro-ordinateur, modem et logiciel du fournisseur d'accès, a contribué à mettre le réseau à la portée du grand public.

- L'Internet représente une solution souvent plus économique que les méthodes classiques pour obtenir, envoyer, recevoir et stocker des informations. Nul ne peut aujourd'hui ignorer la société de l'information.

- De nombreuses entreprises, de la PME à la grosse multinationale, expérimentent sur l'Internet de nouvelles approches pour la gestion du personnel, la communication externe, la promotion de leurs produits ou services et les transactions commerciales. D'autres sociétés, ne voyant pas de rentabilité immédiate, se contentent d'une utilisation plus réduite. Les investissements des grandes banques viennent cependant renforcer la promesse d'un marché électronique. Des entreprises commencent à obtenir des résultats financiers. Selon des chiffres récents, aux États-Unis, les transactions commerciales sur l'Internet s'élèvent à trois milliards de dollars chaque année et ce chiffre ne cesse de croître.

- Même si tous ne l'utilisent pas, l'Internet a modifié nos comportements, dans notre vie professionnelle comme dans notre vie privée. L'Internet est aujourd'hui au cœur de nombreux débats:
  – l'impact de l'évolution technologique sur le monde des affaires, la société et l'État;
  – les nouvelles techniques de marketing et les relations avec la clientèle;
  – la question sociale des laissés-pour-compte du monde de l'information dans une société où l'information est devenue un bien commercial et le savoir un avantage concurrentiel;
  – les implications légales du transfert d'informations au-delà des frontières.

Le Parlement européen et le Sénat américain se penchent aujourd'hui sur les opportunités offertes par l'Internet ainsi que sur les problèmes que son utilisation soulève. Les gouvernements ne peuvent plus ignorer les enjeux stratégiques du réseau.

L'Internet évolue très rapidement, mais une utilisation optimale requiert du temps et des efforts. Il faut en effet envisager de nouvelles approches pour en tirer le meilleur parti. Bien que l'on ne puisse pas affirmer aujourd'hui que ceux qui attendent trop longtemps seront évincés, il est certain qu'ils devront fournir beaucoup d'efforts pour rester compétitifs. En effet, nombreux sont ceux qui voient en l'Internet, et dans les technologies qui en découlent, l'outil d'avenir incontournable de toute stratégie commerciale.

business@harrap.fr

La gestion du réseau

Afin d'exploiter au mieux les possibilités qu'offre l'Internet, il est important de ne pas se laisser influencer par l'attrait de la technologie et de planifier avec soin son utilisation. Il est donc utile dans un premier temps de répondre à certaines questions essentielles:

Pourquoi voulons-nous utiliser l'Internet?

- Par peur d'être dépassé?

- Pour découvrir les opportunités offertes?

- Pour explorer les possibilités commerciales?

- Pour évaluer les avantages que l'entreprise peut en tirer?

Dans quel but voulons-nous utiliser l'Internet?

- Pour améliorer la communication externe de l'entreprise?

- Pour interroger des bases de données? Pour entrer en contact avec des experts? Pour obtenir des informations sur des sociétés et leurs produits?

- Pour tirer parti des possibilités de commercialisation? Pour prendre de l'avance sur la concurrence?

- Pour améliorer les relations avec la clientèle ou attirer de nouveaux clients?

Qui va utiliser l'Internet?

- Quelles sont les compétences requises?

- Est-il nécessaire de recruter du personnel expérimenté ou vaut-il mieux former le personnel interne?

- Est-il préférable de faire appel à un consultant extérieur ou de sous-traiter tout le projet à une société spécialisée?

- Qui doit avoir accès à l'Internet?

- Qui a le temps de s'occuper de l'Internet? Comment trouver le temps nécessaire?

Quel mode d'accès choisir?

- Vaut-il mieux opter pour une ligne spécialisée, une ligne RNIS ou un simple accès commuté?

- Comment choisir le service correspondant le mieux à nos besoins?

Communication

Le *courrier électronique* ["e-mail"] est le service le plus utilisé de l'Internet: des centaines de millions de messages sont échangés chaque jour. Le succès de ce service tient à sa facilité d'emploi, à son faible coût (tarif d'une communication locale) quelle que soit la destination, et à la possibilité de joindre des fichiers informatiques aux messages (graphiques, documents annexes ou même logiciels). Le décalage horaire ou la peur de déranger ne sont plus un problème car le destinataire n'a pas besoin d'être connecté au même moment pour recevoir son message. L'envoi d'un message à de multiples destinataires est une procédure simple et bon marché. Il est également possible d'échanger des informations avec des personnes que l'on ne connaît pas grâce aux groupes d'intérêt appelés *groupes de nouvelles* ou *forums* ["newsgroups"] et *groupes de discussion* ["discussion lists"].

Une adresse électronique se présente généralement sous la forme suivante:
nom@domaine.pays
Par exemple, jdurand@club-internet.fr

Bien que le courrier électronique offre de nombreux avantages, il comporte également des risques qui ne doivent pas être ignorés:

1. Le courrier électronique n'est pas encore totalement sûr. N'importe quelle personne suffisamment déterminée peut intercepter votre courrier. Des enquêtes réalisées au hasard révèlent que jusqu'à un quart des paquets d'information dont sont composés les messages électroniques peuvent ne pas parvenir à leur destinataire, notamment durant les heures de pointe, lorsque les réseaux sont très embouteillés. Dans la plupart des cas cependant, les messages ne sont pas perdus, ils sont renvoyés à l'expéditeur.

2. Le courrier électronique ne garantit pas une réponse immédiate. Certaines personnes lui préfèrent le téléphone pour les informations de nature urgente.

3. La convivialité du courrier électronique encourage une certaine familiarité, que l'on peut parfois regretter après-coup. Cette caractéristique a répandu le sentiment que les messages électroniques sont peu fiables, non durables, voire même inexacts, et ne valent donc pas la peine d'être cités. Il faut savoir pourtant que le courrier électronique est une forme de publication qui est donc soumise en tant que telle à la législation relative aux droits d'auteur et à la diffamation. Un message électronique doit par conséquent être considéré de la même façon que tout autre forme de communication écrite.

4. Les fichiers joints aux messages peuvent contenir des virus. Cependant, il est difficile de savoir si un fichier est infecté ou non tant que l'on ne l'a pas ouvert. Étant donné qu'un virus peut détruire toutes les informations contenues sur le disque dur de l'ordinateur, certaines organisations vérifient tous les fichiers joints avant de les ouvrir; d'autres vont même jusqu'à interdire la réception de fichiers.

Avant d'utiliser le courrier électronique au sein d'une organisation, il est important de tenir compte des points suivants:

1. Utilisation optimale – Il faut diminuer le risque d'utilisation inappropriée, de perte de temps et de surcharge d'information.

business@harrap.fr

2. Priorité – Le courrier électronique doit-il être prioritaire par rapport aux autres moyens de communication? Si tel est le cas, quelle est la procédure à suivre?

3. Responsabilité par rapport au contenu – Cette question ne doit pas être négligée, étant donné la portée du courrier électronique qui permet d'atteindre le plus grand nombre à moindre frais.

Accès à l'information

Sur le *World Wide Web*, ou tout simplement le *Web*, on peut accéder, la plupart du temps gratuitement, à des informations sur une multitude de sujets et sous différentes formes. Ce service permet de consulter des *sites Web* ["Web sites"] contenant des pages de texte, mais aussi des images et du son, à l'aide d'un logiciel spécifique appelé *navigateur* ["browser"]. Il est possible de naviguer d'une page à l'autre grâce à des liens appelés *liens hypertexte* ["hyperlinks"]. Chaque site Web a son adresse, connue sous le nom *d'adresse URL* ["Uniform Resource Locator, URL"], par exemple:http://www.renault.fr

• http:// ["HyperText Transfer Protocol"] signifie protocole de transfert des pages hypertextes;

• www.renault.fr indique le nom du serveur, celui de l'organisme ainsi que le code du pays, dans ce cas la France.

Figure 1: La page d'accueil du site institutionnel de Renault, en français et en anglais (www.renault.com)

Chaque site s'ouvre sur un menu principal ou *page d'accueil* ["home page"]. La plupart des adresses citées correspondent à la page d'accueil, mais il peut arriver que l'adresse renvoie à une section spécifique du site. On appelle *nom de domaine* ["domain name"] la partie de l'adresse comprenant le nom de l'organisation et le code du pays, par exemple*renault.fr*

Il existe un très grand nombre de sites susceptibles d'intéresser une entreprise, il serait impossible de tous les recenser. Le site francophone *(e)-business: la lettre du commerce électronique* (http:\\www.ebusiness.org) représente un bon point de départ pour obtenir des informations sur le commerce électronique. Un lien hypertexte renvoie à une sélection de sites sur le commerce électronique. Il faut s'abonner pour avoir accès à tous les services, mais un espace grand public peut être consulté gratuitement.

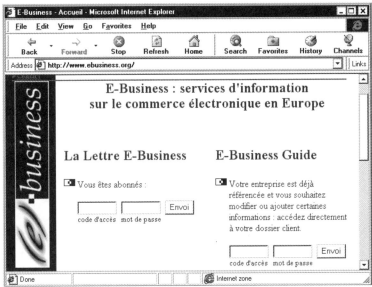

Figure 2: La page d'accueil de (e)-business

Le moyen le plus rapide d'accéder aux informations désirées est d'obtenir les adresses des sites dans la presse ou par le bouche à oreille. Les deux principaux navigateurs, Netscape Navigator et Internet Explorer de Microsoft, permettent de garder en mémoire les adresses des sites désirés, au moyen des options respectives Signets et Favoris. Si vous ne connaissez pas l'adresse du site recherché, vous pouvez utiliser l'un des nombreux outils de recherche proposés sur le Web. Il peut s'agir d'annuaires, où des mots-clés ont été sélectionnés et indexés, ou de moteurs de recherche ("search engines"), programmes explorant régulièrement le Web à la recherche de nouvelles informations.

Il est important de garder à l'esprit qu'une recherche peut déboucher sur des centaines, voire parfois des milliers, de résultats différents, appelés *hits* ou *contacts de page* ["hits"]. En effet, le Web est si vaste que les outils de recherche ne réussissent pas toujours à faire le tri entre les informations pertinentes et celles qui ne le sont pas. Bien que la plupart des outils de recherche classent les informations par catégories (affaires, sports, art, actualité, loisirs, etc.), mieux vaut être le plus précis possible lors d'une recherche.

Les adresses suivantes renvoient à des outils de recherche sur le Web:
    Yahoo – (http://www.yahoo.fr) ou (http://www.yahoo.co.uk)
    Excite – (http://www.excite.fr) ou (http://www.excite.co.uk)
    Altavista – (http://www.altavista.com)
    AltaVista propose également un outil pour la traduction de
    documents en français et en anglais ainsi que dans de nombreuses
    autres langues.
    Ecila – (http://ecila.ceic.com)
    Eureka – (http://www.eureka-fr.com)
    Lokace – (http://lokace.iplus.fr)
    Francite – (http://francite.com)

business@harrap.fr

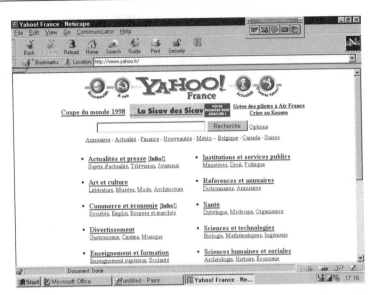

Figure 3: La version française de Yahoo avec les principaux domaines de recherche de l'information

Marketing

Le Web n'est pas qu'une gigantesque source d'informations. C'est également un endroit où particuliers et sociétés peuvent faire connaître et vendre leurs produits ou leurs services. Très vite, des fleurs, des livres et des logiciels ont été commercialisés avec succès. Le Web est un monde égalitaire où les PME côtoient les plus grandes sociétés. Certains sites sont très professionnels, d'autres ont une apparence beaucoup plus artisanale, mais tous en sont encore au stade expérimental.

Le Web est un marché interactif où le client potentiel choisit le lieu, le moment et la durée de sa visite. Ce marché, ouvert 24 heures sur 24 et sept jours sur sept, peut recevoir aussi bien la visite de votre voisin que d'une personne se trouvant à l'autre bout du monde.

Il est possible de commercialiser ses produits sur le Web en plaçant des annonces publicitaires dans d'autres sites Web. Il existe différents types d'annonces:

* *Bandeaux publicitaires*: ces encadrés graphiques ressemblent à des panneaux d'affichage. Ils sont de plus en plus souvent animés et interactifs.

* *Boutons*: semblables aux bandeaux, les boutons affichent en général le nom d'une société, d'une marque ou même d'un secteur d'activité. Il suffit de cliquer sur le bouton pour atteindre le site Web correspondant.

* *Mots-clés*: les annonceurs ont même la possibilité d'acheter des mots. Par exemple, si Moët-Chandon achetait le mot «champagne», à chaque fois que quelqu'un recherche ce mot, le nom Moët-Chandon s'afficherait à l'écran.

La première étape pour se faire connaître consiste à créer un site Web. Le succès d'un site dépend de sa présentation, de l'utilité de son contenu et de la fréquence des mises à jour. L'interactivité du Web permet à une entreprise de découvrir les préférences de ses clients et de développer ses relations commerciales. Pour plus de détails sur la création d'un site Web, reportez-vous au chapitre suivant.

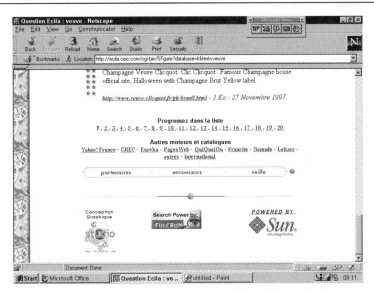

Figure 4: ces "boutons" publicitaires sont situés au bas de la page d'accueil d'Ecila. Les sociétés en question ont acheté cet espace de façon à fournir un lien direct avec leur propre site Web. Reportez-vous à la Figure 3 pour un exemple de bandeau publicitaire pour Sicav.

Accès à l'Internet

Il existe deux façons principales de se connecter à l'Internet: par accès commuté ou par une ligne spécialisée.

Accès commuté

Pour l'accès commuté, c'est-à-dire ponctuel, il suffit d'avoir un modem relié à l'ordinateur, une ligne téléphonique et un abonnement auprès d'un fournisseur d'accès ["Internet Service Provider"]. Ce type d'accès ne requiert pas d'investissement majeur, il convient donc essentiellement aux particuliers et aux sociétés qui n'utilisent pas l'Internet de manière intensive. Son principal inconvénient est qu'il peut être lent, notamment aux heures de pointe lorsque des millions d'utilisateurs se connectent dans le monde entier.

De nombreuses sociétés choisissent d'installer une ligne de type RNIS (Réseau Numérique à Intégration de Service) afin d'obtenir un accès rapide et de qualité supérieure aux lignes téléphoniques. Une ligne RNIS, bien que coûteuse, est tout de même moins chère qu'une ligne spécialisée (voir ci-dessous) et les prix commencent à baisser.

L'efficacité d'une connexion à l'Internet dépend de toute la chaîne qui relie les deux ordinateurs: la puissance des ordinateurs, la rapidité du modem, la capacité des lignes téléphoniques ainsi que la rapidité de la connexion entre le fournisseur d'accès et l'Internet.

Ligne spécialisée

Cet accès se fait au moyen d'un câble fournissant une connexion permanente et rapide à l'Internet. La connexion peut se faire directement à un réseau de l'Internet ou passer par un fournisseur d'accès. L'installation d'une ligne spécialisée est beaucoup plus coûteuse que l'accès commuté et convient par conséquent aux sociétés qui utilisent l'Internet de manière intensive.

business@harrap.fr

1. Définition des objectifs

Pourquoi voulez-vous créer votre propre site?

- Pour élargir votre clientèle?
- Pour vous faire connaître?
- Pour proposer un service?
- À titre expérimental?

Demandez-vous également quels sont les avantages que vous aimeriez tirer de votre site Web tout en tenant compte des ressources financières, techniques et humaines que vous voulez y investir. Définissez les critères qui vous permettront d'évaluer le succès du site. Prévoyez d'analyser les données de fréquentation du site et de consultation des pages.

2. Choix de l'emplacement du site

Une des méthodes les plus utilisées consiste à louer de l'espace auprès d'un fournisseur d'accès à l'Internet. La plupart des fournisseurs d'accès offrent gratuitement à leurs abonnés un espace pour créer quelques pages sur le Web. Cette option, peu coûteuse, permet de faire des essais sans prendre trop de risques. Une fois que vous avez choisi votre fournisseur d'accès, pensez à vous renseigner sur les possibilités d'évolution de votre site, sur les rapports détaillant la consultation du site et sur les transactions commerciales. Une autre possibilité consiste à faire appel à une société spécialisée pour la conception et l'hébergement de votre site, moyennant une redevance.

Beaucoup de grandes entreprises ont leur propre serveur Web. Cette solution cependant requiert des compétences techniques très poussées et un investissement considérable tant au niveau du matériel que des logiciels.

3. Recours à un prestataire ou réalisation en interne?

Le recours à un prestataire doit aboutir à la création d'un site professionnel. Renseignez-vous sur les projets déjà réalisés par la société et sur leur succès. Il vous faudra décider si vous voulez assurer la maintenance et la mise à jour du site ou si vous préférez sous-traiter cet aspect également. Le recours à une société spécialisée n'est pas forcément une solution bon marché car il faut tenir compte des efforts et du temps passés à décrire votre activité au prestataire.

La conception en interne peut également être coûteuse, que vous fassiez appel à des spécialistes ou que vous preniez le temps de créer vous-même le site. Si vous mettez en place un site important en interne, il peut être nécessaire de faire appel à un responsable de site Web ou *webmestre* ("Webmaster") expérimenté. Le webmestre se charge de la conception, de l'évolution et de la maintenance d'un site, aussi bien au niveau du contenu que pour les aspects techniques. Cela nécessite un éventail de compétences rare: maîtrise des aspects techniques et graphiques, connaissance des systèmes d'information et qualités relationnelles.

4. Enregistrement du nom de domaine

Le nom de domaine doit permettre de vous identifier rapidement. Choisissez un nom en rapport avec votre activité ou votre raison sociale. Le nom choisi doit être enregistré avant de pouvoir être utilisé, cela permet de vérifier qu'il n'est pas déjà pris. Le fournisseur d'accès peut généralement se charger de l'enregistrement du nom de domaine pour une somme minime. Les noms sont enregistrés auprès des organisations suivantes:

- En France: AFNIC – Association Française pour le Nommage Internet en Coopération (http://www.nic.fr)

- Au Royaume-Uni: Nominet (http://www.nic.uk).

- Aux États-Unis: Internic (http://www.internic.net).

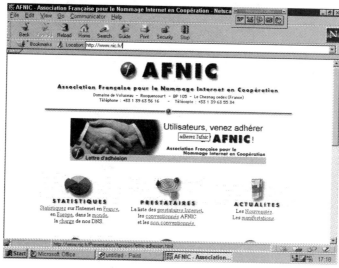

Figure 5: La page d'accueil de l'AFNIC

5. Présentation du site

Lors de la création du site, il est nécessaire de prendre en considération les deux aspects suivants:

- Conception – comment comptez-vous projeter l'image voulue?

- Navigation à l'intérieur du site – combien de fois faut-il cliquer sur la souris avant d'arriver à une information pertinente?

Il peut être utile d'observer les sites Web de différentes organisations et de noter ce qui vous plaît ou non. Consultez également des utilisateurs potentiels, leur avis peut être précieux pour rendre la présentation du site plus pratique.

business@harrap.fr

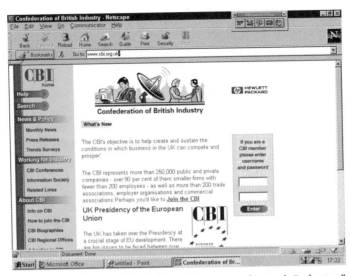

Figure 6: La page d'accueil de la "Confederation of British Industry"

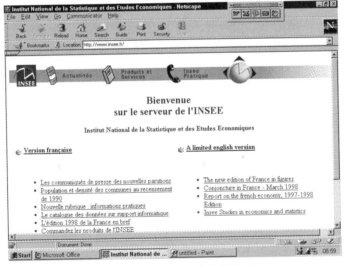

Figure 7: La page d'accueil de l'INSEE

6. Contenu du site

Les suggestions suivantes peuvent aider à rendre votre site plus intéressant et convivial:

- Affichez les réponses aux questions qui reviennent le plus fréquemment.
- Affichez des informations supplémentaires pertinentes.
- Assurez la maintenance et la mise à jour constante du site.

Une utilisation modérée de la couleur et de graphiques peut mettre en valeur votre site. N'en abusez pas cependant car cela pourrait ralentir les temps de consultation. Certains sites Web proposent en option une version texte seulement, d'autres un affichage dans d'autres langues pour toucher une clientèle internationale. Si vous souhaitez intégrer des séquences vidéo et du son, n'oubliez pas que tous les utilisateurs n'y ont pas accès.

business@harrap.fr

Bien que le coût de l'espace disque soit dérisoire, il ne faut pas oublier que la surcharge d'information sur le Web est devenue un problème. Mettez-vous à la place de l'utilisateur afin de créer une présentation qui facilite la lecture et l'assimilation des informations. Prévoyez des espaces blancs et concentrez-vous sur l'essentiel en utilisant un style clair et concis. Privilégiez la qualité plutôt que la quantité.

7. Liens hypertextes et passerelles

La structure d'un site repose sur les liens hypertextes qui permettent de relier différents documents entre eux. D'autres liens peuvent être prévus pour orienter les utilisateurs vers d'autres sites susceptibles de les intéresser. Il s'agit généralement de sites fournissant des informations complémentaires sur un sujet spécifique ou sur une activité similaire (voir l'exemple de lien dans le site *(e)-business: la lettre du commerce électronique* au chapitre précédent).

8. Participation des utilisateurs

Vous pouvez inviter les utilisateurs qui consultent votre site à:

• faire part de leurs commentaires, suggestions ou critiques;

• participer à la conception ou aux tests du produit;

• prendre part à des séances interactives visant à améliorer un produit ou un service

Sachez toutefois que toute réponse demandant une présentation plus élaborée qu'un simple message électronique entraîne du travail supplémentaire au niveau de la programmation et de la conception.

9. Sécurité

Les informations publiées sur le Web s'adressent à un public très vaste, réparti dans le monde entier. À moins de protéger vos documents, il est impossible d'en garder la trace et de savoir ce qu'ils deviennent une fois qu'ils ont été téléchargés par l'un des millions d'ordinateurs connectés. Et ce, malgré les lois internationales en matière de protection des droits d'auteur.

Vous pouvez, si vous le souhaitez, limiter l'accès de certaines sections de votre site à une catégorie spécifique d'utilisateurs ou de clients, en formant un groupe fermé d'utilisateurs dont l'accès est protégé par un mot de passe.

Si vous souhaitez relier votre site Web à des informations très confidentielles, par exemple une base de données clients dont l'accès doit être strictement contrôlé, vous pouvez installer un système de protection appelé *mur coupe-feu* ("firewall"). Ce système, de plus en plus répandu, consiste à utiliser un autre ordinateur pour filtrer les demandes d'accès. Tout demande ne correspondant pas aux critères définis est ainsi rejetée.

10. Promotion du site

Un utilisateur qui ne connaît pas l'URL de votre site, c'est-à-dire son adresse, peut le trouver de différentes façons:

• par l'intermédiaire d'un lien hypertexte dans un autre site;

business@harrap.fr

- en utilisant un moteur de recherche;

- par le bouche-à-oreille;

- dans une publicité;

- par hasard.

Il est donc essentiel que les moteurs de recherche puissent localiser votre site. Ces moteurs utilisent la page d'accueil pour l'indexation du site. Cette page doit donc contenir tous les termes et les concepts que les utilisateurs sont susceptibles d'utiliser pour vous localiser. Ces termes peuvent être cachés, si leur usage est réservé aux moteurs de recherche, ou visibles à l'écran.

Vous pouvez également recourir aux méthodes traditionnelles pour faire connaître votre site: cartes de visite, brochures de vente, rapports d'activité ou campagnes de presse. Un site Web correspondant toutefois à une stratégie marketing, il est conseillé de ne pas abuser de la publicité. En effet, ce n'est pas tant la promotion d'un site que l'intérêt qu'il suscite parmi les utilisateurs qui est garant de son succès.

4: LE COMMERCE ELECTRONIQUE

Au milieu des années quatre-vingt-dix, le président Bill Clinton déclara que l'Internet allait devenir une zone planétaire de libre-échange favorable aux transactions commerciales. Ce jugement s'appuyait sur les nombreuses prévisions du chiffre d'affaires réalisé sur l'Internet, un billion de dollars d'ici 2010 pour certains. Toutes les prévisions ne sont pas si optimistes, mais la plupart s'accordent à prévoir un chiffre d'affaires brut pouvant aller jusqu'à 300 milliards de dollars à l'échelle mondiale, avec plus de 200 milliards de dollars pour les États-Unis et plus de 60 milliards de dollars pour l'Europe, et ceci d'ici l'année 2001 (Source: Forrester Research).

Cependant, nombreux sont ceux qui restent sceptiques quant aux possibilités commerciales de l'Internet. Il y a à cela plusieurs raisons :

- À moins d'être bien informé et de s'armer de patience, on peut encore avoir l'impression que la confusion règne sur l'Internet. Les informations ou les résultats sont souvent longs à obtenir. Le téléchargement des graphiques de certains sites Web peut être lent et les liens ne marchent pas toujours car certains sites peuvent être «en cours de développement». L'encombrement des réseaux peut ralentir les temps de réponse et, dans les cas extrêmes, provoquer des interruptions.

- Des essais réalisés très tôt ont montré que les consommateurs hésitaient à faire leurs achats sur l'Internet. Les raisons avancées étaient qu'ils ne pouvaient pas voir, toucher ou goûter les produits et que le fait de ne pas pouvoir être «sur place» les gênait.

- Les consommateurs hésitent à communiquer leur numéro de carte de crédit sur le Web. En effet, il est impossible de réellement vérifier l'identité du vendeur et de s'assurer que le numéro de la carte ne se retrouvera pas entre les mains d'un escroc. Les transactions commerciales sur le Web dépendent de la vérification de l'identité de l'acheteur et du vendeur.

- Certains produits sont moins adaptés à la vente sur l'Internet que d'autres. Il est ainsi beaucoup plus facile de vendre des services et des produits culturels que des biens matériels. Ceci est dû en partie à la nature de la distribution. Les entreprises qui commercialisent des produits pour lesquels la présence de l'acheteur n'est pas indispensable, tels que des livres, des disques ou des logiciels, sont celles qui actuellement tirent le meilleur parti de l'Internet. Ce type de vente se rapproche de la vente par correspondance.

Cependant, cette situation évolue rapidement, et ce pour plusieurs raisons :

- Le Web se professionnalise grâce à la présence de grands noms et à l'idée qui fait son chemin que le marketing sur l'Internet doit cibler des groupes spécifiques, tout comme pour les autres médias. L'Internet compte de plus en plus d'utilisateurs familiarisés avec le réseau. Les consommateurs savent de mieux en mieux comment trouver les sites qui les intéressent et ce qu'ils vont y trouver. On commence à constater que les sites Web peuvent apporter un plus par rapport aux réseaux traditionnels de la vente.

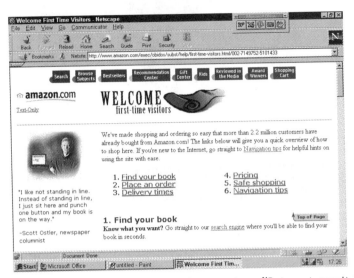

Figure 8: La librairie Amazon, qui fonctionne uniquement par l'Internet, serait d'après ses dirigeants la plus grande librairie du monde. Cet écran renseigne les utilisateurs qui consultent le site pour la première fois, et notamment ceux qui désirent en savoir plus sur les méthodes de paiement.

- Au fur et à mesure du développement de l'infrastructure de l'Internet, les télécommunications s'améliorent et les prix baissent. Des universités américaines testent actuellement Internet2, qui laisse entrevoir des taux de transmission de données 1000 fois plus rapides.

- Les institutions financières du monde entier ont beaucoup investi dans les systèmes de paiement électronique. En Europe et aux États-Unis, les principales sociétés de cartes de crédit, dont Visa et MasterCard, mettent au point des moyens de paiement sûrs, en étroite collaboration avec des éditeurs de logiciels. L'infrastructure nécessaire est encore chère, mais les prix baisseront au fur et à mesure que les entreprises adopteront le système et que les banques amortiront leur investissement.

- L'Internet qui ne connaît pas de contraintes géographiques ou temporelles offre un avantage considérable sur les moyens de vente traditionnels. En effet, la possibilité de demander un produit adapté à ses besoins, de négocier le prix et la livraison, à domicile, 24 heures sur 24, sept jours sur sept, représente un gain de temps et d'argent considérable pour le client comme pour le fabricant.

Le paiement électronique

Le développement du commerce électronique a été freiné par les pirates informatiques qui ont réussi à pénétrer dans certains systèmes qui pourtant promettaient confidentialité et sécurité. Bien que le piratage informatique reste rare, quelques affaires très médiatisées ont souvent suffi à marquer les esprits.

La monnaie électronique

De nombreux petits achats anonymes pour lesquels on n'utilise pas sa carte de crédit, par exemple l'achat de journaux et de magazines, représentent autant de transactions potentielles sur l'Internet. Plusieurs entreprises innovatrices, en collaboration avec des banques et des éditeurs de logiciels, ont mis en place un système de monnaie électronique ("e-cash") pour l'Internet dans le but de sécuriser les transactions.

Le fonctionnement d'un compte électronique est simple. Il suffit d'ouvrir un compte auprès d'une banque électronique, telle que First Virtual, DigiCash ou CyberCash. L'argent électronique est ensuite conservé sur le disque dur du client ou sur l'ordinateur de la banque et l'utilisateur autorise les paiements au moyen de son mot de passe.

Ce système fait encore peu d'adeptes en dehors des particuliers et des vendeurs qui ont pris part aux tests. Il est possible que les consommateurs s'attendent à la gratuité des informations sur le Web ou qu'ils n'aiment pas le système du paiement à la consultation, même pour de petites sommes. Parmi les autres raisons avancées devant le manque de succès de la monnaie électronique, on trouve le peu de publicité fait autour de ces systèmes ainsi que l'hésitation des consommateurs à faire des achats en ligne.

Les paiements par carte de crédit et le cryptage

Le cryptage ("encryption"), c'est-à-dire le codage des informations afin que seul le destinataire puisse les lire, est probablement la solution la plus prometteuse pour payer par carte de crédit en toute sécurité. C'est en tout cas celle qui a reçu le plus de publicité et d'investissements.

Visa et MasterCard ont mis au point conjointement un système de cryptage, SET (Secure Electronic Transaction), qui propose de sécuriser les transactions électroniques par carte de crédit à l'aide d'un cryptage pratiquement inviolable. L'expéditeur et le destinataire doivent être en possession d'un logiciel permettant de vérifier leur identité et fourni par l'organisme de carte de crédit. Le système vérifie que le vendeur est habilité à recevoir des paiements par carte de crédit, sans jamais transmettre le numéro de la carte. Les informations restent cryptées jusqu'à ce qu'elles parviennent à la banque, garantissant ainsi une sécurité maximale pour le vendeur et le client.

Une icône dorée, clef ou cadenas, apparaît en bas et à gauche de l'écran du navigateur. Lorsque l'icône est affichée en surbrillance, toute information sur la carte de crédit est cryptée avant d'être transmise. Seuls le commerçant ou la banque autorisés détiennent la clef pour décoder le message.

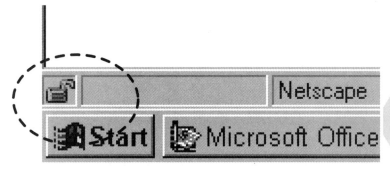

Figure 9: L'icône représentant un cadenas ouvert indique que le cryptage est impossible sur le site.

business@harrap.fr

Selon des estimations, 80% des banques européennes offriront leurs services sur l'Internet d'ici l'an 2000. Le commerce électronique a cependant encore besoin de gagner la confiance du public pour prendre son essor et ne plus être uniquement le domaine réservé de quelques pionniers.

Une stratégie commerciale sur le Web

Le nombre de sociétés réalisant des transactions et gagnant de l'argent sur le Web ne cesse de croître. Les banques pourront bientôt sécuriser les paiements électroniques. Mais avant de vendre ou d'acheter sur le Web, il est important d'effectuer un certain nombre de démarches :

- Renseignez-vous sur les préférences de vos clients pour le paiement ainsi que sur leur comportement d'achat. Vérifiez s'ils sont équipés ou non pour le commerce électronique.

- Demandez-vous si vos produits ou vos services sont bien adaptés au commerce électronique et à la vente par correspondance. Si ce n'est pas le cas, sachez qu'une vitrine virtuelle sur le Web est un bon moyen de faire connaître ses produits et d'élargir sa clientèle.

- Vérifiez que vous pouvez vous permettre l'infrastructure nécessaire au commerce électronique. Ceci est particulièrement important lorsque les prix de vente ne sont pas très élevés. Surveillez les coûts d'installation car ils vont certainement baisser.

- Consultez d'autres sites. On assiste, à la fin des années 90, au développement du commerce électronique. De nombreuses organisations sont sans cesse à la recherche de nouveaux moyens de communication interactif; c'est pourquoi certains sites créés il y a seulement deux ans paraissent déjà vieillots aujourd'hui.

- Si vous optez pour le commerce électronique, pensez aux stratégies que vous devrez développer pour créer une communauté commerciale. Pensez aux moyens de rassurer vos clients sur la sécurité des transactions électroniques. En cas de doute, réfléchissez avant de vous lancer ou demandez à vos clients d'utiliser les moyens de paiement traditionnels.

- Consultez votre banque et votre fournisseur d'accès à l'Internet pour connaître leurs projets en matière de commerce électronique et voir comment ils peuvent vous aider. Sans leur aide, mieux vaut vous contenter d'une vitrine virtuelle, que ce soit pour l'achat ou la vente.

L'Internet n'est pas hors du droit, mais sa spécificité rend difficile l'application des lois existantes. Une entreprise désirant créer un site Web doit tenir compte de la législation relative à la publicité mensongère, aux obligations des vendeurs, aux droits des consommateurs et à la propriété intellectuelle. En fonction de la complexité du site, il peut être nécessaire de faire appel à un juriste.

Publicité et vente

Toute organisation qui publie des informations sur le Web, en tant que stratégie marketing ou à des fins publicitaires, doit respecter les codes de conduite en vigueur et vérifier que les informations publiées sont correctes et à jour. Il est dans l'intérêt des entreprises de faire du Web un endroit où les consommateurs peuvent acheter en toute confiance.

En règle générale, la publicité sur le Web est soumise aux lois et à la réglementation du pays d'où se fait l'accès au site. Les entreprises doivent donc respecter les lois nationales. La compagnie aérienne Virgin a dû ainsi payer une amende, conformément à la réglementation de la publicité aux États-Unis, pour avoir affiché sur son site Web des prix qui n'étaient plus actuels. En 1996, un tribunal américain a engagé des poursuites contre une société italienne pour l'utilisation non autorisée d'une marque américaine, simplement parce que l'accès de son site Web était permis aux utilisateurs américains.

Les codes et standards du Bureau de Vérification de Publicité (BVP) en France et ceux de l'Advertising Standards Authority (ASA) au Royaume-Uni, sont valables pour le Web comme pour les autres médias. Bien que ces codes n'aient pas force de loi, la plupart des organisations obtempèrent lorsqu'elles sont rappelées à l'ordre. La loi en France punit d'autre part tout auteur de publicité mensongère. Alors que de plus en plus de sociétés utilisent le Web comme support publicitaire, le débat continue sur la question de la réglementation.

Protection des consommateurs

Au sein de l'Union européenne, les consommateurs sont couverts par la convention de Bruxelles lors de leurs transactions avec des pays membres. Bien que ce soit au consommateur de fournir les preuves, tout citoyen de l'Union européenne peut engager des poursuites dans tout pays membre contre une société située dans tout autre pays membre. Il n'existe pas à l'heure actuelle de réelle protection du consommateur lorsqu'il achète à partir d'un pays membre un bien en provenance d'un pays situé en dehors de l'Union européenne.

La directive européenne pour la vente à distance, adoptée en février 1997 par la Commission européenne, entrera certainement en vigueur avant l'an 2000. Tous les vendeurs sur le Web devront s'assurer que les termes et conditions de la vente sont facilement accessibles à l'écran. Les termes et conditions devront préciser le pays sous la juridiction duquel la vente s'effectue. Les informations suivantes devront être également obligatoirement fournies:

- le nom et l'adresse du vendeur;
- des informations détaillées sur le produit;
- les accords pour la livraison et le paiement;
- la date de livraison et la procédure à suivre en cas de retard;
- à qui incombe la responsabilité en cas de perte ou de dommages.

Pour de nombreux produits, à l'exception des produits d'information tels que des logiciels ou des magazines électroniques, le client aura le droit de résilier tout contrat de vente, à condition de respecter un délai d'une semaine après l'achat. Si un vendeur pense avoir du mal à respecter les conditions de livraison, il devra peut-être préciser clairement sur son site Web que son entreprise n'offre pas des produits en vente mais que le client est invité à faire une offre d'achat.

Taxes

L'emplacement géographique d'une société et le type de produit ou de service vendu déterminent les taxes à payer. Mais l'Internet, qui ne connaît pas de frontières temporelles ou spatiales, est en train de modifier cette conception. La notion de produit ou de service est également en pleine mutation: il ne s'agit plus nécessairement de quelque chose que l'on peut toucher ou sentir.

Le droit fiscal repose en outre sur une distinction entre les biens et les services. Mais cette distinction est loin d'être simple lorsque l'Internet est également le moyen de livraison du produit, lors par exemple du téléchargement d'un film, d'une musique ou d'un livre. Le problème devient encore plus délicat lors de transactions impliquant plusieurs pays puisqu'il faut prendre en considération différentes façons d'appliquer les taxes à l'achat et les taxes sur la valeur ajoutée.

À l'heure actuelle cependant, les responsables de l'Union européenne et des États-Unis s'accordent à vouloir faire de l'Internet une zone de libre-échange. Si l'OMC donne son accord, il n'y aura plus de droits à payer sur les transmissions électroniques.

Une autre solution consisterait à créer une taxe calculée sur le nombre de bits pour toutes les transmissions électroniques, qu'il s'agisse d'une télécopie, d'un appel téléphonique ou d'un message électronique. Une taxe portant sur toute unité numérique transmise sur l'Internet, quel qu'en soit le contenu, représenterait un changement important, en passant d'une taxe sur la valeur ajoutée à une taxe sur la quantité de données transmises.

Droits d'auteur

Suite aux progrès technologiques, la législation sur les droits d'auteur ne suffit plus pour assurer la protection de la propriété intellectuelle. Les juristes de l'Union européenne et des États-Unis continuent de réfléchir à la question, car les droits d'auteur couvrent aussi bien la transmission des documents que leur reproduction.

Dès qu'un produit culturel, qu'il s'agisse de texte, d'images, de graphiques, de vidéo ou de musique, est disponible sur l'Internet, sa valeur est menacée. Lorsqu'un client reçoit par l'intermédiaire de l'Internet un document qu'il a payé, rien à part la législation sur les droits d'auteur ne s'oppose à ce qu'il le reproduise ou le modifie sur le champ. Un document électronique peut ainsi être retransmis à des centaines, voire des milliers, d'autres destinataires par l'intermédiaire du courrier électronique ou d'un site Web. La protection des droits d'auteur, difficile dans le monde réel, est pratiquement impossible sur l'Internet. Les autorités ne peuvent donc que compter sur la bonne volonté des utilisateurs.

Bien que l'on entende généralement par édition la publication d'écrits dans des livres et des magazines, cette vision est bien trop étroite. On peut considérer que toute personne qui envoie un message électronique ou qui publie des informations dans un site Web fait également de l'édition. Par conséquent, toute information ne peut être publiée sans l'accord préalable de l'auteur.

Pour certains la législation sur les droits d'auteur va être transformée par l'Internet, pour d'autres c'est la nature des transactions sur l'Internet qui changera en fonction de la législation sur les droits d'auteur. Le débat reste ouvert.

Respect de la vie privée

En France, la loi du 6 janvier 1978 relative à l'informatique, aux fichiers et aux libertés a pour objectif la protection des droits et des libertés de la personne par rapport à la création et à l'exploitation de fichiers informatiques contenant des données personnelles. Toute personne ou entreprise désirant créer un fichier informatique qui contient des données personnelles doit obligatoirement en faire la déclaration préalable auprès de la Commission nationale de l'informatique et des libertés (CNIL) et s'engager à respecter la loi.

En 1998, une nouvelle directive de l'Union européenne renforce les normes de sécurité concernant l'accessibilité des informations sur les personnes sur tout le territoire de l'UE. Par voie de conséquence, toute information transférée à l'extérieur de l'UE bénéficie du même niveau de protection qu'à l'intérieur, et ceci même lorsque le transfert d'informations s'effectue au sein d'une même organisation.

L'un des principaux avantages du Web est que le propriétaire du site peut obtenir des informations sur les préférences de ses clients et sur leur comportement d'achat. En effet, lorsque quelqu'un consulte un site Web, il laisse son adresse Internet comme carte de visite. La pratique qui consiste à relever les adresses est parfois vue comme une intrusion dans la vie privée. Elle est cependant indissociable du fonctionnement de l'Internet: en effet, le site doit connaître le nom de domaine du visiteur pour pouvoir transmettre les informations requises. Il existe d'autres moyens d'obtenir des informations sur les personnes qui consultent le site, tels que les cartes d'enregistrement ou l'utilisation, controversée, de *cookies*.

Les cookies sont des informations relevées par le site Web et copiées sur le disque dur de l'utilisateur, souvent à son insu. Ces informations qui portent sur les habitudes d'utilisation de l'Internet et sur les activités du client, peuvent ensuite être récupérées par le serveur lors d'une consultation ultérieure du site. Certains navigateurs peuvent être configurés pour avertir de l'envoi d'un cookie et les programmes les plus récents donnent la possibilité de les rejeter. Il existe également des programmes, tels que Cookie Crusher et Cookie Crumbler, qui rejettent automatiquement tous les cookies. Certains sites Web précisent qu'ils n'utilisent pas de cookies.

Propositions pour le commerce électronique mondial

En juillet 1997, le président des États-Unis a exposé les principales règles du commerce électronique international dans un document intitulé *"A Framework for Global Electronic Commerce"*. Ces propositions qui incluent la nécessité de faire de l'Internet une zone de libre-échange pour le commerce électronique, s'organisent autour de cinq principes et neuf thèmes.

Principes

1. La priorité doit être donnée au secteur privé.

2. Les gouvernements doivent s'abstenir de prendre des mesures qui freinent de façon excessive le libre-échange sur l'Internet.

3. Lorsqu'une aide gouvernementale est nécessaire, son objectif devra être de définir un cadre juridique simple, prévisible et cohérent.

4. Les gouvernements doivent reconnaître les qualités propres à l'Internet.

5. Le commerce électronique sur l'Internet doit être facilité au niveau mondial.

Thèmes

1. Douanes et taxes

2. Systèmes de paiement électronique

3. "Code commercial uniforme" pour le commerce électronique

4. Protection de la propriété intellectuelle

5. Respect de la vie privée

6. Sécurité

7. Infrastructure des télécommunications et de l'informatique

8. Contenu: publicité et fraude

9. Normes techniques.

Le document original complet (A Framework for Global Electronic Commerce, The White House, July 1, 1997) peut être consulté à l'adresse suivante: http://www.ecommerce.gov.framewrk.htm

L'intégration de l'Internet dans la stratégie de l'entreprise nécessite une analyse des opportunités et des limites du réseau, des objectifs fixés et du meilleur moyen de les atteindre ainsi que des forces et des faiblesses de l'entreprise. Une gestion efficace repose sur une vision stratégique de l'avenir.

Les limites de l'Internet

Les objectifs à atteindre dépendent en grande partie de la vision que l'entreprise a de l'Internet et des bénéfices qu'elle pense en tirer.

Le nombre de nouveaux utilisateurs, la quantité de nouvelles pages Web et les ventes de produits et de services continuent d'augmenter de plus de 100% par an.

Pour beaucoup cependant l'Internet, encore entouré de mystère, ne signifie pas grand-chose ou reste trop compliqué et confus. Les critiques portent essentiellement sur les aspects suivants:

- le développement anarchique du réseau, où informations sérieuses et sites pornographiques se côtoient;

- la confusion et la surcharge d'information, ainsi que la prédominance d'informations peu intéressantes;

- la lenteur des temps de réponse et des transmissions aux heures de pointe;

- les fréquentes interruptions, dues à la saturation des lignes, dont on entend beaucoup parler;

- la rapidité d'évolution des technologies, trop difficile à suivre pour beaucoup;

- l'absence de preuves réelles de la rentabilité de l'Internet;

- la préférence de la télévision, par câble ou par satellite, en raison de la complexité et des incohérences du Web.

Les opportunités offertes par l'Internet

Cette vision négative ne tient pas compte des nombreux signes d'évolution:

1. La croissance continuelle de l'Internet et sa présence à l'échelle planétaire.

2. Les développements technologiques constants, tels que Internet2, pour répondre aux besoins des entreprises.

3. Les investissements faits par les principales banques et éditeurs de logiciels pour développer le commerce électronique sur le Web.

4. Le succès commercial rapide que de nombreuses entreprises ont connu.

5. La promotion, les injections de fonds publics et les efforts législatifs réalisés par l'Union européenne et les États-Unis ainsi que par différents États.

business@harrap.fr

6. La prédominance de l'esprit d'entreprise qui refuse de construire l'avenir avec les recettes du passé.

D'autres signes vont dans le sens de ce scénario positif:

- La confiance grandissante des consommateurs grâce à la mise en place de systèmes de paiement sécurisés.

- L'adoption de mesures efficaces pour la protection des droits d'auteur.

- L'apparition de standards adoptés par les grands groupes de télécommunications, les éditeurs de logiciels et les sociétés commerciales.

- L'installation de moyens de télécommunication très performants, chez les particuliers et dans les entreprises, suites aux subventions des gouvernements, aux investissements des sociétés de télécommunication et des particuliers.

- La possibilité, pour ceux qui préfèrent payer plus pour un service de qualité, de se connecter à l'Internet par l'intermédiaire de réseaux privés, plus importants et plus fiables.

- La baisse des prix de connexion et d'accès à l'Internet en raison de la concurrence.

- L'intégration progressive de l'Internet dans la vie professionnelle et privée, au même titre que la presse et la télévision.

Modèles économiques

Une entreprise a en gros le choix entre cinq modèles économiques différents pour offrir des services sur l'Internet:

1. *Communication* – L'Internet est dans ce cas principalement utilisé pour bénéficier de la rapidité et de l'efficacité du courrier électronique.

2. *Publicité* – L'entreprise peut utiliser son site Web comme une vitrine commerciale. Elle peut également, moyennant paiement, afficher des bandeaux publicitaires dans d'autres sites Web et dans des moteurs de recherche.

3. *Abonnement* – Il est possible de proposer l'accès illimité à un service ou à un produit, par exemple, un journal, un magazine ou un service de mise à jour, sur abonnement, généralement payable annuellement. Pour être viable, ce modèle nécessite un changement de comportement des utilisateurs du Web, qui jusqu'à présent hésitent à utiliser des services payants.

4. *Marketing* – L'entreprise peut fournir des informations générales ou personnalisées ainsi que des attractions. Dans ce cas, le site Web peut, grâce à son interactivité, offrir aux groupes d'utilisateurs sélectionnés, les communautés, un service supérieur à celui de la télévision.

5. *Cybermagasin* – Une entreprise peut faire de la vente sur le Web. Le commerce électronique doit cependant auparavant surmonter certains obstacles majeurs et gagner la confiance du grand public.

Principes stratégiques

1. Il est essentiel de bien comprendre le fonctionnement de l'Internet et son potentiel, en lisant la presse et les ouvrages spécialisés, en faisant des essais et en discutant avec d'autres utilisateurs.

2. Une vue d'ensemble de l'entreprise et de ses objectifs est indispensable pour comprendre ce que l'Internet peut apporter à l'organisation et à ses clients.

3. L'entreprise doit chercher à connaître ses clients, en analysant les comportements d'achat et le niveau d'interactivité requis. Cette analyse doit également tenir compte de l'attente des clients, des informations que l'entreprise souhaite obtenir sur sa clientèle, et de ce que l'Internet peut apporter aux produits et aux services proposés. Il peut s'agir d'une meilleure information, de nouvelles méthodes de distribution ou bien d'un service personnalisé pour les particuliers et les groupes.

4. La participation de la direction et la contribution du plus grand nombre de personnes sont indispensables au succès de l'utilisation de l'Internet. Le personnel doit pour cela se familiariser avec le fonctionnement du réseau. Des compétences techniques, graphiques et juridiques sont nécessaires. Il est important de déterminer les ressources qu'il est possible, ou souhaitable, de dédier à l'Internet.

5. Mieux vaut ne pas voir trop grand au départ, l'essentiel est de commencer. Il est important de définir des objectifs précis et de prévoir des résultats rapides, sans s'attendre à des miracles. Sachez reconnaître les personnes qui peuvent aider à obtenir ces résultats et prouver ainsi le succès du projet.

6. Le succès d'un site Web ne se mesure pas uniquement au nombre de ventes réalisées. Il ne faut pas négliger toutes les activités qui, en suscitant l'intérêt et les questions d'éventuels clients, peuvent indirectement générer des ventes.

7. Pour la clientèle comme pour le personnel, les activités sur l'Internet doivent refléter les activités réelles de l'entreprise.

8. Des procédures devront être mises en place pour déterminer:

• Les personnes qui ont accès au Web et les critères d'attribution de l'accès.

• Le type d'informations qui pourront être importées du réseau.

• Les auteurs responsables des informations publiées sur le Web.

9. Il est important de suivre de près l'utilisation de l'Internet, en analysant certaines données : niveau d'utilisation du courrier électronique et du Web au sein de l'organisation, économies réalisées sur le temps du personnel, revenus directs ou indirects et réactions des clients.

10. Les services créés sur l'Internet doivent rester flexibles et pouvoir évoluer rapidement. Il est essentiel pour cela d'assurer une veille technologique, d'explorer les nouvelles possibilités et de ne pas hésiter à prendre des risques.

Pour finir, il est important de se tenir au courant des innovations dans le domaine de l'Internet. Au mois de septembre 1998 la société Dixons, le géant britannique de l'électroménager, a innové en proposant l'accès gratuit à l'Internet. L'accès à l'Internet étant de moins en moins cher, il est recommandé de se familiariser avec les multiples possibilités qu'il offre afin de déterminer le genre de services qu'il peut vous rendre.

business@harrap.fr

business@harrap.fr

Table des Matières

Introduction

La correspondance commerciale en anglais, influencée par la brièveté des faxs et du courrier électronique, exige l'emploi d'un style direct et concis, mais toujours soigné. Les exemples suivants sont des lettres simples et précises dont on espère qu'elles susciteront des réponses tout aussi claires!

Il convient de noter les points suivants:

Mise en page

- Une présentation aérée contribue à une meilleure compréhension du message.

Style

- On emploiera de préférence un ton amical mais respectueux. L'utilisation de contractions telles que "don't", "I've" et "she'd" pour "do not", "I have", et "she had/would", réservées à la communication orale, est à éviter. La communication écrite exige ainsi l'emploi de mots dans leur forme non abrégée.

- La correspondance électronique et les faxs se caractérisent par une langue moins soutenue et plus spontanée.

Organisation

- Chaque phrase doit comporter une idée principale de même que chaque paragraphe doit traiter d'un seul sujet. Dans la mesure du possible, on emploiera le même temps à l'intérieur d'une même phrase (le passé composé, par exemple). De plus, afin d'éviter toute confusion, il est recommandé de commencer une nouvelle phrase lorsque l'on souhaite changer de temps (par exemple, le passé puis le présent). Chaque paragraphe doit comporter un maximum de trois ou quatre phrases.

Début et fin

- On portera une attention toute particulière à l'appellation retenue pour s'adresser au destinataire, comme Ms/Mr, Sir or Madam. Rappelons que la formule d'appel Ms est utilisée lorsque le statut marital de la destinataire est inconnu ou lorsque celle-ci s'est précédemment présentée comme telle. En anglais les formules de politesse finales varient en fonction des formules d'appel choisies en début de lettre (voir modèle de lettre i).

- Enfin, la clarté du message doit être privilégiée avant toute chose. Il est en outre essentiel de définir précisément l'impact souhaité du message ainsi que le type de réponse attendu, et ce, préalablement à toute rédaction.

Conseil: Lorsque l'on répond à une lettre, il peut être utile d'utiliser l'original comme support. Ainsi on prendra soin d'y relever les points cruciaux développés par l'expéditeur, les formules à répéter ainsi que les passages mentionnant propositions et dates.

business@harrap.fr

A. Lettres, fax, courrier électronique

Modèles de lettres

i. Présentation générale et style – Proposer un rendez-vous

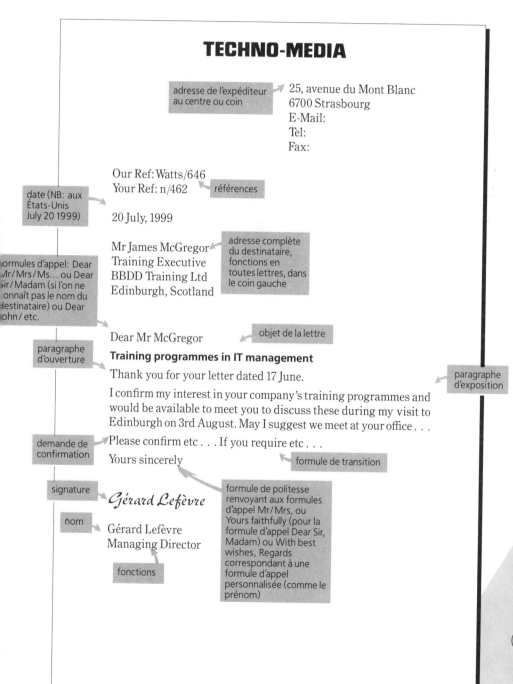

TECHNO-MEDIA

adresse de l'expéditeur au centre ou coin

25, avenue du Mont Blanc
6700 Strasbourg
E-Mail:
Tel:
Fax:

Our Ref: Watts/646
Your Ref: n/462   références

date (NB: aux États-Unis July 20 1999)

20 July, 1999

Mr James McGregor
Training Executive
BBDD Training Ltd
Edinburgh, Scotland

adresse complète du destinataire, fonctions en toutes lettres, dans le coin gauche

ormules d'appel: Dear Mr/Mrs/Ms... ou Dear Sir/Madam (si l'on ne connaît pas le nom du destinataire) ou Dear John/ etc.

Dear Mr McGregor   objet de la lettre

paragraphe d'ouverture

Training programmes in IT management

Thank you for your letter dated 17 June.

paragraphe d'exposition

I confirm my interest in your company's training programmes and would be available to meet you to discuss these during my visit to Edinburgh on 3rd August. May I suggest we meet at your office . . .

demande de confirmation

Please confirm etc . . . If you require etc . . .

Yours sincerely   formule de transition

signature

Gérard Lefèvre

formule de politesse renvoyant aux formules d'appel Mr/Mrs, ou Yours faithfully (pour la formule d'appel Dear Sir, Madam) ou With best wishes, Regards correspondant à une formule d'appel personnalisée (comme le prénom)

nom

Gérard Lefèvre
Managing Director

fonctions

ii. Facture de livraison

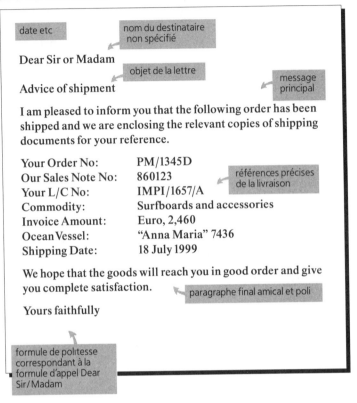

date etc

nom du destinataire non spécifié

Dear Sir or Madam

objet de la lettre

message principal

Advice of shipment

I am pleased to inform you that the following order has been shipped and we are enclosing the relevant copies of shipping documents for your reference.

Your Order No:	PM/1345D
Our Sales Note No:	860123
Your L/C No:	IMPI/1657/A
Commodity:	Surfboards and accessories
Invoice Amount:	Euro, 2,460
Ocean Vessel:	"Anna Maria" 7436
Shipping Date:	18 July 1999

références précises de la livraison

We hope that the goods will reach you in good order and give you complete satisfaction.

paragraphe final amical et poli

Yours faithfully

formule de politesse correspondant à la formule d'appel Dear Sir/Madam

iii. Réponse à une facture

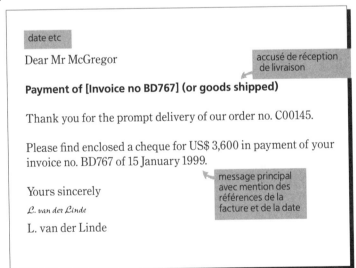

date etc

Dear Mr McGregor

accusé de réception de livraison

Payment of [Invoice no BD767] (or goods shipped)

Thank you for the prompt delivery of our order no. C00145.

Please find enclosed a cheque for US$ 3,600 in payment of your invoice no. BD767 of 15 January 1999.

message principal avec mention des références de la facture et de la date

Yours sincerely

L. van der Linde

L. van der Linde

iv. Publipostage

B R A C O M S A

25 rue Consolat 13100 Aix-en-Provence France Tel. Fax.

Simon Software Inc
291 Howard Street
Santa Fe
New Mexico 87051
USA

> code postal ("zip code" aux États-Unis)

7 February 2000

Dear Sir/Madam

Publishing Opportunities in Europe

> Para 1, 1. présentation de la société
> 2. objet de la lettre

We are an established publisher of European trade and business journals with high visibility throughout the Economic Community, central and eastern Europe. Currently we are offering special advertising rates and benefits to new customers.

> pourquoi faire appel aux services de la société

This is an excellent opportunity for your company to increase its share of the IT market in the dynamic European market place.

Please find enclosed two copies of our journals, with our compliments. If you wish to pursue our offer (attached) or require any further information, please contact our enquiry line on Freefone 0800 3765.

> comment prendre contact avec la société

I look forward to hearing from you and to our possible future partnership.

Yours sincerely

> conclusion positive, ouverture sur l'avenir

J. C. Moreau

J. C. Moreau
Sales Director

business@harrap.fr

v. Réponse à une demande de renseignements

RANDONNEE MATOS

33 Rue Diderot
75012 Paris
France
Tel . . . (E-mail . . .)

(Ms) Laura Little
Rocksport Climbing Ltd
18 New Street
Birmingham
United Kingdom

date à droite

Ms est une formule d'appel de plus en plus utilisée dans la correspondance commerciale pour s'adresser aux femmes

2 March, 1999

Dear Ms Little

On ajoute parfois Re: avant l'objet de la lettre mais cet emploi est déconseillé

Re: Mountaineering wholesale products

Thank you for enquiry of 28 February about our products.
I enclose our current catalogue and price list with details of discounts and delivery dates.

If you require any further information, please contact me. I look forward to hearing from you soon.

Yours sincerely

Angelica Rosetti

Angelica Rosetti

vi. Lettre de réclamation

note: une lettre de réclamation doit être ferme mais polie, autoritaire sans être personnelle dans les reproches ni vindicative dans le ton

Dear Mrs Riddell

objet de la plainte

Order 2789 - failure to deliver

référence de la commande

I am writing to you in connection with your letter of 24 April concerning the above order for new computers (and IT equipment).

Unfortunately, we have not yet received the computers promised with this delivery order.

exposition du problème

As the delivery is now four weeks overdue, we would be grateful if you would forward these goods as soon as possible.

informations supplémentaires éventuelles et demande d'intervention

We look forward to hearing from you.

Yours sincerely

Mr Peter Lang
Manager

on peut être plus ferme encore, en écrivant par exemple: i. We intend to pursue this matter, ii. We look forward to your early reply and action to remedy this fault

vii. Lettre d'excuse/réponse à une lettre de réclamation

note: la lettre d'excuse garde la même structure que la lettre de réclamation

1 June 99

Dear Mr Lang

Order 2789

accusé de réception de la lettre de réclamation du client

Thank you for your letter of 30 May, bringing to our attention the delay in the delivery of your computers (for the above order).

I should like to apologise for the delay and the inconvenience this obviously has caused your company.

We have experienced supply problems from our factory in Warrington which have now been remedied. The computers are expected to arrive at our depot later this week and I shall contact you on their arrival to arrange a speedy delivery.

brève justification et détail des mesures prises pour remédier au problème

Thank you for your patience and I look forward to advising you later this week.

Yours sincerely (etc)

e
ntervention

business@harrap.fr

viii. Fax, notes de service

Quelques conseils et remarques pour une rédaction efficace de fax et de notes de service:

- Ne faire figurer que les informations essentielles, comme les jours et heures, les lieux et les personnes.

- Les phrases peuvent être rédigées dans un style télégraphique: seuls les noms, adjectifs et expressions les plus importants seront ainsi employés.

- Les abréviations et les acronymes sont souvent utilisés pour remplacer des mots voire des expressions entières. Toutefois seules les abréviations reconnues doivent être employées (voir page 11).

- Classer par ordre de priorité les différents points du message au moyen de tirets.

- Les voyelles peuvent parfois être omises. Ainsi, on écrira "yr lttr dtd . . ." pour "your letter dated".

- Veiller au ton général du message — les messages courts et factuels peuvent sembler froids. Il est donc conseillé d'ajouter des formules de politesse informelles, comme, par exemple, "Best Wishes, Clive".

Attn[1]: Miguel Garcia

Date: Monday 18 Sept

Re: Itinerary for visit to France

Arrival date now Tues[2] 19 Sept[3] Flight IB 234 arr[4] Paris CDG[5] 18.40. Please arrange visit to Benefin Wednesday a.m.[6] and meeting at yr[7] office Wed[8] p.m. Flight Paris — Lyon Thurs[9] morning.

Miguel, call Sally a.s.a.p.[10] to confirm.

Thanks and regards.

Hamish Scott

Code

1. Attention
2. Tuesday
3. September
4. arrive
5. Charles De Gaulle airport
6. morning
7. your
8. Wednesday afternoon/evening
9. Thursday
10. as soon as possible

ix. Courrier électronique

- Une adresse électronique comprend deux parties. La première est constituée du nom du destinataire et la seconde du nom de domaine. Les deux parties sont séparées par une arrobase @ (que l'on prononce "at" en anglais). Il est essentiel de taper l'adresse exacte car la moindre faute de frappe empêcherait le message de parvenir à votre correspondant.

- Le courrier électronique étant un moyen de communication rapide, les messages sont souvent rédigés en style télégraphique en utilisant de nombreux acronymes et abréviations. La concision du style et l'utilisation de formes abrégées peuvent parfois créer des problèmes. Il convient de n'utiliser que les abréviations et les acronymes dont vous savez qu'ils seront compris par votre correspondant.

- Pour indiquer que l'on hausse le ton au cours d'un message, on passe des lettres minuscules aux lettres majuscules. Il est donc recommandé d'éviter d'écrire un message en n'utilisant que des lettres majuscules dans la mesure où votre correspondant interprèterait cela comme un signe de mauvaise humeur de votre part.

- La convivialité du courrier électronique encourage une certaine familiarité, que l'on peut parfois regretter après-coup. Cette caractéristique a répandu le sentiment que les messages électroniques sont peu fiables, non durables, voire même inexacts, et ne valent donc pas la peine d'être cités.

- Il faut savoir que le courrier électronique est une forme de publication qui est donc soumise en tant que telle à la législation relative aux droits d'auteur et à la diffamation. Un message électronique doit par conséquent être considéré de la même façon que toute autre forme de communication écrite.

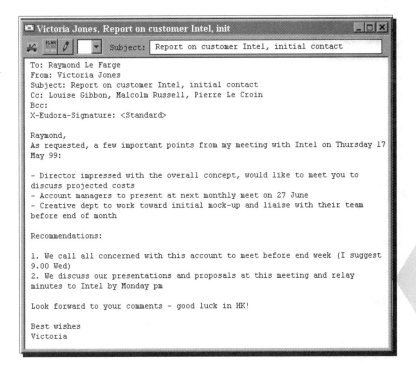

business@harrap.fr

Courrier électronique: abréviations, acronymes et souriants

1. Abréviations et acronymes

On trouvera ci-dessous la liste des abréviations les plus couramment utilisées dans le courrier électronique et les groupes de discussion. Il est recommandé de n'employer ces abréviations que lorsque l'on est sûr que le destinataire connaît leur signification. Certaines d'entre elles appartiennent à un registre plus familier (elles sont suivies ici de la mention *Fam*) et doivent être réservées à une correspondance plus relâchée:

Adv	Advice (conseil)
AFAICT *Fam*	As Far As I Can Tell (Pour autant que je sache)
AFAIK *Fam*	As Far As I Know (Pour autant que je sache)
AFK	Away From Keyboard (indique que l'on va quitter momentanément son poste)
AIUI *Fam*	As I Understand It (si j'ai bien compris)
B4 *Fam*	Before (avant)
BAK	Back At Keyboard (de retour devant l'écran)
BBL *Fam*	Be Back Later (je reviens)
BTW *Fam*	By The Way (à propos)
cld	could
Doc	Document (document)
EOF	End Of File (fin de fichier)
FAQ	Frequently Asked Questions (Foire aux questions)
FOC	Free Of Charge (gratuit, gratuitement)
Foll	following, to follow (suivant, à suivre)
FYI	For Your Information (pour ton/ votre information)
HTH *Fam*	Hope This Helps (j'espère que cela te/vous sera utile)
IIRC *Fam*	If I Recall Correctly (si mes souvenirs sont bons)
IMHO *Fam*	In My Humble Opinion (à mon humble avis)
IMO *Fam*	In My Opinion (à mon avis)
IOW *Fam*	In Other Words (autrement dit)
ISTM *Fam*	It Seems To Me (il me semble que)
ITRO *Fam*	In The Region Of (environ)
NRN *Fam*	No Reply Necessary (réponse facultative)
NW! *Fam*	No Way! (sûrement pas !)
OTOH *Fam*	On The Other Hand (d'un autre côté)
OTT *Fam*	Over The Top (excessif)
PD	Public Domain (domaine public)
prhps	perhaps (peut-être)
TIA *Fam*	Thanks In Advance (merci d'avance)
TNX *Fam*	Thanks (merci)
TVM *Fam*	Thanks Very Much (merci beaucoup)
VR	Virtual Reality (réalité virtuelle)
WRT *Fam*	With Regard To (en ce qui concerne)

2. Souriants

Bien que quelques esprits chagrins en condamnent l'emploi, les souriants (c'est-à-dire des caractères du clavier qui, lorsque l'on penche la tête à gauche, forment des visages) sont fréquemment utilisés dans la correspondance électronique et, chaque jour ou presque, un nouveau souriant apparaît sur les

business@harrap.fr

écrans. Comme les abréviations, les souriants ne doivent être employés qu'à l'occasion d'une correspondance amicale. Les souriants les plus utilisés sont:

:-)	Content; Je plaisante
:-(	Triste
;-)	Clin d'œil
:-O	Choqué
:-I	Froncer les sourcils
:-\	Sceptique

Abréviations et acronymes: correspondance générale

a/c	account (compte)
ack.	acknowledge
add.	addendum (addenda)
ad val.	ad valorem, according to the value (ad valorem, selon la valeur)
AGM	Annual general meeting (assemblée générale annuelle)
am, a.m.	ante meridiem, morning (du matin)
AOB	any other business (questions diverses)
approx.	approximately (approximativement)
appx.	appendix (appendice)
APR	Annual Percentage Rate (taux effectif global)
asap	as soon as possible (dès que possible)
av.	average (moyenne)
Bal	balance (solde)
b/d	banker's draft (chèque bancaire)
bc.	blind copy (of a memo, letter)
bcc.	blind carbon copy
b/e	bill of exchange (lettre de change)
bk	bank; book (banque; livre)
bkcy	bankruptcy (faillite)
bkpt	bankrupt (en faillite)
B/L, bl	bill of lading (connaissement)
b/s	bill of sale (acte, contrat de vente)
BST	British Summer Time (heure d'été en Grande-Bretagne)
c.	circa, approximately (aux alentours de, environ)
CB	Cash book (livre de caisse)
cc	carbon copy (copies to)
CEO	Chief Executive Officer (président-directeur général)
CET	Central European Time (heure de l'Europe centrale)
chq	cheque (chèque)
c.i.f., CIF	Cost, insurance and freight (coût, assurance et fret)
C/O	Care of; carried over; cash order (aux bons soins de; reporté; ordre au comptant)
Co	company; county (entreprise; comté)
COD	Cash on delivery (paiement à la livraison)
Conf	confirm; conference (Confirmez; conférence)
Cons.	consul (consul)
contd, cont'd	continued (suite)
CV	curriculum vitae (curriculum vitae)
Cx	contrast

business@harrap.fr

DD	direct debit (prélèvement automatique)
del.	delivery; delivered (livraison, livré)
Dir	Director (directeur)
Dr	Doctor (docteur, médecin)
E&OE	Errors and omissions excepted (sauf erreur ou omission)
eg	for example (par exemple)
EGM	Extraordinary general meeting (assemblée générale extraordinaire)
enc(s)	enclosure(s) (pièce(s) jointe(s))
ETA	estimated time of arrival (heure d'arrivée prévue)
FAO, fao	for the attention of (à l'attention de)
ff	following (suite à)
ffy	faithfully
HM	His/Her Majesty's (eg: HMC — Her Majesty's Customs) (Sa Majesté le Roi, la Reine)
ie, i.e.	in other words (c'est-à-dire)
Inc., Incorp	incorporated
incl.	included, including (joint(e), y compris)
infm., info	information (information)
inst	of this month (courant, de ce mois)
L/C	letter of credit (lettre de crédit)
Ltd	Limited company (société à responsabilité limitée)
mgr.	manager (directeur, dirigeant, responsable)
mtg.	meeting (réunion)
NB	note well (nota bene)
OD	overdraft (découvert, solde débiteur)
OHP	Overhead projector (rétroprojecteur)
ono	or nearest offer (prix à débattre)
p.a.	per annum, each year (par an)
P&L	profit and loss (pertes et profits)
p&p	postage and packing (frais d'emballage et d'expédition)
PAYE	pay as you earn (retenue de l'impôt sur le revenu à la base ou à la source)
PLC	public limited company (= société anonyme)
pm, p.m.	post meridiem, afternoon/evening (de l'après-midi/du soir)
p.o.	postal order (mandat postal)
pp	post procurationem, on behalf of (au nom de, de la part de)
pps	additional postscript (post postscriptum)
Pres.	president (président)
Prof.	professor (professeur)
ps	postscript (postscriptum)
PTO	please turn over (tournez la page svp)
rc'd	received (reçu)
re	with reference to (objet/à propos de, en référence à)
Ref	reference (référence)
req(d)	required (requis)
retd	retired (retraité)
sae	stamped addressed envelope (enveloppe timbrée)
sase	self-addressed stamped envelope (enveloppe timbrée à son propre nom)
SO	standing order (virement automatique)

tba	to be advised
tbc	to be confirmed (à confirmer)
ult.	ultimo, last (dernier)
viz	namely (à savoir, c'est-à-dire)
VP	Vice-president (vice-président)
yf	Yours faithfully (cordialement)
ys	Yours sincerely (cordialement)

— Abréviations utilisées dans les adresses —

Les abréviations suivantes sont fréquemment utilisées dans les adresses, et peuvent figurer aussi bien en-tête que sur les enveloppes:

Ave	Avenue
Blvd	Boulevard
Cres	Crescent
Ct	Court
Dr	Drive
Gdns	Gardens
Pk	Park
Pl	Place
Rd	Road
Sq	Square
St	Street
Terr	Terrace

B. CV et lettre de motivation

i. CV chronologique

Un bon CV se distingue aujourd'hui par sa concision (deux pages au maximum). En outre, on gardera à l'esprit les exigences et spécificités du poste pour lequel on postule quand il s'agira de sélectionner et mettre en valeur expériences professionnelles et diplômes obtenus.

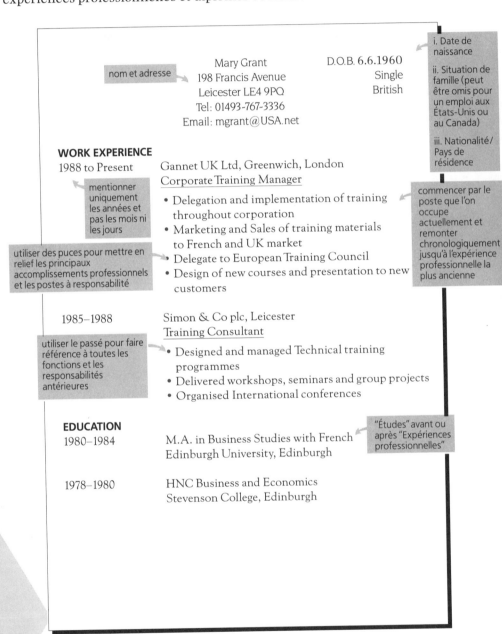

i. Date de naissance

ii. Situation de famille (peut être omis pour un emploi aux États-Unis ou au Canada)

iii. Nationalité/ Pays de résidence

nom et adresse

Mary Grant
198 Francis Avenue
Leicester LE4 9PQ
Tel: 01493-767-3336
Email: mgrant@USA.net

D.O.B. 6.6.1960
Single
British

WORK EXPERIENCE

1988 to Present

mentionner uniquement les années et pas les mois ni les jours

Gannet UK Ltd, Greenwich, London
Corporate Training Manager

commencer par le poste que l'on occupe actuellement et remonter chronologiquement jusqu'à l'expérience professionnelle la plus ancienne

- Delegation and implementation of training throughout corporation
- Marketing and Sales of training materials to French and UK market
- Delegate to European Training Council
- Design of new courses and presentation to new customers

utiliser des puces pour mettre en relief les principaux accomplissements professionnels et les postes à responsabilité

1985–1988

Simon & Co plc, Leicester
Training Consultant

utiliser le passé pour faire référence à toutes les fonctions et les responsabilités antérieures

- Designed and managed Technical training programmes
- Delivered workshops, seminars and group projects
- Organised International conferences

EDUCATION

1980–1984

M.A. in Business Studies with French
Edinburgh University, Edinburgh

"Études" avant ou après "Expériences professionnelles"

1978–1980

HNC Business and Economics
Stevenson College, Edinburgh

ii. CV ciblé

Un CV ciblé est rédigé spécifiquement dans le cadre d'une candidature à une fonction ou à un secteur professionnel précis. On insistera plus sur les compétences et les résultats que sur le parcours.

FRANK RENOIR
22 Mayhew Road
Birmingham BO3 6NK
(0121) 444 7742

D.O.B.: 14/2/64

Status: Married

type de poste
que l'on
souhaite
obtenir

Target: Marketing Consultant/Product Manager

Capabilities:

- Product management experience
- Co-ordinator, marketing teams
- Advertising account handling
- Creative and copy writing experience
- Management of product development teams
- Financial management
- Market research analysis

les compétences
et l'expérience
professionelle
sont privilégiées

Achievements:

- Responsible for marketing new soft drinks brand promotion
- Consulted to BBCO Agency, new sales strategy, customer executives at meetings
- Presented to international advertising conferences, USA and France, on new product issues
- Successful launch of new retail outlets in South of France and Italy

Work History:
1990–1999 Roberts Media Enterprises Inc, London
Seattle, USA (Headquarters)

Education:
1985–1989 MBA Harvard Business School

iii. Lettre de motivation

Une lettre de motivation claire et accrocheuse est le complément indispensable du CV.

Robert Flaubert
46 Rue St.Denis
70689 Paris
France

Ms M Legg
Chief Analyst
Dundonell Investments
Threadneedle Street
London E3 6GP
England

16 May 1999

Dear Ms Legg ← *fonction/poste*

Financial Analyst

référence au CV; on peut aussi écrire: "Please find full career history on my CV (enc.)"

I should like to apply for the above post recently advertised in 'Le Monde', (14.5.99), and I enclose my current CV for your attention.

mettre en valeur ses qualités, en une ou deux phrases ou même un paragraphe →

I am an experienced Financial analyst, consultant and presenter, having worked extensively in this sector in Paris and Brussels, and as a lecturer at the university in The Hague. I am currently looking for a position which will allow me to develop my skills and experience in a small, dynamic commercial team such as Dundonnel Investments. I believe that my financial and academic background would be of benefit to your strategic financial planning and the building of partnerships with investment houses throughout Europe.

paragraphe de développement comportant un résumé du parcours (en une phrase) et expliquant pourquoi l'on postule à ce poste

Thank you for considering this application and I look forward to discussing matters further with you at a future interview. ← *paragraphe final suggérant une rencontre future*

Yours sincerely

R. Flaubert

R. Flaubert
Financial Investment Analyst
Enc.

C. Conversation téléphonique

Comme par écrit, la clarté, la simplicité ainsi qu'un ton formel mais amical, contribuent à une communication efficace en anglais. En outre, il convient de noter les points suivants:

- Parler doucement et distinctement

- Laisser à l'interlocuteur le temps d'assimiler votre message et écouter attentivement les mots-clés utilisés par celui-ci dans sa réponse (heures, dates, lieux, rendez-vous etc)

- Ne pas hésiter à demander à l'interlocuteur de répéter si l'on est pas sûr d'avoir bien compris une information importante

- Etre prêt à épeler des mots en anglais et à demander à votre interlocuteur d'épeler

- Résumer les points importants et repréciser tous les chiffres; être prêt à dicter des chiffres au téléphone

Prononciation des numéros de téléphone

34062	Three four oh six two (*Anglais britannique*)
	Three four zero six two (*Américain*)
95587	Nine, double five, eight, seven

Expressions courantes

1. Demander un interlocuteur:
- Could I speak to . . .?
- Can I speak to . . .?
- I'd like to speak to . . .
- Extension 593 please

2. Répondre à un appel:
- Paul Smith speaking, can I help you?
- Yes, speaking (*confirme que l'on est bien la personne demandée*)
- I'm sorry he/she is not here. Can I take a message?
- Hold on/hold please, I'll get him/her ('to hold' *signifie* 'to wait')
- I'm afraid she's on holiday/off sick (ill)

3. Laisser un message:

A la personne elle-même:

- I'd like to arrange to meet . . .
- I'm returning your call . . .
- I'll be in London, perhaps we can . . .
- Could we meet to discuss . . .

En l'absence de la personne:

- Could you ask him to call me . . .
- Could you tell her that I won't be able to make our meeting
- I'll call back later
- Yes, I need to speak urgently . . .
- Please ask her to confirm . . . thank you

business@harrap.fr

4. Demander une confirmation:

- Could you spell that please?
- Can you speak a little slower please?
- Would you repeat that please?
- Let me just check, 12.00 am Tuesday, meeting in Lyons . . . yes

On peut entendre la phrase suivante:

- I'm sorry, I didn't catch that (*dans ce cas, on répètera ce que l'on vient de dire*)

5. Conclure un appel:

- Thank you, I look forward to seeing you on Tuesday, goodbye
- Thanks for your help, I look forward to your report, 'bye
- Can I summarise/check then?, Wednesday at 3.00 pm, OK?

6. Message de répondeur téléphonique:

La formule la plus couramment utilisée est la suivante:

- We are unable to take your call at the moment. Please leave a message after the tone.

Ne pas oublier que **please** et **thank you** sont très appréciés dans les conversations téléphoniques en anglais et utilisés fréquemment.

LES REUNIONS D'AFFAIRES DANS LES PAYS ANGLO-SAXONS

par Maddy Glas

Maddy Glas, Docteur de la Sorbonne, après avoir travaillé dans plusieurs pays de l'Union européenne, enseigne le français des affaires au département de langues de l'INSEAD en France.

Table des Matières

Illustrations de Jenny Cantwell

business@harrap.fr

Considérations générales

Les réunions tiennent une place essentielle dans l'organisation de la vie de l'entreprise. Une réunion formelle présente certaines, ou toutes les caractéristiques suivantes:

- Un horaire spécifique lui est réservé (habituellement hebdomadaire ou mensuel)

- Généralement, le même groupe de personnes est concerné par la réunion.

- La réunion ne doit pas déranger le cours normal des activités.

Lexique:	
une réunion	**meeting**
le conseil d'Administraton	**board meeting**
la salle de direction	**boardroom**
la salle de réunion	**meeting room**
une réunion de direction	**management meeting**
une réunion de vente	**sales meeting**
une réunion informelle	**informal meeting**
le brainstorming	**brainstorming session**
un comité d'orientation	**planning committee**
le compte-rendu	**minutes**

Chacune des caractéristiques mentionnées ci-dessus implique certains accords tacites:

- La réunion est prioritaire sur toute autre activité d'ordre professionnel ou personnel.

- Les liens créés entre les participants dans le cadre de réunions régulières font naître des réseaux de communication informels entre ceux-ci (le café ou "pub", le club de golf, le country club). Cela n'autorise pas pour autant les familiarités entre les participants; à titre d'exemple, il est exclu de téléphoner à un collègue à son domicile sans y avoir été préalablement invité par celui-ci. En outre, c'est au cours des réunions que doivent être prises les décisions concernant la vie de l'entreprise, et nulle part ailleurs.

- Les réunions doivent être efficaces et permettre d'atteindre le but fixé.

- La réunion doit durer aussi peu de temps que possible.

- Arriver en retard à une réunion d'affaires en Grande-Bretagne est impensable.

1. La Préparation de la Réunion

L'ordre du jour ("the agenda") est préparé à l'avance et envoyé aux personnes dont la présence est requise. Il comporte la liste numérotée des points à l'ordre du jour ("items"). Y figurent les points incrits à l'ordre du jour de la réunion précédente qui n'avaient pas pu être abordés, ainsi que différents points soulevés mais laissés en suspens. Le président de la réunion et les participants ont également la possibilité de faire inscrire à l'ordre du jour tout point qui leur semble devoir être discuté. La personne qui préside la réunion ("chair") est la personne la plus haut placée dans la hiérarchie de l'entreprise, c'est généralement le PDG ("managing director") ou le Directeur des ventes ("sales manager"). En son absence, la fonction de président revient à son adjoint ou à son subordonné immédiat.

Agenda

Meeting held at Transex offices, Milton Keynes

Date:	24 April 2000, 10.00 am
Attending:	DG, JEK, PN, IR, HG, FMcP, MM, Philippe Lebrun, Marie-Hélène Vouvay
Minutes:	EF

1. Minutes of last meeting
2. Report on sales year to date   PN
3. Report on Web site activity and on-line sales   HG
4. Update on French market   Philippe Lebrun
5. Discussion of 2001 projects
6. Staff recruitment   MM
7. Date of next meeting
8. AOB

NB: Le mot "chairman" est considéré comme sexiste. Il est préférable de dire "chairperson" ou encore "chair". Par ailleurs, on utilise souvent les expressions "Mister chairman" ou "Madam chairman" pour s'adresser à la personne qui préside la réunion. Aux États-Unis, les adresses formelles comme celles précédemment mentionnées sont rarement utilisées. S'il s'agit d'une réunion vraiment officielle, comme lors d'un conseil d'administration, on peut utiliser Monsieur/Madame ("Mr/Mrs") suivi du nom propre.

Dans la plupart des entreprises, l'usage est d'appeler ses collègues par leurs prénoms. Puisqu'en anglais la forme unique "you" ne permet pas la distinction entre tutoiement et vouvoiement si familière aux francophones, et que les prénoms sont utilisés presque systématiquement, c'est par le degré d'intimité que l'on montre en public que se manifeste le respect. Être respectueux envers son supérieur ne signifie pas qu'il faille nécessairement épouser les vues de ce dernier.

C'est à l'assistant(e) personnel(le) du président qu'il incombe de préparer la réunion. C'est à cette personne que revient la tâche de taper les convocations ainsi que l'ordre du jour et de les envoyer aux participants au moins 24 heures avant la date prévue pour la réunion. Les participants qui désirent faire inscrire un ou plusieurs points à l'ordre du jour doivent le faire au moins 48 heures avant la réunion. Il n'est pas nécessaire d'avoir l'accord préalable du président pour faire inscrire un point à l'ordre du jour. Le premier et le dernier point abordés sont immuables: toute réunion débute avec la lecture du compte-rendu de la séance précédente ("minutes of last meeting"), et se termine avec l'AOB ("Any Other Business") qui regroupe divers points annexes à traiter. Lorsque la discussion en cours s'écarte du sujet ou traîne en longueur, le président a la possibilité de l'interrompre en demandant aux participants d'intervenir en fin de séance (dans le cadre de la partie "Any Other Business"), de façon à pouvoir traiter en priorité les points les plus importants. Il dit alors:

Bring that up at the end	Mentionnez cela à la fin de la réunion

Toute absence doit être annoncée à l'avance et justifiée. Seul un rendez-vous d'affaires d'une extrême urgence constitue un motif valable (et encore convient-il d'en discuter avec le président au préalable).

Les décisions prises lors d'une réunion sont immédiatement applicables et toutes les informations utilisées lors des débats sont confidentielles.

2. Le Déroulement de la Réunion

Dans une réunion de travail à la française la notion de temps n'est pas primordiale. Le rôle du président est de faire la synthèse des différents points de vue présentés. Dans les pays anglo-saxons, les réunions d'affaires sont très fonctionnelles: les points à discuter sont inscrits à l'ordre du jour à l'avance, et les participants doivent arriver préparés. Les longs discours et les digressions ne sont pas tolérés. Il faut savoir s'en tenir au sujet ("stick to the point") et être le plus concis possible.

Le rôle du président est de permettre à tous ceux qui veulent participer de pouvoir le faire. Il doit interrompre toute discussion qui n'est pas directement liée au sujet à traiter. Il doit également s'assurer que les débats mènent bien à une décision et à une conclusion. Au Royaume-Uni, il est déconseillé de faire signe au président pour lui demander l'autorisation d'intervenir: ce serait faire preuve de faiblesse dans la mesure où le rôle du président est de faire respecter l'ordre du jour et non de donner ou de refuser la parole aux participants. Cependant, la situation est différente aux États-Unis où le rôle du président est précisément de veiller à ce que la réunion se déroule dans la discipline.

Pour signifier son approbation, on peut utiliser des expressions comme:

I agree	je suis d'accord/j'approuve
Hear! Hear!	très bien! très bien!
I think you are absolutely right when you say...	Je suis totalement de votre avis lorsque vous dites que...
Good point	c'est tout à fait vrai
Why didn't I think of that?	Comment n'y ai-je pas pensé?

Les expressions suivantes sont couramment utilisées au cours des discussions pour exprimer le désaccord:

With all due respect...	Soit dit sans vouloir vous offenser
Allow me to disagree...	Permettez-moi de ne pas être de votre avis...
If I might be so bold...	Si je peux avoir la hardiesse de....

La désapprobation est exprimée par des phrases comme:

That's nonsense	c'est complètement absurde
I beg to differ	permettez-moi d'être d'un autre avis
I don't understand why you say...	je ne comprends pas pourquoi vous dites que...

L'un des mots les plus importants en anglais est "sorry" (je suis désolé), qui est rarement utilisé pour exprimer un regret sincère mais qui constitue plutôt une façon d'exprimer poliment un désaccord. Ainsi on peut dire:

I am sorry to disagree with you	je ne suis pas de votre avis

"I am sorry" est la manière la plus commune d'interrompre quelqu'un. On peut également utiliser:

Sorry to interrupt you, but...	Désolé(e) de vous interrompre, mais...

Refuser net d'être interrompu est impoli, mais des expressions comme celles qui suivent sont souvent utilisées:

Can I just finish what I want to say and then you can make your point	Je termine ce que je veux dire puis vous pourrez vous exprimer
Just a moment	Un instant, s'il vous plaît
I've almost finished	J'ai presque terminé

En ce qui concerne l'organisation du plan de table, au Royaume-Uni, la seule place fixe appartient au président/à la présidente de la réunion, son ou sa secrétaire à ses côtés. Cependant, il se crée des habitudes et il vaut mieux les respecter. Aux États-Unis en particulier, les places ne sont pas fixes et les gens choisissent leur place en fonction des rapports qu'ils entretiennent avec leurs collègues, de l'ordre du jour, etc.

On peut "tomber la veste" et desserrer son nœud de cravate, mais le degré d'informalité dans la manière de s'habiller est déterminé par le président et la politique de l'entreprise. Il est parfois possible de fumer mais ce n'est pas toujours le cas. Des boissons non alcoolisées ou chaudes sont à la disposition des participants mais manger est considéré comme incorrect au Royaume-Uni. Aux États-Unis, il n'est pas rare de manger pendant les réunions. Cette pratique est même courante dans certaines entreprises où une personne se charge de commander le dejeuner que les participants prennent pendant la réunion. Le plus simple est de "suivre le mouvement" ou de demander aux anciens quelles sont les habitudes de l'entreprise.

Encore une fois, la règle d'or est d'être rapide et précis. Seul le président, en tant que personne la plus haut placée dans la hiérarchie peut se permettre de ne pas suivre les strictes conventions d'une réunion d'affaires. Les discussions ne doivent jamais dégénérer en disputes: il faut éviter les situations d'hostilité ouverte. L'accent est toujours mis sur "l'esprit d'équipe". On utilise rarement le vote à main levée. Le rôle du président est de clarifier les différents points de vue et de dégager le point de vue majoritaire. La répétition d'un même argument n'est pas acceptable. Pour faire pencher la balance du côté d'une minorité, il est nécessaire d'introduire de nouveaux arguments et de nouveaux faits.

Le président clôt la discussion concernant un point particulier et ouvre la discussion sur le point suivant de l'ordre du jour. Une fois le débat clos sur un point, le rouvrir est considéré comme incorrect. Au Royaume-Uni, la réunion est un forum qui appuie la politique de l'entreprise. L'utilisation d'une réunion pour faire avancer ses propres projets est un art. Il est inopportun de solliciter l'appui d'autres membres du groupe sur un point particulier avant une réunion. La situation est toute autre aux États-Unis, où le contraire se passe. Il est courant de chercher à connaître les participants et d'essayer de les influencer si nécessaire; de nombreux directeurs considéreraient comme dangereux d'assister à une réunion importante sans avoir auparavant "vendu" leur point de vue et sans s'être assurés de l'appui d'un certain nombre de membres du groupe.

3. Le Compte-rendu de la Réunion

Le compte-rendu est tapé et envoyé aux participants en précisant habituellement la date, l'heure et le lieu de la réunion suivante. L'ordre du jour de la réunion suivante inclut la possibilité d'introduire toute correction jugée nécessaire.

Minutes of meeting held at Transex offices, Milton Keynes

Date: 24 April 2000, 10.00 am
Chair: DG
Present: JEK, PN, HG, FMcP, MM, Philippe Lebrun, Marie-Hélène Vouvay
Apologies: IR
Minutes: EF

1. Minutes of last meeting
Approved without alteration
2. Report on sales, year to date
PN distributed sales figures for year to date and explained that the fall from last year's sales is due to several outstanding invoices.
ACTION: PN to ask Accounts department to chase invoices
3. Report on Web site activity and on-line sales
HG reported that there were 2045 hits on the company Web site last week and 56 on-line orders were placed. Redesign of the home page interface is being considered.
(...)

---

4. Pour Conclure

A. *La présentation d'arguments*

Puisqu'il n'y a pas de manière "standard" de présenter des arguments en Grande-Bretagne, il n'y a aucune raison qu'un homme d'affaires français utilise une autre logique que le système de la thèse, antithèse, synthèse. Dans la mesure où les réunions sont courtes, et que l'on rappelle constamment aux participants de ne pas s'écarter du sujet, la personne qui réussit à parler la dernière, soit au moment où un nouveau sujet va être abordé, soit à la fin de la réunion, détient un certain avantage à condition de ne pas trop en profiter.

B. *La notion de responsabilité*

Les hommes d'affaires anglo-saxons assument les conséquences de leurs erreurs. Il serait inacceptable de chercher à se décharger de ses responsabilités sur quelqu'un d'autre. De même, on attend des autres qu'ils admettent franchement leurs erreurs. On considère comme un signe de faiblesse le fait de chercher des excuses, même lorsque certaines de ces excuses sont fondées. Celui qui assume ses décisions et sait tirer les leçons de ses erreurs fait preuve d'intelligence et gagne le respect de ses collègues. On peut dire calmement et sans aucune honte:

I'm sorry, but I made a mistake. It won't happen again.	Je suis désolé mais j'ai fait une erreur. Cela ne se reproduira pas.

C. *L'humour*

L'humour est un moyen efficace de désamorcer les situations de crise au cours d'une réunion. Ce serait se méprendre sur la fonction de l'humour dans la culture britannique que de s'imaginer être la cible des moqueries des autres participants lorsqu'ils plaisantent. La fonction du rire est de faciliter la communication et de détendre l'atmosphère en créant une certaine complicité entre les participants. Il est plus facile de travailler avec des gens avec qui on peut également plaisanter. Très souvent, le contenu d'une remarque peut paraître proche de l'insulte comme par exemple la phrase suivante: "What can you expect from a man/a woman who eats snails?" (Que peut-on attendre d'une personne qui mange des escargots?). Mais l'utilisation de l'insulte dans un contexte qui demande une coopération amicale est l'essence de cet humour. L'utilisation de clichés tels "N'oubliez jamais qui a gagné la bataille de Waterloo" (Don't forget who won the Battle of Waterloo) est une manière de rire de soi-même, pour commencer, puis de la vie en général.

LE TRAVAIL AVEC UN INTERPRÈTE

Avec la mondialisation des échanges économiques et commerciaux, l'interprétation est un moyen de plus en plus fréquemment utilisé pour faciliter la communication entre les gens parlant des langues différentes. Pour se faire comprendre du plus grand nombre, il est indispensable de savoir comment travailler avec un interprète de façon efficace.

Il existe trois sortes d'interprétation:

- L'interprétation simultanée

- L'interprétation consécutive

- Le chuchotage

L'interprétation simultanée est la forme d'interprétation la plus couramment utilisée dans les conférences et les réunions d'affaires. L'intervenant parle dans un micro et sa voix est transmise aux interprètes qui sont installés dans des cabines insonorisées où ils disposent d'écouteurs et d'un micro. Ils interprètent directement dans la langue adéquate et les auditeurs, assis à des pupitres spécialement équipés, écoutent la traduction au moyen d'un casque.

On utilise **l'interprétation consécutive** lorsque l'interprétation simultanée est impossible pour des raisons pratiques, lors de la visite d'une usine ou au cours d'un dîner, par exemple. L'interprète se tient debout ou assis auprès du locuteur et interprète ce que dit celui-ci quand il marque une pause, en s'aidant parfois de notes.

Le chuchotage est la forme d'interprétation la plus rarement utilisée. L'interprète est assis à côté des délégués et traduit simultanément ce qui est dit en chuchotant.

Comment présenter un exposé à un public multilingue

Si vous savez que votre exposé doit être interprété dans d'autres langues, il est important de se souvenir des points suivants:

- Il faut tenir compte du fait que des gens de cultures différentes écouteront votre exposé. Souvenez-vous que plaisanteries et mots d'esprit sont difficilement traduisibles et que tous les peuples n'ont pas le même sens de l'humour. Les références culturelles très spécifiques sont souvent incompréhensibles pour les auditeurs venant d'autres pays que le vôtre, et sont donc à éviter. Essayez dans la mesure du possible de vous exprimer dans une langue simple car les termes familiers ou très techniques posent parfois des problèmes de traduction.

- Si vous avez rédigé votre texte à l'avance, fournissez-en un exemplaire aux interprètes. Il est préférable de le leur faire parvenir deux semaines avant la date de votre exposé, mais si cela s'avère impossible, il est impératif de le leur distribuer avant de prendre la parole, accompagné de copies de tous les documents dont vous vous servirez pendant votre exposé. Il est également utile de fournir à l'avance aux interprètes des informations d'ordre général sur le sujet traité.

- Si vous intervenez dans une conférence où l'on utilise l'interprétation simultanée, vous devrez parler dans un micro. N'oubliez pas que l'interprète se trouve dans une cabine insonorisée et qu'il ne vous entend que grâce au micro. Assurez-vous que votre micro est allumé et que les interprètes vous entendent. Parlez dans la direction du micro sans trop vous en rapprocher. Maintenez une distance constante entre votre bouche et l'appareil de façon à éviter les écarts de volume. Rappelez-vous que si vous tournez le dos au micro pour consulter un tableau ou un écran situé derrière vous, l'interprète n'entendra rien de ce que vous direz. Pour éviter ce genre de problème, la plupart des conférenciers qui utilisent un rétro-projecteur portent un micro-cravate. Si c'est votre cas, sachez qu'à chaque fois que vous frôlerez le micro avec la main ou avec votre veste, seuls des grésillements parviendront aux oreilles des interprètes.

- Lorsque vous vous servez d'un rétro-projecteur, assurez-vous que les interprètes peuvent voir l'écran. Il est important de commenter les documents projetés, sans quoi seuls les gens qui connaissent la langue dans laquelle ils sont rédigés pourront suivre.

- Le défaut le plus courant des conférenciers qui s'adressent à un public multilingue est de parler trop vite. Les interprètes ne se contentent pas de répéter ce que vous dites, ils doivent d'abord traduire vos paroles et il ont donc besoin de plus de temps que vous. D'autre part, il se peut que certains délégués dont la langue maternelle n'est pas celle que vous utilisez vous écoutent sans passer par les interprètes. Il est donc indispensable de ne pas adopter un rythme trop rapide. Plus vous parlerez vite, moins l'on vous comprendra.

- Pour garder un rythme adéquat, il est recommandé de marquer une pause après chaque phrase. Cela permet aux auditeurs d'assimiler ce que vous venez de dire et aux interprètes de finir de traduire. Tout bon conférencier attend que les interprètes aient fini de parler pour continuer son exposé.

- Il est essentiel de s'exprimer distinctement. Si vous marmonnez, les interprètes seront dans l'impossibilité de traduire quoi que ce soit.

Les choses à faire et à ne pas faire lorsqu'on travaille avec un interprète

✔ A faire:

- fournir à l'avance un exemplaire de votre exposé aux interprètes, accompagné de copies de tous les documents dont ils auront besoin, et notamment de ceux qui seront projetés sur écran.

- Allumer votre micro et l'utiliser convenablement.

- Parler lentement et distinctement.

✗ A ne pas faire:

- Inclure de trop nombreuses plaisanteries et références culturelles spécifiques dans votre exposé.

- Tourner le dos au micro lorsque vous commentez des documents projetés sur écran.

- Passer d'une langue à une autre au milieu d'une phrase.

On trouvera le nom anglais des pays dans la deuxième colonne. Pour la traduction anglaise des monnaies et des langues officielles, se reporter au tableau correspondant dans le supplément anglais.

On notera également que les abréviations des monnaies qui figurent dans la cinquième colonne sont les abréviations standards internationales, telles qu'elles ont été définies par l'ISO. Elles diffèrent des abréviations locales et sont utilisées lors des opérations financières internationales.

Nom français	Nom anglais	Nom local	Langue(s) officielle(s)	Monnaie
Afghanistan	Afghanistan	Afghānestān	dari, pachto	1 afghani (AFA) = 100 puls
Afrique du Sud	South Africa	South Africa	anglais, afrikaans	1 rand (ZAR) = 100 cents
Albanie	Albania	Shqīpëri	albanais	1 lek (ALL) = 100 qindarka
Algérie	Algeria	Al-Jazā'ir (arabe), Algérie (français)	arabe	1 dinar algérien (DZD) = 100 centimes
Allemagne	Germany	Bundes-republik Deutschland	allemand	1 Deutsche Mark (DEM) = 100 Pfennig
Andorre	Andorra	Andorra	catalan, français, espagnol	1 franc français (FRF) = 100 centimes; 1 peseta (ESP) = 100 céntimos
Angola	Angola	Angola	portugais	1 nouveau kwanza (AOK) = 100 iwei
Arabie Saoudite	Saudi Arabia	Al-'Arabīyah as Sa'udīyah	arabe	1 riyal (SAR) = 100 halalas
Argentine	Argentina	Argentina	espagnol	1 peso argentin (ARS) = 100 centavos
Arménie	Armenia	Hayastani Hanrape-toutiun	arménien	1 dram (AMD) = 100 louma
Australie	Australia	Australia	anglais	1 dollar australien (AUD) = 100 cents
Autriche	Austria	Österreich	allemand	1 Schilling (ATS) = 100 Groschen
Azerbaïdjan	Azerbaijan	Azerbaijan	Azéri	1 manat (AZM) = 100 kepik
Bahamas	The Bahamas	Bahamas	anglais	1 dollar des Bahamas (BSD) = 100 cents
Bahreïn	Bahrain	Dawlat Al-Bahrayn	arabe	1 dinar de Bahreïn (BHD) = 1000 fils
Bangladesh	Bangladesh	Gana Prajatantri Bangladesh	bengali	1 taka (BDT) = 100 paisa
Barbade	Barbados	Barbados	anglais	1 dollar de la Barbade (BBD) = 100 cents

Nom français	Nom anglais	Nom local	Langue(s) officielle(s)	Monnaie
Belgique	Belgium	Belgique (français), België (flamand)	flamand, français, allemand	1 franc belge (BEF) = 100 centimes
Belize	Belize	Belize	anglais	1 dollar de Belize (BZD) = 100 cents
Bénin	Benin	Bénin	français	1 franc CFA (XOF) = 100 centimes
Bhoutan	Bhutan	Druk-Yul	tibétain	1 ngultrum (BTN) = 100 roupies
Biélorussie	Belarus	Belarus	biélorusse	1 rouble biélorusse (BYB) = 100 kopeks
Birmanie ▶ Myanmar	Burma			
Bolivie	Bolivia	Bolivia	espagnol	1 boliviano (BOB) = 100 centavos
Bosnie-Herzégovine	Bosnia-Herzegovina	Bosnia-Herzegovina	serbo-croate	1 dinar (BAD) = 100 paras
Botswana	Botswana	Botswana	anglais	1 pula (BWP) = 100 thebe
Brésil	Brazil	Brasil	portugais	1 real brésilien (BRL) = 100 centavos
Brunei	Brunei	Brunei	malais	1 dollar de Brunei (BND) = 100 cents
Bulgarie	Bulgaria	Bălgarija	bulgare	1 lev (BGL) (*pl* leva) = 100 stotinki (*sing* stotinka)
Burkina	Burkina Faso	Burkina Faso	français	1 franc CFA (XOF) = 100 centimes
Burundi	Burundi	Burundi	français, rundi	1 franc du Burundi (BIF) = 100 centimes
Cambodge	Cambodia	Preah Reach Ana Pak Kampuchea	khmer	1 riel (KHR) = 100 sen
Cameroun	Cameroon	Cameroon	français, anglais	1 franc CFA (XAF) = 100 centimes
Canada	Canada	Canada	français, anglais	1 dollar canadien (CAD) = 100 cents
Cap-Vert	Cape Verde	Cabo Verde	portugais	1 escudo du Cap-Vert (CVE) = 100 centavos
Centrafricaine, République	Central African Republic	République Centrafricaine	français, sango	1 franc CFA (XAF) = 100 centimes
Chili	Chile	Chile	espagnol	1 peso chilien (CLP) = 100 centavos
Chine	China	Zhongguo	chinois	1 yuan (CNY) = 10 jiao = 100 fen
Chypre	Cyprus	Kipros (grec), Kibris (turc)	grec, turc	1 livre chypriote (CYP) = 1000 mils
Colombie	Colombia	Colombia	espagnole	1 peso colombien (COP) = 100 centavos
Comores	Comoros	Comores	français, comorien	1 franc des Comores (KMF) = 100 centimes
Congo	Congo	Congo	français	1 franc CFA (XAF) = 100 centimes
Congo, République démocratique du	Democratic Republic of Congo	Congo	français, lingala	1 nouveau zaïre (ZRN) = 100 makuta (*sing* likuta)
Corée du Nord	Korea, North	Chosŏn Minjujuŭi In'min Konghwaguk	coréen	1 won (NKW) = 100 chon

Nom français	Nom anglais	Nom local	Langue(s) officielle(s)	Monnaie
Corée du Sud	Korea, South	Taehan-Min'guk	coréen	1 won (KRW) = 100 chon
Costa Rica	Costa Rica	Costa Rica	espagnol	1 colón [Fr colon] (CRC) (pl colones) = 100 céntimos
Côte d'Ivoire	Côte d'Ivoire (Ivory Coast)	Côte d'Ivoire	français	1 franc CFA (XOF) = 100 centimes
Croatie	Croatia	Hrvatska	serbo-croate	1 kuna (HRK) = 100 lipas
Cuba	Cuba	Cuba	espagnol	1 peso cubain (CUP) = 100 centavos
Danemark	Denmark	Danmark	danois	1 krone [Fr couronne danoise] (DKK) (pl kroner) = 100 øre
Djibouti	Djibouti	Djibouti	arabe, français	1 franc de Djibouti (DJF) = 100 centimes
Dominicaine, République	Dominican Republic	República Dominicana	espagnol	1 peso dominicain (DOP) = 100 centavos
Dominique	Dominica	Dominica	anglais, français créole	1 dollar des Caraïbes orientales (XCD) = 100 cents
Égypte	Egypt	Jumhuriyat Misr Al-Arabiya	arabe	1 livre égyptienne (EGP) = 100 piastres
Émirats Arabes Unis	United Arab Emirates	Ittihād al-Imārāt al-'Arabīyah	arabe, anglais	1 dirham (AED) = 100 fils
Équateur	Ecuador	Ecuador	espagnol	1 sucre (ECS) = 100 centavos
Érythrée	Eritrea	Eritrea	tigrinya, arabe	1 birr (ETB) = 100 cents
Espagne	Spain	España	espagnol	1 peseta (ESP) = 100 céntimos
Estonie	Estonia	Eesti Vabariik	estonien	1 kroon [Fr couronne estonienne] (EEK) = 100 senti
États-Unis	United States of America	United States of America	anglais	1 dollar US (USD) = 100 cents
Éthiopie	Ethiopia	Ityopiya	amharique	1 birr (ETB) = 100 cents
Féroé, îles	Faroe Islands	Faroyar/Faeroerne	danois	1 krone [Fr couronne danoise] (DKK) (pl kroner) = 100 øre
Fidji, îles	Fiji	Matanitu Ko Viti	anglais	1 dollar fidjien (FJD) = 100 cents
Finlande	Finland	Suomen Tasavalta	finnois, suédois	1 markka [Fr mark finlandais] (FIM) (pl markkaa) = 100 penniä (sing penni)
France	France	République Française	français	1 franc (FRF) = 100 centimes
Gabon	Gabon	République Gabonaise	français	1 franc CFA (XAF) = 100 centimes
Gambie	The Gambia	Gambia	anglais	1 dalasi (GMD) = 100 bututs
Géorgie	Georgia	Sakartvelos Respublica	géorgien, russe	1 lari (GEL) = 100 tetri
Ghana	Ghana	Ghana	anglais	1 cedi (GHC) = 100 pesewas
Grèce	Greece	Elliniki Dimokratia	grec	1 drachme (GRD) = 100 lepta

Nom français	Nom anglais	Nom local	Langue(s) officielle(s)	Monnaie
Groenland	Greenland	Grønland (danois), Kalaallit Nunaat	danois, groenlandais	1 krone [Fr couronne danoise] (DKK) (pl kroner) = 100 øre
Guatemala	Guatemala	Guatemala	espagnol	1 quetzal (GTQ) (pl quetzales) = 100 centavos
Guinée	Guinea	République de Guinée	français	1 franc guinéen (GNF) = 100 centimes
Guinée-Bissau	Guinea-Bissau	Republica da Guiné-Bissau	portugais	1 peso (GWP) = 100 centavos
Guinée Équatoriale	Equatorial Guinea	Guinea Ecuatorial	espagnol	1 Franc CFA (XAF) = 100 centimes
Guyana	Guyana	Guyana	anglais	1 dollar de la Guyana (GYD) = 100 cents
Guyane	French Guiana	Guyane Française	français	1 franc français (FRF) = 100 centimes
Haïti	Haiti	République d'Haïti	français	1 gourde (HTG) = 100 centimes
Hollande ▶ Pays-Bas	Holland			
Honduras	Honduras	Honduras	espagnol	1 lempira (HNL) = 100 centavos
Hongrie	Hungary	Magyar Koztarsasag	hongrois	1 forint (HUF) = 100 fillér
Inde	India	Bhārat (hindi)	hindi, anglais	1 roupie indienne (INR) = 100 paise
Indonésie	Indonesia	Republik Indonesia	indonésien	1 rupiah (IDR) = 100 sen
Irak	Iraq	Jumhouriya al Iraquia	arabe	1 dinar irakien (IQD) = 1000 fils
Iran	Iran	Jomhoori-e-Islami-e-Iran	persan	1 rial (IRR) = 100 dinars
Irlande	Ireland	Poblacht na hEireann	irlandais, anglais	1 punt [Fr livre irlandaise] (IER) = 100 pence (sing penny)
Islande	Iceland	Ísland	islandais	1 couronne islandaise (ISK) = 100 aurar (sing eyrir)
Israël	Israel	Medinat Israel	hébreu, arabe	1 shekel (ILS) = 100 agorot
Italie	Italy	Repubblica Italiana	italien	1 lira [Fr lire] (ITL) (pl lire) = 100 centesimi (sing centesimo)
Jamaïque	Jamaica	Jamaica	anglais	1 dollar jamaïcain (JMD) = 100 cents
Japon	Japan	Nihon	japonais	1 yen (JPY) = 100 sen
Jordanie	Jordan	Al'Urdunn	arabe	1 dinar jordanien (JOD) = 1 000 fils
Kazakhstan	Kazakhstan	Kazak Respublikasy	kazakh, russe	1 Tenge (KZT) = 100 tiyn
Kenya	Kenya	Jamhuri ya Kenya	swahili, anglais	1 shilling du Kenya (KES) = 100 cents
Kirghizistan	Kyrgyzstan	Kyrgyz Respublikasy	kirghiz	1 som (KGS) = 100 tyiyn
Koweït	Kuwait	Dowlat al-Kuwayt	arabe	1 dinar koweïtien (KWD) = 1 000 fils
Laos	Laos	Lao	laotien	1 kip (LAK) = 100 att

Nom français	Nom anglais	Nom local	Langue(s) officielle(s)	Monnaie
Lesotho	Lesotho	Lesotho	anglais, sotho	1 loti (LSL) (*pl* maloti) = 100 lisente
Lettonie	Latvia	Latvijas Republika	letton	1 lats (LVL) (*pl* lati) = 100 santimi (*sing* santims)
Liban	Lebanon	Al-Lubnān	arabe	1 livre libanaise (LBP) = 100 piastres
Liberia	Liberia	Liberia	anglais	1 dollar libérien (LRD) = 100 cents
Libye	Libya	Lībyā	arabe	1 dinar libyen (LYD) = 1000 dirhams
Liechtenstein	Liechtenstein	Furstentum Liechtenstein	allemand	1 franc suisse (CHF) = 100 centimes
Lituanie	Lithuania	Lietuva	lituanien	1 litas (LTL) (*pl* litai)= 100 centai (*sing* centas)
Luxembourg	Luxembourg	Lëtzebuerg (Letz), Luxembourg (français), Luxemburg (allemand)	français, allemand	1 franc luxembourgeois (LUF) = 100 centimes
Macédoine	Macedonia	Republika Makedonija	macédonien	1 denar (MKD) = 100 paras
Madagascar	Madagascar	Republikan'i Madagasikara	malgache, français	1 franc malgache (MGF) = 100 centimes
Malaisie	Malaysia	Federation of Malaysia	malais	1 ringgit [*Fr* dollar de Malaysie] (MYR) = 100 cents
Malawi	Malawi	Dziko la Malaŵi	chichewa, anglais	1 kwacha (MWK) = 100 tambalas
Maldives	Maldives	Maldives Divehi Jumhuriya	divehi	1 rufiyaa (MVR) = 100 laari
Mali	Mali	Mali	français	1 franc CFA (XOF) = 100 centimes
Malte	Malta	Malta	anglais, maltais	1 livre maltaise (MTL) = 100 cents = 1000 miles
Maroc	Morocco	Mamlaka Al-Maghrebia	arabe	1 dirham (MAD) = 100 centimes
Martinique	Martinique	Martinique	français, créole	1 franc français (FRF) = 100 centimes
Maurice, île	Mauritius	Mauritius	anglais	1 roupie mauricienne (MUR) = 100 cents
Mauritanie	Mauritania	Mauritanie (français), Mūrītāniyā (arabe)	arabe	1 ouguiya (MRO) = 5 khoums
Mexique	Mexico	México	espagnol	1 peso mexicain (MXN) = 100 centavos
Micronésie	Micronesia	Micronesia	anglais	1 dollar US (USD) = 100 cents
Moldavie	Moldova	Republica Moldovenească	roumain	1 leu (MDL) (*pl* lei) = 100 bani (*sing* ban)
Mongolie	Mongolia	Mongol Ard Uls	khalkha	1 tugrik (MNT) = 100 mongo
Mozambique	Mozambique	Republica de Moçambique	portugais	1 metical (MZM)= 100 kobo
Myanmar	Myanmar	Myanmar	birman	1 kyat (MMK) = 100 pyas

Nom français	Nom anglais	Nom local	Langue(s) officielle(s)	Monnaie
Namibie	Namibia	Namibia	anglais	1 dollar namibien (NAD) = 100 cents
Nauru	Nauru	Naeoro (nauruan), Nauru (anglais)	nauruan, anglais	1 dollar australien (AUD) = 100 cents
Népal	Nepal	Nepal Adhirajya	népalais	1 roupie népalaise (NPR) = 100 paisa
Nicaragua	Nicaragua	Nicaragua	espagnol	1 cordoba oro (NIO) = 100 centavos
Niger	Niger	Niger	français	1 franc CFA (XOF) = 100 centimes
Nigéria	Nigeria	Nigeria	anglais, français	1 naira (NGN) = 100 kobo
Norvège	Norway	Kongeriket Norge	norvégien	1 couronne norvégienne (NOK) = 100 øre
Nouvelle-Zélande	New Zealand	New Zealand	anglais	1 dollar néo-zélandais (NZD) = 100 cents
Oman	Oman	Saltanat 'Uman	arabe	1 rial omanais (OMR) = 1 000 baizas
Ouganda	Uganda	Uganda	anglais, swahili	1 shilling ougandais (UGX) = 100 cents
Ouzbékistan	Uzbekistan	Uzbekistan	ouzbek	1 soum (UZS) = 100 tiyin
Pakistan	Pakistan	Pākistān	urdu, anglais	1 roupie pakistanaise (PKR) = 100 paisa
Panamá	Panama	Panamá	espagnol	1 balboa (PAB) = 100 centésimos
Papouasie-Nouvelle-Guinée	Papua New Guinea	Papua New Guinea	anglais, néo-mélanaisien	1 kina (PGK) = 100 tosa
Paraguay	Paraguay	Paraguay	espagnol	1 guaraní (PYG) = 100 céntimos
Pays-Bas	The Netherlands	Koninkrijk der Nederlanden	néerlandais	1 gulden [*Fr* florin] (NLG) = 100 cents
Pérou	Peru	Perú	espagnol	1 nouveau sol (PEN) = 100 centavos
Philippines	Philippines	Pilipinas	tagalog, anglais	1 peso philippin (PHP) = 100 centavos
Pologne	Poland	Rzeczpospolita Polska	polonais	1 zloty (PLN) = 100 groszy (*sing* grosz)
Polynésie Française	French Polynesia	Territoire de la Polynésie Française	polynésien, français	1 Franc CFP (XPF) = 100 centimes
Porto Rico	Puerto Rico	Puerto Rico	espagnol, anglais	1 dollar US (USD) = 100 cents
Portugal	Portugal	Portugal	portugais	1 escudo (PTE) = 100 centavos
Principauté de Monaco	Monaco	Monaco	français	1 franc français (FRF) = 100 centimes
Qatar	Qatar	Dowlat Qatar	arabe	1 riyal (QAR) = 100 dirhams
Roumanie	Romania	Romănia	roumain	1 leu (ROL) (*pl* lei) = 100 bani
Royaume-Uni	United Kingdom	United Kingdom	anglais	1 pound sterling [*Fr* livre sterling] (GBP) = 100 pence (*sing* penny)
Russie	Russia	Rossiya	russe	1 rouble (RUR) = 100 kopeks

Nom français	Nom anglais	Nom local	Langue(s) officielle(s)	Monnaie
Rwanda	Rwanda	Rwanda	rwanda, français, anglais	1 franc rwandais (RWF) = 100 centimes
Saint-Marin	San Marino	San Marino	italien	1 lira [Fr lire] (ITL) (pl lire) = 100 centesimi (sing centesimo)
Salomon, îles	Solomon Islands	Solomon Islands	anglais	1 dollar des îles Salomon (SBD) = 100 cents
Salvador	El Salvador	El Salvador	espagnol	1 colón [Fr colon salvadorien] (SVC) (pl colones) = 100 centavos
Samoa	Samoa	Samoa	samoan, anglais	1 tala (WST) = 100 sene
Sénégal	Senegal	Sénégal	français, ouolof	1 Franc CFA (XOF) = 100 centimes
Seychelles	Seychelles	Seychelles	français, anglais, créole	1 roupie des Seychelles (SCR) = 100 cents
Sierra Leone	Sierra Leone	Sierra Leone	anglais	1 leone (SLL) = 100 cents
Singapour	Singapore	Singapore	chinois, anglais, malais, tamoul	1 dollar de Singapour (SGD) = 100 cents
Slovaquie	Slovakia	Slovenska Republika	slovaque	1 couronne slovaque (CSK) = 100 haleriov
Slovénie	Slovenia	Republika Slovenija	slovène	1 tolar (SIT) =100 centime
Somalie	Somalia	Somaliya	arabe, somali	1 shilling somalien (SOS) = 100 cents
Soudan	The Sudan	As-Sūdān	arabe	1 dinar soudanais (SDD) = 100 piastres
Sri Lanka	Sri Lanka	Sri Lanka	cinghalais, tamoul	1 roupie de Sri Lanka (LKR) = 100 cents
Suède	Sweden	Konungariket Sverige	suédois	1 couronne suédoise (SEK) = 100 öre
Suisse	Switzerland	Schweiz (allemand), Suisse (français), Svizzera (italien)	français, allemand, italien, romanche	1 franc suisse (CHF) = 100 centimes
Surinam	Surinam	Suriname	néerlandais	1 gulden [Fr florin] de Surinam (SRG) = 100 cents
Swaziland	Swaziland	Umbouso we Swatini	swazi, anglais	1 lilangeni (SZL) (pl emalangeni) = 100 cents
Syrie	Syria	As-Sūrīyah	arabe	1 livre syrienne (SYP) = 100 piastres
Tadjikistan	Tajikistan	Jumkhurii Tojikistan	tadjik	1 rouble tadjik (TJR) = 100 tanga
Taïwan	Taiwan	T'aiwan	chinois	1 dollar de Taïwan (TWD) = 100 cents
Tanzanie	Tanzania	Tanzania	swahili, anglais	1 shilling tanzanien (TZS) = 100 cents
Tchad	Chad	Tchad	français, arabe	1 Franc CFA (XAF) = 100 centimes
Tchèque, République	Czech Republic	Česká Republika	tchèque	1 couronne tchèque (CZK) = 100 halé
Thaïlande	Thailand	Prathet Thai	thaï	1 baht (THB) = 100 satang

Nom français	Nom anglais	Nom local	Langue(s) officielle(s)	Monnaie
Togo	Togo	Togo	français	1 franc CFA (XOF) = 100 centimes
Tonga	Tonga	Tonga	anglais, tongan	1 pa'anga (TOP) = 100 seniti
Trinité-et-Tobago	Trinidad and Tobago	Trinidad and Tobago	anglais	1 dollar de Trinité-et-Tobago (TTD) = 100 cents
Tunisie	Tunisia	Tunisiya	arabe, français	1 dinar tunisien (TND) = 1 000 millimes
Turkménistan	Turkmenistan	Turkmenostan	turkmène	1 manat (TMM) = 100 tenesi
Turquie	Turkey	Tūrkiye	turc	1 livre turque (TRL) = 100 kurus
Ukraine	Ukraine	Ukraina	ukrainien, russe	1 hrivna (UAK) = 100 kopiykas
Uruguay	Uruguay	Uruguay	espagnol	1 peso uruguayen (UYU) = 100 centésimos
Vanuatu	Vanuatu	Vanuatu	bichlamar, anglais, français	1 vatu (VUV) = 100 centimes
Vatican, cité du	Vatican City	Citta' del Vaticano	italien	1 lira [*Fr* lire de la cité du Vatican] (ITL) (*pl* lire) = 100 centesimi (*sing* centesimo)
Venezuela	Venezuela	Venezuela	espagnol	1 bolívar (VEB) (*pl* bolívares) = 100 céntimos
Vietnam	Vietnam	Viêt-nam	vietnamien	1 dông (VND) = 10 hao = 100 xu
Yémen	Yemen	Al-Yamaniya	arabe	1 riyal yéménite (YER) = 100 fils
Yougoslavie	Yugoslavia	Jugoslavija	serbo-croate (serbe)	1 dinar yougoslave (YUN) = 100 paras
Zaïre	Zaire			

▶ Congo, République démocratique du

Nom français	Nom anglais	Nom local	Langue(s) officielle(s)	Monnaie
Zambie	Zambia	Zambia	anglais	1 kwacha (ZMK) = 100 ngwee
Zimbabwe	Zimbabwe	Zimbabwe	anglais	1 dollar du Zimbabwe (ZWD) = 100 cents

ETATS-UNIS: LISTE DES ETATS

État	Abréviations	Surnom	Habitants	Capitale
Alabama	Ala; AL	Camellia State, Heart of Dixie	Alabamians	Montgomery
Alaska	AK	Mainland State, The Last Frontier	Alaskans	Juneau
Arizona	Ariz; AZ	Apache State, Grand Canyon State	Arizonans	Phoenix
Arkansas	Ark; AR	Bear State, Land of Opportunity	Arkansans	Little Rock
Californie	Calif; CA	Golden State	Californians	Sacramento
Caroline du Nord	NC	Old North State, Tar Heel State	North Carolinians	Raleigh
Caroline du Sud	SC	Palmetto State	South Carolinians	Columbia
Colorado	Colo; CO	Centennial State	Coloradans	Denver
Connecticut	Conn; CT	Nutmeg State, Constitution State	Nutmeggers	Hartford
Dakota du Nord	N Dak; ND	Flickertail State, Sioux State, Peace Garden State	North Dakotans	Bismarck
Dakota du Sud	S Dak; SD	Sunshine State, Coyote State	South Dakotans	Pierre
Delaware	Del; DE	Diamond State, First State	Delawareans	Dover
District de Columbia	DC	DC, the District	Washingtonians	Washington
Floride	Fla; FL	Everglade State, Sunshine State	Floridians	Tallahassee
Géorgie	Ga; GA	Empire State of the South, Peach State	Georgians	Atlanta
Hawaï	HI	Aloha State	Hawaiians	Honolulu
Idaho	ID	Gem State	Idahoans	Boise
Illinois	Ill; IL	Prairie State, Land of Lincoln	Illinoisans	Springfield
Indiana	Ind; IN	Hoosier State	Hoosiers	Indianapolis
Iowa	IA	Hawkeye State, Corn State	Iowans	Des Moines
Kansas	Kans; KS	Sunflower State, Jayhawker State	Kansans	Topeka
Kentucky	Ky; KY	Bluegrass State	Kentuckians	Frankfort
Louisiane	La; LA	Pelican State, Sugar State, Creole State	Louisianians	Baton Rouge
Maine	ME	Pine Tree State	Downeasters	Augusta
Maryland	Md; MD	Old Line State, Free State	Marylanders	Annapolis

État	Abréviations	Surnom	Habitants	Capitale
Massachusetts	Mass; MA	Bay State, Old Colony	Bay Staters	Boston
Michigan	Mich; MI	Wolverine State, Great Lake State	Michiganders	Lansing
Minnesota	Minn; MN	Gopher State, North Star State	Minnesotans	St Paul
Mississippi	Miss; MS	Magnolia State	Mississippians	Jackson
Missouri	Mo; MO	Bullion State, Show Me State	Missourians	Jefferson City
Montana	Mont; MT	Treasure State, Big Sky Country	Montanans	Helena
Nebraska	Nebr; NE	Cornhusker State, Beef State	Nebraskans	Lincoln
Nevada	Nev; NV	Silver State, Sagebrush State, Battle Born State	Nevadans	Carson City
New Hampshire	NH	Granite State	New Hampshirites	Concord
New Jersey	NJ	Garden State	New Jerseyites	Trenton
New Mexico	N Mex; NM	Sunshine State, Land of Enchantment	New Mexicans	Santa Fe
New York	NY	Empire State	New Yorkers	Albany
Ohio	OH	Buckeye State	Ohioans	Columbus
Oklahoma	Okla; OK	Sooner State	Oklahomans	Oklahoma City
Oregon	Oreg; OR	Sunset State, Beaver State	Oregonians	Salem
Pennsylvanie	Pa; PA	Keystone State	Pennsylvanians	Harrisburg
Rhode Island	RI	Little Rhody, Plantation State	Rhode Islanders	Providence
Tennessee	Tenn; TN	Volunteer State	Tennesseans	Nashville
Texas	Tex; TX	Lone Star State	Texans	Austin
Utah	Utah; UT	Mormon State, Beehive State	Utahans	Salt Lake City
Vermont	Vt; VT	Green Mountain State	Vermonters	Montpelier
Virginie-Occidentale	W Va; WV	Panhandle State, Mountain State	West Virginians	Charleston
Virginie	Va; VA	Old Dominion State, Mother of Presidents	Virginians	Richmond
Washington	Wash; WA	Evergreen State, Chinook State	Washingtonians	Olympia
Wisconsin	Wis; WI	Badger State, America's Dairyland	Wisconsinites	Madison
Wyoming	Wyo; WY	Equality State	Wyomingites	Cheyenne

---

l'Euro

Le 1er janvier 1999, l'euro est devenu la monnaie officielle de onze pays de l'Union européenne. Chacun de ces pays continuera à utiliser son ancienne monnaie concurremment avec l'euro jusqu'en 2002, date à laquelle l'euro deviendra l'unique monnaie de ces onze pays.

Dans la table des états du monde de cet ouvrage, l'euro ne figure pas comme monnaie officielle des pays concernés.

Les taux de change sont les suivants:

Allemagne	=	1,95583 marks
Autriche	=	13,7603 schillings
Belgique	=	40,3399 francs belges
Espagne	=	166,386 pesetas
Finlande	=	5,94573 marks finlandais
France	=	6,55957 francs
Irlande	=	0,787564 livre irlandaise
Italie	=	1 936,27 lires
Luxembourg	=	40,33399 francs luxembourgeois
Pays-Bas	=	2,20371 florins
Portugal	=	200,482 escudos

Français-Anglais
French-English

A3 nm (format de papier) A3

A4 nm (format de papier) A4

abaissement nm (des prix, des taux, d'un impôt) lowering, reduction; (des barrières douanières) lowering; (d'une monnaie) weakening

abaisser vt (prix, taux, impôt) to lower, to reduce; (barrières douanières) to lower

> "
>
> Certains experts n'excluent pas une action concertée des banques centrales pour **abaisser** leurs taux directeurs afin de faire face aux tensions déflationnistes que provoquerait la crise en Asie.
>
> "

abandon nm (**a**) (de marchandises, de droits) renunciation (**b**) (d'un projet) shelving (**c**) ORDINAT abort

abandonner vt (**a**) (marchandises, droits) to abandon, to give up; **abandonner ses biens à ses créanciers** to surrender one's goods to one's creditors; **il a abandonné son poste de directeur** he gave up his post of director (**b**) (projet) to abandon, to shelve (**c**) ORDINAT to abort

abattage nm **à l'abattage** (vente) at knockdown prices

abattement nm FIN (rabais) reduction; (d'impôts) allowance □ **abattement à la base** basic personal allowance; **abattement fiscal** tax allowance; **abattement forfaitaire** fixed-rate rebate

> "
>
> L'amplitude des horaires de travail, pour bénéficier de l'**abattement forfaitaire** de 50% sur les charges sociales, s'étend désormais de 16 à 32 heures par semaine.
>
> "

abîmé, -e adj (articles, marchandises) damaged

abîmer 1 vt (articles, marchandises) to damage, to spoil

2 **s'abîmer** vpr (articles, marchandises) to get damaged

abolir vt (loi, impôt) to abolish

abonné, -e 1 adj (à un journal, à une revue) subscribing; **être abonné à une revue/au Minitel** to subscribe to a magazine/to Minitel

2 nm,f (**a**) (à un journal, à une revue) subscriber (**b**) TÉL **un abonné du téléphone/d'Internet** a telephone/an Internet subscriber; **il n'y a pas d'abonné au numéro que vous avez demandé** ≃ the number you have dialled has not been recognized

abonnement nm (**a**) (à un journal, à une revue) subscription; **prendre** ou **souscrire un abonnement à qch** to take out a subscription to sth □ **abonnement collectif** group subscription; **abonnement à l'essai** trial subscription (**b**) TÉL (au téléphone) line rental; **abonnement à un service en ligne** on-line subscription

abonner 1 vt **abonner qn à un journal/une revue** to take out a subscription to a newspaper/magazine for sb

2 **s'abonner** vpr (**a**) (à un journal, à une revue) to take out a subscription (**à** to) (**b**) TÉL **s'abonner au téléphone** to have a telephone installed

abordable adj affordable, reasonable

aboutir vi (réussir) to be successful; **aboutir à un compromis/à un accord/à un échec** to end or result in compromise/agreement/failure; **l'entreprise n'a pas abouti** the venture fell through

aboutissement nm (conclusion) result, outcome; (résultat positif) success

abrogatif, -ive adj JUR (clause) annulling, rescinding

abrogation nf JUR abrogation, repeal

abrogatoire adj JUR (clause) annulling, rescinding

abroger vt JUR (loi) to abrogate, to repeal, to rescind

absence nf absence; **la réunion commencera en l'absence du directeur** the meeting will begin without the director; **en l'absence du directeur, c'est à M. Dufour qu'il faut s'adresser** while the director is away or during the director's absence, you should speak to Mr Dufour

absent, -e 1 adj absent

2 nm,f absentee

absentéisme nm absenteeism

absenter s'absenter vpr to go away; **s'absenter pour affaires** to go away on business

absorber vt ÉCON (entreprise) to take over, to absorb; **la multinationale va absorber cette entreprise** the multinational is going to take over or absorb this company

absorption nf ÉCON takeover, absorption; **l'absorption d'une petite société par une grosse** the takeover or absorption of a small company by a large one

abus nm JUR **abus de biens sociaux** misappropriation of funds; **abus de confiance** breach of trust; **abus de pouvoir** abuse of power

abuser abuser de vt ind **abuser de son autorité** to abuse one's power

abusif, -ive adj (prix) excessive

ac (a) (abrév **argent comptant**) cash (b) (abrév **année courante**) current year

accabler vt accabler la population d'impôts to overtax the population; **être accablé de dettes** to be burdened with debt

accalmie nf slack period, lull; **le marché financier traverse une période d'accalmie** the financial market is going through a slack period or a lull

accaparement nm (du marché) cornering; (du pouvoir) seizing

accaparer vt (marché) to corner; (pouvoir) to seize; ÉCON **accaparer des marchandises** (pour contrôler le marché) to withhold goods from the market

accéder accéder à vt ind ORDINAT (programme) to access

accélérateur nm ORDINAT accelerator ❑ **accélérateur graphique** graphic(s) accelerator

acceptabilité de la marque nf MKTG brand acceptability or acceptance

acceptable adj (prix, conditions) acceptable

acceptant, -e 1 adj acceptant 2 nm,f acceptant, acceptor

acceptation nf (d'un chèque, d'un effet, d'un contrat, de marchandises) acceptance; **sous réserve d'acceptation du dossier** subject to a favourable report; **bon pour acceptation** (sur effet) accepted bill; **présenter un effet à l'acceptation** to present a bill for acceptance; **refus d'acceptation** non-acceptance; **acceptation par intervention** acceptance for honour

accepté, -e adj (chèque, effet, contrat, marchandises) accepted; **accepté** (sur effet) accepted bill

accepter vt (contrat, marchandises) to accept; (chèque, effet) to accept, to sign, to honour

accepteur, -euse nm,f (d'une facture) acceptor, drawee

accès nm (a) (entrée) access; **avoir accès à qch** to have access to sth; **des marchandises en libre accès** freely available goods; **accès réservé au personnel** (sur panneau) staff only; **accès interdit** (sur panneau) no entry, no admittance; **l'accès au statut de membre de l'Union européenne** entry into the European Union
(b) ORDINAT access; **avoir accès à qch** to be able to access sth; **à accès multiple** multi-access; **accès refusé** access denied ❑ **accès aléatoire** random access; **accès à distance** remote access; **accès sécurisé par mot de passe** password-protected access; **accès séquentiel** sequential access

accessibilité nf (à un produit, à un marché) accessibility; (d'un prix) affordability

accessible adj (produit, marché) accessible; (prix) affordable

accession nf **accession à la propriété** home ownership; **faciliter l'accession à la propriété** to make it easier for people to become home owners; **accession à la monnaie unique** entry into the single currency; **accession au statut de membre de l'Union européenne** entry into the European Union

accessoire de bureau nm ORDINAT desk accessory

accident nm accident ❑ **accident du travail** industrial accident

accidenté, -e nm,f accident victim ❑ **accidenté du travail** victim of an industrial accident

accise nf Can & Belg excise (duty)

accommodant, -e adj **être accommodant en affaires** to be easy to do business with

accommodement nm arrangement, agreement; (avec ses créanciers) composition; **parvenir à un accommodement (avec qn)** to come to an arrangement or agreement (with sb)

accommoder vt to adapt; **accommoder un produit aux désirs des clients** to adapt or tailor a product to the clients' wishes

accompagnateur, -trice nm,f tour guide, courier

accomplir vt (tâche) to perform, to carry out; (formalités) to go through

accord *nm* (**a**) *(convention)* agreement; **signer un accord** to sign an agreement; **conclure un accord** to come to *or* reach an agreement ❑ *accord à l'amiable* private agreement; *(sans procès)* out-of-court settlement; *accord bilatéral* bilateral agreement; *accord de clearing* clearing agreement; *accord commercial* trade agreement; *accord de commercialisation* marketing agreement; *accord de compensation* offset agreement; *accord de distribution exclusive* exclusive distribution agreement; *accord d'exclusivité* exclusivity agreement; *accord de franchise* franchise agreement; *Accord Général sur les Tarifs Douaniers et le Commerce* General Agreement on Tariffs and Trade; *accords d'Helsinki* Helsinki Agreement; *accords internationaux sur les produits de base* international commodity agreements; *accord de libre-échange* Free Trade Agreement; *accord de licence* licensing agreement; *Accord monétaire européen* European monetary agreement; *accord multilatéral* multilateral agreement; *accord de partenariat* partnership agreement; *accord de représentation* agency agreement; *accord de reprise* buyback arrangement; *accord salarial* pay *or* wage agreement; *accord de sous-traitance* subcontracting agreement; *accord tarifaire* tariff agreement; *accord verbal* verbal agreement
(**b**) *(entente)* **être d'accord avec qn/qch** to agree with sb/sth; **d'un commun accord** by common consent, by mutual agreement
(**c**) *(assentiment)* agreement, consent; **avoir l'accord de qn** to have sb's agreement *or* consent; **donner son accord** to agree, to consent

> **❝**
> Le PDG de Total n'a pas caché ses intentions en dévoilant récemment qu'il négociait un **accord de sous-traitance** avec la Kuwait Oil Company.
> **❞**

accord-cadre *nm* outline agreement

> **❝**
> Le 10 juin à l'aube, après une nuit de discussions ... un **accord-cadre** était conclu entre la direction d'Air France et le principal syndicat de pilotes, le SNPL, qui venait de mettre fin à neuf jours de grève.
> **❞**

accorder 1 *vt (découvert bancaire, remise)* to allow, to give; *(dommages-intérêts)* to award; *(prêt)* to authorize, to extend; *(subventions)* to give, to grant; **accorder une** licence à qn to license sb
2 s'accorder *vpr (se mettre d'accord)* to agree, to come to an agreement (**avec qn** with sb; **sur qch** on sth); **s'accorder sur le prix** to agree on the price; **faire s'accorder les livres** to agree the books

> **❝**
> Les subventions que le nouveau gouvernement va **accorder** pour accroître la production bénéficieront aux entreprises les moins efficaces.
> **❞**

accréditation *nf* accréditation d'un produit/d'un service à une norme de qualité awarding of a quality standard to a product/service

accrédité, -e 1 *adj* accredited; **notre représentant dûment accrédité** our duly authorized representative
2 *nm,f* (**a**) ADMIN agent (**b**) FIN holder of a letter of credit (**c**) COMPTA beneficiary, payee

accréditer *vt* (**a**) *(représentant)* to accredit (**b**) FIN *(client)* to open an account for, to open credit facilities for; **être accrédité auprès d'une banque** to have credit facilities at a bank

accréditeur *nm* FIN surety, guarantor

accréditif *nm* (**a**) *(lettre de crédit)* letter of credit; COMPTA credential (**b**) *(crédit)* credit; **loger un accréditif sur une banque** to open credit facilities with a bank ❑ *accréditif permanent* permanent credit

accroche *nf* MKTG slogan

accroissement *nm* growth, increase (**de** in); **les nouveaux équipements ont permis un accroissement de la productivité** the new equipment has led to an increase in productivity ❑ COMPTA, FIN *accroissement global net* aggregate net increment; *accroissement des ventes* sales growth

accroître 1 *vt* to increase; *(productivité)* to increase, to raise
2 s'accroître *vpr* to increase, to rise, to grow

accueil *nm* (**a**) *(lieu)* reception; **passez à l'accueil** go to the reception desk, go to reception; **tenir l'accueil** to be on reception
(**b**) *(façon d'accueillir)* reception, welcome ❑ *cérémonie d'accueil* welcoming speech; *discours d'accueil* welcoming ceremony
(**c**) FIN **faire (bon) accueil à une traite** to meet *or* honour a bill

accueillir *vt* (**a**) *(loger)* to accommodate; **cet hôtel peut accueillir jusqu'à 500 visiteurs** this hotel can accommodate up to 500 guests
(**b**) *(recevoir)* *(personne, décision, proposition)*

to greet; **accueillir qch favorablement/défavorablement** *(idée, projet, décision)* to give sth a favourable/an unfavourable reception; **le projet a été très mal accueilli par la direction** the project got a very cool reception from the management

(**c**) FIN *(traite)* to meet, to honour

> ❝
>
> Les marchés financiers ont bien **accueilli** cette fusion, et malgré la chute des Bourses, les actions de BP et d'Amoco étaient orientées à la hausse.
>
> ❞

accumulation *nf (de marchandises) (action)* stockpiling; *(résultat)* stockpile; *(de stocks)* accumulation, build-up; *(de dettes)* accumulation

accumulé, -e *adj (marchandises)* stockpiled; *(stocks, dettes)* accumulated; FIN *(intérêts)* accrued

accumuler 1 *vt (marchandises)* to stockpile; *(stocks)* to accumulate, to build up; *(dettes)* to accumulate

2 s'accumuler *vpr* to accumulate; FIN *(intérêts)* to accrue

accusé, -e 1 *adj (baisse, hausse)* sharp

2 *nm* **accusé de réception** *(d'une lettre)* acknowledgement (of receipt); *(d'un colis)* receipt; ORDINAT acknowledgement; **envoyer un accusé de réception (à qn)** to send (sb) an acknowledgement

accuser *vt* (**a**) *(bénéfice, perte, baisse, hausse)* to show, to indicate; **la Bourse accuse une forte baisse** the Stock Market is registering big losses (**b**) **accuser réception de qch** to acknowledge (receipt of) sth; **nous accusons réception de votre lettre du 20 juin** we acknowledge receipt of your letter of 20 June

achalandage *nm* (**a**) *(fonds de commerce)* goodwill; **l'achalandage se vend avec l'établissement** the goodwill is to be sold with the business (**b**) *(clientèle)* custom, clientele

achalandé, -e *adj* **bien achalandé** *(qui compte de nombreux clients)* with a large clientele; *(bien approvisionné)* well-stocked; **mal achalandé** *(qui compte peu de clients)* with a small clientele; *(mal approvisionné)* poorly-stocked

achat *nm (action)* purchase, purchasing; *(chose achetée)* purchase; **faire un achat** to make a purchase; **faire l'achat de qch** to purchase sth; **la livre vaut neuf francs à l'achat** the buying rate for sterling is nine francs □ **achat sur catalogue** mail-order purchasing; **achats centralisés** centralized

purchasing; MKTG **achats comparatifs** comparison shopping; **achat au comptant** cash purchase; **achat à crédit** credit purchase, purchase for the account; *(location-achat)* buying on hire purchase *or Am* on the installment plan; **achats directs** direct purchasing; **achats à domicile** teleshopping; **achat en espèces** cash purchase; **achats hors taxes** tax-free shopping; **achat impulsif, achat d'impulsion** impulse buy; **achat juste à temps** just-in-time purchasing; **achat à petits prix** low-cost purchase; **achat spontané** impulse buy; **achat à terme** forward purchase

acheminement *nm (de marchandises) (itinéraire)* flow, routing; *(expédition)* sending, shipping (**sur** *ou* **vers** to); **l'acheminement des marchandises se fait par Calais** the goods are routed through Calais; **acheminement du courrier** mail handling

acheminer 1 *vt (marchandises)* to send, to ship (**sur** *ou* **vers** to)

2 s'acheminer *vpr* **s'acheminer vers qch** *(décision, accord)* to move towards sth; **les syndicats s'acheminent vers une décision en faveur d'une grève** the unions are moving towards a decision to strike

achetable *adj* purchasable

acheter *vt* (**a**) *(acquérir)* to buy, to purchase; **acheter qch à qn** *(faire une transaction)* to buy sth from sb; *(en cadeau)* to buy sth for sb; **acheter qch en gros/au détail** to buy sth wholesale/retail; **acheter qch à crédit/(au) comptant** to buy sth on credit/for cash; **acheter qch à tempérament** to buy sth on hire purchase *or Am* on the installment plan; BOURSE **acheter à terme** to buy forward (**b**) *Fam* **acheter qn** *(soudoyer)* to buy sb off

acheteur, -euse *nm,f* (**a**) *(acquéreur)* buyer, purchaser; JUR vendee; **on n'a pas pu trouver acheteur pour ce produit** there are no buyers for *or* there is no market for this product □ **acheteur anonyme** anonymous buyer; MKTG **acheteur impulsif** impulsive buyer, impulse buyer; **acheteur industriel** business buyer; **acheteur non-identifié** anonymous buyer; **acheteur potentiel** potential buyer

(**b**) *(pour un magasin)* buyer □ **acheteur principal** head buyer

achèvement *nm (d'un travail, d'un projet)* completion

achever *vt (travail, projet)* to complete

acompte *nm (versement régulier)* instalment; *(avance, premier versement)* down payment, deposit; *(sur salaire)* advance; **payer par acomptes** to pay by *or* in instalments;

payer *ou* **verser un acompte de 4 000 francs** *ou* **4 000 francs en acompte (sur qch)** to make a down payment of 4,000 francs (on sth), to pay a deposit of 4,000 francs (on sth); **recevoir un acompte sur son salaire** to receive an advance on one's salary ▫ *acompte de ou sur dividende* interim dividend; FIN *acompte provisionnel* interim payment, advance payment

à-côté *nm Fam (gain d'appoint)* extra; **avoir de petits à-côtés** to make a bit of extra money, to make some money on the side

acquéreur, -euse *nm,f* purchaser, buyer; JUR vendee

acquérir *vt* (a) *(acheter)* to buy, to purchase (b) *(obtenir) (expérience, responsabilités)* to gain, to acquire; **acquérir de la valeur** to go up in value; **l'expérience qu'il a acquise sur le terrain lui a été utile** the experience he gained on the job has been useful

acquis, -e 1 *adj (droits)* acquired, established
2 *nmpl* **acquis sociaux** social benefits, entitlements

> ❝
> Pris de vitesse par l'offensive patronale, les syndicats n'ont réagi jusqu'à présent que par des déclarations convenues sur la défense des **acquis sociaux**.
> ❞

acquisition *nf* (a) *(action)* acquisition; **faire l'acquisition de qch** *(acheter)* to purchase sth (b) *(chose acquise)* acquisition; *(chose achetée)* purchase (c) ORDINAT *acquisition de données* data acquisition

acquit *nm* receipt; **donner acquit de qch** to give a receipt for sth; **pour acquit** *(sur facture, quittance)* received (with thanks), paid ▫ DOUANES *acquit (de douane)* customs receipt; *acquit de paiement* receipt

acquit-à-caution *nm* DOUANES bond note

acquittement *nm (d'une dette)* payment, discharge; *(d'une facture, des droits)* payment

acquitter 1 *vt* (a) *(payer) (dette)* to pay off, to discharge; *(facture, droits)* to pay (b) *(comme preuve de paiement)* to receipt (c) *(chèque)* to endorse
2 **s'acquitter** *vpr* **s'acquitter de qch** *(dette)* to pay sth off, to discharge sth; *(facture, droits)* to pay sth

acte *nm* (a) JUR *(document officiel)* act, deed; **rédiger** *ou* **dresser un acte** to draw up an act or a deed ▫ *acte de cession* deed of transfer; *acte de constitution (d'une société)*

articles of association; *acte déclaratif d'association* statement of intent to work together; *acte hypothécaire* mortgage deed; *acte notarié, acte sur papier timbré* deed executed and authenticated by a notary; *acte de propriété* title deed; UE *acte unique européen* Single European Act; *acte de vente* bill of sale
(b) **actes** *(d'une conférence)* records, proceedings

acteur *nm (participant)* participant, party; **les différents acteurs de la négociation** the different participants in *or* parties involved in the negotiations ▫ *acteur économique* economic agent *or* player; *les acteurs sociaux* = employers, workers and trade unions

actif, -ive 1 *adj* (a) ÉCON *(population)* working ▫ *la vie active* professional life; **entrer dans la vie active** to start working (b) ORDINAT active
2 *nm* COMPTA assets; **excédent de l'actif sur le passif** excess of assets over liabilities ▫ *actif circulant* floating *or* current assets; *actif fictif* fictitious assets; *actif immobilisé* fixed *or* capital assets; *actif réel* real assets; *actif de roulement* current assets

> ❝
> Les taux d'intérêt étant très bas, on devrait assister à une réallocation des **actifs** vers le long terme.
> ❞

action *nf* (a) BOURSE, FIN share; *(document)* share certificate; **actions** shares, equity, *Am* stock; **avoir des actions dans une société, détenir des actions d'une société** to have shares *or* a shareholding in a company; **émettre des actions sur un marché** to issue shares on a market; **les actions ont augmenté/baissé** shares rose/fell ▫ *action d'apport* founder's *or* promoter's share; *action d'attribution* bonus share; *action à dividende cumulatif* cumulative share; *action ordinaire* *Br* ordinary share, *Am* common stock; *action au porteur* bearer share; *action de premier rang, action privilégiée* *Br* preference share, *Am* preferred stock
(b) JUR action, lawsuit; **intenter une action contre qn** to take legal action against sb, to institute proceedings against sb, to take sb to court ▫ *action civile* civil action; *action contractuelle* action for breach of contract; *action en contrefaçon* action for infringement of patent; *action en dommages et intérêts* action *or* claim for damages; *action judiciaire, action en justice* action, lawsuit
(c) *(acte)* MKTG *action commerciale* com-

mercial process; *action de conversion* exchange; *action de vente* sales campaign *or* drive

actionnaire *nmf* BOURSE, FIN *Br* shareholder, *Am* stockholder ❏ *actionnaire majoritaire* majority *Br* shareholder *or Am* stockholder; *actionnaire minoritaire* minority *Br* shareholder *or Am* stockholder

actionnariat *nm* BOURSE, FIN shareholding ❏ *actionnariat ouvrier* employee shareholding

activé, -e *adj* ORDINAT active

activer *vt* (a) *(processus, projet)* to speed up (b) ORDINAT to activate; **activer une option** to select an option

activité *nf* (a) *(occupation)* activity; **activités** *(d'une entreprise)* operations, activities ❏ *activité bancaire* banking; *l'activité commerciale* business activities; *l'activité industrielle* industrial activities; *l'activité professionnelle* professional life (b) **en activité** *(entreprise)* in action, in operation; *(usine)* in production; *(personne)* working; **il est toujours/n'est plus en activité** he's still/no longer working; **en pleine activité** in full operation (c) BOURSE *(du marché)* activity; **sans activité** dull, slack; **en pleine activité** active, brisk

actuaire *nmf* ASSUR, FIN actuary

actualisation *nf* (a) ORDINAT refresh (b) ÉCON discounting

actualisé, -e *adj* (a) ORDINAT refreshed (b) ÉCON discounted

actualiser *vt* (a) ORDINAT to refresh (b) ÉCON to discount

actuariat *nm* ASSUR, FIN *(profession)* actuarial profession

actuariel, -elle *adj* ASSUR, FIN actuarial

actuel, -elle *adj* present, current; **à l'heure actuelle** currently; **le cours actuel du dollar** the current exchange rate for the dollar

actuellement *adv* at present, at the present time, currently

adaptabilité *nf* *(d'une entreprise, de la main-d'œuvre)* adaptability

adapter 1 *vt* to adapt; **adapter la main-d'œuvre aux nouvelles technologies** to adapt the workforce to new technology; **adapté aux besoins du client** adapted *or* tailored to the needs of the customer 2 **s'adapter** *vpr* to adapt; **s'adapter au marché/à la demande** to adapt to the market/to demand

adaptateur *nm* ORDINAT adapter

addition *nf* (a) *(calcul)* adding up, addition; **faire l'addition des chiffres** to add up the figures (b) **en addition au paragraphe 2,...** further to paragraph 2,... (c) *(au restaurant) Br* bill, *Am* check

additionnel, -elle *adj* (a) *(coût, frais)* additional, extra (b) ORDINAT add-on

additionner *vt* to add (up)

adéquation *nf* balance; **l'adéquation entre l'offre et la demande favorise la stabilité des prix** the balance between supply and demand encourages stable prices; **il n'y a pas adéquation entre l'offre et la demande** there is an imbalance between supply and demand

adjoindre 1 *vt* (a) *(associer)* **adjoindre qn à qn** to give sb to sb; **on lui a adjoint un collaborateur** he was given an assistant (b) *(ajouter)* **adjoindre qch à qch** to add sth to sth; **adjoindre des équipements à un ordinateur** to upgrade a computer with add-ons; **adjoindre une pièce à une lettre** to include *or* enclose a document with a letter 2 **s'adjoindre** *vpr* **s'adjoindre qn** to take sb on; **il s'est adjoint un collaborateur** he's taken on an assistant

adjoint, -e 1 *adj* assistant, deputy 2 *nm,f* assistant, deputy ❏ *adjoint au directeur* assistant manager, deputy manager

adjudicataire *nmf* (a) *(pour l'obtention d'un contrat)* successful tenderer; **être déclaré adjudicataire de qch** to secure the contract for sth (b) *(dans une vente aux enchères)* highest *or* successful bidder

adjudication *nf* (a) *(d'un contrat) (appel d'offres)* invitation to tender; *(attribution)* award; **obtenir l'adjudication d'un contrat public** to be awarded a public contract; **mettre qch en adjudication** to invite tenders for sth, to put sth out to tender; **par voie d'adjudication** *(pour l'obtention d'un contrat)* by tender (b) *(de biens) (attribution)* auctioning off; *(vente aux enchères)* (sale by) auction; **mettre qch en adjudication** to put sth up for (sale by) auction; **par voie d'adjudication** by auction

adjuger *vt* **adjuger qch à qn** *(contrat)* to award *or* give sth to sb; *(aux enchères)* to knock sth down to sb; **ils ont adjugé les fournitures de bureau à Corbier** they have awarded *or* given the contract for office supplies to Corbier

admettre *vt* (a) *(autoriser)* to allow; **admettre un recours** to allow a claim (b) *(accueillir)* to admit; **admettre qn au conseil**

d'administration to admit sb to the board of directors; BOURSE **admettre une société à la cote** to list a company

administrateur, -trice *nm,f* (a) *(d'une société, d'une banque)* (non-executive) director; *(d'un journal)* business manager □ **administrateur délégué** managing director; JUR **administrateur judiciaire** *(de biens, d'une entreprise)* (official) receiver (b) ORDINAT **administrateur de réseau** network manager

administratif, -ive 1 *adj* administrative; **détails d'ordre administratif** administrative details

2 *nm,f* administrative worker; **les administratifs** the administrative staff

administration *nf* (a) *(gestion)* administration, direction, management; *(ensemble des directeurs)* board of directors □ **administration du personnel** personnel management; **administration des ventes** sales management

(b) *(service)* **l'administration** the Civil Service; **entrer dans l'administration** to enter the Civil Service, to become a civil servant □ **administration des douanes** *Br* Customs and Excise, *Am* Customs Service; **administration fiscale** tax authorities; **administration portuaire** port authorities

(c) JUR trusteeship

(d) ORDINAT **administration de réseau** network management

administrer *vt (société, biens)* to manage

admissible *adj (à un concours)* eligible; **il a été admissible au concours d'HEC** he qualified for the oral HEC exam

admission *nf* (a) DOUANES *(de marchandises)* **admission (en douane)** entry; **admission en franchise** duty-free entry; **admission temporaire** temporary entry *(of products destined for re-export after processing)*

(b) BOURSE **admission à la cote** admission to quotation, listing; **faire une demande d'admission à la cote** to seek admission to quotation

(c) *(accueil)* entry, admission; **l'admission des pays de l'Est dans l'Union européenne** the entry *or* admission of Eastern European countries into the European Union

adopter *vt (résolution, méthode)* to adopt; *(rapport)* to accept; *(projet de loi)* to pass; **adopté à l'unanimité** carried unanimously

adoption *nf (d'une résolution, d'une méthode)* adoption; *(d'un rapport)* acceptance; *(d'un projet de loi)* passing

adressable *adj* ORDINAT addressable

adressage *nm* ORDINAT addressing; **mode d'adressage** address mode □ **adressage direct** direct addressing

adresse *nf* address; **changer d'adresse** to change one's address; **faire son changement d'adresse** to have one's mail redirected; **inconnu à cette adresse** *(sur lettre)* not known at this address □ **adresse au besoin** *(sur lettre de change)* referee in case of need; **adresse au bureau** office address, business address; ORDINAT **adresse électronique** e-mail address; **adresse de facturation** invoicing address, address for invoicing; ORDINAT **adresse Internet** Internet address; **adresse de livraison** delivery address; *(d'objets volumineux)* shipping address; **adresse personnelle** home address; **adresse professionnelle** business address

adresser 1 *vt* (a) *(courrier, colis)* to address; **adresser qch à qn** to send sth to sb; **cette lettre ne m'est pas adressée** this letter isn't addressed to me (b) ORDINAT to address

2 **s'adresser** *vpr* **s'adresser à qn** *(parler à)* to speak to sb; **veuillez vous adresser au service après-vente** please contact the after-sales department

ad valorem *adj (droit, taxe)* ad valorem

AELE *nf (abrév* **Association européenne de libre-échange***)* EFTA

aérogare *nm* (air) terminal

aérogramme *nm* air letter

affacturage *nm* factoring

affactureur *nm* factor

affaire *nf* (a) **affaires** *(activités commerciales)* business; **entrer dans les affaires** to go into business; **être dans les affaires** to be in business; **faire des affaires avec qn** to do business with sb, to deal with sb; **faire de bonnes affaires** to be successful, to do good business; **faire de mauvaises affaires** to be doing badly, to be in difficulties; **faire des affaires importantes** to do business on a large scale, to have a big turnover; **parler affaires** to talk business; **comment vont les affaires?** how's business?; **les affaires vont mal** business is bad; **je vais à Londres pour affaires** I'm going to London on business □ **affaires courantes** routine business

(b) *(transaction)* deal, transaction; **faire affaire (avec qn)** to do a deal (with sb); **conclure une affaire (avec qn)** to clinch a deal (with sb) □ **affaire blanche** profitless *or* break-even deal; **affaire en or** deal of the century

(c) *(entreprise)* business, firm; **être à la tête**

d'une grosse affaire to be at the head of a large business *or* firm; **son usine est une grande affaire** his factory is a large concern; **administrer** *ou* **gérer** *ou* **diriger une affaire** to run a business; **lancer** *ou* **démarrer une affaire** to start a business

(**d**) *(achat à bon marché)* bargain; **faire une (bonne) affaire** to get a (good) bargain

(**e**) JUR case, lawsuit

(**f**) ADMIN **affaires** affairs □ *affaires publiques* public affairs

affairisme *nm* wheeling and dealing, moneymaking

affairiste *nmf* wheeler-dealer

affectation *nf* (**a**) *(d'une somme, de crédits)* assignment, allocation; **affectation aux dividendes** sum available for dividend □ *affectations budgétaires* budget appropriations; *affectation de fonds* appropriation of funds; *affectation hypothécaire* mortgage charge (**b**) *(des tâches)* assignment (**c**) *(d'un employé)* appointment

affecter *vt* (**a**) *(somme, crédits)* to assign, to allocate (**b**) *(employé)* to appoint (**à** to); **être affecté à un poste** to be appointed to a post

afférent, -e *adj* JUR **afférent à** relating to, pertaining to; **la part afférente à** the portion accruing to

affermage *nm* *(d'un emplacement publicitaire)* contracting

affermer *vt* *(emplacement publicitaire)* to contract for

affichage *nm* (**a**) *(publicitaire)* bill-sticking, bill-posting (**b**) ORDINAT display □ *affichage à cristaux liquides* liquid crystal display; *affichage graphique* graphics display; *affichage numérique* digital display; *affichage tel écran-tel écrit* WYSIWYG

affiche *nf* *(annonce officielle)* public notice; **affiche (publicitaire)** poster, advertisement

afficher **1** *vt* (**a**) *(présenter)* to show; **afficher un déficit/un excédent** to show a deficit/a surplus; **afficher des résultats encourageants** to show encouraging results (**b**) ORDINAT *(message)* to display; **l'écran affiche...** the on-screen message reads..., the screen displays the message...

(**c**) *(mettre en évidence)* to put up, to display; **afficher une vente** to advertise a sale, *Am* to post a sale

2 s'afficher *vpr* ORDINAT *(sur un écran)* to be displayed

afficheur *nm* (**a**) *afficheur publicitaire* billsticker, billposter (**b**) ORDINAT visual dis-play unit, VDU □ *afficheur LCD* LCD display

affidavit *nm* JUR affidavit

affiliation *nf* affiliation

affilié, -e **1** *adj* affiliated □ *société affiliée* *Br* associate *or* affiliated company, *Am* affiliate

2 *nm,f* (affiliated) member, associate

afflux *nm* *(de marchandises, d'or)* inflow, influx □ COMPTA *afflux de capitaux, afflux de fonds* capital inflow

affranchir *vt* *(à la main)* to put a stamp/stamps on; *(à la machine)* to frank; **lettre insuffisamment affranchie** letter with insufficient postage

affranchissement *nm* (**a**) *(à la main)* stamping; *(à la machine)* franking (**b**) *(coût)* postage

affrètement *nm* *(d'un avion, d'un navire)* charter, chartering

affréter *vt* *(avion, navire)* to charter

affréteur *nm* *(d'un avion, d'un navire)* charterer

AFNOR *nf* *(abrév* **Association française de normalisation***)* = French industrial standards authority, *Br* ≃ BSI, *Am* ≃ ASA

AFP *nf* *(abrév* **Agence France-Presse***)* = French international news agency

AG *nf* *(abrév* **assemblée générale***)* GM

AGE *nf* *(abrév* **assemblée générale extraordinaire***)* EGM

agence *nf* (**a**) *(bureau)* agency, bureau □ *agence d'affaires* (general) business agency; *agence conseil en communication* public relations *or* PR consultancy; *agence de distribution* distribution agency; *agence en douane* customs agency; *Agence France-Presse* = French international news agency; *agence immobilière* *Br* estate agent's *or* agency, *Am* real estate agency; *agence d'intérim* temping agency; *agence locale d'aide aux entreprises* regional business development agency; *agence de location* *(de locaux)* letting agency; *(d'équipements)* hire *or* rental company; *agence maritime* shipping *or* forwarding agency; *Agence Nationale Pour l'Emploi* = French national employment bureau, *Br* ≃ Job Centre; *agence de placement* employment agency *or* bureau; *agence de presse* press *or* news agency; *agence de promotion des ventes* sales promotion agency; *agence de publicité* advertising agency; *agence de renseignement(s)* information bureau; *agence de* *réservation* booking agency; ***agence de tourisme*** travel agency *or* agent's; ***agence de travail intérimaire*** temping agency; ***agence de voyages*** travel agency *or* agent's (**b**) *(d'une banque, d'une société)* branch (office); **la maison a plusieurs agences à l'étranger** the company has several branches overseas ▫ ***agence bancaire*** bank branch

agenda *nm* (**a**) diary ▫ ***agenda de bureau*** desk diary; ***agenda électronique*** personal organizer; ***agenda organisateur*** personal organizer, Filofax®; ***agenda de poche*** pocket diary; ***agenda de réservation*** reservations book (**b**) ORDINAT notebook

agent *nm* agent ▫ ***agent d'affacturage*** factoring agent; ***agent d'affaires*** business agent, general agent; ***agent agréé*** registered agent; ***agent d'assurance(s)*** insurance broker *or* agent; ***agent attitré*** appointed agent; ***agent autorisé*** authorized representative; ***agent en brevets*** patent agent; FIN, BOURSE ***agent de change*** stockbroker; ***agent commercial*** sales representative; ***agent commercial exclusif*** sole agent *or* representative; ***agent commissionnaire*** commission agent; ***agent comptable*** accountant; ***agent de contact*** contact; ***agent à demeure*** agent on the spot; ***agent direct*** commission agent; ***agent de distribution*** distribution agent; ***agent en douanes*** customs agent *or* broker; ***agent économique*** economic agent *or* player; ***agent exclusif*** sole agent; ***agent exportateur*** export agent; ***agent de fabrication*** production worker; ***agent de fret*** freight forwarder, forwarding agent; ***agent du fisc*** tax official; ***agent général*** general agent; ***agent immobilier*** *Br* estate agent, *Am* realtor, real estate agent; ***agent importateur*** import agent; ***agent indépendant*** free agent; ***agent intermédiaire*** middleman; ***agent de liaison*** contact; ***agent de ligne*** forwarding agent; ***agent de location*** letting agent; ***agent de maîtrise*** foreman, supervisor; ***agent mandataire*** authorized representative; ***agent maritime*** shipping agent; ***agent de publicité*** advertising agent, publicity agent; ***agent de réceptif*** ground handling agent; ***agent de recouvrement(s)*** debt collector; ***agent de réservation*** reservation agent; ***agent de sécurité*** security officer; ***agent technico-commercial*** sales technician; ***agent de transmission*** runner, messenger; ***agent de voyages*** travel agent

> 66
>
> Les agents resteront la pièce essentielle de la vente d'assurance en France. Le réseau de distribution traditionnel des compagnies d'assurance, dont la force vive est constituée par les **agents généraux**.
>
> 99

agétac *nm* (*abrév* **accord général sur les tarifs douaniers et le commerce**) GATT

agio *nm* (**a**) FIN *(dans un échange de devises)* agio (**b**) BANQUE **agios** *(quand on est à découvert)* bank charges; *(d'un emprunt)* interest payments

agiotage *nm* BOURSE speculating, gambling

agioter *vi* BOURSE to speculate, to gamble

agioteur, -euse *nm,f* BOURSE speculator, gambler

agir *vi* BOURSE **agir sur le marché** to manipulate the market

agitation *nf* (**a**) *(troubles)* unrest ▫ ***agitation sociale*** industrial unrest (**b**) *(sur le marché de la Bourse)* activity

agrafe *nf* staple ▫ ***agrafe antivol*** anti-theft *or* security tag

agrafer *vt* to staple

agrafeuse *nf* stapler

agrandir **1** *vt (entreprise, usine, locaux)* to expand
2 s'agrandir *vpr (entreprise, marché)* to expand; **le marché des logiciels s'agrandit** the market for software is expanding

agréé, -e **1** *adj* recognized, authorized; *(échantillon)* approved
2 *nm* JUR lawyer *(before a ''tribunal de commerce'')*

agréer *vt (fournisseur, équipement, contrat)* to approve; **veuillez agréer** *ou* **je vous prie d'agréer l'expression de mes sentiments distingués, veuillez agréer l'assurance de ma haute considération** *(dans une lettre)* *(à une personne dont on ne connaît pas le nom)* yours faithfully; *(à une personne dont on connaît le nom)* yours sincerely

agrégat *nm* ÉCON aggregate ▫ ***agrégat monétaire*** monetary aggregate

agrément *nm* (**a**) *(accord)* approval; **agir avec l'agrément de ses supérieurs** to act with the approval of one's superiors (**b**) *(d'agence de voyages)* agency appointment (**c**) *(garantie financière)* bonding scheme

agriculture *nf* agriculture, farming

agroalimentaire 1 *adj (industrie, secteur)* food

   2 *nm* **l'agroalimentaire** the food-processing industry

agro-monétaire *adj* agri-monetary

aguiche *nf* MKTG teaser (ad)

AIDA *nm* MKTG *(abrév* **attention-intérêt-désir-action**) AIDA

aide *nf* (**a**) *(assistance)* assistance, help; *(sous forme d'argent)* aid □ ÉCON *aide au développement* foreign aid (to developing countries); *aide économique* economic aid; *aide de l'État* government aid; *aide à l'exportation* export aid; *aide financière* financial aid *or* assistance; COMPTA *aide fiscale* tax credit; *aide gouvernementale* government aid; *aide judiciaire* legal aid; *aide personnalisée au logement* ≃ housing benefit; *aide publique au développement* official development assistance; *aide à la réinsertion professionnelle* help to re-enter the job market; *aide au retour* = voluntary repatriation allowances for immigrant workers leaving France; *aide sociale Br* social security, *Am* welfare

   (**b**) ORDINAT help □ *aide contextuelle* context-sensitive help; *aide en ligne* on-line help

aide-comptable *nmf* bookkeeper

aile *nf* **battre de l'aile** *(entreprise)* to be struggling

AIO *nm* MKTG *(abrév* **activités, intérêts et opinions**) AIO

aire *nf* area □ *aire de chargement* loading bay; *aire d'embarquement* departure lounge

ajournement *nm (d'une décision, d'une réunion, d'un voyage)* postponement; *(après le début d'une séance)* adjournment

ajourner *vt (décision, réunion, voyage)* to postpone; *(après le début d'une séance)* to adjourn

ajout *nm* MKTG *ajout à la gamme* range addition; *ajout à la ligne* line addition

ajouté *nm (à un contrat)* rider, addition

ajouter 1 *vt* (**a**) *(additionner)* to add (**à** to)

   (**b**) ORDINAT to append

   2 s'ajouter *vpr* **s'ajouter à** to be added to; **à cela viennent s'ajouter les frais de transport** on top of this there are travel expenses (to be added)

ajustement *nm (des salaires, d'une monnaie, des prix)* adjustment □ *ajustement fret* bunker adjustment factor; *ajustement saisonnier* seasonal adjustment; MKTG *ajustement stratégique* strategic *or* marketing fit

ajuster *vt (salaires, prix, monnaie)* to adjust

ALE *nf (abrév* **Association de libre-échange**) FTA

aléatoire *adj (contrat)* aleatory; *(sondage, échantillonnage)* random; *(marché, spéculation)* risky

ALENA *nm (abrév* **Accord de libre-échange nord-américain**) NAFTA

> ❝
> L'**ALENA**, cet accord de libre-échange entre les États-Unis, Canada et le Mexique, qui va créer un marché unique de 360 millions de consommateurs, sera-t-il une bonne ou une mauvaise affaire?
> ❞

aliénation *nf* JUR *(de droits, d'une propriété)* transfer

aliéner *vt* JUR *(droits, propriété)* to transfer

alignement *nm* (**a**) COMPTA *(d'un compte)* making up, balancing

   (**b**) FIN alignment (**sur** with); **alignement des prix** alignment of prices, price alignment; **l'alignement des salaires sur le coût de la vie** bringing salaries into line with the cost of living

   (**c**) ÉCON *(d'une monnaie, d'une économie)* alignment □ *alignement monétaire* monetary alignment *or* adjustment

   (**d**) ORDINAT alignment

> ❝
> A court terme, la suppression quasi complète des droits de douane, l'**alignement** sur le tarif extérieur commun de la Communauté, que suppose l'union douanière, ont toute chance de provoquer un choc plutôt rude sur les entreprises turques.
> ❞

aligner *vt* (**a**) COMPTA *(compte)* to make up, to balance (**b**) FIN to align, to bring into line (**sur** with); **les petits commerçants doivent aligner leurs prix sur ceux des grandes surfaces** small shopkeepers have to bring their prices into line with those of hypermarkets (**c**) ÉCON *(monnaie, économie)* to align (**d**) ORDINAT to align

aliment *nm* (**a**) *(nourriture)* food (**b**) ASSUR interest *or* risk value

alimentaire *adj* food □ *l'industrie alimentaire* the food industry; *produits alimentaires* foodstuffs, food products

alimentation *nf* (**a**) *(aliments)* **produits d'alimentation** foodstuffs, food products (**b**) ORDINAT **alimentation feuille à**

feuille cut sheet feed, single sheet feed; *alimentation papier* sheetfeed, paper feed; *alimentation page par page* cut sheet feed, single sheet feed

alimenter *vt (compte bancaire)* to pay money into

alinéa *nm (renfoncement)* indent; *(texte)* paragraph; **faire un alinéa** to indent

allègement *nm (d'impôts, de charges, de dépenses)* reduction ❑ *allègement fiscal* tax relief

alléger *vt (impôts, charges, dépenses)* to reduce

aller *nm* outward journey; **un aller (simple)** *Br* a single (ticket), *Am* a one-way ticket; **un aller (et) retour** *Br* a return (ticket), *Am* a round-trip ticket

alliance *nf* alliance

" La compagnie libanaise Middle East Airlines va conclure une **alliance** commerciale avec Air France à la fin août. "

allier **s'allier** *vpr* to join, to unite (**avec** with)

allocataire *nmf* beneficiary

allocation *nf* (a) ADMIN *(prestation financière)* allowance, *Br* benefit, *Am* welfare ❑ *allocation chômage* unemployment benefit; *allocations familiales* *Br* child benefit, family allowance, *Am* dependents' allowances; *allocation d'invalidité* disability benefit; *allocation logement* housing benefit; *allocation de maternité* maternity benefit; *allocation vieillesse* old-age pension (b) *(attribution) (d'argent)* allocation; *(de dommages-intérêts, d'une indemnité)* awarding (c) BOURSE *(de titres)* allocation, allotment

allouer *vt* (a) ADMIN *(salaire, pension)* to grant, to award (b) *(attribuer) (argent)* to allocate; *(dommages-intérêts, indemnité)* to award; *(dépense, budget)* to allow, to pass (c) BOURSE *(titres)* to allocate, to allot

alourdir 1 *vt (charges, impôts)* to increase 2 **s'alourdir** *vpr (charges, impôts)* to increase

altération *nf* ORDINAT *(d'un fichier)* corruption

altéré, -e *adj* ORDINAT corrupt

altérer ORDINAT 1 *vt* to corrupt 2 **s'altérer** *vpr* to go corrupt

alternance *nf (en politique)* change of government

" Faute d'un développement suffisant de l'**alternance**, on continuera de distribuer ces assignats universitaires qui conduisent tout droit au chômage la catégorie nouvelle des ouvriers diplômés non qualifiés. "

alterner *vi* to alternate, to take turns; **les différents pays alternent à la présidence de l'Union européenne** the different countries alternate the presidency of the European Union

AM *nf* ASSUR *(abrév* **Assurance maladie**) health insurance

amalgamation *nf (d'entreprises)* merger

amalgamer *vt (entreprises, fonctions, postes)* to merge; **amalgamer une entreprise à une autre** to merge one company with another

amateurisme *nm (incompétence)* amateurism

ambulant, -e *adj* itinerant, travelling

AME *nm (abrév* **Accord monétaire européen**) EMA

amélioration *nf* improvement (**de** in) ❑ MKTG *amélioration du produit* product augmentation *or* improvement

améliorer 1 *vt* to improve 2 **s'améliorer** *vpr* to improve

aménagement *nm* (a) ÉCON, ADMIN planning, development ❑ *aménagement du territoire* regional development, town and country planning; *aménagement urbain* town planning; *aménagement urbain et rural* town and country planning (b) *(du temps de travail)* flexibility (c) *(amendement)* adjustment ❑ *aménagement fiscal* tax adjustment

" Axa vient de signer avec tous les syndicats un accord sur l'**aménagement** du temps de travail. "

aménager *vt* (a) *(magasin)* to fit out (b) *(horaire)* to plan, to work out

" Les entreprises du bâtiment ... recherchent surtout à disposer de plus de souplesse pour **aménager** les horaires de travail. "

amende *nf* fine; *(pour retard de livraison)* penalty; **infliger une amende à qn** to fine sb; *(pour retard de livraison)* to penalize sb

amendement *nm* amendment

amender *vt (proposition, loi, texte)* to amend

amiable JUR **1** *adj (accord)* conciliatory ❏ *amiable compositeur* arbitrator
2 à l'amiable *adv* out of court; **régler qch à l'amiable** to reach a private *or* an amicable agreement about sth; *(sans procès)* to settle sth out of court

AMM *nf (abrév* **autorisation de mise sur le marché)** = official authorization for marketing a pharmaceutical product

amont *nm* ÉCON, MKTG upside; **d'amont** *(activités)* upstream; **en amont** *(société)* upstream

amorçage *nm* ORDINAT booting

amorce *nf (début)* beginning; **on assiste à une amorce de reprise économique** we are witnessing the beginnings of economic recovery

amorcer 1 *vt* ORDINAT to boot (up); **amorcer de nouveau** to reboot
2 s'amorcer *vpr* **(a)** ORDINAT to boot (up)
(b) *(commencer)* to begin; **la reprise économique s'amorce** economic recovery has begun

amorti, -e *adj* FIN *(bien)* depreciated; *(frais, investissement, capital)* amortized

amortir 1 *vt* **(a)** FIN *(rentabiliser)* **le matériel a été amorti dès la première année** the equipment had paid for itself by the end of the first year; **il a loué la machine pour en amortir le coût** he rented out the machine to make it pay *or* to recoup the cost
(b) FIN *(dette)* to pay off, to amortize; *(prêt)* to repay; *(obligation)* to redeem
(c) COMPTA *(équipement)* to write off, to amortize, to depreciate
2 s'amortir *vpr (dépenses, investissement)* to pay for itself

amortissable *adj* FIN *(dette)* redeemable

amortissement *nm* **(a)** *(rentabilité)* profitability; **l'amortissement d'un équipement est plus rapide si on emprunte à court terme** equipment pays for itself faster if it's paid for with a short-term loan
(b) FIN *(d'une dette)* repayment, amortization ❏ *amortissement anticipé* redemption before due date
(c) COMPTA *(perte de valeur)* depreciation ❏ *amortissement accéléré* accelerated

depreciation; *amortissement dégressif* sliding scale depreciation

amovible *adj* **(a)** ORDINAT *(disque dur)* removable **(b)** *(personnel)* transferable, mobile

ample *adj (ressources, provisions)* extensive, ample; **pour de plus amples renseignements, veuillez contacter…** for further information, please contact…; **jusqu'à plus ample informé** until further information is available

ampleur *nf (d'un problème, des dégâts, d'une crise)* scale, extent; *(des ressources, des provisions)* abundance ❏ MKTG *ampleur de gamme* breadth of range

an *nm* year; **par an** yearly, per year; FIN per annum; **un prêt sur vingt ans** a loan over twenty years

analogique *adj* ORDINAT analog

analyse *nf* analysis ❏ *analyse des attraits et des atouts* opportunity and issue analysis; *analyse des besoins* needs analysis; *analyse des concurrents* competitor analysis; *analyse des coûts* cost analysis; *analyse de coût et d'efficacité* cost-effectiveness analysis; *analyse coût-profit* cost-benefit analysis; *analyse des coûts et rendements* cost-benefit analysis; *analyse de la demande* demand analysis; *analyse de données* data analysis; *analyse des écarts* variance analysis; ÉCON *analyse économique* economic analysis; *analyse des forces et faiblesses* strengths and weaknesses analysis; *analyse des forces, faiblesses, opportunités et menaces* SWOT analysis; *analyse du marché* market analysis; *analyse des marchés* market research; *analyse de portefeuille* portfolio analysis; *analyse prévisionnelle* predictive analysis; *analyse du prix de revient* cost analysis; *analyse du rendement* rate-of-return analysis; *analyse des risques* risk analysis; *analyse par segment* cluster analysis; *analyse du style de vie* lifestyle analysis; ORDINAT *analyse de système, analyse systémique* systems analysis; *analyse des tâches* job analysis; *analyse des ventes* sales analysis

analyser *vt (résultats, chiffres)* to analyse

analyste *nmf* analyst ❏ *analyste financier* financial analyst; MKTG *analyste du marché* market analyst

analyste-programmeur, -euse *nm,f* ORDINAT systems analyst

analytique *adj* analytical

ancien, -enne *adj* **(a)** *(d'autrefois) (emploi, directeur)* former, old **(b)** *(vieux)* old; **je suis plus ancien que vous dans la profes-**

sion I've been in the profession longer than you; **il n'est pas assez ancien dans l'entreprise** he hasn't worked for the company for long enough

ancienneté *nf* seniority; **être promu à l'ancienneté** to be promoted by seniority

ancrage *nm* ORDINAT justification; **ancrage à droite/gauche** right/left justification

animateur, -trice *nm,f* MKTG *(d'une réunion de groupe)* leader, moderator □ **animateur des ventes** marketing executive

animation *nf* **(a)** FIN *(du marché)* briskness, buoyancy **(b)** MKTG promotion; **faire des animations dans les supermarchés** to promote products in supermarkets □ **animation des ventes** sales drive *or* promotion

animé, -e *adj* FIN *(marché)* brisk, buoyant

année *nf* year □ **année budgétaire** *Br* financial year, *Am* fiscal year; COMPTA **année civile** calendar year; **année comptable** accounting year; **année en cours** current year; **année d'exercice** *Br* financial year, *Am* fiscal year; **année fiscale** tax year; **année d'imposition** tax year; **année record** peak year; **année de référence** base year; **année sabbatique** sabbatical year

> " ————————
>
> Les créances douteuses ont augmenté au cours du premier semestre de l'**année fiscale** et les fonds propres ont fondu avec la chute du Nikkei.
>
> ———————— "

annexe 1 *adj (document, pièce)* attached; *(industries)* subsidiary; *(revenus)* supplementary

2 *nf* **(a)** *(de contrat)* annexe; *(de projet de loi)* rider; *(de loi)* schedule; *(de livre, de rapport)* appendix; *(de lettre)* enclosure; *(document joint)* attached document; **en annexe à ma lettre** enclosed with my letter; **en annexe veuillez trouver…** please find enclosed… **(b)** COMPTA **annexes** notes to the accounts

annexer *vt (document, pièce)* to append, to attach

annonce *nf* advert, advertisement; **demander qch par voie d'annonces** to advertise for sth; **insérer** *ou* **mettre une annonce dans un journal** to put an advertisement in a newspaper □ **annonces classées** classified ads; **annonce publicitaire** advert, advertisement; **petites annonces** *Br* small ads, *Am* want ads; **petites annonces d'emploi** classified job ads

annonceur *nm (de publicité)* advertiser

annuaire *nm (d'un organisme)* yearbook; *(liste d'adresses)* directory □ **annuaire du commerce** commercial directory; **annuaire électronique** electronic telephone directory *(on Minitel)*; **annuaire du téléphone, annuaire téléphonique** telephone directory

annualisation *nf* annualization; **l'annualisation du temps de travail permettra de répondre à une demande saisonnière** calculating working hours across the year will enable us to meet seasonal demand

> " ————————
>
> L'accord conclu dans le secteur du sucre va permettre à une grande partie des salariés de passer aux 35 heures dès le 1er juin 1999. En échange … d'une plus grande flexibilité (sous forme d'**annualisation**).
>
> ———————— "

annualiser *vt* to annualize

annualité *nf* yearly recurrence □ **annualité budgétaire** yearly *or* annual voting of the budget

annuel, -elle *adj* annual, yearly

annuellement *adv* annually, yearly

annuitaire *adj (dette)* redeemable by yearly payments

annuité *nf* **(a)** FIN *(dans le remboursement d'un emprunt)* annual instalment *or* repayment □ COMPTA **annuité d'amortissement** annual depreciation *or* writedown; COMPTA **annuité constante** *(de remboursement)* fixed annual payment **(b)** *(année de service)* year of service **(c)** *(rente)* annuity

annulable *adj (contrat)* voidable, revocable

annulation *nf* **(a)** *(d'une réservation, d'une commande, d'un projet)* cancellation; *(d'une dette)* cancellation, writing off; *(d'un marché, d'une grève)* calling off □ **annulation de dernière minute** late cancellation; **annulation rétroactive** retroactive cancellation **(b)** ORDINAT cancel □ **annulation d'entrée** *(commande)* cancel entry; **annulation des révisions** *(commande)* undo changes **(c)** JUR *(d'un jugement)* quashing; *(d'un contrat)* annulment, invalidation

annuler *vt* **(a)** *(réservation, commande, projet)* to cancel; *(dette)* to cancel, to write off; *(marché, grève)* to call off **(b)** ORDINAT to cancel **(c)** BANQUE *(chèque)* to cancel **(d)** *(remplacer)* to supersede, to cancel; **ce catalogue annule les précédents** this catalogue supersedes all previous issues

(e) JUR *(jugement)* to quash; *(contrat)* to annul, to invalidate

ANPE *nf (abrév* **Agence Nationale pour l'Emploi)** = French national employment bureau, *Br* ≃ Job Centre

antécédents *nmpl (d'un employé, d'une société)* previous history, track record

antémémoire *nf* ORDINAT cache (memory)

anticipation *nf* **payer par anticipation** to pay in advance ❑ **paiement par anticipation** advance payment, prepayment

anticipé, -e *adj (remboursement)* before due date; *(dividende, paiement)* advance; *(ventes)* expected; *(retraite)* early; **avec mes remerciements anticipés** *(dans une lettre)* thanking you in advance

anticiper *vt* **anticiper un paiement** to pay in advance; **anticiper un paiement de dix jours** to pay ten days early

anticommercial, -e *adj (attitude)* unbusinesslike

antidater *vt* to backdate, to antedate

anti-discriminatoire *adj (mesures, politique)* anti-discriminatory

antidumping *adj (loi, législation)* antidumping

antiéconomique *adj* contrary to economic principles, uneconomic

antigrève *adj (loi, législation)* anti-strike

anti-inflationniste *adj* ÉCON anti-inflationary

antiprotectionniste **1** *adj* antiprotectionist, free-trade
 2 *nmf* anti-protectionist, free-trader

antireflet *adj* ORDINAT non-reflecting, anti-glare

antitrust *adj (loi) Br* anti-monopoly, *Am* antitrust

antivirus *nm* ORDINAT antivirus *m*

AOC *nf (abrév* **appellation d'origine contrôlée)** = guarantee of quality

apaisement *nm (du marché)* calming down

apaiser **s'apaiser** *vpr (marché)* to calm down

APE *nf (abrév* **Assemblée parlementaire européenne)** EP

APEC *nf (abrév* **Association pour l'emploi des cadres)** = employment agency for executives and graduates

aperçu avant impression *nm* ORDINAT print preview

apériteur *nm* ASSUR leading underwriter

APL *nf (abrév* **Aide personnalisée au logement)** ≃ housing benefit

appareil *nm* **(a)** *(machine)* apparatus, appliance ❑ **appareil de démonstration** demonstration model
 (b) *(téléphone)* telephone; **qui est à l'appareil?** who's speaking?
 (c) *(système)* apparatus, machinery ❑ **l'appareil administratif** administrative machinery; **l'appareil législatif** the machinery of the law; **appareil de production** production facilities

appartement *nm Br* flat, *Am* apartment ❑ **appartement de fonction** company *Br* flat *or Am* apartment; **appartement témoin** *Br* show flat, *Am* model apartment

appartenir **appartenir à** *vt ind (être la propriété de)* to belong to; *(être membre de)* to belong to, to be a member of

appauvrir **1** *vt* to impoverish
 2 s'appauvrir *vpr* to become impoverished, to grow poorer

appauvrissement *nm* impoverishment

appel *nm* **(a)** FIN call; **faire un appel de fonds** to call up capital ❑ **appel d'offres** invitation to tender; **faire un appel d'offres** to invite bids *or* tenders
 (b) **appel (téléphonique)** (telephone) call, phone call; **prendre un appel** to take a (telephone) call; **recevoir un appel** to receive a (telephone) call; **il y a eu un appel pour vous** there was a (telephone) call for you ❑ **appel automatique** automatic dial; **appel gratuit** *Br* Freefone® call, *Am* toll-free call; **appel en PCV** *Br* reverse-charge call, *Am* collect call; **appel de réveil** wake-up *or* alarm call
 (c) *(demande)* call, demand; **appel à la grève** call to strike; **faire appel aux services de qn** to call on sb's services
 (d) ORDINAT call; *(de commande)* selection

> 73 000 salariés, de l'État du Maine à celui de Virginie, ont décidé hier de cesser le travail à l'**appel** du syndicat du secteur de la communication.

appelé, -e *adj* FIN *(capital)* called-up

appeler **1** *vt* **(a)** **appeler qn (au téléphone)** to ring sb (up), to call sb
 (b) *(inciter)* **appeler les salariés à un arrêt de travail/à la grève** to call a stoppage/a strike

(c) JUR appeler qn à comparaître devant un tribunal to summon sb to appear before a court
(d) ORDINAT *(fichier)* to call up
2 *vi (inciter)* **appeler à un arrêt de travail/à la grève** to call a stoppage/a strike

appellation d'origine contrôlée *nf* = guarantee of quality

applicable *adj* applicable; **le règlement est applicable immédiatement** the ruling will take effect immediately

application *nf* **(a)** *(des sanctions, d'un règlement, des mesures)* application; **entrer en application** to take effect, to come into force; **mettre qch en application** to enforce sth, to apply sth **(b)** ORDINAT application ▫ *application bureautique* business application; *application graphique* graphics application; *application en service* current application

appliquer 1 *vt (sanctions, règlement, mesures)* to enforce, to apply
2 s'appliquer *vpr (sanctions, règlement, mesures)* to apply **(à** to)

appoint *nm (revenu supplémentaire)* additional income

appointements *nmpl* salary; **toucher ses appointements** to draw one's salary

appointer *vt* **appointer qn** to pay sb a salary

apport *nm* **(a)** *(fait d'apporter)* contribution; ÉCON inflow, influx; **cette région bénéficie de l'apport (en devises) du tourisme** this area benefits from the financial contribution made by tourism; **sans apport extérieur nous étions perdus** without outside financial help we'd have been ruined ▫ *apport d'argent frais* injection of new money; COMPTA *apport en capital* capital contribution; *apport en espèces (dans un investissement)* cash contribution; COMPTA *apport en numéraire* cash contribution **(b)** FIN *(dans une entreprise)* initial share

---

"

Il est vrai qu'au Cetelem, la fourchette de taux pour l'achat d'une voiture neuve, avec 25% d'**apport**, qui allait encore de 11,88% à 15% en avril, est passé en septembre de 9% à 13,92%.

"

---

apporter *vt (capitaux)* to contribute

apposer *vt (sceau, cachet, scellés)* to affix **(à** to); **apposer sa signature au bas d'une lettre** to put one's signature to a letter

apposition *nf (d'un sceau, d'un cachet, de scellés, d'une signature)* affixing

appréciateur, -trice *nm,f* appraiser, valuer

appréciatif, -ive *adj* evaluative

appréciation *nf* **(a)** *(estimation)* valuation, estimation; *(d'un préjudice)* estimation, assessment; **faire l'appréciation de qch** to value sth ▫ *appréciation du personnel* staff appraisal; *appréciation des risques* risk assessment
(b) *(augmentation)* appreciation; **l'appréciation de la livre par rapport au dollar freine les exportations britanniques** the rise of the pound against the dollar is curbing British exports

apprécier 1 *vt (estimer)* to value, to estimate; *(préjudice)* to estimate, to assess
2 s'apprécier *vpr (augmenter)* to rise; **le franc s'est apprécié par rapport au dollar** the franc has risen against the dollar

apprenti, -e *nm,f* apprentice

apprentissage *nm* apprenticeship; **mettre qn en apprentissage chez qn** to apprentice sb to sb; **faire son apprentissage chez qn** to serve one's apprenticeship with sb

approbation *nf (d'un document, des comptes, de comptes-rendus)* approval; **pour approbation** *(sur document administratif)* for approval, subject to approval; **soumettre qch à l'approbation (de qn)** to submit sth for approval (by sb); **donner son approbation (à qch)** to give (sth) one's approval

approche *nf* MKTG *approche directe* cold calling; *approche personnalisée* person-to-person approach

appropriation *nf* appropriation ▫ *appropriation de fonds* embezzlement, misappropriation of funds

approuver *vt (document, comptes, comptes-rendus)* to approve; *(appel)* to endorse; *(décision)* to approve of; ADMIN *(nomination)* to confirm; **approuver et contre-argumenter** to agree and counter; **lu et approuvé** *(sur document)* read and approved

approvisionnement *nm* **(a)** *(action)* supplying **(en** with); *(d'un magasin)* stocking **(en** with); **l'approvisonnement du pays en pétrole/en matières premières est compromis par l'embargo** the supply of oil/raw materials to the country has been jeopardized by the embargo
(b) *(réserve)* supply, stock; **faire un approvisionnement de qch** to stock up with sth, to lay in a supply of sth ▫ *approvisionnements de réserve* reserve stocks

(c) *(dans l'industrie de transformation)* raw materials and component parts

approvisionner 1 *vt* (a) BANQUE *(compte)* to pay money into; **son compte en banque n'est plus approvisionné** his bank account is no longer in credit (b) *(fournir)* to supply (**en** with); **cette entreprise nous approvisionne en pièces détachées** this company supplies us with spare parts
2 **s'approvisionner** *vpr* to get in supplies (**en** of); **s'approvisionner chez qn** to get one's supplies from sb

approvisionneur, -euse *nm,f* supplier

approximatif, -ive *adj (calcul, devis, estimation)* approximate, rough; **ce chiffre est très approximatif** this figure is only a rough estimate

approximation *nf* approximation

appui *nm (soutien)* backing, support; **il a apporté son appui à notre projet** he backed *or* supported our project □ *appui financier* (financial) backing; **la société ne bénéficie pas d'un appui financier suffisant** the company does not have sufficient financial backing

appuyer *vt* to back, to support; **appuyer qn financièrement** to back sb (financially), to give sb financial backing; **appuyer la candidature de qn** to back *or* support sb's application

après-vente *adj* after-sales

aptitude professionnelle *nf* ability, aptitude

apurement *nm* (a) *(des comptes)* auditing (b) *(d'une dette, du passif)* discharge

apurer *vt* (a) *(comptes)* to audit (b) *(dette, passif)* to discharge

AR *nm (abrév* **accusé de réception***)* acknowledgement (of receipt)

arbitrage *nm* (a) JUR *(dans un conflit social)* arbitration; **recourir à l'arbitrage** to go to arbitration; **soumettre une question à un arbitrage** to refer a question to arbitration; **soumettre un litige à l'arbitrage d'un tiers** to take a dispute to arbitration by a third party □ *arbitrage à l'amiable* out-of-court settlement (b) FIN, BOURSE arbitrage □ *arbitrage de change* arbitration of exchange

arbitragiste *nmf* FIN, BOURSE arbitrager

arbitral, -e *adj* JUR arbitral □ *procédure arbitrale* procedure by arbitration; *solution arbitrale* settlement by arbitration

arbitralement *adv* JUR by arbitration

arbitre *nm* JUR arbitrator, adjudicator □ *arbitre rapporteur* referee (in commercial suit)

arbitrer *vt* JUR to arbitrate

arborescence *nf* ORDINAT *(structure)* tree diagram; *(chemin)* directory path

arbre *nm* (a) ORDINAT tree (b) MKTG *arbre de décision* decision tree

archivage *nm* filing

archive *nf* (a) ORDINAT archive (b) **archives** archives, records

archiver *vt (documents officiels)* to archive; *(dossiers, factures)* to file

archiviste *nmf (fonction publique)* keeper of public records; *(employé de bureau)* filing clerk

ardoise électronique *nf* ORDINAT notepad computer

argent *nm* (a) *(richesse)* money; **payer en argent** to pay (in) cash; **placer son argent** to invest one's money; **trouver de l'argent** to raise money □ *argent à bon marché* cheap money; COMPTA *argent en caisse* cash in hand; *(recettes)* takings; *argent comptant* cash; ORDINAT *argent électronique* e-cash, electronic money; *argent frais* new money; *argent au jour le jour* call money, day-to-day money; *argent liquide* cash (in hand); *argent mal acquis* dirty money; *argent sale* dirty money; ORDINAT *argent virtuel* e-cash, electronic money (b) *(métal)* silver

> " ────────────
> Les privatisations ont fait rentrer de l'**argent frais**, venu essentiellement de l'etranger.
> ──────────── "

argument de vente *nm* selling point

argumentaire *nm* promotion leaflet; **l'argumentaire est très convaincant** the sales pitch is very convincing

argus *nm* = guide to used car prices; **acheter/vendre qch à l'argus** to buy/sell sth for the book price; **valeur à l'argus** book price

armateur *nm* shipowner

armement *nm (profession)* merchant shipping

arr. *nm (abrév* **arrondissement***)* = administrative subdivision of Paris, Lyons and Marseilles

arrangement *nm* agreement, settlement; *(avec ses créanciers)* composition; **parvenir à un arrangement** to come to an agreement; **sauf arrangement contraire** unless otherwise agreed

arranger s'arranger *vpr* to come to an agreement (**avec** with); **s'arranger à l'amiable avec ses créanciers** to come to an amicable agreement with one's creditors

arrérager 1 *vi* to be in arrears
2 **s'arrérager** *vpr* to fall into arrears

arrérages *nmpl* arrears

arrêt *nm* stoppage ❏ *arrêt maladie* sick leave; **être en arrêt maladie** to be on sick leave; *arrêt de paiement* (d'un chèque) stopping; *arrêt de travail* (grève) stoppage; (congé) sick leave; (certificat) doctor's or medical certificate; **être en arrêt de travail** to be on sick leave

arrêté *nm* (a) ADMIN, JUR order, decree ❏ *arrêté d'exécution* decree providing for the enforcement of a law; *arrêté ministériel* ministerial order; *arrêté municipal* by-law; *arrêté préfectoral* bylaw
(b) BANQUE *arrêté de compte* (fermeture) settlement of account; (bilan) statement of account

arrêter 1 *vt* (a) (cesser) (production, fabrication) to stop
(b) BANQUE (compte) to close, to settle; COMPTA (comptes de l'exercice) to close
(c) (décider de) (date, prix) to fix; (plan, procédure, marché) to decide on, to settle on
2 **s'arrêter** *vpr* (a) (cesser) to stop; **l'entreprise s'est arrêtée de fonctionner** the company has closed down; **il s'est arrêté de travailler l'an dernier** he stopped work last year
(b) ORDINAT (système) to shut down

arrhes *nfpl* deposit; **verser des arrhes** to pay a deposit

arriéré, -e 1 *adj* (a) (dû) late, behind, in arrears; (paiement) overdue, outstanding; (intérêts) outstanding, in arrears
(b) ÉCON (pays) underdeveloped, backward
2 *nm* (a) (dette) arrears; **avoir des arriérés** to be in arrears; **arriéré de loyer** rent arrears, back rent; **arriéré d'impôts** tax arrears, back taxes
(b) (retard) (de commandes, de correspondance, de travail) backlog; **j'ai beaucoup d'arriéré dans mon travail** I have a large backlog of work

arrière-plan *nm* ORDINAT background

arriérer *vt* (paiement) to postpone, to delay, to defer

arrière-saison *nf* (dans le domaine du tourisme) low season

arrivage *nm* (de marchandises) consignment, delivery; FIN (de fonds) accession; **nous attendons un arrivage venant de France** we're expecting a consignment or delivery from France

arrivant, -e *nm,f* arrival; **un nouvel arrivant sur le marché de l'informatique** a new arrival on the IT market

arrivée *nf* (de marchandises, d'un avion, d'une personne) arrival

arriver *vi* (a) (venir) to arrive; **arriver à échéance** (paiement) to fall due; (contrat) to expire (b) (parvenir) **arriver à faire qch** to manage to do sth

arrondir *vt* (somme) (vers le haut) to round up; (vers le bas) to round down; **vous pouvez arrondir à deux cents francs** you can round it up to two hundred francs; **arrondir au franc supérieur/inférieur** to round up/down to the nearest franc; *Fam* **arrondir ses fins de mois** to supplement one's income, to make a bit extra on the side

arrondissement *nm* = administrative subdivision of Paris, Lyons and Marseilles

art. *nm* (abrév **article**) article

article *nm* (a) (produit) article, item; **faire l'article (pour qch)** to make a sales pitch (for sth); **nous ne suivons** ou **faisons plus cet article** we don't stock that item any more ❏ MKTG *article d'appel* loss leader; *article bas de gamme* bottom-of-the-range item; *articles de bureau* office supplies; *articles de consommation courante* consumer goods; *article démarqué* markdown; *articles d'exportation* export goods, exports; *article en fin de série* discontinued item; *article à forte rotation* fast mover; *articles de grande consommation* consumables, consumer goods; *article haut de gamme* top-of-the-range item; *articles de luxe* luxury goods; *article de marque* branded article; *article de première nécessité* basic commodity; *article en réclame* special offer; *articles de voyage* travel goods
(b) (d'une facture) item; (d'un compte) entry; (d'un loi, d'un contrat) article ❏ COMPTA *articles de dépense* items of expenditure; *articles divers* sundries
(c) ORDINAT (d'un menu) command

artisan *nm* craftsman, *f* craftswoman

artisanal, -e *adj* (activité, travaux) traditional; (à la main) hand-made

artisanat *nm* craft industry

ASBL *nf* (*abrév* **association sans but lu-cratif**) *Br* non-profit-making *or Am* not-for-profit organization

ascenseur *nm* ORDINAT scroll box

ASCII *nm* ORDINAT (*abrév* **American Standard Code for Information Interchange**) ASCII

ASE *nf* (*abrév* **Agence spatiale européenne**) ESA

assainir *vt* (*budget, monnaie, économie*) to stabilize; (*bilan*) to balance; (*finances*) to reorganize

> 66
>
> L'organisme chargé d'aider les banques japonaises à **assainir** leurs bilans a annoncé vendredi à Tokyo leur avoir racheté pour 1866 milliards de yens de créances douteuses.
>
> 99

assainissement *nm* (*d'un budget, d'une monnaie, de l'économie*) stabilization; (*d'un bilan*) balancing; (*des finances*) reorganization□ **assainissement monétaire** stabilization of the currency

ASSEDIC *nf* (*abrév* **Association pour l'emploi dans l'industrie et le commerce**) = French unemployment benefit department, *Br* ≃ Unemployment Benefit Office, *Am* ≃ Unemployment Office; **toucher les ASSEDIC** to get *Br* unemployment benefit *or Am* welfare

assemblage *nm* (*dans l'industrie*) assembly

assemblée *nf* (a) (*réunion*) meeting □ **assemblée extraordinaire** extraordinary meeting; **assemblée générale** general meeting; **assemblée générale d'actionnaires** general meeting of shareholders; **assemblée générale annuelle** annual general meeting; **assemblée générale extraordinaire** extraordinary general meeting (b) (*élus*) **Assemblée parlementaire européenne** European Parliament

assentiment *nm* assent; **donner/refuser son assentiment (à qch)** to give/withhold one's assent (to sth)

asseoir *vt* FIN **asseoir un impôt** to calculate the basis for a tax; **asseoir l'impôt sur le revenu** to base taxation on income

assesseur *nm* JUR assessor

assiduité *nf* (a) (*application*) assiduity (b) (*ponctualité*) regularity

assiette *nf* (*d'un impôt, d'un taux*) base; (*d'une hypothèque*) = property or funds on which a mortgage is secured □ **assiette de** *l'amortissement* depreciation, depreciable base; **assiette fiscale, assiette de l'impôt** taxable income

assignation *nf* (a) FIN (*de parts, de fonds*) allotment, allocation (**à** to) (b) (*d'une tâche, d'un poste*) assignment (**à** to) (c) BOURSE exercise notice

assigner *vt* (a) FIN (*parts, fonds*) to allot, to allocate (**à** to) (b) (*tâche, poste*) to assign (**à** to)

assistance *nf* assistance □ **assistance judiciaire** legal aid; **assistance maritime** salvage; **assistance technique** technical assistance *or* backup; ORDINAT **assistance à l'utilisateur** user support

assistant, -e *nm,f* assistant □ **assistant de direction** personal assistant, PA

assisté, -e **1** *adj* (a) ADMIN (*personne*) on *Br* social security *or Am* welfare (b) ORDINAT **assisté par ordinateur** (*conception, enseignement, fabrication, production*) computer-aided, computer-assisted
2 *nm,f* ADMIN person on *Br* social security *or Am* welfare

assister **1** *vt* (*soutenir financièrement*) to help (financially)
2 assister à *vt ind* to be present at, to attend

association *nf* (a) (*organisation*) association □ **association sans but lucratif, association à but non lucratif** *Br* non-profit-making *or Am* not-for-profit organization; **association capital-travail** profit-sharing scheme; **association de consommateurs** consumer association; **Association européenne de libre-échange** European Free Trade Association; **Association Française des Banques** French Bankers' Association; **Association de libre-échange** Free Trade Agreement; **association loi 1901** = type of non-profit-making organization
(b) (*collaboration*) partnership; **entrer en association avec qn** to enter into partnership with sb□ **association de fait** partnership at will

associé, -e **1** *adj* joint, associate
2 *nm,f* associate, partner; **prendre qn comme associé** to take sb into partnership □ **associé commanditaire** sleeping partner; **associé commandité** active partner; **associé fondateur** founding partner; **associé gérant** managing partner; **associé majoritaire** senior partner; **associé minoritaire** junior partner; **associés à part égale** equal partners; **associé passif** sleeping partner; **associé principal** senior partner; **associé en second** junior partner

associer 1 *vt* *(joindre, lier)* to associate; **associer les travailleurs aux profits de leur entreprise** to allow workers to share in their company's profits; **son entreprise est associée au projet** his company is taking part in the project

2 **s'associer** *vpr* to enter *or* go into partnership; **s'associer à** *ou* **avec qn** to enter *or* go into partnership with sb; **s'associer qn** to take sb on as a partner

assortiment *nm* *(de marchandises)* assortment, selection, range

assorti, -e *adj* **bien/mal assorti** *(magasin)* well-/poorly-stocked

assortir *vt* *(magasin)* to stock, to supply

assouplir *vt* *(réglementation, contrôle, conditions, crédit)* to relax

assouplissement *nm* *(de la réglementation, du contrôle, des conditions, du crédit)* relaxing

assujetti, -e 1 *adj* **être assujetti à l'impôt/aux droits de douane** to be liable for tax/customs duty

2 *nm,f* = person liable for tax

assujettir *vt* **assujettir qn à qch** *(taxe, impôt, règlement)* to subject sb to sth

assujettissement *nm* *(à l'impôt)* liability

assumer *vt* *(risque)* to take; *(responsabilité)* to take on; *(dépenses)* to meet

assurable *adj* ASSUR insurable

assurance *nf* (a) ASSUR insurance; **contracter une assurance** to take out insurance, to take out an insurance policy; **il est dans les assurances** he's in insurance; *Fam* **je vais écrire à mon assurance** I'm going to write to my insurance company ❑ *assurance annulation* cancellation insurance; *assurance à capital différée* endowment insurance; *Suisse assurance casco* comprehensive insurance, all-risks insurance; *assurance chômage (payé par le patron et le salarié)* unemployment insurance; *assurance coface* = standard export guarantee insurance; *assurance à cotisations* contributory insurance; *assurance cumulative* double insurance; *assurance décès-invalidité* whole life and disability insurance; *assurance habitation* buildings insurance; *assurance insolvabilité* insurance against bankruptcy; *assurance maladie* health insurance; *assurance médicale* medical insurance; *assurance multirisque* comprehensive insurance; *assurance responsabilité civile* public liability insurance; *assurance au tiers* third party insurance; *assurance tous risques* comprehensive insurance, all-risks insurance

(b) ADMIN *assurance chômage* unemployment benefit; *assurance invalidité* disability pension; *assurance maladie* sickness benefit; *assurance maternité* maternity benefit; *assurances sociales* Br ≃ National Insurance, Am ≃ welfare

assurance-vie *nf* ASSUR life insurance *or* assurance; **prendre une assurance-vie** to take out life insurance *or* assurance

assuré, -e 1 *adj* ASSUR insured

2 *nm,f* (a) ASSUR policyholder, insured person; **les assurés** the insured (b) ADMIN *assuré social* ≃ member of *Br* the National Insurance scheme *or* *Am* the Social Security scheme

assurer 1 *vt* (a) ASSUR **assurer qn** to insure sb; **la Compagnie n'assure pas contre les dégâts causés par la pluie** the Company will not insure against damage caused by rain; **assurer un immeuble contre l'incendie** to insure a building against fire; **assurer qch pour deux millions de francs** to insure sth for two million francs

(b) *(garantir)* to ensure, to guarantee; **assurer une rente à qn** to settle an annuity on sb

(c) *(se charger de)* to be in charge of; **assurer un service** to provide a service; **une permanence est assurée le samedi après-midi** there is someone on duty on Saturday afternoons

2 **s'assurer** *vpr* ASSUR to take out insurance *or* an insurance policy (**contre** against); **s'assurer sur la vie** to take out life insurance *or* assurance

assureur *nm* underwriter; *(agent)* insurance agent; *(compagnie)* insurance company; *(courtier)* insurance broker

assureur-conseil *nm* insurance adviser

astreinte *nf* JUR = daily fine for delay in payment of debt

atelier *nm* (a) *(lieu)* (work)shop; **il est devenu contremaître après cinq ans d'atelier** he became a foreman after five years on the shopfloor ❑ *atelier de montage* assembly (work)shop (b) *(personnel)* workshop staff (c) *(groupe de travail)* work group

atermoiement *nm* *(délai de paiement)* = arrangement with creditors for extension of time for payment; *(d'une lettre de change)* renewal

atout *nm* asset, advantage; **la connaissance d'une langue étrangère est un atout** knowledge of a foreign language is an asset *or* an advantage; **l'abondance des ressources naturelles est un atout pour la région** the abundance of natural resources is an asset to the area

attaché, -e *nm,f* attaché □ *attaché commercial (d'une ambassade)* commercial attaché; *(d'une entreprise)* sales representative; *attaché de presse* press attaché

attaché-case *nm* attaché case

attaquer *vi* (**a**) MKTG *(marché)* to attack (**b**) JUR *(décision)* to contest, to appeal against; **attaquer qn en justice** to bring an action against sb

atteindre *vt (objectifs)* to attain, to achieve; **le nombre des chômeurs a atteint la barre des deux millions** unemployment has reached the two million mark

atteinte *nf (à un droit, une liberté)* violation; **cette nouvelle mesure constitue une atteinte au droit des salariés** this new measure violates employees' rights

attente *nf* (**a**) ORDINAT **liste de fichiers à imprimer en attente** print queue (**b**) **dans l'attente de votre réponse** *ou* **d'une réponse de votre part** *(dans une lettre)* I look forward to receiving your reply

attention *nf* **à l'attention de** *(sur un document)* for the attention of

attentisme *nm* wait-and-see policy; **l'attentisme des investisseurs explique le ralentissement du marché boursier** the wariness of investors explains why the Stock Market is so sluggish

attentiste 1 *adj (attitude, politique)* wait-and-see
2 *nmf* = person who adopts a wait-and-see policy

attestation *nf* certificate □ *attestation d'assurance* insurance certificate; *attestation de conformité* certificate of conformity; *attestation médicale* medical certificate

attirer *vt (investissements, acheteurs)* to attract

attitré, -e *adj (fournisseur, représentant)* appointed

attractif, -ive *adj (prix)* attractive

attraction *nf (pour un produit)* attraction; **les automobiles allemandes suscitent une attraction très marquée chez les Britanniques** German cars are very popular with the British

attrait commercial *nm* MKTG market appeal; **ce produit présente un attrait commercial certain** this product has definite market appeal

attribuer *vt (salaire, prime)* to assign, to allocate (**à** to); BOURSE *(actions, dividendes)* to allocate, to allot; **l'entreprise a attribué une part de ses actions au personnel** the company has allocated *or* allotted some of its shares to its employees

attribut *nm* MKTG *(caractéristique)* attribute □ *attribut du produit* product attribute

attributaire *nmf* JUR beneficiary; BOURSE *(d'actions, de dividendes)* allottee

attribution *nm (d'un salaire, d'une prime)* assigning, allocation; BOURSE *(d'actions, de dividendes)* allocation, allotment

aubaine *nf* Can *(achat avantageux)* bargain

audiotypiste *nmf* audio-typist

audit *nm* (**a**) *(service)* audit; **être chargé de l'audit d'une société** to audit a company □ *audit consommateur* consumer audit; MKTG *audit des détaillants* retail audit; *audit externe* external audit; *audit général* general audit; *audit interne* internal audit; *audit marketing, audit mercatique* marketing audit; *audit social* management consultancy report; *audit de vente* sales audit
(**b**) *(personne)* auditor □ *audit externe* external auditor; *audit interne* internal auditor

auditeur, -trice *nm,f* (**a**) *(chargé de l'audit)* auditor □ *auditeur externe* external auditor; *auditeur interne* internal auditor; *auditeur marketing, auditeur mercatique* marketing auditor
(**b**) ADMIN *auditeur à la Cour des Comptes* = junior official at the French Audit Office

augmentation *nf* (**a**) *(des dépenses, du chômage, des effectifs, de la consommation, de l'inflation)* increase (**de** in); **une augmentation de 3%** a 3% increase; **être en augmentation** to be on the increase, to be rising; **le chiffre d'affaires est en augmentation sur l'année dernière** the turnover is showing an increase *or* is up on last year's; **demander une augmentation** to ask for *Br* a (pay) rise *or* *Am* a raise □ *augmentation du capital* increase in capital; *augmentation de prix* price increase; *augmentation du prix de vente* mark-up; *augmentation de salaire, augmentation salariale* *Br* (pay) rise, *Am* raise
(**b**) ORDINAT *augmentation de puissance* upgrade, upgrading

augmenter 1 *vt (impôts, taux d'intérêt, prix)* to increase, to put up, to raise; *(dé-*

penses) to increase; **augmenter qn** to raise or increase sb's salary, to give sb Br a (pay) rise or Am a raise; **augmenter les ventes de 10%** to increase sales by 10%

2 vi (impôts, taux d'intérêt, prix) to increase, to go up, to rise; (dépenses) to increase; **augmenter de valeur** to increase in value; **tout a augmenté de prix** everything has gone up in price; **le chiffre d'affaires a augmenté de 10% par rapport à l'année dernière** the turnover has increased by 10% or is 10% up on last year

aujourd'hui adv today; **aujourd'hui en huit** a week today; **à compter** ou **à dater d'aujourd'hui** from today

austérité nf ÉCON austerity

autarcie nf autarky □ **autarcie économique** direct production

autarcique adj autarkic

authenticité nf (d'une signature, d'un document) authenticity

authentification nf (**a**) (d'une signature, d'un document) authentication (**b**) ORDINAT authentication

authentifier vt (signature, document) to authenticate

authentique adj (signature, document) authentic, genuine

autocorrecteur, -trice adj ORDINAT self-correcting

autofinancé, -e adj FIN self-financed; **8 milliards de francs autofinancés à un tiers seulement** 8 billion francs, only a third of which was self-financed

autofinancement nm FIN self-financing

> La chute de l'investissement en 1993, la baisse du coût de l'argent et la forte capacité d'**autofinancement** des entreprises atténuent fortement les tensions inflationnistes que pourrait exercer la reprise de l'activité.

autofinancer s'autofinancer vpr FIN to be self-financing

autogérer 1 vt (entreprise, usine) to self-manage
2 s'autogérer vpr (entreprise, usine) to be self-managing

autogestion nf self-management

autogestionnaire adj based on workers' self-management

autolimitation nf setting of voluntary limits

autolimiter vt to set voluntary limits to; **les Japonais autolimitent leurs exportations de voitures** the Japanese set voluntary limits to their car exports

automation nf automation

automatique adj automatic

automatisation nf automation

automatiser vt to automate

autonome adj (organisme, gestion) autonomous; (syndicat) independent

autonomie nf autonomy

autorégulation nf self-regulation

autorisation nf (**a**) (permission) authorization, permission; **donner à qn l'autorisation de faire qch** to authorize sb to do sth, to give sb permission to do sth; **demander l'autorisation de faire qch** to ask permission to do sth; **avoir l'autorisation de vendre qch** to be licensed to sell sth □ ORDINAT **autorisation d'accès** access authorization
(**b**) (document) licence, permit □ **autorisation d'exporter** export permit; **autorisation spéciale** special permit

autorisé, -e adj (transfert, découvert, dépenses, transaction) authorized; **les milieux autorisés** official circles

autoriser vt (transfert, découvert, dépenses, transaction) to authorize; **autoriser qn à faire qch** to authorize sb to do sth, to give sb permission to do sth

autorité nf (**a**) (pouvoir) authority; **agir de pleine autorité** to act with full powers
(**b**) (organisation) **les autorités** the authorities □ **autorités financières** financial authorities; **l'autorité fiscale** the (income) tax authorities

autoroute nf ORDINAT **autoroute de l'information** information superhighway; **autoroute interactive** interactive highway

autosuffisance nf ÉCON self-sufficiency

autosuffisant, -e adj ÉCON self-sufficient

autotest nm ORDINAT self-test

autotester s'autotester vpr ORDINAT to self-test

auxiliaire nmf (**a**) (aide) auxiliary, assistant (**b**) ADMIN (employé temporaire) temporary worker

AV nm BANQUE (abrév **avis de virement**) (bank) transfer advice

aval nm (**a**) FIN (d'un effet de commerce) endorsement, guarantee; **donner son aval à un billet** to endorse or guarantee or back a bill

❑ *aval bancaire* bank guarantee
 (b) *(accord)* approval; **donner son aval à qn/qch** to give sb/sth one's approval; **pour aval** *(sur document)* for approval
 (c) ÉCON, MKTG downside; **d'aval** *(activités)* downstream; **en aval** *(société)* downstream

avaliser *vt* FIN *(effet de commerce)* to endorse, to guarantee, to back

avaliseur, -euse *nm,f* FIN endorser, guarantor, backer

avaliste *nmf* FIN endorser, guarantor, backer

à-valoir *nm* advance (payment)

avance *nf* **(a)** FIN *(d'argent)* **avance (de fonds)** advance; **par avance, à titre d'avance** as an advance; **faire** *ou* **accorder une avance de mille francs à qn** to give sb an advance of a thousand francs, to advance sb a thousand francs; **demander une avance sur son salaire** to ask for an advance on one's salary ❑ *avance bancaire* bank advance; *avances en devises* foreign currency loan; *avance de trésorerie* cash advance
 (b) *(avantage)* lead; **conserver son avance sur ses concurrents** to retain one's lead over one's competitors; **être en avance sur la concurrence** to be ahead of the competition
 (c) **d'avance** in advance; **payé d'avance** paid in advance, prepaid; **payable à l'avance** payable in advance
 (d) ORDINAT *avance automatique* automatic feed

avancé, -e *adj (économie, technologie)* advanced

avancement *nm* **(a)** *(d'un projet, des travaux)* progress; **compte-rendu de l'avancement des travaux** progress report; **paiements proportionnels à l'avancement des travaux** progress payments
 (b) *(promotion)* promotion; **obtenir de l'avancement** to be promoted
 (c) ORDINAT *avancement par friction* friction feed

avancer *vt* **(a)** *(dans le temps)* to advance, to bring forward; **la réunion a été avancée du 14 au 7** the meeting has been brought forward from the 14th to the 7th
 (b) *(financièrement)* **avancer de l'argent à qn** to advance money to sb; *(prêter)* to lend sb money; **avancer un mois d'appointements à qn** to advance sb a month's salary, to pay sb a month's salary in advance

avantage *nm* advantage ❑ *avantages accessoires* fringe benefits; *avantage comparatif* comparative advantage; *avantages en espèces* cash benefits; *avantage fiscal* tax benefit, tax incentive; *avantages en nature* payments in kind; *avantages sociaux* financial benefits

avantager *vt* to advantage, to favour; **la faiblesse du franc avantage les exportateurs français** the weak franc gives French exporters an advantage

avantageux, -euse *adj (contrat, affaire)* profitable; *(prix)* reasonable, attractive; *(conditions)* favourable

avant-contrat *nm* preliminary contract

avant-projet *nm* draft

avarie *nf* ASSUR average, damage *(sustained by a ship)* ❑ *avaries communes* general average

avarié, -e *adj (marchandises)* damaged

avarier *vt (marchandises)* to damage

avenant *nm (de police d'assurance)* endorsement, additional clause

avenir *nm* future; **d'avenir** *(métier, secteur, marché)* up-and-coming; **les nouveaux procédés techniques ont de l'avenir** the new technical processes have a promising future

avertissement *nm* **(a)** *(avis préalable)* warning; **renvoyer qn sans avertissement préalable** to dismiss sb without notice
 (b) ORDINAT *avertissement de réception (de message)* acknowledgement; *avertissement à réception d'un courrier* mail received message

avili, -e *adj (biens)* depreciated

avilir **1** *vt (monnaie)* to depreciate, to devalue; *(prix)* to bring down
 2 s'avilir *vpr (biens)* to depreciate, to decrease in value

avilissement *nm (d'une monnaie)* depreciation, devaluation; *(des biens)* depreciation; *(de prix)* fall, drop

avion *nm* aircraft, *Br* aeroplane, *Am* airplane; **en avion** by air, by plane; **par avion** *(sur lettre)* (by) airmail ❑ *avion commercial* commercial aircraft; *avion de transport de marchandises* freighter, *Am* freight plane

avion-cargo *nm* freighter, *Am* freight plane

avis *nm (pour informer)* notice, notification; **jusqu'à nouvel avis** until further notice; **suivant avis** as per advice; **avis par écrit** notice in writing; **donner avis de qch** to give notice of sth; **donner avis que...** to give notice that... ❑ BOURSE *avis d'attribution* letter of allotment; *avis de la banque* bank notification *or* advice; *avis de crédit* credit advice; *avis de débit* debit advice; *avis de domici-*

liation domiciliation advice; BOURSE *avis d'exécution* contract note; *avis d'expédition* dispatch *or* consignment note; *avis d'imposition* tax assessment; *avis de licenciement* redundancy notice; *avis de livraison* delivery note; *avis de paiement* payment advice; *avis de prélèvement* direct debit advice; *avis de réception* acknowledgement (of receipt); *avis de rejet* notice of returned cheque; BANQUE *avis de virement* (bank) transfer advice

aviser *vt* to inform, to notify; **aviser qn de qch** to advise *or* inform sb of sth; **aviser qn de faire qch** to give sb notice to do sth

avocat, -e *nm,f* JUR lawyer, *Am* attorney; **consulter un avocat** to take legal advice ❏ *avocat d'affaires* business lawyer

avocat-conseil *nm* JUR counsel

avoir *nm* (**a**) *(bien)* property, possessions; *(capital)* capital; *(sur compte)* credit; **doit et avoir** debit and credit; **obtenir un avoir** to be given credit, to obtain *or* to get credit ❏ *avoir en banque* bank credit; *avoir en devises* foreign currency holding; *avoir fiscal* tax credit (**b**) **avoirs** assets ❏ *avoirs disponibles* liquid assets (**c**) *(attestation de crédit)* credit note

avoir-client *nm* COMPTA customer credit

avoir-fournisseur *nm* COMPTA supplier credit

avoué *nm* JUR *Br* ≃ solicitor, *Am* ≃ attorney

ayant-compte *nm* BANQUE account holder

ayant droit *nm* beneficiary (**à** of)

bac¹ nm (a) ORDINAT *bac d'alimentation* sheet feed; *bac de feuilles* paper tray; *bac de ou à papier* paper tray (b) *bac à correspondance, bac à courrier* correspondence tray

bac² nm (abrév **baccalauréat**) = secondary school examination qualifying for entry to university, *Br* ≃ A-levels, *Am* ≃ high-school diploma; **bac + 3** *(dans une annonce)* = three years of higher education required

baccalauréat nm = secondary school examination qualifying for entry to university, *Br* ≃ A-levels, *Am* ≃ high-school diploma

badge nm (a) *(d'identité)* name badge (b) *(d'accès)* swipe card, key card

baie nf ORDINAT bay

bail nm lease; **prendre une maison à bail** to take out a lease on a house; **céder** *ou* **donner une maison à bail** to lease (out) a house, to let a house; **bail à céder** *(sur panneau)* lease for sale; **signer un bail** to sign a lease; **renouveler un bail** to renew a lease; **résilier un bail** to cancel a lease □ *bail commercial* commercial lease; *bail emphytéotique* 99-year lease; *bail à long terme* long lease; *bail à loyer* rental agreement, lease

bailleur, -eresse nm,f (a) *bailleur de fonds (investisseur)* (financial) backer; *(associé passif) Br* sleeping partner, *Am* silent partner (b) JUR lessor

baisse nf (a) *(des prix, du chômage, du taux de l'inflation)* fall, drop (**de** in); **la baisse du franc** the fall in the value of the franc; **le marché des obligations a connu une baisse sensible** the bond market has dropped considerably; **être en baisse** *ou* **à la baisse** to be falling (b) BOURSE *(des cours, des valeurs)* fall; **spéculations à la baisse** bear speculations; **jouer** *ou* **spéculer à la baisse** to bear, to go a bear, to speculate for a fall; **acheter en baisse** to buy on a falling market; **les actions sont en baisse** shares are falling

baisser 1 vt *(prix, loyer)* to lower, to reduce, to bring down; **faire baisser le coût de la vie** to lower *or* reduce *or* bring down the cost of living; **la concurrence fait baisser les prix** competition brings prices down

2 vi *(prix, actions)* to fall; *(stocks)* to be running low; **le dollar a baissé** the dollar has weakened

baissier, -ère BOURSE 1 adj *(marché)* bearish

2 nm,f bear

balance nf COMPTA *(d'un compte)* balance; **la balance est en excédent** there is a surplus; **faire la balance** to make up the balance sheet; **balance de l'actif et du passif** credit and debit balance, balance of assets and liabilities □ *balance de caisse* cash balance; ÉCON *balance du commerce, balance commercial* balance of trade; *balance générale des comptes, balance des paiements* balance of payments; *balances sterling* sterling balances

balancer vt *(compte)* to balance; **balancer les comptes** to balance *or* make up the books

balise nf ORDINAT tag

baliser vt ORDINAT to tag

balles nfpl Fam *(francs)* francs; **200 balles** 200 francs

banc nm (a) *banc d'essai* benchtest; **mettre une idée au banc d'essai** to test out an idea (b) ORDINAT *banc de mémoire* memory bank

bancable adj FIN bankable

bancaire adj *(chèque, commission, crédit, dépôt, frais, prêt)* bank; *(opération)* banking

bancarisation nf **la bancarisation de l'économie** the growing role of banks in the economy; **la bancarisation de la population française** the spread of the use of banking services among the French population

bancarisé, -e adj **être bancarisé** to have an account with a bank, to use the banking system; **presque toutes les PME sont bancarisées** almost all small businesses have accounts with a bank *or* use the banking system

bancassurance nf bancassurance

bande *nf* ORDINAT *bande audionumérique* digital audio tape, DAT; *bande de défilement* scroll bar

banquable = **bancable**

banque *nf* (**a**) *(établissement, organisation)* bank □ *banque d'acceptation* Br accepting or Am acceptance house; *banque d'affaires* Br merchant bank, Am investment bank; *banque centrale* central bank; *Banque centrale européenne* European central bank; *banque de clearing* clearing bank; *banque commerciale* commercial bank; *banque compensatrice* clearing bank; *banque confirmatrice* confirming bank; *banque de crédit* credit bank; *banque de dépôt* deposit bank; *banque de détail* retail bank; *banque d'émission* issuing bank or house; *banque d'épargne* savings bank; *banque d'escompte* discount house; *Banque européenne d'investissement* European Investment Bank; *la Banque de France* the Bank of France; *banque de gestion de patrimoine* trust bank; *banque de gros* wholesale bank; *banque hypothécaire* mortgage bank; *Banque internationale pour la reconstruction et le développement* International Bank for Reconstruction and Development; *banque d'investissement* Br merchant bank, Am investment bank; *la Banque Mondiale* the World Bank; *banque notificatrice* advising bank; *banque de placement* issuing bank or house; *banque privée* private bank

(**b**) *(activité)* banking □ *banque à distance* remote banking; *banque à domicile* telebanking, home banking; *banque d'entreprise* corporate banking

(**c**) *(secteur)* banking; **elle travaille dans la banque** she works in banking; **la haute banque** high finance

(**d**) ORDINAT *banque de données* data bank; *banque d'images* image bank

banqueroute *nf* JUR bankruptcy; **faire banqueroute** to go bankrupt □ *banqueroute frauduleuse* fraudulent bankruptcy; *banqueroute simple* bankruptcy *(with irregularities amounting to a breach of the law)*

banqueroutier, -ère *adj & nm,f* bankrupt

banquier, -ère *nm,f* banker □ *banquier d'affaires* Br merchant banker, Am investment banker; *banquier escompteur* discounting banker; *banquier prêteur* lending banker

barème *nm* (**a**) *(tableau)* ready reckoner (**b**) *(de salaires)* scale; *(de prix)* list □ *barème d'imposition* tax schedule

baril *nm* *(de pétrole)* barrel

barre *nf* (**a**) *(niveau)* level; **en dessous de la barre des 3%** below the 3% mark

(**b**) ORDINAT bar □ *barre de défilement* scroll bar; *barre d'espacement* space bar; *barre d'état* status bar; *barre d'icônes* icon bar; *barre de menu* menu bar; *barre oblique* oblique, slash; *barre oblique inversée* backslash; *barre d'outils* tool bar; *barre de sélection* menu bar; *barre de style* style bar; *barre de titre* title bar

> **"**
>
> A la fin de 1998, la **barre** de 10 millions d'abonnés au téléphone mobile devrait être franchie.
>
> **"**

barré, -e *adj (chèque)* crossed

barrer *vt (chèque)* to cross

barrière *nf* barrier □ *barrière d'accès* access barrier; *barrière commerciale* trade barrier; *barrières douanières* trade barriers; *barrière à l'entrée* entry barrier; *barrière non tarifaire* non-tariff barrier; *barrière à la sortie* exit barrier; *barrière tarifaire* tariff barrier

BAS *nm (abrév* **Bureau d'aide sociale***)* welfare office

bas¹, basse **1** *adj (prix, taux de change, taux d'intérêt)* low; **acheter/vendre qch à bas prix** to buy/sell sth cheap; **leurs actions sont au niveau le plus bas** their shares have reached an all-time low

2 *nm* BOURSE **les hauts et les bas** the highs and lows

3 *adv* low; BOURSE **les cours sont tombés très bas** prices have fallen very low

bas² *nm bas de laine* nest egg; **le bas de laine des Français** the savings of small-time French investors

bascule *nf* ORDINAT toggle

basculer *vi* ORDINAT to toggle

basculeur *nm* ORDINAT toggle (key)

base *nf* (**a**) *(fondement)* basis; **sur une base nette** on a net basis; **de base** *(prix, salaire)* basic □ COMPTA *base amortissable* basis for depreciation; COMPTA *base de calcul* basis of calculations; *base hors taxe* amount exclusive of VAT; *base d'imposition* taxable base

(**b**) *(dans une entreprise)* shop floor; **le patron ne sait pas communiquer avec la base** the boss can't communicate with the shop floor

(**c**) ORDINAT *(d'imprimante laser)* engine □ *base de données* database; **mettre qch dans une base de données** to enter sth into a database; *base de données client-serveur* client-server database; *base de données de consommateurs* customer database; *base de données relationnelle* relational database

basé, -e *adj* être basé à to be based in; **leur entreprise est basée à Sophia Antipolis** their company is based in Sophia Antipolis

Basic *nm* ORDINAT BASIC

bâtiment *nm* (**a**) *(édifice)* building; **nous avons une cantine dans le bâtiment** we have a canteen in the building *or* on the premises □ *bâtiment administratif* administration building (**b**) *(secteur)* **le bâtiment, l'industrie du bâtiment** the building trade *or* industry

battage *nm* *(publicité)* battage (publicitaire) hype; **faire du battage autour de qn/qch** to hype sb/sth up □ *battage médiatique* media hype

baud *nm* ORDINAT baud; **à (une vitesse de) 1200 bauds** at 1200 baud

BBS *nm* ORDINAT *(abrév* **bulletin board system)** BBS

BCE *nf (abrév* **Banque centrale européenne)** European central bank

BD *nf* ORDINAT *(abrév* **base de données)** dbase

BEI *nf (abrév* **Banque européenne d'investissement)** European Investment Bank

bénef *nf Fam (abrév* **bénéfice)** profit

bénéfice *nm* (**a**) *(gain)* profit; **bénéfice de ou pour l'exercice 1999** profits for the year 1999; **rapporter des bénéfices** to yield a profit; **donner un bénéfice** to show a profit; **réaliser** *ou* **dégager un bénéfice** to make a profit; **vendre qch à bénéfice** to sell sth at a profit □ *bénéfice par action* earnings per share; *bénéfice avant l'impôt* pre-tax profit; *bénéfice brut* pre-tax profit, gross profit; *bénéfice cumulé* cumulative profit; *bénéfices distribuables* distributable profits; *bénéfice escompté* desired profit; *bénéfice d'exploitation* operating *or* trading profit; *bénéfices financiers* interest received; *bénéfice fiscal* taxable profit; *bénéfice imposable* taxable profit; *bénéfice marginal* marginal profit; *bénéfice net* after-tax profit, net profit; *bénéfices non distribués* undistributed profits, retained earnings; *bénéfice transféré* profit transferred

(**b**) *(avantage)* benefit; **petits bénéfices** perks □ MKTG *bénéfice consommateur (d'un produit)* consumer benefit

bénéficiaire **1** *adj (entreprise)* profit-making; *(compte)* in credit; *(bilan)* showing a profit

2 *nmf* (**a**) ASSUR, JUR beneficiary (**b**) *(d'un chèque)* payee

bénéficier *vt ind* bénéficier de qch to benefit by *or* from sth; **ils bénéficient de la nouvelle politique fiscale du gouvernement** they are benefitting from the government's new tax policy

bénévole **1** *adj (travail)* voluntary; **être employé à titre bénévole** to do voluntary work

2 *nmf* volunteer, voluntary worker

BEP *nm (abrév* **brevet d'études professionnelles)** = vocational diploma

besoin *nm* need, requirement □ COMPTA *besoins en fonds de roulement* working capital requirements; *besoins de trésorerie* cash requirements

BF *nf (abrév* **Banque de France)** Bank of France

bibliothèque *nf* ORDINAT library □ *bibliothèque de programmes* program library

biclic *nm* ORDINAT double click

bicliquer *vi* ORDINAT to double-click

bidirectionnel, -elle *adj* ORDINAT bidirectional

bidon *adj Fam (société)* phoney; *(chèque)* dud

bien *nm* possession; JUR assets; **biens** possessions, property □ *biens capitaux* capital goods *or* items; *bien de consommation* consumer product *or* good; *bien de consommation durable* consumer durable; *biens corporels* tangible assets; *biens durables* (consumer) durables, durable goods; *biens d'équipement* capital equipment *or* goods; *biens fonciers* landed property; *biens immeubles, biens immobiliers* real estate; *biens industriels* industrial goods; *biens intermédiaires* semi-finished goods; *biens manufacturés* manufactured goods; *biens meubles, biens mobiliers* personal property *or* estate, movables; *biens personnels* personal property; *biens de première nécessité* staples; *biens de production* capital goods; COMPTA **biens sociaux** corporate assets or funds

bien-être nm (material) well-being □ **l'économie du bien-être** the welfare economy

bien-fonds nm real estate

bilan nm (a) COMPTA statement; **bilan (comptable)** balance sheet; **dresser** ou **établir** ou **faire un bilan** to draw up a balance sheet □ **bilan condensé** summary balance sheet; **bilan consolidé** consolidated balance sheet; **bilan de l'exercice** end-of-year balance sheet; **bilan financier** financial statement; **bilan de fin d'exercice** end-of-year balance sheet; **bilan de groupe** consolidated balance sheet; **bilan intérimaire** interim statement; **bilan d'ouverture** opening balance sheet; **bilan prévisionnel** forecast balance sheet

(b) (appréciation) appraisal, assessment; **dresser le bilan de ses pertes** to add up one's losses; **faire le bilan de santé d'une entreprise** to assess or evaluate the state of a company □ **bilan de carrière** = summary of one's employment record; **bilan de compétence** = summary of one's skills

(c) (rapport) report □ MKTG **bilan commercial** market report; **bilan hebdomadaire** weekly trading report; **bilan social** social report

(d) FIN (de l'actif, des responsabilités) schedule; **déposer son bilan** to file one's petition (in bankruptcy)

(e) BANQUE (d'un compte) balance

bilatéral, -e adj (accord, contrat) bilateral

bilatéralisme nm bilateralism

billet nm (a) (pour voyager) ticket □ **billet d'abonnement** season ticket; **billet d'aller** Br single or Am one-way ticket; **billet d'aller (et) retour** Br return or Am round-trip ticket; **billet d'avion** plane ticket; **billet circulaire** Br return or Am round-trip ticket; **billet open** open ticket; **billet de retour** Br return or Am round-trip ticket; **billet simple** Br single or Am one-way ticket; **billet de transport** ticket

(b) FIN (effet) note, bill □ **billet de complaisance** accommodation bill; **billet à ordre** note of hand, promissory note; **billet au porteur** bearer bill; **billet de reconnaissance de dettes** IOU; **billet du Trésor** Treasury bill; **billet de trésorerie** commercial paper

(c) (argent) **billet (de banque)** Br (bank)-note, Am bill; **un billet de cent francs** a hundred-franc Br note or Am bill □ **billet vert** dollar

billétique nf BANQUE, ORDINAT cash dispenser technology

billion nm trillion

bip nm (appareil) pager, beeper

biper vt to page

BIRD nf (abrév **Banque internationale pour la reconstruction et le développement**) IBRD

BIT nm (abrév **Bureau international du travail**) ILO

bit nm ORDINAT bit; **bits par seconde** bits per second

bitmap adj & nm ORDINAT bitmap

blâme nm ADMIN (sanction) reprimand; **donner un blâme à qn** to reprimand sb; **recevoir un blâme** to be reprimanded

blâmer vt ADMIN to reprimand

blanc, blanche 1 adj ORDINAT blank
2 nm (dans un document) blank (space)

blanchiment nm (de l'argent) laundering

blanchir vt (argent) to launder

blindage nm ORDINAT shield

blister nm blister pack; **être vendu sous blister** to be sold in blister packs

bloc nm (a) (ensemble) (de marchandises) job lot; (de titres) parcel; **acheter qch en bloc** to buy the whole stock of sth

(b) (zone) bloc □ **bloc monétaire** currency bloc; **bloc sterling** sterling bloc

(c) (groupe d'actionnaires) shareholding □ **bloc de contrôle** controlling shareholding

(d) (au sein d'une entreprise) department

(e) ORDINAT (de texte) block

blocage nm (a) ÉCON (des tarifs, des fonds, des crédits) freeze; **blocage des prix et des salaires** price and wage freeze (b) ORDINAT **blocage majuscule** caps lock

bloc-notes nm notepad, memo pad □ ORDINAT **bloc-notes électronique** electronic notepad

blocus nm (economic) blockade

bloquer vt (chèque) to stop; (compte) to block, to stop; (prix, salaires, crédits) to freeze

blue chip nm blue chip

BO nm (abrév **Bulletin officiel**) = official listing of all new laws and decrees

BOCE nm (abrév **Bulletin officiel des communautés européennes**) = official listing of all new EC directives

bogue nf ORDINAT bug □ **bogue de l'an 2000** millennium bug; **bogue de logiciel** software bug

bogué, -e adj ORDINAT bug-ridden

boîte *nf* (a) *(pour ranger)* box ◻ *boîte archive* archive file; *boîte de classement* box file
  (b) *(pour le courrier)* *boîte à* ou *aux lettres* Br post box, Am mail box; *boîte postale* post office box
  (c) ORDINAT *boîte de dialogue* dialogue box; *boîte à* ou *aux lettres électronique* mailbox; *boîte à outils* toolbox
  (d) *Fam (entreprise)* firm

boîtier *nm* ORDINAT case ◻ *boîtier de commande* command box; *boîtier vertical* tower

bon¹, bonne *adj* (a) *(investissement, crédit)* good; *acheter qch à bon marché* to buy sth cheap (b) *(valable)* valid; *ce billet est bon pour trois mois* this ticket is valid for three months

bon² *nm* (a) *(papier)* voucher, coupon ◻ *bon d'annulation* cancellation form; *bon de caisse (justifiant sortie de fonds)* cash voucher; COMPTA interest-bearing note; *bon de commande* order form, purchase order; *bon d'entrée* stock received form; *bon d'épargne* savings certificate; *bon d'expédition* dispatch note, consignment note; FIN *bon pour francs (sur chèque)* = letters printed on cheque before amount to be written in figures; *bon de garantie* guarantee, guarantee slip; *bon de livraison* delivery note; *bon de réception des marchandises* receipt note; *bon de réduction* money-off coupon *or* voucher; *bon de remboursement* money-off voucher; *bon de réservation* reservation form; *bon de sortie* stock issued form
  (b) FIN bond ◻ *bon d'épargne* savings bond *or* certificate; *bon nominatif* registered bond; *bon au porteur* bearer bond; *bon de souscription d'actions* equity warrant; *bon du Trésor* treasury bond

bonification *nf* (a) *(rabais)* reduction (b) *(prime)* bonus ◻ ASSUR *bonification pour non sinistre* no-claims bonus

> ❝
> Dans le financement automobile, il n'est pas rare de voir des offres à 7,5% environ. Dans de telles situations, ce sont les constructeurs qui assument une **bonification** d'environ 3 points.
> ❞

bonifié, -e *adj (prêt)* soft, at a reduced rate of interest

bonus *nm* ASSUR no-claims bonus; *j'ai un bonus de 35% sur mon assurance* I have a 35% no-claims bonus on my insurance

bonus-malus *nm* ASSUR no-claims bonus system

boom *nm* FIN boom

boomerang *nm* *faire boomerang* to boomerang ◻ *effet boomerang* boomerang effect; *avoir un effet boomerang* to boomerang

bordereau *nm* note, slip; *(formulaire)* form; *(de marchandises)* invoice, account; *(dans un devis)* list, schedule; *suivant bordereau ci-inclus* as per enclosed statement ◻ *bordereau d'achat (dans le commerce)* purchase note; BOURSE bought note; COMPTA *bordereau de caisse* cash statement; COMPTA *bordereau de compte* statement of account; *bordereau de débit* debit note; *bordereau de dépôt* paying-in slip; *bordereau de douanes* customs note; *bordereau d'encaissement* paying-in slip; *bordereau d'envoi* dispatch note, consignment note, waybill; *bordereau d'escompte* list of bills for discount; *bordereau d'expédition* dispatch note, consignment note, waybill; *bordereau de livraison* delivery note; *bordereau (des) prix* price list; BANQUE *bordereau de remboursement* withdrawal slip; *bordereau de remise (d'espèces* ou *de chèques)* paying-in slip; *bordereau de réservations* reservation sheet; *bordereau de salaire* wage slip, salary advice; *(liste des salaires payés)* wages sheet; *bordereau de vente* list of sales; *bordereau de versement* paying-in slip

bouché, -e *adj (marché)* clogged

boucler *vt* BOURSE *(position)* to close (out)

bouder *vt (produits)* to refuse to buy

bouillon *nm Fam boire le bouillon (faire faillite)* to go under

boule *nf* (a) ORDINAT *boule de commande* trackball (b) *effet boule de neige* snowball effect; *les analystes craignent l'effet boule de neige de la crise asiatique* the analysts are afraid of the snowball effect of the Asian crisis

bourgeois, -e *adj* middle-class

bourgeoisement *adv* ADMIN *occuper bourgeoisement un local* to occupy premises for residential purposes only

bourgeoisie *nf* middle class

bourrage papier *nm* ORDINAT paper jam

bourse *nf* (a) *la Bourse (des valeurs)* the Stock Exchange, the Stock Market; *la Bourse de Londres* the London Stock Exchange; *la Bourse monte/est calme* the market is rising/is quiet; **en** *ou* **à la Bourse** on the Stock Exchange *or* Stock Market; **jouer à la Bourse** to play the market, to speculate on the Stock Market; **coup de Bourse** deal on the Stock Exchange ❑ *Bourse de commerce, Bourse de(s) marchandises* commodities exchange

(b) *(lieu) bourse de l'emploi* = employment exchange; *bourse du travail (réunion)* = meeting of local trade unions for the purpose of reaching agreement on how best to defend their interests and provide community services; *(endroit)* = local trade union centre

boursicotage *nm* BOURSE dabbling *or* speculating on the Stock Market

boursicoter *vi* BOURSE to dabble *or* speculate on the Stock Market

boursicoteur, -euse, boursicotier, -ère *nm,f* BOURSE speculator

boursier, -ère BOURSE **1** *adj (opérations)* Stock Exchange, Stock Market
  2 *nm,f* (Stock Exchange) operator

boutique *nf Br* shop, *Am* store; **tenir boutique** to run a shop; **fermer boutique** to close down, to shut up shop; **parler boutique** to talk shop ❑ *boutique hors taxe* duty-free shop

boutiquier, -ère *nm,f Br* shopkeeper, *Am* storekeeper

bouton *nm* ORDINAT button ❑ *bouton de réinitialisation* reset button; *bouton de souris* mouse button

boycott, boycottage *nm* boycott

boycotter *vt* to boycott

BP *nm (abrév* **boîte postale**) PO Box

BPA *nm (abrév* **bénéfice par action**) EPS

BPF *nm* FIN *(abrév* **bon pour francs**) *(sur chèque)* = letters printed on cheque before amount to be written in figures

bps *nmpl* ORDINAT *(abrév* **bits par seconde**) bps

brader *vt* to sell off, to sell cheaply

braderie *nf* clearance sale

brainstorming *nm* brainstorming

branche *nf (de l'industrie)* branch, sector

branchement *nm* ORDINAT connection

bras droit *nm (personne)* right-hand man

brevet *nm* (a) *(d'invention)* patent; **demande de brevet déposée** *(sur produit)* patent pending; **prendre un brevet** to take out a patent ❑ *brevet d'inventeur, brevet d'invention* (letters) patent (b) *(diplôme)*

diploma ❑ *brevet d'études professionnelles* = vocational diploma; *brevet de technicien supérieur* = advanced vocational training certificate

breveté, -e *adj (invention)* patented; *(personne)* holding letters patent

breveter *vt (invention)* to patent; **faire breveter qch** to take out a patent for sth

briefing *nm* briefing

brique *nf Fam (dix mille francs)* ten thousand francs

briseur, -euse *nm,f briseur de grève* strikebreaker

broche *nf* ORDINAT pin

brochure *nf* brochure ❑ *brochure publicitaire* publicity brochure

brouillard *nm* day book ❑ COMPTA *brouillard de caisse* cash book

brouillon *nm* (a) *(ébauche)* (rough) draft ❑ *(papier) brouillon Br* scrap *or Am* scratch paper (b) ORDINAT *version brouillon* draft version

brut, -e **1** *adj* (a) *(pétrole, minerai)* crude (b) *(bénéfice, valeur, poids)* gross
  2 *nm* crude (oil)
  3 *adv* gross; **gagner 20 000 francs brut** to earn 20,000 francs gross, to gross 20,000 francs

BTP *nm (abrév* **bâtiment et travaux publics**) construction industry

BTS *nm (abrév* **brevet de technicien supérieur**) = advanced vocational training certificate

Buba *nf (abrév* **Bundesbank**) Bundesbank

budget *nm* budget; **inscrire qch au budget** to budget for sth ❑ *budget des approvisionnements* purchase budget; *budget des charges* overhead budget, cost budget; *budget commercial* sales budget; *budget des dépenses* expense budget; *budget équilibré* balanced budget; *budget de l'État* state budget; *budget familial* household budget; *budget de fonctionnement* operating budget; *budget global* master budget, overall budget; COMPTA *budget des investissements* capital budget; *budget marketing* marketing budget; *budget mensuel* monthly budget; *budget mercatique* marketing budget; *budget prévisionnel* provisional budget; *budget de production* production budget; *budget publicitaire, budget de publicité* advertising *or* publicity budget; *budget des recettes* revenue budget; *budget de trésorerie* cash budget; *budget des ventes* sales budget

budgétaire *adj (année) Br* financial, *Am* fiscal; *(contrainte, contrôle, gestion)* budgetary

budgétisation *nf* budgeting

budgétiser *vt* to include in the budget, to budget for

bug *nm* ORDINAT bug

bulle boursière *nf* surge on the Stock Market

> **"**
> L'évolution des indices boursiers sur les douze derniers mois ressemble fort à un phénomène de **bulle boursière** dont on sait qu'elle ne peut durer éternellement.
> **"**

bulletin *nm (communiqué)* bulletin; *(d'entreprise)* newsletter; *(formulaire)* form □ *bulletin d'abonnement* subscription form; *bulletin d'annulation* cancellation form; *bulletin de bagages Br* luggage ticket, *Am* baggage check; *bulletin de commande* order form; BOURSE *Bulletin de la Cote Officielle* Stock Exchange Daily Official List; BOURSE *bulletin des cours* official (Stock Exchange) price list; *bulletin d'expédition* dispatch note, consignment note, waybill; *bulletin de garantie* (certificate of) guarantee; *bulletin d'inscription* registration form; *Bulletin officiel* = official listing of all new laws and decrees; *Bulletin officiel des communautés européennes* = official listing of all new EC directives; *bulletin de paie* pay (advice) slip, salary advice note; *bulletin de salaire* pay (advice) slip, salary advice note; *bulletin de souscription d'actions* share subscription form, share application form; *bulletin de vente* sales note; *bulletin de versement* paying-in slip *or* form

bulletin-réponse *nm* reply form

bureau *nm* (a) *(agence)* office □ *Bureau d'aide sociale* welfare office; *bureau d'affaires* business centre; *bureau des brevets* patent office; *bureau du cadastre* Land Registry Office; *bureau de change* bureau de change; *Can Bureau du Contrôleur Général* Office of the Controller General; *bureau de cotation* credit *Br* agency *or Am* bureau; *bureau de douane* custom(s) house, customs office; *bureau d'enregistrement* registration office; *bureau d'évaluation* credit *Br* agency *or Am* bureau; *bureau d'expédition* forwarding office, shipping office; *bureau d'exportation* export office; *bureau d'information* information office; *Bureau international du travail* International Labour Office; *bureau de placement* employment agency *or* bureau; *bureau de poste* post office; *bureau de publicité* advertising agency; *bureau de renseignements* information office; *bureau de tourisme* tourist office; *bureau de traduction* translation agency; *Bureau de vérification de la publicité* = French advertising standards authority, *Br* ≃ ASA

(b) *(lieu)* office □ *bureau central* head office; *bureau informatisé* electronic office, paperless office; *bureau paysager* open-plan office; *bureau principal* head office

(c) *(meuble)* desk □ *bureau d'inscriptions* registration desk; *bureau de renseignements* enquiry *or* information desk

(d) *(personnel)* (office) staff

(e) *(commission)* committee; **constituer le bureau** *(d'une société)* to set up a committee

(f) *(service)* department □ *bureau d'achat* purchase department; *bureau d'études* design *or* planning department; *(de recherche)* R&D department; *bureau d'étude technique* engineering and design department

(g) *(port)* port □ *bureau de départ* port of departure; *bureau de destination* port of destination; *bureau d'entrée* port of entry; *bureau de passage* port of transit

(h) ORDINAT *(écran)* desktop □ *bureau électronique* electronic desktop

bureaucrate *nmf* bureaucrat

bureaucratie *nf (système)* bureaucracy; *(ensemble des fonctionnaires)* bureaucrats

bureaucratique *adj* bureaucratic

bureaucratiser *vt* to bureaucratize

Bureautique® *nf* office automation

bus *nm* ORDINAT bus □ *bus d'adresses* address bus; *bus de contrôle* control bus; *bus de données* data bus

business *nm Fam* business; **faire du business** to be in business; **il est dans le business** he's in the business

but *nm* goal, aim; **à but lucratif** profit-making; **à but non lucratif** *Br* non-profit-making, *Am* not-for-profit

BVP *nm (abrév* **Bureau de vérification de la publicité**) = French advertising standards authority, ≃ *Br* ASA

c *n* (*abrév* **centime**) centime

CA *nm* (**a**) (*abrév* **chiffre d'affaires**) turnover (**b**) *Can* (*abrév* **comptable agréé**) *Br* ≃ CA, *Am* ≃ CPA

C&A (*abrév* **coût et assurance**) C & I

cabinet *nm* office; (*de juge*) chambers □ **cabinet d'affaires** business consultancy; **cabinet d'assurances** insurance firm; **cabinet d'audit** audit company; **cabinet conseil** consultancy; **cabinet de conseil en gestion** management consultancy; MKTG **cabinet d'études** market research firm; **cabinet d'expertise comptable** accounting firm; **cabinet d'experts-conseils** consultancy; **cabinet juridique** law firm; **cabinet de recrutement** recruitment agency; **cabinet de traduction** translation agency

câble *nm* ORDINAT cable □ **câble d'imprimante** printer cable; **câble parallèle** parallel cable; **câble série** serial cable

câblé, -e *adj* ORDINAT hard-wired

CAC *nf* (*abrév* **Compagnie des agents de change**) **l'indice CAC 40, le CAC 40** the CAC 40 (index) (*Paris Stock Exchange Index*)

cache *nm* ORDINAT cache □ **cache du disque dur** hard disk cache; **cache externe** external cache

caché, -e *adj* (*fonds*) hidden

cachet *nm* (*sceau*) seal; (*tampon*) stamp □ **cachet de douane** customs seal; **cachet de fabrique** maker's trademark; **cachet de la poste** postmark; **le cachet de la poste faisant foi** date of postmark will be taken as proof of postage

cacheter *vt* to seal; **envoyer qch sous pli cacheté** to send sth in a sealed envelope

CAD *nm* (*abrév* **Comité d'aide au développement**) DAC

c.-à-d. (*abrév* **c'est-à-dire**) i.e.

cadastrage *nm* ADMIN land registration

cadastral, -e *adj* ADMIN cadastral

cadastre *nm* ADMIN (*registre*) land register, cadastre; (*administration*) cadastral survey office, ≃ land registry

cadastrer *vt* ADMIN to enter in the land register

cadeau *nm* MKTG **cadeau (publicitaire)** free gift, freebie

cadence *nf* rate □ **cadence de production** rate of production; **cadence de travail** work rate

cadencé, -e *adj* ORDINAT **cadencé à** running at

cadrage *nm* ORDINAT positioning

cadre *nm* (**a**) (*dans une entreprise*) **cadre (d'entreprise)** executive, manager; **les cadres** the managerial staff, the management; **jeune cadre** junior executive; **passer cadre** to become an executive, to be promoted to management □ **cadre commercial** sales executive; **cadres dirigeants** senior executives, top management; **cadres moyens** middle management; **cadres supérieurs** senior executives, top management

(**b**) (*registre*) list of staff; **rayé des cadres** dismissed; **hors cadre** seconded, on secondment

(**c**) (*dans un formulaire*) space, box; ORDINAT (*pour graphique*) box; **cadre réservé à l'administration** (*sur formulaire*) for official *or* office use only

(**d**) (*domaine*) framework; **dans le cadre de ce programme d'expansion** as part of this expansion programme; **cela n'entre pas dans le cadre de mes fonctions** it falls outside the scope of my responsibilities, it's outside my remit

(**e**) (*environnement*) environment □ **cadre de travail** working environment

cadrer **1** *vt* ORDINAT to position
2 *vi* to be consistent (**avec** with); **les chiffres que vous nous avez communiqués ne cadrent pas avec les nôtres** the figures you gave us don't tally with *or* are not consistent with ours

caduc, caduque *adj* JUR (*legs*) null and void; (*accord, contrat*) lapsed; (*dette*) barred by the Statute of Limitations

caducité *nf* JUR lapsing

CAF **1** *adj* (*abrév* **coût, assurance, fret**) CIF □ **vente CAF** sale on CIF basis
2 *nf* (*abrév* **Caisse d'allocations familiales**) = child benefit office

cage *nf* ORDINAT scroll box

cahier *nm* (**a**) (*livre*) notebook □ COMPTA **cahier des achats** bought ledger (**b**) (*liste*) **cahier des charges** (*d'un contrat*) terms and conditions; (*d'une vente*) specifications;

cahier des revendications syndicales claims register

CAHT *nm* (*abrév* **chiffre d'affaires hors taxes**) pre-tax turnover

caisse *nf* (a) FIN (*coffre*) cash box; (*dans un magasin, un garage*) cash desk; (*dans un supermarché*) checkout; **les caisses de l'État** the coffers of the State; **payez à la caisse** pay at the (cash) desk *or* at the till; **tenir la caisse** to be in charge of the cash; **passer à la caisse** to go to the cash desk; (*dans un supermarché*) to go through the checkout; (*payer*) to pay; (*se faire payer*) to be paid; (*se faire licencier*) to be paid off □ *caisse (comptable)* cash register, till; *caisse électronique* electronic billing machine, electric service till; *caisse enregistreuse* cash register, till

(b) (*argent*) cash (in hand); (*recette*) takings; **faire la** *ou* **sa caisse** to balance the cash, to do the till, *Br* to cash up; **avoir 4 000 francs en caisse** to have 4,000 francs in hand □ *caisse d'amortissement* sinking fund; *caisse noire* slush fund

(c) (*pour marchandises*) case, box; **mettre des marchandises en caisse** to case *or* crate goods

(d) (*organisme*) fund □ *caisse de chômage* unemployment fund; *caisse de compensation* = equalization fund for payments such as child benefit, sickness benefit, pensions; *caisse de garantie* credit guarantee institution; *Can caisse populaire* credit union; *caisse de prévoyance* provident fund; *caisse de retraite* pension fund

(e) BANQUE *Caisse des Dépôts et Consignations* = public financial institution which manages National Savings Bank funds and local community funds; *caisse d'épargne* savings bank; *caisse d'épargne-logement Br* ≃ building society, *Am* ≃ savings and loan association; *Caisse nationale d'Épargne* ≃ National Savings Bank; *caisse régionale* ≃ local (bank) branch

(f) ADMIN *caisse d'allocations familiales* = child benefit office; *Caisse nationale d'assurance vieillesse* = French government department dealing with benefit payments relating to old age; *caisse primaire d'assurance maladie* = French government department dealing with health insurance; *caisse de la Sécurité sociale* social security office

caissier, -ère *nm,f* (*dans un restaurant, un magasin*) cashier; (*dans un supermarché*) checkout operator; (*dans une banque*) cashier, teller □ *caisse de nuit* (*dans un hôtel*)

night auditor; **caissier principal** chief *or* head cashier

calcul *nm* calculation; **faire** *ou* **effectuer un calcul** to make a calculation; **faire une erreur de calcul** to miscalculate

calculable *adj* (*prix*) calculable; (*dégâts*) estimable

calculateur, -trice 1 *nm* ORDINAT (desktop) calculator □ *calculateur électronique* electronic computer
2 *nf* **calculatrice** calculator □ *calculatrice de bureau* desk calculator; *calculatrice imprimante* print-out calculator; *calculatrice de poche* pocket calculator

calculer 1 *vt* to calculate, to work out
2 se calculer *vpr* to be calculated (**sur** on)

calculette *nf* (pocket) calculator

calendrier *nm* (a) (*tableau*) calendar (b) (*emploi du temps*) timetable, schedule; **établir un calendrier** to draw up a timetable *or* schedule; **mon calendrier ne le permet pas** my timetable *or* schedule does not allow it

calibrage *nm* (*de vis, de boulons*) grading

calibrer *vt* (*vis, boulons*) to grade

calme *adj* (*marché, Bourse*) quiet, calm; **nos affaires sont calmes en août** business is quiet in August

cambial, -e *adj* FIN exchange

cambiste FIN **1** *adj* (*marché*) foreign exchange
2 *nmf* foreign exchange dealer *or* broker

camembert *nm Fam* pie chart

camion *nm Br* lorry, *Am* truck □ *camion frigorifique* refrigerated *Br* lorry *or* *Am* truck; *camion semi-remorque Br* articulated lorry, *Am* trailer truck

camion-citerne *nm* tanker

camionnage *nm* (*prix, service*) haulage, carriage, *Am* truckage; **une entreprise de camionnage** a haulage firm, *Am* a trucking business

camionner *vt* to carry, to haul, *Am* to truck

camionnette *nf Br* van, *Am* panel truck

camionneur *nm* (a) (*entrepreneur*) *Br* haulier, *Am* trucker (b) (*chauffeur*) *Br* lorry driver, *Am* truck driver

camoufler *vt* COMPTA **camoufler un bilan** to window-dress the accounts

campagne *nf* campaign; **lancer une campagne** to launch a campaign □ *campagne d'affichage* poster campaign; *campagne commerciale* marketing campaign; *cam-*

pagne de dénigrement countermarketing; *campagne de presse* press campaign; *campagne de productivité* productivity campaign or drive; *campagne de promotion* promotion campaign; *campagne publicitaire, campagne de publicité* advertising campaign; *campagne de vente* sales drive

>
> Aux heureux élus, l'Etat offre les services des meilleures firmes de marketing, et paie des **campagnes de promotion** dans les médias nationaux.
>

canal *nm* ÉCON, MKTG channel □ *canal de communication* communications channel; *canal de communication commerciale* marketing communications channel; *canal de distribution* distribution channel; *canal de distribution court* one-level channel; *canal de distribution long* two-level/three-level channel, conventional marketing channel

candidat, -e *nm,f* candidate, applicant (**à** for); **se porter candidat à un poste** to apply for a job

candidature *nf* application (**à** for); **faire acte de candidature** *ou* **poser sa candidature à un poste** to apply for a post; **retirer sa candidature** to withdraw one's application; **date limite de dépôt de candidatures** closing date for applications □ *candidature spontanée* unsolicited application

cannibalisation *nf (d'un produit)* erosion of the market share

cannibaliser *vt (produit)* to eat into the market share of

CAO *nf* ORDINAT *(abrév* **conception assistée par ordinateur***)* CAD

CAP *nm (abrév* **certificat d'aptitude professionnelle***)* = vocational training certificate

cap *nm (étape)* mark; **notre usine a passé le cap des mille employés** our factory has passed the thousand-employee mark

capacité *nf* (**a**) *(possibilité)* capacity □ *capacité d'achat* purchasing power; *capacité d'emprunter* borrowing power or capacity; *capacité d'endettement* borrowing capacity; *capacité d'exportation* export potential; *capacité de financement* financing capacity; *capacité d'hébergement (d'un hôtel)* accommodation capacity; *capacité d'importation* import potential; *capacité d'imposition* ability to pay tax; *capacité de production* manufacturing capacity

(**b**) *(aptitude)* capacity; **la survie de l'entreprise dépendra de sa capacité à innover** this company's survival will depend on its capacity for innovation

(**c**) *(d'un tonneau)* content, capacity □ *capacité linéaire* shelf-space

(**d**) ORDINAT capacity □ *capacité de mémoire* memory capacity; *capacité de stockage* storage capacity; *capacité de traitement* throughput

capitaine d'industrie *nm* captain of industry

capital *nm* FIN capital, assets; **une société au capital de cinq millions de francs** a company with a capital of or capitalized at five million francs; **avoir des capitaux dans une affaire** to have vested interests in a business; **fournir les capitaux pour un projet** to fund or finance a project; **investir** *ou* **mettre des capitaux dans une affaire** to invest or put capital into a business; **posséder un capital** to have some capital; **les capitaux qui circulent** the capital in circulation; **capital et intérêt** capital and interest □ *capital actions* share capital, equity; *capital appelé* called-up capital; *capital d'apport* initial capital; *capital circulant* circulating capital; *capital de départ* start-up capital; *capital disponible* available capital; *capital émis* issued capital; *capital d'emprunt* loan capital; *capital engagé* tied-up capital, capital employed; *capital d'établissement* invested capital; *capital exigible* current liabilities; *capital d'exploitation* Br working capital, Am operating capital; *capital fixe* fixed assets; *capitaux flottants* hot money, floating capital; *capitaux frais* new capital; *capitaux gelés* frozen assets; *capital humain (d'une entreprise)* manpower; *capital improductif* idle capital, unproductive capital; *capital initial* start-up capital; *capitaux propres* shareholders' or stockholders' equity; *capital roulant* circulating capital; *capital de roulement* Br working capital, Am operating capital; *capital social* (issued) share capital; *capital souscrit* subscribed capital; *capital technique* (technical) equipment; *capital versé* paid-up capital

>
> Près de 49% du **capital** de BMW est solidement placé entre les mains de la famille Quandt, le reste est placé entre les mains de quelques actionnaires.
>

capitalisable *adj* capitalizable

capitalisation *nf (des intérêts, des revenus)* capitalization □ *capitalisation boursière* market capitalization

> "
> Le nouveau géant, dont la **capitalisation** boursière dépasse les 110 milliards de dollars, s'appellera au moins dans un premier temps BP-Amoco.
> "

capitaliser *vt* to capitalize

capitalisme *nm* capitalism □ *capitalisme sauvage* ruthless capitalism

capitaliste *adj & nmf* capitalist

capitalistique *adj* capital-intensive

capital-risque *nm* venture capital, risk capital

captif, -ive *adj (marché)* captive

caractère *nm (signe)* character, letter; ORDINAT character; *écrivez en caractères d'imprimerie* please write in block letters □ *caractère accentué* accented *or* accent character; *caractère gras* bold character; *caractère majuscule* upper-case character; *caractère minuscule* lower-case character

caractéristique *nf (d'un produit)* characteristic, feature □ *caractéristiques techniques* specifications

carence *nf* ÉCON insolvency

cargaison *nf* cargo □ *cargaison d'aller* outward cargo; *cargaison mixte* mixed cargo; *cargaison de retour* homeward cargo

cargo *nm (navire)* freighter □ *cargo mixte* passenger and cargo ship

carnet *nm* **(a)** *(petit cahier)* notebook □ *carnet d'adresses* address book; *carnet ATA* ATA carnet; BANQUE *carnet de banque* pass book, bank book; *carnet de commandes* order book; *carnet communautaire* community carnet; *carnet de dépenses* account book; *carnet de dépôt* deposit book; *carnet de passage en douanes* carnet; *carnet de rendez-vous* appointments book; *carnet de versements* paying-in book **(b)** *(ensemble)* *carnet de chèques* chequebook; *carnet de voyage* travel documents

carrière *nf* career; *faire carrière dans qch* to pursue a career in sth

carriérisme *nm* careerism

carriériste *nmf* careerist

carte *nf* **(a)** *(document officiel)* card □ *carte d'abonnement (pour les transports)* season ticket; *carte accréditive* charge card; *carte d'adhérent* membership card; *carte American Express®* American Express® card; *carte Amex* Amex card; *carte bancaire* bank card; *carte bancaire à puce* smart card *(used as a bank card)*; *carte Bleue* = bank card with which purchases are debited directly from the customer's bank account; ADMIN *carte de commerce* trading licence; *carte de crédit* credit card; *carte de débarquement* landing card; *carte de débit* debit card; *carte d'échantillons* sample card; *carte d'embarquement* boarding pass; *carte de fidélité* loyalty card; *carte d'identité* identity card; *carte Mastercard®* Mastercard®; *carte à mémoire* smart card; *carte de paiement* debit card; TÉL *carte Pastel* phone card *(use of which is debited to one's own phone number)*; *carte perforée* punch card; *carte de presse* press card; *carte à puce* smart card; *carte de réduction* discount card; *carte de représentant* sales representative's official identity card; *carte de retrait* bank card; *carte de Sécurité Sociale* ≃ National Insurance Card; *carte de séjour* residence permit; *carte syndicale* union card; *carte T* reply-paid card; *carte de téléphone* phonecard; ASSUR *carte verte* green card; *carte Visa®* Visa® card; *carte de visite (d'une entreprise)* business card

(b) ORDINAT card □ *carte accélérateur graphique* graphics accelerator card; *carte d'affichage* display card; *carte bus* bus board; *carte à circuit(s) intégré(s)* integrated circuit board, IC board; *carte contrôleur de disque* disk controller card; *carte d'extension* expansion card *or* board; *carte d'extension mémoire* memory expansion card *or* board; *carte fax* fax card; *carte graphique* graphics card; *carte magnétique* magnetic card; *carte mémoire* memory card; *carte mère* motherboard; *carte modem* modem card; *carte réseau* network card; *carte son* sound card; *carte de télécopie* fax card; *carte unité centrale* CPU board

(c) *avoir carte blanche (pour faire qch)* to have carte blanche (to do sth); *donner carte blanche à qn* to give sb carte blanche

> "
> Malgré le développement de la monnaie scripturale (**cartes de paiement**, virements, etc…) les Français restent attachés à leurs pièces et à leurs billets.
> "

carte-adaptateur *nf* ORDINAT adapter card

cartel *nm* ÉCON cartel □ *cartel de l'acier* steel cartel; *cartel de prix* price cartel

cartellisation nf ÉCON cartelization

carte-réponse nf reply card

carton nm (boîte) cardboard box

cartouche nf cartridge □ **cartouche d'encre** ink cartridge; ORDINAT **cartouche d'enregistrement sur bande audionumérique** DAT cartridge; **cartouche de toner** toner cartridge

case nf (a) (sur un formulaire) box; **cocher la case correspondante** tick the appropriate box
(b) ORDINAT button; (en forme de boîte) box □ **case d'aide** help button; **case 'annuler'** cancel button; **case de fermeture** close box; **case de pointage** check box; **case de redimensionnement** size box; **case de saisie** input box
(c) Suisse **case postale** post office box

cash and carry 1 adj cash-and-carry
2 nm cash-and-carry (store)

cash-flow nm cash flow □ **cash-flow actualisé** discounted cash flow; **cash-flow marginal** incremental cash flow; **cash-flow net** net cash flow

cassation nf JUR annulment, cassation

casse nf (a) (objets cassés) breakages; **payer la casse** to pay for breakages (b) **mettre qch à la casse** to scrap sth; **vendre qch à la casse** to sell sth for scrap

casser vt **casser les prix** to slash prices

cassette nf **cassette d'alimentation** (de copieuse) paper tray; ORDINAT **cassette numérique** digital audio tape; **cassette de toner** (d'imprimante) toner cassette

catalogage nm cataloguing

catalogue nm catalogue □ **catalogue illustré** illustrated catalogue; **catalogue des prix** price list; **catalogue de vente par correspondance** mail-order catalogue

cataloguer vt (produits) to catalogue

catégorie nf category □ **catégorie socio-professionnelle** socio-professional group

cause nf **pour cause de** owing to, because of; **fermé pour cause d'inventaire** closed for stocktaking; **absent pour cause de maladie** absent due to ill-health; **bail à céder pour cause de départ** for sale due to relocation

caution nf FIN (a) (gage) security, guarantee; **demander une caution** to ask for security; **fournir caution** to give security □ **caution bancaire, caution de banque** bank guarantee; **caution de soumission** bid bond
(b) (garant) surety, guarantor; **être caution de qn, se porter caution pour qn** to stand surety or security for sb
(c) (pour appartement) deposit; **verser une caution** to pay a deposit; **il faut verser 1000 francs de caution** a deposit of 1,000 francs must be paid

cautionnement nm FIN (a) (garantie) surety, bond, guarantee (b) (somme) security, caution money

cautionner vt FIN (personne) to stand surety for, to act as guarantor for

CB nf (abrév **Carte Bleue**) = bank card with which purchases are debited directly from the customer's bank account

CC nm BANQUE (abrév **compte courant**) CA

CCI nf (abrév **Chambre de commerce et d'industrie**) Chamber of Commerce and Industry

CCP nm (abrév **compte chèque postal**) = post office account, Br ≃ Giro account, Am ≃ Post Office checking account

CD nm (a) (abrév **comité directeur**) board of directors (b) (abrév **corps diplomatique**) CD

CDD nm (abrév **contrat à durée déterminée**) fixed-term contract

CDI nm (abrév **contrat à durée indéterminée**) permanent contract

CD-I nm (abrév **Compact Disc Interactif**) CDI

CD-ROM nm (abrév **Compact Disc read only memory**) CD-ROM

CE 1 nm (a) (abrév **Conseil de l'Europe**) Council of Europe (b) (abrév **comité d'entreprise**) works council
2 nf (abrév **Communauté européenne**) EC

cédant, -e 1 adj (partie) granting, assigning
2 nm,f (d'actions) grantor, assignor

céder vt (a) (droit) to give up, to surrender; **les droits à eux cédés** the rights granted to them
(b) (commerce) to sell; (bail) to dispose of, to sell; **céder qch à bail** to lease sth

cédétiste nmf = member of the CFDT trade union

Cedex nm (abrév **courrier d'entreprise à distribution exceptionnelle**) = postal code ensuring rapid delivery of business mail

CEE nf (abrév **Communauté économique européenne**) EEC

cégétiste nmf = member of the CGT trade union

CEL *nm* (*abrév* **compte épargne logement**) savings account (*for purchasing a property*)

cellulaire *adj* (*gestion*) divisional

cellule *nf* (a) ORDINAT (*dans un tableur*) cell (b) *cellule d'achat* purchasing unit

CEN *nm* (*abrév* **Comité européen de normalisation**) European Standards Commission

cent[1] *nm* hundred; **pour cent** percent; **intérêt de sept pour cent** seven percent interest; **cent pour cent** one hundred percent

cent[2] *nm* (*pièce de monnaie*) cent

centime *nm* centime

central, -e 1 *adj* (*banque*) central; (*bureau*) head, main
2 *nm* **central (téléphonique)** (telephone) exchange □ *central numérique* digital exchange
3 *nf* **centrale d'achat(s)** central purchasing office *or* group; (*au sein d'une entreprise*) central purchasing department; **centrale électrique** power station; **centrale de réservations** central reservations unit *or* office; **centrale syndicale** group of affiliated trade unions

> **"**
>
> Dès 1988, plus des 2/3 des lignes téléphoniques françaises étaient raccordés à un **central numérique**, contre moins d'un quart des lignes britanniques.
>
> **"**

centralisateur, -trice *adj* centralizing

centralisation *nf* centralization

centraliser *vt* to centralize

centre *nm* centre □ *centre d'accueil* (*pour touristes*) visitor centre; *centre d'affaires* business centre; (*dans aéroport, hôtel*) business lounge; *centre administratif* administrative building; COMPTA *centre d'analyse* cost centre; COMPTA *centre d'analyse auxiliaire* secondary cost centre; COMPTA *centre d'analyse opérationnel* operational cost centre; COMPTA *centre d'analyse principal* main cost centre; *centre d'appels* call centre; *centre de chèques postaux* PO cheque account centre; *centre commercial* shopping centre; *centre de conférences* conference centre; *Centre d'études sur les revenus et les coûts* = government body carrying out research into salaries and the cost of living; *centre des impôts* tax centre *or* office; *centre industriel* industrial centre; *centre d'information* information centre; *centre d'intérêt*

touristique tourist *or* visitor attraction; *centre de tourisme* tourist centre; *centre de traitement de l'information* data processing centre; *centre de tri* sorting office

CERC *nm* (*abrév* **Centre d'études sur les revenus et les coûts**) = government body carrying out research into salaries and the cost of living

cercle de qualité *nm* ÉCON quality circle

CERN *nm* (*abrév* **Centre européen pour la recherche nucléaire**) CERN

certain, -e 1 *adj* (*prix, date*) definite, fixed
2 *nm* FIN fixed *or* direct rate of exchange; **le certain de la livre est de 8,68 francs** the rate of exchange for the pound is 8.68 francs

certificat *nm* certificate □ *certificat d'actions* share certificate; *certificat d'aptitude professionnelle* = vocational training certificate; *certificat d'assurance* insurance certificate; ASSUR *certificat d'avarie* certificate of damage; *certificat de capacité* (*d'employé*) certificate of proficiency; *certificat de chargement* certificate of receipt; *certificat de conformité* certificate of compliance, clear report of findings; *certificat de dépôt* (*de marchandises*) warehouse warrant; *certificat de dividende provisoire* scrip dividend; DOUANES *certificat d'entrepôt* warehouse warrant; *certificat d'expertise* expert's report; *certificat de garantie* guarantee; *certificat d'homologation* certificate of approval; *certificat d'investissement* investment certificate; *certificat d'investissement privilégié* preferential investment certificate; *certificat médical* medical certificate; *certificat nominatif d'actions* registered share certificate; *certificat de non-paiement* (*de chèque*) notification of unpaid cheque; (*de lettre de change*) certificate of dishonour; *certificat d'origine* certificate of origin; FIN *certificat provisoire* share certificate, (provisional) scrip; ASSUR *certificat provisoire d'assurance* cover note; *certificat de qualité* certificate of quality; *certificat de résidence* certificate of residence; *certificat de titres* share certificate; *certificat de transfert* transfer certificate; *certificat de travail* (*pour certifier qu'on est employé*) attestation of employment; (*pour certifier qu'on a été employé*) employer's reference; FIN *certificat de trésorerie* treasury bond; *certificat de valeur* certificate of value

certification *nf* JUR certification, authentication; (*d'une signature*) witnessing

certifier vt JUR to certify, to attest; *(signature)* to witness

cessation nf stoppage, termination; *(d'un contrat)* termination □ ***cessation d'activités*** termination of business; ***cessation de paiements*** suspension of payments; **être en état de cessation de paiements** to have suspended all payments; ***cessation de travail*** stoppage

cesser vt *(activité, paiement)* to stop

cessibilité nf JUR *(de biens)* transferability, assignability; *(d'une traite, d'une pension retraite)* negotiability

cessible adj JUR *(biens)* transferable, assignable; *(traite, pension retraite)* negotiable

cession nf JUR cession, transfer; *(document)* deed of transfer □ ***cession de bail*** leaseback; ***cession de biens*** assignment of property; ***cession de licence de marque*** corporate licensing; FIN ***cession de parts*** stock transfer; ***cession de parts en blanc*** blank transfer; ***cession en pleine propriété*** renunciation

cession-bail nf leaseback

cessionnaire **1** adj JUR cessionary **2** nm (a) JUR *(de biens)* transferee, assignee; *(d'un effet de commerce, d'une créance)* holder (b) *(d'un chèque)* endorser

césure nf ORDINAT break, hyphenation

cf. *(abrév* **confer***)* cf

CFAO nf ORDINAT *(abrév* **conception et fabrication assistées par ordinateur***)* CAD/CAM

CFDT nf *(abrév* **Confédération française et démocratique du travail***)* = French trade union

CFTC nf *(abrév* **Confédération française des travailleurs chrétiens***)* = French trade union

CGC nf *(abrév* **Confédération générale des cadres***)* = French trade union for managerial staff

CGT nf *(abrév* **Confédération générale du travail***)* = French trade union *(linked to the French Communist Party)*

chaînage nm ORDINAT chaining; *(de commandes)* piping

chaîne nf (a) *(de magasins, de restaurants)* chain □ ***chaîne volontaire de détaillants*** voluntary retailer chain (b) *(dans l'industrie)* ***chaîne de fabrication*** production line; ***chaîne de montage*** assembly line (c) ORDINAT string □ ***chaîne de caractères*** character string

chaîner vt ORDINAT to chain; *(commandes)* to pipe

chambre nf (a) *(organisation)* FIN ***chambre de clearing*** clearing house; ***Chambre de commerce*** Chamber of Commerce; ***Chambre de commerce et d'industrie*** Chamber of Commerce and Industry; ***Chambre de commerce internationale*** International Chamber of Commerce; ***chambre de compensation*** clearing house; ***Chambre des métiers*** Chamber of Trade; ***chambre syndicale*** employers' federation; ***chambre syndicale des agents de change*** stock exchange committee (b) *(local)* ***chambre des criées*** auction room, Br saleroom, Am salesroom

champ nm (a) *(portée)* ***champ d'action*** field or sphere of activity (b) ORDINAT field □ ***champ mémo*** memo field; ***champ numérique*** numeric field; ***champ de texte*** text field

change nm FIN exchange; **le change est avantageux/défavorable** the exchange rate is good/bad; **au change du jour** at the current rate of exchange □ ***change du dollar*** dollar exchange

changement nm (a) *(modification, substitution)* change □ ***changement d'adresse*** change of address; ***changement d'hypothèque*** transfer of mortgage; ***changement de propriétaire*** *(sur panneau)* under new ownership; ***changement stucturel*** structural change (b) ORDINAT ***changement de ligne*** line feed; ***changement de page*** page break

changer vt FIN *(argent)* to change, to exchange; **changer un billet de banque** to change a banknote; **changer des dollars contre des francs** to change dollars into francs

changeur nm (a) *(personne)* money changer (b) ***changeur de monnaie*** *(machine)* change machine

chantier nm (a) *(pour entreposer)* depot (b) ***chantier (de construction)*** building site; ***chantier de construction navale, chantier naval*** shipyard

charge nf (a) *(obligation financière)* charge, expense; *(impôt)* tax; **le loyer plus les charges** rent plus service charge; **être à la charge de qn** *(personne)* to be dependent on sb; *(transport, réparations)* to be chargeable to sb; **les frais de transport sont à notre charge** the cost of transport is chargeable to us; **les réparations sont à la charge du locataire** the repairs are to be paid for by the tenant ◻ *charges courantes* current expenses; *charge d'une dette* Br debt servicing, Am debt service; *charges d'exploitation* running costs; *charge fictive* fictitious cost; *charges financières* financial expenses; *charges fiscales* tax (burden); *charges fixes* fixed costs; *charges nettes* net costs; *charge opérationnelle* overhead, operating cost; *charges patronales* employer's contributions; *charge à payer* sum payable; COMPTA *charges à payer* accrued expenses, accruals; *charges publiques* public expenditure; *charges sociales* Br national insurance contributions *(paid by the employer)*, Am social security charges *(paid by the employer)*; *charges sociales salariales* employee's contributions; *charges variables* variable costs

(b) *(cargaison) (d'un camion)* load; *(d'un navire)* cargo; **prendre charge d'une cargaison** to load (up), to take in cargo ◻ *charge admise* load limit; *charge admissible* safe load; *charge complète* Br lorry load, Am truck load; *charge maximale* maximum load; *charge utile* capacity (load)

(c) *(responsabilité)* charge, responsibility; **avoir la charge de qch** to be in charge of sth

(d) *(fonction)* office ◻ *charge d'avoué* solicitor's practice

> ❝
> Le Premier Ministre envisage au printemps d'alléger les **charges patronales** d'assurance maladie qui pèsent sur les emplois non qualifiés.
> ❞

chargé, -e 1 *adj* (a) *(véhicule, navire)* loaded, laden; *(emploi du temps)* busy (b) *(responsable)* **être chargé de qch/de faire qch** to be responsible for sth/for doing sth
2 *nm* *chargé de budget* account executive; *chargé de clientèle* account manager; *chargé de comptes* account executive; *chargé de dossier* project manager; MKTG *chargé d'étude* market researcher; *chargé de mission* official representative; *chargé de relations clients* customer relations manager

chargement *nm* (a) *(action) (de camion)* loading; *(de cargaison)* shipping, loading (b) *(marchandises)* load, consignment; **prendre chargement** to take on cargo ◻ *chargement complet* full load; *chargement réglementaire* regulation load (c) *(de lettre, colis)* registration; *(lettre)* registered letter; *(colis)* registered parcel

charger 1 *vt* (a) *(donner la responsabilité à)* **charger qn de qch/de faire qch** to put sb in charge of sth/of doing sth
(b) *(camion, navire)* to load (up); **charger des marchandises sur un train** to load goods onto a train
(c) BANQUE *(compte)* to overcharge (on)
2 *vi* ORDINAT to load up
3 se charger *vpr* (a) *(prendre la responsabilité)* **se charger de qch** to take sth on; **se charger de faire qch** to undertake to do sth
(b) ORDINAT to load; **se charger automatiquement** to load automatically, to autoload

charte *nf* charter ◻ *charte commerciale* commercial charter

charte-partie *nf* charter party

charter *nm* *(avion)* charter plane; *(vol)* charter flight

chartiste *nmf* ÉCON chartist

chasser *vt* BOURSE **chasser le découvert** to raid the bears

chasseur de têtes *nm* headhunter

chef *nm* *(responsable)* head ◻ *chef des achats* purchasing manager; *chef d'atelier* shop foreman; *chef de bureau* office manager; *chef de chantier* site foreman; *chef comptable, chef de la comptabilité* chief accountant; *chef d'entreprise* company manager; *chef d'équipe* team leader; *chef d'établissement* works manager; *chef de fabrication* production manager; *chef de file* leader; *chef du groupe* group leader; *chef du personnel* personnel manager; *chef de produit* product manager; *chef de projet* project manager; *chef de rayon (d'un magasin)* department manager; *chef de service* department manager; *chef des traitements* data processing manager; *chef des ventes* sales manager; *chef de zone* area manager

chemin *nm* (a) *(moyen de transport)* **chemin de fer** Br railway, Am railroad; **envoyer des marchandises par chemin de fer** to dispatch goods by rail (b) ORDINAT path ◻ *chemin d'accès* path

chemise *nf* chemise (cartonnée) folder

chèque *nm* Br cheque, Am check; **émettre** *ou* **faire un chèque** to write a cheque; **encaisser** *ou* **tirer** *ou* **toucher un chèque** to cash a cheque; **établir** *ou* **libeller un chèque à l'ordre de qn** to make a cheque out to sb; **faire opposition à un chèque** to stop a cheque; **payer** *ou* **régler par chèque** to pay by cheque; **refuser d'honorer un chèque** to refer a cheque to drawer; **remettre** *ou* **déposer un chèque à la banque** to pay a cheque into the bank; **un chèque de 600 francs** a cheque for 600 francs ❏ **chèque bancaire** cheque; **chèque de banque** banker's cheque, banker's draft; **chèque barré** crossed cheque; **chèque en blanc** blank cheque; *Fam* **chèque en bois** rubber cheque; **chèque de caisse** credit voucher; **chèque certifié** certified cheque; **chèque non barré** uncrossed cheque; **chèque à ordre** cheque to order; **chèque ouvert** open cheque; **chèque périmé** out-of-date cheque; **chèque au porteur** cheque made payable to bearer, bearer cheque; **chèque postal** post office cheque; **chèque postdaté** post-dated cheque; **chèque sans provision** bad cheque; **chèque de voyage** traveller's cheque

> ❝
> Les émetteurs de **chèques sans provision** pourraient en effet bénéficier d'un délai plus important pour régulariser leur situation.
> ❞

chèque-cadeau *nm* gift token

chèque-dividende *nm* FIN dividend warrant

chèque-repas, chèque-restaurant *nm Br* luncheon voucher, *Am* meal ticket

chéquier *nm Br* cheque book, *Am* check book

cher, chère **1** *adj* (**a**) *(onéreux)* dear, expensive; **ce magasin est trop cher** this shop is too expensive; **c'est trop cher pour moi** I can't afford it (**b**) *(dans une lettre)* **Cher client** Dear customer; **Cher Monsieur** Dear Mr X; *(officiel)* Dear Sir
2 *adv* **acheter qch cher** to pay a high price for sth; **se vendre cher** to fetch a high price; **ça ne vaut pas cher** it's not worth much

cherté de la vie *nf* high cost of living

chevalier *nm (dans une OPA)* **chevalier blanc** white knight; **chevalier gris** grey knight; **chevalier noir** black knight

chiffre *nm* (**a**) *(nombre)* figure, number; **en chiffres ronds** in round figures ❏ ORDINAT **chiffre ASCII** ASCII number; ÉCON **chiffres bruts** unweighted figures
(**b**) *(total)* amount, total; **les dépenses de la société atteignent un chiffre de quatre millions de francs** the company's spending has reached a figure of four million francs ❏ **chiffre d'affaires** turnover; **la société a ou fait un chiffre d'affaires d'un million de francs** the company has a turnover of a million francs; **chiffre d'affaires consolidé** group turnover; COMPTA **chiffre d'affaires critique** breakeven point; **chiffre d'affaires à l'exportation** total export

sales; COMPTA **chiffre d'affaires global** total sales; COMPTA **chiffre d'affaires prévisionnel** projected turnover, projected sales revenue; **chiffre de vente** sales figures

> ❝
> Valéo a limité à 4,6% la baisse de son **chiffre d'affaires consolidé** au premier semestre 1993.
> ❞

chiffrement *nm* ORDINAT *(de message)* encoding, encryption ❏ **chiffrement de données** data encryption

chiffrer **1** *vt (coût, dégâts, dommages)* to estimate, to assess; **chiffrer des travaux** to draw up an estimate of the cost of work; **il est trop tôt pour chiffrer le montant des dégâts** it's too early to put a figure to the damage
2 se chiffrer *vpr* **se chiffrer à** to add up to, to amount to; **leurs pertes se chiffrent en centaines de millions de francs** their losses add up to *or* amount to hundreds of millions of francs

chiffreur *nm* ORDINAT encoder, encrypter

chiffrier *nm* counter cash book

chirographaire *adj* FIN *(créance, créancier)* unsecured

choc pétrolier *nm* ÉCON oil crisis

choix *nm* (**a**) *(gamme)* choice, selection; **au choix de l'acheteur** at the buyer's option (**b**) *(qualité)* **de choix** choice, selected; **de tout premier choix** first-class, high-grade; **de second choix** second grade

chômage *nm* unemployment; **au chômage** out of work, unemployed; **s'inscrire au chômage** to sign on; **mettre qn au chômage** to put sb out of work ❏ **chômage conjoncturel** cyclical unemployment; **chômage déguisé** concealed unemployment; **chômage de longue durée** long-term unemployment; **chômage de mobilité** frictional unemployment; **chômage partiel** short-time working; **être en chômage partiel** to work short time; **chômage résiduel** frictional unemployment; **chômage saisonnier** seasonal unemployment; **chômage structurel** structural unemployment; **chômage technique** lay-off; **être en chômage technique** to have been laid off

chômer *vi (personne)* to be unemployed; *(entreprise, machine)* to stand idle, to be at a standstill; **les usines chôment** the factories are at a standstill; **laisser chômer son argent** to let one's money lie idle

chômeur, -euse *nm,f* unemployed person; **les chômeurs** the unemployed; **le nombre des chômeurs est très important** the unemployment figures are very high; **les chômeurs de longue durée** the long-term unemployed ❏ *chômeur partiel* short-time worker

chronique *adj* (*chômage, déficit*) chronic

chronomètre *nm* ORDINAT timer

chute *nf* (*d'une monnaie, des exportations, des ventes*) fall, drop (**de** in)

chuter *vi* to fall, to drop; **faire chuter les cours** to cause a heavy fall *or* drop in prices

CI *nm* (*abrév* **certificat d'investissement**) investment certificate

ci-après *adv* below; JUR hereinafter; **les dispositions ci-après** the provisions set out below; **ci-après dénommé l'acheteur** hereinafter referred to as the Buyer

ciblage *nm* MKTG targeting ❏ *ciblage stratégique* strategic targeting

cible *nf* MKTG target ❏ *cible commerciale* marketing target; *cible de communication* promotional target; *cible publicitaire* advertising target

cibler *vt* MKTG to target

ci-contre *adv* opposite; COMPTA **porté ci-contre** as per contra

ci-dessous *adv* below; **voir le tableau ci-dessous** see the table below

ci-dessus *adv* above; **voir le graphique ci-dessus** see the above diagram

CIDEX *nm* (*abrév* **courrier individuel à distribution exceptionnelle**) = system grouping letter boxes in country areas

Cie (*abrév* **compagnie**) Co

ci-inclus, -e **1** *adj* enclosed; **la copie ci-incluse** the enclosed copy
2 *adv* (**vous trouverez**) **ci-inclus copie de votre lettre** (please find) enclosed a copy of your letter

ci-joint, -e **1** *adj* enclosed; **les pièces ci-jointes** the enclosed documents
2 *adv* (**veuillez trouver**) **ci-joint mon chèque** please find enclosed my cheque

circonscription *nf* ADMIN division, district ❏ *circonscription téléphonique* telephone code area

circuit *nm* (**a**) ÉCON channel ❏ *circuit commercial* commercial channel; *circuit de commercialisation* marketing channel; *circuit de distribution* distribution network; *circuits de vente* commercial chan-

nels (**b**) ORDINAT circuit ❏ *circuit de commande* command circuit

circulaire **1** *adj* (*lettre*) circular
2 *nf* circular

circulant, -e *adj* FIN (*billets, devises*) in circulation; (*capitaux*) circulating

circulation *nf* (**a**) FIN (*des billets, des capitaux, des devises*) circulation ❏ *circulation monétaire* circulation of money, money in circulation (**b**) ÉCON movement, circulation; **la libre circulation des personnes/des biens/des capitaux** the free movement of people/goods/capital

circuler *vi* FIN (*billets, devises*) to be in circulation; (*capitaux*) to be circulating; **faire circuler des effets** to keep bills afloat

citoyen, -enne *nm,f* citizen

classe *nf* (**a**) (*rang*) class; ADMIN rank, grade; **de première classe** (*produits*) top-quality; (*hôtel*) first-class
(**b**) (*dans la hiérarchie sociale*) class ❏ *classes dirigeantes* ruling classes; *classes moyennes* middle classes; *classes ouvrières* working classes; *classes supérieures* upper classes
(**c**) (*dans les transports*) class ❏ *classe affaires* business class; **voyager en classe affaires** to travel business class; *classe club* club class; *classe économique* economy class; *classe touriste* tourist class
(**d**) COMPTA group of accounts ❏ *classe de revenu* income bracket

classement *nm* (*de documents*) filing

classer *vt* (**a**) (*ordonner*) to class, to classify (**b**) (*documents*) to file; **classer qch par ordre alphabétique** to file sth in alphabetical order (**c**) JUR **classer une affaire** to close a case

classeur *nm* (*meuble*) filing cabinet; (*dossier*) folder; ORDINAT filer ❏ *classeur à anneaux* ring binder; ADMIN *classeur des entrées et sorties* tally file; *classeur à fiches* card-index file

classification *nf* classification ❏ *classification de fonctions* job classification

clause *nf* clause ❏ *clause additionnelle* additional clause, rider; *clause d'annulation* cancellation clause; *clause d'arbitrage* arbitration clause; JUR *clause compromissoire* arbitration clause; *clause conditionnelle* proviso; *clause contractuelle* clause of a contract; *clause de dédit* penalty clause; *clause échappatoire* escape clause; *clause d'exclusivité* exclusivity clause; *clause d'exonération* exemption clause; *clause de franchise* excess clause; COMPTA *clause d'indexation* escalation clause, indexation clause; JUR **clause limitative** limiting clause; **clause de non-concurrence** non-competition clause; **clause pénale** penalty clause; FIN **clause au porteur** pay to bearer clause; ASSUR **clause de régularisation** = clause stating that insurance starts after payment of the first premium; **clause de réserve de propriété** retention of title clause; **clause de résiliation** termination clause, cancellation clause; **clause résolutoire** avoidance clause; **clause restrictive** restrictive clause; **clause de sauvegarde** safety clause

> ❝
> L'employeur s'assurera que le candidat est libre de tout engagement et qu'il n'est pas soumis à une **clause de non-concurrence**.
> ❞

clausé, -e adj (connaissance) dirty

clavier nm (d'ordinateur, de machine à écrire) keyboard; ORDINAT **introduire des données par clavier** to key (in) data ▫ **clavier alphanumérique** alphanumeric keypad; **clavier AZERTY** AZERTY keyboard; **clavier multi-fonction** multifunctional keyboard; **clavier numérique** numeric keypad; **clavier QWERTY** QWERTY keyboard

claviste nmf ORDINAT keyboarder

clé 1 nf (a) ORDINAT key; (du DOS) switch (b) BANQUE **clé RIB** bank details 2 adj (très important) key ▫ **industrie clé** key industry; **poste clé** key post; **secteur clé** key sector

clearing nm FIN clearing

clef = **clé**

clic nm click; **double clic** double click

client, -e nm,f client, customer; (d'un hôtel) guest; (dans la publicité) account; **c'est un bon client** he's a good customer; **la France est un gros client du Japon pour la robotique** France is one of Japan's big customers for robotics ▫ **client actuel** existing customer; COMPTA **client douteux** doubtful debt, possible bad debt; **client imprévu** chance customer; **client mystère** mystery shopper; **client de passage** passing customer; **client potentiel** potential customer; **client régulier** regular customer; **client sans réservation** (dans un hôtel) chance guest, walk-in

clientèle nf (clients) customers; (fait d'acheter) custom; **attirer la clientèle** to attract custom; **avoir une grosse clientèle** to have a large clientele; **accorder sa clientèle à qn** to patronize sb, to give sb one's custom ▫ **clientèle de passage** passing trade

clignotant nm ÉCON signal, indicator; **le clignotant de la hausse des prix** the warning light or signal that prices are rising

climat nm (économique, social) climate

clipart nm ORDINAT clip art

cliquer vi ORDINAT to click (**sur** on); **cliquer deux fois** to double-click; **cliquer et glisser** to click and drag

clone nm ORDINAT clone

clore vt (séance, réunion) to close; ORDINAT **clore une session** to log off, to log out

clos, -e adj (achevé) finished, concluded; **les inscriptions seront closes le 3 mars** the closing date for applications is 3 March; COMPTA **exercice clos le 31 déc 1998** year ended 31 Dec 1998

clôture nf (a) (d'une réunion) conclusion, end; (d'un débat) closure; **clôture des inscriptions le 3 mars** closing date for applications is 3 March; **prononcer la clôture des débats** to end the discussion, to bring the discussion to a close

(b) BOURSE close; **être ferme en clôture** to close firm; **la valeur du mark en clôture** the closing value of the mark, the value of the mark at the close

(c) ORDINAT close ▫ **clôture de session** logging off

(d) (d'un compte) closing ▫ COMPTA **clôture annuelle des livres** year-end closing of accounts; COMPTA **clôture de l'exercice** end of the financial year

clôturer 1 vt (a) (séance, débat) to close, to end, to conclude; JUR **clôturer une faillite** to close a bankruptcy (b) COMPTA (comptes, livres) to close
2 vi BOURSE (valeur, indice) to close; **le CAC 40 a clôturé en baisse/hausse de 9 points** the CAC 40 closed 9 points down/up; **le dollar a clôturé à 11,35F** the dollar closed at 11.35F

club d'investissement nm investment club

CM nf (abrév **Chambre des métiers**) Guild Chamber

CNAM nf (abrév **Caisse nationale d'assurance maladie**) French goverment department dealing with health insurance and sickness benefit

CNAV nf (abrév **Caisse nationale d'assurance vieillesse**) = French government department dealing with benefit payments relating to old age

CNC *nm* (*abrév* **Comité national de la consommation**) = consumer protection organization

CNCE *nm* (*abrév* **Centre national du commerce extérieur**) = national export organization

CNE *nm* (*abrév* **Caisse nationale d'Épargne**) ≃ National Savings Bank

CNPF *nm* (*abrév* **Conseil national du patronat français**) = national council of French employers, *Br* ≃ CBI

CNRS *nm* (*abrév* **Centre national de la recherche scientifique**) = national organization for scientific research, *Br* ≃ SRC

CNUCED *nf* (*abrév* **Conférence des Nations Unies pour le commerce et l'industrie**) UNCTAD

coacquéreur, -euse *nm,f* joint purchaser

coacquisition *nf* joint purchase

coadministrateur, -trice *nm,f* co-director

coalition *nf* coalition

coassocié, -e *nm,f* joint partner

coassurance *nf* coinsurance

coassurer *vt* to co-insure

COB *nf* BOURSE (*abrév* **Commission des opérations de Bourse**) = French Stock Exchange watchdog

cobol *nm* ORDINAT COBOL

coche *nf Br* tick, *Am* checkmark

cocher *vt Br* to tick, *Am* to check; **cocher la case correspondante** (*sur formulaire*) *Br* tick *or Am* check the appropriate box

cocontractant, -e JUR **1** *adj* contracting **2** *nm,f* contracting partner

cocréancier, -ère *nm,f* joint creditor

codage *nm* ORDINAT encoding, coding

code *nm* (a) (*symboles*) code ❑ **code assujetti TVA** VAT registration number; **code client** customer code, customer reference number; **code confidentiel** security code; (*pour carte bancaire*) personal identification number, PIN number; **code général des impôts** general tax code; BANQUE **code guichet** bank branch code; BANQUE **code personnel** (*pour carte bancaire*) personal identification number, PIN number; BANQUE **code porteur** personal identification number, PIN number; **code postal** *Br* postcode, postal code, *Am* zip code
  (b) ORDINAT code ❑ **code d'accès** access code; **code ASCII** ASCII code; **code**

d'identification identification code
  (c) (*ensemble de lois*) code ❑ **code de commerce** commercial law; **code du travail** employment regulations

code-barre *nm* bar code

codébiteur, -trice *nm,f* joint debtor

codemandeur, -eresse *nm,f* JUR joint plaintiff

coder *vt* ORDINAT to encode, to code

codétenteur, -trice *nm,f* JUR joint holder

CODEVI *nm* (*abrév* **Compte pour le développement industriel**) = type of instant-access government savings account

codification *nf* JUR (*des lois*) codification, classification

codifier *vt* JUR (*lois*) to codify, to classify

codirecteur, -trice *nm,f* joint manager

codirection *nf* joint management

coefficient *nm* (*proportion*) ratio ❑ **coefficient d'activité** activity ratio; **coefficient de capital** output ratio; **coefficient de capitalisation des résultats** price-earnings ratio; **coefficient d'erreur** margin of error; COMPTA **coefficient d'exploitation** performance *or* operating ratio; **coefficient de liquidité** liquidity ratio; **coefficient de rotation** stock turnover ratio; **coefficient saisonnier** seasonal index; **coefficient de solvabilité** risk asset ratio, solvency coefficient; **coefficient de trésorerie** cash ratio

coentrepreneur *nm* joint venturer

coentreprise *nf* joint venture

coéquation *nf* ADMIN proportional assessment

COFACE *nf* (*abrév* **Compagnie française d'assurances pour le commerce extérieur**) = export insurance company, ≃ ECGD

coffre *nm* BANQUE safe-deposit box; **les coffres de l'État** the coffers of the State

coffre-fort *nm* safe

cofinancement *nm* joint venture

cofinancer *vt* to finance jointly

cofondateur, -trice *nm,f* co-founder

cogérance *nf* joint management

cogérant, -e *nm,f* joint manager

cogérer *vt* to manage jointly

cogestion *nf* joint management

col *nm* **col blanc** white-collar worker; **col bleu** blue-collar worker; **col doré** gold-collar worker

colicitant, -e *nm,f* JUR co-vendor

colis *nm* parcel, package; **envoyer qch par colis postal** to send sth by parcel post □ **colis contre remboursement** *Br* cash on delivery parcel, *Am* collect on delivery parcel; **colis exprès** special delivery parcel

collaborateur, -trice *nm,f* assistant

collaboration *nf* collaboration; **travailler en étroite collaboration (avec qn)** to work in close collaboration (with sb)

collaborer *vi* (entreprises) to collaborate; **collaborer à qch** (projet) to take part in sth; (journal) to contribute to sth

collecte *nf* □ **collecte de données** data collection; **collecte de fonds** fundraising

collecter *vi* to raise funds

collectif, -ive **1** *adj* (action, travail, responsabilité) collective; (licenciements) mass **2** *nm* (a) FIN **collectif budgétaire** interim budget (b) (association) collective

collection *nf* (d'échantillons) line

collectivisme *nm* ÉCON collectivism

collectivité *nf* group □ **collectivités locales** local authorities

collègue *nmf* colleague, *Am* co-worker □ **collègue de travail** work colleague, *Am* co-worker

coller *vt* ORDINAT to paste

collusion d'intérêts *nf* merging of interests

colocataire *nmf* joint tenant, co-tenant

colonne *nf* (de chiffres) column □ COMPTA **colonne créditrice** credit column; **colonne débitrice** debit column

combler *vt* (perte) to make good; (découvert) to pay off

comestible **1** *adj* (aliments, denrées) consumable **2** *nm* **comestibles** consumables

comité *nm* committee □ **comité de conciliation** arbitration or conciliation board; **comité consultatif** advisory board; **comité directeur, comité de direction** board of directors; **comité d'enquête** board of enquiry; **comité d'entreprise** works council or committee; **Comité européen de normalisation** European Standards Commission; **comité d'hygiène et de sécurité** health and safety committee; **comité de**

restructuration steering committee; MKTG **comité synectique** idea committee

commande *nf* (a) (de produit) order; **faire** *ou* **passer une commande** to put in *or* place an order; **exécuter une commande** to fill an order; **livrer une commande** to deliver an order; **fait sur commande** made to order; **payable à la commande** payment with order, cash with order; **conformément à votre commande** as per (your) order □ **commande d'essai** trial order; **commande export, commande pour l'exportation** export order; **commande ferme** firm order; **commande par ordinateur** teleorder; **commandes par quantités** bulk orders; **commande renouvelée** repeat order; **commande téléphonique, commande par téléphone** telephone order

(b) ORDINAT command □ **commande d'annulation** undo command; **commande à bascule** toggle switch; **commande de copie** copy command; **commande DOS** DOS command; **commande d'effacement** delete command; **commande d'insertion** insert command; **commande de recherche** find command; **commande système d'exploitation** operating system command; **à commande vocale** voice-activated

commander *vt* (a) (marchandises) to order; **commander qch chez qn** to order sth from sb; **commander ferme** to place a firm order; **commander qch par téléphone** to order sth by telephone; **commander qch par ordinateur** to teleorder sth (b) ORDINAT to drive; **commandé par menu** menu-driven; **commandé à la voix** voice-activated

commanditaire **1** *adj* **associé commanditaire** *Br* sleeping *or Am* silent partner **2** *nm* (a) (d'une entreprise) *Br* sleeping *or Am* silent partner (b) MKTG (d'un tournoi, d'un spectacle) sponsor

commandite *nf* (a) **commandite par actions** partnership limited by shares; **(société en) commandite simple** limited partnership, mixed liability company (b) (fonds) = capital invested by sleeping partner(s)

commandité, -e **1** *adj* **associé commandité** active partner **2** *nm,f* active partner

commanditer *vt* (a) (soutenir financièrement) to finance (as a limited partner) (b) MKTG (tournoi, spectacle) to sponsor

commerçant, -e **1** *adj* (quartier) commercial, business; **être commerçant** (personne) to have business acumen

2 *nm,f* trader; *(qui tient un magasin)* shop-keeper; **petit commerçant** small trader ❑ *commerçant en détail* retailer; *commerçant en gros* wholesaler

commerce *nm* (**a**) *(activité, secteur)* commerce, trade; **le petit commerce** *(petits commerçants)* small traders; **être dans le commerce, faire du commerce** to be in trade, to run a business; **faire du commerce avec qn/un pays** to do business with sb/a country; **faire le commerce de qch** to trade in sth ❑ *commerce de biens* visible trade; *commerce de demi-gros* cash and carry; *commerce de détail* retail trade; ORDINAT *commerce électronique* electronic commerce, e-commerce; *commerce d'exportation* export trade; *commerce extérieur* foreign trade; *commerce de gros* wholesale trade; *commerce d'importation* import trade; *commerce intérieur* domestic trade; *commerce intermédiaire* middleman's business; *commerce international* international trade; *commerce maritime* maritime trade; *commerce de services* invisible trade

(**b**) *(circuit de distribution)* market; **on ne trouve pas encore ce produit dans le commerce** this item is not yet available on the market; **cela ne se trouve plus dans le commerce** this item has gone off the market

(**c**) *(magasin)* Br shop, Am store; **commerce à céder** *(sur panneau)* business for sale; **tenir un commerce** to run a business

commercer *vi* to trade, to deal (**avec** with)

commercial, -e 1 *adj (activité, attaché, droit, effet)* commercial; *(balance, embargo, tribunal)* trade; *(délégué, direction, service)* sales; **avoir des contacts commerciaux avec qn** to have trading links with sb

2 *nm,f (personne)* salesman, *f* saleswoman

commercialement *adv* commercially

commercialisable *adj* marketable

commercialisation *nf* marketing

commercialiser *vt* (**a**) *(mettre dans le commerce)* to market; **le produit sera commercialisé en janvier** the product will be coming onto the market in January (**b**) FIN *(effet)* to negotiate

commettant *nm* JUR principal; **commettant et mandataire** principal and agent

commis *nm* (**a**) *(dans un magasin)* Br sales assistant, Am sales clerk

(**b**) *(dans une banque, une administration)* clerk; BOURSE floor trader; **premier commis** chief clerk ❑ *commis d'agent de change* stockbroker's clerk; FIN *commis aux*

comptes government auditor; *commis aux écritures* accounting clerk; *commis principal* chief clerk

commissaire *nm* (**a**) *(membre d'une commission)* commissioner ❑ *commissaire européen* European commissioner

(**b**) FIN *commissaire aux comptes* government auditor

> ❝
> Le Conseil d'Administration d'Alcatel Alsthom a examiné le rapport sur l'activité et les résultats du premier semestre qui ont été attesté par les **commissaires aux comptes**.
> ❞

commissaire-priseur *nm* auctioneer

commissariat *nm* commissionership ❑ *commissariat aux comptes* auditorship

commission *nf* (**a**) *(comité)* commission, committee ❑ *commission administrative* management committee; *commission arbitrale* board of referees; *commission de comptabilité* audit committee; *commission d'enquête* board of inquiry; *Commission européenne* European Commission; *commission de normalisation* standards commission; *Commission des opérations de Bourse* = French Stock Exchange watchdog; *commission paritaire* joint commission

(**b**) *(pourcentage)* commission, percentage; FIN brokerage; **3% de commission** 3% commission; **il reçoit** *ou* **touche une commission de 5% sur chaque vente** he gets a commission of 5% on each sale; **être payé à la commission** to be paid on a commission basis ❑ *commission d'affacturage* factoring charges; *commission d'arrangement* over-riding commission; *commission de bourse* transaction costs; *commission de change* agio; *commission de chef de file* management fee; *commission de désintéressement* drop dead fee; *commission de gestion* agency fee

commissionnaire *nm* (commission) agent, broker ❑ *commissionnaire d'achat* buyer; FIN *commissionnaire en banque* outside broker; *commissionnaire en douane* customs agent *or* broker; *commissionnaire expéditeur* forwarding agent, carrier; *commissionnaire à l'export, commissionnaire exportateur* export agent; *commissionnaire en gros* factor; *commissionnaire à l'import, commissionnaire importateur* import agent; *commissionnaire de transport* forwarding agent, carrier

commissionner *vt (projet)* to commission

commun, -e *adj* common; **faire bourse commune** to pool resources; **créer une société en commun avec qn** to start a company in partnership with sb

communautaire *adj* UE *(de la Communauté européenne)* Common Market, Community

communauté *nf* (a) UE **la Communauté (économique) européenne** the European (Economic) Community
(b) *(collectivité)* community □ **communauté financière** financial community; **communauté internationale** international community
(c) JUR **communauté de biens** joint estate

commune *nf* ADMIN commune *(smallest territorial division)*

communication *nf* (a) *(échange)* communication; **se mettre en communication avec qn** to get in touch with sb; **avoir communication d'un dossier** to get hold of a file, to have had a file passed on to one; **demander communication d'un dossier** to ask for a file □ **communication commerciale** business correspondence
(b) ORDINAT communication □ **communication de données** data communications, datacomms; **communication en ligne** online communication
(c) TÉL **communication (téléphonique)** telephone call; **mettez-moi en communication avec M. Martin** put me through to Mr Martin; **je vous passe la communication** I'll put you through; **vous avez la communication** you're through; **la communication est mauvaise** the line is bad □ **communication internationale** international call; **communication locale** local call; **communication longue distance** long-distance call; **communication en PCV** *Br* reverse-charge call, *Am* collect call; **communication télématique** datacommunications, datacomms
(d) MKTG *(publicité)* promotion □ **communication événementielle** event promotion; **communication institutionnelle** corporate promotion; **communication sur le lieu de vente** point-of-sale promotion; **communication produit** product promotion
(e) *(message)* communication, message; **transmettre une communication à qn** to pass on a message to sb
(f) *(dans un congrès, une conférence)* paper; **faire une communication** to give a paper

communiqué *nm* communiqué □ **communiqué de presse** press release

communiquer 1 *vt (renseignements, statistiques, données)* to communicate, to give
2 *vi* to communicate (**avec** with); **communiquer par téléphone/fax/courrier électronique** to communicate by telephone/fax/e-mail

commutatif, -ive *adj* JUR commutative

commutation temporelle asynchrone *nf* ORDINAT asynchronous transfer mode

compagnie *nf* company; **Thomas et Compagnie** Thomas and Company □ **compagnie par actions** joint-stock company; **compagnie aérienne** airline; **compagnie d'assurances** insurance company; **compagnie bancaire** bank; **compagnie captive** daughter company, subsidiary company; **compagnie à charte** chartered company; **compagnie de navigation** shipping line; **compagnie mère** parent company

comparabilité *nf* comparability

comparatif, -ive *adj (tests, publicité, étude)* comparative

compatibilité *nf* ORDINAT compatibility

> **❝**
> D'abord, la **compatibilité** entre les deux versions pour Macintosh et PC est parfois boiteuse et gêne l'échange de données entre les deux environnements.
> **❞**

compatible 1 *adj* (a) *(non contraire)* compatible (**avec** with); **cela n'est pas compatible avec mon emploi du temps** that won't fit into my schedule
(b) ORDINAT compatible; **ces deux applications ne sont pas compatibles** these two functions are incompatible *or* not compatible; **compatible vers le haut/vers le bas** upward/downward compatible
2 *nm* ORDINAT **compatible (PC)** (PC) compatible

compensable *adj* FIN *(chèque)* clearable, payable; **être compensable à Paris** to be cleared at Paris, to be domiciled in Paris

compensateur, -trice *adj* FIN compensatory

compensation *nf* FIN compensation; *(de chèque)* clearing

compensatoire *adj* FIN compensatory

compenser *vt (perte)* to make up for, to offset; FIN *(chèque)* to clear

compétence *nf* (**a**) *(capacité)* competence; **ses compétences en informatique font de lui le candidat idéal** his computing skills make him the ideal candidate ❑ **compétence technique** technical skill (**b**) JUR area of jurisdiction

compétent, -e *adj* (**a**) *(capable) (personne)* competent (**b**) *(approprié)* appropriate, relevant; **adressez-vous au service compétent** apply to the appropriate *or* relevant department, apply to the department concerned (**c**) JUR *(tribunal, autorité)* competent; **seul le maire est compétent en la matière** only the mayor is competent in this matter

compétiteur, -trice *nm,f* competitor

compétitif, -ive *adj (prix)* competitive

compétition *nf* competition; **il existe une compétition féroce sur le marché de l'informatique** there is fierce competition within the IT market

compétitivité *nf (d'une entreprise, d'une économie)* competitiveness

complément *nm* **un complément d'information est nécessaire** further information is required; **demander un complément d'enquête** to order a more extensive inquiry ❑ **complément (de) retraite** supplementary pension

complémentaire *adj* (**a**) *(supplémentaire)* additional, further; **pour tout renseignement complémentaire s'adresser à...** for further information apply to... (**b**) COMPTA *(écriture)* supplementary

compléter *vt* (**a**) *(remplir) (formulaire)* to complete (**b**) *(ajouter à)* to add to; **compléter une gamme de produits** to add to a range of products

complexe *nm* ÉCON complex; **le complexe industriel de la vallée du Rhône** the Rhone valley industrial complex ❑ **complexe commercial** shopping centre *or* complex; **complexe hôtelier** hotel complex; **complexe industriel** industrial complex

comportement *nm* (**a**) MKTG behaviour ❑ **comportement d'achat** buying *or* purchasing behaviour; **comportement de l'acheteur** buyer *or* purchaser behaviour; **comportement du consommateur** consumer behaviour (**b**) BOURSE, FIN *(du marché, des cours, des actions)* performance

comporter **se comporter** *vpr (fonctionner)* to perform; **ses actions se sont bien comportées** his shares have performed well

composé, -e *adj* FIN *(intérêts)* compound

composer *vt (numéro de téléphone)* to dial

composition *nf (d'un portefeuille)* building up

compostage *nm (d'un billet de transport)* punching

composter *nm (billet de transport)* to punch

comprendre *vt (englober)* to include; **le prix comprend les frais d'envoi** the price includes postage; **la TVA est-elle comprise dans le total?** does the total include VAT?

compresseur de données *nm* ORDINAT data compressor

compression *nf* (**a**) *(réduction)* reduction ❑ **compressions budgétaires** budget cuts; **compression des dépenses** spending cuts; **compression des dépenses budgétaires** budget cuts; **compression du personnel** staff cutbacks (**b**) ORDINAT *(de données)* compression

comprimer *vt* (**a**) *(réduire)* to cut down, to reduce (**b**) ORDINAT *(données)* to compress

> **❝**
> Elles **compriment** leurs marges afin de vendre à un consommateur qui craint toujours pour son travail, qui n'achète que le nécessaire et qui privilégie les premiers prix.
> **❞**

compris, -e *adj (inclus)* included; **service compris/non compris** service included/not included; **six mille francs par mois tout compris** six thousand francs a month all inclusive *or* all in

compromis *nm* compromise, arrangement; **mettre une affaire en compromis** to submit a case to arbitration; **obtenir** *ou* **arriver à un compromis avec ses créanciers** to compound with one's creditors ❑ ASSUR **compromis d'avarie** average bond

> **❝**
> On notera que cette fois, les syndicats ont pris les devants sans attendre l'apparition de ces "coordinations" ... souvent incapables de négocier des **compromis**.
> **❞**

compta *nf* Fam *(abrév* **comptabilité***)* accounts, accounting

comptabilisation *nf* COMPTA posting, entering in the accounts; *(dénombrement)* counting; **faire la comptabilisation de qch** to enter sth in the accounts

comptabiliser *vt* COMPTA to post, to enter in the accounts; *(dénombrer)* to count

comptabilité *nf* (a) *(livres)* accounts; *(technique)* bookkeeping, accounting; **passer qch en comptabilité** to put sth through the books *or* accounts; **tenir la comptabilité** to keep the books *or* the accounts ❑ **comptabilité analytique** cost accounting; **comptabilité budgétaire** budgeting; **comptabilité commerciale** business accounting; **comptabilité de la dépréciation** depreciation accounting; **comptabilité financière** financial accounting; **comptabilité générale** general accounts; *(système)* financial accounting; **comptabilité de gestion** management accounting; **comptabilité informatisée** computerized accounts; **comptabilité en partie double** double-entry bookkeeping; **comptabilité en partie simple** single-entry bookkeeping; **comptabilité de prix de revient** cost accounting; **comptabilité publique** public finance

(b) *(service)* accounts department; **adressez-vous à la comptabilité** apply to the accounts department

comptable 1 *adj (travail)* accounting, bookkeeping; *(machine, méthode, plan)* accounting

2 *nmf* accountant ❑ *Can* **comptable agréé** *Br* chartered accountant, *Am* certified public accountant

comptant 1 *adv* **payer comptant** to pay (in) cash; **payer cent francs comptant** to pay a hundred francs in cash; **acheter/vendre qch comptant** to buy/sell sth for cash

2 *nm* cash; **acheter/vendre qch au comptant** to buy/sell sth for cash; **payable au comptant** *(lors d'un achat) Br* cash *or Am* collect on delivery; *(sur présentation de titre, de connaissement)* payable on presentation; **comptant contre documents** cash against documents

compte (a) COMPTA account; **comptes** *(comptabilité)* accounts; **tenir les comptes** to keep the accounts *or* the books; **faire ses comptes** to make up *or* do one's accounts; **vérifier les comptes** to audit the books ❑ **compte accréditif** charge account; **compte d'achats** purchase account; **compte d'agence** agency account; **comptes analytiques d'exploitation** operational cost accounts; **comptes annuels** annual accounts; **comptes approuvés** certified accounts; **compte bloqué** frozen account, *Am* escrow account; **compte (de) caisse** cash account; **compte de capital** capital account; **compte centralisateur** central account; **compte de charges** expense account; **comptes clients** accounts receivable, *Am* receivables; **compte à créd-** it credit account; **compte créditeur** account in credit, credit account; **compte débiteur** debit account; **compte des dépenses et recettes** income and expenditure account; **compte détaillé** itemized account; **compte d'exploitation** *Br* trading account, *Am* operating account; **comptes de gestion** management accounts; **compte de pertes et profits** appropriation account; **compte de régularisation** *(de l'actif)* prepayments and accrued income; *(du passif)* accruals and deferred income; **compte de résultat** profit and loss account, *Am* income statement; **compte de résultat prévisionnel** interim profit and loss account, *Am* interim income statement; **comptes semestriels** interim accounts; **compte de stock** inventory account; **comptes trimestriels** interim accounts

(b) *(chez un commerçant)* account; **avoir un compte chez qn** to have an account with sb; **(se faire) ouvrir un compte chez qn** to open an account with sb; **mettre** *ou* **inscrire qch sur le compte de qn** to enter sth to sb's account; **mettez-le** *ou* **inscrivez-le à mon compte** charge it to my account; **régler un compte** to settle an account; **pour règlement de tout compte** *(sur facture)* in full settlement ❑ **compte d'abonnement** budget account; **compte client** customer account; **compte crédit** budget account; **compte permanent** *Br* credit account, *Am* charge account

(c) BANQUE account; **ouvrir un compte (en banque)** to open a bank account; **verser de l'argent à son compte, alimenter son compte** to pay money into one's account ❑ **compte bancaire, compte en banque** *Br* bank account, *Am* banking account; **compte de caisse d'épargne** savings account; **compte chèques** *Br* current account, *Am* checking account; **compte chèque postal** = account held at the Post Office, ≃ *Br* giro account; **compte commercial** office *or* business account; **compte conjoint** joint account; **compte courant** *Br* current account, *Am* checking account; **compte créditeur** account in credit, credit balance; **compte débiteur** account in debit, debit balance; **compte à découvert** overdrawn account; **compte de dépôt** deposit account; **compte de dépôt à vue** drawing account; **compte en devises étrangères** foreign currency account; **compte d'épargne** savings account; **compte épargne logement** savings account *(for purchasing a property)*; **compte étranger** foreign account; **compte individuel** personal account; **compte joint** joint account; **compte (sur) livret** savings account; **compte numéroté** numbered account; **compte professionnel** business account; **compte rémunéré** interest-bearing account

(d) **être** *ou* **travailler à son compte** to have one's own business; **s'installer** *ou* **se mettre à son compte** to start one's own business

(e) *(calcul)* calculation; **faire le compte de qch** to add sth up, to calculate sth; **le compte y est** the amount is correct ❑ **compte rond** round sum

(f) *(fonds)* fund ❑ **compte sous mandat de gestion** discretionary fund

"
La crise touche également les banquiers qui doivent eux aussi rétablir leurs **comptes d'exploitation** et leurs bilans à un moment où les contraintes du ratio Cooke se font plus rigoureuses.
"

compte-clé *nm* key account

compter 1 *vt* (a) *(calculer)* to count, to add up (b) *(faire payer)* to charge; **compter qch à qn** to charge sb for sth; **je vous compterai cent francs pour cet article** I'll charge you a hundred francs for this article

2 *vi (calculer)* to count; **à compter de** as from or of; **à compter du 1 janvier** as from 1 January, with effect from 1 January

compte-rendu *nm* report; *(d'une réunion)* minutes

compteur *nm* ORDINAT counter

comptoir *nm* (a) *(bureau)* desk ❑ **comptoir d'enregistrement** check-in desk; **comptoir d'information** information desk; **comptoir de réception** reception desk; **comptoir de vente** sales counter (b) ÉCON *(cartel)* trading syndicate (c) FIN bank; *(de banque)* branch ❑ **comptoir d'escompte** discount house

comptoir-caisse *nm* cash desk

concéder *vt (délai, réduction)* to grant

concentration *nf* ÉCON integration ❑ **concentration horizontale** horizontal integration; **concentration verticale** vertical integration

concepteur, -trice *nm,f* designer ❑ **concepteur rédacteur** copywriter

conception *nf* design ❑ **conception assistée par ordinateur** computer-aided *or* computer-assisted design; **conception des produits** product design

concerner *vt* to concern; **en ce qui concerne** as regards, concerning; **les salariés concernés par cette mesure** the employees concerned *or* affected by this measure

concerté, -e *adj (action, développement)* concerted

concession *nf* concession ❑ **concession exclusive et réciproque** tied outlet

concessionnaire 1 *adj (société)* concessionary

2 *nmf* agent, dealer; *(de licence)* licensee; *(de brevet)* patentee; *(de contrat de franchisage)* franchisee ❑ **concessionnaire exclusif** sole agent *or* dealer; **concessionnaire export** export concessionaire

concevoir *vt (produit)* to design

conciliation *nf* arbitration, conciliation

conclure *vt* (a) *(discours, réunion)* to conclude, to end **(par** with) (b) *(accord, pacte)* to finalize; *(marché)* to clinch; *(vente)* to close; *(entente)* to reach

conclusion *nf (d'un accord, d'un pacte)* finalizing

concordat *nm* composition ❑ **concordat préventif (à la faillite)** composition, legal settlement *(between owners and creditors)*

concordataire *adj (failli)* certified

concours *nm* (a) *(pour obtenir un poste)* competitive examination ❑ **concours externe** external competitive examination; **concours interne** internal competitive examination

(b) *(participation)* participation; **ce projet a été réalisé avec le concours d'Air France** this project was realized with the participation of *or* in association with Air France

concurrence *nf* (a) ÉCON *(concept)* competition; **la concurrence** *(les entreprises concurrentes)* the competition; **faire concurrence à qn/qch** to compete with sb/sth; **être/entrer en concurrence avec qn** to compete with sb; **faire jouer la concurrence** to shop around; **nos prix défient toute concurrence** our prices are unbeatable; **la libre concurrence** free *or* open competition ❑ **concurrence acharnée** cut-throat competition; **concurrence déloyale** unfair competition; **concurrence parfaite** perfect competition; **concurrence pure** pure competition

(b) **à concurrence de, jusqu'à concurrence de** up to, up to the limit of; **vous pouvez être à découvert jusqu'à concurrence de 5 000 francs** your overdraft limit is 5,000 francs

concurrencer *vt* to compete with; **leur nouvelle gamme ne peut concurrencer la nôtre** their new line can't compete with ours; **ils nous concurrencent dangereusement** they're very dangerous *or* serious competitors for us

concurrent, -e **1** *adj (industries, produits)* competing, rival
2 *nm,f* competitor, rival; *(pour un poste)* candidate ◘ *concurrent principal* major competitor; MKTG *concurrent tardif* late entrant

concurrentiel, -elle *adj* competitive

condition *nf* (**a**) *(stipulation)* condition, stipulation; **sans condition** *(offre)* unconditional; **acheter des marchandises sous condition** to buy goods on sale or return; **signer qch sans condition/sous condition** to sign sth unconditionally/conditionally *or* provisionally; **envoyer des marchandises à condition** to send goods on approval; **conditions** *(d'une vente, d'un accord, d'un contrat)* terms; **faire de meilleures conditions** to give sb better terms ◘ *conditions d'admission* admission requirements; *conditions d'emploi* conditions of employment; *conditions de livraison* terms of delivery; *conditions de paiement* terms (of payment); *condition préalable* prerequisite; *condition provisionnelle* proviso
(**b**) **conditions** *(circonstances)* conditions ◘ *conditions économiques (du marché)* economic situation; *conditions de travail* working conditions; *conditions de vie* living conditions
(**c**) *(état)* condition; **les marchandises nous sont parvenues en bonne condition** the goods arrived in good condition

conditionné, -e *adj* prepacked, prepackaged

conditionnel, -elle *adj (vente, offre)* conditional; *(acceptation, endos)* qualified; *(clause)* provisory

conditionnement *nm (fait d'emballer, emballage)* packaging

conditionner *vt* to package

conditionneur, -euse *nm,f* packer

confectionner *vt* to manufacture; **confectionné sur demande** made up to order

conférence *nf (congrès)* conference; *(réunion)* meeting; **il est en conférence** he's in a meeting ◘ *conférence de presse* press conference; *conférence au sommet* summit (conference)

conférencier, -ère *nm,f* speaker

confidentialité *nf* confidentiality ◘ ORDINAT *confidentialité des données* data privacy

confidentiel, -elle *adj (dossier, rapport, information)* confidential; **confidentiel** *(sur document)* private and confidential

confier *vt* **confier qch à qn** *(mission, tâche, dossier)* to entrust sth to sb, to entrust sb with sth

configurable *adj* ORDINAT configurable

configuration *nf* ORDINAT configuration ◘ *configuration par défaut* default setting; *configuration matérielle* hardware configuration

configurer *vt* ORDINAT to configure

confirmation *nf* confirmation

confirmer *vt* to confirm; **les derniers chiffres confirment cette tendance** the latest figures confirm this trend; **confirmer qch par écrit** to confirm sth in writing

confisquer *vt* to confiscate, to seize

conflit *nm* dispute ◘ *conflits sociaux, conflits du travail* industrial *or* labour disputes

conforme *adj* **conforme à la demande** as per order; **conforme à la description** as represented; **conforme à l'échantillon** true to sample

conformément à *prép* in accordance with; **conformément à votre demande du 13 avril** in accordance with *or* as per your request of 13 April

conformer **se conformer** *vpr* **se conformer à qch** *(décision, règlement)* to abide by sth, to comply with sth

conformité *nf (d'un produit aux normes)* compliance (**à** with); **en conformité avec** in accordance with

conforter *vt* **conforter ses positions** to consolidate one's position

confrère *nm (de profession)* colleague; *(d'association)* fellow member

congé *nm* (**a**) *(arrêt de travail)* leave (of absence) ◘ *congé pour convenance personnelle* compassionate leave; *congé de longue durée* extended leave; *congé de maladie* sick leave; *congé de maternité* maternity leave; *congé de naissance* paternity leave; *congé parental d'éducation* = unpaid maternity or paternity leave; *congé de paternité* paternity leave; *congé sabbatique* sabbatical
(**b**) *(vacances) Br* holiday, *Am* vacation; **être en congé** to be on *Br* holiday *or Am* vacation;

prendre un congé d'une semaine to take a week off; **un après-midi de congé** an afternoon off ▢ *congé annuel Br* annual leave, *Am* vacation leave; *congés payés Br* paid leave *or* holidays, *Am* paid vacation; *congé sans solde Br* unpaid leave *or* holidays, *Am* unpaid vacation

(c) *(avis de renvoi)* notice; **demander son congé** to hand in one's resignation, to give in one's notice; **donner (son) congé à qn** *(à un employé)* to give sb his/her notice, to dismiss sb; **donner congé à qn** *(à un locataire)* to give sb notice to quit; *(à un propriétaire)* to give sb notice of leaving

congédiement *nm* dismissal

congédier *vt* to dismiss

conglomérat *nm* ÉCON conglomerate

congrès *nm* congress ▢ *congrès annuel* annual congress

congressiste *nmf* participant *(at a congress)*

conjoint, -e 1 *adj (dette, compte, responsabilité)* joint

2 *nm,f* ADMIN spouse; **il faut l'accord des deux conjoints** the agreement of both husband and wife is necessary

conjointement *adv* jointly; **conjointement et solidairement** jointly and severally

conjoncture *nf* ÉCON **conjoncture (économique)** economic situation, economic circumstances; **on assiste à une dégradation de la conjoncture économique** a deterioration in the economic situation is taking place

>
> Morosité de la **conjoncture**, tassement des revenus, menaces sur l'emploi, toutes les conditions sont réunies depuis quelques années pour que les ménages réduisent leur train de vie.
>

conjoncturel, -elle *adj* ÉCON *(chômage, fluctuations)* cyclical; *(prévisions, stratégie, politique)* economic

conjoncturiste *nm* ÉCON economic analyst *or* planner

connaissance *nf* **(a) prendre connaissance de qch** *(dossier, rapport)* to acquaint oneself with sth **(b)** MKTG *connaissance de la marque* brand familiarity, brand awareness

connaissement *nm* bill of lading, waybill ▢ *connaissement aérien* air waybill; *connaissement clausé* dirty bill of lading; *con-naissement direct* through bill; *connaissement net* clean bill of lading

connecter ORDINAT **1** *vt* to connect; **connecté en anneau/bus/étoile** in a ring/bus/star configuration; **connecté en série** series-connected

2 se connecter *vpr* **se connecter à un système** to log on to a system

connectivité *nf* ORDINAT connectivity

connexion *nf* ORDINAT connection

conquérir *vt (marché, part de marché)* to conquer; **l'entreprise a réussi à conquérir de nouvelles parts de marché en dépit de la récession** the company has managed to conquer new market shares despite the recession

conquête *nf (d'un marché, d'une part de marché)* conquest; **la conquête de nouveaux marchés en Asie est une des priorités de l'entreprise** conquering new Asian markets is one of the company's priorities

consacrer *vt (budget, fonds)* to devote (**à** to); **avez-vous dix minutes à me consacrer?** can you spare me ten minutes?

conseil *nm* **(a)** *(personne)* consultant ▢ *conseil en communication* media consultant; *conseil financier* financial consultant *or* adviser; *conseil fiscal* tax consultant; *conseil en gestion* management consultant; *conseil juridique* legal adviser; *conseil en marketing, conseil en mercatique* marketing consultant; *conseil en promotion, conseil en publicité* advertising consultant; *conseil en recrutement* recruitment consultant

(b) *(assemblée)* council, committee; *(d'une entreprise)* board; *(réunion)* meeting; **la banque fait partie du conseil** the bank is represented on the board ▢ *conseil d'administration* board of directors; *conseil d'arbitrage* conciliation *or* arbitration board; *conseil de direction* management committee; *conseil économique* economic council; *conseil d'entreprise* works committee; *Conseil de l'Europe* Council of Europe; *conseil général* regional council; *Conseil national du crédit* National Credit Council; *conseil des prud'hommes* industrial tribunal; *conseil régional* regional council; *Conseil de sécurité (de l'ONU)* Security Council; *conseil de surveillance* supervisory board; *conseil syndical* trade union council

(c) *(pour aider)* advice ▢ *conseil en placements* investment advice

> Le **Conseil d'administration** de TOTAL, réuni le 7 septembre 1993, a examiné les comptes consolidés du premier semestre 1993 du Groupe.

conseiller¹, -ère *nm,f* (**a**) *(spécialiste)* adviser, consultant ☐ *conseiller de clientèle* consumer adviser; *conseiller commercial* marketing *or* sales consultant; *conseiller de direction* management consultant; *conseiller économique* economic adviser; *conseiller fiscal* tax consultant; *conseiller en gestion (d'entreprise)* management consultant; *conseiller juridique* legal adviser; *conseiller en marketing, conseiller en mercatique* marketing consultant; *conseiller en placements* investment adviser; *conseiller professionnel* careers adviser *or* counsellor; *conseiller technique* technical adviser (**b**) *(membre d'un conseil)* councillor ☐ *conseiller municipal* local councillor

conseiller² *vt* to advise; **conseiller qch à qn** to recommend sth to sb; **conseiller à qn de faire qch** to advise sb to do sth

consentement *nm* consent; **donner son consentement à qch** to consent to sth ☐ *consentement exprès* formal consent

consentir 1 *vt (prêt)* to grant; *(remise)* to allow; **on m'a consenti une remise de 10%/un délai supplémentaire de quinze jours** I was allowed a 10% discount/another two weeks
2 *vi* to consent, to agree (**à** to)

conservateur, -trice *nm,f conservateur des hypothèques* registrar of mortgages

consignataire *nmf* (**a**) *(dépositaire)* depository (**b**) *(destinataire)* consignee

consignateur, -trice *nm,f* consigner, shipper

consignation *nf* (**a**) *(d'argent)* deposit (**b**) *(de marchandises)* consignment; **en consignation** on consignment; **envoyer qch à qn en consignation** to consign sth to sb, to send sth to sb on consignment

consigne *nf* (**a**) *(pour les bagages) Br* left-luggage office, *Am* checkroom ☐ *consigne automatique* lockers
(**b**) DOUANES **laisser des marchandises en consigne** to consign goods; **il a dû laisser des marchandises en consigne à la douane** his goods were held up at customs
(**c**) *(d'emballage)* deposit

(**d**) *(ordres)* orders, instructions; **suivre les consignes** to follow orders

consigné, -e *adj (emballage)* returnable

consigner *vt* (**a**) *(bagages) Br* to leave at the left-luggage office, *Am* to check
(**b**) DOUANES *(marchandises)* to consign (**à** to); **ses marchandises ont été consignées par la douane car il n'avait pas les documents requis** his goods were held up at customs because he didn't have the necessary papers
(**c**) *(emballage)* to charge a deposit on
(**d**) *(argent)* to deposit
(**e**) *(noter)* to record, to put down

console *nf* ORDINAT console ☐ *console de visualisation* visual display unit, VDU

consolidation *nf* FIN *(d'une dette)* funding, financing; *(des bénéfices, des fonds, d'un bilan)* consolidation ☐ MKTG *consolidation de ligne* line filling

consolidé, -e FIN 1 *adj (dette)* funded, financed; *(bénéfices, fonds, bilan)* consolidated
2 *nm* **consolidés** consols

consolider *vt* FIN *(dette)* to fund, to finance; *(bénéfices, fonds, bilan)* to consolidate; **le franc a consolidé son avance à la Bourse** the franc has strengthened its lead on the Stock Exchange

consommable 1 *adj* consumable
2 *nm* ORDINAT **consommables** consumables

consommateur, -trice *nm,f* ÉCON consumer; **producteurs et consommateurs** producers and consumers ☐ *consommateur cible* target consumer; MKTG *consommateur final* end-user

consommation *nf* ÉCON consumption ☐ COMPTA *consommations de l'exercice* total annual expenses; *consommation intérieure* home consumption; *consommation de masse* mass consumption; *consommation des ménages* household consumption; *consommation mondiale* world consumption; *consommation par tête* per capita consumption

consommatique *nf* consumer research

consommatisme *nm* consumerism

consommer *vt* to consume

consomptible *adj* consumable

consortial, -e *adj* consortium, syndicated

consortium *nm* consortium, syndicate ☐ *consortium de banques* banking consortium

constant, -e *adj* FIN constant; **en francs/dollars constants** in constant francs/dollars

constat nm JUR certified statement *or* report; **dresser** *ou* **faire un constat** to draw up a report ❑ ***constat amiable*** = report of road accident agreed by the parties involved

constatation nf (**a**) ASSUR ***constatation des dommages*** assessment of damages (**b**) COMPTA ***constatation de stock*** stocktake

constaté, -e adj FIN *(valeur)* registered; **constaté d'avance** *(charge)* prepaid

constater vt (**a**) *(observer) (augmentation, hausse, baisse)* to note (**b**) ASSUR *(dommages)* to assess

constituer 1 vt (**a**) *(créer) (société, comité, association)* to form, to set up; *(capital, stocks)* to build up (**b**) *(représenter)* to constitute, to represent; **ceci constitue une faute professionnelle grave** this constitutes serious professional misconduct; **ceci constitue un excellent résultat pour l'entreprise** this represents an excellent result for the company **2 se constituer** vpr **se constituer en SARL** to form a limited company; **se constituer un portefeuille de clients** to build up a client portfolio

constitutif, -ive adj JUR constitutive

constitution nf *(d'une société, d'un comité, d'une association)* formation, setting up; *(du capital, des stocks)* building up

constructeur nm builder ❑ ***constructeur automobile*** car manufacturer

constructeur-promoteur nm property developer

constructible adj *(terrain)* suitable for building on

construction nf building, construction; **être en construction** to be under construction

construire vt to build, to construct

consultant, -e nm,f consultant

consultatif, -ive adj *(comité, conseil, document)* consultative, advisory; **avoir une voix consultative** to be present in an advisory capacity; **à titre consultatif** in an advisory capacity

consulter vt to consult

contact nm (**a**) *(personne)* contact; **il a de nombreux contacts dans la profession** he has a lot of contacts in the industry (**b**) *(lien)* contact; **prendre contact** *ou* **se mettre en contact avec qn** to get in touch *or* in contact with sb

contacter vt *(personne)* to contact; **ils l'ont contacté pour un entretien** they contacted

him to arrange an interview; **on peut me contacter par téléphone au bureau** I can be reached by phone at the office

container = **conteneur**

contaminé, -e adj ORDINAT **contaminé par un virus** virus-infected

conteneur nm container

conteneurisation nf containerization

conteneuriser vt to containerize

contenir vt *(inflation)* to control, to check

contentieux nm *(conflit)* dispute; JUR litigation; *(service)* legal department; **avoir un contentieux avec qn** to be in dispute with sb; **les contentieux en cours** the claims being disputed ❑ ***service du contentieux*** legal department

> Plus les emprunteurs bénéficient d'un investissement initial important, plus le risque de **contentieux** est faible.

contenu nm *(d'un colis)* contents; *(d'une lettre, d'un document)* content

contestation nf (**a**) *(d'une loi, d'un testament, d'un document)* contesting; *(d'un droit)* contesting, questioning (**b**) *(litige)* dispute

contester vt *(loi, testament, document)* to contest; *(droit)* to contest, to question

contingent nm quota ❑ ***contingents d'exportation*** export quotas; ***contingents d'importation*** import quotas

> Si la signature de FO semblait quasiment acquise depuis jeudi, elle bloquait hier matin sur l'ampleur du **contingent** des heures supplémentaires. L'UIMM voulait, au départ, le voir porter à 280 heures annuelles.

contingentement nm (**a**) *(imposition de quotas)* fixing of quotas; **le contingentement des importations** the fixing of import quotas (**b**) *(système)* quota system of distribution

contingenter vt *(importations, exportations)* to fix quotas on, to limit ❑ ***produits contingentés*** fixed quota products

continuité d'exploitation nf FIN going-concern status

contractant, -e JUR **1** adj contracting **2** nm,f contracting party

contracter vt *(dette)* to incur, to contract; *(emprunt)* to contract; **contracter une assu-**

rance to take out insurance *or* an insurance policy

contraction *nf (de l'activité, de la demande, du crédit)* reduction (**de** in)

contractuel, -elle **1** *adj (main-d'œuvre, garantie)* contractual; *(droits)* granted by contract
2 *nm,f* contract employee

> ... une stabilisation **contractuelle** des relations de travail peut être le vecteur d'une grande souplesse d'adaptation.

contrat *nm (accord)* contract; **être lié par contrat** to be bound by contract; **passer un contrat (avec qn)** to enter into a contract (with sb); **rédiger** *ou* **dresser un contrat** to draw up a contract; **résilier un contrat** to cancel a contract ❑ ADMIN *contrat aidé* = employment contract whereby part of an employee's salary is paid by the state; *contrat d'apprentissage* contract of apprenticeship; *contrat d'assurance* insurance policy; *contrat d'assurance-vie* life insurance policy; *contrat de bail* lease agreement; *contrat de base* principal contract; *contrat collectif* group contract; *contrat à durée déterminée* fixed-term contract; *contrat à durée indéterminée* permanent contract; *contrat d'embauche Br* employment contract, contract of employment, *Am* labor contract; *contrat d'emploi-solidarité* = short-term contract subsidized by the government; *contrat exclusif* sole contract; *contrat de location* rental agreement; *contrat de mission d'intérim* temporary contract; *contrat notarié* notarized contract; *contrat à plein temps* full-time contract; *contrat de prêt* loan agreement; *contrat de qualification* employment and training contract; *contrat de représentation exclusive* sole agency contract; *contrat de service* service contract; *contrat social* social contract; *contrat temporaire* temporary contract; *contrat à temps partiel* part-time contract; *contrat à temps plein* full-time contract; FIN, BOURSE *contrat à terme* forward contract, futures contract; *contrat de transport* contract of carriage; *contrat de travail Br* employment contract, contract of employment, *Am* labor contract; *contrat de travail temporaire* temporary contract; *contrat de vente* bill of sale, sales contract, sales agreement

> Les **contrats de qualification** et **d'apprentissage** permettront au Crédit Agricole d'accroître la qualification initiale de ses nouveaux salariés sans pour autant tomber dans un travers désormais dénoncé par l'ensemble de la profession bancaire: la surqualification.

contre-analyse *nf* check analysis

contre-assurance *nf* reinsurance

contre-attaque *nf* countermove

contrebalancer *vt* to offset; **les bénéfices ne contrebalancent plus les pertes** profits are no longer balancing losses

contrebande *nf (activité)* smuggling; *(marchandises)* contraband; **faire de la contrebande** to smuggle goods; **faire entrer des marchandises en contrebande** to smuggle in goods; **de contrebande** smuggled

contre-écriture *nf* COMPTA contra-entry

contre-épreuve *nf* cross-check

contre-expertise *nf* second valuation

contrefaçon *nf* (**a**) *(d'une marque)* counterfeiting; *(d'un brevet, d'un droit de reproduction)* infringement
(**b**) *(d'un billet de banque, de monnaie)* forgery; *(d'un produit)* imitation

> Les industriels sont d'accord sur un point: l'urgence d'une action à l'encontre des pays bafouant le droit du travail ou qui laissent libre cours à la **contrefaçon**.

contrefacteur, -trice *nm,f* (**a**) *(d'une marque)* counterfeiter; *(d'un brevet, d'un droit de reproduction)* infringer (**b**) *(d'un billet de banque, de monnaie)* forger; *(d'un produit)* imitator

contrefaire *vt* (**a**) *(marque)* to counterfeit; *(brevet, droit de reproduction)* to infringe (**b**) *(billet de banque, monnaie)* to forge; **contrefaire des produits de luxe** to manufacture imitation luxury goods

contremaître, -esse *nm,f* foreman, *f* forewoman

contremarché *nm* countermove

contre-offensive *nf* counter-offer

contre-OPA *nf* counter-bid

contre-ordre *nm* counter-order; **sauf contre-ordre de votre part** unless we hear from you to the contrary

contrepartie *nf* (**a**) *(compensation)* compensation; **en contrepartie** in return (**de** for) ❏ *contrepartie financière* financial compensation; **vous aurez la contrepartie financière de la perte subie** you will be financially compensated for the loss incurred
(**b**) FIN *(dans une transaction)* other party
(**c**) COMPTA contra; *(d'une inscription)* counterpart; *(d'un registre)* duplicate; **en contrepartie** per contra
(**d**) *(de document)* counterpart, duplicate
(**e**) BOURSE hedging, market making; **faire (de) la contrepartie** to operate against one's client

contre-passation *nf* (**a**) COMPTA journal entry, contra-entry; *(d'un article, d'une entrée)* reversing, transferring (**b**) FIN *(d'un effet)* return, endorsement, backing

contre-passer *vt* (**a**) COMPTA *(article, entrée)* to reverse, to transfer (**b**) FIN *(effet)* to return, to endorse, to back

contreseing *nm* counter-signature

contresigner *vt* to countersign

contretemps *nm* hitch, mishap; **nous vous prions de nous excuser de ce contretemps** please excuse us for this unexpected inconvenience

contre-valeur *nf* FIN exchange value; **pour la contre-valeur de 300 francs** in exchange for 300 francs

contribuable *nmf* taxpayer

> ❝
> Nec plus ultra de la défiscalisation, la location en meublé professionnel permet d'alléger sensiblement l'impôt sur le revenu pour les **contribuables** les plus imposés.
> ❞

contribuer contribuer à *vt ind* to contribute to; **ceci a contribué à faire baisser l'inflation** this helped to bring down inflation

contributeur *nm* UE contributor ❏ *contributeur net* net contributor

contribution *nf* ADMIN *(impôt)* tax; **contributions** *(à l'État)* taxes; *(à la collectivité locale) Br* ≃ council tax, *Am* ≃ local taxes; **(bureau des) contributions** tax office, *Br* ≃ Inland Revenue, *Am* ≃ Internal Revenue; **lever** *ou* **percevoir une contribution** to collect *or* levy a tax; **payer ses contributions** to pay one's taxes ❏ *contributions directes* direct taxation; *contribution foncière* land tax; *contributions indirectes* indirect taxation; *contribution sociale généralisée* = income-based tax deducted at source as a contribution to paying off the French social security budget deficit

contrôlable *adj* *(inflation, chômage)* controllable

contrôle *nm* (**a**) *(de l'information, de déclarations)* checking, verification; *(des employés, du travail, des marchandises)* inspection; COMPTA *(des comptes)* checking, auditing ❏ *contrôle bancaire* banking controls; COMPTA *contrôle du bilan* audit; *contrôle budgétaire* budgetary control; FIN *contrôle des changes* (foreign) exchange control; *contrôle de la comptabilité* accounting control; FIN *contrôle de comptes* audit; MKTG *contrôle continu* monitoring; *contrôle de douanes, contrôle douanier* customs control; *contrôle d'efficacité du marketing ou mercatique* marketing efficiency study; *contrôle financier* financial control; FIN *contrôle fiscal* tax inspection; *contrôle de gestion* management control; *contrôles à l'importation* import controls; *contrôle des points de ventes* store audit; *contrôle de présence* timekeeping; *contrôle des prix* price control; *contrôle de (la) qualité* quality control; *contrôle de la qualité totale* total quality control; *contrôle des stocks Br* stock *or Am* inventory control
(**b**) *(maîtrise)* control: **prendre le contrôle d'une entreprise** to take over a company
(**c**) ORDINAT control ❏ *contrôle d'accès* access control; *contrôle du curseur* cursor control

> ❝
> Dans l'espoir d'enrayer la chute du rouble, la Banque centrale russe vient de mettre en place un **contrôle des changes.**
> ❞

contrôler *vt* (**a**) *(information, déclarations)* to check, to verify; *(employés, travail, marchandises)* to inspect; COMPTA *(comptes)* to check, to audit; **contrôler les livres** to check the books
(**b**) *(prix, inflation, chômage)* to control
(**c**) *(entreprise)* to control; **ce groupe contrôle 10% de notre entreprise** this group controls 10% of our company
(**d**) ORDINAT **contrôlé par le logiciel** software-controlled; **contrôlé par menu** menu-driven, menu-controlled; **contrôlé par ordinateur** computer-controlled

contrôleur, -euse 1 *nm,f* (**a**) *(des comptes)* auditor ❏ *contrôleur des contributions* tax inspector, inspector of taxes; *contrôleur du crédit* credit controller; *contrôleur des douanes* customs inspector; *contrôleur financier* financial con-

troller; **contrôleur de gestion** management controller; **contrôleur des impôts** tax inspector, inspector of taxes; **contrôleur aux liquidations** controller in bankruptcy (**b**) *(du travail)* supervisor
   2 *nm* ORDINAT **contrôleur d'affichage** display *or* screen controller; **contrôleur de bus** bus controller; **contrôleur de disque** disk controller

convenir convenir de *vt ind* to agree on, to come to an agreement on; **convenir d'un prix/d'une date (avec qn)** to agree on a price/date (with sb)

convention *nf* agreement; JUR *(d'un contrat)* article, clause ❏ **convention collective** collective (bargaining) agreement; **convention écrite** written agreement; **convention monétaire** monetary agreement; **convention verbale** verbal agreement

> ❝
>
> Les fabricants de sucre avaient partiellement dénoncé la **convention collective** qui régit les droits des salariés dans la branche.
>
> ❞

conventionné, -e *adj (médecin, clinique)* registered with the health system, *Br* ≃ NHS; *(prix, honoraires)* agreed, set

convenu, -e *adj (prix, honoraires)* agreed, set; **comme convenu, les marchandises commandées seront livrées le 22 courant** as agreed, the goods ordered will be delivered on the 22nd

conversion *nf* (**a**) FIN *(d'argent, de devises étrangères, de titres, d'un emprunt)* conversion ❏ **taux de conversion** rate of exchange, exchange rate (**b**) ORDINAT *(de données)* conversion ❏ **conversion de fichier** file conversion

convertibilité *nf* FIN convertibility

convertible FIN **1** *adj (obligation, monnaie)* convertible (**en** into)
   2 *nf* convertible

> ❝
>
> Rappelons que les **convertibles** sont des obligations à taux fixe émises par des entreprises privées pour une durée de 5 à 8 ans et pouvant être échangées à tout moment contre des actions.
>
> ❞

convertir *vt* (**a**) FIN *(argent, devises étrangères, titres, emprunt)* to convert (**en** into); **convertir des valeurs en espèces** to convert securities into cash; **convertir des rentes** to convert stock (**b**) ORDINAT *(données)* to con-

vert; **convertir un système en numérique** to digitize a system

convertissement *nm* FIN *(de valeurs en espèces)* conversion (**en** into)

convertisseur analogique numérique *nm* ORDINAT digitizer

convivial, -e *adj (ordinateur, machine)* user-friendly

convivialité *nf (d'un ordinateur, d'une machine)* user-friendliness

convocation *nf* (**a**) *(d'une assemblée)* convening (**b**) *(d'un employé, d'un candidat)* summoning

convoquer *vt* (**a**) *(assemblée)* to call together, to convene; **convoquer les actionnaires** to call *or* summon the shareholders to a meeting; **convoquer une assemblée générale** to call a general meeting
   (**b**) *(employé, candidat)* to call in; **le directeur m'a convoqué** the manager called me in; **elle m'a convoqué dans son bureau** she called me into her office; **ils m'ont convoqué pour passer un entretien** they've called me in for an interview

coopératif, -ive ÉCON **1** *adj (société, banque)* co-operative
   2 *nf* **coopérative** co-operative, co-op ❏ **coopérative agricole** agricultural co-operative; **coopérative ouvrière** workers' co-operative; **coopérative de production** producers' co-operative; **coopérative vinicole** wine co-operative

coopération *nf* ÉCON co-operation ❏ **société de coopération** co-operative society

coopératisme *nm* ÉCON co-operation, co-operative system

cooptation *nf* co-option

coopter *vt* to co-opt

coordinateur, -trice **1** *adj* coordinating
   2 *nm,f* coordinator

coordination *nf (d'ouvriers)* committee

> ❝
>
> on notera que cette fois, les syndicats ont pris les devants, sans attendre l'apparition de ces **coordinations**, plus ou moins noyautées par l'ultragauche et souvent incapable de négocier des compromis.
>
> ❞

coordonnées *nfpl* name, address and telephone number; **laissez-moi vos coordonnées et je vous contacterai** leave me your details and I'll contact you

coparticipant, -e *nm,f* JUR copartner

coparticipation *nf* JUR copartnership; **coparticipation des employés dans les bénéfices** profit-sharing

co-patronage *nm* co-sponsoring, co-sponsorship

copie *nf* (**a**) *(d'un document, d'une lettre)* copy; **faire une copie de qch** to copy sth, to make a copy of sth □ ADMIN, JUR **copie authentique** certified copy; **copie au carbone** carbon copy; **copie certifiée conforme** certified copy; **copie conforme (à l'original)** true *or* exact copy; **pour copie conforme** *(sur document)* certified true copy; **copie papier** paper copy; MKTG **copie stratégie (créative)** (creative) copy strategy; **copie de travail** working copy
(**b**) ORDINAT copy □ **copie de bloc** copy block; **copie en clair** hard copy, printout; **copie de disquette** *(commande DOS)* disk copy; **copie sur papier** hard copy, printout; **copie de sauvegarde** backup copy; **copie de sûreté** backup copy

copier *vt* ORDINAT to copy; **copier qch sur le disque dur** to copy sth onto hard disk

copier-coller *nm* ORDINAT copy-and-paste

copieur *nm* (photo)copier

coporteur *nm* FIN joint holder

coposséder *vt* JUR to own jointly, to have joint ownership of

copossesseur *nm* JUR joint owner

copossession *nf* JUR joint ownership

copreneur, -euse *nm,f* JUR co-lessee, co-tenant

coprésidence *nf* co-chairmanship

coprésident, -e *nm,f* co-chairman, *f* co-chairwoman

coprocesseur *nm* ORDINAT co-processor □ **coprocesseur arithmétique** maths co-processor

coproducteur, -trice *nm,f* coproducer, joint producer

coproduction *nf* coproduction

copropriétaire *nmf* JUR joint owner, co-owner

copropriété *nf* JUR joint ownership, co-ownership

copyright *nm* copyright

corbeille *nf* (**a**) BOURSE trading floor □ **corbeille des obligations** bond-trading ring (**b**) ORDINAT wastebasket, *Am* trash

(**c**) *(panier)* **corbeille à courrier** desk tray; **corbeille à papier** paper tray

corporatif, -ive *adj (institution, système)* corporative; *(image, esprit)* corporate

corporation *nf* corporate body □ **corporation professionnelle** professional body

corps *nm* **corps constitué** corporate body; **corps de métier** trade

correcteur *nm* ORDINAT checker □ **correcteur liquide** correcting fluid, *Br* Tippex®, *Am* whiteout; ORDINAT **correcteur d'orthographe, correcteur orthographique** spellchecker

correction *nf* (**a**) **correction des variations saisonnières** seasonal adjustment (**b**) ORDINAT **correction d'orthographe, correction orthographique** spellcheck

correspondance *nf* correspondence; **être en correspondance avec qn** to be in correspondence with sb; **référence à rappeler dans toutes les correspondances** please quote this reference number in all correspondence □ **correspondance commerciale** business correspondence

corriger *vt* to correct; **corriger qch à la hausse/à la baisse** *(chiffre)* to round sth up/down; **en données corrigées des variations saisonnières** seasonally-adjusted

cosignataire *nm* co-signatory

cosignature *nf* co-signature

cosigner *vt* to co-sign

cotation *nf* BOURSE quotation, listing □ **cotation en continu** continuous trading; **cotation à la corbeille** floor trading; **cotation au cours du marché** market quotation; **cotation de l'or** gold fixing; **cotation par téléphone** telephone dealing

cote *nf* (**a**) BOURSE *(valeur)* quotation; *(liste)* share index; **inscrit** *ou* **admis à la cote** listed *or* quoted on the Stock Exchange; **retirer qch de la cote** *(société, actions)* to delist sth; **hors cote** *(actions)* unlisted; *(marché) Br* unofficial, *Am* over-the-counter □ **cote de clôture** closing price; **cote officielle** official list; **cote des prix** official list, official share list
(**b**) JUR *(d'un document)* (classification) mark (**c**) ADMIN assessment □ **cote foncière** assessment on land; **cote mobilière** property assessment
(**d**) *(de dépenses, d'impôts)* quote, share, proportion

coté, -e *adj* BOURSE listed, quoted; **non coté** unlisted, unquoted; **être coté à 100 francs** to be trading at 100 francs

"

Tant qu'il n'est pas **coté** en Bourse, Amadeus reste discret sur ses bénéfices.

"

coter vt (**a**) BOURSE to list, to quote; **des valeurs qui seront cotées en Bourse demain** shares which will go on the Stock Exchange tomorrow; **coter à l'ouverture/à la clôture** to open/close (**b**) JUR (documents) to classify; **coté, daté et paraphé** numbered, dated and signed

cotisant, -e nm,f (**a**) (à une organisation) subscribing member (**b**) (à une caisse, à une mutuelle) contributor

cotisation nf (**a**) (à une organisation) subscription (**b**) (à une caisse, à une mutuelle) contribution □ **cotisations maladie** health insurance contributions; **cotisation ouvrière** employee's contribution; **cotisation patronale** employer's contribution; **cotisations à la Sécurité sociale** ≃ National Insurance contributions; **cotisations sociales** ≃ National Insurance and National Health contributions; **cotisation syndicale** union dues

"

Dans l'Hexagone, les **cotisations sociales** constituent 45% des prélèvements obligatoires, contre 38,6% en Allemagne.

"

cotiser vi (**a**) (à une organisation) to subscribe (**à** to) (**b**) (à une caisse de retraite, à une mutuelle) to contribute, to pay one's contributions (**à** to); **cotiser à la Sécurité sociale** ≃ to pay one's National Insurance (contributions)

coulage nm (perte) wastage; (vol) petty theft; (fuite) leakage

couler 1 vt (affaire, entreprise) to bring down, to cause to go under
2 vi (affaire, entreprise) to go under

coulisse nf BOURSE outside market, kerb

coulissier nm BOURSE outside broker, kerb broker

coupe nf cut □ **coupes budgétaires** budget cuts; **coupe claire** drastic cut; **coupe sombre** drastic cut

"

… les **coupes claires** dans les dépenses de santé, dans les pensions et les retraites ponctionneront encore le pouvoir d'achat.

"

coupe-papier nm letter opener

couper-coller nm ORDINAT cut-and-paste

coupon nm FIN coupon □ **coupon d'action** coupon; **coupon attaché** cum dividend or coupon; **coupon détaché, coupon échu** ex dividend or coupon; **coupon de vol** flight coupon

couponing, couponnage nm FIN couponing

coupon-prime nm gift voucher

coupon-réponse nm reply coupon □ **coupon-réponse international** international reply coupon

coupure nf FIN denomination; **coupure de 50 francs** 50-fránc note; **50 000 francs en petites coupures** 50,000 francs in small notes or denominations; **en coupures usagées** in used notes

"

Les banques, particulièrement concernées par la circulation des **coupures**, ne verraient pas d'un mauvais œil l'avènement d'une monnaie sans papier.

"

cour nf (tribunal) court □ **Cour d'Appel** Br ≃ Court of Appeal, Am ≃ appelate court; **Cour de cassation** ≃ Supreme Court of Appeal; **la Cour des comptes** ≃ the Audit Office; **Cour européenne des droits de l'homme** European Court of Human Rights

courant, -e 1 adj (**a**) (en cours) current; **l'année courante** the current year; **le cinq (du mois) courant** the fifth of this month; **fin courant** at the end of this month (**b**) (marque, taille) standard
2 nm trend; **le courant économique actuel** the present economic situation

courbe nf curve; (graphe) graph □ COMPTA **courbe des coûts** cost curve; ÉCON **courbe de croissance** growth curve; MKTG **courbe du cycle de vie** (d'un produit) lifecycle curve; MKTG **courbe de la demande** demand curve; MKTG **courbe d'expérience** experience curve; **courbe d'investissement** investment curve; MKTG **courbe de l'offre** supply curve; **courbe des prix** price curve; **courbe des salaires** salary curve; **courbe des taux** yield curve; **courbe des ventes** sales chart

courir vi (intérêts) to accrue; (bail) to run; **les intérêts qui courent** the accruing interest; **le bail n'a plus qu'un an à courir** the lease has only one more year to run; **le mois qui court** the current month

courrier nm mail, *Br* post; **par retour du courrier** by return of post; **dépouiller son courrier** to go through *or* open one's mail □ *courrier de départ* outgoing mail; *courrier électronique* electronic mail, e-mail; *courrier interne* internal mail

cours nm (**a**) *(d'argent)* currency; **avoir cours** to be legal tender □ *cours forcé* forced currency; *cours légal* legal tender; **avoir cours légal** to be legal tender
(**b**) FIN, BOURSE *(d'une action)* price, quotation; *(de devises)* rate; **au cours (du jour)** at the current daily price; **quel est le cours du sucre?** what is the price *or* quotation for sugar?; **premier cours** opening price □ *cours en Bourse* official price; *cours du change* rate of exchange, exchange rate; *cours de clôture* closing price; *cours des devises* foreign exchange rate; *cours du disponible* spot rate; *cours étranger* foreign exchange; *cours hors Bourse, cours hors cote* unofficial price; *cours du marché* market price *or* rate; *cours du marché au comptant* current market spot rate; *cours officiel* official exchange rate; *cours d'ouverture* opening price; *cours de rachat* buying-in price; *cours spot* spot price; *(de devises)* spot rate; *cours à terme* forward rate; *cours vendeur* offer price; *cours à vue* spot rate
(**c**) **en cours** *(affaires)* in hand, outstanding; *(travaux, négociations)* in progress; *(année)* current; **en cours de production** in production

coursier, -ère nm,f *(d'une entreprise quelconque)* messenger; *(de messageries)* courier

court, -e adj *(titres, obligations)* short-dated; **à court terme** short-term; **à courte échéance** short-dated

courtage nm *(profession)* brokerage, broking; *(commission)* brokerage, commission; **être vendu par courtage** to be sold on commission; **faire le courtage** to be a broker □ *courtage en immeubles* real estate agency; *courtage officiel* official brokerage

courtier, -ère nm,f broker □ *courtier d'assurances* insurance broker; *courtier de Bourse* stockbroker; *courtier de change* exchange broker *or* dealer; *courtier de commerce* general broker; *courtier à la commission* commission agent; *courtier libre* outside broker; *courtier de marchandises* commercial broker; *courtier maritime* ship broker; *courtier en valeurs mobilières* stockbroker

coût nm cost □ *coût d'accroissement* incremental cost; *coût d'achat* purchase cost; *(sur bilan)* cost of goods purchased; *coût d'acquisition* acquisition cost; *coûts administratifs* administrative costs; *coût assurance fret* cost insurance freight; *coût du capital* capital cost; *coût complet unitaire* total unit cost; *coûts constants* fixed costs *or* expenses; *coûts cumulés* cumulative costs; *coûts de développement* development costs; *coût (total) de distribution* (total) distribution cost; *coût économique* economic cost; *coût de l'élaboration du produit* product development cost; *coût d'entretien* maintenance cost; *coûts d'exploitation* operational costs; *coût fixe (total)* (total) fixed cost; *coûts fonciers* landed costs; *coût de fonctionnement* operating *or* running cost; *coût de fret* freight cost; *coût et fret* cost and freight; *coût global* total cost; *coût kilométrique* cost per kilometre; *coût de main-d'œuvre* labour cost; *coût marginal* marginal cost; *coût moyen unitaire* average unit cost; *coûts opératoires* operating costs; *coûts prévisionnels* estimated costs; *coût de production* production cost; *coût de remplacement* replacement cost; *coût de revient* cost price; *coût salarial* labour cost; *coût unitaire (de travail)* unit (labour) cost; *le coût de la vie* the cost of living

coûtant adj **au** *ou* **à prix coûtant** at cost price

coût-efficacité nf cost-effectiveness

coûter vi to cost; **combien ça coûte?** how much is it?, how much does it cost?; **cela coûte mille francs** it costs a thousand francs; **coûter cher** to be expensive

coûteux, -euse adj costly, expensive; **peu coûteux** inexpensive

couvert, -e *adj* (a) ASSUR *(risque, personne)* covered; **je suis couvert contre l'incendie** I'm covered against fire (b) FIN **être à couvert** *(pour un crédit)* to be covered; BOURSE **vendre à couvert** to hedge, to sell for futures

couverture *nf* (a) FIN cover; BOURSE margin, hedge; **une commande sans couverture** an order without security or cover; **exiger une couverture de 20% en espèces** to claim a margin of 20% in cash; **opérer avec couverture** to hedge □ *couverture (boursière) obligatoire* margin requirement
(b) ASSUR cover □ *couverture d'assurance* insurance cover; *couverture santé* health cover
(c) MKTG coverage □ *couverture du marché* sales coverage; *couverture médiatique* media coverage

> 66
> Face au désengagement progressif de la Sécurité sociale remis à l'ordre du jour par le Plan Veil, une **couverture santé** complémentaire s'avère de plus en plus indispensable.
> 99

couvrir **1** *vt* (a) *(frais, dépenses)* to cover; **le prix de vente couvre à peine les frais** the selling price barely covers the cost; **prière de nous couvrir par chèque** *(sur facture)* kindly remit by cheque
(b) ASSUR *(risque, personne)* to cover; **cette assurance ne couvre pas les risques de vol** this insurance doesn't cover us/you against theft
(c) FIN *(emprunt)* to cover, to secure
(d) *(enchère)* to bid higher than, to outbid
2 se couvrir *vpr* BOURSE to cover (oneself), to hedge; **se couvrir en achetant à long terme** to hedge by buying at long date; **se couvrir en rachetant** to cover oneself by buying back

covendeur, -euse *nm,f* co-vendor, joint seller

CPAM *nf* ADMIN *(abrév* **caisse primaire d'assurance maladie***)* = French government department dealing with health insurance

cpp *(abrév* **caractères par pouce***)* ORDINAT cpi

cps *(abrév* **caractères par seconde***)* ORDINAT cps

cpt *(abrév* **comptant***)* cash

CR *nm (abrév* **compte-rendu***) (d'une réunion)* minutes

crayon *nm* (a) *(pour écrire)* pencil (b) ORDINAT *crayon lumineux, crayon optique* light pen

crayonné *nm* MKTG rough layout

CRDS *nf (abrév* **contribution au remboursement de la dette sociale***)* = income-based tax deducted at source as a contribution to paying off the French social security budget deficit

créance *nf* debt; JUR claim; **amortir une créance** to write off a debt □ *mauvaise créance* bad debt; *créance chirographaire* unsecured debt; *créance contractuelle* contractual claim; *créance douteuse* bad debt; *créance exigible* debt due; *créance garantie* secured debt; *créances gelées* frozen credits; *créance hypothécaire* debt secured by a mortgage; *créance irrécouvrable* bad debt; *créance litigieuse* contested claim; *créance privilégiée* preferential or preferred debt

> 66
> Les **créances douteuses** ont augmenté au cours du premier semestre de l'année fiscale, et les fonds propres composés en partie des gains latents sur les portefeuilles de titres, ont fondu avec la chute du Nikkei.
> 99

créancier, -ère *nm,f* creditor □ *créancier chirographaire* unsecured creditor; *créancier d'exploitation* trade creditor; *créancier hypothécaire* mortgagee; *créancier entièrement nanti* fully-secured creditor

créateur, -trice **1** *adj* créateur d'emplois *(industrie, secteur)* job-creating
2 *nm,f (d'un nouveau produit)* designer □ *créateur d'entreprise(s)* entrepreneur

> 66
> Les quelques industries qui se sont implantées dans l'ex-RDA ont créé des usines ultramodernes, peu **créatrices d'emplois**.
> 99

créatif, -ive *nm,f* MKTG *(de publicité)* designer

création *nf* (a) *(d'un nouveau produit)* creation, designing; *(d'une société)* founding, establishment □ *création d'emplois* job creation; **il y a eu 3000 créations d'emplois en mai** 3,000 new jobs were created in May (b) *(chose créée)* new product; **nos dernières créations** our latest creations

crédirentier, -ère *nm,f* JUR recipient of an allowance

crédit *nm* (a) *(prêt)* credit; **acheter/vendre qch à crédit** to buy/to sell sth on credit *or* on hire purchase *or Am* on the installment plan; **faire crédit à qn** to give sb credit; **ouvrir un crédit à qn** to open a credit account in sb's favour *or* in sb's name; **ouvrir un crédit chez qn** to open a credit account with sb ❑ *crédit back to back* back-to-back credit; *crédit bancaire, crédit en banque* bank credit; *crédit bloqué* frozen credit; *crédit commercial* trade credit; *crédit à la consommation, crédit au consommateur* consumer credit; *crédit consortial* syndicated credit; *crédit (à) court terme* short-term credit; BOURSE *crédit croisé* swap; *crédits de développement* development loans; *crédit différé* deferred credit; *crédit documentaire* documentary credit, letter of credit; *crédit dos à dos* back-to-back credit; *crédit de droits* = delay in payment of indirect taxes; *crédits d'équipement* equipment financing; *crédits à l'exportation* export credit; *crédit foncier* = government-controlled building society; *crédit fournisseur* supplier's credit, trade credit; *crédit gratuit* interest-free credit; *crédit immobilier* mortgage, home loan; *crédits à l'importation* import credit; *crédit d'impôt* *(abattement)* tax rebate; *(report)* tax credit; *crédit irrévocable* irrevocable letter of credit; *crédit (à) long terme* long-term credit; *crédit (à) moyen terme* medium-term credit; *crédit permanent Br* revolving *or Am* revolver credit; *crédit personnel* personal credit; *crédit ponctuel* spot credit; *crédit renouvelable Br* revolving *or Am* revolver credit; *crédit révocable* revocable letter of credit; *crédit revolving Br* revolving *or Am* revolver credit; *crédit à taux réduit* low-interest loan; *crédit transférable* transferable letter of credit; *crédits de trésorerie* (short term) credit facilities; *crédit de TVA* VAT credit (b) *(en comptabilité)* credit side; **porter une somme au crédit de qn** to credit sb with a sum

> **❝**
> La Caixabank vient de procéder à une nouvelle baisse de l'ensemble des taux fixes de ses **crédits immobiliers**.
> **❞**

crédit-bail *nm* leasing ❑ *crédit-bail mobilier* equipment leasing

créditer *vt (compte)* to credit (**de** with); **créditer qn de 4000 francs** to credit sb *or* sb's account with 4,000 francs; **faire créditer son compte d'une somme** to pay a sum into one's account

créditeur, -trice 1 *adj (compte, solde)* credit
2 *nm,f* person whose account is in credit

crédit-relais *nm Br* bridging loan, *Am* bridge loan

Credoc *nm (abrév **crédit documentaire**)* documentary credit, letter of credit

créer 1 *vt (emplois, nouveau produit, hypothèque)* to create; *(entreprise)* to set up
2 **se créer** *vpr* (a) *(emplois, nouveau produit, hypothèque)* to be created; *(entreprise)* to be set up (b) *(pour soi-même)* **se créer une clientèle** to build up a clientele

créneau *nm* (market) niche, gap in the market; **exploiter un nouveau créneau** to fill a new gap *or* niche in the market; **trouver un bon créneau** to find a good gap *or* niche in the market ❑ *créneau horaire* time slot; *créneau porteur* big gap in the market

creux, -euse 1 *adj (période, marché)* slack; *(heures)* off-peak
2 *nm* **une période de creux** a slack period

criée *nf (vente)* auction; *(salle)* auction room

crier *vt* to put up for auction, to auction

crise *nf* crisis, slump; **traverser une période de crise** to go through a crisis (period) ❑ *crise économique* economic crisis; *crise de l'emploi* unemployment crisis; *crise financière* financial crisis; *crise du logement* housing shortage; *crise pétrolière* oil crisis

> **❝**
> La **crise** asiatique avec ses nouveaux développements a eu hier un effet dévastateur sur les places financières européennes.
> **❞**

critère *nm* criterion ❑ *critères de sélection* selection criteria

croissance *nf* growth; **notre entreprise est en pleine croissance** our company is growing rapidly ❑ *croissance démographique* population growth; *croissance économique* economic growth; *croissance par habitant, croissance par tête* per capita economic development; *croissance zéro* zero growth

croissant, -e *adj (chiffre d'affaires, production, chômage)* increasing

croître *vi (chiffre d'affaires, production, chômage)* to grow, to increase

crypter *vt & vi* ORDINAT to encrypt

CSG *nf* (*abrév* **contribution sociale généralisée**) = income-based tax deducted at source as a contribution to paying off the French social security budget deficit

> **"**
> Le gouvernement pioche copieusement dans la poche des ménages avec l'augmentation de la **CSG** et la baisse de certains remboursements.
> **"**

culbute *nf Fam* **faire la culbute** (*entreprise*) (*échouer*) to go bust *or* belly up; (*faire un bénéfice*) to make a huge profit

culminer *vi* BOURSE (*cours*) to reach its highest level, to peak

culture d'entreprise *nf* ÉCON enterprise culture

cumul *nm* (*de fonctions, de mandats, de pouvoirs*) concurrent holding; (*de salaires*) concurrent drawing

cumulard, -e *nm,f Fam* (*directeur*) = person making money as the head of several companies; (*employé*) holder of several jobs

cumulatif, -ive *adj* (*actions, dividende*) cumulative

cumulé, -e *adj* (*intérêts*) accrued

cumuler *vt* (**a**) (*fonctions, mandats, pouvoirs*) to hold concurrently; (*salaires*) to draw concurrently (**b**) (*intérêts*) to accrue

curriculum vitae *nm Br* curriculum vitae, *Am* résumé

curseur *nm* ORDINAT cursor

CV *nm* (*abrév* **curriculum vitae**) *Br* CV, *Am* résumé

CVS *adj* (*abrév* **corrigé des variations saisonnières**) seasonally adjusted

cyberespace *nm* ORDINAT cyberspace

cybertexte *nm* ORDINAT cybertext

cycle *nm* cycle ❑ **cycle des affaires** business cycle; MKTG **cycle commande-livraison-facturation** order-to-remittance cycle; MKTG **cycle de commercialisation** trade cycle; **cycle conjoncturel** economic *or* business cycle; MKTG **cycle de la distribution** distribution cycle; **cycle économique** economic *or* business cycle; **cycle d'exploitation** operating cycle; ORDINAT **cycle d'exécution** execute cycle; MKTG **cycle de vie** lifecycle; **cycle de vie du produit** product lifecycle, PLC

cyclique *adj* (*économie, crise*) cyclical

DAB *nm* BANQUE *(abrév* **distributeur automatique de billets**) ATM

dactylo 1 *nmf (abrév* **dactylographe**) typist □ *dactylo intérimaire* temp
2 *nf (abrév* **dactylographie**) typing

dactylographie *nf* typing

dactylographié, -e *adj (lettre, document)* typed, typewritten

dactylographier *vt (lettre, document)* to type

DAS *(abrév* **domaine d'activite stratégique**) SBU

datation *nf (d'un contrat)* dating

date *nf* date; **sans date** *(lettre)* undated; **la lettre porte la date du 5 mai** the letter is dated 5 May; **mettre la date sur une lettre** to date a letter; **à date fixe** on a fixed date; **à trente jours de date** thirty days after date; **la facture n'a pas été payée à la date prévue** the bill wasn't paid on time; **prendre date** *ou* **fixer une date pour qch** to fix a date for sth □ *date d'achèvement* completion date, date of completion; *date butoir* deadline, cutoff date; *date de clôture* closing date; *date contractuelle* date of agreement; *date d'échéance (de dû)* maturity date, due date; *(de terme)* expiry date; *date d'émission* date of issue; *date d'entrée en vigueur* effective date; *date d'exigibilité* due date; *date d'expiration* expiry date; *date de facturation* date of invoice; *date de jouissance* date from which interest begins to run; *date limite* deadline; *date limite de consommation* best-before date; *date limite de paiement* deadline for payment; *date limite de remise de documents* copy deadline; *date de naissance* date of birth; *date d'ouverture de l'exercice* first day of the financial year; *date de péremption* use-by date; *date de la poste* date as postmark; *date prévue d'achèvement* target date; *date de signature* date of signature; BANQUE *date de valeur* value date; *date de validité* expiry date

dater 1 *vt (lettre)* to date; **votre lettre datée d'hier/du 13 mars** your letter dated yesterday/13 March
2 *vi* to date **(de** from); **à dater de ce jour** *(d'aujourd'hui)* from today; *(de ce jour-là)* from that day; **à dater du 15** on and after the 15th

dation *nf* JUR gift *(made to an heir in the course of one's lifetime to avoid inheritance tax)* □ *dation en paiement* payment in kind

DD ORDINAT 1 *adj (abrév* **double densité**) DD
2 *nm (abrév* **disque dur**) HD

DEA *nm (abrév* **diplôme d'études approfondies**) = post-graduate qualification which is a prerequisite for PhD candidates

débâcle *nf* FIN **débâcle (financière)** crash

déballage *nm (de marchandises)* unpacking; *(exposition)* display

déballer *vt (marchandises)* to unpack; *(exposer)* to display

débarquer 1 *vt (marchandises)* to unload; *(passagers)* to land, to disembark
2 *vi (passagers)* to land, to disembark

débat *nm* debate; JUR **débats** proceedings

débattre *vt* to discuss; **à débattre** *(prix)* to be agreed; *(salaire)* negotiable

débauchage *nm* **(a)** *(licenciement)* laying off **(b)** *(embauche d'employés d'autres entreprises)* poaching

débaucher *vt* **(a)** *(licencier)* to lay off, to make redundant **(b)** *(employés d'autres entreprises)* to poach

débit *nm* **(a)** COMPTA debit; *(sur un compte)* debit side; **inscrire** *ou* **porter un article au débit** to debit an entry; **porter une somme au débit de qn** to debit sb *or* sb's account with an amount □ *débit de caisse* cash debit; *débit cumulé* cumulative debit; *débit différé* deferred debit; *débit immédiat* immediate debit
(b) *(ventes)* sale; **des marchandises de bon débit** marketable *or* saleable goods; **ces marchandises ont peu de débit** there is little demand for these goods
(c) *(commerce)* shop
(d) ORDINAT rate □ *débit en bauds* baud rate; *débit de données* data throughput
(e) *(d'une machine)* output □ *débit horaire* hourly output

> ❝
> Les cartes de paiement sont destinées au règlement chez un commerçant affilié, soit par **débit immédiat**, soit par **débit différé**.
> ❞

débitant, -e *nm,f* retailer

débiter *vt* (**a**) COMPTA *(compte)* to debit; **débiter une somme à qn, débiter qn d'une somme** to debit sb with an amount; **débiter une somme d'un compte** to debit an account with an amount, to debit an amount to an account; **débiter les frais de poste au client** to charge the postage to the customer (**b**) *(vendre)* to sell (**c**) *(produire)* to yield; **cette usine débite 250 voitures par jour** this factory produces 250 cars a day

débiteur, -trice 1 *adj (compte, solde)* debit; **mon compte est débiteur de plusieurs milliers de francs** my account is several thousand francs overdrawn
2 *nm,f* debtor □ *débiteur hypothécaire* mortgagor

déblocage *nm* FIN *(de crédits, de capitaux)* unfreezing; *(des prix, des salaires)* decontrolling; *(de fonds)* releasing, making available

débloquer *vt* FIN *(crédits, capitaux)* to unfreeze; *(prix, salaires)* to decontrol; *(fonds)* to release, to make available

> 66
>
> Le directeur général du FMI, Michel Camdessus, a rendu public un communiqué insistant sur la nécessité de mener à bien les réformes économiques afin que le fonds puisse **débloquer** en septembre la seconde tranche de son aide financière de 11,2 milliards de dollars.
>
> 99

débogage *nm* ORDINAT debugging

déboguer *vt* ORDINAT to debug

débogueur *nm* ORDINAT debugger

débouché *nm* (**a**) MKTG outlet, market, opening; **créer de nouveaux débouchés pour un produit** to open up new markets *or* to create new outlets for a product (**b**) *(de carrière)* job opportunity; **cette formation n'offre aucun débouché** this training does not lead to any career openings

> 66
>
> L'Amérique latine est plus proche et elle représente le **débouché** naturel des industriels américains: 20% du commerce des États-Unis et 6% du profit net des entreprises américaines.
>
> 99

déboursement *nm* outlay, expenditure

débourser *vt (somme, argent)* to spend, to lay out

début *nm (commencement)* beginning, start; **être en début de carrière** to be at the start of one's career; **être à ses débuts** *(société)* to be in its infancy

décaissement *nm* (**a**) *(retrait)* cash withdrawal; **faire un décaissement** to make a withdrawal (**b**) *(somme)* sum withdrawn

décaisser *vt* (**a**) *(marchandises)* to unpack (**b**) *(somme)* to withdraw

décalage *nm* (**a**) *(écart)* gap; **il existe un décalage entre l'évolution des prix et celle des salaires** there is a delay between price and salary increases; **le décalage entre l'offre et la demande fait évoluer les prix à la baisse** the gap between supply and demand lowers prices
(**b**) *décalage horaire* time difference; **tenez compte du décalage horaire si vous leur téléphonez** remember the time difference if you're phoning them; **souffrir du décalage horaire** to suffer from jet lag

décentralisation *nf* (**a**) ADMIN decentralization □ *décentralisation administrative* devolution (**b**) *(des bureaux, des services)* relocation *(away from large towns)*

décentraliser *vt* (**a**) ADMIN to decentralize (**b**) *(bureaux, services)* to relocate *(away from large towns)*

décharge *nf* (**a**) JUR *(d'une obligation)* discharge (**b**) *(attestation)* receipt; **il faut signer une décharge avant de prendre livraison** you have to sign a receipt before accepting delivery (**c**) FIN (tax) rebate; **porter une somme en décharge** to mark a sum as paid

déchargement *nm (d'un navire, de marchandises)* unloading

décharger *vt* (**a**) FIN *(compte)* to discharge; **décharger qn de qch** *(dette)* to discharge sb from sth; *(impôt)* to exempt sb from sth (**b**) *(navire, marchandises)* to unload

déchéance *nf* (**a**) FIN *(de droits, de titres, d'un brevet)* forfeiture; *(d'une police)* expiry (**b**) COMPTA **tomber en déchéance** to lapse

déchet *nm (de poids, valeur)* loss, decrease; **il y a du déchet** there is some wastage □ *déchet de route* loss in transit

déchiffrement *nm* ORDINAT decryption □ *déchiffrement de données* data decryption

déchiffrer *vt* ORDINAT to decrypt

décideur, -euse 1 *adj* decision-making
2 *nm,f* decision-maker

décision *nf (choix)* decision; JUR ruling; **prendre/arriver à une décision** to make/to reach a decision (**quant à** *ou* **au sujet de** about); **prise de décision** decision-making;

soumettre une question à la décision de qn to submit a matter for sb's decision ▫ **décision d'achat** buying decision; **décision arbitrale** arbitration ruling; **décision autonome** autonomous decision; **décision collective, décision commune** joint decision; JUR **décision de justice** court ruling

déclarant, -e nm,f JUR, ADMIN declarant ▫ **déclarant de TVA** VAT-registered person

déclaratif, -ive adj JUR declaratory

déclaration nf (**a**) (annonce) declaration, announcement; **faire une déclaration** to make an announcement ▫ **déclaration de changement de domicile** notification of change of address; **déclaration d'intention** declaration of intent; **déclaration de principe** statement or declaration of principle; **déclaration sous serment** sworn statement, affidavit
(**b**) COMPTA return ▫ **déclaration annuelle de résultats** annual statement of results; **déclaration de cessation de paiement** declaration of bankruptcy; **déclaration de faillite** declaration of bankruptcy; **déclaration fiscale** income tax return; **déclaration d'impôts** tax return; **remplir sa déclaration d'impôts** to Br make or Am file one's tax return; **déclaration de résultats** statement of results, financial statement; **déclaration de revenu** income tax return; **déclaration de TVA** VAT return
(**c**) DOUANES declaration ▫ **déclaration de ou en douane** customs declaration, bill of entry; **déclaration d'entrée** declaration or clearance inwards; **déclaration d'entrée en entrepôt** warehousing entry; **déclaration d'exportation** export declaration; **déclaration d'importation** import declaration; **déclaration de sortie** declaration or clearance outwards; **déclaration de transit** transit entry
(**d**) ASSUR **déclaration d'accident** accident claim; **déclaration d'avarie** (ship's) protest; **déclaration d'incendie** fire claim; **déclaration de sinistre** (d'une assurance) damage report; (réclamation) notice of claim, insurance claim; **déclaration de vol** theft claim
(**e**) BOURSE **déclaration de valeur** declaration of value
(**f**) ADMIN **déclaration d'utilité publique** = government decision that a large public works project is vital and should therefore go ahead despite public protest

déclaré, -e adj (**a**) (valeur) declared; (transferts) certified (**b**) ADMIN **déclaré d'utilité publique** (entreprise) declared vital by the government despite public protest

déclarer 1 vt (**a**) (annoncer) to declare; (employé) to register; **je déclare la séance levée** I declare the meeting closed
(**b**) DOUANES to declare; **marchandises à déclarer** goods to declare; **avez-vous quelque chose à déclarer?** have you anything to declare?; **rien à déclarer** nothing to declare
(**c**) COMPTA (dividende) to declare; **déclarer ses revenus au fisc** to Br make or Am file one's tax return
(**d**) ORDINAT (valeur) to define
2 **se déclarer** vpr (**a**) (se prononcer) **se déclarer pour ou en faveur de/contre qch** to declare oneself in favour of/against sth
(**b**) BOURSE **se déclarer acheteur** to call the shares; **se déclarer vendeur** to put the shares

déclassé, -e adj (**a**) BOURSE (valeurs) displaced (**b**) (emploi, produit, hôtel) downgraded

déclassement nm (**a**) BOURSE (de valeurs) displacement (**b**) (d'emploi, de produit, d'hôtel) downgrading

décliner 1 vt (**a**) (refuser) (offre, invitation) to decline; **décliner toute responsabilité** to accept no liability; **décliner une juridiction** to refuse to acknowledge a jurisdiction
(**b**) MKTG to produce; **notre produit est décliné dans une large gamme de couleurs** our product is available in a wide range of colours
2 **se décliner** vpr MKTG to be available

décodeur nm ORDINAT decoder

décommander 1 vt (commande, livraison) to cancel; (réunion) to cancel, to call off
2 **se décommander** vpr to cancel

décomposer vt (**a**) COMPTA (compte, résultats) to analyse, to break down; (dépenses) to break down (**b**) (tâches) to break down

décomposition nf (**a**) COMPTA (d'un compte, des résultats) analysis, breakdown; (des dépenses) breakdown (**b**) (des tâches) breakdown

décompte nm (**a**) (déduction) deduction; (calcul) calculation; **j'ai fait le décompte de ce que vous m'avez payé et de ce que vous**

me devez I've deducted what you've paid from what you owe me
(**b**) (*solde*) balance; **payer le décompte** to pay the balance due (*on an account*)
(**c**) (*relevé d'une opération*) detailed account, breakdown

décompter *vt* to deduct

déconcentration *nf* (*de bureaux, d'entreprises*) relocation (*away from large towns*)

déconcentrer *vt* (*bureaux, entreprises*) to relocate (*away from large towns*)

déconfiture *nf* financial collapse; JUR insolvency

déconnecté, -e *adj* ORDINAT (*imprimante*) off-line

déconsignation *nf* deconsignment

déconsigner *vt* (**a**) (*emballage*) to return (**b**) (*bagages*) to collect from the *Br* left-luggage office *or Am* checkroom

décote *nf* (**a**) (*d'impôt*) tax relief (**b**) FIN below par rating (**c**) (*baisse*) depreciation, loss in value

> **"**
> Si les SCPI plus anciennes souffrent moins de cette brutale **décote**, celles ayant procédé à des réévaluations conséquentes du prix des parts durant les années fastes sont également contraintes de revoir leurs prix à la baisse.
> **"**

découpage *nm* (**a**) MKTG breakdown; **découpage des ventes par pays** breakdown of sales by country (**b**) ORDINAT (*de fichier, d'image*) splitting

découper *vt* ORDINAT (*fichier, image*) to split

découvert *nm* (**a**) BANQUE **découvert (bancaire)** overdraft; **demander une autorisation de découvert** to apply for an overdraft; **accorder à qn un découvert** to allow sb an overdraft; **avoir un découvert** *ou* **être à découvert de 2 000 francs** (*autorisé*) to have a 2,000 franc overdraft; (*non autorisé*) to be overdrawn by 2,000 francs; **mettre un compte à découvert** to overdraw an account ❑ **découvert en blanc** unsecured overdraft; **découvert de la balance commerciale** trade gap
(**b**) ASSUR things not covered by insurance
(**c**) BOURSE **vendre à découvert** to go a bear, to sell short

décret *nm* decree; **promulguer un décret** to issue a decree ❑ ADMIN **décret prési-**

dentiel *Br* ≃ order in council, *Am* ≃ executive order

décréter *vt* (*mesure, nomination*) to decree, to order; (*loi*) to enact; (*grève*) to call, to order; JUR (*moratoire*) to declare

décrocher *vt* (**a**) (*combiné téléphonique*) to pick *or* lift up; **décrocher le téléphone** (*pour ne pas être dérangé*) to take the phone off the hook; (*pour répondre*) to pick up the phone (**b**) (*contrat, commande*) to land

DECS *nm* (*abrév* **diplôme d'études comptables supérieures**) = postgraduate qualification in accounting

dédit *nm* forfeit, penalty; **dédit en cas d'inexécution du contrat** penalty for breaking a contract

dédommagement *nm* compensation, damages; **réclamer un dédommagement** to claim compensation; **recevoir une somme en dédommagement** *ou* **à titre de dédommagement** to receive a sum in *or* by way of compensation

dédommager **1** *vt* to indemnify, to compensate (**de** for); **dédommager qn d'une perte** to compensate sb for a loss
2 se dédommager *vpr* **se dédommager de ses pertes** to recoup one's losses

dédouanage *nm* DOUANES (*à la douane*) customs clearance; (*de l'entrepôt*) taking out of bond

dédouané, -e *adj* DOUANES (*marchandises*) duty-paid

dédouanement = **dédouanage**

dédouaner *vt* DOUANES (*faire passer à la douane*) to clear through customs; (*récupérer de l'entrepôt*) to take out of bond

déductible *adj* (*dépense*) deductible; **déductible de l'impôt** tax-deductible

déduction *nf* deduction, allowance; **après déduction des impôts** after deduction of tax; **faire déduction de qch** to deduct *or* allow for sth; **sous déduction de 10%** less 10%, minus 10%; **entrer en déduction de qch** to be deductible from sth; **sans déduction** terms net cash; **déduction faite des frais d'essence** after deduction of petrol costs ❑ **déduction pour dons** deduction for donations; **déduction fiscale** tax allowance; **déduction forfaitaire** (*d'impôts*) standard allowance

déduire *vt* to deduct; **déduire 5%** to deduct 5%; **les frais de poste sont à déduire du prix total** the postage is to be deducted from the total price; **tous frais déduits** after deduction of expenses

défaillance *nf* (**a**) *défaillance d'entreprise* business failure (**b**) JUR default

> Les **défaillances d'entreprises** ont augmenté de 11% en Europe au cours des six premiers mois de l'année.

défaillant, -e JUR **1** *adj* defaulting
2 *nm,f* defaulter, absconder

défalcation *nf* deduction; *(d'une mauvaise créance)* writing off; **défalcation faite des frais** after deducting the expenses

défalquer *vt* to deduct (**de** from); *(mauvaise créance)* to write off

défaut *nm* (**a**) *(imperfection)* defect ❑ **défaut apparent** visible defect; **défaut caché** hidden defect; **défaut de fabrication** manufacturing fault *or* defect; **défaut de fonctionnement** malfunction
(**b**) *(manque)* lack ❑ **défaut de provision** *(sur chèque)* refer to drawer, insufficient funds; **le chèque a été refusé pour cause de défaut de provision** the cheque was refused because of insufficient funds
(**c**) JUR default; **faire défaut** to fail to appear, to default; **jugement par défaut** judgement by default ❑ **défaut de comparution** failure to appear; **défaut de livraison** non-delivery; **défaut de paiement** failure to pay, non-payment
(**d**) ORDINAT default; **clavier par défaut** default keyboard; **lecteur par défaut** default drive

défavorable *adj (balance commerciale)* adverse; *(change)* unfavourable

défectueux, -euse *adj* imperfect, faulty

défendeur, -eresse *nm,f* JUR defendant

défendre *vt* (**a**) JUR *(accusé)* to defend; *(cause)* to defend, to champion; *(droit, opinion)* to defend, to uphold (**b**) *(protéger)* to defend, to guard (**contre** against *or* from); **défendre ses intérêts** to protect one's interests

défense *nf* **défense des consommateurs** consumer protection, consumerism; MKTG **défense contre-offensive** counter-offensive defence; MKTG **défense mobile** mobile defence; MKTG **défense préventive** pre-emptive defence

déficit *nm* FIN deficit; **être en déficit** to be in deficit; **accuser un déficit** to show a deficit; **combler un déficit** to make up a deficit ❑ **déficit de la balance commerciale** trade deficit; **déficit budgétaire** budget deficit; **déficit de caisse** cash deficit; **déficit commercial** trade deficit *or* gap; **déficit d'exploitation** operating deficit; **déficit ex-** **térieur** external deficit, balance of payments deficit; **déficit fiscal remboursable** negative income tax; **déficit fiscal reportable** tax loss; COMPTA **déficit reportable** loss carry forward; **déficit de trésorerie** cash deficit

> La reprise d'une très forte croissance … va aggraver le **déficit commercial** du pays, qui pourrait atteindre, selon les estimations, 9 à 12 milliards de dollars.

> Ces dépenses supplémentaires pourraient déséquilibrer le budget de l'état allemand, voire faire passer le **déficit budgétaire** au-dessus du maximum autorisé par les critères de convergence européens de Maastricht.

déficitaire *adj (entreprise)* loss-making; *(compte)* in debit; *(budget)* in deficit, adverse; *(balance, solde)* adverse; *(bilan)* showing a loss; **être déficitaire** to show a deficit

défilement *nm* ORDINAT scrolling

défiler *vi* ORDINAT **faire défiler un document** to scroll through a document; **défiler vers le bas** to scroll down; **défiler vers le haut** to scroll up

défini, -e *adj* ORDINAT **défini par l'utilisateur** user-defined

définition de fonction *nf* job description

défiscalisé, -e *adj* tax free

défiscaliser *vt* to exempt from tax

déflation *nf* ÉCON deflation

> Le Japon continue de s'enfoncer, la puissance de la **déflation** financière dans le pays interdisant toute dépense aux entreprises comme aux ménages.

déflationniste *adj* ÉCON deflationary

défragmentation *nf* ORDINAT defragmentation

défrayer *vt* **défrayer qn** to pay sb's expenses

dégagement *nm* FIN *(de fonds, de crédits)* release

dégager 1 *vt* FIN (**a**) *(fonds, crédits)* to release (**b**) *(bénéfices, excédent)* to show
2 se dégager *vpr* **se dégager d'une dette** to discharge *or* pay off a debt

dégât *nm* damage; **les dégâts occasionnés au matériel se chiffrent en millions de francs** the damage to the equipment amounts to several million francs; **limiter les dégâts** to limit the damage

dégeler *vt* FIN *(avoir, crédits)* to unfreeze, to unblock

dégonflement *nm (des dépenses)* cutback (**de** in); *(du marché)* collapse (**de** of)

dégrader 1 *vt (matériel, outil de production)* to damage
  2 se dégrader *vpr (situation économique, relations)* to deteriorate, to get worse; **les relations entre les salariés et le patronat se dégradent** relations between management and staff are deteriorating *or* getting worse

degré *nm* degree □ **degré de liquidité** degree of liquidity, liquidity ratio; **degré de solvabilité** credit rating

dégressif, -ive 1 *adj (impôt, amortissement)* graded, graduated; *(tarif)* tapering
  2 *nm* discount □ **dégressif sur le volume** bulk discount

dégrèvement *nm (remise)* reduction □ **dégrèvement (fiscal)** tax relief

dégrever *vt (produits)* to reduce tax on; *(contribuable)* to grant tax relief to; *(industrie)* to derate; *(propriété)* to reduce the assessment on

dégriffé, -e 1 *adj* = with its designer label removed and reduced in price
  2 *nm* = reduced-price designer item with its label removed

dégringolade *nf (d'une entreprise, d'une monnaie)* collapse; *(des prix, des valeurs)* slump (**de** in)

dégringoler *vi (entreprise, monnaie)* to collapse; *(prix, valeurs)* to slump

déguisé, -e *adj (impôt, chômage)* hidden

délai *nm* time allowed; **dans un délai de trois ans** within three years, within a three year limit; **dans les plus brefs délais, dans le plus court délai, dans les meilleurs délais** as soon as possible; **un délai franc de 5 jours** 5 clear days' grace; **sans délai** without delay; **dans les délais prescrits** *ou* **impartis** within the required time □ **délai d'attente** waiting period; **délai de carence** waiting period;

délai de chargement loading time; **délai de commercialisation** *(d'un produit)* launching period; **délai de congé** term of notice; **délai de crédit** credit period; **délai d'embarquement** loading time; **délai d'exécution** deadline; *(de livraison, de production)* lead time; **délai garanti de livraison** guaranteed delivery period; **délai de garantie** guarantee period, term of guarantee; **délai de grâce** extension; **délai de livraison** delivery time, lead time; **délai de paiement** *(fixé par contrat)* term of payment; **demander un délai de paiement** to request a postponement of payment; **délai de préavis** term of notice; **délai de production** production lead time; **délai de réachat** repurchase period; **délai de recouvrement des sommes** period for debt recovery; **délai de récupération du capital investi** payback period; **délai de réflexion** cooling-off period; **délai de règlement** settlement period; **délai de remboursement** payback period; **délai de rigueur** strict deadline; **avant le 20 février, délai de rigueur** by 20 February at the very latest; **délai de validité** period of validity

délai-congé *nm* term of notice

délaissé, -e *adj* BOURSE *(valeurs)* neglected

délaissement *nm* (a) JUR *(d'un droit, d'une succession)* relinquishment (b) ASSUR abandonment

délaisser *vt* (a) JUR *(droit, succession)* to relinquish, to forego (b) ASSUR *(à l'assureur)* to abandon

délégation *nf* (a) *(de pouvoirs, d'autorité)* delegation; **agir par délégation** to act on the authority invested in one □ **délégation de signature** power of attorney
  (b) JUR *(d'une créance)* assignment, transfer
  (c) *(groupe de personnes)* delegation; **une délégation commerciale japonaise** a Japanese trade delegation

délégué, -e 1 *adj* acting
  2 *nm,f* delegate, representative □ **délégué d'atelier** shop steward; **délégué commercial** sales representative; **délégué général** managing director; **délégué du personnel**

staff representative; **délégué syndical** union representative

> " Les entreprises de moins de 100 salariés ne devraient plus être obligées de mettre en place des **délégués du personnel** (DP) et un comité d'entreprise (CE). "

déléguer vt (**a**) *(personne, pouvoir, autorité)* to delegate (**b**) JUR *(créance)* to assign, to transfer

délit nm JUR *Br* offence, *Am* misdemeanor; **en flagrant délit** red-handed; JUR in flagrante delicto; **prendre qn en flagrant délit** to catch sb red-handed *or* in the act ❑ FIN **délit d'initié** insider dealing *or* trading

délivrance nf *(d'un certificat, d'un reçu)* delivery, issue; *(d'un brevet)* granting

délivrer vt *(certificat, reçu)* to deliver, to issue; *(brevet)* to grant

délocalisation nf *(d'une entreprise, de la production)* relocation; *(des capitaux)* expatriation

> " L'agressivité commerciale des Chinois pourrait bien avoir raison des stratégies de **délocalisation** opérées ces dernières années. "

délocaliser **1** vt *(entreprise, production)* to relocate; *(capitaux)* to expatriate
2 se délocaliser vpr to relocate

> " Le syndicat accuse Bell Atlantic, premier opérateur régional aux États-Unis, de **délocaliser** peu à peu les emplois dans des filiales non syndiquées où les gens sont moins payés et plus flexibles. "

déloyal, -e adj *(procédé, concurrence, pratique commerciale)* unfair

demande nf (**a**) *(requête)* request (**de** for); **faire la demande de qch** to ask for sth; **faire qch à** *ou* **sur la demande de qn** to do sth at sb's request; **travailler à la demande** to work to order; **adresser une demande** to apply in writing; **faire une demande de qch par écrit** to write off for sth, to send for sth; **il faut remplir une demande** you must fill in an application form; **faire une demande de remboursement** to request repayment; **suite à votre demande** as requested, further to your request; **sur demande** on application,

on request; **payable sur demande** *(chèque)* payable on demand *or* at sight ❑ **demande d'emploi** job application; **demandes d'emploi** *(dans un journal)* situations wanted; ASSUR **demande d'indemnité** claim; **demande de prêt** loan application; **demande de renseignements** enquiry, request for information

(**b**) ÉCON demand; **l'offre et la demande** supply and demand; **répondre à la demande** to meet demand; **la demande est en hausse/en baisse** demand is up/down ❑ **demande des consommateurs** consumer demand; **demande excédentaire** overdemand; **demande du marché** market demand; **demande prévisionnelle** projected demand; **demande soutenue** full demand

(**c**) JUR claim ❑ **demande accessoire** related claim; **demande compensatoire** counterclaim; **demande de dommages-intérêts** claim for damages; **demande principale** main claim; **demande en renvoi** request for referral to another court; **demande subsidiaire** subsidiary claim

demander vt (**a**) *(réclamer)* to ask for; *(dommages-intérêts)* to claim; *(emploi)* to apply for; **combien demandez-vous de l'heure?** how much do you charge per hour?; **demandez notre catalogue** send for our catalogue; **on vous demande au téléphone** you're wanted on the phone, there's a call for you

(**b**) *(chercher)* to want; **être très demandé** *(produit, article)* to be in great demand

demandeur¹, -eresse nm,f JUR plaintiff, claimant ❑ **demandeur en appel** appellant

demandeur², -euse nm,f (**a**) **demandeur d'emploi** job seeker (**b**) *(d'un produit, d'un service)* customer

démantèlement nm *(des barrières douanières)* removal, lowering; *(du marché)* breaking up ❑ **démantèlement d'entreprise** asset stripping

> " Le NAFTA prévoit le **démantèlement** des barrières douanières et la disparition des droits de douanes sur quinze ans entre les trois partenaires. "

démanteler vt *(barrières douanières)* to remove, to lower; *(marché)* to break up

démarchage nm *(porte-à-porte)* door-to-door selling; *(prospection)* canvassing; **faire du démarchage** to do door-to-door selling, to sell door-to-door ❑ *démarchage à distance* telephone prospecting

démarche *nf* (**a**) *(initiative)* step; **faire une démarche auprès de qn** to approach sb; **faire les démarches nécessaires pour faire qch** to take the necessary steps to do sth ❑ *démarche collective* joint representation (**b**) *(approche)* approach ❑ *démarche marketing* marketing approach

démarcher **1** *vt (prospecter)* to canvass for **2** *vi (faire du porte-à-porte)* to do door-to-door selling, to sell door-to-door

démarcheur, -euse *nm,f* (**a**) *(représentant)* door-to-door salesman, *f* saleswoman ❑ *démarcheur en assurances* insurance agent (**b**) *(prospecteur)* canvasser ❑ *démarcheur en publicité* advertisement canvasser

démarque *nf* marking down, markdown ❑ *démarque inconnue* shrinkage

démarqué, -e *adj* marked down

démarquer *vt* to mark down

démarrage *nm* (**a**) *(d'une entreprise)* start-up; *(d'une affaire, d'une campagne publicitaire, d'un projet)* start (**b**) ORDINAT *démarrage à chaud* warm start; *démarrage à froid* cold start

démarrer *vt* (**a**) *(affaire, campagne publicitaire, projet)* to start up (**b**) ORDINAT to boot (up), to start up

démembrement *nm (d'une entreprise)* breaking up

démembrer *vt (entreprise)* to break up

démettre **1** *vt* (**a**) *(renvoyer)* **démettre qn de ses fonctions** to remove sb from his/her post (**b**) JUR *(débouter)* **démettre qn de son appel** to dismiss sb's appeal **2 se démettre** *vpr (démissionner)* to resign; **se démettre de ses fonctions** to resign one's post

demeure *nf* JUR **mettre qn en demeure de payer** to give sb notice to pay

demi-gros *nm* cash and carry

demi-produit *nm* semi-finished product

demi-salaire *nm* half-pay

démission *nf* resignation; **donner sa démission** to hand in one's resignation

démissionner *vi* to resign (**de** from)

démographie *nf* demography

démographique *adj* demographic

démonétisation *nf* FIN demonetization

démonétiser *vt* FIN to demonetize

démonstrateur, -trice *nm,f* demonstrator

démonstration *nf (d'article)* demonstration ❑ *démonstration sur le lieu de vente* in-store demonstration

dénationalisation *nf* denationalization

dénationaliser *vt* to denationalize

déni *nm* JUR denial, refusal ❑ *déni de justice* denial of justice

dénier *vt* JUR to deny, to refuse

deniers *nmpl* money, funds ❑ *deniers de l'État* public funds

dénombrement *nm* counting ❑ *dénombrement de la population* population count

dénombrer *vt* to count

dénomination *nf (d'une société)* name ❑ *dénomination sociale* corporate name

> ❝
> La déclaration préalable à l'embauche doit contenir la **dénomination sociale** de l'entreprise (ou les nom et prénom de l'entrepreneur individuel).
> ❞

dénommer *vt* to name; **ci-après dénommé...** *(dans un contrat)* hereinafter referred to as... ❑ ASSUR *personne dénommée* nominee

denrée *nf* commodity; *(aliment)* foodstuff ❑ *denrées alimentaires* food products, foodstuffs; *denrées de consommation courante* basic consumer goods; *denrées marchandes* saleable goods; *denrées du pays* home produce; *denrées périssables* perishable goods; *denrées de première nécessité* staple commodities

densité *nf* (**a**) ORDINAT **à double densité** double-density (**b**) MKTG *densité publicitaire* advertising density

déontologie *nf* professional code of ethics

dépannage *nm* ORDINAT troubleshooting

dépareillé, -e *adj (articles)* odd

départ *nm* (**a**) *départ entrepôt* ex warehouse; *départ usine* ex works (**b**) *(du travail)* departure ❑ *départ en préretraite* early retirement; *départ en retraite* retirement; *départ volontaire* voluntary redundancy (**c**) *(d'un compte)* opening date

département *nm* ADMIN (**a**) *(dans un ministère)* department (**b**) *(de la France)* department *(division of local government)* ❑ *départements et territoires d'outre-mer*

= French overseas departments and territories

dépassement nm exceeding, excess; **il y a un dépassement de crédit de plusieurs millions** the budget has been exceeded by several million □ *dépassement budgétaire* overspending; ORDINAT *dépassement de capacité* overflow; COMPTA *dépassement de coût* cost overrun

dépasser vt *(excéder)* to exceed; **la demande dépasse l'offre** demand exceeds supply; **les ventes ont dépassé le chiffre de l'an dernier** sales figures have overtaken last year's; FIN **dépasser un crédit** to exceed a credit limit

dépens nmpl cost, expenses; JUR costs; **être condamné aux dépens** to be ordered to pay costs

dépense nf expenditure, expense; **dépenses** expenses; **contrôler les dépenses** to check expenditure; **faire des dépenses** to incur expenses; **faire trop de dépenses** to overspend □ COMPTA *dépenses de caisse* cash expenditure; *dépenses en capital* capital expenditure; ÉCON *dépenses de consommation* consumer expenditure; *dépenses courantes* current expenditure; COMPTA *dépenses de création* above-the-line costs; COMPTA *dépenses diverses* sundry expenses; *dépenses d'équipement* capital expenditure; COMPTA *dépenses d'exploitation* operating costs; *dépenses extraordinaires* extras; COMPTA *dépenses de fonctionnement* operating costs; *dépenses d'investissement* capital expenditure; ÉCON *dépenses des ménages* household expenditure; ÉCON *dépense nationale* national expenditure, government spending; *dépenses non prévues au budget* unforeseen expenses; *dépenses prévues au budget* foreseen expenses; *dépenses publicitaires* publicity expenses; *dépenses publiques* public spending, government spending

dépenser vt to spend; **dépenser de l'argent inutilement** to waste money

déplacement nm **(a)** *(d'un fonctionnaire, d'un service)* transfer
(b) *(voyage)* trip, journey; **déplacements** travel; **être en déplacement** to be on a (business) trip; **le directeur est en déplacement à l'étranger** the manager is abroad on business
(c) ÉCON **déplacement de l'offre et de la demande** shift *or* swing in supply and demand
(d) FIN *(de fonds)* movement

déplacer vt **(a)** *(fonctionnaire, service)* to transfer **(b)** FIN *(fonds)* to move

déplafonnement nm *(d'un prix)* removal of the upper limit *or* the ceiling

déplafonner vt *(prix)* to remove the upper limit *or* the ceiling on; FIN **déplafonner un crédit** to raise the ceiling on a credit, to raise a credit limit

dépliant nm leaflet

déplombage nm ORDINAT decoding, decrypting

déplomber vt ORDINAT to decode, to decrypt

déposant, -e nm,f **(a)** FIN depositor **(b)** JUR deponent

déposer vt **(a)** *(faire enregistrer)* *(marque, brevet)* to register; **déposer une demande de brevet** to file an application for a patent; **déposer son bilan** to file one's petition in bankruptcy
(b) *(verser)* **déposer une caution** to leave a deposit; **déposer de l'argent (à la banque)** to deposit money (at the bank)
(c) JUR **déposer une plainte (contre qn)** to lodge a complaint (against sb)

deposit nm FIN initial margin

dépositaire **1** adj *(établissement)* which holds securities on trust
2 nmf **(a)** *(de papiers confidentiels)* trustee, depository □ ADMIN *dépositaire de l'autorité publique* = officer of the state; ADMIN *dépositaire public* = government official with responsibility for the management of public funds; *dépositaire de valeurs* holder of securities on trust
(b) *(de produits)* agent □ *dépositaire agréé* authorized agent; *dépositaire exclusif* sole agent

déposition nf JUR statement, deposition *(made by witness)*; **faire/recueillir une déposition** to make/take a statement

dépositionner vt MKTG to deposition

dépôt nm **(a)** BANQUE deposit; **faire un dépôt** *(d'argent)* to make a deposit; **mettre qch en dépôt dans une banque** to deposit sth with a bank; **dépôt à sept jours de préavis** deposit at seven days' notice □ *dépôt bancaire* bank deposit; *dépôt en coffre-fort* safe-deposit; *dépôt à court terme* call money; *dépôt à échéance fixe* fixed deposit; *dépôt d'espèces* cash deposit; *dépôt de garantie* deposit; *dépôt initial* initial margin; *dépôt interbancaire* interbank deposit; *dépôt de marge* initial margin; *dépôt à terme* short-term investment; *dépôt à terme fixe* fixed deposit; *dépôt à vue* demand deposit
(b) *(d'une marque, d'un brevet)* registration; **effectuer le dépôt d'une marque** to register

a trademark ❏ **dépôt légal** registration of copyright

(**c**) *(entrepôt)* depot; DOUANES **être en dépôt** to be in bond ❏ **dépôt d'expédition** sending depot; **dépôt de marchandises** goods depot, warehouse

(**d**) FIN **en dépôt** *(argent, document, marchandises)* in trust; **avoir qch en dépôt** to hold sth in trust

(**e**) COMPTA **dépôt de bilan** *(d'une entreprise)* (filing of petition in) bankruptcy

dépouillement *nm (d'un compte, d'un rapport)* breakdown, analysis; *(du courrier)* opening; *(des données)* processing; *(d'appels d'offres)* checking

dépouiller *vt* (**a**) *(compte, rapport)* to break down, to analyse; *(courrier)* to open; *(données)* to process; *(appels d'offres)* to check (**b**) JUR **dépouiller qn de ses droits** to strip sb of his rights

dépréciation *nf* (**a**) *(dévaluation)* depreciation, fall in value ❏ COMPTA **dépréciation de créances** write-down of accounts receivable; **dépréciation fonctionnelle** *(du matériel)* wear and tear

(**b**) *(mauvaise évaluation)* underrating, undervaluing

> ❝
> Depuis la **dépréciation** de la lire qui a restauré la compétitivité des produits italiens, les commandes étrangères adressées aux industriels de la Péninsule affluent.
> ❞

déprécier **1** *vt* (**a**) *(dévaluer)* to depreciate (**b**) *(mal évaluer)* to undervalue

2 se déprécier *vpr* to depreciate, to fall in value

déprédateur, -trice *nm,f* FIN *(de fonds)* embezzler

déprédation *nf* FIN *(de fonds)* embezzlement

dépression *nf* BOURSE depression ❏ **dépression économique** economic slump; **dépression du marché** market depression

déprimé, -e *adj* BOURSE *(marché)* depressed

déprogrammer *vt* (**a**) *(rendez-vous)* to cancel (**b**) ORDINAT to remove from a program

DEPS *nm (abrév* **dernier entré, premier sorti**) LIFO

dérangement *nm* (**a**) TÉL *(panne)* **la ligne est en dérangement** the line is out of order, there's a fault on the line (**b**) *(gêne)* distur-

bance, trouble; **excusez-moi pour le dérangement** I'm sorry to disturb *or* trouble you; **je vous envoie un coursier, cela vous évitera un dérangement** I'll send a courier so as not to put you to any trouble

déranger *vt (gêner)* to disturb; **ne pas déranger** *(sur panneau)* do not disturb; **excusez-moi de vous déranger** I'm sorry to disturb *or* trouble you; **si cela ne vous dérange pas** if it's no trouble to you

déréglementation *nf* deregulation

> ❝
> **Déréglementation** et baisse des tarifications faisant loi, toutes les compagnies aériennes sont condamnées à changer de stratégie.
> ❞

déréglementer *vt* to deregulate

dérégulation *nf* deregulation

déréguler *vt* to deregulate

dérivé, -e **1** *adj* **produit dérivé** by-product

2 *nm* by-product

dernier, -ère *adj (ultime)* last, final ❏ **dernier cours** closing price; **dernier délai** deadline; **dernier paiement** final payment; **dernier prix** final offer; BOURSE **dernière proposition** final offer; **dernier rappel** *(de facture)* final demand

dérogation *nf* exemption (**à** from); JUR waiver; *(à une loi)* derogation, impairment (**à** of); **dérogation à un règlement** departure from a rule, exception to a rule; **par dérogation au règlement** notwithstanding the rules

dérogatoire *adj* JUR derogatory

dérouler **1** *vt* ORDINAT *(menu)* to pull down

2 se dérouler *vpr (avoir lieu)* to take place; **la réunion du conseil d'administration s'est déroulée au siège social du groupe** the board meeting took place at the company's headquarters; **les événements qui se déroulent à Paris risquent d'affoler les investisseurs** the events that are unfolding *or* taking place in Paris are likely to scare off investors

désactivation *nf* ORDINAT deactivation

désactiver *vt* ORDINAT to deactivate, to disable

désaisonnalisé, -e *adj* seasonally adjusted

désaisonnaliser *vt* to seasonally adjust

descendre *vi (prix)* to come down, to fall; BOURSE *(actions)* to drop, to fall; **descendre en flèche** to plummet

description nf description ❑ *description de brevet* patent specification; *description de poste* job description

désencadrement nm (des crédits) unblocking

désencadrer vt (crédits) to unblock

désendettement nm degearing, clearing of debts

désendetter se désendetter vpr to clear one's debts

déséquilibre nm imbalance; **il existe dans ce pays un déséquilibre très important entre les secteurs secondaire et tertiaire** there is a considerable imbalance between the secondary and tertiary sectors in this country; **déséquilibre de la balance commerciale** unfavourable or adverse trade balance ❑ *déséquilibre financier* financial imbalance

désescalade nf (de prix, des actions) downturn

désétatiser vt (industrie) to denationalize

déshypothéquer vt to free from mortgage

désignation nf (a) (de marchandises) description (b) (nomination) appointment; **la désignation de qn à un poste** the appointment of sb to a post

designer nm designer

désigner vt (a) (marchandises) to describe (b) (nommer) to appoint; (représentant, fondé de pouvoir) to nominate; **désigner qn à un poste** to appoint sb to a post

désindexation nf removal of index-linking

> **"**
> La **désindexation** des salaires sur les prix a limité les effets inflationnistes de la dépréciation de la lire.
> **"**

désindexer vt to stop index-linking; **ces pensions ont été désindexées** these retirement schemes are no longer index-linked

désinflation nf ÉCON disinflation

désinflationniste adj ÉCON deflationary

désinstallateur n ORDINAT deinstaller

désinstallation n ORDINAT deinstallation

désinstaller vt ORDINAT to deinstall

désintéressement nm (de partenaire) buying out; (de créditeur) paying off

désintéresser vt (partenaire) to buy out; (créditeur) to pay off

désinvestir vt FIN to disinvest in

désinvestissement nm FIN disinvestment ❑ *désinvestissement marginal* marginal disinvestment

désistement nm JUR (d'une demande) waiver; (d'une poursuite) withdrawal

désister se désister vpr JUR **se désister d'une demande** to waive a claim; **se désister d'une poursuite** to withdraw an action

DESS nm (abrév **diplôme d'études supérieures spécialisées**) = postgraduate diploma

dessaisir 1 vt (a) JUR **dessaisir un tribunal d'une affaire** to remove a case from a court (b) ADMIN **dessaisir qn d'un dossier** to remove sb from a project
2 se dessaisir vpr **se dessaisir de qch** to relinquish sth, to part with sth

dessaisissement nm (a) JUR **dessaisissement d'un tribunal d'une affaire** removal of a case from a court (b) ADMIN relinquishment

dessin nm design; (représentation) drawing ❑ *dessin assisté par ordinateur* computer-aided design; *dessin industriel* industrial design; *dessin du produit* product design

déstabilisant, -e, déstabilisateur, -trice adj destabilizing

déstabilisation nf destabilization

déstabiliser vt to destabilize

destinataire nmf (de courrier) addressee, recipient; (de marchandises) consignee

destination nf (a) (lieu) destination; **marchandises à destination de la province et de l'étranger** goods for consignment to the provinces and abroad; **navire à destination de Bordeaux** ship bound for Bordeaux (b) (usage) (de capitaux, de fonds) use

destiner vt (a) (affecter) **destiner des fonds à qch** to allot or assign funds to sth; **cet argent est destiné à la recherche** this money is earmarked for or is going towards research
(b) (réserver) **marchandises destinées à l'exportation** goods intended for export
(c) (concevoir pour) **ces mesures sont destinées à réduire le chômage** these measures are designed to reduce unemployment

déstockage nm destocking, reduction in stocks ❑ COMPTA *déstockage de production* (poste de bilan) decrease in stocks

déstocker *vt* to destock, to reduce stocks of

> "
>
> Nous avons constaté la reprise du stockage au troisième trimestre, notamment dans les biens intermédiaires, mais si l'activité ne redémarre pas rapidement, les entreprises **déstockeront**, ce qui entraînera un nouveau décrochage de la croissance dans les prochains mois.
>
> "

destructeur de documents *nm* shredder

désuet, -ète *adj* obsolete

désuétude *nf* disuse; **tomber en désuétude** to fall into disuse; JUR *(droit)* to lapse; *(loi)* to fall into abeyance ▫ *désuétude calculée* planned *or* built-in obsolescence

détacher 1 *vt* (**a**) BOURSE **détacher un coupon d'une action** to detach a coupon from a share (**b**) *(employé)* to second; **c'est un cadre détaché dans le secteur public** he's a manager who has been assigned *or* seconded to the civil service

2 se détacher *vpr* BOURSE **le coupon de ces actions se détache le 1 août** this stock goes ex-coupon on l August

détail *nm* (**a**) *(élément)* detail; **donner tous les détails** to go into all the details, to give full details; **pour de plus amples détails, s'adresser à...** for more details, please contact... (**b**) *(énumération)* *(d'un compte, d'un inventaire)* items; *(d'une facture)* breakdown; **faire le détail de qch** to itemize sth, to break sth down (**c**) *(dans la vente)* retail; **vendre qch au détail** to sell sth retail

détaillant, -e *nm,f* retailer, shopkeeper ▫ *détaillant indépendant* independent retailer; *détaillant spécialisé* specialist retailer

détaillé, -e *adj (facture, relevé de compte)* itemized

détailler *vt* (**a**) *(marchandises)* to retail, to sell retail (**b**) *(facture, relevé de compte)* to itemize

détaxe *nf* (**a**) *(suppression)* lifting of tax *or* duty; *(diminution)* reduction of tax *or* duty; **vendus en détaxe** duty-free; **la détaxe des marchandises à l'exportation** the lifting of duty on exports (**b**) *(remboursement)* **cela m'a fait 500 francs de détaxe** the reduction of duty saved me 500 francs ▫ *détaxe postale* refund on postage paid in error

détaxé, -e *adj (produits, articles)* duty-free

détaxer *vt (supprimer)* to lift the tax *or* duty on; *(diminuer)* to reduce the tax *or* duty on

détecteur *nm* **détecteur de faux billets** forged banknote detector; ORDINAT **détecteur de virus** virus detector

détection *nf* ORDINAT **détection d'erreurs** error detection; **détection virale** virus detection

détenir *vt (valeurs, titres, compte)* to hold; **société détenue à 50%** 50%-owned company; **ils détiennent 30% des parts de la société/des parts de marché** they have a 30% shareholding in the company/a 30% market share; **détenu par des intérêts privés** privately-held

détente *nf (des taux d'intérêt)* lowering, easing

> "
>
> En réduisant l'écart de rendement avec les autres produits de placement, la **détente** des taux (d'intérêt) redonne un peu d'oxygène au livret A.
>
> "

détenteur, -trice *nm,f (d'argent, d'un compte)* holder ▫ *détenteur d'actions, détenteur de titres* Br shareholder, Am stockholder

> "
>
> Les **détenteurs** de Sicav monétaires ou obligataires ont la possibilité de soustraire leurs plus-values à l'impôt en réinvestissant le produit de la vente dans l'immobilier d'habitation.
>
> "

détérioration *nf* deterioration

détériorer 1 *vt* to damage
2 se détériorer *vpr* to deteriorate

déterminer *vt* to determine, to ascertain; **déterminer le revenu imposable** to assess taxable income; **déterminer les conditions d'un contrat** to fix the conditions of a contract

détournement *nm* FIN **détournement d'actif** embezzlement of assets; **détournement de fonds** misappropriation of funds, embezzlement

détourner *vt (fonds)* to misappropriate, to embezzle

dette *nf* debt; **avoir des dettes** to be in debt (**envers** to); **faire des dettes** to run into debt; **avoir 10 000 francs de dettes** to be 10,000 francs in debt; **s'acquitter d'une dette** to pay off a debt; **assurer le service d'une dette** to service a debt ▫ COMPTA **dettes actives** accounts receivable; **dettes bancaires**

bank debts; *dette caduque* debt barred by the Statute of Limitations; *dettes compte* book debts; *dette consolidée* consolidated or funded debt; *dette non consolidée* unfunded debt; *dette courante* floating debt; COMPTA *dette à court terme* short-term debt; COMPTA *dettes à court terme* current liabilities; *la dette de l'État* the National Debt; *dette exigible* debt due for (re)payment; *dettes d'exploitation* trade debt; *dette extérieure* foreign debt, external debt; *dette flottante* floating debt; *dette foncière* property charge; COMPTA *dettes fournisseurs* accounts payable; *dette d'honneur* debt of honour; *(hypothécaire)* mortgage debt; *dette inexigible* unrecoverable debt; *la dette inscrite* the Consolidated Debt; *dette liquide* liquid debt; COMPTA *dettes à long terme* long-term liabilities; COMPTA *dettes passives* accounts payable, liabilities; *dette privilégiée* preferred or privileged debt; *la dette publique* the National Debt; *dette véreuse* bad debt

DEUG nm (abrév **diplôme d'études universitaires générales**) = degree gained after a two-year course

DEUST nm (abrév **diplôme d'études universitaires scientifiques et techniques**) = university degree awarded after a two-year course of study in science and/or technical subjects

Deutsche Mark nm Deutschmark

deuxième 1 adj second; **de deuxième choix, de deuxième qualité** *(marchandises, articles)* inferior
 2 nm *deuxième de change* second of exchange

dévalorisation nf (a) *(action) (de la monnaie)* devaluation; *(de marchandises)* marking down (b) *(résultat) (de la monnaie)* fall in value, depreciation; *(de marchandises)* markdown

dévaloriser 1 vt *(monnaie)* to devalue; *(marchandises)* to mark down; **dévaloriser une monnaie de 10%** to devalue a currency by 10%
 2 se dévaloriser vpr *(monnaie)* to depreciate; *(marchandises)* to lose value

dévaluation nf *(de la monnaie)* devaluation

dévaluer 1 vt *(monnaie)* to devalue
 2 se dévaluer vpr *(monnaie)* to drop in value

devancement nm FIN *(d'une échéance)* payment before the due date, prepayment

devancer vt (a) FIN **devancer une échéance** to settle an account early, to pay a bill before the due date (b) *(concurrence)* to get ahead of; **sur ce marché, nous ne sommes plus devancés que par les Japonais** now only the Japanese are ahead of us in this market

devanture nf (a) *(vitrine)* Br shop window, Am store window (b) *(façade)* Br shop front, Am store front (c) *(étalage)* window display

développement nm *(d'une entreprise, de l'économie)* development, growth; *(d'un produit)* development; **être en plein développement** to be growing fast; **ce produit n'est qu'au stade de son développement** this product is only at the development stage ❑ *développement durable (d'une économie)* sustainable development; *développement régional* regional development; *développement des ventes* sales expansion

développer 1 vt *(entreprise, économie, produit)* to develop
 2 se développer vpr *(entreprise, économie)* to develop, to grow; *(produit)* to develop; **les usines Viaut cherchent à se développer** Viaut are seeking to expand

déverrouiller vt ORDINAT to unlock; *(majuscules)* to lock off; **déverrouiller un fichier en écriture** to unlock a file, to remove the read-only lock on a file

devis nm estimate, quotation; **établir un devis** to draw up an estimate or a quotation; **faire faire un devis pour qch** to get an estimate or a quotation for sth; **le devis des réparations s'élève à trois mille francs** the estimate or quotation for the repairs comes to three thousand francs ❑ *devis appréciatif* estimate, quotation; *devis descriptif* specification; *devis estimatif* estimate, quotation

devise nf FIN currency ❑ *devise convertible* convertible currency; *devise non convertible* non-convertible currency; *devise(s) étrangère(s)* foreign currency; *devise faible* soft or weak currency; *devise forte* hard or strong currency; *devise internationale* international currency; *devise soutenue* firm currency

devises-titres nf FIN foreign security, exchange currency

devoir vt **devoir qch à qn** to owe sb sth; **il me doit mille francs** he owes me a thousand francs; **la somme qui m'est due** the amount owing to me or due to me; **reste à devoir** *(sur facture)* balance due

diagnostic d'autotest *nm* ORDINAT self-test diagnosis

diagramme *nm* diagram; *(graphique)* graph □ **diagramme à bâtons** bar chart; **diagramme de circulation** flow chart; **diagramme à secteurs** pie chart

dialogue *nm* (a) *(négociations)* dialogue, talks □ **dialogue Nord-Sud** dialogue or talks between North and South (b) ORDINAT **dialogue d'établissement de liaison** handshaking

dialoguer *vi* (a) *(négocier)* to hold talks; **les syndicats vont de nouveau dialoguer avec le ministre** the unions are to resume talks with the minister (b) ORDINAT to interact

dictaphone® *nm* Dictaphone®

dictée *nf* dictation; **écrire qch sous la dictée de qn** to write sth at sb's dictation

dicter *vt* (a) *(courrier, lettre)* to dictate (**à** to) (b) *(imposer)* to dictate; **ces mesures ont été dictées par la conjoncture économique** these measures were dictated by the economic situation

didacticiel *nm* ORDINAT tutorial

différé, -e **1** *adj (paiement, crédit)* deferred **2** *nm* ORDINAT **en différé** *(traitement)* off-line

différence *nf (entre deux prix)* difference; BOURSE *(entre le cours offert et le cours demandé)* spread

différenciation *nf* MKTG differentiation □ **différenciation de ligne** line differentiation; **différenciation du produit** product differentiation

différend *nm* difference of opinion, disagreement (**entre** between); JUR dispute

différentiel, -elle **1** *adj* differential **2** *nm* differential □ **différentiel d'inflation** inflation differential; **différentiel de prix** price differential; **différentiel de taux** interest rate differential

différer *vt (jugement, paiement, réunion)* to defer, to postpone; **différer l'échéance d'un effet** to let a bill lie over

difficulté *nf* difficulty; **être en difficulté** *(entreprise, économie, secteur)* to be in difficulties or trouble □ **difficultés financières, difficultés de trésorerie** financial difficulties; **nous connaissons actuellement quelques difficultés financières** we are currently experiencing some financial difficulties

diffuser *vt (produits, livres)* to distribute; *(rapport)* to circulate; **leurs produits sont diffusés sur une grande échelle** their products are widely available

diffusion *nf (de produits, de livres)* distribution; *(d'un journal)* circulation; **ce sont des articles de grande diffusion** they are widely available products □ **diffusion de masse** *(d'un journal)* mass circulation

digraphie *nf* COMPTA double-entry book-keeping

dilapider *vt (fortune)* to waste, to squander; *(fonds publics)* to embezzle

diluer *vt* FIN *(capital, actions)* to dilute; **diluer le bénéfice par action** to dilute equity; **diluer entièrement des actions** to fully dilute shares

dilution *nf* FIN *(du capital, des actions)* dilution □ **dilution du bénéfice par action** dilution of equity

diminuer **1** *vt* to cut, to reduce; **montant net diminué du prix de vente** net amount less purchase price **2** *vi* to fall, to drop

diminution *nf* reduction, decrease (**de** in); **la diminution des charges patronales est censée encourager l'embauche** it is hoped that the reduction of employer's contributions will stimulate employment; **faire une diminution sur un compte** to allow a rebate on an account

dire *nm* JUR allegation; **au dire de l'expert** according to expert opinion or to the experts

direct, -e *adj (impôts, ligne téléphonique)* direct; **être en rapport** *ou* **contact direct** *ou* **en relations directes avec qn** to be in direct contact with sb

directeur, -trice **1** *adj (équipe, instances)* management, executive; *(force)* directing, managing **2** *nm,f (qui fait partie du conseil d'administration)* director; *(d'un magasin, d'un service)* manager □ **directeur des achats** purchasing manager; **directeur adjoint** deputy director/manager; **directeur administratif** executive director; **directeur administratif et financier** administrative and financial manager; **directeur d'agence** branch manager; **directeur de banque** bank manager; **directeur de chantier** site manager; **directeur de la clientèle** customer relations manager; **directeur commercial** sales director/manager; **directeur de la communication** communications director/manager; **directeur des comptes-clients** accounts director/manager; **directeur de la création** creative director; **directeur du crédit** credit manager; **directeur de division** *(au siège)* divisional director; **directeur exécutif** executive director; **direc-**

teur d'exploitation operations director/manager; **directeur export** export director/manager; **directeur financier** financial director/manager; **directeur général** *(d'une entreprise)* Br managing director, Am chief executive officer; *(d'une organisation internationale)* director general, general manager; **directeur général adjoint** Br deputy managing director, Am vice-president; **directeur gérant** executive director; **directeur hiérarchique** line manager; **directeur (de l') informatique** computer manager; **directeur intérimaire, directeur par intérim** acting manager; **directeur juridique** legal director; **directeur de marché** market manager; **directeur du marketing** marketing director/manager; **directeur de marque** brand manager; **directeur du personnel** personnel director/manager; **directeur de production** production manager; **directeur de produit** product manager; **directeur de projet** project director/manager; **directeur de la publicité** advertising director/manager; **directeur de recherche et développement** director of research and development, R&D director; **directeur de recherche mercatique** marketing research director/manager; **directeur régional** regional director/manager, area director/manager; **directeur des relations publiques** public relations director/manager; **directeur des ressources humaines** human resources manager; **directeur de service** head of department; **directeur des services techniques** technical director; **directeur de succursale** branch manager; **directeur technique** technical manager; **directeur des ventes et du marketing** sales and marketing director/manager; **directeur des ventes** sales director/manager; **directeur de zone** regional manager

direction *nm* (a) *(d'une entreprise, d'un magasin, d'un service)* management; **la direction** *(bureau)* the director's office; *(locaux)* head office; **avoir la direction d'une entreprise** to manage a company; **il a confié la direction du service clientèle à son fils** he put his son in charge of the customer services department ▫ **direction commerciale** sales management; **direction des crédits** credit management; **direction des entreprises** business management; **direction de l'exploitation** operations management; **direction export** export management; **direction financière** financial management; **direction générale** general management, senior management; **Direction générale des Impôts** Br ≃ Inland Revenue, Am ≃

Internal Revenue; **direction multiple** multiple management; **direction par objectifs** management by objectives; **direction du personnel** personnel management; **direction de la production** production control; **direction de projet** project management; **direction régionale** regional headquarters; **direction des ressources humaines** human resources management; **direction des ventes** sales management

(b) *(service)* department ▫ **direction du contentieux** legal department; ADMIN **Direction départementale de l'action sanitaire et sociale** = office administering health and social services at regional level; **direction de l'exploitation** operations department; **direction financière** finance department; ADMIN **Direction générale de la santé** = central administrative body for health and social services; ADMIN **Direction des hôpitaux** = central government office for hospital administration; **direction marketing, direction mercatique** marketing department; **direction du personnel** personnel department; **direction du trésor** finance department

(c) *(ensemble des cadres)* management; *(conseil d'administration)* board (of directors)

(d) ORDINAT **direction systématisée** systems management

directoire *nm* board of directors

directorial, -e *adj* directorial, managerial

dirigé, -e *adj (économie)* controlled, planned; *(monnaie)* managed, controlled

dirigeant, -e 1 *adj (cadres)* managing; *(classes)* ruling
2 *nm,f* manager; **les dirigeants** management ▫ **dirigeant syndical** union leader

diriger 1 *vt (entreprise, équipe)* to manage, to run; *(production)* to control; *(investissements, fonds)* to channel (**vers** to)
2 se diriger *vpr* **se diriger vers** to head for, to move towards; **l'économie se dirige vers la reprise/la récession** the economy is picking up/heading for recession

dirigisme *nm* ÉCON state control

dirigiste ÉCON **1** *adj* interventionist
2 *nmf* advocate of state control

discount *nm* discount; **un discount de 20%** a 20% discount

discounter[1] *nm* discounter

discounter[2] *vt & vi* to sell at a discount

disparaître *vi* **tout doit disparaître** *(sur panneau)* everything must go

disponibilité *nf* (**a**) ADMIN leave of absence; **mettre qn en disponibilité** *(au chômage)* to lay sb off; **prendre une disponibilité** to take leave of absence; **demander une mise en disponibilité** to ask for leave of absence (**b**) FIN **disponibilités** available funds, liquid assets ◻ *disponibilités en caisse* cash in hand; *disponibilités monétaires* money supply (**c**) *disponibilités du stock* items available in stock

disponible **1** *adj* (**a**) ADMIN *(fonctionnaire)* on leave of absence (**b**) FIN *(fonds, capital, solde)* available (**c**) *(article)* available; **ces articles sont disponibles en magasin** these items can be supplied from stock
2 *nm* (**a**) FIN **le disponible** available assets, liquid assets (**b**) **le disponible** *(articles)* items available in stock

disposer disposer de *vt ind* to have at one's disposal; **disposer de capitaux importants** to have a large capital at one's disposal; **nous disposons d'une large gamme de produits** we offer a wide range of products; **le directeur va vous recevoir, mais sachez qu'il ne dispose que de trente minutes** the manager can see you now, but he only has half an hour

dispositif *nm* (**a**) *(mesures)* system, plan; **il s'agit d'un dispositif gouvernemental pour favoriser l'emploi des jeunes** it's a government plan to stimulate youth employment (**b**) ORDINAT *dispositif d'alimentation* power unit; *(pour papier)* sheet feed; *dispositif d'alimentation feuille à feuille* cut sheet feed, stacker; *dispositif d'alimentation papier* sheet feed, paper feed; *dispositif de sortie* output device; *dispositif de stockage* storage device (**c**) *(appareil)* device ◻ TÉL *dispositif de redirection d'appel* call-forwarding device

disposition *nf* (**a**) *(disponibilité)* **avoir qch à sa disposition** to have sth at one's disposal; **mettre qch à la disposition de qn** to put *or* place sth at sb's disposal, to make sth available to sb; **je suis à votre disposition** I am at your disposal; **ils ont mis une secrétaire à la disposition du directeur** a secretary has been made available for the manager ◻ *disposition fiscale* tax provision (**b**) **dispositions** *(préparatifs)* arrangements; **prendre des dispositions pour faire qch** to make the necessary arrangements to do sth (**c**) *(d'un texte, d'un clavier)* layout (**d**) *(tendance)* tendency; *(du marché)* tone, trend (**e**) JUR clause, stipulation

disque *nm* ORDINAT disk ◻ *disque amovible* removable disk; *disque cible* target

disk; *disque de démarrage* boot disk; *disque de destination* destination disk; *disque dur* hard disk; *disque laser* laser disk; *disque optique* optical disk; *disque optique compact* CD-ROM; *disque souple* floppy disk; *disque source* source disk; *disque système* system disk; *disque vidéo numérique* digital video disk

disquette *nf* ORDINAT diskette, floppy (disk); **sur disquette** on diskette, on floppy ◻ *disquette cible* target disk; *disquette de copie* copy disk; *disquette de démarrage* boot disk, start-up disk; *disquette de démonstration* demo disk; *disquette de destination* destination disk; *disquette (à) double densité* double density disk; *disquette d'installation* installation disk, installer; *disquette optique* optical disk, floptical disk; *disquette programme* program disk; *disquette (à) simple densité* single density disk; *disquette source* source disk; *disquette système* system disk

dissimulation d'actif *nf* JUR *(fraudulent)* concealment of assets

dissolution *nf* JUR *(d'un contrat)* dissolution, termination; *(d'une entreprise)* winding up

dissoudre *vt* JUR *(contrat)* to dissolve, to terminate; *(entreprise)* to wind up

distance *nf* ORDINAT **à distance** remote

distribuable *adj* *(bénéfice)* distributable

distribuer *vt* (**a**) MKTG *(produits, marchandises)* to distribute (**b**) *(fonctions, tâches)* to allocate, to allot (**c**) *(actions, bénéfices)* to distribute; *(dividendes)* to pay (**d**) *(courrier)* to deliver

distributaire *nmf* JUR distributee

distributeur, -trice *nm,f* (**a**) *(vendeur)* distributor, dealer ◻ *distributeur agréé* authorized stockist *or* distributor; *distributeur en gros* wholesaler (**b**) *(machine)* *distributeur automatique de billets* cash dispenser, automatic teller machine; *distributeur de monnaie* change machine

distribution *nf* (**a**) *(de produits)* distribution; **la grande distribution** large-scale distribution ◻ *distribution d'échantillons* sampling; *distribution exclusive* exclusive distribution; *distribution à flux tendus* just-in-time distribution; *distribution en gros* wholesale distribution; *distribution de masse* mass distribution; *distribution numérique* stock holding distribution (**b**) *(de fonctions, de tâches)* allocation, allotment

(c) *(d'actions, de bénéfices)* distribution; *(de dividendes)* payment ❑ **distribution des richesses** distribution of wealth
(d) *(du courrier)* delivery

divers, -e 1 *adj* sundry, miscellaneous
2 *nmpl* sundries

diversification *nf* diversification; **l'entreprise a adopté une stratégie de diversification** the company has adopted a policy of diversification; **la diversification de l'entreprise est la condition de sa survie** the company must diversify if it is to survive ❑ **diversification industrielle** diversification, lateral integration of industry; **diversification des produits** product diversification

diversifier 1 *vt (production, activités, économie)* to diversify
2 se diversifier *vpr (entreprise)* to diversify; *(produits, activités, économie)* to become diversified

dividende *nm* dividend; **toucher un dividende** to draw a dividend; **déclarer** *ou* **annoncer un dividende** to declare *or* announce a dividend; **avec dividende** cum div(idend), *Am* dividend on; **sans dividende** ex div(idend), *Am* dividend off ❑ **dividendes accrus** accrued dividends; **dividende d'action** share dividend, dividend on shares; **dividende par action** dividend per share; **dividende anticipé** advance dividend; **dividende brut** gross dividend; **dividende cumulatif** cumulative dividend; **dividende fictif** sham dividend; **dividende final** final dividend; **dividende intérimaire, dividende par intérim** interim dividend; **dividende net** net dividend; **dividende prioritaire, dividende de priorité** preference dividend; **dividende prioritaire cumulatif** preference cumulative dividend; **dividende privilégié** preference dividend

diviser *vt (répartir)* to divide; FIN, BOURSE *(actions)* to split

division *nf* **(a)** *(répartition)* division; FIN, BOURSE *(des actions)* split ❑ **division du marché** market division; **division du travail** division of labour
(b) *(partie)* division, department ❑ **division des exportations** export division; **division de formation professionnelle** training division; **division internationale** international division

DLC *nf* (abrév **date limite de consommation**) best-before date

DOC *nm* ORDINAT (abrév **disque optique compact**) CD-ROM

dock *nm* **(a)** *(bassin)* dock, dockyard **(b)** *(entrepôt)* warehouse ❑ **dock entrepôt** dock-warehouse; **dock frigorifique** cold storage dock

docker *nm Br* docker, *Am* longshoreman

document *nm* document; **rédiger un document** to draw up a document ❑ UE **document administratif unique** unique data folder; ORDINAT **document de base** source document; **documents contre acceptation** documents against acceptance; **documents contre paiement** documents against payment; **document d'embarquement** shipping document; **document d'expédition** shipping document; **document interne à l'entreprise** internal company document; **document maître** master document; **documents maritimes** shipping documents; **document d'offre** tender document; MKTG **document de publicité directe** direct mailing; **document source** source document; COMPTA **document de synthèse** financial statement; **document transmissible** transferable document; **document de transport combiné** combined transport document; **document de travail** working document; **document type** standard document; **documents de voyage** travel documents

documentaire *adj* documentary; **ce rapport vous est fourni à titre documentaire** this report is supplied for information only

documentaliste *nmf* ADMIN information officer

documentation *nf* **(a)** *(technique)* documentation **(b)** *(publicités)* literature, documentation

documenter 1 *vt* to document; **bien documenté** *(rapport)* well-documented; *(personne)* well-informed
2 se documenter *vpr* to gather information or material (**sur** on)

doit *nm* debit, liability; *(d'un compte)* debit side; **doit et avoir** debits and credits; *(personnes)* debtors and creditors

dollar *nm* dollar; **un billet de cinq dollars** a five-dollar *Br* note or *Am* bill ❑ **dollar américain** US dollar

domaine *nm* **(a)** *(propriété)* estate, property; **Domaine (de l'État)** State property ❑ **domaine public** public property; **être dans le domaine public** to be out of copyright; **tomber dans le domaine public** to come into the public domain
(b) *(secteur d'activité)* field, domain; **c'est du domaine du service commercial** that's for the marketing department to deal with

❏ MKTG *domaine d'activité stratégique* strategic business unit; *domaine concurrentiel* competitive scope

domicile *nm* (place of) residence, home; **sans domicile fixe** of no fixed abode; **travailler à domicile** to work from home; **le chéquier sera renvoyé à votre domicile** the chequebook will be sent to your home address; **ils livrent à domicile** they have a delivery service ❏ JUR *domicile conjugal* marital *or* matrimonial home; *domicile fiscal* tax domicile

domiciliataire *nmf* paying agent

domiciliation *nf* domiciliation ❏ *domiciliation bancaire* payment *(by banker's order)*

domicilié, -e *adj* (**a**) *(personne)* resident, domiciled (**à** at); **être domicilié à Londres** to be domiciled in London (**b**) *(salaire)* paid directly into one's bank account

domicilier *vt* to domicile

dominer *vt (secteur, marché)* to dominate

dommage *nm* (**a**) *(dégâts matériels)* damage; **subir un dommage** to suffer damage; **réparer les dommages** to repair *or* to make good the damage (**b**) JUR *(préjudice)* harm ❏ *dommage corporel* personal *or* physical injury; *dommages et intérêts* damages; *dommage matériel* damage to property, material damage; *dommages punitifs* punitive damages

dommages-intérêts *nmpl* JUR damages; **fixer les dommages-intérêts** to fix damages; **poursuivre qn en dommages-intérêts** to sue sb for damages, to bring an action for damages against sb; **verser/obtenir des dommages-intérêts** to pay/to be awarded damages ❏ *dommages-intérêts compensatoires* compensation

DOM-TOM *nmpl* (abrév **Départements et Territoires d'Outre-mer**) = French overseas departments and territories

donation *nf* JUR donation ❏ *donation inter vivos* gift inter vivos; *donations parents-enfants* donations from parents to children

> 66
> Parce qu'on constate une répartition des patrimoines aux âges élevés, on aspire à la possibilité d'une transmission plus précoce – possibilité d'ailleurs ouverte sur le plan fiscal et de plus en plus utilisée, à en juger par la fréquence croissante des **donations parents-enfants**.
> 99

donnée *nf* piece of information; ORDINAT piece of data; **données** information; ORDINAT data; **je n'ai pas toutes les données du problème** I don't have all the information on the problem ❏ *données de base* background data; *données brutes* raw data; *en données corrigées des variations saisonnières* seasonally adjusted; ORDINAT *données numériques* digital data

> 66
> L'excédent de la balance commerciale française est retombé en juin à un niveau plus sage : 4,4 milliards de francs (en **données corrigées des variations saisonnières**).
> 99

donneur, -euse *nm,f* FIN *donneur d'aval* guarantor *or* backer of bill; *donneur de caution* guarantor; *donneur d'ordre* principal

doper *vt (exportations, ventes)* to boost; **la dépréciation de la lire a dopé les ventes à l'étranger** the depreciation in the value of the lira has boosted export sales

dormant, -e *adj* FIN *(compte)* dormant; *(marché, capital)* unproductive, lying idle

DOS *nm* ORDINAT DOS

dos *nm* FIN *(d'un effet, d'un chèque)* back; **signer au dos d'un chèque** to endorse a cheque, to sign the back of a cheque; **voir au dos** see over *or* overleaf

dossier *nm* (**a**) *(pièces, documents)* file, dossier; *(chemise)* folder, file; **verser une pièce au dossier** to file a document; **constituer un dossier sur qn/qch** to build up a file on sb/sth ❏ *dossier d'appel d'offres* tender documents; *dossier de candidature* application; *dossier client* client file; *dossier crédit* credit file; *dossier de demande de prêt* loan application form; *dossier de domiciliation* domiciliation papers, domiciliation file; *dossier de douane* customs papers, customs file; *dossier de lancement (d'un produit)* product launch file; *dossier de presse* book of press cuttings; MKTG press pack; *dossier suspendu* suspension file; *dossier de voyage* travel documents

(**b**) *(sujet)* question, matter; **le dossier du GATT** the GATT question; **s'occuper du dossier de l'environnement** to be responsible for environmental matters

(**c**) ORDINAT file ❏ *dossier actif* active file; *dossier archivé* archive file; *dossier clos* closed file; *dossier ouvert* open file; *dossier sauvegardé* saved file; *dossier système* system file

dotation nf (**a**) *(fonds) (d'hôpital, de collège)* endowment, foundation; *(à un chef d'État)* allowance

(**b**) *(subvention)* grant

(**c**) Can ADMIN **dotation en effectifs** staff increase

(**d**) COMPTA provision ◻ **dotation aux amortissements** depreciation provision, allowance for depreciation; **dotation en capital** capital contribution; **dotation au compte de provisions** appropriation to the reserve; **dotation aux provisions** charge to provisions

> **"**
>
> En 1992, sur 65 milliards de **dotations aux provisions**, 20 étaient dus aux défaillances d'entreprises.
>
> **"**

doter vt (**a**) *(hôpital, collège)* to endow (**b**) *(équiper)* to equip (**de** with)

douane nf DOUANES (**a**) *(à la frontière)* customs; **passer à la douane** ou **au bureau de douane** to go through customs; **passer qch en douane** to clear sth through customs; **passer qch en fraude à la douane** to smuggle sth through customs; **marchandises en douane** bonded goods; **soumis aux droits de douane** dutiable ◻ **douane volante** mobile customs unit (**b**) *(administration)* **la douane** Br ≃ Customs and Excise, Am ≃ Customs Service (**c**) *(taxe)* customs duty; **exempté de douane** duty-free

douanier, -ère 1 *adj* customs
2 *nm,f* customs officer

double 1 *adj* double; **à double revenu** *(foyer, ménage)* two-income; **en double exemplaire** in duplicate ◻ ORDINAT **double densité** double density; COMPTA **double emploi** duplication (of entry); **double imposition** double taxation; BOURSE **double marché des changes** dual exchange market; BOURSE **double option** double option, put and call option
2 *nm (exemplaire)* duplicate, copy; ORDINAT backup; **veuillez nous adresser un double de la facture** please send us a copy of the bill; **j'ai tous mes papiers en double** I have duplicates *or* copies of all my papers

double-clic *nm* ORDINAT double-click; **faire un double-clic** to double-click

double-cliquer *vi* ORDINAT to double-click

DPO nf *(abrév* **direction par objectifs**) management by objectives

drachme *nf* drachma

drainage *nm (de capital, de ressources)* tapping

drainer *vt (capital, ressources)* to tap

dresser *vt (plan, contrat, bilan, liste)* to prepare, to draw up; *(facture)* to make out

DRH 1 *nm (abrév* **directeur des ressources humaines**) human resources manager
2 *nf (abrév* **direction des ressources humaines**) human resources management

droit *nm* (**a**) *(prérogative)* right; **tous droits (de reproduction) réservés** *(sur livre)* all rights reserved; **avoir droit à qch** to have a right to sth, to be entitled to sth; **avoir des droits sur qn/qch** to have rights over sb/sth; JUR **de droit et de fait** de facto and de jure; **à qui de droit** *(sur lettre)* to whom it may concern; **s'adresser à qui de droit** to apply to an authorized person; **faire droit à une demande** to comply with *or* accede to a request ◻ **droit d'accès** right of entry; **droits d'achat** purchasing rights; **droit d'auteur** copyright; **droit au bail** right to a lease; **droits contractuels** rights granted by contract; **droits de distribution, droits de diffusion** *(d'un produit)* distribution rights; **droits étrangers** foreign rights; **droits exclusifs** sole rights; **droits d'exclusivité** exclusive rights; **droits d'exploitation pour le monde entier** worldwide rights; **droits de fabrication** manufacturing rights; **droit de grève** right to strike; **droits internationaux** international rights; **droit de licenciement** right to dismiss; **droit de préemption** right of first refusal, pre-emptive right; **droit de préférence** right of first refusal; **droit préférentiel de souscription** rights issue; JUR **droit de rachat** repurchase right, buyback right; **droit de recours** right of appeal; **droits de reproduction** reproduction rights; **droit de souscription** subscription rights; **droits statutaires** statutory rights; FIN **droits de tirage spéciaux** special drawing rights; **droits de vente exclusifs** exclusive selling rights

(**b**) *(en argent)* fee; *(imposition)* duty; *(taxe)* tax; **droits à la charge du vendeur/de l'acheteur** duty to be paid by the seller/purchaser ◻ **droits ad valorem** ad valorem duty; **droits d'auteur** royalties; **recevoir des droits d'auteur de 10%** to receive royalties of 10%; **droit de courtage** brokerage (fee); **droits différentiels** differential duties; **droits de dock** dock dues; **droits de douane** customs duty; **droits d'enregistrement** registration fees; **droit d'entrée** import duty; **droit d'exportation** export duty; COMPTA **droit fixe** fixed rate of duty;

droits de greffe registry dues; *droit d'immatriculation* registration fee; *droit d'importation* import duty; *droits de mutation* capital transfer tax; *droits de navigation* shipping dues; *droits de port* harbour dues; *droit de sortie* export duty; *droits de succession* inheritance tax; *droit de timbre* stamp duty

(**c**) JUR law ❏ *droit administratif* administrative law; *droit bancaire* banking law; *droit de brevet* patent law; *droit cambial* exchange law; *droit civil* civil law; *droit commercial* commercial law; *droit communautaire* Community law; *droit constitutionnel* constitutional law; *droit des contrats* contract law; *droit douanier* customs legislation; *droit écrit* statute law; *droit fiscal* tax law; *droit international* international law; *droit maritime* maritime law; *droit des obligations* law of contract; *droit social* employment law; *droit des sociétés* corporate law; *droit du travail* labour law

> **❝**
>
> Les **droits de mutation** sur les immeubles d'habitation (parfois appelés frais de notaire) sont allégés de 20%.
>
> **❞**

DTS *nmpl* (*abrév* **droits de tirage spéciaux**) special drawing rights

dû, due 1 *adj* (**a**) *(que l'on doit)* due, owing; **en port dû** carriage forward (**b**) JUR *(approprié)* **en bonne et due forme** in due form
2 *nm* due; **payer son dû** to pay the amount owed

ducroire *nm* del credere; *(agent)* del credere agent

dûment *adv* duly; **dûment expédié/reçu** duly dispatched/received; **dûment accrédité** *(représentant)* duly authorized

dumping *nm* ÉCON dumping; **faire du dumping** to dump ❏ *dumping social* social dumping

duopole *nm* duopoly

duplicata *nm* duplicate (copy) ❏ *duplicata de reçu* duplicate receipt

duplication *nf* *(d'un document, d'un logiciel)* copying

dupliquer *vt* *(document, logiciel)* to copy, to make a copy of

durée *nf* *(d'un bail)* duration, term; *(de crédit)* term; *(d'un prêt)* life; **les syndicats essaient de faire baisser la durée hebdomadaire de travail** the unions are trying to have the working week shortened ❏ COMPTA *durée d'amortissement* depreciation period; ORDINAT *durée de connexion* on-line time; *durée (utile) de vie* *(d'un produit)* life expectancy, shelf-life

DUT *nm* (*abrév* **diplôme universitaire de technologie**) = qualification awarded after a two-year course of study in technology

DVD *nm* ORDINAT (*abrév* **Digital Video Disk, Digital Versatile Disk**) DVD

dynamique 1 *adj* *(concurrence)* brisk
2 *nf* dynamics ❏ *dynamique d'équipe* team dynamics; *dynamique du marché* market dynamics; *dynamique des produits* product dynamics

EAO nm (abrév **enseignement assisté par ordinateur**) CAL

écart nm (entre deux chiffres) difference; COMPTA spread, variance; BOURSE spread; MKTG gap; **il y a un écart de cent francs entre les deux comptes** there is a discrepancy of a hundred francs between the two accounts; BOURSE **l'écart entre le prix d'achat et le prix de vente** the spread between bid and asked prices; **l'écart se creuse entre les pays riches et les pays pauvres** there is a growing gap between the rich and poor countries □ **écart budgétaire** budgetary variance; **écart de caisse** cash shortage; FIN **écarts de conversion** exchange adjustments; **écarts de cours** price spreads; **écart des coûts** cost variance; **écart déflationniste** deflationary gap; **écart inflationniste** inflationary gap; **écart net** net variance; BOURSE **écart de prime** option spread; **écart de prix** price differential; **écart de salaire** wage differential; **écart sur stock** inventory shortage; **écart type** standard deviation

échange nm (a) FIN exchange; (commerce) trade; **les échanges entre la France et l'Allemagne ont connu une progression spectaculaire** trade between France and Germany has increased spectacularly □ **échanges commerciaux** trade; **échanges industriels** industrial trade; **échanges internationaux** international trade; **échanges en valeurs** turnover; **échanges en volume** tonnage

(b) BANQUE, BOURSE swap □ **échange d'actions** share swap; **échange cambiste** treasury swap; **échange de créances** debt swap; **échange de créances contre actifs** debt equity swap; **échange de dette** debt swap; **échange de devises** currency swap; **échange financier** swap; **échange de taux d'intérêt** interest rate swap

(c) MKTG **échange standard** (de produit) replacement

(d) ORDINAT **échange de données** data exchange; **échange de données dynamique** dynamic data exchange; **échange de données informatisé** electronic data exchange

échangeable adj exchangeable (**contre** for)

échanger 1 vt to exchange; **les marchandises ne sont ni reprises ni échangées** goods cannot be returned or exchanged

2 s'échanger vpr BOURSE to trade; **ces titres s'échangent à 70 francs** these securities are trading at 70 francs

échantillon nm (a) MKTG (pour un sondage) sample □ **échantillon aléatoire** random sample; **échantillon aréolaire** cluster sample; **échantillon modèle** standard sample; **échantillon normal** average sample; **échantillon probabiliste** probability sample; **échantillon par quotas** quota sample; **échantillon représentatif** true or fair sample; **échantillon témoin** check sample; **échantillon type** representative sample

(b) (d'un produit) sample □ **échantillon gratuit** free sample; **échantillon promotionnel** promotional sample

échantillonnage nm (a) MKTG (action) sampling; (groupe de personnes) sample; **l'échantillonnage se fait sur un produit sur cent** one product in a hundred is sampled or tested □ **échantillonnage aléatoire** random sampling; **échantillonnage empirique** purposive or non-random sampling; **échantillonnage probabiliste** probability sampling; **échantillonnage par zone** area sampling

(b) (série d'échantillons) range of samples

échantillonner vt (a) MKTG (population) to sample (b) (préparer des échantillons de) to prepare samples of (c) (comparer) to verify or to check by the samples

échantillonneur, -euse nm,f MKTG (personne) sampler

échappatoire nf loophole □ **échappatoire comptabilité** accounting loophole

échappement nm ORDINAT escape

échauffement nm FIN (de l'économie) overheating

échéance nf (a) FIN (de dû) maturity date, due date; (de terme) expiry date; **avant échéance** (paiement, règlement) before the due date; **à trois mois d'échéance** at three months' date; **emprunter à longue/à courte échéance** to borrow long/short; **prêter à longue/à courte échéance** to lend long/short; **venir à échéance** to fall due, to mature; **faire face à ses échéances** to meet one's financial commitments; **avoir de**

lourdes **échéances** to have heavy financial commitments; **l'intérêt n'a pas été payé à l'échéance** the interest is overdue ❑ *échéance commune* equation of payment; *échéance à court terme* short-term maturity; COMPTA *échéances de fin de mois* end-of-month payments; *échéance fixe* fixed maturity; *échéance à long terme* long-term maturity; *échéance moyenne* average due date; *échéance à moyen terme* medium-term maturity; BOURSE *échéance proche* near month; *échéance à vue* sight bill *or* maturity **(b)** *(d'un bail, d'un contrat)* expiration

échéancier *nm* FIN bill book; COMPTA due date file ❑ *échéancier de paiement* payment schedule

échelle *nf* scale; **à l'échelle mondiale/nationale** on a world/national scale; **de grande échelle** large-scale ❑ MKTG *échelle d'attitudes* attitude scale; MKTG *échelle de classement* rating scale; MKTG *échelle d'importance* importance scale; *échelle mobile (des prix, salaires)* sliding scale; *échelle des prix* price range; *échelle des salaires* salary scale; *échelle des traitements* salary scale

> ❝
> Le démantèlement de l'**échelle mobile** des salaires, qui indexait les rémunérations sur les prix … [dissuade] les ménages de … dépenser.
> ❞

échelon *nm* **(a)** *(degré d'une hiérarchie, d'une organisation)* grade; **monter/descendre d'un échelon** to go up/down a grade; **le dernier/premier échelon** the bottom/top grade; **il a gravi rapidement tous les échelons** he quickly climbed to the top of the ladder ❑ *échelon salarial* salary level **(b)** *(niveau)* level; **à l'échelon ministériel/directoriel** at ministerial/managerial level; **à l'échelon régional/national** on a regional/national level; **à tous les échelons** on every level ❑ BOURSE *échelon de cotation* tick size

échelonnement *nm* **(a)** *(de paiements)* spreading **(b)** *(de vacances)* staggering

échelonner *vt* **(a)** *(paiements)* to spread (out); **les versements sont échelonnés sur dix ans** the instalments are spread (out) over ten years **(b)** *(vacances)* to stagger

échoir *vi* **(a)** FIN *(dette)* to fall due; *(investissement)* to mature; **le terme échoit le 20 de ce mois** the date for payment is the 20th of

this month; **le délai est échu** the deadline has expired **(b)** *(bail)* to expire

échu, -e *adj* FIN due; *(intérêts)* outstanding

école *nf* school ❑ *École nationale d'administration* = prestigious university level college preparing students for senior posts in the civil service and public management; *École supérieure de commerce de Paris* = prestigious business and management school

économat *nm* **(a)** *(magasin)* staff (discount) store **(b)** *(fonction d'économe)* bursarship; *(bureau)* bursar's office

économe *nmf* bursar

économétrique *adj* econometric

économie *nf* **(a)** *(système)* economy; **l'économie de la France** the French economy ❑ *économie d'actionnariat populaire* share economy; *économie capitaliste* capitalist economy; *économie de dimension* economy of scale; *économie dirigée* controlled *or* planned economy; *économie d'échelle* economy of scale; *économie libérale* free-market economy; *économie de marché* market economy; *économie mixte* mixed economy; *économie non monétaire* natural economy; *économie parallèle* black economy; *économie planifiée* planned economy; *économie de plein emploi* full-employment economy; *économie politique* political economy; *économie à ressources sous-exploitées* sleeping economy; *économie salariale* wage economy; *économie souterraine* black economy; *économie de troc* barter economy **(b)** *(discipline)* economics **(c)** *(gain)* saving; **faire une économie de temps** to save time; **vous faites une économie de 20%** you make a saving of 20% ❑ *économie de main-d'œuvre* labour saving **(d)** **économies** *(épargne)* savings; **faire des économies** to save money

économique *adj* **(a)** *(relatif à l'économie)* economic **(b)** *(avantageux)* economical

économiquement *adv* **(a)** *(du point de vue de l'économie)* economically; **les économiquement faibles** the lower-income groups **(b)** *(à moindre frais)* inexpensively

économiser *vt* *(argent, temps)* to economize, to save; **économiser sur qch** to economize on sth

économiseur d'écran *nm* ORDINAT screen saver

économiste *nmf* (political) economist ❑ *économiste d'entreprise* business economist

écoulé, -e *adj* (a) *(du mois dernier)* of last month; **votre lettre du 25 écoulé** your letter of the 25th of last month; **payable fin écoulé** due at the end of last month (b) *(passé)* **l'exercice écoulé** the last financial year

écoulement *nm (de marchandises, d'un surplus, des stocks)* sale; **d'écoulement facile/difficile** fast-/slow-moving

écouler 1 *vt (marchandises, surplus, stocks)* to sell (off); **écouler qch à bas prix** to sell sth off cheaply; **écouler qch à perte** to sell sth at a loss; **facile/difficile à écouler** easy/difficult to sell

2 **s'écouler** *vpr* (a) *(marchandises, surplus, stocks)* to sell; **notre stock s'écoule rapidement** our stock is selling fast (b) *(délai)* to expire; **le délai de grâce que nous vous avions consenti s'est écoulé** the extension we agreed to has expired

> **"**
> Les producteurs de jouets chinois n'hésitent pas à copier les créations européennes pour mieux les **écouler**, à prix cassés, dans les réseaux de la grande distribution occidentale.
> **"**

écran *nm* (a) ORDINAT screen; **à l'écran** on screen ❑ *écran d'aide* help screen; *écran antireflet* antiglare screen; *écran couleur* colour screen *or* display; *écran à cristaux liquides* liquid crystal screen; *écran divisé* split screen; *écran haute résolution* high-resolution screen; *écran tactile* touch *or* touch-sensitive screen; *écran de visualisation* visual display unit, VDU (b) *écran publicitaire* commercial break

écraser *vt* (a) *(accabler)* **écraser qn d'impôts** to overburden sb with taxes; **écraser le marché** to glut *or* flood the market; **écraser les prix** to slash prices (b) ORDINAT *(fichier)* to zap

écrémage *nm* MKTG *(du marché)* skimming

écrémer *vt* MKTG *(marché)* to skim

écrire *vt* to write; *(noter)* to write down; **écrire à qn** to write to sb; **écrire une lettre à la machine** to type a letter; ORDINAT **écrire qch sur un disque** to write sth to disk; COMPTA **écrire la comptabilité** to write up the books

écrit, -e 1 *adj (convention, déclaration)* written; **écrit à la main** handwritten; **écrit à la machine** typewritten, typed 2 *nm* (a) **par écrit** in writing; **consigner** *ou*

coucher qch par écrit to put sth down in writing; **confirmez-le nous par écrit** give us written confirmation, confirm it to us in writing (b) *(document)* (written) document; **signer un écrit** to sign a document

écriture *nf* (a) COMPTA *(opération)* entry, item; **passer une écriture** to make an entry ❑ *écriture de clôture* closing entry; *écriture complémentaire* supplementary entry; *écriture comptable* accounting entry; *écriture conforme* corresponding entry; *écriture d'inventaire* closing entry; *écriture d'ouverture* opening entry; *écriture rectificative* corrected entry; *écriture de régularisation* adjusting entry; *écriture regroupement* consolidated entry; *écriture de virement* transfer entry (b) COMPTA **écritures** *(comptes)* accounts; **tenir les écritures** to keep the accounts *or* the books; **arrêter les écritures** to close the accounts; **passer les écritures** to post (up) the books ❑ *écritures en partie double* double-entry bookkeeping; *écritures en partie simple* single-entry bookkeeping (c) *écriture abrégée* speedwriting

ÉCU, écu *nm* FIN *(abrév* **European currency unit***)* ECU, ecu

EDI *nm* ORDINAT *(abrév* **échange de données informatisé***)* EDE

éditer *vt* ORDINAT to edit

éditeur *nm* (a) *(qui publie)* (book) publisher (b) ORDINAT *(de programme)* editor ❑ *éditeur d'icônes* icon editor; *éditeur de liens* linker, link editor; *éditeur de logiciel* software company; *éditeur de texte* text editor

édition *nf* (a) *(activité)* (book) publishing (b) ORDINAT editing

effaçable *adj* ORDINAT *(mémoire)* erasable

effacement *nm* ORDINAT deletion

effacer *vt* ORDINAT *(données)* to erase, to delete; *(écran)* to clear

effectif, -ive 1 *adj* (a) FIN *(coût, monnaie, taux)* effective; *(valeur, revenu)* real; *(circulation)* active; *(rendement)* actual (b) *(règlement, mesures)* in effect; **cette loi sera effective au 1 janvier** this law will come into effect on 1 January 2 *nm* (a) *(employés)* staff; **l'usine emploie un effectif de 49 personnes** the factory employs 49 people *or* has a staff of 49; **à effectif réduit** short-staffed (b) FIN *effectif budgétaire* budgetary strength, *Am* authorized strength (c) *effectif de série économique* economic batch quantity

effectuer **1** vt *(paiement, calculs, réservation)* to make; *(dépenses)* to incur; *(étude)* to carry out; *(commande)* to place
2 **s'effectuer** vpr *(paiement, voyage)* to be made

effet nm (**a**) *(résultat, conséquence)* effect; **les effets de la crise économique** the effects of the economic crisis; **facture avec effet rétroactif** backdated bill; **nul et sans effet** null and void; **prendre effet** to take effect ❑ FIN **effet balançoire** see-saw effect; **effet boomerang** boomerang effect; **effet de dilution** dilutive effect; **effet de levier** gearing, leverage; ORDINAT **effet de transition** transition
(**b**) FIN bill ❑ **effet bancaire** bill, draft; **effet de cavalerie** kite; **effet de commerce** bill of exchange; **effet de complaisance** accommodation bill; **effet à courte échéance** short, short-dated bill; **effet à date fixe** fixed-term bill; **effet en devise(s)** bill in foreign currency; **effet domicilié** domiciled bill; **effet à l'encaissement** bill for collection; **effets à encaisser** accounts receivable; **effet endossé** endorsed bill; **effet escompté** discounted bill; **effet libre** clean bill; **effet à longue échéance** long, long-dated bill; **effets nominatifs** registered stock; **effet à ordre** promissory note; **effets à payer** bills payable; **effet au porteur** bearer bill, bill made out to bearer; **effets publics** government stock *or* securities; **effets à recevoir** bills receivable; **effet en souffrance** overdue bill; **effet à taux flottant** floating rate note, FRN; **effet à vue** sight bill *or* draft
(**c**) ASSUR commencement
(**d**) JUR **effets mobiliers** personal effects

efficace adj *(méthode)* effective; *(personne)* efficient

efficacement adv *(avec succès)* effectively; *(de façon productive)* efficiently

efficacité nf *(d'une méthode)* effectiveness; *(d'une personne)* efficiency ❑ **efficacité du coût** cost effectiveness; **efficacité économique** economic efficiency; **efficacité parfaite** absolute efficiency; **efficacité publicitaire** advertising effectiveness; **efficacité relative** relative efficiency; **efficacité de vente** sales performance

efficience nf *(d'une entreprise)* efficiency

effleurement nm ORDINAT **à effleurement** *(clavier)* touch-sensitive

effondrement nm *(des prix, des marchés, des cours, des bénéfices)* slump (**de** in); *(d'une monnaie)* collapse

effondrer **s'effondrer** vpr *(prix, marchés, cours, bénéfices)* to slump; *(monnaie)* to collapse; **le marché s'est effondré** the bottom has fallen out of the market

effort nm effort ❑ MKTG **effort de commercialisation** marketing effort; **effort financier** financial outlay; **effort de marketing, effort de mercatique** marketing effort; **effort de promotion** promotional campaign; **effort publicitaire** advertising campaign

effritement nm BOURSE *(des cours)* crumbling

effriter **s'effriter** vpr BOURSE *(cours)* to crumble

égalité nf equality; **égalité devant l'emploi** equal opportunities for employment ❑ **égalité des chances** equal opportunities; **égalité des salaires** equal pay

élaboration nf *(d'un plan, d'une idée, d'une stratégie)* working out, development; *(d'une constitution, d'une loi, d'un budget)* drawing up ❑ **élaboration de concept** concept development; MKTG **élaboration de produit** product development

élaborer vt *(plan, idée, stratégie)* to work out, to develop; *(constitution, loi, budget)* to draw up

élargir **1** vt *(gamme de produits, activités, clientèle)* to expand; *(marché)* to expand, to broaden
2 **s'élargir** vpr *(entreprise, marché, organisation)* to expand

élargissement nm *(d'une gamme de produits, d'activités, de clientèle)* expansion; *(du marché)* expansion, broadening

élasticité nf *(de l'offre, de la demande, du marché, des prix)* elasticity

élastique adj *(offre, demande, marché, prix)* elastic

électronique **1** adj *(réservation, traitement de données, point de vente, argent)* electronic
2 nf electronics

élément nm (**a**) ORDINAT *(d'un menu)* item (**b**) *(donnée)* factor; **éléments** data, information ❑ **élément du prix de revient** cost factor (**c**) COMPTA *(d'un compte)* item

élevé, -e *adj (prix, taux)* high; **les dépenses sont élevées** expenditure is running high

élever **1** *vt (prix, taux)* to raise, to put up; **élever qn à un rang supérieur** to promote sb
2 **s'élever** *vpr* **s'élever à** to come to, to amount to; **la facture s'élève à mille francs** the bill comes to *or* amounts to a thousand francs

éluder *vt (loi, règlement)* to elude; **éluder le paiement de l'impôt** to evade payment of tax

émargement *nm (d'un document, d'un compte)* initialling *(in the margin)*

émarger **1** *vt (document, compte)* to initial *(in the margin); (signer)* to sign; *(courrier)* to sign for
2 *vi* to draw one's salary; **il émarge aux fonds secrets** he's paid out of the secret funds

emballage *nm* (**a**) *(contenant)* packaging; **l'emballage est consigné** there is a deposit on the packaging; **emballage compris** packaging included; **emballage gratuit** packaging free of charge □ *emballage géant* giant pack; *emballage d'origine* original packaging; *emballage perdu* non-returnable packaging; *emballage réutilisable* recyclable packaging; *emballage transparent* blister pack; *emballage sous vide* vacuum pack
(**b**) *(action)* packing, packaging

emballage-bulle *nm* blister pack

emballement *nm (des cours, du marché)* boom (**de** in); **on a assisté à l'emballement de la demande pour ce genre de produits** we have witnessed the boom in demand for this type of product

emballer **1** *vt (dans une boîte)* to pack; *(dans du papier)* to wrap up; **emballé sous vide** vacuum-packed
2 **s'emballer** *vpr (cours, marché)* to spiral out of control

embargo *nm* embargo; **lever l'embargo** to lift the embargo; **mettre l'embargo sur qch** to put an embargo on sth □ *embargo commercial* trade embargo; *embargo économique* economic embargo

embarquement *nm* (**a**) *(de marchandises)* loading (**b**) *(de personnes)* boarding

embarquer **1** *vt* (**a**) *(marchandises)* to load (**b**) *(personnes)* to board
2 **s'embarquer** *vpr (aller à bord)* to go on board, to board

embarras *nm* difficulty, trouble; **l'entreprise connaît des embarras financiers** the company is in financial difficulty

embauchage, embauche *nf* taking on, hiring

embaucher *vt* to take on, to hire

emblème de marque *nm* MKTG brand mark

émergent, -e *adj (marché)* emerging

émetteur, -trice FIN **1** *adj (banque, organisme)* issuing
2 *nm,f (de billets, d'actions, d'une carte)* issuer; *(d'un chèque)* drawer

émettre *vt* FIN *(chèque, actions, billets de banque, timbres)* to issue; *(emprunt)* to float; *(lettre de crédit)* to open

> **"**
> France Télécom va acquérir 2% du capital de Deutsche Telekom, qui achètera 2% des actions du groupe français . Pour financer cette opération, France Telecom **émettra** de nouvelles actions en Bourse, représentant 5% de son capital.
> **"**

émission *nf* FIN *(d'un chèque, d'actions, de billets de banque, de timbres)* issue; *(d'un emprunt)* flotation; *(d'une lettre de crédit)* opening □ BOURSE *émission d'actions* share issue; *émission d'actions gratuites* scrip issue; *émission boursière* share issue; *émission obligataire, émission d'obligations* bond issue; *émission par séries* block issues

> **"**
> Ces emprunts n'ont jamais réellement servi à renflouer les caisses de l'État, ni même à financer des investissements: ils servaient de plus en plus à payer les intérêts des **émissions** précédentes...
> **"**

emmagasinage *nm* (**a**) *(de marchandises)* storage (**b**) *(frais)* storage charges

emmagasiner *vt (marchandises)* to store

émoluments *nmpl (d'un employé)* salary, pay; **percevoir des émoluments** to receive payment

empaquetage *nm (action)* packing, packaging; *(emballage)* packaging; **poids net à l'empaquetage 250g** net weight when packed, 250g □ *empaquetage automatique* automatic packaging

empaqueter *vt* to pack, to package

emplacement *nm* (**a**) *(site)* site, location; **ce serait l'emplacement idéal pour notre nouvelle usine** that would be the ideal site *or* location for our new factory □ *emplace-*

ment d'affichage hoarding site; *emplacement publicitaire* advertising space

(b) ORDINAT slot □ *emplacement pour carte* card slot; *emplacement pour carte d'extension* expansion slot; *emplacement d'évolutivité* upgrade slot; *emplacement (pour) périphériques* extension slot

emploi *nm* (a) *(situation)* job; *(embauche)* employment, work; **être sans emploi** to be out of work *or* unemployed; **chercher un emploi, être à la recherche d'un emploi** to be looking for work *or* a job; **solliciter un emploi** to apply for a job; **créer de nouveaux emplois** to create new jobs □ *emplois jeunes* = state-subsidized jobs created specifically for young people as part of the French government's drive to combat unemployment; *emploi à mi-temps* part-time job; *emploi à plein temps* full-time job; *emplois de proximité* = jobs created at local community level *(typically involving childminding, caring for the elderly etc)*; *emploi à temps partiel* part-time job

(b) *(utilisation)* use; *(des capitaux)* deployment □ *emploi du temps* timetable, schedule

employé, -e *nm,f* employee □ *employé d'administration* government employee; *employé de banque* bank clerk; *employé de bureau* office worker; *employé aux écritures* accounts clerk; *employé de l'expédition* shipping clerk; *employé de magasin* Br sales assistant, Am clerk; *employé occasionnel* casual worker; *employé de la régie* Br ≃ Customs and Excise officer, Am ≃ Customs Service officer

employer *vt* (a) *(faire travailler) (personne)* to employ; **employer qn comme secrétaire** to employ sb as a secretary; **employé à plein temps/à temps partiel** employed full-time/part-time

(b) *(utiliser)* to use; **employer les grands moyens** to take drastic measures

(c) COMPTA to enter; **employer qch en recette** to enter sth in the receipts

employeur, -euse *nm,f* employer

emporter *vt (marché)* to close; *(contrat)* to land

emprunt *nm* (a) *(somme)* loan; **faire un emprunt** *(auprès d'une banque)* to take out a loan; **emprunt à 8%** loan at 8%; **procéder à un nouvel emprunt** to make a new loan issue; **amortir un emprunt** to redeem a loan; **contracter un emprunt** to raise a loan; **couvrir un emprunt** to cover a loan; **émettre un emprunt** to float a loan; **placer un emprunt** to place a loan; **rembourser un emprunt** to repay a loan; **souscrire un emprunt** to subscribe a loan □ *emprunt consolidé* consolidated loan; *emprunt à court terme* short-term loan; *emprunt à découvert* unsecured loan; *emprunt en devises* currency loan; *emprunt d'État* government loan; *emprunt forcé* forced loan; *emprunt sur gage* loan against security; *emprunt garanti* secured loan; *emprunt indexé* indexed loan; *emprunt à long terme* long-term loan; FIN *emprunt à lots* lottery loan; *emprunt obligataire* bond issue, loan stock; *(titre)* debenture bond; *emprunt obligataire convertible* convertible loan stock; *emprunt or* gold loan; *emprunt perpétuel* perpetual loan; *emprunt personnel* personal loan; *emprunt public* public loan; *emprunt remboursable sur demande* call loan, loan repayable on demand; *emprunt de remboursement* refunding loan; *emprunt à risques* nonaccruing loan; *emprunt à terme* term loan; *emprunt sur titres* loan on securities *or* stock

(b) *(action)* borrowing

emprunter *vt* to borrow; **emprunter qch à qn** to borrow sth from sb; **la société a dû emprunter pour s'acquitter de ses dettes** the company had to borrow to pay off its debts; **emprunter sur hypothèque** to borrow on mortgage; **emprunter sur titres** to borrow on securities; **emprunter à long/à court terme** to borrow long/short; **emprunter à intérêt** to borrow at interest

emprunteur, -euse 1 *adj* borrowing

2 *nm,f* borrower

émulation *n* ORDINAT emulation

ENA *nf (abrév* **École nationale d'administration**) = prestigious university-level college preparing students for senior posts in the civil service and in public management

encadrement *nm* (a) ADMIN *(fonction)* management; *(cadres)* executives (b) ÉCON control □ *encadrement du crédit* credit control *or* restrictions; *encadrement des loyers* rent control; *encadrement des prix* price control

encadrer *vt* (a) ADMIN *(personnel, équipe)* to manage; **nous sommes bien encadrés** we have a good management team (b) ÉCON *(prix, loyers, crédit)* to control

encaissable *adj* FIN *(chèque)* cashable; *(argent, traite)* collectable, receivable; **ce chèque est encaissable à la banque** this cheque can be cashed at the bank

encaisse *nf* cash (in hand), cash balance; *(d'un magasin)* money in the till □ *encaisse disponible* cash in hand; *encaisse métallique, encaisse or et argent* gold and silver reserves, bullion

encaissement *nm* FIN *(d'un chèque)* cashing; *(d'argent, d'une traite)* collection, receipt □ *encaissements et décaissements* cash inflows and outflows

encaisser *vt* (a) FIN *(chèque)* to cash; *(argent, traite)* to collect, to receive (b) *(marchandises)* to pack (in boxes)

encaisseur, -euse FIN **1** *adj (banque, établissement)* collecting
2 *nm (d'un chèque)* payee; *(de l'argent, d'une traite)* collector, receiver

enchère *nf* bid; **les enchères** bidding; **mettre** *ou* **porter une enchère** to make a bid; **mettre qch aux enchères** to put sth up for auction; **couvrir une enchère** to make a higher bid; **faire monter les enchères** to up *or* raise the bidding; **l'enchère a monté jusqu'à deux cents francs** the bidding rose to two hundred francs □ *enchères publiques* public auction; *enchères au rabais* Dutch auction

enchérir *vi* to make a higher bid; **enchérir de mille francs** to bid another thousand francs; **enchérir sur qn** to outbid sb

enchérisseur, -euse *nm,f* bidder; **vendre au (plus offrant et) dernier enchérisseur** to sell to the highest bidder

encodage *nm* ORDINAT encoding

encoder *vt* ORDINAT to encode

encodeur *nm* ORDINAT encoder.

encombré, -e *adj (marché)* glutted, flooded

encombrement *nm* (a) ORDINAT **faible encombrement sur le disque dur** low use of hard disk space (b) *(de marchandises)* glut

encombrer *vt (marché)* to glut, to flood

encouragements *nmpl* incentives □ *encouragements à l'exportation* export incentives; *encouragements à la production* production incentives

encourir *vt (frais)* to incur

encours, en-cours *nm* (a) BANQUE loans outstanding; **l'encours de la dette** the outstanding debt □ *encours de crédit* outstanding credits; *encours débiteur autorisé* authorized overdraft facility
(b) COMPTA *encours de production de biens* work-in-progress
(c) *encours de fabrication* material undergoing processing; *encours de route*

stock awaiting transfer *(to another department)*

endetté, -e *adj (pays, personne, entreprise)* in debt

endettement *nm* (a) *(action)* running *or* getting into debt; *(état)* debt □ *endettement des consommateurs* consumer debt; *endettement extérieur* foreign debt; *endettement intérieur* internal debt (b) COMPTA indebtedness, gearing

endetter 1 *vt* **endetter qn** to get sb into debt; **l'acquisition de nouvelles machines a endetté la société** the purchase of new machinery has got the company into debt
2 s'endetter *vpr* to get into debt

endiguement *nm* BOURSE, FIN hedging

endiguer *vt (montée des prix, inflation, chômage)* to contain

endommager *vt* (a) *(abîmer)* to damage (b) ORDINAT to corrupt

endos *nm (sur effet, chèque)* endorsement □ *endos en blanc* blank endorsement

endossataire *nmf* endorsee

endossement *nm (sur effet, chèque)* endorsement □ *endossement en blanc* blank endorsement

endosser *vt (effet, chèque)* to endorse

endosseur, -euse *nm,f* endorser

énergétique *adj (ressources, besoins)* energy

engagement *nm* (a) *(promesse)* undertaking, commitment; **contracter** *ou* **prendre un engagement** to enter into an undertaking *or* a commitment; **prendre l'engagement de faire qch** to undertake to do sth; **rompre ses engagements** to fail to honour one's commitments; **sans engagement (de votre part)** with no obligation (on your part) □ *engagement écrit* written undertaking
(b) FIN *(de capital, d'investissements)* locking up, tying up; *(de dépenses, de frais)* incurring □ *engagement bancaire* (bank) commitment; *engagement de dépenses* commitment of funds; *engagement hors bilan* contingent liabilities
(c) *(mise en gage) (au mont-de-piété)* pawning; *(auprès de créanciers)* pledging; *(d'une*

propriété) mortgaging
(**d**) *(embauche)* appointment
(**e**) *(de négociations)* beginning, start; JUR *(de poursuites)* institution

engager 1 *vt* (**a**) FIN *(capital, investisse-ments)* to lock up, to tie up; *(dépenses, frais)* to incur
(**b**) *(mettre en gage) (au mont-de-piété)* to pawn; *(auprès de créanciers)* to pledge; *(pro-priété)* to mortgage
(**c**) *(embaucher)* to hire, to take on
(**d**) *(négociations)* to begin, to start; JUR **engager des poursuites (contre)** to take legal action (against), to institute proceed-ings (against)
(**e**) *(lier)* to bind, to commit; **votre signature vous engage à respecter les termes du contrat** signature of the contract obliges you to respect its terms; **cela n'engage à rien** it doesn't commit you to anything
2 **s'engager** *vpr* (**a**) *(promettre)* **s'engager à faire qch** to undertake to do sth; **s'engager par contrat à faire qch** to contract to do sth; **s'engager vis-à-vis de qn** to contract with sb
(**b**) *(se lancer)* **s'engager dans une affaire** to get involved in a deal

engorgement *nm (du marché)* flooding, glutting

> ❝
>
> Les services téléphoniques dédiés aux clients peinent à suivre le rythme des nouvelles souscriptions. France Télé-com reconnaît l'**engorgement** de ses services.
>
> ❞

engorger *vt (marché)* to flood, to glut

enlèvement *nm (de marchandises)* collec-tion; **enlèvement et livraison** collection and delivery

enlever 1 *vt* (**a**) *(marchandises, actions)* to snap up (**b**) *(contrat, affaire)* to get, to land
2 **s'enlever** *vpr (marchandises)* to sell quickly, to get snapped up

énoncé *nm (d'un contrat, d'une loi)* text, wording

enquête *nf* (**a**) MKTG survey ❑ **enquête auprès des consommateurs** consumer survey; **enquête fiscale** tax survey; **en-quête sur les lieux** field study; **enquête de marché** market survey; **enquête omni-bus** omnibus survey; **enquête d'opinion** opinion poll; **enquête pilote** pilot survey; **enquête postale** postal survey; **enquête sur les prix** price survey; **enquête par questionnaire** questionnaire survey; **en-quête sociologique** sociological survey;

enquête de solvabilité credit enquiry; **en-quête par sondage** opinion poll; **enquête téléphonique** telephone interview *or* sur-vey
(**b**) JUR inquiry, investigation ❑ **enquête administrative** public inquiry

enquêter *vi* MKTG *(faire un sondage)* to conduct a survey (**sur** into)

enquêteur, -trice *nm,f* MKTG pollster

enrayer *vt (montée des prix, inflation, chô-mage)* to curb

enregistrement *nm* (**a**) *(d'une société)* registration, incorporation; **faire l'enregis-trement d'une société** to register a company
(**b**) *(d'une commande)* booking, entering (up) ❑ COMPTA **enregistrement comptable** accounting entry
(**c**) ADMIN **l'Enregistrement** the Registra-tion department
(**d**) ORDINAT *(de données)* logging, record-ing; *(article de base de données)* record
(**e**) *(dans un aéroport)* check-in; **se présenter à l'enregistrement** to check in

enregistrer 1 *vt* (**a**) *(commande)* to book, to enter (up); **les meilleures ventes enregis-trées depuis des mois** the best recorded sales for months
(**b**) *(afficher)* to show; **enregistrer le cour-rier** to log the mail
(**c**) ORDINAT *(données, programme)* to store
(**d**) *(dans un aéroport)* **(faire) enregistrer ses bagages** to check in one's baggage

enseignement assisté par ordi-nateur *nm* computer-aided learning

ensemble *nm* (**a**) *(totalité)* **ces mesures concernent l'ensemble du personnel** these measures concern the entire staff (**b**) *(groupe)* set ❑ MKTG **ensemble de besoins** need set; MKTG **ensemble de considéra-tions** consideration set, product choice set
(**c**) ORDINAT *(de caractères, d'informations)* set

entamer *vt* (**a**) *(travail, recherche, négocia-tions)* to begin, to start; *(démarches)* to initi-ate; **entamer une vente** to open a sale; JUR **entamer des poursuites (contre)** to take legal action (against), to institute proceed-ings (against) (**b**) *(capital, profits)* to eat into

> ❝
>
> Mais Boeing rencontre d'énormes difficultés pour respecter ses délais de livraison, et ces commandes, arra-chées à des prix très serrés pour maintenir coûte que coûte la part de marché du groupe, ont fortement **entamé** les profits.
>
> ❞

entente *nf* *(accord)* agreement, understanding (**entre** between) ❑ *entente industrielle* combine, cartel

en-tête *nm* *(d'une lettre, d'un document)* heading; *(papier)* letterhead; ORDINAT header ❑ *en-tête de facture* billhead

entièrement *adv* entirely, completely; **entièrement versé** *(capital)* fully paid-up

entité *nf* COMPTA item

entrée *nf* (**a**) *(action)* entry, entrance; **l'entrée de l'Autriche dans l'Union européenne** Austria's entry into the European Union ❑ *entrée en fonction* assumption of one's duties; **l'entrée en fonction du nouveau directeur est prévue pour le 1 mai** the new director is scheduled to take up his post on 1 May; *entrée en jouissance* taking possession; *entrée en séance* opening of a meeting; *entrée en vigueur* coming into force (**b**) *(de marchandises)* import ❑ *entrée de capitaux* capital inflow; *entrée en douane* inward customs clearance, clearance inward; *entrée en franchise* free import (**c**) ORDINAT *(processus)* input, entry; *(information)* entry; *(touche)* enter (key) (**d**) *(voie d'accès)* way in, entrance (**e**) COMPTA *(dans un livre de comptes)* entry

entrée/sortie *nf* ORDINAT input/output

entreposage *nm* warehousing, storing; DOUANES bonding

entreposer *vt* to warehouse, to store; DOUANES to bond, to put in bond

entreposeur *nm* (**a**) *(qui tient un entrepôt)* warehouseman; DOUANES officer in charge of a bonded store (**b**) *(commerçant)* = wholesaler selling goods under a government monopoly

entrepositaire *nmf* warehousekeeper

entrepôt *nm* (**a**) warehouse; DOUANES bonded warehouse; DOUANES **mettre des marchandises en entrepôt** to bond goods, to put goods in bond; **à prendre à l'entrepôt** *ou* **en entrepôt** at warehouse ❑ *entrepôt de (la) douane* bonded warehouse; *entrepôt fictif* unbonded warehouse; *entrepôt frigorifique* cold store; *entrepôt maritime* wharf; *entrepôt réel* bonded warehouse (**b**) *(port)* entrepôt; **Londres est un grand centre d'entrepôt** London has a large entrepôt trade

entreprendre *vt* to undertake; **entreprendre de faire qch** to undertake to do sth

entrepreneur, -euse *nm,f* (**a**) *(de travaux)* contractor ❑ *entrepreneur (en bâtiments)* building contractor; *entrepreneur de roulage, entrepreneur de transport* haulage contractor; *entrepreneur de travaux publics* public works contractor (**b**) *(chef d'entreprise)* entrepreneur

entreprise *nf* (**a**) *(firme)* company, business; **les grandes entreprises** big business ❑ *entreprise artisanale* small-scale enterprise; *entreprise commerciale* business enterprise; MKTG *entreprise défendable* tenable firm; *entreprise dominante* dominant firm; *entreprise exportatrice* export company; *entreprise de factage* delivery service; *entreprise familiale* family business; *entreprise individuelle* one-man business, sole trader; *entreprise industrielle* manufacturing company; MKTG *entreprise innovatrice* innovator, market pioneer company; *entreprise marginale* firm with only a marginal profit; *entreprise de messageries* parcel delivery company; *entreprise multinationale* multinational company; *entreprise nationale* national business; *entreprise en participation* joint venture; *entreprise phare* leading company; *entreprise prestataire de services* service company; *entreprise privée* private company; *entreprise publique* public corporation; *entreprise de roulage* road haulage company; *entreprise de service public* public utility company; *entreprise de transports* haulage *or* carrying company; *entreprise de travail intérimaire* temp agency; *entreprise de travaux publics* civil engineering company; *entreprise unipersonnelle* one-man business, sole trader; *entreprise unipersonnelle à responsabilité limitée* sole trader with limited liability; *entreprise de vente par correspondance* mail-order company (**b**) *(action, initiative)* enterprise, undertaking, venture (**c**) JUR *(louage)* contracting; **mettre qch à l'entreprise** to put sth out to contract; **prendre qch à l'entreprise** to contract for sth

entrer **1** *vt* (**a**) *(introduire)* **entrer des marchandises en contrebande** *ou* **en fraude** to smuggle in goods (**b**) ORDINAT *(données)* to enter, to input; *(au clavier)* to key in
2 *vi* (**a**) *(marchandises)* to enter, to be imported; **entrer dans un marché** to enter a market; **les marchandises qui entrent en France sont soumises à des droits de douane** goods entering France are subject to customs duty; **ces marchandises sont entrées en fraude sur le territoire** these goods were smuggled into the country (**b**) *(commencer)* **entrer en association avec qn** to form a partnership with sb; **entrer en**

concurrence avec qn to go into competition with sb; **entrer en fonction** to take up one's duties; **entrer en liquidation** to go into liquidation; **entrer en relation avec qn** to get in contact with sb; **entrer dans la vie active** to start one's working life; **entrer en vigueur** to come into force, to take effect

(**c**) ORDINAT to log in or on

entretenir *vt* (**a**) COMPTA *(comptes)* to keep in order (**b**) *(garder en bon état)* to maintain; **entretenir de bonnes relations avec qn** to remain on friendly or good terms with sb

entretien *nm* (**a**) *(conversation)* conversation, talk; *(entre employeur et candidat)* interview; **avoir des entretiens avec le patronat** to hold talks or discussions with the employers; **convoquer qn à un entretien** to call sb for interview ▫ *entretien d'embauche* job interview

(**b**) MKTG interview ▫ *entretien assisté par ordinateur* computer-assisted interview; *entretien de groupe* group interview; *entretien libre, entretien non structuré* unstructured interview; *entretien organisé* arranged interview; *entretien spontané* intercept interview; *entretien structuré* structured interview; *entretien par téléphone, entretien téléphonique* telephone interview

(**c**) *(de matériel)* maintenance; **entretien et réparations** servicing and repairs ▫ *entretien systématique* planned maintenance

envahir *vt (marché)* to flood

enveloppe *nf* (**a**) *(pour le courrier)* envelope; **mettre une lettre sous enveloppe** to put a letter in an envelope ▫ *enveloppe à fenêtre* window envelope; *enveloppe timbrée* stamped addressed envelope

(**b**) *(somme)* sum; *(budget)* budget ▫ FIN *enveloppe budgétaire* budget (allocation); *enveloppe salariale* wages bill

> Paris négocie avec Ankara la vente de six navires chasseurs de mines pour une **enveloppe** de l'ordre de 4 milliards de francs.

envelopper *vt* to wrap (up)

enveloppe-réponse *nf* reply-paid envelope

environnement *nm* (**a**) *(milieu)* environment ▫ *environnement institutionnel* corporate environment; *environnement du marché* market environment; *environnement marketing, environnement*

mercatique marketing environment (**b**) ORDINAT environment

envoi *nm* (**a**) *(action)* sending; **faire un envoi tous les mois** to send goods every month ▫ *envoi exprès* express delivery; *envoi de fonds* remittance (of funds); **faire un envoi de fonds à qn** to send or remit funds to sb; *envoi en groupage, envoi groupé* grouped consignment; *envoi par mer* shipment; *envoi en nombre* mass mailing; *envoi contre paiement* cash with order; *envoi postal* postal delivery; *envoi contre remboursement* cash on delivery; *envoi recommandé* recorded delivery; *envoi à titre d'essai* sent on approval (**b**) *(ce qui est envoyé) (colis)* parcel; *(lettre)* letter; *(marchandises)* consignment (**de** of); **j'ai bien reçu votre envoi du 10 octobre** I acknowledge receipt of your consignment of 10 October

envolée *nf (hausse rapide)* rapid rise; **l'envolée du dollar** the rapid rise in the dollar

envoler s'**envoler** *vpr (cours, prix)* to soar

> Grâce aux cours du bacon -dites : pork belly-qui **s'envolent** au très officiel Chicago Board of Trade, le voilà depuis un an milliardaire en dollars.

envoyer *vt* to send; *(fonds, mandat)* to send, to remit; **envoyer une lettre à qn** to send sb a letter; **envoyer qch par fax/par télex** to send sth by fax/by telex; **envoyer qch par chemin de fer** to send sth by rail; **envoyer qch par la poste** *ou* **par courrier** to mail sth, Br to post sth; **je lui ai envoyé un chèque par la poste** I sent him a cheque by post

envoyeur, -euse *nm,f (de lettre, de marchandises)* sender

épargnant, -e *nm,f* saver, investor

épargne *nf (action)* saving; *(sommes)* savings; *(épargnants)* savers, investors ▫ *épargne complément de retraite* pension fund savings; *épargne des entreprises* company reserves; *épargne institutionnelle* institutional savings; *épargne investie* investments; *épargne liquide* on-hand savings; *épargne mobilière* fixed savings; *épargne négative* negative saving; *l'épargne privée* private investors; *l'épargne productive* re-invested savings

> La nécessité de leur trouver des financements, bloque les taux d'intérêt à long terme à un niveau élevé et détourne l'**épargne privée** au détriment des investissements productifs.

épargne-logement *nm* **plan d'épargne-logement** home savings plan; **prêt d'épargne-logement** home loan

épargner *vt* to save

épargne-retraite *nf* pension fund, retirement fund

éponger *vt* FIN *(déficit)* to mop up, to absorb; **éponger le pouvoir d'achat excédentaire** to mop up excess purchasing power

épuisé, -e *adj* (a) *(marchandises)* sold out, out of stock; *(ressources, réserves, stocks)* exhausted (b) *(lettre de crédit)* invalid

épuisement *nm (de marchandises)* selling out; *(de ressources, de réserves, de stocks)* exhaustion; **jusqu'à épuisement des stocks** while stocks last

épuiser 1 *vt (marchandises)* to sell out of; *(ressources, réserves, stocks)* to exhaust
2 **s'épuiser** *vpr* to run out

équation *nf* (a) COMPTA equation □ **équation de bénéfice** profit equation; **équation de coût** cost equation (b) MKTG equation □ **équation de la demande** demand equation; **équation de réponse de marché** sales-response function; **équation de vente** sales equation

équilibration *nf (d'un budget)* balancing

équilibre *nm* **en équilibre** *(budget)* balanced □ **équilibre budgétaire** balanced budget

équilibrer *vt (budget)* to balance

équipe *nf* team; **travailler par équipes** to work in shifts; **faire équipe avec qn** to team up with sb □ MKTG **équipe commando** venture team; **équipe commerciale** marketing team; **équipe de création** creative team; **équipe de direction, équipe dirigeante** management team; **équipe de jour** day shift; **équipe de nuit** night shift; **équipe de vente** sales team

équipement *nm (machines)* equipment; *(installations)* facilities □ **équipements collectifs** public facilities *or* amenities; **équipement industriel** industrial plant; ORDINAT **équipement informatique** computer equipment; **équipement lourd** heavy equipment; **équipement portuaire** harbour facilities

ergonomie *nf* ergonomics

ergonomique *adj* ergonomic

érosion monétaire *nf* depreciation of money

erreur *nf* (a) *(faute)* error, mistake; **faire** *ou* **commettre une erreur** to make a mistake; **par erreur** by mistake; **induire qn en erreur** to mislead sb; **il y a une erreur dans votre compte** there is a mistake in your account; **sauf erreur ou omission** errors and omissions excepted; **sauf erreur de notre part** unless we are mistaken □ **erreur de calcul** miscalculation; **erreur de gestion** management error; **erreur typographique** printing error (b) ORDINAT error □ **erreur aléatoire** random error; **erreur disque** disk error; **erreur de logiciel** software error; **erreur système** system error

E/S *nf* ORDINAT *(abrév* **entrée/sortie)** I/O

escalade *nf (des prix, des taux d'intérêt)* escalation

escomptable *adj* COMPTA discountable

escompte *nm* (a) *(de commerce)* discount; **accorder** *ou* **faire un escompte sur qch** to allow *or* give a discount on sth; **à escompte** at a discount; *Can* **50% d'escompte sur toute la marchandise** 50% discount on all goods □ **escompte sur les achats en gros** bulk discount, quantity discount; **escompte de caisse** cash discount; **escompte commercial** trade discount; **escompte au comptant** cash discount; **escompte à forfait** forfaiting; **escompte professionnel** *(au détaillant)* trade discount; **escompte d'usage** trade discount
(b) FIN discount; **prendre à l'escompte un effet de commerce** to discount a bill of exchange; **présenter une traite à l'escompte** to have a bill discounted □ **escompte de banque** bank discount; **escompte de créances** invoice discounting; **escompte en dedans** true discount; **escompte en dehors** bank discount; **escompte officiel** *Br* bank discount rate, *Am* prime rate; **escompte de règlement** discount for early payment; **escompte de traites** invoice discounting
(c) BOURSE *(de valeurs)* call for delivery before settlement

escompter *vt* (a) FIN *(traite)* to discount (b) BOURSE *(valeurs)* to call for delivery of before settlement

escompteur *nm* FIN discount broker

ESCP *nf (abrév* **École Supérieure de Commerce de Paris)** = prestigious business and management school

escroc *nm* crook, swindler

escroquer *vt* to swindle; **escroquer qch à qn, escroquer qn de qch** to swindle *or* cheat sb out of sth

escroquerie *nf (action)* swindling; *(résultat)* swindle; *(délit)* fraud

escudo *nm* escudo

espace *nm* (**a**) ORDINAT space ❑ *espace disque* disk space; *espace mémoire* memory space

(**b**) MKTG *espace d'exposition* display area; *espace de PLV* in-store advertising space; *espace publicitaire* advertising space; *espace de vente* sales area

(**c**) *espace économique* economic area; UE *Espace économique européen* European Economic Area; UE *espace judiciaire européen* common European legal framework; UE *espace social européen* common European social legislation

> ❝
> Les grands **espaces économiques** régionaux-l'Asie, l'Amérique et l'Europe en particulier-sont liés entre eux, ils ont néanmoins chacun une dynamique propre.
> ❞

espacement arrière *nm* ORDINAT backspace

espèces *nfpl* (*argent*) cash; **payer en espèces** to pay in cash ❑ COMPTA *espèces en caisse* cash in hand

espérance de vie *nf* (*d'un produit*) life expectancy, shelf life

esprit *nm* **esprit d'entreprise** entrepreneurship; **esprit d'équipe** team spirit

essai *nm* (**a**) (*de produit*) trial, test; **à l'essai** on a trial basis; **à titre d'essai** subject to approval; **acheter qch à l'essai** to buy sth on approval; **faire l'essai de qch** to test sth ❑ *essai à banc* bench test; *essais comparatifs* comparative tests; *essai gratuit* free trial; ORDINAT *essai de performance* benchmark; *essais de produit* product testing

(**b**) (*d'employé*) trial; **prendre** *ou* **engager qn à l'essai** to take sb on for a trial *or* probationary period

essayer *vt* (*produit, méthode*) to try (out), to test

ESSEC *nf* (*abrév* **École Supérieure des Sciences Économiques et Commerciales**) = university-level business school

essor *nm* (*d'un secteur, de l'économie*) rapid growth; **en plein essor** (*secteur, économie*) booming ❑ *essor économique* economic boom

estampillage *nm* (*d'un document*) stamping; (*de marchandises*) marking

estampille *nf* (*sur document*) (official) stamp; (*sur marchandises*) mark

estampiller *vt* (*document*) to stamp; (*marchandises*) to mark

estimateur, -trice *nm,f* appraiser, valuer

estimatif, -ive *adj* (*valeur, état*) estimated

estimation *nf* (**a**) (*détermination*) (*d'un prix*) estimation; (*de marchandises, d'une propriété*) valuation; (*de dommages, de besoins*) assessment ❑ MKTG *estimation des besoins* needs assessment; COMPTA *estimation des frais* estimate of costs (**b**) (*valeur, quantité estimée*) estimate

estimer *vt* (*prix*) to estimate; (*marchandises, propriété*) to value; (*dommages, besoins*) to assess

établir **1** *vt* (**a**) (*entreprise*) to establish, to set up (**b**) (*budget*) to draw up, to establish; (*compte, contrat*) to draw up; (*prix*) to fix; (*objectifs*) to determine

2 s'établir *vpr* to set up in business; **s'établir à son compte** to start one's own business, to become self-employed

établissement *nm* (**a**) (*d'une entreprise*) establishing, setting up

(**b**) (*d'un budget*) drawing up, establishing; (*d'un compte, d'un contrat*) drawing up; (*des prix*) fixing; (*d'objectifs*) determining ❑ TÉL *établissement d'appel* call connection; *établissement des prix de revient* costing

(**c**) (*institution*) establishment, institution ❑ *établissement bancaire* bank; *établissement de crédit* credit institution; COMPTA *établissement déclarant* company making the return; *établissement dépositaire* financial institution holding securities on trust; *établissement financier* financial institution; FIN *établissement payeur* paying bank

(**d**) (*entreprise*) business, firm; **les établissements Martin** Martin & Co ❑ *établissement affilié* affiliated company, *Am* affiliate; *établissement commercial* commercial premises; *établissement industriel* factory, manufacturing firm; *établissement principal* main branch *or* office; *établissement d'utilité public* public utility

étalage *nm* (**a**) (*de marchandises*) display; (*dans une vitrine*) window display; **faire l'étalage** to put goods on display; (*dans une vitrine*) to dress the window(s); **mettre qch à l'étalage** to display sth in the window (**b**) (*impôt*) tax paid by street trader

étalager *vt* to display, to put on display

étalagiste *nmf* (**a**) (*marchand*) street trader (**b**) (*dans un magasin*) window dresser

étalement *nm* (**a**) *(de marchandises)* displaying (**b**) *(de paiements)* spreading (out); *(de vacances)* staggering

> 66
>
> La crainte d'un **étalement** des paiements ou d'un abandon total ou partiel des créances devait en particulier inciter les banques à faire preuve de plus de discernement.
>
> 99

étaler *vt* (**a**) *(marchandises)* to display (**b**) *(paiements)* to spread (out); *(vacances)* to stagger; **étalez vos versements sur deux ans** spread your payments out over two years

étalon *nm* *(de poids et mesures)* standard □ *étalon de change-or* gold exchange standard; *étalon devise* currency standard; FIN *étalon monétaire* monetary standard

étalonnage, étalonnement *nm* standardization

étalonner *vt* to standardize

étalon-or *nm* gold standard □ *étalon-or lingot* gold bullion standard

état *nm* (**a**) *(rapport)* form; *(des dépenses, ventes)* statement, list; *(des paiements, marchandises)* schedule, list □ *état appréciatif* evaluation, estimation; *état financier* financial statement; JUR *état de frais* bill of costs; *état imprimé* printed statement *or* form; *état des lieux* inventory of fixtures *(in rented premises)*; **faire l'état des lieux** to inspect the premises; *état nominatif* list of names; *état périodique* progress report; ADMIN *états de service* service record; *état de situation* status *or* state-of-play report; *état des ventes* statement of sales figures

(**b**) COMPTA *état de caisse* cash statement; *états comptables* accounting records; *états comptables et commerciaux* internal company records; *état de compte* bank statement, statement of account; COMPTA position on an account; *état détaillé (d'un compte)* breakdown; *état néant* nil return; *état récapitulatif* final assessment, adjustment account; *état TVA* VAT statement *or* return

(**c**) *(autorité centrale)* **l'État** the State

(**d**) *(nation, territoire aux États-Unis)* state □ *État membre* member state; *état tampon* buffer state

(**e**) *(condition)* state, condition □ *état financier, état de fortune* financial standing *or* situation

(**f**) ADMIN *état civil (d'une personne)* (civil) status; *(lieu)* registry office

(**g**) ORDINAT report

étatisation *nf* state control

étatisé, -e *adj* state-controlled

étatiser *vt* to bring under state control

état-major *nm* *(d'entreprise, d'usine)* top management

État-patron *nm* **l'État-patron** the State as an employer

État-providence *nm* **l'État-providence** the welfare state

étendre **1** *vt* ORDINAT *(mémoire)* to upgrade

2 **s'étendre** *vpr* *(grève)* to spread; *(fortune, entreprise)* to expand, to grow larger

étiquetage *nm* *(de bagages, de marchandises)* labelling □ *étiquetage du prix* price labelling

étiqueter *vt* *(bagages, marchandises)* to label

étiquette *nf* label □ *étiquette à bagages* luggage label; *étiquette de calibrage (d'un produit)* grade label; *étiquette d'identification (d'un produit)* identification label; *étiquette magnétique* security tag; *étiquette porte-prix* price label; *étiquette de prix* price ticket *or* tag; *étiquette d'un produit* product label; *étiquette promotionnelle* promotional label; *étiquette de qualité* quality label

étranger, -ère **1** *adj* *(d'un autre pays)* foreign

2 *nm,f* *(d'un autre pays)* foreigner; ADMIN alien

3 *nm* **l'étranger** *(pays étrangers)* foreign countries; **à l'étranger** abroad; **aller/vivre à l'étranger** to go/live abroad

Ets *nmpl* *(abrév* **établissements***)* Ets Legrand Legrand

étude *nf* study; **le projet est encore à l'étude** the project is still at the development stage □ MKTG *étude AIO* AIO research; *étude d'audience* audience research; *étude des besoins* needs study *or* analysis; *étude de cas* case study; *étude des charges* cost analysis; *étude commerciale* marketing study; *études commerciales (dans école de commerce)* business studies; *étude de communication* communications study; *étude comparative* comparative study; *étude du comportement* behavioural study *or* analysis; *étude du comportement du consommateur* consumer behaviour study; *étude de conception* design engineering; *étude auprès des consommateurs* consumer *or* customer survey; *étude documentaire* desk research; *étude économique* economic research; *étude de faisabilité* feasibility study; *étude d'impact* impact study; *étude de marché* market study; **faire une étude**

de marché to do market research; *étude de marché standard* omnibus survey; *étude marketing* marketing study; *étude de mémorisation* recall study; *étude mercatique* marketing study; *étude des méthodes* methods analysis; *études de motivation* motivational research; *étude préliminaire* preliminary *or* pilot study; *étude de produit* product analysis; *étude de projet* project analysis; *étude de projet d'investissement* capital project evaluation; *étude prospective du marché* market study; *études et recherches* research and engineering; *étude de satisfaction de la clientèle* customer satisfaction survey; *étude des temps et des méthodes* time and methods study; *étude des temps et des mouvements* time and motion study; *étude sur le terrain* field study; *études sur les ventes* sales research

> ❝ ———————————————
>
> Peaudouce fait réaliser un ''tracking'' ... qui compare l'effet de chaque campagne sur un certain nombre de points clés de la marque. Cela revient à poser deux questions: la cible a-t-elle été atteinte, a-t-elle vu ou lu le message? Les **études d'impact** sont utilisées dans ces 2 cas et coûtent entre 30 000 et 80 000 francs.
>
> ——————————————— ❞

EURL *nf* (*abrév* **entreprise unipersonnelle à responsabilité limitée**) trader with limited liability

euro *nm* UE *(monnaie)* euro

eurochèque *nm* Eurocheque

eurocrate *nmf* eurocrat

eurodevise *nf* euro-currency

eurodollar *nm* eurodollar

euromarché *nm* euromarket

euromonnaie *nf* euro-currency

euro-obligation *nf* eurobond

Europe *nf* Europe ❑ *l'Europe des quinze* the fifteen member states of the European Union; *l'Europe sociale* social Europe (*a united Europe committed to a progressive social and welfare policy*); *l'Europe Verte* (European) Community agriculture *or* farming

évaluable *adj* (*marchandises, propriété*) appraisable, assessable

évaluation *nf* (**a**) *(action)* evaluation; *(d'une propriété, de biens)* valuation, appraisal; *(des dommages)* assessment; *(de risques, d'une quantité)* estimation ❑ *évaluation approximative* rough estimate; *évaluation du coût* cost assessment; *évaluation des coûts* cost analysis; *évaluation de la demande* demand assessment; *évaluation d'un emploi* job evaluation; *évaluation du marché* market appraisal; *évaluation des performances* (*d'un employé*) performance appraisal
(**b**) *(quantité, valeur)* (*d'une propriété, de biens*) valuation; *(des dommages)* assessment; *(de risques, d'une quantité)* estimate

évaluer *vt* to evaluate; *(propriété, biens)* to value, to appraise; *(dommages)* to assess (**à** at); *(risques, quantité)* to estimate; FIN **évaluer les coûts de qch** to cost sth

évasion *nf* **évasion des capitaux** flight of capital; **évasion fiscale** tax evasion

> ❝ ———————————————
>
> Le gouvernement a également décidé de créer, à titre provisoire, une taxe minimale, qui sous la forme d'un forfait imposé à tous les revenus non salariés, vise à contrer une **évasion fiscale** énorme.
>
> ——————————————— ❞

éventail *nm* range ❑ *éventail des prix* price range; *éventail de produits* range of products; *éventail des salaires* salary range

éventuel, -elle *adj* possible; *(client)* potential, prospective

évolué, -e *adj* (**a**) *(marché, économie, demande)* developed (**b**) ORDINAT *(langage)* high-level

évoluer *vi* (**a**) *(marché, économie, demande)* to develop (**b**) ORDINAT **faire évoluer qch** to upgrade sth

évolutif, -ive *adj* (**a**) ORDINAT upgradeable (**b**) *(poste)* with prospects (for promotion)

évolution *nf* (*du marché, de l'économie, de la demande*) development

évolutivité *nf* ORDINAT upgradeability

examen *nm* examination; *(des comptes)* inspection; **la question est à l'examen** the question is under consideration ❑ *examen financier* financial review

examiner *vt* to examine; *(comptes)* to go through, to inspect; *(question)* to look into, to consider

excédent *nm* (*d'un budget, d'une balance*) surplus; **dégager un excédent** to show a surplus; **la balance commerciale est en excédent** the trade balance shows a surplus; **il y a un excédent des exportations sur les importations** there is an excess of exports over imports ❑ *excédent budgétaire* budget surplus; COMPTA *excédent de caisse* cash overs; *excédents et déficits* overs and shorts; *excédent de dépenses* deficit; **nous avons un excédent de dépenses** we are overspending; *excédent d'exploitation* operating profit; *excédent de main-d'œuvre* overmanning; *excédent de production* surplus produce

" Après avoir atteint un niveau record en mai, l'**excédent** de la balance commerciale française est retombé en juin à un niveau plus sage. "

excédentaire *adj (production)* excess; *(budget)* surplus; **écouler la production excédentaire sur les marchés extérieurs** to dump excess production on foreign markets

excéder *vt* to exceed; **excéder le montant de son compte** to overdraw one's account; **nos pertes excèdent nos bénéfices** our losses are greater than our profits

exceptionnel, -elle *adj* (a) *(taxe)* exceptional (b) *(année)* exceptional; *(prix)* special

excès *nm* excess; **excès des dépenses sur les recettes** excess of expenditure over revenue; **excès de l'offre sur la demande** excess of supply over demand

exclusif, -ive *adj (droit, produit, distributeur)* exclusive

exclusivité *nf (droit)* sole *or* exclusive rights (**de** to); **avoir un contrat d'exclusivité** to have an exclusive contract; **nous avons l'exclusivité de la vente de ce produit** we have the (sole) rights for this product

ex-coupon *adv* FIN ex coupon

ex-dividende *adv* FIN ex dividend

ex-droit *adv* FIN ex rights

exécutable *adj* feasible; ORDINAT *(programme)* executable

exécuter *vt* (a) *(effectuer) (travail, plan)* to execute, to carry out; *(ordres, décision, opération comptable, commande)* to carry out (b) ORDINAT *(programme)* to execute, to run; *(commande)* to execute, to carry out (c) JUR *(débiteur)* to distrain upon; *(jugement, mandat)* to enforce; *(contrat)* to fulfil the terms of (d) BOURSE *(spéculateur)* to hammer; *(client)* to sell out against

exécuteur, -trice *nm,f (d'un ordre)* executor □ *exécuteur testamentaire* executor

exécutif, -ive 1 *adj (comité, pouvoir)* executive

2 *nm (comité exécutif)* executive committee; **un exécutif de cinq membres** an executive of five

exécution *nf* (a) *(d'un travail, d'un plan)* execution, carrying out; *(d'ordres, d'une décision, d'une opération comptable, d'une commande)* carrying out; **en voie d'exécution** in progress (b) ORDINAT *(d'un programme)* execution, running; *(d'une commande)* execution, carrying out (c) JUR *(d'un jugement, d'un mandat)* enforcement; *(d'un contrat)* fulfilment (d) BOURSE *(d'un spéculateur)* hammering; **exécution au prix du marché** execution at market

exécutoire JUR 1 *adj (contrat, jugement, mandat)* enforceable

2 *nm* writ of execution □ *exécutoire des dépens* order to pay costs

exemplaire *nm (unité)* copy; **en double exemplaire** in duplicate; **en triple exemplaire** in triplicate □ ADMIN *exemplaire d'archives* file copy

exempt, -e *adj* **exempt d'impôts** tax-exempt; DOUANES **exempt de droits** duty-free; **exempt de frais** free of charge

exempter *vt* to exempt sb (**de** from)

exemption *nf* exemption (**de** from) □ *exemption fiscale* tax exemption

exercer *vt* (a) BOURSE *(option)* to exercise; **exercer par anticipation** to exercise in advance (b) JUR **exercer des poursuites (contre)** to take legal action (against) (c) *(profession)* to practise; **exercer ses fonctions** to carry out one's duties

exercice *nm* (a) COMPTA *Br* financial year, *Am* fiscal year; **l'exercice de ce mois** this month's trading □ *exercice budgétaire* budgetary year; *exercice comptable* accounting year; *exercice en cours* current *Br* financial *or Am* fiscal year; *exercice financier Br* financial *or Am* fiscal year; *exercice fiscal* tax year (b) *(d'une profession)* practice; **dans l'exercice de ses fonctions** in the exercise of one's duties

" Pour l'**exercice budgétaire** clos en mars dernier, la compagnie a enregistré un bénéfice net de 16,3 milliards de yens. "

" Sur les deux derniers **exercices fiscaux**, les pertes nettes cumulées du fabricant des Macintosh se sont élevées à 1,8 milliards de dollars. "

exigence *nf* demand, requirement; **il n'est pas à la hauteur des exigences du poste** he is not up to the requirements of the job; **la marchandise répond à toutes les exigences** the goods are up to standard in every way; **satisfaire aux exigences de ses clients** to meet one's customers' requirements

exiger *vt* to demand, to require (**de** from)

exigibilité *nf* **exigibilités** current liabilities; **exigibilité immédiate** immediately due ◻ FIN *exigibilité de taxe* tax liability

exigible *adj* (*paiement*) due; (*dette, impôt*) due for payment, payable; **exigible à vue** payable at sight

existant, -e **1** *adj* existing; **majorer les tarifs existants** to increase existing tariffs
2 *nm* COMPTA **existant en caisse** cash in hand; **l'existant en magasin, les existants** stock (in hand)

existence *nf* COMPTA *existences en caisse* cash in hand; *existence en magasin* stock (in hand)

exister *vi* (*article*) to be available; **ce modèle existe aussi en bleu** this model is also available in blue

ex-navire *adv* ex ship

exonération *nf* exemption (**de** from) ◻ *exonération des droits* exemption from duty; *exonération fiscale* tax exemption; *exonération partielle* partial exemption; *exonération totale* total exemption

> ❝
> Le propriétaire d'un immeuble à usage d'habitation bénéficie d'une **exonération** de la taxe foncière au cours des 2 années qui suivent l'achèvement de la construction de son bien.
> ❞

exonérer *vt* (**a**) (*personne, entreprise*) to exempt (**de** from); **exonérer qn de l'impôt sur le revenu** to exempt sb from income tax (**b**) (*marchandises*) to exempt from import duty

expansion *nf* (*d'une ville, d'une industrie*) expansion; **être en pleine expansion** to be booming ◻ *expansion économique* economic growth; *expansion monétaire* currency expansion

expansionnisme *nm* expansionism

expansionniste *adj & nmf* expansionist

expatriation *nf* FIN (*d'argent, de capitaux*) movement abroad

expatrier *vt* FIN (*argent, capitaux*) to invest abroad

expédier *vt* (**a**) (*envoyer*) (*marchandises*) to dispatch, to ship; (*lettre, colis*) to send; DOUANES **expédier des marchandises en douane** to clear goods through customs; **expédier des marchandises par navire** to send goods by sea, to ship goods; **expédier des marchandises par fret aérien** to airfreight goods; **expédiez ceci par le premier courrier** get this off by the first post; **expédier un colis par la poste** to mail *or Br* to post a parcel
(**b**) (*s'occuper de*) to deal with; **expédier les affaires courantes** to deal with the day-to-day matters
(**c**) JUR (*contrat, acte*) to draw up

expéditeur, -trice **1** *adj* (*bureau, compagnie, gare*) shipping, dispatching
2 *nm,f* (**a**) (*de courrier*) sender (**b**) (*de marchandises*) shipper, consigner; (*par bateau*) shipper

expédition *nf* (**a**) (*envoi*) (*de marchandises*) dispatch, shipment; **expéditions** (*service*) dispatch department, shipping department; **expédition franco à partir de 1000 francs** orders of 1,000 francs and over delivered free ◻ *expédition par avion* airfreighting; *expédition par bateau* shipping; *expédition par chemin de fer* sending by rail, railfreighting; *expédition par courrier* mailing, *Br* posting; *expédition de détail* retail shipment; *expédition exclusive* exclusive shipment; *expédition maritime* maritime shipment; *expédition par mer* shipping, shipment; *expédition partielle* part shipment *or* consignment; *expédition port à port* port to port shipment; *expédition par la poste* mailing, *Br* posting
(**b**) (*marchandises*) consignment, shipment
(**c**) JUR (*de contrat, d'acte*) copy; **première expédition** first authentic copy; **en double expédition** in duplicate

expéditionnaire *nmf* shipping clerk

expert, -e **1** *adj* expert, skilled (**en/dans** in); **la main-d'œuvre la plus experte** the most highly-skilled labour
2 *nm* (**a**) (*chargé d'expertise*) expert ◻ *expert en communication* communications expert; *expert en gestion* management expert (**b**) (*en assurances*) valuer, appraiser; (*en bâtiment*) surveyor ◻ *expert en assurances* claims adjuster

expert-comptable *nm Br* ≃ chartered accountant, *Am* ≃ certified public accountant

expert-conseil *nm* consultant

expertise *nf* (**a**) ASSUR *(des dégâts)* (expert) assessment; **faire l'expertise de qch** to appraise *or* value sth; *(dégâts)* to assess sth ❑ **expertise d'avarie** damage survey (**b**) *(rapport)* expert's report

expertiser *vt* ASSUR *(dégâts)* to assess; **faire expertiser qch** to have sth appraised or valued; *(dégâts)* to have sth assessed

expert-répétiteur *nm* ASSUR loss *or* average adjuster

expiration *nf* *(de bail, de contrat)* expiry, expiration; **arriver à expiration** to expire

expirer *vi (bail, contrat)* to expire

exploit *nm* JUR writ

exploitant, -e *nm,f* **exploitant (agricole)** farmer; **les petits exploitants** small farmers

exploitation *nf* (**a**) *(d'une entreprise)* running, operation
  (**b**) *(d'un brevet)* commercialization; *(d'une invention)* utilization
  (**c**) *(entreprise)* concern; **petite exploitation** smallholding ❑ **exploitation agricole** farm; **exploitation commerciale** business (concern); **exploitation familiale** family business; **exploitation industrielle** industrial concern; **exploitation minière** mine

exploiter *vt* (**a**) *(entreprise)* to run (**b**) *(brevet)* to commercialize; *(invention)* to utilize

expomarché *nm* trade mart

export *nm* exportation ❑ ORDINAT **export de données** data export

exportable *adj* exportable

exportateur, -trice **1** *adj (pays)* exporting; *(secteur)* export; **être exportateur de qch** to export sth; **les pays exportateurs de pétrole** the oil-exporting countries
  2 *nm,f* exporter

exportation *nf* (**a**) *(action)* export, exportation; *(produit)* export; **faire de l'exportation** to export; **le montant des exportations a augmenté de 10% cette année** exports have risen by 10% this year; **ce produit marche très fort à l'exportation** this product is doing very well on the export market; **réservé à l'exportation** reserved for export, for export only ❑ **exportation de capitaux** export of capital; **exportations invisibles** invisible exports; **exportation kangourou** piggybacking; **exportations visibles** visible exports
  (**b**) ORDINAT *(d'un fichier)* exporting; *(données exportées)* exported data

exporter **1** *vt* (**a**) *(marchandises)* to export (**vers** to) (**b**) ORDINAT to export (**vers** to)
  2 s'exporter *vpr (marchandises)* to be exported (**vers** to); **ce genre de produit s'exporte mal** this type of product is not good for exporting

exposant, -e *nm,f* (**a**) *(dans une foire)* exhibitor (**b**) JUR petitioner, deponent

exposé *nm* account, statement ❑ **exposé verbal (de mission)** briefing

exposer *vt (produits, marchandises)* to display; **exposer des marchandises en vente** to display goods for sale

exposition *nf* (**a**) *(foire)* exhibition, show ❑ **exposition commerciale** trade exhibition; **exposition interprofessionnelle** trade exhibition; **l'Exposition universelle** the World Fair
  (**b**) *(de marchandises)* display ❑ MKTG **exposition sur le lieu de vente** point of sale display; MKTG **exposition sur le marché** market exposure
  (**c**) FIN **exposition aux risques** exposure

exposition-vente *nf* display *(where the items are for sale)*

exprès *adj* express; **par exprès** by special delivery; **envoyer qch en exprès** to send sth special delivery

expression *nf* **veuillez agréer l'expression de nos sentiments les meilleurs** *(à quelqu'un dont on connaît le nom)* yours sincerely; *(à quelqu'un dont on ne connaît pas le nom)* yours faithfully

expropriation *nf* JUR *(d'une personne)* expropriation; *(d'une propriété)* compulsory purchase

exproprier *vt* JUR *(personne)* to expropriate; *(propriété)* to place a compulsory purchase order on

expulser *vt (locataire)* to evict

expulsion *nf (d'un locataire)* eviction

ex-répartition *adv* FIN ex allotment

extensible *adj* ORDINAT upgradeable; *(mémoire)* expandable, upgradeable

extension *nf* (**a**) ORDINAT expansion ❑ **extension mémoire** memory expansion *or* upgrade; **extension de nom de fichier** file name extension
  (**b**) MKTG expansion, extension ❑ **extension de la gamme** range stretching; **extension de la ligne** line stretching; **extension de marché** market expansion; **extension de la marque** brand extension

extérieur **1** *adj* (**a**) *(étranger)* *(échanges, commerce)* foreign, external (**b**) *(étranger à la chose considérée)* **le travail a été accompli par des personnes extérieures à l'entreprise** the work was done out of house

2 *nm* **l'extérieur** foreign countries; **à l'extérieur** abroad; **de l'extérieur** from abroad

externalisation *nf* outsourcing

externaliser *vt* to outsource

extinction *nf* JUR *(d'un droit)* extinguishment; *(d'un contrat)* termination; *(d'une hypothèque)* redemption; COMPTA *(d'une dette)* discharge

extrabudgétaire *adj* FIN extrabudgetary

extra-comptable *adj* COMPTA *(ajustement)* off-balance sheet

extrait *nm* JUR, FIN *(d'un acte, d'un compte-rendu, d'un titre, d'un bilan)* abstract ◻ **extrait cadastral** land registration certificate; **extrait de compte** COMPTA statement of account; BANQUE bank statement

extraordinaire *adj (assemblée, réunion)* extraordinary

FAB *adj (abrév* **franco à bord**) FOB

fabricant, -e *nm,f* maker, manufacturer

fabrication *nf (construction)* manufacture, production; *(qualité)* workmanship; **de fabrication française** made in France, French-made □ *fabrication assistée par ordinateur* computer-assisted manufacture; *fabrication à la chaîne* mass production; *fabrication par lots* batch production; *fabrication en série* mass production

fabrique *nf* factory, works □ *fabrique de vêtements* clothing factory

fabriquer *vt* to manufacture; **fabriquer qch à la chaîne** to mass-produce sth; **fabriqué en France** made in France; **fabriquer qch en grande série** to mass-produce sth; **fabriqué sur commande** made to order; **fabriqué sur mesure(s)** made to measure

FAC *adj* ASSUR *(abrév* **franc d'avarie commune**) FGA

façade *nf* ASSUR fronting

facilité *nf* **(a)** *(possibilité)* facility □ BANQUE *facilités de caisse* overdraft facilities; *facilités de crédit* credit facilities; *facilité d'endettement* borrowing capacity; *facilités de paiement* payment facilities, easy terms; *facilité de reprise (d'un produit)* trade-in facility
 (b) *(simplicité)* MKTG *facilité d'écoulement* saleability; *facilité d'emploi (d'un ordinateur)* user-friendliness; *facilité de vente* saleability

facob *nm* ASSUR *(abrév* **facultatif obligatoire**) open cover

façon *nf (qualité de travail)* workmanship; *(main-d'œuvre)* labour; **façon et fournitures** labour and material

fac-similé *nm* facsimile, exact copy; ORDINAT hard copy

factage *nm* **(a)** *(livraison)* carriage and delivery, transport; **payer le factage** to pay the carriage **(b)** *(du courrier)* delivery

facteur *nm* factor □ *facteur de charge* load factor; *facteur coût* cost factor; *facteur de déséquilibre* destabilizing factor; *facteur économique* economic factor; *facteur humain* human factor; *facteur de production* production factor; MKTG *facteur de situation* situational factor

factoring *nm* factoring

facturation *nf* COMPTA invoicing, billing
 □ *facturation détaillée* itemized invoicing or billing

facture *nf* invoice, bill; **faire** *ou* **dresser** *ou* **établir une facture** to make out an invoice; **payer** *ou* **régler une facture** to settle an invoice, to pay a bill; **selon** *ou* **suivant facture** as per invoice; ÉCON **la facture pétrolière de la France** France's oil bill □ *facture d'achat* purchase invoice; *facture de consignation* consignment invoice; *facture détaillée* itemized invoice or bill; *facture originale* original invoice; *facture pro forma, facture provisoire* pro forma invoice; *facture de vente* sales invoice

facturer *vt (personne)* to invoice, to bill; *(produit, service)* to charge for; **facturer qch à qn** to invoice sb for sth, to bill sb for sth; **le papier nous a été facturé 60 francs** we were charged 60 francs for the paper; **je ne vous ai pas facturé les pièces détachées** I haven't invoiced you for the spare parts

facturette *nf* credit card sales voucher

facturier, -ère 1 *nm,f* invoice clerk
 2 *nm* sales book
 3 *nf* **facturière** invoicing machine

faculté *nf* **(a)** *(droit)* option, right; **louer un immeuble avec faculté d'achat** to rent a building with the option of purchase □ BOURSE *faculté du double* call of more
 (b) ASSUR **facultés** cargo □ *facultés assurées* insured cargo
 (c) *(capacité)* ability □ *facultés contributives* ability to pay

faible *adj (demande, prix, revenu)* low; *(quantité)* small

failli, -e 1 *adj (commerçant)* bankrupt
 2 *nm* (adjudicated) bankrupt □ *failli concordataire* certified bankrupt; *failli déchargé* discharged bankrupt; *failli non déchargé* undischarged bankrupt; *failli réhabilité* discharged bankrupt

faillite *nf* bankruptcy, insolvency; **être en (état de) faillite** to be bankrupt *or* insolvent; **faire faillite** to go bankrupt, to fail; **déclarer** *ou* **mettre qn en faillite, prononcer la faillite de qn** to declare sb bankrupt; **se mettre en faillite** to file a petition in bankruptcy □ *faillite frauduleuse* fraudulent bankruptcy; *faillite simple* bankruptcy

faire *vt* (**a**) *(paiement, versement)* to make; *(chèque)* to make out; **faire un chèque de 100 francs** to make out a cheque for 100 francs (**b**) *(vendre)* to sell; **nous ne faisons que le gros** we only deal wholesale; **nous ne faisons plus cet article** we no longer sell this article (**c**) *(s'élever à)* to come to; **combien cela fait-il?** how much does that come to?

faisabilité *nf* feasibility

falsification *nf* *(de documents, de comptes)* falsification; *(d'une signature)* forgery

falsifier *vt* *(documents, comptes)* to falsify; *(signature)* to forge, to fake

familial, -e *adj* (**a**) *(entreprise)* family-run, family-owned (**b**) MKTG *(paquet, emballage, format)* family-size(d)

famille *nf* (**a**) *(ménage)* household (**b**) MKTG *(de produits)* family, line

FAO *nf* (*abrév* **fabrication assistée par ordinateur**) CAM

faussaire *nmf* counterfeiter, forger

faute *nf* (**a**) *(erreur)* mistake, error □ ORDINAT **faute de frappe** keying error; **faute professionnelle** professional misconduct (**b**) *(manque)* **faute de** for lack of; **faute de paiement sous quinzaine, nous serons dans l'obligation de majorer notre facture de 10%** should payment not be made within fourteen days, we shall be obliged to add a 10% surcharge to your bill

faux, fausse **1** *adj* *(chèque)* forged; *(bilan)* fraudulent; *(money)* counterfeit; *(déclaration)* false □ **fausse écriture** false entry; **fausse facture** false bill; **faux frais** incidental expenses; **faux fret** dead freight **2** *nm* JUR *(objet, activité)* forgery; **s'inscrire en faux contre qch** to dispute the validity of sth; **inculper qn pour faux et usage de faux** to prosecute sb for forgery □ COMPTA **faux en écritures** forgery

faveur *nf* **en faveur de qn** *(à l'avantage de)* in favour of sb; **le solde est en votre faveur** the balance is in your favour

favorable *adj* *(balance commerciale, taux de change)* favourable; **à des conditions favorables** on favourable terms; **notre demande a reçu un accueil favorable** our request was favourably received

favoriser *vt* *(croissance, emploi, exportations)* to encourage, to promote

fax *nm* *(appareil)* fax (machine); *(message)* fax; **envoyer qch par fax** to send sth by fax, to fax sth □ ORDINAT **fax modem** fax modem

faxer *vt* to fax

fco *adv* (*abrév* **franco**) franco

FCP *nm* FIN (*abrév* **fonds commun de placement**) investment trust, mutual fund

FDR *nm* (*abrév* **fonds de roulement**) working capital

FECOM *nm* (*abrév* **Fonds européen de coopération monétaire**) EMCF

FED *nm* (*abrév* **Fonds européen de développement**) EDF

FEDER *nm* (*abrév* **Fonds européen de développement régional**) ERDF

fédération *nf* federation □ **fédération syndicale** Br trade or Am labor union; **fédération de syndicats** amalgamated union

femme d'affaires *nf* businesswoman

fenêtre *nf* ORDINAT window □ **fenêtre activée** active window; **fenêtre d'aide** help window; **fenêtre déroulante** pull-down window; **fenêtre de dialogue** dialogue window; **fenêtre d'édition** editing window; **fenêtre graphique** graphics window

férié, -e *adj* **lundi prochain est férié** next Monday is a (public) holiday

ferme¹ **1** *adj* (**a**) *(stable)* firm, steady; **maintenir les prix fermes** to keep prices steady; **le marché reste très ferme** the market remains very steady (**b**) *(acheteur, commande, offre, valeur)* firm **2** *adv* **vendre/acheter ferme** to sell/buy firm

> ❝
> La transaction porte sur 59 avions court-courriers de la famille A320 achetés **fermes**, et sur une série d'options et de droits d'achats préférentiels pour 129 autres appareils de la même famille.
> ❞

ferme² *nf* JUR farming lease; **prendre une terre à ferme** to rent a piece of land; **donner qch à ferme** to farm sth out

fermer **1** *vt* (**a**) *(compte)* to close; *(usine, entreprise)* to close down; **fermer ses portes** to close down (**b**) ORDINAT *(fichier, fenêtre)* to close; *(commande)* to end **2** *vi* (**a**) *(usine, entreprise)* *(temporairement)* to close, to shut; *(définitivement)* to close down (**b**) BOURSE *(actions)* to close; **les actions ont fermé à 55 francs** shares closed at 55 francs

fermeté *nf* steadiness

fermeture *nf* (**a**) *(d'un compte)* closing; *(d'une usine, d'une entreprise)* closure; **fermeture pour travaux** *(sur panneau)* closed for repairs (**b**) ORDINAT (d'un fichier, d'une fenêtre) closing; (d'une commande) ending

ferroviaire adj (réseau, ligne) railway; (transports) rail

fête nf fête légale Br bank holiday, Am legal holiday; la fête du Travail Labour Day

feuille nf (imprimé) form □ feuille d'accompagnement covering document; COMPTA feuille d'avancement flow sheet; ORDINAT feuille de calcul spreadsheet; feuille d'émargement payroll; feuille d'impôt tax return; COMPTA feuille de liquidation settlement note; feuille de maladie = medical expense claim form; feuille de paie payslip; feuille de présence (d'un employé) time sheet; feuille de réservation reservation form, booking form; feuille de route waybill; feuille de service (duty) roster; feuille de soins medical expense claim form; ORDINAT feuille de style style sheet; feuille de travail worksheet; BANQUE feuille de versement paying-in slip

FF nm (abrév **franc français**) French Franc

fiche nf (**a**) (formulaire) form; (papier) sheet, slip; remplir une fiche to fill in or fill out a form □ fiche d'accueil registration form; fiche d'appréciation customer satisfaction questionnaire; fiche d'arrivée registration form; fiche client customer record; (d'un hôtel) guest file; fiche de compte accounts card; fiche de contrôle docket; fiche courrier mail checklist or file; fiche d'entretien service record; fiche de facture account card; fiche fournisseur supplier file; COMPTA fiche d'imputation data entry form; fiche d'inscription registration form; fiche d'observations (questionnaire d'évaluation) comment card; fiche de paie payslip; fiche perforée perforated card; fiche de pointage clocking-in card; fiche de poste task sheet; fiche de présence (de salarié) attendance sheet; fiche prospect potential-customer file; fiche de renseignements information card; fiche de stock stock sheet; fiche technique specifications sheet, data sheet; fiche voyageur (d'un hôtel) registration card for foreign guests

(**b**) (carte) (index) card; mettre qch sur fiches to card-index sth □ fiche cartonnée index card

fichier nm (**a**) (boîte) card-index file; (meuble) card-index cabinet (**b**) (ensemble de fiches) card-index file (**c**) ORDINAT file □ fichier d'adresses mailing list, address file; fichier joint (de courrier électronique) attachment; fichier maître master file;

fichier principal master file; fichier de sauvegarde backup file; fichier texte text file

fictif, -ive adj (compte) impersonal; (société) fictitious

fidéicommis nm JUR trust

fidéicommissaire nm JUR trustee

fidèle 1 adj (client) loyal; rester fidèle à un produit to stick with a product; MKTG fidèle à la marque brand-loyal
2 nmf regular or loyal customer

fidélisation nf building of customer loyalty

fidéliser vt to win the loyalty of; fidéliser la clientèle to develop customer loyalty

> ❝
> Aux petits soins pour un consommateur fuyant comme le savon, les hypers rivalisent dans les promotions, les offres qu'on ne peut pas refuser, les cadeaux qui **fidélisent** l'inconstant client.
> ❞

fidélité nf (d'un client) loyalty □ fidélité du consommateur consumer loyalty; fidélité à la marque brand loyalty

fiduciaire 1 adj (prêt, devise) fiduciary; en dépôt fiduciaire in escrow, in trust; avoirs en monnaie fiduciaire (d'une banque) cash holdings; une circulation fiduciaire excessive entraîne l'inflation too much paper money in circulation leads to inflation
2 nm JUR fiduciary, trustee

fiduciairement adv JUR in trust

fiducie nf JUR trust

figer vt (salaires) to freeze

figurer vi to appear, to figure; ces articles figurent dans le catalogue these articles appear or are listed in the catalogue

file d'attente nf ORDINAT print queue or list; mettre en file d'attente to spool

filiale nf subsidiary (company) □ filiale commune jointly-owned subsidiary; filiale consolidée consolidated subsidiary; filiale de distribution marketing subsidiary; filiale étrangère foreign subsidiary; filiale de vente sales subsidiary

filialiser vt to affiliate

filière nf (**a**) (procédures) channels; passer par ou suivre la filière (pour obtenir quelque chose) to go through official channels; (comme employé) to work one's way up □ la filière administrative the official channels (**b**) FIN filière électronique electronic

transfer
(**c**) BOURSE **établir la filière** to trace the succession of previous shareholders
(**d**) *(secteur)* sector ❑ *filière agro-alimentaire* food-processing sector

film publicitaire *nm (à la télévision)* commercial; *(au cinéma)* cinema advertisement

fin *nf* (**a**) *(de contrat, de bail)* expiry, expiration; **mettre fin à un contrat** to terminate a contract; **être en fin de droits** = to be nearing the end of the period in which one is entitled to benefits; **fin courant** at the end of the current month; **fin prochain** at the end of next month ❑ *fin d'année* year end; *fin d'exercice* year end
(**b**) *fin de série (d'articles)* discontinued line
(**c**) BANQUE **sauf bonne fin** under reserve
(**d**) ORDINAT *fin de ligne* line end; *fin de page* page break; *fin de page obligatoire* hard page break; *fin de paragraphe* paragraph break; *fin de session* logoff

final, -e *adj (règlement, solde)* final

finance *nf* (**a**) *(domaine)* finance; **le monde de la finance** the financial world; **la haute finance** *(milieu)* high finance; *(personnes)* the top bankers ❑ *finance d'entreprise* corporate finance (**b**) **finances** *(argent)* finances; **les finances de la compagnie vont mal** the company's finances are in a bad state ❑ *finances publiques* public funds

financement *nm* financing, funding; **le financement du projet sera assuré par la compagnie** the company will finance *or* fund the project ❑ *financement par emprunt* debt financing; *financement initial* start-up capital; *financement à taux fixe* fixed-rate financing

financement-relais *nm* bridge financing

financer *vt (projet)* to finance, to fund; *(personne)* to back; **l'opération a été entièrement financée par emprunt** the transaction was 100% financed through borrowing; **BP financera le projet à 50%** BP will put up half of the funding for the project

financier, -ère 1 *adj* financial; **solide au point de vue financier** financially sound
2 *nm,f* financier ❑ *financier d'entreprise* corporate finance manager

financièrement *adv* financially

firme *nf* business, firm, concern

fisc *nm Br* ≃ Inland Revenue, *Am* ≃ Internal Revenue; **les employés du fisc** tax officials; **frauder le fisc** to evade tax

fiscal, -e *adj* fiscal, tax; **dans un but fiscal** for tax purposes

fiscaliser *vt* to tax

fiscaliste *nmf* tax consultant

fiscalité *nf* tax system ❑ *fiscalité excessive* excessive taxation; *fiscalité indirecte* indirect taxation

fixation *nf (d'une date, d'une heure, d'un rendez-vous)* fixing, arranging; *(des impôts, des dommages-intérêts)* assessment; *(d'un prix, d'un taux, d'un salaire)* fixing, setting; *(des conditions, des objectifs)* setting; *(des indemnités)* determination

> **❝**
> L'opinion, et en particulier l'électorat de la majorité, peineront peut-être à admettre que la **fixation** du taux de TVA sur leurs abonnements d'électricité suffit à caractériser une politique d'équité.
> **❞**

fixe 1 *adj (capital, actif, prix, coûts, traitement)* fixed; *(adresse)* permanent
2 *nm* fixed salary; **toucher un fixe** to be on a fixed salary

fixer *vt (date, heure, rendez-vous)* to fix, to arrange; *(impôts, dommages-intérêts)* to assess; *(prix, taux, salaire)* to fix, to set (**à** at); *(conditions, objectifs)* to set; *(indemnités)* to determine; BOURSE **fixer un cours** to make a price

flambée *nf (des prix)* leap

FLB *adv (abrév* **franco long du bord***)* FAS

flèche *nf* (**a**) **monter en flèche** *(prix)* to shoot up, to rocket (**b**) ORDINAT pointer, arrow

fléchir *vi (marché, devises)* to weaken; *(prix, cours, demande)* to fall, to drop; **les prix des actions fléchissent** share prices are down

fléchissement *nm (du marché, des devises)* weakening; *(des prix, des cours, de la demande)* fall, drop

flexibilité *nf* FIN *(d'une entreprise, de la main-d'œuvre)* flexibility

> **❝**
> Grâce à des accords salariaux modérés, une **flexibilité** accrue dans l'organisation du travail et l'appréciation du dollar en 1997, l'Allemagne commence à récolter les fruits de ses efforts.
> **❞**

flexible *adj* flexible

florin *nm* florin

flottaison *nf* = **flottement**

flottant, -e 1 *adj (dette, capitaux, taux de change, police d'assurance)* floating
  2 *nm* BOURSE float

flottement *nm (d'une monnaie)* floating, fluctuation

flotter *vi (prix)* to fluctuate; *(monnaie)* to float; **faire flotter la livre** to float the pound

> La banque centrale russe dépensait un milliard de dollars par semaine, dans la dernière période, pour soutenir le rouble. L'équipe au pouvoir a donc décidé d'élargir la bande de fluctuation de la monnaie, qui pourra désormais **flotter** entre 6 et 9,5 roubles pour un dollar.

flouze *nm Fam* cash

fluctuation *nf* FIN *(du marché, des cours)* fluctuation (**de** in) □ *fluctuations saisonnières* seasonal fluctuations

fluctuer *vi* FIN *(marché, cours)* to fluctuate

fluidité *nf* fluidity

> Les experts relèvent une hausse des démissions, bon indicateur de la confiance des salariés et de la **fluidité** du marché du travail.

flux *nm (de fonds)* flow; **à flux tendus** *(transport, distribution, production)* just-in-time □ *flux financier* flow of money, monetary flow; *flux monétaire* flow of money, monetary flow; *flux réel* flow of goods; *flux de trésorerie* cashflow

> Du point de vue des **flux financiers**, un effondrement russe serait beaucoup moins grave qu'un effondrement de certains pays asiatiques, comme la Corée du Sud, ou d'Amérique latine, comme le Brésil.

FMI *nm (abrév* **Fonds monétaire international)** IMF

FNE *nm (abrév* **Fonds national de l'emploi)** = French national employment fund

FO *nf (abrév* **Force Ouvrière)** = French trade union

FOB *adj (abrév* **free on board)** FOB

focalisation *nf* MKTG targeting □ *focalisation stratégique* strategic targeting

focaliser *vt* MKTG to target

foi *nf* (a) **un texte qui fait foi** an authentic text; **la lettre doit partir avant le 29, le cachet de la poste faisant foi** the letter must be postmarked no later than the 28th (b) JUR **en foi de quoi** in witness whereof; **de bonne foi** bona fide; **de mauvaise foi** mala fide

foire *nf* (trade) fair □ *foire du livre* book fair

foire-échantillon, foire-exposition *nf* trade fair

foncier, -ère 1 *adj (impôt, rente)* land
  2 *nm* land tax □ *foncier bâti* landed property; *foncier non bâti* land for development

fonction *nf* (a) *(poste)* office; **entrer en fonction, prendre ses fonctions** to take up one's duties; **être en fonction** to be in office; **se démettre de ses fonctions** to resign one's post; **cela ne fait pas partie de mes fonctions** that's not part of my duties □ *la fonction publique* the public *or* civil service
  (b) *(rôle)* function; **les fonctions de président** the functions of a chairman; **faire fonction de gérant** to act as manager □ *fonctions complémentaires* support activities; ÉCON *fonction de demande* demand function; *fonctions de direction* managerial functions; *fonctions d'encadrement* executive functions
  (c) ORDINAT *fonction de comptage de mots* word count facility; *fonction 'couper-coller'* cut-and-paste facility; *fonction multimédia* multimedia facility; *fonction de sauvegarde* save function
  (d) **en fonction de** according to, with respect to; **les salaires offerts seront en fonction de l'expérience** the salary offered will be commensurate with experience

fonctionnaire *nmf* government official, *Br* civil servant; **haut fonctionnaire** senior government official *or Br* civil servant; **petit fonctionnaire** junior government official *or Br* civil servant; **fonctionnaire de l'Union européenne** European Union official

fonctionnariser *vt* to make part of the civil service

fonctionnarisme *nm* officialdom, red tape

fonctionnel, -elle *adj (organisation, responsabilité)* functional

fonctionnement *nm* (a) *(d'une entreprise)* running, functioning; **pour le bon fonctionnement du service, il est préférable que tous les employés aient les mêmes horaires** if the department is to run efficiently it is preferable that all staff have the same working hours (**b**) *(d'une machine)* running, working; **en (bon) état de fonctionnement** in (good) working order

(**c**) ORDINAT *fonctionnement en réseau* networking

fonctionner *vi* (**a**) *(entreprise)* to run, to function; **cette entreprise fonctionne 24 heures sur 24** the company functions round the clock (**b**) *(machine)* to run, to work (**c**) ORDINAT to run

fondateur, -trice *nm,f* founder

fondé, -e de pouvoir *nm,f* JUR agent *(holding power of attorney)*; *(mandant)* proxy; *(directeur de banque)* manager with signing authority; **il est le fondé de pouvoir (de)** he holds power of attorney (for)

fonder *vt* (**a**) *(commerce)* to start, to set up; **fondé en 1928** established in 1928 (**b**) FIN *(dette)* to fund

fondre 1 *vt (compagnies)* to amalgamate, to merge

2 **se fondre** *vpr (compagnies)* to amalgamate, to merge

fonds 1 *nm* (**a**) *(organisme)* fund ❑ *Fonds européen de coopération monétaire* European Monetary Cooperation Fund; *Fonds européen de développement* European Development Fund; *Fonds européen de développement régional* European Regional Development Fund; *Fonds monétaire international* International Monetary Fund; *Fonds national de l'emploi* = French national employment fund; *Fonds national de garantie des salaires* national guarantee fund for the payment of salaries; *Fonds social européen* European Social Fund

(**b**) *(capital)* fund, funds ❑ *fonds d'amortissement* sinking fund; *fonds commun de placement* investment fund, mutual fund; *fonds de capital-risque maison, fonds dédié* captive fund; *fonds de dotation* endowment fund; *fonds à faible frais d'entrée* low-load fund; *fonds fédéraux* federal funds; *fonds de garantie (d'un emprunt)* guarantee fund; *fonds géré* managed fund; *fonds à gestion indicielle, fonds indiciel* index fund; *fonds d'investissement* investment fund; *fonds monétaire* money market fund; *Can fonds de parité* equalization fund; *fonds de placement sur le marché monétaire* money market fund; *fonds de prévoyance* contingency fund; *fonds de réserve* reserve fund; *fonds de retraite maison ou d'entreprise ou de groupe* occupational pension scheme; *fonds de roulement* working ca-

pital; *fonds de stabilisation des changes* exchange equalization account

(**c**) BOURSE stocks, securities ❑ *fonds consolidés* consolidated stock, *Br* consols

(**d**) *fonds de commerce* goodwill; *fonds (de commerce) à vendre* business for sale *(as a going concern)*

2 *nmpl (ressources)* funds; **réunir des fonds** to raise funds; **je n'ai pas les fonds suffisants pour ouvrir un magasin** I don't have the (necessary) funds *or* capital to open a shop; **rentrer dans ses fonds** to get one's money back; **être en fonds** to be in funds; **faire** *ou* **fournir les fonds de qch** to put up the funds for sth; **mettre des fonds dans qch** to invest money in sth ❑ *fonds de caisse* cash in hand; *fonds communs* pool; *fonds disponibles* liquid assets, available funds; *fonds d'État* Government stocks; *fonds liquides* available funds; *fonds offshore* offshore funds; *fonds perdus* annuity; **placer son argent à fonds perdus** to purchase an annuity; *fonds propres* shareholders' equity, equity (capital); *fonds publics* Government stocks; *fonds social* company funds

> ❝
> La première banque française pour le montant des **fonds propres**, qui se dispute également la première place avec le Crédit Lyonnais pour le montant total des actifs (1647 millions de francs en 1992) ressent de plein fouet, comme l'ensemble de la profession bancaire, la chute brutale des crédits.
> ❞

> ❝
> Asher Edelman, à travers quatre **fonds d'investissement** américains, n'a acquis aujourd'hui que 11% du capital et 4% des droits de vote de la Société du Louvre.
> ❞

fonte *nf* ORDINAT font

force *nf* (**a**) *(puissance)* ASSUR *(cas de) force majeure* force majeure, act of God; *forces économiques* economic forces; ÉCON *les forces du marché* market forces; *force de vente* sales force

(**b**) MKTG *forces, faiblesses, opportunités et menaces* strengths, weaknesses, opportunities and threats, SWOT

forcé, -e *adj (emprunt)* forced, compulsory; *(cours, vente)* forced; *(liquidation)* compulsory

forclore *vt* to foreclose

forclusion *nf* foreclosure

forfait *nm* *(contrat)* fixed-rate contract; *(somme)* lump sum; **être au forfait** to be taxed on estimated income; **travailler au forfait** to work for a flat rate; **payer qn au forfait** to pay sb a flat rate; **verser un forfait** to pay a fixed sum □ *forfait de port* carriage forward

> Dans l'immédiat ce sont les assurés qui sont mis à contribution à hauteur de 10Mds/an avec deux mesures principales : un relèvement du **forfait** hospitalier de 50F à 55F et une baisse de cinq points des remboursements pour tous les soins.

> L'accord stipule ainsi que salariés peuvent toujours convenir avec leurs employeurs que leurs horaires sont rémunérés au **forfait.**

forfaitaire *adj* *(prix)* inclusive, fixed; *(indemnités)* basic

forfaitairement *adv* in a lump sum; *(facturer)* in a lump sum, in one amount

formalité *nf* formality □ *formalités administratives* administrative formalities; *formalités douanières* customs formalities

format *nm* **(a)** *(dimension)* format, size; **papier format A4** A4 paper; **grand format** large-sized; **petit format** small-sized □ *format de poche* pocket-sized **(b)** ORDINAT format □ *format ASCII* ASCII format; *format de fichier* file format; *format d'impression* print format; *format de page* page format *or* layout

formatage *nm* ORDINAT formatting

formater *vt* ORDINAT to format

formation *nf* **(a)** *(constitution)* development, formation; **la formation des prix sur le marché** market pricing; **en voie de formation** *(société)* developing □ *formation de réserves* building up of reserves
(b) *(des employés)* training; **suivre une formation** to get training, to take a training course; **être en formation** to be undergoing training □ *formation continue* = day release or night school education for employees provided by companies; *formation dans l'entreprise* in-house training; *formation du personnel* staff training; *formation professionnelle* professional *or* vocational training; *formation sur le tas* on-the-job training

> Si les entreprises (premiers pourvoyeurs et premiers consommateurs de **formation continue**) ont les moyens de tester la qualité et la pertinence des formations qui leur sont proposées, les demandeurs d'emploi, eux, sont moins armés.

forme *nf* **en bonne et due forme** *(reçu, contrat)* bona fide; **faire une réclamation en bonne et due forme** to use the correct procedure in making a complaint

former *vt* **(a)** *(constituer)* to form **(b)** *(donner une formation à)* to train; **former qn à qch** to train sb in sth; **formé à la gestion** trained in management techniques

formulaire *nm* *(imprimé)* form; **remplir un formulaire** to fill in *or* out a form □ *formulaire d'appréciation* customer satisfaction questionnaire; *formulaire d'assurance* insurance form; *formulaire de candidature* (job) application form; *formulaire de demande* application form; *formulaire de détaxe* tax-free shopping form; ORDINAT *formulaire de saisie* input form

formule *nf* **(a)** *(texte)* *(d'un contrat)* wording □ *formule de politesse* *(au début d'une lettre)* standard opening; *(à la fin)* standard ending
(b) *(méthode)* option; **nous avons aussi une formule à 1 000 francs** we also have a 1,000 franc option □ *formules de crédit* credit options; *formules de paiement* methods of payment; *formules de remboursement* repayment options
(c) ADMIN *(formulaire)* form; **remplir une formule** to fill in *or* out a form □ *formule de chèque* cheque form, *Am* blank check; *formule de demande de crédit* credit application form; *formule d'effet de commerce* form for bill of exchange; *formule de réponse* reply form; *formule de soumission* tender form

formuler *vt* *(réclamation, demande)* to formulate; *(acte)* to draw up

fort, -e *adj* **(a)** *(important)* *(hausse, baisse)* sharp, big; *(perte, consommation, demande)* heavy; *(somme)* large; **avoir un fort salaire** to have a high salary, to be highly paid; **payer le prix fort pour qch** to pay the full price for sth; **les prix sont en forte hausse** prices are soaring **(b)** FIN *(devise)* strong

fortement *adv* *(rémunéré)* highly; *(taxé)* heavily

fortune *nf* fortune, wealth; **faire fortune** to make one's fortune; **avoir une fortune personnelle** to have independent means

forum de discussion *nm (sur l'Internet)* newsgroup

fourchette *nf (écart)* bracket, range; **une fourchette de 10 à 20%** a 10 to 20% band; **une fourchette comprise entre 1000 et 1500 francs** prices ranging from 1,000 to 1,500 francs ▫ BOURSE *fourchette de cotation* trading range; BOURSE *fourchette de cours de clôture* closing range; BOURSE *fourchette de cours d'ouverture* opening range; *fourchette d'imposition* tax bracket; *fourchette de prix* price bracket *or* range; *fourchette de salaire* wage bracket; *fourchette de taux* rate band

fourni, -e *adj (approvisionné)* **bien/mal fourni** well-/poorly-stocked

fournir 1 *vt* **(a)** *(approvisionner)* to supply; **fournir qch à qn** to supply sb with sth; **ce magasin nous fournit tout le matériel de bureau** this shop supplies us with all our office equipment
(b) FIN *(lettre de crédit)* to issue (**sur** on); *(traite, chèque)* to draw (**sur** on); **fournir qch en nantissement** to lodge sth as collateral
2 *vi* **fournir aux dépenses** to contribute to the expenses
3 **se fournir** *vpr* **il se fournit chez nous** he is a customer of ours, he's one of our customers

fournisseur, -euse 1 *adj* **les pays fournisseurs de la France** the countries that supply France (with goods)
2 *nm,f* supplier; **quel est votre fournisseur habituel?** who's your usual supplier? ▫ ORDINAT *fournisseur d'accès* access provider; *fournisseur exclusif* sole supplier; *fournisseur principal* prime supplier; *fournisseur secondaire* secondary supplier

fourniture *nf* **(a)** *(action)* supplying, providing **(b)** **fournitures** *(choses fournies)* supplies ▫ *fournitures de bureau* office supplies

foyer *nm (domicile)* home, household; MKTG household unit ▫ FIN *foyer fiscal* household *(as a tax unit)*

fraction *nf* fraction; **par 10 francs ou fraction de 10 francs** for each 10 francs or fraction thereof ▫ COMPTA *fraction imposable* part subject to tax; *fraction d'intérêt* interest accrued

fractionnement *nm* dividing up; *(des paiements)* spreading (out); BOURSE, FIN *(des actions)* split

fractionner *vt* to divide up; *(paiements)* to spread (out); BOURSE, FIN *(actions)* to split

frais *nmpl* expenses, costs; JUR costs; **tous frais payés** all expenses paid; **tous frais déduits** all expenses deducted; JUR **être condamné aux frais** to be ordered to pay costs; **sans frais** free of charge; *(sur une lettre de change)* no expenses; **à grands frais** at great cost, expensively; **à peu de frais** at little cost, inexpensively; **couvrir ses frais, rentrer dans ses frais** to get one's money back, to recover one's expenses, to break even; **menus frais** petty *or* incidental expenses ▫ *frais accessoires* incidental costs *or* expenses; *frais d'achat* purchase costs; *frais d'adhésion* membership charge; *frais administratifs, frais d'administration* administrative costs; *(en échange d'un service)* handling charge; *frais d'administration générale* *Br* general overheads, *Am* general overhead; *frais d'agence* agency fee; *frais d'amortissement* amortization *or* depreciation charges; *frais d'annulation* cancellation charge; *frais d'assurance* insurance charges; *frais bancaires, frais de banque* bank charges; *frais de Bourse* transaction costs; *frais de camionnage* haulage; *frais de constitution* *(de société)* start-up costs; *(de compte)* set-up fee; *frais consulaires* consular fees; *frais de courtage* brokerage, commission; *frais dégressifs* decreasing costs; *frais de déplacement* travelling expenses; *frais de désistement* rupture of contract costs; *frais directs* direct costs; *frais divers* sundry charges, sundries; *frais de dossier* administrative costs; *frais de douane* customs duties; *frais d'emballage* packaging costs; *frais d'entrée* *(d'une sicav)* front-end *or* front-load fees; BOURSE commission on purchase of shares; *frais d'entreposage* storage charges; *frais d'entretien* *(de matériel)* maintenance expenses; *frais d'envoi* carriage costs; *frais d'établissement* start-up costs; *frais d'expédition* shipping costs *or* charges; *frais d'expertise* consultancy fees; *frais d'exploitation* operating costs; *frais extraordinaires* extraordinary expenses; *frais de fabrication* production costs; *frais financiers* interest charges, financial costs; *frais fixes* fixed charges; *frais de fonctionnement* operating costs; *frais généraux* *Br* overheads, *Am* overhead; *frais de gestion* administration costs; *frais d'inscription* membership fee; *frais d'installation* initial expenses; *frais judiciaires, frais de justice* legal costs; *frais de lancement* set-up *or* start-up costs; *frais de liquidation* closing-down costs; *frais de magasinage* warehouse charges; *frais de main-d'œuvre* labour costs; *frais de manutention* handling charges *or* costs; *frais de pilotage* pilotage; *frais de port* *(de marchandises)* carriage; *(de lettres, de colis)* postage; *frais de portage* porterage; *frais de port et d'emballage* postage and packing; *frais portuaires* port charges; *frais de publicité* advertising costs; *frais de recouvrement* collection charges; *frais de représentation* expense account, entertainment allowance; *frais de réservation* booking fee, reservation charge; *frais de tenue de compte* account charges; *(de compte bancaire)* bank charges; *frais de transport* transport charges, carriage; *frais de trésorerie* finance costs; *frais variables* variable costs

> 🙶
> C'est dans les pays où la réglementation est le plus avancée, où la loi sanctionne les écarts par des pénalités de retard, des **frais de recouvrement** et des dommages et intérêts à payer par le débiteur indélicat, que le marché est mieux régulé et les délais plus courts.
> 🙶

franc[1] *nm* franc; **pièce de cinq francs** five-franc coin □ *franc belge* Belgian franc; *franc français* French franc; *franc lourd* new franc; *franc luxembourgeois* Luxembourg franc; *franc or* gold franc; *franc suisse* Swiss franc; *franc vert* green franc

franc[2]**, franche** *adj* (a) *(gratuit)* free; **franc d'avaries** free of average; **franc de douane** duty paid; **franc de tout droit** duty-free, free of duty; **franc d'impôts** tax-exempt; **franc de port** carriage paid
(b) *(complet)* complete, whole; **huit jours francs** eight clear days

franchisage *nm* franchising

franchise *nf* (a) *(exonération)* exemption; **importer** *ou* **faire entrer qch en franchise** to import sth duty-free; **en franchise d'impôt** exempt from tax, tax free; **(en) franchise postale** postage paid □ *franchise de bagages* luggage *or* baggage allowance; *franchise fiscale* tax exemption
(b) *(d'assurance) Br* excess, *Am* deductible □ *franchise d'assurance Br* excess or *Am* deductible clause
(c) *(de commerce)* franchise; **ouvrir un magasin en franchise** to open a franchise

> 🙶
> … les autorités polonaises ont supprimé la **franchise** dont l'entreprise bénéficiait sur l'importation des composants.
> 🙶

> 🙶
> Les frères McDonald exploitent leur concept par le système de la **franchise** depuis un certain temps: ils laissent à d'autres le soin de griller les steaks et empochent les royalties.
> 🙶

franchisé, -e *nm,f* franchisee

franchiser *vt* to franchise

franchiseur, -euse *nm,f* franchisor

franco *adv* **franco (de port)** free, carriage paid; **livré franco** delivered free; **livraison franco frontière française** delivered free as far as the French frontier; **franco (à) domicile** delivery free, carriage paid; **échantillons franco sur demande** free samples available on request; **franco allège** free over side **franco (de** *ou* **à) bord** free on board; **franco de douane** free of customs duty; **franco d'emballage** free of packing charges; **franco frontière** free at frontier; **franco gare** free on rail; **franco gare de réception** free on rail; **franco long du bord** free alongside ship; **franco long du navire** free alongside ship; **franco long du quai** free alongside ship, free on quay *or* wharf; **franco de port et d'emballage** postage and packing paid; **franco rendu** free at; **franco de tous frais** free of all charges; **franco transporteur** free carrier; **franco wagon** free on rail

frappe *nf (dactylographie)* typing; *(sur un clavier d'ordinateur)* keying □ ORDINAT *frappe en continu* type-ahead; ORDINAT *frappe au kilomètre* continuous input; ORDINAT *frappe de touche* keystroke

frapper *vt (affecter)* to hit; **la crise frappe surtout les PME** small businesses are particularly badly hit by the crisis; **frapper un produit d'une taxe** to impose a duty on a product

fraude *nf* fraud; **faire entrer** *ou* **introduire qch en fraude** to smuggle sth through customs □ *fraude civile* fraud, wilful misrepresentation; *fraude douanière* illegal importation, smuggling; *fraude fiscale* tax fraud

frauder *vt (État, douane)* to defraud; **frauder le fisc** to evade tax

fraudeur, -euse *nm,f* (a) *(escroc)* defrauder (b) *(à la douane)* smuggler (c) *(du fisc)* tax dodger

frauduleusement *adv* fraudulently

frauduleux, -euse *adj* fraudulent

free-lance 1 *adj (travail)* freelance
2 *nmf (personne)* freelancer, freelance

3 *nm (travail)* freelance work; **elle travaille en free-lance** she's a freelancer

freeware *nm* ORDINAT freeware; **free-wares** freeware programs

freinage *nm (de l'inflation)* curbing; *(de production)* cutting back; *(des importations, des salaires)* reduction

freiner *vt (inflation)* to curb; *(production)* to cut back; *(importations, salaires)* to reduce

freinte *nf* wastage, loss in volume or weight *(during transit or manufacture)*

fréquence *nf* frequency ❑ MKTG *fré-quence d'achat* purchase frequency; ORDI-NAT *fréquence d'horloge* clock speed; *fréquence de rafraîchissement* refresh rate

fret *nm* (**a**) *(cargaison)* freight; **prendre du fret** to take in freight ❑ *fret aérien* air-freight; *fret d'aller* outward freight; *fret payé* freight paid; *fret au poids* freight by weight; *fret de retour* home freight (**b**) *(location)* chartering; **donner un navire à fret** to freight (out) a ship; **prendre un navire à fret** to charter a ship (**c**) *(coût du transport)* freight (charges); **payer le fret** to pay the freight (charges) ❑ *fret forfaitaire* lump-sum freight (charges)

fréter *vt (navire)* to freight (out); *(voiture, camion)* to hire; *(avion)* to charter

fréteur *nm* shipowner; **fréteur et affréteur** owner and charterer

fric *nm Fam* cash

front-office *nm* BANQUE front office

fructifier *vi (capital)* to yield a profit; **faire fructifier son argent** to make one's money yield a profit

> ❝
> Dans l'intervalle, la marchandise aura tourné 3 ou 4 fois, et les distributeurs auront largement eu le temps de faire **fructifier** leur argent.
> ❞

FS *nm (abrév* **franc suisse***)* Swiss Franc

FSE *nm (abrév* **Fonds social européen***)* ESF

fuite *nf* *fuite des capitaux* flight of capital; *fuite des cerveaux* brain drain

fusion *nf* (**a**) *(de sociétés)* merger, amalgamation; **opérer une fusion** to merge ❑ *fusions-rachats* mergers and acquisitions (**b**) ORDINAT *fusion de fichiers* file merge

fusionnement *nm (de sociétés)* merger, amalgamation

fusionner **1** *vt* (**a**) *(sociétés)* to merge, to amalgamate (**b**) ORDINAT *(fichiers)* to merge **2** *vi (sociétés)* to merge, to amalgamate

> ❝
> A la veille du mois d'août, le gouvernement Jospin a frappé un gros coup hier en annonçant la signature d'un protocole d'accord avec Jean-Luc Lagardère en vue de **fusionner** les groupes Aérospatiale et Matra.
> ❞

G7 *nm* (*abrév* **Groupe des Sept**) G7

G8 *nm* (*abrév* **Groupe des Huit**) G8

gadget publicitaire *nm* advertising gimmick

gage *nm* security; *(chez le prêteur sur gages)* pledge; **laisser qch en gage** to leave sth as security; **mettre qch en gage** to pawn *or* pledge sth; **rester en gage** to remain as security ▫ JUR *gage mobilier* mortgage over assets *or* over property

gagé, -e *adj* (*emprunt*) guaranteed, secured

gager *vt* (*emprunt*) to guarantee, to secure

gagiste *nmf* secured creditor, pledgee

gagner 1 *vt* (a) *(acquérir)* to earn; **gagner de l'argent** to earn money; **gagner dix mille francs par mois** to earn ten thousand francs a month; **il gagne bien sa vie** he earns a good salary, he makes good money (b) *(part de marché)* to capture; **nos concurrents gagnent du terrain** our competitors are gaining ground (c) BOURSE to gain; **l'indice a gagné deux points** the index has gained two points 2 *vi* to increase; **notre production gagne en qualité** the quality of our product is improving

gain *nm* (a) *(profit)* gain, profit; **les gains et les pertes** the profits and the losses ▫ COMPTA *gain latent* unrealized gain (b) *(rémunération)* earnings (c) *(économie)* saving; **un gain de temps** a saving of time ▫ *gains de productivité* productivity gains

> "
> Nous devons réaliser des **gains de productivité** en augmentant les synergies entre les pays afin d'avoir une approche marketing commune.
> "

galerie marchande *nf* shopping centre, *Am* shopping mall

gamme *nf* *(de produits)* range, series; *(de prix)* range; **étendre sa gamme de produits** to widen one's product range; **bas de gamme** bottom-of-the-range; **haut de gamme** top-of-the-range; **milieu de gamme** middle-range

garant, -e *nm,f* guarantor, warrantor, surety; **se porter garant pour qn, servir de garant à qn** to stand surety *or* guarantor for sb

garantie *nf* (a) *(d'un produit)* guarantee, warranty; **sous garantie** under guarantee ▫ *garantie illimitée* unlimited warranty; *garantie légale* legal guarantee; *garantie limitée* limited warranty; *garantie pièces et main-d'œuvre* parts and labour warranty; *garantie prolongée* extended warranty; *garantie totale* full warranty

(b) FIN *(d'une émission d'actions, d'un contrat)* underwriting; *(d'un emprunt)* backing, security ▫ *garantie accessoire* collateral security; *garantie bancaire* bank guarantee; *garantie de bonne exécution, garantie de bonne fin* performance bond; *garantie contractuelle* contractual guarantee; *garantie conventionnelle* contractual cover; *garantie de crédit acheteur* buyer credit guarantee; *garantie de crédit à l'exportation* export credit guarantee; *garantie d'exécution* contract bond; *garantie hypothécaire* mortgage security; *garantie offre* bid bond

(c) *(de l'exécution d'un contrat)* guarantee, pledge; *(d'un paiement)* security, guarantee

garantir *vt* (a) *(produit, service)* to guarantee; **nous garantissons un délai de livraison d'une semaine** we guarantee delivery within seven days

(b) *(dette)* to guarantee; **garantir le paiement d'une dette** to guarantee a debt

(c) FIN *(émission d'actions, contrat)* to underwrite; *(emprunt)* to back, to secure

(d) ASSUR to cover; **son assurance le garantit contre le vol** his insurance covers him against theft

garde *nf* **déposer qch en garde** to place sth in safe custody ▫ *garde en dépôt* safe custody

Garde des Sceaux *nm* French Minister of Justice

gare *nf* *(de chemin de fer)* (*Br* railway *or* *Am* railroad) station ▫ *gare d'arrivée* *(pour passagers)* arrival station; *(pour marchandises)* receiving station; *gare de départ* *(pour passagers)* departure station; *gare expéditrice, gare d'expédition* forwarding station, dispatch station; *gare de marchandises* goods station, *Am* freight depot; *gare maritime* harbour station; *gare routière* *(pour passagers)* bus station; *(de camions)* road haulage depot

gaspillage *nm* waste

gaspiller *vt* to waste

gâter *vt* to spoil, to damage

GATT *nm* ÉCON (*abrév* **General Agreement on Tariffs and Trade**) GATT

géant, -e **1** *adj* (*carton, paquet*) giant-size **2** *nm* giant; **un géant de l'informatique/de l'électroménager** a major player *or* giant in the computer/household appliances business

gel *nm* FIN (*blocage*) freeze □ **gel des crédits** credit freeze; **gel des prix** price freeze; **gel des salaires** wage freeze

gelé, -e *adj* FIN (*bloqué*) frozen

geler *vt* FIN (*bloquer*) to freeze

générateur, -trice **1** *adj* **un secteur générateur d'emplois/de capitaux** a job-creation/capital growth sector **2** *nm* ORDINAT generator

génération *nf* ORDINAT generation

générer *vt* (*profits, emplois*) to generate

génie *nm* engineering □ **génie civil** civil engineering; **génie électronique** electronic engineering; **génie industriel** industrial engineering

gérance *nf* (**a**) (*fonction*) management; **donner la gérance d'un commerce à qn** to appoint sb manager of a business □ FIN **gérance de portefeuille** portfolio management (**b**) (*période*) managership; **pendant sa gérance** during his time as manager

gérant, -e *nm,f* manager □ **gérant de fonds** fund manager; **gérant d'immeubles** property manager; **gérant de portefeuille** portfolio manager

gérer *vt* (*entreprise*) to manage, to run; (*finances*) to manage

gestion *nf* (**a**) FIN (*d'une entreprise, de travaux, des comptes*) management; (*d'affaires*) conduct; **mauvaise gestion** bad management, mismanagement □ **gestion administrative** administration; **gestion des affaires** business management; **gestion autonome** independent administration; **gestion budgétaire** budgetary control; **gestion cellulaire** divisional management; **gestion de la communication** communications management; **gestion de comptes-clés** key-account management; **gestion par consensus** consensus management; **gestion par département** divisional management; **gestion de la distribution physique** physical distribution management; **gestion de division** divisional management; **gestion des effectifs** manpower management; **gestion d'entreprise** business management; **gestion financière** financial management, financial administration; **gestion indicielle** indexed portfolio; **gestion indicielle répliquée** passive management; **gestion des investissements** investment management; **gestion logistique** logistics management; **gestion du marketing** marketing management; **gestion de marque** brand management; **gestion des matières** materials management; **gestion mercatique** marketing management; **gestion par objectifs** management by objectives; **gestion des opérations** operations management; **gestion paritaire, gestion participative** participative management; **gestion passive** passive management; **gestion du personnel** personnel management; **gestion de portefeuille** portfolio management; **gestion prévisionnelle** budgetary control; **gestion de la production** production control; **gestion de produits** product management; **gestion qualité** quality control, quality management; **gestion de la qualité totale** total quality management; **gestion des ressources humaines** human resources management; **gestion des sociétés** business management; **gestion de stocks** inventory management, inventory *or* stock control; **gestion stratégique** strategic management; **gestion des systèmes d'information** informations systems management; **gestion de trésorerie** cash management; **gestion zéro-défaut** total quality management (**b**) ORDINAT management □ **gestion de bases de données** database management; **gestion de données** data management; **gestion de fichiers** file management; **gestion de parc réseau** network management

> ❝ ───────────────
>
> Ces recrutements seront rendus possibles par un système de **gestion prévisionnelle** des effectifs.
>
> ─────────────── ❞

gestionnaire **1** *adj* administrative **2** *nmf* (*dirigeant*) administrator; (*d'un service*) manager □ **gestionnaire de fonds** fund manager; **gestionnaire de portefeuille** portfolio manager; **gestionnaire de(s) stock(s)** *Br* stock controller, *Am* inventory controller **3** *nm* ORDINAT manager, driver □ **gestionnaire de fichiers** file manager; **gestionnaire de fichiers et de répertoires** filer; **gestionnaire de mémoire** memory manager; **gestionnaire de projets** project management package; **gestionnaire de réseau** network manager

GIE *nm* (*abrév* **groupement d'intérêt économique**) economic interest group

gigaoctet *nm* ORDINAT gigabyte

gisement de clientèle *nm* pool of customers, potential customers

glissement *nm (d'une monnaie, des salaires)* slide

> **❝**
>
> L'inflation suisse a reculé en septembre, étant revenue à 3,4% en **glissement** annuel contre 3,6% en aôut.
>
> **❞**

glisser **1** *nm* ORDINAT *glisser d'icônes* icon drag
2 *vi* **(a)** ORDINAT **faire glisser** *(pointeur)* to drag **(b)** *(salaires, monnaie)* to slip, to slide; **le pays glisse vers la crise économique** the country is heading towards recession

glisser-lâcher *nm* ORDINAT drag and drop ❑ *glisser-lâcher d'icônes* icon drag and drop

global, -e *adj (montant, somme, budget, demande)* total; *(résultat)* overall; *(production)* aggregate; *(revenu)* gross; **le budget global de publicité excède les coûts de production** the total publicity budget is higher than the production costs

globalisation *nf* globalization

Go *nm* ORDINAT *(abrév* **gigaoctet***)* GB

gondole *nf* MKTG *(présentoir)* gondola

gonfler *vt (prix, chiffres)* to inflate; *(résultats)* to exaggerate

gouffre financier *nm* MKTG *(produit)* financial disaster, dog

gouvernement *nm* government

gouverner *vt* to govern, to rule

gouverneur *nm* governor

GPAO *nf* ORDINAT *(abrév* **gestion de production assistée par ordinateur***)* computer-aided production management

grâce *nf (dans un délai)* grace; **une semaine de grâce** a week's grace

gracieux, -euse *adj* free (of charge); **à titre gracieux** gratis, free of charge

grade *nm* ADMIN rank; **monter en grade** to be promoted; **il a été promu au grade de chef de service** he was promoted to head of department

grand, -e *adj* big ❑ *grand magasin* department store; ORDINAT *grand réseau* wide area network; *grande surface* superstore, hypermarket

grand-livre *nm* COMPTA ledger; **porter qch au grand-livre** to enter an item in the ledger ❑ *grand-livre d'achats* purchase ledger; *grand-*

livre de la dette publique National Debt register; *grand-livre de ventes* sales ledger

graphe *nm* graph, chart ❑ *graphe en ligne* line chart

grapheur *nm* ORDINAT graphics package

graphique *nm (schéma)* graph, chart; **tracer un graphique** to plot a graph; ORDINAT **graphiques** graphics ❑ *graphique d'acheminement* flow (process) chart; *graphique des activités* activity chart; *graphique à ou en barres* bar chart; *graphique circulaire* pie chart; *graphique en colonnes* bar chart; *graphique d'évolution* flow chart; *graphique financier* financial chart; *graphique de gestion* management chart; *graphique à secteurs* pie chart; *graphique à tuyaux d'orgue* bar chart; *graphique de type camembert* pie chart; *graphique de type lignes* line chart

graphismes *nmpl* ORDINAT graphics

grappe *nf* ORDINAT *(de terminaux)* cluster

gratification *nf (pourboire)* gratuity, tip; *(prime)* bonus

gratis **1** *adj* free
2 *adv* gratis, free (of charge)

gratuit, -e *adj (échantillon, livraison)* free; *(crédit)* interest-free; **à titre gratuit** free of charge

gratuitement *adv* free of charge

gré *nm* **au gré de l'acheteur** at buyer's option; **au gré du vendeur** at seller's option; **le bail est renouvelable au gré du locataire** the tenant has the option of renewing the lease; **de gré à gré** by (mutual) agreement; **vendre de gré à gré** to sell by private contract, to sell privately

greffe *nm* FIN *(de société par actions)* registry

greffier *nm* FIN registrar

grève *nf* strike, walkout; **faire grève** to (be on) strike; **lancer un ordre de grève** to call a strike; **se mettre en grève** to (go on) strike ❑ *grève d'avertissement* token strike; *grève bouchon* disruptive strike; *grève générale* general strike; *grève perlée* go-slow; *grève avec préavis* official strike; *grève sauvage* unofficial strike, wildcat strike; *grève de solidarité* sympathy strike; *grève surprise* lightning strike, walkout; *grève symbolique* token strike; *grève sur le tas* sit-down strike, sit-in; *grève tournante* staggered strike; *grève du zèle* work to rule; **faire la grève du zèle** to work to rule

> **❝**
>
> En tout cas, les **grèves d'avertissement** ne coûtent rien au syndicat, puisqu'il ne prend pas en charge, dans ce cas, les heures chômées.
>
> **❞**

grever *vt* (**a**) *(pouvoir d'achat)* to restrict; **grevé d'impôts** weighed down *or* burdened with tax (**b**) JUR *(propriété)* to mortgage

> **"**
> En baissant sensiblement les taxes locales **grevant** les ventes d'immeubles, Jospin aligne la fiscalité française sur celle de nos partenaires de l'UE.
> **"**

gréviste *nmf* striker

GRH *nf* (*abrév* **gestion des ressources humaines**) HRM

griffe *nf (marque)* label

grille *nf* grid ❑ **grille d'analyse par fonction** functional analysis chart; **grille d'avancement** career structure; **grille de gestion** managerial grid; COMPTA **grille d'imputation** table of account codes; **grille indiciaire** salary structure *or* scale; **grille de rémunération** salary scale; ORDINAT **grille de saisie** input grid; **grille des salaires** salary scale

gros, grosse **1** *adj (bénéfices, somme)* big; **la plus grosse partie de nos affaires** the bulk of our business; **le nouvel impôt touchera principalement les gros salaires** the new tax will have the biggest effect on top wage earners; **on a réussi à récupérer plusieurs de leurs gros clients depuis leur faillite** we have managed to pick up some of their biggest customers since they went bankrupt; **un gros consommateur** a heavy user ❑ ORDINAT **gros système** mainframe

2 *adv* **gagner gros** to make a lot (of money); **cette opération m'a rapporté gros** the deal made me a lot of money *or* a healthy profit

3 *nm* (**a**) *(majorité)* bulk; **le gros de la cargaison** the bulk of the cargo

(**b**) *(en commerce)* wholesale (trade); **acheter en gros** to buy wholesale; *(en grosse quantité)* to buy in bulk; **vendre en gros** to sell wholesale; **faire le gros et le détail** to sell wholesale and retail; **de gros** *(prix, commerce)* wholesale

4 *nf* **grosse** *(douze douzaines)* gross

grossiste *nmf* wholesaler

grossoyer *vt* JUR *(document)* to engross

grouillot *nm* BOURSE messenger

groupage *nm (de paquets)* bulking; *(de commandes, d'envois, de livraisons)* groupage, consolidation

groupe *nm* group; BOURSE crowd ❑ ÉCON **groupe de consommateurs** consumer group; ORDINAT **groupe de discussion** discussion group; **groupe d'étude** study group; **groupe financier** financial group; **groupe hôtelier** hotel group; **Groupe des Huit** Group of Eight; **groupe industriel** industrial group; **groupe multimédia** multimedia group; ORDINAT **groupe de nouvelles** newsgroup; **groupe de presse** press group, newspaper group; **groupe de pression** pressure group; **groupe de prix** price bracket; MKTG **groupe de prospects** prospect pool; **Groupe des Sept** Group of Seven; **groupe socio-économique** socio-economic group; **groupe stratégique** strategic group; MKTG **groupe suivi** control group; **groupe test de consommateurs** consumer test group; **groupe de travail** working party, work group; **groupe volontaire** voluntary group

groupé, -e *adj (commandes, envois, livraisons)* grouped, consolidated

groupe-cible *nm* MKTG target group

groupement *nm* (**a**) *(association)* group ❑ **groupement d'achat** purchasing group, bulk buying group; **groupement de consommateurs** consumer group; **groupement de détaillants** retailers' group; **groupement à l'export** consolidation for export; **groupement financier** financial pool; **groupement d'intérêt économique** economic interest group; **groupement professionnel** trade association; **groupement syndical** *Br* trade *or Am* labor union bloc

(**b**) *(action) (d'intérêts, de ressources)* pooling

grouper *vt (intérêts, ressources)* to pool; *(paquets)* to bulk; *(commandes, envois, livraisons)* to group, to consolidate

groupe-témoin *nm* MKTG focus group

groupeur *nm* consolidator ❑ **groupeur de fret aérien** air freight consolidator; **groupeur maritime** maritime freight consolidator; **groupeur routier** road haulage consolidator

guelte *nf* commission, percentage *(on sales)*

guerre *nf* **guerre économique** economic warfare; **guerre des prix, guerre des tarifs** price war

guichet *nm* BANQUE position, window, *Am* wicket; **payer au guichet** to pay at the counter; **guichet fermé** *(sur panneau)* position closed ❑ BANQUE **guichet automatique (de banque)** cash dispenser *or* machine, automatic teller machine

guichetier, -ère *nm,f (dans une banque)* counter clerk, teller

gulden *nm* guilder

habiliter *vt* JUR to empower, to entitle; **être habilité (à faire qch)** to be empowered *or* entitled (to do sth); **habilité à signer** *(employé de banque)* authorized to sign

habillage *nm* **(a)** *(de marchandises)* packaging ❏ **habillage transparent** blister pack **(b)** COMPTA *(d'un bilan)* window-dressing

habiller *vt* **(a)** *(marchandises)* to package **(b)** COMPTA *(bilan)* to window-dress

habitant, -e *nm,f* inhabitant; **par habitant** per person, per capita

halle *nf* (covered) market

hardware *nm* ORDINAT hardware

hausse *nf* **(a)** *(des prix, du chômage, du coût de la vie)* increase, rise (**de** in); **une hausse de 4%** a 4% rise; **accuser une hausse** to show a rise; **être à la hausse** to go up; **les prix ont subi une forte hausse** prices have increased sharply, prices have shot up ❏ **hausse de prix déguisée** hidden price increase
(b) BOURSE *(des cours, des valeurs)* rise; **à la hausse** *(tendance, marché, position)* bullish; **en hausse** *(actions)* rising; **jouer** *ou* **spéculer à la hausse** to speculate on a rising market, to bull the market; **pousser les actions à la hausse** to bull the market; **les cours sont orientés à la hausse** there is an upward trend in share prices; **provoquer une hausse factice** to rig the market

hausser **1** *vt (prix, taux de l'escompte)* to raise, to put up; **le prix a été haussé de 10%** the price has gone up by 10%
2 *vi* to rise; **faire hausser les prix** to force up prices

haussier, -ère BOURSE **1** *adj (marché)* bullish
2 *nm,f* bull

haut, -e **1** *adj* **(a)** *(prix, salaire)* high ❏ ORDINAT **haute densité** high density; **haute saison** *(dans le domaine du tourisme)* high season
2 *nm* **(a)** MKTG *(du marché)* high end, top end **(b)** COMPTA **haut de bilan** *(fonds propres)* shareholders' funds

hauteur *nf* **participer à hauteur de 30%** to contribute up to 30%; **un actionnaire à hauteur de 5%** a shareholder with 5% of the shares

HD *adj* ORDINAT *(abrév* **haute densité***)* HD

hebdomadaire **1** *adj* weekly
2 *nm (journal, revue)* weekly

HEC *nfpl (abrév* **Hautes Études Commerciales***)* = prestigious business school in Paris

héritage *nm* inheritance

hériter **1** *vt* to inherit
2 **hériter de** *vt ind* to inherit

héritier, -ère *nm,f* heir, *f* heiress

heure *nf* hour; **engager qn à l'heure** to employ sb by the hour; **être payé à l'heure** to be paid by the hour; **il est payé 55 francs (de) l'heure** he is paid 55 francs an hour ❏ **heures d'affluence** rush hour; **heure d'arrivée** arrival time, time of arrival; **heures de bureau** office *or* business hours; BOURSE **heures de cotation** trading time; **heures creuses** off-peak hours; **heure de départ** departure time, time of departure; **heure d'embarquement** boarding time; **heure de fermeture** *(d'un magasin)* closing time; *(d'une usine, d'un bureau)* finishing time; **heures d'ouverture, heures ouvrables** *(d'un magasin, d'une agence)* opening hours; *(d'un bureau)* business *or* office hours; **heures de pointe** rush hour; **heures de réception** *(dans une administration)* opening hours; **heures supplémentaires** *ou Fam* **sup'** overtime; **faire des heures supplémentaires** to do *or* work overtime; **heures de travail** working hours

hiérarchie *nf* hierarchy

hiérarchique *adj (organisation, structure)* hierarchical; **c'est mon supérieur hiérarchique**

he's my immediate superior; **passer par la voie hiérarchique** to go through the official channels

hiérarchisation *nf* (**a**) *(structure)* hierarchical structure (**b**) *(de tâches)* prioritization

hiérarchiser *vt* (**a**) *(personnel)* to grade; **hiérarchiser les salaires** to create a salary structure (**b**) *(tâches)* to prioritize

histogramme *nm* histogram

historique *nm* ORDINAT *(de document)* log

holding *nm* FIN holding company

homme *nm* **homme d'affaires** businessman; **homme de métier** expert, professional

homologation *nf* *(d'un prototype)* approval, certification; *(d'un prix)* authorization; *(d'un accord, d'une décision, d'un document)* ratification; *(d'un testament)* probate

homologué, -e *adj (prix)* authorized

homologuer *vt (prototype)* to approve, to certify; *(prix)* to authorize; *(accord, décision)* to ratify *(document)* to obtain legal ratification of; *(testament)* to probate

honneur *nm* **faire honneur à qch** *(facture, chèque, traite)* to honour, to meet; **nous avons l'honneur de vous informer que...** we are pleased to inform you that...

honorable *adj (entreprise)* of high standing

honoraire 1 *adj (membre)* honorary
2 *nmpl* **honoraires** fee, fees

honorer *vt (facture, chèque, traite)* to honour, to meet; *(signature)* to honour

horaire 1 *adj* hourly
2 *nm* timetable, schedule; *(d'un magasin)* opening hours ▫ *horaires à la carte, horaires flexibles* flexitime; *horaires de travail* working hours

horizontal, -e *adj (concentration, intégration)* horizontal

horloge *nf* **horloge horodatrice** time clock; **horloge pointeuse** time clock; ORDINAT **horloge du système** system clock; **horloge en temps réel** real-time clock

horodaté, -e *adj* stamped with time and date

horodateur *nm* time and date stamp

hors *prép* **hors bilan** off-balance sheet; **hors Bourse** after hours; **hors budget** not included in the budget; **hors commerce** not for sale to the general public; **hors pointe** off-peak; **hors saison** off-season; **hors série** made-to-order, custom-built; **hors taxe** exclusive of tax; *(à la douane)* duty-free; **hors TVA** net of VAT

hors-cote BOURSE 1 *adj* unlisted
2 *nm* unlisted securities market

hôtel *nm* (**a**) *(pour l'hébergement)* hotel (**b**) *(bâtiment)* ADMIN **hôtel des impôts** tax office; **l'Hôtel de la Monnaie** ≃ the Royal Mint; **hôtel des ventes** sale room, auction room; **hôtel de ville** town hall

hôtelier, -ère 1 *adj* **l'industrie hôtelière** the hotel industry *or* trade
2 *nm,f* hotel keeper, hotelier

hôtellerie *nf* **l'hôtellerie** the hotel trade

HT *adj (abrév* **hors taxe**) exclusive of tax

HTML *nm (abrév* **Hyper Text Markup Language**) HTML

huissier *nm* bailiff

huit 1 *adj* **dans huit jours** in a week's time
2 *nm* **lundi en huit** a week next Monday

hyperinflation *nf* hyperinflation

hypermarché *nm* hypermarket

hypermédia *nm* ORDINAT hypermedia

hypertexte *adj & nm* ORDINAT hypertext

hypothécable *adj* mortgageable

hypothécaire *adj* mortgage

hypothèque *nf* mortgage; **franc** *ou* **libre d'hypothèques** unmortgaged; **prendre une hypothèque** to take out a mortgage; **emprunter sur hypothèque** to borrow on mortgage; **avoir une hypothèque sur une maison** to have a mortgage on a house, to have one's house mortgaged; **purger une hypothèque** to pay off *or* clear *or* redeem a mortgage; **propriété grevée d'hypothèques** encumbered estate ▫ *hypothèque générale* blanket mortgage; *hypothèque de premier rang* first legal mortgage

hypothéquer *vt* (**a**) *(propriété, titres)* to mortgage (**b**) *(dette)* to secure by mortgage

icône *nf* ORDINAT icon

idée de vente *nf* MKTG selling idea

identificateur *nm* (**a**) ORDINAT identifier (**b**) MKTG *identificateur de marque* brand identifier

identification *nf* (**a**) ORDINAT *identification de l'utilisateur* user identification (**b**) MKTG *identification de marque* brand recognition

identité *nf* (**a**) ADMIN identity (**b**) MKTG *identité graphique* logo

IEP *nm* (*abrév* **Institut d'études politiques**) = higher education institute of political science

IGP *nf* (*abrév* **indication géographique protégée**) = designation of a product which guarantees its authentic origin and gives the name protected status

illégal, -e *adj* illegal, unlawful

illégalement *adv* illegally, unlawfully

illégalité *nf* (*caractère*) illegality, unlawfulness; (*acte*) unlawful act

illicite *adj* (*profits, transactions*) illicit

illimité, -e *adj* (*crédit, responsabilité*) unlimited

illisible *adj* ORDINAT unreadable

îlot *nm* MKTG gondola □ *îlot de vente* (display) stand, island

image *nf* image □ MKTG *images à compléter* picture completion; ORDINAT *image digitalisée* digitized image; MKTG *image de l'entreprise* corporate image; COMPTA *image fidèle* true and fair view; *image institutionnelle* corporate image; *image de marque* (*d'un produit*) brand image; (*d'une société*) corporate image *or* identity; *image de produit* product image; *images de synthèse* computer-generated images, CGI

imbattable *adj* (*prix*) unbeatable

IME (*abrév* **Institut monétaire européen**) EMI

imitation *nf* (*d'un produit*) imitation; (*d'une signature, d'un billet*) forgery

imiter *vt* (*produit*) to imitate; (*signature, billet*) to forge

immatériel, -elle *adj* FIN (*actif, valeurs*) intangible

immatriculation *nf* (*d'un document, d'une société, des marchandises*) registration

immatricule *nf* registration

immatriculer *vt* (*document, société, marchandises*) to register; **être immatriculé à la Sécurité Sociale** to have a Social Security number

immeuble **1** *adj* JUR real, fixed
2 *nm* (**a**) (*bâtiment*) building □ *immeuble de bureaux* office block; *immeuble (à usage) commercial* business premises; *immeuble locatif, immeuble de rapport* rental property
(**b**) JUR real estate, landed property, *Am* realty; **placer son argent en immeubles** to invest in property □ *immeuble de rapport* rented property

immobilier, -ère **1** *adj Br* property, *Am* real-estate
2 *nm* **l'immobilier** the *Br* property *or Am* real-estate business; **l'immobilier d'entreprise** the commercial *Br* property *or Am* real-estate business; **l'immobilier locatif** the *Br* property *or Am* real-estate rental business

immobilisation *nf* (**a**) COMPTA asset; **immobilisations** fixed *or* capital assets; **faire de grosses immobilisations** to carry heavy stocks □ *immobilisation de capitaux* tied-up capital, capital assets; *immobilisations corporelles* tangible (fixed) assets, capital assets; *immobilisations financières* long-term investments; *immobilisations incorporelles* intangible (fixed) assets; *immobilisations non financières* physical fixed assets
(**b**) JUR conversion into real estate
(**c**) FIN (*de capital*) locking up, tying up, immobilization; (*d'actif, de valeurs*) freezing

immobilisé, -e *adj* FIN (*capital*) locked-up, tied up, immobilized; (*actif, valeurs*) frozen

immobiliser *vt* (**a**) JUR to convert into real estate (**b**) FIN (*capital*) to lock up, to tie up, to immobilize; (*actif, valeurs*) to freeze

immunité *nf* immunity □ *immunité fiscale* immunity from taxation

impartir *vt* (**a**) JUR (*droit, faveur*) to grant (**à** to) (**b**) (*délai*) to grant, to allow; **faire qch dans les délais impartis** to do sth to schedule

impasse *nf* (**a**) *(blocage)* impasse, deadlock; **être** *ou* **se trouver dans une impasse** to be at a dead end; **sortir de l'impasse** to break the deadlock; **les négociations sont dans l'impasse** the talks have reached a deadlock *or* are deadlocked (**b**) FIN *impasse budgétaire* budget deficit

impayé, -e 1 *adj* (**a**) *(dette, facture)* unpaid, outstanding; *(comptes)* unsettled (**b**) *(effet)* dishonoured
     2 *nm* outstanding payment

> "
> De même, des actions tendant à réduire les **impayés** de loyers et à renforcer les droits des petits propriétaires seront entreprises.
> "

impératif, -ive 1 *adj* JUR *(loi, disposition)* mandatory
     2 *nm* *(exigence)* requirement; **nous avons des impératifs de livraison** we have delivery dates that we must respect

implantation *nf* (**a**) *(installation)* setting up, establishment; *(d'un produit sur le marché)* establishment (**b**) *(d'une usine, du matériel)* layout ◻ *implantation fonctionnelle* functional layout

implanter 1 *vt* *(installer)* to set up, to establish, to locate; **cette entreprise japonaise a plusieurs usines implantées en France** this Japanese company has a number of factories located in France
     2 **s'implanter** *vpr* to be set up, to be located, to be sited; **l'usine s'est finalement implantée au Mexique** the factory was eventually sited in Mexico; **s'implanter sur un marché** to establish oneself in a market

impliquer *vt* *(dépenses)* to entail

import *nm* import ◻ ORDINAT *import de données* data import

importable *adj* importable

importance *nf* (**a**) *(d'une somme, d'un projet)* size; **une usine de moyenne importance** a medium-sized factory (**b**) *(des dégâts)* extent (**c**) *(d'une société)* position, standing

important, -e *adj* (**a**) *(grand)* large, considerable; **nous ne pouvons pas vous accorder un crédit plus important** we cannot allow you credit beyond this limit (**b**) *(sérieux)* *(rôle, négociations)* important

importateur, -trice 1 *adj* importing; **les pays importateurs de pétrole** the oil-importing countries
     2 *nm,f* importer; **c'est l'importateur exclusif**

de cette marque pour la France they are the sole French importers of this brand

importation *nf* (**a**) *(activité)* importing ◻ *importation en franchise* duty-free import (**b**) *(produit)* import ◻ *importations invisibles* invisible imports; *importations visibles* visible imports

importer *vt* (**a**) *(marchandises)* to import; **importer des marchandises des États-Unis en France** to import goods from the United States into France (**b**) ORDINAT to import (**depuis** from)

import-export *nf* import-export; **travailler dans l'import-export** to work in the import-export business

imposable *adj* *(personne, marchandises)* taxable, liable to tax; *(propriété)* rateable

imposé, -e 1 *adj* *(soumis à l'impôt)* taxed; **être lourdement imposé** to be heavily taxed
     2 *nm,f* taxpayer; *(d'une propriété)* ratepayer

imposer *vt* *(personne, marchandises)* to tax; *(propriété)* to levy a rate on; **imposer des droits sur qch** to tax sth

imposition *nf* taxation ◻ *imposition en cascade* cascade taxation; *imposition forfaitaire* basic-rate taxation; *imposition progressive* progressive taxation; *imposition à la source* taxation at source

impôt *nm* tax; **avant impôt** before tax; **après impôt** after tax; **frapper qch d'un impôt** to tax sth; **payer 5000 francs d'impôts** to pay 5,000 francs in tax(es) ◻ *impôt sur les bénéfices* profit tax; *impôt sur le capital* capital tax; *impôt sur le chiffre d'affaires* turnover tax; *impôt à la consommation* output tax; *impôt dégressif* sliding scale taxation, degressive taxation; *impôt déguisé* hidden tax; *impôt différé* deferred taxation; *impôt direct* direct tax; *impôt sur les dividendes* dividend tax; *impôt sur les donations et les successions* gift and inheritance tax; *impôt extraordinaire* emergency tax; *impôt foncier* land tax, property tax; *impôt indiciaire* wealth tax; *impôts locaux* *Br* council tax, *Am* local taxes; *impôt de luxe* tax on luxury goods; *impôt sur la masse salariale* payroll tax; *impôt sur les plus-values* capital gains tax; *impôt à la production* input tax; *impôt progressif* progressive tax; *(sur le revenu)* graduated income tax; *impôt de quotité* coefficient tax; *impôt retenu à la base* *ou* *à la source* tax deducted at source, *Br* pay-as-you-earn tax, *Am* pay-as-you-go tax; *impôt sur le revenu* income tax; *impôt sur les sociétés* *Br* corporation tax, *Am* corporation income tax; *impôt de solidarité* *sur la fortune* wealth tax; *impôt du timbre* stamp duty; *impôt sur le travail* payroll tax

> **❝**
> Le taux maximal de l'**impôt sur le revenu** sera relevé de 31 à 36% dès l'an prochain, tandis que l'**impôt sur les sociétés** passera de 35 à 36%.
> **❞**

imprescriptibilité *nf* JUR imprescriptibility, indefeasibility

imprescriptible *adj* JUR imprescriptible, indefeasible

impression *nf* ORDINAT printing ▫ *impression en arrière-plan* background (mode) printing; *impression écran* screen dump; *impression ombrée* shadow printing; *impression en qualité brouillon* draft quality printing

imprévu, -e 1 *adj (dépenses)* unforeseen, incidental
2 *nm* hidden expense, contingency

imprimante *nf* printer ▫ *imprimante à bulles* bubble-jet printer; *imprimante couleur* colour printer; *imprimante feuille à feuille* sheet-fed printer; *imprimante à jet d'encre* ink-jet printer; *imprimante (à) laser* laser printer; *imprimante à marguerite* daisy-wheel printer; *imprimante matricielle* dot-matrix printer; *imprimante parallèle* parallel printer; *imprimante série* serial printer

imprimé, -e 1 *adj* printed
2 *nm* (a) *(formulaire)* form; **remplir un imprimé** to fill in *or* out a form ▫ *imprimé publicitaire* advertising leaflet, publicity handout (b) **imprimés** *(journaux, prospectus)* printed matter

imprimer *vt* ORDINAT to print (out)

improductif, -ive *adj* unproductive, idle

imputable *adj* FIN chargeable (**sur** to)

imputation *nf* FIN *(des dépenses)* charge, charging; **imputation d'un paiement** appropriation of money *(to the payment of a debt)*; **imputation à** charge to; **imputation d'une somme au crédit/débit d'un compte** crediting/debiting an amount to an account ▫ *imputations budgétaires* budget allocations; *imputation des charges* cost allocation

imputer *vt* (a) *(déduire)* to deduct; **imputer qch sur qch** to deduct sth from sth
(b) FIN *(attribuer)* to charge sth to sth; **imputer des frais à un compte** to charge expenses to an account; **imputer une somme à un budget** to allocate a sum to a budget

inabordable *adj (prix, produit, service)* unaffordable

inacceptation *nf (d'un effet)* non-acceptance

inacquitté *adj (effet)* unreceipted

inactif, -ive 1 *adj* (a) ÉCON *(personne)* non-working; **la population inactive** the non-working population (b) *(marché)* sluggish, dull (c) *(fonds)* unemployed, idle
2 *nm,f* ÉCON **un inactif** a person without paid employment; **les inactifs** the non-working population

inactivité *nf (du marché)* sluggishness, dullness

inamical, -e *adj (offre publique d'achat)* hostile

inamovible *adj (fonctionnaire, poste)* permanent

inanimé, -e *adj (marché)* sluggish, dull

INC *nm (abrév* **Institut national de la consommation**) = French consumer research organization

incapacité *nf* (a) *(incompétence)* **incapacité (professionnelle)** inefficiency, incompetence (b) *(invalidité)* disablement, disability ▫ *incapacité de travail* (industrial) disablement (c) *(impossibilité)* incapacity, inability; **nous sommes dans l'incapacité de satisfaire à votre demande** we are unable to meet your request

incertain *nm* BOURSE, FIN variable exchange; **coter** *ou* **donner l'incertain** to quote on the exchange rate

incertifié, -e *adj* uncertified

incessibilité *nf* FIN non-transferability

incessible *adj* FIN non-transferable

inchangé, -e *adj* unchanged

incidence *nf* impact, repercussions; **l'incidence d'un impôt sur le consommateur** the impact of a tax on the consumer; **l'incidence des salaires sur les prix de revient** the impact *or* repercussions of wage levels on production costs

incitation *nf* incentive ▫ *incitation à l'achat* buying incentive; *incitation fiscale* tax incentive; *incitation à la vente* sales incentive

inclure *vt* (a) *(dans un courrier)* to enclose (**dans** with *or* in) (b) *(comprendre)* to include (c) JUR *(clause)* to insert

inclus, -e *adj* (**a**) *(dans un courrier)* enclosed; **le chèque est inclus dans la lettre** the cheque is enclosed with the letter (**b**) *(compris)* inclusive, included; **jusqu'au 30 juin inclus** until 30 June inclusive, *Am* through 30 June; **les frais de main-d'œuvre pour l'installation sont inclus dans la somme totale à payer** the labour costs for installation are included in the total sum due

inclusivement *adv* inclusively; **du vendredi au mardi inclusivement** from Friday to Tuesday inclusive, *Am* Friday through Tuesday; **jusqu'au 30 avril inclusivement** until 30 April inclusive, *Am* through 30 April

incompensé, -e *adj* uncompensated

incompétent, -e *adj* (**a**) JUR *(tribunal)* not competent, incompetent (**b**) *(incapable)* incompetent

inconvertible *adj* FIN inconvertible

incorporation *nf* FIN **incorporation des réserves au capital** capitalization of reserves

incorporel, -elle *adj* *(actif, valeurs, biens)* intangible

incoté, -e *adj* BOURSE unquoted

incoterms *nmpl* incoterms

indemnisable *adj* entitled to compensation

indemnisation *nf* (**a**) *(action)* compensating (**b**) *(paiement)* compensation, indemnity

indemniser *vt* to compensate, to indemnify (**de** for); **indemniser totalement qn** to compensate sb in full; **indemniser qn de ses frais** to reimburse sb his/her expenses, to pay sb's expenses

indemnitaire **1** *adj* compensatory
2 *nmf* beneficiary of compensation

indemnité (**a**) *(pour perte encourue)* compensation, indemnity; *(pour délai, non-livraison)* penalty; **à titre d'indemnité** by way of compensation; **recevoir une indemnité** to receive compensation; **demander une indemnité** to put in a claim ❑ **indemnité en argent** cash compensation; **indemnité de clientèle** compensation for loss of custom; **indemnité compensatrice** compensation; **indemnité compensatrice de congés payés** pay in lieu of holidays; **indemnité contractuelle de départ** ou **de licenciement** golden parachute; **indemnité de départ, indemnité de licenciement** severance pay; **indemnité de retard** late payment penalty; **indemnité de rupture** severance pay; **indemnité de rupture abusive** compensation for breach of contract

(**b**) *(allocation)* allowance, grant ❑ **indemnité de cherté de vie** cost-of-living allowance, *Br* weighting; **indemnité de chômage** unemployment benefit; **indemnité complémentaire** additional allowance; **indemnité conventionnelle** contractual allowance; **indemnité de déménagement** relocation grant or allowance; **indemnité de déplacement** travel or transport allowance; **indemnité de fonction** entertainment allowance; **indemnité journalière** daily allowance; **indemnité kilométrique** ≃ mileage allowance; **indemnité de logement** accommodation allowance; **indemnité de maladie** sickness benefit; **indemnité de représentation** entertainment allowance; **indemnité de résidence** housing allowance; **indemnité de séjour** living expenses; **indemnité de transport** travel or transport allowance; **indemnité de vie chère** cost-of-living allowance, *Br* weighting

> ❝
> Aujourd'hui, on verse les **indemnités de chômage** ou de revenu minimum d'insertion (RMI) en demandant comme seule contrepartie la recherche active d'emploi.
> ❞

indépendant, -e **1** *adj* *(travailleur)* self-employed; *(traducteur, journaliste, photographe)* freelance
2 *nm,f* *(travailleur)* self-employed worker; *(traducteur, journaliste, photographe)* freelancer

indépensé, -e *adj* unspent

indexation *nf* ÉCON index-linking, indexation; **l'indexation des salaires sur les prix** the index-linking of salaries to prices

> ❝
> Les augmentations salariales ralentissent depuis que l'**indexation** des rémunérations sur le coût de la vie a été abandonnée.
> ❞

indexé, -e *adj* ÉCON index-linked, indexed

indexer *vt* (**a**) ÉCON to index-link, to index (**sur** to) (**b**) ORDINAT *(base de données)* to index

indicateur *nm* indicator ❑ **indicateurs d'alerte** economic indicators, business indicators; **indicateur clef** key indicator; FIN **indicateur (d'activité) économique** economic indicator; **indicateur de marché** market indicator; **indicateur statistique**

statistical indicator; *indicateur de ten-dance* market indication

indicatif, -ive 1 *adj (prix)* approximate; **à titre indicatif** for information only

2 *nm* (**a**) TÉL **indicatif (téléphonique)** *Br* dialling code, *Am* dial code ▢ *indicatif du pays* international *Br* dialling code *or Am* dial code (**b**) ORDINAT prompt ▢ *indicatif (du) DOS* DOS prompt

indication *nf* indication; **il n'y a aucune indication de prix dans ce catalogue** there is no indication of the price in the catalogue; **sauf indication contraire** unless otherwise stated ▢ *indication d'origine, indication de provenance* place of origin

indice *nm* index ▢ MKTG *indice ad hoc* specific indicator; BOURSE *indice boursier* share index; BOURSE *l'indice CAC 40* the CAC 40 index; ÉCON *indice corrigé des variations saisonnières* seasonally adjusted index; BOURSE *indice des cours d'actions* share price index; ÉCON *indice du coût de la vie* cost-of-living index; ÉCON *indice de croissance* index of growth; BOURSE *l'indice Dow Jones* the Dow Jones index; BOURSE *l'indice FTSE des 100 valeurs* the FTSE 100 share index; BOURSE *l'indice Hang Seng* the Hang Seng index; BOURSE *l'indice Nikkei* the Nikkei index; ÉCON *indice non-corrigé des variations saisonnières* non-seasonally adjusted index; *indice des prix* price index; *indice des prix à la consommation* consumer price index; *indice (des prix) de détail* retail price index; *indice (des prix) de gros* wholesale price index; *indice des prix et des salaires* wage and price index; *indice de profit* profit indicator; BOURSE *indice des valeurs boursières* share index

indirect, -e *adj (coûts, vente)* indirect

indisponibilité *nf (de fonds)* unavailability, non-availability

indisponible *adj (fonds)* unavailable

individuel, -elle *adj* individual; *(fortune)* private

individuellement *adv* JUR severally; **responsables individuellement** severally liable

indivis, -e *adj* JUR undivided, joint

indivisaire *nmf* JUR joint owner

indivisément *adv* JUR jointly

indivision *nf* JUR joint possession

indu *nm* **l'indu** money not owed

induit, -e *adj (demande, investissement)* induced

industrialisation *nf* industrialization

industrialiser 1 *vt* to industrialize

2 **s'industrialiser** *vpr* to become industrialized; **l'agriculture s'est fortement industrialisée et a augmenté sa production** agriculture has become highly mechanized and has increased output

industrialisme *nm* industrialism

industrie *nf* ÉCON industry, manufacturing; **travailler dans l'industrie** to work in industry *or* in manufacturing ▢ *industrie agro-alimentaire* food-processing industry; *industrie artisanale* cottage industry; *industrie automobile* car *or* motor industry; *industrie de base* basic industry; *industrie du bâtiment* building trade *or* industry; *industrie de consommation* consumer goods industry; *industrie en croissance rapide* growth industry; *industrie électronique* electronics industry; *industrie légère* light industry; *industrie lourde* heavy industry; *industrie de luxe* luxury goods industry; *industrie manufacturière* manufacturing industry; *industrie mécanique* engineering; *industrie des métaux* metal industry; *industrie nationalisée* nationalized *or* state-owned industry; *industrie de pointe* advanced technology industry; *industrie pétrochimique* petrochemical industry; *industrie pétrolière* oil industry; *industrie de précision* precision industry; *industrie primaire* primary industry; *industrie de transformation* processing industry

industrie-clef *nf* key industry

industriel, -elle 1 *adj* industrial

2 *nm,f* manufacturer, industrialist

industriellement *adv* industrially

inemployé, -e *adj* unemployed, unused

inescomptable *adj* FIN undiscountable

inexact, -e *adj* incorrect, wrong

inexécuté, -e *adj (contrat)* unfulfilled; *(travaux)* not carried out

inexécution *nf (d'un contrat)* non-fulfilment; **inexécution des travaux** failure to carry out work

inexigible *adj (remboursement, dette)* irrecoverable

inférieur, -e 1 *adj* (**a**) *(dans une hiérarchie)* inferior; **d'un rang inférieur** of a lower rank; **être rétrogradé à l'échelon inférieur** to be demoted to the grade below; **de qualité inférieure** inferior quality

(**b**) *(dans une comparaison)* **inférieur à** *(qualité)* inferior to; *(quantité)* less than; **les bénéfices réalisés sont inférieurs aux**

prédictions the profits are lower than predicted or forecast; **votre paiement est inférieur de 1000 francs à la somme prévue** your payment falls short of the agreed amount by 1,000 francs
  2 nm,f subordinate

inflation nf inflation; **contenir l'inflation** to contain or curb inflation; **le gouvernement a eu recours à l'inflation** the government resorted to inflation □ *inflation par les coûts* cost-push inflation; *inflation par la demande* demand-pull inflation; *inflation fiduciaire* inflation of the currency; *inflation galopante* galloping or rampant inflation; *inflation monétaire* monetary inflation; *inflation rampante* creeping inflation; *inflation des salaires* wage inflation

inflationnisme nm inflationism

inflationniste 1 adj inflationary
  2 nmf inflationist

> ❝ ... l'extension du chômage... [favorise] un ajustement retardé et **inflationniste** qui rend nécessaire des politiques d'austérité. ❞

infléchir 1 vt (faire diminuer) to cut, to reduce
  2 s'infléchir vpr (diminuer) (cours) to fall

inflexion nm,f (diminution) reduction, fall

informaticien, -enne nm,f computer scientist

information nf (**a**) (renseignement) piece of information; **informations** information; **(devoirs d')information financière** disclosure; **nous vous adressons ce catalogue à titre d'information** we are sending you this catalogue for your information □ MKTG *information sur le lieu de vente* point-of-sale information; *informations primaires* primary data
  (**b**) ORDINAT data, information
  (**c**) JUR (enquête) inquiry; (instruction préparatoire) preliminary investigation; **ouvrir une information** to set up a preliminary investigation

informatique nf ORDINAT data processing; (science) computer science, computing; **elle travaille dans l'informatique** she works in computing □ *informatique d'entreprise* business data processing; *informatique de gestion* administrative data processing; *informatique individuelle* personal computing

informatisation nf ORDINAT computerization

informatiser vt ORDINAT to computerize

infraction nf JUR offence □ *infraction pénale* criminal offence

infrastructure nf infrastructure

infructueux, -euse adj (investissements) unprofitable

ingénierie nf engineering; (service) engineering department □ ORDINAT *ingénierie assistée par ordinateur* computer-aided engineering; FIN *ingénierie financière* financial engineering

ingénieur nm engineer □ *ingénieur civil* civil engineer; *ingénieur commercial* sales engineer; *ingénieur constructeur* civil engineer; *ingénieur d'études* design engineer; *ingénieur informaticien* computer engineer; *ingénieur de méthodes* methods engineer; *ingénieur en organisation* work study engineer; *ingénieur projecteur* design engineer; *ingénieur des travaux publics* civil engineer

ingénieur-conseil nm engineering consultant, consultant engineer

initial, -e adj (coût, capitaux) initial

initialiser vt ORDINAT to initialize

initié, -e nm,f BOURSE insider

injecter vt (argent, capitaux) to inject (**dans** into); **il faudrait injecter quelques idées nouvelles dans ce projet** we need to inject a few fresh ideas into the project; **injecter des millions dans une affaire** to inject or pump millions into a business

injection nf (d'argent, de capitaux) injection (**dans** into)

innovateur, -trice 1 adj (entreprise, procédé) ground-breaking, innovative
  2 nm,f MKTG innovator □ *innovateur continu* continuous innovator

innovation nf innovation □ MKTG *innovation continue* continuous innovation; *innovation de produit* product innovation

innover vi to innovate; **c'est l'incapacité de notre entreprise à innover qui nous empêche de gagner des parts de marché** it's our inability to innovate that is preventing this company from gaining a market share

inondation nf (du marché) flooding

inonder vt (marché) to flood; **le marché des produits de luxe est inondé de contrefaçons** the luxury goods market is flooded with imitation products; **nous sommes inon-**

dés de réclamations we have been inundated with complaints

> France Telecom a en effet cessé depuis décembre dernier de commercialiser une assurance: le marché n'était pas assez mûr et on était **inondés** de fausses déclarations.

inopérant, -e *adj* JUR inoperative

inscription *nf* (**a**) *(action) (de renseignements, d'un nom, d'une date)* writing down, noting down; *(dans un journal, un registre)* entering, recording (**b**) COMPTA *(dans un livre de comptes)* entry ▫ *inscription comptable* accounting entry (**c**) *(à un organisme)* registration (**d**) FIN scrip ▫ *inscription sur le grand-livre* Treasury scrip (**e**) BOURSE *inscription à la cote* quotation on the (official) list; **faire une demande d'inscription à la cote** to apply for admission to the official list, to seek a share quotation

inscrire **1** *vt (renseignements, nom, date)* to write down, to note down; *(dans un journal, un registre)* to enter, to record; **inscrire une adresse sur qch** to address sth; **inscrire une question à l'ordre du jour** to put *or* place a question on the agenda; **inscrire une dépense au budget** to include an item in the budget
2 s'inscrire *vpr* (**a**) *(sur une liste)* to register, to put one's name down; **s'inscrire au chômage** to register as unemployed (**b**) *(faire partie de)* **s'inscrire dans** to come within the framework of; **ces licenciements s'inscrivent dans la stratégie globale de restructuration de l'entreprise** these redundancies are in keeping with *or* are part of the overall restructuring policy of the company (**c**) BOURSE **s'inscrire en baisse** to fall; **s'inscrire en hausse** to rise; **les valeurs industrielles s'inscrivent en baisse de 13 points à la clôture** industrial shares are closing 13 points down

inscrit, -e *adj* BOURSE **inscrit à la cote officielle** listed; **non inscrite** unlisted

INSEE *nm* (*abrév* **Institut national de la statistique et des études économiques**) = French national institute of statistics and information about the economy

insérer *vt* (**a**) *(inclure)* to insert; **insérer une clause dans un contrat** to insert a clause in an agreement; **insérer une annonce dans un journal** to put an advertisement in a newspaper (**b**) ORDINAT to insert

insertion *nf* (**a**) MKTG **tarif des insertions** advertising rates ▫ *insertion publicitaire* advertisement (**b**) *(intégration)* integration; **l'insertion professionnelle des jeunes est de plus en plus tardive** it is taking longer and longer for young people to enter the job market ▫ *insertion sociale* social integration (**c**) ORDINAT insertion

insolvabilité *nf* insolvency

insolvable *adj* insolvent

inspecter *vt* to inspect, to examine

inspecteur, -trice *nm,f* inspector; *(dans un magasin)* supervisor; *(dans une usine)* foreman ▫ *inspecteur des contributions directes* tax inspector; *inspecteur des contributions indirectes* customs and excise official; *Inspecteur des Finances* ≃ general auditor *(of the Treasury)*; *inspecteur du fisc, inspecteur des impôts* tax inspector; *inspecteur du travail* factory inspector; *inspecteur de la TVA* VAT man

inspection *nf* inspection, examination; **faire l'inspection de qch** to inspect sth, to examine sth ▫ *inspection du travail* factory inspection

instabilité *nf (du marché, du change, des prix)* instability

instable *adj (marché, change, prix)* instable

installation *nf* (**a**) *(d'une machine)* installation, setting up; *(d'un logiciel)* installation; *(d'une usine, d'un atelier)* fitting out, equipping (**b**) **installations** *(d'un atelier)* fittings ▫ *installations électriques* electrical fittings *or* equipment; *installations portuaires* port installations; *installations techniques* plant and machinery; *installations touristiques* tourist facilities

installer *vt (machine)* to install, to set up; *(logiciel)* to install; *(usine, atelier)* to fit out, to equip

instance *nf* (**a**) *(organisme)* authority ▫ *instances communautaires* EC authorities; *instances économiques* economic authorities (**b**) JUR (legal) (proceedings) (**c**) **en instance** *(dossier, affaire)* pending; *(courrier)* ready to go out

institut *nm (organisme)* institute ▫ *Institut d'études politiques* = higher education institute of political science; *institut monétaire* lender of last resort; *Institut monétaire européen* European Monetary Institute; *Institut national de la consommation* = French consumer research organization; *Institut national de la statistique et des études économiques* = French national institute of statistics and information about the economy; ***institut de sondage*** polling company; ***Institut universitaire de technologie*** = vocational higher education college

institution *nf* (**a**) *(création)* institution, establishment; *(d'une loi)* introduction (**b**) *(organisme)* institution ▫ ***institution financière*** financial institution

institutionnel, -elle **1** *adj* institutional **2** *nmpl* institutional investors

instruction *nf* (**a**) *(ordre)* instruction; **instructions** *(mode d'emploi)* instructions; **conformément aux instructions** as directed, according to instructions; **nous attendons vos instructions** we await your instructions ▫ ***instructions permanentes*** standard operating procedure (**b**) *(circulaire)* (official) memo, circular (**c**) ORDINAT instruction

instruire *vt* (**a**) *(informer)* **instruire qn de qch** to inform sb of sth (**b**) JUR **instruire un dossier** to set up a preliminary enquiry

instrument *nm* (**a**) *(document)* instrument; JUR (legal) instrument ▫ ***instrument de commerce*** instrument of commerce; ***instrument de couverture*** hedging instrument; ***instrument de crédit*** instrument of credit; ***instrument de négociation*** trading instrument; ***instrument de placement*** investment instrument (**b**) *(moyen d'évaluation)* tool; **c'est un instrument d'analyse de l'inflation** it's a tool for analysing inflation

insuffisance *nf* insufficiency ▫ ***insuffisance de capitaux*** insufficient capital; ***insuffisance de personnel*** staff shortage; ***insuffisance de provision*** insufficient funds *(to meet cheque)*; ***insuffisance de ressources*** insufficient resources

insuffisant, -e *adj* insufficient; **nous avons des effectifs insuffisants** we're understaffed, our workforce is too small; **c'est insuffisant pour ouvrir un compte** it's not enough to open an account with

intégral, -e *adj* complete; **la somme intégrale de vos dépenses s'élève à 800 francs** your expenses amount to 800 francs

intégralement *adv* completely, in full; **rembourser intégralement une somme** to repay a sum in full; **intégralement libéré, intégralement versé** *(capital)* fully paid-up

intégration *nf* ÉCON integration ▫ ***intégration en amont*** backward integration; ***intégration en aval*** forward integration; ***intégration économique*** economic inte-

gration; ***intégration horizontale*** horizontal integration; ***intégration verticale*** vertical integration

intégré, -e *adj* ORDINAT *(fax, modem)* integrated

intenter *vt* JUR **intenter un procès à** *ou* **contre qn** to institute proceedings against sb; **intenter une action contre qn** to bring an action against sb

intention d'achat *nf* MKTG intention to buy

interactif, -ive *adj* ORDINAT interactive

interbancaire *adj* interbank

interdiction *nf* ban ▫ ***interdiction de commerce*** trade ban; ***interdiction d'exportation*** export ban; ***interdiction d'importation*** import ban

interdire *vt* to forbid, to prohibit; **l'exportation de l'or est formellement interdite** the export of gold is strictly prohibited

interdit, -e **1** *adj* (**a**) *(défendu)* forbidden, prohibited (**b**) ORDINAT **interdit d'écriture** *(disquette)* write-protected **2** *nm* **interdit bancaire** ban on writing cheques

> ❝ ⎯⎯⎯⎯⎯⎯⎯⎯⎯⎯⎯⎯⎯
> La loi sur le chèque frappe d'un **interdit bancaire** toute personne ayant émis un chèque sans provision.
> ⎯⎯⎯⎯⎯⎯⎯⎯⎯⎯⎯⎯ ❞

interenterprises *adj* inter-company

intéressé, -e **1** *adj* (**a**) *(financièrement)* **être intéressé dans une entreprise** to have a financial interest in a business (**b**) *(concerné)* **les parties intéressées** the interested parties, the persons concerned **2** *nm,f* **l'intéressé** the interested party, the person concerned

intéressement *nm* profit-sharing scheme; **l'intéressement des salariés aux bénéfices de l'entreprise devrait avoir un effet bénéfique sur la productivité** profit-sharing should have a positive effect on productivity

intéresser *vt* **intéresser qn aux bénéfices** to give sb a share of the profits; **notre personnel est intéressé aux bénéfices** our staff gets a share of the profits, we operate a profit-sharing scheme

intérêt *nm* (**a**) FIN interest; **emprunter à intérêt** to borrow at interest; **laisser courir des intérêts** to allow interest to accumulate; **payer des intérêts** to pay interest; **rapporter des intérêts** to yield *or* bear interest; **placer**

son argent à **7% d'intérêt** to invest one's money at 7% interest; **sans intérêt** interest-free ❏ *intérêt bancaire* bank interest; *intérêt du capital* interest on capital; *intérêts compensatoires* damages; *intérêts composés* compound interest; *intérêts courus* accrued interest; *intérêts pour défaut de paiement* default interest; *intérêts à échoir* accruing interest; *intérêts échus* accrued interest; *intérêts exigibles* interest due and payable; *intérêt fixe* fixed interest; *intérêts moratoires* default interest, penalty interest; *intérêts à payer* interest charges; *intérêt sur prêt* interest on a loan; BOURSE *intérêt de report* contango; *intérêt de retard* interest on arrears; *intérêt simple* simple interest; *intérêt variable* variable-rate interest

(**b**) *(dans une entreprise, une affaire)* share, stake; **avoir des intérêts dans une société** to have a financial interest in a company; **les intérêts économiques de notre pays dans cette région** our country's economic interests in that region; **mettre qn hors d'intérêt** to buy sb out

(**c**) *(avantage)* interest, advantage; **agir dans l'intérêt de la société** to act in the interests of the company ❏ MKTG *intérêt du consommateur* consumer welfare

interface *nf* ORDINAT interface ❏ *interface graphique* graphic interface; *interface parallèle* parallel interface; *interface série* serial interface; *interface utilisateur* user interface; *interface utilisateur graphique* graphical user interface

intérieur, -e *adj (national)* home, domestic

intérim *nm (travail intérimaire)* temporary work, temping; **par intérim** *(fonction, employé, personnel)* temporary; *(directeur)* acting; **faire de l'intérim** to do temporary work, to temp; **assurer** *ou* **faire l'intérim (de qn)** to deputize *or* stand in (for sb)

intérimaire **1** *adj (fonction, employé, personnel)* temporary; *(directeur)* acting

2 *nmf* (**a**) *(employé)* temporary worker, temp; **travailler comme intérimaire** to temp, to work as a temp (**b**) *(fonctionnaire)* official holding a temporary appointment

interlignage *nm* ORDINAT line spacing

intermédiaire **1** *adj (biens, produits)* intermediate

2 *nmf* (**a**) *(personne)* intermediary, go-between; *(dans une transaction)* middleman; **sans intermédiaire** directly; **je préfère vendre sans intermédiaire** I prefer to sell directly to the customer ❏ *intermédiaire*

agréé authorized dealer; *intermédiaire financier* financial intermediary

(**b**) BOURSE market maker

3 *nm* **par l'intermédiaire de qn/qch** through (the intermediary of) sb/sth

international, -e **1** *adj* international

2 *nm* **l'international** *(l'étranger)* world markets; **notre entreprise est très tournée vers l'international** our company is very export-oriented

internaute *nmf* ORDINAT Internet user, Net surfer

interne *adj* internal; *(de l'entreprise)* in-house

Internet *nm* ORDINAT Internet; **naviguer sur l'Internet** to surf the Internet

interprétariat *nm (dans une autre langue)* interpreting; **faire de l'interprétariat** to work as an interpreter

interprétation *nf (dans une autre langue)* interpreting

interprète *nmf (dans une autre langue)* interpreter; **servir d'interprète (à qn)** to interpret (for sb) ❏ *interprète de conférence* conference interpreter

interpréter *vt (dans une autre langue)* to interpret

interprofessionnel, -elle *adj* interprofessional

interrogation *nf* ORDINAT *(d'une base de données)* inquiry, query; *(activité)* interrogation ❏ *interrogation à distance* remote access

interrogeable à distance *adj* TÉL *(répondeur)* with a remote-access facility

interroger *vt* (**a**) MKTG to interview, to question; **60% des personnes intérrogées ont déclaré n'avoir jamais entendu parler de ce produit** 60% of those questioned said that they had never heard of this product (**b**) ORDINAT *(base de données)* to query, to interrogate

intersyndical, -e *adj* inter-union

intervenant, -e *nm,f* (**a**) *(dans une conférence, un débat)* speaker, contributor (**b**) JUR *(dans une transaction)* intervening party (**c**) MKTG *intervenant sur le marché* market participant

intervenir *vi* (**a**) *(avoir lieu)* to happen, to occur; **un accord est intervenu entre la direction et les syndicats** an agreement has been reached between management and unions

(**b**) *(prendre la parole)* to speak up, to intervene; **le délégué syndical est intervenu**

plusieurs fois pendant la réunion the union representative intervened several times during the meeting

  (c) *(agir)* to intervene; **l'État a dû intervenir pour renflouer la société** the state had to intervene to keep the company afloat

intervention *nf* **(a)** *(action)* intervention; **l'intervention d'un médiateur n'a pas été suffisante pour régler le conflit** the intervention of a mediator was not enough to resolve the dispute

  (b) *(prise de parole)* intervention; **j'ai approuvé son intervention** I agreed with what he said

  (c) JUR intervention

interventionnisme *nm* interventionism

interventionniste *nmf* interventionist

intestat 1 *adj* **décéder** *ou* **mourir intestat** to die intestate

  2 *nm* intestacy

intitulé *nm* **(a)** *(d'un compte)* name **(b)** JUR *(d'un acte)* premises

Intranet *nm* ORDINAT Intranet

intransférable *adj* not transferable; JUR *(droit)* unassignable

introduction *nf* **(a)** *(importation)* importing

  (b) BOURSE *(de valeurs)* introduction □ **introduction en Bourse** flotation, listing on the Stock Market, *Am* initial public offering

  (c) *(de mesures, de nouveaux produits)* introduction

  (d) ORDINAT **introduction de données** data input

introduire 1 *vt* **(a)** *(importer)* to bring in, to import **(b)** BOURSE *(valeurs)* to introduce, to bring out **(c)** *(mesures, nouveaux produits)* to introduce; **nous allons bientôt introduire un nouveau produit sur le marché** we are soon going to launch a new product on the market **(d)** ORDINAT **introduire des données** to input *or* enter data

  2 s'introduire *vpr* ORDINAT **s'introduire en fraude dans un réseau** to hack into a network

invalidation *nf* JUR invalidation

invalide *adj* **(a)** JUR invalid **(b)** ORDINAT *(mot de passe, nom du fichier)* invalid

invalidité *nf* JUR invalidity

invendable *adj* unsaleable

invendu, -e 1 *adj* unsold

  2 *nm* unsold item

inventaire *nm* **(a)** *(de marchandises) (procédure)* stocktaking; *(liste) Br* stocklist, *Am* inventory; **faire** *ou* **dresser un inventaire** *Br*

to stocktake, *Am* to take the inventory □ **inventaire d'entrée** ingoing inventory; **inventaire intermittent** periodical inventory; **inventaire des marchandises** inventory of goods; **inventaire périodique** periodic inventory; **inventaire permanent** perpetual inventory; **inventaire physique** physical inventory; **inventaire de sortie** outgoing inventory; **inventaire de stock** physical inventory; **inventaire théorique** theoretical inventory

  (b) *(liste)* inventory; **faire** *ou* **dresser un inventaire** to draw up an inventory; **faire l'inventaire des ressources d'un pays** to assess a country's resources

  (c) COMPTA **inventaire (comptable)** book inventory □ **inventaire de fin d'année** accounts for the end of the *Br* financial *or Am* fiscal year

  (d) FIN *(d'un portefeuille de titres)* valuation

invention *nf* invention □ **invention brevetée** patented invention

inventorier *vt* to make an inventory of; *(marchandises)* to make a *Br* stocklist *or Am* inventory of

investi, -e *adj (argent, capitaux)* invested

investir 1 *vt* **(a)** *(argent, capitaux)* to invest **(dans** in); **investir des capitaux à l'étranger** to invest capital abroad

  2 *vi* to invest **(dans** in); **investir à court terme** to make a short-term investment; **investir à long terme** to make a long-term investment

investissement *nm* investment; *(action)* investing, investment; **faire des investissements** to invest (money) □ **investissement de capitaux** capital investment; **investissement à court terme** short-term investment; **investissement direct** direct investment; **investissements à l'étranger** outward *or* foreign investment; **investissement de l'étranger** inward investment; **investissement immobilier** investment in real estate, property investment; **investissement indirect** indirect investment; **investissement industriel** investment in industry; **investissements initiaux** initial investment; **investissement institutionnel** institutional investment; **investissement locatif** investment in rental property; **investissement lourd** heavy investment; **investissement privé** private investment; **investissement de productivité** productivity investment; **investissement à revenu fixe** fixed-rate investment; **investissement à revenu variable** floating-rate investment; **investissement en**

valeurs de redressement ou *de retour-nement* failure investment

> ❝
> Le problème du choix du cadre fiscal le plus favorable ne se pose en réalité que pour les personnes procédant à un **investissement locatif**.
> ❞

> ❝
> Ces emprunts n'ont jamais réellement servi à renflouer les caisses de l'État, ni même à financer des **investissements**: ils servaient de plus en plus à payer les intérêts des émissions précédentes...
> ❞

investisseur *nm* investor ❑ *investisseur institutionnel* institutional investor; *investisseur privé* private investor

invisible ÉCON **1** *adj (exportations, importations)* invisible
  2 *nm* **invisibles** invisibles

invite *nf* ORDINAT prompt ❑ *invite (du) DOS* DOS prompt

irréalisable *adj* FIN *(valeurs)* unrealizable

irrécouvrable *adj (argent, créance)* irrecoverable

irrégularité *nf (infraction)* irregularity; **il y a des irrégularités dans les comptes** there are some irregularities in the accounts ❑ *irrégularité comptable* accounting irregularity

ISF *nm (abrév* **impôt de solidarité sur la fortune**) wealth tax

ISO *nf (abrév* **International Standards Organization**) ISO

itératif, -ive *adj* ORDINAT iterative

IUT *nm (abrév* **Institut universitaire de technologie**) = vocational higher education college

jargon *nm* jargon ❏ *jargon administratif* administrative jargon; *jargon publicitaire* advertising jargon

JAT *adj* (*abrév* **juste à temps**) JIT

jauge *nf* (*de navire*) tonnage ❏ *jauge brute* gross registered tonnage; *jauge nette* net registered tonnage

jaugeage *nm* measurement (*of tonnage*)

jauger 1 *vt* (*mesurer la capacité de*) to gauge, to measure the capacity of; (*navire*) to measure the tonnage of
2 *vi* **un pétrolier qui jauge quarante mille tonneaux** a forty thousand-ton tanker

Java *nm* ORDINAT Java

jetable *adj* (*emballage, produit*) disposable

jeter *vt* (*mettre au rebut*) to throw away; **jeter des marchandises sur le marché** to throw goods onto the market

jeton de présence *nm* (*honoraires*) director's fees

jeu *nm* (**a**) BOURSE speculating ❏ *jeu de Bourse* gambling on the Stock Exchange, Stock Exchange speculation; *jeu sur les reports* speculating in contangos
(**b**) (*série*) (*de connaissances, de lettres de change*) set ❏ ORDINAT *jeu de caractères* character set; *jeu de fiches* card index
(**c**) COMPTA *jeu d'écritures* paper transaction
(**d**) (*marge de manœuvre*) leeway
(**e**) (*action*) force; **laisser faire le jeu de la concurrence** to allow the free play of competition; **le jeu de la concurrence ne peut pas s'exercer si seules certaines entreprises sont subventionnées par l'État** the forces of competition cannot come into play if only some companies receive State grants

JO *nm* ADMIN (*abrév* **Journal Officiel**) = French government publication giving information to the public about new laws, government business, new companies etc, *Br* ≃ Hansard, *Am* ≃ Federal Register

joindre *vt* (**a**) (*ajouter*) to add (**à** to); (*dans une lettre, dans un colis*) to enclose, to attach; **joindre l'intérêt au capital** to add the interest to the capital; **l'échantillon joint à votre lettre** the sample attached to your letter; **veuillez joindre CV et photo d'identité** please attach a copy of your *Br* CV *or Am* resumé and a photograph
(**b**) (*contacter*) to get in touch with; **joindre qn par téléphone/par lettre** to contact sb by phone/in writing; **j'ai téléphoné, mais je n'ai pas réussi à le joindre** I phoned but I couldn't get hold of him; **où pourrai-je vous contacter?** how can I get in touch with you *or* contact you?

joint, -e *adj* (*documents, échantillons*) enclosed, attached

joint-venture *nf* FIN joint venture

> **❝**
> Elle offrira à une clientèle française et internationale des études d'implantations industrielles et commerciales en **joint-venture** et du conseil en privatisation.
> **❞**

joker *nm* ORDINAT wildcard

jouer 1 *vt* BOURSE **jouer la livre à la baisse/à la hausse** to speculate on a falling/rising pound
2 *vi* (**a**) BOURSE to speculate, to play the market; **jouer à la Bourse** to speculate *or* gamble on the Stock Exchange; **jouer à la hausse** to gamble on a rise in prices, to bull the market; **jouer à la baisse** to gamble on a fall in prices, to bear the market
(**b**) (*s'appliquer*) to be operative, to operate; **l'augmentation des salaires joue depuis le 1 janvier** the rise in salaries has been operative since 1 January
(**c**) (*fonctionner*) to work; **une livre forte joue contre les exportateurs britanniques** a strong pound puts British exporters at a disadvantage

joueur, -euse *nm,f* BOURSE speculator ❏ *joueur à la baisse* bear; *joueur à la hausse* bull

jouissance *nf* (**a**) JUR (*usage*) use; **avoir la jouissance de qch** to have the use of sth; **avoir la (pleine) jouissance de ses droits** to enjoy one's (full) rights; **à vendre avec jouissance immédiate** (*sur panneau*) for sale with vacant possession; **la période de jouissance est de sept ans** the period of tenure is seven years ❏ *jouissance en commun* (*d'un bien*) communal tenure; *jouissance locative* tenure
(**b**) FIN *jouissance d'intérêts* entitlement to interest

jour *nm* (**a**) (*journée*) day; **quinze jours** *Br* a fortnight, *Am* two weeks ❏ *jour d'action* day of action; ADMIN *jour chômable, jour chômé* public holiday; *jour de congé* day off; *jour de l'échéance* due date; *jour férié* public holiday; *jour franc* clear day; FIN *jours d'intérêt* interest days; *jour non-ouvrable* non-trading day; *jour ouvrable* working day; *jour de paie* pay day; *jour plein* clear day; *jour de repos* day off

(b) *(date)* day; **à ce jour** up until now, to date; **à ce jour la facture que nous vous avons envoyée reste impayée** to date the invoice we sent you remains unpaid; **intérêts à ce jour** interest to date ▫ *jour de livraison* delivery date

(c) **à jour** up to date; **notre catalogue n'est pas à jour** our catalogue is not up to date; **mettre qch à jour** to bring sth up to date, to update sth; **tenir les livres à jour** to keep the books *or* the accounts up to date

(d) BOURSE day ▫ *jour de Bourse* trading day; *jour de la déclaration des noms* ticket day; *jour de grâce* day of grace; *jour de la liquidation* account day, settlement day; *jour d'option* option date; *jour de paiement, jour de règlement* payment day, settlement day; *jour de valeur* value day

journal *nm* (a) *(publication)* paper, newspaper ▫ FIN *journal de banque* bank book; *journal électronique* electronic newspaper; *journal interne d'entreprise* in-house *or* staff newsletter, company magazine; ADMIN *Journal officiel* = French government publication giving information to the public about new laws, government business, new companies etc, *Br* ≃ Hansard, *Am* ≃ Federal Register; *journal professionnel* trade journal

(b) COMPTA ledger, account book ▫ *journal des achats* purchase ledger, bought ledger; *journal analytique* analysis ledger; *journal de caisse* cash book; *journal des effets à payer* bills payable ledger; *journal des effets à recevoir* bills receivable ledger; *journal factures-clients* sales invoice ledger; *journal factures-fournisseurs* purchase invoice ledger; *journal de paie* wages ledger; *journal des rendus* returns ledger *or* book; *journal de trésorerie* cash book; *journal des ventes* sales ledger

(c) ORDINAT log

journalier, -ère *adj (production, recette, salaire)* daily

journaliser *vt* COMPTA to enter, to write up in the books

journée *nf* day; **faire la journée continue** *(magasin)* to remain open at lunchtime; *(per-*sonne)* to work through lunch; **être payé à la journée** to be paid by the day *or* on a daily basis; **travailler à la journée** to work on a daily basis ▫ *journée portes ouvertes Br* open day, *Am* open house; *journée de travail (quantité de travail)* day's work; *(durée)* working day; *journées de travail perdues* lost working days

judiciaire *adj* JUR *(pouvoir, enquête, acte)* judicial; *(aide, autorité)* legal; *(vente)* court-ordered, by order of the court

judiciairement *adv* JUR judicially

juge *nm* JUR judge ▫ *juge consulaire* judge in commercial court; *juge d'instance* conciliation magistrate *(in commercial cases)*; *juge d'instruction Br* examining magistrate, *Am* committing magistrate; *juge des référés* judge in chambers

jugement *nm* JUR (a) *(décision)* judgement, decision, ruling; *(dans une cause criminelle)* sentence ▫ *jugement contentieux* judgement in disputed matter; *jugement déclaratif de faillite* adjudication in bankruptcy; *jugement exécutoire* enforceable judgement; *jugement mis en délibéré* reserved judgement

(b) *(d'une affaire)* trial; **passer en jugement** to stand trial

juger *vt* JUR (a) *(affaire, prévenu)* to try (b) *(demande, litige)* to adjudicate

juguler *vt (inflation, chômage)* to check, to curb

juré, -e *nm,f* JUR juror

juridiction *nf* JUR (a) *(compétence)* jurisdiction; **tomber sous la juridiction de** to come under the jurisdiction of ▫ *juridiction commerciale* commercial jurisdiction (b) *(tribunaux)* courts

juridique *adj (système, environnement)* judicial, legal; *(texte, frais)* legal

juriste *nm* lawyer ▫ *juriste d'entreprise* company lawyer

jury *nm* jury ▫ MKTG *jury des consommateurs* focus group

juste 1 *adj* (a) *(équitable) (prix, salaire)* fair (b) *(exact)* correct, accurate
2 *adv* exactly, precisely; **prix calculé au plus juste** minimum price

justice *nf (système judiciaire)* law, legal proceedings; **recourir à la justice, aller en justice** to go to law; **poursuivre qn en justice** to institute legal proceedings against sb, to take legal action against sb; **être traduit en justice** to be tried, to be taken to court

justificatif, -ive 1 *adj* supporting, jusitifi-catory
  2 *nm* written proof

justification *nf* (**a**) *(preuve)* proof □ *justi-fication de paiement* proof of payment
  (**b**) ORDINAT justification □ *justification à droite* right justification; *justification à gauche* left justification

justifier 1 *vt* (**a**) *(légitimer)* to justify, to warrant (**b**) ORDINAT to justify; **justifié à gauche/à droite** left/right justified
  2 *vi* **justifier de qch** to prove sth

juteux, -euse *adj Fam (transaction)* juicy, lucrative; **une affaire juteuse** a money spinner, a goldmine

KF *nm* (*abrév* **kilofranc**) thousand francs; **son salaire annuel est de 200 KF** she earns 200,000 francs a year

kilobaud *nm* ORDINAT kilobaud

kilofranc *nm* thousand francs

kilomètre-passager *nm* (*en avion*) passenger-kilometre

kilo-octet *nm* ORDINAT kilobyte

kit *nm* ORDINAT kit ❑ *kit d'accès, kit de connexion* connection kit; *kit d'évolution, kit d'extension* upgrade kit; *kit de téléchargeur* download kit

KO *nm* ORDINAT (*abrév* **kilo-octet**) K, KB; **une disquette de 720 KO** a 720K disquette

ko/s ORDINAT (*abrév* **kilo-octets par seconde**) kbps

krach *nm* (financial) crash ❑ *krach boursier* Stock Exchange crash

> 〝
> Lassés par les **krachs boursiers** et la chute du rendement des sicav monétaires, les épargnants rêvent d'un placement idéal, performant mais pas trop risqué.
> 〞

label *nm* (**a**) *(étiquette)* label ◽ *label d'exportation* export label; *label de garantie* guarantee label; *label NF, label norme française* *(délivré par l'AFNOR)* = French industry standards label; *label d'origine* certificate of origin; *label de qualité* quality label (**b**) ORDINAT *label de volume* volume label

laboratoire d'idées *nm* think tank

lâcher ORDINAT **1** *nm* *lâcher d'icônes* icon drop
   2 *vt (icône)* to drop

laissé-pour-compte **1** *adj (article, marchandise)* rejected, returned
   2 *nm (article, marchandise)* reject

laissez-faire *nm* ÉCON laissez-faire

laissez-passer *nm* pass, permit; DOUANES transire

lancement *nm* (**a**) *(d'un projet, d'une société, d'un produit, d'un modèle)* launch ◽ MKTG *lancement sur le marché* market entry
   (**b**) BOURSE *(d'une société)* flotation; *(de titres boursiers, d'un emprunt)* issuing, issue; *(d'une souscription)* start
   (**c**) ORDINAT *(d'impression)* start; *(de programme)* running

lancer **1** *vt* (**a**) *(projet, société, produit, modèle)* to launch; **lancer un appel d'offres** to invite tenders
   (**b**) BOURSE *(société)* to float; *(titres boursiers, emprunt)* to issue; *(souscription)* to start; **lancer des titres sur le marché** to issue shares
   (**c**) ORDINAT *(impression)* to start; *(programme)* to run, to start (up)
   2 se lancer *vpr* **se lancer dans les affaires** to set oneself up in business; **se lancer sur le marché** to enter the market

langage *nm* ORDINAT language ◽ *langage machine* machine language; *langage naturel* natural language; *langage de programmation* programming language; *langage utilisateur* user language

languissant, -e *adj (marché)* dull, sluggish; *(affaires, activité)* slow

l/c *nf* FIN *(abrév* **lettre de crédit***)* L/C

LCR *nf* FIN *(abrév* **lettre de change relevé***)* bills of exchange statement

leader *nm* MKTG leader; **cette entreprise est le leader mondial de la micro-informatique** this firm is the world leader in microcomputing

leasing *nm* lease financing; **acheter qch en leasing** to lease sth, to buy sth on lease

lèche-vitrines *nm* window-shopping; **faire du lèche-vitrines** to window-shop

lecteur *nm* ORDINAT reader; *(de disque, de disquettes)* drive ◽ *lecteur de carte à mémoire* smart card reader, card reader; *lecteur de carte à puce* smart card reader; *lecteur de CD-ROM* CD-ROM drive; *lecteur DAT* DAT drive; *lecteur par défaut* default drive; *lecteur de destination* destination drive; *lecteur de disque dur* hard disk drive; *lecteur de disque optique* CD-ROM drive; *lecteur de disquettes* disk drive, floppy (disk) drive; *lecteur de documents* document reader; *lecteur OCR* OCR reader; *lecteur optique de caractères* optical character reader

lectorat *nm (d'un journal)* readership

lecture *nf* ORDINAT read; **en lecture seule** in read-only mode; **mettre un fichier en lecture seule** to make a file read-only ◽ *lecture sur disque* reading to disk; *lecture optique* optical reading; *lecture au scanneur* scan

lecture-écriture *nf* ORDINAT read-write (mode); **être en lecture-écriture** to be in read-write (mode)

légal, -e *adj* legal; *(action)* legal, lawful; **avoir recours aux moyens légaux** to take legal action, to institute legal proceedings; **suivre la procédure légale** to follow the legal procedure; **par les voies légales** legally, by legal means

légalement *adv* legally, lawfully

légalisation *nf* (**a**) *(d'un produit, d'une pratique)* legalization (**b**) *(d'une signature)* authentication, certification

légaliser *vt* (**a**) *(produit, pratique)* to legalize (**b**) *(signature)* to authenticate, to certify

légalité *nf* legality, lawfulness; **ils ont réussi à échapper à cet impôt tout en restant dans la légalité** they managed to avoid paying the tax by legal means

légataire *nmf* legatee, heir

légende *nf (commentaire)* caption

léger, -ère *adj (amélioration, reprise)* slight

législation *nf* legislation ❑ *législation anti-dumping* anti-dumping laws; *législation antitrust* *Br* anti-monopoly *or* *Am* antitrust legislation; *législation bancaire* banking legislation; *législation douanière* customs legislation; *législation fiscale* tax laws; *législation du travail* industrial *or* labour legislation

légitime *adj* legitimate

legs *nm* JUR legacy, bequest; **faire/recevoir un legs** to leave/receive a legacy ❑ *legs particulier* personal *or* private legacy; *legs universel* residuary legacy

léguer *vt* JUR to leave, to bequeath

lettre *nf* (a) *(courrier)* letter; **adresser une lettre à qn** *(écrire l'adresse sur)* to address a letter to sb; *(écrire)* to write a letter to sb ❑ *lettre d'accompagnement* covering letter; *lettre accréditive* letter of credit; *lettre d'affaires* business letter; *lettre d'agrément* letter of consent; BOURSE *lettre d'allocation* letter of allotment; *lettre d'avis* advice note; FIN *lettre de change* bill of exchange; *lettre de change à l'extérieur* foreign bill; *lettre de change relevé* bills of exchange statement; *lettre circulaire* circular; *lettre commerciale* business letter; *lettre de confirmation* letter of confirmation; *lettre de couverture* cover note; *lettre de créance* letter of credit; BANQUE *lettre de crédit* letter of credit; **émettre une lettre de crédit** to open a letter of credit; *lettre de crédit circulaire* circular letter of credit; *lettre de crédit documentaire* documentary letter of credit; *lettre de crédit irrévocable* irrevocable letter of credit; *lettre de démission* resignation letter; *lettre d'embauche* written offer of employment; *lettre d'envoi* covering letter, advice note; *lettre d'excuse* letter of apology; DOUANES *lettre d'exemption* bill of sufferance; *lettre exprès* express letter; *lettre de gage* debenture bond; *(pour hypothèque)* mortgage bond; FIN *lettre de garantie* letter of guarantee; *lettre de garantie bancaire* bank guarantee; *lettre de garantie d'indemnité* letter of indemnity; *lettre d'intention* letter of intent; *lettre de licenciement* letter of dismissal; *lettre de motivation* covering letter *(with curriculum vitae)*; *lettre de nantissement* letter of hypothecation; *lettre notificative* letter of notification; *lettre de poursuite* letter threatening legal action, chasing letter; *lettre de rappel* reminder; *lettre de réclamation* letter of complaint; *lettre de recommandation* letter of recommendation, reference; *lettre*

recommandée registered letter; *lettre recommandée avec accusé de réception* registered letter with confirmation of receipt; *lettre de relance* follow-up letter; *lettre de relance des impayés* debt-chasing letter; *lettre de transport aérien* air waybill; *lettre type* *(pour mailing)* form letter; *lettre de vente* sales letter; *lettre de voiture* waybill, consignment note

(b) *(de l'alphabet)* letter; **écrire une somme en (toutes) lettres** to write an amount in words (not figures) ❑ *lettres majuscules* capital letters, capitals, upper case; *lettres minuscules* small letters, lower case

levée *nf* (a) *(du courrier, des impôts)* collection; **quand la levée du courrier a-t-elle lieu?** when is the mail *or Br* post collected? (b) *(d'embargo, de sanctions)* lifting; *(de séance)* closing, adjourning (c) FIN, BOURSE *(des actions, d'une option)* taking up ❑ BANQUE *levées de compte* personal withdrawals

lever *vt* (a) *(courrier, impôts)* to collect (b) *(embargo, sanctions)* to lift; *(séance)* to close, to adjourn (c) FIN, BOURSE *(actions, option)* to take up

levier *nm* ÉCON leverage

liaison *nf* (a) *(dans les transports, dans les télécommunications)* link ❑ *liaison aérienne* air link; *liaison ferroviaire* rail link; *liaison maritime* sea link; *liaison postale* postal link; *liaison rail-aéroport* rail-air link; *liaison routière* road link; *liaison téléphonique* telephone link *or* communications (b) *(contact)* contact, liaison; **travailler en liaison avec qn** to liaise with sb, to work closely with sb; **assurer la liaison entre deux personnes/services** to liaise between two people/departments; **les différents services sont en liaison** the various departments are in contact *or* liaise closely (with each other); **être en liaison permanente (avec)** to be constantly in touch (with); **se mettre en liaison avec qn** to get in touch with sb; **rester en liaison avec qn** to stay in touch with sb (c) ORDINAT connection

> ❝ ────
> Les **liaisons** entre pays asiatiques, en pleine expansion, progressent d'environ 10% par an.
> ──── ❞

liasse *nf* *(de billets de banque)* wad; *(de documents)* bundle

libellé *nm* wording; COMPTA *(d'une écriture)* particulars

libeller *vt* (**a**) ADMIN *(document, acte, contrat)* to word, to draw up; **libellé comme suit...** worded as follows... (**b**) *(chèque, facture)* to make out; **chèque libellé à l'ordre de Y. Mourier** cheque made out *or* payable to Y. Mourier; **libellé en francs** *(chèque)* made out in francs; *(cours)* quoted *or* given in francs; **être libellé au porteur** to be made out to bearer, to be made payable to bearer

libéral, -e ÉCON **1** *adj (économie, doctrine)* free-market
2 *nm,f* free-marketeer

libéralisation *nf* ÉCON *(de l'économie, des échanges commerciaux)* liberalization □ **libéralisation du commerce** easing of trade restrictions, liberalization of trade; **libéralisation du cours du franc** freeing of the franc

libéraliser *vt* ÉCON to liberalize

libéralisme *nm* ÉCON (economic) liberalism, laissez-faire

libération *nf* (**a**) *(déréglementation) (des prix)* deregulation □ **libération des changes** relaxing of foreign exchange controls; **libération des échanges commerciaux** deregulation of trade, relaxing of exchange controls (**b**) *(d'une dette)* payment in full, discharge; *(d'un engagement)* release; *(d'une action, du capital)* paying up; *(d'un débiteur)* discharge, release; *(d'un garant)* discharge □ FIN **libération intégrale** *(d'une action)* payment in full

libératoire *adj* **avoir force libératoire** to be legal tender

libéré, -e *adj* FIN *(action)* (fully) paid-up; **non (entièrement) libéré, partiellement libéré** partly paid-up; **un titre de 1000 francs libéré de 750 francs** *ou* **libéré à 75%** a 1,000-franc share of which 750 francs are paid up; **libéré d'impôt** tax paid

libérer **1** *vt* (**a**) *(déréglementer) (prix, échanges commerciaux)* to deregulate (**b**) *(dette)* to free; *(engagement)* to release; *(action, capital)* to pay up; *(débiteur)* to discharge, to release; *(garant)* to discharge; **libérer entièrement une action** to make a share fully paid-up, to pay up a share in full; **libérer qn de la responsabilité légale** to relieve sb of legal liability
2 se libérer *vpr (se dégager)* **se libérer de qch** *(dette)* to redeem sth, to liquidate sth; *(engagement)* to free oneself from sth

liberté *nf (déréglementation) (des prix, des échanges commerciaux)* freedom □ **liberté du commerce** freedom of trade; **liberté d'entreprise** (right of) free enterprise; **liberté**

syndicale freedom to join a union, union rights

libre *adj* (**a**) *(non réglementé)* free □ **libre circulation** *(des marchandises, des personnes, des capitaux)* free movement; **libre concurrence** free competition; **libre entreprise** free enterprise
(**b**) *(disponible)* free; **la ligne n'est pas libre** the line's *Br* engaged *or* *Am* busy □ **libre possession** vacant possession
(**c**) **libre d'hypothèque** free from mortgage; **libre d'impôt** tax-free

libre-échange *nm* ÉCON free trade

libre-échangisme *nm* ÉCON free trade

libre-échangiste ÉCON **1** *adj (politique, théorie)* free trade
2 *nmf* free trader

libre-service *nm* self-service; *(magasin)* self-service shop

licence *nf* (**a**) *(permis)* licence; *(pour l'utilisation d'un logiciel)* registration card; **obtenir une licence** to obtain a licence; **fabriqué sous licence** manufactured under licence □ **licence de débit de boissons** licence to sell beer, wines and spirits, *Am* liquor license; **licence exclusive** exclusive licence; **licence d'exploitation d'un brevet** licence to use a patent; **licence d'exportation** export licence; **licence de fabrication** manufacturing licence; **licence d'importation** import licence; ORDINAT **licence individuelle d'utilisation** single user licence; **licence de vente** selling licence
(**b**) *(diplôme)* degree; **une licence en droit/en économie** a law/economics degree

licenciement *nm (pour raisons économiques)* redundancy; *(pour faute professionnelle)* dismissal □ **licenciement abusif** unfair dismissal; **licenciement collectif** mass redundancy; **licenciement économique** redundancy; **licenciement sans préavis** dismissal without notice

> "
> Face à la hausse des coûts salariaux, plus de la moitié des firmes manufacturières ont déjà procédé à des **licenciements**.
> "

licencier *vt* **licencier qn** *(pour raisons économiques)* to make sb redundant; *(pour faute professionnelle)* to dismiss sb

licite *adj* licit, lawful

licitement *adv* licitly, lawfully

lié, -e *adj (marchés)* related; *(opérations)* combined; *(emprunts)* tied; **tous les emplois**

liés à l'industrie automobile sont affectés par cette grève this strike has affected all jobs connected with the motor industry

lien *nm* ORDINAT link □ *lien hypertexte* hypertext link

lier *vt* to bind; **ce contrat vous lie** you are bound by this agreement; **votre contrat ne vous lie pas à la société** your contract does not bind you to the company

lieu *nm* (**a**) *(endroit)* place; **vider les lieux** to vacate the premises □ *lieu de livraison* place of delivery, point of delivery; *lieu de naissance* place of birth; *lieu de paiement* place of payment; *lieu de rendez-vous* meeting place; *lieu de travail* place of work; **sur le lieu de travail** in the workplace; *lieu de vente* point of sale
(**b**) **avoir lieu** *(se dérouler)* to take place; **la réunion aura lieu vendredi** the meeting will take place *or* will be held on Friday

ligne *nf* (**a**) TÉL line; **être en ligne** to be on a call; **la ligne est occupée** the line is *Br* engaged *or Am* busy; **la ligne a été coupée** I've/we've/*etc* been cut off; **il y a quelqu'un sur la ligne** there's someone on the line; **vous êtes en ligne** you're connected, you're through; **il est déjà en ligne** he's on another line; **la ligne est en dérangement** the line is out of order □ *ligne directe* direct line; *ligne directe accessible 24 heures sur 24* 24-hour hotline; *ligne extérieure* outside line; *ligne ouverte* open line; *ligne privée* private line; *ligne téléphonique* telephone line; *ligne téléphonique directe* direct dial telephone
(**b**) MKTG *(de produits)* line, range □ *ligne pour hommes* range for men; *ligne de produits* line of products, product line
(**c**) FIN *ligne de crédit, ligne de découvert* line of credit
(**d**) *(principe)* **les grandes lignes, les lignes directrices** *(d'un projet)* the guiding principles
(**e**) COMPTA **au-dessus de la ligne** *(dépenses)* above-the-line
(**f**) *(dans les transports)* line □ *ligne aérienne* airline; *ligne intérieure* domestic route; *ligne maritime, ligne de navigation* shipping line
(**g**) ORDINAT line; **en ligne** on line; **sur ligne** on line; **hors ligne** off line

limitatif, -ive *adj* JUR *(clause)* limiting, restrictive

limitation *nf* limitation, restriction; **ils appliquent une limitation volontaire de leurs exportations** they set voluntary limits on their exports □ *limitation des prix* price

control; *limitation de responsabilité* limitation of liability; *limitation des salaires* wage restraint

limite *nf* (**a**) *(maximum ou minimum)* limit; **dans la limite des stocks disponibles** while stocks last □ *limite d'âge* age limit; *limite de crédit* credit limit; *limite d'endettement* borrowing limit; *limite de poids* weight limit; *limite de prix* price limit
(**b**) BOURSE limit □ *limite de la baisse* limit down; *limite de la hausse* limit up; *limite inférieure* limit down; *limite de position* position limit; *limite supérieure* limit up

limité, -e *adj* limited; *Can* **Desrochers et Cie Limitée** Desrochers and Co. Ltd.

linéaire **1** *adj (programmation)* linear
2 *nm* shelf space; **ce produit n'apparaît pas dans les linéaires de magasins non spécialisés** non-specialist shops do not stock this product

> Mes bouteilles sont vendues 70 centimes au départ. Elles coûtent 1,10 francs à leur arrivée sur les **linéaires** mais elles seront étiquetées à 1,50 francs.

lingot *nm* ingot □ *lingot d'or* gold ingot *or* bar; *lingots en or* gold bullion

liquidateur, -trice *nm,f* JUR liquidator □ *liquidateur judiciaire* official liquidator; ST EXCH *liquidateur officiel* official assignee

liquidatif, -ive *adj* JUR pertaining to liquidation

liquidation *nf* (**a**) JUR liquidation; **être en liquidation** to have gone into liquidation; **entrer en liquidation** to go into liquidation; **mettre en liquidation** to put into liquidation, to liquidate □ *liquidation des biens* liquidation of assets; *liquidation forcée* compulsory liquidation; *liquidation (par décision) judiciaire* official receivership; *liquidation volontaire* voluntary liquidation
(**b**) *(d'un compte, d'une dette)* settlement, clearing
(**c**) BOURSE settlement; *(d'une position)* liquidation □ *liquidation en espèces* cash settlement; *liquidation de fin de mois* end-of-month settlement; *liquidation de quinzaine* fortnightly settlement, fortnightly account
(**d**) *(de stocks)* selling off, clearance □ *liquidation totale* *(sur panneau)* closing down sale, everything must go

> Nombre d'entreprises affichent des pertes, ne respectent pas les normes de solvabilité ou ont arrêté leur activité de crédit. Deux, celles de Picardie et de Lorraine, sont en **liquidation**. La BZ est proche de la liquidation pour cause de pannes en série et de chute du prix de la cellulose.

liquide 1 *adj* FIN liquid; **peu liquide** illiquid 2 *nm (espèces)* (ready) cash; **je n'ai pas assez de liquide** I haven't enough cash; **vous payez par chèque ou en liquide?** are you paying by cheque or cash?

liquider (**a**) JUR *(entreprise)* to liquidate (**b**) *(compte, dette)* to settle, to clear (**c**) BOURSE *(position)* to liquidate (**d**) *(stocks)* to sell off, to clear

liquidité *nf* FIN liquidity; **être à court de liquidité** to be short of funds; **liquidités** liquid assets □ *liquidités excédentaires* excess liquidities; *liquidité du portefeuille* portfolio liquidity

> La Réserve fédérale ne remontera pas ses taux d'intérêt, bien qu'elle souhaite retirer de la circulation une partie des **liquidités** injectées depuis trois ans.

lire[1] *nf (unité monétaire)* lira

lire[2] *vt* ORDINAT *(disquette)* to read; **lire au scanneur** to scan

lisible *adj* ORDINAT **lisible par ordinateur** machine-readable

liste *nf* list; **faire** *ou* **dresser** *ou* **établir une liste** to draw up *or* to make out a list □ *liste d'adresses* mailing list, address list; *liste des arrivées* arrivals list; *liste d'attente* waiting list; *liste de clients* customer *or* client list; *liste de colisage* packing list; *liste de contrôle* checklist; *liste des départs* departure list; *liste de diffusion* mailing list; *liste d'émargement* payroll; *liste d'envoi* mailing list; ORDINAT *liste de fichiers à imprimer* print list, print queue; *liste des importations* import list; DOUANES *liste des marchandises importées en franchise* free list; *Can liste de paie* payroll; *liste de prix* price list; *liste de publipostage* mailing list; ORDINAT *liste rapide* draft; **être sur la liste rouge** to be *Br* ex-directory *or Am* unlisted; *liste des signatures autorisées* authorized signatory list; FIN *liste des souscripteurs* list of applications; *liste des tarifs* price list, tariff

listing *nm* ORDINAT listing, printout

litige *nm (conflit)* dispute; *(procès)* lawsuit; **être en litige** to be in dispute; **régler un litige** to settle a dispute □ *litige commercial* commercial dispute

litigieux, -euse *adj (question)* contentious

livrable *adj* (**a**) *(marchandises)* ready for delivery; **marchandises livrables à domicile** goods delivered to your home (**b**) FIN deliverable

livraison *nf* (**a**) *(action, marchandises)* delivery; **faire** *ou* **effectuer une livraison** to make a delivery; **faire la livraison de qch** to deliver sth; **prendre livraison de qch** to take delivery of sth □ *livraison à domicile (sur panneau)* door-to-door delivery, we deliver; *livraison échelonnée* staggered delivery; *livraison franco* free delivery, delivered free; *livraison franco à domicile* free home delivery; *livraison franco par nos soins* carriage paid; *livraison gratuite* free delivery, delivered free; *livraison immédiate* immediate delivery; *livraison le jour même* same-day delivery; *livraison lendemain* next-day delivery; *livraison contre remboursement* Br cash on delivery, Am collect on delivery (**b**) FIN, BOURSE *(des titres)* delivery □ *livraison à terme* future delivery, forward delivery

livre[1] *nf (unité monétaire)* pound; **un billet de cinq livres** a five-pound note □ *livre irlandaise* Irish pound, punt; *livre sterling* pound (sterling)

livre[2] *nm (registre)* book; COMPTA **tenir les livres** to keep the accounts *or* the books; **vérifier les livres** to check the books □ COMPTA *livre d'achats, livre des achats* bought ledger, purchase ledger; *livre d'actionnaires* register of shareholders; *livre blanc* official report; *(publié par le gouvernement)* white paper; *livre de caisse* cash book; *livre de commandes* order book; *livre de commerce, livre de comptabilité, livre de comptes* ledger, account book; *livre des créanciers* accounts payable ledger; *livre des débiteurs* accounts receivable ledger; *livre de dépenses* cash book; *livre d'échéance* bill book; *livre des effets à payer* bills payable ledger; *livre des effets à recevoir* bills receivable ledger; *livre des entrées* purchase ledger; *livre fractionnaire* day book, book of prime entry; *livre des inventaires* stock book; *livre journal* journal, day book; *livre de magasin* warehouse book; *livre de paie* wages ledger; *livre de petite caisse* petty cash book; *livre* *des réclamations* claims book; *livre des rendus* returns ledger; *livre des sorties* sales ledger; *livre de stock* stock book; *livre de trésorerie générale* general cash book; *livre des ventes* sales ledger

livrer *vt* (a) *(marchandises)* to deliver; **nous avons bien été livrés** we have received the delivery; **livrer une commande** to deliver an order; **nous livrons à domicile** we deliver to your door; **vous serez livrés dès demain** you'll receive delivery tomorrow; **livré franco domicile** delivered free at domicile; **livrer une usine clés en mains** to hand over a turnkey factory
  (b) FIN, BOURSE to deliver; **livrer à terme fixe** to deliver at a fixed term; **prime pour livrer** seller's option; **vente à livrer** sale for delivery

livret *nm* book ◻ BANQUE *livret de caisse d'épargne* bank book, passbook; *livret de compte* bank book; *livret de dépôt* deposit book, passbook; *livret d'épargne logement* *Br* ≃ building society passbook, *Am* ≃ savings and loan association passbook

livreur, -euse *nm,f* (a) *(qui effectue des livraisons)* delivery man, *f* delivery woman
  (b) FIN, BOURSE deliverer

LJM *nf (abrév* **livraison le jour même)** same-day delivery

LOA *nf (abrév* **location avec option d'achat)** lease financing

local, -e **1** *adj (autorités, industrie, personnel)* local
  2 *nm* premises ◻ *locaux commerciaux* business premises, commercial property; *locaux à louer* premises to let; *local professionnel* premises used for professional purposes; *locaux à usage commercial* business premises, commercial property

locataire *nmf (de logement)* tenant; *(pensionnaire)* lodger ◻ JUR *locataire à bail* lessee, leaseholder

location *nf* (a) *(de voiture, d'équipement) (par le locataire)* renting, *Br* hiring; *(par le propriétaire)* renting out, *Br* hiring out; **prendre qch en location** to rent sth, *Br* to hire sth; **donner qch en location** to rent sth out, *Br* to hire sth out ◻ *location d'équipement* plant hire; *location de voitures* car rental, *Br* car hire
  (b) *(de logement) (par le locataire)* renting; *(par le propriétaire)* renting out, *Br* letting (out); **prendre qch en location** to rent sth; **donner qch en location** to rent sth out, *Br* to let sth (out) ◻ *location avec option d'achat* lease financing; *location à vie* life tenancy
  (c) *(appartement, maison)* rented accommodation

> Nec plus ultra de la défiscalisation, la **location** en meublé professionnel permet d'alléger sensiblement l'impôt sur le revenu pour les contribuables les plus imposés.

location-gérance *nf* = agreement with a liquidator to manage a company in liquidation

location-vente *nf* hire purchase, *Am* installment plan; **acheter qch en location-vente** to buy sth on hire purchase *or Am* on the installment plan

lock-out *nm* lockout

lock-outer *vt (personnel)* to lock out

logement *nm* accommodation ◻ *logement locatif* rented accommodation

logiciel *nm* ORDINAT software; **un logiciel** a software package; *(programme)* a piece of software ◻ *logiciel d'application* application software; *logiciel de bureautique* business software; *logiciel de communication* communications package, comms package; *logiciel de comptabilité* accounts package, accounts software; *logiciel de conception assistée par ordinateur* computer-aided design package; *logiciel de conversion* conversion software; *logiciel convivial* user-friendly software; *logiciel de dessin* art package, drawing program; *logiciel d'exploitation* system software; *logiciel grapheur, logiciel graphique* graphics software; *logiciel intégré* built-in software; *logiciel de mise en page* desktop publishing package; *logiciel multi-utilisateur* multi-user software; *logiciel de navigation* browser; *logiciel de présentation* presentation software; *logiciel de réseau* network software; *logiciel système* system software; *logiciel de système d'exploitation* operating system software; *logiciel de télémaintenance* remote-access software; *(pour base de données)* server software; *logiciel de traitement de texte* word-processing software, word-processing packages; *logiciel utilisateur* user software

> Le champion mondial du **logiciel** se contente, cette année, d'adapter 2 de ses succès américains. Concepteurs et éditeurs de **logiciels** informatiques sont complémentaires et poursuivent un même objectif: concevoir des **logiciels de bureautique** capables de communiquer entre eux.

logistique 1 *adj* logistic
   2 *nf* logistics

logo *nm* logo

loi *nf* law □ *loi antitrust* *Br* anti-monopoly *or* *Am* antitrust law; *loi de Finances* Finance Act; *la loi de la jungle* the law of the jungle; *loi de l'offre et de la demande* law of supply and demand; *loi parlementaire* Act of parliament; *loi des rendements décroissants* law of diminishing returns

loi-programme *nf* framework legislation

long, longue *adj* long; **à longue échéance** long dated; **à long terme** long-term; **emprunter à long terme** to borrow long

longévité *nf (d'un produit, des capitaux)* life

lot *nm* (a) *(de marchandises)* batch □ *lot d'envoi* consignment (b) *(aux enchères)* lot (c) *(de terrain)* plot, lot (d) BOURSE *(d'actions)* parcel

lotir *vt* (a) *(marchandises)* to divide into batches (b) *(terrain à bâtir)* to divide into building plots

lotissement *nm* (a) *(fait de diviser)* *(de marchandises)* dividing into batches; *(de terrain à bâtir)* division into plots (b) *(terrain à bâtir)* building plot (c) *(ensemble d'habitations)* housing estate *or* development

lotisseur, -euse *nm,f* property developer

louage *nm* **prendre qch à louage** to rent sth □ *louage de services* contract of employment

louer 1 *vt* (a) *(donner en location) (logement)* to rent out, *Br* to let (out) (**à** to); *(voiture, équipement)* to rent out, *Br* to hire out (**à** to); **maison à louer** house *Br* to let or *Am* for rent

(b) *(prendre en location) (logement)* to rent (**à** from); *(voiture, équipement)* to rent, *Br* to hire
   2 se louer *vpr (logement)* to be rented *or Br* let; *(voiture, équipement)* to be rented *or Br* hired; **les locaux situés au centre de la capitale se louent à prix d'or** city centre premises are very expensive to rent

loueur, -euse *nm,f* renter, *Br* hirer

lourd, -e *adj (industrie, investissement)* heavy; **la crise en Asie est lourde de conséquences pour bien des entreprises en Europe** the crisis in Asia has serious consequences for many European companies

loyal, -e *adj* honest, fair; **bon et loyal inventaire** true and accurate inventory; **c'est quelqu'un de parfaitement loyal en affaires** he's a scrupulously fair businessman

loyalement *adv* honestly, fairly

loyauté *nf* honesty, fairness

loyer *nm* (a) *(de logement)* rent; **être en retard sur son loyer, avoir des arriérés de loyer** to be behind with one's rent; **devoir trois mois de loyer** to owe three months' rent; **prendre une maison à loyer** to rent a house □ *loyer de bureau* office rent; *loyer trimestriel* quarterly rent
   (b) FIN **le loyer de l'argent** the interest rate, the price of money

> **"**
> Depuis 9 mois, les taux d'intérêt ont très fortement reculé en France: 4% au total pour **le loyer de l'argent** à court terme.
> **"**

lucratif, -ive *adj (travail, activité, commerce)* lucrative, profitable

luxe *nm* luxury; **de luxe** *(produits)* luxury

machine nf (**a**) (de bureau) machine; **écrire** ou **taper une lettre à la machine** to type a letter ❑ **machine à additionner** adding machine; **machine à affranchir** Br franking machine, Am postal meter; **machine à calculer** calculator; **machine à écrire** typewriter; **machine à facturer** invoicing machine; **machine de traitement de texte(s)** word processor

(**b**) (dans l'industrie, l'agriculture) machine; **les machines** (the) machinery; **fait à la machine** machine-made

(**c**) (organisation) machinery ❑ **machine administrative** administrative or bureaucratic machinery

machine-outil nf machine-tool

machinerie nf machinery

macro-commande nf ORDINAT macro (command)

macro-économie nf macroeconomics

macro-économique adj macroeconomic

macro-instruction nf ORDINAT macro instruction

macrolangage nm ORDINAT macro language

Madame nf (titre) Mrs; (au début d'une lettre) Dear Madam

Mademoiselle nf (titre) Miss; (au début d'une lettre) Dear Madam

magasin nm (**a**) (commerce) shop, Am store; **tenir un magasin** to keep a shop ❑ **magasin de détail** retail shop; **magasin détaxé** duty-free shop; **magasin de discount** discount store; **magasin d'exposition** showroom; **magasin franchisé** franchise; **magasin sous franchise exclusive** tied outlet; **magasin à grande surface** hypermarket; **magasin libre-service** self-service store; **magasin de luxe** shop selling luxury goods; **magasin minimarge** discount store; **magasin à prix unique** one-price store; **magasin à succursales multiples** chain store; **magasin d'usine** factory shop, factory outlet; **magasin de vente au détail** retail shop

(**b**) (entrepôt) store, warehouse; **avoir qch en magasin** to have sth in stock ❑ **magasins généraux** bonded warehouse

(**c**) MKTG **magasin laboratoire** = model test-shop used to monitor consumer behaviour

magasinage nm (**a**) (de marchandises) warehousing, storing; (frais) warehouse or storage charges (**b**) Can shopping

magasiner vi Can **aller magasiner** to go shopping

magasinier nm warehouseman

magazine nm magazine

magnat nm magnate, tycoon ❑ **magnat du pétrole** oil magnate or tycoon; **magnat de la presse** press baron or tycoon

magouiller vi Fam to scheme, to wheel and deal

magouilles nfpl Fam scheming, wheeling and dealing

mailing nm (**a**) (procédé) mailing (**b**) (envoi de prospectus) mailshot; **faire un mailing** to do or send a mailshot

main nf (**a**) (membre) hand; **faire/fabriquer qch à la main** to do/to make sth by hand; **fait (à la) main** hand-made; **payer de la main à la main** to pay cash in hand; **passer la main** to stand down (**à** in favour of); **changer de mains** (entreprise, propriété) to change hands; **camion d'occasion de première main** second-hand truck (with only one previous owner)

(**b**) COMPTA **main courante** cash book; **main courante de caisse** counter cash book; **main courante de dépenses** paid cash book; **main courante de recettes** received cash book

main-d'œuvre nf manpower, workforce; ÉCON labour; **embaucher de la main-d'œuvre** to take on workers; **cela vous coûtera 10 000 francs, main-d'œuvre comprise** that will cost 10,000 francs, including labour costs; **main-d'œuvre et fournitures** labour and material ❑ **main-d'œuvre contractuelle** contractual labour; **main-d'œuvre directe** direct labour; **main-d'œuvre étrangère** foreign labour; **main-d'œuvre féminine** female labour; **main-d'œuvre indirecte** indirect labour; **main-d'œuvre occasionnelle** casual labour; **main-d'œuvre productive** productive labour; **main-d'œuvre qualifiée** skilled labour; **main-d'œuvre spécialisée** semi-skilled labour; **main-d'œuvre temporaire** temporary labour

mainlevée *nf* JUR withdrawal; *(d'une hypothèque)* withdrawal, release ▫ **mainlevée de saisie** restoration of goods *(taken in distraint)*, replevin

mainmise *nf (sur une propriété)* seizure (**sur** of); **la mainmise d'une seule société sur le marché du logiciel en inquiète plus d'un** many people are worried about a single company having a stranglehold on the software market ▫ **mainmise économique** economic stranglehold

maintenance *nf (de matériel)* maintenance (service) ▫ **maintenance à la demande, maintenance périodique** routine maintenance

maintenir 1 *vt* to maintain, to keep; **dividende maintenu à 5%** dividend maintained at 5%; **maintenir le change au-dessus du gold-point** to maintain the exchange above the gold-point; **maintenir les prix fermes** to keep prices firm *or* steady

2 **se maintenir** *vpr* to hold up; **la hausse des prix se maintient à 4%** the rise in prices remains at 4%; **la livre se maintient par rapport au dollar** the pound is holding its own against the dollar; BOURSE **ces actions se maintiennent à 57,5 francs** these shares remain firm at 57.5 francs

> ❝
> Mais Boeing rencontre d'énormes difficultés pour respecter ses délais de livraison, et ces commandes, arrachées à des prix très serrés pour **maintenir** coûte que coûte la part de marché du groupe, ont fortement entamé les profits.
> ❞

maintien *nm (à un niveau donné)* maintenance; **maintien continu du plein emploi** continuous full employment; **le maintien du franc** maintaining the level of the franc; **le maintien du pouvoir d'achat des salariés doit être une priorité** maintaining wage-earners' purchasing power must be a priority; **on accuse le gouvernment de maintenir cette entreprise en activité de façon artificielle** the government has been accused of using artificial means to keep the company operating

maison *nf (entreprise)* maison (de commerce) firm, company, business; **notre comptable a 25 ans de maison** our accountant has been with the firm for 25 years; **elle n'a pas l'esprit maison** she's got no company spirit ▫ BANQUE **maison d'acceptation** *Br* accepting house, *Am* acceptance house; **maison affiliée** affiliated company, *Am* af-

filiate; **maison de commission** commission agency; **maison de courtage** brokerage house; **maison de détail** retail company; **maison d'édition** publishing company *or* house; **maison d'escompte** discount house; **maison d'expédition** forwarding house; **maison d'exportation** export firm; **maison de gros** wholesale firm; **maison d'importation** import firm; **maison mère** parent company; **maison de prêt** loan office *or* company; **maison de rabais** discount store; **maison à succursales multiples** chain store; FIN **maison de titres** securities firm

> ❝
> Résultat: une perte de plus de 1,5 milliard de francs et une contribution négative au résultat de la **maison mère** de 104 milliards de francs.
> ❞

maître *nm (artisan)* skilled tradesman; **être maître du marché** to lead the market ▫ **maître d'œuvre** chief architect, project manager; **maître d'ouvrage** works owner; ORDINAT **maître des postes** postmaster

> ❝
> Première étape: un jury est formé. Il représente de façon paritaire l'ensemble des acteurs: les architectes (**maîtres d'œuvre**), les élus (**maître d'ouvrage**), et les administratifs (usagers).
> ❞

maîtrise *nf* (a) *(dans une entreprise)* supervisory staff (b) *(diplôme)* ≃ master's degree

majeur, -e *adj (important)* major; **la majeure partie de nos exportations** the major part of our exports

majoration *nf* (a) *(de prix)* increase, mark-up
(b) *(sur une facture)* additional charge, surcharge; **frapper un immeuble d'une majoration de cinq pour cent** to put five percent on the valuation of a building ▫ **majoration fiscale, majoration d'impôt** surcharge on taxes
(c) *(d'actif)* overestimation, overvaluation

> ❝
> Le pouvoir d'achat en Allemagne sera amputé par les **majorations fiscales**, tandis que les pertes d'emploi et le freinage des salaires se poursuivront.
> ❞

majorer *vt* (a) *(prix, tarif)* to increase, to raise (**de** by)

(b) *(facture)* to make an additional charge on; **majorer une facture de 10%** *(faire payer en plus)* to put 10% on an invoice; *(faire payer en trop)* to overcharge by 10% on an invoice; **tous les impôts impayés avant la fin du mois seront majorés de 5%** there will be a 5% additional charge on all taxes not paid by the end of the month
(c) *(actif)* to overestimate, to overvalue

majoritaire FIN, BOURSE **1** *adj* majority; **se rendre (largement) majoritaire** to acquire a majority interest *or* shareholding; **il a une participation majoritaire dans la société** he has a majority interest *or* shareholding in the company
2 *nmf* majority shareholder

majorité *nf* majority; **une majorité de(s) deux tiers** a two-thirds majority; **décision prise à la majorité (des voix)** majority decision; **la majorité des consommateurs se sont déclarés satisfaits de ce produit** most customers said that they were happy with the product □ *majorité absolue* absolute majority; *majorité qualifiée* supermajority; *majorité simple* simple majority

mal *adv* badly; **mal calculer un compte** to miscalculate an account; **mal gérer une affaire** to mismanage a business; **mal renseigner qn** to misinform sb; **il est très mal payé** he is very badly paid

maladie professionnelle *nf* occupational disease

malfaçon *nf* **(a)** *(travail de mauvaise qualité)* bad workmanship **(b)** *(défaut)* defect

malus *nm* ASSUR surcharge, extra premium

malversation *nf* embezzlement, corrupt administration (of funds)

management *nm* management □ *management des ressources humaines* human resource management

manager¹ *nm* manager

manager² *vt* *(projet, équipe commerciale)* to manage

mandant, -e *nm,f* JUR principal *(in transaction)* □ *mandant et mandataire* principal and agent

mandat *nm* **(a)** *(mission)* *(de député)* mandate; *(de président)* term of office; **exercer un mandat** to fill an elected position
(b) JUR *(ordre)* warrant □ *mandat d'action* receiving order (in bankruptcy); *mandat d'amener* ≃ summons; *mandat de dépôt* committal order
(c) *(mode de paiement)* order; **toucher un mandat** to draw on *or* to cash a money order;

mandat sur la Banque de France order on the Bank of France □ *mandat international* international money order; *mandat de paiement* order to pay; *mandat postal, mandat poste* Br postal order, Am money order; FIN *mandat du Trésor* Treasury warrant; *mandat de virement* transfer order
(d) *(autorité)* mandate
(e) JUR *(procuration)* power of attorney, proxy; **donner mandat à qn** to give sb power of attorney

mandataire *nmf* **(a)** *(représentant)* proxy, representative **(b)** JUR authorized agent, assignee □ *mandataire général* general agent; *mandataire liquidateur* official receiver

mandat-carte *nm* Br postal order, Am money order *(in postcard form)*

mandat-contributions *nm* Br postal order, Am money order *(for paying income tax)*

mandatement *nm* = payment by means of a money order

mandater *vt* **(a)** *(représentant)* to appoint, to commission **(b)** *(somme)* to pay by Br postal order *or* Am money order

mandat-lettre *nm* Br postal order, Am money order *(which may be sent as a letter in an envelope)*

mandat-poste *nm* Br postal order, Am money order

maniement *nm* *(d'une affaire, de fonds)* handling, management

manier *vt* *(affaire, fonds)* to handle, to manage

manifeste *nm* manifest □ *manifeste de chargement* manifest; *manifeste de douane* customs manifest; *manifeste d'entrée* inward manifest; *manifeste de fret* freight manifest; *manifeste de sortie* outward manifest

manipulation *nf* **(a)** FIN, BOURSE manipulation, rigging □ *manipulation monétaire* currency manipulation **(b)** ORDINAT *manipulation de documents* document handling; *manipulation de données* data manipulation

manœuvre¹ *nf* **(a)** BOURSE *manœuvre boursière* Stock Market manipulation **(b)** JUR *manœuvres frauduleuses* swindling

manœuvre² *nm* unskilled labourer *or* worker; **travail de manœuvre** unskilled labour *or* work □ *manœuvre qualifié* skilled worker; *manœuvre spécialisé* semi-skilled worker

manquant *nm* shortfall, shortage ❑ *manquant en caisse* cash shortage; *manquant en stock* stock shortage

manque *nm* (a) *(pénurie)* lack, shortage ❑ *manque à l'embarquement* short-shipped goods; *manque à gagner* loss of profit *or* earnings; *manque à la livraison* short delivery (b) COMPTA shortfall ❑ *manque de caisse* cash unders; *manque de capitaux* capital shortfall

manquement *nm* breach ❑ *manquement à la discipline* breach of discipline, misconduct; *manquement à l'obligation de prudence* negligence

manquer 1 *vt (occasion)* to miss, to lose; **manquer une affaire** to miss one's chance of doing business; **manquer un contrat** to lose a contract
  2 *vi* (a) *(faire défaut)* to be lacking; **manquer en magasin** to be out of stock (b) *(être absent)* to be missing (**à** from); **manquer à un rendez-vous** to fail to keep an appointment
  3 **manquer de** *vt ind (argent, main-d'œuvre)* to be short of, to lack
  4 *v impersonnel* **il nous manque les capitaux nécessaires** we are short of the necessary capital

manuel¹, -elle 1 *adj (travail, travailleur)* manual
  2 *nm,f (personne)* manual worker

manuel² *nm* manual, handbook ❑ *manuel d'entretien* service manual; *manuel d'utilisation* user manual

manufacturé, -e *adj* manufactured, factory-made

manufacturer *vt* to manufacture

manufacturier, -ère *adj (industrie)* manufacturing

manutention *nf (de marchandises)* handling ❑ *manutention industrielle* industrial handling

manutentionnaire *nmf* warehouseman, *f* warehousewoman

manutentionner *vt (marchandises)* to handle

maquette *nf* (a) *(de livre)* dummy (b) *(d'une construction architecturale)* (scale) model; *(de mise en page)* paste-up (c) *(dans l'industrie)* mock-up

maquignonnage *nm* shady dealing, wheeling and dealing

maquignonner *vi* to wheel and deal

maquillage *nm (d'un chèque, d'un document, d'un bilan)* falsification

maquiller *vt (chèque, document, bilan)* to falsify

marasme *nm* ÉCON stagnation, slump; **le marasme économique actuel** the present economic slump; **le marasme des affaires** the slump in business; **l'économie des pays d'Asie traverse actuellement une période de marasme** Asian economies are currently going through a period of stagnation

marchand, -e 1 *adj (quartier, ville)* commercial
  2 *nm,f (dans un magasin)* Br shopkeeper, Am storekeeper; *(de tableaux, de meubles)* dealer ❑ *marchand de biens* Br ≃ estate agent, Am ≃ realtor, real estate agent; *marchand au détail* retailer; *marchand en gros* wholesaler, wholesale dealer

marchandage *nm* (a) *(sur le prix d'un article)* bargaining, haggling (b) JUR illegal subcontracting of labour *(whereby the worker receives less than a fair wage)*

marchander 1 *vt* (a) *(prix, article)* to bargain over, to haggle over (b) JUR to subcontract illegally
  2 *vi* to bargain, to haggle

marchandeur, -euse *nm,f* (a) *(sur le prix d'un article)* haggler, bargainer (b) JUR illegal subcontractor of labour

marchandisage *nm* marketing, merchandising

marchandise *nf* merchandise, commodity; **marchandises** goods, merchandise ❑ BOURSE *marchandises et biens physiques* actuals; *marchandises au détail* retail goods; *marchandises en entrepôt* warehoused goods, goods in storage; DOUANES bonded goods, goods in bond; *marchandises à l'export* export goods; *marchandises en gros* wholesale goods; *marchandises à l'import* import goods; BOURSE *marchandises livrables au comptant* spot goods; *marchandises en magasin* stock in hand; *marchandises d'origine* = goods of guaranteed origin; *marchandises sur palette(s)* palletized goods; *marchandises périssables* perishable goods, perishables; *marchandises en souffrance* unclaimed goods; *marchandises en transit* goods in transit; *marchandises de vente courante* goods that have a ready sale; *marchandises en vrac* bulk goods

marche *nf* (a) *(fonctionnement)* running, working; **en état de marche** in working order; **la bonne marche d'une entreprise**

the smooth running of a firm **(b)** *marche à suivre* procedure

marché *nm* **(a)** ÉCON market; **mettre** *ou* **lancer un nouveau produit sur le marché** to put *or* to launch a new product on the market; **ce produit n'a pas de marché** there is no market for this product; **conquérir un marché** to break into a market ▢ *marché d'acheteurs* buyers' market; BOURSE *marché des actions* share market, stock market; *marché à la baisse* sellers' market; BOURSE *marché baissier* bear market; *marché boursier* stock market; *marché cambiste* foreign exchange market; *marché de capitaux* capital market; *marché captif* captive market; BOURSE *marché des changes* currency (exchange) market, foreign exchange market; BOURSE *marché des changes à terme* forward exchange market; *le Marché commun* the Common Market; FIN *marché au comptant* spot market; *marché des consommateurs, marché de consommation* consumer market; BOURSE *marché des contrats à terme* futures market; *marché en coulisse* outside market; FIN *marché des denrées et matières premières* commodity market; *marché des devises (étrangères)* foreign exchange market; FIN *marché du disponible* spot market; *marché effectif* available market; *marché de l'emploi* job market; *marché des entreprises* business market; *marché environnant* substitution market; *marché d'équipement* capital goods market; *marché de l'eurodevise* euromarket; *marché à l'exportation* export market; *marché extérieur* foreign market, overseas market; *marché financier* money *or* financial market; *marché grand public* consumer market, mass market; *marché de gré à gré entre banques* interbank wholesale market; *marché gris* grey market; *marché à la hausse* buyers' market; BOURSE *marché haussier* bull market; BOURSE *marché hors cote* unlisted securities market, *Am* over-the-counter market; *marché hypothécaire* mortgage market; *marché de l'immobilier* property market; *marché industriel* industrial market; *marché de l'information* information market; *marché interbancaire* interbank market; *marché intérieur* home market, domestic market; *marché libre* free market; *marché libre des capitaux* open money market; *marché locatif* rental market; FIN *marché des matières premières* commodity market; *marché mondial* world *or* global market; *marché monétaire* money market;

marché national national market, home market; BOURSE *marché du neuf* primary market; *marché noir* black market; **faire du marché noir** to buy and sell on the black market; BOURSE *marché des nouvelles émissions* new issue market; BOURSE *marché obligataire, marché des obligations* bond market; *marché officiel* official market; *marché à ou des options* options market; *marché de l'or* gold market; *marché d'outre-mer* overseas market; *marché parallèle* parallel *or* black market; *marché primaire* primary market; *marché à primes* options market; *marché principal* core market; JUR *marché public* market overt; *marché de référence* core market; *marché secondaire* secondary market; *marché témoin* control market, test market; *marché à terme* futures market; *marché à terme d'instruments financiers* financial futures market; *marché des transactions hors séance* *Br* unlisted securities market, *Am* over-the-counter market; BOURSE *marché des titres* securities market; *marché du travail* labour market; *le Marché unique (européen)* the Single (European) Market; MKTG *marché utile* addressable market; *marché des valeurs mobilières* stock exchange, securities market; *marché vendeur* seller's market; *marché visé* target market

(b) *(accord)* deal, bargain; *(plus officiel)* contract; **faire** *ou* **conclure un marché** to strike a deal *or* bargain, to clinch a deal ▢ *marché compensatoire* compensation deal; *marché de gré à gré* mutual agreement, private contract

> **"**
> Les **marchés des changes** semblent vouloir à nouveau forcer les banques centrales à prendre les mesures nécessaires pour sortir les économies européennes de la récession.
> **"**

> **"**
> De nombreuses SCPI qui n'ont pas baissé le prix de leur part en 1993 enregistrent néanmoins des échanges sur le **marché gris**, c'est à dire le marché de gré à gré entre particuliers à moins 20%, voire moins 30% par rapport au prix officiel.
> **"**

marchéage *nm* MKTG marketing mix, marketing spectrum ▢ *marchéage de distribution* retailing mix

marché-cible *nm* target market

marcher *vi* (**a**) *(travail, projet)* to be going well; *(entreprise, nouveau produit)* to do well; **les affaires marchent/ne marchent pas fort** business is brisk/slack; **notre nouveau modèle marche bien/mal** our new model is doing well/badly; **ça fait marcher le commerce** it's good for business (**b**) *(machine, appareil)* to work, to run; **faire marcher qch** to work *or* operate sth

marché-test *nm* test market

marge *nf* margin; **avoir une faible/forte marge** to have a low/high (profit) margin; **nous faisons 30% de marge sur ce produit** we make a 30% margin on this product □ *marge bénéficiaire* profit margin; *marge brute* gross (profit) margin; COMPTA *marge brute d'autofinancement* cash flow; *marge commerciale* trading profit; *marge commerciale brute* gross profit margin; *marge de crédit* credit margin; *marge du détaillant* retailer margin; *marge du distributeur* distributor's margin; *marge d'erreur* margin of error; *marge étroite* fine price; *marge de fluctuation (d'une monnaie)* margin of fluctuation; *marge du grossiste* wholesaler margin; *marge de l'importateur* importer margin; *marge avant impôt* pre-tax margin; *marge initiale* initial margin; *marge d'intérêt* margin of interest; *marge nette* net (profit) margin; *marge nette d'exploitation* operating margin; *marge de profit* profit margin; *marge de sécurité* safety margin; *marge de tolérance* tolerance margin

> Pour préserver leurs **marges**, les groupes d'assurance doivent réduire leurs coûts, notamment ceux de l'intermédiation, quitte à provoquer des hoquets sociaux.

marger ORDINAT **1** *vt (page)* to set the margin(s) for
2 *vi* to set the margin(s); **marger à droite/à gauche** to set the right/left margin

marginal, -e *adj* ÉCON marginal

margoulin *nm Fam* (**a**) *(à la Bourse)* petty speculator (**b**) *(escroc)* shark, swindler

maritime *adj (droit, législation, risque)* maritime

mark *nm* (**a**) *(monnaie allemande)* (German) mark, Deutschmark (**b**) *(monnaie finlandaise)* markka

marketing *nm* marketing □ *marketing après-vente* after-sales marketing; *marketing ciblé* niche *or* target marketing; *mar-*

keting commercial trade marketing; *marketing de contact, marketing direct* direct marketing; *marketing écologique* green marketing; *marketing de grande consommation* mass marketing; *marketing sur mesure* customized marketing; *marketing mix* marketing mix; *marketing non lucratif* not-for-profit marketing; *marketing de relance* remarketing; *marketing relationnel* relationship *or* direct marketing; *marketing de stimulation* stimulation *or* incentive marketing; *marketing stratégique* strategic marketing; *marketing téléphonique* cold calling, telemarketing

> Le **marketing direct** permet de réduire d'environ 15 à 20% tant les coûts d'opérations commerciales et administratives que ceux des infrastructures (immobilier et technologie).

marquage *nm* branding, marking

marque *nf* (**a**) *(de produit)* brand; *(de voiture)* make; *(sur l'article)* trademark; **grande marque** famous make, well-known brand; **de marque** *(produit)* branded □ *marque d'appel* brand on offer; *marque collective* label; *marque de commerce* trademark, brand (name); *marque déposée* registered trademark; *marque de distributeur* distributor's brand name; *marque dominante* dominant brand; *marque économique* budget *or* economy brand; *marque de fabricant* manufacturer's brand name; *marque de fabrique* trademark, brand (name); *marque de garantie* certification mark; *marque générique* generic brand; *marque grand public* consumer brand; *marque d'origine* maker's mark; *marque de service* mark of quality, quality guarantee *(on range of services offered by company or manufacturer)*
(**b**) *(cachet)* stamp
(**c**) ORDINAT marker, flag, tag □ *marque d'insertion* insertion marker

marquer *vt* (**a**) *(article, produit)* to label, to mark (**b**) ORDINAT to mark, to flag, to tag

marqueur *nm* (**a**) *(feutre)* marker pen (**b**) ORDINAT marker, flag, tag □ *marqueur de fin de texte* end-of-text marker

masse *nf* FIN fund, stock; *(de personnes)* body □ *masse active* assets; *masse des créanciers* (general) body of creditors; *masse monétaire* money supply; *masse des obligataires* body of debenture holders *or* bondholders; *masse passive* liabilities; *masse salariale* wage bill

> "
> Cet automne, E. Balladur fait voter une loi quinquennale de la **masse salariale** plus flexible, plus proche de l'évolution des carnets de commandes.
> "

mass(-)média *nmpl* mass media

matérialiser *vt* FIN to realize

matériel, -elle **1** *adj* material
2 *nm* (**a**) *(équipements)* equipment □ *matériel de bureau* office equipment; *matériel à longévité élevée* long-life equipment; *matériel lourd* heavy equipment *or* plant; *matériel et main-d'œuvre* material and labour
(**b**) MKTG material □ *matériel de PLV* point-of-sale material; *matériel de présentation* display material; *matériel publicitaire* advertising material
(**c**) ORDINAT hardware □ *matériel informatique* computer hardware

matière *nf* (**a**) *(substance)* material □ *matière brute* unprocessed material; *matière et façon* material and labour; *matière non travaillé* unrefined material; *matières premières* raw materials; BOURSE *matières premières et denrées* commodities
(**b**) *(domaine)* matter □ *matière juridique* legal matter
(**c**) *matière imposable* taxable income

MATIF *nm* (*abrév* **marché à terme d'instruments financiers**) financial futures market

matinée de Bourse *nf* morning session

matraquage publicitaire *nm* MKTG plugging, hype

matrice *nf* ADMIN register

maturité *nf* maturity; **économie en pleine maturité** mature economy; **mon compte d'épargne n'est pas encore arrivé à maturité** my savings account hasn't matured yet

mauvais, -e *adj* bad; **en mauvais état** in bad condition; **de mauvaise qualité** poor-quality, inferior; **faire de mauvaises affaires** to be doing badly (in business); **faire de mauvais placements** to make bad investments, to invest unwisely □ *mauvaise administration* mismanagement; *mauvaise créance* bad debt; *mauvaise gestion* mismanagement; *mauvais payeur* bad payer

maximal, -e *adj* maximum

maximalisation *nf* maximization, maximizing

maximaliser, maximiser *vt* to maximize

maximum **1** *adj* *(prix, tarif, cours)* maximum
2 *nm* maximum; **maximum de rendement** highest performance, maximum efficiency; **au maximum** *(au plus)* at the most; *(le plus possible)* to the highest degree; **porter la production au maximum** to maximize production

MBA *nf* COMPTA (*abrév* **marge brute d'autofinancement**) cash flow

mécanisation *nf* mechanization

mécanisé, -e *adj* mechanized

mécaniser *vt* to mechanize

mécanisme *nm* mechanism □ *mécanisme administratif* administrative machinery; *mécanisme bancaire* banking machinery *or* mechanism; *mécanisme budgétaire* budgetary mechanism; *mécanismes économiques* economic machinery; *mécanisme du marché* market mechanism; *mécanisme de l'offre et de la demande* supply and demand mechanism; *mécanisme des prix* price mechanism

mécénat *nm* patronage □ *mécénat d'entreprise* corporate sponsorship

mécompte *nm* miscalculation, error in reckoning

média *nm* medium; **les médias** the media

médialogie *nf* media research

médiateur, -trice **1** *adj* mediatory, mediating
2 *nm,f* mediator; ADMIN ombudsman; *(dans l'industrie)* arbitrator, conciliator; **agir en médiateur** *ou* **servir de médiateur (entre)** to act as mediator (between) □ *médiateur d'entreprises* arbitrator

médiation *nf* *(de conflit, de crise)* mediation

médiatique *adj* media; *(personne)* media-friendly

médiatisation *nf* media coverage

médiatiser *vt* to give media coverage to

méga *nm* ORDINAT megabyte, meg

mégabit *nm* ORDINAT megabit; **mégabits par seconde** megabits per second

méga-fusion *nf* mega-merger

mégaoctet *nm* ORDINAT megabyte

meilleur, -e *adj* (**a**) *(comparatif de* **bon***)* better; **meilleur marché** cheaper, less expensive; **acheter qch (à) meilleur marché** to buy sth cheaper; **payer qch meilleur marché** to pay less for sth; **ce produit est de meilleure qualité** this product is of better quality (**b**) *(superlatif de* **bon**) best; **veuillez nous faire profiter de votre meilleur prix** please give us your best price

membre 1 *adj (pays, État)* member
2 *nm (participant)* member ❑ *membre associé* associate member; BOURSE *membre de compensation* clearing member; *membre fondateur* founding member; *membre honoraire* honorary member; *membre permanent* permanent member; *membre suppléant* deputy member

mémoire 1 *nm* (**a**) *(note)* account, bill; **présenter un mémoire** to send a detailed account *or* bill
(**b**) COMPTA report
2 *nf* (**a**) ORDINAT memory; **cet ordinateur possède 32 mégaoctets de mémoire RAM** this computer has 32 megabytes of RAM; **mettre un dossier en mémoire** to write a file to memory ❑ *mémoire cache* cache memory; *mémoire centrale* main memory; *mémoire disponible* available memory; *mémoire à disque* disk memory; *mémoire de masse* mass storage; *mémoire morte* read-only memory; *mémoire tampon de texte* text buffer; *mémoire vive* random access memory; *mémoire vive dynamique* dynamic random access memory; *mémoire vive statique* static random access memory
(**b**) **pour mémoire** for the record

mémorandum *nm* (**a**) *(circulaire)* memorandum, memo (**b**) *(à un fournisseur)* written order

mémorisation *nf* (**a**) ORDINAT writing to memory (**b**) MKTG recall ❑ *mémorisation un jour après* day after recall; *mémorisation de la marque* brand name recall

mémoriser *vt* ORDINAT to write to memory

ménage *nm* ÉCON household; **les revenus des ménages** household incomes

> ❝
> Dans un récent rapport, le Conseil des impôts notait que 10% des **ménages** détenait plus de la moitié du patrimoine français. ❞

ménager, -ère *adj* household

mener *vt* (**a**) *(groupe, équipe)* to lead (**b**) *(négociation, étude)* to carry out

meneur, -euse *nm,f* leader ❑ *meneur de grève* strike leader

mensualisation *nf (d'un salaire, d'un paiement)* paying by the month, monthly pay-

ment; **pour vos règlements, pensez à la mensualisation** don't forget that you can pay in monthly instalments

> ❝
> L'UGTG réclame "la **mensualisation** des travailleurs précaires et la garantie d'emploi liée à la carte professionnelle." ❞

mensualiser *vt* to pay monthly; **il est payé au trimestre mais il a demandé à être mensualisé** he is paid quarterly but has asked to be paid monthly

mensualité *nf* (**a**) *(paiement)* monthly payment; **payer par mensualités** to pay by monthly instalments; **il a payé son ordinateur en 36 mensualités** he paid for his computer in 36 monthly instalments ❑ *mensualité de remboursement* monthly repayment (**b**) *(salaire)* monthly salary

> ❝
> Pour les 50 000 francs sur 36 mois, les **mensualités de remboursement** ne varient que de 117 francs entre un taux de 15% et un taux de 10%. ❞

mensuel, -elle 1 *adj (rapport, publication, relevé)* monthly
2 *nm,f (employé)* employee paid monthly

mensuellement *adv (tous les mois)* monthly, every month; *(une fois par mois)* once a month

mention *nf* (**a**) *(fait de citer)* mention; **faire mention de qn/qch** to mention sb/sth, to refer to sb/sth (**b**) *(indication)* note, comment; ADMIN **rayer les mentions inutiles** *(sur formulaire)* delete where inapplicable; **le dossier porte la mention "confidentiel"** the file is marked "confidential"

mentionner *vt* to mention; **mentionné ci-dessus** above-mentioned, aforementioned

menu *nm* ORDINAT menu ❑ *menu d'aide* help menu; *menu déroulant* pull-down menu; *menu fichier* file menu; *menu d'impression* print menu; *menu local* pop-up menu; *menu principal* main menu

mercantile *adj* mercantile, commercial

mercantilisme *nm* mercantilism

mercaticien, -enne *nm,f* MKTG marketing expert, marketing consultant

mercatique *nf* marketing

merchandising *nm* merchandising

mercuriale *nf* BOURSE commodity *or* market price list

message *nm* (a) *(communication)* message; **prendre un message** to take a message; **veuillez laisser un message après le signal sonore** please leave a message after the tone; **laisser un message à l'attention de qn** to leave a message for sb □ *message électronique* e-mail; **envoyer un message électronique à qn** to e-mail sb; *message enregistré* recorded message; MKTG *message publicitaire* advertisement; *message téléphonique* telephone message; *message télex* telex (message)

(b) ORDINAT message □ *message d'accueil* welcome message; *message d'aide* help message; *message d'alerte* warning message, alert box; *message d'attente (du système)* (system) prompt; *message d'erreur* error message; *message d'invite* prompt

messagerie *nf* (a) *(service de transports)* courier company □ *messageries aériennes* air freight company; *messageries maritimes* shipping company

(b) ORDINAT *(service télématique)* *messagerie électronique* electronic mail service, e-mail; *messagerie vocale* voice mail

(c) *(entreprise de routage)* *messagerie de presse* newspaper distributing service

mesure *nf* (a) *(initiative)* measure, step; **le gouvernement a pris des mesures pour réduire le chômage des jeunes** the government has taken measures to reduce youth unemployment □ *mesures déflationnistes* deflationary measures; *mesures préventives* preventive measures; *mesures protectionnistes* protectionist measures; *mesures provisoires* temporary measures; *mesures de sécurité* safety measures *or* precautions; **par mesure de sécurité** as a safety precaution; *mesures d'urgence* emergency measures

(b) *(estimation)* measurement; **la mesure de la productivité a été améliorée grâce à de nouvelles techniques** productivity measurement has been improved thanks to new techniques

(c) **être en mesure de faire qch** to be in a position to do sth, to be able to do sth; **l'entreprise n'est pas en mesure de fournir les quantités nécessaires** the company is unable to supply the necessary quantities

mesurer *vt* (a) *(déterminer la dimension de)* to measure (b) *(estimer)* to assess; **mesurer l'ampleur d'un problème** to assess the size of a problem (c) *(adapter)* **mesurer ses dépenses sur ses profits** to gear one's expenditure to one's profits (d) *(limiter)* to limit; **on nous mesure les crédits** our funds are limited

métal *nm* FIN metal □ *métal en barres* bullion; *métal en lingots* ingots

métallique *adj* FIN *(monnaie)* metallic

méthode *nf* *(façon de procéder)* method □ *méthodes administratives* systems and procedures; *méthode d'amortissement linéaire* straight line depreciation method; *méthode d'analyse statistique* method of statistical analysis; MKTG *méthode de la boule de neige* referral system; FIN *méthode de capitalisation du coût entier* full cost accounting (method); *méthode du chemin critique* critical path method; *méthode de classement* filing system; *méthode des coûts marginaux* cost pricing; *méthode des coûts variables* direct costing; COMPTA *méthode par* *ou* *à échelles* daily balance interest calculation; *méthode expérimentale* experimental method; *méthode d'exploitation* method of working *or* operation; *méthode de fabrication* manufacturing method; *méthode linéaire* straight line method; *méthodes et organisation* organization and methods; *méthode prospective* projected benefit valuation method; MKTG *méthode des quotas* quota sampling method; *méthode de sondage* polling method

métier *nm* (a) *(profession)* profession, occupation; **exercer** *ou* **faire un métier** to carry on a trade *or* a profession; **il exerce le métier de comptable** he is an accountant; **il est du métier** he's in the trade *or* the business □ *métier manuel* manual trade (b) *(savoir-faire)* experience; **avoir du métier** to have experience, to be experienced; **manquer de métier** to lack experience, to be inexperienced

métrage *nm* ≃ yardage

métrer *vt* (a) *(mesurer)* to measure (in metres) (b) *(dans le bâtiment)* to survey

mettre *vt* (a) *(placer)* to put, to place; **mettre son argent à la banque** to put *or* deposit one's money in the bank; **mettre sa signature à un contrat** to put one's signature to a contract, to sign a contract

(b) *(investir)* to put, to invest; **mettre son argent en immeubles** to put *or* to invest one's money in property; **je ne peux pas y mettre tant que ça** I can't afford as much as that

(c) *(établir)* **mettre une maison en vente** to put a house up for sale

(d) ORDINAT **mettre en forme** to format

meuble 1 *adj* movable

2 *nm* (a) *(élément du mobilier)* piece of furniture; **meubles** furniture □ *meubles de bu-*

reau office furniture (**b**) JUR movable; **meubles** movables, personal property □ *meubles corporels* tangible assets *or* movables; *meubles à demeure* fixtures; *meubles gagés* furniture under distraint; *meubles incorporels* intangible assets *or* movables

mévente *nf* slump (in sales), slack period; **c'est une période de mévente dans l'immobilier** there is a slump in the property market

micro ORDINAT **1** *nm* (*abrév* **micro-ordinateur**) micro(computer)
2 *nf* (*abrév* **micro-informatique**) micro-computing

microéconomie *nf* microeconomics

microéconomique *adj* microeconomic

microédition *nf* ORDINAT desktop publishing, DTP

microfiche *nf* microfiche

microfilm *nm* microfilm

micro-informatique *nf* ORDINAT microcomputing, microprocessing

micro-ordinateur *nm* ORDINAT micro (computer) □ *micro-ordinateur de bureau* desktop computer; *micro-ordinateur portable* laptop (computer)

microprocesseur *nm* ORDINAT microprocessor

mieux **1** *adv* BOURSE **acheter/vendre au mieux** to buy/sell at best
2 *nm* (*amélioration*) improvement; **on constate un léger mieux par rapport aux ventes du mois dernier** a slight improvement on last month's figures can be observed

milieu *nm* (*entourage*) environment; **dans les milieux autorisés, on s'accorde à dire que la société n'est plus viable** informed sources are agreed that the company is no longer viable □ *milieux commerciaux* business circles; *milieux financiers* financial circles

millésime *nm* (**a**) (*sur une monnaie*) date (**b**) (*d'un produit*) year of manufacture

milliard *nm* billion; **10 milliards de dollars** 10 billion dollars

milliardaire *adj & nmf* billionaire

million *nm* million; **un million de francs** a million francs; **un chiffre d'affaires de deux millions** a turnover of two million

millionnaire *adj & nmf* millionaire

mine *nf* mine □ *mine de charbon* coal mine; *mine d'or* gold mine

minerai *nm* ore □ *minerai de fer* iron ore

mineur *nm* miner

minier, -ère *adj* (*industrie, secteur*) mining

minimal, -e *adj* minimum

minimarge *nm* discount store

minimisation *nf* minimization, minimizing

minimiser *vt* (*pertes, dépenses, coûts*) to minimize

minimum **1** *adj* minimum
2 *nm* minimum; **au minimum** (*au moins*) at least; (*le moins possible*) to a minimum; **il y en aura 5 au minimum** there will be a minimum of 5, there will be at least 5; **réduire les frais au minimum** to reduce expenses to a minimum □ *minimum imposable* tax threshold; *minimum vieillesse* = basic old-age pension; *minimum vital* minimum living wage

mini-ordinateur *nm* minicomputer

ministère *nm* department, *Br* ministry □ *le ministère du Commerce Br* ≃ the Department of Trade and Industry, *Am* ≃ the Department of Commerce; *le ministère du Commerce extérieur* Overseas Trade Department, *Br* ≃ the Department of Trade and Industry; *le ministère de l'Économie et des Finances Br* ≃ the Treasury, *Am* ≃ the Treasury Department; *le ministère de l'Industrie Br* ≃ the Department of Trade and Industry, *Am* ≃ the Department of Industry; *le ministère de l'Intérieur Br* ≃ the Home Office, *Am* ≃ the Department of the Interior; *le ministère de la Santé et de la Sécurité Sociale Br* ≃ the Department of Social Security, *Am* ≃ the Department of Health and Human Services; *le ministère des Transports Br* ≃ the Department of the Environment, Transport and the Regions, *Am* ≃ the Department of Transportation; *le ministère du Travail Br* ≃ the Department of Education and Employment, *Am* ≃ the Department of Labor

ministre *nm* minister, *Am* secretary □ *ministre du Commerce Br* ≃ Secretary of State for Trade and Industry, *Am* ≃ Secretary of Commerce; *ministre du Commerce extérieur* Overseas Trade Minister, *Br* ≃ Secretary of State for Trade and Industry; *ministre de l'Économie et des Finances* Finance Minister, *Br* ≃ Chancellor of the Exchequer, *Am* ≃ Secretary of the Treasury; *ministre de l'Industrie Br* ≃ Secretary of State for Trade and Industry, *Am* ≃ Industry Secretary; *ministre de l'Intérieur Br* ≃ Home Secretary, *Am* ≃ Secretary of State; *ministre de la Santé et de la Sécurité Sociale Br* ≃ Secretary of State for Social Security, *Am* ≃ Secretary for Health and

Human Services; *ministre des Transports Br* ≃ Secretary of State for the Environment, Transport and the Regions, *Am* ≃ Transportation Secretary; *ministre du Travail Br* ≃ Secretary of State for Education and Employment, *Am* ≃ Labor Secretary

mini-tour *nf* ORDINAT mini tower

minoritaire *adj* minority

minorité *nf* minority; **être en minorité** to be in the *or* a minority □ *minorité de blocage* blocking minority

minutage *nm* (*d'un contrat*) drafting

minute *nf* (*d'un contrat*) minute; (*d'un acte notarié*) record; **faire la minute d'un contrat** to minute *or* draft a contract

minuter *vt* (a) (*contrat*) to minute, to draft; (*acte notarié*) to record (b) (*chronométrer*) to time; **sa journée est soigneusement minutée** his day is carefully planned, his day is run to a tight schedule

MIPS *nm* ORDINAT (*abrév* **million d'instructions par seconde**) mips

mise *nf* (a) (*placement*) putting □ *mise en application* implementation; *mise en circulation* (*de l'argent*) circulation; *mise en commun de fonds* pooling of capital; *mise en demeure* formal demand; *mise en demeure de payer* final demand; *mise en dépôt* warehousing; *mise en disponibilité* leave of absence; *Can* layoff; *mise en distribution* distribution; *mise en examen* indictment; *mise de fonds* investment; **faire une mise de fonds** to put up capital; **ma première mise de fonds a été de 1000 livres** my initial outlay was £1,000; *mise en gage* pawning, pledging; *mise en garde* warning; *mise hors* (*action*) disbursement; (*somme*) sum advanced; *mise à jour* updating; *mise en œuvre* implementation; *mise en paiement* (*d'un dividende*) payment; FIN *mise en pension* borrowing against securities, pledging; *mise à pied* suspension; *Can* layoff; *mise sur pied* setting up; *mise en place* putting into place; *mise au point* (*d'une technique*) perfecting; (*d'un document, d'un rapport, d'un produit*) finalization; *mise à la retraite anticipée* early retirement; *mise en route* start-up; *mise en service* (*d'une machine*) commissioning, putting into service; *mise sociale* = capital brought into a business by a partner; *mise en valeur* (*d'un investissement*) turning to account; (*d'une propriété, d'un terrain*) development; *mise en vente* (*d'une propriété*) putting up for sale; (*d'un produit*) bringing onto the market, launching; *mise en vigueur* implementation

(b) (*à une vente aux enchères*) bid; **doubler la mise** to double the stakes □ *mise à prix* reserve price, upset (price)

(c) MKTG *mise en avant* special display

(d) TÉL *mise en attente d'appels* call holding

(e) ORDINAT *mise en attente des fichiers à imprimer* printer spooling; *mise en forme* formatting; *mise en mémoire* saving; *mise à niveau* upgrade; *mise en relation* (*avec un service*) log-on; *mise en réseau* networking; *mise hors tension* power-down; *mise sous tension* power-up; *mise sur pied* setting up

miser **1** *vt* (*somme*) to bid
2 miser sur *vt ind* (a) (*parier sur*) to bet on; BOURSE **miser sur une hausse/une baisse** to speculate on a rising/falling market (b) (*compter sur*) to count on; **nous misons sur une reprise des exportations** we are counting on a recovery in exports

mission *nf* (a) (*groupe*) mission, delegation; **une mission commerciale japonaise** a Japanese trade mission (b) (*tâche*) assignment; **partir en mission** to go away on business

mi-temps *nm* part-time job; **travailler à mi-temps** to work part-time

mix *nm* MKTG (*marchéage*) mix □ *mix de produits* product mix

mixte *adj* (*cargaison, économie*) mixed; (*commission*) joint

Mo *nm* ORDINAT (*abrév* **mégaoctet**) MB

mobile **1** *adj* mobile; **la main-d'œuvre en Europe est moins mobile qu'aux États-Unis** the European workforce is less mobile than the workforce in the US
2 *nm* MKTG *mobile d'achat* buying inducement, purchasing motivator; *mobile (publicitaire)* (advertising) mobile

mobilier, -ère **1** *adj* JUR movable
2 *nm* furniture □ *mobilier de bureau* office furniture

mobilisable *adj* FIN (*capital*) realizable; (*actif, biens immobiliers*) mobilizable

mobilisation *nf* FIN (*de capital*) realization, (*d'actif, de biens immobiliers*) mobilization; (*de fonds*) raising

mobiliser *vt* FIN (*capital*) to realize; (*actif, biens immobilier*) to mobilize; (*fonds*) to raise

mobilité *nf* (*du capital, des travailleurs*) mobility □ *mobilité sociale* upward mobility

modalité *nf* method; FIN **modalités** (*d'une émission*) terms and conditions □ *modalités d'application de la loi* means of enforcing the law; *modalités de financement* financing terms *or* conditions; *modalités de paiement, modalités de règlement* methods *or* terms of payment; *modalités de souscription* conditions of application

> 66
>
> Grâce à leur alliance, Francfort et Londres vont former le duo qui dominera cette Europe des Bourses et en dictera les **modalités**.
>
> 99

mode *nm* (a) *(manière)* method ❑ COMPTA *mode d'amortissement linéaire* straight line depreciation method; *mode de classement* filing system; *mode d'emploi* directions for use; *mode de fabrication* manufacturing method; *mode de fonctionnement* method of operation; *mode de gestion* management method *or* style; COMPTA *mode linéaire* straight line method; *mode de paiement, mode de règlement* method *or* means of payment

(b) ORDINAT mode ❑ *mode autonome* off-line mode; *mode brouillon* draft mode; *mode connecté* on-line mode; *mode démarrer* start-up mode; *mode de dialogue* dialogue mode; *mode graphique* graphics mode; *mode d'insertion* insert mode; *mode paysage* landscape mode; *mode portrait* portrait mode; *mode de superposition* overwrite mode; *mode survol* browse mode; *mode texte* text mode

modèle 1 *adj (usine, employé)* model

2 *nm* (a) *(exemplaire)* model; **le nouveau modèle de chez Renault** the new model from Renault; **ce modèle existe aussi en rouge** this model also comes in *or* is also available in red; **petit/grand modèle** small-scale/large-scale model ❑ *modèle de démonstration* demonstration model; *modèle déposé* registered design; *modèle familial* family model

(b) *(représentation schématique)* model ❑ *modèle du chemin critique* critical path model; *modèle de décision, modèle décisionnel* decision model; *modèle de décision en arborescence* decision-tree model; *modèle déterministe* decision model; *modèle économique* economic model; *modèle d'entreprise* corporate model; *modèle de lettre* standard letter; *modèle prévisionnel* econometric model; MKTG *modèle de prise de décision* decision-making model; *modèle de signature* specimen signature

(c) *(référence)* model; **prendre modèle sur qch** to use sth as a model; **le modèle américain/japonais** the American/Japanese model

modem *nm* ORDINAT modem; **envoyer qch à qn par modem** to modem sth to sb, to send sth to sb by modem ❑ *modem externe* external modem; *modem interne* internal modem

modération *nf* reduction ❑ *modération de droit* tax reduction *or* rebate

modéré, -e *adj* moderate; **une baisse, même modérée, des taux d'intérêt permettrait de relancer la consommation** even a moderate drop in interest rates would boost consumption

modernisation *nf* modernization

moderniser 1 *vt* to modernize

2 **se moderniser** *vpr (industrie, secteur)* to modernize

modeste *adj (salaires, revenus, prix)* modest, low

modicité *nf (des salaires, des revenus, des prix)* lowness

modification *nf* modification, alteration; *(d'un loi)* amendment; **apporter des modifications à qch** to modify sth, to alter sth

modifier *vt* to modify, to alter; *(loi)* to amend

modique *adj (salaires, revenus, prix)* modest, low

module d'extension *nm* ORDINAT plug-in

moins *adv* (a) *(comparatif)* less; **je gagne moins que vous** I earn less than you (do); **moins de** *(argent)* less; *(travailleurs, magasins)* fewer; *(avec un nombre)* less than; **celui-ci coûte dix francs de moins que l'autre** this one costs ten francs less than the other one; **il y a eu 20% de clients de moins** *ou* **en moins par rapport à l'année dernière** there have been 20% fewer customers than last year

(b) *(superlatif)* **le moins** the least; **le moins disant** the lowest bidder; **c'est le produit le moins cher de tous** it's the cheapest product of all

moins-perçu *nm* amount due, outstanding amount

moins-value *nf* FIN depreciation, drop in value; *(après une vente)* capital loss

> 66
>
> Les sicav monétaires offrent l'avantage de ne supporter que des frais très faibles et, surtout, de mettre les montants investis à l'abri de tout risque de **moins-value**.
>
> 99

mois *nm* (a) *(période)* month; **au mois d'août** in the month of August, in August; **le 12 de**

ce mois the 12th of this month; **le mois dernier** last month; **un mois de crédit** a month's credit; **être payé au mois** to be paid by the month; **elle gagne 25 000 francs par mois** she earns 25,000 francs a month ❑ *mois civil* calendar month; BOURSE *mois d'échéance* trading month; *mois légal* thirty days

(**b**) *(salaire mensuel)* monthly salary; **toucher son mois** to receive one's (month's) salary ❑ *mois double* = extra month's salary paid as an annual bonus

moitié *nf* half; **à moitié prix** at half price; **réduit de moitié** reduced by half; **être de moitié dans une entreprise** to have a half share in a business; **partager les frais moitié-moitié** to share the cost fifty-fifty

monde *nm (univers, milieu)* world; **ce produit est disponible dans le monde entier** this product is available worldwide *or* all over the world ❑ *le monde des affaires* the business world *or* community; *le monde de la haute finance* the world of high finance, the financial world; *le monde de la publicité* the advertising world, the world of advertising

mondial, -e *adj (cours, prix, production)* world, worldwide; *(commerce, consommation)* worldwide, global; **à l'échelle mondiale** on a worldwide scale; **leur réseau de distribution mondial est leur atout principal** their worldwide distribution network is their main asset

mondialisation *nf* globalization

mondialiser **1** *vt* to globalize
2 se mondialiser *vpr* to become globalized

monétaire *adj (circulation, politique, système, zone)* monetary; *(marché, masse)* money

monétarisme *nm* ÉCON monetarism

monétariste *adj & nmf* ÉCON monetarist

Monétique® *nf* FIN electronic money, e-money

moniteur *nm* ORDINAT monitor ❑ *moniteur couleur* colour monitor; *moniteur à écran plat* flat screen monitor; *moniteur SVGA* SVGA monitor

monnaie *nf* (**a**) FIN *(argent)* money; *(d'un pays)* currency ❑ *monnaie d'appoint* fractional money; *monnaie d'argent* silver money; *monnaie de banque* bank money, deposit money; *monnaie de compte* money of account; *monnaie courante* legal currency; *monnaie dirigée* managed *or* controlled currency; *monnaie divisionnaire* divisional money; *monnaie électro-*

nique electronic money, e-money; *monnaie étrangère* foreign currency; *monnaie faible* soft currency; *monnaie fiduciaire* paper money, *Am* fiat money; *monnaie flottante* floating currency; *monnaie forte* hard currency; *monnaie légale* legal tender; *monnaie de marchandise* commodity money; *monnaie d'or* gold money; *monnaie de papier* paper money; *monnaie de réserve* reserve currency; *monnaie scripturale* bank money, deposit money; *Fam monnaie de singe* Monopoly money; UE *monnaie unique* single currency; *monnaie verte* green currency

(**b**) *(pièces)* change; **donner la monnaie de 50 francs** to give change for 50 francs *or* a 50-franc note; **faire de la monnaie** to give change ❑ *petite monnaie, menue monnaie* small change

> “
> Le chancelier Kohl a réitéré sa volonté de voir maintenir le calendrier de l'union économique et monétaire, qui prévoit la création d'une **monnaie unique** d'ici 1999.
> ”

> “
> "Les obligations seront remboursées en **monnaie de singe**, car le rouble va continuer à se déprécier", redoute un économiste.
> ”

monnayable *adj* convertible into cash

monnayer *vt (terrains, biens, actif)* to convert into cash

monnayeur *nm* change machine

monopole *nm* monopoly; **avoir le monopole de qch** to have a monopoly on sth; **exercer un monopole sur un secteur** to monopolize a sector ❑ *monopole d'émission* issuing monopoly; *monopole d'État* State monopoly; *monopole d'exploitation* operating monopoly; *monopole de fabrication* manufacturing monopoly; *monopole des prix* price ring; *monopole de vente* sales monopoly

monopoleur, -euse **1** *adj* monopolistic
2 *nm,f* monopolist

monopolisateur, -trice **1** *adj* monopolistic
2 *nm,f* monopolist

monopolisation *nf* monopolization

monopoliser *vt* to monopolize, to have a monopoly on

monopoliste 1 *adj* monopolistic
  2 *nmf* monopolist

monopolistique *adj* monopolistic

monoposte *nm* ORDINAT standalone

monotâche *adj & nm* ORDINAT single-tasking

Monsieur *nm* (*titre*) Mr; (*au début d'une lettre*) Dear Sir

montage *nm* (**a**) ÉCON *montage finan-cier* financial arrangement; **le montage fi-nancier a été difficile** it wasn't easy getting the money together; **le montage financier du projet sera le suivant** money for the project will be provided as follows
  (**b**) (*fabrication*) assembling, assembly

montant *nm* (*somme*) amount, sum; **quel est le montant du chèque/de la facture?** how much is the cheque/invoice for?; **cinq versements d'un montant de 500 francs** five payments of 500 francs (each); **j'ignore le montant de mes dettes** I don't know what my debts amount to □ *montant brut* gross amount; UE *montants compensatoires (monétaires)* subsidies, compensatory amounts; *montant exonéré de TVA* VAT exempt amount; *montant forfaitaire* lump sum; *montant net* net total; *montant pré-visionnel des ventes* forecast sales level; COMPTA *montant à reporter* amount brought forward; *montant du retour net* net return; *montant total* total (amount)

monté, -e *adj* (*équipé*) **être bien monté (en qch)** to be well stocked (with sth)

monte-charge *nm* hoist, *Br* goods lift, *Am* goods elevator

montée *nf* (*des prix, des salaires*) increase, rise (**de** in); **face à la montée en flèche des prix du pétrole** faced with rocketing *or* soaring oil prices

monter 1 *vt* (**a**) (*atelier*) to fit out, to equip; (*machine*) to assemble (**b**) (*entreprise, affaire*) to set up; (*opération financière, campagne publicitaire*) to arrange, to set up
  2 *vi* (*cours, prix*) to rise, to go up, to increase (**de** by); **empêcher les prix de monter** to keep prices down; **faire monter les prix** to raise prices, to send prices up; **les prix mon-tent en flèche** prices are soaring
  3 se monter *vpr* **se monter à** to amount to; **les frais se montent à des milliers de francs** the expenses amount to thousands of francs; **la facture se monte à mille francs** the bill amounts *or* comes to a thousand francs

mops *nmpl* ORDINAT (*abrév* **mégaoctets par seconde**) MBps

morale *nf* ethics □ *morale profession-nelle* business ethics

moratoire FIN **1** *adj* (*paiement*) delayed by agreement
  2 *nm* moratorium; **décréter un moratoire** to declare a moratorium; **le moratoire des loyers** the moratorium on rents

    „
> Le Crédit maritime mutuel (CMM) envisage un projet de **moratoire** de trois ans sur les dettes des pêcheurs bretons en difficulté.

    „
> Un député travailliste, Ian Gibson, lui-même biologiste, a demandé un **moratoire** sur la commercialisation des aliments génétiques.

moratorium *nm* moratorium

mort, -e *adj* (*marché*) dead; (*argent*) lying idle

morte-saison *nf* slack season, off season

mot de passe *nm* ORDINAT password

moteur de recherche *nm* ORDINAT search engine

motif *nm* (**a**) MKTG (*intention*) motive □ *motif d'achat* buying motive (**b**) (*raison*) reason (**de** for); **c'est sa troisième absence sans motif valable** it's the third time that he has been absent without a good reason □ *motif de licenciement* grounds for dis-missal

motion *nf* motion, proposal; **faire une mo-tion** to propose a motion; **adopter une mo-tion** to carry a motion; **appuyer une motion** to second a motion; **présenter une motion** to present *or Br* to table a motion; **ajourner une motion** to defer *or Am* to table a motion; **rejeter une motion** to reject a motion □ *motion de censure* vote of no confidence

motivation *nf* motivation, incentive □ MKTG *motivation d'achat* buying motive; *motivation de consommateur* consumer motivation; *motivation du personnel* staff motivation; *motivation par le profit* profit motive

mouchard électronique *nm* ORDI-NAT cookie

mouvement *nm* (**a**) (*déplacement*) move-ment; (*tendance*) trend □ *mouvement as-censionnel* upward trend; *mouvement de baisse* downward trend; COMPTA *mouve-ment de caisse* cash transaction; FIN

mouvement de capitaux movement or flow of capital; COMPTA **mouvement d'espèces** cash transaction; FIN **mouvement de fonds** movement or flow of capital

(b) *(fluctuation)* fluctuation □ **mouvement boursier** Stock Market fluctuation; BOURSE **mouvement des cours** price fluctuation; **mouvement des devises** currency fluctuation; **mouvement du marché** market fluctuation; **mouvement des prix** change or fluctuation in prices; **mouvement des valeurs** share fluctuation

(c) *(renouvellement)* turnover □ **mouvement du personnel** staff turnover; **mouvement des stocks** stock turnover

(d) *(dans un port, un aéroport)* traffic □ **mouvement des marchandises** goods or freight traffic

(e) *(groupe)* movement □ **mouvement de défense des consommateurs** consumer protection movement; **mouvement syndical** Br trade union or Am labor union movement

moyen¹, -enne *adj* (a) *(prix, salaire, consommation)* average; **de taille moyenne** medium-sized (b) *(ni bon ni mauvais)* average

moyen² *nm* (a) *(façon, possibilité)* means □ **moyens de communication** means of communication; **moyens de paiement** means of payment; **moyens de production** means or method of production; **moyens de transport** means of transport (b) **moyens** *(financiers)* means; **vivre au-dessus de ses moyens** to live beyond one's means □ **moyens financiers** financial means; **moyens liquides** liquid resources; **moyens de trésorerie** financial means

moyennant *prép* (in return) for; **moyennant paiement de 500 francs** on payment of 500 francs; **moyennant finance** for a fee

moyenne *nf* average, mean; **en moyenne** on average; **il gagne en moyenne 100 francs (de) l'heure** on average he earns 100 francs an hour; **établir la moyenne de qch** to average sth □ **moyenne horaire** hourly average; **moyenne mobile** moving average; **moyenne pondérée** weighted average

multifonctions *adj* multipurpose

multilatéral, -e *adj* multilateral

multimédia *adj & nm* multimedia

multimillionnaire *adj & nmf* multimillionaire

multinational, -e 1 *adj* multinational
2 *nf* **multinationale** multinational

> ❝
> Pour convaincre les **multinationales** européennes de lui confier la gestion de leurs communications spécialisées, BT a mis le paquet.
> ❞

multiple *adj* multiple

multiplier *vt* to multiply (**par** by); **notre chiffre d'affaires a été multiplié par deux en cinq ans** our turnover has doubled in five years

multiposte *adj* ORDINAT multi-station

multipropriété *nf* time-share

multirisque *adj (assurance)* all-in, all risk; *(pour un véhicule)* comprehensive

multitâche *adj & nm* ORDINAT multitasking

> ❝
> Un système d'exploitation est dit **multitâche** à partir du moment où il permet de faire fonctionner plusieurs applications simultanément.
> ❞

multitraitement *nm* ORDINAT multiprocessing

multi-utilisateur *adj* ORDINAT multi-user

mûr coupe-feu *nm* ORDINAT firewall

mutation *nf* (a) *(de personnel)* transfer; **demander/obtenir sa mutation** to ask for/be given a transfer (b) DOUANES **mutation d'entrepôt** transfer of bonded goods *(to another bonded warehouse)* (c) JUR change of ownership, transfer

muter *vt (personnel)* to transfer

mutualisme *nm* ASSUR mutual insurance

mutualiste ASSUR 1 *adj (caisse, banque)* mutual
2 *nmf* member of a mutual insurance company

mutualité *nf* ASSUR mutual insurance

mutuel, -elle ASSUR 1 *adj (service, assurance)* mutual
2 *nf* **mutuelle (d'assurance)** mutual insurance company, Br ≃ friendly society, Am ≃ benefit society

> ❝
> Que ce soit du côté des assurances ou des **mutuelles**, le langage est le même : le Plan Veil va entraîner une augmentation des tarifs de l'ordre de 10 à 15%.
> ❞

nantir *vt* FIN, JUR *(créancier)* to give security to, to secure; *(valeurs)* to pledge; **entièrement/partiellement nanti** *(créancier)* fully/partly secured

nantissement *nm* **(a)** *(action)* pledging **(b)** *(gage)* pledge, collateral; **déposer des titres en nantissement** to lodge stock as security; **emprunter sur nantissement** to borrow on security ❑ **nantissement d'actions** lien on shares; BANQUE **nantissement flottant, nantissement général** floating charge

nation *nf* nation ❑ *les Nations Unies* the United Nations

national, -e *adj (produit, dette, fortune, grève)* national; *(marché)* domestic

nationalisation *nf* nationalization

nationalisé, -e *adj* nationalized

nationaliser *vt* to nationalize

nationalité *nf* ADMIN nationality; **prendre la nationalité française** to take French nationality

nature *nf* **(a)** ADMIN **nature du contenu** nature of contents **(b) payer en nature** to pay in kind

navette *nf* shuttle; **faire la navette (entre sa résidence et son travail)** to commute; **il y a une navette entre la gare et l'aéroport** there is a shuttle between the station and the airport

navetteur, -euse *nm,f Belg* commuter

navigateur *nm* ORDINAT browser

navigation *nf* navigation, shipping ❑ *navigation côtière* coastal trade

naviguer *vi* ORDINAT **naviguer sur l'Internet** to surf the Net, to browse the Web

navire *nm* ship ❑ *navire de charge* freighter, cargo ship; *navire de commerce* merchant ship; *navire frigorifique* refrigerated vessel; *navire marchand* merchant ship; *navire mixte* mixed passenger and cargo ship; *navire de passagers* passenger ship; *navire porte-conteneurs* container ship

navire-citerne *nm* tanker

néant *nm* ADMIN none, nil

négatif, -ive *adj (balance, impôt)* negative

négligence *nf* JUR negligence; **par négligence** through negligence ❑ *négligence*

coupable, négligence criminelle criminal negligence; **négligence grave** gross negligence; **négligence professionnelle** professional negligence, malpractice

négoce *nm* **(a)** *(commerce)* trade; **faire le négoce de qch** to trade in sth **(b)** BOURSE *(de titres, d'actions)* dealing

négociabilité *nf* FIN negotiability

négociable *adj* **(a)** *(salaire, prix, conditions d'emploi)* negotiable; **non-négociable** not negotiable, non-negotiable **(b)** FIN *(bon, traite)* negotiable, transferable, trad(e)able; **négociable en banque** bankable; **négociable en Bourse** negotiable on the Stock Exchange

négociant, -e *nm,f* **(a)** *(dans le commerce)* wholesale merchant *or* dealer, wholesaler ❑ *négociant en vins* wine merchant **(b)** BOURSE trader ❑ *négociant courtier* broker dealer

> **"**
>
> Chaque **négociant** dispose d'un certain quota: tant de caisses pour le marché français, tant pour l'exportation.
>
> **"**

négociateur, -trice *nm,f* negotiator

négociation *nf* **(a)** *(de traité, de paix)* negotiation (**sur** on); **entamer des négociations** to enter into negotiations; **rompre des négociations** to break off negotiations; **en négociation** *(conditions)* under negotiation; **nous sommes en négociation avec la direction** we are negotiating *or* we are in negotiation with the management ❑ *négociations (de conventions) collectives* collective bargaining; *négociations commerciales* trade negotiations; *négociations paritaires* joint negotiations

(b) BOURSE *(transaction)* negotiation, transaction; FIN *(d'un effet)* negotiation ❑ *négociations de bloc* block trading; *négociations de Bourse* Stock Exchange transactions; *négociations de change* exchange transactions; *négociation au comptant* cash transaction; *négociations à prime* options trading; *négociations à terme* futures trading

négocier 1 *vt* **(a)** *(traité, paix, salaire, prix)* to negotiate; **modalités/prix à négocier** terms/price negotiable **(b)** BOURSE to trade

2 *vi* (*traiter, discuter*) to negotiate (**avec with**)

3 se négocier *vpr* to be negotiated

Net *nm* ORDINAT **le Net** the Net

net, nette **1** *adj* (**a**) (*bénéfice, valeur, poids*) net; **il reçoit un salaire net de 250 livres par semaine** he nets £250 a week; COMPTA **net après cessions** net of disposals; **net d'impôt** tax-free; **net de tout droit** exempt of *or* free from duty

2 *adv* **cent francs net** a hundred francs net; **cela m'a rapporté 100 francs net** I cleared *or* netted 100 francs, I made a net profit of 100 francs

3 *nm* net; **net à payer** (*sur bulletin de paie*) net pay, net payable □ COMPTA *net commercial* net profit; *net financier* net interest income; (*à payer*) net interest charges

netiquette *nf* ORDINAT (*sur l'Internet*) netiquette

neuf, neuve **1** *adj* (*machine, matériel, locaux*) new; **à l'état neuf** as new

2 *nm* **remettre qch à neuf** (*machine, matériel*) to recondition sth; (*locaux*) to do sth up

NF *nf* (*abrév* **norme française**) = label indicating compliance with official French standards, *Br* ≃ BS, *Am* ≃ US standard

niche *nf* (*market*) niche

niveau *nm* (**a**) (*degré*) level; **l'indice des actions est descendu à son plus bas niveau/est monté à son plus haut niveau** the share index has reached an all-time low/an all-time high; **maintenir les prix à un niveau élevé** to maintain prices at a high level; **les bénéfices ont atteint un niveau record** profits have reached a record level; **ces deux candidats ont un niveau de qualification équivalent** the two candidates have the same level of ability □ ORDINAT *niveau d'accès* (*dans un réseau*) access level; *niveau de cours des actions* stock price level; BOURSE *niveau de dépôt requis* margin requirement; ORDINAT *niveau de sécurité* security level; *niveau de vie* standard of living

(**b**) (*échelon*) level; **c'est au niveau de la distribution qu'il nous faut faire un effort** we need to make an effort at the distribution level

niveler *vt* (*prix, taux, salaires*) to level, to even up; **niveler par le bas** to level down

nivellement *nm* (*des prix, des taux, des salaires*) levelling; **nivellement par le bas** levelling down

N° (*abrév* **numéro**) No.

noir *nm* **acheter au noir** to buy on the black market; **vendre au noir** to sell on the black market; **travailler au noir** to moonlight

nolisement *nm* (*de navire, d'avion*) chartering

noliser *vt* (*navire, avion*) to charter

nom *nm* name; **nom... prénoms...** (*sur formulaire*) surname... first name...; **nom et prénoms** full name; **agir au nom de qn** to act on behalf of sb; **les actions sont à mon nom** the shares are in my name; **le chèque est libellé au nom de M. Dufour** the cheque is made out to M. Dufour; **un nom bien connu dans le monde des affaires** a big name in the business world; **se faire un nom** to make a name for oneself □ *nom du bénéficiaire* name of the payee; ORDINAT *nom de champ* field name; *nom commercial* company name; *nom déposé* registered (trade) name; *nom de famille* surname; MKTG *nom de famille global* blanket family name; ORDINAT *nom de fichier* file name; *nom de jeune fille* maiden name; ORDINAT *nom de l'utilisateur* user name

nombre *nm* number; **nombre à trois chiffres** three-digit number; **un grand nombre de** a large number of, many □ *nombre index* index number

nomenclature *nf* list □ *nomenclature douanière* customs classification

nominal, -e FIN, BOURSE **1** *adj* nominal, par

2 *nm* (*d'une action*) nominal value; (*d'une obligation*) par value

nominatif, -ive **1** *adj* (**a**) (*carte d'adhérent, billet*) non-transferable (**b**) BOURSE (*liste*) nominal; (*titres, actions*) registered

2 *nm* BOURSE **dividende au nominatif** dividend on registered securities

nomination *nf* (*à un poste*) appointment (**à** to); **elle a obtenu** *ou* **reçu sa nomination au poste de directrice** she was appointed (to the post of) manager

nommer *vt* (*à un poste*) to appoint (**à** to); **nommer qn président** to appoint sb chairman *or* president; **il a été nommé à Lille** he was appointed to a post in Lille

non-acceptation *nf* (*de marchandises*) refusal; BANQUE (*d'une lettre de change*) non-acceptance

non-accomplissement *nm* (*d'un contrat*) non-fulfilment

non-autorisé, -e *adj* ORDINAT (*nom de fichier*) illegal

non-connecté, -e *adj* ORDINAT off-line

non-consigné, -e *adj* non-returnable

non-coté, -e *adj* BOURSE unquoted

non-disponibilité *nf* non-availability

non-exécution *nf* *(d'un contrat)* non-fulfilment, non-performance

non-formaté, -e *adj* ORDINAT unformatted

non-garanti, -e *adj* unsecured

non-initialisé, -e *adj* ORDINAT uninitialized

non-lieu *nm* JUR *(d'une affaire)* withdrawal, dismissal; **bénéficier d'un non-lieu** to be discharged through lack of evidence

non-livraison *nf* non-delivery

nonobstant *prép* JUR notwithstanding, in spite of; **nonobstant toute clause contraire** notwithstanding any provision to the contrary

non-paiement *nm* non-payment

non-réception *nf* non-delivery

non-reconduction *nf* ADMIN *(de contrat)* failure to renew

non-récupérable *adj* ORDINAT non-recoverable

non-résident, -e *adj* non-resident, non-domiciled

non-responsabilité *nf* JUR non-liability

non-salarié, -e 1 *adj* self-employed **2** *nm,f* self-employed person

non-syndiqué, -e 1 *adj* non-union **2** *nm,f* non-union worker

non-valeur *nf* **(a)** *(créance)* bad debt; BOURSE worthless security **(b)** JUR *(caractère improductif)* unproductiveness

non-vente *nf* no sale

non-vérifié, -e *adj* COMPTA unaudited

normal, -e 1 *adj* **(a)** *(dans la norme)* normal **(b)** *(moyen)* standard **2** *nf* **normale** standard; **au-dessus/au-dessous de la normale** above/below standard

normalisation *nf* *(de produits, de procédures)* standardization

normaliser *vt* *(produits, procédures)* to standardize

norme *nf* norm, standard □ **norme d'application** relevant standard; **normes d'application obligatoires** compulsory standards; **normes européennes** European standards; **normes financières** financial standards; **norme française** French standard, *Br* ≃ British standard, *Am* ≃ US standard; **norme de prix de revient** cost standard; **norme de production** production norm; **norme de** productivité productivity norm; **normes publicitaires** advertising standards; **normes de sécurité** safety standards; **norme technique** technical standard; **norme de travail** work standard

notaire *nm* JUR notary (public); **dressé par-devant notaire** drawn up before a notary

notarial, -e *adj* JUR notarial

notarié, -e *adj* JUR legally drawn up

notation *nf* **(a)** *(évaluation)* rating □ **notation du personnel** personnel rating, merit rating **(b)** BOURSE rating □ **notation AAA** triple-A rating

❝

Il a déploré les systèmes de **notation** des salariés en fonction de leurs résultats et la concurrence entre les services, les jugeant contraires à un esprit de collaboration.

❞

note *nf* **(a)** *(facture)* bill; *(dans un hôtel)* *Br* bill, *Am* check; **régler** *ou* **payer une note** to pay a bill □ **note de frais** expense account; *(présentée après coup)* expenses; **mettre qch sur sa note de frais** to put sth on one's expense account; **note de rappel** reminder; **note de téléphone** phone bill **(b)** *(communication écrite)* note, memo; **prendre qch en note** to note sth down □ **note d'avis** advice note; **note d'avoir** credit note; FIN **note de commission** commission note, fee note; **note de couverture** cover note; **note de crédit** credit note; **note de débit** debit note; DOUANES **note de détail** details, description *(of parcel)*; **note d'information** memo; **note de poids** weight note; **note de service** memo **(c)** *(annotation)* note □ **note explicative** explanatory note; **note marginale** marginal note **(d)** ORDINAT **note de fin de document** end note

noté, -e *adj* BOURSE rated; **noté AAA** triple-A rated

notebook *nm* ORDINAT notebook

noter *vt* **(a)** *(écrire)* to note down, to make a note of **(b)** *(évaluer)* to rate, to evaluate; **c'est l'employé le mieux noté du service** he's the highest-rated employee in the department

notice *nf* *(mode d'emploi)* instructions □ **notice explicative** directions for use; BOURSE **notice d'information** information prospectus; **notice publicitaire** advertising brochure; *(dans un journal)* advertisement; **notice technique** technical instructions, technical handbook

notificatif, -ive *adj* notifying

notification *nf* notification, notice; **donner à qn notification de qch** to notify sb of sth, to give sb notification of sth; **recevoir notification de qch** to be notified of sth

notifier *vt* **notifier qch à qn** to notify sb of sth; **veuillez notifier par écrit** please inform us in writing

notoriété *nf* MKTG **notoriété de la marque** brand awareness; **notoriété publicitaire** advertising awareness

nouveau, -elle *adj* new; **créer de nouveaux débouchés au commerce** to open up new channels for trade; **jusqu'à nouvel ordre** until further notice; BOURSE until cancelled; **pour une nouvelle période de trois mois** for a further three months □ *nouveaux emprunts* new borrowings; ÉCON *nouveau pays industrialisé* newly industrialized country

nouveauté *nf* new product, innovation; **il est allé voir les nouveautés au salon de l'informatique** he went to see the latest innovations at the computing fair

nouvelle *nf* piece of news; **nouvelles** news

novation *nf* JUR novation, substitution □ *novation de créance* substitution of debt

nover *vt* JUR to novate, to substitute

noyau *nm* (a) ORDINAT node (b) BOURSE *noyau dur* = group of stable shareholders chosen for a company by the government on its flotation

NPI *nmpl* (*abrév* **nouveaux pays industrialisés**) newly industrialized countries, NIC

nue-propriété *nf* JUR bare ownership

nuit *nf* night; **être de nuit** to be on night shift, to work nights

nul, nulle *adj* JUR **nul et de nul effet, nul et non avenu** null and void; **considérer une lettre comme nulle et non avenue** to consider a letter cancelled; **rendre qch nul** to invalidate sth, to render sth void

nullité *nf* JUR invalidity, nullity; **frapper qch de nullité** to invalidate sth, to render sth null and void

numéraire 1 *adj* **espèces numéraires** legal tender
2 *nm* cash; **payer en numéraire** to pay in cash □ *numéraire fictif* paper currency

numérique *adj* (a) (*analyse, valeur, liste*) numerical (b) ORDINAT (*calculateur, ordinateur*) digital; (*données, pavé*) numerical

numériquement *adv* (a) (*en nombres*) numerically (b) ORDINAT digitally

numérisation *nf* ORDINAT digitization

numériser *vt* ORDINAT to digitize

numériseur *nm* ORDINAT digitizer □ *numériseur d'image* image digitizer

numéro *nm* (a) (*chiffre*) number; **le numéro un du verre** the number one company in the glass industry □ *numéro de chèque* cheque number; *numéro de commande* order number; BANQUE *numéro de compte* account number; *numéro d'enregistrement* booking number; *numéro de fabrication* serial number; *numéro d'immatriculation* registration number; ORDINAT *numéro IP* IP number; *numéro de lot* batch number; *numéro de nomenclature* catalogue number, inventory number; *numéro d'ordre* serial number; *numéro de référence* reference number; *numéro de série* serial number
(b) TÉL number; **composer** *ou* **faire un numéro** to dial a number □ *numéro azur* = special telephone number for which users are charged at the local rate irrespective of the actual distance of the call; *numéro de fax* fax number; *numéro de poste* extension number; *numéro de téléphone* telephone number; *numéro d'urgence* hot-line, emergency number; *numéro vert* *Br* ≃ Freefone® number, 0800 number, *Am* ≃ 800 number, toll-free number
(c) (*d'un journal, d'une magazine*) issue

numérotation *nf* (a) (*attribution d'un numéro*) numbering □ ORDINAT *numérotation alphanumérique* alphanumeric numbering (b) TÉL dialling □ *numérotation abrégée* speed dial

numéroter *vt* to number

nu-propriétaire *nmf* JUR bare owner

obérer *vt (entreprise, pays)* to burden with debt; **la facture pétrolière obère le budget de l'État** the oil bill is a burden on the country's budget

objectif *nm* objective, goal, aim □ *objectif global* overall objective; *objectif lointain* long-term objective; *objectif de production* production target; *objectif de profit* profit target; *objectif de vente* sales target

objet *nm* **(a)** *(objectif)* object, aim; **la société a pour objet de...** the aim of the company is to...
(b) *(dans une lettre)* **objet: confirmation de commande** re: confirmation of order
(c) *(sujet)* *(d'une dispute, d'une discussion)* subject; *(d'un contrat)* purpose; **cette société fait l'objet d'une liquidation** this company is currently in liquidation
(d) *(article)* article □ *objet de luxe* luxury item *or* article; *objet de valeur* valuable, article of value
(e) ORDINAT object

obligataire FIN **1** *adj (créancier, émission, intérêts, marché)* bond; *(dette, emprunt)* debenture
2 *nmf* bondholder, debenture holder

obligation *nf* **(a)** FIN *(titre)* bond, debenture □ *obligation amortissable* redeemable bond; *obligation à bon de souscription d'actions* bond with share warrant attached; *obligation cautionnée* guaranteed bond; *obligation chirographaire* simple debenture; *obligations convertibles* convertible bonds, convertibles; *obligation d'État* government bond, Treasury bond; *obligation garantie* guaranteed bond; *obligation hypothécaire* mortgage bond; *obligation indemnitaire* indemnity bond; *obligation indexée* indexed *or* index-linked bond; *obligation à intérêt variable* floating-rate bond; *obligations longues* long-dated securities, longs; *obligation à lots* prize bond, *Br* ≃ premium bond; *obligation nominative* registered bond; *obligation or* gold bond; *obligation au porteur* bearer bond; *obligation de premier ordre* prime bond; *obligation remboursable* redeemable bond; *obligations remboursables en actions* redeemable bonds; *obligation à revenu fixe* fixed-rate bond; *obligation à revenu variable* variable-income bond, floating-rate bond; *obligation de société* corporate bond

(b) *(engagement)* obligation, binding agreement; **contracter une obligation (envers qn)** to enter into a binding agreement (with sb); **honorer ses obligations** to honour *or* meet one's obligations; **avoir des obligations financières** to have financial obligations □ *obligation contractuelle* privity of contract; *obligation d'information* disclosure

> 〞
> Non seulement les **obligations convertibles** permettent de profiter de la hausse de la Bourse mais elles offrent en outre la sécurité d'une obligation classique.
> 〞

obligatoire *adj* compulsory, obligatory; JUR *(ayant force)* binding

obligé, -e **1** *adj (reconnaissant)* grateful, obliged; **nous vous serions obligés de bien vouloir nous régler dans les meilleurs délais** we would be grateful *or* obliged if you would send us payment as soon as possible
2 *nm,f* **(a)** JUR obligee **(b)** FIN obliger *(guaranteeing a bill)*

OBSA *nf* FIN *(abrév* **obligation à bon de souscription d'actions**) bond with share warrant attached

obsolescence *nf* obsolescence; **le taux d'obsolescence des ordinateurs est très élevé** the obsolescence rate of computers is very high, computers very quickly become obsolescent □ *obsolescence calculée, obsolescence planifiée, obsolescence prévue* built-in *or* planned obsolescence

obsolescent, -e *adj* obsolescent

obtenir *vt (augmentation de salaire, avancement, contrat, délai, poste)* to get; *(prêt)* to get, to secure; *(accord)* to reach; **où peut-on obtenir ce produit?** where can you get this product?; **l'entreprise a obtenu d'excellents résultats l'année dernière** the company achieved excellent results last year; **les salariés ont réussi à obtenir de meilleures conditions de travail** the staff succeeded in obtaining better working conditions; **obtenir sa mutation** to be given a transfer

occasion *nf* **(a)** *(bonne affaire)* bargain **(b)** *(article de seconde main)* second-hand item; **acheter qch d'occasion** to buy sth second-hand

occasionnel, -elle *adj (travail, ouvrier)* casual; *(clientèle)* occasional

occulte *adj* secret

occupant, -e 1 *adj* occupying
2 *nm,f* occupier, occupant ❑ JUR **premier occupant** occupant

occupation *nf (d'un lieu)* occupancy; **grève avec occupation des locaux** sit-in (strike)

occupé, -e *adj (ligne téléphonique)* Br engaged, Am busy

occuper 1 *vt (détenir) (poste, fonction)* to have, to hold; **occuper un poste important** to hold an important post; **cette entreprise occupe une position enviable sur la marché** this company has an enviable market position
(b) *(employer)* to employ; **occuper vingt ouvriers** to employ twenty workmen
(c) *(lieu)* to occupy, **occuper des locaux/une usine** *(lors d'une grève)* to occupy premises/a factory
2 s'occuper *vpr* **s'occuper de** to take care of; *(avoir pour responsabilité)* to be in charge of; **est-ce qu'on s'occupe de vous?** *(dans un magasin)* are you being attended to?; **c'est lui qui s'occupe de la comptabilité de l'entreprise** he is in charge of the company's accounts

OCDE *nf (abrév* **Organisation de coopération et de développement économique)** OECD

octal, -e *adj* ORDINAT octal

octet *nm* ORDINAT (eight-bit) byte

octroi *nm (de crédits, de subventions, d'un délai supplémentaire, d'un prêt)* granting

octroyer *vt (crédits, subventions, délai supplémentaire, prêt)* to grant (**à** to)

offert, -e *adj* offered

office *nm* **(a)** *(poste)* office, post; **faire office de secrétaire** to act as secretary
(b) *(organisation)* agency ❑ **office de publicité** advertising agency; **office de régularisation de vente** marketing board; **office du tourisme** tourist board
(c) **d'office** ex officio; **être nommé d'office** to be automatically appointed; **être mis à la retraite d'office** to be automatically retired

officiel, -elle 1 *adj* official; **à titre officiel** officially, formally
2 *nm,f* official

officiellement *adv* officially

officieusement *adv* unofficially, off the record

officieux, -euse *adj* unofficial; **à titre officieux** unofficially

off-line *adj* ORDINAT off-line

offrant, -e *nm,f (à une vente aux enchères)* **le plus offrant (et dernier enchérisseur)** the highest bidder; **vendre au plus offrant** to sell to the highest bidder

offre *nf* **(a)** *(proposition)* offer, proposal; **recevoir/accepter une offre** to receive/accept an offer ❑ **offre d'emploi** job offer, offer of employment; **offres d'emploi** *(dans un journal)* situations vacant; FIN **offre publique d'achat** takeover bid; **faire** *ou* **lancer une offre publique d'achat (sur)** to make *or* launch a takeover bid (for); **offre publique d'échange** exchange offer, takeover bid for shares; **offre publique de vente** offer by prospectus
(b) MKTG offer; **cette offre est valable jusqu'au 30 juin** this offer is valid until 30 June ❑ **offre de base** basic offer; **offre de bon de réduction** coupon offer; **offre d'échantillon gratuit** sampling offer; **offre d'essai** trial offer; **offre de lancement** introductory offer; **offre à prix réduit** reduced-priced offer; **offre promotionnelle** promotional offer; **offre spéciale** special offer
(c) ÉCON supply; **l'offre et la demande** supply and demand; **lorsque l'offre excède la demande, les prix ont tendance à baisser** when supply exceeds demand, prices have a tendency to fall
(d) *(à une vente aux enchères)* bid
(e) *(dans un appel d'offres)* tender, bid

> **"**
> A quatre jours de la clôture des souscriptions, **l'offre publique de vente** des actions de la BNP s'annonce comme un grand succès populaire.
> **"**

offrir *vt* **(a)** *(proposer)* to offer; **offrir ses services** to offer one's services; **offrir un emploi à qn** to offer sb a job; **offrir sa démission (à qn)** to tender *or* offer one's resignation (to sb)
(b) *(présenter)* to offer; **combien m'en offrez-vous?** how much will you offer *or* give me for it?; **offrir des marchandises à la vente** to offer goods for sale; **enchérir sur les prix offerts** to improve on the prices offered; **être offert à...** to be on offer at...; **ce genre d'investissement n'offre aucune garantie** this kind of investment offers no guarantee whatsoever; **ce placement offre un meilleur**

rendement this investment gives *or* offers a better return

offshore *adj* offshore

oisif, -ive *adj (capital)* uninvested, idle

OIT *nf (abrév* **Organisation internationale du travail)** ILO

oligopole *nm* ÉCON oligopoly

OMC *nf (abrév* **Organisation mondiale du commerce)** WTO

omission *nf* **sauf erreur ou omission** errors and omissions excepted; **sauf erreur ou omission de notre part, notre facture du 16 janvier reste impayée à ce jour** unless we are mistaken, our invoice of 16 January remains unpaid

omnium *nm* ÉCON combine

onduleur *nm* ORDINAT UPS

onéreux, -euse *adj* costly, expensive; JUR **à titre onéreux** subject to payment, for a consideration

ONG *nf (abrév* **organisation non gouvernementale)** NGO

on-shore *adj* onshore

ONU *nf (abrév* **Organisation des nations unies)** UNO

OP *nm (abrév* **ouvrier professionnel)** skilled worker

OPA *nf* FIN *(abrév* **offre publique d'achat)** takeover bid; **lancer une OPA (sur)** to make *or* launch a takeover bid (for) □ *OPA amicale* friendly takeover bid; *OPA hostile, OPA inamicale, OPA sauvage* hostile takeover bid

OPCVM *nm* BOURSE *(abrév* **organisme de placement collectif en valeurs mobilières)** *Br* unit trust, *Am* mutual fund □ *OPCVM actions* equity-based *Br* unit trust *or Am* mutual fund

OPE *nf* FIN *(abrév* **offre publique d'échange)** exchange offer, takeover bid for shares

opéable *adj* vulnerable to takeover bids

open-market *nm* open market

OPEP *nf (abrév* **Organisation des pays exportateurs de pétrole)** OPEC

opérateur, -trice **1** *nm,f* **(a)** FIN trader; BOURSE operator, dealer □ *opérateur à la baisse* operator for a fall, bear; *opérateur boursier* Stock Exchange dealer; *opérateur à la hausse* operator for a rise, bull **(b)** TÉL operator **(c)** ORDINAT *opérateur de saisie* keyboard operator, keyboarder **2** *nm* ORDINAT operator

---

❝

Le syndicat accuse Bell Atlantic, premier **opérateur** régional aux États-Unis, de délocaliser peu à peu les emplois dans des filiales non syndiquées où les gens sont moins payés et plus "flexibles".

❞

---

opération *nf* **(a)** BANQUE, FIN *(transaction)* transaction, deal, operation □ *opération blanche* break-even transaction; COMPTA *opération de caisse* counter transaction; COMPTA *opération en capital* capital transaction; *opération de clearing* clearing transaction; *opération en commun* joint venture; *opération comptable* accounting operation; *opération au comptant* cash transaction; COMPTA *opérations courantes* normal business transactions; *opération d'escompte* discount operation; *opération de face à face* back-to-back loan; *opération financière* financial transaction; *opération imposable* taxable transaction; *opération de prêt* loan transaction

(b) BOURSE transaction, deal □ *opération à la baisse* bear transaction; *opération de Bourse* Stock Exchange transaction; *opération de change* exchange transaction, swap; *opération de change à terme* forward exchange transaction; *opérations de clôture* late trading, trading at the finish; *opération au comptant* spot deal *or* transaction; *opération de couverture* hedging; *opération à découvert* short position; *opération à la hausse* bull transaction; *opération de journée* day trade; *opérations à option* option dealing *or* trading; *opération à terme* futures transaction

(c) ORDINAT operation

(d) *(activité)* operation; **le procédé comporte trois opérations** the process involves three operations □ *opération commerciale* business *or* commercial operation

(e) *(campagne)* operation, campaign □ *opération escargot (grève)* go-slow (strike); *opération publicitaire* advertising campaign

---

❝

Il résoud leur problème de capital par des architectures et des **opérations financières** audacieuses qui ne se soucient guère de transparence, ni des actionnaires minoritaires.

❞

---

opérationnel, -elle *adj* **(a)** *(coûts, efficacité)* operational **(b)** *(en service)* operational; **ce système sera opérationnel en**

2008 this system will be operational *or* will be in operation in 2008

opérer 1 *vt* (*virement, paiement*) to make, to effect; (*changement*) to carry out, to implement; **opérer une restructuration au sein d'une entreprise** to restructure a company; **le pays tente d'opérer un redressement économique** the country is attempting to bring about an economic recovery

2 *vi* BOURSE **opérer à découvert** to take a short position, to go short

3 s'opérer *vpr* (*changement, transformation*) to take place

opinion *nf* opinion (**de/sur** of/about) ▫ *opinion publique* public opinion

opposition *nf* **faire opposition à un chèque, faire opposition au paiement d'un chèque** to stop (payment of) a cheque

optimal, -e *adj* optimum, optimal

optimalisation *nf* optimization ▫ *optimalisation du profit* ou *des profits* profit optimization

optimaliser *vt* to optimize

optimisation *nf* optimization ▫ *optimisation du* ou *des profits* profit optimization

optimiser *vt* to optimize

> " Et pour **optimiser** la rentabilité de son investissement, on peut gonfler le déficit en recourant à l'emprunt pour financer l'immobilier et même les meubles. "

optimiseur *nm* ORDINAT optimizer

optimum 1 *adj* optimum, optimal
2 *nm* optimum

option *nf* (**a**) BOURSE option; **lever une option** to take up an option ▫ *option d'achat* call option, option to buy; *option sur actions* option on shares; *option américaine* American-style option; *option à l'argent* at-the-money option; *option de change* foreign currency option; *option cotée* traded option; *option au cours* at-the-money option; *option en dedans* in-the-money option; *option en dehors* out-of-the-money option; *option du double* call of more; *option européenne* European-style option; *option sur indice* index option; *option à la monnaie* at-the-money option; *option négociable* traded option; *option de titres* stock option; *option de vente* put option, option to sell

(**b**) (*choix*) option; **prendre une option sur qch** to have the option of purchase on sth

▫ *option d'achat* option to buy; *option de vente* option to sell

(**c**) (*accessoire*) optional extra; **le fax est en option sur ce portable** a fax is an optional extra with this laptop

(**d**) ORDINAT option ▫ *option d'impression* print option; *option de menu* menu option; *option de sauvegarde* save option

optionnel, -elle *adj* optional

optique *nf* outlook ▫ MKTG *optique marketing, optique mercatique* marketing orientation; *optique produit* product orientation; *optique publicitaire* advertising approach; *optique vente* sales orientation, sales philosophy

OPV *nf* FIN (*abrév* **offre publique de vente**) offer by prospectus

or *nm* gold ▫ *or en barre* gold bars, gold bullion; *Fam* **ces actions, c'est de l'or en barre** these shares are a rock-solid investment; *or monnayé* gold coins

ORA *nfpl* (*abrév* **obligations remboursables en actions**) redeemable bonds

ordinateur *nm* computer; **mettre qch sur ordinateur** to put sth on computer, to computerize sth ▫ *ordinateur autonome* stand-alone (computer); *ordinateur bloc-notes* notebook (computer); *ordinateur de bureau* business computer, desktop (computer); *ordinateur central* mainframe (computer); *ordinateur à écran tactile* touch-screen computer; *ordinateur de gestion* business computer; *ordinateur individuel* personal computer; *ordinateur de poche* palmtop (computer); *ordinateur portable* laptop (computer)

ordonnance *nf* JUR order, ruling ▫ *ordonnance de mise sous séquestre* receiving order; FIN *ordonnance de paiement* order or warrant for payment, order to pay; *ordonnance de saisie* writ of execution; *ordonnance de saisie-arrêt* garnishee order

ordonnancement *nm* (**a**) (*de production, de commandes*) scheduling, sequencing (**b**) FIN order to pay

ordonnancer *vt* (**a**) (*production, commandes*) to schedule, to sequence (**b**) FIN (*paiement*) to authorize, to order; (*compte*) to initial, to pass for payment; (*dépense*) to sanction

ordonnateur, -trice *nm,f* ADMIN = official in charge of public expenditure and authorization of payment

ordre *nm* (**a**) (*classement*) order; **il faut traiter les affaires par ordre de priorité** the items must be dealt with in order of priority

❑ *ordre alphabétique* alphabetical order; *ordre de date* order of date; *ordre hiérarchique* hierarchical order; *ordre du jour* (*d'une réunion*) agenda; **inscrire qch à l'ordre du jour** to add sth to the agenda; JUR *ordre utile* ranking (of creditor)

(**b**) (*catégorie*) class, category; **de premier ordre** first-class, first-rate; **la hausse de l'inflation sera de l'ordre de 5%** the rise in inflation will be in the region of 5%

(**c**) BANQUE, BOURSE order; **exécuter un ordre** to fill an order; **payez à l'ordre de J. Martin** pay to the order of J. Martin; **libeller** *ou* **faire un chèque à l'ordre de qn** to make a cheque payable to sb, to make out a cheque to sb; **c'est à quel ordre?** who should I make it out to?, who should I make it payable to?; **non à ordre** (*sur chèque*) not negotiable ❑ *ordre d'achat* purchase order; BOURSE buy order; BOURSE *ordre de Bourse* Stock Exchange order; FIN *ordre au comptant* cash order; BOURSE *ordre conditionnel* contingent order; BOURSE *ordre environ* discretionary order; *ordre limite, ordre limité* limit order; BOURSE *ordre de négociation* trading order; FIN *ordre de paiement* payment order; BANQUE *ordre permanent* standing order; BANQUE *ordre de prélèvement (permanent)* direct debit; BOURSE *ordre à révocation* good-till-cancelled order; BOURSE *ordre stop* stop order, stop loss order; BOURSE *ordre à terme* futures order; BOURSE *ordre "tout ou rien"* all-or-none order; BANQUE *ordre de transfert permanent* banker's order, standing order; BOURSE *ordre de vente* order to sell; BOURSE *ordre de vente stop* stop-loss selling; FIN *ordre de virement* transfer order; BANQUE *ordre de virement automatique* banker's order, standing order

organe *nm* ADMIN *organe distributeur* distributing agency; *organe de publicité* advertising agency

organigramme *nm* organization chart, organigram; ORDINAT (data) flow chart, flow diagram ❑ *organigramme de production* production flow chart

organisateur, -trice 1 *adj* organizing

2 *nm,f* organizer ❑ *organisateur de conférences* conference organizer; *organisateur de voyages* tour operator

organisateur-conseil *nm* time and motion consultant

organisation *nf* (**a**) (*groupement*) organization ❑ *organisation à but lucratif* profit-making organization; *organisation à* *but non lucratif* Br non-profit-making organization, Am not-for-profit organization; *Organisation de coopération et de développement économique* Organization for Economic Cooperation and Development; *Organisation internationale de normalisation* International Standards Organization; *Organisation internationale du travail* International Labour Organization; *Organisation mondiale du commerce* World Trade Organization; *Organisation des nations unies* United Nations Organization; *organisation non gouvernementale* non-governmental organization; *organisation patronale* employers' organization; *Organisation des pays exportateurs de pétrole* Organization of Petroleum Exporting Countries; *organisation politique* political organization; *organisation syndicale* Br trade-union *or* Am labor-union organization

(**b**) (*façon de s'organiser*) organization ❑ ORDINAT *organisation des données* data organization; *organisation fonctionnelle* functional organization; *organisation hiérarchique* line organization; *organisation horizontale* staff organization; *organisation mixte* line and staff organization; *organisation de la production* production engineering; *organisation scientifique du travail* organization and methods; *organisation verticale* line organization

organisé, -e *adj* organized

organiser 1 *vt* (*réunion, voyage d'affaires*) to organize

2 **s'organiser** *vpr* to organize (oneself), to get organized; **la main-d'œuvre s'est organisée en syndicat** the workforce has organized itself into a Br trade union *or* Am labor union

organisme *nm* (*organisation*) organization, body ❑ *organisme de crédit* credit organization; *organisme de défense des consommateurs* consumer organization; *organisme international* international organization; *organisme de placement* investment fund; *organisme de placement collectif en valeurs mobilières* Br unit trust, Am mutual fund; *organisme professionnel* professional body

orientation *nf* (**a**) (*tendance*) trend ❑ *orientation du marché* market trend; *orientation du marché à la baisse* downward market trend; *orientation du marché à la hausse* upward market trend (**b**) (*conseil*) *orientation professionnelle* vocational *or* careers guidance

orienté, -e *adj* (**a**) BOURSE **orienté à la baisse** bearish; **orienté à la hausse** bullish (**b**) *(économie, entreprise)* orientated; **une économie orientée vers les exportations** an export-orientated economy (**c**) ORDINAT **orienté ligne** line-orientated; **orienté objet** object-orientated

original, -e 1 *adj* original

2 *nm (d'un document, d'une facture)* original *(d'un fichier, d'une disquette)* master copy; **copier qch sur l'original** to copy sth from the original

origine *nf (d'un produit)* origin

OS *nm (abrév* **ouvrier spécialisé**) semi-skilled worker

oscillant, -e *adj* FIN fluctuating

oscillation *nf* FIN fluctuation, variation; **les oscillations du marché** the fluctuations of the market, the ups and downs of the market □ *oscillations saisonnières* seasonal fluctuations

osciller *vi* FIN to fluctuate

oseille *nf Fam (argent)* cash, *Br* dosh, *Am* bucks

OST *nf (abrév* **organisation scientifique du travail**) organization and methods, O & M

outil *nm* tool □ *outil d'aide à la décision* decision-making tool; *outil de gestion* management tool; ORDINAT *outil de navigation sur le Web* Web browser; *outil de production* production tool; *outil de spéculation* trading instrument; *outil de travail* tool

outillage *nm (d'une usine)* plant, equipment, machinery

outre-mer *adv* overseas

ouvert, -e *adj* open; **les bureaux sont ouverts de dix heures à cinq heures** the offices are open from ten to five

ouverture *nf* (**a**) *(d'un magasin, d'une entreprise, des frontières)* opening (up); *(d'un compte, d'un crédit, des négociations)* opening; **l'ouverture de nouveaux débouchés** the opening up of new markets □ ORDINAT *ouverture de session* log-on

(**b**) MKTG window of opportunity

(**c**) BOURSE start of trading; **à l'ouverture, le dollar était à 5,98 francs** at the start of trading, the dollar was at 5.98 francs

ouvrage *nm* (**a**) *(travail)* work (**b**) *(œuvre)* piece of work, product

ouvrier, -ère 1 *adj* working

2 *nm,f* worker □ *ouvrier hautement qualifié* highly-skilled worker; *ouvrier à la journée* day labourer; *ouvrier aux pièces* pieceworker; *ouvrier professionnel* skilled worker; *ouvrier qualifié* skilled worker; *ouvrier spécialisé* semi-skilled worker; *ouvrier syndiqué* worker belonging to a union

ouvrir 1 *vt* (**a**) *(magasin, entreprise, frontières)* to open (up); *(compte, crédit, négociations)* to open; **ouvrir un nouveau débouché à un produit** to open up a new market for a product

(**b**) ORDINAT *(fichier, répertoire)* to open; **ouvrir une session** to log on

2 *vi* (**a**) *(magasin, entreprise)* to open; **nous ouvrons tous les jours à huit heures** we open every day at eight (o'clock); **les banques n'ouvrent pas les jours de fête** the banks do not open on public holidays

(**b**) BOURSE to open; **ouvrir en baisse/en hausse** to open down/up; **les valeurs pétrolières ont ouvert ferme** oils opened firm

3 s'ouvrir *vpr* to open up; **leur pays s'ouvre peu à peu au commerce extérieur** their country is gradually opening up to foreign trade

PAC *nf* UE *(abrév* **politique agricole commune)** CAP

package *nm* ORDINAT package

pacson *nm Fam* **toucher le pacson** *(dans une affaire)* to make a bundle

pacte *nm* agreement □ *le pacte pour l'emploi* = job creation scheme for young people; JUR *pacte de paiement* pay agreement; *pacte de préférence* preference scheme

PAG *nf* DOUANES *(abrév* **procédure accélérée générale de dédouanement)** accelerated customs clearance procedure

page *nf* (a) *(feuille)* page □ *page de garde (d'un fax)* cover(ing) sheet; TÉL *les pages jaunes* the Yellow Pages® (b) ORDINAT page □ *page d'accueil* home page; *page précédente* page up; *page suivante* page down; *page Web* Web page (c) *page de publicité* commercial break

page-écran *nf* ORDINAT screen page

paie *nf* pay, wages; **toucher sa paie** to draw one's wages, to get paid

paiement *nm* payment; *(d'un compte)* payment, settlement; **effectuer** *ou* **faire un paiement** to make a payment; **recevoir un paiement** to receive a payment; **contre paiement de 100 francs** on payment of 100 francs; **suspendre** *ou* **cesser les paiements** to stop payments □ *paiement par anticipation* payment in advance, advance payment; *paiement arriéré* payment in arrears; *paiement d'avance* payment in advance, advance payment; BANQUE *paiement par carte* card payment, payment by card; *paiement par chèque* payment by cheque; *paiement à la commande* cash with order; *paiement (au) comptant* cash payment, payment in cash; *paiement différé* deferred payment; *paiement contre documents* payment against documents; *paiement échelonné* staggered payment; *paiement électronique* electronic payment, payment by electronic transfer; *paiement en espèces* payment in cash, cash payment; *paiement intégral* payment in full; *paiement par intervention* payment on behalf of a third party; *paiement libératoire* payment in full discharge from debt; *paiement en liquide* payment in cash, cash payment; *paiement à la livraison* cash on delivery, COD; *paiement en nature* payment in kind; *paiement partiel* partial *or* part payment; *paiements périodiques* periodic payments; *paiement préalable* prepayment; *paiement progressif* graduated *or* increasing payments; *paiement au prorata* payment pro rata; *paiement en souffrance* overdue *or* outstanding payment; *paiement à tempérament* payment by *or* in instalments; *paiement à terme* payment by *or* in instalments; *paiement par versements échelonnés* staggered payment

pair *nm* FIN par; **au-dessous/au-dessus du pair** below/above par; **au pair** at par □ *pair du change* par of exchange; *pair commercial* par

palette *nf* (a) ORDINAT palette □ *palette graphique* graphics palette; *palette d'outils* tool palette (b) *(pour la manutention)* pallet

palette-avion *nf* air-freight pallet

palettisation *nf* palletization

palettiser *vt* to palletize

palier *nm* stage, level; **l'inflation a atteint un nouveau palier** inflation has reached a new level; **taxes imposées par paliers** graduated taxation

panel *nm* MKTG panel □ *panel de consommateurs* consumer panel, shopping panel; *panel de détaillants* retail panel; *panel de distributeurs* distributor panel; *panel d'essayeurs de produits* product testing panel; *panel de téléspectateurs* television viewing panel

panier *nm* (a) ÉCON **le panier de la ménagère** the shopping basket; **avec des conséquences sur le panier de la ménagère** with consequences for the food bill (b) MKTG dump bin □ *panier de présentation en vrac, panier présentoir* dump bin; *panier à la sortie* checkout display (stand); *panier vrac* dump bin (c) ÉCON *panier de devises, panier de monnaies* basket of currencies (d) BOURSE *(d'actions)* basket

panne *nf* (a) *(de machine)* breakdown; **tomber en panne** to break down (b) ORDINAT failure, crash □ *panne logicielle* software failure; *panne matérielle* hardware crash; *panne du système* system crash

panneau *nm* board □ *panneau d'affichage* Br notice board, Am bulletin board;

ORDINAT bulletin board; *panneau publici-taire Br* hoarding, *Am* billboard

PAO *nf* ORDINAT (*abrév* **publication assis-tée par ordinateur**) DTP

paperasserie *nf* (a) *(documents)* papers, paperwork (b) *(d'un système bureaucratique)* red tape

papeterie *nf (produits)* stationery

papier *nm* (a) *(matière)* paper □ *papier à en-tête* headed notepaper; *papier à let-tres* writing paper, notepaper; *papier libre* plain paper; *papier machine, papier pour machine à écrire* typing paper

(b) *(document)* document, paper □ *papiers de bord* ship's papers; *papiers d'expédi-tion* clearance papers; *papiers d'identité* identity papers; *papier libre* = official paper on which stamp duty has not been paid; *papier timbré* = official paper on which stamp duty has been paid

(c) FIN bill; **papiers à trois mois (d'échéance)** bills at three months □ *papier bancable* bankable paper; *papier non bancable* un-bankable paper; *papier de commerce, pa-pier commercial* commercial *or* trade paper; *papier sur l'étranger* foreign bill; *papier fait* guaranteed paper, backed bill; *papier négociable* negotiable paper; *pa-pier à ordre* instrument to order; *papier au porteur* bearer paper; *papiers valeurs* pa-per securities; *papier à vue* sight paper

(d) ORDINAT paper □ *papier à bandes per-forées* perforated paper; *papier continu* continuous paper *or* stationery; *papier couché* coated paper; *papier à étiquettes* sheets of labels; *papier d'impression* prin-ter paper; *papier listing* listing paper; *pa-pier multiple* multi-part stationery; *papier peint* wallpaper

papier-monnaie *nm* paper money, paper currency

paquet *nm* (a) *(à expédier)* parcel, package; **expédier un paquet par la poste** to post a parcel, to send a parcel by post

(b) *(marchandise emballée)* packet, pack □ MKTG *paquet échantillon* sample pack-et; *paquet économique* economy pack; *paquet familial* family-size pack; *paquet géant* giant pack; *paquet individuel* indi-vidual pack; *paquet de présentation* dis-play pack

(c) BOURSE *(d'actions, de valeurs)* parcel, block

(d) ORDINAT packet

paradis fiscal *nm* tax haven

parafe = **paraphe**

parafer = **parapher**

parafiscal, -e *adj* parafiscal

parafiscalité *nf* = taxes paid to the state and used for administrative purposes

paragraphe *nm* (a) *(de lettre)* paragraph (b) *(de contrat)* sub-clause, paragraph

parallèle *adj* (a) *(marché)* unofficial (b) ORDINAT *(imprimante, interface)* parallel

paralyser *vt (pays, industrie, économie)* to paralyse; **la grève des routiers a paralysé le pays pendant plusieurs jours** the *Br* lorry *or Am* truck drivers' strike paralysed the country for several days

paramétrable *adj* ORDINAT configur-able; **paramétrable par l'utilisateur** user-definable

paramétrage *nm* ORDINAT configuration

paramètre *nm* ORDINAT parameter, set-ting; *(du DOS)* switch

paramétrer *vt* ORDINAT to configure

paraphe *nm* ADMIN initials; **mettre son paraphe au bas d'une page** to initial a page

parapher *vt* ADMIN to initial

parc *nm* (a) *(ensemble)* **parc automobile** *(d'un pays)* number of cars on the road; *(d'une entreprise)* fleet (of cars); *parc locatif* rental dwellings; *parc d'ordinateurs* computer population, total number of computers in service (b) *(zone)* park □ *parc d'activités* business park; *parc industriel* industrial park, *Br* industrial estate; *parc technologi-que* technology park

parcage *nm* (a) ORDINAT *(de disque dur)* parking (b) BOURSE *(d'actions)* warehousing

parcourir *vt* ORDINAT *(document)* to scroll through

parité *nf* FIN, BOURSE parity; **à parité** at parity, at the money; **change à (la) parité** exchange at par *or* parity □ *parité du change* exchange rate parity; *parité à crémaillère* sliding peg; *parité fixe* fixed parity; *parité franc-mark* franc-mark parity; *parité des monnaies* monetary parity; *parité du pou-voir d'achat* purchasing power parity; *pa-rité rampante* crawling peg

parquer *vt* ORDINAT *(disque dur)* to park

parquet *nm* BOURSE **le parquet** *(lieu)* the trading floor; *(personnes)* the Stock Exchange

parrain *nm* MKTG promoter, sponsor

parrainage *nm* MKTG sponsoring

parrainer *vt* MKTG to sponsor

part *nf* (a) FIN share, part □ *part d'associa-tion* partnership share; *part bénéficiaire* founder's share; **part de fondateur** founder's share; **part de marché** share of the market, market share; **part patronale** employer's contribution; **part salariale** employee's contribution; **part sociale** share of capital, capital share

(b) **avoir part aux bénéfices** to have a share in the profits, to share in the profits; **mettre qn de part (dans une affaire)** to give sb a share in the profits

(c) **faire part de qch à qn** to inform sb of sth; **de la part de** on behalf of; **c'est de la part de qui?** *(au téléphone)* who's calling, please?

> Apple, qui bénéficie du succès du "G3", la dernière génération de Macintosh commercialisée depuis novembre, a commencé à regagner un peu de terrain. Aux États-Unis, sa **part de marché** est remontée de 3,4% à 4%.

> La **part de marché** de ces produits varie d'une enseigne à l'autre et d'un marché à l'autre (plus de 20% pour les produits alimentaires contre 10% pour les articles d'entretien ménager).

partage *nm (répartition)* division; *(de marchandises, de biens)* allotment, distribution; *(de tâches, de responsabilités)* sharing out; JUR *(d'une propriété)* partition □ **partage des bénéfices** profit sharing; ORDINAT **partage des données** data sharing; **partage de l'emploi** job sharing; ORDINAT **partage de fichiers** file sharing; **partage d'imprimantes** printer sharing; **partage de temps** time sharing; **partage du travail** job sharing

partager *vt* (a) *(répartir)* to divide; *(marchandises, biens)* to allot, to distribute; *(tâches, responsabilités)* to share out; JUR *(propriété)* to parcel out; FIN **partager proportionnellement** to divide pro rata (b) *(utiliser en commun)* to share; **il partage les bénéfices avec son partenaire** he shares the profits with his partner

partenaire *nm* partner □ **partenaire commercial** business partner; **partenaire financier** financial partner; **partenaires sociaux** workers and management

> La chaîne française vient de signer trois accords avec des **partenaires** locaux pour l'ouverture de grands magasins à Shanghai et à Bangkok.

partenariat *nm* (trading) partnership □ MKTG **partenariat télévision** television tie-in

participant, -e 1 *adj* FIN *(action, obligation)* participating
2 *nm,f* participant (**à** in)

participation *nf* (a) *(fait de participer)* participation (**à** in); **nous comptons sur votre participation à la prochaine réunion** we are counting on your attendance at the next meeting
(b) *(argent)* contribution □ **participation aux frais** contribution towards costs
(c) FIN holding, share, interest (**à** in); **notre groupe a une participation de 25% dans cette société** our group has a 25% holding *or* share *or* interest in the company □ **participation aux bénéfices** profit sharing; **participation majoritaire** majority holding *or* interest; **participation minoritaire** minority holding *or* interest; **participation ouvrière** worker participation; **participation des salariés aux bénéfices** profit-sharing scheme

participer **participer à** *vt ind* (a) *(prendre part à)* to take part in, to participate in; **participer à la gestion d'une entreprise** to take part in the running of a firm; **participer à une réunion** to attend a meeting
(b) *(financièrement)* to contribute to; **participer aux frais** to pay one's share of the costs, to contribute towards the costs
(c) *(partager)* **participer aux bénéfices** to share in the profits

particulier, -ère 1 *adj (compte)* private, personal
2 *nm,f* (private) individual; **vente de particulier à particulier** private sale

partie *nf* (a) *(portion)* part; **faire partie du personnel** to be on the staff, to be a member of staff
(b) JUR party □ **partie concernée** interested party; **partie contractante** contracting party; **partie défaillante** defaulting party; **partie lésée** aggrieved party; **partie signataire** signatory
(c) **partie prenante** FIN payee; *(de biens)* recipient; **être partie prenante dans des discussions** to be a party to the discussions
(d) COMPTA **en partie double** double-entry; **en partie simple** single-entry

partiel, -elle *adj* part, partial

partiellement *adv* partially, in part; **payer partiellement** to pay in part

partir *vi* (a) *(s'en aller)* to go, to leave; **ceux qui partiront volontairement de l'entreprise recevront une prime** those who leave the company voluntarily will receive a bonus

(b) **à partir de** starting from; **à partir d'aujourd'hui** starting from today, from today (onwards); **le directeur sera libre à partir de 10 heures** the manager will be free from 10 (o'clock) onwards; **imposé à partir de 30 000 francs** taxable from 30,000 francs upwards

parvenir parvenir à *vt ind (endroit, accord)* to reach; **faire parvenir qch à qn** to send *or* to forward sth to sb; **votre lettre m'est parvenue hier** I received your letter yesterday; **votre demande doit nous parvenir avant la fin du mois** your application must reach us by the end of the month

pas-de-porte *nm* JUR *(somme d'argent)* key money

> **❝**
> Naguère de règle, le versement d'un **pas-de-porte**, c'est à dire d'une avance au propriétaire sur le loyer versé, se fait plus rare.
> **❞**

passage *nm (à l'euro, à l'économie de marché)* changeover, transition (**à** to)

passager, -ère 1 *adj (crise, problèmes)* temporary
2 *nm,f* passenger

passation *nf* (a) COMPTA *(d'une écriture)* entering □ *une passation d'écriture* a journal entry; *passation par pertes et profits* write-off
(b) *(d'un accord, d'un contrat)* signing; *(d'une commande)* placing
(c) FIN *(d'un dividende)* payment
(d) *passation de pouvoirs* handover *or* transfer of power

> **❝**
> La **passation de pouvoirs** à la tête de la Bundesbank exclut toute baisse des taux d'intérêt dans l'immédiat.
> **❞**

passe de caisse *nf* allowance to cashier for errors

passeport *nm* passport

passer 1 *vt* (a) *(introduire)* **passer des marchandises à la douane** to clear goods through customs; **passer des marchandises en fraude** to smuggle in goods
(b) TÉL **passer qn à qn** to put sb through to sb; **passez-moi M. Lecuyer** put me through to *or* get me Mr Lecuyer; **je vous passe le directeur** I'll put you through to the manager
(c) *(accord, contrat)* to enter into, to sign; *(commande)* to place (**de qch** for sth; **à qn** with sb); **passer un acte par-devant notaire**

to draw up a document before a solicitor
(d) COMPTA to enter, to post; **passer un article au grand-livre** to post an entry in the ledger; **passer écriture d'un article** to post an entry; **passer une somme au débit/au crédit** to debit/credit an account with a sum; **passer une somme en perte** to charge an amount to an account; **passer une somme en profit** to credit an amount to an account; **passer par pertes et profits** to transfer to profit and loss, to write off
(e) *(devenir)* **il est passé contremaître** he has been promoted to foreman
2 *vi* (a) *(aller)* **passer à la douane** to go through customs
(b) *(changer)* **passer de qch à qch** to go from sth to sth; **notre chiffre d'affaires est passé de deux à trois millions en cinq ans** our turnover has increased from two million to three million in five years
(c) *(représentant)* **passer chez un client** to call on a client

passerelle *nf* ORDINAT **passerelle (de connexion) (avec)** gateway (to)

passible *adj (d'une amende)* liable (**de** to); *(d'un impôt, d'une taxe)* liable, subject (**de** to)

passif *nm* FIN, COMPTA liabilities, debts; **l'actif et le passif** assets and liabilities; **inscrire** *ou* **passer une dette au passif** to enter a debt on the liabilities side □ *passif circulant* current liabilities; *passif éventuel* contingent liabilities; *passif exigible* current liabilities; *passif à long terme* long-term liabilities; *passif reporté* deferred liabilities

patentable *adj* subject to a licence, requiring a licence

patente *nf* (a) *(licence)* licence *(to exercise a trade or profession)*; **payer patente** to be duly licensed (b) *(impôt)* tax *(paid by self-employed people)*

patenté, -e *adj* licensed

patenter *vt* to license

patienter *vi* to wait; **faire patienter qn** *(au téléphone)* to ask sb to hold; **est-ce que vous désirez patienter?** would you like to hold?

patrimoine *nm* FIN *(d'un individu)* property, wealth, personal assets; *(actif net)* net assets □ *patrimoine immobilier Br* property assets, *Am* real-estate assets; BANQUE *patrimoine social* social assets

> **❝**
> Les français sont endettés, inquiets et d'autant moins tentés de réduire leur épargne qu'ils ont le sentiment d'être appauvris par la dévalorisation de leur **patrimoine immobilier**.
> **❞**

patron, -onne *nm,f* **(a)** *(d'une entreprise)*
(directeur) employer; *(propriétaire)* owner;
les patrons *(le patronat)* employers
  (b) *Fam (responsable)* boss
  (c) *(d'un hôtel)* proprietor

patronage *nm* MKTG sponsorship, sponsoring; **placé sous le patronage de...** spon-
sored by...; **sous le patronage de** under the
sponsorship of

patronal, -e *adj* employers'

patronat *nm* employers; **le patronat et les
syndicats** employers and unions

patronner *vt* MKTG to sponsor

pavé *nm* ORDINAT keypad □ *pavé numérique* numeric keypad

pavillon *nm* flag; **battre pavillon libérien**
to sail under a Liberian flag □ *pavillon de
complaisance* flag of convenience

payable *adj* payable; **effet payable au 1
juillet** bill due on 1 July; **payable à 30 jours**
payable at 30 days' date; **payable en 12
mensualités** payable in 12 monthly instalments; **payable à l'arrivée** payable on arrival;
payable à la banque payable at the bank;
payable à la commande cash with order,
payable with order; **payable comptant** payable in cash; **payable sur demande** payable
on demand; **payable à l'échéance** payable at
maturity; **payable à la livraison** payable on
delivery; **payable au porteur** payable to
bearer; **payable sur présentation** payable
on demand *or* on presentation; **payable à
vue** payable on sight

payant, -e *adj* **(a)** *(non gratuit) (agence)*
charging a fee; *(service)* with a charge
(b) *(qui rapporte)* profitable

paye = **paie**

payement = **paiement**

payer *vt (facture, impôts, intérêts, loyer, personne)* to pay; *(marchandises, service)* to pay
for; *(dette)* to pay (off), to settle; *(effet)* to
honour; **payer qch à qn** to buy sth for sb;
payer qch cher to pay a lot of money for sth;
payer qch bon marché to buy sth cheaply;
payer d'avance to pay in advance; **comment
désirez-vous payer?** how are you paying?,
how would you like to pay?; **payer par carte
de crédit** to pay by credit card; **payer par
chèque** to pay by cheque; **payer comptant**
ou **en liquide** to pay cash; **payer à l'échéance**
to pay at maturity *or* due date; **payer en
espèces** to pay (in) cash; **payer intégralement** *ou* **en totalité** to pay in full; **payer à la
livraison** to pay on delivery; **payer à l'ordre
de...** *(sur chèque)* pay to the order of...; **payez
au porteur** pay to bearer; **payer à présenta-**
tion to pay on presentation; **payer à vue** to
pay at sight; **être payé à l'heure/à la se-
maine/au mois** to be paid by the hour/by
the week/by the month; **être payé à la pièce**
to be on piecework; **c'est une entreprise qui
paie mal** that firm pays badly; **travail bien
payé** well-paid job

payeur, -euse 1 *nm,f* payer; **c'est un bon/
mauvais payeur** he is a good/bad payer
  2 *nm* ADMIN pay clerk

pays *nm* country; **les pays d'Europe de l'Est**
Eastern European countries □ *pays créditeur* creditor country; *pays débiteur*
debtor country; *pays exportateur* exporting country; *pays importateur* importing
country; *pays industrialisé* industrialized
country; *pays membre* member state; *pays
d'origine* country of origin; *pays pétrolier*
oil-producing country; *pays de provenance*
country of origin; *pays signataires (d'un
accord)* signatory countries; *pays en voie
de développement* developing country

paysage *nm* **(a)** *(situation)* scene, landscape; **le paysage politique/économique
d'un pays** the political/economic landscape
of a country **(b)** ORDINAT **(mode)** paysage
landscape (mode); **imprimer qch en paysage**
to print sth in landscape

PC 1 *nm* ORDINAT *(abrév* **personal computer)** PC
  2 *nf* FIN *(abrév* **pièce de caisse)** cash voucher

PCG *nm* COMPTA *(abrév* **plan comptable
général)** chart of accounts

PCV *nm* TÉL *(abrév* **payable chez vous)
(appel en) PCV** *Br* reverse-charge call, *Am*
collect call; **appeler en PCV, faire un appel
en PCV** *Br* to reverse the charges, *Am* to call
collect

P-DG *nm* *(abrév* **président-directeur
général)** *Br* Chairman and Managing Director, *Am* CEO

PEA *nm* FIN *(abrév* **plan d'épargne en
actions)** investment trust, *Br* ≃ PEP

pécuniaire *adj* financial; **améliorer sa situation pécuniaire** to improve one's financial
situation

PEE *nm* FIN *(abrév* **plan d'épargne d'entreprise)** company savings scheme

peine *nf* penalty □ *peine contractuelle*
penalty for non-performance (of contract)

PEL *nm* *(abrév* **plan épargne-logement)**
Br ≃ building society account, *Am* ≃ savings
and loan association account

pénal, -e *adj (système, droit)* penal

pénaliser vt (punir, désavantager) to penalize; **cette mesure pénalise les petits épargnants** this measure penalizes small savers

pénalité nf penalty □ FIN **pénalité libératoire** full and final penalty payment; **pénalité de retard** late payment penalty; (pour livraison tardive) late delivery penalty

pendant, -e adj JUR pending; **la question est toujours pendante** the matter is still pending or in abeyance

pénétration nf (d'un marché) penetration

pénétrer vt (marché) to penetrate, to enter into

pension nf (allocation) pension □ **pension d'invalidité** invalidity pension; **pension de retraite** (retirement or old-age) pension; **pension de réversion** survivor's pension; **pension viagère** life annuity

> " Ils sont à la fois très réticents à l'idée d'une baisse des **pensions**, attachés à la sécurité (une rente plutôt qu'un capital) et plutôt individualistes que redistributeurs. "

pensionné, -e **1** adj (employé) pensioned; **elle est pensionnée à 75%** her pension represents 75% of her income
2 nm,f pensioner

pensionner vt to grant a pension to

pénurie nf (de matières premières, de capitaux, de devises) shortage, scarcity □ **pénurie de main-d'œuvre** labour shortage

PEP nm FIN (abrév **plan d'épargne populaire**) special savings account

pépinière d'entreprises nf enterprise zone

PEPS nm (abrév **premier entré, premier sorti**) FIFO

PER nm FIN (abrév **plan d'épargne retraite**) retirement savings scheme

percée nf breakthrough; **leur société a fait une percée sur le marché de la micro-informatique** their company has broken into the microcomputer market □ **percée commerciale** market thrust; **percée technologique** technological breakthrough

percepteur nm ADMIN collector of taxes, tax collector

perceptible adj ADMIN (impôt) collectable

perception nf ADMIN (d'impôts, de droits, de loyer) collection, receipt □ FIN **perception de dividende** receipt of a dividend; **percep-**

tion douanière collection of customs duties; **perception à la source** tax deduction at source

percer vi **percer sur un marché** to break into a market

percevable adj ADMIN (impôt) collectable

percevoir vt ADMIN (impôts, droits, loyers) to collect; (revenus, indemnités, intérêts, commission) to receive, to be paid; **percevoir l'allocation chômage** to receive unemployment benefit; **cotisations à percevoir** contributions still due; **percevoir les impôts à la source** to collect tax at source

perdre vt (argent, procès, client, emploi) to lose; **perdre de sa valeur** to lose value; **le franc a encore perdu par rapport à la livre** the franc has slipped further against the dollar

péremption nf lapsing

péréquation nf (des impôts, des salaires) equalization; **faire la péréquation des salaires** to equalize wages

perfectionnement nm (a) (d'une machine, d'une méthode, d'un procédé) perfecting; **notre but est le perfectionnement de nos techniques** our aim is to perfect our techniques (b) (formation) (further) training; **faire un stage de perfectionnement** to do an advanced training course

perfectionner **1** vt (machine, méthode, procédé) to perfect
2 se perfectionner vpr (personne) to improve oneself; (technologie) to improve, to advance

perforation nf ORDINAT (a) (action) punching (b) (trou) punch (hole)

perforatrice nf ORDINAT card punch, (key) punch

perforer vt ORDINAT (carte, bande) to punch

perforeuse nf ORDINAT card punch, (key) punch

performance nf performance, achievement; **il faut améliorer les performances de notre entreprise/économie** we must improve the performance of our company/economy

performant, -e adj (employé) efficient; (investissement) profitable, high-yield; (entreprise) successful

péril de mer nm ASSUR risk and peril of the seas, sea risk

périmé, -e adj (coupon) out-of-date; (passeport) expired; (ticket) no longer valid; (mandat) lapsed

périmer se **périmer** *vpr (document)* to lapse, to expire

période *nf* period; **pendant une période de trois mois** for a period of three months, for a three month period ◻ *période d'activité (d'une personne)* period of active employment; FIN *période d'amortissement* depreciation period; *période comptable* financial period, accounting period, *Am* fiscal period; *période d'essai* probation *or* trial period; *période d'essor* boom; *période de grâce* tax holiday; *période d'inactivité* period of inactivity; *période de liquidation* phase-out period; *période de prospérité* boom, period of prosperity; *période de recouvrement* collection period; *période de remboursement* payback period

périodique *adj (inventaire, résultats)* periodical

périphérique ORDINAT **1** *adj* peripheral **2** *nm* peripheral ◻ *périphérique d'entrée* input device; *périphérique d'entrée-sortie* input/output device; *périphérique externe* external device; *périphérique d'impression* printer peripheral; *périphérique de sortie* output device

périssable *adj* perishable

permanence *nf* (**a**) *(lieu)* (duty) office (**b**) *(service)* **il y a une permanence le dimanche** there is a 24-hour service on Sundays; **être de permanence** to be on duty; **en l'absence du directeur, M. Lenoir assure la permanence au conseil d'administration** in the director's absence, Mr Lenoir will head the board of directors

permanent, -e 1 *adj (emploi)* permanent; *(comité)* standing **2** *nm,f (d'une organisation)* paid worker, worker on the payroll

permettre *vt* to allow, to permit

permis *nm* permit ◻ *permis de chargement* loading permit; *permis de construire* planning permission; *permis de débarquement* landing permit; *permis de douane* customs permit; *permis d'embarquement* shipping note; *permis d'entrée (pour marchandises)* import permit *or* licence; *(pour bateau)* clearance inwards; *permis d'exportation* export permit *or* licence; *permis de séjour* residence permit; *permis de sortie (pour marchandises)* export permit *or* licence; *(pour bateau)* clearance outwards; *permis de transit* transit permit; *permis de travail* work permit

perquisition *nf* search

> La possibilité pour les agents du fisc d'effectuer des **perquisitions** au domicile privé des contribuables est très strictement encadrée.

personnalisation *nf (d'un service, d'une assurance, d'un produit)* personalization, customization

personnaliser *vt (service, assurance, produit)* to personalize, to customize

personnalité juridique *nf* JUR legal status

personne *nf* person; **par personne** per person, per capita; **le prix est de 200 francs par personne** it costs 200 francs a head *or* per person; **les deux tiers des personnes interrogées ont déclaré ne pas connaître ce produit** two-thirds of those people interviewed said that they hadn't heard of the product ◻ JUR *personne à charge* dependent; JUR *personne morale* legal entity, corporate body; *personne physique* individual entity

> Tous les employés, **personnes physiques** ou **morales**, sont visés par la procédure de déclaration préalable à l'embauche.

personnel, -elle 1 *adj (entreprise, lettre)* personal; **personnel** *(sur document)* private and confidential **2** *nm (d'une entreprise, d'un hôtel, d'une boutique)* personnel, staff, employees; *(d'une usine)* workforce; **faire partie du personnel** to be on the staff, to be a member of staff, to be on the payroll; **manquer de personnel** to be understaffed *or* shorthanded ◻ *personnel administratif* administrative staff; BANQUE *personnel de back-office* back office staff; *personnel de bureau* office staff; *personnel dirigeant* managerial staff; *personnel d'encadrement* management; *personnel d'entretien* maintenance staff; *personnel intérimaire* temporary staff; *personnel réduit* reduced *or* skeleton staff; *personnel saisonnier* seasonal staff; *personnel de service* staff on duty; MKTG *personnel de soutien commercial* sales support staff; *personnel à temps partiel* part-time staff; *personnel de vente* sales personnel

personnellement *adv* personally, in person

perspective *nf* prospect, outlook ◻ *perspectives de carrière* job prospects; *per-*

spectives *commerciales* market prospects; *perspectives de croissance* prospects for growth; *perspectives économiques* economic prospects; *perspectives de profit* profit outlook

perte *nf (de marché, de clientèle, d'argent)* loss; ASSUR loss, damage; **travailler** *ou* **fonctionner à perte** to operate at a loss; **vendre qch à perte** to sell sth at a loss; **passer une perte par profits et pertes** to write off a loss; **subir de lourdes pertes** to suffer heavy losses; **il s'agit d'un secteur en perte de vitesse** it's a sector that's going downhill □ *perte de bénéfice* loss of profit; FIN *perte brute* gross loss; *perte en capitaux* capital loss; FIN *perte de change* (foreign) exchange loss; ORDINAT *perte de données irréparable* irretrievable data loss; FIN *perte d'intérêts* loss of interest; FIN *perte latente* unrealized loss; FIN *perte nette* net loss; *perte partielle* partial loss; *perte présumée* presumptive loss; COMPTA *pertes et profits exceptionnels* extraordinary items; FIN *perte sèche* dead loss; COMPTA *perte supportée* loss attributable; FIN *perte totale* total loss; COMPTA *perte transférée* loss transferred

peser *vt (entreprise)* to be worth; **cette entreprise pèse 20 millions de dollars** this company is worth 20 million dollars

> ❝
> Douze ans après sa création cette société cotée au second marché depuis 1996 **pèse** environ 2 milliards de francs. ❞

peseta *nf* peseta

petit, -e *adj* small □ *petites annonces* classified advertisements, small ads; *petite caisse* petty cash; *petit commerçant* small trader, shopkeeper; *le petit commerce* the small retail trade; *petite entreprise* small firm; *petits épargnants, la petite épargne* small savers; *la petite industrie* small-scale industry; *petites et moyennes entreprises* small (and medium-sized) businesses; *petites et moyennes industries* small (and medium-sized) industries; FIN *petit porteur* small investor *or* shareholder

pétrodollar *nm* petrodollar

pétrole *nm* oil, petroleum; BOURSE les pétroles oils, oil shares □ *pétrole brut* crude oil

pétrolier, -ère 1 *adj (prix, produits, marché)* oil; **les grandes sociétés pétrolières** the big oil companies
2 *nm* (oil) tanker

pétromonarchie *nf* oil kingdom

pétromonnaie *nf* petrocurrency

pèze *nm* cash, *Br* dosh, *Am* bucks

phase *nf* phase, stage □ *phase de commercialisation* marketing stage; *phase de croissance* growth phase; **être en phase de croissance** to be growing; *phase de déclin* phase of decline; **être en phase de déclin** to be on the decline; *phase de fabrication* manufacturing stage

phoning *nm* MKTG telesales

> ❝
> Efficaces et bon marché, le **phoning** et le couponing réduisent les frais de démarchage. ❞

photocopie *nf* photocopy

photocopier *vt* to photocopy

photocopieur *nm* photocopier, photocopying machine

photocopieuse *nf* photocopier, photocopying machine

photostyle *nm* ORDINAT light pen

PIB *nm* ÉCON (*abrév* **produit intérieur brut**) GDP

> ❝
> Après un premier semestre morose, l'économie américaine a doublé de rythme au troisième trimestre avec une hausse annualisée du **PIB** de 2,8%. ❞

pic *nm (d'une courbe)* peak

pièce *nf* (**a**) *(monnaie)* pièce (de monnaie) coin; **pièce de deux francs** two-franc coin □ *pièce d'or* gold coin
(**b**) *(exemplaire)* piece; **ils coûtent dix francs la pièce** they cost ten francs each; **ils se vendent à la pièce** they are sold separately *or* singly; **être payé à la pièce** to be paid piecework (rates); **travailler à la pièce** *ou* **aux pièces** to be on piecework, to do piecework
(**c**) *(document)* document, paper; **pièce à joindre...** *(à une lettre)* please enclose... □ *pièce annexe* attachment; *pièce à l'appui* supporting document; COMPTA *pièce de caisse* cash voucher; *pièce d'identité* proof of identity; *pièce jointe (à une lettre)* enclosure; *pièce justificative* written proof, supporting document
(**d**) *(de machine) pièces détachées, pièces de rechange* spare parts, replacement parts

pignoratif, -ive *adj* FIN with a repurchase option

pilote 1 *adj (usine, échantillon, étude, prix)* pilot 2 *nm* ORDINAT driver ❏ *pilote de mise en file d'attente* spooler

piloter *vt* ORDINAT to drive; **piloté par menu** menu-driven

pilule empoisonnée *nf (contre-OPA)* poison pill

piquet *nm* picket ❏ *piquets de grève* pickets; *piquets de grève volants* flying pickets

piratage informatique *nm* ORDINAT (computer) hacking

pirate informatique *nm* ORDINAT hacker

pirater *vt* to pirate

piste *nf* ORDINAT *piste d'amorçage* boot track; *piste magnétique (sur carte)* magnetic strip

piston *nm Fam* string-pulling; **avoir du piston** to have friends in high places; **il a eu le poste par piston** someone pulled some strings to get him the job

pistonner *vt Fam* to pull strings for

pixel *nm* ORDINAT pixel

pixélisé, -e *adj* ORDINAT bit-mapped, bitmap

placard *nm* poster, bill ❏ *placard publicitaire* advertisement *(in newspaper)*

place *nf* (a) *(emploi, poste)* job, post, position; **quitter/perdre sa place** to leave/to lose one's job; **il a trouvé une place de comptable** he found a job as an accountant; **le gouvernement en place** the government in office *or* power

(b) *(endroit)* place, location; **engager du personnel sur place** to hire staff locally; **s'approvisionner sur place** to use local suppliers; **avoir du crédit sur la place** to have credit (facilities) locally; **chèque encaissable sur la place** cheque cashable locally

(c) BOURSE market ❏ *place boursière* stock market; *place financière* money market; **le dollar est à la hausse sur la place financière de New York** the dollar has risen on the New York exchange

> **❝**
> La baisse de 5,4% de Francfort est la plus forte subie par cette **place financière** depuis le début de l'année.
> **❞**

> **❝**
> Pendant des années, les responsables de la Bourse de Francfort ont souffert d'un sentiment d'infériorité par rapport aux grandes **places** du monde.
> **❞**

placement *nm* (a) FIN *(action)* investment, investing; *(argent)* investment; **faire des placements** to invest (money), to make investments; **faire un bon placement** to make a good investment ❏ *placement à court terme* short-term investment; *placement financier* Stock Market investment; *placement à long terme* long-term investment; *placement obligataire* bond investment; *placement de père de famille* gilt-edged investment, blue chip; *placement privé* private investment *or* placement; *placement à revenus fixes* fixed-income investment, fixed-yield investment; *placement à revenus variables* variable-income investment

(b) MKTG placement ❏ *placement de produit* product placement

(c) *(fait de donner un emploi)* placement, placing

> **❝**
> Lassés par les krachs boursiers et la chute du rendement des sicav monétaires, les épargnants rêvent d'un **placement** idéal, performant mais pas trop risqué.
> **❞**

placer 1 *vt* (a) *(procurer un emploi à)* to find a job for; **placer qn comme apprenti chez qn** to apprentice sb to sb; **elle a été placée à la direction commerciale** she was appointed head of the sales department

(b) *(vendre)* to sell; **facile/difficile à placer** easy/difficult to sell

(c) FIN *(argent)* to invest; *(actions)* to place; **placer de l'argent dans les pétroles** to invest in oils; **placer à court terme/à long terme** to invest short-term/long-term; **placer à intérêts** to invest at interest; **placer de l'argent sur un compte** to put *or* deposit money in an account

2 **se placer** *vpr* (a) *(trouver un emploi)* to get *or* find a job; **se placer comme analyste-programmeur** to get a job as a systems analyst

(b) *(se vendre)* to sell; **ces marchandises se placent facilement** these goods sell easily

placier *nm* (a) *(représentant de commerce)* sales representative (b) *(qui fait du porte-à-porte)* door-to-door salesman

plafond *nm (limite)* ceiling; **le franc a atteint son plafond** the franc has reached its ceiling *or* upper limit; **crever le plafond** to exceed the limit, to break the ceiling; **fixer un plafond à un budget** to put a ceiling on a budget, to cap a budget ❏ BANQUE *plafond d'autorisation de retrait* withdrawal limit; *plafond des charges budgétaires* spending limit, budgetary limit; **plafond du crédit** credit ceiling or limit; **plafond de découvert** overdraft limit; **plafond de l'impôt** tax ceiling

plafonnement *nm* **le plafonnement des salaires** the ceiling imposed on salaries

plafonner 1 *vt* (salaires, prix, dépenses) to cap, to put a ceiling on; **être plafonné à** to have a ceiling of
2 *vi* to have reached a ceiling (**à** of); **la production plafonne** output has reached its ceiling; **cette année, l'inflation a plafonné à 3%** inflation this year peaked at 3%

plage *nf* (éventail) range, band □ **plage de prix** price range; **plage de taux** rate band

plaider *vt & vi* JUR to plead

plaignant, -e *nm,f* JUR plaintiff

plaindre se plaindre *vpr* to complain

plainte *nf* complaint

plan *nm* (a) (projet) plan, project □ **plan d'action** plan of action; MKTG **plan d'activité** business plan; COMPTA **plan d'amortissement** depreciation schedule; **plan d'assainissement** stabilization plan; FIN, ÉCON **plan d'austérité** austerity programme; **plan de campagne** campaign plan; **plan de carrière** career plan; COMPTA **plan comptable** accounting plan; COMPTA **plan comptable général, plan de comptes** chart of accounts; **plan de développement** development plan; **plan directeur** master plan; **plan d'échantillonnage** sampling project; **plan d'échéances** instalment plan; **plan économique** economic plan; **plan d'embauche** recruitment plan; FIN **plan d'épargne** savings scheme or plan; FIN **plan d'épargne en actions** investment trust, Br ≃ personal equity plan; FIN **plan épargne-logement** Br ≃ building society account, Am ≃ savings and loan association account; FIN **plan d'épargne populaire** special savings account; FIN **plan d'épargne retraite** retirement savings plan or scheme; COMPTA **plan de financement** funding plan, financial plan; **plan d'investissement** investment plan; MKTG **plan de marketing** marketing plan; **plan média** media planning; BOURSE **plan d'options sur titres** stock option plan; **plan optionnel d'achat d'actions** stock option plan; **plan prévisionnel** forecast plan; ÉCON **plan quinquennal** Five Year plan; **plan de redressement de l'entreprise** company recovery plan; **plan de relance** revitalisation plan; **plan de restructuration** restructuring plan; **plan social** (du gouvernement) = corporate restructuring plan, usually involving job losses; MKTG **plan stratégique d'entreprise** strategic business plan; **plan de travail** planning; **plan de trésorerie** cash flow forecast (b) (point de vue) **sur le plan de** as regards; **sur le plan économique** economically, as far as the economy is concerned

> 44
> Ce n'est pas parce que les temps sont plus propices aux **plans sociaux** qu'aux **plans d'embauche** qu'il faut se désintéresser des lois sur le recrutement.
> 77

> 44
> Hier, lorsque les banquiers occidentaux et russes ont pris connaissance des détails du **plan de restructuration** de la dette intérieure annoncée mardi soir par le nouveau Premier ministre, Viktor Tchernomyrdine, la tornade financière a été d'une violence sans précédent.
> 77

planche à billets *nf* **faire fonctionner la planche à billets** to print money

plancher *nm* floor, lower limit □ **plancher des salaires** wage floor

planifiable *adj* ÉCON plannable

planificateur, -trice 1 *adj* (autorité, mesures) planning
2 *nm,f* ÉCON planner

planification *nf* ÉCON planning □ **planification budgétaire** budget planning; **planification à court terme** short-term planning; **planification économique** economic planning; **planification de l'emploi** manpower planning; **planification de l'entreprise** company or corporate planning; **planification financière** financial planning; **planification à long terme** long-term planning; **planification des opérations** operational planning; **planification du produit** product planning; ORDINAT **planification des systèmes** systems engineering; **planification des ventes** sales planning

planifié, -e *adj* ÉCON (économie) planned

planifier *vt* to plan

planigramme *nm* MKTG flowchart

planning *nm* plan, schedule; (programme d'activités, de travail) schedule; **nous avons un planning très chargé cette semaine** we have a very busy schedule this week □ COMPTA **planning des charges** expenditure planning; **planning de distribution** distribution planning; **planning de la production** production planning

plaquette publicitaire *nf* advertising brochure

plate-forme *nf* ORDINAT platform

plein, -e *adj* full; **agir de plein droit** to act by right; **avoir plein(s) pouvoir(s)** to have full power; JUR to have power of attorney; **être en plein travail** *(usine)* to be in full production; **payer plein tarif** to pay the full rate; **la pleine saison** the high season; **travailler à plein temps** to work full-time

plein-emploi *nm* ÉCON full employment

pli *nm* *(enveloppe)* envelope; **sous pli cacheté** in a sealed envelope; **sous pli séparé** under separate cover; **nous vous envoyons sous ce pli…** please find enclosed…, herewith…; **sous pli recommandé** by registered letter

plomber *vt* DOUANES *(colis, wagon de marchandises)* to seal

plus 1 *adv* **(a)** *(davantage)* more; **le plus** the most; **gagner plus de mille francs** to earn more than *or* over a thousand francs; **le taux le plus élevé** the top *or* highest rate of interest **(b) en plus** in addition, extra; **la TVA est en plus** there is VAT on top

2 *conj* plus; **deux cents francs d'amende plus les frais** two hundred francs fine plus costs; **le prix du produit plus la TVA** the price of the product plus VAT

3 *nm* plus, bonus; **le service après-vente est un plus que nous offrons à notre clientèle** the after-sales service is a plus that we offer all our customers

plus-value *nf* ÉCON, FIN *(augmentation de la valeur)* appreciation, increase in value; *(bénéfice)* profit; *(excédent) (d'impôts)* surplus; **réaliser une plus-value sur la vente d'un produit** to make a profit on the sale of a product; **les recettes présentent une plus-value de…** the receipts show an increase of…; **nos actions ont enregistré une plus-value** our shares have increased in value ▫ **plus-value sur titres** paper profit

> Le premier semestre s'est en effet terminé sur une perte de 140 millions de francs malgré une **plus-value** liée à la cession de 49% de Cofinoga.

PLV *nf* *(abrév* **publicité sur le lieu de vente)** point-of-sale promotion

PME *nf* *(abrév* **petite et moyenne entreprise)** small business, SME

PMI *nf* *(abrév* **petite et moyenne industrie)** small industrial firm, SMI

PNB *nm* ÉCON *(abrév* **produit national brut)** GNP

PO *(abrév* **par ordre)** by order

poids *nm* **(a)** *(masse)* weight; **vendre au poids** to sell by weight; **vendre à faux poids** to give short weight ▫ **poids brut** gross weight; **poids insuffisant** short weight; MKTG **poids mort** *(produit)* dog, dodo; **poids net** net weight; **poids rendu** delivered weight; **poids de taxation** chargeable weight

(b) *(dans un chargement)* load ▫ **poids en charge** laden weight; **poids mort** dead weight; **poids net à l'emballage** net weight when packed; **poids net embarqué** loaded net weight; **poids normal** standard weight; **poids utile** load-carrying capacity

(c) poids lourd *Br* heavy goods vehicle, HGV, *Am* heavy goods truck

(d) *(charge)* burden ▫ **poids de la fiscalité** tax burden

poinçon *nm* *(sur l'or et l'argent)* hallmark

point *nm* **(a)** *(endroit)* point, place ▫ **point de chargement** loading point *or* place; **point de déchargement** unloading point *or* place; **point de destination** destination; MKTG **point de distribution** distribution outlet; **point d'entrée de l'or** import gold-point; **point d'expédition** place of shipment; BANQUE **point retrait** cashpoint; **point de sortie de l'or** export gold-point; MKTG **point de vente** point of sale, POS; *(magasin)* sales outlet; **disponible dans votre point de vente habituel** available at your local stockist; **point de vente au détail** retail outlet; **point de vente électronique** electronic point of sale

(b) *(dans un pourcentage, dans une échelle)* point; **amélioration de trois points** improvement of three points, three-point improvement; **l'indice CAC 40 a perdu un point hier** the CAC 40 index fell by a point yesterday ▫ **point de retraite** pension point

(c) *(stade)* point ▫ **point critique** break-even point; FIN **point mort** break-even point; **l'activité est au point mort dans ce secteur** activity is at a standstill in this sector; **point de saturation** saturation point

(d) *(élément)* point, item; **il a présenté un plan de redressement en trois points** he presented a three-point recovery plan ▫ **point faible** weak point; **point fort** strong point

(e) mettre qch au point *(produit)* to finalize sth; *(procédé, technique)* to perfect sth; **mettre les choses au point** *(clarifier la situation)* to get things straight, to make things clear; **faire le point (sur qch)** to take stock (of sth)

(f) ORDINAT *point de césure* breakpoint, hyphenation point

(g) MKTG *point d'interrogation* question mark

> **❝**
> Baisser d'un **point** le taux de la TVA, c'est amputer les recettes budgétaires de plus de 25 milliards.
> **❞**

pointage *nm* **(a)** *(d'articles, de noms)* checking, ticking off **(b)** *(au travail) (à l'arrivée)* clocking in; *(à la sortie)* clocking out

pointer 1 *vt* **(a)** *(articles, noms)* to check, to tick off; **pointer un compte** to tick off items on an account **(b)** ORDINAT *(curseur)* to position **(sur** on)
2 *vi (à l'arrivée)* to clock in; *(à la sortie)* to clock out; **pointer à l'ANPE** *ou* **au chômage** to register unemployed

pointeur *nm* ORDINAT pointer

pointeuse *nf (machine)* time clock

pôle *nm* ÉCON **les pôles de croissance** the main centres of economic growth ▫ *pôle de reconversion* development *or* reconversion zone

police *nf* **(a)** ASSUR policy; **établir une police** to draw up *or* make out a policy ▫ *police d'assurance* insurance policy; **souscrire à** *ou* **prendre une police d'assurance** to take out an insurance policy; *police d'assurance maritime* marine insurance policy; *police d'assurance (sur la) vie* life (assurance) policy; *police de chargement* bill of lading; *police conjointe* joint policy; *police à forfait* policy for a specific amount; *police générale* master *or* general policy; *police individuelle crédit acheteur* individual buyer credit policy; *police individuelle crédit fournisseur* individual supplier credit policy; *police ouverte* open policy; *police au porteur* policy to bearer; *police tous risques* fully comprehensive policy; *police type* standard policy; *police universelle* worldwide policy
(b) ORDINAT **police (de caractères)** (character) font ▫ *police bitmap* bitmap font; *police par défaut* default font; *police pixelisée* bitmap font

politique *nf (stratégie)* policy; **suivre** *ou* **adopter une nouvelle politique** to follow *or* adopt a new policy; **pratiquer la politique de la chaise vide** to make a political point by not attending meetings ▫ *politique d'accommodement* give-and-take policy; *politique d'achats centralisés* centralized purchasing; UE *politique agricole commune* Common Agricultural Policy; MKTG *politique d'assortiment diversifié* mixed merchandising; *politique d'austérité* austerity policy; *politique budgétaire* budgetary policy; *politique commerciale* trade policy; MKTG *politique de communication* promotional policy; *politique conjoncturelle* economic policy *(responding to changes in the business cycle)*; *politique de crédit* credit policy; *politique de déflation, politique déflationniste* deflationary policy; *politique de distribution* distribution policy; *politique de dividendes* dividend policy; *politique économique* economic policy; *politique de l'emploi* employment policy; *politique de l'entreprise* company policy; *politique extérieure* foreign policy; FIN *politique fiscale* fiscal policy; *politique de gestion* business policy; *politique d'inflation, politique inflationniste* inflationary policy; *politique intérieure* domestic policy; *politique d'investissement* investment policy; *politique du laissez-faire* laissez-faire policy; *politique de libre-échange* free-trade policy; *politique de la main tendue* policy of the outstretched hand; **pratiquer la politique de la main tendue** to make friendly overtures, to be conciliatory; *politique en matière de change* exchange policy; *politique monétaire* monetary policy; *politique d'open-market* open-market policy; *politique de plein emploi* policy of full employment; *politique de la porte ouverte* open-door policy; *politique des prix* pricing policy; *politique des prix et des salaires* prices and incomes policy; *politique de promotion* promotional policy; *politique salariale, politique des salaires* wages policy; *politique de la terre brûlée* scorched earth policy; *politique de vente* sales policy

polycopie *nf (procédé)* duplication; *(document)* duplicate

polycopié *nm* (duplicated) copy

polycopier *vt* to duplicate

polyvalence *nf (d'un employé)* adaptability, versatility

polyvalent, -e 1 *adj (produit)* multipurpose; *(employé)* adaptable, versatile
2 *nm* ADMIN tax inspector

ponction *nf (retrait)* withdrawal; **faire une grosse ponction sur un compte** to withdraw a large sum from an account; **c'est une ponction importante sur mes revenus** it makes a big hole *or* dent in my income; ADMIN *ponction fiscale* taxation; *ponction sociale* =

contributions to the social security scheme, *Br* ≃ National Insurance contributions

ponctionner *vt (économies, pouvoir d'achat)* to make a hole *or* dent in; **on nous ponctionne un tiers de notre salaire en impôts** a third of our salary goes in tax

> " ⎯⎯⎯⎯⎯⎯⎯⎯
> ... les coupes claires dans les dépenses de santé, dans les pensions et les retraites **ponctionneront** encore le pouvoir d'achat.
> ⎯⎯⎯⎯⎯⎯⎯⎯ "

ponctuel, -elle *adj* (**a**) *(paiement, impôt)* one-off; **l'État accorde une aide ponctuelle aux entreprises en difficulté** the state gives backing to companies to see them through periods of financial difficulty (**b**) *(employé)* punctual

pondérateur, -trice *adj* ÉCON balancing, stabilizing; **les éléments pondérateurs du marché** the stablizing factors of the market

pondération *nf* ÉCON *(d'un indice, d'une moyenne)* weighting

pondéré, -e *adj* ÉCON *(indice, moyenne)* weighted

pondérer *vt* ÉCON *(indice, moyenne)* to weight

pont *nm* (**a**) *pont d'or* golden hello; **faire un pont d'or à qn** to offer a golden hello to sb (**b**) *(congés)* long weekend; *(jour)* = day off granted by an employer to fill the gap between a national holiday and a weekend; **faire le pont** to take a long weekend

pool *nm* (**a**) ÉCON pool, common stock ▫ *pool d'assurances* insurance pool; *pool bancaire* banking pool; *pool de l'or* gold pool (**b**) *(équipe)* pool ▫ *pool de dactylos, pool dactylographique* typing pool; *pool de secrétaires* secretarial pool

population *nf* population ▫ *la population active* the working population; MKTG *population cible* target population; *population mère* basic population; *population prévue* projected population

port¹ *nm* ORDINAT port ▫ *port de communication* comms port, communications port; *port d'extension* expansion port; *port d'imprimante* printer port; *port modem* modem port; *port parallèle* parallel port; *port série* serial port; *port souris* mouse port

port² *nm (pour bateaux)* port, harbour; **le port du Havre** the port of Le Havre ▫ *port d'arrivée* port of arrival; *port d'attache*

home port, port of registry; *port autonome* independent *or* autonomous port; *port de commerce* commercial port; *port pour conteneurs* container port; *port de déchargement* unloading port; *port de départ* port of departure; *port de destination* port of destination; *port d'embarquement* port of loading; *port d'entrée* port of entry; *port d'entrepôt* entrepôt port; *port d'escale* port of call; *port d'expédition* port of shipment; *port fluvial* river sea; *port franc* free port; *port marchand* commercial port; *port maritime* sea port; *port ouvert* open port; *port pétrolier* oil port; *port de relâche* port of call; *port de transit* transit port

port³ *nm (de marchandises)* carriage; *(de paquet, de lettre, de télégramme)* delivery; **en port dû** carriage forward, freight collect ▫ *port avancé* carriage forward, freight collect; *port compris* postage included; *port et emballage* postage and packing; *port franc (de revue, de journal)* postage paid; *(de marchandises)* carriage paid *or* free; *port en lourd* deadweight; *port payé (de revue, de journal)* postage paid; *(de marchandises)* carriage paid; *port payé, assurance comprise* carriage insurance paid

portable **1** *adj (machine à écrire)* portable; *(ordinateur)* laptop; *(téléphone)* mobile
2 *nm (ordinateur)* laptop; *(téléphone)* mobile (phone)

portage *nm* (**a**) *(transport) (de marchandises)* porterage, transport; *(de bateau)* portage (**b**) BANQUE piggy-backing

portatif, -ive **1** *adj (machine à écrire)* portable; *(ordinateur)* laptop
2 *nm (ordinateur)* laptop

porte-à-porte *nm* door-to-door selling; **faire du porte à porte** to be a door-to-door salesman, *f* saleswoman

porte-conteneurs *nm (avion)* container aircraft; *(navire)* container ship

porte-documents *nm* document case

portée *nf* (**a**) *(d'un navire)* burden, tonnage ▫ *portée en lourd* deadweight (capacity); *portée utile* load-carrying capacity (**b**) *(impact) (d'une décision, de mesures)* impact, effect; **il est encore trop tôt pour évaluer la portée de cette brusque hausse des taux d'intérêt** it is still too early to judge the impact of this sudden rise in interest rates

portefeuille *nm* FIN portfolio ▫ *portefeuille d'actions* share portfolio; MKTG *portefeuille d'activités* business portfolio, portfolio mix; *portefeuille d'assurances* insurance portfolio; **_portefeuille effets_** bills in hand, holdings; **_portefeuille indexé_** indexed portfolio; **_portefeuille avec mandat_** discretionary portfolio; **_portefeuille de marques_** brand portfolio; **_portefeuille de produits_** product portfolio; **_portefeuille de titres_** securities portfolio

> «
> Les créances douteuses ont augmenté au cours du premier semestre de l'année fiscale, et les fonds propres, composés en partie des gains latents sur les **portefeuilles de titres**, ont fondu avec la chute du Nikkei.
> »

porte-parole _nm_ spokesperson, spokesman, _f_ spokeswoman

porter 1 _vt_ (**a**) _(signature, date)_ to bear; **la lettre porte la date du 28 novembre** the letter is dated 28 November; **l'enveloppe portait la mention "confidentiel"** the envelope was marked "confidential"
(**b**) _(intérêts)_ to bear
(**c**) _(transmettre)_ **porter qch à la connaissance de qn** to bring sth to sb's attention; **je porterai votre proposition à la connaissance du conseil d'administration** I shall bring your suggestion to the notice of the board
(**d**) _(inscrire)_ to enter, to inscribe; **porter un achat sur un compte** to enter a purchase on an account; **portez cela sur** _ou_ **à mon compte** put that on my account, charge it to my account; **portez-le sur la note** put it on the bill; **porter une somme au crédit de qn** to credit sb's account with a sum
2 **porter sur** _vt ind_ _(avoir pour sujet)_ to concern, to be about; **les négociations portent sur la possibilité de fusion des deux sociétés** the negotiations concern a possible merger of the two companies; **le détournement de fonds porte sur plusieurs millions de francs** the funds embezzled run into several millions of francs
3 **se porter** _vpr_ JUR **se porter garant de qch pour qn** to stand surety for sb for sth; **se porter acquéreur de qch** to offer to buy sth

porteur, -euse 1 _adj (marché)_ buoyant, flourishing; **l'informatique est un secteur porteur** computing is a flourishing _or_ booming industry
2 _nm,f_ FIN _(d'un chèque)_ bearer, payee; _(d'un effet)_ bearer, holder, payee; **payer au porteur** _(sur chèque)_ pay bearer ❑ **_gros porteur_** big investor; **_petit porteur_** small investor; **_porteur d'actions_** shareholder; **_porteur d'actions nominatives_** registered share-

holder; **_porteur d'obligations_** debenture holder, bondholder; **_porteur de titres_** holder of stock, stockholder

> «
> Satisfaisants pour les **porteurs d'actions**, ces bénéfices fastueux irritent fortement les consommateurs britanniques, qui y voient la preuve que les prix pratiqués par BT sont abusifs.
> »

portrait _nm_ ORDINAT **(mode) portrait** portrait (mode); **imprimer qch en portrait** to print sth in portrait

portuaire _adj_ port; **Montréal est une ville portuaire** Montreal is a port

poser _vt_ **poser sa candidature (à)** to apply (for)

position _nf_ (**a**) FIN _(d'un compte)_ balance; **demander sa position** to ask for one's balance ❑ FIN **_position de compte_** balance; **_position créditrice_** credit balance; **_position débitrice_** debit balance; **_position financière_** financial position; **_position de trésorerie_** cash(flow) situation
(**b**) BOURSE position; **liquider une position** to close (out) a position; **prendre une position inverse sur le marché** to offset ❑ **_position acheteur_** long position, bull position; **_position baissière_** short position; **_position à couvert_** covered position; **_position non couverte_** uncovered position; **_position vendeur_** short position, bear position
(**c**) _(d'une entreprise)_ position ❑ **_position clé_** key position; **_position concurrentielle_** competitive position

positionnement _nm_ (**a**) FIN _(d'un compte)_ calculation of the balance (**b**) MKTG _(sur un marché)_ positioning ❑ **_positionnement concurrentiel_** competitive positioning; **_positionnement de la marque_** brand positioning; **_positionnement de prix_** price positioning; **_positionnement du produit_** product positioning

positionner 1 _vt_ (**a**) ORDINAT _(curseur, graphique)_ to position (**b**) FIN _(compte)_ to calculate the balance of (**c**) MKTG _(produit)_ to position
2 **se positionner** _vpr_ **se positionner à la hausse sur le marché** to move upmarket; **se positionner par rapport à la concurrence** to position oneself in relation to the competition

possesseur _nm_ owner; _(de valeurs, de titres)_ holder

possession _nf_ (**a**) _(de biens, de valeurs, de titres)_ possession; **être en possession de qch**

to be in possession of sth; **entrer en possession de qch** to come into possession of sth, to come by sth; **nous sommes en possession de votre lettre du 4 mars** we are in receipt of *or* have received your letter of 4 March ▫ JUR *possession de fait* actual possession **(b)** FIN **la possession** *(d'une société)* the assets

possibilité *nf* possibility; **achat avec possibilité de versements échelonnés** purchase with the option of payment by instalments; **son poste n'offre guère de possibilités de promotion** there is little possibility for promotion in his job ▫ ORDINAT *possibilités d'extension* upgradeability

possible *adj* possible; **aussitôt que possible, le plus tôt (qu'il vous sera) possible** at your earliest convenience, as soon as possible

post-achat *adj* MKTG post-purchase

postal, -e *adj (tarif, services)* postal

postdater *vt* to postdate

poste[1] *nf* **(a)** *(service)* mail, *Br* post; **la Poste** *Br* ≃ the Post Office, *Am* ≃ the US Postal Service; **par poste aérienne** by airmail; **envoyer qch par la poste** to send sth by mail *or Br* by post; **mettre une lettre à la poste** to mail *or Br* post a letter **(b)** *(endroit)* **(bureau de) poste** post office ▫ *poste restante* poste restante

poste[2] *nm* **(a)** *(emploi)* post, position; **M. Dupont s'est vu confier le poste de directeur général** Mr Dupont was appointed general manager; **c'est un poste à responsabilités** it's a responsible job, it's a position of responsibility ▫ *poste d'encadrement* managerial position; *poste évolutif* job with prospects (for promotion); *poste à pourvoir* (job) vacancy; *poste vacant* vacant post **(b)** *(lieu)* post, station ▫ *poste douanier* customs (post); ORDINAT *poste de travail* workstation **(c)** *(de travail posté)* shift; **un poste de 12 heures** a 12-hour shift ▫ *poste de nuit* night shift **(d)** TÉL extension; **poste 106** extension 106; **le poste est occupé** the extension is *Br* engaged *or Am* busy; **je vous passe le poste** I'm putting you through **(e)** COMPTA entry, item ▫ *poste de bilan* balance sheet item; *poste créditeur* credit item; *poste débiteur* debit item; *poste extraordinaire* extraordinary item

poster *vt (courrier)* to mail, *Br* to post

postulant, -e *nm,f* applicant, candidate

postuler **postuler à** *vt ind (poste)* to apply for

pot-de-vin *nm* bribe; **verser des pots-de-vin à qn** to bribe sb

potentiel, -elle **1** *adj (acheteur, marché, ressources)* potential
2 *nm* potential; **c'est une entreprise qui a du potentiel** it's a company with potential ▫ *potentiel de croissance, potentiel de développement* growth potential; *potentiel industriel* industrial potential; *potentiel du marché* market potential; *potentiel de production* production potential *or* capacity; *potentiel publicitaire* advertising potential; *potentiel de vente* sales potential

poubelle *nf* ORDINAT wastebasket, *Am* trash

pourcentage *nm* percentage; **travailler au pourcentage** to work on a commission basis

pourcompte, pour-compte *nm* = undertaking to sell goods on behalf of a third party

poursuites *nfpl* JUR (legal) proceedings; **engager** *ou* **intenter des poursuites (judiciaires) contre qn** to take *or* to institute proceedings against sb, to take (legal) action against sb ▫ *poursuites judiciaires* legal proceedings

poursuivre *vt* JUR **poursuivre qn (en justice)** to take (legal) action against sb, to sue sb; **poursuivre qn en dommages et intérêts** to sue sb for damages

pourvoi *nm* JUR appeal

pourvoir **1** *vt* **(a)** *(équiper)* **pourvoir qn de qch** to supply *or* provide sb with sth **(b)** *(remplir) (emploi)* to fill; **le poste est toujours à pourvoir** the post is still vacant *or* to be filled
2 pourvoir à *vt ind (besoins)* to provide *or* cater for; *(frais)* to cover, to pay

pourvoyeur, -euse *nm,f* supplier

poussée *nf (des prix, d'une monnaie, de l'inflation)* rise **(de** in) ▫ *poussée inflationniste* inflationary surge

pousser *vt* ÉCON **pousser qch à la hausse/la baisse** to have an inflationary/a deflationary effect on sth; **poussé par les profits** profit-driven; **pousser la vente de qch** to push the sale of sth; **pousser un article aux enchères** to up the bidding for sth; **pousser les enchères** to run up the bidding

pouvoir *nm* **(a)** *(autorité)* power ▫ *pouvoir de décision* decision-making power; *pou-*

voir exécutif executive power; *pouvoir judiciaire* judicial power; *pouvoir législatif* legislative power; *les pouvoirs publics* the authorities (**b**) *(possibilité) pouvoir d'achat* purchasing *or* buying power; *pouvoir de négociation* bargaining power

pratique *nf* (**a**) *(procédé)* practice; **cette commission a été créée pour lutter contre les pratiques discriminatoires à l'embauche** the commission was set up to combat discriminatory recruitment practices; **c'est une pratique courante sur le marché boursier** it's common practice in the Stock Market; **la pratique de ce genre de vente est illégale en France** this kind of sales practice is illegal in France ◻ *pratiques déloyales* unfair trading; *pratiques restrictives* restrictive practices

(**b**) *(expérience)* (practical) experience; **elle a décidé d'embaucher le candidat qui avait le plus de pratique** she decided to employ the candidate with the most experience

pratiquer 1 *vt* **pratiquer des prix trop élevés** to be too expensive; **les prix pratiqués sur le marché** the ruling *or* current market prices

2 **se pratiquer** *vpr (prix, salaires)* to be in force, to apply

préalable 1 *adj (accord, étude, budget)* preliminary; *(conditions)* prerequisite

2 *nm* prerequisite, precondition; **les prix doivent être négociés au préalable** prices must be negotiated beforehand *or* in advance

PréAO *nf* ORDINAT *(abrév* **présentation assistée par ordinateur**) computer-assisted presentation

préavis *nm (notification)* (advance *or* prior) notice; *(au travail)* notice; **il a été licencié sans préavis** he was dismissed without notice; **donner un préavis d'un mois (à qn)** to give (sb) a month's notice; **exiger un préavis de trois mois** to require three months' notice; **préavis de dix jours francs** ten clear days' notice; BANQUE **dépôt à sept jours de préavis** deposit at seven days' notice ◻ *préavis de grève* strike notice; *préavis de licenciement* notice of dismissal

précis *nm (d'un article)* abstract

préciser *vt* to specify, to stipulate

précompte *nm* FIN (**a**) *(d'un compte)* advance deduction (**b**) *(de cotisations, d'impôts)* deduction at source

précompter *vt* FIN (**a**) *(argent d'un compte)* to deduct in advance (**b**) *(cotisations, impôts)* to deduct at source; **précompter la Sécurité Sociale sur le salaire de qn** to deduct social security payments from sb's salary

préconditionné, -e *adj* pre-packed, pre-packaged

préconditionner *vt* to pre-pack, to pre-package

prédécesseur *nm* predecessor

préemballé, -e *adj* pre-packed, pre-packaged

préemballer *vt* to pre-pack, to pre-package

préemption *nf* JUR pre-emption

pré-étude *nf* pilot study

préférence *nf* (**a**) *(d'un créancier)* priority (**b**) ÉCON **préférence pour la liquidité** liquidity preference (**c**) DOUANES *préférences douanières* customs preferential duty

préférentiel, -elle *adj* DOUANES *(tarif, taux)* preferential

préfinancement *nm* FIN advance funding, pre-financing

préfinancer *vt* FIN to fund in advance, to pre-finance

pré-formaté, -e *adj* ORDINAT pre-formatted

pré-formater *vt* ORDINAT to pre-format

pré-installé, -e *adj* ORDINAT pre-installed

pré-installer *vt* ORDINAT to pre-install

préjudice *nm* prejudice, detriment; **sans préjudice de nos droits** without prejudice (to our rights); **subir un préjudice matériel** to sustain damage; **subir un préjudice moral** to suffer mental distress; **porter préjudice à qn** to do sb harm; **au préjudice de qch** to the detriment of sth ◻ *préjudice financier* financial harm

préjudiciable *adj* detrimental

prélèvement *nm* FIN *(action)* deduction (**sur** from); *(somme prélevée)* amount deducted; **faire un prélèvement sur un compte** to debit an account; **le prélèvement sera effectué le dernier jour de chaque mois** the deduction will be made on the last day of each month ◻ UE *prélèvements agricoles* agricultural levies; BANQUE *prélèvement bancaire (automatique)* direct debit; *prélèvement sur le capital* capital levy; *prélèvement à l'exportation* export levy; *prélèvement fiscal* taxation; *prélèvement de l'impôt à la source* taxation at source; *prélèvement libératoire* deduction (of tax) at source; *prélèvements obligatoires* = tax and social security contributions; *prélève-*

ment salarial, **prélèvement sur salaire** deduction from wages; **prélèvement social** social security contribution

>
> Le Japon rechute dans la récession et l'Allemagne risque de suivre la même voie après l'alourdissement des **prélèvements fiscaux**, début 1994.
>

prélever *vt* to deduct in advance; *(compte)* to draw on; **prélever 10% sur qch** to make an advance deduction of 10% from sth, to deduct 10% in advance from sth; **prélever une commission de 2% sur une opération** to charge a 2% commission on a transaction; **dividende prélevé sur le capital** dividend paid out of capital; **prélever une somme sur un salaire** to deduct a sum from a salary; **prélever une somme sur un compte** to withdraw a sum from an account; **prélever qch à la source** to deduct sth at source

premier, -ère 1 *adj* first; **produit de premier choix** *ou* **première qualité** top-quality product; **la France est le premier exportateur de produits agricoles de l'Union européenne** France is the leading exporter of agricultural products in the EU ❑ **Premier Ministre** Prime Minister

2 *nm* **premier entré, premier sorti** first in, first out

prendre *vt* **(a)** *(avion, bateau, train)* to take **(b)** *(faire payer)* to charge; **prendre 40 francs (de) l'heure** to charge 40 francs an hour **(c)** *(embaucher)* to take on, to hire; **prendre un associé** to take on a partner; **prendre qn comme secrétaire** to hire sb as one's secretary **(d)** *(noter)* *(lettre, coordonnées)* to take; **voulez-vous prendre une lettre?** will you take a letter? **(e)** *(charger)* *(marchandises)* to take in **(f)** **prendre qn/qch en charge** to take charge of sb/sth; **prendre des frais en charge** to cover costs **(g)** **prendre date** to fix a date; **prendre rendez-vous** to make an appointment

preneur, -euse *nm,f* buyer, purchaser; *(d'un chèque, d'une lettre de change)* payee; JUR *(d'un bail)* lessee, leaseholder; **nous sommes preneurs** we are interested in buying; **trouver preneur** to find a buyer ❑ JUR **preneur à bail** lessee, leaseholder

prépayer *vt* to prepay

préposé, -e *nm,f* *(employé)* employee ❑ **préposé à la caisse** cashier; **préposé des douanes** customs officer

préposer *vt* **préposer qn à une fonction** to appoint sb to a position; **préposer qn à la direction d'un service** to appoint sb as head of department

préprogrammer *vt* ORDINAT to preprogram

préretraite *nf* early retirement; **partir en préretraite** to take early retirement; **être mis en préretraite** to be given early retirement

>
> Les ... départs en retraite ou **préretraite** n'occupent qu'une place mineure dans les sorties d'emploi.
>

prérogative *nf* prerogative

prescription *nf* FIN **prescription acquisitive** positive prescription; **prescription extinctive** negative prescription

prescrit, -e *adj* stipulated; **dans les délais prescrits par la loi** within the legally required time; **à la date prescrite** on the agreed date

présentateur, -trice *nm,f* *(d'une traite, d'un chèque)* presenter

présentation *nf* **(a)** *(d'une traite, d'un chèque)* presentation; **sur présentation de** on presentation of; **présentation à l'encaissement** BANQUE paying in, *Br* encashment; ADMIN presentation for collection; **présentation au paiement** presentation for payment **(b)** MKTG display ❑ **présentation sur le lieu de vente** point-of-sale display; **présentation en masse** mass display; **présentation du produit** product display; **présentation au sol** floor display; **présentation à la sortie** checkout display; **présentation en vrac** dump display **(c)** *(à un client potentiel)* presentation; **faire une présentation** to make a presentation **(d)** *(d'une lettre)* layout **(e)** *(apparence)* appearance; **excellente présentation exigée** *(dans une offre d'emploi)* excellent presentation required

présenter *vt* **(a)** FIN **présenter une traite à l'acceptation** to present a bill for acceptance; **présenter un chèque à l'encaissement** to present a cheque for payment **(b)** *(proposer)* **présenter une motion à l'assemblée** to put a motion to the meeting **(c)** MKTG to display **(d)** *(montrer)* to show; **votre compte présente un solde créditeur de 50 000 francs** your account shows a credit balance of 50,000 francs

présentoir *nm* MKTG display stand, display unit; *(panier)* dump bin ❑ **présentoir de**

caisse checkout display; *présentoir au sol* floor display, floor stand

présérie *nf* pre-production, pilot run

présidence *nf* chairmanship, presidency; **être nommé à la présidence de qch** to be appointed chairman of sth; **les pays de l'UE se succèdent à la présidence tous les six mois** a different EU member state assumes the presidency every six months; **elle a été élue à la présidence de la société** she was elected chairwoman of the company

président, -e *nm,f* (a) *(d'une réunion, d'une commission)* chairperson, chairman, *f* chairwoman; **être élu président** to be voted into the chair, to be elected chairperson □ *président d'honneur* honorary chairperson *or* president (b) *(d'une entreprise) Br* chairman, *Am* president □ *président du conseil d'administration Br* chairman (of the board), *Am* president; *président-directeur général Br* Chairman and Managing Director, *Am* Chief Executive Officer; *président du directoire Br* chairman (of the board), *Am* president

présider 1 *vt* (réunion, commission) to preside over, to chair
2 *vi* **présider à une réunion** to preside over a meeting, to chair a meeting

presse *nf* **la presse** the press □ *presse nationale* national press; *presse professionnelle* trade press

presse-papiers *nm* ORDINAT clipboard

pression *nf* pressure; **la pression de la demande a entraîné des ruptures de stocks** the pressure on demand has led to stock shortages; **la pression de la concurrence les a contraints à baisser leurs prix** pressure from the competition forced them to lower their prices; **sous la pression des syndicats, la direction a finalement accepté de revoir les salaires à la hausse** under pressure from the unions, the management finally agreed to revise salaries upwards □ *pression fiscale* tax burden; *pression inflationniste* inflationary pressure

prestataire *nmf* (a) ADMIN person receiving benefits *or* allowances (b) *(fournisseur)* *prestataire de service* contractor, service provider

prestation *nf* (a) *(allocation)* benefit, allowance; **verser les prestations** to pay out benefits; **recevoir des prestations** to receive benefits □ *prestations familiales* family benefits; *prestation indemnitaire* allowance, benefit; *prestations maladie* sickness benefit; *prestations sociales* social security benefits (b) *(service)* service □ *prestation de capitaux* provision of capital; *prestation de service* provision of a service

> La majeure partie des régimes de prévoyance mis en place dans les entreprises offrent des **prestations** uniformes en cas de décès, de maladie ou d'invalidité.

prêt loan; **accorder/consentir un prêt** to allow/to grant a loan; **demander** *ou* **solliciter un prêt** to apply for a loan □ *prêt pour l'accession à la propriété* home loan; *prêts d'aide à l'investissement ou au développement des entreprises* loan guarantee scheme; *prêt bail* leasing; *prêt bancaire* bank loan; *prêt de banque à banque* inter-bank loan; *prêt bonifié* loan at reduced rate of interest, soft loan; *prêt conditionnel, prêt à condition* tied loan; *prêt à la consommation* consumer loan; *prêt à court terme* short(-term) loan; *prêt à découvert* overdraft loan; *prêt de démarrage* start-up loan; *prêt d'épargne-logement* home loan; *prêt à fonds perdus* loan without security; *prêt sur gage* loan against security; *prêt garanti* guaranteed loan; *prêt d'honneur* loan on trust; *prêt hypothécaire, prêt sur hypothèque* mortgage loan; *prêt immobilier Br* property *or Am* real-estate loan; *prêt à intérêts* loan at interest, interest-bearing loan; *prêt sans intérêt* interest-free loan; FIN *prêts au jour le jour* loan at call; *prêt à long terme* long(-term) loan; *prêt sur nantissement* loan on collateral; *prêt participatif* equity loan; *prêts aux particuliers* personal loans; *prêt personnalisé, prêt personnel* personal loan; *prêt à la petite semaine* = short-term loan at high rate of interest; *prêt remboursable sur demande* loan at call, loan repayable on demand; *prêt en souffrance* non-performing loan; *prêt à terme* loan at notice; *prêt à terme fixe* term loan; *prêt sur titres* loan against securities

prétendant, -e *nm,f* MKTG challenger

prête-nom *nm* FIN *(société)* dummy company

prétention *nf* (a) *(demande)* claim (**à** to); **exposé détaillé des prétentions du demandeur** detailed statement of claim (b) *(financière)* expected salary; **envoyer curriculum vitae et prétentions (de salaire)** send CV and state salary requirements

prêter *vt* to lend, to loan; **prêter de l'argent à intérêt** to lend money at interest; **prêter à 8%** to lend at 8%; **prêter sur garantie** *ou* **gage(s)** to lend against security; **prêter à la petite semaine** to make a short-term loan at a high rate of interest

prêteur, -euse *nm,f* lender; JUR bailor
❑ *prêteur sur gages* pawnbroker

prêt-relais *nm Br* bridging loan, *Am* bridge loan

préventif, -ive *adj (mesure)* preventive

prévision *nf* forecast; *(activité)* forecasting; **nous avons constitué des stocks en prévision d'une hausse subite de la demande** we have built up stocks in anticipation of a sudden increase in demand; **nos résulats sont inférieurs à nos prévisions** our results are lower than *or* below forecast ❑ BOURSE *prévision boursière* Stock Market forecast; *prévisions budgétaires* budget estimates *or* forecasts; *prévisions conjoncturelles* economic prospects; *prévision du marché* market forecast; *prévision de ventes* sales forecast; *prévision des ventes et profits* sales and profit forecast

prévisionnel, -elle *adj (coût)* estimated; *(budget)* predicted

prévisionniste *nmf* ÉCON forecaster

prévisualisation *nf* ORDINAT print preview

prévoir *vt (augmentation, baisse)* to foresee, to forecast; **les experts prévoient une baisse du chômage dans les mois à venir** the experts are forecasting a drop in unemployment over the coming months; **ventes prévues** projected sales; **il prévoit une baisse de 4% au mois de mai** he's projecting a 4% fall in May; **la mise en service de ces ordinateurs est prévue pour l'année prochaine** these computers are scheduled for installation next year; **la réunion est prévue pour demain** the meeting is arranged for *or* will be held tomorrow; **dépenses prévues au budget** expenses provided *or* allowed for in the budget; **selon les conditions prévues dans le contrat** according to the conditions set out in the contract; **le contrat prévoit une prime de licenciement** the contract provides for a severance payment

prévoyance *nf* FIN contingency, provision for the future ❑ *prévoyance sociale* social security provisions

prier *vt* **nous vous prions de bien vouloir accepter l'assurance de nos sentiments les meilleurs** *(dans une lettre) (à quelqu'un dont on connaît le nom)* yours sincerely; *(à quelqu'un dont on ne connaît pas le nom)* yours faithfully; **nous vous prions de bien vouloir vous présenter à l'accueil à 14 heures** please report to reception at 2 pm

prière *nf (utilisé dans la correspondance)* **prière de nous couvrir par chèque** kindly remit by cheque; **prière de faire suivre** please forward; **prière de bien vouloir confirmer votre commande** please confirm your order

primaire ÉCON **1** *adj (secteur)* primary
2 *nm* primary sector

prime *nf* **(a)** ASSUR premium ❑ *prime annuelle* annual premium; *prime d'assurance* insurance premium; *prime nette* pure premium; *prime de renouvellement* renewal premium; *prime unique* single premium

(b) FIN, BOURSE premium, option; **abandonner la prime** to forfeit *or* surrender the option; **acheter à prime** to give for the call; **donner la réponse à une prime, répondre à une prime** to declare an option; **faire prime** to stand at a premium; **lever la prime** to exercise *or* take up an option ❑ *prime du change* agio; *prime de conversion* conversion premium; *prime sur le dollar* dollar premium; *prime d'émission* issue premium; *prime de fusion* merger premium; *prime de l'or* premium on gold; *prime de remboursement* premium on redemption

(c) *(subvention)* subsidy, grant ❑ *prime de développement* (government) development subsidy *or* grant; *prime à l'exportation* export subsidy; *prime à l'investissement* investment subsidy

(d) *(sur salaire)* bonus ❑ *prime d'ancienneté* = bonus for long service; *prime de déménagement* relocation allowance; *prime de départ* severance pay, golden handshake; *prime d'efficacité* efficiency bonus; *prime d'encouragement* incentive bonus; *prime d'intéressement* reversionary bonus; *prime de licenciement* severance pay; *prime de mérite* merit bonus; *prime de productivité* productivity bonus; *prime de rendement* productivity bonus; *(suite à une mission réussie)* success fee; *prime de risque* danger money; *prime de transport* travel allowance; *prime de vie chère* cost-of-living allowance, *Br* weighting

(e) MKTG free gift; **recette donnée en prime avec ce produit** free recipe when you buy this product ◻ *prime échantillon* free sample

> La modération salariale, la chute des heures supplémentaires et des **primes** amputent leur pouvoir d'achat alors que la baisse des prix immobiliers et la dégradation de l'emploi, renforcent l'incitation à épargner.

principal, -e **1** *adj* principal, main; **le vin est la production principale du pays** wine is the main product of the country; **un des principaux actionnaires** a major shareholder **2** *nm* FIN principal, capital sum; *(de l'impôt)* = original amount of tax payable before surcharges ◻ *principal et intérêts* principal and interest

principe *nm* principle; **c'est un principe directeur de la politique de notre entreprise** it's a guiding principle of our company's policy ◻ *principes économiques* economic principles; COMPTA *principe de la partie double* double-entry method; COMPTA *principe de la partie simple* single-entry method

prioritaire *adj* priority; **être prioritaire** to have priority; **notre projet est prioritaire sur tous les autres** our project has priority over all the others

priorité *nf* priority; JUR priority of claim; **avoir la priorité** to have priority; **il faut établir une liste des priorités pour l'entreprise** we must draw up a list of priorities for the company; **la recherche de nouveaux débouchés est une priorité absolue pour notre société** finding new outlets is an absolute priority for our company

pris, -e *adj* *(occupé)* busy; **elle est très prise en ce moment** she's very busy at the moment; **je suis pris mercredi toute la journée** I'm busy all day Wednesday

prise *nf* FIN *prise de bénéfices* profit-taking; *prise en charge* *(de frais)* payment, covering; *prise de contrôle (majoritaire)* takeover; *prise de décision* decision-making; *prise à domicile* receipt at domicile; *prise de participation* *(dans une entreprise)* acquisition of an interest in a company; BOURSE *prise de position* position taking

privatif, -ive *adj* *(droit)* exclusive, private

privatisation *nf* privatization

> Les **privatisations** des banques en 1992 ont provoqué l'apparition de nouveaux instruments financiers sophistiqués pour répondre aux besoins nouveaux des épargnants.

privatiser *vt* to privatize

privé, -e *adj* *(banque, entreprise, propriété, secteur, investisseur)* private

privilège *nm* **(a)** BANQUE *privilège d'émission* exclusive right to issue banknotes **(b)** FIN, JUR preferential right; **avoir un privilège sur qch** to have a lien *or* charge on sth ◻ *privilège du créancier* creditor's preferential claim; *privilège fiscal* tax privilege; *privilège général* general lien; *privilège spécial* particular lien

privilégier *vt* **(a)** *(personne, groupe)* to privilege; *(facteur, aspect)* to prioritize; **les augmentations en pourcentage privilégient les haut salaires** percentage increases work in favour of high salaries **(b)** *(banque)* to grant a charter to; *(créancier)* to give preference to

prix *nm* **(a)** *(coût)* price; **à moitié prix** half price; **acheter qch à bas prix** to buy sth at a low price *or* cheaply; **je vous ferai un prix (d'ami)** I'll let you have it cheap; **mettre un prix à qch** to price sth, to put a price to sth; **prix à débattre** *(dans une annonce)* price negotiable ◻ MKTG *prix d'acceptabilité* psychological price; *prix d'achat* purchase price; *prix adapté au marché* market-based price; *prix d'adjudication* auction price; *prix affiché* sticker price, displayed price; *prix d'appel* loss leader price; *prix cassés* knock-down prices; *prix catalogue* catalogue price; *prix (au) comptant* cash price; *prix conseillé* recommended retail price; *prix contractuel* contract *or* contractual price; *prix courants du marché* current market prices; *prix coûtant* purchase price, cost price; **acheter/vendre qch au prix coûtant** to buy/sell sth at cost; *prix demandé* asking price; *prix démarqués* double pricing; *prix de demi-gros* trade price; *prix de départ* *(à une vente aux enchères)* upset price; *prix départ usine* price ex-works, factory price; *prix directeur* price leader; *prix d'équilibre* choice price, average price; *prix exceptionnel* bargain price; *prix à l'exportation, prix (à l')export* export price; *prix de fabrique* cost price, manufacturer's price; *prix facturé* invoice *or* invoiced price; *prix de faveur* preferential *or* special price; *prix fixe* fixed price, all-inclusive price; *prix forfaitaire, prix à forfait* fixed price, all-inclusive price; *prix fort (de vente)* full price; *prix de gros* wholesale price; *prix homologué* authorized price; *prix hors taxe* price net of tax, price before tax; *prix à l'importation* import price; *prix imposé* retail price maintenance; *prix indicatif* approximate price; *prix initial* starting price; *prix de* *lancement* introductory price; *prix limite* upper price limit; *prix de liquidation* closing-down price; *prix loco* loco price; MKTG *prix magique* odd numbers price; *prix marchand* trade price; *prix du marché* market price; *prix marqué* marked price; *prix minimum* minimum price; *prix net* net price; *(sur un menu)* price inclusive of service; *prix offert* offered *or* selling price; *prix officiel* standard price; *prix optimum* optimal price; *prix sur place* loco price; ÉCON *prix plafond* ceiling price; *prix plancher* bottom price; *prix pratiqué* current price; *prix préférentiel* preferential price; MKTG *prix de prestige* premium price; *prix à la production* price ex warehouse; *prix promotionnels* promotional pricing; MKTG *prix psychologique* psychological price; *prix public* posted price, list price; *prix de rabais* reduced or discount price; *prix réduit* reduced or discount price; *prix réel* actual price; *prix de référence* reference price; *prix de revient* cost price; ÉCON *prix seuil* floor price; UE *prix du seuil* threshold price; *prix de solde* bargain price; *prix standard* standard price; *prix taxé* standard price; *prix taxe comprise* price inclusive of tax; *prix tout compris, prix tous frais compris, prix toutes taxes comprises* all-inclusive price; *prix de transport* freight price; *prix unique* one price, single price; *prix unitaire* unit price; *prix d'usine* factory price; *prix à la vente* sticker price, displayed price; *prix de vente* selling price

(b) BOURSE, FIN price; **ces actions sont cotées au prix de...** these shares are quoted at the rate of... ▫ *prix acheteur* bid price; *prix de l'argent* price of money; *prix du change* (exchange) premium; *prix (au) comptant, prix du disponible* spot price; *prix d'émission* issue price; *prix d'exercice* exercise price; *(d'option d'achat)* exercise price, strike price; *prix de facture* invoice or Am billing price; *prix du marché* market price; **acheter/vendre au prix du marché** to buy/sell at market price; *prix de négociation* trade price; *prix de l'option* option price; *prix du report* contango rate; *prix à terme* forward price; *prix vendeur* offer price

prix-courant *nm* price list, catalogue

prix-étalon *nm* standard cost *or* price

probatoire *adj (période)* probationary

procédé *nm* process ▫ *procédé comptable* accounting procedure; *procédé de fabrication* manufacturing process; *procédé de travail* operating process

procédure *nf* **(a)** *(méthode)* procedure ▫ ORDINAT *procédure de chargement* loading procedure; *procédure de licenciement* dismissal procedure

(b) JUR proceedings; **engager une procédure contre qn** to institute proceedings against sb ▫ *procédure de faillite* bankruptcy proceedings

procès *nm* proceedings; *(civil)* lawsuit; *(criminel)* trial; **intenter un procès à qn** to institute proceedings against sb

processeur *nm* ORDINAT processor ▫ *processeur central* central processing unit, CPU; *processeur de données* data processor

processus *nm* process ▫ *processus décisionnel, processus de décision* decision-making process; *processus de fabrication* manufacturing process

procès-verbal *nm* (official) report; *(d'une réunion)* minutes; **dresser un procès-verbal** to draw up a report; **tenir le procès-verbal de la réunion** to keep the minutes of the meeting; **le procès-verbal de la dernière séance a été approuvé** the minutes of the last meeting were approved ▫ *procès-verbal des avaries* protest

procuration *nf* JUR proxy, power of attorney; **signé par procuration** signed by proxy; **agir par procuration** to act by proxy; **donner procuration à qn** to give sb power of attorney; **avoir procuration sur un compte** to have power of attorney over an account ▫ *procuration générale* full power of attorney

procurer **1** *vt* to get, to obtain (**à** for); **procurer un emploi à qn** to get sb a job

2 se procurer *vpr* to get *or* obtain for oneself

procureur *nm* JUR prosecutor

producteur, -trice **1** *adj* productive; **producteur d'intérêt** interest-bearing; **les pays producteurs de pétrole** the oil-producing countries

2 *nm,f* producer; **ce pays est le premier producteur d'acier du monde** this country is the world's largest steel producer

productif, -ive *adj* productive; **productif d'intérêts** interest-bearing

production *nf* **(a)** *(fait de produire)* production; *(quantités produites)* production, output; **augmenter la production** to increase production; **ralentir la production** to slow down production ▫ *production à la chaîne* mass production; *production sur ou à la commande* production to order;

production continue continuous flow production; *production dirigée* planned production; *production discontinue* production in batches; *production globale* aggregate production; FIN *production immobilisée* = fixed assets produced for use by the company; *production intérieure brute* gross domestic product; *production juste à temps* just-in-time production; *production par lots* batch production; *production à la machine* machine production; *production manufacturée* secondary production; *production de masse* mass production; *production de matières premières* primary production; *production planifiée* planned production; *production en série* mass production

(b) *(produit)* product □ COMPTA *production stockée* *(poste de bilan)* stored production, production left in stock; COMPTA *production vendue* sales

productivité *nf* productivity, productive capacity

> " ————
> Les patrons préfèrent recourir aux heures supplémentaires et accroître la **productivité** plutôt que d'embaucher.
> ———— "

produire 1 *vt* (a) *(documents)* to produce
(b) *(intérêt)* to bear, to yield
(c) *(marchandise, produit)* to produce, to manufacture; **produire qch en masse** to mass-produce sth; **produire qch en série** *ou* **à la chaîne** to produce sth on an assembly line
2 *vi* ÉCON to produce, to be productive

produit *nm* (a) *(article)* product □ *produits d'achat courant* convenience goods; *produits alimentaires, produits d'alimentation* food products; MKTG *produit d'appel* loss leader; *produit de base* staple commodity *or* product; *produits de consommation courante* consumer goods; *produits en cours* work in progress; MKTG *produits de dépannage* emergency goods; *produits dérivés* by-products, derivatives; MKTG *produit drapeau* own-brand product; *produit écologique* green product; *produits étrangers* foreign produce *or* goods; *produit final* end product; *produit fini* finished *or* end product; MKTG *produit générique* generic product; *produits de grande consommation* consumer products; *produit de haut niveau* high standard product; MKTG *produit d'imitation* imitative product; *produit industriel* industrial product; *produits intermédiaires* semi-finished products;

produits de luxe luxury goods; *produits manufacturés* manufactured goods *or* products; *produit de marque* branded *or* brand-name product; *produit sans marque* unbranded product; MKTG *produit sans nom* no-name product; *produit novateur* innovative product; *produits d'origine nationale* home(-grown) produce; *produit ouvré* finished *or* end product; *produits du pays* home produce; *produits périssables* non-durable goods; *produit de première nécessité* essential *or* staple product; *produits de second choix* seconds, rejects; *produit semi-fini* semi-finished product; *produit semi-ouvré* semi-manufactured product; *produits spécialisés* speciality goods; MKTG *produit substituable* substitutable product; *produit de substitution* substitute product; MKTG *produit tactique* me-too product; MKTG *produit vert* green product

(b) *(profit)* yield; *(recette)* proceeds; **le produit de la journée** the day's takings *or* proceeds □ FIN *produits accessoires* sundry income; COMPTA *produits annexes* incidental income; *produit augmenté* augmented product; COMPTA *produit brut* gross proceeds, gross income; COMPTA *produit constaté d'avance* prepaid income; COMPTA *produits courants* current income; COMPTA *produits exceptionnels* extraordinary income; COMPTA *produits d'exploitation* income from operations; COMPTA *produits financiers* interest received; COMPTA *produits de gestion courante* income from operations; ÉCON *produit intérieur brut* gross domestic product; ÉCON *produit intérieur net* net domestic product; *produit moyen* average revenue; ÉCON *produit national brut* gross national product; *produit net* net earnings *or* proceeds; COMPTA *produits à recevoir* accrued income, accruals
(c) BANQUE *produit bancaire* banking product

> " ————
> Il est vrai que Bruxelles n'a obtenu qu'une obligation de discussion – et non une limitation – concernant l'invasion des **produits de substitution** des céréales.
> ———— "

profession *nf* profession; **être sans profession** to be out of a job

professionnalisme *nm* professionalism

professionnel, -elle *adj & nm,f* professional

profil *nm* profile; **quel est le profil du candidat idéal?** what is the profile of the ideal candidate?; **elle a le profil requis pour ce genre de poste** she has the right profile for this kind of job ❑ MKTG *profil de la clientèle* customer profile; MKTG *profil des consommateurs* consumer profile; *profil d'entreprise* company profile; MKTG *profil du marché* market profile; BANQUE *profil patrimonial* personal assets profile; MKTG *profil de produit* product profile; *profil psychologique* psychological profile

profit *nm* profit; **vendre à profit** to sell at a profit; **profit de 12%** 12% profit ❑ COMPTA *profit brut* gross profit; *profit espéré* anticipated profit; *profits exceptionnels* windfall profits; *profits de l'exercice* year's profits; *profit d'exploitation* operating profit; *profits fictifs* paper profits; *profits non matérialisés* paper profits; *profits mis en réserve* capital reserves; *profit net* clear profit; *profits et pertes* profit and loss; *profit réel* real profit; *profit tout clair* clear profit

profitable *adj* profitable

profiter 1 **profiter de** *vt ind* to take advantage of; **ils ont profité de la baisse des taux d'intérêt** they took advantage of the drop in interest rates
2 **profiter à** *vt ind* to benefit; **la chute du franc a profité aux exportateurs** the fall in the value of the franc benefited exporters

profiteur, -euse *nm,f* profiteer

pro forma *adj* pro forma

progiciel *nm* ORDINAT software package ❑ *progiciel de communication* comms package; *progiciel de comptabilité* accounting package; *progiciel intégré* integrated package

programmateur, -trice *nm,f* ORDINAT programmer

programmation *nf* (a) *(planning)* programming, planning ❑ *programmation de la production* production scheduling (b) ORDINAT programming ❑ *programmation par objets, programmation orientée objet* object-oriented programming

programme *nm* (a) *(planning)* programme, schedule; **arrêter un programme** to draw up *or* arrange a programme ❑ MKTG *programme d'amélioration de la qualité* quality improvement programme; *programme de développement* development programme; *programme de fabrication* production programme *or* schedule; *programme de fidélisation* frequent user programme; *programme de formation* training programme; FIN *programme d'in-*

vestissement investment programme; *programme de maintenance* maintenance programme; *programme de production* production programme *or* schedule; *programme de recherche(s)* research programme; MKTG *programme des ventes* sales programme *or* schedule (b) ORDINAT program ❑ *programme antivirus* antivirus program; *programme de commande d'impression* printer driver; *programme de commande de la souris* mouse driver; *programme de conversion* conversion program; *programme en cours d'éxécution* active program; *programme de dessin* drawing program, paint program; *programme sentinelle* watchdog program; *programme utilitaire* utility program; *programme virus* virus program

programmé, -e *adj* ORDINAT programmed

programmer 1 *vt* (a) ORDINAT to program; **programmer en assembleur** to program in assembly language (b) *(prévoir)* to plan, to schedule
2 *vi* ORDINAT to program

programmeur, -euse *nm,f* ORDINAT programmer

progrès *nm* progress; **faire des progrès** to make progress

progressif, -ive *adj (développement, croissance)* progressive, gradual; *(impôt, taux)* graduated, progressive; **l'amélioration progressive du rendement** the gradual improvement in productivity

progression *nf* (a) *(de la situation économique)* upturn; *(d'un secteur)* expansion; *(des bénéfices)* increase; BOURSE *(des actions)* rise, improvement; **être en progression** *(secteur)* to be growing *or* expanding; **les ventes sont en progression par rapport à l'année dernière** sales are on the increase compared with last year (b) *(dans une carrière)* progress, advancement

progressivement *adv* progressively, gradually; **adopter qch progressivement** to phase sth in

progressivité *nf* progressivity ❑ FIN *progressivité de l'impôt* progressive increase in taxation

prohibé, -e *adj (marchandises)* prohibited

prohibitif, -ive *adj (prix, tarif)* prohibitive

prohibition *nf* prohibition, ban ❑ *prohibition d'entrée, prohibition à l'importation* import prohibition *or* ban; *prohibition de sortie* export prohibition *or* ban

projection *nf* projection ❑ *projection des ventes* sales projection

projet nm plan, project; **être à l'état de projet** to be at the planning stage ❑ **projet de budget** budget estimates; **projet de contrat** draft contract; JUR **projet de loi** bill

projeter vt to plan; **ils projettent d'ouvrir une nouvelle usine au Mexique** they are planning to open a new factory in Mexico

prolongation nf extension; **obtenir une prolongation de congé** to get an extension of leave

prolonger vt (délai) to extend

promesse nf (a) MKTG claim ❑ **promesse mensongère** false claim; **promesse unique de vente** unique selling point, USP (b) FIN undertaking ❑ **promesse d'achat** undertaking or promise to purchase; **promesse écrite** written undertaking; **promesse de vente** undertaking or promise to sell

> ❝
> Les **promesses de ventes** d'appartements anciens à Paris ont progressé respectivement de 7,8 et 12,6% durant les deux premiers trimestres de 1993.
> ❞

promo nf Fam promo

promoteur, -trice nm,f promoter ❑ **promoteur (immobilier)** property developer; **promoteur des ventes** sales promoter

> ❝
> Les **promoteurs immobiliers** regroupés dans la Fédération nationale des promoteurs-constructeurs (FNPC) ne croient pas à une amélioration de la conjoncture en 1994 pour le logement.
> ❞

promotion nf (a) (d'un employé) promotion ❑ **promotion à l'ancienneté** promotion by seniority; **promotion des cadres** executive promotion; **promotion interne** internal promotion
(b) (offre spéciale) promotion; **articles en promotion** items on promotion or Am on special; **notre promotion de la semaine** this week's special offer or Am special; **faire une promotion sur un produit** to promote a product; **faire la promotion de qch** to promote sth ❑ MKTG **promotion d'entreprises** corporate identity; **promotion immobilière** property development promotion; MKTG **promotion sur le lieu de vente** point-of-sale promotion; MKTG **promotion sur point d'achat** point-of-purchase promotion; **promotion spéciale** special promotion; **promotion des ventes** sales promotion

promotionnel, -elle adj (brochure) promotional; (tarif) special; (budget) promotional, publicity

promouvoir vt (a) (donner de l'avancement à) to promote; **être promu** to be promoted (b) (article) to promote, to publicize

pronostic nm forecast ❑ **pronostic du marché** market forecast

propension nf ÉCON propensity ❑ **propension à consommer** propensity to consume; **propension à épargner** propensity to save

proportion nf proportion

proportionnalité nf (rapport) balance; (répartition) equal distribution ❑ FIN **proportionnalité de l'impôt** fixed rate system of taxation

proportionnel, -elle adj proportional (à to); (impôt, droit) ad valorem

proportionnellement adv proportionally (à to)

proposer vt (service, prix) to recommend; (candidat) to nominate; **être proposé pour un emploi** to be recommended for a job; **proposer une motion** to propose a motion

proposition nf (suggestion) suggestion, proposal; (offre) offer; **faire ou formuler une proposition** to make a proposal; **dernière proposition** final offer ❑ **proposition d'affaires** business proposition; **proposition d'assurance** insurance proposal; **proposition de loi** bill; **proposition de paiement** payment proposal; **proposition de prix** price proposal; **proposition de rachat** offer to buy; **faire une proposition de rachat à une entreprise** to make an offer to buy a company; MKTG **proposition unique de vente** unique selling point, USP

propriétaire nmf (d'une entreprise, d'un hôtel) owner, proprietor; (des actions) holder ❑ **propriétaire foncier** landowner; **propriétaire individuelle** individual owner; **propriétaire indivis** joint owner; **propriétaire légitime** rightful or legal owner; **propriétaire occupant** owner-occupier; **propriétaire unique** sole owner

propriété nf (a) (fait de posséder) ownership, proprietorship ❑ **propriété artistique** copyright; **propriété collective** collective ownership; **propriété commerciale** = commercial tenant's right to security of tenure or compensation; **propriété commune** joint ownership; **propriété foncière** land ownership; **propriété individuelle** individual ownership; **propriété indivise** joint ownership
(b) (chose ou terre possédée) property, estate ❑ **propriété de l'État** government property;

propriété foncière landed estate; *propriété immobilière* real estate, *Am* realty; *propriété industrielle* patent rights, industrial property; *propriété intellectuelle* intellectual property; *propriété mobilière* personal estate; *propriété privée* private property; *propriété publique* public property; *propriété à vendre* property for sale

prorata *nm* proportion; **au prorata** proportionately, pro rata; **au prorata de qch** proportionately to sth

prorogation *nf* extension of time limit; *(d'un contrat, d'un bail)* extension, renewal

proroger *vt* to extend; *(contrat, bail)* to extend, to renew; **proroger l'échéance d'un billet** to extend the maturity of a bill

> ❝
> L'exonération des cotisations sociales pour le deuxième et le troisième salarié est **prorogée** jusqu'au 31 décembre 1995.
> ❞

prospect *nm* MKTG prospective customer, prospect □ *prospects à forte potentialité* hot prospect pool

prospecté, -e *nm,f* MKTG prospective customer, prospect

prospecter *vt* *(client)* to canvass; *(marché)* to explore; **prospecter la clientèle** to canvass for new business

prospecteur, -trice *nm,f* canvasser

prospectif, -ive *adj* prospective

prospection *nf* MKTG canvassing, prospecting; **faire de la prospection** to explore the market □ *prospection des marchés* market exploration; *prospection téléphonique* telephone marketing; *prospection sur le terrain* field research

prospectus *nm* **(a)** BOURSE prospectus **(d'émission)** prospectus **(b)** *(de publicité)* leaflet; *(de plusieurs pages)* brochure; *(donnant renseignements de base)* fact sheet

prospère *adj* prosperous, thriving

prospérer *vi* to prosper, to thrive

prospérité *nf* prosperity

protecteur, -trice *adj* ÉCON *(droits, tarif)* protective

protection *nf* **(a)** *(défense)* protection (**contre** from *or* against) □ *protection du consommateur* consumer protection; *protection de l'emploi* job protection; *protection de l'environnement* environmental protection, protection of the environment; *protection sociale* social welfare (system)

(b) ÉCON protection(ism)

(c) ORDINAT protection □ *protection contre la copie* copy protection; *protection contre l'écriture* ou *en écriture* write-protection; *protection de fichiers* file protection; *protection de l'information* data protection; *protection par mot de passe* password protection

protectionnisme *nm* ÉCON protectionism

protectionniste *adj* ÉCON protectionist

protégé, -e *adj* **(a)** protected; **protégé contre l'inflation** inflation-proof **(b)** ORDINAT **protégé contre la copie** copy-protected; **protégé contre l'écriture** ou **en écriture** write-protected; **protégé par mot de passe** password-protected

protéger *vt* **(a)** ÉCON *(industrie)* to protect; BOURSE *(position)* to hedge; **protéger qch par un brevet** to patent sth **(b)** ORDINAT **protéger contre l'écriture** ou **en écriture** to write-protect; **protéger contre la copie** to copy-protect

protestable *adj* FIN *(effet)* protestable

protester *vt* FIN *(effet)* to protest

protêt *nm* JUR protest; **dresser un protêt** to make a protest; **signifier un protêt** to give notice of a protest □ *protêt authentique* certified protest; *protêt faute d'acceptation* protest for non-acceptance; *protêt faute de paiement* protest for non-payment

protocole *nm* **(a)** *(procès-verbal)* protocol □ *protocole d'accord* draft agreement, heads of agreement; *protocole d'intention* statement of intent; *protocole de vente* sale agreement

(b) ORDINAT protocol; *(de réseau)* frame format; *(de traitement)* procedure □ *protocole Internet* Internet protocol; *protocole point à point* point-to-point protocol; *protocole POP* post office protocol, POP; *protocole PPP* PPP; *protocole de téléchargement* download protocol; *protocole de transfert anonyme* anonymous FTP; *protocole de transfert de fichier* file transfer protocol; *protocole de transmission* transmission protocol

(c) *(cérémonial)* protocol, etiquette

> ❝
> A la veille du mois d'août, le gouvernement Jospin a frappé un gros coup hier en annonçant la signature d'un **protocole d'accord** avec Jean-Luc Lagardère en vue de fusionner les groupes Aérospatiale et Matra.
> ❞

prototype *nm* prototype

provenance *nf* origin; **de provenance française** of French origin

provision *nf* (a) FIN, BANQUE funds; **verser une provision** *ou* **des provisions** to deposit funds; **manque de provision** *(sur chèque)* no funds; **provision d'une lettre de change** consideration for a bill of exchange; **faire provision pour une lettre de change** to provide for *or* protect a bill of exchange
(b) COMPTA provision, reserve □ *provision pour amortissement* provision for depreciation, depreciation allowance; *provision pour créances douteuses* provision for bad debts; *provision pour dépréciation* provision for depreciation, depreciation allowance; *provision pour risques et charges* contingency and loss provision
(c) JUR *(payé à un avocat)* retainer
(d) *(stock)* store, stock, supply

> **"**
> Contrairement à la plupart de ses concurrents, le montant de ses **provisions** n'a jamais été obéré par des ventes exubérantes d'actifs mobiliers ou immobiliers.
> **"**

provisionnement *nm* funding

provisionner *vt* FIN, BANQUE *(compte)* to pay money into, to deposit funds into; *(lettre de change)* to provide for, to protect

provisoire *adj (situation, bilan, état des comptes)* temporary; *(gérant)* temporary, acting; **à titre provisoire** on a temporary basis

prud'homme *nm* member of an industrial tribunal; **cette affaire va être portée devant les prud'hommes** this case will be taken to an industrial tribunal

psychologie *nf* psychology □ MKTG *psychologie commerciale* psychology of marketing; *psychologie des consommateurs* consumer psychology; *psychologie industrielle* industrial psychology; *psychologie de la publicité* advertising psychology

psychométrique *adj* psychometric

pub *nf* Fam *(abrév* **publicité***)* (a) *(secteur)* advertising; **elle travaille dans la pub** she works in advertising (b) *(message)* ad

public 1 *adj* public; *(entreprise)* public, government-owned
2 *nm* (a) *(secteur)* **le public** the public sector; **placer des actions dans le public** *(société)* to go public (b) *le grand public* the general public

publication *nf* (a) *(fait de publier)* publication, publishing □ *publication assistée par ordinateur* desktop publishing; *publication des comptes* disclosure (of accounts) (b) *(document)* publication, published work

publicitaire 1 *adj (dépenses, campagne)* advertising
2 *nmf (personne)* advertising executive

publicité *nf (secteur)* advertising; *(message)* advert, advertisement; **être dans la publicité** to be in advertising; **faire de la publicité pour qch** to advertise *or* publicize sth □ *publicité agressive* hard sell; *publicité d'amorçage* advance publicity; *publicité collective* group advertising; *publicité comparative* comparative advertising; *publicité concurrentielle* competitive advertising; *publicité directe* direct advertising; *publicité institutionnelle* corporate advertising; *publicité sur le lieu de vente* point-of-sale promotion; *publicité de marque* brand advertising; *publicité-médias* media advertising; *publicité mensongère* misleading advertising; *publicité de prestige* prestige advertising; *publicité au point de vente* in-store promotion; *publicité subliminale* subliminal advertising; *publicité télévisée* television advertising; *publicité par voie d'affiches* poster advertising

publicité-produit *nf* product advertising

publiphone® *nm* public telephone □ *publiphone à carte* cardphone

publipostage *nm* MKTG mail shot, mailing

puce *nf* ORDINAT (a) *(composant)* (micro)chip □ *puce à mémoire* memory chip (b) *(symbole)* bullet

puissance *nf* power; **une grande puissance économique** a major economic power □ *puissance d'achat* buying power; *puissance de vente* selling power

punaise *nf* Br drawing pin, Am thumbtack

pupitre *nm* ORDINAT *pupitre (de commande)* console (desk); *pupitre de visualisation* visual display unit

purger *vt (hypothèque)* to pay off

put *nm* BOURSE put (option)

PVD *nm (abrév* **pays en voie de développement***)* developing country

pyramide des salaires *nf* wage pyramid

QCM *nm* MKTG (*abrév* **questionnaire à choix multiple**) multiple-choice questionnaire

quadrimestriel, -elle *adj* four-monthly

quai *nm* (**a**) *(dans un port)* quay, wharf; **à prendre** *ou* **livrable à quai** *(marchandises)* ex quay, ex wharf; **rendu** *ou* **livré franco à quai** free on quay
 (**b**) *(dans une gare)* platform □ *quai de chargement* loading platform; *quai de déchargement* off-loading platform; *quai d'embarquement* loading platform

qualification *nf* (**a**) *(compétence)* qualification; **posséder les qualifications nécessaires pour un poste** to have the necessary qualifications for a job □ *qualifications professionnelles* professional qualifications (**b**) FIN, BOURSE qualification *(by acquisition of shares)*

qualifié, -e *adj* qualified; *(ouvrier)* skilled; **être qualifié pour faire qch** to be qualified to do sth

qualité *nf* (**a**) *(d'un produit)* quality; **de bonne qualité, de qualité supérieure** good-quality, high-quality; **de mauvaise qualité, de qualité inférieure** poor-quality; **de première qualité** high-grade, of the best quality □ *qualité loyale et marchande* fair average quality; *qualité marchande* fair average quality; *qualité prescrite* stipulated quality
 (**b**) *(qualification)* qualification, skill; **avoir qualité pour agir** to be qualified *or* authorized to act; **posséder les qualités requises pour un poste** to have the necessary qualifications for a post
 (**c**) *(fonction)* capacity; **en sa qualité de directeur général** in his capacity as managing director
 (**d**) ORDINAT quality □ *qualité brouillon* draft quality; *qualité courrier* (near) letter quality; *qualité d'impression* print quality

quantitatif, -ive *adj* quantitative

quantité *nf* quantity; **acheter qch en grande quantité** to buy sth in bulk *or* in large quantities □ *quantité économique de commande* economic order quantity; *quantité économique de production* economic manufacturing quantity; *quan-*

tité économique de réapprovisionnement economic lot size

quantum *nm* *(montant)* amount; *(proportion)* proportion, ratio; **fixer le quantum des dommages-intérêts** to fix the amount of damages

quartier *nm* area □ *quartier des affaires* business area; *quartier commerçant* shopping area

quasi-contrat *nm* JUR quasi contract, implied contract

quasi-trésorerie *nf* COMPTA cash equivalents

question *nf* question □ MKTG *question à choix multiple* multiple-choice question; *question de confiance* vote of confidence; MKTG *question fermée* closed-ended question; MKTG *question ouverte* open-ended question

questionnaire *nm* MKTG questionnaire □ *questionnaire à choix multiple* multiple-choice questionnaire; *questionnaire pilote* pilot questionnaire

quittance *nf* receipt □ *quittance comptable* accountable receipt; *quittance de douane* customs receipt; *quittance finale, quittance libératoire* receipt in full; *quittance de loyer* rent receipt; *quittance pour solde* receipt in full; BANQUE *quittance pour solde de tout compte* closing account balance; *quittance valable* proper receipt

quittancer *vt* to receipt

quitter *vt* (**a**) ORDINAT **quitter le système** to quit (**b**) *(au téléphone)* **ne quittez pas** hold on, hold the line

quitus *nm* COMPTA (final) discharge

quorum *nm* quorum; **constituer un quorum** to have a quorum; **le quorum n'est pas atteint** we don't have a quorum

quota *nm* quota □ *quota d'exportation* export quota; *quota d'importation* import quota; *quota de ventes* sales quota; *quotas volontaires à l'export* voluntary export restraint

quote-part *nf* share, quota; **apporter** *ou* **payer sa quote-part** to contribute one's share; **quote-part des bénéfices** share in the profits

> **❝**
>
> Les ressources du FMI sont limitées et ne dépasseraient pas aujourd'hui quinze milliards de dollars. Ces ressources proviennent des **quote-parts** versées par les 182 états qui en sont membres et qui disposent de droits de vote directement proportionnels à leurs apports.
>
> **❞**

quotidien, -enne *adj* daily

quotient *nm* quotient, ratio ❑ *quotient familial* = income tax relief system based on number of dependents

quotité *nf* (**a**) *(part)* quota, share; **la quotité du dégrèvement fiscal** the portion of income not subject to taxation ❑ JUR *quotité disponible* disposable portion *(of estate)*; *quotité imposable* taxable portion of income (**b**) FIN, BOURSE *(d'actions)* minimum number

rabais nm reduction, discount; **un rabais de 500 francs** a 500-franc reduction or discount; **acheter/vendre qch au rabais** to buy/sell sth at a discount or at a reduced price; **faire** ou **accorder un rabais sur qch** to give a discount on sth; **certains patrons profitent de la situation pour se procurer de la main-d'œuvre au rabais** some employers are taking advantage of the situation by taking on cheap labour

rabattre vt to take off, to deduct; **il a rabattu 5% sur le prix affiché** he took 5% off the marked price

raccordement nm ORDINAT link

raccorder ORDINAT 1 vt to connect
2 **se raccorder** vpr **se raccorder à** to link up to

raccourci clavier nm ORDINAT keyboard shortcut

rachat nm (a) (par le vendeur) repurchase, buying back; JUR **avec faculté de rachat** with option of repurchase
(b) (de police d'assurance) surrender; (de valeur, de dette, d'obligation) redemption ▫ COMPTA **rachat forfaitaire des créances** lump-sum purchase of accounts receivable
(c) (d'une entreprise) buy-out ▫ **rachat d'une société par la direction** management buy-out
(d) BOURSE (d'actions) repurchase ▫ **rachat gagnant** repurchase at a profit

rachetable adj repurchasable

racheter vt (a) (au propriétaire) to repurchase, to buy back (**à** from) (b) (police d'assurance) to surrender; (valeur, dette, obligation) to redeem (c) (entreprise) to buy out; **racheter les parts de qn** to buy sb out (d) BOURSE (actions) to repurchase, to buy back; **se couvrir en rachetant** to cover a short position by buying back

racine nf ORDINAT root

radiation nf (a) (d'une liste) crossing out; (d'une dette) cancellation (b) BOURSE **radiation de la cote** delisting

radier vt (a) (d'une liste) to cross out; (dette) to cancel (b) BOURSE **radier qch de la cote** (société, actions) to delist sth

raffermir se raffermir vpr (prix, marché) to steady

raffermissement nm (des prix, du marché) steadying

raid nm BOURSE raid; **lancer/financer un raid** to mount/to finance a raid

raider nm FIN (corporate) raider

raison nf (a) (nom) **raison commerciale** trade name; **raison sociale** (company) name (b) **à raison de** at the rate of; **le travail est payé à raison de 120 francs l'heure** the work is paid at the rate of 120 francs an hour

raisonnable adj (prix, revenu) reasonable

rajustement nm adjustment; **les syndicats réclament un rajustement des salaires** the unions are demanding an adjustment of the wage structure

rajuster vt (taux d'intérêt) to adjust, to revise; **rajuster les salaires** to readjust the wage structure

ralentir vt & vi (affaires, production, croissance économique) to slow down

ralentissement nm (des affaires, de la production, de la croissance économique) slowing down

rallonge nf Fam extra money; **une rallonge de 1000 francs** an extra 1,000 francs

RAM nf ORDINAT RAM ▫ **RAM sur carte** on-board RAM

ramassage nm (a) BOURSE (d'actions) buying up (b) (transport) picking up; **service de ramassage et de livraison** pick up and delivery service

ramasser vt BOURSE (actions) to buy up

rang nm (a) (dans une hiérarchie) rank; **cette entreprise occupe le premier rang mondial du marché des composants électroniques** this company is number one in the world in the electronic component market; **l'entre-**

prise a été reléguée au cinquième rang pour la production d'appareils électroménagers the company has slipped to fifth place in the white goods market (**b**) FIN *(d'une créance, d'une hypothèque)* rank

ranger *vt (marchandises)* to stow; ORDINAT **ranger en mémoire** to store

rapidité *nf* ORDINAT speed ◻ *rapidité d'impression* print speed; *rapidité de traitement* processing speed

rappel *nm* (**a**) FIN *rappel (de compte)* reminder; *rappel d'échéance* prompt note; *rappel de salaire* back pay (**b**) *(d'une somme déjà avancée)* calling in (**c**) ORDINAT calling up (**d**) *(de marchandises défectueuses)* recall (**e**) *(en publicité)* follow-up

rappeler *vt* (**a**) *(au téléphone)* to call *or* phone back; **il est en réunion, voulez-vous qu'il vous rappelle?** he's in a meeting, would you like him to call you back?; **je vous rappelle dans une minute** I'll call you back in a minute
(**b**) *(faire figurer)* to quote; **dans votre réponse, veuillez rappeler la référence FK/FJ** when replying please quote reference FK/FJ; **prière de rappeler ce numéro** in reply please quote this number
(**c**) ORDINAT *(faire revenir)* to call up
(**d**) *(marchandises défectueuses)* to recall

rapport *nm* (**a**) *(compte-rendu)* report; **faire** *ou* **rédiger un rapport (sur)** to make *or* to draw up a report (on); **soumettre un rapport à qn** to submit a report to sb ◻ FIN *rapport d'activité* progress report; *rapport des affaires sociales* social report; *rapport annuel* annual report; *rapport d'avancement des travaux (dans la construction)* progress report; *rapport commercial* market report; *rapport du commissaire aux comptes* auditor's report; *rapport d'étude de marché* market study report; *rapport d'expertise* valuation, expert's report; COMPTA *rapport d'exploitation* operating statement; *rapport financier* financial report; *rapport de gestion* management report; *rapport intérimaire* interim report; *rapport périodique* progress report; *rapport du président* chairman's report; *rapport récapitulatif* summary report; *rapport de situation journalière* daily trading report; *rapport de vente* sales report
(**b**) FIN *(profit)* yield, return; **en rapport** *(capital)* interest-bearing, productive; **d'un bon rapport** profitable; **d'un mauvais rapport** unprofitable
(**c**) *(proportion)* ratio, proportion ◻ *rapport*

cours-bénéfice price-earnings ratio; *rapport de parité* parity ratio; *rapport profit sur ventes* profit-volume ratio; *rapport qualité-prix* quality-price ratio, value for money; **être d'un bon rapport qualité-prix** to be good value for money
(**d**) *(relation)* **mettre qn en rapport avec qn** to put sb in touch with sb; **rapports** relations; **avoir des rapports avec qn** to have dealings with sb; **nous avons de bons rapports avec la filiale française** we're on good terms with the French subsidiary ◻ *rapports patrons-syndicats* relations between the employers and the unions

> ❝ ⸻
> Les experts qui travaillent sur la comptabilité de la Sasea doivent rendre un premier **rapport d'expertise** en novembre.
> ⸻ ❞

rapporter 1 *vt* (**a**) *(faire le compte-rendu de)* to report, to give an account of; **vous me rapporterez ses commentaires** let me know what he says
(**b**) FIN *(bénéfices, intérêts)* to yield; **rapporter de l'argent** to be profitable; **le compte d'épargne vous rapporte 7,5%** the savings account carries 7.5% interest
(**c**) COMPTA *(écriture)* to post
2 *vi (être rentable)* to be profitable, to yield a profit; **c'est un métier qui rapporte** it's a profitable career; **l'affaire a beaucoup rapporté à l'entreprise** the deal brought in a lot of money for the company; **ça ne rapporte pas** it doesn't pay, there's no money in it; **ça peut rapporter gros** it can be very profitable

rapprochement bancaire *nm* COMPTA bank reconciliation

rapprocher *vt* COMPTA to reconcile

raquer *vi Fam* to pay up, to fork out

raréfaction *nf (de ressources, d'argent)* growing scarcity

rareté *nf (de ressources, d'argent)* scarcity

rassemblement *nm* ORDINAT *(de données)* gathering

rassembler *vt* ORDINAT *(données)* to gather

ratification *nf* ratification

ratifier *vt* to ratify

ratio *nm* ratio ◻ *ratio de capitalisation* capitalization ratio; *ratio capital-travail* capital-labour ratio; *ratio capitaux empruntés-fonds propres* debt-to-equity ratio; *ratio comptable* accounting ratio; *ratio Cooke* capital adequacy ratio; *ratio* *cours-bénéfices* price-earnings ratio; *ratio de couverture de l'intérêt* interest coverage; *ratio de distribution* distribution ratio; *ratio d'endettement* debt ratio; COMPTA *ratio d'exploitation* performance ratio, operating ratio; *ratio de gestion* financial ratio; *ratio d'intensité de capital* capital-output ratio; *ratio de levier* leverage; *ratio de liquidité* quick ratio, acid test ratio; *ratio de rentabilité (nette)* (net) profit ratio; *ratio de trésorerie* cash ratio

rationalisation *nf* ÉCON *(d'une industrie)* rationalization, streamlining; **rationalisation des choix budgétaires** planning, programming and budgeting system

rationaliser *vt* ÉCON *(industrie)* to rationalize, to streamline

rationnel, -elle *adj* rational; ÉCON **l'organisation rationnelle de l'industrie** the rationalization *or* streamlining of industry

rattrapage *nm* ÉCON adjustment

rattraper *vt* (**a**) *(combler)* to make up (**b**) *(arriver au même niveau que)* to catch up with; **il est impératif que nous rattrapions nos principaux concurrents** we have to catch up with our main competitors (**c**) ÉCON to adjust

rayon *nm* (**a**) **rayon d'action** *(d'une entreprise)* range of activities; *(d'une campagne publicitaire)* range (**b**) *(dans un magasin)* department

rayonnage *nm* shelving, shelves

RCB *nf (abrév* **rationalisation des choix budgétaires**) PPBS

RCS *nm (abrév* **Registre du commerce et des sociétés**) register of companies

R-D *nf (abrév* **recherche et développement**) R & D, R and D

réachat *nm* MKTG rebuy

réacheminement *nm (de marchandises)* rerouting; ORDINAT *(de message)* redirecting

réacheminer *vt (marchandises)* to reroute; ORDINAT *(message)* to redirect

réaction *nf* reaction; *(des consommateurs)* feedback; BOURSE **il y a eu une vive réaction de la livre sterling sur le marché des changes** sterling has reacted sharply on the exchange market ◻ MKTG **réaction émotionnelle** emotional response; **réaction des ventes** sales response

réactique *nf* business intelligence system

réaffectation *nf* (**a**) *(de ressources, de subventions)* reassignment, reallocation

(**b**) *(d'un employé)* reassignment; **il a demandé sa réaffectation à son poste initial** he asked to be reassigned to his original job (**c**) ORDINAT reallocation

réaffecter *vt* (**a**) *(ressources, subventions)* to reassign, to reallocate; **réaffecter une subvention à sa destination première** to reallocate funds to their original use (**b**) *(employé)* to reassign; **réaffecter qn à son poste initial** to reassign sb to his/her original job (**c**) ORDINAT to reallocate

réafficher *vt* ORDINAT to redisplay

réajustement, réajuster = **rajustement, rajuster**

réalignement *nm (des taux de change)* realignment ◻ **réalignement monétaire** realignment of currencies

réaligner *vt (taux de change)* to realign

réalisable *adj* (**a**) FIN, BANQUE *(avoirs)* realizable (**b**) *(projet)* realizable; *(but)* achievable

réalisation *nf* (**a**) FIN, BANQUE realization; *(d'actions)* selling out; *(d'un bénéfice)* making ◻ **réalisation du stock** clearance sale (**b**) *(d'un projet)* realization; *(d'un but)* achievement

réaliser *vt* (**a**) FIN, BANQUE to realize; *(actions)* to sell out; *(bénéfice)* to make; **réaliser un capital** to realize an asset, to convert an asset into cash; **réaliser un chiffre d'affaires de 10 millions de francs** to have a turnover of 10 million francs; **réaliser des économies** to economize (**b**) *(projet)* to realize; *(but)* to achieve

réalité virtuelle *nf* ORDINAT virtual reality

réaménagement *nm (d'un magasin)* refit

réaménager *vt (magasin)* to refit

réamorcer ORDINAT **1** *vt* to reboot **2 se réamorcer** *vpr* to reboot

réapprovisionnement *nm* restocking

réapprovisionner 1 *vt (magasin)* to restock (**en** with); *(personne)* to resupply (**en** with) **2 se réapprovisionner** *vpr* to stock up again (**en** with)

réassortiment *nm* (**a**) *(fait de réassortir)* restocking (**b**) *(nouveau stock)* new stock

réassortir *vt* to restock

réassurance *nf* reinsurance

rebaisser *vi (prix)* to go back down

rebut *nm (article)* reject

recensement *nm (de marchandises)* inventory ▫ *recensement des distributeurs* census of distribution; *recensement des entreprises* company census; *recensement de la production* census of production

recenser *vt (marchandises)* to inventory

recentrage *nm (modification)* reorientating, refocussing

recentrer *vt (modifier)* to reorientate, to refocus; **le nouveau directeur a décidé de recentrer la politique de l'entreprise sur l'exportation** the new manager decided to refocus the company's activities on exporting

récépissé *nm* receipt ▫ *récépissé de dépôt* deposit receipt; *récépissé de douane* customs receipt; *récépissé d'entrepôt* warehouse receipt; *récépissé postal* postal receipt

réceptif précoce *nm* MKTG early adopter

réception *nf* (**a**) *(d'une lettre, d'une commande, de biens)* receipt; **accuser réception de qch** to acknowledge receipt of sth; **à payer à la réception** *Br* cash *or Am* collect on delivery ▫ *réception définitive* final acceptance; *réception des travaux* acceptance of work (**b**) *(accueil)* reception (desk); **demandez à la réception** ask at reception

réceptionnaire *nmf (de marchandises)* consignee, receiving agent

réceptionner *vt (marchandises)* to take delivery of

réceptionniste *nmf* receptionist

réceptivité des consommateurs *nf* MKTG consumer acceptance

récession *nf* ÉCON recession ▫ *récession économique* economic recession

recette *nf* (**a**) FIN takings; **faire recette** to be profitable *or* a success; **recettes et dépenses** receipts and expenditure, incomings and outgoings ▫ *recette annuelle* annual income *or* revenue; *recette brute* gross income *or* earnings; *recettes de caisse* cash receipts; *recettes fiscales* tax revenue; *recettes non gagées* unassigned *or* unpledged revenue; *recette journalière* daily takings; *recette nette* net income *or* receipts; *recettes publiques* government revenue (**b**) *(d'argent dû)* collection; *(bureau)* tax office; **faire la recette de l'argent/des contributions** to collect the money/contributions

> "
> Des déficits budgétaires structurels se sont ainsi installés dans tous les grands pays (c'est à dire des déficits suffisamment importants pour qu'une forte croissance de l'économie, donc des **recettes fiscales**, ne puisse pas les annuler).
> "

recevable *adj (marchandises)* fit for acceptance

receveur, -euse *nm,f* (**a**) *(de marchandises)* receiver (**b**) ADMIN *receveur des contributions* tax collector; *receveur des douanes* customs officer; *receveur des Finances* district tax collector; *receveur des postes* postmaster, *f* postmistress

recevoir *vt (courrier, coup de téléphone)* to get, to receive; *(salaire, somme)* to get, to receive, to be paid; **nous avons bien reçu votre lettre du 20 juin** thank you for your letter of 20 June, we acknowledge receipt of your letter of 20 June; **vous avez reçu un appel de Londres** you've had *or* received a call from London; **recevoir des ordres de qn** to take orders from sb; **recevez, Monsieur, l'assurance de mes sentiments distingués** *(dans une lettre)* *(à quelqu'un dont on connaît le nom)* yours sincerely; *(à quelqu'un dont on ne connaît pas le nom)* yours faithfully; **bien reçu** duly received; FIN **à recevoir** *(effets, intérêts)* receivable

rechange *nm* (**a**) *(remplacement)* replacement; **de rechange** spare (**b**) FIN, BANQUE *(d'un effet)* redraft

recherche *nf* (**a**) MKTG research ▫ *recherches sur les besoins des consommateurs* consumer research; *recherche commerciale* marketing intelligence; *recherche et développement* research and development; *recherche marketing, recherche mercatique* market research; *recherche opérationnelle* *Br* operational research, *Am* operations research; *recherches par panel* panel research; *recherche sur les prix* pricing research; *recherche de produits* product research; *recherche par sondage* survey research; *recherches sur le terrain* fieldwork

(**b**) ORDINAT find, search ▫ *recherche arrière* backward search; *recherche avant, recherche vers le bas* forward search; *recherche documentaire* information retrieval; *recherche de données* data retrieval; *recherche globale* global search; **recherche vers le haut** backward search; **recherche et remplacement** search and replace; **recherche et remplacement global** global search and replace

(**c**) **recherche de personne** paging (service)

recherché, -e adj (produit) in demand, sought-after

recherche-développement nf research and development

rechercher vt ORDINAT to search, to do a search for; **rechercher et remplacer qch** to search and replace sth; **rechercher en arrière** ou **vers le haut** to search backwards; **rechercher en avant** ou **vers le bas** to search forwards

réciproque adj (bénéfices, accord, concessions) reciprocal

réclamation nf (**a**) (plainte) complaint; **faire** ou **déposer une réclamation** to make or lodge a complaint; **toutes réclamations devront être adressées au service clientèle** all complaints should be addressed to the customer services department (**b**) (revendication) claim; **faire** ou **déposer une réclamation** to make a claim ❑ JUR **réclamation en dommages-intérêts** claim for damages; **réclamation d'indemnité** claim for compensation

réclame nf (**a**) (publicité) advertising; (annonce) advertisement; **faire de la réclame pour qch** to advertise sth (**b**) (promotion) **en réclame** on offer

réclamer 1 vt (**a**) (revendiquer) (dommages-intérêts, allocation, indemnité) to claim (**b**) (demander) to ask for; (exiger) to demand; **réclamer son argent** to ask for one's money back; **ils réclament la semaine de 35 heures** they are demanding a 35-hour week

2 vi to complain (**auprès de** to)

reclassement nm (**a**) (de poste) reassignment (**b**) (de personnel, de salaires) regrading

“
Un syndicaliste est venu signer un document par lequel il acceptait son **reclassement** individuel.
”

reclasser vt (**a**) (poste) to reassign (**b**) (personnel, salaires) to regrade

recommandation nf (**a**) (parrainage) recommendation; (lettre) (letter of) reference; **elle a été embauchée sur la recommandation du chef de service** she

was recruited on the recommendation of the head of department (**b**) (d'une lettre, d'un colis) recording

recommandé, -e 1 adj (**a**) (produit, prix) approved, recommended (**b**) (lettre, colis) recorded

2 nm **en recommandé** (lettre, colis) by recorded delivery

recommander 1 vt (**a**) (personne, produit) to recommend (**b**) (lettre, colis) to record

2 **se recommander** vpr **se recommander de qn** (pour un emploi) to give sb's name as a reference

recommercialiser vt to remarket

recomposer vt (numéro de téléphone) to redial

reconduction nf (d'un bail, d'un contrat) renewal

reconduire vt (bail, contrat) to renew

reconfiguration nf (d'une société) reengineering

reconfigurer vt ORDINAT to reconfigure

reconnaissance nf (**a**) ORDINAT **reconnaissance des caractères** character recognition; **reconnaissance optique des caractères** optical character recognition; **reconnaissance de la parole, reconnaissance vocale** speech recognition (**b**) MKTG **reconnaissance des besoins** need recognition; **reconnaissance de dette** (document) IOU

reconstituer vt (**a**) (stocks) to rebuild, to build up again (**b**) (entreprise) to reconstruct

reconstitution nf (**a**) (de stocks) rebuilding (**b**) (d'une entreprise) reconstruction

reconversion nf (**a**) (de l'économie) turnaround; (d'un site industriel, d'une région, d'une entreprise) conversion, changeover (**b**) (d'un salarié) retraining

“
Déjà engagée du temps de Bush, la **reconversion** du secteur industriel militaire vers le civil se poursuit.
”

reconvertir 1 vt (**a**) (économie) to turn around; (site industriel, région, entreprise) to convert, to change over (**b**) (salarié) to retrain

2 **se reconvertir** vpr (**a**) (site industriel, région, entreprise) to convert, to change over (**dans** to) (**b**) (salarié) to retrain; **il s'est reconverti dans la comptabilité** he retrained as an accountant

record *adj (chiffre)* record; **l'inflation a atteint le chiffre record de 45%** inflation has reached an all-time high of 45%

recoupement *nm* cross-checking; **faire le recoupement (de qch)** to cross-check (sth); **moyen de recoupement** cross-reference

recouponnement *nm* FIN, BOURSE renewal of coupons

recouponner *vt* FIN, BOURSE to renew the coupons of

recours *nm* (a) *(utilisation)* recourse, resort; **avoir recours à l'arbitrage** to go to arbitration (b) JUR appeal □ **recours en cassation** appeal; **recours contre des tiers** recourse against third parties; ASSUR **s'assurer contre le recours des tiers** to insure against a third-party claim

recouvrable *adj (argent, dette)* recoverable; *(impôt)* collectable

recouvrement *nm* (a) *(d'argent, d'une dette)* recovery; *(de l'impôt)* collection; **faire un recouvrement** to recover a debt; **l'impôt est mis en recouvrement après le 31 octobre** payment of tax is due from 31 October (b) **recouvrements** *(dettes)* outstanding debts

recouvrer *vt (argent, dette)* to recover; *(impôt)* to collect

recrutement *nm* recruitment; **le recrutement du personnel s'effectue par concours** staff are recruited by competitive examination

> **"**
>
> En conséquence, cette année, les **recrutements** atteignent un niveau plancher, permettant à peine la compensation des départs: la population salariée décroît de 0,4% chaque année.
>
> **"**

recruter 1 *vt* to recruit; **l'entreprise recrute des ingénieurs en informatique** the company is recruiting computer engineers

2 **se recruter** *vpr* to be recruited; **les ingénieurs se recrutent sur diplôme** engineers are recruited on the basis of their qualifications

rectificatif, -ive 1 *adj* rectifying, correcting

2 *nm* rectification, correction

rectification *nf* rectification, correction; FIN, COMPTA *(d'un compte)* adjustment

rectifier *vt* to rectify, to correct; FIN, COMPTA *(compte)* to adjust

recto *nm* front; **recto verso** recto verso, on both sides

reçu *nm* receipt □ *Can* **reçu de caisse** (till) receipt; **reçu certifié** accountable receipt; **reçu en duplicata** receipt in duplicate; **reçu libératoire** receipt in full discharge; **reçu du transitaire** forwarding agent receipt

recueil des données *nm* MKTG data collection

recul *nm* decline, drop; **le recul de l'industrie textile** the decline of the textile industry; **les ventes ont subi un recul** sales have dropped; **le recul du yen par rapport au dollar** the fall of the yen against the dollar

reculer *vi (baisser)* to decline, to drop; **le yen recule par rapport au dollar** the yen is falling against the dollar

récupérabilité *nf* salvage value

récupérable *adj* (a) *(dette)* recoverable; *(TVA)* reclaimable (b) *(marchandises, cargaison)* salvageable (c) *(temps)* recoverable; **les heures supplémentaires sont récupérables** additional time off may be taken in lieu

récupération *nf* (a) *(d'une dette)* recovery; *(de TVA)* reclaiming (b) *(des débours)* recoupment (c) *(de marchandises, de cargaison)* recovery, salvage (d) *(du temps)* making up; **la récupération des heures supplémentaires** time off in lieu (e) ORDINAT *(d'un fichier, de données)* retrieval

récupérer *vt* (a) *(dette)* to recover; *(TVA)* to reclaim (b) **récupérer ses débours** to recoup one's expenditure (c) *(marchandises, cargaison)* to recover, to salvage (d) *(temps)* to make up; **récupérer des heures supplémentaires** to take time off in lieu; **on récupère ce jour férié samedi prochain** we are making up for this public holiday by working next Saturday (e) ORDINAT *(fichier, données)* to retrieve

recyclage *nm* (a) *(du personnel)* retraining; **suivre un stage de recyclage** to retrain (b) *(de matières)* recycling

recycler 1 *vt* (a) *(personnel)* to retrain (b) *(matières)* to recycle

2 **se recycler** *vpr (personnel)* to retrain

rédacteur, -trice *nm,f* editor □ **rédacteur en chef** chief editor; **rédacteur publicitaire** copywriter

rédaction *nf* (a) *(poste)* editorship; *(personnel)* editorial staff; *(département)* editorial department (b) *(fait de rédiger)* drawing up

reddition *nf* FIN *(de comptes)* rendering

redéfinir *vt* ORDINAT *(touche)* to redefine

redémarrage *nm* (**a**) *(de l'économie, du commerce)* recovery (**b**) ORDINAT restart

> ❝
> "C'est le moment d'acheter" : le slogan court depuis plusieurs mois et on attend toujours les signes d'un **redémarrage** de l'immobilier.
> ❞

redémarrer *vi* (**a**) *(économie, commerce)* to recover, to take off again (**b**) ORDINAT to reboot, to restart

redéploiement *nm* ÉCON redeployment

redéployer *vt* ÉCON to redeploy

redevable *adj* **être redevable de qch à qn** to be accountable to sb for sth; **être redevable de l'impôt** to be liable for tax; **vous êtes redevable d'un acompte provisionnel** you are liable for an interim payment

redevance *nf* *(pour un service)* fees ❑ **redevance pétrolière** oil royalty; **redevance téléphonique** rental charge

rédhibition *nf* = cancellation of a sale due to a material defect in the article or product

rédhibitoire *adj* *(prix)* prohibitive; *(conditions, salaire)* unacceptable

rédiger *vt* *(lettre, contrat, facture)* to draw up

redimensionnement *nm* (**a**) *(d'une entreprise)* downsizing, rightsizing (**b**) ORDINAT resizing

redimensionner *vt* (**a**) *(entreprise)* to downsize (**b**) ORDINAT to resize

redressement *n* (**a**) *(d'une erreur)* rectification; COMPTA *(d'un compte)* adjustment ❑ ADMIN **redressement fiscal** tax adjustment (**b**) *(d'une monnaie, de l'économie)* recovery ❑ **redressement économique** economic recovery (**c**) **redressement judiciaire** receivership; **être mis en redressement judiciaire** to go into receivership

> ❝
> Le **redressement** financier qui s'opère est cependant dû également pour une large part aux restructurations engagées par le prédécesseur de M. Jobs.
> ❞

redresser 1 *vt* *(erreur)* to rectify; COMPTA *(compte)* to adjust

2 se redresser *vpr* *(monnaie, économie)* to recover, to rally

redresseur d'entreprise *nm* company doctor

redû *nm* balance due, amount owed

réduction *nf* (**a**) *(des prix, des taux d'intérêt, des impôts)* reduction (**de** in), lowering (**de** of); *(des dépenses, des frais, du personnel, des salaires)* reduction (**de** in), cutting (**de** of); *(des stocks)* running down; FIN *(du capital)* writing down; **on nous a demandé d'accepter une réduction de salaire** we were asked to take a cut in wages; **ils ont promis une réduction des impôts** they promised to reduce *or* lower taxes; **ils nous ont imposé une réduction des dépenses** they've reduced *or* cut our expenditure ❑ **réductions d'impôts** tax cuts (**b**) *(rabais)* reduction; **faire une réduction de 15% (à qn)** to give (sb) a 15% reduction

réduire *vt* *(prix, taux d'intérêt, impôts)* to reduce, to lower; *(dépenses, frais, personnel, salaires)* to reduce, to cut; *(stocks)* to run down; FIN *(capital)* to write down; **la société réduit progressivement ses opérations en Allemagne** the company is winding down its operations in Germany

réduit, -e *adj* *(prix)* reduced; **depuis la vague de licenciements l'entreprise fonctionne avec un effectif réduit** since the wave of redundancies the company is operating with a reduced workforce

rééchelonnement *nm* FIN *(d'une dette)* rescheduling

rééchelonner *vt* FIN *(dette)* to reschedule

réel, -elle *adj* *(coût, revenu)* real

réembaucher *vt* to re-employ; **elle a été licenciée puis réembauchée en tant que freelance** she was made redundant and then re-employed *or* taken on again as a freelancer

réemploi *nm* re-employment

réemployer = **remployer**

rééquilibrer *vt* *(budget)* to rebalance

réescompte *nm* FIN rediscount

réescompter *vt* FIN to rediscount

réévaluation *nf* *(d'une monnaie, de l'actif)* revaluation; *(d'une propriété, des prix, d'un budget)* reassessment; *(des salaires)* reappraisal

réévaluer *vt* *(monnaie, actif)* to revalue; *(propriété, prix, budget)* to reassess; *(salaires)* to reappraise

réexpédier *vt* *(à une autre adresse)* to forward, to send on; *(à l'expéditeur)* to send back, to return

réexpédition *nf (à une autre adresse)* forwarding, sending on; *(à l'expéditeur)* sending back, returning

réexportation *nf (activité)* re-exportation; *(produit)* re-export

réexporter *vt* to re-export; **produits réexportés** re-exports

réf *nf (abrév* **référence)** ref; **N/Réf** our ref; **V/Réf** your ref

réfaction *nf (de biens endommagés ou de qualité inférieure)* allowance, rebate

référence *nf* (**a**) *(sur une lettre, sur un document)* reference; **en référence à** with reference to; **adresser sous référence RL3U, référence à rappeler RL3U** when replying please quote reference RL3U
(**b**) **références** *(recommandation)* reference; **avoir de bonnes références** to have good references; **références exigées** *(sur offre d'emploi)* references required
(**c**) MKTG *(produit)* benchmark
(**d**) COMPTA **référence au meilleur** benchmarking

référencé, -e *adj* **être référencé** to have a reference number; **votre lettre référencée 450/198** your letter reference number 450/198

référencer *vt* (**a**) ORDINAT to reference
(**b**) *(échantillon)* to classify in a sample book

refinancement *nm* refinancing

refinancer *vt* to refinance

reformatage *nm* ORDINAT reformatting

reformater *vt* ORDINAT to reformat

réforme *nf* reform □ **réforme monétaire** monetary reform

refrain publicitaire *nm* (advertising) jingle

refus *nm (d'une invitation, d'une demande)* refusal; *(d'une proposition, d'une offre, des marchandises)* rejection □ **refus d'acceptation** non-acceptance; **refus de paiement** non-payment

refuser *vt (invitation, demande)* to refuse; *(proposition, offre, marchandises)* to reject; *(chèque)* to bounce

regagner *vt (après perte)* to win back; **le dollar a regagné quelques cents sur le marché des changes** the dollar has regained a few cents on the foreign exchange market

régie (**a**) ADMIN *(gestion)* management, control; *(d'un domaine)* administration, stewardship; **en régie** in the hands of trustees
(**b**) *(entreprise publique)* public corporation, state-owned company; **la régie Renault** the Renault company □ **régie publicitaire** advertising sales agency
(**c**) ADMIN **régie des impôts indirects** excise (administration), ≃ *Br* Customs and Excise department; *Can* **Régie des Loyers** rental board

régime *nm (système)* scheme, system □ **régime d'assurance vieillesse** old age pension fund *or* scheme; **régime douanier** customs system; **régime fiscal** tax system; FIN **régime du forfait** standard assessment system, fixed rate tax assessment system; **régime d'imposition** tax system; DOUANES **régime préférentiel** preferential rates of duty; FIN **régime du réel** full assessment system; **régime de retraite** pension scheme; **régime de retraites complémentaires** = graduated pension scheme; **régime de retraite des artisans, commerçants et professions libérales** self-employed pension; **régime de Sécurité sociale** social security system; FIN **régime simplifié** simplified system; **régime de transit** transit system; **le régime du travail** the organization of labour

> ❝
> Les cotisations aux **régimes de retraite** représentent un "placement obligatoire" important, près de 20% du salaire d'un cadre.
> ❞

région *nf* region, area □ MKTG **région test** test area

régional, -e **1** *adj (conseil)* local
2 *nm* TÉL area telephone system

régir *vt* to govern, to rule; **les prix sont régis par la demande** prices are governed by demand; **les conditions régissant votre compte** the terms for the conduct of your account

registre *nm* (**a**) *(de comptes)* account book; *(des délibérations)* minutes book; **inscrire/rapporter un article sur un registre** to enter/to post an item in a register; **signer le registre** *(d'un hôtel)* to sign the register □ **registre du commerce** trade register; **s'inscrire au registre du commerce** to enter oneself in the trade register; **Registre du commerce et des sociétés** register of companies; **registre de comptabilité** account book, ledger; **registre foncier** land register; **registre international des marques** international trademark register; **registre des obligataires** debenture register; **registre des procès-verbaux** minutes book; **registre des salaires** payroll (**b**) ORDINAT register ❑ *registre d'accès mémoire* memory access register

règle *nf* (**a**) *(mesure)* rule ❑ COMPTA *règles comptables* accounting rules; *règles de sécurité* safety regulations (**b**) **en règle** *(document)* in due form; *(papiers, passeport)* in order; **tenir sa comptabilité en règle** to keep one's accounts in order (**c**) ORDINAT *(sur écran)* ruler line

règlement *nm* (**a**) *(d'un compte)* settlement; *(d'une facture, d'une dette)* payment; **en règlement de...** in settlement of...; **faire un règlement par chèque** to pay by cheque; **pour règlement de tout compte** in full settlement ❑ *règlement à la commande* cash with order; *règlement contre documents* cash against documents; *règlement en espèces* cash payment, cash settlement; *règlement en nature* settlement in kind (**b**) *(règles)* regulations ❑ *règlement intérieur* internal regulations (**c**) BOURSE settlement ❑ *(marché du) règlement mensuel* forward market (**d**) JUR *(résolution)* settlement ❑ *règlement à l'amiable* amicable settlement; *(sans procès)* out-of-court settlement; *règlement arbitral, règlement par arbitrage* settlement by arbitration; *règlement de gré à gré* amicable settlement, settlement by negotiation; *règlement judiciaire* liquidation; **être en règlement judiciaire** to be in the hands of the receiver(s); **se mettre en règlement judiciaire** to go into liquidation *or* receivership

réglementaire *adj* statutory, prescribed

réglementation *nf* (**a**) *(fait de réglementer)* control, regulation ❑ *réglementation des changes* exchange control; *réglementation des prix* price control (**b**) *(règlement)* regulations, rules ❑ *réglementation du travail* labour regulations *or* legislation

réglementer *vt* to regulate, to control; *(prix)* to control

régler 1 *vt* (**a**) *(compte)* to settle; *(facture, dette, personne)* to pay; **régler qch en espèces** to pay cash for sth; **régler qch par chèque** to pay for sth by cheque (**b**) JUR *(résoudre)* to settle; **régler qch à l'amiable** to settle sth amicably; *(sans procès)* to settle sth out of court (**c**) ASSUR *(sinistre)* to settle
2 *vi* to pay

réglette *nf* ORDINAT *(pour un clavier)* template

régresser *vi (ventes, production)* to decline

régression *nf (des ventes, de la production)* decline

regrèvement *nm* tax increase

regroupement *nm* (**a**) *(de sociétés)* amalgamation, merger (**b**) FIN *(de comptes)* consolidation

regrouper 1 *vt* (**a**) FIN *(sociétés)* to amalgamate, to merge (**b**) FIN *(comptes)* to consolidate
2 se regrouper *vpr (sociétés)* to amalgamate, to merge

régularisation *nf (d'une situation)* regularizing; FIN *(de dividende)* equalization; *(d'un compte, des stocks, des charges)* adjustment

régulariser *vt (situation)* to regularize; *(document)* to put into proper form; FIN *(dividende)* to equalize; *(compte, stocks, charges)* to adjust

régularité *nf (d'une décision, d'une situation)* legality; FIN **régularité et sincérité des charges** true and fair nature of expenses

régulateur, -trice *adj* regulating

régulation *nf (de la Bourse)* regulation; *(de l'économie)* control; **la régulation du marché des changes** foreign exchange control

réhabilitation *nf* (**a**) JUR *(de failli)* discharge (**b**) *(d'immeuble, de quartier ancien)* rehabilitation, renovation

> ❝
> Les chantiers de logement social, les programmes de **réhabilitation** dans les quartiers ont été l'an dernier un facteur important dans le maintien de l'activité.
> ❞

réhabilité, -e *nm,f* discharged bankrupt

réhabiliter *vt* (**a**) *(failli)* to discharge (**b**) *(immeuble, quartier ancien)* to rehabilitate, to renovate

réimportation *nf* (**a**) *(activité)* re-importation, re-importing (**b**) *(produit)* re-import

réimporter *vt* to re-import

réimposer *vt* FIN *(produit)* to reintroduce tax on, to retax

réimposition *nf* FIN retaxation

réinitialisation *nf* ORDINAT reset; *(de la mémoire)* reinitialization

réinitialiser *vt* ORDINAT to reset; *(mémoire)* to reinitialize

réinjecter *vt (bénéfices)* to plough back (**dans** into)

réinscription *nf* COMPTA re-entry, re-registering

réinscrire *vt* COMPTA to re-enter, to re-register

réinsérer *vt* ORDINAT *(bloc)* to reinsert

réinsertion professionnelle *nf* = getting back into the job market

réinstaller *vt* ORDINAT to reinstall

réintégration *nf (d'un employé)* reinstatement

réintégrer *vt (employé)* to reinstate; **réintégrer qn dans ses fonctions** to reinstate sb

réinvestir *vt* to reinvest; *(bénéfices)* to plough back

rejet *nm (d'une offre)* rejection; *(d'une dépense)* disallowance

rejeter *vt (offre)* to reject; *(dépense)* to disallow

relais *nm* relay, shift; **travail par relais** shift work

relance *nf* (**a**) *(de l'économie, de la production, des ventes, du commerce)* revival (**b**) *(d'un produit)* relaunch ❑ **relance économique** economic revival, reflation (**c**) *(d'un client)* follow-up ❑ **relance téléphonique** telephone follow-up

relancer *vt* (**a**) *(économie)* to boost, to revive; *(production, ventes, commerce)* to boost (**b**) *(produit, projet)* to relaunch (**c**) *(débiteur)* to chase up; *(client)* to follow up (**d**) ORDINAT *(programme)* to rerun; *(logiciel)* to restart

relation *nf* (**a**) *(rapports entre personnes)* relations; **être en relation avec qn** to be in touch with sb; **mettre qn en relation avec qn** to put sb in touch with sb; **être en relations d'affaires avec qn** to have business relations with sb, to deal with sb ❑ **relations industrielles** industrial relations; **relations publiques** public relations; **relations sociales** labour relations (**b**) *(personne)* acquaintance; **avoir des relations** to have contacts ❑ **relation d'affaires** business acquaintance

relevé *nm* statement ❑ **relevé d'achat** purchase report; MKTG **relevé d'achat journalier** diary; **relevé de caisse** cash statement; **relevé de compte** bank statement; **relevé des dépenses** statement of expenditure; **relevé des dettes actives et passives** statement of assets and liabilities; **relevé de factures** statement of invoices; **relevé de fin de mois** end-of-month statement; **relevé d'identité**

bancaire = document giving details of one's bank account; **relevé d'identité postal** = document giving details of one's post office account; **relevé remis** account tendered; **relevé de vente** sales report

relèvement *nm* (**a**) *(des salaires, d'un tarif, d'un impôt, des taux d'intérêt)* raising, increasing (**b**) *(des affaires, de l'économie, d'une industrie)* recovery, revival

relever 1 *vt* (**a**) *(salaires, tarif, impôt, taux d'intérêt)* to raise, to increase; **relever le cours du franc** to raise the value of the franc (**b**) *(affaires, économie, industrie)* to revive (**c**) *(adresse, coordonnées)* to take down; **relever un compte** to make out a statement of account
2 se relever *vpr (affaires, économie, industrie)* to recover, to revive; *(cours)* to recover; **l'entreprise ne s'est jamais relevée de la perte de ce marché** the company has never recovered from the loss of this market

relief *nm* ORDINAT highlight; **mettre en relief** to highlight

relier se relier *vpr* ORDINAT to link up

reliquat *nm* remainder; *(d'un compte)* balance

remballage *nm* repacking

remballer *vt* to repack

rembours *nm* DOUANES drawback

remboursable *adj (prêt)* repayable; *(caution, versement)* refundable; *(obligation, coupon)* redeemable; **remboursable sur une période de 25 ans** repayable over (a period of) 25 years; **remboursable au pair** repayable at par

remboursement *nm (des dépenses)* repayment, reimbursement; *(d'un prêt)* repayment; *(d'une caution, d'un versement, d'un achat, des frais)* refund; *(d'une obligation, d'un coupon)* redemption; *(d'un effet)* retirement ❑ **remboursement anticipé** redemption before due date

rembourser *vt* (**a**) *(dépenses)* to repay, to reimburse; *(prêt)* to repay; *(caution, versement, achat, frais)* to refund; *(obligation, coupon)* to redeem; *(effet)* to retire (**b**) *(personne)* to repay, to reimburse

remembrement *nm* ADMIN *(de terres)* re-allocation, regrouping

remembrer *vt* ADMIN *(terres)* to re-allocate, to regroup

réméré *nm* repurchase

remettant *nm* BANQUE = person who pays money or a cheque into a current account

remetteur, -euse FIN **1** *adj (banque)* remitting
2 *nm,f* remitter

remettre *vt* (**a**) *(donner)* to remit; **remettre un chèque à l'encaissement** to cash a cheque; **remettre sa démission** to hand in one's notice (**b**) *(ajourner)* to postpone, to put off; **la réunion a été remise à lundi** the meeting has been put off *or* postponed until Monday (**c**) *(lettre, colis)* to deliver (**d**) *(dette)* to cancel

remise *nf* (**a**) FIN *(fait de remettre)* remittance; **payable contre remise du coupon** payable on presentation of the coupon; **faire une remise (de fonds) à qn** to send sb a remittance ❑ *remise documentaire* documentary remittance; *remise de fonds* remittance of funds; *remise à vue* demand deposit
(**b**) *(rabais)* discount, reduction; **une remise de 10%** a discount of 10%, 10% off; **faire une remise sur qch** to allow a discount on sth; **faire une remise à qn** to give sb a discount ❑ *remise de caisse* cash discount; *remise de fidélité au client* customer loyalty discount; *remise de marchandisage* merchandising allowance; *remise sur marchandises* trade discount; *remise promotionnelle* promotional discount; *remise quantitative, remise pour quantité, remise sur la quantité* bulk discount, quantity discount; *remise saisonnière* seasonal discount; *remise d'usage* trade discount
(**c**) *(d'une lettre, d'un colis)* delivery
(**d**) *(d'une dette)* cancellation; **faire remise d'une dette** to cancel a debt
(**e**) *(ajournement)* postponement

remisier *nm* BOURSE half-commission man, intermediate broker

remontée *nf (d'une monnaie, des valeurs, des prix)* recovery; **faire une belle remontée** to make a good recovery

remonter *vi (monnaie, valeurs, prix)* to go back up

remplacement *nm* replacement; **de remplacement** *(coût)* replacement; *(produit)* substitute; *(marché)* alternative

remplacer *vt* to replace; **doit-on accepter que l'euro remplace notre monnaie nationale?** should we accept that our national currency be replaced by the euro?; **il a remplacé Luc Leblanc à la direction de l'entreprise** he has replaced Luc Leblanc *or* taken over from Luc Leblanc as manager of the company; ORDINAT **tout remplacer** replace all

remplir *vt* (**a**) *(formulaire, questionnaire)* to fill in, to fill out, to complete; *(chèque)* to write, to make out (**b**) *(condition, obligation)* to comply with, to fulfil

remployer *vt* (**a**) *(personne)* to re-employ (**b**) *(argent, fonds)* to reinvest

remue-méninges *nm* MKTG brainstorming

rémunérateur, -trice *adj* remunerative, profitable; *(placement)* interest-bearing

rémunération *nf* (**a**) *(somme versée)* remuneration, payment (**de** for); **en rémunération de vos services** as payment for your services ❑ *rémunération du capital* return on capital; *rémunération au temps passé* time rate (**b**) *(salaire)* salary ❑ *rémunération de départ* starting salary

> ❝
> L'écart de **rémunération** entre les diplômés et ceux qui ne le sont pas s'élargit fortement dans les premières années de la carrière et, à nouveau, à partir de 40 ans.
> ❞

rémunérer *vt* (**a**) *(travail, services)* to pay for (**b**) *(salaires)* to pay

renchérir **1** *vt (marchandises, main-d'œuvre)* to raise the price of; *(prix)* to raise
2 *vi* (**a**) *(marchandises, main-d'œuvre)* to go up in price; *(prix)* to go up, to increase (**b**) **renchérir sur qn** *(aux enchères)* to outbid sb

> ❝
> Des jours difficiles se préparent: la dévaluation du rouble va certes aider les exportateurs, mais elle va aussi **renchérir** le prix des produits importés.
> ❞

renchérissement *nm (de marchandises, de main-d'œuvre)* price increase; *(d'un prix)* increase

rendement *nm* (**a**) FIN *(d'un investissement, d'une obligation)* yield, return, profit; *(des actions)* earnings; **à gros rendement** *(investissement, obligation)* high-yield; *(actions)* high-earning ❑ *rendement actuariel brut* gross actuarial return; *rendement annuel* annual return; *rendement brut* gross yield *or* return; *rendement constant* fixed yield; *rendement sur fonds propres* return on equity; *rendement réel* inflation-adjusted yield
(**b**) *(d'un ouvrier)* output; *(d'une usine)*

output, production; *(d'un processus, d'un ordinateur)* throughput; **travailler à plein rendement** to work to full capacity; **l'usine tourne à plein rendement** the factory is operating at full capacity ❑ *rendement d'ensemble, rendement global* aggregate output; *rendement à l'heure, rendement horaire* output per hour; *rendement individuel* output per person; *rendement maximum* maximum output; *rendement minimum* minimum output; *rendement optimal* peak output; *rendement total* aggregate *or* total output
  (**c**) *(d'une machine)* efficiency ❑ *rendement économique* commercial efficiency; *rendement effectif* performance rating; *rendement global* overall efficiency

rendez-vous *nm* appointment; **fixer un rendez-vous** *ou* **donner rendez-vous (à qn)** to make *or* fix an appointment (with sb) ❑ *rendez-vous d'affaires* business appointment

rendre *vt* (**a**) *(redonner)* to give back, to return; *(argent)* to repay, to pay back; *(article)* to return
  (**b**) *(sujet: investissement)* to yield
  (**c**) *(livrer)* to deliver; **rendu à domicile** delivered to your door; **rendu franco à bord** (delivered) free on board

rendu *nm* returned article, return; **faire un rendu** to return *or* exchange an article

renflouer *vt (entreprise, personne)* to bail out, to keep afloat

renommer *vt* ORDINAT *(fichier)* to rename

renouvelable *adj (contrat)* renewable

renouveler *vt* (**a**) *(changer) (personnel)* to renew; *(stock, matériel)* to renew, to replace (**b**) *(répéter) (commande)* to repeat; *(passeport, abonnement, demande)* to renew; **renouveler sa candidature** *ou* **sa demande d'emploi** to reapply *(for a job)* (**c**) *(prolonger) (traite, bail, contrat)* to renew, to extend; *(crédit)* to extend

renouvellement *nm* (**a**) *(de personnel)* turnover; *(du stock, du matériel)* renewal, replacement (**b**) *(d'une commande)* repetition (**c**) *(d'une traite, d'un bail, d'un contrat)* renewal, extension; *(d'un crédit)* extension

renseignement *nm* (**a**) *(information)* piece of information; **renseignements** information; **pour tout renseignement complémentaire, veuillez appeler ce numéro** for information *or* if you have any queries, please call this number; **je vous envoie à titre de renseignement...** I am sending you for your information...; **demander/donner des renseignements sur qn/qch** to ask for/to give (some) information about sb/sth; **prendre des renseignements sur qn/qch** to make enquiries *or* to enquire about sb/sth; **aller aux renseignements** to go to find out *or* to make enquiries ❑ FIN *renseignements de crédit* status *or* credit enquiry; *renseignements statistiques* statistical data; *renseignements techniques* data
  (**b**) TÉL **renseignements** *Br* directory enquiries, *Am* information

renseigner **1** *vt* **renseigner qn (sur qch)** to give sb (some) information (about sth), to inform sb (about sth)
  2 se renseigner *vpr* to make enquiries; *(sur un point précis)* to find out (**sur** about)

rentabilisation *nf* making profitable; **la rentabilisation de l'affaire prendra peu de temps** it won't be long before the business becomes profitable *or* starts to make a profit

rentabiliser *vt* to make profitable; **l'industrie exige de gros investissements longs à rentabiliser** industry requires heavy investment which takes a long time to show a profit

> ❝
> Avec deux magasins, le groupe avait peu de chances de **rentabiliser** ses investissements et sa logistique. ❞

rentabilité *nf* profitability, cost-effectiveness (**de** of); *(d'un investissement, des ventes)* return (**de** on) ❑ *rentabilité directe du produit* direct product profitability

rentable *adj* profitable; **l'opération n'a pas été très rentable** the operation has not been very profitable

rente *nf* (**a**) **rentes** *(revenu)* private income; **avoir cent mille francs de rentes** to have a private income of a hundred thousand francs
  (**b**) *(pension)* annuity, pension ❑ *rente annuelle* annuity; *rente à paiement différé* deferred annuity; *rente de situation* guaranteed income; *rente à terme* terminable annuity; *rente viagère* life annuity, life interest
  (**c**) FIN *(emprunt d'État)* government loan *or* bond ❑ *rentes amortissables* redeemable stock *or* loans; *rentes sur l'État* government stock *or* funds; *rentes perpétuelles* irredeemable securities
  (**d**) ÉCON rent ❑ *rente foncière* ground rent

rentier, -ère *nm,f (qui vit de ses rentes)* person of independent means ❑ ***rentier viager*** annuitant

rentrée *nf (d'argent)* receipt; **rentrées** income, money coming in; **avoir des rentrées d'argent** to have a regular income *or* money coming in regularly ❑ COMPTA ***rentrées de caisse*** cash receipts; ***rentrées de devises*** foreign exchange inflows; ***rentrées fiscales*** tax revenue; ***rentrées journalières*** daily takings; COMPTA ***rentrées et sorties de caisse*** cash receipts and payments

rentrer *vi* **rentrer dans ses frais** to recover one's expenses, to get one's money back, to break even

renvoi *nm* (**a**) *(de lettre, de marchandises, de colis)* return, sending back (**b**) *(d'un employé)* dismissal (**c**) *(ajournement)* postponement; JUR adjournment (**d**) JUR *(devant une autre juridiction)* transfer, referral (**devant** to) (**e**) ORDINAT cross-reference

renvoyer *vt* (**a**) *(lettre, marchandises, colis)* to return, to send back (**b**) *(employé)* to dismiss (**c**) *(ajourner)* to postpone; JUR to adjourn (**d**) JUR *(devant une autre juridiction)* to transfer, to refer (**devant** to) (**e**) ORDINAT to cross-refer

réorganisation *nf (du personnel, des ressources)* reorganization

réorganiser *vt (personnel, ressources)* to reorganize

réouverture *nf (d'un magasin, d'un marché)* reopening; *(de négociations)* resumption

réparation *nf* (**a**) *(action)* repairing; *(résultat)* repair; **être en réparation** to be under repair ❑ ***réparation d'entretien*** maintenance; ***réparations locatives*** repairs incumbent on the tenant (**b**) JUR compensation ❑ ***réparation civile*** compensation; ***réparation de dommages*** damages; ***réparation légale*** legal redress

réparer *vt* (**a**) *(appareil, défaut)* to repair (**b**) *(erreur)* to rectify; *(pertes, dommage)* to make good

répartir 1 *vt* (**a**) *(distribuer) (tâches, argent)* to divide, to distribute; *(dividende)* to distribute; *(coûts)* to break down; BOURSE *(actions)* to allot, to allocate (**b**) *(étaler) (versements, dépenses)* to spread (out) (**c**) *(impôts)* to assess; ASSUR *(avarie)* to adjust

répartiteur, -trice *nm,f* ADMIN **(commissaire)** répartiteur tax assessor ❑ ASSUR ***répartiteur d'avaries*** loss adjuster

répartition *nf* (**a**) *(de tâches, d'argent)* division, distribution; *(d'une dividende)* distribution; *(de coûts)* breakdown; BOURSE *(d'actions)* allotment, allocation; **première et unique répartition** first and final dividend; **nouvelle répartition** second dividend; **dernière répartition** final dividend ❑ ***répartition optimale des ressources*** optimal resource allocation (**b**) *(des versements, des dépenses)* spreading (out) (**c**) *(des impôts)* assessment ❑ ASSUR ***répartition d'avarie*** average adjustment

répercuter 1 *vt* to pass on; **la taxe sera répercutée sur les consommateurs** the tax will be passed on to the consumers
2 **se répercuter** *vpr (effets, crise)* to have repercussions (**sur** on)

répertoire *nm* (**a**) ORDINAT directory ***répertoire central, répertoire principal*** main directory (**b**) *(carnet)* address book *(with alphabetical index)*; *(liste)* list ❑ ***répertoire d'adresses*** directory; ***répertoire des métiers*** trade directory

répertorier *vt* to list

répétition *nf* JUR claiming back ❑ ***répétition d'indu*** recovery of payment made in error

repli *nm* BOURSE fall, drop

replier se replier *vpr* BOURSE to fall back, to drop

répondant, -e *nm,f* JUR surety, guarantor

répondeur *nm* **répondeur (automatique** *ou* **téléphonique)** answering machine, answerphone ❑ ***répondeur interrogeable à distance*** answering machine with remote-access facility

répondre répondre à *vt ind* (**a**) *(question, lettre)* to reply to, to answer (**b**) FIN, BOURSE *(prime)* to declare

réponse *nf* (**a**) *(à une question, à une lettre)* answer, reply; **en réponse à votre lettre** in reply *or* response to your letter; **réponse payée** reply paid (**b**) ORDINAT answering ❑ ***réponse automatique*** unattended answering

report *nm* (**a**) *(renvoi à plus tard) (d'un rendez-vous, d'une réunion)* postponement ❑ FIN **report d'échéance** extension of due date; **report de livraison** extension of delivery date
(**b**) COMPTA *(en bas de page)* (balance) carried forward; *(en haut du page)* (balance) brought forward ❑ ***report déficitaire sur les exercices précédents*** loss carry back; ***report déficitaire sur les exercices ultérieurs*** loss carry forward; ***report de***

l'exercice précédent carried forward from the previous financial year; **report à l'exercice suivant** carried forward to the next financial year; **report à nouveau** carried forward

(**c**) COMPTA *(d'une écriture)* entering up, posting

(**d**) BOURSE contango, continuation; **en report** *(actions, titres)* taken in, carried over; **prendre des actions en report** to take in *or* carry over shares

reporté, -e *nm,f* BOURSE *(d'actions)* giver

reporter *vt* (**a**) *(remettre à plus tard) (rendez-vous, réunion)* to postpone

(**b**) COMPTA *(balance, total) (en bas de page)* to carry forward; *(en haut de page)* to bring forward; **solde à reporter** balance carried forward

(**c**) COMPTA *(écriture)* to enter up, to post

(**d**) BOURSE to continue, to contango; **(faire) reporter des titres** to carry stock; **(faire) reporter un emprunteur** to take in stock for a borrower; **se faire reporter** to be carried over

reporteur *nm* BOURSE *(d'actions)* taker

repositionnement *nm* MKTG *(d'un produit)* repositioning

repositionner MKTG **1** *vt (produit)* to reposition

2 se repositionner *vpr* **se repositionner à la baisse** to move downmarket; **se repositionner à la hausse** to move upmarket

reprendre 1 *vt* (**a**) *(employé, marchandises)* to take back (**b**) *(recommencer)* **reprendre le travail** to return to work (**c**) *(acheter) (entreprise)* to take over, to buy out (**d**) ORDINAT *(programme)* to restart

2 *vi (affaires)* to recover, to pick up

> Le groupe d'électronique Raytheon suit … en **reprenant** pour 12,5 milliards les sociétés Hughes et Texas Instrument.

repreneur *nm* purchaser, buyer

représentant, -e *nm,f* representative ❑ **représentant de commerce, représentant commercial** sales representative; **représentant dûment accrédité** duly authorized representative; **représentant exclusif** sole agent; **représentant multi-carte** representative for several companies; **représentant du personnel** staff representative

représentation *nf* representation; *(agence)* agency; **faire de la représentation,**

être dans la représentation to be a (sales) representative ❑ **représentation exclusive** sole agency; **avoir la représentation exclusive de…** to be sole agents for…

représenter *vt* (**a**) *(agir au nom de)* to represent, to act for (**b**) *(correspondre à)* to represent; **ceci représente 10% du budget** this represents 10% of the budget

repris, -e *adj* **non repris** *(emballage)* non-returnable

reprise *nf* (**a**) *(des affaires, des cours)* recovery; *(des travaux)* resumption ❑ **reprise économique** economic recovery, upswing *or* upturn in the economy; **reprise de travail** return to work; **les grévistes ont voté la reprise de travail** the strikers have voted to return to work

(**b**) *(de marchandises invendues, d'articles en solde)* taking back ❑ COMPTA **reprises sur provisions** recovery of provisions, write-back of provisions

(**c**) *(rachat)* takeover ❑ **reprise de l'entreprise par ses salariés** employee buy-out

(**d**) ORDINAT *(d'un programme)* restart

reproduction *nf (d'un document)* reproduction, duplicating

reproduire *vt* (**a**) *(document)* to reproduce, to duplicate (**b**) *(répéter)* to repeat; **la nouvelle direction a reproduit les mêmes erreurs** the new management repeated the same mistakes

reprogrammable *adj* ORDINAT *(touche)* reprogrammable

reprogrammer *vt* (**a**) *(livraison)* to reschedule (**b**) ORDINAT to reprogram

réputation *nf* reputation, standing; **avoir (une) bonne/mauvaise réputation** to have a good/bad reputation

requérant, -e JUR **1** *adj* **partie requérante** claimant

2 *nm,f* claimant

requête *nf* ORDINAT query

requin *nm* **requin (de la finance)** shark, raider

RES *nf* FIN *(abrév* **rachat de l'entreprise par ses salariés)** employee buy-out

réseau *nm* (**a**) *(dans le commerce, dans les télécommunications)* network ❑ **réseau câblé** cable network; **réseau commercial** sales network; **réseau de distribution** distribution network; **réseau multimédia** multimedia network; **réseau téléphonique** telephone system *or* network; **réseau de transport intégré** integrated transport network; **réseau de vente** sales network

(b) ORDINAT network❏ *réseau en anneau à jeton* token ring network; *réseau de communication de données* datacomms network; *réseau connecté en étoile* star network; *réseau de données* data network; *réseau informatique* computer network; *réseau local* local area network, LAN; *réseau longue distance* wide area network, WAN; *réseau neuronal* neural network; *réseau numérique à intégration de services* integrated services digital network; *réseau de télématique* datacomms network; *réseau d'utilisateurs* user network

❝ ───────

France Télécom possède pourtant, avec Numeris, l'un des **réseaux multimédias** les plus performants du monde.

❞

réservation *nf* reservation, booking ❏ *réservation électronique* electronic reservation

réserve *nf* **(a)** *(stock)* reserve; **en réserve** in reserve, set aside; **avoir qch en réserve** to have sth in stock or in reserve; **mettre qch en réserve** to put or set sth aside; **puiser dans les réserves** to draw on the reserves; **sans réserve de retour** non-returnable, no-return; **avec réserve de retour** on a sale or return basis ❏ *réserve d'achat* credit limit; *réserves bancaires* bank reserves; *réserves de change* monetary reserves; *réserve pour créances douteuses* bad debts reserve; *réserves en devises* foreign exchange reserves; *réserve latente* hidden reserve; *réserve légale* legal reserve; *réserve liquide* liquid assets, cash reserve; *réserves mondiales* *(de matières premières)* world reserves; *réserves monétaires internationales* international monetary reserves; *réserves non distribuées* capital reserves; *réserves obligataires* federal fund; *réserve occulte* secret reserve; *réserve de prévoyance* contingency reserve; *réserve statutaire* statutory reserve; *réserve visible* visible reserve

(b) *(restriction)* reservation; JUR **sous toutes réserves** without prejudice; **sous réserve de la signature du contrat** subject to contract **(c)** *(magasin)* storeroom, warehouse

❝ ───────

La devise allemande a terminé la semaine à plus de 3,51 francs. Une mauvaise affaire pour la Banque de France qui continue de reconstituer ses **réserves de change**.

❞

réserver *vt* **(a)** *(chambre, place)* to reserve, to book **(b)** *(mettre de côté)* to set aside; **réserver des fonds pour qch** to put money aside for sth

réservoir de main-d'œuvre *nm* labour pool

résident, -e 1 *adj (personne)* resident **2** *nm,f (personne)* resident

résiliable *adj (bail, contrat)* that may be terminated

résiliation *nf (d'un bail, d'un contrat)* termination

résilier *vt (bail, contrat)* to terminate

résistance des consommateurs *nf* MKTG consumer resistance

résoluble *adj (bail, contrat)* that may be terminated

résolution *nf* **(a)** *(d'un bail, d'un contrat)* termination; *(d'une vente)* cancellation **(b)** *(décision)* resolution; **prendre** *ou* **adopter une résolution** to pass or adopt a resolution **(c)** ORDINAT resolution

résorber *vt (surplus, déficit)* to absorb; *(inflation, chômage)* to reduce, to bring down; *(stocks)* to reduce; *(dettes)* to clear

❝ ───────

Malgré la chute de la production industrielle, les entreprises ne **résorbent** pas leurs stocks, qui progressent toujours plus vite que les livraisons.

❞

résoudre *vt (bail, contrat)* to terminate

respecter *vt* to respect; *(clause)* to comply with

responsabilité *nf (morale)* responsibility **(de** for); JUR *(légale)* liability **(de** for); **avoir la responsabilité de qch** *(en avoir la charge)* to be in charge of sth; **elle a la responsabilité du service après-vente** she's in charge of the after-sales department; **"la direction décline toute responsabilité en cas de vol"** *(sur panneau)* the management accepts no responsibility in case of theft; **on lui a confié de nouvelles responsabilités au sein du groupe** he was given new responsibilities within the group; **il a un poste à responsabilités** he has a position of responsibility ❏ *responsabilité civile* public liability, third party liability, civil liability; **être assuré responsabilité civile** to have public liability insurance; *responsabilité collective* collective responsibility; *responsabilité conjointe et solidaire* joint and several liability; *responsabilité con-*

tractuelle contractual liability; ***responsabilité de l'employeur*** employer's liability; FIN ***responsabilité illimitée*** unlimited liability; ***responsabilité individuelle*** several liability; FIN ***responsabilité limitée*** limited liability; ***responsabilité patronale*** employer's liability; ***responsabilité solidaire et indivise*** joint and several liability; ***responsabilité au tiers*** third-party liability; **être assuré responsabilité au tiers** to carry third-party insurance

responsable 1 *adj (moralement)* responsible (**de** for); *(légalement)* liable (**de** for); **être responsable de qch** *(en avoir la charge)* to be in charge of sth; **elle est responsable du service après-vente** she's in charge of the after-sales department
2 *nmf (coupable)* person responsible (**de** for); *(personne qui a la charge)* person in charge (**de** of) □ ***responsable de budget*** account manager; ***responsable commercial*** business manager; ***responsable du marketing*** marketing manager; ***responsable de projet*** project manager; ***responsable des relations publiques*** public relations officer; ***responsable syndical*** union official

resserrement du crédit *nm* ÉCON credit squeeze

ressort *nm (d'un tribunal)* competence; **cette affaire est du ressort du chef du personnel** this is a matter for the personnel manager; **ce conflit est du ressort du tribunal des prud'hommes** this conflict falls within the jurisdiction of the industrial tribunal

ressources *nfpl* resources □ ***ressources d'appoint*** additional (sources of) income; ***ressources du budget*** budgetary resources; ***ressources de l'État*** government resources; ***ressources financières*** financial resources; ***ressources fiscales*** tax resources; ***ressources humaines*** human resources; ***ressources naturelles*** natural resources; ***ressources personnelles*** private means

restant *nm* rest, remainder; *(d'un compte)* balance □ ***restant en caisse*** cash surplus

restauration *nf* ORDINAT restore

restaurer *vt* ORDINAT to restore

reste *nm* rest, remainder; **vous pouvez payer le reste par mensualités** you can pay the balance in monthly instalments

restituable *adj* repayable

restitution *nf* repayment, refund □ DOUANES ***restitution des droits d'entrée*** drawback; UE ***restitution à l'exportation*** export refund; ***restitution d'impôts*** tax refund; JUR ***restitution d'indu*** return of payment made in error

restreindre *vt (crédit, dépenses, production)* to restrict, to limit

restreint, -e *adj (crédit, dépenses, production)* restricted, limited

restrictif, -ive *adj (pratique, endossement)* restrictive; *(clause)* limitative

restriction *nf* restriction □ ORDINAT ***restriction d'accès*** access restriction; ***restrictions budgétaires*** budget restrictions; ***restriction de concurrence*** trade restraint; ***restriction du crédit*** credit squeeze *or* restrictions; ***restrictions sur les exportations*** export restrictions; ***restrictions sur les importations*** import restrictions; ***restrictions salariales, restrictions des salaires*** wage restraint; FIN ***restrictions de transfert*** transfer restrictions

restructuration *nf* (**a**) *(d'une industrie, d'une entreprise)* restructuring (**b**) *(de dette)* rescheduling

> ❝
> Malgré les **restructurations** auxquelles elles ont procédé, les entreprises sud-coréennes sont incapables de reprendre leur production, leurs banques, japonaises, étant dans l'incapacité de financer leurs achats de matières premières.
> ❞

restructurer *vt* (**a**) *(industrie, entreprise)* to restructure (**b**) *(dette)* to reschedule

> ❝
> Dans l'impossibilité de rembourser les obligations qui arrivent à échéance, l'État a donc décidé de **restructurer** sa dette et de transformer les bons du Trésor à court terme en bons à long terme.
> ❞

résultat *nm* (**a**) COMPTA result □ ***résultat brut*** gross return; ***résultat courant*** profit before tax and extraordinary items; ***résultat économique*** economic profit; ***résultat exceptionnel*** extraordinary profit or loss; ***résultat de l'exercice*** profit or loss for the financial year, statement of income; ***résultat d'exploitation*** operating profit or loss; ***résultat final*** final statement; ***résultat financier*** financial profit or loss; ***résultat***

net net return; *résultat net consolidé* consolidated statement of net income; *résultat de la période* profit or loss for the financial period; *résultats prévisionnels* earnings forecast

(**b**) MKTG performance ❏ *résultats antérieurs* past performance; *résultats perçus* perceived performance

rétablir 1 *vt (économie, échanges commerciaux)* to re-establish, to restore; **rétablir un budget déficitaire** to balance an adverse budget; **rétablir qn (dans ses fonctions)** to reinstate sb

2 **se rétablir** *vpr (économie)* to recover, to pick up again; *(entreprise, monnaie)* to recover

retard *nm* delay; **en retard** *(compte, paiement)* outstanding, overdue; **ils sont en retard dans leurs paiements** they're behind or in arrears with their payments ❏ *retard de livraison* delay in delivery, late delivery; *retard de paiement* delay in payment, late payment

retarder *vt* to delay; *(paiement)* to defer, to delay; **la grève des routiers a retardé les livraisons** deliveries were delayed because of the lorry drivers' strike

retenir *vt* (**a**) *(somme)* to keep back, to deduct (**sur** from) (**b**) *(offre)* to accept (**c**) *(chambre, table, place)* to reserve, to book

retenue *nf (d'une somme)* deduction; **faire une retenue de 5% sur les salaires** to deduct or withhold 5% from salaries ❏ *retenue fiscale* withholding tax; *retenue à la source* payment (of income tax) at source, *Br* ≃ PAYE, *Am* ≃ pay as you go

retirer 1 *vt* (**a**) *(argent)* to withdraw, to take out; **retirer des marchandises de la douane** to take goods out of bond (**b**) *(commande, candidature)* to withdraw; *(ordre de grève)* to call off (**c**) FIN *(effet)* to retire, to withdraw; *(monnaies)* to withdraw from circulation, to call in

2 **se retirer** *vpr* **se retirer des affaires** to retire from business

retombées *nfpl* repercussions; **la grève aura des retombées sur les prix** the strike will have repercussions on prices

retour *nm* (**a**) *(de marchandises, d'une lettre)* return; **marchandises de retour, retours** returns; **vendu avec possibilité de retour** sold on a sale or return basis; **répondre par retour du courrier** to reply by return of post; **retour à l'envoyeur** *ou* **à l'expéditeur** return to sender; **en retour d'une somme de 50 francs** in consideration of a sum of 50 francs ❏ *retour en charge* loaded return; *retour sans frais* return free of charge; *retour*

d'information feedback; *retour à vide* empty return

(**b**) *(amortissement)* return ❏ *retour sur achat* purchase return; *retour sur investissement* return on investment, ROI; *retour sur ventes* return on sales

(**c**) FIN dishonoured bill, bill returned dishonoured

(**d**) ORDINAT *(sur clavier)* return ❏ *retour arrière* backspace

retourner *vt (effet, lettre, colis, marchandises)* to return; **retourner à l'envoyeur** *ou* à **l'expéditeur** to return to sender; **prière de nous retourner l'accusé de réception ci-joint, revêtu de votre signature** please sign and return the enclosed acknowledgement

retrait *nm* (**a**) *(d'argent)* withdrawal; **faire un retrait** to make a withdrawal; **faire un retrait de 5 000 francs** to withdraw 5,000 francs ❏ *retrait d'espèces* cash withdrawal (**b**) *(d'une commande, d'une candidature)* withdrawal; *(d'un ordre de grève)* calling off (**c**) FIN *(d'un effet)* withdrawal; *(de monnaies)* withdrawal from circulation, calling in

retraite *nf* (**a**) *(de la vie active)* retirement (from work); **âge de la retraite** retirement age; **être à la retraite** to be retired; **mettre qn à la retraite** to pension sb off, to retire sb; **prendre sa retraite** to retire; **partir en retraite** to retire, to go into retirement ❏ *retraite anticipée* early retirement; *retraite forcée* compulsory retirement (**b**) *(pension)* pension ❏ *retraite par capitalisation* loanback pension; *retraite complémentaire* private pension; *retraite indexée sur le revenu* earnings-related pension; *retraite minimum* guaranteed minimum pension; *retraite vieillesse* retirement pension

retraité, -e 1 *adj* retired

2 *nm,f* pensioner

retrancher *vt* to deduct, to take off

rétribuer *vt (employé, service, travail)* to pay; **bien rétribué** highly-paid; **mal rétribué** badly-paid

rétribution *nf* payment

rétroactif, -ive *adj* retrospective, retroactive; **augmentation avec effet rétroactif au 1 septembre** increase backdated to 1 September

rétrocéder *vt* to resell

rétrocession *nf* resale

rétro-éclairé, -e *adj* ORDINAT *(écran)* backlit

rétroprojecteur *nm* overhead projector

rétrospective *nf* FIN review

réunion *nf* (**a**) *(assemblée)* meeting; *(d'un comité)* session, sitting; **le directeur est en réunion** the manager is in a meeting ▫ *réunion d'actionnaires* shareholders' meeting; *réunion de comité* committee meeting; *réunion du conseil d'adminis-tration* board meeting; *réunion éléctorale* election meeting; *réunion paritaire* round-table conference; *réunion préparatoire* briefing; *réunion publique* public meeting; MKTG *réunion de remue-méninges* brainstorming session

(**b**) *(de deux services)* merger, amalgamation

réunir **1** *vt* (**a**) *(somme)* to collect, to get together (**b**) *(personnes)* to bring together; **réunir un comité** to convene a committee, to call a committee meeting; **la conférence a réuni les dirigeants de plusieurs multina-tionales** the conference brought together executives from several multinationals

2 se réunir *vpr* (**a**) *(personnes)* to meet, to convene (**b**) *(sociétés)* to amalgamate, to merge

revalorisation *nf* (**a**) FIN *(d'une monnaie)* revalorization, revaluation (**b**) *(des salaires, des retraites)* upgrading

revaloriser *vt* (**a**) FIN *(monnaie)* to revalorize, to revalue (**b**) *(salaires, retraites)* to upgrade

revendable *adj* resaleable

revendeur, -euse *nm,f* retailer; *(d'articles d'occasion)* second-hand dealer

revendicatif, -ive *adj* *(mouvement)* protest

revendication *nf* *(de travailleurs)* claim, demand (**sur** on) ▫ *revendications sala-riales, revendications salaires* wage claims; *revendications syndicales* union demands *or* claims

revendiquer *vt* to claim, to demand; **les salariés revendiquent de meilleures conditions de travail** the employees are demanding better working conditions

revendre *vt* to resell; BOURSE *(titres)* to sell out

revenir *vi* to cost; **revenir cher** to be expensive; **sa maison lui est revenue à 750 000 francs** his house cost him 750,000 francs; **cet article vous reviendra à 100 francs** this item will cost you 100 francs

revente *nf* resale; BOURSE *(de titres)* selling out

revenu *nm* (**a**) *(d'une personne, d'une entreprise)* income; *(de l'État)* revenue; **avoir de gros/petits revenus** to have a large/small income ▫ *revenus accessoires* incidental income; *revenus actuels* current earnings; *revenu annuel* annual income; *revenu brut global* total gross income; *revenu cumulé* cumulative revenue; *revenu disponible* disposable income; *revenus de l'exportation* export revenue; ADMIN *revenu familial* family income; *revenu fixe* fixed income; *revenu imposable* taxable income; *revenu imposable après déduction des abattements fiscaux* taxable income after deduction of tax allowances; *revenu des intérêts* earned interest, interest income; *revenu locatif* rental income; *revenu minimum d'inser-tion* Br ≃ income support, Am ≃ welfare; ÉCON *revenu national brut* gross national income; ÉCON *revenu national net* net national income; *revenu net global* total net income; *revenu personnel disponible* disposable personal income; *revenu réel* real income; *revenu résiduel* residual income; *revenu du travail* earned income

(**b**) *(d'un investissement)* yield, return ▫ *re-venu(s) obligataire(s), revenu(s) des obligations* income from bonds; *revenu variable* income from variable-yield invest-ments

> **"**
> L'objectif est de réduire l'écart … entre le **revenu** net perçu par les salariés et son coût global pour l'entreprise.
> **"**

reversement *nm* FIN transfer *(of funds from one account to another)*

reverser *vt* FIN *(somme)* to transfer (**à** *ou* **sur** to); *(impôt)* to pay

revêtir *vt* *(document)* to sign, to validate

révisable *adj* *(prix)* *(qui peut changer)* subject to alteration *or* to modification; *(négociable)* open to offer, negotiable

réviser *vt* *(clause, contrat)* to revise; *(compte)* to check; **réviser une estimation à la hausse/baisse** to revise an estimate upwards/downwards; **il a fallu réviser à la baisse les prévisions pour l'an prochain** the projected figures for next year have had to be scaled down

réviseur *nm* FIN *réviseur (comptable)* auditor; *réviseur externe* external auditor; *réviseur interne* internal auditor

révision *nf (d'un contrat, des salaires, des prix)* review

révoquer *vt* (**a**) *(commande, contrat)* to revoke, to countermand; *(ordre de grève)* to call off (**b**) *(fonctionnaire)* to dismiss, to remove from office

revue *nf (publication)* magazine; *(spécialisée)* journal, review □ *revue financière* financial journal *or* review; *revue professionnelle* trade journal

RH *nfpl (abrév* **ressources humaines**) HR

RIB *nm (abrév* **relevé d'identité bancaire**) = document giving details of one's bank account

riche **1** *adj* rich, wealthy
2 *nmf* wealthy person; **les impôts indirects touchent davantage les pauvres que les riches** indirect taxes penalize the poor more than the rich

richesse *nf* (**a**) *(d'une personne, d'un pays)* wealth □ MKTG *la richesse vive* consumer purchasing power (**b**) **richesses** *(ressources)* resources

RIP *nm (abrév* **relevé d'identité postale**) = document giving details of one's post office account

risque *nm* FIN, ASSUR risk; **couvrir un risque** to cover a risk; **souscrire un risque** to underwrite a risk; **aux risques et périls du propriétaire** *(sur panneau)* at owner's risk □ *risque accru* overexposure; *risque assuré* risk subscribed *or* taken up; *risque de change* exchange risk; *risque collectif* collective risk; *risque d'incendie* fire risk; *risque locatif* tenant's third-party risk; *risque de marché* market risk; *risque maritime, risque de mer* sea risk; *risques mixtes* mixed risks; *risque de perte et d'avaries* loss risk; *risque du recours du tiers* third-party risk; *risque de vol* theft risk

> ❝
> L'assurance contre le **risque de change** consiste à souscrire une police auprès d'une compagnie privée ou, plus souvent, publique.
> ❞

risque-pays *nm* country risk

ristourne *nf* (**a**) *(rabais)* discount; **une ristourne de 15%** a 15% discount; **faire une ristourne à qn** to give sb a discount □ *ristourne de fidélité* customer loyalty discount; *ristourne de prime* premium discount (**b**) ASSUR repayment, refund

ristourner *vt (réduire)* to give a discount of; **il nous a ristourné 15% du prix** he gave us a 15% discount

RMI *nm (abrév* **revenu minimum d'insertion**) *Br* ≃ income support, *Am* ≃ welfare

RNIS *nm* ORDINAT *(abrév* **réseau numérique à intégration de services**) ISDN

robotique *nf* robotics

ROC *nf* ORDINAT *(abrév* **reconnaissance optique des caractères**) OCR

rôle *nm (liste)* roll, register □ ADMIN *rôle des contributions* tax roll; *rôle d'impôt* tax roll

ROM *nf* ORDINAT *(abrév* **read only memory**) ROM

rompre *vt (négociations)* to break off; *(contrat)* to break

rotation *nf* *rotation des capitaux* turnover of capital; *rotation du personnel* staff turnover; *rotation de portefeuille* churning; *rotation de portefeuille-action* equity switching; *rotation de portefeuille-obligation* gilt switching; *rotation des stocks* *Br* stock turnround, *Am* inventory turn; **le délai de rotation des stocks est de quatre mois** stocks are turned round every four months

rouge *nm* **être dans le rouge** to be in the red; **sortir du rouge** to get out of the red

> ❝
> Rover affiche un résultat opérationnel de 56 millions de livres après deux années **dans le rouge**.
> ❞

roulage *nm (de marchandises)* carriage, haulage

roulant, -e *adj (fonds, capital)* working

roulement *nm* (**a**) FIN *(de fonds)* circulation; *(de capitaux)* turnover (**b**) *(de personnel)* turnover

rouler *vi (argent)* to circulate freely

roulier *nm* RORO (ship)

routage *nm (de documents, de lettres)* sorting and mailing

route *nf (itinéraire)* route; **en cours de route** in transit □ *route commerciale* commercial route, trade route

routeur *nm* ORDINAT router

routier, -ère **1** *adj* road
2 *nm,f Br* long-distance lorry driver, *Am* truck driver

rouvrir *vt (compte)* to reopen

RSVP *(abrév* **répondez s'il vous plaît)** RSVP

ruiner *vt* to ruin, to bankrupt

rupture *nf* (**a**) *(de négociations)* breaking off ❑ *rupture de contrat* breach of contract; *rupture de garantie* breach of guarantee; *rupture de stock* stock outage; **être en rupture de stock** to be out of stock (**b**) *(transbordement)* **rupture de charge** transhipment of cargo

> **❝**
> Victime de son succès, le maillot de l'équipe de France **était en rupture de stock** dès les quarts de finale.
> **❞**

rythme *nm* rate; **à quel rythme dois-je vous les envoyer?** what rate should I send them to you at? ❑ *rythme annualisé* annually compounded rate; *rythme des livraisons* delivery rate; *rythme de production* rate of production

SA *nf* (*abrév* **société anonyme**) *Br* ≃ plc, *Am* ≃ Inc

sacquer *vt Fam* to sack, to fire

sacrifié, -e *adj* (*prix*) rock-bottom; (*article*) at a rock-bottom price

sacrifier *vt* (*marchandises*) to sell at rock-bottom prices

saisie *nf* (**a**) (*de marchandises, de capitaux*) seizure; (*d'un bien pour non-paiement des traites*) repossession ❑ *saisie conservatoire* seizure of goods (*to prevent sale*) (**b**) (*d'une hypothèque*) foreclosure (**c**) ORDINAT *saisie automatique* automatic input; *saisie de données* data capture, keyboarding; *saisie manuelle* manual input

> **"**
> Le service est encore assuré par une équipe de professionnels se consacrant à la **saisie manuelle** des 120 000 bilans des plus grosses entreprises françaises.
> **"**

saisir *vt* (**a**) (*marchandises, capitaux*) to seize (**b**) (*hypothèque*) to foreclose on (**c**) ORDINAT (*données*) to key in (**d**) JUR (*tribunal*) to refer a case to; **la juridiction compétente a été saisie** the case was referred to the appropriate jurisdiction

saison *nf* season; **la haute saison** the busy *or* high season; **la basse saison** the off season, the slack season; **hors saison** off season; **pendant la saison** in season ❑ *saison creuse* off season, slack season; *saison touristique* tourist season

saisonnier, -ère **1** *adj* seasonal
2 *nm,f* seasonal worker

salaire *nm* (*mensuel*) salary; (*hebdomadaire, journalier*) wage ❑ *salaire de base* basic salary *or* pay; *salaire brut* gross salary *or* pay; *salaire de départ* starting salary; *salaire fixe* fixed salary *or* pay; *salaire hebdomadaire* weekly pay *or* wage; *salaire horaire* hourly wage *or* pay; *salaire indexé* index-linked salary; *salaire indirect* fringe benefits; *salaire mensuel* monthly salary; *salaire minimum* minimum wage; *salaire minimum interprofessionnel de croissance* index-linked guaranteed minimum wage; *salaire net* net salary *or* pay; *salaire*

nominal nominal wages; *salaire plafonné* wage ceiling; *salaire réel* real wage

salarial, -e *adj* (*mensuel*) salary; (*hebdomadaire, journalier*) wage

salariat *nm* wage-earning population; **le salariat et le patronat** employees and employers

salarié, -e **1** *adj* (**a**) (*travailleur*) (*payé au mois*) salaried; (*payé à la semaine*) wage-earning (**b**) (*travail*) paid
2 *nm,f* (*payé au mois*) salaried employee; (*payé à la semaine*) wage-earner; **les salariés de l'entreprise se sont mis en grève** the employees went on strike

salarier *vt* (*tous les mois*) to pay a salary to; (*toutes les semaines*) to pay a wage to

salle *nf* room ❑ *salle d'accueil (de la clientèle)* reception room; *salle d'attente* waiting room; BOURSE *salle des changes* trading room; BANQUE *salle des coffres* vaults; *salle de conférence* conference room; *salle du conseil* boardroom; *salle de démonstration* showroom; *salle d'exposition* showroom; (*pour une foire*) exhibition hall; BANQUE *salle des guichets* front office; BOURSE *salle des marchés* trading room; *salle de réception (de la clientèle)* reception room; *salle de réunion* boardroom, meeting room; *salle des ventes* auction room, salesroom

salon *nm* exhibition, trade fair ❑ **le Salon de l'informatique** = information technology trade fair

sanction *nf* (**a**) (*punition*) sanction; **prendre des sanctions contre un pays** to impose sanctions on a country ❑ *sanctions économiques* economic sanctions (**b**) (*approbation*) sanction

sans-emploi *nmf* unemployed person; **les sans-emploi** the unemployed

sans-travail *nmf* unemployed person; **les sans-travail** the unemployed

sapiteur *nm* ASSUR (*de cargaison*) valuer

saquer = **sacquer**

SARL *nf* (*abrév* **société à responsabilité limitée**) limited (liability) company

satisfaction *nf* satisfaction ❑ *satisfaction du consommateur* consumer satisfaction; *satisfaction dans le travail* job satisfaction

satisfaire 1 *vt* to satisfy
2 satisfaire à *vt ind (demande, condition, besoins)* to satisfy; *(règlement, normes de sécurité)* to comply with; *(obligation)* to fulfil

satisfait, -e *adj* satisfied; **j'espère que vous en serez entièrement satisfait** I trust it will give you complete satisfaction

saturation *nf* MKTG *(du marché)* saturation; **arriver à saturation** to reach saturation point

saturé, -e *adj (marché)* saturated

sauf *prép* except; **sauf avis contraire** unless I/we hear to the contrary; **sauf stipulation contraire** unless otherwise stated; COMPTA **sauf erreur ou omission** errors and omissions excepted

sauter *vt* ORDINAT *(commande)* to skip

sauvegarde *nf* **(a)** ORDINAT saving, backup; **faire la sauvegarde d'un fichier** to save a file □ *sauvegarde automatique* automatic backup; *sauvegarde sur bande* tape backup

sauvegarder *vt* **(a)** *(protéger)* to safeguard, to protect; **sauvegarder les intérêts des actionnaires** to protect the interests of shareholders **(b)** ORDINAT *(fichier)* to save, to back up; **sauvegarder un fichier sur disquette** to save a file to disk

SAV *nm (abrév* **service après-vente**) after-sales service

scanner[1] *nm* ORDINAT scanner; **passer qch au scanner** to scan sth

scanner[2] *vt* ORDINAT to scan

scannérisation *nf* ORDINAT scanning

scanneur *nm* ORDINAT scanner; **passer qch au scanneur** to scan sth □ *scanneur à main* handheld scanner; *scanneur optique* optical scanner; *scanneur à plat* flatbed scanner

sceau *nm* seal; **apposer son sceau à qch** to set one's seal to sth

sceller *vt (apposer son sceau à)* to seal

schéma *nm* **(a)** *(dessin)* diagram, plan □ ORDINAT *schéma de clavier* keyboard map; *schéma d'entreprise* organization chart
(b) *(résumé)* summary, outline

schématique *adj* **(a)** *(sous forme de dessin)* diagrammatic **(b)** *(sous forme de résumé)* schematic, simplified

schématiser *vt* **(a)** *(dessiner)* to make a diagram of **(b)** *(résumer)* to schematize, to simplify

schilling *nm* schilling

science *nf* *sciences économiques* economics; *science de la gestion* management science

scinder *vt (société)* to break up, to split

scission *nf (d'une société)* demerger; FIN *(d'actif)* divestment

script *nm* FIN scrip

scriptural, -e *adj* cashless

scrutin *nm* vote, ballot; **dépouiller le scrutin** to count the votes

séance *nf (réunion)* session, meeting; BOURSE (trading) session; **être en séance, tenir séance** to be sitting *or* in session; **la séance s'ouvrira/sera levée à huit heures** the meeting will open/adjourn at eight o'clock; **je déclare la séance ouverte** I declare the meeting open; **en séance publique** at an open meeting □ BOURSE *séance boursière* trading session; *séance de clôture* closing session; *séance de concertation* policy meeting; *séance d'information* briefing (session); *séance d'ouverture* opening session; *séance supplémentaire* additional session

> ❝
> Le mark s'est sensiblement raffermi au cours des dernières **séances**, profitant de l'affaiblissement du dollar.
> ❞

second, -e *adj* second □ *second associé* junior partner; BOURSE *second marché* secondary market, unlisted securities market

secondaire ÉCON **1** *adj (secteur)* secondary
2 *nm* secondary sector

secours *nm* **(a)** *(aide)* help, assistance □ *secours d'argent* financial assistance **(b)** ORDINAT **de secours** *(copie, fichier, disquette)* backup

secret *nm* *secret de fabrication* trade secret; *secret professionnel* professional confidence *or* confidentiality

secrétaire *nmf* secretary □ *secrétaire de direction* personal assistant; *secrétaire général* company secretary; *secrétaire particulier* private secretary

secrétariat *nm* **(a)** *(fonction)* secretaryship **(b)** *(bureau)* secretary's office; *(d'un organisme international)* secretariat **(c)** *(métier)* secretarial work

secteur *nm* **(a)** ÉCON *(d'une activité)* sector □ *secteur d'activité* field *or* sphere of activity; *secteur du bâtiment* building industry *or* sector; *secteur économique*

economic sector; MKTG **secteur de la grande distribution** mass distribution sector; **secteur industriel** branch *or* sector of industry; **secteur primaire** primary sector; **secteur privé** private sector; **secteur privé à but non lucratif** private non-profit sector; **secteur public** public sector; **secteur sanitaire** health sector; **secteur secondaire** secondary sector; **secteur des services** service *or* tertiary sector; **secteur tertiaire** tertiary secteur
  (**b**) *(d'un représentant)* area, patch❏ **secteur de vente** sales area *or* territory
  (**c**) ORDINAT sector ❏ **secteur endommagé** bad sector

❝
Plusieurs **secteurs**, comme l'informatique, la restauration et le bâtiment, ont beaucoup de mal à trouver les salariés qu'ils recherchent.
❞

section *nf* (**a**) *(d'un service, d'un syndicat)* branch (**b**) *(d'un document)* section

sectoriel, -elle *adj (revendications, crise)* sector-based

sécu *nf Fam (abrév* **Sécurité sociale**) = French social security system providing public health benefits, pensions, maternity leave etc

sécuriser *vt (paiement)* to securitize; FIN **sécuriser un financement** to guarantee a loan

sécurité *nf* security ❏ ORDINAT **sécurité des données** data security; **sécurité de l'emploi** job security; ADMIN **Sécurité sociale** = French social security system providing public health benefits, pensions, maternity leave etc

séduction *nf* MKTG appeal ❏ **séduction du client** customer appeal

segment *nm* MKTG segment ❏ **segment démographique** demographic segment; **segment de marché** market segment

segmentation *nf* MKTG segmentation ❏ **segmentation démographique** demographic segmentation; **segmentation stratégique** strategic segmentation

segmenter *vt* MKTG *(marché)* to segment

seing *nm* JUR **acte sous seing privé** private contract

sélecteur *m* ORDINAT chooser

sélectif, -ive *adj* ORDINAT **en mode sélectif** in veto mode

sélection *nf* (**a**) *(fait de choisir)* selection; *(de candidats)* screening, shortlisting (**b**) MKTG *(échantillon)* selection ❏ **sélection au hasard** random selection

sélectionner *vt* (**a**) *(choisir)* to select (**b**) ORDINAT *(texte)* to highlight

self-service *nm* self-service

selon *prép* (**a**) *(d'après)* according to (**b**) *(conformément à)* in accordance with

semaine *nf* (**a**) *(période)* week (**b**)*(rémunération)* week's pay, weekly wages

semainier *nm* (**a**) *(feuille)* weekly time sheet (**b**) *(agenda)* desk diary *(with sections for each day of the week)*

semestre *nm* (**a**) *(période)* half-year, six-month period; **les bénéfices du premier semestre** the first-half profits (**b**) *(rémunération)* six months' pay (**c**) *(loyer)* six months' rent

semestriel, -elle *adj* half-yearly, six-monthly

semestriellement *adv* half-yearly, every six months; **réviser les salaires semestriellement** to review salaries every six months

semi-fini, -e *adj* ÉCON *(produit)* semi-finished

semi-ouvré, -e *adj* ÉCON *(produit)* semi-finished

semi-produit *nm* semi-manufactured product

sensibilité *nf (du marché)* sensitivity ❏ MKTG **sensibilité aux prix** price sensitivity

sensible *adj (hausse, baisse)* marked, noticeable

séparateur *nm* ORDINAT separator

séparation automatique des pages *nf* ORDINAT automatic pagination

séquence *nf* ORDINAT sequence ❏ **séquence de caractères** character string, sequence of characters

séquestre *nm* JUR sequestration; **mettre qch sous séquestre** to sequester *or* seize sth

séquestrer *vt* JUR to sequester, to sequestrate

série **1** *adj* ORDINAT serial
2 *nf (de marchandises)* range, line; **fabriquer qch en série** to mass-produce sth; **hors série** custom-made, custom-built ❏ ÉCON **série économique** economic batch; **série économique de production** economic manufacturing quantity

sérieux, -euse *adj* (**a**) *(offre, acheteur)* genuine, serious (**b**) *(entreprise)* reliable

serpent *nm* UE, FIN (currency) snake ❑ *serpent monétaire européen* European currency snake

serveur *nm* ORDINAT server ❑ *serveur distant* remote server; *serveur de fichiers* file server; *serveur Minitel®* Minitel service provider; *serveur de réseau* network server; *serveur télématique* bulletin board (system); *serveur Web* Web server

service *nm* (**a**) *(département)* department ❑ *service des achats* purchasing department; *service d'action commerciale* marketing department; *service administratif* administrative department; *service après-vente* after-sales department; *service clientèle, service clients* customer service (department); *service des commandes* order department; *service commercial* sales department; *service commercial export* export department; *service de (la) comptabilité* accounts department; *service consommateurs* customer service (department); *service contrôle qualité, service de contrôle de qualité* quality control (department); *service du courrier* mail room; COMPTA *service des émissions* issue department; *service de l'entretien* maintenance department; *service d'études* research department; *service d'étude marketing* market research department; *service des expéditions* forwarding *or* dispatch department; *service export* export department; *service export intégré* integrated export service; *service de facturation* invoice department; *service de groupage* joint-cargo service; *service informatique* computer department; *service juridique* legal department; *service du marketing, service mercatique* marketing department; *service marketing-vente* sales and marketing department; *service des méthodes* methods office; *service du personnel* personnel department; *service de planification, service de planning* planning department; *service de presse* press department; *service (de) production* production department; *service de la prospection* new business department; *service de publicité* advertising *or* publicity department; *service des réclamations* complaints department; *service de relation clientèle* customer service (department); *service des renseignements* information office; *service des renseignements commerciaux* status enquiry department; *service technique* technical department; *service des ventes* sales department

(**b**) *(prestation)* service; **offrir ses services (à qn)** to offer one's services (to sb) ❑ *service après-vente* after-sales service; *service clients* customer service; ORDINAT *service de dépannage* breakdown service; *service d'informations* information services; *service de livraison* delivery service; *service de messageries* courier service; *services du secteur tertiaire* business services; *services de soutien* support services

(**c**) ÉCON **services** *(secteur)* services; **les biens et les services** goods and services

(**d**) *(travail)* duty; **être de service** to be on duty; **prendre/quitter son service** to go on/off duty; **il a été licencié après 25 ans de service** he was dismissed after 25 years' service ❑ *service de jour* day shift; *service de nuit* night shift

(**e**) *(dans un restaurant)* service; **service compris** service included; **service non compris** service not included

(**f**) FIN *(d'un emprunt, d'une dette)* servicing; **assurer le service d'un emprunt/d'une dette** to service a loan/debt

(**g**) ADMIN *service des douanes* customs service; *service postal, service des postes* postal service(s); *service public Br* public utility, *Am* utility

(**h**) *(dans les transports)* service ❑ *service de marchandises* goods *or* freight service; *service de voyageurs* passenger service

(**i**) *(d'une machine)* service; **en service** in service; **hors service** out of order, not in use; **mettre qch en service** to bring sth into service

serviette *adj (cartable)* briefcase

servir *vt* (**a**) *(client)* to serve, to attend to (**b**) *(dette)* to pay, to service; **servir une rente à qn** to pay an annuity to sb

servitude *nf* JUR *(droit d'usage)* easement

seuil *nm* threshold; **la dette a atteint le seuil critique des deux milliards** debt has reached the critical level *or* threshold of two billion ❑ BOURSE *seuil d'annonce obligatoire* disclosure threshold; *seuil d'imposition* tax threshold; *seuil de pauvreté* poverty line; *seuil de prix* price threshold; *seuil de réapprovisionnement* reorder point; *seuil de rentabilité* break-even point

SGAO *nm* ORDINAT (*abrév* **système de gestion assisté par ordinateur**) computer-assisted management system

SGBD *nm* ORDINAT (*abrév* **système de gestion de base de données**) DBMS

SGDBR *nm* ORDINAT (*abrév* **système de gestion de bases de données relationnelles**) RDBMS

SGDG (*abrév* **sans garantie du gouvernement**) without government guarantee

shareware *nm* ORDINAT shareware

SICAF *nf* FIN (*abrév* **société d'investissement à capital fixe**) closed-end investment company

sicav *nf* FIN (*abrév* **société d'investissement à capital variable**) (a) (*organisme*) *Br* ≃ unit trust, *Am* ≃ mutual fund □ *sicav actions* equity-based unit trust; *sicav monétaire* money-based unit trust; *sicav obligataire* bond-based unit trust (b) (*action*) ≃ share in a *Br* unit trust *or Am* mutual fund

> **"**
> La contrainte financière reste très forte: restreintes par les banques, les entreprises se désendettent (l'encours des crédits est encore en baisse à la rentrée) et préfèrent acheter des **sicav monétaires** plutôt qu'investir.
> **"**

SICOB *nm* (*abrév* **salon des industries du commerce et de l'organisation du bureau**) = annual information technology trade fair in Paris

siège *nm* (*d'une organisation, d'une société*) headquarters □ *siège social* head office, registered office

signal *nm* (a) TÉL *signal d'appel* call waiting service (b) ORDINAT *signal numérique* digital signal

signaler *vt* ORDINAT to post

signataire 1 *adj* (*pays*) signatory
2 *nmf* (*d'un contrat, d'un accord*) signatory

signature *nf* signature; **avoir la signature** to be authorized to sign; **la lettre portait la signature du président** the letter was signed by the chairman; **pour signature** (*sur lettre*) for signature □ *signature collective* joint signature; ORDINAT *signature numérique* digital signature; *la signature sociale* the signature of the company

signer *vt* to sign; **signer à la réception de marchandises** to sign for goods on reception; **signez au bas de la page** sign at the bottom of the page

signet *nm* ORDINAT bookmark; **créer un signet sur une page** to bookmark a page

SIM *nm* (*abrév* **système d'information marketing**) MIS

simple *adj* (a) (*intérêts*) simple (b) ORDINAT *simple densité* single density

sinistre *nm* disaster; ASSUR loss; **déclarer un sinistre** to put in a claim □ *sinistre maximum prévisible* maximum foreseeable loss; *sinistre partiel* partial loss

site *nm* ORDINAT site □ *site miroir* mirror site; *site Web* Web site

site-témoin *nm* MKTG test site

situation *nf* (a) (*état*) state, condition; (*d'un compte*) balance; **la situation de l'emploi/de l'économie** the economic/employment situation □ *situation en banque* financial position *or* situation; *situation financière* financial situation *or* position; *situation nette* (*d'une société*) net assets, net worth; *situation de trésorerie* cash flow situation
(b) (*document*) report, return; FIN statement of finances □ *situation de caisse* cash statement; *situation hebdomadaire* (*de la Banque de France*) weekly report
(c) (*emploi*) position, job; **avoir une belle situation** to have a good job; **chercher une situation** to look for a job; **perdre sa situation** to lose one's job

slogan *nm* slogan □ *slogan publicitaire* advertising slogan

SME *nm* (a) (*abrév* **système monétaire européen**) EMS (b) (*abrév* **serpent monétaire européen**) European currency snake

SMIC *nm* (*abrév* **salaire minimum interprofessionnel de croissance**) index-linked guaranteed minimum wage

smicard, -e *nm,f* minimum wage earner

SNC *nf* (*abrév* **société en nom collectif**) partnership

social, -e *adj* (a) (*qui a trait à la société*) social (b) (*qui a trait à une entreprise*) company

socialisation *nf* ÉCON (*du capital, des industries*) socialization, collectivization

socialiser *vt* ÉCON (*capital, industries*) to socialize, to collectivize

sociétaire *nmf* (a) (*membre*) member (b) (*d'une société anonyme*) *Br* shareholder, *Am* stockholder

société *nf* (a) (*entreprise*) company, firm; **se monter en société** to set up in business □ *société par actions* *Br* joint-stock company, *Am* incorporated company; *société d'affacturage* factoring company; *société affiliée* *Br* affiliated company, *Am* affiliate; **société anonyme** Br public limited company, Am corporation; **société d'assurance** insurance company; **société de Bourse** stockbroker, stockbroking firm; **société civile** non-trading company; **société en commandite** limited partnership; **société en commandite par actions** partnership limited by shares; **société en commandite simple** limited partnership; **société de commerce international** international trading corporation; **société commerciale** business firm; **société commune** joint venture; **société de conseil en investissement** investment consultancy; **société coopérative** cooperative; **société cotée en Bourse** listed company; **société cotée à la Cote officielle** quoted company; **société de crédit immobilier** Br ≃ building society, Am ≃ savings and loan association; **société de crédit mutuel** mutual insurance company, Br ≃ friendly society; **société d'économie mixte** semi-public company; **société enregistrée** incorporated company; **société d'État** state-owned or public company; **société d'études** research company or firm; **société d'études de marché** market research company; **société d'exploitation, société exploitante** development company; **société d'exploitation en commun** joint venture; **société d'exportation** export company or house; **société de factoring** factoring company; **société fictive** dummy company; **société fiduciaire** trust company; **société financière** finance company; **société de gestion** holding company; **société de gestion de portefeuille** Br ≃ unit trust, Am ≃ mutual fund; **société immobilière** real-estate company; **société industrielle** manufacturing firm; **société d'investissement** investment company; **société d'investissement à capital fixe** closed-end investment company; **société d'investissement à capital variable** Br ≃ unit trust, Am ≃ mutual fund; **société de location** rental firm; **société de location de voitures** Br car hire company, Am car rental company; **société de marketing, société de mercatique** marketing company or firm; **société mère** parent company; **société multinationale** multinational (company); **société de mutualité** mutual insurance company, Br ≃ friendly society; **société nationale** state-owned or public company; **société de négoce** trading company; **société en**

nom collectif partnership; **société opéable** target company; **société en participation** joint venture; **société de personnes** partnership; **société de placement** investment trust; **société à portefeuille** holding company; **société de prévoyance** provident society; **société privée** private company; **société à responsabilité infinie** unlimited company; **société à responsabilité limitée** limited (liability) company; **société de secours mutuels** mutual insurance company, Br ≃ friendly society; **société de services** service company; **société sœur** sister company; **société de transport** transport company; **société d'utilité publique** Br public utility company, Am utility; **société de vente par correspondance** mail order company (b) (communauté) society □ **société d'abondance** affluent society; **société de consommation** consumer society

> **"**
>
> Les **sociétés d'investissement** américaines redistribuent toutes à leurs clients, à grand renfort de publicité, entre 12% et 14% d'intérêts annuels en moyenne ces cinq dernières années.
>
> **"**

software nm ORDINAT software

solde nm (a) (de compte) balance; **pour solde** in settlement; **pour solde de tout compte** in full settlement; **régler le solde** to pay the balance □ **solde actif** credit balance; **solde bancaire, solde en banque** bank balance; **solde bénéficiaire** credit balance; **solde en caisse** cash balance; **solde créditeur** credit balance; **solde cumulé** cumulative balance; **solde débiteur** debit balance; BANQUE overdraft; **solde à découvert** outstanding balance; **solde déficitaire** debit balance; **solde disponible** available balance; **solde de dividende** final dividend; **solde dû** balance due; **solde de fin de mois** end-of-month balance; COMPTA **solde à nouveau** balance brought forward; COMPTA **solde nul** nil balance; **solde d'ouverture** opening balance; **solde passif** debit balance; COMPTA **solde reporté** balance brought forward; COMPTA **solde à reporter** balance carried forward (b) (promotion) sale; (marchandise) sale item; **en solde** (marchandise) Br in the sale, Am on sale; **acheter** ou **avoir qch en solde** to buy or get sth Br in the sale or Am on sale; **mettre** ou **vendre qch en solde** to sell sth off □ **solde de fermeture** closing-down sale; **solde de**

fin de saison end-of-season sale; *solde après inventaire* stocktaking sale

solder 1 *vt* (**a**) FIN *(compte)* to balance, to close; *(dette)* to settle, to pay (off); **solder l'arriéré** to make up back payments (**b**) *(stock)* to sell off, to clear

2 se solder *vpr* (**a**) FIN **se solder par qch** to show sth; **les comptes se soldent un bénéfice/un déficit de 10 000 francs** the accounts show a profit/a deficit of 10,000 francs (**b**) **se solder par qch** *(avoir pour résultat)* to end in sth; **les négociations se sont soldées par un échec** the negotiations ended in failure

soldeur, -euse *nm,f* discount trader

solidaire *adj* JUR jointly liable *or* responsible

solidairement *adv* JUR **conjointement et solidairement** jointly and severally

solidarité *nf* (**a**) JUR joint and several liability, joint responsibility (**b**) *(soutien)* solidarity; **faire grève** *ou* **débrayer par solidarité** to come out in sympathy

solide *adj (entreprise)* sound, well-established

solidité *nf (d'une entreprise)* soundness

solvabilité *nf* solvency, creditworthiness

solvable *adj* solvent, creditworthy

sommaire *nm (d'un article)* abstract

somme *nf* (**a**) *(d'une addition)* sum, total amount; **la somme s'élève à 100 francs** the total amounts to 100 francs □ *somme due* amount due, total due; *somme en excédent* sum in excess; *somme nette* net amount; COMPTA *sommes payables* sums payable; *somme totale* total amount, sum total (**b**) *(argent)* **somme (d'argent)** sum (of money); **payer une grosse** *ou* **forte somme** to pay a large sum *or* amount of money; **dépenser une somme de 500 francs** to spend (a sum of) 500 francs □ *somme forfaitaire* lump sum

sommier *nm* COMPTA cash book, ledger

sonal *nm* (advertising) jingle

sondage *nm* MKTG *(enquête)* poll, survey; **faire un sondage** to carry out a poll *or* survey □ *sondage aléatoire* random sampling; *sondage d'opinion* opinion poll; *sondage par quotas* quota sampling

sondé, -e *nm,f* MKTG respondent

sonder *vt* to poll; **sonder l'opinion** to carry out *or* to conduct an opinion poll

sortant, -e *adj (élu)* retiring, outgoing

sortie *nf* (**a**) *(d'un nouveau produit)* launch (**b**) ORDINAT exit; *(information)* output □ *sortie (sur) imprimante* printout;

sortie parallèle parallel output; *sortie série* serial output

(**c**) *(de marchandises, de devises)* export; *(de capital)* outflow

(**d**) FIN **sorties** outgoings; **ce mois-ci il y a eu plus de sorties que de rentrées** outgoings have exceeded incomings this month □ *sorties de fonds* expenses, outgoings; *sorties de trésorerie* cash outgoings

sortir 1 *vt* (**a**) *(nouveau produit)* to bring out, to launch (**b**) ORDINAT to output

2 *vi* ORDINAT to exit; **sortir d'un programme** to exit a program

souche *nf (de chèque, de ticket)* counterfoil, stub

souffrance *nf* **en souffrance** *(coupon, dette)* outstanding, unpaid; *(effet)* overdue, outstanding; *(marchandises)* held up, awaiting delivery; *(travail)* pending

soumettre *vt (document, loi)* to submit, to refer; **soumettre un document à la signature** to submit *or* present a document for signature

soumis, -e *adj (à une loi)* subject (**à** to); *(à un impôt)* liable, subject (**à** to); **soumis à l'impôt sur le revenu** liable to income tax; **soumis au (droit de) timbre** subject to stamp duty; **soumis aux fluctuations du marché** subject to fluctuations in the market

soumission *nf* (**a**) *(offre)* tender, bid; **par (voie de) soumission** by tender; **faire une soumission pour un travail** to tender for a piece of work □ *soumission cachetée* sealed tender (**b**) DOUANES *soumission (en douane)* bond; *soumission cautionnée* secured bond

soumissionnaire *nmf* tenderer

soumissionner *vt (travail)* to tender *or* bid for; **soumissionner à une adjudication** to tender *or* bid for a contract

source *nf* source; FIN **imposé à la source** taxed at source □ ORDINAT *source de données* data source; *source de revenus* source of revenue

souris *nf* ORDINAT mouse □ *souris à infrarouge* infrared mouse; *souris optique* optical mouse; *souris sans fil* cordless mouse; *souris tactile* touchpad mouse; *souris à trois boutons* three-button mouse

sous-agence *nf* sub-agency

sous-agent *nm* sub-agent

sous-bail *nm* sublease

sous-capitalisation *nf* ÉCON under-capitalization, underfunding

sous-capitalisé, -e adj ÉCON under-capitalized, underfunded

sous-chef nm assistant manager

sous-comité nm sub-committee

sous-commission nf sub-committee

sous-consommation nf ÉCON under-consumption

sous-contractant, -e nm,f subcontractor

souscripteur, -trice nm,f (**a**) FIN (d'un emprunt) subscriber (**de** to) (**b**) BOURSE (des actions) applicant (**c**) ASSUR policy holder

souscription nf (**a**) FIN (à un emprunt) subscription (**à** to) (**b**) BOURSE (à des actions) application (**à** for) (**c**) ASSUR (d'une police d'assurance) taking out (**d**) (somme) subscription, contribution; **lancer une souscription** to start a fund; **verser une souscription** to pay a subscription

souscrire 1 vt (**a**) (abonnement) to take out (**b**) ASSUR (police d'assurance) to take out (**c**) BOURSE (actions) to apply for
2 **souscrire à** vt ind (**a**) BOURSE (actions) to apply for (**b**) FIN (emprunt) to subscribe to

> 66 ─────
> L'assurance contre le risque de change consiste à **souscrire** une police auprès d'une compagnie privée ou, plus souvent, publique.
> 99

sous-développé, -e adj ÉCON (pays, économie) underdeveloped

sous-développement nm ÉCON underdevelopment

sous-directeur, -trice nm,f assistant manager, deputy manager

sous-emploi nm ÉCON under-employment

sous-employé, -e adj ÉCON under-employed

sous-équipé, -e adj ÉCON under-equipped

sous-équipement nm ÉCON under-equipment

sous-estimation nf undervaluation

sous-estimer vt to undervalue

sous-évaluation nf undervaluation

> 66 ─────
> Les devises des pays du sud ne peuvent que remonter, vu leur **sous-évaluation** manifeste.
> 99

sous-évaluer vt to undervalue

sous-locataire nmf subtenant, sublessee

sous-location nf (**a**) (par le locataire) subletting (**b**) (par le sous-locataire) subrenting

sous-louer vt (**a**) (sujet: locataire) to sublet (**b**) (sujet: sous-locataire) to subrent

sous-menu nm ORDINAT submenu

Sous-ministre nm Can ADMIN Deputy Minister □ **Sous-ministre adjoint** Assistant Deputy Minister

sous-payer vt to underpay

sous-préfet, -ète nm,f ADMIN sub-prefect

sous-production nf ÉCON underproduction

sous-produit nm by-product

sous-programme nm ORDINAT sub-routine, subprogram

sous-répertoire nm ORDINAT subdirectory

sous-seing nm private agreement

soussigné, -e adj & nm,f undersigned; **je soussigné, Gérard Manvussat, déclare que …** I, the undersigned, declare that…

sous-total nm subtotal

sous-traitance nf subcontracting; **donner qch en sous-traitance** to subcontract sth, to contract sth out

sous-traitant, -e 1 adj subcontracting
2 nm,f subcontractor

sous-traité nm subcontract

sous-traiter vt to subcontract

sous-utiliser vt to underutilize

soutenir vt (**a**) (monnaie, économie) to support, to bolster up; **soutenir des cours par des achats** to support prices by buying (**b**) (dépense) to meet

> 66 ─────
> La banque centrale russe dépensait un milliard de dollars par semaine, dans la dernière période, pour **soutenir** le rouble. L'équipe au pouvoir a donc décidé d'élargir la bande de fluctuation de la monnaie, qui pourra désormais flotter entre 6 et 9,5 roubles pour un dollar.
> 99

soutenu, -e adj (marché) steady

soutien nm support □ **soutien de famille** breadwinner; **soutien financier** financial support; ÉCON *soutien des prix* price pegging

spammer *vt* ORDINAT to spam

spamming *nm* ORDINAT spamming

spécialisation *nf* specialization

spécialisé, -e *adj (travail)* specialized; *(ouvrier, main-d'œuvre)* semi-skilled; **non spécialisée** unskilled

spécialiser se spécialiser *vpr* **se spécialiser dans qch** to specialize in sth; **il s'est spécialisé dans l'import-export** he has specialized in import-export

spécialiste *nmf* specialist; **c'est un spécialiste du marketing** he's an expert in marketing □ MKTG *spécialiste produit* product specialist

spécialité *nf Br* speciality, *Am* specialty □ FIN *spécialité budgétaire* budgetary speciality; *spécialité pharmaceutique* patent medicine

spécification *nf* specification □ *spécification de la fonction* job specification

spécifier *vt* to specify; BOURSE **spécifier un cours** to make a price

spécimen *nm* specimen; MKTG *(d'un livre)* specimen copy □ *spécimen de signature* specimen signature

spéculateur, -trice *nm,f* FIN, BOURSE speculator □ *spéculateur à la baisse* bear; *spéculateur sur devises* currency speculator; *spéculateur à la hausse* bull; *spéculateur à la journée* day to day trader, scalper; *spéculateur sur plusieurs positions* position trader

spéculatif, -ive *adj* FIN, BOURSE speculative

spéculation *nf* FIN, BOURSE speculation □ *spéculation à la baisse* bear operations; *spéculation à la hausse* bull operations; *spéculations immobilières* property speculation

spéculer *vi* FIN, BOURSE to speculate; **spéculer en Bourse** to speculate on the Stock Market; **spéculer à la baisse** to speculate for a fall *or* on a falling market, to go a bear; **spéculer à la hausse** to speculate for a rise *or* on a rising market, to go a bull; **spéculer sur les valeurs pétrolières** to speculate in oils

spirale *nf (hausse rapide)* spiral; **monter en spirale** *(prix)* to spiral □ *spirale inflationniste* inflationary spiral; *spirale prix-salaires* wage-price spiral

sponsor *nm* sponsor, backer

sponsoriser *vt* to sponsor

spot *nm* MKTG *spot (publicitaire)* advert, commercial; *spot télé* TV commercial

spouleur *nm* ORDINAT spooler

SS *nf* ADMIN *(abrév* **Sécurité sociale***)* = French social security system providing public health benefits, pensions, maternity leave etc

stabilisateur, -trice *adj* stabilizing; **exercer une action stabilisatrice sur les prix** to have a stabilizing effect on prices

stabilisation *nf (d'une monnaie, des prix, du marché)* stabilization

stabiliser 1 *vt (monnaie, prix, marché)* to stabilize
2 se stabiliser *vpr (monnaie, prix, marché)* to stabilize; **la Bourse a fini par se stabiliser après une chute vertigineuse** the Stock Exchange eventually stabilized after plunging dramatically

stabilité *nf (d'une monnaie, des prix, du marché)* stability, steadiness

stable *adj (monnaie, prix, marché)* stable

stage *nm (cours)* training course; *(expérience professionnelle)* work placement; **faire un stage** *(cours)* to go on a training course; *(expérience professionnelle)* to do a work placement □ *stage de formation* training course; *stage de perfectionnement* advanced training course; *stage de reconversion* retraining course

stagflation *nf* ÉCON stagflation

stagiaire *adj & nmf* trainee

stagnant, -e *adj (économie, prix, marché)* stagnant

stagnation *nf (de l'économie, des prix, du marché)* stagnation; **en stagnation** at a standstill, stagnant

stagner *vi (économie, prix, marché)* to stagnate

stand *nm (d'exposition)* stand □ *stand d'exposition* exhibition stand

standard 1 *adj (modèle, prix)* standard
2 *nm* **(a)** *(critère)* standard □ *standards budgétaires* budgetary standards **(b)** TÉL switchboard

standardisation *nf* standardization

standardiser *vt* to standardize

standardiste *nmf* TÉL (switchboard) operator

stand by *nm* FIN standby agreement

star *nf* MKTG *(produit)* star

station *nf* ORDINAT *(d'un réseau)* station, node ◦ *station d'accueil* docking station; *station de travail* workstation

statisticien, -enne *nm,f* statistician

statistique 1 *adj* statistical
2 *nf* statistics

statuer statuer sur *vt ind* to rule on

statut *nm* (a) JUR *(état)* status ◦ *statut juridique* legal status (b) statuts *(d'une société)* articles of association, statutes; statuts et règlements rules and regulations

statutaire *adj* statutory; *(actions)* qualifying; *(gérant)* appointed according to the articles

statutairement *adv* in accordance with the regulations

stellage *nm* BOURSE put and call (option), double option

sténo 1 *nf (abrév* **sténographie**) shorthand; prendre qch en sténo to take sth down in shorthand
2 *nmf (abrév* **sténographe**) stenographer

sténodactylo 1 *nf* shorthand typing
2 *nmf* shorthand typist

sténodactylographie *nf* shorthand typing

sténographe *nmf* shorthand typist

sténographie *nf* shorthand

sténographier *vt* to take down in shorthand

sterling *adj* sterling

stimulant *nm (pour relancer)* stimulus; *(pour encourager)* incentive ◦ *stimulants de la production* production incentives; *stimulants de vente* sales incentives

stimuler *vt* to stimulate; l'exportation stimule la production exports stimulate production; pour stimuler les employés, la direction a décidé de les intéresser aux bénéfices de la société as an incentive to employees, management has decided to give them a share in the company's profits

stipulation *nf (d'un contrat)* stipulation ◦ *stipulation particulière* special provision

stipuler *vt* to stipulate; le contrat stipule que toutes les réparations seront à la charge du locataire the contract stipulates that the tenant shall be responsible for all repairs

stock *nm (des marchandises)* stock; COMPTA stocks *Br* stock, *Am* inventory; en stock in stock; nous n'avons plus ce modèle en stock we no longer have this model in stock, this

model is out of stock; dans la limite des stocks disponibles while stocks last, subject to availability; constituer des stocks to build up stocks; épuiser les stocks to deplete *or* exhaust stocks ◦ *stock d'alerte* minimum stock level; *stock de dépannage* buffer stock; *stock existant* stock in hand; *stock final* closing stock; *stock en magasin* stock in hand; *stock d'or (d'une Banque d'État)* gold reserve; *stock d'ouverture* opening stock; *stocks régulateurs* buffer stocks; *stocks de réserve* stockpile; *stock de sécurité* safety stock; *stock stratégique* perpetual inventory

stockage *nm* (a) *(des marchandises)* stocking; *(en grande quantité)* stockpiling ◦ *stockage mécanisé* mechanized stocking (b) ORDINAT storage ◦ *stockage de données* data storage; *stockage en mémoire tampon* buffering

stocker *vt* (a) *(marchandises)* to stock; *(en grande quantité)* to stockpile (b) ORDINAT *(informations)* to store

stockiste *nmf Br* stockist, *Am* dealer

stop-vente *nf* BOURSE stop-loss selling

stratégie *nf* MKTG strategy ◦ *stratégie commerciale* business strategy; *stratégie de l'entreprise* corporate strategy; *stratégie financière* financial strategy; *stratégie de mercatique, stratégie de marketing* game plan, marketing strategy; *stratégie de pénétration* market penetration strategy

structure *nf* (a) *(organisation)* structure ◦ *structure des coûts* cost structure; *structure de l'entreprise* corporate *or* company structure; *structure hiérarchique* line organization; *structure du marché* market structure; *structure de(s) prix* price structure; *structure des salaires* wage structure
(b) ORDINAT structure ◦ *structure en anneau* ring structure; *structure arborescente* directory *or* tree structure; *structure en arbre* tree structure; *structure de bloc* block structure; *structure en bus* bus structure; *structure en étoile* star structure; *structure de fichier* file structure

structurer *vt* to structure

stylo *nm* pen ◦ *stylo bille* ballpoint pen; ORDINAT *stylo optique* light pen

subalterne *adj (position)* subordinate; *(employé)* junior

subordonné, -e *nm,f (employé)* subordinate

subrogation *nf* JUR subrogation

subside *nm* subsidy, grant

substitut *nm* substitute □ MKTG *substitut rapproché* close substitute

substitution *nf* substitution

subvention *nf* subsidy, grant □ *subventions en capital* capital grants; *subvention d'équipement* equipment subsidy; *subvention d'exploitation* operating subsidy; *subvention à l'exportation* export subsidy

subventionné, -e *adj* subsidized; **subventionné par l'État** State-aided

subventionner *vt* to subsidize, to grant financial aid to

succéder succéder à *vt ind* to take over from, to succeed

successeur *nm* successor (de to)

succession *nf* (a) JUR *(héritage)* inheritance; *(biens)* estate (b) *(remplacement)* succession; **prendre la succession de qn** to take over from sb; **la succession du poste sera assurée par M. Dupont** Mr Dupont will take over the post

succursale *nf* branch

suite *nf* (a) *(dans une lettre)* **(comme) suite à votre lettre du 15 août** with reference to *or* further to your letter of 15 August; **(comme) suite à notre conversation téléphonique** further to our telephone conversation (b) **donner suite à qch** *(demande, lettre)* to follow sth up; *(commande)* to deal with sth; **pour suite à donner** *(sur document)* (passed to you) for action (c) **sans suite** *(article)* discontinued

suivant¹ *prép (conformément à)* in accordance with; **suivant inventaire** as per stock list

suivant², -e 1 *adj* following; **aux conditions suivantes** on the following terms 2 *nm,f* MKTG follower; *(sur le marché)* market follower □ *suivant immédiat* early follower

suivi, -e 1 *adj (demande)* steady, persistent; *(achats)* consistent 2 *nm* follow-up; **assurer le suivi de qch** *(demande, lettre)* to follow sth up; *(commande)* to deal with sth

suivre 1 *vt* (a) *(dossier)* to follow up; *(commande)* to deal with (b) *(article)* to continue to stock; **nous n'avons pas suivi cet article** we have discontinued this item 2 *vi* **faire suivre une lettre** to forward a letter; **(prière de) faire suivre** *(sur enveloppe)* please forward

sujet, -ette *adj* **sujet à** *(soumis à)* subject or liable to; **ce contrat est sujet au droit de timbre** this agreement is subject to stamp duty

superdividende *nm* FIN surplus dividend

superficie *nf (des locaux)* surface area; **l'entrepôt fait 3000m² de superficie** *ou* **a une superficie de 3000m²** the warehouse has a surface area of 3,000m²

supérieur, -e 1 *adj* (a) *(produit, marchandises)* of superior quality (b) *(rang, grade)* higher; *(cadre)* senior (c) *(offre)* higher 2 *nm,f* superior

supermarché *nm* supermarket

super-ordinateur *nm* ORDINAT supercomputer

superposer *vt* ORDINAT **superposer une écriture** to overwrite

superprofits *nmpl* very large profits

superviser *vt* to supervise

superviseur *nm* supervisor

supplément *nm* (a) *(surcroît)* supplement; **un supplément d'information/de travail** additional *or* extra information/work; **en supplément** extra, additional (b) *(somme)* additional charge, supplement

supplémentaire *adj* supplementary, additional

support *nm* (a) ORDINAT medium, support □ *support de données* data carrier; *support de sortie* output medium; *support de souris* mouse support; *support de stockage* storage medium (b) *(médium)* medium □ *support de publicité, support publicitaire* publicity *or* advertising medium

supporter *vt (frais, coût)* to bear; **l'acheteur supporte les frais** the fees are borne by the purchaser

suppression *nf* (a) *(de crédits, d'aide)* withdrawal; *(d'un impôt)* abolition (b) *(d'emplois)* axing; **il y a eu beaucoup de suppressions d'emploi dans la région** there were many job losses in the area

supprimer *vt* (a) *(crédits, aide)* to withdraw; *(impôt)* to abolish (b) *(emplois)* to shed, to axe (c) ORDINAT to delete

sûr, -e *adj (placement)* safe, secure; *(entreprise)* of good standing

surabondance *nf* surfeit, glut

surassurance *nf* overinsurance

surcapacité *nf* ÉCON overcapacity

surcapitalisation *nf* FIN overcapitalization

surcapitalisé, -e *adj* overcapitalized

surcharge *nf* (**a**) *(d'un véhicule)* overloading □ **surcharge permise** permissible overload (**b**) *(de bagages)* excess weight (**c**) *(surcroît)* **une surcharge de travail** excess *or* extra work (**d**) *(sur un mot)* alteration; **sans rature ni surcharge** *(sur document administratif)* without deletions or alterations

surcharger *vt* (**a**) *(véhicule)* to overload (**b**) *(marché)* to glut, to overload (**c**) *(accabler)* **surcharger qn d'impôts** to overburden sb with taxes (**d**) *(chèque, écriture)* to alter

surchauffe *nf* ÉCON overheating

surconsommation *nf* ÉCON overconsumption

surcoût *nm* extra charge

surcroît *nm* addition, increase; **un surcroît de dépenses/travail** additional *or* extra expenditure/work

surdéveloppé, -e *adj* ÉCON highly developed; *(excessivement)* overdeveloped

surdéveloppement *nm* ÉCON high state of development; *(excessif)* overdevelopment

surdon *nm* (**a**) *(indemnité)* = compensation allowable to purchaser for damage to goods (**b**) *(droit)* = right to non-acceptance of damaged goods

sureffectif *nm* overmanning

surémission *nf* FIN overissue

suremploi *nm* ÉCON overemployment

surenchère *nf* higher bid, overbid; **faire une surenchère sur qn** to outbid sb

surenchérir *vi* to bid higher; **surenchérir sur qn** to outbid sb, to bid higher than sb

surenchérissement *nm* further rise in prices

surenchérisseur, -euse *nm,f* outbidder

surendetté, -e *adj* ÉCON overindebted

surendettement *nm* ÉCON excessive debt; **courir un risque de surendettement** to run a risk of getting into excessive debt

suréquipement *nm* overequipment

suréquiper *vt* to overequip

surestarie *nf* demurrage

surestimation *nf* overestimate, overvaluation

surestimer *vt* to overestimate, to overvalue; **l'entreprise a surestimé ses capacités de production** the company overestimated its production capabilities

sûreté *nf* *(garantie)* surety, guarantee □ **sûreté personnelle** surety; **sûreté réelle** (real) security

surévaluation *nf* overestimate, overvaluation

surévaluer *vt* to overestimate, to overvalue

surexploitation *nf* over-exploitation, excessive exploitation

surexploiter *vt* to overexploit

surface *nf* (**a**) *(aire)* surface □ MKTG **surface d'exposition, surface de présentation** display space; **surface de vente** sales area (**b**) *(état)* FIN **surface financière** financial standing (**c**) ORDINAT **surface d'affichage** display area; **surface d'enregistrement** read-write surface

surfacturation *nf* overbilling

surfaire *vt* *(marchandises)* to overprice

surfait, -e *adj* *(prix)* excessive

surfer *vi* ORDINAT **surfer sur l'Internet** to surf the Internet

surfin, -e *adj* of the highest quality

surimposer *vt* (**a**) *(augmenter l'impôt sur)* to increase the tax on (**b**) *(frapper d'un impôt trop lourd)* to overtax

surimposition *nf* (**a**) *(augmentation de l'impôt)* increase of taxation (**b**) *(excessif)* overtaxation

surindustrialisation *nf* overindustrialization

surinvestissement *nm* FIN overinvestment

surligneur *nm* highlighter (pen)

surmarquage *nm* overpricing

surmarquer *vt* to overprice

surnombre *nm* **en surnombre** excess; **personnel en surnombre** surplus staff

suroffre *nf* (**a**) *(surenchère)* better offer, higher bid (**b**) ÉCON *(surabondance)* excess supply

surpaie, surpaye *nf* overpayment

surpayer *vt* *(personne)* to overpay; *(produit)* to pay too much for

surplus *nm* (**a**) *(excédent)* surplus, excess ❑ **surplus d'importation** import surplus; FIN **surplus monétaire** monetary surplus; **surplus de productivité** productivity surplus (**b**) *(supplément)* *(à un prix)* surcharge; **payer le surplus** to pay the difference

surprime *nf* ASSUR extra *or* additional premium

surprix *nm* excess price

surproduction *nf* ÉCON overproduction

> **"**
> Le marché du nickel souffre depuis plus de deux ans d'une **surproduction** constante en raison de la faiblesse de la demande.
> **"**

surproduire *vt & vi* ÉCON to overproduce

surprofit *nm* ÉCON excessive profit

surréservation *nf* overbooking; **faire une surréservation de qch** to overbook sth

sursalaire *nm* bonus, extra pay

sursis *nm* JUR respite, delay ❑ **sursis de paiement** extension of deadline for payment

sursouscription *nf* FIN oversubscription

sursouscrire *vt* FIN to oversubscribe

sursouscrit, -e *adj* FIN oversubscribed

surtaux *nm* excessive rate

surtaxe *nf* (**a**) *(en sus)* surtax, surcharge ❑ **surtaxe à l'importation** import surcharge; **surtaxe progressive** progressive surtax (**b**) *(taxe excessive)* excessive tax

surtaxer *vt* (**a**) *(frapper d'une taxe supplémentaire)* to surtax, to surcharge; *(lettre)* to surcharge (**b**) *(frapper d'une taxe excessive)* to overtax

survaleur *nf* goodwill

surveillance *nf* *(de travail)* supervision; *(des prix)* monitoring; *(de la production)* control

surveillant, -e *nm,f* *(dans une usine, sur un chantier)* supervisor

surveiller *vt* *(travail)* to supervise; *(prix)* to monitor; *(production)* to control

survendre *vt* to overcharge for

survente *nf* overcharging

survoler *vt* ORDINAT to browse through

sus *adv* **en sus** in addition, extra; **les frais d'expédition sont en sus** postage is extra

suscription *nf* ADMIN *(sur une lettre)* address

susdit, -e *adj & nm,f* above-mentioned, aforesaid

susmentionné, -e *adj & nm,f* above-mentioned, aforesaid

susnommé, -e *adj & nm,f* above-named

suspendre *vt* (**a**) *(paiement, travail)* to suspend, to stop; **suspendre le paiement d'un chèque** to stop a cheque (**b**) *(employé)* to suspend

suspens **en suspens** *adv* pending, outstanding

suspension *nf* (**a**) *(d'un paiement, de travail)* suspension (**b**) *(d'un employé)* suspension

SVP *(abrév* **s'il vous plaît***)* please

swap *nm* BOURSE swap ❑ **swap d'actifs** asset swap; **swap de change** exchange rate swap

symbolique *adj* *(loyer)* nominal; *(paiement, somme)* token; JUR **obtenir le franc symbolique de dommages-intérêts** to be awarded token damages

syndic *nm* (**a**) JUR receiver ❑ **syndic de faillite** trustee in bankruptcy (**b**) ADMIN **syndic d'immeuble** property manager

syndical, -e *adj* *(Br* trade *or Am* labor) union

syndicalisme *nm* (**a**) *(mouvement)* *(Br* trade *or Am* labor) unionism (**b**) *(activité)* **faire du syndicalisme** to be involved in union activities

syndicaliste **1** *adj* *(Br* trade *or Am* labor) union
2 *nmf* *(Br* trade *or Am* labor) unionist

syndicat *nm* (**a**) *(de salariés, d'ouvriers)* *(Br* trade *or Am* labor) union (**b**) *(d'employeurs)* federation; *(de producteurs, de propriétaires)* association; *(de financiers)* syndicate ❑ **syndicat d'en-**

chères tender pool; *syndicat financier* (financial) syndicate; *syndicat de garantie* underwriting syndicate; *syndicat industriel* industrial pool; *syndicat d'initiative* tourist information office; *syndicat patronal* employers' federation; FIN *syndicat de prise ferme* underwriting syndicate; *syndicat de producteurs* producers' association; *syndicat professionnel* trade association

syndicataire 1 *adj* syndicate
  2 *nmf* member of a syndicate

syndiqué, -e 1 *adj* (**a**) *(membre d'un syndicat financier)* belonging to a syndicate (**b**) *(membre d'un syndicat de travailleurs)* belonging to a (*Br* trade *or Am* labor) union; **être syndiqué** to be a member of a (*Br* trade *or Am* labor) union
  2 *nm,f* (*Br* trade *or Am* labor) union member

syndiquer 1 *vt* to unionize
  2 **se syndiquer** *vpr* (**a**) *(se constituer en syndicat)* to form a (*Br* trade *or Am* labor) union (**b**) *(adhérer à un syndicat)* to join a (*Br* trade *or Am* labor) union

syntaxe *nf* ORDINAT syntax

synthétiseur de paroles *nm* ORDINAT voice synthesizer

sysop *nm* ORDINAT (*abrév* **Systems Operator**) SYSOP

systématique *adj* systematic

système *nm* (**a**) *(structure)* system ❑ *système bancaire* banking system; BANQUE *système de compensation* clearing system; *système comptable* accounting system; *système de contrôle de stocks* stock control system; *système*
de direction management system; *système de distribution* distribution system; *système fiscal* tax system; *système d'information mercatique ou marketing* marketing information system; BOURSE *système informatique de cotation* computerized trading system; *système informatisé de transaction* screen-trading system; *système intégré de gestion* integrated management system; *système d'inventaire* inventory method; ÉCON *système monétaire européen* European monetary system; *système de participation aux bénéfices* profit-sharing scheme; *système de primes* bonus scheme; *système de retraite* pension scheme
  (**b**) ORDINAT system ❑ *système expert* expert system; *système d'exploitation* operating system; *système d'exploitation de ou à disques* disk operating system; *système d'exploitation réseau* network operating system; *système de gestion de bases de données* database management system; *système de gestion de fichiers* file management system; *système informatique* computer system; *système informatisé* computerized information system; *système intégré de gestion* integrated management system; *système multi-utilisateur* multi-user system; *système de sauvegarde* backup system; *système de secours* backup system; *système serveur* host system; *système à tour* tower system; *système de traitement de l'information* data processing system

table *nf* (**a**) *(liste, recueil)* table ❑ ASSUR *tables d'actualisation* present value tables; *tables d'espérance de vie* life expectancy tables, actuarial tables; *table des intérêts* interest table; *tables de mortalité* life expectancy tables, actuarial tables; *table des parités* parity table, table of par values; ORDINAT *table de recherche, table de référence* look-up table (**b**) *(meuble)* table ❑ *table des négociations* negotiating table; *s'asseoir à la table des négociations* to get round the negotiating table; *table ronde* round table

> **"**
>
> Avec l'accord annoncé hier, la partie française se présente à la **table des négociations** enfin rassemblée et donc plus puissante.
>
> **"**

tableau *nm* (**a**) *(liste)* list, table; **disposer qch en tableau** to tabulate sth ❑ *tableaux d'activité économique* economic activity tables; *tableau d'affichage* notice board; COMPTA *tableau d'amortissement* depreciation schedule; *tableau d'avancement* promotions list; *tableau d'avancement de commandes* order flowchart; *tableau de bord* management chart; *tableau comptable* (financial) statement; COMPTA *tableau de financement* statement of sources and uses of funds, cashflow statement; *tableau de marche* progress schedule; *tableau de prix* price list; *tableau de service* rota; *tableau statistique* statistical table (**b**) ORDINAT control panel

tablette graphique *nf* ORDINAT graphics tablet

tableur *nm* ORDINAT spreadsheet ❑ *tableur de graphiques* graphics spreadsheet

tâche *nf* (**a**) *(travail)* task, job; **travailler à la tâche** to do piecework (**b**) ORDINAT task ❑ *tâche d'arrière-plan* background task; *tâche de fond* background task *or* job

tacite *adj (convention)* tacit ❑ JUR *tacite reconduction* renewal (of lease) by tacit agreement

tactique **1** *adj* tactical
2 *nf* tactics ❑ *tactique commerciale* marketing tactics; *tactiques de défense contre-OPA* defensive tactics

taille *nf* (**a**) ORDINAT *(de fichier)* size (**b**) BOURSE *taille boursière* market size

talon *nm* (**a**) *(de chèque)* counterfoil, stub (**b**) FIN *(de coupon)* talon

tampon *nm (cachet, instrument)* rubber stamp ❑ *tampon dateur* date stamp; *tampon encreur* ink pad

tantième *nm (de bénéfices)* percentage, quota; *le tantième des administrateurs* the directors' percentage of the profits

taper **1** *vt* (**a**) ORDINAT to key; *tapez entrée ou retour* select enter or return (**b**) *(dactylographier)* *taper qch (à la machine)* to type sth
2 *vi (dactylographier)* *taper (à la machine)* to type; *taper au toucher* to touch-type

tapis de souris *nm* ORDINAT mouse mat *or* pad

tare *nf* (**a**) *(dépréciation)* depreciation, loss in value *(owing to damage or waste)* (**b**) *(pour calculer le poids net)* tare; *faire la tare* to allow for the tare ❑ *tare commune, tare par épreuve, tare moyenne* average tare; *tare réelle* actual tare

tarer *vt (emballage, caisse)* to tare

tarif *nm* (**a**) *(prix)* rate; *(d'un billet d'avion, de train)* fare ❑ *tarif de base* basic rate; *tarif dégressif* sliding-scale tariff, tapering charge; *tarif forfaitaire* fixed rate; *tarif groupage* groupage rate; *tarif (des) imprimés* printed paper rate; *tarif lettres* letter rate; *tarif marchandises* goods *or* freight rate; *tarif normal* ordinary rate, first-class (rate); *tarifs postaux* postal rates; *tarif de la publicité* advertising rates; *tarif réduit* reduced rate; *tarif des salaires* salary scale; *tarif uniforme* flat rate
(**b**) *(tableau des prix)* price list, *Br* tariff
(**c**) DOUANES *(droit)* tariff, rate; *(liste)* list ❑ *tarif ad valorem* ad valorem tariff; *tarif différentiel* discriminating duty; *tarif douanier* customs tariff; *tarif douanier commun* common external tariff; *tarif d'entrée* import list; *tarif préférentiel* preferential rate *or* tariff; *tarif de sortie* export list

tarifaire *adj (accord, lois)* tariff

tarifer *vt* to fix the price of

tarification *nf* pricing

tassement *nm (du marché, des valeurs)* weakening, downturn; **l'augmentation de la TVA a provoqué un léger tassement de nos ventes** the rise in VAT has caused a slight drop in our sales

tasser **se tasser** *vpr (marché, valeurs)* to weaken

taux *nm* **(a)** *(montant, pourcentage)* rate; **à taux fixe** fixed-rate; **taux de 8%** rate of 8%; **emprunter à un taux de 7%** to borrow at 7% □ *taux d'accroissement* rate of increase *or* of growth; ÉCON *taux d'activité* participation rate; COMPTA *taux d'actualisation* net present value rate, rate of discount; COMPTA *taux d'amortissement* rate of depreciation; *taux annualisé* annual percentage rate, APR; FIN *taux de l'argent au jour le jour* overnight rate; *taux d'assurance* insurance rate; *taux d'autofinancement* cash flow rate; *taux bancaire* bank rate; *taux de base (bancaire)* base rate; COMPTA *taux de capitalisation* price-earnings ratio; *taux de change* exchange rate, rate of exchange; *taux de change à l'achat* bank buying rate; *taux de change fixe* fixed exchange rate; *taux de change flottant* floating exchange rate; *taux de change à la vente* bank selling rate; *taux de conversion* conversion rate; *taux de corrélation* relative strength; *taux de couverture* cover ratio; *taux de crédit export* export credit rate; *taux de croissance* growth rate; *taux de déport* backwardation rate; *taux de désintéressement* drop-dead rate; *taux directeur* intervention rate; *taux d'échange* rate of exchange, exchange rate; *taux effectif global* annual percentage rate; BANQUE *taux d'emprunt* borrowing rate; *taux d'épargne* savings rate; *taux d'escompte* discount rate; *taux d'expansion économique* economic growth rate; *taux de faveur* special rate; *taux du fret* freight rates; *taux horaire* hourly rate; *taux d'imposition* rate of taxation; *taux d'imposition effectif* Br effective *or* Am average tax rate; *taux d'inflation* rate of inflation, inflation rate; *taux interbancaire offert* interbank offered rate; *taux d'intérêt* interest rate, rate of interest; *taux d'intérêt à court terme* short-term interest rate; FIN *taux d'intérêt légal* official rate of interest; *taux d'intérêt à long terme* long-term interest rate; *taux d'intérêt nominal* nominal rate; *taux d'intervention* intervention rate; *le taux du jour* today's

rate; *taux légal* legal rate; FIN *taux linéaire* straight-line rate; BANQUE *taux de liquidité* liquidity ratio; BANQUE *taux Lombard* Lombard rate; BOURSE *taux long obligataire* long-term bond rate; *taux de marge, taux de marque* mark-up ratio; *taux maximum* top rate; *taux minimum* minimum rate; *taux normal* standard rate; MKTG *taux de notoriété* *(d'un produit)* rate of awareness; *taux officiel* official rate; *taux officiel d'escompte* minimum lending rate; *taux de panne* failure rate; *taux de pénétration* *(d'un marché)* penetration rate; *taux plafonné* cap; Can BANQUE *taux préférentiel* prime rate; *taux privé* market rate; *taux de production* rate of production; *taux de profit net* net profit ratio; *taux proportionnel* *(d'un crédit)* annual percentage rate; MKTG *taux de réachat* rebuy *or* repurchase rate; FIN *taux réduit* reduced rate; BANQUE *taux de référence* reference rate; *taux de référence interbancaire* interbank reference rate; *taux de rendement* rate of return; FIN *taux de rendement actuariel brut* gross annual interest return; *taux de rentabilité* rate of return; *taux de report* contango rate; FIN *taux des repos* repo rate; *taux de rotation des stocks* rate of turnover; *taux des salaires* wage rate; *taux de TVA* VAT rate; *taux uniforme* uniform *or* flat rate; FIN *taux d'usure* penal rate; *taux zéro* zero rating; **taxer à taux zéro** to zero rate

(b) ORDINAT rate □ *taux de compression* compression rate; *taux de transfert* transfer rate

> **"**
>
> Certains experts n'excluent pas une action concertée des banques centrales pour abaisser leurs **taux directeurs** afin de faire face aux tensions déflationnistes que provoquerait la crise en Asie.
>
> **"**

> **"**
>
> Même en pariant sur une légère baisse du **taux d'épargne**, il est peu probable que les Français augmentent significativement leurs dépenses.
>
> **"**

taxable *adj* dutiable, taxable

taxation *nf (par l'impôt)* taxation; *(contrôle)* assessment □ *taxation d'office* special rate of taxation; *taxation au poids* tax on weight; *taxation à la valeur* tax on value

taxe *nf* (a) *(prélèvement)* tax; **hors taxes** exclusive of tax; **toutes taxes comprises** inclusive of tax ❑ *taxe d'aéroport* airport tax; *taxe d'apprentissage* = tax paid by businesses to fund training programmes; *taxe sur le chiffre d'affaires* turnover tax; *taxe exceptionnelle* exceptional tax, special levy; *taxe à l'exportation* export duty *or* tax; *taxe foncière* property tax; *taxe à l'importation* import duty *or* tax; *taxe d'habitation, taxe locale* local tax; *taxe de luxe* tax on luxury goods; ADMIN *taxe parafiscale* exceptional tax, special levy; *taxe professionnelle* = tax paid by businesses and self-employed people; *taxe à la valeur ajoutée, Can taxe sur les ventes Br* value-added tax, *Am* sales tax (b) *(prix)* charge, rate; TÉL call charge ❑ *taxe forfaitaire* flat rate; *taxe postale* postal charge; *taxe supplémentaire* surcharge (c) *(prix fixé)* controlled price; **vendre des marchandises à la taxe** to sell goods at the controlled price

> La plupart déplore l'aberration du fonctionnement de la **taxe profes-sionnelle** qui pénalise les entreprises qui investissent, donc les plus dynamiques.

taxer *vt* (a) *(personne, alcool, cigarettes)* to tax; **taxer qch à 10%** to put a 10% tax on sth (b) *(prix)* to regulate, to fix; *(salaire)* to regulate the rate of; TÉL *(appel)* to charge for

taylorisme *nm* ÉCON Taylorism, time and motion studies

TCI *nmpl* *(abrév* **termes commerciaux internationaux**) incoterms

technicien, -enne *nm,f* technician

technico-commercial, -e 1 *adj* *(service)* technical sales ❑ *agent technico-commercial* sales technician *or* engineer **2** *nm,f* sales technician *or* engineer

technique 1 *adj* technical; *(service)* engineering **2** *nf* technique ❑ *techniques commerciales* marketing techniques; *techniques de défense contre-OPA* defensive tactics; *techniques de gestion* management techniques; *techniques marchandes* merchandising techniques; *techniques de vente* sales techniques

technologie *nf* technology

TEG *nm* FIN *(abrév* **taux effectif global**) APR

téléachat *nm* teleshopping

téléassistance *nf* ORDINAT remote help

Télécarte® *nf* phonecard

téléchargeable *adj* ORDINAT downloadable

téléchargement *nm* ORDINAT downloading

télécharger *vt* ORDINAT to download

télécommunications *nfpl* telecommunications

téléconférence *nf* teleconference

> L'appareil est équipé de moyens de reconnaissance vocale et peut organiser des **téléconférences** entre plusieurs interlocuteurs.

télécopie *nf* fax

télécopier *vt* to fax

télécopieur *nm* fax (machine)

télécourtage *nm* telebroking

tel écran-tel écrit *adj* ORDINAT WYSIWYG

télédémarchage *nm* MKTG telephone prospecting

télégestion *nf* ORDINAT teleprocessing, remote processing

télégramme *nm* telegram; **envoyer un télégramme à qn** to send a telegram to sb

télégraphe *nm* telegraph

télégraphier *vt & vi* to telegraph

téléimprimeur *nm Br* teleprinter, *Am* teletypewriter; **liaison par téléimprimeur** teleprinting

téléinformatique *nf* ORDINAT teleprocessing

télémarketing *nm* telemarketing

télématique ORDINAT **1** *adj* *(serveur, service, réseau)* data retrieval **2** *nf* telematics

téléphone *nm* telephone, phone; **appeler qn au téléphone, donner un coup de téléphone à qn** to telephone sb, to phone sb; **être abonné au téléphone** to be on the phone; **coup de téléphone** telephone *or* phone call ❑ *téléphone cellulaire* cellular phone; *téléphone mobile* mobile phone; *téléphone portable* mobile phone

téléphoner *vi* to telephone, to phone; **téléphoner à qn** to telephone sb, to phone sb

téléphonique *adj* telephone

téléphoniste *nmf* telephone operator, *Br* telephonist

téléréunion *nf* teleconference

téléscripteur *nm Br* teleprinter, *Am* teletypewriter

télétex *nm* ORDINAT teletex

télétraitement *nm* ORDINAT tele-processing, remote data processing

télétypiste *nmf* teletypist

télévendeur, -euse *nm,f* telesales person

télévente *nf* telephone selling; **téléventes** telesales

télex *nm* telex; **envoyer qch par télex** to send sth by telex, to telex sth

télexer *vt* to send by telex, to telex

télexiste *nmf* telex operator

tel-tel *nm* ORDINAT WYSIWYG

témoignage *nm* (a) JUR testimony (b) MKTG *(publicité)* testimonial advertising

tempérament *nm* **à tempérament** on hire purchase, *Am* on the installment plan **acheter qch à tempérament** to buy sth on hire purchase *or Am* on the installment plan

temporaire *adj (mesures, personnel, travail)* temporary

temps *nm* time; **à plein temps, à temps complet** *(emploi, travail)* full-time; **travailler à plein temps** *ou* **à temps complet** to work full time; **à temps partiel, à mi-temps** *(emploi, travail)* part-time ▫ ORDINAT *temps d'accès* access time; *temps d'accès disque* disk access time; *temps d'arrêt, temps improductif, temps mort* down time, idle time; ORDINAT *temps réel* real time; ORDINAT *temps de réponse* response time; ORDINAT *temps de traitement* processing time

tendance *nf* tendency, trend ▫ *tendance ascensionnelle* upward trend; *tendance à la baisse* downward trend *or* tendency, downtrend; BOURSE bearish tendency; *tendances conjoncturelles* economic trends; *tendance de croissance* growth trend; *tendance générale* general trend *or* tendency; *tendance à la hausse* upward trend *or* tendency; BOURSE bullish tendency; *tendance du marché* market trend

tendu, -e *adj* BOURSE *(cours)* steady, firm

teneur[1] *nf* (a) *(d'un document, d'un discours)* content; *(d'un contrat)* terms (b) *(quantité)* content; **teneur en or** gold content

teneur[2]**, -euse** *nm,f* **teneur de livres** bookkeeper; **teneur de marché** market maker

tenir *vt* (a) *(s'occuper de)* to keep; **tenir la caisse** to be in charge of the cash; **tenir la comptabilité** *ou* **les livres** to keep the accounts (b) FIN **tenir qch à bail** to hold a lease on sth

tenu, -e *adj* BOURSE *(cours)* steady, firm

tenue *nf* (a) *(d'une assemblée)* sitting, session; **pendant la tenue du conseil** during the council meeting
(b) BOURSE *(des cours)* steadiness, firmness; *(du marché)* state; **le franc n'est pas la seule monnaie à souffrir de la bonne tenue du mark** the franc is not the only currency to suffer from the steadiness *or* firmness of the mark
(c) *(fait d'administrer)* COMPTA *tenue de caisse* petty cash management; *tenue des comptes, tenue des livres* bookkeeping; *tenue des stocks* stock keeping

terme *nm* (a) FIN **à court terme** *(effet)* short-dated; *(emprunt, placement, crédit)* short-term; *(argent)* at short notice, at call; **à long terme** *(effet)* long-dated; *(emprunt, placement, crédit)* long-term; **à terme fixe** fixed-term; **arriver à terme** *(plan d'épargne)* to reach fruition
(b) BOURSE settlement; **à terme** *(compte, cours, livraison, marché)* forward; **livrable à terme** for forward delivery; **acheter à terme** to buy forward; **vendre à terme** to sell forward; **placer de l'argent à terme** to invest in futures
(c) *(versement)* instalment; **acheter à terme** to buy on credit; **payable en deux termes** payable in two instalments
(d) *(loyer)* quarter's rent; *(date de paiement d'un loyer)* rent day
(e) **termes** *(d'un accord, d'un contrat)* terms; **aux termes de l'article 12** in accordance with the terms of article 12, under article 12 ▫ *termes commerciaux internationaux* incoterms; *termes d'échange* terms of exchange; *termes de paiement* terms of payment

terminal *nm* (a) ORDINAT terminal, VDU ▫ *terminal distant* remote terminal; *terminal électronique de paiement* electronic payment terminal; *terminal éloigné* remote terminal; *terminal intelligent* smart terminal; *terminal de paiement en ligne* on-line cash desk terminal; **terminal point de vente** point-of-sale terminal (**b**) *(dans un aéroport)* terminal

terminateur *nm* ORDINAT terminator

terminer 1 *vt (discours, réunion)* to end, to close (**par** with)
  2 *vi (actions)* to close
  3 se terminer *vpr* to end, to come to an end

terrain *nm* (**a**) *(terre)* piece *or* plot of ground ▫ **terrain à bâtir** building plot; **terrain à lotir** development site
  (**b**) **perdre du terrain** *(monnaie, entreprise)* to lose ground; **gagner du terrain** *(monnaie, entreprise)* to gain ground; **l'entreprise regagne du terrain sur le marché français** the company is making up lost ground on the French market
  (**c**) MKTG **sur le terrain** in the field

> **"**
> Apple, qui bénéficie du succès du "G3", la dernière génération de Macintosh commercialisée depuis novembre, a commencé à regagner un peu de **terrain**. Aux États-Unis, sa part de marché est remontée de 3,4% à 4%.
> **"**

terre *nf (propriété)* **une terre** a piece of land; **des terres** land ▫ **terres en non-valeur** unproductive land

territoire *nm (d'un représentant)* territory ▫ **territoire de vente** sales territory

tertiaire ÉCON **1** *adj (secteur)* tertiary
  2 *nm* tertiary *or* service sector

tertiairisation, tertiarisation *nf* ÉCON tertiarization, growth of the tertiary *or* service sector

test **1** *adj (zone, département)* test; *(période)* trial
  2 *nm* MKTG test ▫ **test en aveugle** blind product test; **tests auprès des consommateurs** consumer testing; **test de marché** market test; **test de mémoire** memory *or* recall test; **test de performance du produit** product performance test; **test sur place** field testing; **test de préférence** preference test; **test de produit** product test; **test de rappel** recall test; **test de reconnaissance** recognition test; **test de vente** market test

testament *nm* will; **faire un testament** to make a will

tester *vt* MKTG to test; **tester qch sur le marché** to test-market sth

tête *nf* head; **par tête** per capita, per head; **être à la tête de qch** *(à la direction de)* to be in charge *or* at the head of sth

texte *nm* text ▫ ORDINAT **texte de départ** source text; **texte publicitaire** advertising copy

théorie *nf* theory ▫ MKTG **théorie de la décision** decision theory; **théorie de l'information** information theory; MKTG **théorie des jeux** game theory; ÉCON **théorie quantitative** quantity theory

théorique *adj (profits)* paper

thésaurisation *nf* ÉCON building up of capital; *(par des particuliers)* hoarding

thésauriser *vi* ÉCON to build up capital; *(particuliers)* to hoard money

ticket *nm* ticket ▫ **ticket de caisse** till receipt

ticket-repas, ticket-restaurant *nm* Br luncheon voucher, Am meal ticket

tiers, tierce **1** *adj* third ▫ **tiers bénéficiaire** *(d'un chèque, d'un effet)* beneficiary; **tierce caution** contingent liability; **tierce détenteur** third-party holder; ORDINAT **tierce partie de confiance** trusted third party; **tierce personne** third person *or* party; **tierce porteur** second endorser; **tiers possesseur** third-party owner; **tiers souscripteur** third-party subscriber
  2 *nm* (**a**) *(individu)* third party (**b**) FIN *(impôt)* interim tax payment *(equal to one third of tax paid in the previous year)*

tiers-monde *nm* **le tiers-monde** the Third World

tiers-saisi *nm* JUR garnishee

timbre *nm* (**a**) *(pour le courrier)* (postage) stamp (**b**) *(marque)* stamp ▫ **timbre fiscal** revenue stamp; **timbre de quittance** receipt stamp (**c**) *(instrument encreur)* stamp ▫ **timbre dateur** date stamp

> **"**
> Depuis 1979, le prix du permis de conduire est passé de moins de 50 francs à 250 francs, tandis que le **timbre fiscal** nécessaire pour la carte d'identité grimpait de 35 francs à 160 francs.
> **"**

timbre-poste *nm* postage stamp

timbrer *vt* to put a stamp/stamps on

TIOP *nm* BANQUE *(abrév* **taux interbancaire offert à Paris**) PIBOR

TIP *nm* BANQUE (*abrév* **titre interbancaire de paiement**) bank giro transfer

TIR *nm* (*abrév* **transport international routier**) TIR

tirage *nm* (**a**) BANQUE, FIN (*d'un chèque, d'une lettre de change*) drawing, emission; (*d'un prêt*) drawdown ❑ *tirage en l'air, tirage en blanc* kite flying, kiting

(**b**) (*de loterie*) draw (**de** for); **les obligations sont rachetées par voie de tirage** debentures are redeemed by lot ❑ *tirage au sort* drawing lots

(**c**) (*d'un journal*) circulation; **à fort tirage** with a large circulation

(**d**) ORDINAT hard copy

tiré, -e *nm,f* BANQUE, FIN (*d'un chèque, d'une lettre de change*) drawee

tirer **1** *vt* BANQUE, FIN (*chèque, lettre de change*) to draw (**sur** on); **avez-vous tiré des chèques depuis cette date?** have you written any cheques since then?; **ce chèque a-t-il déjà été tiré?** has this cheque cleared yet?

2 *vi* FIN **tirer à découvert** to overdraw; **tirer à vue** to draw at sight

tireur, -euse *nm,f* BANQUE, FIN (*d'un chèque, d'une lettre de change*) drawer

tiroir-caisse *nm* till, cash register

titre *nm* (**a**) FIN, BOURSE (*valeur*) security; (*certificat*) certificate; **titres** stocks and shares, securities, *Am* stock; **prendre livraison de titres** to take delivery of stock; **vendre des titres** to sell stock ❑ *titre d'action* share certificate; *titre de créance* loan note, debt instrument; *titre de crédit* proof of credit; *titres déposés en nantissement* securities lodged as collateral; *titres détenus en garantie* stocks held as security; *titres dilués* watered stock; *titres émis* issued securities; *titres fiduciaires* paper securities; *titres flottants* shares available on the market; *titres libérés* fully paid-up securities; *titres longs* long-dated securities, longs; *titre à lots* lottery loan bond; *titres négociables* negotiable stock; *titre nominatif* registered security; *titre d'obligation* loan *or* bond note; *titre de paiement* document of payment; **le titre de paiement doit être envoyé à...** remittance by cheque or money order to be sent to...; *titre participatif, titre de participation* equity investment *or* loan; *titres de placement* marketable securities; *titres en portefeuille* securities (in portfolio); *titre au porteur* bearer bond, negotiable instrument; *titre de prêt* loan certificate; *titre provisoire* scrip

certificate; *titres ramassés* takeover stock; *titre de rente* government bond; *titres à revenu fixe* fixed-rate securities; *titres à revenu variable* floating-rate securities; *titre sous-jacent* underlying security; *titres subordonnés à durée indéterminée* subordinated perpetuals; *titres à terme* futures; *titre universel de paiement* (*joint à la facture*) payment form, universal payment order

(**b**) **à titre de** by way of; **à titre d'essai** on approval; **à titre gratuit** free (of charge); JUR **à titre onéreux** subject to payment, for a consideration; **à titre provisoire** provisionally

(**c**) JUR title ❑ *titre de propriété* title deed

(**d**) (*d'une personne*) title ❑ *titre de civilité* (*dans une lettre*) salutation

> ❝
> Les détenteurs de **titres au porteur** disposent d'une période de six mois pour faire inscrire leurs **titres** sous forme nominative.
> ❞

titrisation *nf* FIN, BOURSE securitization

titulaire **1** *adj* ADMIN (*fonctionnaire*) with a permanent contract

2 *nmf* (**a**) (*d'un droit, d'un titre, d'un certificat, d'une carte*) holder; (*d'un passeport*) holder, bearer ❑ *titulaire d'action* shareholder

(**b**) (*d'un poste*) incumbent

titularisation *nf* ADMIN (*d'un fonctionnaire*) granting of a permanent contract; **en stage de titularisation** on probation

titulariser *vt* ADMIN **titulariser qn** to grant sb a permanent contract

TJJ *nm* FIN (*abrév* **taux d'argent au jour le jour**) overnight rate

Toile *nf* ORDINAT **la Toile** the Web

tolérance *nf* DOUANES **tolérance (permise)** tolerance, allowance

tomber *vi* (*prix, valeurs*) to fall, to drop

tonalité *nf* TÉL *Br* dialling *or Am* dial tone ❑ *tonalité d'appel* ringing tone

tonnage *nm* tonnage

tonne *nf* metric ton, tonne ❑ *tonne courte* short ton; *tonne métrique* metric ton

tort *nm* (*dommage*) wrong; **la livre forte fait du tort aux exportateurs britanniques** the strong pound is harming British exporters

total, -e **1** *adj* total

2 *nm* total; **le total des recettes et des dépenses** total revenue and expenditure;

faire le total des bénéfices to add up the profits, to calculate the total profit ❏ *total de l'actif* total assets; *total global* grand total; *total du passif* total liabilities; *total à payer* total payable

totaliser *vt* (**a**) *(additionner)* to total up, to add up (**b**) *(avoir au total)* to have a total of

totalité *nf* la totalité de all of; l'entreprise exporte la totalité de sa production the company exports its entire production; payer qch en totalité to pay sth in full

touchable *adj* *(chèque)* that can be cashed; *(effet)* collectable

touche *nf* *(de clavier)* key ❏ ORDINAT *touche d'alimentation* power-on key; *touche alt* alt key; *touche d'arrêt de défilement* scroll lock key; *touche à bascule* toggle key; *touche contrôle* control key; *touche début* home key; *touche de défilement* scroll key; *touche de déplacement du curseur* cursor movement key; *touche de direction* arrow key; *touche d'échappement* escape key; *touche d'effacement* delete key; *touche d'effacement arrière* backspace key; *touche (d')entrée* enter key; *touche d'espacement arrière* backspace key; *touche fin* end key; *touche fléchée, touche (à) flèche* arrow key; *touche flèche vers le bas* down arrow key; *touche flèche vers la droite* right arrow key; *touche flèche vers la gauche* left arrow key; *touche flèche vers le haut* up arrow key; *touche (de) fonction* function key; *touche d'insertion* insert key; *touche d'interruption* break key; *touche majuscule* shift key; *touche multifonction* multifunctional key; *touche numérique* number key; *touche page précédente* page up key; *touche page suivante* page down key; *touche de raccourci* shortcut key; *touche de répétition* repeat-action key; *touche retour* return or enter key; *touche de retour arrière* backspace key; *touche de verrouillage du clavier numérique* num lock key; *touche du verrouillage des majuscules* caps lock key

toucher *vt* *(salaire)* to get, to draw; *(chèque)* to cash; *(intérêts, pot-de-vin)* to receive, to get; *(traite)* to collect

tour[1] *nm* (**a**) BANQUE, FIN *tour de table* pool, backers (**b**) **à tour de rôle** in turn, by rotation

tour[2] *nf* ORDINAT tower

tourisme *nm* tourism

tournée de présentation *nf* MKTG road show

tourniquet *nm* MKTG *(présentoir)* stand, spinner

tour-opérateur *nm* tour operator

TPC *nf* ORDINAT *(abrév* **tierce partie de confiance***)* TTP

traceur *nm* ORDINAT plotter

tract *nm* leaflet

trader *nm* trader

traducteur, -trice **1** *nm,f* translator **2** *nm* ORDINAT translator

traduction *nf* translation (**de/en** from/into) ❏ *traduction assistée par ordinateur* computer-assisted translation, machine translation; *traduction automatique* machine translation; *traduction simultanée* simultaneous translation

traduire **1** *vt* (**a**) *(texte, terme)* to translate (**de/en** from/into) (**b**) ORDINAT to translate **2** se traduire *vpr* se traduire par qch *(avoir pour résultat)* to result in sth; le ralentissement de l'activité économique s'est traduit par de nombreux licenciements the slowdown in economic activity brought about numerous redundancies

trafic *nm* (**a**) *(activité illégale)* trafficking ❏ JUR *trafic d'influence* influence peddling (**b**) *(circulation)* traffic ❏ *trafic aérien* air traffic; *trafic routier* road traffic

traficoter *vi* to be involved in shady deals

trafiquant, -e *nm,f* trafficker

trafiquer *vt* to traffic in

train *nm* (**a**) *(pour le transport)* train ❏ *train de marchandises* goods or freight train; *train mixte* passenger and goods train (**b**) *(ensemble)* set, package; **un train de mesures économiques/fiscales** a set or package of economic/tax measures ❏ *train de propositions* package deal (**c**) *(niveau)* *train de vie* standard of living

"

Certes, cela faisait des mois que François Hollande réclamait un véritable **train de mesures fiscales** et l'amorce de la baisse des prélèvements obligatoires.

"

traite *nf* FIN *(lettre de change)* (banker's) draft, bill (of exchange); **encaisser une traite** to collect a bill; **escompter une traite** to discount a bill; **présenter une traite à l'acceptation** to present a bill for acceptance; **tirer une traite** to draw a bill □ *traite contre acceptation* acceptance bill; *traite en l'air* fictitious bill, kite; *traite avalisée* guaranteed bill; *traite bancaire* bank draft; *traite à courte échéance* short-dated bill; *traite à date fixe* time bill; *traite documentaire* documentary bill; *traite domiciliée* domiciled bill; *traite sur l'étranger, traite sur l'extérieur* foreign bill; *traite sur l'intérieur* inland bill; *traite libre* clean bill; *traite à longue échéance* long-dated bill; *traite de plaisance* accommodation bill; *traite pro forma* pro forma bill; *traite 'sans frais'* bill 'without protest'; *traite à terme* term draft; *traite à vue* sight draft

traité nm (accord) treaty □ ASSUR *traité facultatif obligatoire* open cover

traitement nm (a) ORDINAT processing □ *traitement automatique de l'information* automatic data processing; *traitement de données* data processing; *traitement électronique de l'information* electronic data processing; *traitement d'images* image processing; *traitement de l'information* data processing; *traitement par lots* batch processing; *traitement séquentiel* sequentiel processing; *traitement de textes* word processing; (logiciel) word processor, word processing software; **réaliser qch par traitement de texte** to word process sth
(b) (rémunération des fonctionnaires) pay, salary; **sans traitement** (secrétaire) honorary; (magistrat) unsalaried □ *traitement de base* basic pay or salary; *traitement fixe* fixed salary; *traitement initial* starting salary
(c) (d'une commande, d'une plainte, d'une demande) processing
(d) (de matières premières) processing

traiter 1 vt (a) ORDINAT to process (b) (commande, plainte, demande) to process, to handle (c) (matières premières) to process
2 vi **traiter avec qn** to deal with sb; (créancier) to negotiate with sb

tranche nf (de chiffres) group, block; (d'actions) block, tranche; (d'un crédit, d'un emprunt) instalment; (d'assistance financière internationale) tranche; (d'un programme immobilier) stage, portion; ADMIN **par tranche de 1000 francs ou fraction de 1000 francs** for every complete sum of 1,000 francs or part thereof □ *tranche d'imposition* tax bracket; *tranche de revenus* income bracket

tranquille adj (marché) quiet

transaction nf (opération) transaction, deal; **transactions** transactions, dealings □ *transaction bancaire* bank transaction; *transaction boursière* Stock Exchange transaction; BANQUE *transaction par carte* card transaction; BOURSE *transaction de clôture* closing transaction; *transaction commerciale* business transaction; BOURSE *transaction au comptant* spot or cash transaction; *transaction à crédit* credit transaction; BOURSE *transactions à terme* futures

transbordement nm transshipment

transborder vt to transship

transcription nf (texte) transcript

transcrire vt (recopier) to transcribe; COMPTA **transcrire le journal au grand-livre** to transfer journal entries into the ledger

transférable adj transferable, negotiable

transférer vt (a) (argent, actions, effets) to transfer; **transférer un billet par voie d'endossement** to transfer a bill by endorsement; **il a transféré son argent sur un compte suisse** he's transferred his money into a Swiss account (b) ORDINAT (données) to transfer

transfert nm (a) (d'argent, d'actions, d'effets) transfer □ TÉL *transfert d'appel automatique* automatic call transfer; BANQUE *transfert par CCP* giro transfer; COMPTA *transfert de charges* transfer of charges; COMPTA *transfert de créances* assignment of accounts receivable or of debts; *transfert de devises* currency transfer (b) ORDINAT (de données) transfer □ *transfert de fonds électronique, transfert électronique de fonds* electronic funds transfer

transfert-paiement nm FIN transfer of account (from one savings bank to another)

transformation nf (de matières premières) processing

transformer vt (matières premières) to process

transiger *vi* to compromise, to come to an arrangement (**avec** with); **transiger avec ses créanciers** to come to terms with one's creditors

transit *nm* transit; **en transit** *(marchandises, passagers)* in transit ❑ **transit communautaire** community transit; **transit douanier** customs transit

transitaire **1** *adj* transit
2 *nmf* forwarding agent, transport agent

transiter **1** *vt (marchandises)* to forward
2 *vi (marchandises, voyageurs)* to pass in transit (**par** through)

translation *nf* JUR *(de propriété)* conveyancing

transmettre *vt* JUR *(propriété)* to transfer, to convey; *(actions, brevet)* to assign

transmissible *adj* JUR *(propriété)* transferable; *(actions, brevet)* assignable (**b**) FIN **transmissible par endossement** transferable by endorsement

transmission *nf* (**a**) ORDINAT *(de données)* transmission ❑ **transmission par modem** modem transmission (**b**) JUR *(de propriété)* transfer, conveyance; *(d'actions, d'un brevet)* assignment (**c**) FIN **transmission par endossement** transfer by endorsement

transport *nm* (**a**) *(de marchandises, de passagers)* transport; **cela permet d'effectuer les transports urgents par avion** this enables urgent freight to be sent by air ❑ **transport aérien** air transport; **transports en commun** public transport; **transport ferroviaire** rail transport; **transport maritime** transport by sea, shipping; **transports routiers** road transport *or* haulage; **transport terrestre** surface transport; **transport urbain** urban transport (**b**) JUR *(de droits)* transfer (**c**) BANQUE *(de fonds)* transfer *(from one account to another)* (**d**) COMPTA transfer

transport-cession *nm* JUR transfer, conveyance

transporter *vt* (**a**) *(marchandises)* to transport; **transporter qch par avion/par mer** to transport sth by air/by sea; **transporter par route/par chemin de fer** to transport by road/by rail (**b**) JUR *(droits)* to transfer, to assign (**c**) BANQUE *(fonds)* to transfer *(from one account to another)* (**d**) COMPTA to transfer

transporteur *nm* carrier, forwarding agent

travail *nm* (**a**) *(activité)* work ❑ **travail de bureau** office work; **travail à la chaîne** assembly line work, production line work; **travail en cours** work in progress; **travail à domicile** work done at home; **travail à l'entreprise** contract work, work by *or* on contract; **travail par équipes** shift work; **travail d'équipe** teamwork; **travail à façon** job work; **travail à forfait** fixed-price work; **travail à la machine** machine work; **travail (au) noir** moonlighting; **travail de nuit** night work; **travail à la pièce, travail aux pièces** piece work; **travail à plein temps** full-time work; **travail posté** shift-work; **travail à la tâche** piecework; *(intermittent)* jobbing (work); **travail au ralenti** go-slow; **travail par roulement** shift work; ORDINAT **travail en temps partagé** time sharing; **travail à temps partiel** part-time work; **travaux sur le terrain** fieldwork
(**b**) *(emploi)* employment, job; **être sans travail** to be out of work, to be unemployed
(**c**) *(lieu)* work; **il est à son travail** he's at work
(**d**) *(tâche)* piece of work, job; **entreprendre un travail** to undertake a piece of work, to take on a job
(**e**) **travaux** *(réparations)* work ❑ **travaux publics** *(secteur)* public works

travailler *vi* (**a**) *(effectuer une tâche)* to work; **travailler à son compte** to work for oneself, to be self-employed; **travailler à la pièce** to do piecework; **travailler au ralenti** to go slow; **travailler à la tâche** to do piecework; **travailler à temps partiel** to work part time, to have a part-time job (**b**) *(fructifier)* **faire travailler son argent** to make one's money work for one

travailleur, -euse *nm,f* worker ❑ **travailleur indépendant** self-employed person; **travailleur manuel** manual worker; **travailleur à mi-temps** part-time worker; **travailleur occasionnel** casual worker; **travailleur à la pièce** pieceworker; **travailleur à plein temps** full-time worker; **travailleur posté** shiftworker; **travailleur à la tâche** pieceworker; **travailleur à temps partiel** part-time worker

treizième mois *nm* = extra month's salary paid as an annual bonus

trésor *nm* treasury; **le Trésor (public)** *(institution)* = department dealing with the State budget, ≃ the Treasury; *(finances publiques)* public funds *or* finances

trésorerie *nf* (**a**) *(fonction de trésorier)* treasurership (**b**) *(bureau) (gouvernemental)* public revenue office; *(d'une entreprise)* accounts department **(c)** *(ressources)* funds, finances; **avoir des problèmes de trésorerie** to have cash flow problems **(d)** *(gestion)* accounts

trésorier, -ère *nm,f* treasurer ❑ *trésorier de banque* bank treasurer

tri *nm* **(a)** *(de candidats)* selection, screening; *(de courrier)* sorting **(b)** ORDINAT sort; **effectuer un tri** to do a sort ❑ *tri alphabétique* alphasort; *tri en ordre croissant* ascending sort; *tri en ordre décroissant* descending sort

tribunal *nm* court ❑ *tribunal arbitral* arbitration court; *tribunal de commerce* commercial tribunal *or* court; *tribunal d'instance* ≃ magistrates' court

trier *vt* **(a)** *(candidats)* to select, to screen; *(courrier)* to sort; **trier qn/qch sur le volet** to hand-pick sb/sth **(b)** ORDINAT to sort; **trier par ordre alphabétique** to sort in alphabetical order, to alphasort

trieuse *nf* ORDINAT sorter; *(logiciel)* sort program

trimestre *nm* **(a)** *(période)* quarter, three months; **par trimestre** quarterly **(b)** *(salaire)* quarter's salary; *(loyer)* quarter's rent

trimestriel, -elle *adj* quarterly

trimestriellement *adv* quarterly, every three months

triple *adj* triple; **en triple exemplaire** in triplicate

tripotage *nm Fam* scam, *Br* fiddle

troc *nm* barter; **faire du troc** to barter

trois-huit *nmpl* **les trois-huit** = shift system based on three eight-hour shifts; **ils font les trois huit** they work eight-hour shifts

trombone *nm (agrafe)* paper clip

trop-perçu *nm* FIN *(d'impôts)* excess payment; **rembourser le trop-perçu** to refund the excess payment

troquer *vt* to exchange, to barter

trouver *vt* ORDINAT **trouver et remplacer** to find and replace

trust *nm* FIN trust; **un trust de l'acier/du pétrole** a steel/an oil cartel ❑ *trust commercial* commercial monopoly; *trust industriel* industrial monopoly; *trust de placement* investment trust; *trust de valeurs* holding company; *trust vertical* vertical trust

truster FIN **1** *vt* to monopolize, to form into a monopoly
2 *vi* to form a monopoly

trusteur *nm* organizer *or* administrator of a trust

TTC *(abrév* **toutes taxes comprises**) inclusive of tax, tax inclusive

tuyau *nm Fam (information)* tip ❑ *tuyau de Bourse* Stock Exchange tip

TVA *nf (abrév* **taxe à la valeur ajoutée**) *Br* VAT, *Am* sales tax; **soumis à la TVA** subject to *Br* VAT *or Am* sales tax

type 1 *adj échantillon type* representative sample; *lettre type* standard letter
2 *nm (sorte)* type

UAS *nf* (*abrév* **unité d'activité stratégique**) SBU

UE *nf* (*abrév* **Union européenne**) EU

UEM *nf* (*abrév* **union économique et monétaire**) EMU

ultérieur, -e *adj* (*date*) later; (*commandes*) further

ultracompétitif, -ive *adj* very highly competitive

ultraportatif *nm* ORDINAT mini laptop, palmtop

UME *nf* (*abrév* **union monétaire européenne**) EMU

unanime *adj* (*vote, consentement*) unanimous

unification *nf* FIN (*des crédits*) consolidation

unifié, -e *adj* FIN (*crédits*) consolidated

unifier *vt* FIN (*crédits*) to consolidate

uniforme *adj* uniform, across-the-board

unilatéral, -e *adj* (*contrat*) unilateral

union *nf* (**a**) (*association*) union, association □ **union douanière** customs union; **union économique** economic union; **union économique et monétaire** economic and monetary union; **l'Union européenne** the European Union; **union monétaire européenne** European monetary union (**b**) JUR **union des créanciers** = agreement on the part of creditors to take concerted action in bankruptcy proceedings

unique *adj* sole, single

unitaire *adj* (*prix, coût*) unit

unité *nf* (**a**) (*article*) unit; **actions émises en unités** shares issued in ones; **la production a dépassé les 3000 unités** production has passed the 3,000-unit mark
(**b**) (*département*) unit □ **unité administrative** administrative unit; **unité de fabrication** factory unit; **unité de production** production unit
(**c**) ORDINAT unit, module □ **unité d'affichage** display unit; **unité de bande** tape unit; **unité centrale** central processing unit; (*de disque*) drive; **unité de destination** destination drive; **unité de disque** disk drive; **unité de disquettes** floppy drive; **unité externe** external drive; **unité interne** internal unit; **unité**

périphérique peripheral device *or* unit; **unité de sauvegarde** backup device; **unité de sortie** output device; **unité de stockage** storage device
(**d**) (*étalon*) unit □ ÉCON **unité de compte** unit of account; UE **unité de compte européenne** European currency unit; **unité de consommation** unit of consumption; **unité de coût** cost unit; **unité monétaire** monetary unit, unit of currency; **unité de poids** unit of weight; **unité de production** unit of production; BOURSE **unité de transaction** lot size; **unité de travail** unit of labour, man-work unit

> "
> La délocalisation à l'étranger d'une **unité de production** peut entraîner sur le territoire national de la firme un effet indirect de création d'emplois.
> "

urbanisme *nm* town planning

urbaniste *nmf* town planner

urgence *nf* **d'urgence** immediately; **veuillez répondre d'urgence** please reply without delay *or* immediately

urgent, -e *adj* urgent

URSSAF *nf* (*abrév* **Union de recouvrement des cotisations de Sécurité sociale et d'Allocations familiales**) = organization which collects social security and family allowance payments

usage *nm* (**a**) (*utilisation*) use; **à usages multiples** multi-purpose; **locaux à usage commercial** business *or* commercial premises
(**b**) JUR **avoir l'usage de qch** to have the right to sth
(**c**) (*coutume*) custom, practice; **je peux vous fournir les références d'usage** I can supply you with the usual references; **suivant les usages bancaires** according to normal banking practice

usagé, -e *adj* used

usager *nm* user

usance *nf* usance; **à deux usances** at double usance; **à usance de trente jours** at thirty days' usance

usinage *nm* (**a**) *(fabrication industrielle)* manufacturing (**b**) *(à la machine-outil)* machining, tooling

usine *nf* factory, plant; **travailler en usine** to work in a factory ❑ *usine d'assemblage* assembly plant; *usine d'automobiles* car factory; *usine modèle* model factory

usiner *vt* (**a**) *(fabriquer)* to manufacture (**b**) *(à la machine-outil)* to machine, to tool

usufruit *nm* JUR usufruct

usure[1] *nf (intérêt, délit)* usury

usure[2] *nf (action de s'user)* wear and tear ❑ *usure en magasin* shelf depreciation

usurier, -ère *nm,f* usurer

utile *adj (nécessaire)* necessary; **en temps utile** in (good) time, within the prescribed time; **prendre toutes dispositions utiles** to make all necessary arrangements

utilisable *adj* usable; **utilisable à vue** *(crédit)* available at sight

utilisateur, -trice *nm,f* user ❑ MKTG *utilisateur final* end user; MKTG *utilisateur tardif* late adopter

utilitaire 1 *adj* utilitarian
2 *nm* ORDINAT utility

utilité *nf* ÉCON utility ❑ *utilité marginale* marginal utility

vacance *nf* (a) *(poste)* vacancy; **suppléer à une vacance** to fill a vacancy; **il y a une vacance à la comptabilité** the accounts department has a vacancy (b) **vacances** *Br* holiday(s), *Am* vacation; **un mois de vacances** a month's holiday, a month off

vacant, -e *adj* vacant

vache à lait *nf* MKTG *(produit)* cash cow

vague *nf (mouvement)* wave; **l'annonce a provoqué une vague de protestations** the announcement provoked a wave of protest ❑ **vague de prospérité** boom, wave of prosperity; **vague de spéculation** wave of speculation

valable *adj* valid; **ce billet est valable pour un mois** this ticket is valid for one month; BOURSE **valable jusqu'à nouvel ordre** good until cancelled

valeur (a) *(prix)* value, worth ❑ **valeur d'achat** purchase value; COMPTA **valeur actualisée** present value; COMPTA **valeur actuelle** current value; **valeur actuelle nette** current net value; ÉCON **valeur ajoutée** added value; **valeur assurable** insurable value; **valeur assurée** insured value; **valeur de bilan** book value; **valeur boursière** market value; **valeur brute** gross value; **valeur capitalisée** capitalized value; **valeur à la casse** break-up value; **valeur compensée** cleared value; **valeur comptable** book value; **valeur comptable nette** net book value; BANQUE **valeur en compte** value in account; **valeur déclarée** declared value; **valeur de départ** initial value; **valeur en douane** customs value, value for customs purposes; **valeur d'échange** exchange value; FIN **valeur à l'échéance** maturity value; FIN **valeur à l'encaissement** value for collection; **valeur d'émission** issue price; **valeur extrinsèque** extrinsic value; *(d'une monnaie)* legal *or* fictitious value; **valeur faciale** *(d'une action)* face value, nominal value; **valeur de facture** invoice value; FIN **valeur fictive** *(de la monnaie fiduciaire)* face value; **valeur future** prospective value; **valeur intrinsèque** intrinsic value; COMPTA **valeur d'inventaire** balance sheet value, break-up value; BANQUE **valeur jour** same-day value; **valeur de liquidation, valeur liquidative** value at liquidation; FIN cash-in value; **valeur locative** rental value; **valeur locative imposable** rateable value; **valeur marchande** commercial value, marketable value; **valeur marginale** marginal value; **valeur négociable** market value, commercial value; **valeur nette** net value *or* worth; **valeur à neuf** replacement value; **valeur nominale** *(d'une obligation)* par value; *(d'une action)* nominal value, face value; **valeur numéraire** legal-tender value; **valeur à l'origine, valeur d'origine** original value; **valeur au pair** par value; **valeur perçue** perceived value; **valeur de rachat** *(d'une police)* surrender value; **valeur réelle** real value, actual value; **valeur de remboursement** redemption value; **valeur de remplacement** replacement value; **valeur de rendement** *(d'une entreprise)* profitability value; **valeur de reprise** trade-in allowance; **valeur à la revente** resale value; BOURSE **valeur temporelle** time value; **valeur d'usage** value as a going concern; **valeur vénale** fair market value

(b) BOURSE *(titre)* **valeur (boursière)** security, share ❑ **valeurs bancaires** bank shares; **valeurs de bourse** quoted securities; FIN **valeurs classées** investment stock; **valeurs au comptant** securities dealt in for cash; **valeurs de croissance** growth shares *or* stocks; **valeurs immobilières** property shares; **valeurs industrielles** industrial shares, industrials; **valeurs à intérêt fixe** fixed-interest securities; **valeurs à lot** lottery bonds, prize bonds; **valeurs mobilières** stocks and shares, transferable securities; **valeurs (mobilières) de placement** marketable securities; **valeurs nanties** pledged securities; **valeurs négociables** marketable securities; **valeurs nominatives** registered securities; **valeur non cotée** unlisted security; **valeurs de père de famille** blue chip stock; **valeurs de placement** investment securities; **valeurs de portefeuille** portfolio securities; **valeurs au porteur** bearer securities, bearer bonds; **valeurs de premier choix ou ordre** blue chip stock; **valeurs réalisables** realizable *or* marketable securities; **valeurs de retournement** recovery shares; **valeurs à revenu fixe** fixed-income securities; **valeurs à revenu**

variable floating-rate *or* variable-rate securities; **valeurs du second marché** unlisted securities; **valeurs des sociétés industrielles** industrials; **valeurs spéculatives, valeurs de spéculation** speculative securities; **valeurs à terme** futures; **valeurs de tout repos** gilt-edged securities

(**c**) **valeurs** *(capital)* assets □ **valeurs actives** assets; **valeur en capital** capital assets; **valeurs disponibles** available *or* liquid *or* current assets; **valeur en espèces** cash, bullion; **valeurs immobilisées** fixed assets; **valeurs incorporelles** intangible assets, intangibles; **valeurs liquides** liquid assets *or* securities; **valeurs matérielles** tangible assets, tangibles; **valeurs passives** liabilities

> **"**
> Les **valeurs locatives** tombent à 4000 francs vers l'Etoile, pourtant proche des Champs-Elysées et doté de valeurs vénales élevées.
> **"**

valeur-or *nf* FIN value in gold currency

valeur-temps *nf* extrinsic value

validation *nf* (**a**) *(d'un contrat)* ratification (**b**) *(d'un document)* authentication, validation

valide *adj (contrat, document)* valid

valider *vt* (**a**) *(contrat)* to ratify; *(document)* to authenticate, to validate (**b**) ORDINAT *(option)* to confirm; *(cellule, case)* to select

validité *nf (d'un contrat, d'un document)* validity

valoir *vi* (**a**) *(avoir comme valeur)* to be worth; **valoir cher** *(objet en vente)* to be expensive; *(objet précieux)* to be worth a lot (**b**) *(fructifier)* **faire valoir son argent** to invest one's money profitably (**c**) **à valoir** *(paiement, somme)* to be deducted, on account; **payer 200 francs à valoir** to pay 200 francs on account; **verser un acompte à valoir sur une somme** to pay a deposit to be set off against *or* deducted from a sum

valorisation *nf* (**a**) *(augmentation de la valeur)* FIN increase in value, valorization; COMPTA *(d'un inventaire)* valuation (**b**) ÉCON development

valoriser **1** *vt* (**a**) *(bien, monnaie)* to increase the value of (**b**) ÉCON *(région)* to develop
2 se valoriser *vpr* to increase in value

valse *nf* **valse des étiquettes** constant price rises; **valse des prix** spiralling prices

VAN *nm* COMPTA *(abrév* **valeur actuelle nette***)* current net value

variabilité *nf* variability

variable **1** *adj* variable
2 *nf* ORDINAT variable □ **variable de mémoire** memory variable

variation *nf* variation; *(des cours, du marché)* fluctuation □ **variations annuelles** annual variations; **variation de cours minimale** minimum fluctuation; **variation maximale autorisée** maximum fluctuation; **variations saisonnières** seasonal variations

varier *vi* to vary, to change; *(cours, marché)* to fluctuate; **les prix varient d'un magasin/d'un jour à l'autre** prices vary from one shop/day to another; **les salaires proposés varient suivant l'expérience des candidats** the salaries offered vary according to the experience of the candidates

vedette *nf* MKTG *(produit)* star

véhicule *nm* vehicle □ **véhicule commercial** commercial vehicle; **véhicule industriel** industrial vehicle, goods vehicle; **véhicule utilitaire** commercial vehicle

véhiculer *vt* (**a**) *(transporter)* to transport (**b**) *(transmettre)* to convey; MKTG **véhiculer une image** to convey an image

veille *nf* ORDINAT standby mode; **en veille** in standby mode

vendable *adj* saleable, sellable

vendeur, -euse *nm,f* (**a**) *(particulier)* seller; JUR vendor (**b**) *(dans un magasin)* Br sales assistant, Am (sales) clerk □ **vendeur à domicile** door-to-door salesman; **vendeur export** exporter; **vendeur par téléphone** telesales person (**c**) BOURSE seller; *(d'une prime)* giver □ **vendeur à découvert** short seller, bear seller

vendre *vt* to sell; *(commercialiser)* to market; **vendre qch à qn** to sell sb sth, to sell sth to sb; **vendre moins cher que qn** to undersell sb; **vendre comptant** to sell for cash; **vendre à crédit** to sell on credit; BOURSE **vendre à découvert** to sell short, to go a bear; **vendre au détail** to sell retail, to retail; **vendre en entrepôt** to sell in bonded warehouses; **vendre de gré à gré** to sell privately; **vendre en gros** to sell wholesale; **vendre à perte** to sell at a loss; BOURSE **vendre à terme** to sell forward

vente *nf (transaction)* sale; *(activité)* selling; **réaliser une vente** to make a sale; **elle est**

dans la **vente** she's in sales; COMPTA **ventes** sales, turnover; **en vente** for sale, on sale; **en vente libre** freely available; **mettre qch en vente** to put sth up for sale, to offer sth for sale; **en vente dans tous les grands magasins** on sale at all leading stores □ *Suisse* **vente action** bargain offer; **vente à l'amiable** sale by private agreement, private sale; **vente à l'arrivée** sale at arrival; **vente par catalogue** mail-order (selling); **vente (au) comptant** cash sale; **vente par correspondance** mail-order (selling); **vente à crédit** credit sale; *(à tempérament)* hire purchase, *Am* installment plan; BOURSE **vente à découvert** short sale; **vente au détail** retailing, retail selling; **vente directe** *(méthode)* direct selling; *(occurrence)* direct sale; **vente à distance** in-home shopping; **vente à domicile** door-to-door selling; **vente aux enchères** (sale by) auction; **vente à l'essai** sale on approval; **ventes export, ventes à l'exportation** export sales; **vente ferme** firm sale; **vente forcée** forced sale; **vente à froid** cold selling; **vente de gré à gré** sale by private agreement, private sale; **vente en gros** wholesaling; **vente judiciaire** sale by order of the court; **vente jumelée** twin-pack selling; **vente de liquidation** closing-down sale; BOURSE **vente nue** naked sale; **vente à perte** sale at a loss; **vente de porte-à-porte** door-to-door selling; **vente à prix réduit** sale at a reduced price; **vente promotionnelle** promotional sale; **ventes de prospection** missionary selling; **vente publique** public sale; **vente pyramidale** pyramid selling; **vente rapide** quick *or* ready sale; **vente réclame** bargain sale; **vente à réméré** sale with option of repurchase; **vente sans intermédiaire** direct selling; **vente en semi-gros** small wholesale selling; **vente par téléphone** *(méthode)* telephone selling; **ventes par téléphone** *(transactions)* telephone sales, telesales; **vente à tempérament** hire purchase, *Am* installment plan; BOURSE **vente à terme** forward sale

ventilation *nf* (a) *(décomposition) (des prix, des dépenses)* breakdown (b) *(répartition) (de crédits, d'équipments)* allocation

ventiler *vt* (a) *(décomposer) (prix, dépenses)* to break down (b) *(répartir) (crédits, équipements)* to allocate; **ventiler un lot** to break down bulk

vépéciste *nm* mail order specialist

verbal, -e *adj (convention, offre)* verbal

véreux, -euse *adj (affaires, financier)* shady, dubious

vérificateur, -trice **1** *nm,f* inspector, examiner □ **vérificateur de comptes** auditor; **vérificateur externe** external auditor; **vérificateur interne** internal auditor

2 *nm* ORDINAT **vérificateur orthographique** spellchecker

vérification *nf* (a) *(de déclarations)* checking, verification; *(du travail)* inspection, examination, checking □ COMPTA **vérification de comptes** audit(ing) of accounts; **vérification en douane** customs examination (of goods); **vérification d'écritures** audit(ing) of accounts; **vérification externe** external auditing; **vérification fiscale** tax audit; **vérification interne** internal auditing; COMPTA **vérification à rebours** audit trail; **vérification des stocks** stock control (b) ORDINAT check □ **vérification antivirale** antivirus check; **vérification orthographique** spellcheck

vérifier *vt* to check; *(comptes)* to audit; *(références)* to take up; **vérifié et revérifié** checked and double-checked

verrouillage *nm* ORDINAT lock □ **verrouillage du clavier numérique** num lock; **verrouillage des fichiers** file lock; **verrouillage en lecture seule** read-only lock; **verrouillage en majuscule(s)** caps lock

verrouiller *vt* ORDINAT to lock on; **verrouiller en écriture** *(fichier)* to lock; **verrouillé en majuscule(s)** *(clavier)* with caps lock on

versement *nm (paiement)* payment; *(paiement partiel)* instalment; **en plusieurs versements** by *or* in instalments; **premier versement** down payment □ **versement annuel** yearly payment; **versement à la commande** down payment; **versement comptant** cash payment; **versements échelonnés** staggered payments, instalments; **versement d'espèces** cash deposit; **versement en numéraire** payment in cash; **versement partiel** instalment

verser *vt* (a) *(argent, intérêt, salaire)* to pay; *(sur un compte)* to deposit; **verser qch au crédit de qn** to credit sb with sth; **verser un acompte** to make a down payment; **verser de l'argent sur son compte** to pay money into one's account; BOURSE **verser un premium** to pay *or* deposit a premium (b) *(joindre)* to add; **verser un document au dossier** to add a document to the file

version nf (d'un projet, d'un document) draft

verso nm (d'un effet, d'un chèque) back

vertical, -e adj ÉCON (concentration, intégration) vertical

veto nm veto; **mettre** ou **opposer son veto à qch** to veto sth

vétusté nf obsolescence

VI nf COMPTA (abrév **valeur d'inventaire**) balance sheet value, break-up value

viabilisé, -e adj ADMIN (terrain) serviced, with services

viabiliser vt ADMIN (terrain) to service

viabilité nf (d'un projet, d'un système) viability, workability

viable adj (projet, système) viable, workable

viager, -ère 1 adj (rente) life
2 nm life annuity; **placer son argent en viager** to invest one's money in a life annuity; **acheter une propriété en viager** = to acquire a property by paying pre-determined instalments until the death of the owner(s)

vice nm fault, defect, flaw ▫ **vice apparent** obvious defect; **vice caché** hidden defect; **vice de construction** construction fault; **vice de fabrication** manufacturing defect; **vice de forme** legal flaw; **vice inhérent, vice propre** inherent defect; **vice rédhibitoire** material defect

vice-gérance nf deputy managership

vice-gérant, -e nm,f deputy manager

vice-présidence nf (d'état, d'organisation) vice-presidency; (d'entreprise) vice-chairmanship

vice-président, -e nm,f (d'état, d'organisation) vice-president; (d'entreprise) vice-chairman

vide adj **vide en retour** empty on return

vidéo nf video

vidéoconference nf videoconference; (concept) videoconferencing

vidéotex nm ORDINAT Videotex®, Viewdata®

vider vt (a) ORDINAT **vider l'écran** to clear the screen; **vider la corbeille** to empty the wastebasket or Am the trash (b) Fam (congédier) to kick out

vie nf ÉCON living, livelihood; **gagner sa vie** to earn one's living ▫ **vie économique** (d'un produit) economic life

vierge adj ORDINAT (ligne, espace) blank; (disquette) blank, unformatted

vignette nf manufacturer's label (of quality, guarantee)

vigueur nf **en vigueur** (règlement, loi) in force; **entrer en vigueur** to come into force; **cesser d'être en vigueur** to lapse

village planétaire nm global village

ville nf town ▫ **ville industrielle** industrial town; MKTG **ville test** test city

violation nf infringement, violation; **en violation de la loi** in breach or violation of the law

violer vt (accord, loi) to break, to violate

virement nm (a) BANQUE (credit) transfer ▫ **virement automatique** automatic transfer; **virement bancaire** bank transfer; **virement par courrier** mail transfer; **virement de crédit** credit transfer; **virement interbancaire** interbank transfer; **virement postal** post office transfer; **virement télégraphique** cable transfer; **virement par télex** telex transfer (b) ADMIN **virement de fonds** = transfer (often illegal) of funds from one article of the budget to another

virer vt (a) BANQUE (somme) to transfer; (chèque) to clear; **je vire 1 000 francs tous les mois sur son compte** I transfer 1,000 francs into his account every month (b) Fam (congédier) to sack

virgule flottante nf ORDINAT floating point

virus nm ORDINAT virus

visa nm (a) (pour passeport) visa ▫ **visa de la douane** customs visa (b) (signature) signature; (initiales) initials; (tampon) stamp (c) (de chèque) certification (d) BOURSE **visa de la COB** permission to deal

viser vt (a) (passeport) to visa (b) (document) (signer) to countersign; (apposer ses initiales à) to initial; (tamponner) to stamp (c) (chèque) to certify; COMPTA **viser des livres de commerce** to certify the books (d) MKTG (clientèle, public) to target

visible adj (biens, importations, exportations) visible

visioconférence nf videoconference; (concept) videoconferencing

visiophone nm videophone

visite nf (a) (d'un représentant) call ▫ **visite d'affaires** business call; **visite à froid** cold call (b) (inspection) inspection, examination ▫ **visite de douane, visite douanière** customs inspection

visiter *vt* (**a**) *(client)* to call on (**b**) *(inspecter)* to inspect, to examine

visualisation *nf* ORDINAT display ❑ *visualisation de la page à l'écran* page preview

visualiser *vt* ORDINAT to display

visuel *nm* ORDINAT visual display unit, VDU

vitesse *nf* (**a**) *(rapidité)* speed, rate; **être en perte de vitesse** *(entreprise, économie, monnaie)* to be losing ground ❑ FIN *vitesse de rotation (des stocks)* turnover rate, turnround rate; ÉCON *vitesse de transformation des capitaux* income velocity of capital

(**b**) ORDINAT speed ❑ *vitesse d'affichage* display speed; *vitesse de calcul* processing or computing speed; *vitesse de clignotement* blink rate; *vitesse d'écriture* write speed; *vitesse d'exécution* execution speed; *vitesse de frappe (à la machine à écrire)* keying speed; *vitesse de frappe à la minute/à l'heure* keystrokes per minute/hour; *vitesse d'impression* print speed; *vitesse du processeur* processor speed; *vitesse de traitement* processing speed; *vitesse de transfert* transfer speed

vitrine *nf Br* shop window, *Am* store window; **mettre des marchandises en vitrine** to display goods in the window

VMP *nfpl* FIN *(abrév* **valeurs mobilières de placement***)* marketable securities

voie *nf* (**a**) *(route)* way, road; **par voie aérienne** by air; **par voie ferrée** by rail; **par voie maritime** by sea; **par voie terrestre** by land, overland

(**b**) ADMIN *la voie hiérarchique* the official channels; **suivre la voie hiérarchique** to go through the official channels

(**c**) FIN **voies et moyens** ways and means

(**d**) *(cours)* **en voie d'achèvement** nearing completion

(**e**) JUR *voie de droit* recourse to legal proceedings; *voie de recours* grounds for appeal (to a higher court)

(**f**) ORDINAT *voie d'accès* path; *voie de transmission de données* data link

voiture *nf* (**a**) *(automobile)* car ❑ *voiture de fonction* company car; *voiture de livraison* delivery van; *voiture de location, voiture de louage* rented car, *Br* hire car; *voiture de luxe* de luxe car; *voiture d'occasion* secondhand car, used car; *voiture de société* company car (**b**) *(wagon) Br* coach, *Am* car

voix *nf* (individual) vote; **donner sa voix à qn** to vote for sb; **mettre une question aux voix** to put a question to the vote, to take a vote on a question ❑ *voix prépondérante* casting vote

vol *nm* flight ❑ *vol direct* direct flight; *vol avec escale* flight with stopover

volant, -e **1** *adj (personnel)* mobile
2 *nm* (**a**) FIN, ÉCON reserve ❑ *volant de sécurité* reserve fund; *volant de trésorerie* cash reserve (**b**) *(de carnet)* tear-off portion; **talon et volant** *(de chèque)* counterfoil and leaf

volatil, -e *adj* BOURSE *(option)* volatile

volatilité *nf* BOURSE *(d'une option)* volatility

volet *nm (d'un chèque)* tear-off portion; *(d'un document)* section

volontaire *adj (liquidation)* voluntary

volonté *nf* **payable à volonté** payable on demand

volume *nm* volume ❑ *volume d'achat* purchase volume; *volume d'activité* volume *or* level of activity; *volume d'affaires* trading volume; *volume annuel de production* annual (volume of) production; *volume des échanges commerciaux* volume of trade; *volume des exportations* volume of exports; *volume des importations* volume of imports; *volume de la production courante* volume of current output; *volume des ventes* sales volume, volume of sales

> L'organisation du travail taylorienne et fordienne apparaît de plus en plus rigide face à la variabilité de la demande quant à son **volume**.

votant, -e *nm,f* voter

vote *nm* vote; **déclarer le résultat d'un vote** to declare the result of the voting; **prendre part au vote** to vote, to take part in the voting ❑ *vote de confiance* vote of confidence; *vote par correspondance* postal vote; *vote de défiance* vote of no confidence; *vote majoritaire* majority vote

voter **1** *vt (crédit)* to vote; *(loi)* to pass; *(projet de loi)* to vote for
2 *vi* to vote; **voter à main levée** to vote by a show of hands; **voter par procuration** to vote by proxy

voyage *nm* journey, trip ❑ *voyage d'affaires* business trip

voyager *vi* (**a**) *(personne)* to travel; **voyager pour affaires** to travel on business; **voyager pour une maison de commerce** to represent a firm (**b**) *(marchandises)* to be transported; **le vin voyage mal** wine doesn't travel well

voyageur, -euse *nm,f* traveller; *(passager)* passenger ◻ *voyageur de commerce, voyageur représentant placier* sales representative

voyagiste *nm* tour operator

VPC *nf* (*abrév* **vente par correspondance**) mail order selling

vrac *nm* **en vrac** *(marchandises)* loose; *(cargaison)* bulk; **faire le vrac, transporter le vrac** to transport goods in bulk

vracquier *nm* bulk carrier

VRAM *nf* ORDINAT (*abrév* **video random access memory**) VRAM

VRC *nf* MKTG (*abrév* **vente par réseau coopté**) MLM, multilevel marketing

V/Réf (*abrév* **votre référence**) your ref

VRP *nm* (*abrév* **voyageur représentant placier**) sales rep ◻ *VRP multicarte* freelance rep

vue *nf* (**a**) FIN **à sept jours de vue** seven days after sight (**b**) **en vue** on view; **mettre des marchandises bien en vue** to display goods prominently

W3 *nm* ORDINAT (*abrév* **World Wide Web**) WWW

wagon *nm* (**a**) *(de passagers) Br* carriage, *Am* car; *(de marchandises) Br* wagon, *Am* car ❏ *wagon frigorifique* refrigerated van; *wagon de marchandises Br* goods wagon, *Am* freight car (**b**) *(contenu) Br* wagonload, *Am* carload (**de** of)

warrant *nm* (warehouse) warrant ❏ *warrant hôtelier* hotel warrant; *warrant industriel* industrial warrant; *warrant en marchandises* produce warrant

warrantage *nm* issuing of a warehouse warrant

warranté, -e *adj* covered by a warehouse warrant

warranter *vt* to issue a warehouse warrant for

Web *nm* ORDINAT **le Web** the Web

Webmaître, Webmaster, Webmestre *nm* ORDINAT Web master

World Wide Web *nm* ORDINAT **le World Wide Web** the World Wide Web

WORM ORDINAT (*abrév* **write once read many times**) WORM

WWW *nm* ORDINAT (*abrév* **World Wide Web**) WWW

Wysiwyg *nm* ORDINAT WYSIWYG

yen *nm* yen

ZAC *nf* (*abrév* **zone d'aménagement concerté**) = area developed through cooperation between public and private sectors

ZAD *nf* (*abrév* **zone d'aménagement différé**) = zone for future development

ZEP *nf* (*abrév* **zone d'environnement protégé**) = environmentally protected zone

zéro *nm* zero; **tomber à zéro** *(action)* to fall to zero; **zéro défaut** zero defect

ZI *nf* (*abrév* **zone industrielle**) industrial estate

zinzin *nm Fam* FIN institutional investor

zipper *vt* ORDINAT to zip

zone *nf* (**a**) *(espace)* area, zone □ *zone d'aménagement concerté* = area developed through cooperation between public and private sectors; *zone d'aménagement différé* = zone for future development; *zone de développement* development area; *zone de développement d'entreprises* enterprise zone; *zone dollar* dollar area; *zone sous douane* customs zone; *zone d'environnement protégé* environmentally-protected zone; *zone euro* euro area; *zone franc* franc area; ÉCON *zone franche* free zone; *zone franchise* duty-free zone; *zone frontière* frontier zone; *zone industrielle* industrial estate *or* park; *zone de libre-échange* free-trade area; *zone monétaire* monetary area; *zone postale* postal area; *zone sterling* sterling area; MKTG *zone test* test area; ADMIN *zone à urbaniser en priorité* = priority development area

(**b**) ORDINAT *zone d'affichage* display area; *zone d'amorçage* boot sector; *zone de dialogue* dialogue box; *zone d'écriture* write area; *zone d'état* status box; *zone tampon* *(en mémoire)* (memory) buffer; *zone de travail* work area

(**c**) ADMIN *zone de salaire* wage zone *or* bracket

> **"**
>
> Notre association n'a pas de position officielle sur l'euro mais, avec la moitié de la production de nos membres exportée en Europe, notre entrée dans la **zone euro** améliorerait notre compétitivité et donnerait une nouvelle stabiblité au secteur.
>
> **"**

ZUP *nf* (*abrév* **zone à urbaniser en priorité**) = priority development area

SUPPLEMENT

Contents

*Please note that "business@harrap.eng" is **not** an e-mail address but simply a device to identify that this supplement is for English speakers.*

Remarque: "business@harrap.eng" est une adresse électronique factice dont le rôle est d'indiquer à l'utilisateur du dictionnaire qu'il s'agit du supplément destiné aux anglophones.

business@harrap.eng

DOING BUSINESS ON THE INTERNET

A guide to using the Internet as a business tool, with special reference to French

by Bob Norton and Cathy Smith

Bob Norton is Head of Information Services at the Institute of Management in Corby, England. Cathy Smith is Systems Controller in the Institute's Management Information Centre. They are responsible for managing the Institute's approach to the Internet and putting up its pages on the World Wide Web. Both have written widely on information management and are authors of the book *Understanding Business on the Internet.*

Contents

business@harrap.eng

1: INTRODUCING THE INTERNET

What is the Internet?

The Internet is an open, worldwide network of computer networks interconnected through a mix of private and public telephone lines. The individual networks are owned by various organizations, including government agencies, universities, commercial companies and voluntary bodies, all of which have decided to allow others to connect to their computers often referred to as servers – to share their information.

The most widely used Internet function is e-mail – an alternative to post, telephone and fax. Another is the Newsgroups and Discussion Lists which enable people who are remote from each other to come together on the Internet to debate common interests. The function which has captured the imagination is the World Wide Web, a program which links and retrieves data of all kinds, in various forms, such as text, graphics, video and sound, from the interconnected computers.

There is no one single owner of the Internet. The nearest thing to a governing body is a number of voluntary organizations such as The Internet Society or The Internet Engineering Taskforce, although neither of these bodies exercises control in a regulatory or legislative sense.

How did it start?

The origins of the Internet are in the Cold War in the early 1960s when the US government was searching for an effective communications system in the event of a nuclear attack. The theory was that if vital information was all held in one location, and that location was destroyed, the US defensive capability would be severely damaged. The Rand Corporation proposed that a decentralised network would continue to work even if some of its components were knocked out. Furthermore, information would be routed around the network, not as a complete package, but split into discrete packets that would find their own way through the network and re-assemble at the destination address.

In 1969 ARPANET was formed to put this theory into practice. It linked four universities together using high-speed transmission lines and modems, allowing government scientists and university researchers to communicate by e-mail. The fast telecommunications links proved successful, and other research organizations and companies in the USA and elsewhere began to connect up. The collective grouping became known as the Internet.

In the 1980s, large companies began to use the Internet for communication purposes, and in the 1990s, businesses of all kinds in countries all over the world began to get connected, as did individuals at home.

Recent estimates suggest that there are over 50 million subscribers in the USA, and that numbers are still rising rapidly. European usage is currently put at

business@harrap.eng

around 2-3% of all households. German usage is estimated to be higher than in the UK, where it is 3 million and rising, with Britain being closely followed by France, the Netherlands, Sweden, Italy and Spain. One estimate has suggested that there will be 250 million users by the year 2000; another that, at current growth rates, everyone on the planet will be connected up by the year 2003!

At the end of the 1990s, it is claimed that Internet traffic, particularly e-mail, is doubling every 100 days, and the World Wide Web is doubling in size every six months.

This massive growth in usage can be ascribed to four main factors:

- the convergence of the formerly separate technologies of computing and telecommunications
- the fall in the price, and rise in sales, of personal computers
- the discovery and promotion of the Internet by the media
- the growing user-friendliness of the Internet, especially the advent of the World Wide Web in 1993-4.

The early profile of the Internet user was that of a 35 year-old male described as literate and libertarian, believing in freedom of speech and the right of every group to be heard. By the mid 1990s this had changed to include the company manager, perhaps in his or her 40s, communicating with customers and suppliers in remote locations and using the Internet to search for and send information pertinent to the business.

Why is the Internet important?

There are tremendous benefits to be had in using the Internet for business: improved and cheaper communications, the opportunity to work more efficiently and effectively from a distance and the chance for companies of all sizes to promote themselves more easily and cheaply to a worldwide market.

In the early 1990s, however, many businesses fell for inflated promises of an effortless, electronic market where customers were there for the taking. Hype of another kind was fuelled by press articles creating fears that those who were not soon on the Internet would be out of touch and out of business.

Many companies jumped onto the Internet bandwagon, but they failed to look at the opportunity as a business project which, like any other, needed planning, resourcing, organizing and controlling. Many companies neglected to align and integrate their use of the Internet with their business needs and are now asking what they should do next to turn promise into reality, and how much resource they should put into their Internet operation.

Is the Internet just another passing fad, or is it something worthwhile which can improve the way we work and do business? The answer is that the Internet is here to stay, growing rapidly, and people's knowledge and use of it are becoming more sophisticated.

- The Internet is no longer the preserve of computer nerds. This is partly because the equipment you need – such as PC, modem and appropriate software – is increasingly being packaged as standard.

business@harrap.eng

- It offers an alternative, often a much cheaper alternative, to obtaining, sending, receiving and storing information by traditional methods. We are all in the information business now.

- Many companies – small and large – are experimenting on the Internet to explore new ways of doing business, including the way they manage their workforce, the way they interact with other organizations, the way they promote their products or services, and the way they buy and sell. Others are using it in a more limited way because they can see no direct return on their investment. The promise of an electronic market, however, is now being reinforced by the investment of major banks and some businesses are beginning to derive some bottom-line value. Recent figures suggest that $3 billion worth – and growing – of Internet business transactions are carried out annually in the USA alone.

- The Internet impacts on both our personal and business lives even if we do not use it, and is central to current debates on:
  - the impact of technological progress on business, government and society
  - new forms of marketing and building relationships with customers
  - the social implications of the information 'haves' and 'have-nots' as information becomes a tradeable commodity worldwide and knowledge becomes the key to competitive advantage
  - the legal ramifications of the transfer of information across national borders.

The opportunities – and problems – of the Internet are the subject of debate in the US Senate and the European Parliament as governments struggle to get to grips with the challenges that the Internet poses. The Internet is government business now.

The Internet is evolving very rapidly but it takes time and effort to investigate its promise. It involves new ways of thinking out how best to take advantage of it. There is, at present, little substance for saying that those who leave it late will be out of business, but they will have a lot of learning and catching up to do while others will have stolen a march. The Internet – and Internet-type technology – is foreseen by many to be *the* business medium of the future.

business@harrap.eng

Questions for Management

One of the most important factors is not to let the Internet dictate to your business; it is too easy to get carried away with the attraction of the technology rather than exploit it to help you. So it is important not to rush in, but keep key questions in mind.

Why use the Internet?

- A fear of getting left behind?
- To learn what it can offer?
- To explore its business potential?
- To assess what advantage it will offer our organization?

What are we trying to do on the Internet?

- Improve the external communications of the business?
- Search databases? Contact experts? Look at company and product information?
  - Exploit the marketing potential?
  - Gain a lead over the competition?
  - Deal better with existing customers, or attract new ones?

Who should be doing the Internet work?

- What Internet skills do we need?
- Should we hire new staff with Internet skills, or train ourselves and our staff to learn about the Internet and tackle it?
- Should we hire an expert consultant or contract the whole business out to a specialist?
- And when access is established, to whom shall we allow access?
- Who has the time to devote to the Internet?
- How do we make the time?

How should we set up access?

- Leased line, ISDN, or straightforward dial-up?
- How do we choose a service that provides us with the access that we need?

Communication

Electronic mail (e-mail) ["courrier électronique"] is the main use of the Internet with hundreds of millions of messages sent and received daily. Its huge appeal lies in its ease of use, its low cost to remote places (the price of a local call) and the facility to send electronic attachments (graphics, additional documents, even software) to text messages. E-mail overcomes time zone differences and inconvenience, as the recipient does not have to be "there" to receive it. One-to-many messaging is simple and cheap, and it enables you to exchange information with people unknown to you, through special interest groups, called *newsgroups* ["groupes de nouvelles"] or *discussion lists* ["groupes de discussions"].

An e-mail address usually takes this form:
    yourname@organizationname.organizationtype.countryoforigin
    e.g. jbloggs@inst-mgt.org.uk

Although there are many advantages to be gained, there are also several dangers to be aware of.

1. E-mail is not wholly secure, yet. Anyone can read and intercept your e-mail if they are determined to do so. Random surveys show that up to a quarter of the information packets, of which e-mail messages are composed, can fail to get to their destination, especially at peak periods when networks are heavily congested. Usually, in such cases, the messages are returned to the sender, so they are not actually lost.

2. E-mail is no guarantee of an immediate response. Some people prefer the telephone if information is needed for a deadline.

3. The ease and "friendliness" of e-mail might encourage off-the-cuff replies, which might be regretted later. This informality has generated a feeling that e-mail is an unreliable source, lacking permanence, possibly inaccurate, and not worthy of quoting. E-mail is in fact a form of publication, subject to the laws of libel and copyright. As such, e-mail should be treated in the same way as any other method of committing thoughts to print.

4. File attachments to e-mail can contain viruses. The problem is that it is difficult to know whether an attachment is "infected" or not until it is opened. Given that a virus can wreck the information stored on your computer, some organizations virus-check all attachments before opening them; others ban attachments altogether.

If you are going to use e-mail in your organization, you need to address some policy considerations such as:

1. Reducing the potential for inappropriate use, time-wasting and information overload.
2. Reaction—is e-mail to be regarded as more "urgent" than other forms of communications, and if so, how is it to be handled?
3. Responsibility for content—given the power of e-mail to reach so many so quickly and so cheaply.

Information Searching and Gathering

Information is available on a myriad of topics, in a variety of forms, and largely free of charge, on the *World Wide Web* (WWW) ["le Web"]. This is an application which allows users to view Web sites ["sites Web"]—collections of files of text, graphics and other media—by means of a *browser* ["navigateur"] (a piece of software that sits on your PC) and move to other files by means of links established between them. These links are referred to as *hyperlinks* ["liens hypertexte"]. Each Web site has an address, known as a *Uniform Resource Locator* or *URL* ["adresse URL"]. For example, http://www.renault.fr

business@harrap.eng

http://stands for HyperText Transfer Protocol; www.renault.fr gives us the name of the server and of the organization and the country code—in this case, France.

Figure 1: Renault's Home Page in French and English
(of their corporate site www.renault.com)

Every site has an entrance hall or main menu and this is known as the *home page* ["page d'accueil"]. Most addresses which you will see quoted are for the home page but some lead you to a specific section of a site. The part of the address which contains the name of the organization and the country code is referred to as the *domain name* ["nom de domaine"], such as renault.fr

There are hundreds of thousands of sites of interest to business. Start with a site like The Institute of Management's Management Link at (http://www.inst-mgt.org.uk/external/mgt-link.html) which provides a list of, and links to, a wide selection of management and other business-related sites.

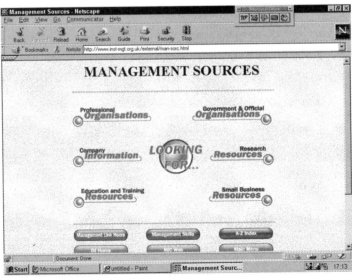

Figures 2 and 3: The Management Link is divided into Skills and Sources. Figure 2 looks at the options for sources, and Figure 3, some of the sites which enable you to explore company information in the UK

business@harrap.eng

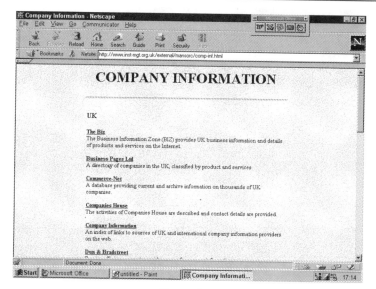

Figure 3

One of the most reliable ways to gather your own information is to pick it up by word of mouth, or tips in the press. Both major browsers (Netscape and Microsoft Internet Explorer) allow you to store frequently used addresses in their respective Bookmarks and Favorites options. If you don't know the address then the next best option is to use one of the many search tools which exist on the Web. Some of these are called directories which are constructed by people who select and apply index terms; others, called search engines, are software programs which trawl the Web at regular intervals for new information.

It is important to remember that you risk retrieving hundreds, maybe thousands, of information items (referred to as *hits* ["hits", "contacts de page"]) simply because the Web is so vast and the search tools often do not distinguish between valuable, worthwhile information and trivia. Many of the search tools classify their information into categories such as business, sport, arts, current affairs, recreation, but be as specific as you can when typing in information requests.

Here are a few of the Web search tools:

> Yahoo - (http://www.yahoo.fr) or (http://www.yahoo.co.uk)
> Excite - (http://www.excite.fr) or (http://www.excite.co.uk)
> Altavista - (http://www.altavista.com)
> > AltaVista allows you to search for documents in English, French and many other languages.
> Ecila - (http://ecila.ceic.com)
> Eureka - (http://www.eureka-fr.com)
> Lokace - (http://lokace.iplus.fr)
> Francite - (http://francite.com)

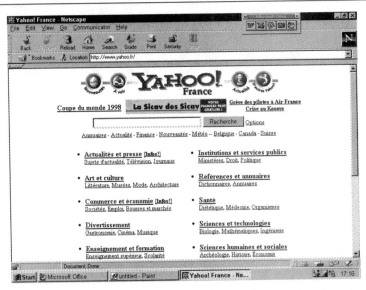

Figure 4: The French version of Yahoo, and some of the main categories for information seaching

Marketing

Just as the Web is a source of information, it is also an arena for individuals and organizations to market their goods and services. Flowers, books and computer software have been early success stories. The WWW is a great leveller: the small business can stand alongside the large. Some marketing is very professional, other attempts are amateurish but all are experimental.

The Web is an interactive medium where the potential consumer chooses where they visit, when and for how long. It is open 24 hours a day, seven days a week and a Web site may receive visitors as easily from the other side of the world as from the person next-door.

Marketing on the WWW can be achieved by taking out advertisements on others' Web sites. These appear in various forms:

- *Banners*: small rectangular graphics like roadside billboards. Once static, they are becoming increasingly animated and interactive.

- *Buttons*: similar to banners, but usually contain a corporate name, the brand, or even the industry. A click on the button will take you to the appropriate Web site.

- *Keywords*: here advertisers can "buy" a term! For example, if Moët-Chandon were to buy the term "champagne', any time that someone does a search for "champagne" on a particular search engine, the name Moët-Chandon will pop up.

Marketing is primarily being tackled by building your own site. The success of a Web site will depend on how attractive it is, how easy it is to find useful information, and how often the site is updated to offer the customer something new. Because the WWW is interactive it can offer great opportunities for discovering customer likes and dislikes and building up relationships. We look at designing a Web site in the next section.

business@harrap.eng

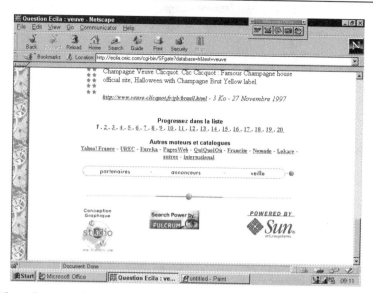

Figure 5: These 'button' advertisements are located at the foot of Ecila's Home Page. They have been paid by those companies to provide a direct link to their corporate Web site. Look back to Figure 4 for an example of a 'banner' advertisement on Le Sicav.

Gaining Access to the Internet

There are basically two ways you can connect to the Internet:

Dial-up
Dial-up access requires a modem attached to your PC and a telephone line. You also need an account with a commercial Internet Access Provider ["fournisseur d'accès Internet"]. Dial-up requires no major capital outlay and is therefore good for home use and for experimentation at work. On the other hand, it can be slow, especially at peak periods when the Internet is used by millions of people all over the world.

Increasingly, many businesses are installing ISDN (Integrated Services Digital Network) to provide faster and better-quality access than the existing telephone lines. It is more expensive but cheaper than leased lines (see below) and costs are falling.

An efficient Internet connection depends on the whole chain which links the two computers — the power of the sending and receiving computers, the speed of the modem and the capacity of the telephone lines.

Leased line
A leased line is a physical cable, providing a fast and permanent connection to the Internet. This connection may be directly to one of the backbone networks on the Internet or made via an Internet Access Provider. A leased line is a much more expensive option than dial-up and is perhaps more suitable for those intending to use the Internet extensively for a number of functions.

business@harrap.eng

3: A CHECKLIST FOR DESIGNING A WEB SITE

1. Decide what you want to achieve

Is your Web site to be:

- A way of attracting new customers?
- A public relations statement?
- A means of providing a service?
- An experiment?

Ask what benefits you expect from a Web site bearing in mind how much time, money, technical and human resource you are going to invest in it. Ask too how you will measure success. You will need to analyse information about who visits your site and what pages they look at.

2. Choose how to host your Web site

Renting space on a computer run by an Internet Access Provider has become an established method of setting up on the Web. Most Internet Access Providers offer some free disk space to start up and experiment with as part of their package. This often provides a cheap and low-risk option. When you identify your Internet Access Provider, remember to ask questions concerning developments for your site, usage reports and commercial transactions.

External design consultants will also usually host your site but they will expect you to buy their design services.

Many large organizations host their Web site on their own server. This requires a significant investment in hardware and software as well as considerable technical knowledge and skill.

3. Consider whether site design should be outsourced or kept in-house

Outsourcing design to a specialist should result in a professional site. Find out what work they have already accomplished and how successful it was. Think about whether you want to update and maintain the site yourself or hand that work over too. Outsourcing is not necessarily a cheap option and involves a considerable amount of time and effort in explaining your business to the outsider.

In-house development may also be costly depending on whether you bring in specialist staff, or spend time and money on the training and development of your own. If you are building an extensive site in-house, you may need to bring in an experienced Webmaster ("webmestre"). A *Webmaster* is responsible for the design, development and maintenance of a site in both the technical and content aspects. This requires a rare combination of IT, information, design and interpersonal skills.

4. Register your domain name

Your domain name is one of the first things by which people identify you. Choose a domain name that reflects your usual business or trading name. It needs to be registered before you can use it, although your first choice may have already been taken. Your Internet Access Provider will register your domain name for you for a nominal extra charge. Domain names are registered with the following organizations:

- The UK: Nominet (http://www.nic.uk).

- The USA: Internic (http://www.internic.net).

- France: AFNIC—Association Francaise pour le Nommage Internet en Cooperation (http://www.nic.fr)

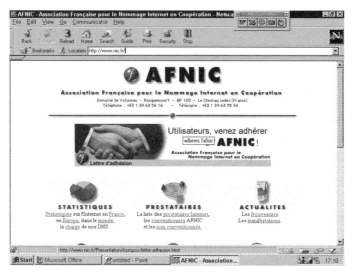

Figure 6: AFNIC's Home Page

5. Think about the layout of your site

When constructing your site you need to think about:

- Design—how will you convey the image you wish to project?

- Navigation around the site—how many mouse-clicks will it take to find something of interest?

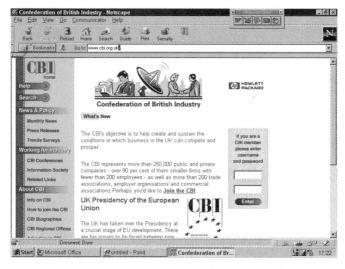

Figure 7: Home Page of the Confederation of British Industry

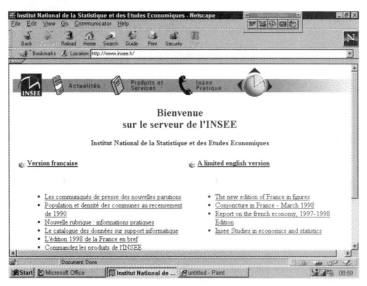

Figure 8: Home Page of the Insitut National de la Statistique et des Etudes Economiques

Look at the Web sites of other organizations, decide what you like and don't like and ask the opinions of potential users to get on the right track. Their view of a helpful layout may differ from yours.

6. Consider the content of the site

How will you try to get visitors to delve deeper into the site?

- Posting up answers to frequently asked questions on your products or services?

- Providing value-added snippets of information?

- Keeping the site fresh and up-to-date?

A moderate use of colour and graphics can greatly enhance the attractiveness of your site. But their over-use can make your site time-consuming to use. Some Web sites offer the alternative of a text-only version, just as others wishing to attract an international clientele, offer alternative language versions. If you want to use video and sound, remember that some users may not have the facilities to take advantage of them.

Although the cost of disc space is very low, information overload for Web users is already a problem. Think of how *you* like to read and absorb new information, perhaps with plenty of white space on the page/screen, in clear, concise and simple-to-understand language. Keep things brief and to-the-point with no long, rambling sentences. Don't be like some Web site producers who think that quantity not quality is the key.

7. Plan related hyperlinks and gateways

Hyperlinks will form the foundation of your site with links from one document to another. It is also useful to point users to other sites which might be of interest to them. These will usually be sites that give more information on a particular topic or cover a complementary activity to which you may want to refer. (See the example of Management Link in the previous section.)

business@harrap.eng

8. Plan to get the customer involved

Enable your Web site visitors to: offer comments, suggestions or criticisms; take part in product design or testing; get involved in interactive sessions for product or service improvement.

Remember that anything more demanding than straightforward e-mail replies requires fairly sophisticated design and programming.

9. Consider security issues

Unless you protect it, information that you put on the Web is for public consumption by a worldwide market. It is virtually impossible to follow and police what might happen to your information once it is downloaded to any of the 60+ million computers linked up, notwithstanding international laws on copyright.

If there are sections of your Web site that you would wish to secure for some categories of user or customer only, then form a closed user group to which only password-holders are allowed access.

If you wish your Web site to link to extremely sensitive information to which access must be even more strictly controlled, for example your customer database, then it is becoming standard practice to protect such information from abuse with a firewall ("mur coupe-feu"). A *firewall* is another computer through which all access traffic is routed and vetted. Anything that does not meet access criteria can be shut out.

10. Promote the site

Unless people know your address — your URL — they will find you in one of a number of ways:

- They will visit your site as a result of a hypertext link from another

- They will use one of the search engines to find you

- Word of mouth recommendation

- They will have seen some of your advertising

- It will be by chance.

It is important that the Search Engines pick up your site. Your Home Page is the principal page that search engines will use for indexing your site and therefore it needs to contain the important concepts and terms that people may use to find you. These may be apparent to the user or hidden away where only the search engines will find them.

Your Web site will also need promotion through more traditional media such as business cards, marketing literature, company reports or press or media campaigns. Remember though that the Web is about marketing, so be wary about using one marketing medium to market another. The real trick to a successful Web site is not how much you promote it but in the value that visitors / customers can derive from it. It will then promote itself.

business@harrap.eng

4: BUYING AND SELLING ON THE INTERNET

In the mid 1990s, President Clinton declared that the Internet was going to turn into 'a global free-trade zone' which would provide a safe environment for people to do business. This was against the background of various forecasts, one of which put Internet turnover at some $1 trillion by the year 2010. Other forecasts have been less ambitious, but most agree that by the year 2001, the Internet will be handling up to $300 billion in gross turnover world-wide, with over $200 billion in the USA, and over $60 billion in Europe (Forrester Research).

Many business people, however, remain sceptical about buying and selling over the Internet, because:

- The Internet can still be a confusing arena for all but the informed and the patient. It can take time to find the information, or results, that you want. Some Web sites contain time-consuming graphics to come through, and some have links that don't work because the 'site is still under development'. Over-congested networks can cause delays and, on occasions, overload can lead to breakdown.

- Early experimentation showed that consumers were reluctant to shop on the Internet. They could not try the goods out by seeing, touching, or tasting, and they missed the social aspect of actually 'being there'.

- Consumers have been hesitant to give their credit card number over the Web. The problem is one of knowing that the seller really is who they say they are, and that your credit card number is not disappearing into a black hole, or into the hands of a fraudster. Trading on the Web depends on the verification and authentication of buyer and seller.

- Not all items are suitable for selling on the Internet. It is far easier to sell information products and services than hard goods. This is due—in part—to the nature of distribution. At the moment, the Web is benefiting those industries which are information-rich like books, music and software, which don't rely on the sense of touch and feel, and which are closest to mail-order.

This picture, however, is changing rapidly because:

- The Web is becoming more professional with the presence of household names and with marketers waking up to the idea that marketing must be tailored to specific groups as in other media. More and more people are using the Internet and are becoming more comfortable with it. Consumers will get better at knowing which sites they want to visit and what they will find when they get there. Web sites are beginning to add value beyond what consumers can find in the terrestrial shopping world.

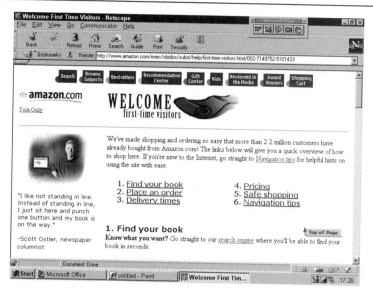

Figure 9: The Amazon Internet Bookshop claims to be the biggest bookshop in the world. This screen offers advice to those using the site for the first time, especially those with worries about paying over the Web.

- Telecommunications are improving and costs are falling as the Internet infrastructure develops. Internet2, with data transmission potential 1,000 times faster than at present, is already being trialled at American Universities.

- Financial institutions world-wide have invested heavily in electronic payment systems. Most major credit card companies in Europe and the USA, including VISA and MasterCard are working with software houses to finalise secure payment systems. The infrastructure for such trading is still expensive but prices will fall as more companies take it up and the banks recoup their investment.

- The Internet can offer greater efficiencies on traditional means of trading by offering a buying medium unconstrained by the barriers of time or place. If you can specify your own requirements for product modification, agree them, and negotiate over price and delivery all from your own back-yard, 24 hours a day, seven days a week, it is much quicker and cheaper for you and for the manufacturer.

Paying electronically

Progress towards full electronic commerce has been slowed by hackers who have broken the systems that promised confidentiality and security. Although these cases have been few and far between, they have nonetheless been rewarded by widespread publicity often out of all proportion to the actual seriousness of what happened.

E-cash

Many potential consumer transactions involve small and anonymous purchases, for example a newspaper or magazine, for which you would not normally use a credit card. For these small purchases, some innovative companies have been working with banks and software houses to devise a currency for the Internet—digital money—as safe and secure as the real thing.

business@harrap.eng

An e-cash account works quite simply. Customers open an account with an e-bank, such as First Virtual, DigiCash, or CyberCash, store their e-cash ("monnaie électronique") on their hard disk or in the bank's computer and use a pass code to authorise payment of goods.

There are comparatively few takers as yet and most of those are the individuals and shops involved in the controlled trials. Perhaps people expect low-cost information to be free—especially on the Web—or they do not like to pay-as-you-go, even for small amounts. Other possible reasons for the slow take-up of e-cash is the failure to publicise such schemes, and consumers' continuing reluctance to shop online.

Credit Card Payments and Encryption

Encryption ("cryptage") is perhaps the most promising way of making credit card payments secure. It is certainly the one which has attracted the most publicity, and investment. Encryption is the term used for scrambling messages so that only the intended recipient can decode and read them.

Visa and MasterCard have collaborated on an encryption technology, Secure Electronic Transaction (SET), that promises to make credit card payments safer than they are in the real world. SET, it is claimed, offers virtually uncrackable encryption. It requires both sender and recipient to have software supplied by the card issuer to prove to each other that they are who they claim to be. SET then verifies that the retailer is qualified to take credit cards and shields the card numbers from the retailer, keeping them coded all the way to the bank, thus providing the security and authentication that buyer and seller require of each other.

An icon representing a golden key or golden padlock should appear in the bottom left of your browser screen. When this symbol is solid—not broken—it indicates that any credit card information supplied will be encrypted. Only the authorised merchant or bank will have the key to unlock the figures at the other end.

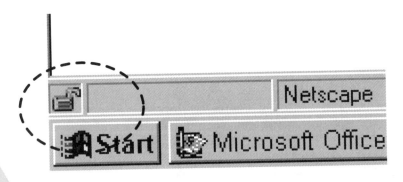

Figure 10: The icon representing an open padlock in a site
that does not support encryption.

It is estimated that some 80% of European banks will offer a full Internet banking service by the year 2000, although electronic trading still needs the boost of public trust and confidence to carry it beyond the pioneer stage into widespread practice.

business@harrap.eng

A Strategy for Buying and Selling on the Web

With a growing number of organizations demonstrating different ways and means of making money on the Web, and with banks on the point of assuring safe and secure payment transactions, how do we go about selling, and buying, on the Web?

- Find out about your customers' preferences for payment along with their buying habits. Find out whether or not they are gearing up for trading on the Web.

- Determine whether or not your products or services are suitable for electronic transactions and mail-order. If not, remember that many firms are winning business from unexpected quarters because their site offers a shop-window to customers who would normally not come across their products.

- Find out whether you can afford the infrastructure necessary for electronic trading. This is particularly important where individual sales are of low value. Keep an eye on these costs as they are likely to drop.

- Look at other sites. The end of the 1990s is witnessing a new wave of initiatives heralding the beginnings of electronic commerce. Innovative organizations are exploring new kinds of interactivity with customers, making sites which were fresh two years ago, now seem cumbersome and dated.

- If you decide to go down the trading route think about the tactics you will need to create a shopping community. Think about how you can reassure your customers that electronic transactions are safe. If there is any doubt, then perhaps you should think twice, or provide customers with a warning that it is better to pay via traditional methods.

- Talk to your bank and your Internet Service Provider about their plans for electronic trading and how they can help you. Without their support and advice, it is probably better to stick to a shop-window, whether selling or buying.

The laws and codes of practice laying down what you can and cannot do in the real world apply just as much to the Internet, even though they may be difficult to interpret and enforce. In particular, a company setting up a Web site should examine legislation applying to misleading advertising, sellers' obligations, buyers' rights and the ownership of information. Depending on the sophistication of your site, the services of a lawyer may be appropriate.

Advertising and Selling

An organization putting information on the Web for marketing and advertising purposes has a duty to respect standard advertising practice, and ensure that the content of their information is accurate and up-to-date. This is because it is in their interests to make the Web a place where consumers can shop in confidence.

As a general rule, Web advertisements are subject to the laws and regulations of the country where the site is accessed. This can lead to liability under local law. Virgin Atlantic Airways was fined under United States advertising regulations for offering out-of-date price information on its Web site. In 1996, a US court held one Italian company to be infringing a US trademark, simply by offering access to its Web site to Americans.

The codes and standards of the Advertising Standards Authority (ASA) in the United Kingdom, and of the Bureau de Vérification de Publicité (BVP) in France, apply equally to the Web and to traditional media. They are not legally binding but most organizations which breach such codes are willing to toe the line when challenged. Further sanctions exist in the form of legislation, in the UK, with the *Control of Misleading Advertisements Regulations 1988*, which enables the Office of Fair Trading to take action against anyone publishing a misleading advertisement. As more and more organizations use the Web to advertise, the issue of regulations continues to be debated.

Consumer Protection

In the European Union, buyers are protected under the Brussels convention in dealings with companies based in other countries of the EU. Although the onus of proof is on the customer, a European Union citizen can take action in any EU country against a company situated in any other member state. Currently, anyone buying within the EU from a country outside it has no real consumer protection.

The European Distance Selling Directive, adopted by the European Commission in February 1997, is likely to come into effect before the year 2000. It will require all Web vendors to ensure that their terms and conditions for trading are easily accessible on screen. These terms and conditions will have to state under which country's legal jurisdiction the sale is made. Other information which must be provided will include:

- the seller's name and address

- detailed information about the product

- arrangements for delivery and payment

- time of delivery and what happens if delivery is late

- who bears the risk if the product is lost or damaged.

For some products – excluding information-rich products such as software or electronic magazines – the customer will have the right to withdraw from any sales contract within one week. If there is a risk of difficulty in meeting stated delivery terms, sellers may be advised to make it clear on the Web site that the company is not making an offer to supply goods, but rather an invitation to the customer to make an offer to purchase.

Taxation

Tax laws are based on geography – where the company is located, or doing business, and on the products and services being sold. But the Internet is changing one's conception of geography – it transcends space and time – and one's notion of a product or service – no longer something you can always touch and feel.

Tax laws are also based on a distinction between goods and services. But if the Internet is also the medium for delivering the product, such as downloading a film, music or a book, then distinctions between goods and services are not so easy to apply. The problem intensifies with cross-border trade and differing applications of purchase or value added tax.

At present, however, both EU and US officials believe that the Internet should be a customs-free zone. If the World Trade Organization agrees, all levies on electronic transmissions will disappear.

Alternatively a 'bit tax', under which each electronic transmission—fax, phone call, e-mail—is logged and taxed, might be the answer. A bit tax, applying to each digital unit sent over the Internet, irrespective of its content, would mean a shift away from value-added tax to one based purely on the quantity of data transmitted.

Copyright

Technological developments have now far outstripped the capacity of copyright legislation to protect intellectual property. This issue continues to stretch the legislative bodies of the EU and of the US Senate as the focus of copyright embraces document transmission as well as reproduction.

As soon as any intellectual property—be it text, images, graphs, video or music—is available through the Internet, then any monetary value attached to it is at risk. When a customer pays for and receives a document on the Internet, it is only copyright law that stands in the way of instant reproduction or modification. An electronic document can be re-transmitted to hundreds or thousands of others via e-mail or a Web site. Copyright transgressions are hard enough to monitor and control in the real world; on the Internet, it is virtually impossible to enforce copyright law without relying on 'good citizenship' to help the aggrieved party.

Although we tend to think of publishing as being about material published in books and magazines, don't take too narrow a view. Anyone who sends an e-mail or puts information on a Web site can be considered to be publishing; so, if it's not your information, you should not use it without permission.

Some have said that the Internet will bring about a massive change to copyright legislation, others that the force of copyright itself will influence the nature of business on the Internet. It is not yet certain what the outcome will be.

Privacy of the Individual

While copyright protects others' intellectual property, the Data Protection Act came into force in the UK in 1984 to provide rights to people about whom personal information is held on others' computers (although the Act is being amended to include personal information held *in all forms*, not just that held on computer). The Act requires those who record and use data about individuals to be open about that use and follow practice laid down by the Data Protection Registrar. In 1998, a European Directive on Data Protection reinforced a personal information safeguards throughout the EU. One of the impacts will be to apply data protection principles to information being transferred outside the EU, even within the same organization.

One of the great advantages of the Web is that site owners can track what customers look at, buy or reject. This is possible because when you visit an Internet site, you leave your own Internet address as a calling-card. This is known as address logging, and some view it as an invasion of privacy. It is, however, fundamental to the way the Internet works; a visitor's domain name has to be known by the host site, otherwise it would not know where to direct any information requested. Information can also be collected in other ways, including visitor registration forms, and, more controversially, cookies.

A *cookie* is a piece of information that a Web site can send out which can be unknowingly stored on your hard drive. It can pick up information on your Internet habits and activities and be collected by the Web site sender at a later date. Some browsers can be configured to alert you to the arrival of a cookie and there are also programs—such as Cookie Crusher and Cookie Crumbler—which will automatically reject all cookies. Some Web site owners announce that theirs is a 'cookie-free' site.

A Framework for Global Electronic Commerce

In July 1997 in a proposal called *'A Framework for Global Electronic Commerce'*, President Clinton outlined the basic rules for international electronic commerce, including making the Internet a duty-free, untaxed zone for electronic buying and selling. The framework—tantamount to a written constitution for the Internet—consists of five principles and nine issues.

Principles

1. The private sector should lead.

2. Governments should avoid undue restrictions on electronic commerce.

business@harrap.eng

3. Where governmental involvement is needed, its aim should be to support and enforce a predictable, minimalist, consistent and simple legal environment for commerce.

4. Governments should recognise the unique qualities of the Internet.

5. Electronic commerce over the Internet should be facilitated on a global basis.

Issues

1. Customs and taxation

2. Electronic payment systems

3. 'Uniform Commercial Code' for electronic commerce

4. Intellectual property protection

5. Privacy

6. Security

7. Telecommunications infrastructure and information technology

8. Content: Advertising and Fraud

9. Technical standards.

The full recommendations are to be found in A Framework for Global Electronic Commerce, The White House, July 1, 1997, at:

http://www.ecommerce.gov.framewrk.htm

business@harrap.eng

6: DEVELOPING AN INTERNET STRATEGY

Developing a strategy for the Internet means assessing the Internet's weaknesses and opportunities, working out what you want to achieve and how best to tackle it, while appraising your own strengths and weaknesses. Strategic management has more do with how you achieve a vision for the future, than sticking to the present or past.

The Internet – its weaknesses

What we want to achieve will depend very much on the view we have formed of the Internet and on exactly what kind of prospects it holds for us.

The number of new users, the number of new Web pages, and spending on products and services all continue to grow at rates in excess of 100% per annum.

For many people, however, the Internet is at worst a non-event, shrouded in mystery, and at best characterized by anarchy and chaos. They point to:

- unregulated anarchy which allows pornography to side by side with respectable information
- information clutter and overload dominated by trivia
- slow response times with delays at popular access points
- much publicized breakdowns because of growing network congestion
- a rate of innovation which seems too rapid for most to keep up with
- a lack of hard evidence that money can be made from the Internet
- a preference for TV – cable or satellite – as a more digestible alternative to the inconsistencies and difficulties of the Web.

The Internet – its opportunities

Such a scenario ignores many influences and signs of progress, such as:

1. The continual growth and use of the Internet in all parts of the world.
2. Continuing technological developments, such as Internet2, offering solutions to business questions.
3. The investment made by major banks and software houses to develop the commercial side of the Web.
4. Early commercial successes that many organizations have enjoyed. The promotion, pump-priming and legislative efforts of national governments and two of the major trading powers – the EU and the US. The entrepreneurial and commercial spirit which will not accept yesterday's way of doing things as valid for tomorrow.

Furthermore, the positive scenario assumes that the Internet will become a reliable platform for conducting business as:

- Consumer purchasing confidence spreads as a result of secure payment systems.

- Adequate and effective protection is given to copyright information.

- Standards emerge from consortia of telecomms, software and trading companies.

- A mix of government subsidy, telecomms investment and consumer payment begins to pipe high performance telecommunications capability into the home and office.

- Private networks, which are more secure and robust, link up to the Internet for those customers willing to pay for premium services.

- Affordable market-based pricing for access and usage emerges.

- The Internet establishes its own identity—or identities—and becomes as integrated in social and business life as the Press and TV.

Models for business

There are currently a number of loose business models in evidence for the Internet:

1. The *Communications* Model using the Internet primarily to allow greater flexibility and efficiency through e-mail.

2. The *Advertising* Model – using the organization's Web site as a shop window, and paying for advertising banners on other sites and search engines.

3. The *Subscription* Model – offering unlimited access to a service or product, for example, a newspaper, magazine or current awareness updating service in return for payment of an annual sum. This third alternative assumes that people will pay for information on the Web. As yet, they generally seem reluctant to do so, however.

4. The *Niche Marketing* Model – packaging personalized information, news and entertainment services. Here, as a superior alternative to TV, the Web provides an experience for selected groups of people—communities— through its interactive, two-way capability.

5. The *Department Store* Model – setting up as a seller on the Web. This option sees the major obstacles to electronic commerce overcome, and confidence in online buying and selling widespread.

Ten strategic principles

1. Understand how the Internet works and what its potential is by experimenting with it, reading about it and discussing it with others.

2. Consider how the Internet can benefit your customers and keep your business moving forward. This means having a full understanding of your business and what it is trying to achieve.

3. Understand your audience—the profile of your best prospect is the profile of your best customer. Keep an eye on customer buying habits and the level of interactivity they are likely to want. Think about what customers most want to know about your organization and what you most want to know

about them. Think about how the Internet can add value to your services and products. This might lie in better information provision, alternative methods of distribution or more customization for individuals and groups.

4. Obtain commitment from senior management and involvement and interest from as many people as possible. You won't get anywhere by making the Internet a sideline that only a few know about and contribute to. Staff need time to feel their way and become familiar with the way the Internet works. Recognise that you will need technical, design and legal expertise. Decide how much resource you can, or are prepared, to put into the Internet.

5. Start small – getting started is more important than getting it perfect straightaway. Go for specific objectives. Look for early wins but not quick fixes. Identify who can help to achieve early success which demonstrates that change is working.

6. Expect your Web site to be a cost-centre. Don't just look for sales. Value also those activities which lead indirectly to sales, such as those which generate interest and enquiries from prospective clients.

7. Align and integrate your Internet activities with all the others you perform in the real world for the benefit of customers and staff alike.

8. Think about control policies and procedures which clarify:

• Who may access the Web and who may not, and why.

• What information may be imported from the Web into the organization's systems.

• Who has ownership and responsibility for information on the Web.

9. Monitor the effects of your Internet strategy. Look at the levels of e-mail and Web activity in the organization, the cost-savings in staff-time, direct or indirect income, and customer reaction.

10. Keep your Internet services adaptable, changing and moving forward. This means taking risks, keeping up with new technological developments and exploring new possibilities.

A final word – watch out for progress taking place in leaps and bounds. In September 1998, Dixons Stores, the giant UK retailer, broke all the newly established industry rules by offering subscription-free access to the Internet. With access getting cheaper, do try it out to see if it can offer a different perspective on how you work, even on what kind of work you do.

Table of Contents

business@harrap.eng

Introduction

Business correspondence in French, although more and more influenced by the Anglo-Saxon style, still tends to be rather formal, as will be seen in the examples that follow.

When sending a letter or other written communication, the appropriate terminology must be used and the grammar must be absolutely correct. Particular attention should be paid to spelling as this is a sensitive topic. French schoolchildren are trained in dictation in order to ensure that they attain proficiency in this area, and people who make spelling mistakes are considered badly educated. Some letters end up in the waste paper basket for this very reason!

The presentation of letters was extremely standardized in the past but with the influence of marketing and Anglo-Saxon business etiquette, writing conventions are somewhat less rigid than they used to be. Nevertheless the formal and extremely codified style of letter-writing in French is still the norm and is probably the one to use when in doubt.

The beginning and the end of letters written in French follow certain well-established rules. (see below)

Each paragraph should deal with one idea only. The idea is presented in the first sentence of the paragraph and is then developed. A new idea is expressed in a new paragraph.

Depending on what needs to be expressed, various grammatical modes and tenses are used and the conditional is particularly useful to make sure that the tone of the letter does not sound impolite.

Layout

- At the top of the letter, centred and usually already printed, the name of the company is given with its address, official registered number, phone number, fax number, e-mail address, and bank details.

- Underneath, on the right, appears the name and address of the addressee, and below that again, on the left, appear the reference numbers of both the sender and the addressee, followed on the next line by the name of the town from which the letter is sent and the date.

- Then comes the main body of the letter and the ending. At the bottom, on the right, the sender's signature appears with their job title typed above it and their name typed under it.

Beginning a letter

- To begin the letter, one uses the forms "Madame" (= Dear Madam), "Monsieur" (= Dear Sir) or "Mademoiselle" (for an unmarried young person). If the letter is addressed to a company rather than to an individual, one uses the plural form "Messieurs". In cases where one is unsure whether the recipient of the letter will be male or female, the form "Madame, Monsieur" (= Dear Sir or Madam) is used.

business@harrap.eng

- If the person to whom the letter is addressed is head of a company or institution, the form "Madame la Directrice/Monsieur le Directeur" may be used. When writing to the head of a specific department within a company (for example the head of the accounts department) one can write "Madame le Chef Comptable/Monsieur le Chef Comptable".

- If the correspondents are known to each other, and get on well or have a good working relationship, the slightly less formal style "Chère Madame/Cher Monsieur" – or, in the case of colleagues, "Chère collègue/Cher collègue" – may be used. In cases where the correspondents are actual friends, the letter can begin: "Cher ami/Chère amie".

Ending a letter

- It should be noted that the endings of French business letters are usually expressed in very formal language which may appear slightly florid or pompous to English speakers unused to the conventions of French correspondence. It must be remembered that this is all part of a "code" of politeness integral to French business etiquette. The ending of the letter will, of course, correspond in terms of form and tone to what was written at the beginning of the letter:

"Veuillez agréer (*or* Nous vous prions d'agréer), Madame la Directrice/ Monsieur le Directeur, nos salutations distinguées."

"Veuillez agréer (*or* Nous vous prions d'agréer), Madame la Directrice/ Monsieur le Directeur, l'expression de nos sentiments distingués."

If a supplier writes to a customer, the usual ending is: "Veuillez agréer, Madame/Monsieur, l'expression de nos sentiments dévoués."

- If the correspondents are friends, they may use: "Veuillez agréer, Cher ami, mes plus cordiales salutations"

However , due to the influence of other countries' more informal style of correspondence, French endings are becoming more simplified in some contexts. It is now possible to find the following types of ending:

"Salutations distinguées"

"Sentiments dévoués"

"Bien à vous"

and for friends: "Cordialement".

However, these more casual endings appear more often on faxes.

A. Letters, faxes, e-mails

Model letters
i. General layout and style – Ordering a catalogue

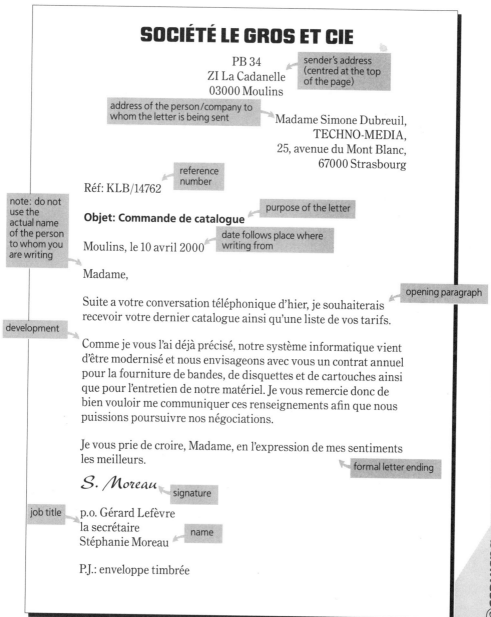

SOCIÉTÉ LE GROS ET CIE

PB 34
ZI La Cadanelle
03000 Moulins

sender's address (centred at the top of the page)

address of the person/company to whom the letter is being sent

Madame Simone Dubreuil,
TECHNO-MEDIA,
25, avenue du Mont Blanc,
67000 Strasbourg

reference number

Réf: KLB/14762

note: do not use the actual name of the person to whom you are writing

purpose of the letter

Objet: Commande de catalogue

date follows place where writing from

Moulins, le 10 avril 2000

Madame,

opening paragraph

Suite a votre conversation téléphonique d'hier, je souhaiterais recevoir votre dernier catalogue ainsi qu'une liste de vos tarifs.

development

Comme je vous l'ai déjà précisé, notre système informatique vient d'être modernisé et nous envisageons avec vous un contrat annuel pour la fourniture de bandes, de disquettes et de cartouches ainsi que pour l'entretien de notre matériel. Je vous remercie donc de bien vouloir me communiquer ces renseignements afin que nous puissions poursuivre nos négociations.

Je vous prie de croire, Madame, en l'expression de mes sentiments les meilleurs.

formal letter ending

S. Moreau

signature

job title

p.o. Gérard Lefèvre
la secrétaire
Stéphanie Moreau

name

P.J.: enveloppe timbrée

ii. Letter of inquiry and answer

Here are some typical beginnings of sentences:

Nous aimerions savoir... (We would like to know...)

Pourriez-vous nous communiquer...? (Could you let us have...?)

Avant de passer une commande, nous souhaiterions... (Before placing an order we would like...)

A typical letter of inquiry might be written as follows:

Monsieur,

Auriez-vous l'obligeance de bien vouloir nous envoyer votre dernier catalogue présentant les nouveaux produits de votre gamme NENUTAM?

> Note use of conditional tense to convey polite tone

Nous vous saurions gré de nous préciser également vos tarifs actuels ainsi que vos conditions et délais de livraison à l'étranger.

Veuillez agréer, Monsieur, l'expression de nos sentiments distingués.

Le Directeur
Jean Martin
Jean Martin

Answer

Basic phrases:

Nous accusons réception de votre lettre du... (We acknowledge receipt of your letter dated...)

Merci de l'intérêt que vous portez à... (Thank you for your interest in...)

Vous trouverez ci-joint... (We enclose...)

Monsieur,

Nous avons bien reçu votre demande de renseignements du 30 août au sujet de la gamme NENUTAM, présentée dans notre nouveau catalogue ci-joint. Monsieur François Dupont, notre directeur régional des ventes, vous contactera prochainement pour prendre rendez-vous et il sera en mesure de vous renseigner de manière plus détaillée et de vous conseiller sur les acquisitions que vous souhaiteriez faire. Nous sommes convaincus que la gamme NENUTAM conviendra parfaitement à vos besoins.

Nous vous prions d'agréer, Monsieur, l'expression de nos sentiments les meilleurs.

Le Directeur commercial

Jean-Pierre LeGoff

Jean-Pierre LeGoff

business@harrap.eng

iii. Order placed by a customer and answer

Basic phrases:

Veuillez nous faire parvenir... (Please forward...)

Nous vous passons commande de... (We enclose our order for...)

Veuillez trouver ci-joint notre bon de commande no... (Please find enclosed our order form no...)

Madame,

Suite à notre entretien téléphonique du 3 octobre dernier, nous vous confirmons notre commande de 300 mallettes de jeux, référence 12345.

Nous vous rappelons que ces articles doivent impérativement nous être parvenus pour le 15 novembre, les courses de Noël commençant de plus en plus tôt.

Nous vous prions de croire, Madame, à l'expression de nos sentiments distingués.

Jacques Dupont

Jacques Dupont
Directeur des achats

Answer

Monsieur,

Nous avons bien reçu votre commande du 9 octobre.

Nous avons le plaisir de vous informer que les 300 mallettes de jeux vous ont été expédiées ce jour selon vos instructions.

Nous vous rappelons que nos délais de livraison sont de 10 jours minimum et que si vous désirez un nouvel envoi avant Noël, il serait prudent de nous prévenir par fax.

Nous vous prions d'agréer, Monsieur, l'expression de nos sentiments dévoués.

Marie-Françoise Durand

Marie-Françoise Durand
Directrice des ventes

---

business@harrap.eng

If it is necessary to cancel or alter an order, one can use the following sentences:

Veuillez annuler la première partie de notre ordre (We must ask you to cancel the first part of our order)

Nous vous serions obligés de remettre la livraison à... (We would be obliged if you would delay delivery until...)

iv. Invoicing and payment

Basic phrases:

Veuillez trouver ci-joint la facture d'un montant de... (We enclose an invoice for...)

Veuillez nous faire parvenir un chèque... (Please send us a cheque...)

Nous vous avisons que nous avons donné l'ordre à notre banque de vous virer la somme restant due. (This is to advise you that our bank has been instructed to remit the sum left uncleared.)

Votre règlement a été crédité à notre compte. (Your remittance has been credited to our account.)

Messieurs,

Nous vous adressons votre relevé trimestriel pour la période du 1.1.99 au 30.03.99.

Nous vous serions obligés de bien vouloir nous couvrir de cette somme dans les meilleurs délais.

Veuillez agréer, Messieurs, nos salutations distinguées.

Le Chef comptable

Eric Leblanc

Eric Leblanc

---

v. Letter of complaint and answer

Here are a few useful phrases to help write a letter of complaint:

Il nous manque (deux caisses) (We are two cases short)

Nous sommes déçus de constater que... (We are disappointed that ...)

Nous vous retournons... (We are returning ...)

Madame,
Objet: Commande n° 2983   concise explanation of
nature of complaint

J'ai le regret de vous faire savoir qu'en ouvrant les colis que vous nous avez envoyés, nous nous sommes aperçus qu'il manquait 20 mallettes de jeux.

Cette situation nous plonge dans un profond embarras et nous vous prions d'effectuer immédiatement un nouvel envoi pour réparer l'erreur commise, faute de quoi nous serions obligés de nous adresser à un autre fournisseur.   demand for action

Nous vous prions de croire, Madame, à l'expression de nos sentiments distingués.

Le Directeur des Achats

Jacques Dupont

Jacques Dupont

Answer

Various sentences can be used as well such as:

Recevez nos excuses pour ce dérangement (Please accept our apologies for the inconvenience caused)

Nous avons pris des mesures pour que cela ne se reproduise plus (We have taken steps to ensure that this will not occur again)

Monsieur,   reference to letter of complaint

Dans votre lettre du 28 octobre, vous nous signalez un défaut de quantité dans notre livraison no 2983. Or, notre agent à Cherbourg qui a personnellement supervisé le chargement à bord du navire nous certifie que la quantité a bien été embarquée.

explanation   Nous considérons donc que nous ne pouvons être tenus pour responsables et qu'il s'agit
of cause of   probablement d'un vol qui a pu se produire en cours de transport ou lors du stockage au
problem   débarquement et nous vous conseillons de prendre contact avec votre assureur.

Nous vous prions d'agréer, Monsieur, l'expression de nos sentiments dévoués.

Marie-Françoise Durand

Marie-Françoise Durand

Directrice des Ventes

---

business@harrap.eng

vi. Mailing

When writing to clients, it is possible to use various terms of address.

The most common ones are: "Cher(s) client(s)/Chère(s) cliente(s)", "Cher Monsieur/Chère Madame" and – for example in the case of a newpaper or trade journal writing to a reader – "Cher Lecteur/Chère Lectrice".

> Cher client,
>
> En raison d'un changement dans notre politique des ventes, notre catalogue ne comportera plus de prix et ces derniers seront fournis sur demande.
>
> Sentiments dévoués
>
> La Direction

vii. Memo

The title of a French memo ("note de service") is usually centred. The purpose of the memo is outlined below the heading with specific indications like "pour affichage" (for circulation), "pour information" (for information) etc.

The sender, the recipient, the subject, the date and the signature are then mentioned successively.

viii. Faxes

Faxes, which are by definition a form of rapid communication, can generally be drafted in a more casual and concise way than letters.

When handwritten, the endings of faxes correspond to the short ones used for letters (see Introduction).

> **A l'attention de :** Nicolas Roche
>
> **Date :** mardi le 16 mai
>
> **Numéro de télécopie:** 01 40 92 97 35
>
> **De la part de:** Pierre Lenoir
>
> **Nombre de pages (y compris cette page) :** 1
>
> Message: La réunion a été reportée au lundi 24 juin. Nous nous chargeons de la réservation de votre billet d'avion ainsi que de votre chambre d'hôtel.
>
> Cordialement,
> P. Lenoir

ix. E-mails

- E-mail addresses are made up of two parts, the first being the user's name and the second being the domain name. The two parts are separated by the symbol

business@harrap.eng

@ (pronounced "arrobase" in French). It is important to type the exact address – get a single character wrong and the e-mail will not get through.

- Because of the nature of the medium, e-mails are not subject to the formal code of letter-writing that is prevalent in French.

- E-mail is becoming more and more widely used in the French working environment, although it is probably not yet as established a method of business correspondence as it is in English.

- E-mails in French are often written in a slightly less telegraphic style than tends to be the case in English, this being mainly due to the fact that French contains fewer of the abbreviated forms that characterize so much of this type of communication in English. Endings are usually rather informal.

- The same rules of "netiquette" apply as in English, so avoid typing entire words in capital letters as this is equivalent to shouting.

- Note that in the model e-mail below, the headings are in English as most French firms use American-manufactured software.

E-mail: abbreviations, acronyms and smileys

1. Abbreviations and acronyms

Below is a list of French abbreviations which are used in e-mail correspondence and in newsgroups. These abbreviations should only be used when you are sure that the person to whom you are sending the message understands what they mean. Some are familiar in register (labelled *Fam*) and therefore should only be used in casual correspondence with friends or very close colleagues.

Note that because English is the main language of the Internet, English abbreviations (see section in French supplement) are much more well established than French ones.

A+ *Fam*	à plus tard (see you/talk to you etc later)
actu *Fam*	actualités (news, current affairs)
alld	allemand (German)
alp *Fam*	à la prochaine (see you!; until we're next in touch!)

ama *Fam*	à mon avis (in my opinion)
amha *Fam*	à mon humble avis (in my humble opinion)
angl	anglais (English)
bcp *Fam*	beaucoup (a lot; many)
BAL	boîte à lettres (mailbox)
B.D.	base de données (database)
dc	donc (then, therefore)
doc.	documents (documents, documentation)
Doss	dossier (file)
ds	dans (in)
envoy.	envoyer (please send)
err	erreur (error)
esp	espagnol (Spanish)
ex.	exemple (example)
fr	français (French)
impr.	impression/imprimer/imprimante (printout; print; printer)
info *Fam*	information
K7 *Fam*	cassette
Ltr	lettre (letter)
m	même (even; same)
Mdr *Fam*	mort de rire (hilarious)
MMS *Fam*	mes meilleurs souvenirs (Best regards)
nvx	nouveaux (new)
p	pour (for)
pb, pbm	problème (problem)
pr	pour (for)
quoi 2/9	*Fam* quoi de neuf? (what's new?)
RAS *Fam*	rien à signaler (nothing to report)
suiv.	suivant (following)
svt	souvent (often)
urgt	urgent
we	weekend

2. Smileys

Smileys are becoming more and more a feature of e-mail correspondence: again, as with abbreviations, they are probably used more in English than in French, but it is worth illustrating some of the most common ones here. It must be remembered of course that these symbols should only ever appear in the context of casual correspondence.

:-)	Happy; I'm making a joke
:-(	Unhappy
;-)	Wink
:-o	Very surprised; shocked
:-ı	Frowning
:-\	Sceptical

Abbreviations and acronyms: general correspondence

ac	argent comptant; année courante; acompte (ready money; current year; on account)
AG	assemblée générale (General Meeting, GM)
arr.	arrondissement (district)

art	article (article)
AV	avis de virement (transfer advice)
bd	boulevard
BP	boîte postale (PO Box)
CA	chiffre d'affaires (turnover)
C&A	coût et assurance (cost and insurance, C and I)
c-à-d.	c'est-à-dire (that is to say)
CAF	coût, assurance, fret (cost, insurance and freight, cif)
c-c.	compte courant (current account)
CCP	compte chèque postal (post office account)
Cedex	courrier d'entreprise à distribution exceptionnelle (postal code for business mail)
Cie	compagnie (company)
cpt	comptant (cash)
CR	compte-rendu (minutes)
CV	curriculum vitae
Dépt	département (administrative subdivision of France)
Dest.	destinataire (recipient)
DRH	Directeur(trice) des Ressources Humaines (Human Resources Manager)
E.O.O.E	erreur ou omission exceptée (errors and omissions excepted)
esc.	escompte (discount)
Ets	établissements (factory; premises)
Exp.	expéditeur (sender)
Fres	Frères (brothers)
F.S.	faire suivre (please forward)
hon.	honorée (''favour''; letter)
HT	hors taxe (exclusive of tax)
id.	idem (ditto)
incl.	inclus (included)
j./jr(s)	jour(s) (day(s))
KF	kilofranc (thousand francs)
l/c	lettre de crédit (letter of credit)
LCR	lettre de change relevé (bills of exchange statement)
LJM	livraison le jour même (same-day delivery)
M	Monsieur (sir)
Me	Maître (title applied to lawyers)
Melle(s)	Mademoiselle/Mesdemoiselles (Miss(es))
MM.	Messieurs (Messrs.)
Mme	Madame (Madam)
Mon, Mson	maison (firm)
n.	notre, nos (our)
NB	Nota Bene
N°	numéro (number, No.)
N/Réf	notre référence (our ref)
p/c	pour compte
P.-D.G.	Président-Directeur Général (Chairman and Managing Director)
p.j.	pièce jointe (enclosure, enc)
PO	par ordre (by order)
p.p	par procuration (by proxy)
P.T.T.	Postes, Télégraphes et Téléphones (General Post Office)

réf	réference (reference, ref)
R.F.	République Française (French Republic)
r.p.	réponse payée (reply paid)
R.S.V.P.	répondez, s'il vous plaît (Please reply)
S.A.	Société Anonyme (Limited Company)
SARL	société à responsabilité limitée (limited (liability) company)
s.e. ou o.	sauf erreur(s) ou omission(s) (errors and omissions excepted)
SS	Sécurité Sociale (social security)
SVP	s'il vous plaît (please)
TEG	taux effectif global (annual percentage rate, APR)
Tél.	téléphone (telephone)
T.S.V.P.	tournez s'il vous plaît (please turn over, PTO)
v.	votre, vos (your)
Ve; Vve	veuve (widow)
V/Réf	votre référence (your ref)

A note on French postal addresses and post codes

- Sometimes in French addresses the forms "bis" and "ter" are used after the street number. For example:

3 bis, rue des Lilas
11 ter, avenue de Bernay

These indicate that there is more than one residence, whether in the form of another self-contained apartment or an annex to the main house or premises, at the address in question. "Bis" is used to indicate that there is a second residential (or business) unit, "ter" a third.

- With regard to the French system of post codes, the first two numbers of a given post code correspond to the administrative code number of the relevant "département" (see table with list of French départements and code numbers on page 65). Thus all postal codes for Paris begin with 75. This system also applies to vehicle licence plates. For example:

20, boulevard Arago, 75013 Paris

In the example above, the first two numbers indicate the city of Paris while the last two figures indicate that the address is located in the thirteenth "arrondissement" (district) of the city.

- The abbreviation **Cédex** is often found in French business addresses. For example:

Société Delacour, 77170 Fontainebleau Cédex

This is a special post code ensuring rapid delivery of mail to businesses and certain institutions. In these cases, the first two figures, as in other post codes, denote geographical location but the following three figures denote an individual code assigned to the company in question.

business@harrap.eng

B. CV and covering letter

i. CV

The CV must give precise information about educational qualifications, professional experience and career path. French CVs should be concise and where possible should fit onto one page. It is often customary to send a photograph, attached to the top right-hand corner of one's CV, when applying for jobs in France.

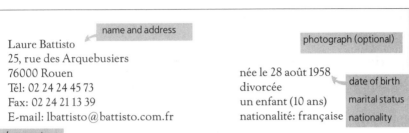

Laure Battisto
25, rue des Arquebusiers
76000 Rouen
Tél: 02 24 24 45 73
Fax: 02 24 21 13 39
E-mail: lbattisto@battisto.com.fr

name and address

photograph (optional)

née le 28 août 1958 — *date of birth*
divorcée
un enfant (10 ans) *marital status*
nationalité: française *nationality*

begin with one's current or most recent job and list one's previous jobs going back in chronological order

Consultante en Ressources Humaines
job title → **13 ans d'expérience**

- **Expérience professionnelle**

1991–1996	Consultante en Ressources Humaines, Cabinet Battisto-Langlade, Rouen: Conseil auprès d'entreprises, Audit, Recrutement
1987–1990	Directrice des Ressources Humaines, Conseil Général, Le Havre: Recrutement, Planification des formations, Suivi du personnel
1985–1986	Assistante du Directeur des Ressources Humaines, Société Pierre et Fils, Le Havre

- **Formation**

1983	Master of Business Administration, Boston University
1981–1982	DEA 'Langage et Médias' (Université de la Sorbonne, Paris III)
1980	Maîtrise d'Histoire (Paris)
1976	Baccalauréat Mathématiques (Lycée Claude Monet, 75015 Paris)

begin with one's most recent degree or qualification

- **Autres expériences**

1984–1985	Voyage en Afrique dans le cadre d'une mission Médecins Sans Frontières

- **Divers**

Bilingue anglais
Espagnol: lu, écrit, parlé
Bonne maîtrise du traitement de texte sur PC et sur Mac
Responsable d'une association bénévole luttant contre l'analphabétisme

mention knowledge of foreign languages (with degree of fluency), computer literacy, interests and activities etc

business@harrap.eng

ii. Covering letter

It is customary to handwrite the covering letter ("lettre manuscrite" = handwritten letter), as this adds a more personal touch and also because it is not unusual for French companies to use the services of graphologists who analyse applicants' handwriting. A letter of application is also quite formal in its presentation. It is short, structured in paragraphs and uses the standard beginning and end formulas. In your letter you should cover the following points:

- Enhance what you consider important in your CV
- Add information about your objectives
- Explain why you are interested in the company
- Convince the reader that you are the right person for the job.

Raoul Chesnier
24, rue d'Écosse
75005 Paris

tél: 01 40 92 97 35

Paris, le 8 novembre 1999

Société INFORAMA
128, boulevard de la Reine
78000 Versailles

Monsieur,

introductory paragraph mentioning where the applicant saw the vacancy advertised

Suite à l'annonce parue dans 'Le Monde' du 30 octobre 1999, j'ai l'honneur de poser ma candidature pour le poste d'analyste de systèmes.

outline of the applicant's current employment situation, qualifications and previous experience

Titulaire d'un diplôme de l'Institut de génie informatique et industriel de Lens, je travaille actuellement dans le service informatique d'une grande maison d'édition à Paris. Je dispose de plusieurs années d'expérience dans différentes entreprises d'informatique de la région parisienne. Je pense donc posséder l'expérience et les qualifications requises pour le poste que vous proposez, comme vous pourrez le constater au vu de mon CV. Je souhaite élargir mon expérience professionnelle tout en acquérant de nouvelles responsabilités et serais donc ravi d'intégrer une entreprise aussi dynamique et réputée que la vôtre.

referring to the information contained in the enclosed CV

indicating the applicant's availability for interview

Je me tiens à votre disposition pour un entretien éventuel, et vous prie d'agréer, Monsieur, l'expression de mes sentiments distingués.

conventional polite conclusion

R. Chesnier
Raoul Chesnier

P.J: un curriculum vitae avec photographie

C. Telephone calls

- When on the phone it is important to speak as clearly as possible to make sure that one is understood.

- Concentrate on the key words (date, place, time of appointment) and don't hesitate to ask the person to repeat what he/she says).

- Knowing the French alphabet and how to say figures may be useful if one needs to spell names or give numbers on the phone.

- When giving their phone numbers, French people say them two by two and you may have to ask them to repeat giving one number at a time:
01 45 67 44 32: zéro un, quarante-cinq, soixante-sept, quarante-quatre, trente-deux

Typical phrases

1. When you phone a company, the person who answers will typically say:
Déménagements Leclerc/Éditions Robinson *etc*, **bonjour** (good morning, Leclerc Removals, Robinsons *etc*)

It is your turn to speak:

Je voudrais parler à Monsieur Dupont (I'd like to speak to Mr. Dupont)

or **Pouvez-vous me passer le service du/des... s'il vous plaît?** (Could you put me through to..?)

or **le poste 321** (pronounced trois cent vingt-et-un) (extension 321)

2. The receptionist may ask you:
Qui dois-je annoncer? (Who's calling, please?)

Once you've given your name, the receptionist will try to connect you and will either say:

Je vous le passe/ne quittez pas, je vous le passe (Hold the line, I'm putting you through)

or if she can't, she will come back to you with messages like:

La ligne est occupée pour l'instant (The line's engaged at the moment)

or **Il est en communication, voulez-vous patienter** (He is on the line, will you hold?

3. If you choose to not stay on the line, she will say:
Voulez-vous lui laisser un message? (Can I take a message?/Would you like to leave a message?)

At that point you may want to ask for Mr. Dupont to phone back:

Pouvez-vous lui demander de me rappeler (Can you ask him to call me back?)

4. At the end of the call one just says:
Au revoir (Goodbye)

5. If you have to deal with the answering machine, the usual recorded message while waiting to get through is:

Nous vous demandons de bien vouloir patienter quelques instants. Nous allons donner suite à votre appel (One moment please. We are trying to connect you)

If you have to leave a message, you will hear the following standard set of sentences:

Vous êtes bien en communication avec .... Nous ne pouvons répondre à votre appel. Veuillez nous laisser votre nom et numéro de téléphone après le signal sonore et nous vous rappellerons dès que possible. Merci (Thank you for calling... We're unable to take your call at the moment. Please leave your name and phone number after the tone and we'll call you back as soon as possible. Thank you)

FRENCH BUSINESS MEETINGS

by Maddy Glas

Maddy Glas, Docteur de la Sorbonne, has worked in many EU countries and now teaches business French in the language department of the French business school INSEAD.

Contents

Introduction

The word "réunion" in French is used to refer to meetings which lie outside the scope of the typical business meeting discussed below: we find in particular, "la réunion d'information" which is more of a conference or a seminar where, without any agenda, a speaker makes a presentation of an issue which may or may not be followed by a question and answer session.

The run-of-the-mill business meeting (with a chairperson, a secretary, an agenda, minutes, a fixed slot in the week's or month's business diary, and largely the concern of the same limited group of colleagues) resembles only superficially the business meeting conducted in the UK and US.

Glossary	
a business meeting	**une réunion d'affaires**
a seminar/conference	**une réunion d'information**
a Board meeting	**un conseil d'Administration**
a sales meeting	**une réunion de vente**
a brainstorming session	**un brainstorming**
a planning committee	**un comité d'orientation**
an informal meeting	**une conférence**
a management meeting	**une réunion de la direction**
the meeting room	**la salle de réunion**
the Board room	**la salle de direction**

1. Preparing the meeting

Preparation implies fixed objectives, thus an agenda ("l'ordre du jour") has to be established and distributed beforehand to those taking part ("les participants"). Usual expressions are:

Je dois assister à une réunion/participer à une réunion	I have to attend/take part in a meeting

The agenda is the responsibility of the chairperson ("président de la réunion/animateur"), so placing an item on the agenda requires his assent.

Practice varies, and in many small businesses ("PME-PMI") the agenda is drawn up at the beginning of the meeting on the basis of the current preoccupations of its participants.

The agenda, on which the date ("la date"), the time ("l'heure"), and the place ("le lieu") are mentioned, acts as a summons ("une convocation"). Should one or another of these parameters be different to normal practice, the chairperson's secretary ("la secrétaire de direction") would normally have informed the participants personally beforehand to confirm their availability.

In French business, hierarchies tend to be strictly formal, so any excuse for absence has to be negotiated with the chairperson in person. Greater latitude is given to the demands of one's private life than in the UK (for example, sick children, or picking up the car from the garage), but repeated absence is not recommended.

The existence of a more formal hierarchy in French business largely explains the different function of the business meeting in the two countries. As, in France, decision-making is the prerogative of the hierarchical superior (the chair – "l'animateur"), the business meeting is more of a forum for the formulation and exchange of ideas. A bad idea, brilliantly proposed, may have more impact than a good idea poorly presented. This has obvious consequences both for the agenda and for the conduct of the meeting.

As far as the agenda is concerned, a reading of the previous minutes is not a formal item, and the idea of AOB tends to be relegated to the realm of non-sense. Responsibility for presenting items on the agenda is often delegated to the participants (thankfully forewarned), leaving the newcomer with the impression of attending a seminar. There is no pressure from the chairperson to get through the agenda, or even to finish the agenda: the wider discussion can range, the better. The agenda, in other words, is no more than an approximation of what the participants are expected to and will in fact discuss. Effective participation thus demands a thorough grasp of company politics, and a high level of preparation for those items relevant to one's interests.

2. Running the meeting

Before the meeting starts, do not forget to shake hands with all those you have not previously shaken hands with that day. The chairperson starts the proceedings by referring to the agenda and suggesting any changes in the order of the items down for discussion. The tone is often stiffly formal, a strange contrast to the generally relaxed atmosphere of such meetings in English-speaking countries. He/she uses such expressions as:

Nous sommes ici pour...	We are here today in order to...
Aujourd'hui, nous allons examiner...	Today, we are going to discuss...
Le but de notre réunion est de...	The purpose of today's meeting is to...

A lot of UK businessmen are surprised by the apparent aimlessness of such meetings compared to the conventions they are used to, where a chairperson guides the participants through the agenda with a firm hand, cuts short speakers who tend not to stick to the point, or who stray from the cut and thrust of opinion and argument the various items demand. Here, the role of the chairperson is to encourage the widest discussion possible with a view to later synthesizing the different positions adopted by the participants. As decisions are the prerogative of the chairperson, his/her aim is to have the possibilities examined from all the conceivable angles. Should you remain reticent, he/she will often explicitly demand your opinion:

Nous n'avons pas encore bénéficié du point de vue de Monsieur...	We haven't heard from Mr... yet
Et vous, Monsieur, quelle est votre opinion à ce sujet?	And what do you think about this, Mr...

First names are rarely used, and in the absence of a lead from the chairperson, "Nous pouvons nous tutoyer, je crois" (I think it is appropriate to use the "tu" form of address), you would be advised to stick to the "vous" form. Even using the "vous" form does not exempt the participant from a formal display of respect which can border on caricature:

Je suis d'accord avec vous, Monsieur	I totally agree with you, sir
Monsieur, avec tout le respect que je vous dois...	With all due respect, sir,...

Even a certain intimacy between participants is subtly suppressed: a close collaborator of the chairperson, on first name terms, would address him/her as "Monsieur"/"Madame" or "Monsieur le Président"/"Madame la Présidente". The use of the blunt "Monsieur"/"Madame" however, to someone with whom you are on close terms, would be taken as a rebuke. French also includes a highly developed form of gestural expression: it is often necessary to catch the chairperson's eye by lifting a finger; opening both palms may express either agreement or disagreement, but above all a desire to speak; putting the thumb and the index finger together underlines the importance of a point, or a desire for precision. By contrast, an open palm pointing upwards means you have made your point, but without conviction.

Most contributors use a common stock of phrases:

A mon avis...	In my opinion/if you ask me
Je trouve que.../Je pense que...	I think that...
Je voudrais préciser mon point de vue...	I'll try to be more clear...
Je désire mettre en évidence...	I'd like to draw your attention to...
J'aimerais suggérer...	May I suggest...
Je tiens à préciser que...	I'd like to point out that...
Je voudrais ajouter un point qui me paraît important...	The essential thing in my opinion is that...

business@harrap.eng

Agreement may be expressed as follows:

Je suis d'accord avec...	I agree with...
Je partage l'idée de...	I like the idea of...
J'approuve ce point de vue...	I'm of the same opinion
Vous avez absolument raison...	You are quite right
Excellente idée	What a good idea

Disagreements on the other hand can be uttered in the following way:

Je ne suis pas d'accord	I don't agree
Je crains que...	What worries me is/I'm afraid...
Je désapprouve l'idée	I'm not happy with the idea
Je ne suis pas de votre avis...	I don't share your viewpoint
Je déplore...	I'm sorry to say...
Je doute que...	I doubt if...

And of course there is always the infamous:

Oui, mais...	Yes, but...

Disagreement would often be preceded by an innocent enough request for further information:

Que voulez-vous dire par...?	What do you mean when you say...?
Qu'entendez-vous exactement par...?	What does... mean exactly?
Pourriez-vous m'expliquer...?	Can you explain...?

Interrupting requires diplomacy:

Je suis désolé(e) de vous interrompre...	Excuse me for butting in...
Si vous me permettez une seconde...	Sorry! but just a second

To which one may retort:

Vous permettez que je termine	Let me finish what I'm saying
Laissez-moi continuer	Please don't interrupt

business@harrap.eng

3. Follow-up

The editing and distributing of minutes ("le compte-rendu") is the responsibility of the secretary. As the reading of the previous minutes does not figure on the agenda, serious complaints should be raised at the start of the following meeting, but in a highly diplomatic form:

Juste un détail sur le compte-rendu de notre dernière réunion... Si ma mémoire est bonne...	Just a small point concerning the minutes... If I remember correctly...

4. General Observations

A. *Punctuality*

The French notion of time is quite different to that in northern Europe. Not only do meetings tend to be open-ended (discussion can continue for hours), but they rarely begin on time. At first, British people may interpret this as sloppiness, or downright rudeness, or some other form of "inefficiency". It is none of these. It is neither better nor worse than a Briton's "respect" of time: it is just different, and reflects deeper aspects of Latin culture. If you start to calculate by how much you can be late for a meeting or an appointment, you have not begun to understand the difference. Nobody arrives late on purpose, but nobody will break off a conversation because it is "time" to be somewhere else.

B. *The presentation of an argument*

Since high school, a particular method for writing and presenting an argument has been drummed into French children: "thèse", "antithèse" and "synthèse". Thus it is not surprising that in business arguments and presentations revolve around this logic: first, the points in favour; second, the points against; and finally, a judicious summing up of the strengths and weaknesses.

Two different strategies can be identified. First, a description of the present situation followed by an analysis of its strong and weak points, leading to suggestions as to how the situation can be improved or reformed. Second, the analysis of a problem in terms of known causes and standard remedies, followed by the recommendation of a particular solution.

C. *Losing face*

Being mistaken, or being responsible for an error, means losing face. Consequently, errors and mistakes are not openly recognised and assumed. This aspect of French culture raises two problems: how to cover up for one's own mistakes, and how to indicate the mistakes of others.

The first requires a certain aplomb. Whereas Britons tend to assume responsibility for the mistakes of others, the French make no reservations in detecting the "culprit" and detailing the disciplinary measures taken to avoid similar mistakes in the future. This is considered "good management". Another tactic is to review the situation prior to the error in order to highlight either a mistake in somebody else's appreciation on which the analysis was based, or a change in the situation which would explain how error was logically induced.

The second requires elegance:

Ne pensez-vous pas que la meilleure solution aurait été de...?	Don't you think with hindsight that it might have been better to...?
Avec les données d'aujourd'hui en main, il aurait peut-être fallu...	Knowing what we know today, don't you think it might have been better to...?

WORKING WITH AN INTERPRETER

In today's international business environment, interpretation is becoming increasingly common as a means of helping people from different countries to communicate. In order to get your message across to an international audience, it is essential to understand how best to work with interpreters.

There are three types of interpreting:

- Simultaneous
- Consecutive
- Whispering

Simultaneous is the most common form for conferences and business meetings. A microphone relays the speaker's voice to the interpreters who are sitting in soundproof booths. They then interpret instantaneously into the relevant language and the delegates listen to the interpretation via headsets.

Consecutive is used when simultaneous interpretation would not be practical, eg for factory visits or over dinner. The interpreter stands or sits next to you and interprets what you have said after you have said it, sometimes taking notes.

Whispering is the least common form of interpretation. The interpreter sits next to the delegates and whispers the translation of the presentation while it is being made.

Making a presentation to an international audience

If you know that your presentation is being interpreted into other languages, bear in mind the following points:

- Adapt the content of your speech to reflect the fact that it will be listened to by people from different cultures. Jokes rarely translate well and may even seem inappropriate to people from certain cultures. Culture-specific references are also usually meaningless to delegates from other countries. Colloquial or very technical language can be hard to translate, so stick to everyday vocabulary wherever possible.

- If you have written your speech out in advance, always provide a copy for the interpreters. Ideally, they should receive it a couple of weeks before the presentation, but if this is impossible, at least distribute it to them just before you speak, along with copies of any overheads or other documents you may be discussing. Background information on the subject of the presentation is also useful if provided in advance of the conference.

- When using simultaneous interpretation, you will be speaking into a microphone. The sound from the microphone is what the interpreters hear, and if they cannot hear what you are saying, they cannot interpret it. First, make sure your microphone is switched on and the interpreters can hear you. Direct your voice towards the microphone, but slightly over the top of it rather than straight at it. Remain at a constant distance from the microphone - if you keep moving towards it and then away, the volume will keep going up and down. When turning to point to a screen behind you, remember that if you speak with your back to the microphone, it will not pick up what you say. To avoid this problem, people using transparencies

business@harrap.eng

often wear a small microphone attached to their tie or lapel. If you are using one of these, remember that if you brush against it with your hand or jacket while speaking, the interpreters will only be able to hear a loud crackling noise.

- When using overheads, make sure the screen is positioned so that the interpreters can see it. It is important to take the audience through the overheads' content, otherwise only those people who speak the language in which they are written will understand them.

- The most common mistake made by people speaking to an international audience is to speak too quickly. Interpreters don't simply repeat what you say, they have to translate it first, so they inevitably need more time than you do. Consider also that many European languages (including French) are up to one third longer than English. Furthermore, there may be delegates listening to your speech in the language you are making it in, even though it is their second language. Do you want the foreign delegates to understand 40% or 99% of your presentation? If the answer is 99%, speak slowly!

- One way to ensure you keep to a reasonable pace is to pause at the end of every sentence. This allows the listeners to digest what you have said and gives the interpreters time to finish translating. A good speaker will wait until he hears that the interpreters have stopped speaking before continuing with his presentation.

- It is essential to speak clearly. Interpreters can only translate what they hear; if you mumble they will not be able to communicate your message.

If you bear all these points in mind next time you attend a multilingual conference or business meeting, you will be doing your bit to improve international communication and understanding.

Do's and don'ts when working with an interpreter

✔ DO:
- Provide your speech, overheads and reference material in advance.
- Switch your microphone on and use it correctly.
- Speak slowly and clearly.

✘ DON'T:
- Use too many jokes or culture-specific references.
- Turn away from the microphone when speaking about overheads.
- Change language in the middle of a sentence.

business@harrap.eng

NATIONS OF THE WORLD

Please note that the French name for the countries has been given in the second column. In order to find the French terms for the currencies and languages, please refer to the corresponding table in the French supplement.

Note also that the abbreviations given for currencies are the internationally recognised standard abbreviations established by the ISO and used in international financial transactions, rather than locally used abbreviations.

English name	French name	Local name	Official language(s)	Currency
Afghanistan	Afghanistan	Afghānestān	Dari, Pushtøu	1 Afghani (AFA) = 100 puls
Albania	Albanie	Shqīpëri	Albanian	1 Lek (ALL) = 100 qindarka
Algeria	Algérie	Al-Jazā'ir (Arabic), Algérie (French)	Arabic	1 Algerian Dinar (DZD) = 100 centimes
Andorra	Andorre	Andorra	Catalan, French, Spanish	1 French Franc (FRF) = 100 centimes; 1 Peseta (ESP) = 100 céntimos
Angola	Angola	Angola	Portuguese	1 New Kwanza (AOK) = 100 weil
Argentina	Argentine	Argentina	Spanish	1 Peso (ARS) = 100 centavos
Armenia	Arménie	Hayastani Hanrape-toutiun	Armenian	1 Dram (AMD) = 100 louma
Australia	Australie	Australia	English	1 Australian Dollar (AUD) = 100 cents
Austria	Autriche	Österreich	German	1 Schilling (ATS) = 100 groschen
Azerbaijan	Azerbaïdjan	Azarbaijan	Azeri (Azerbaijan)	1 Manat (AZM) = 100 gopik
The Bahamas	Bahamas	Bahamas	English	1 Bahamian Dollar (BSD) = 100 cents
Bahrain	Bahreïn	Dawlat Al-Bahrayn	Arabic	1 Bahrain Dinar (BHD) = 1,000 fils
Bangladesh	Bangladesh	Gana Prajatantri Bangladesh	Bengali	1 Taka (BDT) = 100 poisha
Barbados	Barbade	Barbados	English	1 Barbados Dollar (BBD) = 100 cents
Belarus	Biélorussie	Belarus	Belarussian	1 Rouble (BYB) = 100 kopeks
Belgium	Belgique	Belgique (French), België (Flemish)	Flemish, French, German	1 Belgian Franc (BEF) = 100 centimes
Belize	Belize	Belize	English	1 Belize Dollar (BZD) = 100 cents

English name	French name	Local name	Official language(s)	Currency
Benin	Bénin	Bénin	French	1 CFA Franc (XOF) = 100 centimes
Bhutan	Bhoutan	Druk-Yul	Dzongkha	1 Ngultrum (BTN) = 100 chetrum
Bolivia	Bolivie	Bolivia	Spanish	1 Boliviano (BOB) = 100 centavos
Bosnia-Herzegovina	Bosnie-Herzégovine	Bosnia-Herzegovina	Serbo-Croat	1 Dinar (BAD) = 100 paras
Botswana	Botswana	Botswana	English	1 Pula (BWP) = 100 thebe
Brazil	Brésil	Brasil	Portuguese	1 Real (BRL)= 100 centavos
Brunei	Brunei	Brunei	Malay	1 Brunei Dollar (BND) = 100 sen
Bulgaria	Bulgarie	Bălgarija	Bulgarian	1 Lev (BGL) = 100 stotinki
Burkina Faso	Burkina	Burkina Faso	French	1 CFA Franc (XOF) = 100 centimes
Burma ▶ Myanmar	Birmanie			
Burundi	Burundi	Burundi	French, Kirundi	1 Burundi Franc (BIF) = 100 centimes
Cambodia	Cambodge	Preah Reach Ana Pak Kampuchea	Khmer	1 Riel (KHR) = 100 sen
Cameroon	Cameroun	Cameroon	English, French	1 CFA Franc (XAF) = 100 centimes
Canada	Canada	Canada	English, French	1 Canadian Dollar (CAD) = 100 cents
Cape Verde	Cap-Vert	Cabo Verde	Portuguese	1 Escudo Caboverdiano (CVE) = 100 centavos
Central African Republic	République centrafricaine	République Centrafricaine	French, Sango	1 CFA Franc (XAF) = 100 centimes
Chad	Tchad	Tchad	French, Arabic	1 CFA Franc (XAF) = 100 centimes
Chile	Chili	Chile	Spanish	1 Chilean Peso (CLP) = 100 centavos
China	Chine	Zhongguo	Chinese	1 Renminbi Yuan (CNY) = 10 jiao = 100 fen
Colombia	Colombie	Colombia	Spanish	1 Colombian Peso (COP) = 100 centavos
Comoros	Comores	Comores	French, Comorian	1 Comorian Franc (KMF) = 100 centimes
Congo	Congo	Congo	French	1 CFA Franc (XAF) = 100 centimes
Congo, Democratic Republic of	Congo	Congo	French, Lingala	1 New Zaïre (ZRN) = 100 makuta (sing likuta)
Costa Rica	Costa Rica	Costa Rica	Spanish	1 Costa Rican Colón (CRC) = 100 céntimos
Côte d'Ivoire	Côte d'Ivoire	Côte d'Ivoire	French	1 CFA Franc (XOF) = 100 centimes
Croatia	Croatie	Hrvatska	Serbo-Croat	1 Kuna (HRK) = 100 lipas
Cyprus	Chypre	Kipros (Greek), Kibris (Turkish)	Greek, Turkish	1 Cyprus Pound (CYP) = 100 cents
Czech Republic	République tchèque	Česká Republika	Czech	1 Koruna (CZK) = 100 haléřu

English name	French name	Local name	Official language(s)	Currency
Denmark	Danemark	Danmark	Danish	1 Danish Krone (DKK) = 100 øre
Djibouti	Djibouti	Djibouti	Arabic, French	1 Djibouti Franc (DJF) = 100 centimes
Dominica	Dominique	Dominica	English, French Creole	1 East Caribbean Dollar (XCD) = 100 cents
Dominican Republic	République Dominicaine	República Dominicana	Spanish	1 Dominican Republic Peso (DOP) = 100 centavos
Ecuador	Équateur	Ecuador	Spanish	1 Sucre (ECS) = 100 centavos
Egypt	Égypte	Jumhuriyat Misr Al-Arabiya	Arabic	1 Egyptian Pound (EGP) = 100 piastres
El Salvador	Salvador	El Salvador	Spanish	1 Colón (SVC) = 100 centavos
Equatorial Guinea	Guinée Équatoriale	Guinea Ecuatorial	Spanish	1 CFA Franc (XAF) = 100 centimes
Eritrea	Érythrée	Eritrea	Tigrinya, Arabic	1 Ethiopian Birr (ETB) = 100 cents
Estonia	Estonie	Eesti Vabariik	Estonian	1 Kroon (EEK) = 100 sents
Ethiopia	Éthiopie	Ityopiya	Amharic	1 Ethiopian Birr (ETB) = 100 cents
Faroe Islands	îles Féroé	Faroyar/ Faeroerne	Faroese, Danish	1 Danish Krone (DKK) = 100 øre
Federated States of Micronesia		▶ Micronesia		
Fiji	îles Fidji	Matanitu Ko Viti	English	1 Fiji Dollar (FJD) = 100 cents
Finland	Finlande	Suomen Tasavalta	Finnish, Swedish	1 Markka (FIM) = 100 penniä
France	France	République Française	French	1 French Franc (FRF) = 100 centimes
French Guiana	Guyane	Guyane Française	French Creole	1 French Franc (FRF) = 100 centimes
French Polynesia	Polynésie Française	Territoire de la Polynésie Française	Polynesian, French	1 CPA Franc (XPF) = 100 centimes
Gabon	Gabon	République Gabonaise	French	1 CFA Franc (XAF) = 100 centimes
The Gambia	Gambie	Gambia	English	1 Dalasi (GMD) = 100 butut
Georgia	Géorgie	Sakartvelos Respublica	Georgian, Russian	1 Lari (GEL) = 100 tetri
Germany	Allemagne	Bundes-republik Deutschland	German	1 Deutsche Mark (DEM) = 100 pfennig
Ghana	Ghana	Ghana	English	1 Cedi (GHC) = 100 pesewas
Greece	Grèce	Elliniki Dimokratia	Greek	1 Drachma (GRD) = 100 leptae
Greenland	Groenland	Grønland (Danish), Kalaallit Nunaat	Danish, Greenlandic	1 Danish Krone (DKK) = 100 øre
Guatemala	Guatemala	Guatemala	Spanish	1 Quetzal (GTQ) = 100 centavos
Guinea	Guinée	République de Guinée	French	1 Guinea Franc (GNF) = 100 centimes
Guinea-Bissau	Guinée-Bissau	Republica da Guiné-Bissau	Portuguese	1 CFA Franc (GWP) = 100 centimes

English name	French name	Local name	Official language(s)	Currency
Guyana	Guyana	Guyana	English	1 Guyana Dollar (GYD) = 100 cents
Haiti	Haïti	République d'Haïti	French	1 Gourde (HTG) = 100 centimes
Holland ▶ Netherlands, The				
Honduras	Honduras	Honduras	Spanish	1 Lempira (HNL) = 100 centavos
Hungary	Hongrie	Magyar Koztarsasag	Hungarian	1 Forint (HUF) = 100 fillér
Iceland	Islande	Ísland	Icelandic	1 Króna (ISK) = 100 aurar
India	Inde	Bhārat (Hindi)	Hindi, English	1 Indian Rupee (INR) = 100 paisa
Indonesia	Indonésie	Republik Indonesia	Bahasa Indonesia	1 Rupiah (IDR) = 100 sen
Iran	Iran	Jomhoori-e-Islami-e-Iran	Farsi	1 Iranian Rial (IRR) = 100 dinars
Iraq	Irak	Jumhouriya al Iraquia	Arabic	1 Iraqi Dinar (IQD) = 1,000 fils
Ireland	Irlande	Poblacht na hEireann	Irish, English	1 Irish Pound/Punt (IER) = 100 pence
Israel	Israël	Medinat Israel	Hebrew, Arabic	1 Shekel (ILS) = 100 agora
Italy	Italie	Repubblica Italiana	Italian	1 Italian Lira (ITL) = 100 centesimi
Ivory Coast ▶ Côte d'Ivoire				
Jamaica	Jamaïque	Jamaica	English	1 Jamaican Dollar (JMD) = 100 cents
Japan	Japon	Nihon	Japanese	1 Yen (JPY) = 100 sen
Jordan	Jordanie	Al'Urdunn	Arabic	1 Jordanian Dinar (JOD) = 1,000 fils
Jugoslavia ▶ Yugoslavia				
Kampuchea ▶ Cambodia				
Kazakhstan	Kazakhstan	Kazak Respublikasy	Kazakh, Russian	1 Tenge (KZT) = 100 tiyn
Kenya	Kenya	Jamhuri ya Kenya	(Ki) Swahili, English	1 Kenyan shilling (KES) = 100 cents
Korea, North	Corée du Nord	Chosŏn Minjujuüi In'min Konghwaguk	Korean	1 Won (KPW) = 100 chon
Korea, South	Corée du Sud	Taehan-Min'guk	Korean	1 Won (KRW) = 100 chon
Kuwait	Koweït	Dowlat al-Kuwayt	Arabic	1 Kuwaiti Dinar (KWD) = 1,000 fils
Kyrgyzstan	Kirghizistan	Kyrgyz Respublikasy	Kyrgyz	1 Som (KGS) = 100 tiyin
Laos	Laos	Lao	Lao	1 Kip (LAK) = 100 at
Latvia	Lettonie	Latvijas Republika	Latvian	1 Lat (LVL) = 100 santimes
Lebanon	Liban	Al-Lubnān	Arabic	1 Lebanese Pound/ Livre (LBP) = 100 piastres
Lesotho	Lesotho	Lesotho	English, Sesotho	1 Loti (pl Maloti) (LSL) = 100 lisente
Liberia	Liberia	Liberia	English	1 Liberian Dollar (LRD) = 100 cents
Libya	Libye	Lībyā	Arabic	1 Libyan Dinar (LYD) = 1,000 dirhams

English name	French name	Local name	Official language(s)	Currency
Liechtenstein	Liechtenstein	Furstentum Liechtenstein	German	1 Swiss Franc (CHF) = 100 centimes = 100 rappen
Lithuania	Lituanie	Lietuva	Lithuanian	1 Litas (LTL) = 100 centas
Luxembourg	Luxembourg	Lëtzebuerg (Letz), Luxembourg (French), Luxemburg (German)	French, German, Letzebuergesch	1 Luxembourg Franc (LUF) = 100 centimes
Macedonia	Macédoine	Republika Makedonija	Macedonian	1 Denar (MKD) = 100 paras
Madagascar	Madagascar	Republikan'i Madagasikara	Malagasy, French	1 Malagasy Franc (MGF) = 100 centimes
Malawi	Malawi	Dziko la Malaŵi	Chichewa, English	1 Kwacha (MWK) = 100 tambala
Malaysia	Malaisie	Federation of Malaysia	Bahasa Malaysia	1 Malaysian Dollar/Ringgit (MYR) = 100 cents
Maldives	Maldives	Maldives Divehi Jumhuriya	Divehi	1 Rufiyaa (MVR) = 100 laaris
Mali	Mali	Mali	French	1 CFA Franc (XOF) = 100 centimes
Malta	Malte	Malta	English, Maltese	1 Maltese Lira (MTL) = 100 cents = 1,000 mils
Martinique	Martinique	Martinique	French Creole	1 French Franc (FRF) = 100 centimes
Mauritania	Mauritanie	Mauritanie (French), Mūrītāniyā (Arabic)	Arabic	1 Ouguiya (MRO) = 5 khoums
Mauritius	île Maurice	Mauritius	English	1 Mauritian Rupee (MUR) = 100 cents
Mexico	Mexique	México	Spanish	1 Mexican Peso (MXN) = 100 centavos
Micronesia	Micronésie	Micronesia	English	1 US Dollar (USD) = 100 cents
Moldova	Moldavie	Republica Moldove-nească	Moldavian	1 Leu (MDL) (*pl* lei) = 100 bani
Monaco	Principauté de Monaco	Monaco	French	1 French Franc (FRF) = 100 centimes
Mongolia	Mongolie	Mongol Ard Uls	Halh Mongol	1 Tugrik (MNT) = 100 möngö
Morocco	Maroc	Mamlaka Al-Maghrebia	Arabic	1 Dirham (MAD) = 100 centimes
Mozambique	Mozambique	Republica de Moçambique	Portuguese	1 Metical (MZM) = 100 centavos
Myanmar	Myanmar	Myanmar	Burmese	1 Kyat (MMK) = 100 pyas
Namibia	Namibie	Namibia	English	1 Namibian Dollar (NAD) = 100 cents
Nauru	Nauru	Naeoro (Nauruan), Nauru (English)	Nauruan, English	1 Australian Dollar (AUD) = 100 cents
Nepal	Népal	Nepal Adhirajya	Napali	1 Nepalese Rupee (NPR) = 100 paise/pice

English name	French name	Local name	Official language(s)	Currency
The Netherlands	Pays-Bas	Koninkrijk der Nederlanden	Dutch	1 Dutch Guilder (NLG)/Florin = 100 cents
New Zealand	Nouvelle-Zélande	New Zealand	English	1 New Zealand Dollar (NZD) = 100 cents
Nicaragua	Nicaragua	Nicaragua	Spanish	1 Córdoba Oro (NIO) = 100 centavos
Niger	Niger	Niger	French	1 CFA Franc (XOF) = 100 centimes
Nigeria	Nigéria	Nigeria	English, French	1 Naira (NGN) = 100 kobo
Norway	Norvège	Kongeriket Norge	Norwegian	1 Norwegian Krone (NOK) = 100 øre
Oman	Oman	Saltanat 'Uman	Arabic	1 Omani Rial (OMR) = 1,000 baiza
Pakistan	Pakistan	Pākistān	Urdu, English	1 Pakistan Rupee (PKR) = 100 paisa
Panama	Panamá	Panamá	Spanish	1 Balboa (PAB) = 100 centésimos
Papua New Guinea	Papouasie-Nouvelle-Guinée	Papua New Guinea	English, Tok Pïsin, Hiri Motu	1 Kina (PGK) = 100 toea
Paraguay	Paraguay	Paraguay	Spanish	1 Guaraní (PYG) = 100 céntimos
Peru	Pérou	Perú	Spanish	1 New Sol (PEN) = 100 cénts
Philippines	Philippines	Pilipinas	Filipino, English	1 Philippine Peso (PHP) = 100 centavos
Poland	Pologne	Rzeczpospolita Polska	Polish	1 Złoty (PLN) = 100 groszy
Portugal	Portugal	Portugal	Portuguese	1 Escudo (PTE) = 100 centavos
Puerto Rico	Porto Rico	Puerto Rico	Spanish, English	1 US Dollar (USD) = 100 cents
Qatar	Qatar	Dowlat Qatar	Arabic	1 Qatar Riyal (QAR) = 100 dirhams
Romania	Roumanie	Romănia	Romanian	1 Leu (ROL) (pl Lei) = 100 bani
Russia	Russie	Rossiya	Russian	1 Rouble (RUR) = 100 kopeks
Rwanda	Rwanda	Rwanda	(Kinya) Rwanda, French, English	1 Rwanda Franc (RWF) = 100 centimes
Samoa	Samoa	Samoa	Samoan, English	1 Tala (WST) = 100 sene
San Marino	Saint-Marin	San Marino	Italian	1 San Marino Lira (ITL) = 100 centesimi
Saudi Arabia	Arabie Saoudite	Al-'Arabīyah as Sa'ūdīyah	Arabic	1 Saudi Arabian Riyal (SAR) = 20 qursh = 100 halala
Senegal	Sénégal	Sénégal	French, Wolof	1 CFA Franc (XOF) = 100 centimes
Seychelles	Seychelles	Seychelles	Creole French, English, French	1 Seychelles Rupee (SCR) = 100 cents
Sierra Leone	Sierra Leone	Sierra Leone	English	1 Leone (SLL) = 100 cents
Singapore	Singapour	Singapore	Chinese, English, Malay, Tamil	1 Singapore Dollar (SGD) = 1 Ringgit = 100 cents
Slovakia	Slovaquie	Slovenska Republika	Slovak	1 Koruna (CSK) = 100 haléru

English name	French name	Local name	Official language(s)	Currency
Slovenia	Slovénie	Republika Slovenija	Slovene	1 Tolar (SIT) = 100 stotin
Solomon Islands	îles Salomon	Solomon Islands	English	1 Solomon Islands Dollar (SBD) = 100 cents
Somalia	Somalie	Somaliya	Arabic, Somali	1 Somali Shilling (SOS) = 100 cents
South Africa	Afrique du Sud	South Africa	English, Afrikaans	1 Rand (ZAR) = 100 cents
Spain	Espagne	España	Spanish	1 Peseta (ESP) = 100 céntimos
Sri Lanka	Sri Lanka	Sri Lanka	Sinhala, Tamil	1 Sri Lankan Rupee (LKR) = 100 cents
The Sudan	Soudan	As-Sūdān	Arabic	1 Sudanese Dinar (SDD) = 10 pounds
Surinam	Surinam	Suriname	Dutch	1 Surinam Guilder (SRG)/Florin = 100 cents
Swaziland	Swaziland	Umbouso we Swatini	Swazi, English	1 Lilangeni (SZL) (*pl* Emalangeni) = 100 cents
Sweden	Suède	Konungariket Sverige	Swedish	1 Swedish Krona (SEK) = 100 øre
Switzerland	Suisse	Schweiz (German), Suisse (French), Svizzera (Italian)	French, German, Italian, Romansch	1 Swiss Franc (CHF) = 100 centimes = 100 rappen
Syria	Syrie	As-Sūrīyah	Arabic	1 Syrian pound (SYP) = 100 piastres
Taiwan	Taiwan	T'aiwan	Chinese	1 New Taiwan Dollar (TWD) = 100 cents
Tajikistan	Tadjikistan	Jumkhurii Tojikistan	Tajik	1 Tajik Rouble (TJR) = 100 tanga
Tanzania	Tanzanie	Tanzania	(ki)Swahili, English	1 Tanzanian Shilling (TZS) = 100 cents
Thailand	Thaïlande	Prathet Thai	Thai	1 Baht (THB) = 100 satang
Togo	Togo	Togo	French	1 CFA Franc (XOF) = 100 centimes
Tonga	Tonga	Tonga	English, Tongan	1 Pa'anga/Tongan Dollar (TOP) = 100 seniti
Trinidad and Tobago	Trinité-et-Tobago	Trinidad and Tobago	English	1 Trinidad and Tobago Dollar (TTD) = 100 cents
Tunisia	Tunisie	Tunisiya	Arabic, French	1 Tunisian Dinar (TND) = 1,000 millimes
Turkey	Turquie	Türkiye	Turkish	1 Turkish Lira (TRL) = 100 kurus
Turkmenistan	Turkménistan	Turkmenostan	Turkmenian	1 Manat (TMM) = 100 tenesi
Uganda	Ouganda	Uganda	English, Kiswahili	1 Uganda Shilling (UGX) = 100 cents
Ukraine	Ukraine	Ukraina	Ukrainian, Russian	1 Hryvna (UAK) = 100 kopiykas
United Arab Emirates	Émirats Arabes Unis	Ittihād al-Imārāt al-'Arabīyah	Arabic, English	1 Dirham (AED) = 100 fils
United Kingdom	Royaume-Uni	United Kingdom	English	1 Pound Sterling (GBP) = 100 pence

English name	French name	Local name	Official language(s)	Currency
United States of America	États-Unis	United States of America	English	1 US Dollar (USD) = 100 cents
Uruguay	Uruguay	Uruguay	Spanish	1 New Uruguayan Peso (UYU) = 100 centésimos
Uzbekistan	Ouzbékistan	Uzbekistan	Uzbek	1 Sum (UZS) = 100 tiyin
Vanuatu	Vanuatu	Vanuatu	Bislama, English, French	1 Vatu (VUV) = 100 centimes
Vatican City	cité du Vatican	Citta'del Vaticano	Italian	1 Italian Lira (ITL) = 100 centesimi
Venezuela	Venezuela	Venezuela	Spanish	1 Bolívar (VEB) = 100 céntimos
Vietnam	Vietnam	Viêt-nam	Vietnamese	1 Dông (VND) = 10 hào = 100 xu
Western Samoa	▶ Samoa			
Yemen	Yémen	Al-Yamaniya	Arabic	1 Yemeni Riyal (YER) = 100 fils
Yugoslavia	Yougoslavie	Jugoslavija	Serbo-Croat (Serbian)	1 New Dinar (YUN) = 100 paras
Zaire	Zaïre			
▶ Congo, Democratic Republic of				
Zambia	Zambie	Zambia	English	1 Kwacha (ZMK) = 100 ngwee
Zimbabwe	Zimbabwe	Zimbabwe	English	1 Zimbabwe Dollar (ZWD) = 100 cents

FRENCH DEPARTEMENTS

Note: In 1996 a new system was introduced for French telephone numbers. Mainland France (plus Corsica) was divided into five regions. The right-hand column of the table below lists the number that must now prefix all eight-digit telephone numbers for the respective départements.

Département	Code	Administrative centre	Region	Telephone code
Ain	01	Bourg-en-Bresse	Rhône-Alpes	4
Aisne	02	Laon	Picardie	3
Allier	03	Moulins	Auvergne	4
Alpes-de-Haute-Provence	04	Digne-les-Bains	Provence-Alpes-Côte d'Azur	4
Alpes (Hautes-)	05	Gap	Provence-Alpes-Côte d'Azur	4
Alpes-Maritimes	06	Nice	Provence-Alpes-Côte d'Azur	4
Ardèche	07	Privas	Rhône-Alpes	4
Ardennes	08	Charleville-Mézières	Champagne-Ardennes	3
Ariège	09	Foix	Midi-Pyrénées	5
Aube	10	Troyes	Champagne-Ardennes	3
Aude	11	Carcassonne	Languedoc-Roussillon	4
Aveyron	12	Rodez	Midi-Pyrénées	5
Belfort (Territoire de)	90	Belfort	Franche-Comté	3
Bouches-du-Rhône	13	Marseille	Provence-Alpes-Côte d'Azur	4
Calvados	14	Caen	Basse-Normandie	2
Cantal	15	Aurillac	Auvergne	4
Charente	16	Angoulême	Poitou-Charentes	5
Charente-Maritime	17	La Rochelle	Poitou-Charentes	5
Cher	18	Bourges	Centre	2
Corrèze	19	Tulle	Limousin	5
Corse-du-Sud	2A	Ajaccio	Corse	4
Corse (Haute-)	2B	Bastia	Corse	4
Côte-d'Or	21	Dijon	Bourgogne	3
Côtes-d'Armor	22	Saint-Brieux	Bretagne	2
Creuse	23	Guéret	Limousin	5
Dordogne	24	Périgueux	Aquitaine	5
Doubs	25	Besançon	Franche-Comté	3
Drôme	26	Valence	Rhône-Alpes	4
Essonne	91	Évry	île-de-France	1
Eure	27	Évreux	Haute-Normandie	2
Eure-et-Loire	28	Chartres	Centre	2
Finistère	29	Quimper	Bretagne	2
Gard	30	Nîmes	Languedoc-Roussillon	4
Garonne (Haute)	31	Toulouse	Midi-Pyrénées	5
Gers	32	Auch	Midi-Pyrénées	5
Gironde	33	Bordeaux	Aquitaine	5
Hauts-de-Seine	92	Nanterre	île-de-France	1
Hérault	34	Montpellier	Languedoc-Roussillon	4
Ille-et-Villaine	35	Rennes	Bretagne	2
Indre	36	Châteauroux	Centre	2

Département	Code	Administrative centre	Region	Telephone code
Indre-et-Loire	37	Tours	Centre	2
Isère	38	Grenoble	Rhône-Alpes	4
Jura	39	Lons-le-Saunier	Franche-Comté	3
Landes	40	Mont-de-Marsan	Aquitaine	5
Loir-et-Cher	41	Blois	Centre	2
Loire	42	Saint-Étienne	Rhône-Alpes	4
Loire (Haute-)	43	Le-Puy-en-Velay	Auvergne	4
Loire-Atlantique	44	Nantes	Pays de la Loire	2
Loiret	45	Orléans	Centre	2
Lot	46	Cahors	Midi-Pyrénées	5
Lot-et-Garonne	47	Agen	Aquitaine	5
Lozère	48	Mende	Languedoc-Roussillon	4
Maine-et-Loire	49	Angers	Pays de la Loire	2
Manche	50	Saint-Lô	Basse-Normandie	2
Marne	51	Châlons-en-Champagne	Champagne-Ardennes	3
Marne (Haute-)	52	Chaumont	Champagne-Ardennes	3
Mayenne	53	Laval	Pays de la Loire	2
Meurthe-et-Moselle	54	Nancy	Lorraine	3
Meuse	55	Bar-le-Duc	Lorraine	3
Morbihan	56	Vannes	Bretagne	2
Moselle	57	Metz	Lorraine	3
Nièvre	58	Nevers	Bourgogne	3
Nord	59	Lille	Nord-Pas-de-Calais	3
Oise	60	Beauvais	Picardie	3
Orne	61	Alençon	Basse-Normandie	2
Paris (Ville de)	75		île-de-France	1
Pas-de-Calais	62	Arras	Nord-Pas-de-Calais	3
Puy-de-Dôme	63	Clermont-Ferrand	Auvergne	4
Pyrénées-Atlantiques	64	Pau	Aquitaine	5
Pyrénées (Hautes-)	65	Tarbes	Midi-Pyrénées	5
Pyrénées-Orientales	66	Perpignan	Languedoc-Roussillon	4
Rhin (Bas-)	67	Strasbourg	Alsace	3
Rhin (Haut-)	68	Colmar	Alsace	3
Rhône	69	Lyon	Rhône-Alpes	4
Saône (Haute-)	70	Vesoul	Franche-Comté	3
Saône-et-Loire	71	Mâcon	Bourgogne	3
Sarthe	72	Le Mans	Pays de la Loire	2
Savoie	73	Chambéry	Rhône-Alpes	4
Savoie (Haute-)	74	Annecy	Rhône-Alpes	4
Seine-Maritime	76	Rouen	Haute-Normandie	2
Seine-et-Marne	77	Melun	île-de-France	1
Seine-Saint-Denis	93	Bobigny	île-de-France	1
Sèvres (Deux)	79	Niort	Poitou-Charentes	5
Somme	80	Amiens	Picardie	3
Tarn	81	Albi	Midi-Pyrénées	5
Tarn-et-Garonne	82	Montauban	Midi-Pyrénées	5
Val-de-Marne	94	Créteil	île-de-France	1
Val-d'Oise	95	Pontoise	île-de-France	1
Var	83	Toulon	Provence-Alpes-Côte d'Azur	4
Vaucluse	84	Avignon	Provence-Alpes-Côte d'Azur	4
Vendée	85	La-Roche-sur-Yon	Pays de la Loire	2
Vienne	86	Poitiers	Poitou-Charentes	5
Vienne (Haute-)	87	Limoges	Limousin	5
Vosges	88	Épinal	Lorraine	3
Yonne	89	Auxerre	Bourgogne	3
Yvelines	78	Versailles	île-de-France	1

DEPARTEMENTS ET TERRITOIRES D'OUTRE-MER/COLLECTIVITES LOCALES

Département	Code	Administrative centre	Region
Guadeloupe	971	Basse-Terre	DOM
Martinique	972	Fort-de-France	DOM
Guyane	973	Cayenne	DOM
Réunion	974	Saint-Denis	DOM
Nouvelle-Calédonie	98	Nouméa	TOM
Wallis-et-Futuna	98	Mata-Utu	TOM
Polynésie-Française		Papeete	TOM
Terres australes et antarctiques françaises			TOM
Mayotte	976	Mamoudzou	CT
Saint-Pierre-et-Miquelon	97500	Saint-Pierre	CT

── A Note on the Euro ──

Note that as of 1 January 1999, the Euro has been adopted as
the national currency by 11 member states of the EU. They will
continue to use their former currencies alongside the Euro
until 2002 when the Euro will become the sole currency.

In the tables of currencies in this dictionary, the Euro is not
given as the national currency for these countries.

The exchange rates are as follows:

Austria	=	13.7603 schillings
Belgium	=	40.3399 Belgian francs
Finland	=	5.94573 markka
France	=	6.55957 French francs
Germany	=	1.95583 marks
Holland	=	2.20371 guilders
Ireland	=	0.787564 Irish pounds
Italy	=	1,936.27 lira
Luxembourg	=	40.33399 Luxembourg francs
Portugal	=	200.482 escudos
Spain	=	166.386 pesetas

Sources of English Quotes
Sources de Citations Anglaises

A

ABOVE-THE-LINE *Management: Theory and Practice* Cole, G. A.
London: D P Publications Ltd, Date unknown

ACCRUED *Accountancy* London: Institute of Chartered
Accountants, 1992

ACTUAL [Miscellaneous papers], Date and publisher unknown

ADVANCE [Financial leaflets from Midland Bank], Date and
publisher unknown

ADVISORY *Managing Innovation* Date and publisher unknown

AFLOAT *Principles of Modern Company Law* Gower. London:
Sweet & Maxwell Ltd, 1992

AFTER-SALES *Organisational Analysis* London: BPP
Management Education Ltd, 1990

ANTITRUST *Economics* Begg, David; Fischer, Stanley;
Dornbusch, Rudiger. Maidenhead: McGraw-Hill Book
Company, 1991

ARBITRAGE *Computergram International* Date and publisher
unknown

ARTICLE *Principles of Hotel and Catering Law* Pannett, A.
London: Cassell, 1992

ASEAN *The Guardian* 1989

AVAILABLE [Management training course (Business)], 1993

B

BACS [Financial leaflets from Midland Bank], Date and
publisher unknown

BARGAINING *Twenty Ways to Manage Better* Leigh, Andrew.
London: Institute of Personnel Management, 1992

BIG *The Independent* 1989

BORROW AGAINST *Hospitality* London: Hotel Catering & Inst.
Manag., 1993

BRAIN DRAIN *New Scientist* 1991

BREAK-EVEN *Management: Theory and Practice* Cole, G. A.
London: D P Publications Ltd, Date unknown

BULLISH *Art Criticism: A User's Guide* Darracott, Joseph.
London: Bellew Publishing Company Ltd, 1991

BUNDLE *The Guardian* 1989

BUY-OUT *Advice From the Top* Oates, David & Ezra, Derek.
Newton Abbot, Devon: David & Charles Publishers plc, 1989

C

CEILING *The Independent* 1989

CET *Keesings Contemporary Archives* Harlow: Longman Group UK Ltd, 1991

CHARGEABLE *Law for the Haulier* Brown, Largent. London: Kogan Page Ltd, 1987

CHURN *Public Order and Private Lives* Brake, M. & Hale, C. London: Routledge & Kegan Paul plc, 1992

CLUSTER *Methods of Social Investigation* Mann, Peter H. Oxford: Basil Blackwell Ltd, 1985

COLLATERAL *Futures Trading Law and Regulation* Ottino, Peter. Harlow: Longman Group UK Ltd, 1993

COLLECTIVE *Thatcherism and British Politics* Kavanagh, Dennis. Oxford: Oxford University Press, 1990

COMPETITIVE *R&D Management: Managing Projects and New Products* Date and publisher unknown

CONSUMER *Credit Management* Stamford, Lincs: Institute of Credit Management, 1992

CONTROLLED ECONOMY *The British Polity* Norton, Philip. New York: Longman, 1984

COOLING-OFF PERIOD *Accountancy* London: Institute of Chartered Accountants, 1993

COST-PLUS *Problems of Unemployment and Inflation* Hardwick, Philip. Harlow: Longman Group UK Ltd, 1987

CUSTOMER-DRIVEN *ICI Innovation* Date and publisher unknown

CYCLE *The Daily Telegraph* 1992

D

DAILY *The City Share Pushers* Davidson, Alexander. UK: Scope Books Ltd, 1989

DAWN *A Right Approach to Economics?* Hardy, Peter. Sevenoaks, Kent: Hodder & Stoughton Ltd, 1991

DEBENTURE *Law for the Haulier* Brown, Largent. London: Kogan Page Ltd, 1987

DEBTOR *The Americas* Lancaster, A. B. Sevenoaks, Kent: Edward Arnold (Publishers) Ltd, 1984

DECISION-MAKING *Markets* Levacic, Rosalind; Thompson; Mitchell, Jeremy; Frances, Jennifer. London: Sage Publications Ltd, 1993

DECONTROL *The Guardian* 1989

DEEP-DISCOUNT BOND *Accountancy* London: Institute of Chartered Accountants, 1993

DEFAULT *Today* 1992

DEMAND-LED [*Rapid – ESRC Grant Abstracts*], Date and publisher unknown

DEMOGRAPHIC *Management: Theory and Practice* Cole, G. A. London: D P Publications Ltd

DEPRECIATE *Problems of Unemployment and Inflation* Hardwick, Philip. Harlow: Longman Group UK Ltd, 1987

DEPTH *The Sociology of Housework* Oakley, A. Oxford: Blackwell, 1990

DESKILLING *Sociology: Themes and Perspectives* Holborn, M. & Haralambos, M. London: HarperCollins, 1991

DILUTION *The Economist* 1991

DIRTY *Keesings Contemporary Archives* Harlow: Longman Group UK Ltd, 1991

DOLLAR *Twentieth Century British History* Oxford: Oxford University Press, 1991

DOWNSIDE *Accountancy* London: Institute of Chartered Accountants, 1993

E

EARNED *What Every Woman Should Know About Retirement* Donald, V.; Orton, C.; Dudley, C.; Ward, S. Mitcham: Age Concern England, 1987

EBRD *Keesings Contemporary Archives* Harlow: Longman Group UK Ltd, 1990

EEA *Nature* 1993

ELECTRONIC *Management: Theory and Practice* Cole, G.A. London: DP Publications Ltd, Date unknown

EMPLOYMENT *How to Get the Best Deal From Your Employer* Edwards, Martin. London: Kogan Page Ltd, 1991

ENDOWMENT *Accountancy* London: Institute of Chartered Accountants, 1993

ENTERPRISE *The Independent* 1989

ERDF *European Economic Integration* Tomkins, Judith. Harlow: Longman Group UK Ltd, 1992

EURO-CURRENCY *International Finance and Developing Countries* Leslie, James. Harlow: Longman Group UK Ltd, 1987

EXCLUSIVITY *Management Buy-outs* Cooke, Darryl J. Harlow: Longman Group UK Ltd, 1993

EX-GROWTH *Computergram International* Date and publisher unknown

EXPANDING *World Energy* Hedley, Don. London: Euromonitor Publications Ltd, 1986

EXPORTING *European Economic Integration* McDonald, Frank. Harlow: Longman Group UK Ltd, 1992

F

FACTORING [Financial leaflets], Date and publisher unknown

FAT CAT *Here's Health: The Green Guide* Wheater, Caroline & Smyth, Angela. Hemel Hempstead, Herts: Argus Books, 1990

FEATHERBED *The Economist* 1991

FED *The Daily Telegraph* 1992

FEDERAL *The Economist* 1993

FIAT *Involuntary Employment* Trevithick, J.A. Hemel
Hempstead: Harvester & Wheatsheaf, 1992

FIREWALL *Electronic Information Resources and the Historian*
Ross, Seamus & Higgs, Edward, Date and publisher unknown

FIRST-TIME *Accountancy* London: Institute of Chartered
Accountants, 1993

FLEXIBLE [Employment service], Date and publisher unknown

FOCUS GROUP *Methods of Social Investigation* Mann, Peter H.
Oxford: Basil Blackwell Ltd, 1985

FOOTSIE *The Daily Telegraph* 1992

FOREIGN *International Finance and Developing Countries* Leslie,
James. Harlow: Longman Group UK Ltd, 1987

FORTUNE 500 *The Daily Telegraph* 1992

FREE *Disadvantaged Rural Europe* Langholm, Dumfriesshire:
The Arkleton Trust, 1981

FRONT-END *The Scotsman* Date unknown

FUNNELLING *Data Collection in Context* Ackroyd, Stephen.
Harlow: Longman Group UK Ltd, Date unknown

FUTURE *The Daily Telegraph* 1992

G

GAP *Advice From the Top* Oates, David & Ezra, Derek. Newton
Abbot, Devon: David & Charles Publishers plc, 1989

GEAR UP *New Technology at Work* Francis, Arthur. Oxford:
Oxford University Press, 1986

GEARING *The Independent* 1989

GILT-EDGED *The Independent* 1989

GLASS CEILING *Hospitality* London: Hotel Catering & Inst.
Manag., 1993

GLOBALIZE *Introduction to Politics* Gill, Peter & Ponton,
Geoffrey. Oxford: Blackwell, 1984

GOODWILL *The Independent* 1989

GREENFIELD SITE [Miscellaneous unpublished material from
Campaign for the Preservation of Rural Wales], Date unknown

H

HANDS-ON *Environmental Scanning and Business Strategy*
Waters, Judith & Lester, Ray. London: The British Library
Board, 1989

HEADHUNT *Advice From the Top* Oates, David & Ezra, Derek.
Newton Abbot, Devon: David & Charles Publishers plc, 1989

HEDGE *The Independent* 1989

HIGHLY-GEARED *Takeovers* Stedman, Graham. Harlow:
Longman Group UK Ltd, 1993

HOLDING *The Economist* 1991

HOSTILE TAKEOVER BID *Competition and Business Regulation in the
Single Market* S.J. Berwin & co, Date and publisher unknown

I

IFA *Ideal Home* 1991

IMF *The Independent* 1989

IMPREST *The Hotel Receptionist* Paige, Jane & Paige, Grace. London: Cassell Educational, 1992

INDEMNIFY *How to Get the Best Deal From Your Employer* Edwards, Martin. London: Kogan Page Ltd, 1991

INDICATOR *Applied Economics* Griffiths, Alan & Wall, Stuart. Harlow: Longman Group UK Ltd, 1993

INDUSTRIALIZED *Exploring Data* Marsh, Catherine. Cambridge: Polity Press, 1988

INFLATIONARY *Keesings Contemporary Archives* Harlow: Longman Group UK Ltd, 1990

INFORMATION *A Future for the NHS?* Ranade, Wendy. Harlow: Longman Group UK Ltd, 1994

INITIAL *Computergram International* Date and publisher unknown

INSIDER *Financial Conglomerates and the Chinese Wall* McVea, H. New York: Oxford University Press, 1993

INSTANT-ACCESS *Economics* Date and publisher unknown

INTEGRATION *Hospitality* London: Hotel Catering & Inst. Manag., 1993

INTERNATIONAL *The Elements of Nursing* Tierney, Alison J.; Logan, Winifred W.; Roper, Nancy. Harlow: Churchill Livingstone, 1990

INVISIBLE *Sales Technique and Management* Lancaster, G. & Jobber, D. London: Pitman Publishing, 1992

ISDN *Accountancy* London: Institute of Chartered Accountants, 1993

J

JOB *Human Resource Strategies* Salaman, G.; Mabey, C.; Hamblin, H.; Thompson; Cameron, S.; Iles, P. Milton Keynes: Open University Press, 1992

JUNK *Financial Market Analysis* Blake, David. Maidenhead: McGraw-Hill Book Company, 1990

JUST-IN-TIME *The Economist* 1991

K

KERB *The Economist* 1991

L

LAME DUCK *Hotel and Catering Case Studies* Abbott, Peter & Shepherd, John. London: Cassell, 1989

LAUNDER *The Daily Telegraph* 1992

LEARNING CURVE *The Mind at Work* Singleton, W.T. Cambridge: Cambridge University Press, 1989

LEVERAGED *The Independent* 1989

LIFFE *Financial Market Analysis* Blake, David. Maidenhead: McGraw-Hill Book Company, 1990

LIQUIDITY *Economics* Date and publisher unknown

LOCAL *Accountancy* London: Institute of Chartered Accountants, 1993

M

MAILING *Retailing: A Manual for Students* Leach, Helen. Oxford: Basil Blackwell Ltd, 1989

MANAGEMENT *Public Sector Financial Control and Accounting* Glynn, J. Oxford: Blackwell, 1993

MARGINAL *R&D Management: Managing Projects and New Products* Bergen, S.A. Oxford: Basil Blackwell Ltd, 1990

MARKET *Financial Conglomerates and the Chinese Wall* McVea, H. New York: Oxford University Press, 1993

MBI *The Alton Herald* 1992

MEDIA *Marketing Week* 1992

MERCANTILE *Sale of Goods and Consumer Credit* Dobson, A.P. London: Sweet and Maxwell Ltd, 1989

MEZZANINE *The Independent* 1989

MIRAS *Accountancy* London: Institute of Chartered Accountants, 1992

MISSION *Education Management in the 1990s* Osborne, Allan; Davies, Brent; West-Burnham, John; Ellison, Linda. Harlow: Longman Group UK Ltd, 1990

MONETARY *The Economist* 1993

MORTGAGE *The Independent* 1989

MOST-FAVOURED NATION *Keesings Contemporary Archives* Harlow: Longman Group UK Ltd, 1990

MULTIMEDIA *The Guardian* 1989

N

NATURAL *AEA Times* The Atomic Energy Authority, 1993

NEGATIVE *The Scotsman* Date unknown

NICHE *The Economist* 1993

NON-CONTRIBUTORY PENSION *Accountancy* London: Institute of Chartered Accountants, 1993

NORTH AMERICAN FREE TRADE AGREEMENT *Keesings Contemporary Archives* Harlow: Longman Group UK Ltd, 1991

O

OCCUPATIONAL *Accountancy* London: Institute of Chartered Accountants, 1993

OFFSHORE *Accountancy* London: Institute of Chartered Accountants, 1992

OPEN *Markets and Dealers* Leslie, James. Harlow: Longman Group UK Ltd, 1992

ORGANIZATION *Sociology of the Global System* Sklair, Leslie. Hemel Hempstead: Harvester, 1991

OUTPLACEMENT *The Scotsman* Date unknown

OUTSOURCE [*Rapid – ESRC Grant Abstracts*], Date and publisher unknown

OVERDRAFT *Accountancy* London: Chartered Institute of Accountants, 1992

OVERNIGHT *Keesings Contemporary Archives* Harlow: Longman Group UK Ltd, 1991

OVER-THE-COUNTER *UK Financial Institutions and Markets* Pawlet, Michael; Bentley, Patrick; Winstone, David. London: Macmillan Press Ltd, 1991

P

PAID-UP *Principles of Hotel and Catering Law* Pannet, A. London: Cassell, 1992

PARI PASSU [Dawson International plc: Notice of annual general meeting], Date unknown

PATERNITY LEAVE *It's Time to Get Britain Working Again* London: The Labour Party, 1992

PAYE *The Rock File* York, Norton. Oxford: Oxford University Press, 1991

PENSION *The Economist* 1991

PERSONAL *The Scotsman* Date unknown

PIBOR *Markets and Dealers* Leslie, James. Harlow: Longman Group UK Ltd, 1992

PLANNED *Morality and the Market-place* Griffiths, Brian. Sevenoaks, Kent: Hodder & Stoughton Ltd, 1989

POISON PILL *Against a Federal Europe* Cash, William. London: Gerald Duckworth & company Ltd, 1991

POSTER *Marketing Week* 1992

POVERTY LINE *The Economist* 1991

PREFERENTIAL *Keesings Contemporary Archives* Harlow: Longman Group UK Ltd, 1991

PRICE-ELASTIC *Rival States, Rival Firms* Henley, J.; Strange, S.; Stopford, J. Cambridge: Cambridge University Press, 1992

PROBLEM CHILD *Computergram International* Date and publisher unknown

PROFIT *A Right Approach to Economics?* Hardy, Peter. Sevenoaks, Kent: Hodder & Stoughton Ltd, 1991

PRUDENCE CONCEPT *Public Sector Accounting* Pendlebury, Maurice & Jones, Rowan. London, Pitman Publishing, 1992

PURCHASING *KBS Open Learning MBA Programme* London: BPP Publishing Ltd, 1989

Q

QUANGO *The Government and Politics of Britain* Richards P. London: Unwin Hyman Ltd, 1988

QUICK *Human Resource Strategies* Salaman, G.; Mabey, C.; Hamblin, H.; Thompson; Cameron, S.; Iles, P. Milton Keynes: Open University Press, 1992

R

R AND D *The Birmingham Magazine* 1990

REAL *The Independent* 1989

RECALL *Advertising: What It Is And How To Do It* White, R. Maidenhead: McGraw-Hill Book Company, 1993

RECESSIONARY *Clothes Show* London: Redwood Publishing Company, 1991

RED *The Independent* 1989

REFLATION *Social Classes in Marxist Theory* Cottrell, A. London: Routledge & Kegan Paul plc, 1984

REGULATORY *A Right Approach to Economics?* Hardy, Peter. Sevenoaks, Kent: Hodder & Stoughton Ltd, 1991

RELOCATION *Chemistry in Britain* London: Royal Society of Chemistry, 1992

REMUNERATION *Introductory Sociology* Sheard, K.; Stanworth, M.; Buton, T.; Jones, P.; Bonnett, K. Basingstoke: Macmillan Publishers Ltd, 1992

REPOSITION [Dawson International plc: Annual report], 1993

RESERVE *Applied Economics in Banking and Finance* Partington. New York: Oxford University Press, 1989

RETAIL *Consumption, Identity and Styles* Ewen, S.; Cubitt, S.; Tomlinson, A.; Murdock, G. London: Routledge & Kegan Paul plc, 1991

RETRAIN *Microsoft Word: Training Guide* Andralojc, Hari; Lambden, Anne; Walker, Pauline. London: Pitman Publishing, 1990

RETROACTIVE *The Art Newspaper* London: Umberto Allemandi & Company, 1992

REVOLVING *Consumers and Credit* London National Consumer Council, 1980

ROCK BOTTOM *Today* 1992

RSI *Country Living* 1991

S

SALE *Sales Technique and Management* Lancaster, G. & Jobber, D. London: Pitman Publishing, 1992

SATURATION *The Face* 1992

SCHEME *Introduction to English Law, 10th edition* Geldart, William & Yardley D.C.M. Oxford: Oxford University Press, 1991

SEAQ *The Economist* 1998

SECURITY *The Economist* 1991

SELF-LIQUIDATING *International Finance and Developing Countries* Leslie, James. Harlow: Longman Group UK Ltd, 1987

SELLING *Regulation of the Firm and Natural Monopoly* Waterson, Michael. Oxford: Basil Blackwell Ltd, 1988

SERPS *The Guardian* 1989

SET *.net Magazine* 1998

SHAREHOLDER *State and Society in Post-war Japan* Eccleston, Bernard. Cambridge: Polity Press, 1989

SHOPPING *The Alton Herald* 1992

SHORT-TERM *Keesings Contemporary Archives* Harlow: Longman Group UK Ltd, 1990

SIGHT *Accountancy* London: Institute of Chartered Accountants, 1992

SINGLE *The Economist* 1998

SLUSH FUND *Keesings Contemporary Archives* Harlow: Longman Group UK Ltd, 1991

SOFT *In Good Faith* Lamont, Stewart. Edinburgh: St Andrews Press, 1989

SPECIAL *Capitalism Since 1945* Harrison, John; Glyn, Andrew; Armstrong, Philip. Oxford: Blackwell, 1991

SPIN-OFF *The Economist* 1998

SRO *UK Financial Institutions and Markets* Pawlet, Michael; Bentley, Patrick; Winstone, David. London: MacMillan Press Ltd, 1991

STAGFLATION *The Guardian* 1989

STANDSTILL *The Economist* 1998

STEERING COMMITTEE *Keesings Contemporary Archives* Harlow: Longman Group UK Ltd, 1991

STOCK [Dawson International plc: Notice of annual general meeting], Date unknown

STRADDLE *Financial Market Analysis* Blake, David. Maidenhead: McGraw-Hill Book Company, 1990

SUB-AGENT *Bookseller* Uden, Grant. Woodbridge, Suffolk: Antique collectors club, 1993

SUBSIDY *Keesings Contemporary Archives* Harlow: Longman Group UK Ltd, 1991

SUPPORT *Decisions in Geography: the United Kingdom* Farleigh Rice, W. Harlow: Longman Group UK, Ltd, 1985

SWOT *Organisation and Management in the Public Sector* Lawton, Allan & Rose, Aidan. London Publishing, 1991

T

TAKEOVER *The Independent* 1989

TAX *The Guardian* 1989

TELECOMMUTING *New Technology at Work* Francis, Arthur. Oxford: Oxford University Press, 1986

TEMPORARY *Accountancy* London: Institute of Chartered Accountants, 1992

TESSA *The Economist* 1990

TIGER ECONOMY *The Economist* 1998

TOP-HEAVY *Managing Innovation* Date and publisher unknown

TQM *Education Management in the 1990s* Osborne, Allan; Davies, Brent; West-Burnham, John; Ellison, Linda. Harlow: Longman Group UK Ltd, 1990

TRANCHE *The Independent* 1989

TREASURY *The Economist* 1990

TRICKLE-DOWN THEORY *New Statesman and Society* 1992

TRUSTED THIRD PARTY *The Economist* 1998

U

UMBRELLA *Accountancy* London: Institute of Chartered Accountants, 1992

UNCTAD *Rival States, Rival Firms* Henley, J.; Strange, S.; Stopford, J. Cambridge: Cambridge University Press, 1992

UNDERGROUND ECONOMY *The Economist* 1998

UNEARNED INCOME *Introductory Sociology* Sheard, K.; Stanworth, M.; Bilton, T.; Jones, P.; Bonnet, K. Basingstoke: Macmillan Publishers Ltd, 1992

UNLISTED *The Daily Telegraph* 1992

UNSECURED *Principles of Modern Contemporary Law* Gower. London: Sweet & Maxwell Ltd, 1992

UPSWING *Bukharin's Theory of Equilibrium* Tarbuck, Kenneth J. London, Pluto Press, 1989

USP *Advertising: What It Is And How To Do It* White, R. Maidenhead: McGraw-Hill Book Company, 1993

V

VALUE *R&D Management: Managing Projects and New Products* Date and publisher unknown

VERTICAL *Economics* Begg, David; Fischer, Stanley; Dornbusch, Rudiger. Maidenhead: McGraw-Hill Book Company, 1991

VISIBLE *The Economist* 1990

W

WAGE-PRICE SPIRAL *The Daily Telegraph* 1992

WASTING ASSET *Drafting Business Leases* Lewison, Kim. Harlow: Longman Group UK Ltd, 1993

WHEELING AND DEALING *Capitalism Since 1945* Harrison, John; Glyn, Andrew; Armstrong, Philip. Oxford: Blackwell, 1991

WHOLLY-OWNED SUBSIDIARY *Financial Times* Date unknown

WINDOW *Accountancy* London: Institute of Chartered Accountants, 1992

WORKER *Advice From the Top* Oates, David & Ezra, Derek.
  Newton Abbot, Devon: David & Charles Publishers plc, 1989
WORLD *The Economist* 1998
WRONGFUL *Principles of Hotel and Catering Law* Pannett, A.
  London: Cassell, 1992

Z

ZERO *The Scotsman* Date unknown

Sources de Citations Françaises

Sources of French Quotes

A

ABAISSER *Le Monde/Sélection hebdomadaire* 1998
ABATTEMENT *L'Entreprise* 1994
ACCORD *Courrier International* 1994
ACCORD-CADRE *Libération* 1998
ACCORDER *Courrier International* 1994
ACCUEILLIR *Libération* 1998
ACQUIS *L'Expansion* 1994
ACTIF *Le Revenu Français* 1994
AGENT *L'Expansion* 1994
ALENA *L'Expansion* 1994
ALIGNEMENT *Le Monde Économie* 1994
ALLIANCE *Libération* 1998
ALTERNANCE *L'Expansion* 1994
AMÉNAGEMENT *Courrier Cadres* 1994
AMÉNAGER *Libération* 1998
ANNÉE *L'Expansion* 1994
ANNUALISATION *Libération* 1998
APPEL *Libération* 1998
APPORT *L'Expansion* 1994
ARGENT *Le Figaro* 1994
ASSAINIR *Le Figaro* 1994
AUTOFINANCEMENT *La Tribune des Fossés* 1994

B

BAISSE *Libération* 1998
BAISSIER *Libération* 1998
BARRE *Libération* 1998
BÉNÉFICE *Courrier International* 1994
BONIFICATION *L'Expansion* 1994
BULLE BOURSIÈRE *Libération* 1994

C

CAMPAGNE *L'Expansion* 1994
CAPITAL *Libération* 1998
CAPITALISATION *Libération* 1998
CARTE *L'Expansion* 1994
CENTRAL *L'Expansion* 1994
CHARGE *Le Nouvel Observateur* 1994
CHÈQUE *Le Revenu Français* 1994
CHIFFRE *Le Revenu Français* 1994
CLAUSE *L'Entreprise* 1994

COMMISSAIRE *Le Revenu Français* 1994
COMPATIBILITÉ *S.V.M.* 1994
COMPORTEMENT Source non disponible
COMPRIMER *L'Expansion* 1994
COMPTE *L'Expansion* 1994
CONJONCTURE *L'Expansion* 1994
CONSEIL *Le Revenu Français* 1994
CONTENTIEUX *Le Revenu Français* 1994
CONTINGENT *Libération* 1998
CONTRACTUEL *Les Cahiers Français* 1994
CONTRAT *Courrier Cadres* 1994
CONTREFAÇON *L'Entreprise* 1994
CONTRIBUABLE *L'Expansion* 1994
CONTRÔLE *Libération* 1998
CONVENTION *Libération* 1998
CONVERTIBLE *Le Revenu Français* 1994
COORDINATION *L'Expansion* 1994
COTÉ *Libération* 1998
COTISATION *L'Expansion* 1994
COUPE *L'Expansion* 1994
COUPURE *L'Expansion* 1994
COURTIER *L'Expansion* 1994
COÛT *L'Expansion* 1994
COUVERTURE *Le Revenu Français* 1994
COUVRIR *Le Revenu Français* 1994
CRÉANCE *L'Expansion* 1994
CRÉATEUR *Le Monde/Sélection hebdomadaire* 1998
CRÉDIT *Le Revenu Français* 1994
CRISE *Libération* 1998
CSG *Le Nouvel Observateur* 1994

D
DÉBIT *Le Revenu Français* 1994
DÉBLOQUER *Libération* 1998
DÉBOUCHÉ *Le Monde/Sélection hebdomadaire* 1998
DÉCLARATION *L'Entreprise* 1994
DÉCOTE *Le Revenu Français* 1994
DÉFAILLANCE *L'Expansion* 1994
DÉFICIT *L'Expansion* 1994
DÉFLATION *L'Expansion* 1994
DÉGRÈVEMENT *Le Revenu Français* 1994
DÉLAI *Libération* 1998
DÉLÉGUÉ *L'Entreprise* 1994
DÉLOCALISATION *Le Revenu Français* 1994
DÉLOCALISER *Libération* 1998
DÉMANTÈLEMENT *L'Expansion* 1994

DÉNOMINATION *L'Entreprise* 1994
DÉPRÉCIATION *L'Expansion* 1994
DÉRÈGLEMENTATION *Courrier International* 1994
DÉSINDEXATION *L'Expansion* 1994
DÉSTOCKER *L'Expansion* 1994
DÉTENTE *Le Revenu Français* 1994
DÉTENTEUR *Le Revenu Français* 1994
DONATION *L'Expansion* 1994
DONNÉE *Le Figaro* 1994
DOTATION *L'Expansion* 1994
DROIT *Libération* 1998

E
ÉCHELLE *L'Expansion* 1994
ÉCOULER *Le Revenu Français* 1994
EFFONDREMENT *L'Expansion* 1994
ÉMETTRE *Le Monde/Sélection hebdomadaire* 1998
ÉMISSION *Libération* 1998
ENCOURS *L'Expansion* 1994
ENGORGEMENT *Libération* 1998
ENTAMER *Libération* 1998
ENVELOPPE *Le Figaro* 1994
ÉPARGNE *L'Expansion* 1994
ESPACE *Le Monde/Sélection hebdomadaire* 1998
ÉTALEMENT *Le Monde Économie* 1994
ÉTUDE *L'Entreprise* 1994
ÉVASION *L'Expansion* 1994
EXCÉDENT *Le Figaro* 1994
EXERCICE *Courrier International* 1994,
Le Monde/Sélection hebdomadaire 1998
EXONÉRATION *Le Revenu Français* 1994

F
FERME *Libération* 1998
FIDÉLISER *L'Expansion* 1994
FIXATION *Libération* 1998
FLEXIBILITÉ *Le Monde/Sélection hebdomadaire* 1998
FLOTTER *Libération* 1998
FLUIDITÉ *Le Monde/Sélection hebdomadaire* 1998
FLUX *Libération* 1998
FONDS *Courrier Cadres* 1994,
Libération 1998
FORFAIT *Le Revenu Français* 1994,
Libération 1998
FORMATION *Courrier Cadres* 1994
FRAIS *Professions et Entreprises* 1994

FRANCHISE *L'Expansion 1994,*
  Libération 1998
FRUCTIFIER *L'Expansion* 1994
FUSIONNER *Libération* 1998

G

GAIN *L'Expansion* 1994
GESTION *Courrier Cadres* 1994
GLISSEMENT *Le Figaro* 1994
GRÈVE *La Tribune des Fossés* 1994
GREVER *Libération* 1998

H

HAUTEUR *Libération* 1998
HEURE *Libération* 1998

I

IMPAYÉ *Courrier Cadres* 1994
IMPÔT *L'Expansion* 1994
INDEMNITÉ Source non disponible
INDEXATION *L'Expansion* 1994
INFLATIONNISTE *Les Cahiers Français* 1994
INONDER *Libération* 1998
INTERDIT *Le Revenu Français* 1994
INVESTISSEMENT *Le Revenu Français* 1994,
  Libération 1998

J

JOINT-VENTURE *Courrier Cadres* 1994

K

KRACH *L'Expansion* 1994

L

LIAISON *Courrier International* 1994
LICENCIEMENT *L'Expansion* 1994
LINÉAIRE *L'Expansion* 1994
LIQUIDATION *L'Expansion* 1994
LIQUIDITÉ *L'Expansion* 1994
LOCATION *L'Expansion* 1994
LOGICIEL *Le Nouvel Observateur* 1994
LOYER *Le Nouvel Observateur* 1994

M

MAINTENIR *Libération* 1998
MAISON *L'Expansion* 1994

MAÎTRE *Libération* 1998
MAJORATION *L'Expansion* 1994
MARCHÉ *Le Figaro* 1994,
  Le Revenu Français 1994
MARGE *L'Expansion* 1994
MARKETING *L'Expansion* 1994
MASSE *Le Figaro* 1994
MÉNANGE *Libération* 1998
MENSUALISATION *Libération* 1998
MENSUALITÉ *L'Expansion* 1994
MODALITÉ *Le Monde/Sélection hebdomadaire* 1998
MOINS-VALUE *Le Revenu Français* 1994
MONNAIE *L'Expansion* 1994,
  Libération 1998
MORATOIRE *Le Figaro* 1994,
  Libération 1998
MULTINATIONAL *L'Expansion* 1994
MULTITÂCHE *S.V.M.* 1994
MUTUEL *Le Revenu Français* 1994

N
NÉGOCIANT *L'Expansion* 1994
NOTATION *Courrier International* 1994

O
OBLIGATION *Le Revenu Français* 1994
OFFRE *Le Figaro* 1994
OPÉRATEUR *Libération* 1998
OPÉRATION *L'Expansion* 1994
OPTIMISER *L'Expansion* 1994

P
PART *L'Entreprise* 1994,
  Le Monde/Sélection hebdomadaire 1998
PARTENAIRE *L'Expansion* 1994
PAS-DE-PORTE *Le Revenu Français* 1994
PASSATION *Le Figaro* 1994
PATRIMOINE *L'Expansion* 1994
PENSION *L'Expansion* 1994
PERQUISITION *Le Revenu Français* 1994
PERSONNE *L'Entreprise* 1994
PESER *l'Événement du Jeudi* 1998
PHONING *L'Expansion* 1994
PIB *L'Expansion* 1994
PLACE *Le Monde/Sélection hebdomadaire* 1998
PLACEMENT *L'Expansion* 1994

PLAN *L'Entreprise* 1994,
  Libération 1998
PLUS-VALUE *L'Expansion* 1994
POINT *Libération* 1998
PONCTIONNER *L'Expansion* 1994
PORTEFEUILLE *L'Expansion* 1994
PORTEUR *L'Expansion* 1994
PRÉLÈVEMENT *L'Expansion* 1994
PRÉRETRAITE *Les Cahiers Français* 1994
PRESTATION *L'Entreprise* 1994
PRIME *L'Expansion* 1994
PRIVATISATION *L'Expansion* 1994
PRIX *L'Expansion* 1994
PRODUCTIVITÉ *L'Expansion* 1994
PRODUIT *Le Nouvel Observateur* 1994
PROMESSE *Le Revenu Français* 1994
PROMOTEUR *Courrier Cadres* 1994
PROROGER *L'Entreprise* 1994
PROTOCOLE *Libération* 1998
PROVISION *L'Expansion* 1994

Q
QUOTE-PART *Le Monde/Sélection hebdomadaire*
  1998

R
RAFFERMIR *Le Figaro* 1994
RAJUSTEMENT *Le Revenu Français* 1994
RAPPORT *Le Figaro* 1994
RECETTE *L'Expansion* 1994
RECLASSEMENT *Le Nouvel Observateur* 1994
RECONVERSION *L'Expansion* 1994
RECRUTEMENT *Courrier Cadres* 1994
REDÉMARRAGE *L'Expansion* 1994
REDRESSEMENT *Le Monde/Sélection*
  hebdomadaire 1998
RÉGIME *Le Revenu Français* 1994
RÉHABILITATION *La Tribune des Fossés* 1994
RÉMUNÉRATION *L'Expansion* 1994
RENCHÉRIR *Libération* 1998
RENTABILISER *Libération* 1998
RÉSORBER *L'Expansion* 1994
RESTRUCTURATION *Le Monde/Sélection*
  hebdomadaire 1998
RESTRUCTURER *Libération* 1998
REVENU *Les Cahiers Français* 1994

RISQUE *L'Entreprise* 1994
ROUGE *Les Échos* 1994
RUPTURE *Libération* 1998

S
SAISIE *Professions et Entreprises* 1994
SÉANCE *Le Figaro* 1994
SECTEUR *Le Monde/Sélection hebdomadaire* 1998
SICAV *L'Expansion* 1994
SOCIÉTÉ *L'Événement du Jeudi* 1998
SOUSCRIRE *L'Entreprise* 1994
SOUS-ÉVALUATION *Le Revenu Français* 1994
SOUTENIR *Libération* 1998
SUREFFECTIF *L'Expansion* 1994
SURENDETTEMENT *Le Monde Économie* 1994
SURFACTURATION *Libération* 1998
SURPRODUCTION *Le Figaro* 1994

T
TABLE *Libération* 1998
TAUX *L'Expansion* 1994
TAXE *L'Entreprise* 1994
TÉLÉCONFÉRENCE *Le Revenu Français* 1994
TERRAIN *Le Monde/Sélection hebdomadaire* 1998
TIMBRE *Libération* 1998
TITRE *Le Figaro* 1994
TRAIN *Libération* 1998
TRANCHE *Libération* 1998

U
UNITÉ *L'Expansion* 1994

V
VALEUR *Le Revenu Français* 1994
VOLUME *Les Cahiers Français* 1994

Z
ZONE *Libération* 1998

Organization Chart of a Large French Company
Organigramme d'une Grande Entreprise Française

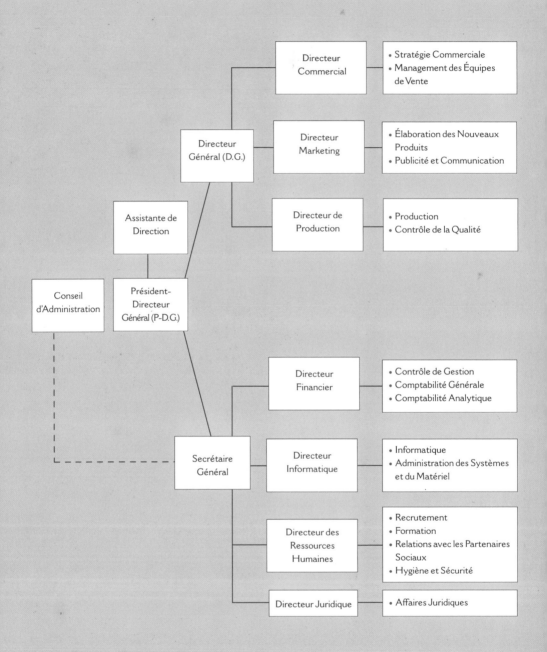